AF884347

SWAHILI-ENGLISH DICTIONARY

SWAHILI-ENGLISH DICTIONARY

Charles W. Rechenbach

Assisted by

Angelica Wanjinu Gesuga
Harold M. Onyango Josiah
Leslie R. Leinone
Florence G. Kuipers

Bureau of Special Research
in Modern Languages

The Catholic University of America Press
Washington, D. C. 20017
1968

THE CATHOLIC UNIVERSITY OF AMERICA PRESS, INC.

Library of Congress Catalog Number 67-31438

INTRODUCTION

The compilers of this Swahili-English dictionary, the first new lexical work for English speakers in many years, hope that they are offering to students and translators a more reliable and certainly a more up-to-date working tool than any previously available. They trust that it will prove to be of value to libraries, researchers, scholars, and governmental and commercial agencies alike, whose interests and concerns will benefit from a better understanding and closer communication with peoples of Africa.

The Swahili language *(Kiswahili)* is a Bantu language spoken by perhaps as many as forty million people throughout a large part of East and Central Africa. It is, however, a native or 'first' language only in a quite restricted area consisting of the islands of Zanzibar and Pemba and the opposite coast, roughly from Dar es Salaam to Mombasa.

Outside this relatively small territory, elsewhere in Kenya, in Tanzania (formerly Tanganyika), and to a lesser degree in Uganda, in the Republic of the Congo, and in other fringe regions hard to delimit, Swahili is a *lingua franca* of long standing, a 'second' (or 'third' or 'fourth') language enjoying a reasonably well accepted status as a supra-tribal or supra-regional medium of communication.

Its chief competitor in this function is English, and English is of course a formidable competitor indeed in Kenya and Tanzania and particularly in Uganda. The competitors are both English and Luganda in Uganda, both French and Lingala in the Congo. In the long view, the future of Swahili is difficult to predict; but, for the present, its position appears to be more stable than that of any other African language.

The older literature of the language, written in Arabic characters, goes back to the seventeenth century and includes a wide range of subject matter and forms, from poetry to chronicles and history. There is an abundance of modern material, including perhaps a thousand titles in short stories, poetry, scholarly works, and text books for elementary and secondary schools. Swahili can no longer be considered in the category of the 'rarer' languages. There are several Swahili newspapers as well as various commercial media in circulation, and there is an abundance of excellent teaching aids, such as E.V. Parrott's *Teach Yourself Swahili* (The English Universities Press Ltd., London). The East African Literature Bureau of Nairobi has published a great many Swahili titles, and Longmans, Green and Company Ltd., London, should also be mentioned as having made much educational material available in the language.

In view of these resources, the compilers of this dictionary have not felt it necessary or advisable to expand the volume with phonetic or grammatical aids. This volume is primarily and specifically a word source for readers and translators. Like all subsequent compilations, it builds gratefully upon the *Standard Swahili-English and English-Swahili Dictionary* in two volumes, prepared under the direction of Frederick Johnson and published by the Oxford University Press in 1939. The present dictionary has critically reappraised the entire word-stock of the language, modernizing and augmenting from many sources. It brings the vocabulary up to date, including the fantastic developments since World War II.

ACKNOWLEDGMENTS

The compilers are moved by piety and by a sense of real and deep indebtedness when they acknowledge the long line of earlier toilers in this particular vineyard: Krapf, Steere, Madan, Johnson (and his many associates), Sacleux, Olderogge, and Höftmann.*

They wish also to acknowledge the very substantial assistance of Miss Barbara Dudley and Mr. Harold A. Goldklang, who furnished lists of new entries and of new senses for old entries drawn from their long experience in reading contemporary Swahili texts of many kinds.

They must finally express their very great obligation to Messrs. Harry Goff and Eugene R. Garnett, who prepared the final text of the dictionary, and to the Right Reverend James A. Magner and other officials of the Catholic University of America Press, who have given it a handsome and practical outward form.

*See Marcel van Spaandonck, *Practical and Systematical Swahili Bibliography, Linguistics 1850-1963.* Leiden (E.J. Brill), 1965.

A NOTE ON THE CONSTRUCTION OF THE DICTIONARY

1. Derivative verb forms (applicative, causative, etc.) are listed under the base form of the verb. When the base form is not in current use, the derivative forms appear as separate entries. In cases where derivative forms are much commoner than, or differ drastically in sense from, the base verb, they also appear as separate entries.

2. Derivative nouns (formed with the prefixes **ki-**, **m-**, **u-**, etc.) appear in the normal alphabetical order *of the prefix,* with a cross-reference to the base word.

3. At the end of the entry for each base word there is an alphabetical list of derivative words (if any) appearing as main entries in this dictionary: *Cf.* ...

4. Words of Arabic origin are likewise cross-referenced to derivative or related words.

5. Common synonyms of rare entries are given in parentheses: (= ...)

6. Each noun is followed by its plural prefix in parentheses or by the indications *sing.* or *pl.* if the entry is commonly used only in the singular or in the plural. The indication (–) after an entry means that the entry is a noun having in the plural the same form as in the singular.

SIGNS AND ABBREVIATIONS

* foreign loanword (from Arabic unless otherwise specified)

(–) plural the same as singular (i.e., without prefix)

< derived from...

= (more or less) synonymous with...

abbr. abbreviation, abbreviated as...

abs. absolute

adj. adjective

adv. adverb(ial)

affirm. affirmative

Afr. Afrikaans

agr., *agric.* agriculture

amplic. amplicative (= augmentative)

anat. anatomical

anth. anthropology

app. approximately

appl. applicative

approx. approximately

Ar. Arabic

arch. archaic

arith. arithmetic

ass. associative

astr., *astron.* astronomy

augm., *augment.* augmentative

auto. automotive term

aux., *auxil.* auxiliary

av. aviation

Bibl. Biblical

biol. biological term

bot. botanical term

caus. causative

chem. chemistry

Christ. Christian (as opposed to Muslim) usage

cl. class

coll. colloquial

collec. collective

comm. communist terminology

conj. conjunction

conn. connective

consec. consecutive

cont. contactive

contr. contrast(ed)

cul. culinary

dem., *demon.* demonstrative

derog. derogatory

det. determinative

dial. dialectal

dimin. diminutive

dur. durative

econ. economics

elec. electricity

emph. emphatic

encl. enclitic

Engl. English

esp. especially

eth., *ethn.* ethnology

euph. euphemism

expr. expression

fem. feminine

fig. figurative(ly)

fin. finance

foll. following

Fr. French

gen. general(ly)

geogr. geographical term

geom. geometry

Germ. German

gramm. grammatical term

hist. historical

id. ideophone

imp., *imper.* imperative

Ind. Indian (Hindi, Gujerati, etc.)

indef. indefinite

inf. infinitive

int. intensive

interj. interjection

interr., *interrog.* interrogative

intr. intransitive

inv. inversive

Isl. (term usually restricted to) Islamic (contexts)

Jap. Japanese

jur. jurisprudence

Lat. Latin

leg. legal term

ling. linguistics

lit. literal(ly)

liter. literary

loc. locative

Lug. Luganda

Mal. Malay

masc. masculine

math. mathematics

mech. mechanics

med. medical term

meteor. meteorology

mil. military

min. mining, mineralogy

mod. modern

mus. music

myth. mythology

n. noun

naut. nautical

neg. negative

num. numeral

obj. object

obs. obsolete

onom. onomatopoeic

opp. (as) opposed (in meaning to...)

opt. optics

orig. originally

ornith. ornithology

parl. parliamentary term

part. particle

pass. passive

pej., *pejor.* pejorative

pers. person, personal

Pers. Persian

pharm. pharmaceutical term

phon. phonetics

phot. photography

phy. physiology

phys. physics

pl., *plur.* (occurring commonly only in the) plural

pol. political term

polyg. (term relating to the practice of) polygamy

Port. Portuguese

poss. possessive

pr. proper (noun)

prep. preposition(al)

prob. probable, probably

pron. pronoun

prov. proverb

psych. psychology

punct. punctuation

railw. railway term

rec. recent

red. reduplicated, reduplication

ref. reference

refl. reflexive

rel. religious

relat. relative

Russ. Russian

sing. (occurring commonly only in the) singular

sl. slang

Span. Spanish

stat. stative

suff. suffix(ed)

tech. technology

tr., *trans.* transitive

Turk. Turkish

typ. typography

us. usually

v. verb

vulg. vulgar

w. with

zool. zoology

Zu. Zulu

A

a, aa, ah *interj. expressing surprise, joy, pain.*

aali* *adj.* good, excellent, first-class.

aasi* *see* **¹asi.**

abadan* 1. *adv.* never. **hawatakuja kwetu —.** They will never come to us. 2. *interj.* 'Make way!'

abadi, abidi *adv., rare* always, constantly. (= **daima, sikuzote, kila mara, milele.**) **kazi yake ni kuiba —.** He is always stealing.

abd* (—) *liter.* servant, slave. *See* **abudu.**

abe* *see* **labeka.**

¹abedari* [*Port. ?*] (—) pulley, block *(used on dhows).*

²abedari* *see* **habedari.**

abidi* *see* **abadi.**

abiri* 1. travel by sea; pass over, cross *(river, lake, sea).* 2. go, travel *(by ship, railway, automobile, airplane). appl.* **abiria.** *intr.* **abirika.** *caus.* **abirisha.** *pass.* **abiriwa.** *Cf.* **²abiria.**

¹abiria* *appl. of* **abiri.**

²abiria* (ma-) passenger. **meli ya —.** passenger ship. **motakaa ya —.** bus. **gari la —.** passenger train. **motokaa ya —.** taxi, bus. *Cf.* **abiri.**

abu* (—) *liter.* father. (= **¹baba.**)

abudi* (—) *see* **budi.**

abudu* pray, worship; serve; fear. **— Mungu.** worship/serve/fear God. *appl.* **abudia.** *caus.* **abudisha.** *Cf.* **ibada, uabudiwaji, maabadi, maabudu, mwabudu.**

Abunuwasi*, Banawasi *liter.* proper name in tales of Arabic origin; one who tells such tales. *Cf.* **kibanawasi.**

acha, *dial.* **ata** leave (behind), desert, abandon; divorce (wife, husband). **Fulani amemwacha mkewe.** X is divorced from his wife. **wameuacha mji wao.** They have left their town. 2. stop, cease, discontinue; fail to do, neglect. 3. release, acquit, pardon. 4. allow, permit. *ass.* **achana.** leave each other, separate, be separated; be different, diverge *(views, opinions). appl.* **achia.** leave something to someone, let someone have something; bequeath. **achia mtu mali.** bequeath property to someone. *double appl.* **achilia.** 1. pardon, forgive. 2. **:achilia mbali.** cease, break off; leave alone, abandon.

double appl.-intr. **achilika.** be excusable/pardonable. *caus.* **achisha.** cause to leave/abandon/divorce; wean *(a child).* *ass.* **achana.** leave each other; diverge, be different.

achali* (—) *see* **achari.**

achana *ass. of* **acha.**

achari*, achali, ajari [*Ind.*] (—) appetizer, relish, chutney.

achisha *caus. of* **acha.**

ada* 1. (—) fee, (customary) payment, gift *(that is expected to be forthcoming).* **— ya mganga.** doctor's fee. **maada ya harusi.** wedding-present. **kiasi cha — tu.** as is fitting/appropriate. **— ya shule.** school fees. 2. (ma-) contribution, payment. **— ya kuingilia.** admission fee.

adabu* (—) politeness, courtesy, consideration; good manners. **Huna —.** You have no manners. *Cf.* **adibu.**

Adamu* (wa-) 1. *pr. n. masc.* 2. *see* **mwanadamu, binadamu.**

adawa* (—) *see* **uadui.**

Aden, Edeni *sing.* (the city of) Aden.

adesi* (—) *bot.* lentils.

adhabu* 1. punishment, penalty. 2. pain, torment. **tia (pa, patisha) —.** punish, chastise. 3. pursuit, persecution. *Cf.* **adhibu.**

adhama*, adhima (—) 1. greatness, grandeur, dignity. 2. fame. 3. power, authority. 4. pomp, splendor. *Cf.* **adhimisho, adhimu, taadhima, taadhimika, uadhimishaji.**

adhana* 1. (—) *Isl.* call to prayer of the muezzin. **piga —.** call to prayer. 2. *see* **adhini.**

adhibisha* *see* **adhibu.**

adhibu*, adhibisha 1. punish, chastise; pass judgment/sentence. 2. cause pain/torment; harass, molest, annoy. **watakapochelewa kurudi kwenye masomo tutawaadhibu.** If they return late to the lessons we shall punish them. *Cf.* **adhabu.**

adhima* (—) *see* **adhama.**

adhimisha* *see* **adhimu.**

adhimisho* (ma-) (*more commonly* **maadhimisho**) celebration, solemnity, ceremony. **— la misa takatifu.** *rel.* celebration of the mass. *Cf.* **adhama.**

adhimu* 1. *adj. & adv., liter.* great, important, significant. 2. (*also caus.* **adhimisha**) praise, honor, glorify, celebrate. **— (adhimisha) sikukuu.** celebrate a holiday. *appl.* **adhimia.** *Cf.* **adhama.**

adhini*, adhana *Isl.* call to prayer. **Mwadhini anaadhini.** The muezzin calls to prayer. *Cf.* **adhana, mwadhini.**

adhiri*, **aziri** find fault with, reprove, criticize; degrade, humiliate; slander, defame. **Usiniadhiri mbele za watu.** Don't criticize me in front of the people.

adhuhuri*, **adhuuri** (–) midday, noon *(between* 12 *and* 2 *o'clock).* **wakati wa –.** noontime. **sala ya –.** *Isl.* time of the second prayers.

adhuuri* (–) *see* **adhuhuri.**

adi* *arch.* go part of the way with someone *(e.g., a guest),* escort. (= [2]**sindikiza.**)

adia*, **hidaya** (–) *arch.* gift, present. *Cf.* **hedaya.**

adibisha* *caus. of* **adibu.**

adibu* (*also* **taadabu**) 1. (*also caus.* **adibisha**) bring up, educate, teach good manners. 2. *adj.* polite, courteous, gracious, well-bred. 3. *interj.* **taadabu**! *or* **– nafsi yako**! Behave yourself! *Cf.* **adabu.**

adili* 1. be just (righteous, impartial); conduct oneself well. 2. (**ma-**, **–**) morality, ethics; good conduct; justice, impartiality. 3. (*also* **adilifu**) *adj.* right, correct; just, righteous, impartial; straightforward, honest. *Cf.* **adilisha, uadilifu.**

adilifu* *see* **adili 3.**

adilisha* cause to be righteous/moral, teach morality/good conduct. *Cf.* **adili.**

adimika*, **hadimika** be rare/unobtainable. *Cf.* **adimu.**

adimu* *adj.* 1. rare, scarce, unobtainable. 2. insufficient, inadequate; deficient, faulty, unsatisfactory. *Cf.* **adimika.**

adinasi*, **wadinasi** (–) 1. *arch.* free man. 2. a man of good birth. *Cf.* [1]**wadi.**

admeli*, **admirali** [*Engl.*] (–) admiral.

adua* *arch.* 1. make offerings/sacrifices. 2. prepare magic charms *(against the evil eye).*

adui* (**ma-**) enemy, opponent. **– mbaya.** *rel.* devil. *Cf.* **uadui.**

aenzi* (–) *see* **enzi.**

afa* (**ma-**) (*more commonly* **maafa**) 1. misfortune, catastrophe, disaster, calamity, mishap, accident, bad luck, damage, injury. 2. danger, peril; threat, menace; horror, terror. 3. injustice.

afadhali*, **afdhali**, **afudhali** *adv.* rather, better, particularly. **ni – kusafiri kuliko kukaa.** It is better to travel than to stay. *Cf.* **fadhili.**

afdhali* *see* **afadhali.**

afendi*, **efendi** [*Turk.*] (–) *mil.* effendi (title of rank).

afia* (–) *see* [1]**afya.**

afikana* *ass. of* **afiki.**

afiki* agree, correspond; be the same as; fit, be fitting; satisfy, appease; (*usually ass.* **afikiana, afikana**) come to an agreement, make a settlement, be reconciled. *ass.-caus.* **afikanisha.** satisfy, appease, reconcile, conciliate. *Cf.* **maafikiano, mwafaka.**

afikiano* (ma-) *see* **maafikiano.**

afisa* [*Engl.*] (ma-) *see* **ofisa.**

afisi*, ofisi [*Engl.*] (—) office, department, bureau.

afiuni* (—) *see* **afyuni.**

Afrika* [*Engl.*] *sing.* **—ya kaskazini.** North Africa. **— ya kusini.** South Africa. **— ya kati** (*or* **katikati**). Central Africa. **— ya magharibi.** West Africa. **— ya mashariki.** East Africa. **nchi ya —.** African continent. *Cf.* **kiafrika, Mwafrika.**

afrikanaizesheni* [*Engl.*] *sing.* Africanization.

afriti* (—) 1. (evil) spirit, devil. 2. wicked/malicious person.

[1]**afu*** (—) flower of the wild jasmine. *Cf.* **mwafu.**

[2]**afu*, afua** 1. forgive, pardon. 2. guard, protect, defend. 3. free, liberate, release. 4. heal, cure. 5. (—, ma-) liberation, redemption, salvation, protection, defense.

afua* *see* [2]**afu.**

afudhali* *see* **afadhali.**

[1]**afya*, afia** (—) health; strength, vigor. **bora —.** The main thing is health. **hana — nzuri** *or* **— yake si nzuri.** He is not in good health.

[2]**afya** *caus. of* **apa.**

afyuni*, afiuni (—) opium. (= **kasumba.**)

[1]**aga** take one's leave, say good-bye, leave. **— dunia.** *euph.* to die. *appl.* **agia.** take leave of, dismiss. *ass.* **agana.** take leave of each other *(for a long period).* **agana buriani.** bid each other a final farewell. *Cf.* [2]**agano, kiago,** [4]**mwago.**

[2]**aga** (*usually ass.* **agana**) agree, come to an agreement, reach a settlement, make a contract. *caus.* **agiza.** charge, order, commission; instruct. **fanya kama nilivyokuagiza.** Do as I have instructed you. *caus.-appl.* **agizia.** order/commission for... *Cf.* [1]**agano, agizo, kiaga,** [3]**mwago, uagizaji.**

[3]**aga** *rare* destroy.

Agami* *see* **Uajemi.**

agana *ass. of* [1]**aga,** [2]**aga.**

[1]**agano** (ma-) (*more commonly* **maagano**) 1. agreement, settlement, contract, treaty, covenant; arrangement,

understanding. **Agano Jipya.** New Testament. **Agano la Kale.** Old Testament. 2. promise, vow. *Cf.* [2]**aga.**

[2]**agano (ma-)** *rare* departure, farewell. *Cf.* [1]**aga.**

aghalabu*, aghlabu *adv.* usually, ordinarily, mostly; mainly, chiefly, as a rule. **maji huchotwa kwa ndoo, – na ng'ombe.** Water is drawn with buckets, but the work is usually done by oxen.

aghlabu* *see* **aghalabu.**

agiza (*caus. of* [1]**aga,** *q.v.*) order, direct, commission, give instructions.

agizo (ma-) (*more commonly* **maagizo**) order, commission, instruction; regulation, directive. *Cf.* [2]**aga.**

Agosti* [*Engl.*] (month of) August.

agua 1. foretell, predict, prophesy; interpret *(a dream or omen).* 2. *med.* treat *(usually with charms or potions). Cf.* **aguzi, mwaguzi, uaguzi.**

aguzi (ma-) (*usually* **maaguzi**) 1. medicine, remedy. 2. interpretation *(of a dream or omen).* 3. prophecy, prediction. *Cf.* **agua.**

ahadi*, wahadi (–) promise, obligation, vow, agreement. **toa (funga, pa) –.** make a promise. **vunja –.** break a promise/vow. **timiza (fikisha, shika) –.** keep a promise/vow. *Cf.* **ahidi, miadi.**

ahali*, ahli (–) 1. relations, family, *(distant)* relative. **ndugu na –.** brothers and (other) relatives. 2. *rare* wife.

ahera*, akhera (–) hereafter, life to come. *fig.* **enda –.** *die. Cf.* **aheri.**

aheri*, akheri (–) end; limit, border. **toka awali hata –.** from beginning to end. **– yako nini?** *or* **– yako kiasi gani?** What is your rock-bottom price? *Cf.* **ahera.**

ahi* (–) *see* **yahe.**

ahidi*, wahidi promise, vow, agree. *Cf.* **ahadi.**

ahiri*, akhiri 1. be put off/postponed. 2. delay, hesitate, procrastinate. *caus.* **ahirisha.** put off, postpone. **mtihani umeahirishwa mpaka kesho.** The examination is postponed until tomorrow. *pass.* **ahiriwa.** *Cf.* **taahari, taahira.**

ahli* (–) *see* **ahali.**

ahsante* *see* **asante.**

aibika* 1. be disgraced/dishonored. 2. be ashamed/abashed. **ameaibika.** He is ashamed. *caus.* **aibisha.** disgrace, dishonor; abash, disconcert. *Cf.* **aibu.**

aibisho* (ma-) *see* **aibu.**

aibu* (–), aibisho (ma-) shame, dishonor, scandal, disgrace. *Cf.* **aibika.**

aidha*, **waaidha** *conj.* then, thereupon; moreover, furthermore.

aili* *(& caus.* **ailisha)** *rare* reproach, criticize. *Cf.* **uaili.**

ailisha* *caus. of* **aili.**

aina* (–) 1. kind, sort, class. **kila – ya...** all kinds of... 2. *biol.* sex. 3. *bot.* species. 4. breed *(of cattle, etc.).* 5. grade *(of merchandise). Cf.* **aini.**

aini* show; explain, define; classify, differentiate, distinguish. *Cf.* **aina.**

aisei* *interj., coll.* [*Engl.*] I say, hello.

aishi* *see* **ishi.**

ajabu*, **ajibu, staajabu** 1. marvel, be surprised/astonished/amazed. 2. (–, ma-) prise, amazement. **ona –.** be astounded. 3. *adj. & adv.* amazing, astonishing, extraordinary. 4. (*reinforcing* **mno & sana**): **nyingi mno –.** extraordinarily many, an amazing number. *See also* **staajabu.**

ajali* (–) 1. fate, destiny; destination; chance. *prov.* **haina kinga wala kafara.** Nothing can avert an impending blow of fate. (*lit.:* Fate has neither defense nor sacrifice.) *prov.* **tabibu hazuii –.** The physician does not delay fate. 2. hour of death. 3. accident. **hapa leo pana –.** An accident occurred there today.

[1]**ajari*** (–) *see* [1]**ayari.**

[2]**ajari*** (–) *see* **achari.**

ajazi* *rare* be weak/infirm/helpless. *intr.* **ajizika.** *Cf.* **ajizi, uajizi.**

Ajemi* *see* **Uajemi.**

ajenti* [*Engl.*] (–) agent, manager, foreman. *Cf.* **uajenti.**

ajibu* *see* **ajabu.**

ajihi* *rare* pay a visit on someone *(at a considerable distance).*

ajili* (–) *arch.* reason, cause. *Now occurring only in the expressions* **kwa – ya** as a result of, thanks to *and* **kwa –** therefore, because of, on the strength of. *Cf.* **minajili.**

ajiri* hire, engage, employ, enlist, recruit *(laborers, soldiers). caus.* **ajirisha.** 1. employ someone for pay. 2. lease, rent. *Cf.* **ijara, ujira.**

ajiza* (–) *see* **ajizi.**

ajizi* (*also* **ajiza**) 1. (–) weakness, limpness, laziness, negligence. 2. (–) delay, indecision, hesitancy. *prov.* **– nyumba ya njaa.** Indecision is the house of hunger. 3. *adj.* weak, slack, hesitant, dilatory. *Cf.* **ajazi, uajizi.**

ajuza* (–) *rare* old woman. (= **kizee.**)

[1]**aka** *interj. expressing amazement, impatience, negation.*

^{2}aka build, erect *(with stone)*. *caus.* **akisha, asha.**

^{3}aka act as if..., pretend to be..., feign. **– kimya.** feign muteness.

akali* 1. (–) *rare* isolation, segregation. 2. *adj.* few, individual, isolated. **– ya vitu** *or* **vitu –.** few things.

akarabu* (–) *see* **akrabu.**

akari* (–) intoxicating drink.

-ake (*rare* **-akwe**) *poss. pron. 3rd pers. sing.* his, her. **kiti chake.** his chair. **viti vyake.** his chairs.

akhera* (–) *see* **ahera.**

akheri* (–) *see* **aheri.**

akhiri* *see* **ahiri.**

akhiyari* *adv., rare* well, better.

akhtari* (–) *see* **aktari.**

aki* (–) *see* **yahe.**

akia* swallow, devour, gulp down; gorge oneself.

akiba* (–) supply, reserve; savings. **vyombo vya –.** spare parts. **– ya wananchi.** savings bonds. **weka –.** lay aside, save. **toa –.** dip into one's savings. *prov.:* **– haiozi.** What is saved does not spoil.

akida* (ma-) 1. chief, leader. 2. official. 3. officer, adjutant. 4. manager, supervisor, foreman.

akidi* *rare* suffice; end, conclude, finish.

akidu* (ma-) contractor.

akifia* entrust with *(a task, money, property)*.

akifu* *see* **wakifu.**

akika* (–) **akika:** 1. ceremony of a baby's first haircut. 2. burial ceremony for a child. *Cf.* **^{2}akiki.**

^{1}akiki* (–) *min.* carnelian.

^{2}akiki* 1. the slaughtering of a goat for the festival of the first hair-cutting. *Cf.* **akika 1.** 2. **soma –.** hold the burial ceremony for a child. *Cf.* **akika 2.**

akili* (–) 1. understanding, reason, intelligence, intellect; judgment, discretion. 2. ability, capability, proficiency, competence. 3. sense, thought. **fanya –.** consider, reflect. *prov.* **– ni mali.** Sense is wealth. 4. trick; *(in a good sense)* plan.

akina*, kina, wakina (–) family; descent, extraction; a person/people like... **– Said.** Said's family. **– sisi.** people like us. **– bibi (bwana).** *collec.* women (men).

-ako *poss. pron. 2nd pers. sing.* your. **tunda lako.** your fruit. **matunda yako.** your fruits.

akrab* *sing., rare:* **— magharibi.** southwest. **— matlai.** southeast.

akraba* (—) relation, relative *(only of the first degree).*

akrabu*, akarabu (—) pointer, indicator, hand. **— ya saa.** hand of a watch or clock.

aksidenti*, eksidenti [*Engl.*] (—) *rare* accident. *Cf.* **ajali.**

aktari*, akhtari (—) crowd, gathering. **— ya watu.** crowd of people.

-akwe *see* **-ake.**

[1]**ala*** *interj. expressing amazement or impatience.*

[2]**ala*** **(nyala, ala, maala)** 1. case, sheath, scabbard *(for knife, sword).* 2. instrument, tool, implement, apparatus, appliance. **kila — ya kazi.** all kinds of instruments/tools. **amekuja na — zake kamili.** He came fully equipped.

alaf* *see* **elfu.**

[1]**alafu*** *see* **elfu.**

[2]**alafu*** *adv., conj.* *see* **halafu.**

alama* (—) 1. sign, mark, symbol. **— ndogo.** dot. **— ya kushangaa.** exclamation mark. **— ya kuuliza.** question mark. **— ya kutaja.** quotation mark. **— ya usawa.** equals mark, sign of equality. 2. indication, marking, trace. **tia —.** mark, indicate. 3. postmark. 4. symptom, prognosis, prediction. *Cf.* **mialamu.**

alamsiki* *interj.* farewell, goodbye.

alamu* (—) 1. flag, banner. 2. signalling flag, warning.

alasiri* (—) 1. afternoon. 2. *Isl.* prayer (between 3 and 5 o'clock).

alau* *see* **walau.**

alfabeti* [*Engl.*] (—) alphabet. (= **herufi.**)

alfafa* (—) alfafa (cloth worn after circumcision to protect the wound).

alfajiri* (—) 1. dawn, daybreak. 2. *Isl.* prayer (at 4:00 A.M.).

alfu* *see* **elfu.**

Alhamdulillahi!* *interj.* Praise be to Allah!

Alhamisi* (—) Thursday. **— kuu.** Maundy Thursday.

alhasil*, alhasir *adv.* 1. then, thereupon; hence, consequently. 2. thus, in this way, similarly. **na —.** and so forth.

alia make marks on the body *(by a blow).*

[1]**alika** 1. splash, ripple *(of water).* 2. go off, explode *(of bombs).* 3. snap, crack. *caus.* **alisha. — vidole.** make the joints of one's fingers crack. *Cf.* [2]**mwaliko,** [2]**mwalishi.**

[2]alika 1. call, invite; challenge. **– karamuni.** invite to a feast. **– vita.** summon to battle, declare war. 2. beckon, entice. 3. inform, explain. *Cf.* **[1]mwaliko, [1]mwalishi.**

[3]alika confine *(a sick person, etc. to a house or room).*

aliki* hang, hang up; fasten, attach.

aliko (ma-) *see* **mwaliko.**

alili *adv., rare* very.

alisa (–) *rare* dancing place.

Allah* God *(usually in Arabic formulas).* **Allah akbar.** Allah is great. **la illahi ila Allah.** There is no God but Allah. **Alhamdulillahi.** Praise be to Allah. **Bismillahi.** In the name of Allah. **wallahi.** By Allah.

almari* (–) chest of drawers.

almaria*, halmaria [*Port.*] **(–)** 1. embroidery. 2. braid.

almasi*, almazi (–) 1. diamond, brilliant. 2. *pr. n. masc.*

almuradi*, mradi *conj.* then, thereupon; hence, consequently.

alowensi* [*Engl.*] **(–)** allowance. (= **kipimo.**)

alwaridi* (–) *see* **halwaridi.**

[1]ama* (*rare* **ima**) *conj.* or. **– ... –.** either ... or. **– hii – hii.** either this or that. **wa –.** yet, however. (= **au.**)

[2]ama!* 1. *interj. expressing amazement or impatience.* 2. *introduction of a question.* **–, huna habari ya baba yako?** It is true that you have no news of your father?

[3]ama *rare* lie prone.

[1]amali* (–) 1. act, action; behavior. 2. activity, work, employment. **– yao ni kujenga nyumba.** Their business is house-building. 3. occupation, business, profession, speciality. *Cf.* **amili, mwamali.**

[2]amali* (–) amali (kind of charm).

amana* (–) vow; pledge, trust, security. **weka –.** leave as a pledge, give as security. *Cf.* **[1]amini.**

amani* (–) peace, security, safety. **mapatano ya –.** peace treaty. *Cf.* **amana, [1]amini.**

amania* *liter.* trust, believe in, depend/rely on. *Cf.* **amana, [1]amini.**

amara* (–) *rare* (= **muhimu**) 1. urgent matter/business. 2. help, aid, assistance. **haja –?** Can I do something for you?

amari* [*Port.*] anchor-chain/cable.

[1]amba 1. *arch.* speak. 2. speak ill of someone, slander. **kumwamba mtu.** talk about someone behind his back. *appl.* *see* **ambia.** *Cf.* **jigamba, kigambo, mgambo, mwambaji.**

[2]**amba** *rare* be in contact, stick together, adhere. *us. intr.* **ambika.** 1. hold/stick together, cohere. 2. prepare a trap for fish; bait, lure. *inv.* *see* **ambua.** *Cf.* **ambata, ambo, ambua, ambukizo, [1]chamba, chambo, chambua, [2]gamba, ngambi, uambukizo, wamba, wambiso.**

[3]**amba** *relat. pron.* who, which, that *(in conj. w. det.).* **wale ambao wamekwenda.** those who have gone.

ambaa come near to without touching, pass by, skirt, hug *(the shore)*; avoid, escape. **waliambaa mji bila ya kuingia.** They went past the town without entering it. **waliambaa hatari.** They escaped from danger. *caus.* **ambaza.** *Cf.* **mwambao, mmwambao.**

ambari* (—) ambergris.

ambata clasp, cling, stick to, adhere. *caus.* **ambatisha.** fix, attach. *ass.* **ambatana. nguo imeambatana na kidonda.** The cloth has adhered to the wound. *Cf.* [2]**amba.**

ambia (*appl. of* [1]**amba**) 1. speak/say something to someone. 2. inform; tell, relate. *pass.* **ambiwa. nimeambiwa.** I was told. *double appl.* **ambilia.** chatter, gossip.

ambika *intr. of* [2]**amba.**

ambo (ma-) gum, glue. *Cf.* [2]**amba.**

ambua (*inv. of* [2]**amba**) 1. loosen, detach, separate, pull off. **— ngozi.** remove skin (rind, bark). **— mchungwa.** peel an orange. 2. profit, benefit. **alisoma miaka mingi lakini hana alichoambua.** He has studied for a long time, but hasn't benefited from it. *intr.* **ambuka.** *intr.-caus.* **ambukiza.** *med.* be infectious/contagious. **ugonjwa wa kuambukiza.** contagious disease. *Cf.* **ambukizo, chambua, uambukizo.**

ambukizo (ma-) *med.* infection, contagion. *Cf.* **ambua.**

amdelahane* (—) amdelahane (soft, silky material). *Cf.* **mdarahani.**

amerikani* [*Engl.*] *see* **merekani.**

ami* (—) *see* [2]**amu.**

amia* protect *(a field or garden from birds and animals).* *Cf.* **mwamizi**; *also* **hami, himaya.**

amili* 1. do, act; complete, accomplish. 2. lead, guide, steer. *Cf.* [1]**amali.**

[1]**amini*** (*also* **staamani**) 1. trust, entrust; believe; prove oneself worthy of trust. **nilimwamini na fedha yangu.** I trusted him with my money. *intr.* **aminika.** be trustworthy/reliable. **mtu huyu haaminiki.** This man is not reliable. *caus.* **aminisha.** inspire confidence, give certainty. 2. (—) faithfulness, fidelity, devotion,

reliability. 3. *adj.* (*also* **aminifu**) faithful, devoted, reliable, trustworthy. *Cf.* **amana, amani, amania, imani, mwamana, mwamini, uaminifu, toamini.**

[2]**amini*, yamini** (—) blood brother. **huyu ni amini yangu.** This man is my blood brother.

aminifu* *adj.* *see* [1]**amini** 3.

[1]**amiri*** (ma-) commander, leader, officer, colonel. **— jeshi.** leader of an army. *Cf.* **amri.**

[2]**amiri*** begin/start something. **— shamba (mji).** lay out a new field (village).

amirisho* (ma-) start, beginning. *Cf.* [2]**amiri.**

amka wake up, stir. *caus.* **amsha.** wake up, rouse. **—** (*usually* **fungua**) **kinywa.** eat breakfast. *Cf.* **amkia, changamka, kiamshakinywa, maamkio.**

amkia, amkua (*appl. of* **amka**) 1. wake up for/because of someone. 2. show someone one's respect/esteem. 3. greet someone. 4. grow light, dawn.

amkua *see* **amkia.**

amri* (—, ma-) 1. order, command, directive. **toa —.** give an order. **shika (fuata) —.** carry out an order, obey a command. 2. authority, rule, mastery, responsibility, power. **ana amri juu yao.** He has power over them. *Cf.* [1]**amiri, amuru.**

amria* *appl. of* **amuru.**

amrisha* *caus. of* **amuru.**

amriwa* *pass. of* **amuru.**

amsha *caus. of* **amka.**

[1]**Amu** (the island of) Lamu.

[2]**amu*, ami** (—) (paternal) uncle. *Cf.* **binamu.**

[1]**amua** end/settle a dispute; adjudge, decide by arbitration; reach a decision; act as an arbitrator. *appl.* **amulia.** *caus.* **amuliza.** *Cf.* **maamuzi, mwamua, uamuzi.**

[2]**amua** = **amwa.**

amulia *appl. of* [1]**amua.**

amuliza *caus. of* [1]**amua.**

amuru* 1. order, command, prescribe, decide, decree **aliniamuru niende.** He ordered me to go. 2. administer, manage, govern, lead. *appl.* **amria.** *pass.* **amriwa.** *caus.* **amrisha.** drill, train *(soldiers).* *Cf.* **amri.**

amuzi (ma-) *(us. pl.)* judgment, verdict. *Cf.* [1]**amua.**

amwa suck. *caus.* **amwisha.** nurse/suckle *(a baby).*

anana *adj.* soft, mild, gentle. **upepo mwanana.** gentle wind. *fig.* **mtu mwanana.** a gentle, modest person.

anasa* (—) 1. pleasure, joy; festive mood. 2. comfort, prosperity, luxury. **maisha ya —.** a life in easy circumstances. *Cf.* **anisi, taanasa.**

andaa prepare, make preparations; cook *(food). appl.* **andalia.** make preparations for. **waliandalia vita (kazi).** They are making preparations for war (work). *Cf.* **andao, andazi, maandalio, mwandaliaji, mwandao, mwandazi.**

andama follow, succeed; accompany. **mwezi umeandama.** new moon. *ass.* **andamana.** follow one another, go together/in a company; walk in a line or row *(procession, demonstration). Cf.* **andamano, andamo, mwandamano, mwandamo, mwandani, uandamano, uandamizi.**

andamano, andamizi (ma-) (*usually* **maandamano, maandamizi**) 1. series, sequence, succession. 2. procession, demonstration. *Cf.* **andama.**

andamizi (ma-) (*usually* **maandamizi**) *see* **andama, andamano.**

andamo *adj.* following, subsequent, consecutive. **mwezi mwandamo.** *rare* new moon. *Cf.* **andama.**

andao (ma-) (*usually* **maandao**) preparation, arrangement, provision, measure; cooking *(of food). Cf.* **andaa.**

andazi (ma-) (*usually* **maandazi**) pastry, confectionery; seasoning, garnishing; pastry/confectionery shop. *Cf.* **andaa.**

andika 1. put in order, arrange. *appl.* **andikia.** arrange something. **— meza.** set the table. 2. write; register, enter; recruit, sign on. *appl.* **andikia.** write to someone. **alimwandikia barua.** He wrote him a letter. 3. draw, sketch. **andikia picha.** draw a picture. *caus.* **andikisha.** cause to write, dictate; have the table set *(for a meal);* (*or* **jiandikisha**) register *(for voting). ass.* **andikiana.** write to each other, correspond. *ass.-caus.* **andikanya.** get each other to write. *Cf.* **andiko, maandiko, maandishi, mwandiko, mwandikaji, mwandishi, uandikishaji, uandishi.**

andikanya *ass.-caus. of* **andika.**

andiko (ma-) (*usually* **maandiko**) 1. what is written: manuscript, text, book, inscription, address, label, heading, title; *recent* (written) statement, communiqué. 2. *pl., rel.* scriptures. **Maandiko Matakatifu.** The Holy Scriptures. 3. preparation, arrangement. *Cf.* **andika.**

[1]**anga, wanga** 1. *rare* hang, be suspended, float *(in the air).* 2. bewitch, enchant, cast a spell. 3. spend the night. *Cf.* **angama, angika, angua,** [3]**chango, kiango.**

[2]**anga** (ma-) 1. brightness, radiance, brilliance. **— la jua.** sunlight. **— la mwezi.** moonlight. 2. *tech.* lighting, illumination. 3. *psych.* intuition, perception. 4. *meteor., av.* sky, space; atmosphere, weather. **hali ya anga.** weather conditions. **anga la juu.** orbit. **angani.** cosmos, space. **chombo cha**

angani. spaceship. safari ya angani. space flight. mwanaanga. cosmonaut. 5. *adj.* = angavu. *Cf.* angaa.

3anga *arch.* compute, count. (= 3wanga.)

angaa shine, be bright; give light, gleam, flash. *appl.* angalia. be alert, watch; look, observe; be careful/cautious; inspect, test, check. angalia! Look! Watch out! *caus.* & *int.* angaza. light up, illuminate; look fixedly, stare. mwezi huangaza usiku. The moon lights up the night. angaza macho. fix one's eyes on something, stare. *Cf.* 2anga, angalifu, angavu, kianga, kiangaza, maangalio, maangalizi, mwanga, mwangalifu, mwangalizi, mwangaza, uangaliaji, uangalifu, uangavu.

angaika *see* hangaika.

angalao *see* angao.

angalia *appl. of* angaa.

angalifu *adj.* cautious, careful; considerate. *Cf.* angaa.

angama (*stat. of* 1anga) hang, be suspended *(in, on)*; hover, float *(in the air)*; be caught on, be stuck/tangled. – mtini. be caught/tangled in the tree. *caus.* angamiza. cause to hang, hang up; *(fig.)* store, stockpile. *Cf.* 2uangamizi.

angamia perish, be ruined; fail, be unsuccessful; be destroyed. *caus.* angamiza. destroy, ruin. *Cf.* maangamizi, maangamizo, mwangamizi, uangamio, 1uangamizi.

angamizi (ma-) (*us. pl.*) destruction, ruin. *Cf.* angamia.

angao, angalao *conj.* 1. although, even if. nipe chakula – ni kidogo tu. Give me food even if it is only a little. 2. so that, in order that.

angavu, anga *adj.* 1. bright, gleaming, shining. 2. transparent, clear. 3. *fig.* intelligent, open-minded, clever. *Cf.* angaa.

angaza *caus.* & *int. of* angaa.

angema 1. be despondent/dejected. 2. be timid/timorous.

angika hang up *(on the wall, on a tree, etc.)*. *Cf.* 1anga, angama, angua.

-angu *poss. pron. 1st pers. sing.* my. mtoto wangu. my child. nyumba yangu. my house.

angua (*inv. of* 1anga) 1. take off/down, throw down, bring down; drop. – nazi. pick coconuts. 2. hatch. – mayai. hatch eggs. 3. pass into a state of..., fall into... – kicheko (machozi). burst out laughing, burst into tears. *appl.* angulia. *intr.* anguka. 1. fall down; drip, trickle; crash *(of an airplane)*. 2. be ruined. 3. be seized by, be overtaken by. *intr.-appl.* angukia. fall down *(into, on, before)*. angukia miguu. prostrate oneself at someone's feet. *caus.* angusha. cause to fall, fell, bring down; ruin. *Cf.* anguko, kiangushio, mwangushi.

anguka *intr. of* angua.

anguko (ma-) (*usually* **maanguko**) 1. fall, drop, collapse, crash. **maanguko ya maji.** waterfall. 2. *fig.* downfall, decay, ruin. 3. ruin(s) *(of a building, etc.).* *Cf.* **angua.**

angusha *caus. of* **angua.**

ania* 1. intend, plan, propose, have in mind. **anaania kazi ya ualimu.** He intends to become a teacher. 2. defend, fight for. **aliania maisha yake.** He fought for his life. *Cf.* **nia, nuia.**

anika, janika put out to dry/air. **– nyama (samaki).** dry meat (fish). **– nguo.** air/dry clothes. *Cf.* **anua.**

anisi* 1. (*also* **taanisi, taanasa**) please, delight, cause pleasure, be pleasing. 2. *adj.* pleasant, delightful; luxurious. *Cf.* **anasa.**

anjili* (–) *see* **injili.**

ankachifu* [*Engl.*] (–) handkerchief.

ankra* [*Ind.*] (–) 1. bill of lading; bill, invoice. 2. label, tag, ticket. 3. mortgage.

anna* [*Ind.*] (–) anna (1/16 of a rupee). *Cf.* **rupia.**

anua (*inv. of* **anika**) remove, take away *(out of the sun)*, take down washing. *intr.* **anuka.** be dry *(of washing)*. *fig.* **kumeanuka sasa.** It has stopped raining. It has cleared up.

anwani* (–) address. **andika – ya barua.** address a letter.

anza begin, start, set about (something). **– kazi.** begin to work. *appl.* **anzia.** *caus.* **anzisha,** *or double appl.-caus.* **anzilisha, anziliza.** found, establish. **anzisha chama.** found a party. *Cf.* **chanzo, maanzilisho, mwanzilishi, mwanzo, uanzishaji.**

anzali* (–) depraved/despised person.

anzilisha, anziliza *double appl.-caus. of* **anza.**

Anzwani* Anjouan (island of the Comoros).

1-ao *poss. pron. 3rd pers. plur.* their. **nchi yao.** their country. **nchi zao.** their countries.

2ao* *see* **au.**

apa swear, take an oath. **– Kurani.** swear by the Koran. *caus.* 1. **apisha,** *(rare)* **afya.** put on oath. *caus. 2. (w. int. force)* **apiza.** swear at, curse. *caus. 1-pass.* **(kw)apishwa.** be sworn in, take an oath (of office). *inv.* **apua.** break an oath. *Cf.* **apizo, kiapo, mwapaji, mwapizi, 1uapo.**

aparati* [*Germ. ?*] (–) apparatus. (= **nyambo vya kufania kazi.**)

apizo (ma-) (*us.* **maapizo**) curse, imprecation, invective. *Cf.* **apa.**

Aprili* [*Engl.*] April.

apua *inv. of* **apa.**

Arabu*: Bara Arabu. Arabia. (= **Uarabu.**) *Cf.* **Mwarabu.**

[1]**Arabuni*** (—) 1. an object of Arabian origin. 2. *sing.* Arabia. *Cf.* **Mwarabu;** *also* [2]**Manga.**

[2]**arabuni*** (—) deposit, advance *(payment).*

araka* (—) arrack; any intoxicating liquor.

arba*, aroba *arch.* four. (= **nne.**) **-a —.** fourth. **arbatashara.** fourteen. **— mia.** four hundred.

arbaini* *see* **arobaini.**

arda lay eggs.

ardhi* (—) ground, earth; (dry) land *(as opp. to sea); (rare)* world, globe.

ari* (—) 1. shame, disgrace, dishonor. 2. special effort exerted to prevent being disgraced, will to succeed/win.

aria* (—) *rare* part, section, party.

aridhia* explain, expound, demonstrate; inform, report; interpret. **aliniaridhia maneno.** He explained (interpreted) the words for me.

aridhilihali* (—) *rare, arch.* request, petition; memorandum.

arifu* 1. state, report, inform *(usually by letter);* tell, relate, say. 2. *adj.* well-informed, educated; experienced, versed, proficient. *Cf.* **maarifa, maarufu, taarifa, umaarufu.**

arithi* *rare* want, wish.

aroba *see* **arba.**

arobaini*, arubaini, arbaini 1. forty. 2. forty days of impurity of a woman after childbirth. *Cf.* **arba.**

arteri* [*Engl.*] (—) *see* **ateri.**

arubaini* *see* **arobaini.**

arufu* *see* **harufu.**

arusi*, harusi (—) wedding *(ceremony and festivity).* **bwana —.** bridegroom. **bibi —.** bride. **fanya —.** get married.

asa*, wasa forbid, prohibit; warn.

asaa* *conj., arch.* if.

asali* (—) honey, syrup. **— ya nyuki.** honey. **— ya miwa.** molasses. *prov.* **fuata nyuki ukale —.** Follow the bee and you will get (eat) honey. (= Attach yourself to the right friend.)

asante*, ahsante thanks. **— sana.** Thank you very much. **toa (sema) —.** thank.

asfari* *adj. rare* yellow. (= **kimanjano.**)

asha *caus. of* [2]**aka.**

ashakum* Excuse it. Pardon the expression. *(Used in apology for a vulgar word or expression).*

ashara* *arch.* ten. (= **kumi.**)

asharati* (–) *see* **asherati.**

ashekali* 1. *rare* improvement. **ona –.** note improvement. 2. *adj.* better, improved *(after an illness).*

asherati*, asharati (–) 1. dissipation, debauch, excess; prodigality, waste; amusement, good time. 2. adultery, immorality, fornication. *Cf.* **mwasherati, uasherati.**

asherini* *see* **ishirini.**

ashiki*, ashki 1. be in love, love passionately, have a passion for, be enamored of. 2. (–) love, passionate desire; feeling, affection, fondness; yearning, longing. **tia –.** evoke affection/yearning. *Cf.* **shauku.**

ashiria* signal, inform promptly, give someone an indication/warning. *Cf.* **ishara.**

ashki* *see* **ashiki.**

asi*, aasi 1. be disobedient, not meet an obligation; revolt, rebel. **wameasia serikali yao.** They have rebelled against their government. *caus.* **asisha.** incite to rebellion, stir up, agitate. 2. (ma-) *(us. pl.)* revolt, rebellion. *Cf.* **maasi, mwasi, uasi.**

asikari* (–) *see* **askari.**

asili* (–) 1. beginning; origin, source, home; foundation, basis; *(gramm.)* root; *(math.)* denominator. 2. ancestor, forebear; descent, ancestry. 3. nature, temperament. 4. essence, basic principle; reason (for something). 5. *adv.* originally, from the beginning, by nature; in old times. **babu –.** of original/proved quality. 6. *adj.:* **-a –.** original. *Cf.* **asilia.**

asilia* *adj.* original, genuine, real, true. *Cf.* **asili.**

asisha* *caus. of* [1]**asi.**

asisiwa found, establish; appoint. *pass.* **asiswa.** be named/appointed.

askafu* (ma-) *see* **askofu.**

askari*, asikari (–) 1. warrior, soldier, military man. 2. guard, overseer. **– polisi.** policeman. **– jela.** prison guard. **– kanzu.** local constable/constabulary *(wearing* **kanzu** *rather than uniform).* **– wapanda farasi.** cavalry. *Cf.* **uaskari.**

askofu*, askafu (ma-) bishop. **– mkuu.** archbishop. **– msaidizi.** auxiliary bishop. *Cf.* **uaskofu.**

askut!* Be still! Silence! *Cf.* **sukutu.**

aspirini* [*Engl.*] (–) *pharm.* aspirin.

astahili* *see* **stahili.**

aste* [*Ind.*] *adv., rare* slowly. (= **polepole.**)

asubuhi*, asubui, asubukhi 1. (–) morning. **– na mapema.** in the early morning. **tangu – hata jioni.** from morning to evening. 2. *adv.* in the morning. *Cf.* **sabahi.**

asubui* (–) *see* **asubuhi.**

asusa* (–) 1. meat dish. 2. something eaten when one is drinking alcoholic beverages.

ata* *see* **acha.**

atamia, tamia, latamia brood, hatch *(eggs). caus.* **atamisha, atamiza.**

ateri*, arteri [*Engl.*] 1. *anat.* artery. 2. *fig.* arterial road, main route.

athari* (–) 1. mark, spot, blemish. 2. scratch, abrasion, wound, scar, sore. 3. *fig.* fault, defect, mistake, omission, deficiency. **ana – ya jicho.** He has only one eye *(euph.)*. 4. influence. 5. *v.:* **(ku)athari.** to influence. *Cf.* **athiri.**

athiri* damage, injure, destroy, disfigure, deface. *pass.* **athiriwa.** be corrupted. *Cf.* **athari.**

ati!, eti! *interj.* 1. *exclamation to attract attention:* Hey! Hey there! **– wewe!** Hey, you! 2. *exclamation introducing a statement:* Say..., Listen... **–! yasemwa watu wale ni wageni!** Say, they tell me those people are strangers. 3. *in requests for for repetition:* **– umesema nini?** What did you say?

atia* *see* **[1]hatia.**

atibu* scold, swear, abuse, insult; blame, find fault with, criticize, reprimand; be dissatisfied. *appl.* **atibia.** *intr.* **atibika.**

atika replant, transplant, plant out *(seedlings, cuttings).*

atikali* *rare* understand, know; estimate.

atilika* *rare* be injured, deformed *(after an accident or illness).*

Atlantiki* [*Engl.*] (–) *geogr.* Atlantic (Ocean).

atlasi* (–) silk cloth. **nguo ya –.** satin.

atomiki* [*Engl.*] *adj.* **–a –.** (*or* **kiatomik**). atomic, nuclear. **bomu la –.** atomic bomb.

atua split, chop *(wood);* tear, crack. *intr.* **atuka.** be split, torn. **nchi imeatuka kwa joto la jua.** The ground is cracked from the heat of the sun. *Cf.* **mwatuko.**

au*, ao *conj.* or. **– ... –.** either ... or. (= **ama.**)

aua 1. inspect, examine, investigate, check on. **– skuli.** inspect a school. 2. survey, mark out, lay out. **– shamba.** survey (mark out) a field. *appl.* **aulia.** *intr.* **auka.** *caus.* **auza** *or* **ausha.**

auka *rare* develop, open up *(plants).*

aula* *adj.* better, superior, more important, more suitable. **jambo hili ni aula...** This matter is better (more important)... **si —.** It is unimportant/inconsequential.

auni*, awuni, awini 1. help, assist, support. *appl.* **aunia.** *intr.* **aunika.** *caus.* **aunisha.** 2. *rare* help, assistance, support. *Cf.* **muawana.**

aunsi* [*Engl.*] (—) ounce (= 28.3 gr.).

auradi* *see* **uradi.**

ausha *caus. of* **aua.**

aushi* (—) *rare* 1. life. 2. permanence, durability. **vyungu vya —.** durable pottery. *Cf.* **ishi.**

ausi *see* **eusi.**

auwali* (—) *see* **awali.**

auza *caus. of* **aua.**

avya *dial.* destroy, waste; squander. **— fedha (mali).** squander money (property).

awa *dial.* go out, go away.

awadha*, awaza *rare* assign, allot; arrange, organize. *Cf.* **mwawazi.**

awali*, auwali 1. (—) beginning, start, inception. **tangu — hata aheri.** from beginning to end. *prov.* **— ni —, hakuna — mbovu.** Take the first or nothing. 2. *adj.* & *adv.* in the first place, at first, in the beginning; earlier, formerly; almost, nearly. 3.: **—** *ya nchi.* border/boundary/frontier of a country *(i.e., where the country begins;* = **asili, mwanzo, kwanza).**

awaza* *see* **awadha.**

awesia* (—) awesia (kind of dhow).

awini* *see* **auni.**

awuni* *see* **auni.**

[1]**aya*** (—) section, part, paragraph *(of a book),* verse *(esp. of the Koran).*

[2]**aya*** (—) (children's) nurse(maid). (= [1]**mlezi.**)

ayala* (—) stag, hart.

[1]**ayari*, ajari** (—) cheat, swindler, rascal, scoundrel. *prov.* **mwangalie — huyu aliyeko mtini.** Watch out for the scoundrel who is in the tree.

[2]**ayari** (—) *naut.* 1. anchor chain. 2. rope for hoisting a sail. 3. pulley, block.

aye *arch.* thank you. (= **asanti.**)

aza *see* **waza.**

azali* *adj., rel.* eternal, without beginning.

azama* (—) *arch.* nose ring.

[1]**azima*** (—) talisman, charm; magic.

2azima lend, borrow; borrow something from someone *(without leaving an equivalent or furnishing security)*. *appl.* **azimia.** *Cf.* **maazimo, mwazimo, uazimaji.**

3azima* (ma-) *rare* = **azimio.**

azimio* (ma-) (*usually* **maazimio**) 1. intention, purpose, resolution; motive. 2. proposal, scheme, project, plan. 3. *parl.* motion. **– la kutokuwa na imani.** no-confidence motion. *Cf.* **azimu.**

azimo (ma-) (*usually* **maazimo**) something borrowed or lent: loan, debt. *Cf.* **azima.**

azimu* 1. do magic, cast spells. 2 intend, determine, propose. *Cf.* **azimio (maazimio).**

aziri* *see* **adhiri.**

azizi* 1. (–) rarity, treasure. 2. *adj.* rare; dear, esteemed *(persons)*.

azur* (–) *see* **2zuri.**

B

baa*, balaa, balia (–) 1. evil; disaster, disturbance, calamity, catastrophe. **mvua hii imetuletea baa na balaa.** This rain has led to a great catastrophe. 2. pestilence, epidemic. 3. person who creates trouble or does damage.

baada* *prep.* after, behind (*usually* **– ya** after). **– ya miaka mingi.** after many years. **– ya kazi.** after work. *Cf.* **baidi.**

baadaye* (< **baada yake**) *adv. & conj.* thereafter, afterwards, after, then; next.

baadhi* (–) part, section *(of a larger whole or number)*; (small) amount/quantity, some. **– ya watu.** some of the people. **Wanafunzi wamegawanyika – mbili.** The students are divided into two sections.

baathi*, buathi *rare* set up, place upright.

1baba (–) 1. father, (paternal) uncle. **– mkubwa (mdogo).** uncle (older/younger brother of one's father). **– Mtakatifu.** Holy Father, Pope. 2. ancestor, forebear. 3. patron, protector. 4. guard, watchman. *Cf.* **ubaba;** *also* **1babu.**

2baba *rare* fasten/tie tightly.

babaika, babayika 1. stutter, stammer *(from fear)*. 2. talk deliriously, rave *(in a fever, etc.)*. *caus.* **babaisha.** deceive, swindle, cheat. *Cf.* **babaiko, ubabaiko.**

babaiko, babayiko (ma-) meaningless words, nonsense; confused/unintelligible explanation. *Cf.* **babaika.**

babaisha *caus. of* **babaika.**

babaje (–) babaje (large marine snail).

babaka 1. prove; argue; convince. 2. fight, struggle.

babakabwela *sing.* proletariat.

babale [?] *adv.* just, then.

babata strike lightly, tap; hammer *(metal)*. *intr.* **babatika.** (**– mbawa**) flutter, beat *(with the wings)*.

babayika *see* **babaika.**

babayiko (ma-) *see* **babaiko.**

babewatoto, babewana (–) *ornith.* (species of) owl.

babia overfeed (someone).

[1]**babu (–, ma-)** 1. grandfather. 2. ancestor, forbear, patriarch. **Mababu wa Kanisa.** the Fathers of the Church. 3. respectful term of address for an old man. *Cf.* [1]**baba.**

[2]**babu* (–)** kind, sort, category; character, quality. **– kubwa (ndogo)** of superior (inferior) quality (character).

babua pull off, strip off, remove *(skin, rind)*; clean, polish. *appl.* **babulia.** *intr.* **babuka.** suffer from a disfiguring skin disease.

[1]**badala* (–)** substitute, replacement, representation. **– ya.** instead of. *Cf.* **badili.**

[2]**badala*** [*Ind.* ?] Badala (name of an Indian sect).

badani*, bidani (–) badani (front or back piece of a kanzu, *q.v.*).

badhiri*, badiri 1. embezzle, misappropriate, defalcate; squander *(money, property)*. 2. *adj. also* **badhirifu** wasteful, extravagant. *Cf.* **badhirifu, budhara, mbadhiri, ubadirifu.**

badhirifu* *adj.* wasteful, extravagant. *Cf.* **badhiri, ubadhirifu.**

badili* 1. change, exchange. **– shauri.** change one's mind. **– hewa.** have a change of air (rest, recuperation). **– fedha.** change money. **– nguo.** change clothes. *appl.* **badilia.** *intr.* **badilika.** *int.* **badilibadili.** 2. **(ma-)** change, alteration, modification; exchange; innovation. *Cf.* [1]**badala, badilifu, badiliko, mbadilishaji, ubadilifu, ubadilishaji.**

badilifu* *adj.* exchangeable, interchangeable; changeable, inconstant; *fig.* unstable, whimsical. *Cf.* **badili, ubadilifu.**

badiliko*, badilisho (*usually* **mabadiliko, mabadilisho**) (ma-) change, alteration, variation, transformation *(conditions, customs, practices). Cf.* **badili.**

badilisho* (ma-) *see* **badiliko.**

[1]**badiri*** (–) 1. *meteor.* celestial phenomenon. 2. omen.

[2]**badiri*** *see* **badhiri.**

bado* *adv.* 1. still. **huyu ni mtoto –.** He is still a child. 2. not yet *(usually w. the negative particle* -ja-*).* **hawajafika –.** They have not yet arrived.

bafe (–) poisonous snake, puff adder *(Bitis arietans).*

bafta*, bafuta (–) bafta (thin, bleached cotton cloth, used for lining clothes).

[1]**bafu*** [*Engl.*] (–) bathtub, bath.

[2]**bafu** (ma-) *see* **pafu.**

bafuta* (–) *see* **bafta.**

bagala* [*Ind.*] (–) bagala (sailing vessel with large stern, usually two-masted).

bagawa use indecent/filthy language.

baghairi*, minghairi 1. *prep., conj.* without, apart from, except. 2. *adv.* exclusively. *Cf.* **ghairi.**

baghala* (–) mule. (= **nyumbu**).

baghami* 1. (–) fool, stupid person. 2. *adj.* foolish, stupid.

bagua separate, detach; discriminate, segregate; divide up; lay aside, put away. *appl.* **bagulia.** *appl.-intr.* **bagulika.** be separated/divided; in disagreement/conflict. *intr.* **baguka.** *intr.-ass.* **bagukana.** dispute with one another; be opposed to one another in hostile camps, be divided *(into parties, factions). Cf.* **ubaguzi.**

bahameli*, mahameli (–) velvet, corduroy.

bahari* (–) 1. sea, ocean. **– ya Sham.** Red Sea. **– ya Atlantiki.** Atlantic Ocean. **– ya Arktiki.** Arctic Ocean. **– ya Hindi.** Indian Ocean. **– Nyeusi.** Black Sea. **– ya Pasifiki.** Pacific Ocean. **safiri/safari (ya) baharini.** navigation. 2. *fig.* something vast or immeasurable. *Cf.* **baharia, ubaharia.**

baharia* (ma-) sailor, seaman. (= **mwanamaji.**) *Cf.* **bahari, ubaharia.**

bahasa* *adj.* cheap, reasonable *(in price),* worth the money.

bahasha* (–, ma-) 1. envelope. 2. bag, sack. 3. package, bundle.

bahashika* be deceived/embarrassed/ confused.

bahati*, bakhti (–) 1. luck, fortune; success. **– nasibu.** lottery. **– njema.** good luck, success. **– mbaya.** bad luck, misfortune. **ana bahati.** He has good luck. He is successful. **hana bahati.** He is unlucky/unsuccessful. 2. lot, fate, destiny. 3. chance, accident. 4. **-a –.** fortunate; *(comm.)* adventuristic. *Cf.* **bahatika, bahatisha, bahatisho.**

bahatika* be lucky/fortunate. *Cf.* **bahati.**

bahatisha* try one's fortune, trust to luck; guess, speculate, hazard. *Cf.* **bahati.**

bahatisho* (–) 1. guesswork. 2. *comm.* adventurism. *Cf.* **bahati, bahatisha.**

bahili* 1. (–, ma-) miser. *prov.* **mali ya – huliwa na wadudu.** The property of a miser is apt to be eaten by insects. 2. *adj.* miserly, parsimonious, stingy, frugal. *Cf.* **ubahili.**

baidi* be apart/separated; be by oneself/ distant/remote. *caus.* **baidisha.** separate, segregate; avoid. *Cf.* **baada.**

baina*, bayana (–) clarity, certainty, incontrovertible fact. **– ya.** between, among, in the midst of. **– ya Tanga na Daressalam.** between Tanga and Dar es Salaam. **– ya watu.** among the people. *Cf.* **baini.**

baini*, bayini 1. see clearly, recognize, know with certainty. **yule mwuaji sasa amebaini.** That murderer is now recognized. 2. make clear, show. *intr.* **bainika** and *intr.-ass.* **bainikana.** be clear/obvious/ irrefutable. *Cf.* **baina, bainifu, bayana, mbayana, ubainifu.**

bainifu* *adj.* clear, plain, apparent, obvious, evident, manifest, generally known. *Cf.* **baini.**

baisikeli*, baiskeli [*Engl.*] (–) bicycle.

baiskeli* (–) *see* **baisikeli.**

bajia* [*Ind.*] bajia (small cake made of flour, ground beans, and pepper).

Bajuni, Bajun (ma-) member of the Bajuni tribe, native of the coast north of Mombasa.

baka* (ma-) mark on the body, birthmark; scar; ringworm; marking *(of animals)*, *(fig.)* stigma.

bakhshishi* (–) *see* **bakshishi.**

bakhti* (–) *see* **bahati.**

baki* 1. remain, be left over, remain behind. *appl.* **bakia.** *caus.* **bakisha, bakiza.** 2. (ma-) remainder, residue, remnant; *(math.)* remainder *(in subtraction)*, balance. 3. *n. & adj.* neutrality, impartiality; neutral, impartial. **mtu –.** a neutral/impartial person *(in a quarrel, etc.)* **siasa ya –.** *pol.* (policy of) neutrality.

bakiza* *caus. of* **baki.**

bakora* (–) 1. stick; walking-stick, cane. **– ya kiaskofu.** *rel.* crozier. 2. blow *(with a stick).* 3. fee *(given by a father to the master who teaches his son a trade).*

bakshishi*, bakhshishi (–) gratuity, gift, alms, tip, donation, bonus.

bakua *see* **bakwia.**

bakuli* (–) (*also* **kibakuli, vi-**) basin, deep dish, tureen. **kibakuli cha chumvi.** saltcellar.

bakwia, bakua take by force, rob, plunder. *Cf.* **ubakuaji.**

balaa* (–) *see* **baa**

balamwezi (–) *see* **mbalamwezi.**

balanga (–) *see* **mbalanga.**

balari* (–) (kind of) chisel.

[1]**balasi*** (–, ma-) balasi (large jug for storing water).

[2]**balasi*** (–) *see* **barasi.**

balbu* [*Engl.*] (–) (electric-light) bulb.

bale (ma-) *augment. of* **ubale** (*larger than* [2]**mbale**).

balegi* *see* **balehe.**

balehe*, balegi 1. be ready for marriage, reach puberty. 2. *bot.* reach the fruit-bearing stage. 3. (ma-) (*also* **mbalehe, wa-**) girl or boy at the age of puberty. **mtoto huyu sasa –.** This girl is now at the age of puberty. *Cf.* **ubalehe.**

[1]**bali*** *conj.* but, however, on the contrary.

[2]**bali*** [*Ind.*] (–) earring.

balia* (–) *see* **baa.**

balozi* (ma-) 1. *hist.* administrator, political agent. 2. representative of a foreign country (ambassador, minister, consul). *Cf.* **ubalozi.**

balungi* [*Ind. Pers. ?*] (–) grapefruit. *Cf.* **mbalungi.**

[1]**bamba** (–) *rare* discussion; affair, matter; advice. (= **shauri.**)

[2]**bamba** 1. arrest, catch, detain. 2. resist, oppose.

[3]**bamba** (ma-) 1. any thin, flat object: sheet metal, cardboard, paper. **– la chuma.** sheet of metal. **– la kobe.** shell of a tortoise. 2. *rare* tin *(container, for gasoline, etc.). Cf.* [1]**bambo,** [2]**bambo,** [2]**mbamba, ubamba, ubambo.**

bambika dip, soak, steep *(in water).*

[1]**bambo** (–) 1. sampling rod *(for examining the contents of sacks).* 2. walking-stick. *Cf.* [3]**bamba.**

[2]**bambo** (ma-) strip of palm-leaf *(used to weave baskets and mats). Cf.* [3]**bamba.**

bambua peel/strip off.

bamia* (ma-) *bot.* okra (lady's fingers, fruit of the mbamia, *Hibiscus esculentus).*

bamvua (ma-) spring-tide.

bana press, squeeze, pinch, crush. *intr.* **banika.** be fixed *(meat, fish)* on a spit; *(w. trans. force)* roast *(on a spit, at a fire),* toast. *caus.* **banza.** *inv.* **banua.** loosen, release pressure, separate, take apart. **– miguu.** spread the legs. *Cf.* **bano, banzi, kibaniko, kibanzi, mbano.**

banada*, **banaderi** [*Pers. ?*] (–) 1. Somali Coast. 2. ports on the coast north of Mombasa. *Cf.* **bandari.**

banaderi* (–) *see* **banada.**

banagiri* (–) *see* **bangili.**

banajili* (–) *see* **bangili.**

Banawasi* *see* **Abunuwasi.**

1**banda** (ma-) 1. hut, shed. 2. workshop, factory. 3. stable. **– la farasi.** horse stable. **– la motakaa.** garage. **– la gari.** railway station. **– la ndege.** hangar. **– la starehe.** shed erected on plantations as a rest place for workers. *Cf.* **kibanda.**

2**banda** (–) flower-stem of the coconut palm.

bandama (–) *anat.* spleen. (= **wengu.**)

bandari*, **bendari** [*Pers.*] (–) harbor, port, anchorage, roadstead. **bandari ya mto.** river port. *Cf.* **mbandarini.**

bandera* (–) *see* **bendera.**

bandi (ma-) stitch *(in sewing);* a row of stitches. **fanya (shona) –.** stitch, sew.

bandia* [*Ind., Ar. ?*] (–) 1. bolt of cloth. 2. **mtoto wa –.** doll.

bandika 1. fit together, join, connect, fasten to, attach, stick on, affix, fasten/ glue down. **– stempu.** affix a stamp. **– dawa.** apply a plaster. 2. *fig.* attach oneself to someone. **amejibandika kwa fulani.** He has taken up with X. 3. load (up). **– mzigo.** put on a load. *caus.* **bandikisha, bandikiza.** *inv.* **bandua.** loosen, remove, strip off (bark, skin). *Cf.* **mbandiko, mbanduko.**

bandikiza *caus. of* **bandika.**

1**bandua** *inv. of* **bandika.**

2**bandua** chop up *(wood).*

banduru* (–) *naut.* bilge, ship's well.

bange (–) bange (kind of fish).

bangi* [*Ind.*] (–) hemp, hashish. **vuta –.** smoke hashish.

bangili*, **banagiri, banajili** [*Ind.*] (–) (chased silver) bracelet. **– za mguu.** ankle ring.

bango (ma-) 1. broad part of the palm-leaf stem. 2. fender, mud-guard *(bicycle, automobile)*. 3. placard, sign.

banguzi (ma-) (large) wound, sore, abscess.

baniani (ma-) *see* **banyani**.

banika (*intr. of* **bana**.) roast, toast. *Cf.* **kibaniko**.

banja crack *(nuts, etc.)*, break, break open. *Cf.* **mbanjo**.

banki* (–) *see* **benki**.

bano (ma-) clamp, vise, press. *Cf.* **bana**.

banua *inv. of* **bana**.

banyani*, **baniani** [*Ind.*] (–) Hindu *(neither Moslem nor Christian)*; Banyan, (Indian) small retail tradesman, craftsman *(carpenter, tinsmith, barber)*.

banza *caus. of* **bana**.

banzi (ma-) 1. rod, pole; spit *(for roasting meat)*. 2. peg, pin; stick of wood. 3. *med.* splint. *Cf.* **bana**.

bao, **bau** (ma-) (*also* **mbao**, **mi-**) 1. board, plank. **– la kuruka**. diving-board, trampoline. 2. divining board. **piga –**. prophesy, tell fortunes. 3. **bao** *or* **bao la mtaji**. game played on a board. 4. *fig.*, *sport* goal, score. **tuliwafunga** (*coll.* **tuliwapiga**) **mabao sita**. We scored six goals. 5. platform *(at railroad stations)*. *Cf.* **kibao**, **kimbaombao**, **ubao**.

bapa (ma-) 1. flat or slightly curved surface. **– la mpanga**. flat (side) of a sword. **– la kisu**. blade of a knife. 2. *adj.* flat, level. **sura –**. level surface. *Cf.* **ubapa**.

bara* (–) 1. land, mainland, interior *(as opp. to coast)*. 2. territory, continent. **– ya Afrika (Ulaya)**. continent of Africa (Europe). **– Arabu**. Arabia.

baraba* *see* [2]**barabara**.

[1]**barabara*** 1. (–) wide road, highway. **kanuni za barabarani**. traffic regulations. *av.* runway, landing strip. 2. *coll.* prostitute.

[2]**barabara***, **baraba** [*Pers.*] *adj. & adv.* proper, right, regular, correct.

baradhuli*, **bardhuli** (–, ma-) 1. ordinary person. 2. stupid person, fool. 3. rascal. 4. fop, dandy. *Cf.* **ubaradhuli**.

barafu* [*Pers.*] (–) ice. **mto wa –**. glacier.

baragumu* (–, ma-) 1. horn (used as an instrument for giving signals, 'warhorn'). 2. name of a newspaper appearing in Tanganyika.

baraji* (–) *naut.* halyard.

baraka* (–) 1. blessing, benefaction. 2. fortune, luck. **hana –**. He has had bad luck. 3. prosperity, advantage. 4. *rare* gift. *Cf.* **bariki**, **kibaraka**, **tabaruki**.

barakinya* [*Port.*] (–) *rare, naut.* brig, schooner.

barakoa* (–) veil, mask.

barangeni*, **burangeni** [*Pers.*] (–) two-colored dhow.

barare (–) *see* **parare.**

barasati* [*Ind.*] (–) multicolored woven fabric.

barasi*, **balasi** (–) *med.* eruption, rash; leprosy.

barawaji* [*Ind.*] (–) barawaji (fabric with gold threads).

baraza* (–) 1. *orig.* reception room, entrance hall. 2. *recent* assembly, meeting; council, committee. **– ya mawaziri.** cabinet *(of ministers).* **– la kufanya sheria.** legislative assembly. **– la Amani la Dunia.** World Peace Council. **– la Usalama.** Security Council. **– kuu.** parliament. **– Kuu la Jumuiya ya Madola.** General Assembly of the United Nations. 3. members of a council or cabinet; elders of a tribe. *Cf.* **barizi.**

barazahi* (–) *rel.* paradise. (= **peponi, ferdausi.**)

bardhuli* (--, ma-) *see* **baradhuli.**

baridi* (–) 1. cold, frost; damp. **vita –.** cold war. **pata –.** catch cold. **ugonjwa wa –.** cold, chill, ague. 2. wind, air. 3. coolness, refreshment. 4. *fig.* mildness, gentleness. **maneno ya –.** gentle words. 5. *med.* (intermittent) fever. **– yabis(i).** rheumatism. *Cf.* **buruda, burudi, kiburudishaji, kiburudisho, maburudisho, ubaridi, uburudisho.**

bariki* bless; bloom, thrive, prosper, be successful. *appl.* **barikia.** 1. bless someone. 2. accept a final bid, knock down *(at an auction). pass.* **barikiwa.** be approved/ratified *(by a government). Cf.* **baraka.**

bariyo* (–) leftover *(food saved for the following morning).*

barizi* 1. receive guests, give an audience; convene a council. 2. attend a meeting. 3. sit (together) out of doors. *appl.* **barizia.** *ass.* **bariziana.** *Cf.* **baraza.**

barua* (–) 1. letter, document. **– ya ndege.** airmail letter. **– ya mtengenezaji.** editorial, leading article. **andikiana –.** correspond (with each other). 2. document, testimonial, certificate. **– ya fedha.** (postal) money-order. *Cf.* **kibarua.**

barubaru* (ma-) vigorous young man. *Cf.* **beberu**(?).

barudi* (–) *see* **baruti.**

baruti*, **barudi** [*Turk.*] (–) gunpowder.

bas* *see* [1]**basi.**

basbas* (–) *see* **basibasi.**

basbasi* = **basibasi.**

basha* [*Turk.*] (–) *cards* king.

bashiri* 1. predict, announce; interpret. 2. report, bring news; deliver, convey *(a report, news).* – **heri**! I hope it is good news. *Cf.* **mbashiri, ubashiri.**

[1]**basi*, bassi, bas** *conj.* 1. *at the beginning of a clause:* well, and then, so. – **twende.** Well, let's go. 2. *alone:* very well, agreed, OK; stop.

[2]**basi*** [*Engl.*] (ma-) (motor)bus.

basibasi* (–) nutmeg *(the spice). Cf.* **kungumanga, mkungumanga.**

bassi* *see* [1]**basi.**

bastola*, pistola [*Port.*] (–) pistol, revolver.

basua* (–) confusion *(of ideas),* weakness *(of intellect). Cf.* **mbasua.**

bata (ma-) 1. duck. – **Bukini.** goose. – **mzinga.** turkey. 2. (*also* **batabata, batua**) walk like a duck, waddle, walk flatfooted.

batabata *see* **bata** 2.

batela*, betela [*Port. ?*] (–) batela (small boat).

bateri* (–) *see* **betri.**

bathdei* [*Engl.*] (–) birthday.

bati (ma-) 1. tin, zinc. **tia –.** coat or line with tin. 2. sheet-metal, galvanized iron, corrugated iron. **nyumba ya – (mabati).** corrugated-iron hut. **fundi wa –.** sheet-metal worker.

batili* 1. revoke, declare invalid, cancel, annul. *appl.* **batilia.** *caus.* **batilisha.** 2. (*also* **batilifu**) *adj.* invalid, worthless, ineffective; dishonest, insincere, deceitful. *Cf.* **mbatilifu, ubatili.**

batilifu *see* **batili** 2.

batini* (–) *rare* innermost thoughts/intentions.

batiza* [*Engl.*] *rel.* baptize. *Cf.* **mbatizaji, ubatizo.**

batli* (–) *naut.* (ship's) log(-book).

bato (ma-) 1. *med.* ringworm *(on the head).* 2. spot, mark *(on the skin).*

[1]**batobato** (ma-) (*also* **kibatobato,** vi-) marking(s), spot, stripe *(of animals).*

[2]**batobato** (ma-) open, level place; *(rare)* dancing place.

batua *see* **bata** 2.

bau (ma-) *see* **bao.**

baura* [*Engl.* bower ?] (–) anchor *(with two flukes).*

[1]bavu, mbavu (ma-) strength, power; force, violence. *coll.* usiniletee –! Don't force me!

[2]bavu (ma-) *augment. of* ubavu.

bavuni, ubavuni *adv.* along, alongside, sidewards, at the side; on the other side. *Cf.* ubavu.

bawa (ma-) (*augment. of* ubawa) wing *(of a bird or airplane)*.

bawaba* (ma-) hinge *(of a door, etc.)*. *Cf.* bawabu.

bawabu* (ma-) doorkeeper, porter. – wa gereza. guard in a prison. *Cf.* bawaba, ubawabu.

bawasili*, bawasiri (–) *med.* hemorrhoids, piles.

bawasiri (–) *see* bawasili.

baya 1. *adj.* bad, evil, wicked. mtu mbaya. bad person. chakula kibaya. bad food. 2. *adv.* vibaya, kubaya. leo – nje. The weather is bad today. 3. (ma-) *see* mabaya. *Cf.* ubaya.

[1]bayana* *adj., adv.* clear, plain, obvious; legible; well-known, famous. *Cf.* baina, baini, mbayana.

[2]bayana* (–) *see* baina.

bayini* *see* baini.

bazazi* (ma-), mbazazi (wa-) 1. dealer, trader; speculator, gambler. 2. cheat, sharper, swindler. *Cf.* ubazazi.

beba 1. carry, transport *(in gen.)*. *caus.* bebesha. put a load on the back/head; *(fig.)* steal, swipe. 2. *recent* tune *(a radio, etc.)*.

bebea *see* pepea.

beberu 1. (ma-) billy goat; male animal *(especially of certain domestic varieties)*; *(fig.)* strong man. 2. *adj.* hard, strong; *recent* dictatorial, imperialistic. serikali ya kibeberu. dictatorial government. *Cf.* ubeberu, barubaru (?).

bebesha *caus. of* beba.

bedani*, behedani [*Pers.*] (–) 1. bedani (sticky substance used for dressing women's hair). 2. seed of the bedani plant.

bedari *see* habedari.

bedawi (ma-) *see* bedui.

bedeni* (ma-) bedeni (Arab sailing vessel with cut-water and sharp stern).

bedui*, bedawi (ma-) 1. bedouin, nomad. 2. vagrant, tramp.

bee *see* labeka.

bega (ma-) shoulder *(of man or animal)*. chukua begani. carry on the shoulder.

– kwa –. shoulder to shoulder, hand in hand, closely (inter-)connected, inseparable.

begi* [*Engl.*] (–) bag, sack.

behedani (–) *see* **bedani.**

behewa* (ma-) 1. *orig.* inner court of Arab houses. 2. empty space *(in gen.).* **nyumba hii ni –.** This house consists of a single room *(i.e., is not divided up by partitions).* 3. railroad car. **– la abiria (bidhaa).** passenger (freight) car. 4. storage area.

bei* (–) value, price. **fanya –.** set a price. **pandisha –.** push up the price. **piga –.** bargain, dicker. **hati ya –.** bill of sale, contract.

beit* *rare* house. **– al mal.** treasury.

beja scorn, disdain, treat with contempt. *Cf.* **beza.**

beki* [*Engl.*] (ma-) *sport* back.

bekua 1. keep off, divert. **– mpira.** (receive and) return a ball. **lazima ubekue mbu.** Mosquitos must be kept off. 2. treat with contempt. 3. take by force.

belaghami*, belghami, belghamu (–) 1. mucus, saliva, phlegm. 2. *med.* discharge, excretion.

beled* (–) *see* **buldani.**

beleko (ma-) *see* **mbeleko.**

belenga strut, show off; boast, brag.

belewasi* (–) kind of ape.

belghamu* (–) *see* **belaghami.**

beluwa* [*Ind., Pers. ?*] (–) difficulty, trouble, care, worry.

bemba 1. carry tales, meddle in someone's affairs. 2. flatter; wheedle, coax; flirt. 3. annoy, pester. *appl.* **bembea.** *double appl.-int.* **bembeleza.** pet, caress *(a child); (fig.)* coax, persuade. *Cf.* **bembe, bembejea, [1]mbembe, ubembelezi.**

bembe (ma-) confectionery, dessert *(presented as a gift during Ramadhan and on visits).* *Cf.* **bemba.**

bembea *rare* *see* **pembea.**

bembejea obtain by coaxing; curry favor, ingratiate oneself. *Cf.* **bemba.**

bendari* (–) *see* **bandari.**

bendera*, bandera [*Port.*] (–) flag, banner. **tweka –.** hoist the flag. **bendera hufuata upepo.** The flag flutters in the wind. *fig.* **yeye ni – hufuata upepo.** He turns like a flag in the wind (= he is fickle/unreliable).

bendi*, beni [*Engl.*] (–) (jazz-)band, orchestra.

beneti* [*Engl.*] (–) bayonet. (= **singe.**)

bengi* (–) *see* **benki.**

beni* (–) *see* **bendi.**

benibeni* sideways, edgeways; askew, wrong, amiss.

benki*, banki, bengi [*Engl.*] (–) (savings-) bank. **– ya shirika.** cooperative bank. **– ya akiba kwa njia ya posta.** postal savings bank. **– ya ugawaji.** bank of issue.

benua, binua stick out, protrude, put forward. **– kifua.** throw out one's chest, swagger. *appl.* **benulia.** *caus.* **benusha.** *Cf.* **mbenuko, mbinu.**

benusha *caus. of* **benua.**

bepari* [*Ind.*] (ma-) *rare* (dishonest) merchant; hoarder, monopolist. *Cf.* **kibepari, ubepari.**

bera despise, scorn, disdain; treat disdainfully, contemptuously.

beramu* [*Port.*] (–) flag. (= **bendera.**)

berenge* (ma-) *rare.* railway car. *Cf.* **kiberenge.**

beresati* [*Ind.*] (–) beresati (kind of cloth).

bereu* [*Port.*] (–, ma-) 1. *orig.* mixture of oil and lime for caulking boats. 2. *mod.* tar, asphalt, pitch.

beseni* [*Engl.*] (–) basin, dish.

besera* [*Ind.*] (–) besera (frame for mosquito-netting).

bet* (–) *see* **beti.**

betabeta twist, wind, meander *(of a road or river);* turn, rotate.

betela* (–) *see* **batela.**

beteri* (–) *see* **betri.**

[1]**beti*, bet** (–) *rare* house. *Cf.* **ubeti.**

[2]**beti*** *pl. of* **ubeti.**

[3]**beti*** [*Engl.* belt ?] (ma-) (cartridge) pouch.

betri*, beteri [*Engl.*] (–) *elec.* battery.

beua scorn, disdain, despise; disregard, slight; detest, abhor; displease, offend. *appl.* **beulia.** *caus.* **beusha.**

beusha *caus. of* **beua.**

beza think little of, scorn, despise; disregard, slight, neglect. *Cf.* **bezo, mbezi.**

bezo (ma-) scorn, contempt *(usually of words or admonitions).* *Cf.* **beza.**

[1]**bi*** *arch., prep.* by, in, with; by means of. *Cf.* **bila, bilashi, binafsi, bismillahi.**

[2]**bi** *see* **bibi.**

[1]**bia** (ma-) clay vessel, basin.

[2]**bia*** (–) cooperation, partnership; business company. **changa –.** assume an equal share of expenses. **hili ni duka letu la –.** This is our joint business.

[3]**bia*** [*Engl.*] (–) beer.

biabia be industrious, diligent; like to do something.

biashara* (–) business, trade, commerce; business company, concern. **fanya –.** engage in trade, carry on business. **mali ya –.** merchandise. **tangaza –.** advertise. **– ya nje.** foreign trade. **– ya nchi(ni).** domestic trade.

bibi*, bi [*Pers.*] (ma-) 1. madam, miss *(term of polite address)*; lady, mistress *(of a household)*. **– mkubwa.** madam *(showing a higher degree of respect than* **bibi** *alone)*. **– harusi.** bride. 2. grandmother. *Cf.* **kibibi.**

bibidia show contempt *(by protruding the lower lip)*.

biblia* [*Port.*] (–) Bible. *Cf.* **agano.**

bibo* [*Port.*] (–) bibo (cashew fruit). *Cf.* **mbibo.**

bichboi* [*Engl.*] (–) beach boy *(who assists passengers in the harbor)*.

bichi (*dial.* **biti**) *adj.* 1. unripe, raw, fresh. 2. young, immature. 3. damp, moist *(earth)*. *Cf.* **ubichi.**

bidaa* (–) *see* **bidhaa.**

bidani* (–) *see* **badani.**

bidhaa*, bidaa (–) goods, merchandise.

bidhalik(a)* *see* **kadhalika.**

bidi* strain, exert pressure; obligate, compel, force *(always used impersonally)*. **inabidi.** It is necessary. It must be. **imembidi kwenda.** He had to go. *appl.* **bidia.** *caus. & intr.* **bidisha.** *refl.* **jibidisha.** exert oneself, make a special effort. *Cf.* **bidii.**

bidii* (–) exertion, effort; diligence, industry; energy, activity, alacrity. **fanya –.** exert oneself, display energy. **kwa –.** diligent, energetic, industrious. *Cf.* **bidi.**

bighairi* ya..., baghairi ya... without, except, apart from. *Cf.* **ghairi.**

bihi* 1. forego, renounce, abdicate; revoke, repudiate, withdraw. 2. forgive *(a debt, etc.)*.

bikari* (–) compass *(for drawing circles)*.

bikira* (ma-) 1. virgin, virginity. 2. something untouched or newly begun. *Cf.* **bikiri, ubikira.**

bikiri* deflower. *pass.* **bikiriwa.** *Cf.* **bikira.**

bila* *prep.* without. **– ruhusa (udhuru).** without permission (excuse). **– idadi.** without number, numberless. **– kusita.** constantly. *Cf.* **bilashi.**

biladia* (–) (anything relating to a) town.

bilahi*, billahi! *interj.* by Allah!

bilashi*, bileshi *adv.* in vain, for nothing, gratuitously. **alimpiga –.** He struck him without reason. *Cf.* **bila.**

bilau* (–) [*Pers.*] pilau (rice boiled with meat). *Cf.* **pilau.**

bilauli* (–) *see* **bilauri.**

bilauri*, bilauli (–) glass, crystal; drinking-glass.

bildi* (–) 1. *naut.* (sounding) lead. **tia (piga) –.** take soundings. 2. weight *(of a clock).*

bileshi* *see* **bilashi.**

bilimbi*, birimbi [*Port.*] (–) bilimbi (fruit of the cucumber tree). *Cf.* **mbilimbi.**

bilingani*, biringani, biringanya (–, ma-) (fruit of the) eggplant. *Cf.* **mbilingani.**

bilioni* [*Engl.*] (ma-) billion.

bilisi* 1. tempt, entice; stir up, incite. 2. (–) temptation, enticement. *coll.* **ana – ya mpira.** He is a fanatical football fan. 3. (–) *see* **ibilisi.**

1biliwili (–) biliwili (kind of fish).

2biliwili (–) *bot.* thistle.

billahi* *see* **bilahi.**

bilula*, bulule [*Ar. ?*] (–, ma-) (water-) faucet, tap.

bima* [*Ind.*] (–) 1. insurance. **– ya maisha.** life-insurance. **– ya kitaifa ya afya.** national health insurance. **mwenye kupiga –.** insurance agent. 2. lottery, raffle. **fanya –.** organize a lottery. **cheza –.** hold a lottery, take a chance in a lottery.

bimbashi* [*Turk.*] (–) *mil.* bimbashi (rank of noncommissioned officer).

bimbiriza flame up, flare up. *ass.* **bimbirizana.** quarrel with each other, provoke/exasperate each other.

bimbirizana *ass. of* **bimbiriza.**

bin* (–) son *(only in proper names).* **bin Zaid.** Son of Zaid. *Cf.* **binadamu, binamu, 2ubini.**

binadamu* (–) (**bin + adamu**) human being, man; fellow. *Cf.* **kibinadamu, ubinadamu.**

binafsi* [bi + nafsi] 1. *adv.* personally, by myself, *etc.* **Mimi nimefika hapa kwa matembezi yangu binafsi.** I have come here on my own personal business. 2. *n.* personality (= **ubinafsi**).

binamu* [bin + 2amu] (–) cousin.

1binda* [*Ind.*] (ma-) *bot.* okra, lady's-finger *(Hibiscus esculentus).*

2binda* [*Engl.*] bind, hem, enclose.

bindo (ma-) *see* **kibindo.**

bingiria roll *(a stone, etc.)* *intr.* **bingirika.** *caus.* **bingirisha.**

bingwa 1. (ma-) capable/competent person (worker); specialist, expert. 2. *adj.* capable, competent. *Cf.* **ubingwa.**

bini* 1. forge, hammer. 2. forge, counterfeit, fake. *Cf.* **mbini, 1ubini.**

binti* (ma-) 1. daughter *(only in proper names.* **– Ali.** Daughter of Ali. 2. *forming names of certain birds and plants.* **– Athmani/Ali.** (varieties of) cassava. **– Chuma.** Kersten's weaver finch (= **kinanda**).

binua *see* **benua.**

binya pinch, nip, tweak.

binzari* (–) spice, (*us.* =) curry powder.

biri* [*Ind.*] (–) tobacco leaf *(rolled up for smoking).*

biriani (–) *see* **birinzi.**

Birigiji* [*Fr.* Belgique] 1. *adj.* Belgian. **Kongo –.** Belgian Congo. 2. *sing.* **birigiji** (a kind of cloth of a light brownish yellow color).

birika* (ma-) 1. (metal) vessel for water. 2. kettle. 3. tank, cistern.

birimbi* [*Port.*] (–) *see* **bilimbi.**

biringa *see* **viringa.**

biringani*, biringanya (–, ma-) *see* **bilingani.**

birinzi*, biriani [*Pers.*] (–) birinzi (highly spiced dish of meat and rice).

bisari (–) bisari (annual edible plant).

bisbis* (–) *see* **bisibisi.**

bisha 1. knock, rap *(on a door).* **– mlango (hodi).** ask admittance. 2. resist, oppose; quarrel. 3. joke, jest. 4. *naut.* tack. *ass.* **bishana.** argue, dispute, quarrel *(with each other);* tease *(each other).* *Cf.* **bishi, bisho, mabishano, 1mbishi, ubishi.**

bishaushi* [*Turk.* ?] (ma-) sergeant.

bishi *adj.* 1. quarrelsome; nagging, grumbling, fault-finding; obstinate. 2. humorous, fun-loving. *Cf.* **bisha.**

bisho (–) 1. blow, knock *(on the door).* 2. *naut.* tacking. **upepo ya –.** head wind. *Cf.* **bisha.**

bisi* [?] (–), **mbisi** (mi-) roasted/ parched corn, maize; popcorn.

bisibisi*, **bisbis** [*Ind. ?*] (–) screw-driver, wrench.

biskiti* (–) *see* **biskuti.**

biskuti*, **biskiti** [*Engl.*] (–) biscuit, cracker.

bismillahi!* *interj.* in the name of Allah! *Cf.* **simile.**

bitana* (–) thin fabric, lining *(of clothing).*

bitarehe *see* **tarehe.**

biti *see* **bichi.**

bivu *adj.* ripe *(of fruits)*; cooked, well done. *Cf.* **iva, ubivu.**

biwi (ma-) heap, pile *(of weeds, leaves, refuse).*

bizari* (–) 1. seed, grain *(of pepper, coriander, etc.).* 2. *(pl.)* curry powder.

bizi* [*Engl.*] *adj.* busy.

bizimu* (–) 1. buckle. 2. brooch, clasp, fastener. (= **kifungo.**)

blangeti* *see* **blanketi.**

blanketi*, **blangeti**, **bulangeti** [*Engl.*] (ma-) blanket.

bluu* *see* **buluu.**

boba *rare* bind, tie.

bobari* (–) chisel, gouge. (= **ngabu.**)

bobo* (–) *see* **popoo.**

boboka talk indiscreetly, blabber, let the cat out of the bag.

1**bodi*** [*Engl.*] (–) body *(of an automobile).*

2**bodi*** [*Engl.*] (–) board. **– ya taifa.** national board.

bodoa *obs.* *see* **jibodoa.**

bofu (ma-) (*augment. of* **kibofu**) 1. *anat.* bladder. 2. *fig.* balloon.

bofulo* [*Port. ?*] *sing.* (European type of) bread.

bofya *caus. of* **bopa.**

boga (ma-) pumpkin, gourd. *Cf.* **mboga.**

bohara* (ma-) *see* **bohora.**

bohari*, **bokhari** (–, ma-) 1. storehouse, warehouse; large store, department store. 2. *rare* chronicle, annals.

bohora*, **bohara** [*Ind.*] (ma-) member of the Bohora (sect of Indian Moslems).

boi* [*Engl.*] (ma-) boy, house-servant, waiter.

boji* (–) 1. intoxicating beverage, new beer. 2. oatmeal porridge.

bokhari* (–) *see* **bohari.**

boko (ma-) *augment. of* [1]**kiboko.**

bokoa 1. penetrate forcibly; decompose, disintegrate; break in, invade. 2. have a good harvest.

bokoboko (–) something soft/gelatinous: 1. a kind of meat pie. 2. a variety of banana. 3. a kind of sugarcane.

bokoka fall off, come loose, come off *(button, etc.)*; be separated/detached.

boma* [*Pers.*] (ma-) 1. pile of earth/stones; mound, wall; palisade, enclosure. 2. fort, fortress. **fanya (tia) –.** fortify, enclose, fence in. 3. (government) administrative office. 4. *rare* framework (*of a house*). 5. stable (*for cattle*). 6. *fig.*: **– kubwa.** mainstay.

bomba* [*Port.*] (–, ma-) 1. (water) pump. 2. (large) pipe. **– la mafuta.** petroleum pipeline. **mabomba.** piping. 3. (water) tap, faucet. 4. chimney, smokestack, stack *(of a ship)*. 5. *med.* syringe, hypodermic needle.

bombo* *sing.* 1.: **suruali –.** short, baggy trousers. 2. *see* **bombom** 2.

bombom*, **bombomu** [*Engl.*] (–) 1. bomb, shell. **(mzinga wa) –.** machine gun. 2. (*also* **bombo**) **(homa ya) –.** *dial., med.* influenza, grippe, pneumonia.

bombwe (ma-) 1. carving, sculpture, ornament. 2. pattern, model. **kata mabombwe.** carve figures/ornaments.

bomoa break down, tear down, demolish; break through, pierce. **– ukuta.** tear down/pierce a wall. *appl.* **bomolea.** *intr.* **bomoka.** *caus.* **bomosha.** *Cf.* **bomoko, mbomoshi.**

bomoko (ma-) *(us. pl.)* 1. (act of) destroying/demolishing, destruction. 2. collapse, landslide. 3. ruins. *Cf.* **bomoa.**

bomolea *appl. of* **bomoa.**

[1]**bomu** (ma-) 1. *id.* a loud noise *(shot, drum)*. 2. *rare* a kind of dance.

[2]**bomu***, **bom** [*Engl.*] (ma-) bomb. **– la atomiki.** atom bomb. **– la kutoa moshi.** smokepot.

bonas* [*Engl.*] (–) bonus, premium, prize, dividend.

bonde (ma-) valley, hollow, low ground. **– la mto.** river bed.

bonge (ma-) 1. clod *(of earth)*; ball *(of yarn)*. 2. *pharm.* (*us.* **kibonge**) tablet.

bongo (ma-) *coll.* brain. **hana –.** He is stupid. *Cf.* **ubongo.**

bong'oa 1. bend down, stoop, bow. 2. *fig.* show one's respect for someone.

bonyea be soft/yielding, yield to pressure, give way. *caus.* **bonyeza, bonyesha.**

squeeze out *(also fig., of examinations, etc.:* 'put through the wringer').

bonyeza *caus. of* **bonyea.**

boosa *rare* be lame.

bopa 1. be soft to the touch, feel soft *(fruit, sores).* **ndizi zikibopa zimeiva.** When the bananas feel soft they are ripe. 2. sink in, become hollow. *caus.* **bofya.** *Cf.* **bopo.**

bopo (ma-) hole, pit, groove, furrow; dent, depression. *Cf.* **bopa.**

bora* *adj.* excellent, first-class; best. **– afya.** The best thing is good health. *Cf.* **ubora.**

[1]**bori*** [*Pers.*] (–) 1. bowl of a pipe. 2. *dial.* (ma-) fruit of the mkunazi tree.

[2]**bori*** (–) *see* **buri.**

boriti* [*Port. ?*] (–, ma-) 1. (mangrove) post. 2. *(in gen.)* post, beam, girder.

borohoa* [*Pers.*] (–) native dish of cooked beans.

boromoka *intr. of* **poromoa.**

boronga 1. botch, bungle, do sloppy work. 2. confuse, throw into disorder. *Cf.* **borongo.**

borongo (ma-) disorder, confusion, muddle, mess. *Cf.* **boronga.**

bovu *adj.* 1. bad, spoiled, decayed, unwholesome. 2. *fig.* unhealthy; worthless, unreliable. **mtu mbovu.** unreliable person. *Cf.* **ubovu.**

boya* [*Port.*] (ma-) *naut.* buoy.

boza* [*Pers.*] (–) 1. intoxicating beverage, beer. 2. narcotic.

bozi* 1. (ma-) fool, idiot, useless person. 2. *red.:* **bozibozi** *adj.* stupid, useless. *Cf.* **ubozi.**

bozibozi *see* **bozi** 2.

bradha* [*Engl.*], **bruda*** [*Germ.*] (wa-) *rel.* brother.

brashi*, **burashi** [*Engl.*] (–) brush. **piga –.** to brush.

breki* [*Engl.*] (–) brake *(of automobile, etc.).* **tia (piga) –.** put on the brake.

bruda* [*Germ.*] (wa-) *see* **bradha.**

bua (ma-) *bot.* stem, stalk *(millet, maize, grass).*

buabua cut/hew/slice *(a little off the top of something).*

buana (–, ma-) *see* **bwana.**

buathi *see* **baathi.**

buba (ma-) *med.* frambesia, yaws.

[1]**bubu, bubwi** 1. (ma-) mute person. 2. *adj.* dumb, mute. *Cf.* **ububu.**

[2]**bubu** (ma-) *anat.* nipple.

bubujika, buguika 1. gush/stream out, foam up, burst out. **maji yanabubujika.** The water gushes out. **— maneno.** burst out with a flood of words. 2. burst, explode. *Cf.* **bubujiko.**

bubujiko (ma-) spring *(of water). Cf.* **bubujika.**

buburusha 1. scrape, scratch, paw *(of animals).* 2. push, shove. *ass.* **buburushana. watu walibuburushana.** The people were pushing and shoving (each other).

bubuta *rare* strike, hit. *Cf.* **buta.**

bubwi (ma-) *see* [1]**bubu.**

buchari* [*Ind.*] (—) (large) knife.

budaa become lumpy *(soup, etc.).*

buddi (—) *see* **budi.**

budhara* (—) extravagance. *Cf.* **badhiri.**

budi*, buddi, abudi (—) way out, loophole, evasion, alternative. *usually in neg. expressions:* **hapana —.** There is no alternative. One must...

bueta (ma-) *see* **bweta.**

bufuu, bupu, bupura, bupuru (ma-) empty shell/husk. **— la kichwa.** skull.

buga 1. hunt for, gather, collect, glean. 2. sponge, cadge.

buge (ma-) person or animal missing a finger or toe.

bughudha* (—) 1. aversion, dislike, repugnance, abhorrence, hatred, hostility. 2. slander, calumny. *Cf.* **bughudhi.**

bughudhi*, bughudhu hate, abhor; insult, slander. *Cf.* **bughudha.**

bughudhu* *see* **bughudhi.**

bugia, bwakia, bwia bite off, put into the mouth. *Cf.* **mbuge, ubuge.**

bugu (ma-) flexible twig/wand *(used for weaving baskets).*

buguika *see* **bubujika.**

buheri*: — wa afya. recovery *(of health, after an illness). Cf.* **heri.**

buhumu* (ma-) *anat.* lung. (= **pafu, pumu.**)

buhuri* (—) 1. incense; fumigation. 2. steam bath *(for invalids).*

bui (—) 1. large spider, tarantula. 2. **mchezo wa —.** children's game (a kind of hide-and-seek). *Cf.* **buibui.**

buibui (**–**, **ma-**) 1. spider. **utando wa –.** spider's web, cobweb. 2. buibui (a black veil for women). *Cf.* **bui.**

bujua press out, squeeze out.

buka (–) *rare* care, worry, grief.

¹**Buki, Bukini** Madagascar. **komba wa –.** lemur. *Cf.* **Mbuki.**

²**buki** (**ma-**) kidney. (= **nso, figo.**)

Bukini *see* ¹**Buki.**

¹**buku** (**ma-**) large rat *(Cricetomys gambianus).*

²**buku** [*Engl.*] *rare* (large) book. (= **kitabu.**)

bukua uncover, discover, reveal *(secret, scandal). appl.* **bukulia.** *intr.* **bukuka.** *Cf.* **mbukulia, ubukuzi.**

bulangeti* (**ma-**) *see* **blanketi.**

buldani*, beled (–) district *(of a city).*

buli* [*Port.*] (**ma-**) teapot.

bulibuli* (–): **kofia ya –** embroidered white cap.

bulula (**–**, **ma-**) *see* **bilula.**

buluu*, bluu, kibuluu [*Engl.*] 1. *adj.* blue. 2. *sing.* bluing, bleach.

bumani* (–) building, structure.

bumba, pumba (**ma-**) 1. lump, heap. **– la nyuki.** swarm of bees. 2. package, pack, **– la sigara.** pack of cigarettes.

bumbi (–) *bot.* kind of salad herb, cress *(Barbarea vulgaris).*

bumbuasa *adj.* lumpy.

bumbuaza 1. confuse/perplex someone, cause someone discomfort. 2. startle, frighten, astonish. 3. drive a person into a corner; disconcert, embarrass. *Cf.* **bumbuazi.**

bumbuazi (**–**, **ma-**) confusion, consternation, dismay, embarrassment, perplexity. **shikwa na –.** be perplexed/dismayed. *Cf.* **bumbuaza.**

bumbura* [*Ind.*] (–) edible sea-fish; dried fish.

bumburuka be startled, be scared away; run away, bolt. *caus.* **bumburusha.** start up, scare away *(birds).*

bumbwi (–) *see* **bwimbwi.**

bumia* [*Pers. ?*] (–) *naut.* sternpost *(of a native boat).*

bumunda (**ma-**) bumunda (dumplings made of flour and bananas).

bunda* [*Engl.*] (**ma-**) 1. bundle, package. **– la tumbaku (chai).** a package of tobacco (tea). **– la noti.** a bundle of banknotes. 2. bale. 3. knot.

bunde (–) empty coconut.

bundi (–, **ma-**) *ornith.* (species of) owl.

bunduki* (–) gun, rifle. **piga –.** shoot. **elekeza –.** aim. **– ya marisaa.** shotgun. **– ya midomo miwili.** double-barreled gun. **– ya kupigia vifaru.** antitank gun. **– ya mtombo.** machine gun. **– ya nusu mtombo.** submachine gun.

bunga *adj.:* **mtu –.** feeble-minded/foolish/silly person.

Bungala* *geogr.* Bengal. **mpunga (muhogo) wa –.** Bengal rice, manioc.

bunge *sing.* parliament. *Cf.* **mbunge.**

[1]**bungo** (–) bungo (small dish).

[2]**bungo** (**ma-**) *bot.* bungo (fruit of the rubber liana).

bungu (–) 1. a stinging insect which bores holes in wood. 2. kind of caterpillar. *Cf.* **bungua.**

bungua bore *(of insects which bore holes in wood). intr.* **bunguka.** be eaten away by insects *(wood, grain). Cf.* **bungu.**

bunguu (**ma-**) large earthenware cooking-pot.

[1]**buni*** (–) coffee-bean, coffee. *Cf.* **mbuni.**

[2]**buni*** 1. construct, put together, arrange; write (fiction). **– kitabu.** write a book. 2. invent; fabricate, start false rumors. **– maneno.** fabricate statements. *appl.* **bunia.** *Cf.* [3]**mbuni.**

bunju (–) round, inedible fish. *prov.* **mimi –, akili yangu kichwani.** I am like a bunju. I am clever. (= I overcome all difficulties.)

bunta* [*Engl.*] (–) pontoon, landing-stage, pier.

[1]**bunzi** (**ma-**) large stinging fly.

[2]**bunzi** (**ma-**) *see* **gunzi.**

bupu (**ma-**) *see* **bufuu.**

bupura, bupuru (**ma-**) *see* **bufuu.**

[1]**buraa*** (–) buraa (Arab garment).

[2]**buraa*** (–) forgiveness, exemption. *Cf.* **burai.**

buraha* (–) rest, comfort. *Cf.* **burahi.**

burahi* rest, make oneself comfortable, take it easy. *Cf.* **buraha.**

burai* forgive, remit *(debts);* release, absolve *(from obligations);* vindicate, exculpate, acquit. *appl.* **buraia.** *Cf.* [2]**buraa.**

buraia *appl. of* **burai.**

burangeni* (–) *see* **barangeni.**

burashi* (–) *see* **brashi.**

burda* (–) *see* **buruda.**

bure* *adv.* 1. for nothing, free of charge, gratis. 2. uselessly, without purpose, fruitlessly, in vain. **fanya kazi –.** do work to no purpose. 3. without cause/reason. **tukana –.** scold/swear without reason. 4. rashly, frivolously. **sema maneno ya –.** make rash statements. *Cf.* **ubure.**

buri*, **bori** (–) buri (medium-sized elephant tusk).

buriani* (–) leave-taking, farewell *(only before a journey of some length).* **peana –.** take leave, say farewell. **agana –.** exchange farewells.

buru (ma-) *rare* calabash *(used for churning butter).*

buruda*, **burda, burudai** (–) *Isl.* prayer *(in distress, illness, etc.). Cf.* **baridi, burudi.**

burudai* (–) *see* **buruda.**

burudi* be cool/cold. *usually intr.:* **burudika.** *fig.* be soothed, appeased, pacified. *caus.* **burudisha** (*also* **tabaradi, tabaridi, tabarudu**). cool, refresh; calm, sooth, appease. *Cf.* **baridi, maburudisho.**

buruga 1. stir up, mix *(foods).* 2. turn up the ground *(hoe, weed, etc., preparatory to planting).* 3. *fig.* confuse, complicate *(affairs). ass.-caus.* **buruganya.** mix together. *Cf.* **mburugo;** *also* **vuruga.**

buruganya *ass.-caus. of* **buruga.**

buruhani* (–) 1. test, evidence, proof. 2. power of efficacious prayer.

[1]**buruji*** (–) *arch.* battlement.

[2]**buruji*** [*Engl. ?*] (–) bugle.

buruma* (–) water-pipe, hookah. (= **kikororo.**)

burunga make balls of earth/clay.

burura, buruta 1. pull, haul, drag. 2. fan *(a fire).* **mama anaburuta moto.** Mother is fanning the fire. (= **pepea**). *Cf.* **kiburuta, maburuzo, mburuzo.**

buruta *see* **burura.**

busa* (–) busa (Arab beer, made of barley and millet).

busara* (*rare* **tabasuri**) (–) 1. sense, prudence, sagacity, foresight, astuteness, skill, adroitness. **tumia –.** act shrewdly, astutely. **leta –.** display sagacity. 2. intention, plan. 3. trick, stratagem.

busati* (–, ma-) (kind of) mat *(used chiefly in mosques).*

busha*, **fusha** (–) 1. *mil.* wad, swab. 2. *med.* elephantiasis of the scrotum.

bushashi* (–) bushashi (thin cotton fabric similar to muslin). (= **shashi.**)

bushti* (–, ma-) *see* **bushuti.**

bushuti*, bushti (–, ma-) bushuti (Arab cloak).

bustani* [*Pers.*] (–) (flower) garden *(us. a small plot in the back yard, for raising flowers or vegetables).*

busu* [*Ar., Pers.*] 1. (–) kiss. 2. to kiss. *appl.* **busia.** *appl.-ass.* **busiana. busiana mikono.** kiss each other's hands.

busuri* take care, be careful; worry.

buta, puta *rare* strike, hit. *Cf.* **bubuta.**

butaa* (–) surprise, amazement.

butu 1. (ma-) stump, stub. 2. *adj.* dull, obtuse. **kisu –.** a dull knife. **pembetatu –.** an obtuse-angled triangle. *fig.* dull-witted, feeble-minded. *Cf.* **butua, kibubutu, ubutu.**

butua 1. cut off, knock off *(the end of something),* dull. 2. *fig.* amputate. *Cf.* **butu.**

¹buu! *interj.* Be quiet!

²buu (ma-) *zool.* grub, maggot, larva.

buyu (ma-) 1. *bot.* buyu (fruit of the baobab). 2. calabash *(made from the shell of the fruit). Cf.* **mbuyu, ubuyu.**

buyuka burst, explode; open up *(of an ulcer).*

buza* (–) intoxicating beverage *(made with honey).*

bwabwaja, bwata *id.* talk confusedly/meaninglessly.

bwaga 1. throw off/down. 2. *fig.* free oneself of something. **– moyo.** free the heart, be comforted. 3. *fig., sport.:* **Wanderers iliwabwaga Brazil kwa mabao matatu.** The Wanderers defeated (the) Brazil (team) by three goals. *Cf.* **mbwago.**

bwakia 1. put/toss into the mouth *(e.g., nuts, tobacco).* 2. *see* **bugia, bwia.**

bwakua tear away, take away by force; *fig.* snatch.

bwana, buana (–, ma-) 1. sir, Mr. *(term of address).* **bwana mkubwa.** sir *(showing a higher degree of respect than bwana alone, but sometimes humorous or contemptuous, especially when used of women).* 2. owner, proprietor. **– shamba.** landlord; supervisor of a shamba; *(sometimes used in a derogatory way to refer to the former)* colonial landowners. 3. *arch.* **– arusi.** bridegroom. 4.: **– shauri.** administrative officer (Tanganyika). 5. *rel.* Lord. *Cf.* **kibwana, ubwana.**

bwata *see* **bwabwaja.**

bwawa (ma-) swamp, fen, bog, quagmire.

bweha, mbweha (–) jackal.

bweka bark *(of dogs).* *appl.* **bwekea.** bark at. *Cf.* **mbweko.**

bwende (ma-) bwende (garment worn by those working in the fields).

bweni (–) 1. sleeping quarters of unmarried young men or girls. 2. *sport* junior team. 3. boarding-school pupil.

bwenzi (–) tuft of hair *(left on top of the shaven head).*

bweshu (ma-) unpleasant, ill-disposed person.

bweta*, bueta [*Port.*] (ma-) small box, case.

bwimbwi, bumbwi (–, ma-) bwimbwi (rice-flour mixed with sugar and coconut milk; eaten uncooked).

CH

[1]**cha** *conn.* ki-/ch- *class:* **kitabu – mwanafunzi.** the pupil's book.

[2]**cha** fear, be afraid of; tremble. *appl.* **chea.** *double appl.* **chelea.** *intr.* **cheka.** *caus.* **chesha.** *ass.* **chana.** *Cf.* **kicho, macheleo, mcha, mchea, mchelea, uchaji.**

[3]**cha** dawn, become light. **kunakucha.** It is growing light. Day is breaking. *appl.* **chea.** *double appl.* **chelea.** *double appl.-caus.* **cheleza.** cause to remain *(all night, for a long time),* delay. *pass.* **chewa.** be surprised/overtaken by sunrise. *caus.* **chesha.** remain until morning. **tumechesha tukiimbi.** We sang the whole night through. *appl.-pass.* **chelewa.** oversleep, be late. *appl.-pass.-caus.* **chelewesha.** let someone wait. *Cf.* [2]**chelezo, kichea,** [1]**kucha, macheo, uchao, ucheachea, uchelewaji.**

[4]**cha** *see* **ja.**

[1]**chaa** (–) chaa (edible sea-fish).

[2]**chaa** (–) group of people who cultivate land in common.

[3]**chaa** (–) *dial.* cattle-pen.

[1]**chacha** (–) chacha (kind of grass which grows in damp places).

[2]**chacha** be stormy *(of the sea).*

[3]chacha turn sour, ferment, foam; *(fig.)* be angry. *caus.* **chachisha.** make sour; *(fig.)* challenge, provoke someone. *inv.* **chachua.** allow something to ferment. *inv.-intr.* **chachuka.** = **chacha.** *Cf.* **chachu, uchachu.**

chachachika be pounded/crushed.

chachaga wash *(clothes).*

chachaniza *see* **chachawiza.**

chachari (ma-) (*usually* **machachari**) 1. unrest, excitement, restlessness. 2. stubbornness, obstinacy. 3. difficulty.

chacharika, chachatika 1. tingle, sizzle. 2. insist strongly, persist. 3. gesticulate. 4. run quickly back and forth. *appl.* **chacharikia.**

chachatika *see* **chacharika.**

chachawa 1. jump, leap; be delighted, enjoy oneself. 2. emulate someone, make a strong effort.

chachawi (–) confused speech.

chachawiza (*rare* **chachaniza**) interrupt/disturb someone *(with noises).* *Cf.* **chachawizo.**

chachawizo (ma-) 1. noise. 2. interruption, delay. 3. embarrassment. *Cf.* **chachawiza.**

chache *adj.* 1. little, few; insufficient, incomplete; unimportant. 2. distant, remote. 3. rare, scarce. *Cf.* **uchache.**

chachi* (–) *see* **shashi.**

chachia 1. be difficult, complicated; be too much. 2. confuse, involve in difficulties. *pass.* **chachiwa.**

chachili (ma-) ignorant person; timid person.

chachu (–) leaven, yeast. -a –, sour. *Cf.* **[3]chacha.**

chachua *inv. of* **[3]chacha.**

[1]chachuka surge, roll, heave *(of the sea).*

[2]chachuka *inv.-intr. of* **[3]chacha.**

chadi* *see* **[2]jadi, [3]jadi, [4]jadi.**

[1]chafi, tasi (–) chafi (kind of fish).

[2]chafi (–) chafi (kind of insect).

chafia *see* **chafya.**

[1]chafu *adj.* 1. dirty, unclean. 2. *fig.* indecent, obscene. *Cf.* **chafua, uchafu.**

[2]chafu (–) chafu (basket, pannier).

[3]chafu (ma-) *see* **shavu.**

chafua 1. soil, pollute; spoil; *(fig.)* disturb, disarrange; ruin, destroy. 2. smoke, blacken. 3. be disorderly, messy. 4. surge, be rough *(of the sea)*. *appl.* **chafulia.** *intr.* **chafuka. bahari ilichafuka sana.** The sea was very rough. *caus.* **chafusha.** *Cf.* **chafu, chafuko, machafuko, mchafuko, mchafuzi, uchafuko, uchafuzi.**

chafuka *intr. of* **chafua.**

chafuko (ma-), **mchafuko** (mi-) 1. unrest, disorder, movement; crisis. **– wa kilimwengu.** international crisis. 2. *naut.* wave, surge, surf. *Cf.* **chafua.**

chafulia *appl. of* **chafua.**

chafuo (–) tsetse fly (= ^{2}**mbungo.**)

chafusha *caus. of* **chafua.**

chafya, chafia *sing.* sneezing. **piga (enda) –.** to sneeze.

^{1}**chaga** 1. be excited/startled. 2. begin something *(work)*. 3. emulate (someone). 4. be prevalent *(disease, etc.)*. *caus. & int.* **chagiza.** annoy, pester, be insistent; press one's point; be talkative/garrulous.

^{2}**chaga** *pl. of* **uchaga.**

chagernati* [*Ind.*] chagernati (bleached cotton cloth).

chagina 1. (–) brave, courageous person; bold, daring, impudent person. 2. *adj.* brave; bold, audacious, impudent.

chagiza *caus. of* **chaga.**

^{1}**chago** (–, ma-) (*also* **mchago, uchago**) head end of a bedstead.

^{2}**chago** (–) land-crab.

chagua 1. seek out, select, choose. **– kwa kura.** 2. *pol.* elect. 3. distort, deform; be unjust/unfair/prejudiced. *appl.* **chagulia.** *caus.* **chaguza.** *Cf.* **chaguzi, mchagua, mchaguo, mchaguzi, uchaguzi.**

chagulia *appl. of* **chagua.**

chaguza *caus. of* **chagua.**

chaguzi *adj.* fastidious, critical. *Cf.* **chagua.**

chai* [*Chin.-Ar.*] (–) tea *(the beverage)*. *Cf.* **mchai.**

chaji* [*Eng.*] (–) charges, expenditure, cost.

^{1}**chaka** (ma-) 1. hot season *(December to February)*. 2. heat, blazing sun.

^{2}**chaka** (ma-) thicket, bushes, undergrowth; clump of trees.

chakaa grow old, be worn out/used up/ exhausted; use up, wear out. *appl.* **chakalia.** *caus.* **chakaza.** use up, spend, consume. *Cf.* **chakavu.**

chakaazi (–) *bot.* a succulent tree *(Euphorbia tirucalle).*

chakacha 1. rustle *(of grass, when one walks through it),* crackle, murmur. **– menoni.** gnash the teeth. 2. crush, grind. *Cf.* **chakarisha, mchakacho, uchakacho.**

chakari 1. *adv.* much, very, to a high degree. 2. *fig., coll.* be drunk. **alikuwa –.** He was drunk.

chakarisha, charakisha frighten, startle, start *(game);* make a rustling sound *(in dry grass). Cf.* **chakacha.**

chakavu, chakafu *adj.* old, worn-out, shabby, ragged. *Cf.* **chakaa.**

chakaza *caus. of* **chakaa.**

chake *see* **-ake.**

chakeleti* (–) *see* **chokoleti.**

chaki* [*Engl.*] (–) *see* **choki.**

chakleti* (–) *see* **chokoleti.**

chako *see* **-ako.**

chakogea (vyakogea) *see* **chakugea.**

chakua 1. stir *(foods).* 2. chew. 3. clean the teeth. 4.: **– matakataka.** *(of fowl)* peck, pick up *(grains).*

chakubimbi (vi-) liar, slanderer.

chakugea, chakogea (vyakugea) bathtub. (<**cha kogea**; *cf.* [1]**oga.**)

chakula (vyakula) food, nourishment, victuals; something edible. **– cha asubuhi (mchana, jioni).** breakfast (lunch, dinner). **vyakula vikavu.** food *(as opp. to drink).* (<**cha kula**; *cf.* [1]**la.**)

chakura 1. scrape, scratch, paw *(of horses).* 2. *fig.* search carefully, spy. *Cf.* **mchakuro.**

chakuzidishwa (vy-) *math.* multiplicand. (<**cha kuzidishwa**; *cf.* [1]**zidi.**)

[1]**chale** (–, ma-) cut, scratch; tattooing *(tribal marks).* **chanja –.** tattoo. *Cf.* **uchale.**

[2]**chale: – cha pwani.** sea-urchin.

[3]**chale** (–) chale (kind of fish).

chali, chani, tani *adv., arch.* backwards, on the back. **lala –.** lie on one's back. *Cf.* **kichali.**

chama (vyama) 1. association, society, club. **– cha biashara.** business company. **– cha ushirika.** cooperative.

2. organization, party. – cha wafanya kazi. labor union, trade union. – cha siasa. political party. utawala wa – kimoja. one-party rule. – cha Msalaba Mwekundu. Red Cross Society. – Kikuu cha Dunia. United Nations Organization.

chamanda* (–) *see* **jamanda.**

[1]**chamba** (vyamba) 1. *bot.* bark *(of a tree).* 2. *anat.* cornea. *Cf.* [2]**amba.**

[2]**chamba** wash *(esp. after using the toilet). caus.* **chambiza.** wipe up.

chambi, chamvi (–) movement in dancing, dance-step.

chambo (vyambo) 1. bait, lure. *prov.* **mtego bila – haunasi.** A trap without bait catches nothing. 2. *fig.* temptation. *Cf.* [2]**amba.**

chambua, chamvua 1. clean *(fruits, meat);* husk, shell *(grain, beans);* pull off, pluck out, tease *(fibers).* 2. *fig.* criticize. *appl.* **chambulia.** *Cf.* **ambua.**

chambulia *appl. of* **chambua.**

chamburo (–) flat-nosed pliers *(used by silversmiths).*

chamchela (–) whirlwind; hurricane, cyclone, tornado.

chamia* *rare* gather, collect.

chamka 1. be repeated, recur *(of disease).* 2. open up, break *(wounds, abscesses). Cf.* **chamko.**

chamkano (ma-) 1. separation, division, partition. 2. fraction; section, department.

chamko (–) return, repetition; recurrence, relapse *(diseases). Cf.* **chamka.**

championi* [*Engl.*] (ma-) *sport* champion.

chamshakinywa (vy-) *see* **kiamshakinywa.**

chamvi *see* **chambi.**

chamvua *see* **chambua.**

[1]**chana** (–) bundle; cluster, bunch *(of large fruits).*

[2]**chana** (–) larva of the bee. *Cf.* **jana.**

[3]**chana** separate, slit, split, cleave, cut up, dissect. **kitambaa.** tear cloth. – **miyaa.** slit leaves *(for plaiting).* – **nywele.** comb the hair. *intr.* **chanika.** be torn/cut up. *inv.* **chanua.** comb, smooth out; loosen, detach. *inv.-appl.* **chanulia.** *inv.-intr.* **chanuka.** *Cf.* **chane, chanuo, kichane.**

[4]**chana** *ass. of* [2]**cha.**

chanaba* (–) *see* **janaba.**

[1]**chanda** (**ma-**) chanda (leaf of the coconut palm).

[2]**chanda** (**vyanda**) *arch.* finger, toe. (= **kidole.**) *Only in the prov.* **chanda na kidole.** stick together (= be inseparable like fingers or toes).

chandalua*, **chandarua**, **tandarua**, **jandaru** [*Ind.*] (–, **vyandalua**) (protective) covering: 1. mosquito-net. 2. tarpaulin, awning, canopy. 3. hood *(of an automobile)*.

chandarua* (–) *see* **chandalua.**

chando (–) kind of dance; dance-step.

chane (–) 1. strip of leaf *(for weaving mats)*. 2. bundle. *Cf.* [3]**chana.**

[1]**changa** 1. bring together, gather, collect; recruit *(soldiers)*. – **fedha.** collect *(voluntary contributions of)* money, take up a collection. 2. shuffle *(cards)*. *caus.* **changisha, changiza.** *ass.* **changana.** *ass.-caus.* **changanya.** gather, assemble; mix, mingle; jumble, confuse. **changanya maneno.** jumble words. *ass.-double caus.* **changanyisha.** *ass.-caus.-intr.* **changanyika.** be mixed/jumbled/confused. *ass.-int.* **changaniza.** falsify, forge; produce utter confusion. *stat.-ass.* **changamana** (*dial.* **tangamana**) be in a condition of mixture; mix with *(people)*; adjoin, border on. *inv.* **changua.** take apart, dismember. *ass.-inv.* **changanua.** take apart, dissect; analyse. *Cf.* **changamano,** [1]**chango, kichango, kichanganyiko, machanganyiko, machanganyo, mchanganuo, mchanganyaji, mchanganyiko, mchanganyo,** [2]**mchango, uchanganuo.**

[2]**changa** 1. chop up *(firewood, etc.)*. 2. *fig.* damage, injure; cause pain.

[3]**changa, janga** *adj.* young, immature, undeveloped, in an early stage of growth. **mwezi mchanga.** new moon. *Cf.* [2]**uchanga.**

changamana *stat.-ass. of* [1]**changa.**

changamano (*dial.* **tangamano**) (**ma-**) union, association; connection, contact; mixture, blend. *Cf.* [1]**changa.**

changamfu *adj.* gay, cheerful, good-humored, amiable; enlivening, animating, encouraging. *Cf.* **changamka, uchangamfu.**

changamka (*dial.* **chanjamka**) 1. wake up *(from sleep)*. 2. be gay/cheerful/merry; look happy. *caus.* **changamsha, chanjamsha.** 1. wake someone up. 2. please, make happy, cheer up, cause pleasure. *intr.* **changamuka, changanuka, chanjanuka.** 1. be awake. 2. *fig.* be enlightened/progressive. *Cf.* **amka, changamfu, changamko, kichangamsha, uchangamfu.**

changamko (ma-) (*also* **kichangamko**, vi-) 1. entertainment, amusement; play, game. 2. annoyance, nuisance. *Cf.* **changamka.**

changamsha *caus. of* **changamka.**

changaniza *ass.-int. of* [1]**changa.**

changanua *ass.-inv. of* [1]**changa.**

changanya *ass.-caus. of* [1]**changa.**

changanyika *ass.-caus.-intr. of* [1]**changa.**

changarawe, changawe (–, vi-; *us. pl.*) pebbles, gravel.

changawe (–, vi-) *see* **changarawe.**

[1]**chango** (–, ma-) 1. contribution *(of money, food, etc.)*. 2. fee, subscription *(to a newspaper or magazine)*. 3. recruitment, levy *(of soldiers)*. *Cf.* [1]**changa.**

[2]**chango** (–, ma-) 1. small intestine (= **uchengelele**). 2. intestinal worm.

[3]**chango** (vi-) hook, (wooden) peg/pin, dowel; cross-beam, railing. *Cf.* [1]**anga.**

[1]**changu** *see* **-angu.**

[2]**changu** (–) changu (small edible fish).

[1]**changua** (–) *rare* wilderness, desert. *Cf.* **jangwa.**

[2]**changua** *inv. of* [1]**changa.**

[1]**chani** *see* **chali.**

[2]**chani, chanui** (–) sea-urchin, sea-porcupine.

chania (–) *rare* comb. (= **chanuo.**)

chanikiwiti *adj., rare* *see* **janikiwiti.**

[1]**chanja** (–), **kichanja** (vi-) 1. basketwork, wickerwork, grill, screen. **– ya chuma.** iron grillwork, wire netting. 2. stand for storing grain *(in a house)*.

[2]**chanja** 1. cut in pieces, cut up; make a cut/incision in something. **– kuni.** chop up firewood. 2. *fig.* inoculate, give a hypodermic injection. **– ndui.** vaccinate against smallpox. *appl.-ass.* **chanjiana.** make cuts in each other. **chanjiana uchale.** conclude blood-brotherhood. *Cf.* **chanjo, mchanjo.**

chanjamka *see* **changamka.**

chanjanuka *intr. of* **changamka.**

chanjari *see* **sanjari.**

chanje (–) (variety of) crab.

chanjo (ma-) 1. cut, incision; slit, scratch, gash, slash. 2. inoculation, vaccination. 3. tattooing. *Cf.* [2]**chanja.**

chano (vyano) 1. wooden trough, board for carrying mortar. 2. serving-tray.

[1]**chanua** *inv. of* [3]**chana.**

[2]**chanua** unfold, open *(of buds).*

chanui *see* [2]**chani.**

chanuka *inv.-intr. of* [3]**chana.**

chanulia *inv.-appl. of* [3]**chana.**

chanuo (*also* **shanuo**) (–) 1. wooden comb *(with long teeth).* 2. comb *(in gen.). Cf.* [3]**chana.**

chanyata 1. cut up, slice *(fruits).* 2. wash carefully/gently *(fine fabrics). Cf.* **mchanyato.**

chanyatia (–) chanyatia (kind of fish, appearing usually in mangrove swamps).

chanzi (ma-, –) *see* **ganzi.**

chanzo (vya-) start, beginning; source; basis, foundation; cause. **– cha dharuba.** storm center. *Cf.* **anza.**

[1]**chao** *see* [1]**-ao.**

[2]**chao** (–) *naut.* roller *(used for launching).*

[1]**chapa*** [*Ind.?*] 1. strike, stamp. **– miguu.** stamp the feet, walk heavily. 2. *fig.* print, stamp. **– magazeti.** print newspapers. *inv.* **chapua.** strike; run fast. *intr.* **chapuka.** 3. (–) blow, stroke; stamp, impression, printing; trademark, brand. **piga –.** stamp, print. *Cf.* **mchapaji, mchapo, uchapaji, uchapishaji.**

[2]**chapa** *adj.* many, numerous.

[3]**chapa, chapara** be very drunk.

chapara *see* [3]**chapa.**

chapeo* (–) *see* **chepeo.**

chapua *inv. of* [1]**chapa.**

chapuchapu 1. *adv.* quickly, speedily, briskly. 2. *interj.* hurry up!

chapukia be delicious/appetizing.

chapuo (–) chapuo (small drum).

chapwa *adj.* 1. tasteless, insipid, flat. 2. repulsive, nasty; unpleasant, painful.

charahani* (–) *see* **cherehani.**

charakisha *see* **chakarisha.**

charaza 1. play *(an instrument);* dance; beat time. 2. *fig.* do something skilfully or energetically.

charo (vyaro) caravan, party of travelers. (= **msafara.**)

charuka 1. begin something over again, start anew. 2. emulate someone.

chasasa (–) chasasa (kind of pearl).

chasi (vi-) abundance, plenty, a great many.

chasiri* venture, dare, risk. *Cf.* **jasiri.**

chata hiss; hum, buzz.

chati* [*Engl.*] (–) chart.

chatu (–) python, boa constrictor.

[1]**chavu** (–) *rare* net. *Cf.* **wavu.**

[2]**chavu** (ma-) *see* **shavu.**

chawa (–) louse. *prov.* **kidole kimoja hakivunji –.** A single finger kills no louse.

chaza*, **shaza** [*Pers.?*] (–) oyster.

chazi (–) *bot.* (kind of) liana (*Cissus rotundifolia).*

chazo (–) sucker-fish.

chea *appl. of* [2]**cha,** [3]**cha.**

checha 1. divide, cut up. 2. object, contradict; forbid; criticize. *Cf.* [1]**cheche.**

[1]**cheche, chechi** (–, ma-) (*and* **mcheche,** mi-) small piece, slice *(of cassava, etc.).* **– ya (la) moto.** spark, ray. **– ya (la) umeme (stimu).** electric spark. *Cf.* **checha.**

[2]**cheche** (–), **kicheche** (vi-) a small animal resembling a mongoose.

chechea walk carefully; be lame, limp. *stat.-appl.* **chechemea.** be lame, limp. *caus.* **chechesha, checheza.** support, help someone walk.

chechele (–) forgetfulness, absentmindedness.

chechemea *stat.-appl. of* **chechea.**

chechemua stimulate.

chechesha *caus. of* **chechea.**

chechevu, kekevu (–) hiccup.

checheza *caus. of* **chechea.**

chechi (–) *see* **cheche.**

chefua cause nausea. *intr.* **chefuka.** have a feeling of nausea. *Cf.* **kichefuchefu.**

chega shave off, shave; cut off, dock, clip; cut the hair.

chegama *see* **egama.**

[1]**chege** (ma-) *see* tege.

[2]**chege, tege** *adj.* 1. moist, damp, watery. muhogo mchege. watery manioc. 2. *fig.* feebleminded, inane, stupid, foolish.

chegema *see* egama.

chego (ma-) *see* gego.

[1]**cheka** 1. laugh; smile, grin. 2. *(also appl.* chekelea, chekerea) laugh at, deride, mock, tease. *caus.* chekesha. make someone laugh; amuse, stimulate. *Cf.* chekeshaji, cheko, [1]cheshi, kichekesho, kicheko, mchekeshi, mcheko, mcheshi, ucheshi.

[2]**cheka** *intr. of* [2]cha.

chekeamwezi (–) *ornith.* stone curlew.

chekecha sift, select; shake; reduce. *Cf.* chekecheke, mchekecho.

chekechea (–) *ornith.* bishop-bird *(Euplectes hordacea).*

chekecheke (–) 1. sieve. 2. *fig.* retrenchment, frugality, economy, thrift. *Cf.* chekecha.

chekehukwa (–) *ornith.* golden plover, dotterel.

chekelea, chekerea *appl. of* [1]cheka.

chekenene (–) *rare, med.* sty. (= chokea.)

chekerea *see* chekelea.

chekeshaji *adj.* gay, jolly, amusing. ni mtu mchekeshaji. He is an amusing person. *Cf.* [1]cheka.

cheki* [*Engl.*] (–) *fin.* check.

cheko (–, ma-) laugh, laughter. *Cf.* [1]cheka.

chekua dig out.

[1]**chekwa, chekwachekwa** *adj.* many, in great numbers.

[2]**chekwa** *pass. of* [1]cheka.

chekwachekwa *see* [1]chekwa.

chelebi* (–) chelebi (kind of light pastry).

chelema *adj.* watery *(of fruit after cooking). Cf.* mchelema.

[1]**cheleo** (ma-) (*usually* macheleo) 1. fear, terror. 2. *fig.* awe, reverence. *Cf.* [2]cha.

[2]**cheleo** (ma-) delay, postponement. *fig., fin.* respite, delay of payment. *Cf.* [3]cha.

[1]**chelewa** *see* [3]cha.

^{2}**chelewa** (–) rattle *(used in dances).*

^{3}**chelewa** (–) vein in a leaf.

^{1}**cheleza** *see* ^{3}**cha.**

^{2}**cheleza** unload, discharge cargo *(ships).*

^{1}**chelezo** (vyelezo) buoy; life-belt; float *(on a fishing-line). Cf.* **elea.**

^{2}**chelezo** (ma-) hindrance, obstacle, disturbance; delay. *Cf.* ^{3}**cha.**

chembamba (vyembamba) chembamba (a small, thin worm).

^{1}**chembe** (–) (*and* **kichembe**, vi-) grain *(cereal, sand),* tiny particle. **chembechembe** *adj.* granular, granulated. **sukari chembechembe.** granulated sugar.

^{2}**chembe** (vyembe) point, head *(of arrow, spear, harpoon). Cf.* **jembe, kijembe.**

^{1}**chembeu** (vi-) *rare* chisel.

^{2}**chembeu** (–) *anat.* diaphragm.

chemchemi (–) spring *(of water). Cf.* **chemka.**

chemka, chemuka bubble, seethe, effervesce, boil; boil over; be hot. *caus.* **chemsha, chemusha.** boil/cook something, heat (up). *Cf.* **chemko, chemchemi.**

chemko (–), **mchemko** (mi-) bubbling, seething, effervescence; boiling, cooking. *Cf.* **chemka.**

chemne*, chemni, chemli [*Engl.*] (–, ma-) chimney *(of a lamp).*

chemni (–, ma-) *see* **chemne.**

chemsha *caus. of* **chemka.**

chemua sneeze.

chemuka *see* **chemka.**

chemusha *caus. of* **chemka.**

chena (–) chena (kind of haddock).

chenene (–) (kind of) cricket.

cheneo, kieneo (vi-) *rare, usually* **eneo,** *q.v.*

cheneta itch, irritate; become inflamed; smart, hurt.

chenezo, kienezo (vi-) measure *(measuring-rod, yardstick, tape-measure, etc.) Cf.* **enea.**

^{1}**chenga, shenga** 1. cut/saw/hack/chop off, split. **–kuni.** chop firewood. *Cf.* **mchengo.** 2. (–) (*also* **chenge**, –; **chengechenge**, vi-) grain, particle, chip, shaving, splinter. **chengachenga.** *adv.* in small particles, granular. **unga wa –.** flour that is not well ground.

[2]**chenga** 1. deceive. 2. (–) excuse, evasion. **piga –.** *sport* dribble *(a football)*, avoid, dodge.

chengachenga *see* [1]**chenga.**

chengechenge (vi-) *see* [1]**chenga.**

chengelele (ma-) *see* **jengelele.**

chengeu (vi-) lampshade.

chengo (vyengo) (dwelling-)house, residence; stopping-place, camp; village.

chengua *rare* tear down, demolish *(buildings)*.

chenji* [*Engl.*] 1. (–) substitute. *fin.* change, exchange. **fedha ya –.** (small) change. 2. *v.* to change/exchange.

chenu *see* **-enu.**

chenza (ma-) chenza (kind of Mandarin orange). *Cf.* **mchenza.**

cheo (vyeo) 1. *rare* measure, measurement, dimension(s); scale. 2. *fig.* rank, degree, status, title; class *(railway)*. **abiria wa – cha kwanza.** first-class passenger.

chepe 1. (ma-) rude, ill-bred person. 2. *adj.* rude, coarse, rough, ill-bred.

chepechepe *adj.* wet, moist, damp, watery. *Cf.* **uchepechepe.**

chepeo*, chapeo, chepeu [*Port.*] (–) (European) hat.

cherahani* (–) *see* **cherehani.**

cheraka* (–) *see* **jeraha.**

cherehani*, cherahani, charahani [*Pers.*] (–) small machine. **– ya kushonea.** sewing machine. **kazi ya –.** machine-sewn work. **fundi –.** tailor. **shona kwa –.** sew with the sewing machine. **– ya barafu.** refrigerator.

cherehe* [*Pers.*] (–) grindstone, whetstone.

cheruhi* *see* **jeruhi.**

chesha *caus. of* [2]**cha.**

[1]**cheshi** *adj.* funny, amusing, comical. *Cf.* [1]**cheka.**

[2]**cheshi** (ma-) *see* **jeshi.**

chete (–) *dial.* market-place, market-day.

chetezo (–) incense burner, censer.

chethamu* (–) *see* **jethamu.**

cheti* [*Ind.*] (–, vyeti) 1. chit, note, paper. 2. certificate, receipt, ticket. 3.: **– cha njia.** passport. 4. testimonial, document.

chetu *see* **-etu.**

cheu (–) 1. ruminating, chewing the cud. 2. belch(ing). *Cf.* **cheua.**

cheua 1. chew the cud *(cattle).* 2. belch. *intr.* **cheuka.** *caus.* **cheusha.** *Cf.* **cheu, cheuo.**

[1]**cheuka** *dial.* boil, bubble.

[2]**cheuka** *intr. of* **cheua.**

cheuo (–) cud *(of ruminants). Cf.* **cheu, cheua.**

cheusha *caus. of* **cheua.**

cheuzi* (**vyeuzi**) pair *(of shoes, etc.). Cf.* [1]**jozi.**

chewa (–) chewa (large sea-fish; kind of rock-cod with very large mouth). *coll.* **kinywa kama –.** very large mouth *(of a person).*

cheyaman* [*Engl.*] (**vyeaman**) chairman. (= **mwenye kiti.**)

cheyo (**ma-**) *see* **gego**

cheza 1. play, amuse oneself; dance; engage in sports; waste time. 2. set in motion, start *(a mechanism). int.* **chezacheza.** dally, joke. *appl.* **chezea.** play with; make fun of, tease. *intr.* **chezeka.** *Cf.* **chezo, mcheza, mchezo, uchezaji.**

chezacheza *int. of* **cheza.**

chezo (–) 1. game. 2. sport. *Cf.* **cheza, mchezo.**

chiazi* (–) *mil.* cartridge. *Cf.* [2]**kiasi.**

chibene (–) *see* **jibini.**

chiboa (–) *rare* young dog. *Cf.* **mbwa.**

[1]**chicha** (–, **ma-**) oilcake (flesh of a ripe coconut after the oil has been pressed out).

[2]**chicha** *coll.* very drunk. **alikuwa –.** He was very drunk.

chichiri (–), **kijiri** (**vi-**) bribe. (= **rushwa, hongo.**)

chifu* [*Engl.*] (**ma-**) chief, leader, chairman. *Cf.* **uchifu.**

chigi (–) chigi (a small yellow bird).

chika (–) chika (kind of plant: Abyssinian dock, sorrel).

chikicha, tikita *rare* cut *(as with a dull knife),* saw away at something. *Cf.* **tikisa.**

chikichi (–) *bot.* palm-nut *(fruit of the oil-palm). Cf.* **mchikichi.**

chiku (–) *see* **chiriku.**

chikwaya (–) *bot.:* – dume. *Dichapetalum mosambicense.* – jike. *Dichapetalum macrocarpum.*

chimba (*dial.* **timba**) 1. dig, excavate. – **kisima.** dig a well. *fig.* injure, damage. *inv.* **chimbua.** *inv.-intr.* **chimbuka.** appear, come up *(sun, moon).* *inv.-int.(-caus.).* **chimbuza.** force its way out, make its appearance, appear through the clouds *(sun).* 2. *fig.* cause trouble/misfortune *(to one's parents).* *Cf.* **chimbo, chimvu, mchimbaji, mchimbi, uchimbaji, uchimvi.**

chimbi (ma-) *dial.* cook.

chimbo, chimbuko (ma-) 1. hole. 2. *min.* shaft, pit. 3. excavation, ditch, trench. *Cf.* **chimba.**

chimbua *inv. of* **chimba.**

chimbuko (ma-) 1. *see* **chimbo.** 2. source; beginning, start.

chimbule (–) chimbule (kind of bird).

chimbuza *inv.-int. of* **chimba.**

chimvi (ma-) (*rare* **mtimbi, wa-**) 1. unlucky person *(with certain peculiarities which are regarded as bad omens),* one who brings misfortune, jinx, troublemaker. 2. medicine man *(who prepares charms). Cf.* **chimba, mchimbi, uchimvi.**

china 1. be late, be delayed, fail to show up. 2. stay on the shelf, find no takers *(merchandise).* 3. *(of a girl)* fail to find a husband at the proper age *(the girl is not only disappointed because she has not met the expectations of her society, but is actually considered to be delinquent).*

chindi (–) *dial. see* **kindi.**

chingirisha pour off *(water, etc., gently so as to leave the sediment).* (= **gida.**)

chini 1. (–) underside, lower part; ground, floor; *(euph.)* the genital organs. – **ya utawala wa ...** under the domination/rule of... 2. *adv.* below, underneath; on the ground; downstairs; at the feet; on foot. **enda –.** go on foot. – **kwa –.** very far below, underground; *(fig.)* secretly. **weka –.** underestimate. 3. **–a –.** *adj.* low; inferior, humble. *Cf.* **kichinichini.**

chinja (*dial.* **tinda**) slaughter, cut the throat, stick *(pigs, etc.). Cf.* **chinjo, chinyango, kichinja, mchinjoni, mchinjaji, mchinjo.**

chinjo (ma-) 1. slaughter(ing). 2. *fig.* massacre, carnage, bloodshed. *Cf.* **chinja.**

chinjoni *see* **machinjoni.**

chinusi, chunusi (ma-) 1. *liter.* sea-monster, water-sprite. **liwa na —.** be eaten by the sea-monster (*i.e.*, drown). 2. (swimmer's) cramp.

chinyango (—) piece of meat *(prepared for cooking). Cf.* **chinja.**

chipua grow, bud, sprout. *intr.* **chipuka.** *caus.* **chipukisha, chipuza.** *Cf.* **chipukizi, kichipukizi, mchipukizi, uchipuko.**

chipukizi, chipuko (ma-) sprout, shoot. *Cf.* **chipua.**

chipuko (ma-) *see* **chipukizi.**

chira, chura do harm (*e.g.*, to a child) by failure to observe taboos and traditional restrictions, cause bad luck (to someone). *Cf.* **chirwa, churo, uchuro.**

chiriku, chiku (—) 1. *ornith.* finch *(Fringilla coelebs)*, canary. 2. *fig.* talkative person, chatterbox.

chiririka (*dial.* **tiririka**) 1. drip, trickle; lick; flow, run. 2. glide *(of snakes). Cf.* **chirizi, mchiririko, mchirizi.**

chiriwa (—) *see* **jiriwa.**

chirizi *adj.* dripping, trickling. **machozi machirizi.** trickling tears. *Cf.* **chiririka.**

chiroko (—) *see* **choroko.**

chirwa (—) *med.* rickets (= **nyongea**). *Cf.* **chira.**

chisi* (—) *see* **chizi.**

chizi*, chisi [*Engl.*] (—) cheese. (= **jibini.**)

cho *det.* **ki-** *cl.:* **kitu — chote.** anything whatsoever.

choa (—) *med.* 1. growth, tumor. 2. skin disease, ringworm.

chobea (*and ass.* **chobeana**) stand opposite each other *(in dancing).*

chobeana *see* **chobea.**

chocha prod, urge forward *(animals);* stir, poke, stir up. *appl.* **chochea.** stir *(a fire).* **chochea matata (ugomvi).** stir up unrest (conflict), incite, inflame. *double appl.* **chochelea.** *caus. & int.* **chocheleza.** enrage, provoke, excite, irritate, challenge. *Cf.* **kichocheo, kichocho, mchocheaji, mchocheo, mchochezi, uchochezi.**

chochoro (ma-) *see* **kichochoro.**

chochota feel, suffer *(severe pain);* burn/scald oneself. *Cf.* **chonyota, mchochota.**

chogoe (—) 1. hooked stick (used to pull down branches in fruit-picking). 2. golf-club.

[1]choka grow tired, be exhausted; be tired of/disgusted with something; be impatient. **– safari (kazi).** be tired of a trip (job). *fig.* lose strength (or good properties), be exhausted (*e.g., the soil). caus.* **chokesha, chokeza, chosha.** tire out, exhaust. *caus.-ass.* **choshana.** tire/weary each other. *Cf.* **choshi, chovu, mchoshi, uchovu.**

[2]choka (ma-) *see* **joka.**

[3]choka (ma-) *see* **shoka.**

chokaa (–) lime, mortar, plaster, stucco. **choma –.** prepare lime by burning.

chokea (–) *med.* sty.

chokesha, chokeza *caus. of* **[1]choka.**

[1]choki (–) *bot.* liana *(Strophanthus kombe,* the seeds of which are used for preparing arrow poison).

[2]choki*, chaki [*Engl.*] (–) chalk, whiting, pipeclay. *Cf.* **chokaa.**

choko (vyoko) *rare* oven.

chokoa, chokocha, chokora pick at, clear out, take out the contents *(e.g., the meat of a coconut);* stir up. **– meno.** pick the teeth. *appl.* **chokolea.** *caus.* **chokoza.** tease, irritate, annoy; deceive, cheat. *Cf.* **chokochoko, kichokoo, mchokocho, mchokoo, mchokozi, uchokozi.**

chokocha *see* **chokoa.**

chokochoko (–) difficulty, trouble, annoyance; dispute, disagreement, provocation. *Cf.* **chokoa.**

chokolea *appl. of* **chokoa.**

chokoleti*, chakeleti, chakleti [*Engl.*] (–) chocolate.

[1]chokora (ma-) *see* **chotara.**

[2]chokora *see* **chokoa.**

chokoza (*caus. of* **chokoa**) tease, annoy; deceive, cheat.

[1]chole (–) chole (edible fish).

[2]chole (–) chole (kind of bird).

[1]choma stick, stab, pierce; hurt, injure. *fig.* stimulate, excite, spur on, impel. *appl.* **chomea.** *intr.* **chomeka.** be stuck/pierced/stimulated (*also tr.:* stick/thrust into something). *inv.* **chomoa** (*rare* **shumua**). pull out; borrow. **chomoa kisu.** pull out/borrow a knife. **chomoa fedha (nguo).** borrow money (clothes). *inv.-appl.* **chomolea.** pull out for/from someone; *(fig.)* steal from. *inv.-caus.* **chomoza.** appear, come out *(sun). Cf.* **[1]chomeo, [1]chomo, kichomi, [2]mchoma, [2]mchomo, uchomozi.**

[2]choma burn, be on fire; set fire to; smoke out *(bees, etc.).* **jua linachoma.** The sun is very hot. *Cf.* [2]**chomeo**, [2]**chomo**, **kichoma**, [2]**kichomo**, [1]**mchoma**, **mchomaji**, [1]**mchomo**, **uchomaji**.

chombo (**vyombo**) 1. tool, implement, instrument, utensil, apparatus; item of household goods, piece of furniture. **cha kufanyia kazi.** tool, implement *(used in working).* **vyombo vya akiba.** spare parts. 2. cooking-pot, pan, jar, jug, cup. 3.: **vyombo.** household goods, personal belongings; gear, machinery. 4. sailing-vessel *(of various kinds). loc.* **chomboni.** on board. **– cha angani.** spaceship. **– cha kuandikishia maneno.** tape-recorder. **– cha kunyunyizia.** pulverizer, atomizer. **– cha kukuzia sauti.** microphone. **– cha simu.** telephone booth.

[1]**chomeo** (**ma-**) 1. pointed object (stick, awl, etc.). 2. pain. 3. small wound, prick *(left after removing a thorn, etc.)* *Cf.* [1]**choma.**

[2]**chomeo** (**ma-**) something used for cooking: frying-pan, grill, etc. *Cf.* [2]**choma.**

[1]**chomo** (**ma-**) blow, cut, stab, prick. *Cf.* [1]**choma.**

[2]**chomo** (**ma-**) 1. burn, scar from burning. 2. product of combustion, slag. **– la chuma.** iron slag. *Cf.* [2]**choma.**

chomoa *inv. of* [1]**choma.**

chomolea *inv.-appl. of* [1]**choma.**

chomoza *inv.-caus. of* [1]**choma.**

[1]**chondo** (**–**) 1. musical instrument *(kind of xylophone).* 2. signaling drum.

[2]**chondo** (**vyondo**) chondo (small traveling-bag).

[3]**chondo** (**vyondo**) chondo (small sea-mussel).

chonga 1. cut *(with an instrument),* chop, carve. **– sanamu.** carve a statue. 2. cut to a point, sharpen. **– kalamu.** sharpen a pencil. *appl.* **chongea.** cut, sharpen something. 3. *fig.* slander. **chongea kwa maneno mabaya.** bring someone into discredit by spreading tales about him. *inv.* **chongoa.** shape, round off. *inv.-intr.* **chongoka.** *Cf.* **chonge, chongelezo, mchongezi, mchongo, uchongezi.**

chonge (**–**) *anat.* canine tooth; tooth filed to a point. *Cf.* **chonga.**

chongelezo (**ma-**) slander, calumny, gossip. *Cf.* **chonga.**

[1]**chongo** (**–**) *see* **mchongo.**

[2]**chongo** (**–**) hump *(on the back).*

[3]**chongo** (**–**) condition of having only one eye. **mwenye –.** one-eyed person. **ana –.** He has only one eye. *Cf.* **uchongo.**

[4]**chongo** (–) chongo (purulent discharge from the eye).

chongoa *inv. of* **chonga.**

chongoe (vi-) chongoe (large fish).

chongoo (ma-) *see* [1]**jongoo.**

chonjo (–) incitement *(to quarrel, combat). Cf.* **chonjomoa.**

chonjomoa incite, instigate, stimulate, impel. *Cf.* **chonjo.**

chonyota prickle, sting, burn. **pilipili inachonyota ulimini.** The pepper burns on the tongue. *Cf.* **chochota.**

chonza (–) discord, unrest. **tia –.** cause unrest.

choo (vyoo) 1. toilet, privy, water closet. **enda chooni.** go to the toilet. 2. need to relieve oneself; bowel movement, urination. **– yabisi.** constipation. **vyoo** excreta. **– kidogo.** urine. **– kikubwa.** feces.

chooko (–) *see* **choroko.**

chopa 1. take *(a small amount, a handful);* engage in business on a small scale, vend, hawk. *inv.* **chopoa.** pull out; snatch away, seize; *(fig.)* steal. *inv.-intr.* slip away; *(fig.)* be stolen. 2. (ma-) handful, bundle *(of firewood). Cf.* **kichopa, mchopozi.**

chopi *adj./adv.* 1. crooked, lopsided. **enda –.** be lame, limp. 2. *fig.* drunk, intoxicated.

chopoa *inv. of* **chopa.**

chopoka *inv.-intr. of* **chopa.**

[1]**chora** 1. scratch, carve; cut/carve in stone. 2. *int.* **chorachora.** scribble, write illegibly. *Cf.* **choro, kichoro, mchorachora, mchoraji, mchoro, mchorochoro, uchoraji.**

[2]**chora*** (–) *see* **shura.**

chorachora *int. of* **chora.**

choro (–, ma-) scratch; drawing, engraving; (**chorochoro**) scribble, scrawl. *Cf.* [1]**chora.**

choroa (–) *zool.* fringe-eared oryx.

chorochoro (ma-) *see* **choro.**

choroko, chooko, chiroko (–) choroko (small green bean).

chosha *caus. of* [1]**choka.**

choshi *adj.* tiring, exhausting. *Cf.* [1]**choka.**

chosho (ma-) *see* **josho.**

chosi (–) chosi (kind of bird).

chota take a little of something. — **maji.** draw water *(by the bucketful). caus.* **chotesha, choteza.** *fig.* **alinichota akili.** He deceived/cheated me. *Cf.* **choto, mchoto.**

chotara*, chokora (ma-) 1. half-breed, mestizo. 2. person who works at odd jobs, servant performing heavy/dirty work. 3. *fig.* hanger-on.

chote *see* **-ote.**

choto (ma-) small amount: piece, bit, fragment, morsel. *Cf.* **chota.**

chovu *adj.* 1. tired, exhausted. 2. tiring, boring, annoying. *Cf.* **1choka.**

chovya put/dip/plunge into a liquid; submerge. *appl.* **chovyea.** *pass.* **chovywa.** *Cf.* **chovyo, mchovya, mchovyo.**

chovyo (ma-) dipping, plunging, submerging. *Cf.* **chovya.**

chovywa *pass. of* **chovya.**

choyo (—) greed, avarice; parsimony, stinginess; meanness, pettiness. **mwenye —.** miser. **ana —.** He is stingy. *Cf.* **moyo.**

1chozi, jozi (ma-) tear. **lia (toka) machozi.** shed tears.

2chozi (—) *ornith.* sunbird. *Cf.* **kichozi.**

1chua, tua rub, rub in, massage; clean, polish *(by rubbing); (fig.)* flatter, deceive. *appl.* **chulia.** rub something. **jiwe la kuchulia.** pestle, grindstone. *ass.* **chuana.** rub/massage each other; *(fig.)* quarrel. *caus.* **chusha.** irritate, anger, provoke. *refl.* **jichua.** masturbate.

2chua (vyua) *see* **chura.**

chuakari (—) *rare* precious stone. jewel. *Cf.* **johari.**

chub! *interj.* Be quiet!

chubua abrade, rub off *(skin),* rub sore, bruise badly, gall. — **miguu.** get sore feet. *appl.* **chubulia.** *intr.* **chubuka.** *Cf.* **chubuko.**

chubui (—) *see* **chubwi.**

chubuko (ma-) abrasion. bruise, sore. *Cf.* **chubua.**

chubwi, chubui (—) 1. *naut.* lead. 2. sinker *(on a fishing line),* plumb-line.

chucha *see* **2chicha.**

chuchia shake, move back and forth, swing. — **mtoto.** rock a child.

[1]**chuchu** (ma-) *rare* dwarf, pygmy.

[2]**chuchu** (–, **ma-**) *anat.* nipple. (= titi.)

chuchumaa squat, crouch. *caus.* **chuchumaza.**

chuchumaza *caus. of* **chuchumaa.**

chuchumia stretch, stand on tiptoe or hind legs *(animals).*

chuchunge (–) swordfish *(Nemiramphus far).* (= **mchumbururu.**)

chudi (–) *see* [3]**jadi.**

chugachuga be uneasy, feel uncomfortable; be confused, unprepared. *Cf.* **machugachuga.**

chuguu (–) (*augment. of* **kichuguu**) 1. anthill, termite-heap. 2. pile of ashes or refuse.

chui (–) leopard. *comm.* **chui wa karatasi.** paper tiger.

chuja filter, strain; press out; cleanse, purify; *fig.* separate, isolate, pick out, select, sort, refine. – **watu wengine.** pick out a few people. *inv.* **chujua.** thin, dilute, water down. *inv.-intr.* **chujuka.** be washed-out/faded; fade *(of colors).* *appl.* **chujia. chujia mvuke.** liquefy. *Cf.* **chujio, chujo, uchujo.**

chujio (–, **ma-**), **kichujio** (**vi-**) filter, strainer. *Cf.* **chuja.**

chujo (–, **ma-**) 1. = **chujio.** 2. product of filtering/straining: residue, deposit, precipitate. *Cf.* **chuja.**

chujua *inv. of* **chuja.**

chujuka *inv.-intr. of* **chuja.**

chuki (–) 1. bad humor/mood, dissatisfaction. 2. dislike, aversion, contempt. **ona –.** be in a bad humor. **– na majivuno ya kitaifa.** chauvinism. *Cf.* **chukia, chukio, uchukivu.**

chukia hate, despise, abhor, loath. *caus.* **chukiza.** offend, insult. *refl.-caus.* **jichukiza.** be annoyed with oneself. *ass.* **chukiana.** *Cf.* **chuki.**

chukio, chukizo (**ma-**) (*usually* **machukio, machukizo**) hatred, disgust; offense, insult. *Cf.* **chuki, chukia.**

chukiza *caus. of* **chukia.**

chukizo (ma-) *see* **chukio.**

chuku (–) 1. *med.* cupping-glass. **piga –.** cup, bleed; *(fig.)* exaggerate, tell unbelievable stories. 2. *rare* lie, falsehood; something invented, fiction; nostrum. **hadithi ya –.** story, fiction.

chukua 1. carry, take along; take, take away, remove. **maji yanachukua mchanga.** The water washes the sand away. 2. *fig.* bear, endure. – **taabu.** endure hardships. 3. last. – **muda mkubwa.** last a long time. *appl.* **chukulia.** 1. carry to/for someone. 2. *fig.* have sympathy, feel for. *appl.-intr.* **chukulika. haichukuliki.** It is unbearable. *ass.* **chukuana.** support each other, agree together, conform. *appl.-ass.* **chukuliana.** *caus.* **chukuza.** employ someone to carry something, hire as a bearer. *ass.-caus.* **chukuzana.** 1. carry by turns. 2. accompany each other, go together. *Cf.* **mchukuzi, uchukuzi.**

chukulia *appl. of* **chukua.**

chukuti *pl. of* **uchukuti.**

chukuza *caus. of* **chukua.**

chula (**vyula**) *see* **chura.**

[1]**chuma** (**vyuma**) 1. (piece of) iron. – **cha pua.** steel. **mabamba ya –.** sheet iron. – **cha noti.** tuning-fork. **bao la –.** iron bar. – **cha reli.** rail. **chuma cha pua kisioganda/kisichoingia kutu.** stainless steel. 2. *fig.* hardness, severity. **mtu huyu ni –.** This man is steady/reliable.

[2]**chuma** (*dial.* **tunda**) 1. gather, pick *(fruit).* 2. *fig.* earn, make a profit. *Cf.* **chumi, chumo, uchumaji, uchumi.**

chumba (**vyumba**) room (*of a house*). – **cha mwendesha ndege.** cockpit, turret *(of an airplane).* – **cha dwa.** drugstore. – **cha kuni.** shed, barn. – **cha kulala.** bedroom. – **cha kulia.** dining-room. – **cha maktaba.** reading-room. *Cf.* **chumbisha, jumba, kichumba, kijichumba, mchumba, nyumba, uchumba, unyumba.**

chumbe (**vyumbe**) *see* **kiumbe.**

chumbisha bring about an engagement. *pass.* **chumbishwa.** be engaged *(of a girl). Cf.* **chumba, mchumba, uchumba.**

chumi (–) cowrie-shell(s) *(used in playing games). Cf.* [2]**chuma.**

chumo (**ma-**) total product, yield; *(fig.)* receipts, earnings, profits. *Cf.* [2]**chuma.**

chumu (**vi-**) *rare* good luck.

chumvi (–) salt; saltiness, salinity; sharpness, pungency. – **ya haluli.** Epsom salts, sulphate of magnesia. *fig.* **tia –.** exaggerate, boast. *coll.* **kula – nyingi.** have a long life.

chuna (*and inv.* **chunua**) skin, flay *(animals);* strip off *(bark),* scrape off. *Cf.* [1]**chuno, mchunaji.**

[1]**chunga** sift, screen; shake; *(fig.)* tremble *(from fear). inv.* **chungua.** *inv.-appl.* **chungulia.** *inv.-caus. (int.)* **chunguza.** examine/investigate carefully; *(fig.)* pry into/meddle in someone else's affairs. *Cf.* **chungio, mchunguzi, uchunguzi.**

²**chunga, shunga** watch over, take care of, tend, take to pasture *(cattle, sheep, etc.)*. *Cf.* **machunga, mchungaji, uchungaji.**

³**chunga** (–) hull, pod, shell.

chungio (–) sieve. *Cf.* ¹**chunga.**

¹**chungu** (vyungu), **ungu** (nyungu) clay vessel, cooking pot. **kufinyanga vyungu.** pottery. *Cf.* ⁴**kichungu, jungu,** ¹**mkungu.**

²**chungu, kichungu** *adj.* 1. bitter, sharp, acrid. 2. *fig.* unpleasant, angry, harsh. **maneno machungu.** bitter/harsh words. *Cf.* **uchungu.**

³**chungu** (–, ma-), **kichungu** (vi-) heap, pile; quantity; mass, crowd. – **nzima.** a great deal, a lot (of...). **mkutanoni walikuwapo watu – nzima.** There were a lot of people in the gathering. **chunguchungu.** *adv.* in great quantity/number.

⁴**chungu** (–) (black) ant.

chungua *inv. of* ¹**chunga.**

chunguchungu *see* ³**chungu.**

chungulia *inv.-appl. of* ¹**chunga.**

chunguza *inv.-caus. & int. of* ¹**chunga.**

chungwa (ma-) orange. *Cf.* **mchungwa.**

chuni (–) chuni (waterfowl).

chunjua (–) *med.* wart.

¹**chuno** (ma-) (*usually* **machuno**) skinning, flaying. *Cf.* **chuna.**

²**chuno** (–) *see* **kiuno.**

chunua *inv. of* **chuna.**

chunuka favor/encourage someone, be well-disposed toward someone. *See also* **tunuka.**

¹**chunusi, kinusi** (–) *med.* acne.

²**chunusi** (ma-) *see* **chinusi.**

chunyu (–) salt-deposit/incrustation *(from sea-water)*; salinity. **ardhi ina –.** saliferous earth. *Cf.* **chumvi, munyu.**

¹**chuo** (vyuo) 1. school. – **kikuu.** university. **enda chuoni.** go to school. **mwana chuoni.** learned man, scholar. 2. *rare* book (= **kitabu**). – **cha sala.** prayer-book.

²**chuo** (vyuo) chuo (pointed stick used for opening coconuts).

¹**chupa** (–, ma-) 1. bottle. 2. jar *(for jam, etc.)*. 3. *anat.* uterus, womb. **kuvunja –.** first stages of childbirth.

[2]**chupa** 1. jump, hop. **chura anachura.** The frog jumps. 2. *fig.* become too short/small *(of clothes).* **suruali yangu imechupa.** My trousers have become too small for me. *appl.* **chupia.** move fast, gallop.

[1]**chura** (vyura) (*rare* **chula, chua**) frog, toad.

[2]**chura** *see* **chira.**

churo *adj.* unlucky, ill-omened. **mtoto mchuro.** child who is supposed to bring misfortune to his family because of omens *(marks, etc.). Cf.* **chira, uchuro.**

churua *see* **surua.**

churupuka flee, run away, escape; slip from one's hand.

churura (*and int.* **churuza, chuuza**) drip, trickle; run, flow (off), drain. *intr.* **chururika** (*and int.* **chururiza**). *fig.* be wasted away, emaciated *(after an illness). Cf.* **chururu.**

chururika *intr. of* **churura.**

chururiza *int. of* **churura.**

chururu (–) efflux, trickle; leak, seepage. *Cf.* **churura.**

churusi (vyurusi) chisel.

churuwa* (–) *med* measles *Cf.* **surua.**

churuza *int. of* **churura.**

chusa*, chussa [?] (vyusa) harpoon *(for large fish).*

chusha *caus. of* **chua.**

chussa* (vyussa) *see* **chusa.**

chut! *interj.* = [1]**kefu!**

chutama squat, crouch.

[1]**chuuza** *int. of* **churura.**

[2]**chuuza** engage in business in a small way, be a hawker/peddler, have a small shop. *Cf.* **mchuuzi, uchuuzi.**

chuzuu* (–) *see* **tuzuu.**

chwa (*also* **twa**) go down, set *(sun).* **kumekuchwa.** The sun has gone down. It is evening. **mchana kutwa.** the whole day long. **kutwa kucha.** every day and every night. **kucha hata (mpaka) kuchwa.** from morning till evening, the whole day through. **kesho kutwa.** day after tomorrow. *appl.* **chwea.** *double appl.-pass.* **chwelewa.** be overtaken by darkness. *Cf.* **machwa.**

chwelewa *double appl.-pass. of* **chwa.**

D

daa (–) daa (kind of worm used for fish-bait).

daawa*, **dai** (–, **ma-**) lawsuit, (legal) action, (civil) suit, claim. *Cf.* **dai, mdaawa, mdai, mdaiwa.**

¹daba* (**ma-**) simpleton, fool.

²daba (–, **ma-**) *see* **debe.**

dabaulo* *see* **tabawali.**

dabiku* (–) *rare* sacrifice, offering. *Cf.* **dhabihu.**

dabiri* *rare* find (again).

dabwadabwa, debwedebwe *adj.* fluid, watery, diluted. **wali wa –.** watery rice.

¹Dachi* [*Engl.*] *adj.* Dutch.

²Dachi* [*Germ.*] *adj., arch.* German. (= **-a kijeremani.**) *Cf.* **Kidachi, Mdachi, Udachi.**

dada (–, **ma-**) 1. sister. 2. *form of polite address among women.*

dadisa gird, wind around.

dadisi* besiege with questions, pump; spy on. *intr.* **dadisika.** be curious/inquisitive. *appl.* **dadisia.** *caus.* **dadisiza.** *Cf.* **mdadisi, udadisi.**

dadisika* *intr. of* **dadisi.**

dadisiza* *caus. of* **dadisi.**

dado* (–, **ma-**) *see* **dadu.**

dadu*, dado [*Port.*] (–, **ma-**) 1. die, dice. 2. any game played with dice.

dafi* (–) tambourine.

dafina* (–) 1. something valuable/precious. 2. hidden treasure, find, treasure trove. 3. unexpected gift, windfall.

dafrao*, dafurao 1. (–) collision, impact, clash; accident. **motakaa mbili ziligongona (pigana) –.** Two automobiles collided. 2. *adv.* face to face. **piga (pigana) –.** fight hand to hand.

daftari*, deftari (–) 1. ledger, account book, catalogue, index, list. **– ya hesabu.** account book. 2. notebook, exercise book.

dafu (–) dafu (coconut in the unripe stage, with much milk). **dafu** *or* **maji ya –.** coconut milk.

dafurao* (–) *see* **dafrao.**

daga* (–) *see* **dagaa.**

dagaa*, **daga** (–) 1. dagaa (small fish, anchovy, sardine). 2. *fig.* trifle, inconsequential thing.

daghadagha* 1. (–) confusion *(of mind)*, uncertainty. 2. *v.* be uncertain. *Cf.* **dukuduku.**

dagla* [*Ind.*] (ma-) cloth coat *(decorated with ornaments).*

daha* *see* **dai.**

dahabu* (–) *see* **dhahabu.**

dahari* 1. (–) epoch, century, age. 2. *adv.* always, constantly.

dahi *dial.* offer, sacrifice.

dahili* 1. be well informed about a person. 2. (ma-) inquiry, investigation. *Cf.* **mdahalo.**

dai*, **daha** 1. demand, claim; *(leg.)* press claims, bring action, sue. *appl.* **daia.** demand in someone else's name, act as attorney/solicitor. *ass.* **daiana.** *refl.* **jidai.** demand something for oneself *(without justification, falsely).* 2. (ma-) (*also* **daawa**) demand, claim. **madai ya fedha.** claim for money, amount due, debt. *Cf.* **daawa, mdaawa, mdai, mdaiwa.**

daifu* *see* **dahifu.**

daima*, **dawamu**, **dawama** 1. *adv.* always, constantly, continually. *emph.* **– dawamu.** 2. *adj.* **-a –.** permanent, constant, lasting. 3. *mil.* regular. **afisa wa –.** regular officer. *Cf.* [2]**dumu.**

[1]**daka** 1. grasp, seize; catch. **– mpira.** catch a ball. 2. *fig.* catch at *(an idea).* **– maneno.** make a quick/shrewd reply, contradict. *appl.* **dakia.** jump over/across *(water, from tree to tree).* *caus.* **dakiza.** retort, object, contradict, interrupt *(a conversation).* *inv.* **dakua.** talk foolishly, chatter, gossip. **dakua siri.** divulge secrets, blab. *inv.-appl.-caus.* **dakuliza.** protest, object to, demur, disavow. *Cf.* **dakizo, mdakizi, mdako, mdakulizi, udakaji, udaku, udakuzi;** *also* **dukiza, dukizi.**

[2]**daka** (ma-) 1. hiding-place, niche. 2. shelf *(on a wall)*, cupboard. *Cf.* [2]**kidaka.**

dakalika *rare* be tired/exhausted.

dakawa* (–) *naut.* tow-rope, hawser. **vuta –.** to tow.

dakika* (–) minute, (brief) period of time. **kwa – moja.** in a moment, immediately, at once. **ndani ya – chache.** in a few minutes.

dakiza *caus. of* [1]**daka.**

dakizo (ma-) objection, protest, contradiction; interruption *(of a conversation).* *Cf.* [1]**daka.**

dakta* (ma-) *see* **daktari.**

daktari*, dakta [*Engl.*] (ma-) doctor, physician. *Cf.* **mganga. – wa kupasuwa.** *rare* surgeon. (= **kuchinja.**) *Cf.* **udaktari.**

daku* (–) feast of Muhammadans at the conclusion of Ramadhan.

dakua *inv. of* [1]**daka.**

dakuliza *inv.-appl.-caus. of* [1]**daka.**

dalali* (ma-) agent, broker, auctioneer. *Cf.* **udalali.**

dalasini*, dallasini [*Pers.*] cinnamon. *Cf.* **mdalasini.**

dalia* (–) powder *(cosmetic).*

dalili*, delili (–) 1. sign, trace, signal, indication. **– ya mguu.** footprint. *prov.:* **– ya mvua ni mawingu.** Clouds are the signs of rain (= one can always tell when there is something wrong with someone whom one knows well). 2. omen. **– mbaya.** a bad omen. **si hata –.** not a bit, not in the least.

dalji* *adv.* **kuenda –.** walk gracefully; amble *(of horses).*

dalki* *see* **telki.**

dallasini* (–) *see* **dalasini.**

[1]**dama*** (–) *see* **tama.**

[2]**dama*** [*Port.*] (–) game played on a board. (= **bao 3.**)

dambwa (ma-) dambwa (secret place where preparations are made for the circumcision ceremonies).

damisi* *adj.* cheerful, jolly. *Cf.* **udamisi.**

damka *obs.* *see* **jidamka.**

damu* (–) 1. blood. **toa –.** bleed. 2. *fig.* menstruation. **ingia damuni.** menstruate. 3. blood relationship. *coll.* **– yangu mwenyewe.** my own flesh and blood (*i.e.*, child). **watu wenye – moja.** blood relatives. *prov.* **– ni nzito kuliko maji.** Blood is thicker than water.

danda *rare* *see* **panda.**

dandalo (–) dandalo (a kind of dance).

[1]**danga: – maji** dip up water *(carefully, in small quantities).*

[2]**danga** (–) (white) yam *(Dioscorea alata).*

dang'a (–) dang'a (the first milk of an animal after having given birth; beestings).

danganya lie to someone, deceive, cheat, swindle. *appl.* **danganyia.** *caus.* **danganyisha.** *Cf.* **danganyifu, danganyo, mdanganyi, udanganyifu.**

danganyifu *adj.* deceitful, fraudulent. **mtu mdanganyifu.** a deceitful person. **mke mdanganyifu.** an unfaithful wife. *Cf.* **danganya.**

danganyo (ma-) (*usually* **madanganyo**) deceit, deception, fraud; hypocrisy. *Cf.* **danganya.**

dangro* (ma-) *see* **danguro.**

danguro*, **dangro** [*Port.*] (ma-) 1. house of ill fame, brothel. *loc.* **danguroni.** section of a city where brothels are located. 2. *rare* prostitute, whore.

dansi*, **densi** [*Engl.*] (–) (European) dance.

danzi (ma-) bitter orange. *Cf.* **mdanzi.**

dapa *see* **tapa.**

dara* [*Pers.*] 1. touch, feel. 2. *fig.* try out, put to the test.

daraba* (–) lavatory space (on a dhow).

darabi* (ma-) rose apple. *Cf.* **mdarabi.**

daraja* (ma-, –) 1. bridge. **– ya reli.** railroad bridge. 2. *fig.* rank, degree, social status. **amepewa – ya juu.** He has been promoted. 3. terrace *(in agriculture)*. 4. *pl.* steps, (flight of) stairs; ladder (= **ngazi**). *Cf.* **kidaraja.**

daraka* (ma-) (*usually* **madaraka**) 1. arrangement, regulation, precept. 2. obligation, responsibility, duty. **chukua –.** have responsibility, be responsible. **madaraka ya kiasi.** limited responsibility/liability. **madaraka bila kiasi.** unlimited responsibility/liability. 3. pledge, security, guarantee. 4. full responsibility, plenary powers; *(pol.)* self-government, autonomy. *Cf.* **diriki.**

darasa* (ma-, –) instruction; lesson, class; classroom. **madarasa** *rare* school. *Cf.* **durusi.**

darau* *see* **dharau.**

daraza* *see* **darizi.**

darbini* (–) *see* **darubini.**

dari* [*Pers.*] (–) 1. roof, attic; upper floor; ceiling *(of a room)*; (flat) roof. *(Originally the space under the roof where clothing and food were stored.)* **anakaa katika nyumba ya –.** He lives in a house of more than one floor/story. 2. *fig., naut.* deck of a boat/ship.

darii* (–) *see* **deraya.**

darizi*, **daraza, tarizi, taraza** 1. embroider *(a border, edging)*. 2. (–) (*also* **tarazo**) embroidery, decoration. **kanzu ya –.** a kanzu decorated with embroidery. 3. *adj.* decorated, ornamented.

darubini*, **durubini**, **darbini** [*Pers.*] (–) telescope, binoculars. **– ya vidudu.** microscope.

darumeti* [?] (–) interior framework of a (native) ship.

darzeni* (–) *see* **dazani.**

[1]**dasi*** [*Pers.?*] (–) *naut.* rope (sewed into the edge of a sail).

[2]**dasi*** (–) *med.* dasi (disease of donkeys).

dasili* (–) dasili (a powder used as a remedy for skin diseases; prepared from the leaves of the mkunazi tree).

[1]**dasturi*** (–) *naut.* bowsprit.

[2]**dasturi*** (–) *see* **desturi.**

data *rare* crack, crackle *(noise of twigs breaking).*

datama crouch down, bend over.

dau* (–) dhow (sailing vessel).

dauati* (–) *see* **dawati.**

daula* (–, ma-) *see* **dola.**

dausi*, **tausi** (–) *ornith.* peacock.

dawa* (–, ma-) 1. medicine, remedy, drug. **– ya homa.** febrifuge. **– ya kuhara (kuharisha).** purgative, laxative. **– ya kupatisha.** emetic. **– ya kunywa.** medicine for internal use. **– ya kupaka.** salve, ointment. **– ya sindano.** vaccine, serum. 2. (*also* **nyumba ya –** *or* **nyumba ya kutoa –**) pharmacy, drugstore.

dawaa* *see* **duwaa.**

dawama*, **dawamu*** *see* **daima.**

dawati*, **dauati** (–) (*also* **kidawati**) writing desk. (= **meza.**)

dazani*, **dazeni**, **darzeni** [*Engl.*] (–) dozen.

dazeni* (–) *see* **dazani.**

debe*, **daba** [*Ind.*] (–, ma-) 1. tin can, tank *(for gasoline or kerosine).* 2. sheet metal.

debwani* (–) turban cloth.

debwedebwe *see* **dabwadabwa.**

dede *adv.:* **simama –.** stand unsteadily *(as an infant first learning to walk).*

defa* (–) *rare* time, occasion. **– mbili.** twice. (= **mara.**)

deftari* (–) *see* **daftari.**

dega *see* **tega.**

[1]**dege** (ma-) *see* **ndege.**

^{2}**dege** (–) dege (kind of moth).

^{3}**dege** (–) *med.* cramps, convulsions *(esp. of small children).*

^{4}**dege** (ma-): – **la watoto.** *bot.* kind of fern *(Pteris longifolia).*

deheni* 1. (–) deheni (waterproof mixture for caulking boats). 2. *v.* to caulk with deheni.

deheri* *rare* be plain/evident.

deka put on airs, be presumptuous/arrogant. *caus.* **dekeza.** spoil *(a child).*

dekua (*dial.* **dengua**) bring down, knock down *(birds with stones).* – **kichwa.** behead, decapitate. *appl.* **dekulia.** *Cf.* **udekuaji.**

delali* [?] (ma-) *rare* peddler (= **mchuuzi**).

dele*, deli (–) (*also* **mdele, mi-**) coffeepot *(made of metal).* (= **mdila.**)

deli* (–) *see* **dele.**

delili* (–) *see* **dalili.**

dema, ndema (–) wickerwork fish-trap.

demani* (–) 1. season (of the year; period of the southeast monsoon from August to October), autumn. 2. *naut.* sheet. 3. *naut.:* (**upande wa** –) lee side.

demokrasi* [*Engl.*] (–) democracy. – **yenye kiini kimoja.** *comm.* democratic centralism. **jamhuri ya** –. democratic republic. **kidemokrasi.** *adj.* democratic.

demu (ma-) work clothes *(for field work).*

^{1}**denge** (–) denge (a style of wearing the hair: the head is shaved leaving only a patch on top). *Cf.* ^{2}**dengua.**

^{2}**denge** (–) 1.: – **ya mbuzi.** billy goat. (= **beberu.**) 2. goat pen *(on poles, raised off the ground).*

dengezi (–) dengezi (kind of fish).

dengo* (–) *see* **dengu.**

dengu*, dengo [*Ind.*] (–) 1. *bot.* lentil. (= **adesi.**) 2. *(us.)* the thick soup made of lentils (or of beans or peas). *Cf.* **mdengu.**

^{1}**dengua** *see* **dekua.**

^{2}**dengua** shave off *(the hair, for a particular hair-style).* *Cf.* ^{1}**denge.**

deni* (–, ma-) debt, (financial) obligation. **fanya (ingia)** –. run into debt. **lipa** –. pay debts. *Cf.* **mdeni.**

densi* (–) *see* **dansi.**

deraya*, darii, dirii, durui (–) armor, armament.

derereka drip, trickle, flow.

dereva*, dreva [*Engl.*] **(ma-)** 1. driver, chauffeur. **– wa ndege.** pilot. 2. machinist, mechanic. *Cf.* **udereva.**

Desemba* [*Engl.*] (–) December.

deski* [*Engl.*] (–) (school) desk.

deste* (ma-) deste (vessel in which halua is stored).

desturi*, dasturi (–) custom, usage, practice; customary/prescriptive law; routine. **ni –.** it is customary. **kama –.** according to custom. **fuata –.** comply with customs.

dete, detepwani (–) *ornith.* (species of) kingfisher.

detea *rare* limp, hobble.

detepwani (–) *see* **dete.**

deua 1. take down/off *(a pot from the fire).* 2. *fig.* turn *(the head, scornfully).*

deuli* [*Ind.?*] (–) 1. silk sash or waistband. 2. cloth for covering a bier, pall.

devu (ma-) *augment. of* **udevu.**

dhabihu*, *(rare)* **dabiku** 1. sacrifice *(things or animals).* 2. (–) sacrifice. *Cf.* **madhabahu, madhabuha.**

dhahabu*, dahabu (–) *min.* gold. **-a –.** golden.

dhahiri* *adj. & adv.* (well) known, clear, plain, evident, obvious. *Cf.* **dhihiri, dhihirifu.**

dhaifu*, daifu *adj.* 1. weak, sickly, infirm, feeble, powerless. 2. insignificant, slight, poor *(in quality)*; unsuitable, useless. 3. bad-tempered. *Cf.* **dhoofika, udhaifu.**

dhaka* (–) *rare* jest, joke; mockery, ridicule.

dhakari* (–) *anat.* penis. (= **uume, mboo.**)

dhalika* *see* **kadhalika.**

dhalili* *adj.* deplorable, pitiful, miserable, wretched; humble, meek, obsequious.

dhalimu* 1. **(ma-)** swindler, cheat; oppressor, tyrant; unjust person. 2. *adj.* unjust, cruel, oppressive, violent. *Cf.* **mdhalimu, udhalimu.** 3. *v., see* **dhulumu.**

dhaluma* (–) *see* **dhuluma.**

dhamana* (–) pledge, guarantee, security, bail. **weka –.** give a guarantee, go bail. **– ya maisha.** social security. *Cf.* **dhamini.**

dhamani* *sing.* last month of the south monsoon.

dhambi* (–, ma-) transgression, offense, crime; *(rel.)* sin. **mwenye – tupu.** constant offender/sinner, incorrigible criminal. **– ya asili.** original sin.

dhambu* (–) *see* **tambuu.**

dhamini* 1. (–) guarantee, bail. 2. *v.* vouch for, go bail for, stand up for, guarantee, sponsor. *appl.* **dhaminia.** *caus.* **dhaminisha.** *Cf.* **dhamana, mdhamini, udhamini.**

dhamira* (–) *see* **dhamiri.**

dhamiri*, **dhamira** 1. (–) thought, wish; (innermost) conviction, intention; conscience. **ni – ya Waafrika kupata uhuru.** It is the desire of the Africans to achieve independence. 2. *v.* think, intend. *appl.* **dhamiria.** reflect *(about something);* intend, contemplate; *(urgently)* desire.

dhamiria* *appl. of* **dhamiri** 2.

dhamisa* *rare* bring to an end, conclude.

dhana* (–) 1. thought, idea; opinion; suggestion, proposal. 2. suspicion, conjecture, surmise. *Cf.* **dhani, 1udhani.**

dhani* think, consider, reflect; believe, imagine; assume, conjecture. *appl.* **dhania.** think of/about, suspect. *pass.* **dhaniwa.** *Cf.* **dhana, 1udhani.**

dhara* (ma-) (*usually* **madhara**) damage, injury, harm, loss; misfortune, accident. **pata –.** come to harm, be damaged/injured. **–a –.** *adj.* injurious, harmful. *Cf.* **dhuru.**

dharau*, **darau** 1. despise, disregard, have a low opinion of, scorn; deride, ridicule. *appl.* **dharaulia.** 2. (–) contempt, scorn; derision.

dharba* (–) *see* **dharuba.**

dhariri* (–) radioactive dust.

dharuba*, **dharba** (–) 1. pressure; impact, shock; blow, stroke *(of an ax, etc.).* 2. storm, gust of wind. 3. *rare, arith.* multiplication.

dharura* (–) 1. (sudden, unexpected) event, occurrence; confusion, commotion. 2. *rare* business transaction, deal.

dhati* (–) 1. intention, plan, purpose, goal, aim. 2. essence, nature, character. 3. *adv.* doubtless, definitely.

dhiaka* (ma-) 1. bait, lure. 2. alertness, readiness *(to meet a danger).*

dhiba* (–) *arch.* auxiliary troops, auxiliaries.

dhibiti* defend, protect from; manage, control. *caus.* **dhibitisha.** *Cf.* **madhubuti, udhibiti.**

dhidi* **ya...** *adv.* anti-, against.

dhifa* (–) guesthouse; feast.

dhihaka* (–) derision, mockery, laughter, joking, teasing. **sema (fanya) –.** make fun of, mock, deride. *Cf.* **dhihaki.**

dhihaki* joke, mock, deride, tease. *appl.* **dhihakia.** *caus.* **dhihakisha.** *Cf.* **dhihaka.**

dhihiri*, dhahiri be clear, obvious, apparent. *prov.* **kweli ikidhihiri uwongo hujitenga.** When the truth is obvious, falsehood usually gives way. *appl.* **dhihiria.** *caus.* **dhihirisha** explain, show, reveal, expose. *Cf.* **dhahiri, dhihirifu, udhahirifu.**

dhihirifu* *adj.* clear, plain, obvious, apparent, well known. *Cf.* **dhahiri, dhihiri.**

dhii* dwindle, waste away *(strength, powers);* grow weak, pine away, perish; grieve. *intr.* **dhiika.** *caus.* **dhiisha.**

dhiika* *intr. of* **dhii.**

dhiisha* *caus. of* **dhii.**

dhiki* 1. be in need, be poor; be in distress/difficulty; oppress, afflict. *appl.* **dhikia.** *intr.* **dhikika.** be in distress. 2. (ma-) difficulty, want, need, misfortune. **ana – gani?** What kind of difficulties does he have? *Cf.* **udhiki.**

dhikiri*, dhukuru, zikri (–) *Isl.* mention of the name of God.

dhila* *see* **dhili.**

dhili*, dhila 1. degrade, humiliate, despise. 2. (–) humiliation, disparagement, distress. 3 (*also* **dhilifu**) *adj.* low, abject, humiliated, degraded. *Cf.* **madhilifu, udhalifu.**

dhilifu* *see* **dhili 3.**

dhima* (–) responsibility.

dhiraa* (–) ell, cubit *(unit of measure: about 18 inches or half a yard).*

dhoofika*, dhoofu become weak/feeble/infirm. *caus.* **dhoofisha.** *Cf.* **dhaifu.**

dhoofisha *caus. of* **dhoofika.**

dhoofu *see* **dhoofika.**

dhoruba* (–) storm, hurricane.

dhuha* (–) 1. period between sunrise and noon. 2 *Isl.* prayer of this time.

dhuku* *rare* taste, try.

dhukuru* 1. remember, think, consider; praise *(the name of Allah).* 2. (–) *see* **dhikiri.**

dhulu* *rare* be discovered, come to light.

dhuluma*, **dhaluma** (–) injustice, oppression, tyranny, exploitation. *Cf.* **dhulumu, dhalima.**

dhulumu* 1. treat unjustly, exploit, oppress; do wrong, deceive. *appl.* **dhulumia.** 2. (–, ma-) injustice, oppression, tyranny. *Cf.* **dhuluma, dhalimu.**

dhumna* (–) dice game, dominoes.

dhuria* (–) descendants, progeny.

dhurisha* *caus. of* **dhuru.**

dhuru* damage, hurt, injure. **haidhuru.** It does no harm. It does not matter. All right, OK. *appl.* **dhuria.** *caus.* **dhurisha.** *Cf.* **dhara.**

dia* (–) punishment, penalty, fine; atonement *(for homicide)*; ransom; *(rel.)* retribution. **toa (lipa) –.** pay a penalty.

dibaji* (–) style *(of writing)*; introduction *(to a letter or book)*. *Cf.* **udibaji.**

didima, didimia sink in/down, be submerged, be swallowed up. *intr.* **didimika** & *intr.-appl.* **didimikia.** bore, pierce, penetrate *(with an implement)*. *caus.* **didimisha.** put/stuff into.

didimia *see* **didima.**

difensi* [*Engl.*] *sport* 1. (–) defense. 2. (ma-) fullback *(football)*.

difu* (ma-) (*also* **kidifu, kilifu,** vi-) fiber *(of young coconut leaves)*.

digali* (–) stem of a hookah. *Cf.* **mdakale.**

digrii* [*Engl.*] (–, ma-) 1. (academic) degree, rank. 2. degree *(of temperature, etc.)*. (= **daraja.**)

dike* *see* **tike.**

diko* (ma-) *naut.* landing-place, moorings.

dikteshin*, diktesheni (–) [*Engl.*] dictation *(in school)*. *Cf.* **imla.**

dikteta* [*Engl.*] (–) dictator. *Cf.* **udikteta.**

dila* (–) dipper, bailer.

dili (–) dili (kind of snake).

dimba (ma-) dimba (camp at which initiation rites are performed).

dimbwi (ma-) pool, puddle. *Cf.* **kidimbwi.**

dimu (–) *see* **ndimu.**

dinari* (–) *arch.* dinar *(gold coin)*.

dinda 1. be firm/taut. 2. *phy.* be erect, have an erection *(of the penis)*. 3. be lasting/durable. 4. be contrary/opposed.

dindi (ma-) *see* **lindi.**

dindia sink down, go to the bottom; penetrate.

dini* (–) religion, creed, faith, worship.

[1]dira* cut the hair, shave the head.

[2]dira* (–, ma-) 1. *naut.* compass. 2. *elec.* meter.

[3]dira (–) dira (kind of bird).

dirabu* *arch.* spin.

diradira* talk evasively, beat around the bush. *Cf.* duara, duru.

dirhamu* (–) *arch.* dirhem *(coin).*

dirii* (–) *see* deraya.

diriki* (*also* tadariki, tadaraki) be able, be in time *(for something);* manage, achieve, attain; be successful, have possibilities; undertake, venture. *appl.* dirikia. *Cf.* daraka.

dirisha* [*Pers.*] (ma-) 1. square, rectangle. -a madirisha. checkered, checked; divided into squares. 2. window. *Cf.* kidirisha.

[1]dirizi* [*Fr.* diriger?] direct, lead *(singing, dancing).*

[2]dirizi* (–) *arch.* iron armor.

disa *vulg.* be erect *(of the penis).* (= dinda.)

dishi*, disi [*Engl.*] (ma-) dish, tureen; *(rare)* dishes, crockery.

diski* [*Engl.*] (–) *rare* disc, phonograph record.

dispensari* [*Engl.*] (–) 1. dispensary, pharmacy. 2. public health service.

divai* [*Fr.* du vin] (–) wine.

divisheni* [*Engl.*] (–) division, part, section.

diwani* (ma-) 1. adviser. 2. public servant; civil leader, dignitary. 3. collection of poems. 4. *arch.* court/council of a king.

doa 1. (ma-) spot, blot. – la mafuta. grease spot. 2. *pl.* madoa (*also red.* madoadoa *w. adj. sense:* spotted, varicolored.

doana (ma-) *see* ndoana.

[1]dobi* [*Ind.*] (ma-) laundryman. *Cf.* udobi.

[2]dobi *adj.* heavily laden *(a vessel, etc.).*

doda 1. turn bad *(of perishable goods),* become cold *(of foods). appl.* dodea. *caus.* dodesha. 2. fail to get something which one has long desired. 3. drop, drip, trickle.

dodi (ma-), udodi (dodi) 1. wire *(iron or brass).* 2. bracelet *(made of such wire).*

dodo (ma-) 1. breast *(of a young woman).* 2.: embe –. large mango.

dodoa *rare* preserve, keep, lay aside.

dodofu (–) dodofu (kind of fish).

dodoki* (ma-) *bot.* (fruit of the) luffah *(Luffa acutangula). Cf.* **mdodoki.**

[1]**dodosa** 1. hesitate, drawl; falter, stammer *(in speaking or reading).* 2. cross-examine.

[2]**dodosa** strike, beat, knock, rattle; scratch, scrape.

doea 1. interfere, meddle; spy; observe, investigate, study; pursue. 2. *mil.* engage in reconnaissance. *appl.* **doelea.** *Cf.* **doya, mdoezi.**

dofara*, **dofra** (ma-) dofara (sailmaker's measure).

dofra* (ma-) *see* **dofara.**

dogo *adj./adv.* 1. small, little; young. **mtoto mdogo.** a small child. *red.* **dogo-dogo.** very small, tiny. 2. *fig.* sub-, junior, deputy. **komiti ndogo.** sub-committee. **waziri mdogo.** deputy minister. 3. slight, insignificant, unimportant. 4.: **kidogo** *adv.* a little, somewhat, not much. *Cf.* **kidogo, udogo.**

dogori (ma-) dogori (kind of drum).

dohani*, **dokhani** (–) 1. smoke-vent, chimney. 2. smoke, soot. 3. long, narrow basket *(for carrying fruit).*

dohori* (–) 1. *rare* midday, noon. 2. *Isl.* time of prayer.

dokeza 1. indicate, suggest, hint; tell something secretly. 2. use something in small amounts *(e.g.,* medicine). *Cf.* **dokezo, dokoa, kidokezo,** [1]**kidoko.**

dokezi (ma-) hindrance, obstacle, impediment.

dokezo (ma-) suggestion, hint, recommendation. *Cf.* **dokeza.**

dokhani* (–) *see* [1]**dohani.**

dokoa 1. break/bite off a small amount of something. 2. = **dokeza.** *appl.* **dokolea.** report, tell *(news). Cf.* **dokeza.**

dokolea *appl. of* **dokoa.**

dokua (–) dokua (kind of beer).

[1]**dola***, **daula, daulati** (–, ma-) government, state, power. **Jumuia ya Madola.** United Nations. **mkuu wa –.** chief of state.

[2]**dola*** [*Engl.*] (–) dollar.

dole (ma-) 1. *augment. of* **kidole.** 2. (single) banana. 3. clumsy person.

doli* [*Engl.*] (–) doll.

dolola 1. dribble, drool, slaver *(of saliva).* 2. be unsuccessful *(in getting something).* 3. take a long time *(in agreeing on the price, when making a purchase).*

dominika* [*Lat.*] (–) *rel.* Sunday (= **siku ya Bwana**). – **ya Matawi.** Palm Sunday.

domo (ma-) (*augment. of* **mdomo**) 1. (large) lip/beak. 2. *fig.* talkativeness, boasting. **ana –.** He talks constantly/ chatters. **piga –.** boast, brag. 3. *fig.* projection, crag; promentory, cape.

dona 1. pick at, peck, pick up; bite *(fish, at bait).* **kuku wanadona nafaka.** Chickens pick up grain. **sar aki wanadona sasa.** The fish are biting now (it is a good time for fishing). *appl.* **donea.** *caus.* **donesha.** *ass.* **donana.** peck each other *(chickens, etc.), inv.* **donoa.** peck, sting, bite; *(fig,)* kiss. 2. (ma-) grain of poor quality. *Cf.* **mdono.**

donda (ma-) (large) ulcer, sore. – **ndugu.** sore that refuses to heal. *Cf.* **[2]dondoa, kijidonda.**

[1]dondo (ma-) 1. (large) cowrie-shell. 2. starch *(for clothing)*, gloss.

[2]dondo, dondoo (ma-) (*usually* **madondo**) excerpt, quotation, extract; note(s). *Cf.* **[1]dondoa.**

[1]dondoa 1. pick up a little at a time. 2. (*also caus.* **dondosha**) drop (one object after another). 3. make a selection. 4. quote.

[2]dondoa form/cause sores; wound, injure. *Cf.* **donda.**

[1]dondoo (ma-) *see* **[2]dondo.**

[2]dondoo (–) *see* **[1]dondoro.**

[1]dondoro, dondoo (–) dondoro (kind of antelope, steinbuck).

[2]dondoro (–) dondoro (stinging insect, hornet).

donge (ma-) 1. lump, ball. – **la uzi.** ball of yarn. – **la damu.** clot of blood. 2. *coll.* money; winnings; bonus, raise in pay. *Cf.* **tonge, kidonge.**

dongo *see* **udongo.**

dongoa (–) mass, lump.

donoa *inv. of* **dona.**

dopa* (ma-) sailmaker's palm *(of leather or canvas, to protect the hand when sewing heavy material).*

dopoa *rare see* **toboa.**

[1]doria* [*Ind.*] (–) doria (bleached muslin).

[2]doria* (–) *mil.* patrol, advance guard. **askari –.** outpost, picket. **linda –.** to patrol.

dosari* (–) *rare* error, mistake; fault, defect.

doti* [*Ind.*] (–) 1. loincloth (= **¹shuka.**) 2. measure of length (4 yards). **– ya kanga.** a part of the kanga (*see* **²kanga**).

dovuo (–) dribble of saliva *(during sleep)*.

doya, doyadoya reconnoiter, spy, investigate; sponge (*a free meal, although uninvited*). *caus.* **doyeza.** *Cf.* **doea, mdoezi.**

doyadoya *see* **doya.**

doyeza *caus. of* **doya.**

drammeja* [*Engl.*] (–) drummer.

dresa* [*Engl.* dresser] (ma-) orderly, nurse's aide. *Cf.* **udresa.**

dreva* (ma-) *see* **dereva.**

dua* (–) 1. prayer; plea, petition. **omba –.** pray. *prov.* **– ya kuku haimpati mwewe.** The prayer of the hen does not reach the hawk. 2. curse, spell, incantation.

duala* *see* **duwaa.**

duara*, duwara (–, ma-) 1. circle. 2. wheel; windlass, winch. **– ya maji.** waterwheel. **– ya meno.** cogwheel. **– kamili.** *elec.* circuit. 3. *adj.* round, circular. **usukani ni mduara.** The steering wheel is round. *Cf.* **diradira, duru, mduara.**

duazi*, duwazi (ma-) a person who is speechless from amazement. *Cf.* **duwaa.**

duba* *rare* be partially/ not quite full/ filled.

¹dubu* *rare* improve, correct.

²dubu* (–) *zool.* bear.

dubwana* [*Ind.*] 1. (ma-) giant. 2. *adj.* huge, gigantic; extreme, excessive.

dubwasha* [*Ind.*] (–) loud (dull, reverberating) sound *(report of a shotgun, noise of an ax striking wood, etc.)*. *Cf.* **dubwana.**

dude* (ma-) 1. anything the name of which one does not know or cannot remember, what's-its-name, thingumbob. **– gani hili?** What kind of a thing is that? 2. *coll.* worthless person, good-for-nothing. *Cf.* **kidude;** *also* **¹dudu** (?).

dudia *rare* fill in *(a hole)*; fill up, pour on.

¹dudu* (ma-) 1. *augment. of* **¹mdudu.** 2. *(fig.)* parasite *(term of abuse)*.

²dudu (ma-) *med.* infectious disease; smallpox. **– mai.** chicken pox. *Cf.* **duduka.**

duduka (*also* **dudulika**) be deformed, disfigured *(as a result of illness or an accident)*. **– uso.** have a pockmarked face. *Cf.* **²dudu, duduvule, kidudusi.**

dudulika *see* **duduka.**

dudumi (–) dudumi (large horn).

dudumia pierce, puncture, perforate. *caus.* **dudumiza.** *intr.* **dudumika.** *intr.-ass.* **dudumikana.** cause each other embarrassment. *intr.-caus.* **dudumikiza.** press, squeeze.

dudumikiza *intr.-caus. of* **dudumia.**

dudumizi (ma-) dudumizi (kind of bird, coucal). (= **tipitipi.**)

duduvule (–) duduvule (kind of wood-boring hornet). *Cf.* [1]**dudu.**

dufi (–) dufi (kind of sea-tortoise).

dufu* 1. (ma-) simplicity, folly, stupidity. **– la mtu** *or* **mtu –.** foolish/stupid person. 2. *adj.* stupid, foolish, silly; dull, narrow-minded; useless, uninteresting; *(fig.)* insipid, in bad taste. *Cf.* **udufu.**

dugi *adj.* dull, blunt. **kisu kidugi.** a dull knife. *Cf.* **dugika.**

dugika be dull/blunt. *Cf.* **dugi.**

dugu (–) dugu (round mat).

duguda shake, jog, jolt.

duhushi* search out; look into, investigate; spy.

duka* (ma-) shop, store, business. **weka (anza) –.** open up a business. **weka dukani.** display for sale. **vunja –.** give up a business. **tembea madukani.** go on a shopping trip. **– la vitabu (mboga).** book (vegetable) store.

dukisa *see* **dukiza.**

dukisi (ma-) *see* **dukizi.**

dukiza, dukisa impose oneself, intrude; listen (secretly), eavesdrop. *appl.* **dukizia.** *Cf.* [1]**daka** (?), **dukizi.**

dukizi, dukisi (ma-) eavesdropping, gossip-mongering. *Cf.* **dukiza.**

dukuduku* (–) 1. confusion, embarrassment; amazement, speechlessness; unrest, excitement; alarm, apprehension. 2. urgent request. *Cf.* **daghadagha.**

dulabu* (–) spinning wheel.

duma (–) *zool.* cheetah.

dumaa be stunted, underdeveloped, atrophied; be backward, retarded (mentally).

dumbu *dial.* *see* **umbu.**

dume (ma-) male animal, male sex. **– la farasi** *or* **farasi –.** stallion. *fig.* **amezaa –.** She has given birth to a boy. **sauti –.** bass voice. *Cf.* [1]**ume.**

dumiliza* go through the ceremony of blood-friendship. *Cf.* **dumilizo;** *also* [2]**dumu, dumisha.**

dumilizo* (ma-) (ceremony of) blood-friendship. *Cf.* **dumiliza.**

dumisha* conclude a blood-friendship. *Cf.* **2dumu** *caus.*

1dumu (ma-) can, jug, mug, pot. (= **mdumu.**)

2dumu* remain, keep on, last (a long time), continue. **– daima.** last forever. *caus.* **dumisha.** *Cf.* **daima.**

dunda strike forcibly against something. *Cf.* **mdundo.**

1dundu (ma-) dried gourd or pumpkin used as a container for liquids, calabash.

2dundu (–) scavenger beetle.

dundua be deformed/mutilated.

dunduiza begin to ripen *(of fruit).*

unduliza put aside, lay away, save, keep in reserve.

dundumio (ma-) *anat.* larynx, Adam's apple. (= **kikoromeo.**)

1dunga bore, pierce *(usually the ears, for ornaments); (fig.)* administer a hypodermic injection. *Cf.* **kidungadunga.**

2dunga (ma-) dunga (covered basket).

dunge (ma-) (green) cashew apple. *See also* **bibo, mbibo.**

dungu (ma-) hut or shelter for a watchman guarding crops against birds; scaffolding; *(rel.)* pulpit. **– la ndege.** cockpit *(of an airplane).*

dungudungu (ma-) 1. deformity. 2. deformed person. 3. something badly made. 4. confusion of mind.

dungumaro (–) 1. evil spirit. 2. drum for warding off such a spirit. **ngoma ya –.** ceremony for exorcising an evil spirit.

duni* *adj.* insignificant, low, mean, inferior; unimportant, useless. **jambo –.** an unimportant matter, lowness, vulgarity. **mtu –.** an insignificant person.

dunia* (–) universe, world, globe, earth. **sehemu ya –.** continent. **fariki/aga –.** *euph.* depart from the world, die.

dunzi (ma-) *see* **mdunzidunzi.**

1dupa step/jump over, cross; press forward, push one's way through.

2dupa (ma-) *see* **tupa.**

dura* (–) parrot. (= **kasuku.**)

duriani* [*Mal.*] (–) fruit of the breadfruit tree. *Cf.* **mduriani.**

duru* 1. surround, encircle; go around. *fig.* **akili zimemduru.** He has lost his mind. 2. (–) turn, revolution, rotation; *(fig.)* drinking by turn. *coll.* **sasa ni – yangu.** Now it is my turn (to drink). *Cf.* **duara.**

durubini* (–) *see* **darubini.**

durufu (ma-) canvas cover.

durui* (–) *see* **deraya.**

durusi* *rare* attend a school, learn, study. *Cf.* **darasa.**

dusa* (& *appl.* **dusia**) sponge, live at others' expense. *Cf.* **mdusi.**

dusamali* (–) *see* **dusumali.**

dusumali*, dusamali [*Pers.*] (–) (colored) kerchief or scarf (worn by women).

duta rebound, bounce back *(a ball);* reverberate; return, reflect *(light).*

dutu (–, ma-) 1. form, shape, appearance, constitution. 2. *fig.* spot, blemish; pimple, wart.

duvi *pl. of* **uduvi.**

duwaa*, dawaa, duala be dumbfounded, shocked, unnerved; be silent *(from astonishment);* be in a difficult situation; become confused. *Cf.* **duazi.**

duwara* (–, ma-) *see* **duara.**

duwazi* (ma-) *see* **duazi.**

[1]**duzi** (ma-) *rare* eavesdropper, gossip.

[2]**duzi*** (ma-) (semi-wild) tomcat.

E

ebee* *see* **labeka.**

ebu!* *see* [2]**hebu!**

eda* (–, ma-) eda (ritual seclusion of a woman after the death of her husband or after divorce).

edaha* (–) edaha (a sacrifice).

edashara*, hedashara (–) *arch.* eleven. **-a –.** eleventh.

Edeni* *see* **Aden.**

edita* [*Engl.*] (–) editor.

ee! *interj.* oh! **– walla.** certainly, all right.

eewaa*, eewala *interj.* *see* **ewaa.**

efendi* (–) *see* **afendi.**

efya *caus. of* **epa.**

egama, chegama, egema, chegema lean on, rest on, be supported; approach. *prov.* **mwega haanguki ela mwega kugwa.** Who supports himself does not fall, unless his support falls. *appl.* **egamia, egemea.** *intr.* **egamika, egameka.** *caus.* **egesha, egamisha, egamiza, egamesha, egameza.** support, prop up; establish, confirm. *caus.-ass.* **egeshana.** bring together, connect. *Cf.* **egesha, egemeo, mchegamo, mwegamo.**

egema *see* **egama.**

egemeo (ma-) 1. prop, support; railing, banister. 2. *fig.* support, assistance. *Cf.* **egama.**

egesha bring up close, bring into contact with; secure, moor. **meli imeegesha.** The ship is moored (at the wharf). *appl.* **egeshea.** *ass.* **egeshana.** *Cf.* **egama,** *caus.-ass.*

ehee! enhee! *interj. expressing agreement or approval:* yes.

ehsani* (–) *see* **hisani.**

ehuka be a lunatic, be seized with madness. *Cf.* **mwehu.**

eidi* (–) *see* **idi.**

eka* [*Engl.*] (–) acre.

ekevu *see* **elekevu.**

ekeza *rare intr.-appl.-caus. of* **elea.**

eksidenti* [*Engl.*] (–) *see* **aksidenti.**

ekua, wekua break (down), destroy, knock to pieces. *intr.* **ekuka.**

ekuka *intr. of* **ekua.**

ekundu *adj.* red *(all shades from yellow-red to red-brown).* – **kidogo.** reddish.

ekwata* [*Engl.*] (–) *see* **ikweta.**

ela* *see* [2]**ila.**

elafu* *see* **elfu.**

elea 1. be on the surface, float, swim. **samaki wanaelea.** Fish swim. 2. *fig.* be clear/plain/evident. **maneno yako yamenielea.** Your words are clear/obvious to me. *caus.* **eleza.** 1. cause to float. 2. make clear, explain. *caus.-appl.* **elezea.** *appl.-caus.* **eleleza.** imitate, copy. *intr.-appl.* **elekea.** point to, be directed toward; incline toward, tend to. *intr.-appl.-ass.* **elekeana.** be face to face, confront each other, be opposite; agree, correspond. *intr.-ass.-caus.* **elekeanisha.** *intr.-appl.-caus.* **elekeza.** show, show the way; order, direct. **elekeza chombo.** steer a ship. *intr.-appl.-caus.-ass.* **elekezana.** reach an agreement. *ass.-caus.* **elekanya.** put one object on top of another, pile up. *See also* **elekea, elewa,** *and cf.* [1]**chelezo elekevu, elezo, kieleaji, kielekezo, kielezo, maelekeo, maelezi, maelezo, mwelewa, mwelezaji, mwelezo, ueleano, uelekeo, uelekevu, uelekezo, uelezaji.**

eleka carry (a child on one's hip/back). *Cf.* **mbeleko, mweleko.**

elekanya *ass.-caus. of* èlea.

elekea, lekea 1. point to, be directed toward. nyumba yangu inaelekea kusini. My house faces south. 2. appear, seem. inaelekea kuwa atakuja. It seems that he will come. 3. realize, understand. sasa wanaanza kuelekea. Now they are beginning to understand. *Cf.* elea *(intr.-appl.),* elekevu, kielekezo, maelekeo, mwelekeo, uelekeo, uelekevu, uelekezo.

-elekeana, -a kuelekeana *adj.* opposite. mistari inayoelekeana. opposite lines/sides. *Cf.* elea.

elekevu, lekevu, ekevu *adj.* clear, sensible, reasonable, intelligent, understanding; *(fig.)* enlightened, open-minded. *Cf.* elekea, uelekevu.

elekeza *intr.-appl.-caus. of* elea.

elektrisiti* [*Engl.*] (–) electricity. (= umeme.)

eleleza *appl.-caus. of* elea.

elemea *see* lemea.

elementi* [*Engl.*] (–) *chem.* element.

elemisha* *see* elimisha.

elewa *(pass. of* elea, *used actively)* understand. sielewi maana. I don't understand. simuelewi kamwe. I don't understand him. naelewa kwamba hatafika tena. I understand that he will not come again. *Cf.* mwelewa.

eleza *caus. of* elea.

elezo (ma-) (*usually* maelezo) explanation, description, commentary. *Cf.* elea, mwelezo.

elfeen* (–) *arch.* two thousand.

elfu*, elafu, alfu, alaf, alafu (ma-) thousand. *red.* elfu elfu. great number.

eliki*, elki, iliki, hiliki [*Ind.*] (–) cardamom *(Elettaria cardamomum).*

elimika* be well informed/educated. *Cf.* elimu.

elimisha*, elemisha impart knowledge, teach, instruct, train, drill. *appl.* elimishia. teach something to someone. *pass.* elimishwa. *Cf.* elimu.

elimu*, ilmu, ilimu (–) knowledge, education, science. – ya hesabu. arithmetic, mathematics. – ya afya. hygiene. – ya roho (*or* nafsi). psychology. – ya ukulima. agricultural science. *Cf.* elimika, elimisha, maalum, mwalimu, taalamu, taalimu, mtaalamu, utaalamu, uwalimu.

Eljuma* *see* Ijumaa.

elki* (–) *see* eliki.

[1]ema *adj.* good *(in gen.).* chakula chema. good food. moyo mwema. a good heart. upepo mwema. pleasant breeze. *Cf.* mema, vema, wema.

[2]ema (–) *dial.* weir-basket, fishing-net.

embamba *adj.* 1. thin, narrow; slender, slim. **bonde jembamba.** a narrow valley. **mtu mwembamba.** a slim/slender person. 2. *fig.* fine, delicate. **nafaka nyembamba.** fine grain. **nguo nyembamba.** fine material, gauze.

embe* [*Ind.*] (–) mango (fruit). *Cf.* **mwembe.**

emboe (–) *see* **embwe.**

embwe, emboe (–) resin, gum (of the baobab).

enchini* (–) *see* **injini.**

enda 1. go *(in gen.)*, move, progress. **– kwa miguu.** go on foot. **– kwa motokaa.** go by automobile, drive. **– kwa farasi.** ride (a horse). **– nyumbani.** go into a house. **– mbio.** run, gallop. **tikiti ya kwenda na kurudi.** round-trip ticket. 2. go forward, proceed. 3. do, act. **– chafya.** sneeze. **– miayo.** yawn. *in conj. w. poss. pron.:* **naenda (njia) zangu.** I go my own way. *imp. sing.* **nenda, enenda;** *pl.* **nendeni. nendeni zenu.** Go about your business. *appl.* **endea.** go for/with. **endea kuni.** go to collect firewood. *appl.-refl.* **jiendea.** go by oneself, take a walk for pleasure. *double appl.* **endelea.** go forward, move ahead; make progress; continue. **habari inaendelea.** The story will be continued. *double appl.-caus.* **endeleza.** develop; spell (words). *intr.* **endeka. njia haiendeki.** The street is impassable. *intr.-caus.* **endekeza.** fit, adapt, adjust; pay attention; spoil *(a child)*. **usimwendekeze maneno yake.** Pay no attention to his words. *caus.* **endesha, enza.** set in motion, start; steer, conduct, lead *(a meeting)*; manage, operate *(a business)*; carry out *(a plan)*. **endesha** (*rare* **enza**) **gari (motakaa).** drive a wagon (an automobile). **endesha eropleni.** pilot an airplane. *Cf.* **endapo, endeleo, enenzi, huenda, kiendeleo, kujiendesha, mwenda, mwendeleo, mwendelezi, mwendesha, mwendeshaji, mwendo, mwenenzi, mwenzi, uendelezo, uendeshaji, wenzo.**

endapo *conj.* in case, in the event that... *Cf.* **enda.**

endelea *double appl. of* **enda.**

endeleo, endelezo (ma-, *us. pl.*) 1. (act of) advancing, proceeding. 2. increase, growth, expansion, development. 3. improvement, enhancement, progress. 4. *rare* success. *Cf.* **enda.**

endeleza *double appl.-caus. of* **enda.**

endesha *caus. of* **enda.**

enea spread, expand; become known. *caus.* **eneza.** spread, expand (something); make known; compare. **eneza habari.** spread news, advertise. *caus.-ass.* **enezana.** *Cf.* **eneo, enezi, chenezo, maenezo, mwenea, mweneza, mwenezi.**

enenda *imper.* *see* **enda.**

enenza *see* [1]**enza.**

enenzi (ma-) (*usually* **maenenzi**) gait, pace. **maenenzi ya pole pole (haraka).** slow (rapid) gait. *Cf.* **enda.**

eneo, cheneo, kieneo (ma-) 1. expansion, area, range, extent; *(fig.)* sphere of influence, zone. **— la nchi hii.** the extent of this country. **— la kushilia kwa majeshi.** military occupation zone. 2.: **-a eneo.** *adj.* square *(as a measure of area).* **inchi za enea nne.** four square inches. *Cf.* **enea.**

eneza *caus. of* **enea.**

enezi (ma-) extension, distribution. *Cf.* **enea.**

[1]**enga** split, slit, cut up *(e.g., manioc).*

[2]**enga** spoil, pamper. *red. (int.)* **engaenga.** overwhelm someone with affection.

engua remove foam/cream. **— siagi katika maziwa.** separate the cream from the milk.

enhee! *see* **ehee!**

enjili* (—) *see* **injili.**

enjine* (—) *rare* *see* **injini.**

-enu *poss. pron. 2nd pers. pl.* your. **nyumba yenu.** your house. **nyumba zenu.** your houses.

-enye, -enyi possessing, having, containing. *used in conj. w. other parts of speech to form adjectives.* **— giza.** dark. **— maji.** moist, watery. **— watu wengi.** thickly populated. **— kutawala.** governing, ruling. *Cf.* **kienyeji, kimwenye, mwenye, mwenyeji.**

-enyewe *adj.* -self *(emphasizing identity).* **mtu mwenyewe.** the man himself. **mimi mwenyewe.** I myself, my very self. **sehemu inayojitawala wenyewe.** autonomous region (*i.e.*, self-governing, which governs itself).

[1]**enyi** *see* **-enye.**

[2]**enyi!** *interj.* (< **ee ninyi**) *exclamation referring to 2nd pers. pl.* Hey, you there!

[1]**enza, enenza, eza** measure, survey; compare.

[2]**enza** *caus. of* **enda.**

enzi*, aenzi, ezi 1. (—) power; rule, dominion, sovereignty. **kiti cha —.** throne. **katika — ya...** during the reign of... 2. invest with power; install, inaugurate *(as ruler)*; exalt, glorify.

epa turn aside, get out of the way; go round, make a detour; deviate, diverge; reflect; avoid, evade; *(fig.)* make excuses, wriggle out of something; shirk (something), make oneself scarce. *caus.* **epesha, efya.** *inv.* **epua.** put out of the way, clear away, remove. **epua chungu motoni.** take a pot off the fire. *inv.-intr.* **epuka.** *same senses as* **epa.** *inv.-ass.* **epukana.** pass by each other, avoid each other; be at variance, disagree. *inv.-caus.* **epusha.** keep at a distance, reject. **nimeepushwa.** I am kept from (doing something). **-siyoepukika.** unavoidable, inevitable.

epesi *adj.* 1. light *(in weight).* **kiatu chepesi.** slipper. 2. quick, fast, swift; *(fig)* energetic; hasty, impatient. 3. unimportant, of no consequence, not serious.

eproni* [*Engl.*] (–) apron.

epua *inv. of* **epa.**

epuka *inv.-intr. of* **epa.**

epusha *inv.-caus. of* **epa.**

erevu *adj.* clever, shrewd, talented, capable, ingenious; crafty, sly. *Cf.* **erevuka, mwerevu, werevu.**

erevuka be shrewd, intelligent, enlightened. *caus.* **erevusha.** make wise, open someone's eyes, enlighten. *Cf.* **erevu.**

erevusha *caus. of* **erevuka.**

eria* [*Engl.*] (–) area.

erieli* [*Engl.*] (–) *elec.* aerial, antenna.

eropleni* [*Engl.*] (–) airplane. **endesha –.** pilot an airplane. **njia ya –.** airline.

esha* (–) *see* **²isha.**

esi* (–) *rare* *see* **hesi.**

espesheli* [*Engl.*] *adv.* especially.

¹eti *conj.* as if.

²eti! *see* **ati!**

-etu *poss. pron. 1st pers. pl.* our. **kitabu chetu.** our book. **vitabu vyetu.** our books.

eua 1. cleanse, purify. *fig., rel.* purify by prayer or magic. 2. *med.* disinfect. *appl.* **eulia.**

eupe *adj.* 1. white, light *(in color);* light bright, transparent, clean, clear. 2. *fig.* open, free. **nchi nyeupe.** open land *(without trees).* **moyo mweupe.** an open/honest character.

eusi, ausi *adj.* 1. black, dark *(in color).* 2. *fig.* dark, gloomy.

ewaa*, eewaa, eewala *interj. of assent or approval:* yes.

ewe! *interj.* (< ee wewe) Hey there!

ewedeka *see* **weweseka.**

eza *see* **¹enza.**

ezeka 1. cover. **– nyumba.** cover a roof *(with grass, straw).* 2. *fig.* beat, thrash. *Cf.* **ezeko, ezua, mwezekaji, mwezeko.**

ezeko (ma-) 1. (act of) covering a roof, thatching. 2. material for roof covering. *Cf.* **ezeka.**

ezi* (–) *see* **enzi.**

ezua uncover; remove roofing *(grass, straw).* *Cf.* **ezeka.**

F

fa 1. die, perish. **– njaa (baridi).** die of hunger (cold), be very hungry (cold). **– kucheka.** die laughing, split one's sides. **– maji.** drown. 2. lose strength, suffer loss of..., come to an end. **– macho.** become blind, lose one's eyesight. **saa imekufa.** The clock has stopped. **desturi hizi zimekufa.** These practices are no longer observed. *appl.* **fia. amefia wapi?** Where did he die? *double appl.* **filia.** *pass.* **fiwa. amefiwa na mtoto wake.** His child has died. *caus.* **fisha.** *refl.-caus.* **jifisha.** commit suicide. *Cf.* **fu, ²kifa, kifo, ¹kifu, mafa, mafu, mfisha, mfiwa, mfu, ufu.**

faa be good, be of use; fit, suit, be suitable/appropriate; be sufficient/adequate; help. **haifai.** It is useless/unsuitable/inappropriate/improper. *appl.* **falia.** *ass.* **faana.** be useful to/help each other. *Cf.* **fana, fanana, fanya, kifaa, kifano, mafaa, mfano, mfanya, mfanyaji, mfanyizaji, ufananaji, ufanyaji.**

fadhaa*, fazaa, fatha (–) difficulty, excitement, confusion. **shikwa na (patwa na) –.** be involved in difficulties, be thrown into confusion. *Cf.* **fadhaika.**

fadhaika* be confused/terrified. *caus.* **fadhaisha.** *Cf.* **fadhaa.**

fadhili* 1. show kindness/favor; lay under an obligation, put in one's debt. *appl.* **fadhilia.** *intr.* **fadhilika.** be well-disposed, show good will. 2. (–) kindness, favor, amiability; preference, privilege; gratitude. *prov.* **– ya punda (ni) mashuzi** The donkey's gratitude is stench. *Cf.* **afadhali, mfadhili, tafadhali, ufadhili.**

fafanisha contrast, compare; explain. *Cf.* **fafanua.**

fafanua recognize, understand, see clearly. *appl.* **fafanulia.** make clear to someone. *caus.* **fafanusha.** explain, make clear. *intr.* **fafanuka.** be recognizable, clear, plain. *Cf.* **fafanusi, mfafanusi, ufafanuzi;** *also* **fafanisha.**

fafanusha *caus. of* **fafanua.**

fafanusi (–) theory. *Cf.* **fafanua.**

fagia sweep, brush, remove *(dirt). appl.* **fagilia.** *caus. (int.)* **fagiza.** *pass.* **fagiwa.** *Cf.* **fagio, mfagiaji, mfagio, ufagio.**

fagio (ma-), **kifagio** (vi-) broom, brush. *Cf.* **fagia.**

fagiza *caus. (int.) of* **fagia.**

fahali* (–, ma-) 1. bull. *prov.* **mafahali wawili hawakai zizi moja.** Two bulls cannot live in the same herd (farmyard). 2. *adj., fig.* manly, brave, strong.

fahamivu*, fahamifu *adj.* 1. intelligent, quick, acute. 2. understood, implied. **sharti –.** implied condition. *Cf.* **fahamu.**

fahamu* 1. know, be acquainted with, understand. **fahamu!** Pay attention! **kutofahamu.** misunderstand. *appl.* **fahamia.** *intr.* **fahamika.** be understood/ understandable; remember. *caus.* **fahamisha.** inform, remind. 2. (–) (*also* **ufahami** *sing.*) understanding, intelligence; consciousness; memory, recollection. **potea –.** lose consciousness. *Cf.* **fahamivu, ufahamikiano, ufahamivu.**

faharasa*, fahirisi (–) list, index, catalog, table of contents.

fahari*, fakhari 1 boast, brag, show off, plume oneself. *appl.* **faharia.** *caus.* **faharisha, fahari.** *refl.* **jifaharisha.** boast, pride oneself. 2. (–) dignity, glory, magnificence, pomp, ostentation, pride, arrogance. **fanya –.** give oneself airs, be haughty/arrogant. 3. *adj.* **kwa –.** splendid, magnificent; proud, pompous, ostentatious.

fahirisi* (–) *see* **faharasa.**

fahuwa* *see* **fauwa.**

faida*, fayida (–) gain, earnings, profit; *(coll.)* interest *(on a loan).* **mkopo bila ya –.** interest-free loan. **– ghafi.** gross profits. **– safi.** net profits. **– ya hesa.** dividend. *Cf.* **faidi.**

faidi* profit/benefit from something; bear interest; prosper, thrive. *appl.* **faidia. biashara imemfaidia.** He made a profit on the business. *Cf.* **faida.**

faili* [*Engl.*] (ma-) file *(of papers).*

fainali* [*Engl.*] (–) *sport* final *(round or match).*

faini* [*Engl.*] (–) fine, penalty. **toza –.** charge/exact a fine. **lipa –.** pay a fine.

faiti*, fawiti hinder, check; delay, detain; keep someone waiting. *intr.* **faitika.** be delayed, be prevented *(from going somewhere).*

faja* (–) *rare* stable. (= [1]**zizi.**)

fajaa* *adv., rare* suddenly, unexpectedly.

fakaika*, fakefu *adv., rare* much more, much less; not to speak of. *Cf.* **fauka.**

fakefu* *see* **fakaika.**

fakhari* *see* **fahari.**

fakiri*, fukara 1. (–) beggar, poor person. 2. *adj.* poor. *Cf.* **fukarika, ufukara.**

Falada*, **Faladi** *sing., arch.* Mombasa.

falaki* (–) astronomy, astrology. **piga –.** prophesy, tell fortunes; cast a horoscope.

falani* (–) *see* **fulani.**

fali* (–) omen, augury; fate, chance.

faliti* (–) faliti (children's game: tag).

falka*, **faluka** (–) *naut.* hold *(of a ship).*

falme *pl. of* **ufalme.**

falsafa* (–) *rare* philosophy. (= **hekima.**)

faluda* (–) porridge made of corn (maize).

faluka* (–) *see* **falka.**

fana prosper, succeed. *ass.* **fanana,** *q.v. caus.* **fanya,** *q.v. Cf.* **faa.**

fanaka* (–) prosperity, success, benefit. *Cf.* **fanikia, fanikio.**

fanana be similar, resemble. *caus.* **fananisha.** compare, contrast. *Cf.* **faa, fana.**

faneli*, **fanel** [*Engl.*] (–) *rare* funnel *(of a ship),* chimney.

fanguru* [*?*] (–) clamp, vise.

fani* *adj.* worthy, valuable; favorable, successful.

fania *see* **fanya.**

fanicha* [*Engl.*] (–) furniture.

fanidi* choose, select *(by comparing).*

fanikia* succeed in something, attain *(a goal). pass.* **fanikiwa.** be successful. *Cf.* **fanaka, fanikio, mafanikio, ufanikivu.**

fanikio* (ma-) success. *Cf.* **fanaka, fanikia.**

fanikiwa* *see* **fanikia.**

fanusi* (–) lantern, lamp; headlight, searchlight.

fanya, fania make, do, perform, produce. **– shamba.** prepare a field *(for planting).* **– amani.** make peace. **– biashara.** carry on trade. **– dawa.** give medical treatment. **– kazi.** work. **– kelele.** be noisy. **– mali.** accumulate wealth, make a profit. **– matata.** cause trouble. **– shauri.** advise, negotiate, discuss. **– serikali.** form a government. *appl.* **fanyia.** *appl.-refl.* **jifanyia.** do something without purpose/unsystematically. *intr.* **fanyika.** be done, take place; be feasible, practicable. *caus.* **fanyiza, fanza.** repair, put in order; complete, perfect. *ass.* **fanyana.** act together/jointly, cooperate. *refl.* **jifanya.** pretend, pose, feign. *pass.* **fanywa.** *Cf.* **fa, fana.**

fanza *caus. of* **fanya.**

fara*, **farafara, furifuri** *adj./adv.* brimful. **jaa –.** be full to the brim. *Cf.* **fori, fura.**

faradhi*, faridha (–) 1. immutability. 2. obligation, necessity. kula ni – ya kila mtu. Every human being must eat.

farafara* *see* fara.

faragha* (*rare* feraga) 1. (–) seclusion, privacy; secrecy, secret. nilisema naye kwa –. I have spoken with him privately. *coll.* amekwenda –. He has gone to the toilet. 2. *adv.* personally, privately, secretly.

faragua* boast, brag.

faraja* (–) rest, comfort, consolation, relief, support. pata –. get relief/rest. *coll.* amepatikana na –. He is dead. *Cf.* fariji, mfariji.

faraji* *see* fariji.

¹faraka* (–) wool-comb, weaver's comb. *Cf.* fariki.

²faraka* (–) division, sect. *Cf.* fariki.

³faraka* *see* fariki.

farakana* *ass. of* fariki.

farakano* (ma-) 1. separation, division, split, faction, sect. – la dini. religious sect. – la chama. splitting up of a party. 2. segregation. *Cf.* fariki.

¹faranga* (ma-) franc *(unit of currency)*.

²faranga* [*Port.*] (ma-) (*also dimin.* kifaranga, vi-) young bird, nestling, chick. (= kinda, mtoto.)

farangi* (–) *med., rare* syphilis. (= kaswende.)

Faransa* 1. *adj.* French. 2. *sing.* France (= Ufaransa). *Cf.* Mfaransa, Kifaransa.

farasi* (–) 1. horse. enda kwa –. ride. panda –. mount a horse. shuka juu ya –. dismount. 2. frame, framework, support. – ya baisikeli. frame of a bicycle. 3. knight *(chess)*. *Cf.* kifarasi.

farasila* (–) *see* frasila.

faridha* (–) *see* faradhi.

fariji*, faraji comfort, console, relieve, help. *appl.* farijia. *intr.* farijika. *Cf.* faraja.

fariki*, faraka *rare* separate from, be divorced from. *fig.* – dunia. die. *appl.* farikia. *caus.* farikisha. *ass.* farakana, farikiana. be separated from each other. *Cf.* ¹faraka, ²faraka, farakano, mfariki, mfaruku.

farikiana* *ass. of* fariki.

Farisayo* (ma-) *Bibl.* Pharisee.

farisi* *adj.* experienced, skilful, expert, capable. *Cf.* ufarisi.

faritha* *rare* pay (for).

faru (–) (*augment. of* **kifaru**) 1. (large) rhinoceros. 2. *fig., mil.* tank, armored car.

faruma*, foroma [*Port.*] (–) form /last for blocking caps *(after washing).*

farumi*, farumu, furumi (–) *naut.* ballast. *Cf.* **furumiza.**

farumu* (–) *see* **farumi.**

fasaha*, fasihi *adj.* pure, correct *(style);* faultless, lucid. **lugha yake – sana.** His language is very correct. *Cf.* **ufasaha.**

faseha* (–) *rare* cleanliness, purity. *Cf.* **fasaha.**

fashini* [*Pers. ?*] (–) *naut.* rudder-block.

fasihi* *see* **fasaha.**

fasiki* (–) immoral/dissolute person. *Cf.* **ufasiki.**

1**fasili*** (–) 1. shoot, sprout. 2. *fig.* offspring, descendant. **hana asili wala –.** He has no family connections.

2**fasili*** cut, tailor *(clothes).*

fasiri* 1. explain, interpret; translate *(languages).* *appl.* **fasiria.** *caus.* **fasirisha.** 2. (–) explanation, exposition, interpretation; translation. *Cf.* **mfasiri, tafsiri.**

fata *see* **fyata.**

fataki* (–) 1. *mil.* percussion cap. 2. fireworks. 3. *elec.* fuse.

fatha* (–) *see* **fadhaa.**

fathali* *adv.* excellently.

fatiha* (–) 'Opener' = first sura of the Koran.

fatiisha* be curious, inquisitive; search, spy on. *Cf.* **tafiti, tafuta.**

fauka*, foko: – ya. *rare* more than. *Cf.* **fakaika.**

faulu* 1. succeed, be successful, reach one's goal. **bila kufaulu.** unsuccessfully. 2. *naut.* get past, get round *(a point, etc.),* weather *(a storm).* 3. (–) success (= **ufaulu**).

fauwa!*, fahuwa! *interj., rare* good! all right! it doesn't matter.

fawiti* *see* **faiti.**

fayida* (–) *see* **faida.**

fazaa* (–) *see* **fadhaa.**

Februari* [*Engl.*] (–) February.

fedeha* (–) *see* **fedheha.**

fedha* (–) silver; money, currency, coin. **-a –.** (made of) silver. **– taslimu (mkononi tayari).** ready money, cash. **mambo ya –.** financial matters. **– za mkopo.** loan, credit. **waziri wa (mambo ya) –.** minister of finance. *prov.* **– fedheha.** Money does not make happiness.

fedhaluka*, **fethaluka** (–) 1. *min.* carnelian. 2. **marijani ya –.** red coral.

fedheha*, **fedeha** (–) shame, disgrace, insult, scandal. *Cf.* **fedhehi.**

fedhehi* put someone to shame, disgrace, dishonor. *Cf.* **fedheha.**

fedhuli* **(ma-)** *see* **fidhuli.**

fedhulika* *see* **fidhulika.**

fefe (–) fefe (variety of perennial grass, often used for thatching roofs).

feguli* **(ma-)** *see* **fidhuli.**

feka* *see* **fyeka.**

felefele, ferefere (–) felefele (inferior kind of millet).

felegi* (–) *see* **1feleji.**

1feleji*, **felegi** [*Pers.*] (–) steel *(of good quality).*

2feleji* **(ma-)** *see* **fereji.**

feleti* free, discharge, absolve, release *(from an obligation or promise).*

1feli* [*Engl.*] *rare* fail, be unsuccessful. **alifeli mtihani wake.** He failed the examination. *Cf.* **anguka** (*sub* **angua**).

2feli* 1. surprise, catch, discover, detect. **alimfeli mumewa na bibi mwingine.** She caught her husband with another woman. **alimfeli alipokuwa anaoga.** He surprised him while he was bathing. 2. (–) misdeed, mishap.

fenesi*, **finesi** [*Ind.*] **(ma-)** 1. jackfruit; durian, breadfruit. *Cf.* **mfenesi.** 2. *proper name (fem.) (chiefly in Mombasa).*

feraga (–) *rare* *see* **faragha.**

ferdausi* [*Pers.*] (–) *rel.* paradise.

ferefere (–) *see* **felefele.**

fereji*, **feleji** **(ma-)** channel, canal; ditch, sewer; pipe. *Cf.* **mfereji.**

feruzi* (–) 1. turquoise. 2. *masc. pr. n.*

fesheni* [*Engl.*] (–) fashion, style; (modern) manners, way of life. **hii ni – ya sasa.** This is the latest fashion.

feta* *see* **fetwa.**

fetwa*, **feta** 1. pass judgment, make a legal decision. 2. (–) (legal) decision, judgment, verdict.

feuli* (–) *naut.* (ship's) hold.

fezuli* (ma-) *see* **fidhuli.**

fezulika* *see* **fidhulika.**

fi* *prep.* in, on, with, by.

[1]**fia** (–) fia (kind of snake).

[2]**fia** *appl. of* **fa.**

fianda *see* **fyanda.**

fiata *see* **fyata.**

ficha (*dial.* **fita**) hide, conceal; put aside; keep secret. *refl.* **jificha.** conceal oneself, hide. **jificha mvua.** seek shelter from the rain. *stat.* **fichama.** be hidden/concealed. *inv.* **fichua.** 1. uncover, reveal, take out. 2. pay someone for something. *Cf.* **ficho, fichuo, kifichoficho, maficho, mfichaji.**

ficho (ma-) (*us.* **maficho** *or* **kificho,** vi-) concealment, screen, hiding-place. **kaa mafichoni.** remain in hiding. *Cf.* **ficha.**

fichua *inv. of* **ficha.**

fichuo (ma-) 1. discovery, revelation. 2. present given by bridegroom to bride. *Cf.* **ficha.**

fidhuli*, fedhuli, fezuli, feguli, fudhali. 1. (ma-) impudent/insolent person. 2. (*also* **fidhulika**) *adj.* impudent, insolent, shameless; rude, unmannerly, boorish; provoking, defiant. *Cf.* [1]**fidhulika, mfidhuli, ufidhuli.**

[1]**fidhulika*, fedhulika, fezulika.** boast, talk big; be arrogant. *Cf.* **fidhuli.**

[2]**fidhulika*** *see* **fidhuli 2.**

fidi* redeem, ransom; pay a ransom, put up bail, post bond. *appl.* **fidia. fidia mtu.** to ransom someone. *pass.* **fidiwa.** *Cf.* **fidia, ufidio.**

fidia* (–) (*also* **kifidio,** vi-) 1. ransom, fine, reparation; bail, bond. 2. *rel.* redemption. *Cf.* **fidi.**

fidla* [*Engl.*] (–) fiddle, violin.

fido (–) wand, sapling, switch.

fidua, fudua 1. uncover, take out, turn inside out. 2. expose the glans (of the penis); wash after circumcision.

fieka *see* **fyeka.**

fieko (ma-) *see* **fyeko.**

fifia disappear, die away; wilt, wither; fade *(of colors).* *appl.* **fifilia.** *pass.* **fifiwa.** *caus.* **fifisha, fifiliza.** cause to disappear; *(fig.)* pretend not to hear or understand, feign forgetfulness. *Cf.* **ufifi.**

figa (ma-) (*usually* **mafiga**) cooking-stone *(one of three, supporting a pot).* *prov.*

mafiga mawili hayaivishi chungu. You can't cook with only two cooking-stones.

figili* (–, ma-) (kind of) radish. *Cf.* mfigili.

figo (ma-) *anat.* kidney. (= [2]buki, nso.)

figu* [*?*] (–) quarrel, dispute.

figuta *rare* work a bellows. *Cf.* vukuta.

figuto (ma-) *rare* heat, sweat. *Cf.* fukuto.

fihi*, fii (–) discord, dispute, dissension, difference of opinion.

fika arrive, get to..., reach. – mjini. arrive in a city. amesafiri kufika Tanga. He traveled to Tanga. *appl.* fikia. reach someone. *intr.* fifika. be accessible; *(fig.)* be hospitable. *caus.* fikisha. cause to reach, lead to, escort. *double appl.-caus.* fikiliza, fikilisha. cause to reach someone, send to, bring upon. *ass.* fikana. *appl.-ass.* fikiana. arrive/meet at the same place. *double appl.-ass.* fikiliana. come to the same result/conclusion, agree. *Cf.* kifiko, kufika, mfiko.

fikara* (–) *see* fikira.

fikicha break into small pieces, crumble; rub. – macho. rub the eyes. *intr.* fikichita. be friable/brittle.

fikira*, fikara, fikra (–) thought, idea; sudden idea, theory, brainstorm; reflection. yuko katika – zake. He is deep in thought. kwa (katika) – yake. in his opinion.

fikiri* (*also* tafakari) think, reflect, consider; meditate, ponder; examine. *appl.* fikiria.

fikra* (–) *see* fikira.

filam* (–) *see* film.

filifili* (–) angle iron, carpenter's square.

[1]filimbi (–) *ornith.* hornbill.

[2]filimbi, firimbi (ma-) (kind of) flute, whistle.

filisi*, firisi 1. go bankrupt, declare bankruptcy. 2. make the highest bid *(at an auction)*. 3. win all the money *(in gambling)*. *appl.* filisia. *intr.* filisika. mwenye kufilisika. bankrupt (person). *caus.* filisisha. *pass.* filisiwa. be overcome/obsessed by a particular desire/ambition. moyo wake ulifisiliwa na tamaa kubwa ya kutumikia Mwenyezi Mungu. He was overcome by the desire to serve God. *Cf.* mfilisi, mfilisika, muflisi, ufilisi.

film*, filmu, filam [*Engl.*] (–) film, movie. tia – katika kamera. put film in a camera. safisha –. develop a film.

filmu* (–) *see* film.

filosofia* [*Engl.*] (–) philosophy. (= hekima, falsafa.)

fimbi (–) *ornith.* crowned hornbill. (= **kwembe.**)

fimbo (–) stick, cane. **piga –.** beat someone with a stick.

finesi* (ma-) *see* **fenesi.**

finga protect by magic *(field, house). caus.* **fingiza.** prevent, forbid. *Cf.* **fingo.**

finginyika (*also* **vinginyika, vivinyuka**) writhe, wriggle; coil, twist, wind.

fingirika, vingirika turn, roll (along), turn somersaults. *appl.* **fingirikia.** *caus.* **fingirisha.** turn/roll something. **fingirisha chuma cha pua.** roll steel. *Cf.* **ufingirishaji.**

fingo (ma-) charm, spell *(as a protection against evil). Cf.* **finga.**

finika *see* **funika.**

finya pinch, nip, tweak; press, squeeze. **kiatu kinamfinya.** His shoes are too tight. *fig.* **– uso.** scowl. *red. (int.)* **finyafinya.** crumble, break into small pieces. *ass.* **finyana.** be drawn/pinched/wrinkled *(the face). dur.* **finyaa.** shrivel, become thin/emaciated, lose weight. *Cf.* **finyo, mfinyo.**

finyanga knead clay, make pottery. *appl.* **finyangia.** *caus.* **finyangiza.** *Cf.* **mfinyanzi, ufinyanzi.**

finyo (ma-) (*usually* **mafinyo**) 1. fold, wrinkle. **mafinyo ya uso.** wrinkles on the face. 2. narrowness. *coll.* **njia ya –.** narrow street. *Cf.* **finya.**

fio (–) *arch.* rein(s).

fioa *see* **fyoa.**

[1]**fira** (–) cobra.

[2]**fira*** practice sodomy/pederasty. *Cf.* **mfiraji.**

firaha*, firaka, firari (–) *anat.* penis.

firangi* (–) *rare, med.* measles. (= **surua.**)

firari* (–) *see* **firaha.**

firashi* (–) bedspread, quilt.

firidi* *rare* have a pleasant smell, be fragrant.

firigisi* (–) crop, craw, gizzard *(of birds).*

firimbi (ma-) *see* **filimbi.**

firisi* *see* **filisi.**

fisadi* (ma-), **mfisadi** (wa-) corrupter, seducer, immoral person, libertine. *Cf.* **fisidi, ufisadi.**

fisha *caus. of* **fa.**

fisi (–) (common) hyena. *Cf.* **kifisifisi.**

fisidi* destroy, ruin, corrupt; *(fig.)* seduce; violate, rape. *Cf.* **fisadi, ufisadi.**

fisifisi* (–) *see* **fusfus.**

fita *see* **ficha.**

fitina*, fitna 1. (–) discord, strife; intrigue; rebellion, mutiny, revolt. **fanya (leta, tia) –.** make trouble, cause dissension, agitate. 2. (ma-) mischief-maker, agitator. *Cf.* **fitini, ufitina.**

fitini* agitate; slander; cause trouble, do damage. *appl.* **fitinia.** *appl.-ass.* **fitiniana.** *caus.* **fitinisha.** *Cf.* **fitina, mfitini, ufitina.**

fitiri* (–) *see* **futari.**

fitna* (–) *see* **fitina.**

fito *pl. of* **ufito.**

fiwa *pass. of* **fa.**

fiwi (–) lima bean. *Cf.* **mfiwi.**

fizi *pl. of* **ufizi.**

flana* (–) *see* **fulana.**

flotile* (–) *see* **furutile.**

foadi* (ma-) *see* **fowadi.**

fofofo *adv.* completely, totally, absolutely. **kufa –.** be dead as a doornail. **lala –.** sleep very soundly.

foka overflow, run over *(of liquids). fig.* bubble over, gush *(in speaking). appl.* **fokea.** *Cf.* **mfoko.**

foko* *see* **fauka.**

fola* (–) a gift given by a person who holds a baby for the first time *(both to wish the infant good luck and to indicate that the person holding the child has no ill-feelings toward it).*

fomu* [*Engl.*] (–) form, pattern; *(printed)* form, blank, questionnaire. **jaza –.** fill out a form/questionnaire.

fora* 1. defeat someone *(in a game)*, win, be successful. 2. (–) victory; *(sport)* goal. **katika mashindano timu yetu imetia –.** Our team won in the contest. **piga –.** win out, top the list.

fordha* (–) *see* **forodha.**

fori* *adv.* (*also, rare* **fulifuli**) abundantly, in great quantities. *Cf.* **fara.**

forodha*, fordha, furdha (–) customhouse. *loc.* **forodhani.** ship's cargo, reloading place.

foroma* [*Port.*] (–) *see* **faruma.**

foromali* (–) *naut.* yard, spar.

foronya* [*Port.*] (–) pillowcase.

forosadi*, forsadi (–) mulberry. *Cf.* **mforsadi.**

forota* snore. *Cf.* **korota.** **²koroma.**

forsadi* (–) *see* **forosadi.**

foto* [*Engl.*] (–) photo(graph).

fotoa* [*Engl.*]: **– foto.** take a photo-(graph).

fowadi*, foadi [*Engl.*] **(ma-)** *sport* forward; *(mil.)* attacker, aggressor.

frasila*, farasila (–) unit of weight *(about 16 kg, 35 lb.)*

fremu* [*Engl.*] (–) frame *(of a bicycle, etc.)*.

fu *adj.* dead. **Waislamu hawali nyamafu.** Moslems do not eat the meat of dead animals. *Cf.* **fa, kifu, mafu, mfu, ufu.**

¹fua 1. strike, beat, hammer. **– chuma (fedha).** hammer iron (silver). **– nazi.** break open a coconut. **– nguo.** wash (= pound) laundry. *appl.* **fulia.** *caus.* **fulisha.** *caus. & int.* **fuliza.** *fig.* keep on, continue doing something. *pass.* **fuliwa, fuawa.** 2. **(–, ma-)** washtub. *Cf.* **fuawe, fuliza, ¹fuo, kifuo, mfua, mfulizo, mfululizo, ²mfuo, ufuaji.**

²fua (ma-) *see* **mafua.**

³fua (–, ma-) wooden bowl.

fuama, fulama, furama lie prone. *caus. & int.* **fuamisha, fuamiza.** put down flat.

fuasa *caus. of* **fuata.**

fuata 1. follow, succeed, pursue; accompany; obey, comply with. **– sheria.** obey the law. 2. imitate, copy. **– mfano.** take as an example. *caus.* **fuatisha, fuatiza, fuasa.** copy, trace. *ass.* **fuatana.** accompany one another, go together *(in a crowd)*; be a (natural) result of, ensue. **namba zinazofuatana.** numbers in sequence. *Cf.* **kifuasi, mafuatano, mfuasi, mfuatano, ufuasi, ufuataji, ufuatano.**

fuatano (ma-) *see* **mafuatano.**

fuawe (--, ma-) anvil. *Cf.* **¹fua.**

fubaa *see* **fuwaa.**

fudhali* (ma-) *see* **fidhuli.**

fudifudi, fulifuli, kifudifudi, kifulifuli *adv.* on the face, face down, upside down. **lala –.** lie face down. *Cf.* **fudikiza.**

fudikiza turn over, turn upside down/inside out, turn face downwards *(e.g., playing cards)*. *Cf.* **fudifudi.**

fudua *see* **¹fidua.**

fufua 1. wake up, revive, renew. **– desturi.** revive (old) customs. **– deni.** ask for payment of a forgotten debt. 2. **– mtu.** *rel.* bring someone back from the dead. *intr.* **fufuka (katika wafu).** rise from the dead, be resurrected/revived. *Cf.* **mfufuaji, ufufuko.**

fufuliza *see* **fuliza.**

fufurika *rare* boil over, overflow.

fufutende *adj.* lukewarm, tepid.

fuga keep in captivity; tame *(animals);* raise, breed *(livestock).* **– ng'ombe (mbuzi).** keep/raise cattle (goats). *fig.* protect. *intr.* **fugika. farasi huyu hafugiki.** This horse is not tameable. *Cf.* **fugo, mfuga, mfugo, ufugaji.**

fugo (ma-) breeding *(of animals);* breaking in, training; domestication. *Cf.* **fuga.**

fuja confuse, bring into confusion, make a mess of something; overturn, turn upside down; waste, squander. *Cf.* **fujo, mfujaji.**

fujo (–, ma-) disorder, confusion, unrest; noise, tumult. **fanya (tia) –.** throw into disorder. *red.* **fujofujo.** extreme disorder, total confusion. *Cf.* **fuja.**

[1]**fuka, vuka** smoke, give off smoke/fumes/vapor. **jiko linafuka moshi.** The stove is smoking. *appl.* **fukia.** *caus.* **fukiza, fukisha.** smoke *(something),* fumigate, burn incense. *Cf.* **fukizo, fukuto, fusho, kifukizo, kifuku, mfukuto, mvuke, ufukizo, ufukuto.**

[2]**fuka (–)** fuka (oatmeal porridge with pepper and cardamom).

fukara* (–) *see* **fakiri.**

fukarika* become impoverished, be ruined. *Cf.* **fakiri.**

fukia dig in, fill up *(with earth).* **– kaburi.** fill in a grave. *appl.* **fukilia.** *caus.* **fukiza, fukisha.** *inv.* **fukua.** dig out, dig up. **– mizizi.** dig up roots. *fig.* rummage through, ransack. *Cf.* [2]**fuko, fukuo, mfukuaji.**

fukizo, vukizo (ma-) vapor, steam, fumes, smoke; something used for fumigation, incense, etc. *Cf.* [1]**fuka.**

[1]**fuko (ma-)** 1. *augment. of* mfuko. 2. *rare* womb.

[2]**fuko (ma-)** 1. hole, pit, ditch, trench, excavation. 2. dam, embankment; mole, pier. 3. *zool.* mole. *Cf.* **fukia.**

fukombe (–) *see* **furukombe.**

fukua *inv. of* **fukia.**

fukuo (ma-) cavity, excavation. *Cf.* **fukia.**

fukuta *see* **vukuta.**

fukuto, vukuto (ma-) 1. vapor, exhalation, (smell of) perspiration. 2. heat, temperature. 3. stuffiness, closeness *(of a room).* *Cf.* [1]**fuka.**

fukuza drive out, drive/chase away; reject, expel, banish; discharge *(from a job).* **– katika nchi.** expel/banish/exile from a country. *Cf.* **fukuzano,** [2]**mfukuzi.**

fukuzano (ma-) (*us.* **mafukuzano**) expulsion, banishment; persecution, molestation. *Cf.* **fukuza.**

fulama *see* **fuama.**

fulana*, flana [*Engl.*] (–) 1. sweater, cardigan. 2. undershirt, vest. 3. flannel.

fulani* (*rare* **falani**) 1. (–) so-and-so, what's-his-name. **– amefika.** What's-his-name has arrived. 2. *adj.* such and such, some or other, any, a given... **bidhaa –.** such and such goods. **namba –.** a given number.

[1]**fulifuli** *see* **fudifudi.**

[2]**fulifuli*** *adv., rare* *see* **fori.**

fuliza, fululiza, fuuza, fuuliza, fufuliza (*caus. & intr. of* [1]**fua**) do something uninterruptedly/continuously. **mvua imefuliza siku tano.** It rained continuously for five days.

fululiza *see* **fuliza.**

fulusi* (–) 1. fulusi (kind of fish). 2. *coll.* money, cash.

[1]**fuma** weave, knit, crochet, embroider; plait, braid; sew together. *inv.* **fumua.** loosen, untie, unravel, undo, unroll. *fig.* 1. release. **fumua vita.** start war. 2. uncover, reveal. *inv.-appl.* **fumulia.** *inv.-intr.* **fumuka.** *inv.-intr.-ass.* **fumukana.** separate, scatter, disperse *(after assemblies).* *Cf.* **fumukano, mfuma, mfumi,** [1]**mfumo, mfumua.**

[2]**fuma** pierce, penetrate. *Cf.* **fume, fumo.**

fumania 1. surprise, appear unexpectedly, take by surprise, catch unawares. 2. discover someone in a wrongful act *(e.g., adultery).* *intr.* **fumanika.** *caus.* **fumaniza.**

[1]**fumba** 1. bring together, close. **– macho (kinywa).** close the eyes (the mouth). 2. disguise, mystify, make a secret of. **– maneno.** speak mysteriously (in riddles). *refl.* **jifumba.** be wrapped up in oneself, live in a world of one's own. *stat.* **fumbama.** be in a state of confusion. **fumbama akili.** lose one's senses, not be in one's right mind. *cont.* **fumbata.** embrace, grasp, seize, clutch. *inv.* **fumbua.** open. *coll.* **kufumba na kufumbua (macho).** in a moment. *fig.* reveal, disclose; explore. *inv.-intr.* **fumbuka.** reveal oneself, appear. *Cf.* [1]**fumbo, mfumba, mfumbua, ufumbuzi;** *also* **vumbua.**

[2]**fumba** (–) bag made of matting. **mkeka wa –.** 1. woven sleeping bag. 2. shroud. *Cf.* **kifumba, kifumbu.**

[3]**fumba** (ma-) heap, lump.

[1]**fumbi** (ma-) stream, brook; drain, gutter; ditch. **– la (kupandia) mpunga.** furrow for planting rice.

[2]**fumbi** (–) *see* **vumbi.**

[1]fumbo (ma-) 1. mystery; puzzle, riddle; problem. 2. mysterious/veiled language, hidden/obscure meaning; hint, allusion. **sema kwa —.** use veiled language, speak in riddles (hints, allusions). **mwandiko wa —.** code, cipher. 3. *dial.*: **jina la —.** pseudonym. *Cf.* **[1]fumba.**

[2]fumbo (ma-) fumbo (title of a chief). *Cf.* **fumo.**

fumbua *inv. of* **[1]fumba.**

fume (ma-) person wounded *(by a spear).* *Cf.* **[2]fuma.**

[1]fumi (—) fumi (kind of fish).

[2]fumi (—) *see* **vumi.**

fumo (ma-) 1. *rare* spear. 2. fumo (title of a chief). *Cf.* **[2]fuma, [2]fumbo.**

fumua *inv. of* **[1]fuma.**

fumukano (ma-) (*us.* **mafumukano**) separation, dispersal, breaking up *(of a meeting, etc.)*; spreading, diffusion. *Cf.* **[1]fuma.**

funa *see* **vuna.**

[1]funda pound, pulverize *(grain)*; break up, crush *(by pounding)*. *red.* **fundafunda** *(w. int.-dur. force)* pound thoroughly, keep on pounding. **— unga.** to mix several kinds of meal or flour. *Cf.* **funde.**

[2]funda learn. *caus.* **fundisha, funza.** teach, instruct, educate. *caus.-ass.* **funzana.** teach each other, study together. *refl.* **(ku)jifundisha, jifunza.** teach oneself, learn, study. *Cf.* **fundi, funzo, kifundi, mafundisho, mfundishaji, mkufunzi, mwanafunzi, uanafunzi, ufundi.**

[3]funda (ma-) mouthful, swallow. **— ya maji.** a mouthful of water. **piga mafunda.** to take large bites of food.

[4]funda *rare* tie in a knot. (= **fundika.**)

fundarere (—) fundarere (kind of snake).

funde (ma-) something pounded; powder. *Cf.* **[1]funda.**

fundi, funzi (—) craftsman, skilled worker; expert, master *(of something)*; instructor. **yeye ni — kwa kucheza mpira.** He is a master at football-playing. **— cherehani.** tailor. **— wa cherehani.** sewing-machine repairman. *Cf.* **[2]funda.**

fundika tie a knot, draw tight, tie up. *Cf.* **[4]funda, fundo, fundua, kifundo, mfundo.**

fundisha *caus. of* **[2]funda.**

fundisho (ma-) *see* **mafundisho.**

fundo (ma-) 1. knot; thickening, swelling. **— la uzi.** knot in thread. **— la mti.** knot in wood (a tree). **— la ua.** bud. **— la mguu.** ankle. 2. bundle. **— la nguo.**

bundle of clothes. 3. *fig.* difficulty, complication, confusion. **— la moyo.** bad humor, grudge. *Cf.* [4]**funda, fundika.**

fundua untie, loosen. **— chupa.** open/uncork a bottle. *fig.* overcome difficulties. *Cf.* [4]**funda, fundika.**

[1]**funga** 1. tie (on, up). **— (kwa) kamba.** tie with a cord or string. 2. fasten, secure; close, shut, lock. **— mlango.** shut/lock a door. **— barua.** seal up a letter. **— choo.** *med.* be constipated. **— (piga) breki.** put on the brake. **— maneno.** clench the teeth. 3. imprison. **— gerezani.** put in jail. 4. conclude. **— mapatano ya biashara.** make a business deal, conclude a contract. 5. decide on. **— safari (vita).** decide on/begin a journey (war), make preparations. **funga virago vyake.** pack one's bags, close out one's affairs. 6. *sport* win. 7. *elec.*: **— stimu.** turn off. 8. fast. *refl.* **jifunga.** 1. devote oneself to, give special attention to. 2. become involved in a difficult situation. *intr.* **fungika.** be closeable. *ass.* **fungana.** *ass.-caus.* **funganya.** pack up, get ready for a trip. *stat.* **fungama.** be tight/firm/dense. *stat.-ass.* **fungamana.** be intertwined, be impenetrable *(forest).* **siasa ya fungamana.** policy of alignment. *inv.* **fungua.** 1. untie, unfasten, loosen. 2. open. **fungua mlango.** open a door. 3. open, start, inaugurate. **fungua mkutano.** open/begin a meeting. **fungua kinywa.** eat breakfast. 4. free, liberate, release *(from prison).* *appl.* **fungulia.** *caus.* **funguza.** *inv.-refl.* **jifungua.** free oneself, be opened; give birth. **amejifungua mtoto wa kike.** She has given birth to a girl. *Cf.* **fungasha,** [1]**fungo, kifunga, kifungo, kifungua, kifunguo, mafungia, mafungulia, mfunga, mfungizo, mfungo, mfungua, mfunguo, mfungwa, ufunguaji, ufunguo.**

[2]**funga** *pl. of* **ufunga.**

fungasa *see* **fungasha.**

fungasha, fungasa (*caus. of* [1]**funga**) take someone (something) in tow, pull along.

fungate (—) 1. *arch.* seven. 2. the first seven days after a wedding (when food is supplied to the newly-weds by their relatives), honeymoon.

[1]**fungo** (—) *Isl.* period of fasting. *Cf.* [1]**funga.**

[2]**fungo** (—) civet cat.

[1]**fungu** (ma-) 1. part, share; piece. **— la nyama.** a piece of meat. *gramm.*: **— la maneno.** sentence. *liter.*: verse. 2. heap, pile; quantity, group; *(mil.)* small unit, company; *(sport)* league. 3. *naut.* sandbank, reef. *Cf.* **kifungu.**

[2]**fungu** (ma-) *bot.* cockscomb *(Celosia argentea* and *Celosia cristata).*

fungua *inv. of* **funga.**

funguo *pl. of* **ufunguo.**

funika, finika cover, close. **— chungu.** put a lid on a pot. **— fumba.** get into a sleeping bag. *fig.:* conceal, keep secret. **— maneno.** express oneself unclearly. *refl.* **jifunika.** cover oneself. *caus.* **funikisha, funikiza.** have something covered. *fig.:* **maji yameifunikisha nchi.** The water has flooded the land. *Cf.* **funua, kifuniko, mfuniko.**

funiko (ma-) *augment. of* **kifuniko.**

funo (—) funo (kind of antelope, common duiker; *cf.* **mindi**).

funua 1. open, uncover. **— mabawa.** spread the wings. **— kitabu.** open a book. 2. *fig.:* reveal, expose, discover. **— taksiri.** discover a crime. *appl.* **funulia.** disclose/explain to someone. *intr.* **funuka.** be open; be obvious/plain. *Cf.* **funika, funuo, kifunuo, mafunuo, ufunuo.**

fununu* (—) rumor, report.

funuo (—) opening. *Cf.* **funua.**

funutu (—) *see* **tunutu.**

[1]**funza** (—) chigger; grub, maggot; caterpillar. (= [1]tekenywa.)

[2]**funza** *caus. of* [2]**funda.**

funzi (—) *see* **fundi.**

funzo (ma-; *us. pl.*) teaching, doctrine; instruction, training. **mafunzo ya kiaskari.** military training. *Cf.* [2]**funda.**

[1]**fuo** (ma-) 1. place for washing clothes. 2. place where a dead body is washed. *Cf.* [1]**fua.**

[2]**fuo** (ma-) 1. foam. **mafuo ya bahari.** seafoam. 2. *fig.* scum, dregs.

fupa (ma-) *augment. of* **mfupa.**

fupi *adj.* 1. short, low. **mti mfupi.** a low tree. **watu wafupi.** short/undersized people. 2. brief, terse, concise. **maneno mafupi.** brief/terse words. *Cf.* **fupika, kifupi, ufupi, ufupisho.**

fupika be short/low, be brief/abbreviated. *caus.* **fupisha, fupiza.** make short, abbreviate, abridge, condense. *Cf.* **fupi, ufupisho.**

fura 1. rise/swell up; effervesce. 2. *fig.* become excited, be furious, rage. *intr.* **furika.** flow over, flood, inundate; boil over. *caus.* **furisha.** cause a flood. *Cf.* **furufuru, mafuriko, ufurufuru.**

furaha* (—) joy, pleasure, gaiety, delight, enthusiasm. **fanya(ona) —.** be happy/delighted. **kwa —.** with joy/enthusiasm. **pokea kwa —.** greet cordially. *Cf.* **furahi, furahivu, mfurahivu, ufurahi.**

furahi* be glad/happy/pleased; enjoy oneself, have a good time. *appl.* **furahia.** *intr.* **furahika.** *caus.* **furahisha.** please someone. *Cf.* **furaha, furahivu, mfurahivu, ufurahi.**

furahifu* *adj., rare* happy, gay. *Cf.* **furaha, furahi.**

furama *see* **fuama.**

furdha* (–) *see* **forodha.**

furifuri *adj./adv.* *see* **fara.**

furika *intr. of* **fura.**

furiko (ma-) *see* **mafuriko.**

furkani* (–) 1. *Isl.* Furkani (name applied to the Koran). 2. *rare* Bible.

fursa* (–) 1. incident, accident. 2. convenient time, favorable moment, opportunity. **toa –.** give an opportunity.

furufuru (–) confusion, disorder. *Cf.* **fura.**

furukobe (–) *see* **furukombe.**

furukombe, furukobe, fukombe (–) sea eagle.

furukuta be in constant motion, turn, twist, move back and forth restlessly, roll, toss. **alikamata sawasawa hata hakuweza kufurukuta.** He was so tightly bound that he could not move a limb.

furumi* (–) *see* **farumi.**

furumiza* *rare* throw away. *Cf.* **farumi.**

[1]**furungu*** (ma-) *bot.* shaddock, pomelo. *Cf.* **mfurungu.**

[2]**furungu*** [*Pers.*] (ma-) anklet.

furusha scare away *(birds)*; scatter, disperse *(enemies)*.

furushi* (ma-) package, parcel, bundle.

furutile*, flotile [*Germ.* Flotille?] (–) 1. shipyard, dockyard. 2. (**– la kiwanda**). workshop. **– la kurekibisha.** assembly shop.

[1]**fusa** 1. knock, hit, strike; beat until soft. 2. fall upon, attack. *Cf.* [1]**fusi, fusia, ufusio.**

[2]**fusa*** release, let off air *(from tires, etc.)*.

fusfus*, fusus, fisifisi (–) incrustation.

fusha* (–) *see* **busha.**

fusho (ma-) something burnt/producing smoke *(e.g., fumigant, charm)*. *Cf.* [1]**fuka.**

[1]**fusi** (ma-), **kifusi** (vi-) rubble, debris, rubbish. *Cf.* [1]**fusa.**

[2]**fusi*** (ma-) *rare* *see* **fuzi.**

fusia (*appl. of* **fusa**) lay the foundation/bed *(of a house or street)*.

fusus* (–) *see* **fusfus.**

fususi* (–) precious stone, gem.

[1]**futa** 1. wipe (off), clean (up). – **kamasi.** wipe the nose. 2. *fig.:* clear off, remove, abolish, cancel; steal from. *intr.* **futika.** be wiped away; *(fig.)* be erased/eradicated *(from one's memory). Cf.* **mfuto.**

[2]**futa** (ma-) *see* **mafuta.**

[3]**futa** (–) futa (variety of large snake).

futahi* 1. *sing.* good luck. 2. *v.* have a lucky escape. *caus.* **futusha.** save, rescue.

futari*, fitiri (–) evening meal after a day's fasting. *Cf.* **futuru.**

[1]**futi*** [*Engl.*] (–) foot (unit of measurement, 30 cm.).

[2]**futi** (ma-) knee. (= **goti.**)

futika tuck into *(the waistcloth, girdle, etc.),* put into the pocket. *Cf.* **futua.**

futua 1. take out *(of the pocket, a bundle, etc.);* undo, open up. 2. *fig.* be exposed/revealed/brought to light. *intr.* **futuka.** be revealed/exposed; stick out *(of the pocket, etc.); (fig.)* be annoyed/angry. *intr.-appl.* **futukia.** be angry with someone. *Cf.* **futika.**

[1]**futuri*** (–) span (unit of measure, 22.5 cm.).

[2]**futuri*** (–) hemorrhoids.

futuru* eat the first meal after fasting. *Cf.* **futari.**

futusha* *rare* save, rescue, come to the aid of. *Cf.* **futahi.**

[1]**fuu, fuvu** (ma-) 1. (empty) shell. – **la yai.** eggshell. 2. (– **la kichwa**) cranium, skull. 3. cuttlefish bone. *Cf.* **kifuu, ufuu.**

[2]**fuu** (–) kind of small berry. *Cf.* **mfufu.**

fuuliza *see* **fuliza.**

fuuza *see* **fuliza.**

fuvu (ma-) *see* [1]**fuu.**

fuwaa, fubaa be retarded *(in growth),* be stunted/shrivelled.

fuya *rare* spoil, ruin; waste, squander *(money, property). Cf.* **fuja.**

fuzi*, fusi (ma-) *anat.* shoulder, shoulder blade.

fuzu* be successful, win *(in gambling),* pass *(an examination).*

fyanda, fianda crush, squash; hurt, injure.

fyata, fiata, fata press, squeeze *(between the legs). fig.:* be discreet in one's speech, have one's tongue under control. *inv.* **fyatua.** loosen one's grip, release. **fyatua mota.** start an engine. **fyatua mtego.** release a trap. **fyatua mkiki (shuti).** *sport* score a goal. **fyatua bunduki.** release the trigger, discharge a gun. *inv.-appl.* **fyatulia.** *caus.* **fyatusha.** *Cf.* **fyatuko, fyusa, mfyuso.**

fyatua *inv. of* **fyata.**

fyatuko (ma-), mfyatuko (mi-) (act of) releasing, opening. *Cf.* **fyata.**

fyeka, fieka, feka, fyekua clear *(land),* reclaim, make arable; *(fig.)* clear away, eliminate. **– mwitu.** clear a forest. *appl.* **fyekea.** *caus.* **fyekesha.** *Cf.* **fyeko, mafyeko, mfyeka.**

fyeko, fieko (ma-; *us. pl.*) clearing, reclamation *(of land). Cf.* **fyeka.**

fyekua *see* **fyeka.**

fyeruka become irritated/angry.

fyoa, fioa 1. cut *(only of grain).* 2. *fig.* be subtle, ingenious, keen. 3. use abusive/insolent language. *caus.* **fyoza.** treat with contempt, deride. *Cf.* **fyozi, mfyozaji, ufyozi.**

fyonda *see* **fyonza.**

fyonya, sonya make a hissing sound *(as a sign of contempt.) Cf.* **msono.**

fyonza, fyonda suck. *Cf.* **mfyonza.**

fyozi *adj., dial.* derisive, scornful, contemptuous. *Cf.* **fyoa.**

fyusa set a trap *(for animals). Cf.* **fyata, mfyuso.**

fyuzi* [*Engl.*] (–) *elec.* fuse.

G

gaagaa, galagala, garagara 1. turn, toss, roll. 2. *fig.* be idle, lazy; stretch oneself. *Cf.* **mgaagaa.**

gabi (–) *rare* roller, pulley, block(-and-tackle). (= **kapi.**)

[1]**gadi*** (ma-) prop, support, stay, brace; pillar. *Cf.* **gudi, gadimu.**

[2]**gadi*** [*Engl.*] (ma-) 1. guard, watch; protection. 2. watchman.

[3]**gadi*** (–) lump of clay.

gadimu* support, prop up *(with posts, braces).* *Cf.* [1]**gadi.**

gadiwana* [*Engl.*] (–) *rare, mil.* guard of honor.

gae, gai (ma-) 1. potsherd, splinter *(of glass, pottery).* 2. *fig.* **nyumba ya vigae.** a house roofed with tiles. *Cf.* **kigae.**

gafi* *see* **ghafi.**

[1]**gaga** (ma-) crust, coating; *(med.)* scurf, scab; tartar *(on the teeth).* *Cf.* **kigaga, ugaga.**

[2]**gaga** (–) gaga (a spell cast on a house to keep wild animals away).

[3]**gaga** turn, roll, toss (from one side to the other).

gagamiza penetrate, push in *(forcibly);* press/roll together.

gai (ma-) *see* **gae.**

[1]**gaidi*** [*Engl.*] (ma-) guide.

[2]**gaidi, mgaidi** (ma-) 1. robber, thief. 2. *mil.* guerrilla. *Cf.* **ugaidi.**

gala (ma-) gala (kind of wild cat).

galagala *see* **gaagaa.**

galani* (–) *see* **galoni.**

galawa (–) *see* **ngalawa.**

gale (ma-) *see* **ugale.**

galili (ma-) armor, shell *(tortoise, turtle, crab).*

galme*, kalme (–) small sail of a dhow. **mlingoti wa –.** mast for this sail.

galoni*, galani [*Engl.*] (–) gallon *(liquid measure,* 4.54 *l).*

[1]**gamba** (*us. refl.:* **jigamba**) boast, show off. **– kwa nguo mpya.** show off new clothes.

[2]**gamba** (ma-) scale, shell, armor. **– la kobe.** tortoise-shell. **magamba ya samaki.** fish scales. *fig.:* **– la kitabu.** cover/jacket of a book. *Cf.* [2]**amba,** [1]**chamba.**

gambia (–) *rare* dagger. (= **jambia.**)

[1]**gambusi, kambusi** (–) gambusi (musical instrument similar to a banjo).

[2]**gambusi, kambusi** (–) gambusi (kind of fish).

gamdra* (–) *naut.* hatch(way).

gamti* [*Ind.*] (–) gamti (inferior kind of unbleached cotton cloth).

gana* (–, ma-) *see* [2]**kana.**

ganda 1. thicken, congeal, coagulate *(blood, milk); (fig.)* freeze, be frozen. **maziwa ya kuganda.** curdled milk. 2. stick fast, hold tight, clasp. *stat.* **gandama.** be congealed; be stuck together; be sticky. **gandama na.** stick to something. *stat.-appl.* **gandamia.** adhere, stick to; rely on something/someone; *(fig.)* be faithful/devoted. *stat.-caus.* **gandamiza.** press heavily on, crush. *stat.-ass.* **gandamana.** harden, thicken; freeze (solid). *inv.* **gandua.** loosen, pull off, separate; escape (*from a danger*). **gandua stempu.** pull off a stamp *(from an envelope).* *inv.-appl.* **gandulia.** *inv.-intr.* **ganduka, gandulika.** 3. (ma-) rind, husk, shell, crust. **— la mkata.** bread crust. **— la limau.** lemon rind. **— la yai.** eggshell. *Cf.* **gandalo, [1]gando, [2]mganda, mgando, ugandamano, ugandisho.**

gandalo (ma-) leg-fetter *(made of wood),* stocks. *Cf.* **ganda.**

gandama *stat. of* **[1]ganda.**

gandamana *stat.-ass. of* **[1]ganda.**

gandamia *stat.-appl. of* **[1]ganda.**

gandamiza *stat.-caus. of* **ganda.**

[1]gando (ma-) claw, pincers *(of a crab, etc.) Cf.* **ganda.**

[2]gando (ma-) *see* **ganjo.**

gandua *inv. of* **[1]ganda.**

gane (–) gane (sleeping place for unmarried boys or girls).

ganga bind up, splice; mend, repair; *(fig.)* bandage. **— kidonda.** bandage a wound, treat (medically), cure. *inv.* **gangua.** untie, remove (a bandage); free from *(a charm, taboo, etc.).* *inv.-appl.* **gangulia.** *Cf.* **gango, [1]mganga, mgango, uganga.**

gange (ma-) *min.* chalk stone, (soft) limestone.

gango (ma-) 1. clamp, brace; hoop. **— la pipa.** barrel-hoop. 2. *med.* bandage, sling, splint. *Cf.* **ganga.**

gangua *inv. of* **ganga.**

gani *interr. (invariable)* what kind of? **sababu —?** for what reason? why? **wakati —?** at what time? when? **habari gani?** What's the news? **mahali —?** where? in what place?

ganja (ma-) *see* **kiganja.**

ganjo (ma-) 1. abandoned village. 2. *fig.* ruin, impoverishment.

gano (–) *rare* sinew, tendon, nerve. (= **kano, [1]mkano.**)

ganza (*red.* **ganzaganza**) hesitate, falter, stammer. *fig.* be clumsy, awkward. *caus.* **ganzisha.** *med.* give a local anesthetic.

ganzi, chanzi (–) numbness. **– la meno.** numbness of the teeth *(produced by an anesthetic)*. **mguu wangu umekufa –.** My foot is asleep. *fig.* stupefaction, narcosis. *med.* **sindano ya –.** local anesthetic.

[1]**gao** (ma-) 1. palm *(of the hand)*. 2. handful. **– moja la unga.** a handful of flour.

[2]**gao** (ma-) *augment. of* **ngao.**

garafuu* (–) *see* **karafuu.**

garagara *see* **gaagaa.**

gari* [*Ind.*] (ma-) *in gen.* vehicle, wagon, car. **– la farasi.** horse-drawn wagon. **– la miguu.** *arch.* bicycle. **– la moshi.** locomotive. **– la mizigo (abiria).** freight (passenger) car. **chumba cha –.** compartment (of a railroad carriage). **tikiti ya –.** railway ticket. **mkubwa wa magari.** driver, engineer. **– la kulimia.** *rare* tractor. **– la maji.** watering-machine. **– la mtoto.** baby-carriage, perambulator. **enda kwa –.** go by train/car. **endesha –.** drive *(a car)*. *Cf.* **kijigari.**

gashi (ma-) *coll.* woman.

gati* [*Ind.*] (–, ma-) *naut.* landing stage, pier, dock.

gaugau, geugeu (–) gaugau (kind of bird).

gauni* [*Engl.*] (ma-) (woman's) gown, dress. **vaa – la kisasa.** wear modern clothes.

gavana* [*Engl.*] (ma-) *rare* governor. (= **balozi.**)

gawa divide, distribute, pass/hand out. **– chakula.** pass out/serve food. **– karata.** deal cards. **– nusu kwa nusu.** divide in equal parts, halve. *ass.* **gawana.** *ass.-caus.* **gawanya.** divide up, share. *ass.-caus.-intr.* **gawanyika.** be divided up. *Cf.* **gawio, gawo, kigawanye, kigawanyo, mgao, mgawaji, mgawanya, mgawanyiko, mgawanyo, ugawaji, ugawanyaji.**

gawanya *ass.-caus. of* **gawa.**

gawio (ma-) 1. division, distribution, apportionment. 2. *math.* divisor. *Cf.* **gawa.**

gawo (ma-) part, share, portion. *Cf.* **gawa.**

gayagaya (ma-) gayagaya (kind of mat).

gazeti* [*Engl.*] (ma-) newspaper, magazine, periodical. **– la jimbo.** provincial/local newspaper. *coll.:* **usinipige magazeti.** Don't talk such nonsense.

gea throw; leave behind, abandon, give up.

gebali* (ma-) *see* **jabali.**

gefyagefya *see* **gofyagofya.**

gego, chego, cheyo (ma-) *anat.* molar (tooth). **wa na –.** have a toothache.

gelada* (–) *see* **jalada.**

[1]**geli** (–) geli (children's game similar to tipcat).

[2]**geli** (–) large knife.

gema cut, slit, tap *(the bark of trees, to obtain resin).* **– mpira (tembo).** tap rubber (palm-wine). *prov.:* **mgema akisifiwa tembo hulitia maji.** If the palm-wine tapper is praised for his wine, he dilutes it with water. *Cf.* **mgema, mgemo, ugema, ugemo.**

[1]**genge** (ma-) (steep) slope, declivity, cliff, crag, escarpment; edge, brink.

[2]**genge*** [*Engl.*] (–) gang *(of workers),* group, troop.

[3]**genge** (ma-) coral.

geni *adj.* strange, foreign; unusual, extraordinary. **sema maneno ya kigeni.** speak in a remarkable/unusual way. **jambo –.** a remarkable affair. *Cf.* **kigeni, mgeni, ugeni.**

gensi* (–) *see* **jinsi.**

gereji* [*Engl.*] (–) garage, repair shop.

gereza*, greza [*Port.*] (–) fort, prison. **tia (funga, peleka) gerezani.** imprison. **toa (fungua, ondoa) gerezani.** release from prison. **bawabu (mngojezi) wa –.** (prison) guard.

gesa *rare* turn (on a lathe). *Cf.* **kereza.**

geshi* (–) *rare* *see* **jeshi.**

geso (–) *rare* lathe. *Cf.* **gesa.**

geua *rare* change, avoid. *appl.* **geulia.** *caus.* **geuza.** change, alter; interchange, exchange; change position, turn around; *(fig., elec.)* transform *(current). intr.* **geuka.** be changeable/interchangeable, be transformed; *(fig.)* treat with scorn. *Cf.* **geugeu, geuzi, kigeugeu, mageuzi, mgeuzo, ugeuzi.**

[1]**geugeu** *adj.* changeable, fickle, uncertain. *Cf.* **geua.**

[2]**geugeu** (–) *see* **gaugau.**

geuko (ma-) *see* **mageuko.**

geuza *caus. of* **geua.**

[1]**geuzi** 1. (ma-) (*us.* **mageuzi**) change, alteration, transformation. 2. *adj.* changeable, fickle, inconstant, uncertain. *Cf.* **geua.**

[2]**geuzi** *pl. of* **ugeuzi.**

geuzo (ma-) *see* **mgeuzo.**

geza* [*Pers.*] try on *(an article of clothing)*. *Cf.* **kigezo.**

ghadhabika*, ghadhibika be angry, irritated. *caus.* **ghadhabisha.** anger, irritate, provoke, exasperate. *Cf.* **ghadhabu.**

ghadhabu* (–) anger, vexation, irritation. **ona (ingia) –.** be annoyed, lose one's temper. **ingiwa (patwa, shikwa) na –.** be vexed, irritated. *Cf.* **ghadhabika.**

ghadhia* (–) unrest, disorder, tumult, rebellion.

ghadhibika* *see* **ghadhabika.**

ghafala* (–) *see* **ghafula.**

ghafalika* *see* **ghafilika.**

ghafi*, gafi 1. *sing.* gross weight. 2. short weight. 3. *adj., fig.* (*also* **ghafighafi**) inferior *(in quality)*; insignificant, worthless.

ghafilika*, ghafalika be forgetful, absentminded; be surprised, amazed. *caus.* **ghafilisha.** divert; neglect; astonish. *Cf.* **ghafula.**

ghafilisha* *caus. of* **ghafilika.**

ghafula*, ghafala 1. (–) suddenness, abruptness, (unexpected) occurrence. **kwa –.** sudden, abrupt, unexpected. **maradhi ya –.** *med.* apoplexy. **kifo cha –.** a sudden death. 2. *adv.* suddenly, unexpectedly. *Cf.* **ghafilika, mghafala, taghafali.**

ghaibu* (–) absence; lack, deficiency; distance, remoteness. **soma kwa –.** recite from memory. *Cf.* **ghibu, ughaibu.**

ghaidhi*, ghaidi (–) 1. (sudden fit of) anger. 2. exertion, (strong) effort, determination.

ghaidi* (–) *see* **ghaidhi.**

ghairi* 1. consider, change one's mind, do something unexpected. *appl.* **ghairia.** *caus.* **ghairisha.** 2. (–) change, surprise. **tia –.** surprise, disappoint. 3. *prep.* **ghairi ya –.** without; except, exclusive of, apart from. *Cf.* **baghairi.**

ghala* (–, ma-) 1. storage place, storeroom. **– chini ya nyumba.** cellar, basement. **– ya bidhaa.** warehouse, stock(room). **weka ghalani.** put in storage, store away. 2. *bot.:* **– ya mbegu.** seed-lobe, cotyledon.

ghalati* (–) lie, falsehood; fault, mistake, transgression.

ghali* *adj.* scarce, rare; costly, expensive. *Cf.* **ghalika.**

ghalibu* *see* **ghilibu.**

ghalika* be scarce, be in short supply; be expensive; rise in price. *caus.* **ghalisha.** raise the price. *Cf.* **ghali.**

ghalisha* *caus. of* **ghalika.**

ghamma* be unusual/rare.

ghamu*, ghammu (–) sadness, sorrow, grief, melancholy, **tia –.** grieve. **ingiwa na –.** be caused grief/distress.

ghangi* (–) ghangi (kind of ship).

ghani* 1. sing *(songs of a serious character). Cf.* **mghani.** 2. (ma-) song.

ghanima* (–) success, good fortune, prosperity, advantage, benefit. **pata –.** derive benefit, make a profit; win *(in a lottery).*

gharadhi* (–) 1. *rare* aim, intention, desire (= **kusudi, nia.**) 2. usual/ routine tasks, odds and ends *(of business, etc.)*

gharama* (–) expense(s), expenditure; payment; amount due, fee, charges, costs. **fanya (toa) –.** spend money, go to expense. *Cf.* **gharimu.**

gharika* (–) 1. flood, inundation. **mvua ya –.** heavy rain, cloudburst. 2. *fig.* wreck, ruin, downfall. *Cf.* **ghariki, gharikisho, mafuriko.**

ghariki* be flooded/inundated, sink into the water. *caus.* **gharikisha.** flood, inundate. **– nchi.** flood a country. *Cf.* **gharika.**

gharikisho* (ma-) flood, inundation. *Cf.* **ghariki.**

gharimu* cost. **imegharimu paundi ishirini.** It cost 20 pounds. *appl.* **gharimia.** spend for/on, pay out (money), pay expenses. **nimemgharimia safari yake.** I have paid his travel expenses. *Cf.* **gharama.**

ghashi* (–) deceit, guile, trickery, fraud.

ghasi* confuse, complicate; create a disturbance. *appl.* **ghasia.** *caus.* **ghasisha.** *pass.* **ghasiwa.** *Cf.* **1ghasia.**

1ghasia* (–) confusion, disorder; haste, excitement. **kwa –.** hurried, restless, agitated. **fanya –.** cause/produce confusion. *Cf.* **ghasi.**

2ghasia *appl. of* **ghasi.**

ghera* (–) 1. *rare* jealousy, distrust. 2. = **ari.**

ghibu* be absent; be lost, disappear. *Cf.* **ghaibu.**

ghiliba* (–) deception, cheating, fraud. *Cf.* **ghilibu.**

ghilibu*, ghalibu compete; get the better of *(by underhanded means),* come out ahead; take advantage of, cheat, defraud. *appl.* **ghilibia.** *appl.-ass.* **ghilibiana.** *pass.* **ghilibiwa.** *Cf.* **ghiliba, mghalaba.**

ghofira* (–) *rel.* forgiveness, pardon, absolution. (= **msamaha.**)

ghofiri*, **gofiri** *rel.* forgive, pardon, absolve. *appl.* **ghofiria.** *caus.* **ghofirisha.** *pass.* **ghofiriwa.**

ghorofa* *see* **orofa.**

ghoshi*, **ghushi** cheat, deceive; falsify, adulterate. *appl.* **ghoshia.** *caus.* **ghoshisha.** *pass.* **ghoshiwa.** *Cf.* **ughoshi.**

ghosubu* swindle, cheat.

ghuba*, **ghubba** (**ma-**) bay, gulf, inlet.

ghubari* (**ma-**) cloud *(of rain, vapor, dust).*

ghubba* (**ma-**) *see* **ghuba.**

ghulamu* (–) 1. young man. 2. *cards* knave, jack. (= **mzungu wa tatu.**)

ghumia* lose consciousness, grow weak; *(fig.)* be disconcerted/frightened; be speechless from amazement. *caus.* **ghumisha.** *pass.* **ghumiwa.**

ghuri* deceive, cheat, mislead; falsify. *intr.* **ghurika, ghururika.** be conceited/ arrogant; be deluded. *Cf.* **ghururi.**

ghurubu* (–) *see* **magharibi.**

ghururi* (–, **ma-**) vanity, conceit, presumption, arrogance; self-deception. *Cf.* **ghuri.**

ghururika* *intr. of* **ghuri.**

[1]**ghushi*** *see* **ghoshi.**

[2]**ghushi*** be sufficient/adequate.

ghusubu* force, compel, coerce; take by force. *appl.* **ghusubia.**

gia* [*Engl.*] (–) gear, mechanism. *auto.* gear. **tia –.** shift (gears).

gida pour off, decant *(a liquid, leaving the sediment).* (= **chingirisha.**)

gidam* (–) *see* **gidamu.**

gidamu*, **gidam** (–) leather strap *(on sandals).*

gilasi* [*Engl.*] (–) *see* **glasi.**

gilidi* bind *(a book in leather).* *Cf.* **jalidi.**

giligilani* (–) *bot.* coriander seed *(Coriandrum sativum).* *Cf.* **mgiligilani.**

gimbi (–) *see* **ugimbi.**

ginsi* (–) *see* **jinsi.**

gisi* *rare* suppose, guess, believe. *Cf.* **kisi.**

gisikafiri (–) gisikafiri (kind of lizard).

gita* [*Engl.*] (–, **ma-**) *see* **gitaa.**

gitaa*, gita [*Engl.*] (–, **ma-**) guitar. **piga –.** play the guitar.

giza, kiza, jiza (–, **ma-**) dark(ness), gloom. **– la usiku.** the dark of night. **fanya –.** become dark. *fig.:* ignorance. *prov.:* **moyo wa mwenzio ni msitu wa giza.** The heart of another person is a dark forest *(i.e., an unfathomable mystery).* **–a –.** *adj.* dark *(= not light).*

glasi*, gilasi [*Engl.*] (–) (drinking) glass, wineglass.

globu* [*Engl.*] (–) *elec.* (light) bulb.

[1]**goba** (–) dried manioc.

[2]**goba** *rare* end, conclude.

goboa, koboa break, break off, pluck off. **– pamba.** pick cotton. *appl.* **gobolea.** *intr.* **goboka.**

gobolea *appl. of* **goboa.**

gobori* [?] (–) *mil., arch.* muzzle-loader. (= [1]**koroboi.**)

goda (*us. refl.* **jigoda**) make an effort, exert oneself, work hard for *(one's children, parents).*

godoro* [*Ind.*] (**ma-**) mattress, bolster, cushion.

goe *sing.* *see* **ugoe.**

gofi (–) 1. rind, bark. 2. skin.

gofia* [?] (–) roller, pulley.

gofiri* *see* **ghofiri.**

gofu 1. (**ma-**) ruin(s). **– la nyumba.** ruins of a house. *fig.* an emaciated person, human wreck. 2. *adj.* destroyed, collapsed; thin, emaciated. *Cf.* **gofua.**

gofua fall down, collapse *(buildings). fig.* become thin, emaciated; weaken, debilitate. **ugonjwa umemgofua sana.** The illness has greatly weakened him. *intr.* **gofuka.** *caus.* **gofusha.** *Cf.* **gofu.**

gofyagofya, gefyagefya drive, impel.

gogadima (–) *bot.* kind of shrub *(Capparis corymbosa).*

gogo (**ma-**) log. *Cf.* **kigogo.**

gogoreka cackle, cluck, chatter.

gogoroda force, compel.

gogota 1. strike, tap, beat, hammer *(metal).* 2. pull, drag. **– mti.** drag off a tree. *appl.* **gogotea.** *caus.* **gogoteza. gogoteza maneno.** speak imperfectly/haltingly *(with a poor pronunciation). red. (int.)* **gotagota.**

gotagota maneno. use a mixture of words from different dialects. 3. (–) *zool.* woodpecker. (= **kigogota.**) *Cf.* **gota.**

gogoteza *caus. of* **gogota.**

goigoi 1. (–) laggard, lazy person. 2. *adj.* inactive, idle, lazy, indolent. *Cf.* **ugoigoi.**

goka *rare* gag, retch, choke *(in vomiting).* (= **kokomoka, tapika.**)

goko (ma-) *anat.* shinbone. (= [1]**muundi.**)

[1]**gole*** [*Pers.*] (ma-) 1. mucus, phlegm, saliva. 2. crop, craw *(of a bird).*

[2]**gole*** [*Ind.*] (ma-) pellet of opium *(for smoking).*

golegole, goregore, goligoli (–) *ornith.* Tanganyika kakelaar, hoopoe *(Phoeniculus purpureus).*

goli* [*Engl.*] (–) *sport* goal.

goligoli (–) *see* **golegole.**

golikipa* [*Engl.*] (ma-) *sport* goalkeeper.

gololi* [*Pers.*] (–) 1. ball of glass, marble *(for playing).* 2. *tech.* ball bearing.

[1]**goma** refuse *(to do something),* stand up for one's rights, strike. **watu wamegoma hawataki kufanya kazi kabla ya kuongezwa mshahara.** The people are on strike; they won't work until they receive a pay increase. *Cf.* **mgomaji, mgomo, ugomaji.**

[2]**goma** *see* [2]**gomba.**

[3]**goma** (ma-) *see* **ngoma.**

[1]**gomba** (ma-) fiber of the banana leaf. *Cf.* [1]**mgomba, ugomba.**

[2]**gomba, goma** 1. quarrel, squabble, wrangle; oppose, contradict; refuse. 2. go on a strike, strike. *appl.* **gombea.** quarrel, argue *(about something);* stand up for, lay claim to. **gombea cheo.** insist on one's social position, claim the privileges due one's rank or class. **gombea uchaguz** run for office *(in an election). caus.* **gombeza.** forbid. **tumegombezwa tusiende (kwenda).** We are forbidden to go. *caus. intr.* **gombezeka.** be reprehensible. *ass.* **gombana.** quarrel, fall out, have words (with each other). *Cf.* **gomvi, magombano, magombezi, mgombea, mgombezi, mgomvi, ugomvi.**

gombeza *caus. of* **gomba.**

gombo (ma-) *dial.* page of a book. (= **ukurasa.**)

gomboa (*dial.* = **komboa**) liberate. *pass.* **gombowa.** be liberated.

gome (ma-) 1. bark, rind, peel. **ambua — la mti (tunda).** peel the bark off a tree (the rind from a fruit). 2. shell *(of a crab, etc.).* 3. *coll.* shilling.

gomea (*appl. of* **¹goma**) boycott.

¹gomvi *adj.* quarrelsome. *Cf.* **²gomba, mgomvi, ugomvi.**

²gomvi *pl. of* **ugomvi.**

gona *rare* sleep, lie down. *appl.* **gonea** (*also* **gonia**). soothe, appease, pacify. *caus.* **gonya, goneza.** *Cf.* **kigono, mgoni, ngono, nyono, ugoni.**

gonda (—) gonda (kind of small lizard).

gondi (ma-) claw *(of a crab, etc.).* (= **¹gando.**)

goneza *caus. of* **gona.**

gonga strike, tap, knock. **— mlango.** knock at a door. *appl.* **gongea.** *appl.-ass.* **gongeana. gongeana bilauri.** touch glasses *(when drinking together).* *ass.* **gongana.** strike against each other, collide *(ships, automobiles).* *inv.* **gongoa.** *inv.-stat.-appl.* **gongomea.** hammer, drive *(nails).* *Cf.* **¹gongo.**

¹gongo (ma-) stick, club, knocker. *Cf.* **gonga.**

²gongo (ma-) (*amplic. of* **mgongo**) 1. height, pinnacle, top. **— la mlima.** mountaintop. 2. *rare* hump *(on the back).* 3.: **— la mwitu.** dense forest, heavy undergrowth.

gongoa *inv. of* **gonga.**

gongomea *inv.-stat.-appl. of* **gongo.**

gongonola (—) woodpecker. (= **gogota, kigogota.**)

gong'ota *see* **kong'ota.**

gonia *appl. of* **gona.**

gonjwa 1. *adj.* ill, sick, unwell. 2. (ma-) *rare see* **ugonjwa.** *Cf.* **gonjweza, mgonjwa.**

gonjweza make ill. *refl.* **jigonjweza.** feign illness. *Cf.* **gonjwa.**

gonya *caus. of* **gona.**

goo: mtondo (mi-) **—.** the fourth day from today. (= **kushinda —.**)

gora* (—) *see* **jora.**

goregore (—) *see* **golegole.**

gorofa* (—) *see* **orofa.**

goromoe (—) goromoe (kind of lizard).

gorong'ondo (ma-) leg *(of an animal).*

gorong'ondwa 1. (—) gorongondwa (kind of lizard). 2. move in a zigzag, twist, crawl.

goshi* (—) *see* **¹joshi.**

gota rap, knock. – **mlango.** knock at a door. *appl.* **gotea.** *caus.* **gotesha, goteza.** *red.* **gotagota.** rap continuously, beat a drum. *Cf.* **mgoto;** *also* **gogota.**

gotagota *see* **gota.**

goti (ma-) *anat.* knee. **piga magoti.** kneel down, fall to one's knees. **kunja magoti.** draw up the knees. **pia ya –.** *anat.* kneecap.

govi (ma-), **ngovi** (–) *anat.* foreskin, prepuce (= **zunga**). **mwenye –.** uncircumcised person.

goya *sing.* *see* **ugoe.**

1**gozi** (ma-) *sport* (game of) football. **mcheza –.** football player.

2**gozi** (ma-) *pejor.* negro, black *(used by Arabs of Africans).*

gramafoni* [*Engl.*] (–) gramophone, record player. **sahani ya –.** (phonograph) record.

gredi* [*Engl.*] (–) 1. grade, rank, position. **ana – gani?** What kind of a position *(social, occupational)* does he have? 2. quality, level. **kahawa ya – ya chini.** coffee of inferior quality. **mshahara wake ni wa – ya juu.** His salary is very high.

greza* (–) *see* **gereza.**

guama *see* **gwama.**

guba* (–) *see* **kuba.**

gubari* (–) heavy black cloud, dust-cloud.

gubeti* (–, ma-) *naut.* prow, bow; figurehead.

gubi (ma-) leaf-stem of the coconut palm.

gubigubi *red. of* **gubika.**

gubika cover, cover over, cover up; wrap up. *caus.* **gubisha.** *inv.* **gubua.** uncover, open; *(fig.)* discover, reveal, bring to light. *red. (int.).* **gubigubi.** cover oneself from head to foot.

gubiti* [*Pers.*] (–) stick of sugar candy.

gubu* (–) 1. ill humor, annoyance, vexation, anger. 2. forwardness, importunity, obtrusiveness, pushiness. **mwenye –.** a forward/pushy person, nuisance, bore.

gubua *inv. of* **gubika.**

gude (–) 1. awl. 2. gude (kind of bird, coucal; = **dudumizi, tipitipi, shundi**).

gudi* (–, ma-) *naut.* dock, dockyard, shipyard. *Cf.* 1**gadi.**

gudulia* (–, ma-) water-jar.

gugu (ma-) weed; undergrowth, brush, thicket. **vunja (ng'oa) magugu.** clear out a thicket. **magugu.** bush. **maguguni.** in the bush. **–a –.** wild, uncultivated *(plants).*

gugumia 1. swallow, gulp. *caus. & int.* **gugumiza.** 2.: **gugumiza maneno.** stutter, stammer. *Cf.* **gugumizi, kigugumizi.**

gugumizi (ma-) person with a speech-defect, one who stutters. *Cf.* **gugumia.**

gugumu (–) body odor; sweat, perspiration.

gugumua (–) (kind of) reed *(Phragmites communis).*

guguna 1. gnaw, nibble; bite, chew, munch. 2. *fig.* find fault, nag, pester. *caus.* **guguniza.**

gugurusha, gurugusha 1. pull/drag/haul along *(on the ground, with a scraping or rustling sound).* 2. rustle, scrape, rasp. *appl.* **gugurushia.**

guguta (–, ma-) corncob *(without grains). Cf.* **gunzi.**

guia *see* **gwia.**

gulabi* [*Pers.*] **(ma-)** litchi (*fruit of the* **mgulabi**).

gulegule (–) gulegule (kind of fish; porpoise).

gulio (ma-) *rare, dial.* (weekly) market. (= **soko.**)

guma, gumia growl, bark *(dog). Cf.* **gumio.**

gumba *adj.* 1. alone, solitary, isolated. 2. childless, sterile. *only in certain expressions:* **kidole –.** thumb, big toe. **mtu mgumba.** childless/solitary man. *Cf.* **mgumba.**

gumbizi (–) dizziness, fainting spell. **ana –.** He is dizzy.

gumbo (ma-) *dial.* need, distress; shortage *(of food supplies);* crop failure, poor harvest.

gumbu (–) musical instrument *(made of a calabash).*

gumegume (–) *arch.:* **bunduki ya –.** flintlock musket.

gumia *see* **guma.**

gumio (ma-) (*also* **mgumio, mi-**) barking, yelping *(of a dog). Cf.* **guma.**

gumu *adj.* 1. hard, firm, strong, tough; severe. **mkate mgumu.** hard bread. 2. *fig.* hard, difficult. **kazi ngumu.** hard work. **moyo mgumu.** hardhearted. 3. unyielding, obstinate, stubborn. 4. brave, courageous. *Cf.* **ugumu, vigumu.**

guna grumble, growl; be cross/irritable. *fig.* protest, find fault, criticize. *Cf.* **mguno.**

[1]**gunda** (ma-) gunda (musical instrument, horn).

[2]**gunda** be short *(in stature)*. *Cf.* **kundaa.**

gundi* [*Ind.*] (–) glue, paste. (= **sherisi.**)

gundua discover, expose, disclose, hunt out; *(fig.)* surprise, catch. – **siri.** divulge a secret. *appl.* **gundulia.** approach stealthily, sneak up on. *caus.* **gundulisha, gunduza.** *intr.* **gunduka.** *ass.* **gunduana.**

gunga 1. abstain from, give up *(certain foods, as tabu)*; resist a temptation. 2. *med.* observe a diet. 3. warn. 4. coax.

gungu (–) gungu (kind of dance)

[1]**guni*** [*Ind.*] (ma-) bag made of matting *(for transporting dates)*.

[2]**guni*** (ma-) carpenter's square.

[3]**guni*** (–) unrhymed/blank verse.

gunia* [*Ind.*] (ma-) 1. grain-sack. 2. sacking, burlap.

guno (ma-) *see* **mguno.**

gunzi, bunzi (ma-) corncob. *Cf.* **kigunzi;** *also* **guguta.**

gura *dial.* change one's residence, move. (= **hama.**) *caus.* **gurisha.** drive away, expel.

guru* [*Ind.*] (–): **sukari –.** unrefined sugar.

gurudumu* [*Pers.*] (ma-) wheel. **– la mbele (nyuma).** front (back) wheel. **jino la –.** sprocket. **– zenye ndewe.** lobed wheels. **– la mzinga.** *mil.* gun carriage.

gurufa* [*Engl.?*] (–) curve. **katika reli pana – ya hatari.** In this section there is a dangerous curve.

gurufu* (–, ma) *rare* highway. (= [1]**barabara.**)

[1]**guruguru** (ma-) large lizard *(Gherrosaurus major)*.

[2]**guruguru** (–) guruguru (kind of fish, sole).

gurugusha 1. *see* **gugurusha.** 2. do badly, bungle, spoil.

gururu* (–) curdled milk, whey.

guruta press, flatten, smooth, roll; mangle *(clothes)*. *Cf.* **guruto, mguruto.**

guruto (ma-) press, mangle. *Cf.* **guruta.**

gusa touch, feel, handle. *ass.* **gusana.** *fig.* get acquainted. *Cf.* **mguso.**

[1]**guta** push, gore, fight *(cattle).*

[2]**guta** shout, yell, call. *appl.* **gutia.** call out for (someone).

gutu 1. (**ma-**) stump *(of a leg, etc.).* **ana mguu (kidole) –.** He has lost a leg (finger). **– la mti.** tree-stump. 2. *adj.* blunt, dull; broken off, chopped of. **kisu kigutu.** a dull knife. **majani magutugutu.** stubble.

[1]**gutua** 1. do something suddenly; startle, frighten. 2. *med.* set (reduce) a broken or dislocated arm or leg. *appl.* **gutulia.** *intr.* **gutuka.** *caus.* **gutusha.** receive an electric shock; shock, astound, horrify. *Cf.* **mgutusho.**

[2]**gutua** *see* **kutua.**

guu (**ma-**) *amplic. of* **mguu. tia –.** cause trouble.

guya *rare* seize, grasp, hold fast.

gwa *rare* fall.

gwafua bare the teeth, snarl.

gwama, guama press, squeeze.

gwanda (**ma-**) man's outer garment *(knee-length).*

gwaraza rub, grind. **– meno.** grind/gnash the teeth.

gwaride* (**ma-**) *mil.* 1. parade, review; drill exercises. 2. military music, band. 3. guard. **– la heshima.** honor guard. **cheza (piga) –.** play military music; drill *(to music).* **nyumba ya –.** barracks.

gwaru* [*Ind.*] (–) bean *(Cyamopsis psoraloides). Cf.* **mgwaru.**

gwase (**ma-**) *see* **gwasi.**

gwasi, gwase (**ma-**) warthog. (= **ngiri, mbango.**)

gwaya tremble, quiver *(from fear, cold).*

gwia, guia 1. catch, seize, hold fast. **– mnyama mtegoni.** catch an animal in a trap. 2. *fig.* surprise, take by surprise, catch unawares. *appl.* **gwilia.** *caus.* **gwiza.** *pass.* **gwiwa. gwiwa na giza.** be overtaken by darkness.

gwiji *adj. & n.* (–) brave, clever (person) *(chiefly in reference to witch doctors).*

H

[1]**haba*** *adj.* little, slight, insignificant; scarce, in short supply. **siku –.** a few days. *prov.* **– na – hujaza kibaba.** Little by little fills the measure. *Cf.* **uhaba.**

[2]**haba*, huba, hubba** (–, **ma-**) love, devotion, friendship, affection. *Cf.* [1]**hebu, muhebi, stahabu.**

hababi* (**ma-**) *a term of respect used in addressing persons of high rank:* Your Excellency.

habali* *adj., rare* 1. irresponsible. 2. hot-tempered, irritable.

habari* (–) 1. report, message, information, news. **toa –.** give a report, pass out information. **– gani?** What's the news? How are you? 2. material; tradition, history; event. *Cf.* **hubiri, mhubiri.**

habedari!* abedari! bedari! *interj.* Watch out! Look out! Take care! *Cf.* **hadhari.**

Habeshi* (**ma-**) *see* **Mhabeshi.**

habibu* *adj., liter.* dear, beloved.

habithi* (–) 1. wickedness, cruelty, malice, dishonesty. 2. a malicious/dishonest person.

habu* *see* [1]**hebu.**

hadaa* 1. deceive, cheat, trick. *appl.* **hadai.** *intr.* **hadaika.** *pass.* **hadaiwa.** *ass.* **hadaana.** 2. (–) deception, fraud, trickery.

hadai* *appl. of* **hadaa.**

hadaika* *intr. of* **hadaa.**

hadaiwa* *pass. of* **hadaa.**

hadaya* (–) *see* **hedaya.**

haddi* (–) *see* **hadi.**

hadhara* *adv.:* **– ya...** in the presence of... **– ya watu.** in public. **mkutano hadharani.** public/open meeting. *Cf.* **hadhiri,** [1]**hudhuria, hudhirio.**

hadhari*, hathari (*also* **tahadhari**) 1. be cautious/watchful, avoid, evade. *appl.* **hadharia.** *refl. (interj.).* **jihadhari!** Watch out! Take care! 2. (–) caution, discernment. **kuwa na –.** be on one's guard. **tia (fanya) –.** warn. 3. (–) tenseness, tension. **– ya hali ya kisasa.** the tenseness of the present situation.

hadhi* (–) 1. respect, honor. 2. title. **– ya heshima.** honorary title.

hadhiri*, **hadhirisha** make known, announce, publish. *Cf.* **hadhara.**

hadhirisha* *see* **hadhiri.**

hadi*, **haddi** 1. (–) boundary, limit; rule. 2. (–): – **mfundo.** children's jumping game. 3. *prep. & conj.* until, as far as, so far as to...; so, then. **tangu asubuhi – jioni.** from morning to evening. **nilingoja – akaja.** I waited until he came. – **nitampiga.** I will even go so far as to beat him. – **asubuhi.** Well then, until tomorrow. 4. *conj.* so as to, so that, in order that. **Nitafanya akili gani hadi tugawe sawasawa?** What arrangements shall I make so that we may divide equally?

hadima*, **hedima** (**ma-**) service. *Cf.* **hadimu, huduma.**

hadimika* *see* **adimika.**

hadimu* (**ma-**) 1. servant. 2. (freed) slave. *Cf.* **hadima, huduma, hudumu, mhadimu.**

hadithi* 1. (*us. appl.* **hadithia**) tell, relate, report; describe, explain. *pass.* **hadithiwa. nimehadithiwa.** I was told. 2. (–) report, narrative, story, legend; myth. **ni – tu.** It is only a story *(i.e., something made up).*

hafifisha* 1. reduce, diminish, decrease; minimize, disparage; lessen *(in value);* weaken, debilitate, exhaust. 2. *fig.* behave in a careless/frivolous way. *Cf.* **hafifu.**

hafifu* (*also* **tahafifu**) *adj.* trivial, worthless, insignificant. *Cf.* **hafifisha, uhafifu.**

hafisi* (–) *see* **afisi.**

hafla*, **halfa** (**ma-**) ceremony, party, feast.

hafu* [*Engl.*] (–) half. *sport* half-time.

hafukasti* [*Engl.*] (–) half-caste.

hafutaimu* [*Engl.*] (–) *sport* half-time.

hai*, **hei** *adj.* living, alive, existent. *Cf.* **hayati, hui, uhai.**

haiba*, **heiba, heba** (**ma-**, –) 1. beauty, charm, grace *(of external appearance or of character).* 2. good reputation/character.

haidhuru* *see* **dhuru.**

haini* 1. betray, divulge *(a secret),* deceive. 2. (–) (*also* **mhaini, wa-**) traitor, deceiver, informer, deserter, renegade. *Cf.* **uhaini.**

haja* (–) 1. need, desire; necessity. **sina – nayo.** I have no need of that. 2. request, demand, petition. 3. need to relieve oneself. **kwenda –.** go to the toilet. *Cf.* **hitaji, hoja, hoji, uhaji.**

hajambo *sing.* *see* ujambo.

haji* 1. (–) pilgrimage *(to Mecca).* **enda –.** go on the pilgrimage. 2. (ma-) pilgrim. *Cf.* **hiji.**

hajiri*, hujuru change one's residence, move; emigrate. *appl.* **hajiria.** *appl.-ass.* **hajiriana.** *intr.* **hajirika.** live far away, be an emigrant. *caus.* **hajirisha.** expel, deport. *Cf.* **mhajiri.**

hajivale (–) (kind of) hawk *(Gymnogenis/polyboroideo typicus).*

haka*, hakali (–) payment, price, (entrance) fee; fine *(for violating the rules of a club, etc.).* **shika –.** pay the entrance fee.

hakali* (–) *see* **haka.**

hakama*, hakma (ma-) *rare* (law-)court. *Cf.* **hukumu, hakimu.**

haki*, hakki (–) 1. law, legality; (legal) claim. **– ya kuchagua.** right to vote, active suffrage. **– ya kuchaguliwa.** eligibility. 2. justice, love of truth. **shika (fanya) –.** be just/upright. **mtu mwenye –.** a just/upright/righteous person. 3. (lawful, just) right, privilege, claim. **nipe – yangu.** Give me what is coming to me *(i.e., what is mine by right).* **takia –.** take legal action on someone's behalf. *Cf.* **stahika, stahiki, ustahiki.**

hakika* 1. (–) certainty, reality, fact, truth, correctness, accuracy. **mambo haya ni –.** These are facts. This is the truth of the matter. **sina –.** I have no certainty. 2. *adv.* undoubtedly, of course, for certain, positively. *Cf.* **hakiki, hakikisho, uhakikisho.**

hakiki* make sure, prove, ascertain, check on, determine the truth. *appl.* **hakikia.** ask after someone. *caus.* **hakikisha.** 1. have inquiries made. 2. *(int.)* attest, certify, vouch for; convince. *pass.* **(ku)hakikishwa.** be convinced. *Cf.* **hakika.**

hakikisho* (ma-) proof, evidence; deposition, testimony. *Cf.* **hakiki.**

hakimu* (ma-) 1. judge. 2. *rare* leader, chief. *Cf.* **hukumu.**

hakiri* *rare* scorn, despise, treat with contempt, deprecate, humiliate, vilify. (= **dharau, tweza.**) *appl.* **hakiria.** *caus.* **hakirisha.** abuse, revile, insult.

hakki* (–) *see* **haki.**

hakma* (ma-) *see* **hakama.**

hakuna there is/are not.

[1]halafa*, hilafu (–) dissension, difference, quarrel; rupture, cleavage; opposition. *Cf.* **[1]halifu.**

[2]halafa*, halfa (–) oath.

halafu*, hilafu, alafu 1. *adv.* afterwards, later; subsequently, in future.

(= **baadaye, nyumaye.**) 2. *conj.* and then... *Cf.* **²halifu.**

halahala!* *interj.* 1. immediately! 2. Don't forget! (= **upesi, sasa hivi.**)

halali* 1. (–) *Isl.* law, lawfulness. **ni – yako kula nyama hii.** You are permitted to eat this meat. 2. *adj.* lawful, permitted. *Cf.* **halalika.**

halalika* be lawful, be permitted. *caus.* **halalisha.** permit, legalize; declare to be lawful. *Cf.* **halali.**

halasa* (–) 1. profit *(from business).* 2. *arch.* payment, wages *(of seamen).* *Cf.* **²halisi.**

¹halfa* (–) *see* **²halafa.**

²halfa* (ma-) *see* **hafla.**

hali* (–) (*also* **uhali, ilhali**) 1. condition, state *(of health).* **– gani?** *in address.* How are you? 2. situation. **– ya kisasa.** the present situation. **– ya hatari.** state of emergency. **kwa kila –.** under all circumstances. **– ya anga.** weather conditions *(for flight purposes).* **– ya maisha.** standard of living.

halifa*, khalifa (–) *hist., Isl.* successor, caliph. *Cf.* **halafu, ²halifu.**

¹halifu* 1. act contrary to, disobey, infringe, violate. **– amri (sheria).** disobey an order (the law). **– kwa serikali.** oppose/resist the government. *caus.* **halifisha.** incite (to rebellion). 2. (**ma-**) mutineer, rebel, insurgent; lawbreaker. 3. *adj.* disobedient, rebellious, seditious. *Cf.* **¹halafa, uhalifu.**

²halifu* leave, bequeath. *Cf.* **halafu.**

halili* (–) beloved/esteemed/distinguished person.

¹halisi* *adj.* exact, definite; real, genuine.

²halisi* 1. make a profit *(from business).* 2. *rare* receive wages. *Cf.* **halasa.**

halitumwa (–) halitumwa (variety of sweet potato).

halkumu* (–) *anat.* carotid artery, jugular vein.

halmaria* (–) *see* **almaria.**

halmashauri*, halmshauri (–) council, committee, organization. **– ya kufanya sheria.** legislative body. **– ya udhamini.** trust company. **– ya Umoja wa Mataifa.** United Nations Organization. **– ya Usalama.** Security Council (of the United Nations). **ya kuwaajiri wafanya kazi.** committee for public services. **– kuu.** central committee. **– ya taifa kusimamia mazao.** National Agricultural Products Board. **– Kuu ya serikali ya nchi ya Urusi.** Supreme Soviet of the USSR. *Cf.* **shauri.**

halmshauri* (–) *see* **halmashauri.**

halua* (–) kind of candy, Turkish delight.

halula* (–) *med.* abscess, swelling in the throat, quinsy.

haluli* (–) laxative, Epsom salts.

halwaridi*, alwaridi (–) attar of roses. *Cf.* **waridi.**

halzeti* (–) (*also* **mafuta ya –**) olive oil. *Cf.* **zeituni.**

hama change one's residence; migrate; move out, emigrate. *appl.* **hamia.** emigrate/immigrate *(from/to a country). caus.* **hamisha.** expel; resettle. *Cf.* **hamaji, hame, hamiji, hamio, kihame, mahame, mhamiaji, mhamishi, uhamaji, uhamisho.**

hamaji *adj.* unsettled, homeless, nomad. *Cf.* **hama, uhamaji.**

hamaki* 1. act heedlessly (suddenly, unexpectedly). 2. (–) rash/inconsiderate act, burst of temper.

hamali* (ma-) 1. carrier, porter. 2. load, burden, freight. **gari la –.** cart for transporting goods. *Cf.* **himila, himili, mhimili, stahimili, stahimilivu, ustahimilivu.**

hamamu* (–) public bath.

hamanika be confused, disconcerted, dismayed; be irritated/excited.

hamarawi* (–) *naut.* rope for attaching a yard.

hamaya* (–) *see* **himaya.**

hamdi*, hemdi (–) *see* **hamdu.**

hamdu*, humdu, himdu, hamdi, hemdi (–) *rel.* praise. **al – lilahi.** Praise be to Allah. *Cf.* **himidi.**

hame (ma-) deserted place *(village, town).* (= **kihame, mahame, [1]tongo.**) *Cf.* **hama.**

hami* protect, defend; show favor. *Cf.* **amia, himaya, mahamia.**

hamia *appl. of* **hama.**

hamidi*, hemidi (–) *see* **hamdu.**

hamiji (wa-) 1. homeless person, nomad, vagrant. 2. *rel.* pilgrim. *Cf.* **hama, hamaji.**

hamio (ma-) move, removal, emigration. *Cf.* **hama.**

hamira* (–) yeast, leaven.

hamisha *caus. of* **hama.**

hamna there is not. *Cf.* **mna.**

hamsa* *arch.* five. (= **tano.**) **– mia.** five hundred. *Cf.* **hamsini, hamstashara, hamsauishirini.**

hamsauishirini* *arch.* twenty-five. (= **ishirini na tano.**)

hamsini* fifty.

hamstashara* *arch.* fifteen. (= **kumi na tano.**)

[1]**hamu*** (–) desire, (urgent) wish; anxiety. **ona (kuwa na) –.** desire, wish/yearn for.

[2]**hamu*** be alert/on one's guard. **jihamu.** defend oneself. *Cf.* **ujihamu.**

hamumi* (–) hamumi (kind of smoking tobacco).

hanamu* 1. (–) slope, slant, bevel, edge; *(math.)* diagonal. **– ya chombo.** *naut.* bow, cutwater. 2. *adj.* diagonal, slanting, oblique.

handaki* (–) trench, ditch, channel; *(sport)* sector.

hando* [*Ind.*] (–) (copper) water-vessel.

hangaika, angaika be excited/restless; be disconcerted/upset; be irresolute; be impatient. *fig.* rock, swing. *caus.* **hangaisha.** confuse, worry (someone). *Cf.* **hangaiko.**

hangaiko (ma-) restlessness, excitement; worry; noise, commotion. *Cf.* **hangaika.**

hangwe, hangue (–) hook, bend.

hani* comfort, show sympathy; condole.

hanithi* (–, ma-) 1. pervert, homosexual. 2. (sexually) impotent man. 3. *adj.* homosexual, perverted; shameful.

hanjari* (–) scimitar, dagger. (= **jambia.**)

hanziri* (–) *rare* pig. (= **nguruwe.**)

hanzua* (–) sword dance.

hao *det. 3rd pers. pl.* these/those mentioned (already referred to). **watu –.** the people referred to.

hapa 1. *dem. pron.* this. **mjini –.** at this town. 2. *adv.* here, to this place. **aje –.** He should come here. **toka – mpaka pale.** from here to there. **papa –.** at this very place.

hapana *adv.* no (lit.: there is no...).

hapo 1. *demon.* that (already mentioned). **mahali –.** at the place referred to. 2. *adv.* there, to/from that place. **ningojee –.** Wait for me there. **papo –.** at that (very) place *(previously mentioned)*. **– kale.** then, in ancient times, once upon a time *(at the beginning of stories)*.

[1]**hara*** purge, evacuate; have diarrhea. **dawa ya kuhara.** laxative. *caus.* **harisha.** 1. produce diarrhea. **dawa hii inaharisha.** This medicine has a

laxative effect. 2. *(intr.)* be terribly frightened *(e.g., when caught in wrong-doing)*. *Cf.* **harisho.**

[2]**hara*** (–) *rare* (*us. loc.* **harani**) district, quarter *(of a town)*.

harabu* 1. (–, ma-) (*also* **mharabu**, wa-) destroyer, spoiler, vandal. *prov.* **nazi mbovu – ya nzima.** A bad coconut spoils the good ones. 2. *adj.* destructive, pernicious; violent, brutal. *Cf.* **haribu.**

haradali* (–) mustard. (= **mastadi.**)

haragi* (ma-) *see* **haragwe.**

haragwe*, **haragi** [*Pers.*] (ma-) bean *(Phasealis communis)*. *Cf.* **mharagwe.**

haraja* 1. (–) expense, expenditure, outlay, consumption; loss. 2. incur expenses, spend money recklessly. *Cf.* **hariji.**

haraka* 1. (–) hurry, haste, speed, rapidity, excitement. **fanya –.** hurry up, hasten. **enda kwa –.** go fast, be in a hurry. *prov.* **– – haina baraka.** Haste brings no blessing. 2. *adj.* hasty, fast, excited, feverish. *Cf.* **harakisha, taharaki.**

harakisha*, **harikisha** urge, press, hurry. *Cf.* **haraka.**

haram*, **ihramu** *pl.* the Pyramids. *Cf.* **haramu, harimu.**

haramia* (ma-) robber, bandit, pirate, outlaw. *Cf.* **haramu, uharamia.**

haramu* 1. (–) *rel.* prohibition, avoidance *(of something unlawful)*. **ni – kula nyama ya nguruwe.** It is forbidden to eat pork. **mtoto wa –.** an illegitimate child. 2. *adj.* undesirable, forbidden, prohibited. *Cf.* **harimu, uharamu, haramia.**

harara* (–) 1. warmth, heat, temperature. *med.* fever, inflammation; erythema. 2. *fig.* zeal, enthusiasm, passion. **ana –.** He is passionate/temperamental. *Cf.* **hari, uharara.**

hari*, **harri** (–) 1. heat, fervor. **– ja jua.** heat of the sun. 2. *rare* sweat. **toka –.** sweat, perspire. *Cf.* **harara.**

haria* *see* **heria.**

haribifu*, **haribivu** *adj.* destructive, pernicious; extravagant, wasteful. *Cf.* **haribu, uharibifu.**

haribivu* *see* **haribifu.**

haribu* destroy, ruin, damage. *fig.* demoralize. **– mimba.** procure abortion. *appl.* **haribia.** *pass.* **haribiwa.** *intr.* **haribika.** be destroyed, ruined, dilapidated. *caus.* **haribisha.** bring misfortune, ruin. *Cf.* **harabu, haribifu, uharibifu.**

hariji* spend, waste, squander *(money)*. *appl.* **harijia.** 1. spend money on *(someone)*, be generous. 2. donate, contribute to. *Cf.* **haraja.**

[1]harijia* *appl. of* **hariji.**

[2]harijia* (–): **waziri –.** foreign minister.

harikisha* *see* **harakisha.**

harimu* 1. forbid, prohibit. *appl.* **harimia.** *caus.* **harimisha.** pronounce unlawful, declare taboo. 2. (ma-) harimu (a taboo: person or thing). 3. (ma-) Harimu (name used by a sister for her brother). *Cf.* **haram, haramu, ihramu, maharimisho.**

hariri* (–) silk.

harisha* *caus. of* [1]**hara.**

harisho (ma-) 1. *med.* diarrhea. 2. (strong) laxative. *Cf.* [1]**hara.**

harita* (–) seeds of the soapberry tree. *Cf.* **mharita.**

haro* [*Engl.*] (–) *rare* harrow.

harri* (–) *see* **hari.**

harufi* (–) *see* **herufi.**

harufu* (–) smell *(good or bad)*, aroma, scent.

harusi* (–) *see* **arusi.**

[1]**hasa***, **hassa** *adv.* 1. especially, exactly, just. 2. completely, wholly, very much. *Cf.* **husu, hususa, mahsusi.**

[2]**hasa*** (–) *rare* castrated man or animal, eunuch. *Cf.* **hasi, mhasi.**

hasada* (–) hasada (kind of porridge).

[1]**hasama*** (–) nose ring. (= **kipini.**)

[2]**hasama*** (ma-) *see* **hasimu** 2.

[3]**hasama*** (ma-) = **uhasama, husuma.**

hasanati* (–) *see* **hisani.**

hasara*, **khasara** (–) loss, damage, injury. **pata –.** lose. **lipa –.** pay for damage incurred, compensate. *Cf.* **hasiri.**

hasha!* *interj.* by no means! impossible! of course not!

hasharati* 1. (–) excess, dissipation, intemperance; extravagance, wastefulness. 2. (ma-) dissolute person, hard drinker; spendthrift.

hashiki* (–) *liter.* ardor, passion.

hasho* (ma-), **kihasho** (vi-) *naut.* piece of wood for repairing a boat, patch, plug.

hasi* 1. castrate, geld. *pass.* **hasiwa.** 2. *fig.:* **mtu huyu ni –.** This man is an outcast/outlaw. *Cf.* [2]**hasa, hasua, maksai, mhasi,** [1]**uhasi.**

hasidi* 1. (**ma-**) envious/malicious person; enemy. 2. (–) envy, ill will. 3. *v.* (*also* **husudu**) envy, hate, hold a grudge. *Cf.* **husuda, husudu, uhasidi.**

hasimu* 1. *see* **husumu.** 2. (**ma-**) (*also* **hasama**) opponent, rival; a person with whom one is not on speaking terms; wrangler, quarrelsome person. *Cf.* **husuma, husumu, uhasama.**

hasira* (–) vexation, anger. **pata** (**wa na**) **–.** be vexed/angry.

hasiri* do harm, damage, wrong, injure. **– mtu katika ugomvi.** injure someone in a dispute. *appl.* **hasiria.** *intr.* **hasirika.** decay, deteriorate. *Cf.* **hasara.**

hassa* *see* **hasa.**

hasua* (–) *anat.* testicles. *Cf.* **hasi.**

hata* 1. *prep.* until, as far as. **tangu asubuhi – jioni.** from early to late. 2. *prep.* since. 3. *conj.* so, so that, in order that; even if. **tutasoma kitabu gani – tujue maneno yenu?** What kind of a book should we read so that we may understand your words? **– akija.** even if he comes. 4. *adv.* (*or* **– kidogo**, *usually after negation*) (not ...) at all, in the least. **maneno haya si kweli –.** These words are absolutely untrue.

hatamu* (–) bridle, rein.

hatari* (–) danger, risk. **hali ya –.** state of emergency. *Cf.* **hatarisha.**

hatarisha*, hatirisha imperil, endanger, risk, jeopardize. *refl.* **jihatarisha.** expose oneself to danger. *Cf.* **hatari.**

hathari* *see* **hadhari.**

hati*, hatti (–) (prepared) document; form, blank. **– ya maombi.** application form. **– ya deni.** promissory note. **– ya uwakala.** power of attorney. **– ya mkono.** handwriting, manuscript. **– ya utambulishi.** credentials.

[1]**hatia*** (–) error, transgression, violation, crime, guilt. **tia hatiani.** accuse, find guilty. **tiwa hatiani.** be convicted. **ana –.** He is guilty. **patikana na hatia.** be found guilty.

[2]**hatia*** (–) *rare* gift, gratuity, tip. (= **bakshishi.**)

hatibu* (**ma-**) *Isl.* preacher. *Cf.* **hutubu.**

hatima* 1. (–) end, conclusion, termination. 2. *adv.* (*also* **hatimaye**) finally; then, later, afterwards; *(conj.)* after. *Cf.* **hitima, hitimu.**

hatimaye* *see* **hatima.**

hatimisha* *caus. of* **hitimu.**

hatimu* *see* **hitimu.**

hatirisha* *see* **hatarisha.**

hatta* *see* **hata.**

hatti* (–) *see* **hati.**

hatua* (–) 1. step, pace. **pima kwa –.** measure in paces. **ni – tu.** It is only a short distance. 2. *fig.* progress, development; possibility, opportunity.

haula* *see* **lahaula.**

[1]**hawa*** (–) 1. longing, yearning, desire. 2. (passionate) love/attraction. **– ya moyo.** deep/fervent love. 3. lust. 4. (ma-) concubine. 5. *pr. n. fem.* (*also* Ewa) Eve.

[2]**hawa*** (–) *see* **hewa.**

[3]**hawa** *dem. pron. pl.* these. **watu –.** these people.

hawaa* (ma-) *see* **hawara.**

hawai* (ma-) *rare* whore. (= **hawara.**)

hawala* (–) check, draft; money order, bill of exchange. *Cf.* **hawili.**

hawara*, **hawaa** (ma-) lover, paramour, concubine, mistress. *Cf.* **uhawara.**

hawili* change, exchange, convert; transfer *(funds).* **– hawala.** refund a note, repay a debt. *caus.* **hawilisha.** *jur.* convey, make over. *Cf.* **hawala.**

[1]**haya*** (–) 1. shame, modesty, bashfulness, timidity. **tia (ingiwa na) –, ona –.** feel shame. 2. subservience, humility. 3. esteem, respect, reverence, awe. *Cf.* **tahayari, tahayuri.**

[2]**haya!*** *interj.* Come on! Now then! Get a move on!

[3]**haya** *demon. pron.* (*pl. of* **hili**) these.

hayati* (–) deceased (person). *Cf.* **hai.**

hayawani* (–) *rare* 1. animal, beast. 2. monster. 3. feeble-minded person, imbecile, idiot. *Cf.* **uhayawani.**

hayo *det.* **ma-** *cl.* those (mentioned, referred to). **maneno –.** those words (which have been mentioned).

hazama* (–) hazama (ornament, ring, etc. worn in the nose). (= **kikero, kishaufu.**)

hazamu* (ma-) *see* **mahazamu.**

hazina* (–) 1. treasure *(money, jewelry),* valuables. 2. treasury, exchequer.

heba* (ma-, –) *see* **haiba.**

[1]**hebu***, **habu** love, like; be content/happy. *Cf.* [2]**haba. muhebi, stahabu.**

[2]**hebu!*** **ebu! hela!** *interj.* well! come now!

hedashara* (–) *see* **edashara.**

hedaya*, **hidaya, hadaya** (–) (valuable) gift.

hedhi*, **hidhi, hethi** (–) menstruation. **kuwa na –.** menstruate.

hedikwota* [*Engl.*] (–) headquarters.

hedima* (ma-) *see* **hadima.**

hedimasta* [*Engl.*] (ma-) headmaster, principal *(of a school).*

hehema *see* ²**hema.**

hei* *see* **hai.**

heiba* (ma-, –) *see* **haiba.**

hekaheka* (–) 1. confusion, unrest, noise. 2. *fig., sport* cheers, cheering. *Cf.* **heko.**

hekalu* (ma-) *rel.* 1. temple *(esp. the Temple of Jerusalem).* 2. pagoda *(China, India).*

hekaya*, **hikaya** (–) 1. tale, story, anecdote. 2. remarkable occurrence, wonder, miracle.

hekemua 1. stretch oneself. 2. *rare* sneeze. (= **chemua.**)

hekima* (–) wisdom, knowledge; philosophy; (power of) judgment, discernment. **wa na –.** be wise/shrewd. **mwenye –.** philosopher, well-informed/educated person. *Cf.* **hukumu.**

hekimiza* impart knowledge, inform, instruct. *Cf.* **hukumu, hekima.**

heko* 1. *interj.* hurrah! bravo! well done! 2. *sing.* compliments, congratulations. *Cf.* **hekaheka.**

¹**hela**!* *see* ²**hebu.**

²**hela*** [*Germ.*] (–) *arch.* heller, money.

¹**hema*** (–) tent. **piga –.** pitch a tent. **ng'oa –.** strike a tent.

²**hema, hehema** be out of breath, pant, breathe heavily, gasp. *appl.* **hemea.** *pass.* **hemewa.** *fig.* be very busy, be overworked.

hemaya* (–) *see* **himaya.**

hemdi* (–) *see* **hamdu.**

hemera buy (or go hunting for) food.

hemidi* (–) *see* **hamdu.**

henezi *adv.* slowly, gradually.

henza* (–) *naut.* halyard.

henzarani*, **henzerani, henzirani, hinzirani** (–) 1. cane, rattan, bamboo. 2. plaited belt/sash.

heri* 1. (–) good luck, success, advantage. **mtu wa –.** fortunate/successful person. **jaliwa (na) –.** have good luck. *salutation:* **kwa —!** *or* **kwa — ya kuonana!** Good-bye! 2.: **—a —.** *adj.* fortunate, successful. 3. *adv.* better, rather. *prov.* **— adui mwerevu kama rafiki mpumbavu.** Better a clever enemy than a stupid friend. *Cf.* **buheri, uheri.**

heria*, haria [*Port.* arrier] 1. *naut.* take in *(a sail).* 2. lower! *(direction to crane operators, etc.)*

herimu* (—) *see* **hirimu.**

herini* [*Engl.*] (—) *coll.* earring. (= ²**bali, kipuli.**)

hero (ma-) hero (small wooden serving dish). *Cf.* **kihero.**

heroe (—) flamingo.

herufi*, harufi (—) letter *(of the alphabet).* **— za kiarabu.** Arabic letters.

hesabu* 1. count, calculate; estimate, appraise; consider. *appl.* **hesabia.** settle an account with someone; consider, regard as. **alihesabiwa kuwa ana hekima.** He was regarded as/had the reputation of being a clever man. *intr.* **hesabika.** be countable/calculable. 2. (*also* **hisabu**) (—) arithmetic, mathematics (= **elimu ya —**); account, bill; number, sum; settlement; calculation, computation; *(bank)* account, credit; rate. **— ya biashara.** balance of trade. **— ya mapato na matumizi.** balance of income and expenditures. **neno la —.** *gramm.* numeral. **fanya —.** work a sum, draw up an account. **tia katika —.** put to (someone's) account. **—a —.** mathematical.

heshima* (—) honor, respect, courtesy, esteem. **wekeana —.** treat each other with respect. **shika kwa —.** receive someone with courtesy. *prov.* **— huuzwa bure.** Politeness costs you nothing. *Cf.* **heshimu, mahashumu, muhashamu.**

heshimu* honor, respect, esteem; be polite. *appl.* **heshimia.** *caus.* **heshimisha.** *Cf.* **heshima, mahashumu, mheshimiwa, muhashamu.**

hesi*, hessi, esi (—) screw, bolt; peg *(of a musical instrument).*

hethi* (—) *see* **hedhi.**

heti* [*Engl.*] (—) hat, cap.

hewa*, hawa (—) 1. air, atmosphere; climate, weather; sky. **punga —.** take a walk, get a breath of fresh air; enjoy a change of air, take a trip. **utabiri wa —.** weather forecasting, meteorology. **kujilinda hewani.** air defense. 2. gas. **— ya kutoa machozi.** tear gas.

hezaya* (—) *see* **hizaya.**

¹**hiana*, hiyana** 1. (—) treachery, betrayal, deceit. 2. (ma-) betrayer,

traitor, renegade. 3. *adj.* faithless, disloyal, treacherous. **mtu –.** a treacherous person. **mfanya –.** *pol.* renegade. *Cf.* **hini, uhiana.**

[2]**hiana*** (–) *rare* hardness *(of wood).*

hiari*, hiyari 1. choose, select; prefer. 2. (*also* **hitiari, ihtiari, ikhtiari**) (–) wish, choice, (free) will, pleasure, discretion, judgment. **– yako.** at your discretion, as you see fit. **kwa –.** at one's own discretion, voluntarily. **kazi ya –.** voluntary work.

hiba* (–) gift, present, donation; legacy.

hibia* please/delight *(someone). Cf.* [1]**hebu.**

hicho *det.* **ki-** *cl.* that (previously mentioned/referred to). **kitabu –.** the book referred to.

hidaji* *see* **hitaji.**

[1]**hidaya*** (–) *see* **hedaya.**

[2]**hidaya*** (–) *see* **adia.**

[3]**hidaya*** *adj.* beautiful, desirable.

hidhi* (–) *see* **hedhi.**

hidi* persuade, convert.

hidima* *adv.* quickly, promptly; diligently, carefully.

hifadhi* 1. keep, save; put aside, keep in reserve; preserve. 2. guard, protect; rescue. **– hadithi.** preserve stories/traditions. **– maziwa.** store up milk. *appl.* **hifadhia.** *intr.* **hifadhika.** *refl.* **jihifadhi.** protect oneself. 3. (–) guarding, protection.

hii *dem. pron.* 1. **mi-** *cl.* these. **miti –.** these trees. 2. **n-** *cl.* this. **nyumba –.** this house.

hijabu* (–) *med.* 1. neuralgia. 2. swelling of glands in the neck.

hiji* *Isl.* go on the pilgrimage (to Mecca). *Cf.* **haji.**

hikaya* (–) *see* **hekaya.**

hiki *dem. pron.* **ki-** *cl.* this. **kitu –.** this thing.

hila* (–) trick, strategem, pretext, subterfuge, deceit, cunning. **kwa –.** craftily, deceitfully. **fanya –.** employ a trick. **-a –.** *adj.* crafty, deceitful.

[1]**hilafu*** *adv.* *see* **halafu.**

[2]**hilafu*** (–) *see* [1]**halafa.**

hilali* (–) crescent.

hili *dem. pron.* **ji-** *cl.* this. **tunda –.** this fruit.

[1]**hiliki*** (–) *see* **eliki.**

[2]hiliki* be destroyed, be lost; *(fig.)* die. *pass.* **hilikiwa.**

hilo *det.* ji- *cl.* this *(previously mentioned).* **jina —.** the name referred to.

hima* 1. (—) haste, hurry, precipitation. 2. (—) stubbornness, obstinacy; persistence, perseverance; energy, stamina. 3. *adv.* hastily, hurriedly, quickly; persistently. *Cf.* **himia, himiza, muhimu.**

himaya*, hamaya, hemaya (—) protection; guardianship, tutelage. *Cf.* **amia, hami.**

himdu* (—) *see* **hamdu.**

himia* drive, impel; force, urge. *Cf.* **hima.**

himidi* *rel.* 1. to praise (God). 2. (—) = **hamdu.**

himila* (—) 1. load, burden; freight, cargo. 2. *fig.* pregnancy. *Cf.* **hamali.**

himili* 1. bear, endure, hold out. 2. *fig.* be pregnant. *appl.* **himilia.** *intr.* **himilika.** *caus.* **himilisha.** *Cf.* **hamali.**

himiza*, himu urge (to haste); speed up, drive on. *refl.* **jihimiza.** make haste, hurry. **— mtu kazi.** urge someone to speed up his work. *Cf.* **hima.**

himu* *see* **himiza.**

hina*, hinna (—) henna *(a red dye used for staining the nails and hair). Cf.* **mhina.**

[1]Hindi* adj.: **Bara Hindi.** India (= **Uhindi**). *Cf.* **[2]hindi, Kihindi, Mhindi, [1]muhindi, Uhindi.**

[2]hindi* (ma-) single grain of corn, maize. **mahindi.** corn, maize. **unga wa mahindi.** cornmeal. *Cf.* **[1]Hindi, [1]muhindi.**

hini* withhold, keep back; refuse. *refl.* **jihini.** refrain, abstain; restrain oneself. *appl.* **hinia.** *refl.-caus.* **jihinisha.** deny oneself, practice self-denial/abstinence. *Cf.* **[1]hiana, uhiana.**

hinikiza break off, interrupt *(a conversation);* be bored.

hinna* (—) *see* **hina.**

hinzirani* (—) *see* **henzarani.**

hirimia* intend, decide.

hirimu*, herimu (—) 1. time of life, age. 2. *eth.* age-group. **huyu — yangu.** This man belongs to my age-group. 3. a contemporary.

hirizi* (—) amulet, talisman.

[1]hisa* (—) 1. part, share. 2. *math.* quotient. 3. *econ.* share of stock.

[2]**hisa***, **hissa** (–) forgiveness, pardon.

hisabu* (–) *see* **hesabu** 2.

hisani*, **ehsani, ihsani, hasanati** (–) kindness, complaisance, favor, benefaction, preference. **fanyia –.** show favor to someone, treat preferentially. *Cf.* **mhisani.**

hisi* recognize; feel, perceive, sense. *Cf.* **hisiya.**

hisiya* (–) feeling. *Cf.* **hisi.**

hissa* (–) *see* [2]**hisa.**

historia* [*Engl.*] (–) history. **– ya Afrika.** African history.

hitaji*, **hidaji, ihtaji** 1. be lacking; want, desire; be necessary; need, require. **yahitaji.** It is necessary. *appl.* **hitajia.** *intr.* **hitajika.** 2. (ma-) *(usually* **mahitaji**) necessity, need, requirement, requisite; request, petition. *Cf.* **haja, mhitaji, uhitaji.**

hitiari* (–) *see* **hiari** 2.

hitilafu*, **ihtilafu** 1. distinguish, differentiate; differ, be different. *appl.* **hitilafia.** *appl.-ass.* **hitilafiana.** be different/distinct; disagree, contradict. 2. (–) difference; exception, contradiction, discrepancy; fault, defect.

hitima* (–) *Isl.* 1. reading from the Koran. 2. funeral sermon. 3. feast at the conclusion of a funeral service. *Cf.* **hatima, hitimu.**

hitimu*, **hatimu** end, stop; complete, finish, conclude *(esp. school, courses, etc.).* **mtoto huyu amehitimu.** This child has finished school. *appl.* **hitimia.** *caus.* **hitimisha, hatimisha.** *Cf.* **hatima.**

hivi 1. *dem. pron.* vi- *class.* these. **vitu –.** these things. 2. *adv.* thus, in this way, of this sort; just. **ameniambia –.** This is what he told me. **leo –.** just today. **– juzi (karibu).** recently, just now. **sasa – (– sasa).** immediately, directly.

hivyo 1. *det.* vi- *cl.* these/those *(mentioned).* **vitu –.** the things mentioned. 2. *adv.* thus, in this way. **vivyo –.** just so, in this very way.

hiyana* (–) *see* **hiana.**

hiyari* (–) *see* **hiari.**

hiyo 1. *det.* mi- *cl.* that/those *(previously mentioned).* **miti –.** those trees which were mentioned. 2. *det.* n- *cl.* this. **nyumba –.** the house referred to. 3. *adv.* in this way. **kwa –.** therefore.

hizaya*, **hezaya** (–) disgrace, dishonor; disfavor, misfortune, curse. *Cf.* [1]**hizi.**

[1]**hizi*** (*rare* **stihizai**) abuse, insult, disgrace, put to shame; curse, execrate;

dishonor, debase. *appl.* **hizia.** *intr.* **hizika.** be disgraced/dishonored. *caus.* **hizisha.** *Cf.* **hizaya.**

²**hizi** *dem. pron.* **n-** *cl. pl.* these. **nyumba –.** these houses. **siku –.** these days. *fig.* recently, today. **zizi –.** *emph.* these very...

hobe!* *interj.* Go! Get out! Get started!

hobela*: – – *adv.* somehow or other, any old way, hastily and badly.

hodari* *adj.* 1. strong, powerful. 2. firm, stable. 3. active, energetic. 4. diligent, skilful, capable. **mtu –.** a capable person. *Cf.* **uhodari.**

hodhi* (–) 1. water-tank, boiler. 2. waste land adjoining a cultivated field (and claimed by its owner).

hodi!* *interj.* May I come in? *(before entering a house/room.)* **piga –.** call 'hodi,' ask for admission.

hoduma* (–) *see* **huduma.**

hofia* *appl. of* **hofu.**

hofu* 1. fear, be afraid. *appl.* **hofia.** be afraid of (someone/something). *intr.* **hofika.** *pass.* **hofiwa.** *caus.* **hofisha.** frighten/intimidate (someone). 2. (–) fear, fright, terror. **wa na (patwa na, shikwa na) –.** be afraid, dread. **kwa –.** from fear.

hogo* (ma-, –) *see* **muhogo.**

hohehahe* [*Pers.*] (–) lonely/solitary person. *Cf.* **hoi.**

hoho (–) 1.: **pilipili –.** red pepper. 2. a kind of cake *(flavored with red pepper).*

hoi* [*Pers.*] *adj.* helpless.

hoihoi* [*Pers.*] (–) noise, shouting. **– ya karamu.** mirth at a feast or festival.

hoja*, huja (–, ma-) 1. necessity; wish. 2. affair, matter; reason, motive; evidence, argument. **hapana – ya kugombana.** There is no reason to quarrel. **una –?** *jur.* Do you have a question? 3. (trumped-up) excuse, evasion. **usinipe –.** Don't make excuses to me! *Cf.* **haja.**

hoji*, huji *jur.* question, examine, investigate; argue; compel, press. *appl.* **hojia.** *ass.* **hojiana.** argue. *pass.* **hojiwa.** *red. (int.).* **hojihoji.** keep on asking questions, cross-examine. *Cf.* **haja.**

hojihoji* *red. (int.) of* **hoji.**

hokumu* *see* **hukumu** 1.

homa* (–) *med.* fever. **imenishika** *or* **nimeshikwa na –.** I have a fever/temperature. **– ya malaria.** an attack of malaria. **kipimo cha –.** fever thermometer.

hombwe (–) hombwe (kind of snail).

homu* (–) steady wind.

homugadi* [*Engl.*] *sing.* home guard.

hondo, hondohondo, horohoro (–) *ornith.* crowned hornbill. (= **kwembe.**)

hondohondo (–) *see* **hondo.**

honga 1. pay *(toll, tribute).* 2. congratulate. 3. bribe, corrupt. *appl.* **hongea, hongela, hongera.** 1. pay for something. 2. recover *(esp. after childbirth).* 3. *jur.* be acquitted/cleared of a charge. *caus.* **hongeza.** make someone pay, ask for a bribe/blackmail. *refl.* **jihongeza.** rid oneself of something. *Cf.* **hongera, hongo.**

hongera 1. (–) congratulations; gift, present *(birthday, holiday).* 2. *appl. of* honga. *Cf.* honga.

hongo (ma-, –) exaction, tribute; bribe, blackmail. *Cf.* **honga.**

honi* [*Engl.*] (automobile) horn.

[1]**hori*** (–) *geogr.* bay, inlet.

[2]**hori*** [*Pers.*] (–) 1. watering trough, feed-trough *(for animals).* 2. a kind of canoe.

horji*, horiji (–) saddlebag.

horohoro (–) *see* **hondo.**

horuma* (–) *see* **huruma.**

horumia* *see* **hurumia.**

hospitali* [*Engl.*] (*also* **sipitali**) (ma-, –) hospital, clinic. *Cf.* **kiji-hospitali.**

hosumu* (–) *see* **husuma.**

hota treat, give medicine to *(against sterility or to encourage the growth of teeth in infants).* *Cf.* **hoto.**

hoteli* [*Engl.*] (–) hotel, restaurant.

hoto (ma-) medicine against sterility. **dawa ya – la uzazi.** medicine for inducing pregnancy. *Cf.* **hota.**

hotuba* (–) *see* **hutuba.**

hoza (–) hoza (medicine for teething children).

hozahoza remove, eliminate *(doubts, difficulties).*

hozi* 1. acquire, have, possess. **mwenye kuhozi.** monopolist. 2. (–) *jur.* property.

hozuni* (–) *see* **huzuni.**

hua (–) *ornith.* wild dove *(Streptopelia semitorquata).*

huba* (–) *see* [2]**haba.**

hubba* (–) *see* [2]**haba.**

hubiri* 1. say, tell, report, inform, announce. 2. **(ma-)** communication, report, message; *(rel.)* sermon. *Cf.* **habari, mhubiri.**

hudhud* (–) *ornith.* hoopoe.

hudhuni* *see* **huzuni.**

[1]**hudhuria*** be present, attend, participate. **– katika mkutano.** attend a meeting. *caus.* **hudhurisha.** summon, convene, convoke; invite. *Cf.* **hadhara, hudhurio.**

[2]**hudhuria*** risk, venture.

hudhurio* **(ma-)** presence, attendance, participation. *Cf.* **hadhara, [1]hudhuria.**

hudhurungi* 1. (–) light-brown cotton cloth *(for making* kanzu) 2. *adj.* light brown, yellow.

huduma*, hoduma (–) service, attention, assistance. *med.* **– ya kwanza.** first aid. *Cf.* **hadimu, hudumu.**

hudumia* *see* **hudumu.**

hudumu*, hudumia serve, attend, wait on; take care of, nurse. *Cf.* **hadimu, huduma.**

huduru* gather, assemble. *Cf.* **hadhara.**

huenda *adv.* possibly, perhaps. **– akaja.** Possibly he will come. *Cf.* **enda.**

hui* be revived. *caus.* **huisha.** revive, resuscitate, revivify. *Cf.* **hai.**

huja* **(–, ma-)** *see* **hoja.**

hujambo *see* **[1]jambo, ujambo.**

huji* *see* **hoji**

hujuma* *rare* attack.

hujuru* *see* **hajiri.**

huko 1. *dem. pron.* this *(previously mentioned).* **kucheza –.** the game referred to. **shambani –.** in the field mentioned. 2. *adv.* there, to that place; here, to this place. **huko –.** in that very place. 3. *conj.* **– nyuma.** while, as when.

huku 1. *dem. pron.* this. **kucheza –.** this game. **nyumbani –.** at his house. 2. *adv.* here, to this place. **toka – mpaka huko.** from here to there.

hukumu*, hokumu 1. judge, dispense justice, sentence; decide; rule, govern. *appl.* **hukumia.** pass judgment on. *caus.* **hukumiza, hukumisha.** 2. (–) administration of justice, judgment, sentence, decision; trial; decree, ordinance, regulation; jurisdiction, authority, power. **– ya mwisho.** *rel.* last judgment. **hana – hapa.** He has no authority here. **– ya saa kumi.** at the tenth hour. *Cf.* **hakama, hakimu, hekima, hekimiza, mahakma.**

huliwa* (–) fish-roe, caviar.

hulka*, huluka (–) status, natural condition, nature, quality, characteristic. *Cf.* **huluki, huluku, mahluki.**

hulu* 1. cease, desist. 2. allow, permit.

huluka* (–) *see* **hulka.**

huluki* (–) 1. creation. 2. creature, being. *Cf.* **hulka.**

huluku* *rel.* create. *Cf.* **hulka.**

humdu* (–) *see* **hamdu.**

humo 1. *dem. pron.* in this... *(previously mentioned).* **nyumbani –.** in the house referred to. 2. *adv.* here, in this place. **mumo –.** at/in this very place.

[1]**humu** 1. *dem. pron.* this, in this... **nyumbani –.** in this house. 2. *adv.* here, in this place. **mumu –.** in this very place.

[2]**humu*** (–) *rare* sorrow, grief.

humuda (–) help, assistance. **– ya kwanza.** first aid.

humusi* (–) a fifth.

hundi* [*Ind.*] (–) bill, draft, check, money order.

huni* 1. wander around, be idle. 2. do wilful damage, commit acts of vandalism/robbery. 3. be unstable/flighty, change about *(e.g., from one political party to another).* 4. be disobedient. *Cf.* **mhuni, uhuni.**

huntha* (–) *rare* hermaphrodite.

huo *dem. pron.* **m-** *and* **u-** *cl.* this *(previously mentioned).* **mti –.** the tree mentioned. **upanga –.** the sword referred to.

huri*, hurri, huria, huru (ma-) free person, freedman. *Cf.* **huria, huru, uhuru.**

huria* 1. (–) freedom *(of action, choice).* 2. (ma-) = **huri.** *Cf.* **huri, uhuru.**

hurijia* *rare* invite *(to a celebration).*

hurri* (ma-) *see* **huri.**

hurru* *see* **huru.**

huru*, hurru 1. *adj.* free; liberated, emancipated. **sisi ni watu –.** We are free people. 2. (ma-) *see* **huri.** *Cf.* **huri, uhuru.**

hurulaini*, huruleini (ma-) *Isl.* houri.

huruma*, horuma (–) sympathy, compassion; affection, generosity, humanity. **wa na (patwa na, shikwa na, ona, fanya) –.** show sympathy, be sympathetic/generous. *Cf.* **rehema, hurumia.**

hurumia*, horumia show sympathy toward someone, have pity/mercy. *Cf.* **huruma.**

hurunzi* (–) *see* **kurunzi.**

husiana/kuhusiana na... according to... *Cf.* **husu.**

husiano* (ma-) relationship. *Cf.* **husu.**

husika* *intr. of* **husu.**

husisha* *caus. of* **husu.**

husu* (*and appl.* **husia**) give someone a share, divide up; belong to, be due to. **alimhusu katika damu.** He belonged to him (was related to him). *fig.* concern, pertain to, affect; befit, be suitable; be in accordance with. **maneno haya yalimhusu kila mtu.** These words concerned everyone. *intr.* **husika.** *caus.* **husisha.** *ass.* **husiana.** concern each other, be pertinent. **(ku)husiana na...** according to... *Cf.* [1]**hasa, hususa, husiano, husuniano, kihusiano, kuhusu, mahsusi, uhusiano.**

husuda* (–) envy, ill will, jealousy, hostility. *Cf.* **hasidi, husudu.**

husudu*, hasidi be envious, envy. **– fulani kwa mali yake.** envy someone for his wealth. *appl.* **husudia.** *pass.* **husudiwa.** *Cf.* **hasidi, husuda.**

husuma*, hosumu, hasama (–) enmity, antipathy, antagonism, hostility; quarrel, dispute. *jur.* lawsuit, action. **ana – na mwenzake.** He is having a quarrel with his friend. *Cf.* **hasima, husumu.**

husumu*, hasimu quarrel, dispute. *fig.* compete, be rivals. *appl.* **husumia.** *appl.-ass.* **husumiana.** quarrel with each other. **amehusumiana na mwenzangu.** He has quarreled with my friend. *Cf.* **hasimu, husuma.**

husuni* (–) fort, fortress, castle.

husuniano* (ma-) relationship, connection. *Cf.* **husu.**

husuru* suppress, subjugate, oppress. *fig., mil.* besiege. *fig.* press, assail *(with words).*

hususa* 1. *adj.* special, particular. 2. *adv.* especially, exactly, extremely, fully, completely. *Cf.* [1]**hasa, husu, mahsusi.**

hutuba*, hotuba (–) 1. *Isl.* reading from the Koran, sermon. 2. *recent.* speech, address. *Cf.* **hutubu.**

hutubu* 1. *Isl.* read the Koran, preach. 2. *recent* make a report, give a speech/lecture. *appl.* **hutubia.** speak before..., address. *Cf.* **hatibu, hutuba.**

huu *dem. pron.* **m-** *and* **u-** *cl.* this. **mti –.** this tree. **utawala –.** this government.

huwa *adv.* usually, ordinarily, as a rule; perhaps, possibly. *Cf.* [1]**wa.**

huyo *dem. pron.* **m-** *cl.* this *(previously mentioned).* **mtu –.** the person mentioned.

huyu *dem. pron.* **m-** *cl.* this. **mtu –.** this person.

huzuni*, **hudhuni**, **hozuni** (–) mourning, sorrow, grief. **kwa – kubwa**. in deep mourning. **wa na –**. be worried/distressed. **ona (shikwa na, pata) –**. grieve, worry. *Cf.* **huzunia**.

huzunia* grieve, worry; regret. *intr.* **huzunika**. be sad. *caus.* **huzunisha**. make sad, sadden. *Cf.* **huzuni**.

I

iba embezzle, misappropriate, defalcate; steal, purloin. *appl.* **ibia**. steal from someone, rob someone. **tumeibiwa**. We have been robbed. *caus.* **ibisha**, **ibiza**. *Cf.* **jizi**, **kijivi**, **mwivi**, **wivi**.

ibada* (–) 1. *rel.* reverence, worship; liturgy, divine service. 2. cult. **– ya ubinafsi**. personality cult. (= **uabudiwaji**.) *Cf.* **abudu**.

Ibadhi* (–) *Isl.* (sect of the) Ibadites.

ibara* (–) paragraph, clause.

ibilisi*, **iblisi**, **bilisi** (–) devil, satan.

iblisi* (–) *see* **ibilisi**.

ibura* (–) 1. marvel, miracle, (remarkable) occurrence. 2. sign, mark, characteristic. 3. spot, speck, blot.

idadi* (–) 1. number, quantity, amount. **bila –**. without number, numberless. 2. counting, computing.

idara* (–) (government) office, department, ministry. **– ya posta**. post-office department. **– ya elimu (ukulima)**. ministry of education (agriculture). **– ya utibabu wa wanyama**. veterinary service.

idhaa* (–) program. **– ya redio**. radio program, broadcast.

idhara* 1. (–) slander, calumny; shame, disgrace, discredit. 2. *v.* slander, cause disgrace.

idhini* 1. allow, permit; approve, confirm; empower, authorize; assent, concur. *appl.* **idhinia**. *intr.* **idhinika**. *caus.* **idhinisha**. *pass.* **idhiniwa**. 2. (–) permission, approval, confirmation, concurrence, authorization. **taka –**. request approval. **toa –**. give approval/consent.

idi*, **eidi** (–) *Isl.* festival. **siku kuu ya –**. Bairam festival. **– ndogo**. festival at the end of Ramadhan. **pa mkono wa –**. to visit and shake hands on Bairam holiday.

idili* 1. (–) exertion, effort; perseverance; enthusiasm. 2. *v.* learn good conduct; teach someone good manners.

iftari* (–) iftari (a talisman).

ifu (–, **ma-**) *rare, dial.* 1. ashes. 2. remainder, residue. *Cf.* **jivu.**

ifuifu *rare, adj.* gray, ash-color. (= **jivujivu.**) *Cf.* **ifu.**

ifya be vexed/angry *(at someone).*

iga imitate, copy. **– maneno ya kigeni.** imitate a foreign language. **hodari wa kuiga.** imitator, mimic. *appl.* **igia.** imitate someone. *caus.* **igiza. jina la kuigiza.** pseudonym. *Cf.* **igizo, mwigaji,** [1]**mwigo, uigaji.**

igizo (**ma-**) imitation. **matendo ya maigizo.** stage setting. *Cf.* **iga.**

ihramu* (–) 1. *Isl.* clothing worn on the pilgrimage to Mecca. 2. the Pyramids. (= **haram.**) *Cf.* **haramu, harimu.**

ihsani* (–) *see* **hisani.**

ihtaji* *see* **hitaji.**

ihtiari* (–) *see* **hiari** 2.

ihtilafu* *see* **hitilafu.**

ihtinsa* end, conclude *(apprenticeship, education).*

ijapo, ijapokuwa *conj.* even if, although.

ijara* (–) 1. payment, rent. 2. pay, wages, earnings. *Cf.* **ajiri.**

ijaza* (–) 1. reward. 2. requital, retribution, punishment. *Cf.* [2]**jaza.**

Ijumaa*, Eljuma Friday. **– kuu.** Good Friday.

ika *rare* put, place. (= **weka, ikiza.**)

ikhiari* *adv.* better.

ikhtiari* (–) *see* **hiari** 2.

ikibali* *sing.* *see* **ukubali.**

ikirahi* (–) *see* **kirahi.**

ikirari* (–) *jur.* plea. *Cf.* [1]**kiri.**

ikiwa *conj.* if.

ikiza lay across, place crossways, spread out over. **ikiza nyumba boriti.** build the roof of a house.

iko *loc.* be. **minazi iko shambani.** The coconut palms are in the plantation. **nyumba yake – wapi?** Where is his house? **sukari –?** Is there sugar there?

iktikazi* (–) increase.

iktisadi* (–) thrift, economy. **-a –.** economic.

Ikulu Ikulu (the State House in Dar es Salaam).

ikweta*, ekwata [*Engl.*] (–) equator.

[1]**ila*** (–) fault, defect, shortcoming; shame, disgrace. **tia mtu –.** to attribute a failing/fault to someone.

[2]**ila*, illa, ela** *conj.* except, apart from; unless; but; otherwise, or else.

ilakini* *see* **lakini.**

ilani* (–) announcement, publication, (public) statement, declaration, proclamation. **– ya ulimwengu kuhusu haki za binadamu.** universal declaration of human rights.

ile *dem. pron.* 1. **mi-** *cl.* those. **miti –.** those trees. 2. **n-** *cl.* that. **kazi –.** that work.

ilhali* *see* **hali.**

ili* *conj.* (so)that, in order that, (in order) to.

iliki* (–) *see* **eliki.**

ilimu* (–) *see* **elimu.**

ilizi* (–) ilizi (charm against lions).

ilkanun* (–) measure, standard.

illa* *see* [2]**ila.**

ilmu* (–) *see* **elimu.**

[1]**ima** *see* **wima.**

[2]**ima** *rare* eat up *(food intended for others).*

[3]**ima* ... ima** *conj., rare* either ... or. (= [1]**ama.**)

imaima *adv.* *see* **kiwimawima.**

imamia fall upon, attack.

imamu* (–) *Isl.* imam.

imani* (–) belief; (religious) faith, creed; confidence, honesty. **hana – na mwenziwe.** He has no confidence in his friend. **– ya kithaura.** revolutionary spirit. *Cf.* **amana,** [1]**amini.**

imara* 1. (–) strength, power; *(fig.)* firmness, steadfastness; stubbornness, persistence, perseverance, stamina, endurance. **kipa –.** *rel.* confirmation (*lit.* that which gives strength). 2. *adj.* strong, powerful; *(fig.)* firm, steadfast, persistent. *Cf.* **imarika, uimara, uimarisho.**

imarika* be strong/firm, be steadfast/persistent. *caus.* **imarisha.** strengthen, establish, confirm. *Cf.* **imara.**

imarisha* *caus. of* **imarika.**

imba sing. *appl.* **imbia.** *appl.-ass.* **imbiana.** sing together/ in chorus. *caus.* **imbisha, imbiza:** 1. lead singing, direct a chorus. 2. study singing. *Cf.* **mwimba, mwimbishi, wimbaji, wimbo.**

imla* (–) dictation *(in school)*.

imo *loc.* be. **mizizi imo mchangani.** The roots are in the sand. **nguo imo sandukini.** The clothes are in the chest.

ina*, **inna** *adv.* truly, surely, certainly, positively.

inadi* (–) *see* **inda.**

inama 1. bend, decline, sink. **– macho.** cast down the eyes. 2. bow, bend over; crouch. *appl.* **inamia.** bow to someone; lean/depend on someone. *fig.* insist on something. *caus.* **inamisha. – kichwa.** lower the head *(from shame, embarrassment)*. *Cf.* **jinamizi, kiinamizi, mwinamishi, mwinamo;** *also* **inika, inua.**

[1]**inchi*** [*Engl.*] (–) inch (2.5 cm).

[2]**inchi** (–) *see* **nchi.**

[1]**inda***, **inadi** (–) obstinacy; tactlessness, troublesomeness.

[2]**inda** *see* **winda.**

inde (–) *bot.* Guinea grass *(Panicum maximum)*.

ingawa, ingawaje *conj.* although, even if, notwithstanding.

ingi *adj.* many, numerous. **watu wengi.** many people. **wale wengi.** majority. **miaka mingi.** many years. **matunda mengi.** much fruit. **vitu vingi.** many things. **nyumba nyingi.** many houses. *Cf.* [1]**wingi.**

ingia 1. come/go in, enter. **– nyumba/nyumbani.** enter a house. 2. have a share in, take part in, join. **– safarini.** start a journey; join an expedition. 3. get, become. **– baridi (kutu).** get cold (rusty). **– hofu.** become/be afraid. 4. be imported. *appl.* **ingilia.** 1. enter with a purpose, go in for..., pry into... 2. cohabit, have sexual intercourse with (*pass.* **ingiliwa,** *ass.* **ingiliana**). *stat.* **ingika.** *caus.* **ingiza.** cause/permit to enter, effect entry; insert; import. *appl.-caus.* **ingiliza.** introduce someone to *(a new job, etc.)*, break in; install *(in office)*; import *(merchandise)*. *ass.* **ingiana.** *caus.-ass.* **ingizana.** *Cf.* **kiingilio, maingiano, maingiliano, mwingilizi, mwingizaji, uingizaji.**

ingine *adj.* 1. other, second; different. **watu wengine.** other people. **miti mingine.** other trees. **matunda mengine.** other fruits. **vilima vingine.** other mountains. **nyumba nyingine.** other houses. **ingine ... ingine.** some ... others. 2. some, a few. **watu wengine.** some people. 3. next. **saba nyingine.** next week. *Cf.* **kwingineko, pengine, vingine, vinginevyo.**

ingua scare, frighten.

ini (ma-) 1. *anat.* liver. 2. heart *(as the seat of emotions)*. **maneno yale yalimkata –.** Those words cut him to the quick. (= **moyo.**)

inika 1. bend, bend down; lower the head *(from shame)*. 2. lower, pull down. **— tawi.** pull down a branch. 3. overturn, lay on one side. 4. *fig.* humble/abase oneself. *caus.* **inikisha, inikiza.** humble/humiliate someone. *Cf.* **kiini-kizo;** *also* **inama, inua.**

injili*, anjili, enjili (—) *rel.* gospel, New Testament. (= **maandiko ya Agano Jipya.**)

injini* (*rare* **enjine, enchini**) [*Engl.*] (—) engine, machine, motor. **— ya moshi.** steam engine.

injinia* [*Engl.*] (—) engineer. *Cf.* **uinjinia.**

inkishafi* (—) 1. *rel.* revelation. 2. Inkishafi *(name of a poem)*.

inna* *see* **ina.**

insaidi* [*Engl.*] (—) *sport* inside *(foot-ball)*. **— kuume (wa raiti).** inside right. **— kushoto (wa lefti).** inside left.

insha* (—) 1. essay; theme, composition *(school)*. 2. (written) draft, version. 3. work *(of literature or music)*.

inshallah!* *interj. of assent* Yes, certain-ly. *(If Allah wills it.)*

inspekta* [*Engl.*] (ma-) inspector. **— wa polisi.** police inspector.

insurensi* [*Engl.*] (—) insurance. **— ya maisha.** life insurance.

inua 1. raise, lift, elevate. **— mizigo.** raise/pick up a load. **— macho.** raise the eyes. 2. *fig.* heal, cure. *intr.* **inuka.** raise oneself, rise; be raised. **nchi inainuka.** The country is a highland. *intr.-appl.* **inukia.** get better, improve; pick up, start to thrive. *Cf.* **kiinua, mwinuko;** *also* **inama, inika.**

inuka *intr. of* **inua.**

inya *see* **nya.**

inzi (ma-, —) (common house-) fly.

iowe* (—) *see* **yowe.**

1**ipi** *see* **pi.**

2**ipi** (—) *rare* fist. (= **ngumi.**)

ipo *loc.* be. **miti ipo shambani.** The trees are there in the field.

ipu (—) *see* **jipu.**

ipua *inv. of* **epa.**

irabu* (—) vowel sign *(in the Arabic script)*.

iriba* (—) *rare see* **riba.**

iriwa (—) (bench-)vise.

1**isa*** *rare* love, like.

2**Isa*** *pr. n. masc.* **Isa (bin Mariamu).** Jesus (son of Mary) *(when spoken of by Moslems)*.

[1]**isha** end, conclude; stop, cease; complete. **ugomvi umekwisha.** The dispute has been ended. **kazi imekwisha fanywa.** The work is already done. *appl.* **ishia.** *double appl./int.* **ishilia.** *double appl.-caus.* **ishiliza.** *Cf.* **kisha, mwisho,** [2]**maishilio.**

[2]**isha*, esha** (–) *Isl.* evening prayer (6:30 - 8:30).

ishara*, taashira (–) 1. sign, indication, symptom; phenomenon. 2. something strange/remarkable. *Cf.* **ashiria.**

ishi*, aishi live, exist; last, remain. **– milele.** last forever. **kuishi pamoja kwa amani.** peaceful coexistence. *appl.* **ishia.** *Cf.* **aushi, maisha,** [1]**maishilio.**

ishirini*, asherini twenty.

isilahi* (–) *see* **suluhu.**

isimu*, ismu (–) 1. name. 2. essence, character; person. **– ya mtu.** everyone, each person. 3. *gramm., rare* subject.

isipokuwa 1. *prep.* except, with the exception of. 2. *conj.* if not, unless.

Islamu* 1. (–) Islam. **ingia –.** accept Islam. 2. (ma-) Moslem, Mohammedan. *Cf.* **silimu, Kiislamu, Mwislamu.**

ismu* (–) *see* **isimu.**

Israfil* *see* **Izraili** 2.

Israili* *see* **Izraili.**

istakabadhi* (–) *see* **stakabadhi.**

istiimari* *sing.* colonialism, imperialism.

istiska* (–) *med.* dropsy.

istiwai* *sing., rare* equator. (= **ikweta.**)

ita call, summon; name, mention; call upon, invite. *intr.* **itika.** be called; respond to a call/summons/invitation. *intr.-appl.* **itikia.** answer someone, respond to something; agree with someone. *caus.* **itisha.** summon someone, have someone called. *pass.* **itwa. anaitwa Saidi.** He is called Said. His name is Said. **kama inavyoitwa.** so-called. *Cf.* **itikio, itiko, kiitikio, mwitaji, mwito.**

itakadi* *rel.* believe. *Cf.* **itikadi.**

itatubwaga bring a curse upon oneself, suffer the bad effects of one's own action. *Cf.* **bwaga.**

ithibari* (–) *see* **itibari.**

ithibati* (–) confirmation, evidence, proof.

itibari*, ithibari (–) confidence; esteem, respect; faith, fidelity.

itifaki* (–) agreement, concord, harmony.

itikadi* (–) 1. belief, faith *(religion, tradition)*. 2. endurance, perseverance. *Cf.* **itakadi.**

itikio (ma-) 1. answer, echo. 2. *liter.* refrain. 3. consent, acceptance. *Cf.* **ita.**

itiko (ma-) answer. *Cf.* **ita.**

ituri* (–) odor, fragrance, perfume. (= **manukato, marashi.**)

itwa *pass. of* **ita.**

iva, wiva 1. ripen, become ripe; be cooked/done. **embe zinaiva.** The mangoes are ripening. **nyama imeiva.** The meat is done. 2. be ready/prepared. *coll.* **mambo yote yameiva.** Everything is prepared/ready. *Cf.* **bivu.**

ivu, ivo (–) *see* **jivu.**

iwapo *conj.* if, even if; although.

iza* *rare* refuse, decline, reject *(assistance);* not like, not favor. (= **chukia, kanusha, zia.**)

izara* (–) disgrace, shame, dishonor. (= **aibu, fedheha.**)

Izraili*, Israili 1. Israel. 2. (*also* **Israfil**) the angel of death.

J

ja (*dial.* **cha**) 1. come, arrive. **– mbio.** come running. 2. occur, happen, turn out. **nitakuja kusafiri.** It will turn out that I will have to go on a trip. *appl.* **jia.** *intr.* **jika.** be accessible/passable. **njia hii haijiki.** This road is impassable. *Cf.* **jio, kijakazi, kijio, kinjia, mja, mjakazi, mjio, njia, ²ujaji, ujia, ujio.**

¹jaa 1. be/become full. **mtungi umejaa maji.** The jug is full of water. **maji ya kujaa.** flood. 2. *fig.* be abundant/plentiful; have plenty of something, be abundantly supplied. **amejaa ujanja.** He has very great skill. *appl.* **jalia.** *caus.* **jaza.** fill (up, out). **jaza hati.** fill out a form. *fig.* **saa imejaza.** The clock is wound up. *caus.-ass.* **jazana.** push, crowd (one another). *Cf.* **²jazi, kijaa, ujalivu, ujazi.**

²jaa (–) rubbish-heap, dunghill. *Cf.* **jalala.**

³jaa* (–) *rare* north. (= **kaskazi, kibla.**)

jaahiri* (ma-) *see* **jahili.**

jaali* 1. be powerful. 2. favor.

jaamati* (–) 1. mosque. 2. meeting-place. *Cf.* **jamii.**

jabali*, jibali, gebali (ma-) 1. mountain, mountain range; rock, crag, cliff. 2. *fig.* prominent/exceptional person. **mtu huyu – sana.** This is a fearless person. 3. *fig.* raised embroidery on the back of a kanzu.

jabari* (–) 1. almighty, omnipotent *(a title of Allah).* 2. proud, fearless person. 3. martyr *(to a cause). Cf.* **jabali.**

jaddi* (–) *see* **[4]jadi, [5]jadi.**

[1]jadi* (–) 1. ancestor, forebear. 2. family tree, genealogy. (= **nasaba, asili, ukoo, kabila.**) **watu hawa hawana – nasi.** The people are not related to us.

[2]jadi* 1. wish, desire (strongly); demand. 2. (ma-) (*usually* majadi) desire; effort, exertion; persistence. 3. *adv.* very much; exorbitantly.

[3]jadi*, chadi (–) *astr.* Capricorn.

[4]jadi*, jaddi (–) *rare* hunger, famine. (= **njaa.**)

[5]jadi*, jaddi (–) kafir corn.

jadili* discuss, argue, debate. *appl.* **jadilia.** *ass.* **jadiliana.** prove/demonstrate something to each other. *Cf.* **jadiliano.**

jadiliano* (ma-) (*usually* **majadiliano**) discussion, argument, debate. **shirikiana –.** take part in a debate. *Cf.* **jadili.**

jafi* (–) jafi (kind of insect).

jafu (–) weir-basket *(for crabs).*

jagi* [*Engl.*] (–) jug. **– la maji.** water-jug. **– la maziwa.** milk-can. **– la maua.** flower-vase.

jaha* (–) 1. dignity, honor, fame, glory. 2. good luck, success. (= **utukufu, ukuu, usitawi, heshima.**) **mtu aliyeshushiwa –.** a person who has been granted good fortune. *fig.* **kilango cha –.** the gate of paradise. **nyota ya –.** *astr.* comet. **ameona nyota ya –.** He has a happy/successful future before him. **pa –.** show honor *(to someone);* raise in rank, promote; appoint *(to a responsible post).*

jahabu* 1. shore up *(a ship for repairs).* 2. (ma-) *naut.* brace, stay; slipway. *Cf.* **majahabu.**

jahanum*, jahinu, jehannum, jehena (–) *rel.* hell.

jahazi* (–, ma-) sailing ship *(in gen.).*

jahi* (–) *geogr.* North Pole.

jahili*, jaahiri *rare* 1. (ma-) rough, insensitive person. 2. *adj.* cruel; ignorant, uncivilized. (= **katili, jinga, pumbavu.**) *Cf.* **ujahili.**

jahina* *adj.* bold, brave, courageous.

jahinu* (–) *see* **jahanum.**

jaja (–) jaja (perennial plant, *Aneilema aequinoctiale).*

jajaga *rare* wash *(cloth, by rubbing between the hands).*

[1]**jaji*** [*Engl.*] (ma-) judge. *Cf.* [1]**ujaji.**

[2]**jaji** (ma-) *see* **yai.**

jajua make sour.

jalada*, jelada, gelada (–) bookbinding, cover. – **ya karatasi.** cardboard, pasteboard; case/folder *(for documents). Cf.* [1]**jalidi.**

jalala (–) rubbish-heap, dump. *Cf.* [2]**jaa.**

jalali* (–) almighty, omnipotent *(title of Allah).*

jali* 1. honor, respect. 2. pay attention to, observe, regard. **bila kujali.** inattentive.

[1]**jalia*** grant, empower, enable; lend support. *pass.* **jaliwa. tutasafiri tukijaliwa.** We will make the trip if we are able (if it is granted to us). *Cf.* **majaliwa.**

[2]**jalia** *appl. of* **jaa.**

[1]**jalidi*, jelidi** 1. bind *(a book).* 2. beat, whip. *Cf.* **jalada, mjelidi.**

[2]**jalidi*** (–) (black) frost, killing frost. *Cf.* **sakitu.**

jaliko (ma-) *see* [1]**mwaliko.**

jaluba*, jaruba (–), **kijaluba** (vi-) metal box *(usually for betel).*

jamaa* (–) 1. family, relatives. **mtu wa –.** a member of the family, a relative; *(fig.)* companion, comrade. *interj.* **jamani twendeni.** Let us go, friends. 2. company, gathering, meeting; coöperation. *Cf.* **jamii, ujamaa.**

jamadari* (ma-) *see* **jemadari.**

jamala* (–) 1. courtesy, manners, propriety, decorum. **hana jamaa wala –.** He has neither breeding *(lit.* family*)* nor manners. 2. kindness, complaisance. *Cf.* **tajamala, tajamali.**

jamanda*, chamanda (–) (round) covered basket. *Cf.* **kijamanda.**

jamba 1. break wind loudly. 2. (ma-) (intestinal) wind.

jambazi* (ma-) 1. tramp, beggar. 2. rogue, cheat, sharper.

jambeni* (–) crosscut saw *(two-handed).*

jambia*, jamvia (–) dagger (curved, broad-bladed). *Cf.* **shembea.**

[1]**jambo** (**mambo**) 1. matter, affair, condition, circumstance. **katika mambo ya sasa.** under the present circumstances/conditions. – **gumu.** difficult matter. 2. fact, actual state of affairs. **hili ni – wazi.**

This is an obvious fact. 3. *general formula of greeting.* **jambo**! Good Day, Hello *(to a single person).* **jamboni**! *(to several persons).* **hujambo**? How are you? **jambo** *or* **sijambo.** Good, thank you. *Cf.* **ujambo.**

²**jambo** (–) (fishing-)bait.

jambua *rare* clean, cleanse.

jamda (–) cumin, caraway. *Cf.* **kisibiti.**

jamdani* [*Pers.*] (–) (white) brocade, ribbon.

jamei* unnatural sexual relations.

jamhuri* (–) 1. republic. **– ya Sudan.** the Republic of the Sudan. **– ya Muungano, – ya Waarabu.** United Arab Republic. **tangaza –** (*or* **nchi kuwa –**). proclaim a republic. 2. accumulation, gathering, assembly. **– ya watu.** a gathering of people, crowd; *(comm.)* People's Republic.

jamia* (–) *see* **jamii** 3.

jamii* 1. gather, collect, assemble. 2. (*also ass.* **jamiiana**) copulate, have sexual intercourse. *caus.* **jamiisha.** 3. (*also* **jamia**) (–) mass, group, body; company, community; number, sum; totality. **– ya manowari.** navy. **– ya ndege.** air force. **– ya mizinga.** battery. 4. *gramm.* substantive. **– ya dini.** religious community. **– ya mali.** sum (total) of money. 5. *adv.* in mass, together. **wote –.** all together. *Cf.* **jaamati, jamaa, jumuiya, ujamaa.**

jamvi* (–) (plaited floor-)matting.

jamvia* (–) *see* **jambia.**

¹**jana** (ma-) 1. large/healthy child. 2. young person, young man/woman (= **kijana**). 3. larva of insects. **majana ya nyuki.** bees in the larval stage. *Cf.* **mwana.**

²**jana** 1. (–) time past/previous. **siku ya –.** the previous day. **wiki (ya) –.** last week. 2. *adv.* yesterday. **tumefika –.** We arrived yesterday.

janaa* (–) *see* **janaha.**

janaba* (*rare* **chanaba**) (–) *Isl.* (ritual) impurity, pollution, uncleanliness *(after sexual intercourse).*

janaha*, janaa (–) shame, dishonor, disgrace. (= **aibu, haya, fedheha.**)

janda (ma-) *rare* leaf, foliage.

jandala (–) leaving, leftover *(after a meal).*

jandaru* [*Ind.*] (–) *see* **chandalua.**

jando (ma-) 1. (rite of) initiation/circumcision. 2. secret place where initiation rites are performed.

¹**janga** 1. (ma-) torment, pain, annoyance; failure. **patwa na –.** be beset by pain/

failure. 2. *v.* grumble, complain; blame, accuse. *Cf.* **mjango.**

[2]**janga** *adj.* *see* [3]**changa.**

jangwa (ma-) desert, wilderness, desolate place. (= **nyika, pori, pululu, wangwa.**)

jani (*usually* **majani**) (ma-) 1. leaf, grass; leaves, foliage, bush. **ingia majanini.** go into the bush. 2. *adj.* green. **majani mabichi.** dark green.

janibu* (–) side; district, region; direction.

janika *see* **anika.**

janikiwiti (*rare* **chanikiwiti**) *adj.* green, grass-green.

janja 1. (ma-) (*augment. of* **mjanja**) thief, swindler, rogue. **– na janjuzi.** a great rogue outwitted by a still more artful rogue. 2. *adj.* clever, crafty, cunning, artful, deceitful. *Cf.* **mjanja, ujanja.**

janjuzi *see* **janja.**

janna* (–) *rare* paradise. (= **peponi, ferdausi.**)

jano (–) footstool.

jansi (–) *med.* cramp, spasm, convulsion.

Januari* [*Engl.*] (–) January.

japo *conj.* although, even if. **– hakuja...** although he did not come... *Cf.* **ijapo.**

jarabati*, mjarabati, mjaribati *adj.* tried, tested, attested, certified. *Cf.* **jaribu.**

jaraka* (–) *rare* *see* **jeraha.**

jarari* (–) *naut.* halyard.

jaribio*, jaribu (ma-) (*usually* **majaribio**) attempt, trial, test, experiment; effort. **– ya makombora ya atom.** atomic test. *Cf.* **jaribu.**

jaribosi* (ma-) tinfoil.

jaribu*, jeribu 1. try out, test; taste *(foods)*. *appl.* **jaribia.** *intr.* **jaribika.** *caus.* **jaribisha.** 2. (ma-) *see* **jaribio.** *Cf.* **jarabati, jaribio, majaribu, mjaribu.**

jarida*, jerida (ma-) *rare* newspaper. (= **gazeti.**) **– la serikali.** official gazette.

jarifa* (ma-) dragnet *(for fishing)*.

jaruba* (–) *see* **jaluba.**

jasho* (ma-) 1. heat, temperature. 2. sweat, perspiration. **fanya (toa) –.** sweat, perspire. **kazi ya –.** heavy physical labor. **jitia –.** work up a sweat.

[1]**jasi*** (ma-) *rare* jasi (ear-ornament, a round silver disc). (= **kipali, kipini.**)

[2]**jasi*** (ma-) white limestone *(used on the fingers when plaiting mats and as a face-powder)*.

jasiri*, jusiri 1. be reckless, foolhardy; be bold, brave. *appl.* **jasiria.** *intr.* **jasirika.**

caus. **jasirisha.** 2. (**ma-**) *see* **mjasiri.** 3. *adj.* brave, courageous. *Cf.* **mjasiri, ujasiri.**

jasisi* 1. find, locate. 2. *rare* investigate, go into thoroughly, pursue *(a subject);* shadow, spy on (someone). (= **mpelelezi, mdoya, haini, saliti.**) *appl.* **jasisia.** *caus.* **jasisisha.** *Cf.* **mjasusi, ujasusi.**

jasmini* (–) *see* **yasmini.**

jasusi* (**ma-**) *see* **mjasusi.**

jauri* (–) *see* **jeuri.**

jawabu* (**ma-**) 1. answer. *math.* product. 2. matter, affair. **– liwe lote.** be it (the matter) as it may. *Cf.* [1]**jibu, majibizano.**

[1]**jaza** *caus. of* [1]**jaa.**

[2]**jaza*** 1. reward, give a present to; maintain, support. 2. punish. *Cf.* **jazi, jazua.**

[1]**jazi*** 1. reward, requite; compensate, indemnify. *appl.* **jazia.** *caus.* **jazisha.** 2. (**ma-**) reward, compensation; gift. *Cf.* [2]**jaza.**

[2]**jazi, jazo** (**ma-**) enlargement, increase, augmentation, increment; abundance, profusion; excess, surplus. *Cf.* [1]**jaa.**

jazo (**ma-**) *see* [2]**jazi.**

jazua*, jezwa, jizya (–) indemnification, compensation; reward; gift, present. *Cf.* [2]**jaza.**

je *interr.* how? what? **nifanyeje?** What shall I do?

jebu* [*Ind.*] (**ma-**) woman's ornament (of gold or silver, worn under the chin).

jedhamu* (–) *see* **jethamu.**

jedwali* (–) list, table, plan, schedule.

jefua* *rare* abhor, feel repugnance/loathing.

jefule* (–) roughness, brutality, violence, coercion; tyranny, despotism.

jehannum* (–) *see* **jahanum.**

jehena* (–) *see* **jahanum.**

jeki* [*Engl.*] (–) 1. jack. **kutia –.** jack up *(e.g., an automobile, for repairs).* 2. *coll.* money. **nipige (tie) –.** Lend me some money.

jela* [*Engl.*] (–) 1. jail. 2. jailer.

jelada* (–) *see* **jalada.**

jelidi* *see* [1]**jalidi.**

jem* [*Engl.*] (–) jam, marmalade.

jemadari*, jamadari [*Ind., Pers.*] (**ma-**) commander, general. **– mkuu.** commander-in-chief.

jembe (**ma-**) 1. *agric.* hoe, mattock, spade, plow. **– la meno.** harrow. **– Ulaya.** plow. **piga –.** hoe, plow. 2.: **majembe.**

naut., *av.* screw, propeller (= **rafardha**). *Cf.* **²chembe, kijembe, wembe.**

jenabu* (–) jenabu (title of address in Arabic letters).

jeneral* [*Engl.*] (ma-) general.

jeneza* (–) bier.

jenga build, construct, erect. *appl.* **jengea.** *intr.* **jengeka.** *caus.* **jengesha.** *inv.* **jengua.** cut down, tear down, destroy. **sisi kazi yetu kujenga, sio kujengua.** It is our task to build up, not to destroy. *inv.-appl.* **jengulia.** *inv.-intr.* **jenguka.** *inv.-caus.* **jengusha.** *Cf.* **jengo, jenzi, mjengo, mjenzi, ujenzi.**

jengelele, chengelele (ma-) (*also* **ujengelele**, –) *anat.* 1. small intestine. 2. *(vulg.)* penis.

jengo (ma-) (*usually* **majengo**) 1. building, construction. **toa (andika) –.** draw a plan for a building. 2. building material. 3. scaffolding, enclosure, shed. *Cf.* **jenga.**

jengua *inv. of* **jenga.**

jenzi (ma-) (*usually* **majenzi**; *also* **ujenzi**) style/method of building. *Cf.* **jenga.**

jera* (ma-) *rare* *see* **jeraha.**

jeraha* (*rare* **jera, jeraka**) (ma-) 1. mark, marking. 2. wound, injury; ulcer, sore. (= **kidonda.**) **pata –.** be wounded. *Cf.* **jeruhi, majeruhi.**

jeraka* (ma-) *rare* *see* **jeraha.**

jeribu* *see* **jaribu.**

jerida* (ma-) *see* **jarida.**

jeruhi* wound, injure. *pass.* **jeruhiwa.** *Cf.* **jeraha, majeruhi.**

jeshi* (*rare* **geshi, cheshi**) (ma-) 1. *mil.* army. **– la ukombozi la umma.** People's Liberation Army. **fanya (kusanya) –.** muster/levy an army. **majeshi.** armed forces. **majeshi ya kanuni.** regular army/troops. 2. mass, crowd, host. *Cf.* **kijeshi.**

jeta* [*Ind.*] (–) loafer, lazybones.

jetea, nyetea 1. rely on, count on *(someone, something)*. 2. be arrogant/overbearing. *refl.* **jijetea.** be self-assured/conceited.

jethamu*, jedhamu, chethamu (–) *med.* 1. leprosy. 2. elephantiasis.

jeuri* (*rare* **jore**) 1. (–) (*also* **ujeuri**) injustice, brutality, oppression. **mwenye –.** tyrant, oppressor. **fanya (leta, toa) –.** act unjustly/arbitrarily/tyrannically. 2. *adj.* unjust, arbitrary, violent, tyrannical.

jezi* [*Engl.*] (–) jersey, knitted jacket.

jezwa* (–) *see* **jazua.**

jia *appl. of* **ja.**

jibali* (ma-) *see* **jabali.**

jibene* (–) *see* **jibini.**

jibini*, **jibene** (*dial.* **chibene**) (–) cheese. (= **chizi.**)

jibio* (ma-) *see* 1**jibu** 2.

jibiza *caus. of* 1**jibu.**

jibodoa praise oneself, boast.

1**jibu*** 1. answer, reply, respond. *appl.* **jibia.** answer someone. *intr.* **jibika. swali hili halijibika.** This question is not answerable. *caus.* **jibiza, jibisha.** 2. (ma-) (*also* **jibio**; *usually* **majibu** & **majibio**) answer, response. **pata (pokea) –.** receive an answer. **kupa (toa) –.** give an answer. *Cf.* **jawabu, majibizano.**

2**jibu*** [*Engl.*] (–) *naut.* jib.

jibwa (ma-) large dog. *Cf.* **mbwa.**

jicho (macho) eye. **fumba (fumbua) macho.** open (close) the eyes. **angaza –.** fix the eye on, look fixedly at. **pepesa –.** wink, blink. **kaa macho.** be/keep awake. **ana (yu) macho.** He is awake. **tazama kwa macho.** observe, inspect. **macho kwa macho.** eye to eye, face to face. *fig.* **– la maji.** spring *(of water).* **– la ua.** (opening) bud. *rel.* **Jicho la Mungu.** God Almighty. *Cf.* **kijicho, kimacho.**

jidai* *refl. of* **dai.**

jidamka *dial.* get up *(very early in the morning).*

jifia (ma-) *see* **jifya.**

jifu (ma-) *see* **jivu.**

jifundisha *refl.-caus. of* 2**funda.**

jifya, jifia (mafya) cooking-stone. *(Three of these stones form the cooking place).*

jigamba boast, show off. *Cf.* 1**amba.**

jigonjweza *see* **gonjweza.**

jiguzo (–) 1. pillar, post *(in house construction).* 2. *fig.* support, comfort. *Cf.* **nguzo.**

jihadhari* *refl. (interj.) of* **hadhari.**

jihifadhi* *refl. of* **hifadhi.**

jihongeza *caus.-refl. of* **honga.**

jijetea *refl. of* **jetea.**

jiji (ma-) *rare* big town/city. *Cf.* **mji, kijiji.**

1**jika** make an effort; press, strain *(in giving birth).* *Cf.* **mjiko.**

2**jika** *intr. of* **ja.**

jikalia *refl.-appl. of* 1**kaa.**

jikalifu* *refl. of* **kalifu.**

jikania *refl.-appl. of* **[1]kana.**

jike (**ma-**) female animal. **farasi —.** mare. *Cf.* **ke.**

jikimbiza *refl.-caus. of* **kimbia.**

jiko (**meko**) fireplace, cooking-place, stove. **kazi ya kijungu —.** a job which affords a bare subsistence. **—** *or loc.* **jikoni.** kitchen. **— la umeme.** electric cooker; dynamo *(on a bicycle).* **mkaa jikoni.** stay-at-home.

jikohoza *refl.-caus. of* **kohoa.**

jikunjua *refl.-inv. of* **kunja.**

jikweza *refl.-caus. of* **kwea.**

jilio (**ma-**) 1. *(us. pl.)* arrival, occurrence, approach. 2. (**majilio**, *usually rel.*) advent. *Cf.* **ja.**

jilisi* sit down. *Cf.* **majilisi.**

jiliwa*, jiriwa (*rare* **chiriwa**) (**—**) vise.

[1]jimbi (**ma-**) cock, rooster. (= **jogoo.**) **— lawika.** The cock crows.

[2]jimbi (**—**) 1. taro root *(Colocasia antiquorum). Cf.* **myugwa, mayugwa.** 2. (*also* **mjimbi, vi-**) fern, bracken *(Pteridium aquilinum).*

[1]jimbo (**ma-**) 1. (inhabited) territory, district, province. 2. *rel.* diocese.

[2]jimbo (**ma-**) medicine made from tamarind leaves *(used for washing new-born babies).*

jina (**ma-**) name, proper name; appellation, designation; *(gramm.)* substantive, noun. **— lako nani?** What is your name? **— la kupanga (dhihaka, utani).** nickname. **— la fumbo.** pseudonym. *Cf.* **kijina.**

jinai* (**—**) crime, delict. **kesi ya —.** criminal case.

jinaki* think well of oneself, be proud, boast. *Cf.* **nakawa.**

jinamisi (**—**) jinamisi (kind of fish).

jinamizi (**ma-**) (*also* **ujinamizi**) 1. twist, bend, curve. 2. bow, (act of) bending over/bowing. 3. humility, self-abasement. 4. nightmare. **— limenilemea.** I had nightmares. *Cf.* **inama.**

jinga *adj. & adv.* stupid, ignorant, foolish. *Cf.* **kijinga, mjinga, ujinga.**

[1]jingi (**ma-**) quantity, (great) number.

[2]jingi (**ma-**) one of the uprights of a frame for rope-making *(supporting a cross-board,* **bao la —**).

jingizi *see* **zingizi.**

jini* (**ma-**) spirit *(chiefly in children's stories: beneficent, but sometimes frightening).* (= **zimwi,** *not* **shetani.**) *Cf.* **ujini.**

jino (meno) 1. tooth. **– la mbele.** front tooth, incisor. **– la nyuma.** molar. **meno ya juu.** upper teeth. **meno ya chini.** lower teeth. **ng'oa –** *(or, in the case of a child,* **ota –***).* pull a tooth. **toa meno.** show/bare the teeth. **umwa na –.** have a toothache. **meno ya msumeno.** saw-teeth. **-a meno meno.** notched, serrated, crenelated. 2. *something toothlike:* prong *(of a fork, etc.),* cog. 3. strand *(of rope, etc.);* plug, twist *(of tobacco).* **– zima la tumbako.** plug of pressed tobacco. *Cf.* **kimenomeno, msumeno.**

jinsi*, ginsi (–) 1. kind, sort; class, quality. 2. manner, procedure, method. **– gani?** in what way? how?

jinywa (ma-) (*augment. of* **kinywa**) big mouth *(as a term of opprobrium). Cf.* **nywa.**

jio (ma-) 1. *rare* approach, arrival. 2. *fig.* evening. *usually loc.* **jioni.** (in the) evening. **jioni leo.** this evening. *Cf.* **ja.**

jiografia* [*Engl.*] (–) geography.

jioni (*loc. of* **jio**) (in the) evening.

jipu (ma-) *med.* abscess, tumor, boil. **tumbua –.** lance a boil.

jira (–) caraway, cumin. *Cf.* **kisibiti.**

jirani* (–, ma-) 1. neighbor. *prov.* **heri – karibu kuliko ndugu mbali.** A neighbor nearby is better than a relative far away. 2. neighborhood, vicinity. **nchi hii ni – na kwetu.** This country is close to ours. 3. *adv.* near, close by. **shamba –.** an adjacent field. **tunakaa –.** We live near each other. *Cf.* **majirani, ujirani.**

jiri* 1. start, set in; happen, occur. 2. flow *(of water);* pass, elapse *(of time); (fig.)* circulate *(of money). caus.* **jirisha.** carry out, execute *(laws, etc.).*

jiriwa* (–) *see* **jiliwa.**

jisima* (ma-) *rare* form, figure, (external) appearance.

jisu (ma-) (*augment. of* **kisu**) large knife.

jitahidi*, jitihadi 1. exert oneself, try hard, take pains. *caus.* **jitahidisha.** 2. (ma-) *see* **jitihadi.**

jiti (ma-) (*augment. of* [1]**mti**) large tree, tree trunk; (large) piece of wood.

jitihadi*, jitahidi, jitihada (ma-) (*also* **ujitahidi**) exertion, effort, industry, zeal. *Cf.* **jitahidi, juhudi.**

jitimai* (–) sorrow, grief, sadness, melancholy, affliction. **kuwa na –.** grieve.

jito, juto (ma-) (*augment. of* [1]**mto**) (large, broad) river, lake.

jitu (ma-) (*augment. of* **mtu**) giant.

jituka be frightened/startled/confused; be anxious/uneasy. *Cf.* **shtua** (?).

[1]jivi (ma-) *see* **jizi.**

[2]jivi (ma-) wild hog.

jivu, jifu (ma-) ash(es). **jivujivu, -a kijivu.** *adj.* ash-colored, ashen, gray.

jivujivu *adj.* *see* **jivu.**

jivuna be proud; put on airs, boast. *Cf.* **vuna.**

jiwe (mawe) 1. stone. **nyumba ya mawe.** stone house. **mchongaji wa mawe.** stonemason. **– la thamani.** precious stone. **– la msingi.** cornerstone. *fig., interj.* mawe! Nonsense! 2. (*us. pl.:* **mawe ya mizani**) weights *(of scales).* *Cf.* **kiwe, mbwe.**

jiza (–, ma-) *see* **giza.**

jizi, jivi (ma-) (*augment. of* **mwivi, mwizi**) a well-known/habitual thief. *Cf.* **iba.**

jizla* (–) jizla (unit of weight: 166 kg).

jizya* (–) *see* **jazua.**

jodari* (–) jodari (kind of dried fish).

jogoo (ma-) cock, rooster. **– la kwanza.** first cock-crow (2:00 A.M.). **– la pili.** second cock-crow (4:00 A.M.). *Cf.* **kijogoo, ujogoo.**

johari* (–) jewel, precious stone; valuable thing. *fig.* **– ya mtu.** valuable human quality.

joho* (–) 1. woolen cloth. 2. a kind of Arab cloak.

joka, choka (ma-) (*amplic. of* **nyoka**) large snake.

joko (ma-) potter's kiln. *Cf.* **oka.**

jongea move, come near, approach. *appl.* **jongelea.** *caus.* **jongeza.**

jongo (ma-) 1. *amplic. of* **mgongo.** 2. (strong, heavy) seam *(in sewing).* 3.: **ugonjwa wa –.** *med.* gout, rheumatism.

jongomeo (–) *myth.* hereafter, life to come.

[1]**jongoo** (ma-) millipede. **– la pwani.** bêche-de-mer, large sea slug (= **babaje, kojojo**).

[2]**jongoo: – halipandi mtungi.** *coll.* impotent man.

jora* [*Ind.*] (–) 1. cotton, calico. 2. piece of calico about 30 yards long.

[1]**jore** (–) jore (kind of bird, *Eurystomus afer).*

[2]**jore*** (–) *see* **jeuri.**

[1]**joshi*, goshi** (–) *naut.* weather/windward side.

[2]**joshi** *adv.* (ride) at a gallop. **alimpanda farasi –.** He rode the horse at a gallop.

3**joshi** (**ma-**) (*augment. of* **moshi**) thick/copious smoke.

josho, chosho (**ma-**) 1. place for washing/bathing. 2. place for washing corpses. *Cf.* **osha.**

joto (**ma-**) (*augment. of* 1**moto**) 1. (intense) heat. 2. *med.* inflammation, high fever. **pima —.** take the temperature *(of a person). Cf.* **ujotojoto.**

joya (**ma-**) joya (coconut with spongy shell). **kama —.** spongy, porous.

1**jozi*** (**—, ma-**) 1. pair. **— ya viatu.** a pair of shoes. 2. things belonging together *(in a set, etc.).* **— ya karata.** a deck of playing cards.

2**jozi*** (**—**) (kernel of a) nut, almond, walnut. *Cf.* **lozi.**

3**jozi** (**ma-**) *see* 1**chozi.**

1**jua** (**ma-**) 1. sun, sunshine. **— kucha.** sunrise. **— kuchwa.** sunset. **— kichwani.** midday, noon ('sun on the head'). **— kali.** hot sun. 2. clear, sunny weather.

2**jua** know, be acquainted with; recognize; grasp, understand. **— jambo.** know a thing, know about something. **— kuandika.** know how to write. **kwa kujua.** intentionally, on purpose. *appl.* **juia, julia.** *intr.* **julika.** *intr.-ass.* **julikana.** be known/recognizable/understandable. *caus.* **julisha** (*rare* **juza**). let know, announce, inform. *Cf.* **juvi, kijuvi, mjuvi, mjuzi, ujuvi, ujuzi.**

1**juba*** (**—**) chisel.

2**juba*** (**—, ma-**) linen shirt/coat.

3**juba*** *adj., rare* fearless, brave.

juburu* 1. force, compel. 2. encourage.

jugumu* talk contemptuously/derisively/ironically.

jugwe* [*Engl.*] (**—**) *sport* tug-of-war.

juha* (**ma-**) *rare* stupid person, fool. (= **mjinga, mpumbavu, baradhuli.**)

juhudi* (**—**) effort, exertion, zeal. **mwenye —.** *comm.* activist. *Cf.* **jitihadi.**

jukumu* [*Ind.*] (**—**) insurance, guarantee, warranty; responsiblity; rôle, task. **lipa —.** insure *(commercial goods).* **chukua —.** bear the responsibility, guarantee. **jichukulia —.** take/assume responsiblity.

jukwaa*, jukwari (**ma-**) 1. scaffold(ing), platform. 2. gallows, scaffold. 3. rostrum.

jukwari* (**ma-**) *see* **jukwaa.**

Julai* [*Engl.*] (**—**) July.

juma* (ma-) 1. week. — **moja.** a week. — **nzima.** the entire week. 2. *(usually* **jumaa, ijumaa)** Friday. 3. *pr. n. masc.*

Jumamosi Saturday.

Jumanne Tuesday.

Jumapili Sunday.

Jumatano Wednesday. — **ya majivu.** Ash Wednesday.

Jumatatu Monday.

jumba (ma-) (*augment. of* **nyumba**) (large) house, mansion, palace. — **la kufanyia majiribio.** laboratory, experimental station. — **la ukumbusho.** National Museum.

jumbe (ma-) village elder, headman, chief. *Cf.* **kijumbe, mjumbe, ujumbe.**

jumla* 1. (–) final result. *math.* sum (total). *fig.* — **ya maneno ni.** in brief ('the result of the words is...'). **kwa —.** in general. 2. *adv.* all together, as a whole. *Cf.* **jumlisha, ujumla.**

jumlisha* 1. put together, count up. 2. *math.* add, plus. *pass.* **jumlishwa.** *Cf.* **jumla.**

jumu*, nujumu (–) luck, fate, chance.

jumuiya*, jumuia (–) 1. society, association. — **ya michezo.** sports/athletic association. — **ya taaluma ya Kiswahili.** Society for the Study of Swahili. 2. alliance. — **ya madola.** commonwealth; United Nations. *Cf.* **jamii.**

jungu, kungu (ma-) (*augment. of* [1]**chungu**) large cooking pot.

Juni* [*Engl.*] (–) June.

jura (ma-) 1. (*amplic. of* **chura**) large frog. 2. *rare* stupid person, fool. (= **mjinga, mpumbavu, baradhuli.**)

jurawa (–) *ornith.* (species of) sparrow.

jusiri* *see* **jasiri.**

juta* regret, deplore; be ashamed/dejected. *Cf.* [1]**juto.**

[1]**juto*** (ma-) (*usually* **majuto**) regret, pangs of conscience, contrition. **ona (fanya) majuto.** have regrets, feel pangs of conscience. **shikwa (patwa) na —.** be overcome by regret/pangs of conscience. *Cf.* **juta.**

[2]**juto** (ma-) *see* **jito.**

juu 1. (–) top, upper part; sky. — **ya nyumba.** the top of the house. — **yako.** You are responsible. It is your business. 2. *adv.* up, above. **panda —.** go upstairs. — **kwa —.** at the top, uppermost. **weka —.** overestimate. *red.* **juujuu.** 1. *adv.* (high) up, aloft. 2. proud, arrogant. 3. shallow, superficial; perplexed. *Cf.* **kijuujuu, ujuu.**

juvi curious, inquisitive, impudent. *Cf.* [2]**jua, kijuvi, mjuvi, ujuvi.**

juya* (ma-) *rare* fishing net (made of coconut fiber).

juzi (ma-) day before yesterday. **tangu majuzi yale.** for some time. **mwaka** (wa) **—.** year before last. **— hivi.** not long ago, recently.

juzijuzi *adv.* *see* **majuzi.**

juzu* be permissible/admissible; be suitable/proper. **inajuzu kwenda.** It is permissible to go.

juzuu* (ma-) part, section, paragraph; chapter *(of the Koran).*

ka *consec. part.:* **akaenda.** (and) he went.

[1]**kaa** 1. be; live, stay, dwell, settle; wait. **— mjini.** live in town. 2. exist; continue, last, endure, remain. **mitungi hii imekaa sana.** These earthenware pots have lasted for a long time. **itakaa siku nyingi.** It will continue for many days. 3. sit. **— kitako.** sit down, be seated. *appl.* **kalia.** *intr.* **kalika.** *caus.* **kalisha.** settle someone, make someone a resident. *pass.* **kaliwa. nchi hii imekaliwa na watu.** This country is settled. *refl.-appl.* **jikalia.** be idle/inactive. *intr.-ass.* **kalikana.** be habitable. **nyumba hizi hazikaliki.** These houses are uninhabitable. 4. *red.:* **kaakaa.** wait a while (before doing something), be dilatory. *Cf.* **kaza** (?), **kikalio, kikao, makao, makazi,** [1]**mkaa, mkalio, ukaaji, ukao, ukazi.**

[2]**kaa** (—) crab.

[3]**kaa** (ma-) (*usually* **makaa**): **makaa ya mawe.** coal. **makaa ya miti.** charcoal. **— la moto.** glowing embers. **choma makaa.** burn charcoal.

Kaaba* Kaaba (in Mecca).

[1]**kaakaa, kaka** (ma-) *anat.* palate.

[2]**kaakaa** *see* [1]**kaa** 4.

[1]**kaanga, karanga** fry, roast, bake, stew. **— nyama.** roast meat. **mayai ya kuka anga.** fried eggs. *caus. (rare)* **kaanza, kanza;** *usually* **kaanza moto.** warm at a fire, warm up. *Cf.* **kaango, kanzo, kikanza, ukaango.**

[2]**kaanga, kanga** (ma-) branch bearing fruit.

kaango, kango (**ma-**) cooking pot, frying pan. *Cf.* **¹kaanga.**

kaanza *caus. of* **¹kaanga.**

kaanzo (**ma-**) *see* **kanzo.**

¹kaba* 1. press, squeeze. **nguo hii inamkaba.** This garment is too tight for him. *fig.* **– roho.** choke, throttle. 2. (–): **hana – ya ulimi.** He talks too much.

²kaba* (–) 1. lining of kanzu. 2. collar.

kabadhi* *see* **kabidhi.**

kabaila*, kabaili 1. (**ma-**) important person, person in high position or much respected. 2. *hist.* one born of free parents, nobleman. *Cf.* **kikabaila, ukabaila.**

kabaili* (–) *see* **kabaila.**

kabaka* [*Lug.*] 1. kabaka (title of the king of Buganda). 2. *(humorous or ironical)* one who behaves as if he were a king.

kabari*, kabali (–) wedge *(of wood or iron).* **kaza kwa –.** to wedge tightly.

kabati* [*Engl.*] (–, **ma-**) cupboard, cabinet.

kabe* [*Engl.*] (–) *elec.* cable.

kabeji* (–) *see* **kabichi.**

kabibu* *adj.* narrow.

kabichi*, kabeji [*Engl.*] (–) cabbage, lettuce.

kabidhi*, kabadhi 1. seize; accept, receive; lay hand on something. **– mali.** keep, save. 2. *(in a caus. sense)* hand over, deliver. **– fedha (mali) warithi.** leave money (property) to heirs. *appl.* **kabidhia.** *intr.* **kabidhika.** *caus.* **kabidhisha.** 3. (–) care, attention; guardianship. 4. *adj.* economical, thrifty, frugal. *fig.* greedy, avaricious; penurious, stingy, miserly. *Cf.* **mkabidhi, stakabadhi, takabadhi, ukabidhu.**

kabila* (–, **ma-**) tribe *(a smaller division than* **taifa,** *but larger than* **ufungu, jamaa**). *Cf.* **kikabila, ukabila.**

¹kabili* 1. go and stand before/face someone; approach; be directed toward. **– uso kwa uso.** stand face to face with someone. *naut.* **kuikabili bahari ile.** shape a course for that sea. *appl.* **kabilia.** *appl.-ass.* **kabiliana.** go and face each other, have relations with each other. *intr.* **kabilika.** *caus.* **kabilisha.** **– mtu.** introduce someone. 2. *adj.* honest, upright. *Cf.* **kabla, kibla, mkabala.**

²kabili* (–) *see* **kabiri.**

kabiri*, kabili (–) flute player.

kabisa* *adv.* 1. completely, totally. **mji huu umeharibika –.** This city is totally destroyed. **nyuma –.** right at the end, far to the rear. 2. very, extremely.

kwenda mbio —. run very fast. 3. absolutely. definitely. **lazima — aende.** He definitely has to go. (= **kamwe, hasa, hasili.**)

kabla*, kabula 1. *conj.* before. **— hajaja (bado).** before he will come. 2.: **— ya.** *prep.* before, ago. **— ya siku nyingine.** several days ago. *Cf.* **kabili.**

kabsa* (—) *see* **kamsa.**

kabula* *see* **kabla.**

[1]**kabuli*** [*Ind.*] (—) a dish prepared with rice and curry.

[2]**kabuli*** *see* **kubali.**

[3]**kabuli*** (—) *see* **ukubali.**

kaburi* (ma-) grave, mound. *loc.* **makaburini.** burial-place, cemetery. *prov.* **kama hujui kufa tazama —.** Even though you don't know what dying means, keep an eye out for a grave. **— kubwa.** tomb, mausoleum.

kaburu* [*Afr.*] (ma-) *(us. pl.)* 1. Boor(s); Government of South Africa; *(comm.)* imperialist, colonialist. 2. *(in gen.)* European settler/farmer in Africa.

kabwela (ma-) 1. (unfair, arbitrary) use of force/power. **hakimu wa korti amenipa kabwela kubwa ya nguvu kushinda mastaka yangu.** The magistrate fined me heavily for nothing, for he has the power. 2. *fig.* a person who conceals his true motives/acts on false pretenses (who claims to need something which he really does not need, etc.), hypocrite, deceiver, fraud. **Hassan ni kabwela usisadiki yote asemayo.** Hassan is a deceiver; don't believe anything he tells you. **Nchi yetu imepoteza viongozi, sasa twatawaliwa na makabwela.** Our country has lost (real) leaders and is now run by frauds and hypocrites.

kabwiri (—) kabwiri (kind of anchovy).

kachala*, kachara *adj.* old, worn-out; of inferior quality.

kachara* *see* **kachala.**

kachumbari* (—) [*Ind.*] pickle(s).

kada* [*Engl.*] (—) *comm.* cadre.

kadamisha*, kadimisha precede, send ahead/in advance. *Cf.* **kadamu.**

kadamnasi* *adv.* in public, publicly *(lit.: before the people; cf.* **kadamu).**

kadamu* 1. *adv., rare* before (= **mbele).** 2. (ma-) (*also* **mkadamu, mtakadamu,** wa-) *rare* foreman, supervisor. *Cf.* **kadamisha, kadamnasi,** [1]**kidamu, takadamu.**

kadha* *adj. & adv.* so and so many, several *(an indefinite number).* **— wa —.** so and so many, and many more, and so on, *etcetera.* **miaka — wa —**

imepita. so and so many years have passed. (= **vivi hivi, vivyo hivyo.**)

kadhabu*, kedhabu (–) *rare* liar. (= **mwongo.**) *Cf.* **kadhibisha.**

kadhalika*, dhalika, bidhalika *adv.* likewise, similarly; at the same time; again. **na –** (*abbr.:* **n k**). and so forth, etc.

kadhi*, kadi (ma-) *rare* judge. (= **hakimu, mwamuzi.**)

kadhia* (–) *rare* matter, affair; occurrence, event.

kadhibisha* deny, reject, refute. *Cf.* **kadhabu.**

[1]**kadi*** (ma-) *see* **kadhi.**

[2]**kadi*** [*Engl.*] (–) 1. card. **– ya kutambulisho.** identification card. 2. invitation.

kadimisha* *see* **kadamisha.**

kadinali*, kardinali [*Engl.*] (ma-) 1. *rel.* cardinal. 2. *math.* cardinal (number). **namba ya kikadinali.** cardinal number.

kadiri* 1. reckon, calculate, estimate, assess. **– kiasi.** estimate/establish the value of something. *fig.* judge, appraise, consider, form an opinion of something. **– maneno.** weigh words. *appl.* **kadiria.** appraise/consider something. *intr.* **kadirika.** be limited/measurable. *caus.* **kadirisha.** 2. (–) measure, calculation; amount; extent; *(arith.)* numerator. **– gani.** What amount? How much? **pima –.** take a measurement. **– ya miaka kumi.** in the course of ten years. 3. *(also* **– ya***) adv. & conj.* to the extent that, in accordance with; about, on the average. **– upendavyo.** as much as you please. **lipa (toa) – ya shilingi ishirini.** pay on the average 20 shillings. *Cf.* **kadirifu, makadirio, ukadirifu.**

kadirifu* *adj., rare* moderate, temperate; abstemious, continent; careful, anxious. *Cf.* **kadiri, ukadirifu.**

kadirio* (ma-) *see* **makadirio.**

kadogo 1. *adj. (dial. emph. of* **kidogo**) extremely small, tiny; *(fig.)* insignificant. 2. *adv.* to a very slight extent.

kafala* (–) *rare* security, bail.

kafara* (ma-) 1. animal sacrifice, expiatory offering; atonement, penalty. **toa (fanya) –.** make a sacrifice. *rare:* **chinja –.** slaughter a sacrificial animal. 2. amulet, charm.

kaffi (ma-) *see* **kafi.**

kafi, kaffi (ma-) *naut.* paddle, oar. **piga –.** to paddle, row.

kafila* (–) *rare* caravan. (= **safari, msafara.**)

kafini* *rare* cover, wrap. **– (kwa) sanda.** wrap (a corpse) in a shroud.

kafiri* (ma-) *Isl.* unbeliever, non-Moslem, atheist. *Cf.* **kufuru, makufuru, ukafiri.**

kaftani* (–) caftan (outer garment of Arabs).

kafu *see* **kavu.**

kafua *rare* thresh (grain). (= **pura, piga.**)

kafuri* (–) camphor.

[1]**kaga** *dial.* protect, ward off evil *(by magic).* – **shamba.** protect a field by magic. *Cf.* [1]**kago, ukago.**

[2]**kaga** (–) *med.* swelling, tumor.

[1]**kago** 1. protect someone or something by magic. 2. (–) *(dial.)* protective magic. – **la simba.** charm against lions. *Cf.* [1]**kaga, ukago.**

[2]**kago*** [*Engl.*] (–) *naut.* 1. cargo. 2. dock.

kagua inspect, superintend; examine, check. – **skuli.** inspect a school. – **askari.** review troops. – **hesabu.** check accounts. *appl.* **kagulia.** *intr.* **kaguka.** *appl.-caus.* **kagulika.** *Cf.* **mkagua, mkaguo, mkaguzi, ukaguzi.**

kaha (ma-) *rare* pod, shell. – **la yai.** *rare* eggshell. (= [2]**kaka.**)

kahaba* (ma-) (*and* **mkahaba,** wa-) prostitute. *Cf.* **ukahaba.**

kaharabu* [*Pers.*] (–) amber.

kahawa* (–) coffee. – **ya tangawizi.** a ginger beverage. *Cf.* **kahawia, mkahawa.**

kahawia* *adj.* coffee-colored. *Cf.* **kahawa.**

kahini*, kuhani (ma-) 1. *Bibl.* priest, prophet. 2. *rare:* soothsayer.

kahuni* (–) *rare* law. *Cf.* **kahini.**

kai* [?] 1. hand over, deliver, surrender. (= **angukia, miguuni, shika miguu.**) 2. *rare* be timid.

[1]**kaida*** (–) *see* **kawaida.**

[2]**kaida*** Kaida (the second month after Ramadhan).

kaidi* 1. be intractable/obstinate/disobedient; contradict; offer resistance. *appl.* **kaidia.** *caus.* **kaidisha.** incite someone to disobedience; dare someone to contradict. 2. *adj.* intractable, disobedient, obstinate. **mtoto mkaidi.** disobedient child. *Cf.* **mkaidi, ukaidi.**

kaimia* force oneself to do something.

[1]**kaimu*** (ma-) 1. representative, substitute, deputy. – **wa president.** vice-president. 2. manager, agent, legal adviser. **kuwa – wa shughuli.** act as legal adviser in a matter. *Cf.* **makamu, ukaimu.**

[2]**kaimu*** (ma-) exorcist, necromancer.

kajayeye (–) kajayeye (kind of manioc).

kajekaje (–) *naut.* (thin) rope (for fastening sails to the yards).

kajia (vi-) *see* **kinjia.**

[1]**kaka** (–) elder brother, brother *(in gen.).*

[2]**kaka,** *(rare)* **kaha** (ma-) shell *(of an egg),* rind *(of fruit),* husk *(of grain).*

[3]**kaka** (ma-) *dial., med.* circulation.

[4]**kaka** (ma-) *see* **kaakaa.**

[5]**kaka** (ma-) *rare* leech. (= **ruba.**)

kakaka (–) kakaka (variety of vegetable).

kakakaka *adv.* hastily, precipitately, headlong, head over heels. *Cf.* **kikaka.**

kakakuona (–) kakakuona (animal resembling an armadillo; it is believed that burning its scales will ward off wild animals).

kakamavu *adj.* sly, cunning, crafty, deceitful. *Cf.* **kakamia, mkakamavu, ukakamavu.**

kakamia strive after something, work hard, exert/strain oneself. *inv.* **kakamua** = **kakamia.** *inv.-intr. (w. intr. force).* **kakamuka, kakamka.** make great exertions, take great pains; groan, moan. *Cf.* **kakamavu, kakamizi, mkakamavu, ukakamavu.**

kakamizi *adj.* stubborn, obstinate, unyielding, inflexible, uncompromising. *Cf.* **kakamia.**

kakamka *inv.-intr. of* **kakamia.**

kakamua *inv. of* **kakamia.**

[1]**kakara*** (–) struggle, combat, hand-to-hand fighting, scuffle. *Cf.* **kikiri, kukuru.**

[2]**kakara** (–) kakara (variety of vegetable).

kakasi (–) *see* **ukakasi.**

kakata feel pain, be in pain.

kakatua break, break off; tear off *(with the teeth). appl.* **kakatulia.** *intr.* **kakatuka.**

kakawana 1. be strong/powerful/muscular. 2. (ma-) athlete.

[1]**kaki*** [*Pers.*] (–) kaki (kind of cloth).

[2]**kaki*** [*Pers.*] (–) kaki (kind of pastry made of rice-flour and sugar).

kakindu (–) kakindu (variety of plant, *Striga pubiflora*).

[1]**kala** (–) large mongoose.

[2]**kala*, kola** [*Engl.*] (–) collar. (= **ukosi.**)

[3]**kala*** (–) *rare, liter.* word.

kalab* (–) rabies, hydrophobia. *Cf.* **kelb.**

kalafati*, kalfati 1. *naut.* caulk. *appl.* **kalafatia.** *pass.* **kalafatiwa.** 2. (–) caulking material.

kalakonje (–) kalakonje (kind of wild cat).

[1]**kalala, karara** (ma-) woody covering of the flower-stem of the coconut *(used as firewood).*

[2]**kalala** (ma-): **– la nyuki.** honeycomb; *(fig.)* grill, gridwork *(something resembling a honeycomb).*

kalambezi (–) kalambezi (kind of mackerel).

kalamka, karamka be alert/intelligent/quick-witted. *interj.* –! Watch out! Look sharp! *appl.* **kalamkia.** outwit/get the better of someone, cheat. *caus.* **kalamsha.** enliven, revive, cheer up. *appl.-pass.* **kalamkiwa.** be cheated.

kalamu* (–) 1. pen, penholder. 2.: **– ya lisasi** (mate). pencil. **chonga –.** sharpen a pencil. **– ya wino.** (fountain-)pen.

kalamzi *adj.* quick-witted, witty, sharp-tongued. *Cf.* **kalamka.**

kalanga (–, ma-) *see* **karanga.**

kalasha* (–) small elephant-tusk.

kalasia*, karasia [*Ind.*] (–) small metal jug.

kale 1. (–) the past, past ages, antiquity. **watu wa –.** ancestors. *prov.* **mavi ya – hayanuki.** The filth of ancient times does not smell. 2. *adv.* earlier, formerly. **hapo –.** long ago, once upon a time. **zamani za –.** in ancient times. **tangu –.** long since, long ago. **– na –.** a very long time ago. *Cf.* **kikale, mkale.**

kalenda* [*Engl.*] (–) calendar. *coll.* **– iko mbali.** There's a long time to go until payday.

kalfati* *see* **kalafati.**

kali *adj.* 1. sharp. **kisu kikali.** a sharp knife. 2. sharp, hot, sour, strong *(of foods, etc.).* **siki ni –.** The vinegar is sour. **tembo –.** strong palm-wine. 3. strong, scorching, intense. **jua –.** a scorching sun. 4. *fig.* violent, cruel, wild, vehement, severe. **simba ni nyama mkali.** The lion is a wild animal/a beast of prey. **hukumu –.** a severe verdict. 5. distressing, urgent. **swali –.** sore point/subject, urgent matter. *Cf.* **makali, ukali,** *and also* **karipia, karipio.**

kalia *appl. of* [1]**kaa.**

kalibu* (–) 1. mold, form, matrix *(for casting metal, concrete, etc.).* 2. heating pot, furnace.

kalifu*, kilifu (*usually refl.* **jikalifu**) force/drive oneself; torment oneself. *Cf.* **takalifu, ukalifu, utakalifu.**

kalika *intr. of* [1]**kaa.**

kalikana *intr.-ass. of* **¹kaa.**

kalima* (–) *arch.* word. *Cf.* **mkalimani, mkalimu, ukalimani.**

kalipia *see* **karipia.**

kalisha *caus. of* **¹kaa.**

kaliwa *pass. of* **¹kaa.**

kalme* (–) *see* **galme.**

kaltiveta* [*Engl.*] (–) *agric.* cultivator.

kalua* [*Ind.?*] **(ma-)** Kalua (name of a sect of Indian fishermen).

¹kama* (*rare* **kana**) *conj. & adv.* 1. if. **– ukitaka.** if you wish. **– ningemwambia angefanya.** If I told him, he would do it. 2. as, like; about, approximately. **lia – mtoto.** scream like a child. **– upendavyo.** as you like. **– hivi.** like this; for example. **– maji.** watery, fluid. **– nini** (*rare* **kamani**). extraordinarily (*lit.:* like what). **anakimbia – nini.** He ran extraordinarily fast. **– shilingi kumi.** about ten shillings. 3. than *(in comparisons)*. **bora dhahabu – fedha.** Gold is more valuable than silver. 4. (*also* **ya –**) that *(conj.)*. **tumeona – aliondoka.** We have seen that he went away. 5. whether. **walimwambia (kama) aje.** They called to him (and asked) whether he was coming. **kama ... kama.** whether ... or.

²kama press, press out; milk. *appl.* **kamia.** squeeze someone dry (*i.e.*, extort something from him). *fig.* extort, demand insistently, threaten. *appl.-ass.* **kamiana.** *intr.* **kamika.** *caus.* **kamisha, kamiza.** *inv.* **kamua.** press (out), squeeze, crush. **kamua mafuta.** extract oil. **kamua maziwa.** milk. **kamua nguo.** wring out clothes. *inv.-appl.* **kamulia.** *inv.-intr.* **kamulika.** *inv.-caus.* **kamulisha.** *inv.-pass.* **kamuliwa.** *Cf.* **kamio, kikamulio, ukamio.**

¹kamani *see* **¹kama 2.**

²kamani* [*Pers.*] (–) watch spring, mainspring.

kamari* (–) game of chance *(in gen.: any game played for money)*. **cheza –.** play for money, gamble.

kamasi (ma-) (*usually* **makamasi**) 1. mucus discharge from the nose. **futa –.** blow one's nose. **vuta –.** breathe heavily, pant. 2. cold in the head, sniffles. **siwezi –.** I have a cold in the head. **toa (penga) –.** blow one's nose.

kamata 1. seize, grasp; catch, detain. **– kwa mtego.** catch in a trap. **– mwizi.** catch a thief. *appl.* **kamatia.** *intr.* **kamatika.** be seizable/tangible, palpable. **hewa haikamatiki.** Air is not palpable. 2. *sing.* influenza, pneumonia.

¹kamba* (–) rope, cord, twine, string. **– ya nazi.** rope made of coconut fibers. **– ya ulayiti.** rope of European manufacture. **funga (piga) –.** tie/lace up. **suka (sokota) –.** make rope. *sport:* **mvutano wa –.** tug-of-war. *fig.:* **mvutano**

wa – ya siasa. political wire-pulling. *Cf.* **ukambaa.**

^{2}**kamba** (–), **mkamba** (mi-) lobster, crayfish, crab, shrimp. **meno ya –.** crab's claws. **– wa pwani (bahari).** land (sea) crab. **– mdogo.** shrimp, prawn.

^{3}**kamba** (ma-): **– ya asali.** honeycomb.

kambaa* (ma-) 1. rope *(braided with strips of leaves).* 2. whip. (= **ukambaa.**) *Cf.* ^{1}**kamba.**

kambare (–, ma-) (kind of) catfish, barbel, mudfish.

kambi* [*Engl.*] (–) 1. camp, camping-place. **piga (panga) –.** pitch camp. **vunja –.** break camp. 2. *recent, pol.* camp, bloc. **– ya (ki)soshialisti.** socialist camp/bloc.

kambo (–) relationship by remarriage, step-relationship. **mtoto wa –.** stepchild. **baba (mama) wa –.** stepfather (stepmother). **kikambo.** *adj. & adv.* typical of a step-parent, in the way a stepparent typically behaves.

kambuka 1. dry up, wither. 2. *fig.* lose strength, become weak.

kambusi (–) *see* ^{1}**gambusi,** ^{2}**gambusi.**

kame *adj.* desolate, waste, empty, uncultivated, uninhabited. *Cf.* **ukame.**

kamera* [*Engl.*] (–) camera. **kazi ya –.** photography.

kamia *appl. of* ^{2}**kama.**

kamili* 1. end, complete, perfect. *appl.* **kamilia.** *intr.* **kamilika.** be whole/complete/perfect. *caus.* **kamilisha.** 2. (*also* **kamilifu**) *adj.* complete, perfect, whole, intact. *Cf.* **takamali, ukamilifu.**

kamilifu* *see* **kamili** 2.

kamio (ma-) (*usually* **makamio**) *rare* 1. threat, demand. 2. reproach, reprimand; criticism. *Cf.* ^{2}**kama.**

kamisheni* [*Engl.*] (–) *see* **komisheni.**

kamiti* (–) *see* **komiti.**

kamo (–) *arch.* sieve. (= **chekecheke, chungio.**)

kampuni*, kumpuni (*rare* **kompania**) [*Engl.*] (–, ma-) 1. (business) company, firm. **– ya biashara.** business company. **– ya kuchimba barabara.** street railway company. 2. *mil.* company.

kamsa*, kabsa (–) 1. alarm, danger signal. **piga –.** sound an alarm. 2. *mil.* reveille.

kamua *inv. of* ^{2}**kama.**

kamus* (–) *see* **kamusi.**

kamusi*, kamus (–) 1. dictionary, glossary. 2. encyclopedia.

kamwe *adv.* *(at the end of neg. sentences)* not at all, by no means, absolutely not, never. **sitaki –.** I definitely do not want that.

[1]**kana** deny, reject, repudiate, refuse to recognize. **– deni.** repudiate a debt. **– rafiki.** disown a friend. *appl.* **kania.** *appl.-refl.* **jikania.** justify oneself. *caus.* **kanya.** reprove, censure; refuse. *inv.-caus.* **kanusha.** dare someone to disagree; *(in an int. sense)* deny, refute. *Cf.* [2]**kano, mkana, mkanya, mkanyo.**

[2]**kana*, gana** [*Port.?*] (–, ma-) *naut.* tiller.

[3]**kana*** *see* [1]**kama.**

Kanani* Palestine.

kanchiri* (–) cloth worn by women to support the breasts, *(recent)* brassiere (= **sidiria.**)

[1]**kanda** (–, ma-) (*also* **kikandi, vi-**) grain-sack *(made of matting).*

[2]**kanda** *pl. of* **ukanda.**

[3]**kanda** knead, press. **– unga (udongo)** knead dough (clay). *fig.* massage. **– mwili.** massage the body. *appl.* **kandia.** *intr.* **kandika,** *usually used transitively:* plaster a house with clay. *stat.-int.* **kandamiza.** impress, compress, exert pressure; oppress. *stat.-caus.* **kandamisha.** *Cf.* **kandiko, mkandaji, mkandamizo,** [1]**mkando, ukandamizwaji.**

kandamiza *stat.-int. of* [3]**kanda.**

kandanda (–) *rare* 1. football game. 2. football.

kandarinya*, kanderinya [*Port.*] (–) *arch.* teakettle. (= **birika, buli.**)

[1]**kande** (–) 1. *dial.* supply of food, provisions. 2. *rare* industry.

[2]**kande** (–) kande (a special dish prepared for New Year's Day [Nairuzi] in which seven kinds of grain are included).

kanderinya* (–) *see* **kandarinya.**

kandika *intr. of* [3]**kanda.**

kandiko (ma-) *rare* clay coating (on the walls of a house). *Cf.* [3]**kanda.**

kandili* (ma-) lantern, lamp.

kando 1. (–) (*also* **ukando**) side, corner, edge. **– ya mto.** bank of a river. **– zote.** on all sides. 2. (*also* **– ya**) *adv.* sideways, along, aside; by, next to. **simama –.** stand aside. **– ya nyumba.** at the side of the house. *red.* **kandokando** (*or* **kandokando ya**): **– ya mto.** along the river.

kandokando *see* **kando.**

[1]**kanga** (–) *ornith.* (common) guinea fowl *(Numida mitrata).*

[2]**kanga** (–) cotton cloth *(with designs in several colors)* worn by women.

[3]**kanga** (ma-) *see* **kaanga.**

kang'a *see* **kanganya.**

kangaga (ma-) 1. (species of) reed, flag. 2. (species of) fern.

[1]**kangaja** (ma-) kangaja (small mandarin orange). *Cf.* **mkangaja.**

[2]**kangaja** (–) kangaja (kind of fish).

[3]**kangaja** (–) kangaja (variety of tall grass growing usually in stagnant water).

kanganya, kang'a confuse, surprise; intrigue.

kangara (–) beer made from corn-husks and sweetened with honey.

kang'ata 1. feel pain. 2. (–) rheumatic pains.

kango (ma-) *see* **kaango.**

kani* (–) 1. strength, energy. **penda kwa –.** to love passionately. 2. vexation, anger.

kaniki* (–) 1. (dark blue) cotton cloth. 2. kaniki (article of women's clothing).

kanisa* (–, ma-) 1. (Christian) church, chapel. 2. *rare* mosque.

kanji (–) starch, starch-flour. (= [1]**wanga.**)

kanju* [*Ind.*] (ma-) fruit of the cashew tree. *Cf.* **mkanju.**

[1]**kano** (ma-) *augment. of* [1]**mkano.**

[2]**kano, karo** (ma-) *rare* 1. refusal, denial, disavowal. 2. sudden fit of anger. *Cf.* [1]**kana.**

kanseli* [*Germ.* Kanzlei?] (–) chancery *(of an embassy)*, consulate.

kantara* (–) *rare* bridge. (= **daraja.**)

kantini* [*Engl.*] (–) canteen, bar.

kanu (ma-) 1. wild cat. 2. marten, weasel.

kanuni* (–) rule, regulation, precept; (essential) condition, principle; theory. **– za barabarani.** traffic regulations. **majeshi ya –.** regular army/troops. **– tano za kuishi pamoja kwa amani.** the five principles of peaceful coexistence. **hana – ya kuja.** He doesn't come as a rule. **sina –.** I am not certain. **– ya sheria.** lawbook. **–a –.** unalterable, irrevocable, necessary.

kanusha *inv.-caus. of* [1]**kana.**

kanwa (vi-) *see* **kinywa.**

kanya *caus. of* [1]**kana.**

kanyaga 1. step/tread/stamp on, trample down. *Cf.* **kanyagio.** 2. copulate *(of a male bird).*

kanyagio (ma-) (bicycle) pedal. *Cf.* **kanyaga.**

kanyo (ma-) *see* **mkanyo.**

kanza *caus. of* [1]**kaanga.**

kanzi* (–) (hidden) treasure, valuable.

kanzo, kaanzo (ma-) heating, warming (up). (= **akiba, hazina, dafina.**) *Cf.* [1]**kaanga.**

kanzu* (–) kanzu (long, white outer garment, the old traditional costume of Swahili men). – **ya mfuto.** simple kanzu. – **ya darizi.** embroidered kanzu.

kao (ma-) (*usually* **makao**) dwelling, residence. *Cf.* [1]**kaa.**

[1]**kapa** (–) sleeveless shirt. *Cf.* **kwapa?**

[2]**kapa** *adv.*: **enda –.** lose *(in a card-game). coll.* **amekwenda –.** He owns nothing.

kapani* [*Pers.*] (–) (kind of) scales, balance.

kapatula (–) *see* [1]**kaputula,** [2]**kaputula.**

kapela, kapera (ma-) unmarried man. (= **mvulana, mseja.**)

kapera (ma-) *see* **kapela.**

[1]**kapi** (ma-) chaff, husks. **makapi ya mpunga.** rice husks.

[2]**kapi** (–, ma-) pulley.

kapilari* [*Engl.*] (–) 1. *phy.* capillary action. 2. *anat.* capillary (vessel).

kapile (–) any kind of cooked food sold in the market.

kapteni*, kepteni [*Engl.*] (ma-) *naut.* & *sport* captain. – **wa manowari.** captain of a warship.

kaptura (–) *see* [1]**kaputula.**

kapu (ma-) *augment. of* **kikapu.**

kapungu (–) kapungu (1. kind of eagle. 2. variety of shark).

kaputa (–) kaputa (kind of dance performed in exorcising spirits).

kaputi* [*Germ.?*] *adj.*: **nusu –.** stunned, stupefied.

[1]**kaputula, kaptura, kapatula** (–) (short) trousers, shorts.

[2]**kaputula, kapatula** (–) *med.* grippe, influenza.

[1]**kara*** (ma-) splinter, shaving.

[2]**kara*** (ma-) *Isl.* reading from the Koran.

karabai* (–) 1. lamp (burning gasoline, kerosine). 2. *recent* electric light bulb.

karabu* *see* **karibu.**

karadha* (–) loan, credit *(without interest)*. **omba –.** raise a loan. **pa –.** give a loan. *Cf.* **karidhi.**

karafuu*, **karofuu, garafuu** (–) clove(s). *Cf.* **mkarafuu.**

karagosi* (–) *see* **karangosi.**

karaha*, **ikirahi** (–) aversion, distaste, antipathy, abhorrence, rejection, disfavor. *Cf.* **kirahi, kirihi, makuruhi.**

karai (ma-) 1. (metal) washbasin. 2. cooking-pot. **– la kukaanga.** frying-pan.

karakana*, **karkana** [*Pers.*] (–) workshop, factory.

karakoli*, **karakoni** (–) *see* **korokoroni.**

[1]**karama*** (–) 1. honor, respect, esteem, favor. **ana –.** He enjoys respect. 2. worth, value, importance, weight. **maneno yake yana karama.** His words have importance/carry weight. *Cf.* [1]**kirimu, karimu.**

[2]**karama*** *see* **karimu.**

karamka *see* **kalamka.**

karamu* (–) party, festival, festivity, celebration; feast, banquet. **fanya –.** give a feast. **enda karamuni.** go to a festival. **– ya kiserikali.** state banquet. *Cf.* **kirimu, karimu.**

[1]**karanga, kalanga** (–, ma-) 1. peanut, groundnut *(usually when roasted)*. 2.: **– mwitu.** a perennial herb *(Desmodium adscendens)*.

[2]**karanga** *see* [1]**kaanga.**

karangosi*, **karagosi** [*Turk.*] (–) puppet.

karani*, **kerani** (ma-) clerk, secretary, office-worker, bookkeeper. (= **katibu, mwandishi.**) **– wa kodi.** tax-official. *Cf.* **ukarani.**

karantini* [*Engl.*] (–) *med.* quarantine.

karara (ma-) *see* [1]**kalala.**

karasa (–) mongoose, ichneumon *(Herpestes ichneumon)*.

karasia* (–) *see* **kalasia.**

karata* [*Port.*] (–) playing card. **gawa –.** deal cards. **cheza –.** play cards.

karatasi*, **kartasi** (–) paper, list. **kipande cha –.** a piece of paper. **– ya kukaushia wino.** blotting paper. **– ya kunakilisha.** tracing paper, carbon paper. **– ya shashi.** tissue paper. *Cf.* **kikaratasi.**

kardinali* (ma-) *see* **kadinali.**

karela* [*Ind.*] (–) karela (an annual plant, *Momordica morgose/charantia)*.

karema be sterile/barren.

Kariakoo* [*Port.*] Kariakoo (center of Dar es Salaam).

karibia*, **kurubia** come closer, approach; be near. *ass.* **karibiana.** meet. *caus.* **karibisha.** bring closer, approximate; invite, make welcome. **karibisha chakula.** offer food. **karibisha kiti.** invite someone to sit down. *pass.* **karibiwa.** *Cf.* **karibisho, karibu, mkaribishaji.**

karibisho* (ma-) welcome. *Cf.* **karibia.**

karibu* (*rare* **karabu**) 1. (–) (close) relative. **watu hawa ni ndugu zangu wa –.** These people are my close relatives. 2. *also* – ya [na]) *adv.* near, in the vicinity. **– yangu.** near me. **tunakaa – ya (na) mji huu.** We live near the city. 3.: **hivi – (karibuni).** recently, not long ago; soon. 4. **karibu!** *interj.* (*plur.* **karibuni!**) Come in! Welcome! *(in response to the query* Hodi?). **karibu kitini!** Please be seated. *Cf.* **karibia.**

karidhi*, **kiridhi** *rare* 1. lend *(money).* 2. borrow *(money). appl.* **karidhia.** *pass.* **karidhiwa.** *Cf.* **karadha.**

karii* (ma-) (recognized) expert/authority on poetry/literature, literary critic. **alitoa vyeti na tuzo kwa washindi wa mashairi, naye akiwa – wa washairi.** He awarded the prizes to the winners of the poetry contest, for he is an authority on poetry.

karimu*, **kerimu, kirimu, karama** *adj.* generous, magnanimous; hospitable. *Cf.* [1]**kirimu, mkarimu, ukarimu.**

karini* (–) *see* **karne.**

karipia, kalipia scold/reproach/reprimand someone; be vexed with/angry at someone. *pass.* **karipiwa.** *Cf.* **kali.**

karipio (ma-) scolding, rebuke, reprimand. *Cf.* **kali, karipia.**

kariri* say again, repeat; recite. *appl.* **kariria.** *caus.* **karirisha.** *pass.* **kaririwa.** *Cf.* **kikariri.**

karkana* [*Pers.*] (–) *see* **karakana.**

karne*, **karini, karni** (–) century. **– ya sasa.** the present century, modern times.

karni* (–) *see* **karne.**

[1]**karo*** (–) pay, remuneration, fee *(usually in kind);* recompense, reward.

[2]**karo*** (–) *see* [2]**kano.**

karofuu* (–) *see* **karafuu.**

karoti* [*Engl.*] (–) carrot.

kartasi* (–) *see* **karatasi.**

[1]**kasa***, **kassa** [*Pers.?*] (–) kassa (sea-tortoise).

[2]**kasa*** *adv.* less (than), shorter (than). **saa sita – robo.** 11:45 o'clock (*lit.:* sixth hour less a quarter).

[3]**kasa** *see* **kaza.**

kasabu* (–) cloth of gold, brocade.

[1]**kasama*** (–) *see* [1]**mkasama.**

[2]**kasama*** (–) kasama (an oath).

kasarobo* *see* [2]**kasa.**

kasha* [*Port.*] (ma-) box, chest, case. **– la fedha.** strongbox, safe.

kashabi* [*Pers.*] *rare* crush, squeeze out, press *(sugarcane).*

kashabu* (–) 1. wooden rod *(on a loom).* 2. hollow bead *(of gold, silver, or glass).*

kashata* (–) kashata (a confection made of burnt sugar and grated coconut).

kashida* (–) shawl, scarf, neckerchief.

kashifa* (–) 1. unveiling, exposure. 2. slander, libel; false statements about a person, or secret facts the revelation of which is injurious to him. (= **aibisha, chongea, singizia**). *Cf.* **kashifu, ukashifu.**

kashifu* unveil, reveal, expose; slander, offend, insult; throw suspicion on someone. *appl.* **kashifia.** *intr.* **kashifika.** *pass.* **kashifiwa.** *Cf.* **kashifa.**

[1]**kasi*** (–) 1. intensity, energy, exertion, effort. 2. hurry, haste, speed. **tia (piga) –.** make an effort, exert oneself. 3. *adv.* quickly, speedily; energetically, vigorously. **enda (kwa) –.** run very fast. *red. (int.).* **kasikasi.** *adj.* distorted.

[2]**kasi** (–, ma-) calabash *(for storing milk or palm-wine).*

[1]**kasia** (ma-) *naut.* oar. **piga (vuta) makasia.** row. **– la nyuma.** steering-oar, rudder.

[2]**kasia** (ma-) kasia (species of antelope, oribi).

kasiba* (–) pipe, tube. **– ya bunduki.** *mil.* rifle-barrel. *fig.* **mdomo kama –.** small, round mouth *(evidence of female beauty).*

kasida* (–) *see* **kusudi** 2.

kasidi* *see* **kusudi.**

kasikasi *red. (int.) of* [1]**kasi.**

[1]**kasiki*** (ma-) 1. robe, gown *(of a clergyman).* 2. *rel.* chalice, communion-cup.

[2]**kasiki*** (–, ma-) large earthenware jug *(for storing water).*

kasimile* (–) coconut oil.

kasimu* *rare* divide (up). (= **gawa, gawanya.**) *Cf.* [1]**mkasama.**

kasirani* (–) anger, annoyance, vexation. *Cf.* [1]**kasiri.**

[1]**kasiri*** (*usually caus.* **kasirisha**) irritate, vex, annoy; make angry, infuriate. *appl.* **kasiria.** *intr.* **kasirika.** be annoyed/irritated/angry. *intr.-appl.* **kasirikia.** be annoyed with/angry at someone. *pass.* **kasiriwa.** *Cf.* **kasirani.**

[2]**kasiri*** (–) *rare* end. (= **mwisho, hatima.**)

kasirisha* *caus. of* [1]**kasiri.**

kasisi* (**ma-**) priest. (= **padre.**) *Cf.* **ukasisi.**

kaskazi* (–) 1. north wind, northeasterly wind. 2. north. **kaskazini.** in a northerly direction. 3. time of the northeast monsoon, hot season of the year (December-March).

kasoro* 1. (–) fault, defect. **gari hii ina –.** This car has something wrong with it. 2. *adv.* less, except, but. **nimepata vitabu vyote – vitabu vitatu.** I have received all the books but three. *Cf.* [2]**kasa.**

kasri* (–) palace.

kassa* (–) *see* [1]**kasa.**

kassi* (–) twined thread. **tia (piga) –.** twist, twine.

kastabini*, kustabini, kustabani, kustubani (–) thimble.

kasuku (–) parrot. (= **dura.**)

kasumba* [*Ind.*] (–) opium. (= **afyuni.**)

kaswende (–) *med.* syphilis.

[1]**kata*** 1. cut (off). **– kwa kisu.** cut with a knife. **– nguo.** cut out a garment. 2. chop, fell. **– mti.** chop down/fell a tree. **– kuni.** chop firewood. 3. cut up, divide up; reduce, abbreviate; (*math.*) subtract. 4. buy, purchase, order. *fig.* **– njia.** shorten/block a road. **– mshahara.** reduce/cut wages. **– kiu (njaa).** appease thirst (hunger). **– shauri.** decide, conclude. **– hukumu (maneno).** make a decision. **– tamaa.** lose hope. **– shauri.** frustrate a plan. *red. (int.).* **katakata.** cut into small pieces. *appl.* **katia.** *appl.-ass.* **katiana.** settle accounts (with each other), strike a balance. *intr.* **katika. ukuni huu haukatiki.** This wood cannot be cut. *caus.* **katiza.** 1. interrupt. **katiza maneno.** interrupt a conversation, break in. 2. do away with, end. *Cf.* [2]**kataa, kato, mkata, mkataji, mkate, mkato, mkatizo, ukata.**

[2]**kata** (–, **ma-**) dipper, ladle *(made of a coconut shell or of wood).*

[3]**kata** (–, **ma-**) pad *(made of grass)* serving as a rest for loads carried on the head.

[4]**kata*** (–, **ma-**) *see* [2]**kataa.**

[1]**kataa*** 1. refuse, decline, reject (something); refuse to do something. *appl.* **katalia. nimemkatalia.** I have refused him/turned him down. *intr.* **katalika.** *pass.* **kataliwa.** *caus.* **kataza.** forbid, prohibit; prevent. **kataza watu wasiende.** forbid the people to go. 2. *adj.* final, definitive. **neno hili –.** This is the final word. *Cf.* **katao, katavu, katazo, makataa, mkataa, mkatavu, ukatavu, ukatazaji.**

[2]**kataa***, **kata** (–, ma-) part, section, division. – **ya nchi.** district. – **ya nyumba.** room. – **la kitabu.** section/chapter of a book; page. *Cf.* [1]**kata.**

katabahu* *at the end of letters, preceding the signature* (*lit.* 'he wrote it'). *Cf.* **kitabu, katibu.**

katadole (–) *ornith.* grosbeak weaver (= **yombiyombi**).

katakata *red. (int.) of* [1]**kata.**

katani* (–) sisal, hemp *(the fiber). Cf.* **mkatani.**

katao* (ma-) *rare* refusal, rejection, denial. *Cf.* [1]**kataa.**

katara (–) 1. old/dilapidated vehicle. 2. *coll.* motor bus.

katavu* *adj., rare* stubborn, argumentative. *Cf.* [1]**kataa, mkatavu.**

kataza* (*caus. of* [1]**kataa.**) forbid, prohibit; prevent. *Cf.* **katazo.**

katazo* (ma-) (*usually* **makatazo**) 1. prohibition. 2. refusal, denial. 3. embargo. *Cf.* [1]**kataa, kataza.**

kati, katikati 1. (–) middle, center. – **ya mahali.** in the middle of the place. **wakati wa –.** interval, interim, interregnum. 2. (*also* – **ya**) *adv. & prep.* in the middle/midst of, between. **weka –.** put/place in middle. 3.: **-a –.** central. **komiti ya kati.** central committee.

katiba* (–) text, piece of writing, document; decree; decision, declaration; *(pol.)* constitution. *Cf.* **kitabu.**

katibu* 1. write. *appl.* **katibia.** *appl.-ass.* **katibiana.** correspond (with each other), make a settlement/contract/treaty. 2. (ma-) writer, clerk, secretary. – **mwenezi.** secretary for propaganda. *Cf.* **kitabu, ukatibu.**

[1]**katika** *prep.* in, at, with, from, to, on; during; concerning. **ingia – mji.** go to/into a city. **toka – nchi.** come from a country. **panda – mlima.** climb (up) a mountain. – **kuenda.** while going. – **wakati wote.** during the whole time. – **habari zile.** concerning those reports.

[2]**katika** *intr. of* [1]**kata.**

katikati *see* **kati.**

katili* 1. (ma-) murderer. 2. *adj.* murderous; *(fig.)* bloodthirsty, cruel. *Cf.* **mkatili, ukatili.**

katiti 1. *adj.* very small, tiny. 2. *adv.* very little, not much.

katiza *caus. of* [1]**kata.**

kato* (ma-) section, fragment. *Cf.* [1]**kata.**

katoliki* [*Engl.*] *adj.* Catholic. **kanisa (ya) –.** Catholic church. *Cf.* **kikatoliki.**

[1]**katu*** [*Ind.*] (–) katu (gum for chewing with betel).

[2]**katu*** *interj.* no! *(emph.)*

katua clean, polish, shine up. **– fedha.** polish silver. *appl.* **katulia.** *intr.* **katuka.** *Cf.* **kwatua.**

kauka become dry, dry up. **nchi imekauka.** The ground is dried up. *fig.* **sauti imemkauka.** He is hoarse (*lit.:* his voice has dried up). *fig., coll.* **nimekauka,** I am broke. I have no money. *caus.* **kausha.** dry something. **wamekausha matunda.** They have been drying fruit. *Cf.* [2]**kausha,** [1]**kavu, kikausho, kikavu, mkavu, ukavu.**

kaule* [*Ind.*] *sing.* china, porcelain, imported earthenware. **sahani za –.** (imported) crockery. *Cf.* **kauri.**

kauleni* **(ma-)** deceitful/untrustworthy person.

kauli* **(–)** 1. expression, voice. **kwa – moja.** unanimous. 2. advice; prescription, regulation; report.

kaumu* **(–)** 1. crowd, mass. **– ya watu.** a gathering of people. 2. representative, delegate.

kaumwa **(ma-)** kaumwa (root of the mkaumwa tree, serving as a medicine for dysentery).

kauri*, kaure [*Ind.*] **(–)** cowrie shell. **vyombo vya –.** porcelain, china. *Cf.* **kaule.**

[1]**kausha** *caus. of* **kauka.**

[2]**kausha** **(wa-), kikausha** **(vi-)** one who brings bad luck, ill-omened person. *Cf.* **kauka.**

kauta **(–)** dust, grit.

[1]**kavu, kafu** *adj.* 1. dry, dried up. **kuni –.** dry firewood. **mto mkavu.** a dried-up stream. 2. *fig.* sarcastic; deceitful, cunning; impudent, insolent. **mtu mkavu wa macho.** a deceitful, insolent person. *Cf.* **kauka, kikavu, mkavu, ukavu.**

[2]**kavu*** [*Engl.*] **(–)** curve. (= **mstari uliopinda.**) **– kuelekea kulia.** curve to the right.

[1]**kawa, kawili** **(–, ma-)** a plaited cover or lid *(for covering foods). prov.* **tulingane sawasawa kama sahani na –.** We want to be like dish and lid (*i.e.*, live in harmony with each other).

[2]**kawa** **(–)** mold, mildew, blight.

[3]**kawa** (*and appl.* **kawia**) be delayed, tarry, linger, be late, be in arrears. *appl.-caus.* **kawilisha.** keep back, hold up, delay. *caus.* **kawisha.** put off, postpone, adjourn. *Cf.* **ukawiaji.**

kawadi*, kuwadi **(–)** procurer, pimp. *Cf.* **kawadia, mkuwadi.**

kawadia* procure, pander. *Cf.* **kawadi.**

kawaida*, **kaida** (–) 1. rule, habit, regulation; custom, usage; system, form, scheme. 2. norm, standard. **mambo ya –.** an ordinary, everyday matter. **fuata –.** follow/comply with a rule/custom. **–a –, kwa –.** regular, ordinary, usual. **kamiti ya –.** standing committee. *Cf.* **kiada.**

kawe (vi-) *see* **kiwe.**

kawia *see* ^{3}**kawa.**

kawili (–, ma-) *see* ^{1}**kawa.**

^{1}**kaya** (ma-) kaya (kind of shellfish).

^{2}**kaya*** [*Zu.?*] (–) town, village.

^{3}**kaya** *pl. of* **ukaya.**

kayamba (–) rattle.

kayaya (–) *rare* trouble, difficulty. (= **matata.**)

kaza, kasa (*caus. of* ^{1}**kaa?**) 1. fasten, tighten, make fast, hold tight. **– kamba.** fasten, pull tight a rope/cord. **– sukurubu.** exert pressure. 2. exert oneself, intensify one's efforts. **– (mwendo) mbio.** move faster, run. *fig.* persist, insist on. *appl.* **kazia macho.** fix the eyes on something. *ass.* **kazana.** hold together. *Cf.* **kikaza, kikazo, mkazo.**

kazi (–) 1. work, employment, occupation; (military) service. **– ya kulima.** agricultural work. **– ya hiari.** voluntary work. **– ya kibaharia.** service in the navy. **mfanya –.** worker. **fanya –.** to work. **shika –.** go to work. *loc.* **kazini.** at work. 2. business, affairs. **– ya bahari.** naval affairs. 3. product of (skilled) work, art, decoration. **kanzu ya –.** decorated (embroidered) kanzu. 4. duty, obligation. 5. specialty. *Cf.* **kaza (?).**

kazo (ma-) *see* **mkazo.**

kazoakazoa (–) *term of abuse* (scavenger? *Cf.* **zoa**).

ke *adj.* female, feminine. *Cf.* **jike, kike, kuke, mke, mwanamke, uke.**

kebe (ma-) *see* **mkebe.**

kebehi* insult, abuse, offend, injure.

kecha (–) jealousy, envy.

kedhabu* (–) *see* **kadhabu.**

kefiakefia *see* **kefyakefya.**

^{1}**kefu!*** (*also* **kefule, sefule**) *interjection of surprise/disgust/indignation.* 1. Shame! You scoundrel! 2. It is not worth mentioning.

^{2}**kefu*** *see* ^{2}**kifu.**

kefule!* *interj.* *see* ^{1}**kefu.**

kefyakefya, kefiakefia torment, annoy, vex, tease; nag; discourage, depress (= **sumbua, tesa, chokoza, udhi.**)

kejekeje *adj., rare* loose, slack. (= **pwaya, legea.**)

kejeli* deride, mock, make fun of someone; slander, malign.

[1]**kekee** (–) drill, auger, brace and bit.

[2]**kekee** (–) broad silver bracelet. (= **kikuku, bangili, urembo.**)

keketa cut (by sawing back and forth, as with a dull knife). – **meno.** grit/grind one's teeth. *Cf.* **mkeketo.**

kekevu, chechevu (–) hiccup(s). **fanya –.** have the hiccups.

keki* [*Engl.*] (–) cake, pastry.

kelb* (–) *rare* dog. (= **mbwa.**) *Cf.* **kalab.**

kelele (**ma-**) (*also* **ukelele, –, ma-**) noise, shouting, tumult, uproar. **piga –.** be noisy, shout, scream. **nena kwa –.** interrupt, interject. *interj.* **kelele!** Quiet! **sema kwa –.** talk loudly.

keleti *see* **keti.**

keleza *see* **kereza.**

kem* *adv.* how much? how many? what amount?

[1]**kema** *dial.* shout, roar, yell, scream. *appl.* **kemea.** scold. *caus.* **kemesha, kemeza.**

[2]**kema** take off, peel *(fruits).*

keme (–) call, shout. *Cf.* **kemea.**

kemea scold, reprimand (someone). *Cf.* [1]**kema, keme, kemeo, ukemi.**

kemeo (**ma-**) *rare* rebuke, reprimand; warning, threat. *Cf.* **kemea.**

[1]**kenda** *num. (arch., dial.)* nine. **–a –.** ninth. (= **tisa.**)

[2]**kenda** (< **ka-enda**) *see* **ka** *and* **enda.**

kende (**ma-**) *anat.* scrotum, *(pl.)* testicles.

kenga deceive, dupe, cheat, hoax, bamboozle. *appl.* **kengea.** *intr.* **kengeka.** *caus.* **kengeza.**

kenge, mburukenge (–) monitor lizard *(Varanus niloticus).*

kengee (–) (*also* **ukengee**) 1. blade *(of a knife or sword),* spearhead. 2. ray of the sun, sunbeam. **– za jua.** sunrise.

kengele (–, **ma-**) bell. **piga (gonga) –.** ring (a bell).

kengemeke *rare* rebuke, reprimand; accuse. (= **suta, laumu, shutumu, shtaki.**)

kengeua deviate, diverge, turn aside/off. **– njia.** depart from/turn off a path/road. *intr.* **kengeuka.** *caus.* **kengeusha.** *pass.* **kengeuliwa.** *Cf.* **ukengefu.**

kengewa (–) *ornith.* African kite. (= **mwewe.**)

[1]**kengeza** 1. squint. 2. (ma-) cross-eyed condition, convergence. **mtu mwenye makengeza.** a squinting/cross-eyed person. 3. *adj.* squinting/cross-eyed. **macho makengeza.** squinting eyes. *Cf.* **makengeza.**

[2]**kengeza** *caus. of* **kenga.**

kenyekenye *adv.* completely, absolutely, unconditionally.

kenyo (–) *rare* excuse, evasion. (= **danganyo, zuzuio.**)

Kepi* [*Engl.*] *sing.* Cape (of Good Hope).

kepteni* [*Engl.*] (ma-) *see* **kapteni.**

kera torment, bother, tease, worry. *Cf.* **kero, mkero.**

kerani* (ma-) *see* **karani.**

[1]**kereketa** scratch, cause irritation, prickle, cause a rough feeling *(in the throat). fig.* irritate, vex, anger. **habari hii inanikereketa sana** This report made me very angry. *appl.* **kereketea.**

[2]**kereketa** (–) rancid oil.

keremkerem (–) *ornith.* keremkerem (kind of bird, *Merops).*

[1]**kereng'ende** (–) *ornith.* (kind of) partridge, francolin.

[2]**kereng'ende** (–) dragonfly.

kereza, keleza 1. saw, file, rasp, abrade, grind. *fig.* **– meno.** grind the teeth. 2. turn *(on a lathe). Cf.* **kerezo, mkereza.**

kerezo (ma-) lathe. *Cf.* **kereza.**

kerimu* *see* **karimu,** [1]**kirimu.**

kero (ma-) unrest, disturbance; annoyance, teasing. *Cf.* **kera.**

kerosini* [*Engl.*] (–) *rare* kerosine, lamp oil.

kesha 1. be awake, not sleep, have insomnia. **nimekesha usiku kucha nikisoma.** I spent the whole night reading. *appl.* **keshea.** stay up with, watch over. **keshea na mgonjwa.** stay up with a sick person. *caus.* **keshesha, kesheza.** 2. (ma-) insomnia; night-watch, vigil. *Cf.* **kesho,** [2]**mkesha.**

kesho 1. (–) the next day. 2. *adv.* tomorrow. **– kutwa.** day after tomorrow. *Cf.* **kesha.**

kesi* [*Engl.*] (–) case (*at law*). **– ya jinai.** criminal case.

keta *rare* knock someone down, injure someone.

kete (–) 1. small cowrie shell. 2. a game played with these shells. **meno kama –.** teeth like cowrie shells *(a high compliment).*

keti (*rare* **keleti**) sit down. – **kitini.** sit down in a chair. **tafadhali –.** Please be seated. *appl.* **ketia.** *caus.* **ketisha.** keep someone from leaving; preserve, protect. *pass.* **ketiwa.** *Cf.* [1]**kaa** (?).

[1]**keu:** **kupiga –.** chew the cud. *Cf.* **cheu.**

[2]**keu** a cut made with an ax *(in order to straighten a pole; see* **keua**).

keua cut a notch *(in a pole, in order to straighten it and make it serviceable for building after a wedge has been inserted).*

khalifa* (–) *see* **halifa.**

khasara* (–) *see* **hasara.**

[1]**kia** (vi-) 1. bolt, latch *(on a door).* 2. *anat.* joint.

[2]**kia, kiwa** step over, pass, cross. **isiokia.** impassable. *Cf.* **kiuka.**

kiada* *adj.* plain, clear, distinct. **sema –.** speak slowly and clearly. *Cf.* **kawaida.**

kiafrika* [*Engl.*] *adj.:* **–a –.** African. *Cf.* **Afrika.**

kiaga (vi-) *dial.* promise, agreement, contract. *Cf.* [2]**aga.**

kiagano (vi-) *see* **agano.**

kiago (vi-) *rare* departure, farewell. *Cf.* [1]**aga.**

Kiajemi* 1. *sing.* Persian language. 2. *adv.* in the Persian manner. *Cf.* **Mwajemi, Uajemi.**

kiama* (–) *see* **kiyama.**

kiamba (vi-) *see* **mwamba.**

kiambaza, kiwambaza, kiyambaza (vi-) (outer) wall *(made of earth and rubble); (in gen.)* wall *(of a house).* *Cf.* **wamba.**

kiambo (vi-) *rare* 1. household, housekeeping, household furnishings. 2. village.

kiamerika*, kiamerikani, kimarekani [*Engl.*]: **–a –.** *adj.* American.

kiamerikani* *see* **kiamerika.**

kiamshakinywa (vi-), **chamshakinywa** (vy-) breakfast. *Cf.* **amka, kinywa.**

Kiamu *sing.* Old Swahili *(the language of Lamu preserved in literary works).*

kianga, kiangazi (vi-) clearing up *(of the weather, after rain).* **pigwa na –.** clear up. *Cf.* **angaa.**

kiangaza (vi-): – **macho.** reward for finding something lost (*lit.:* eye-brightener). *Cf.* **angaa.**

kiangazi (vi-) *see* **kianga.**

kiango (vi-) *arch.* lampstand, lamp holder. *Cf.* [1]**anga.**

kiangu (vi-) kiangu (kind of fish).

kiangushio (vi-) parachute. *Cf.* **angua.**

kiapo (vi-) 1. oath. **apa (fanya, shika) –.** swear an oath. **– cha uwongo.** perjury. *also* **lia –.** take an oath. *Cf.* **[1]la.** 2. *myth.* test, trial by ordeal. **la –.** subject oneself to a trial by ordeal. **– cha moto.** trial by fire. *Cf.* **apa.**

Kiarabu* 1. *sing.* the Arabic language. 2. *adv.* in the Arab manner. 3.: **–a –.** *adj.* Arabic, Arabian, Arab. *Cf.* **Mwarabu, Uarabu.**

kiarifa* (vi-) *gramm.* verb. *Cf.* **arifu.**

kiarusi* *sing.:* **ana –.** He trembles. *Cf.* **arusi.**

[1]kiasi* (–) 1. measure, price, value, amount. **– gani?** What is the price? How much does it cost? **– cha sehemu.** *math.* numerator. **bila –.** without measure, inexact; immoderate. 2. *fig.* moderation, temperance. **kwa –.** moderately, temperately. 3. *adv.* a little, somewhat; for a short time. **tembea –.** go walking for a short time.

[2]kiasi* (–) *mil.* charge, round *(of ammunition);* cartridge. *Cf.* **risasi.**

kiaskari*: **–a –.** *adj.* military. **utumishi wa –.** military service. *Cf.* **askari.**

kiatomiki* [*Engl.*]: **–a –.** atomic. *Cf.* **atomiki.**

kiatu (vi-) sandal, shoe. **– cha ngozi.** leather shoe. **– chepesi.** slipper. **mshona (mshoni wa) –.** shoemaker. *Cf.* **[1]kwata, kwato, liwata.**

kiazi (vi-) sweet potato. **– sena (kindoro).** white (red) sweet potato. **– kikuu.** yam. **– cha kizungu.** European potato.

[1]kibaba* (vi-) kibaba (unit of weight or capacity: about 700 g. or .56 liters). *prov.:* **haba na haba hujaza –.** Little by little fills the measure.

[2]kibaba (vi-) *dimin. of* **[1]baba.**

kibafute (vi-) kibafute (a children's game in which the identity of an object hidden in the hand must be guessed at).

kibago (vi-) stool.

kibahaluli* (vi-) *rare* 1. small torch, paper spill. 2. foolish/stupid person.

kibakuli* (vi-) *see* **bakuli.**

[1]kibali* *see* **kubali.**

[2]kibali* *sing. see* **ukubali.**

kibama (vi-) kibama (cake made of flour and bananas).

kibanawasi* (vi-) *liter.* rabbit, hare. *Cf.* **Abunuwasi.**

kibanda, kijibanda (vi-) (*dimin. of* **banda**) 1. hut, shed, lean-to; pavilion. 2.: **– cha uso.** *rare.* forehead.

kibaniko (vi-) 1. (roasting) spit. 2. *recent* toaster. *Cf.* **bana.**

kibano (vi-) *see* **mbano** 3.

Kibanyani* [*Ind.*] *sing.* language of the Banyani *(q.v.)*.

kibanzi (vi-) 1. splinter, chip, shaving. *rare:* **vibanzi vua msumeno.** sawdust. 2. *fig.* pointed instrument: skewer, etc. *Cf.* **bana.**

kibao (vi-) (*dimin. of* **bao**) 1. small board, tray, salver. 2. slate *(used by schoolchildren)*.

kibapara (vi-) 1. old, worn-out article of clothing. 2. *pejor.* poor person, beggar. 3. kind of cap.

kibaraka* (vi-) vassal, lackey; *(comm.)* reactionary. *Cf.* **baraka.**

kibaramwezi (vi-) windmill *(children's toy)*. (= **kititia** 2.)

kibarango (vi-) (*dimin. of* **mbarango**) 1. short, thick stick. 2. short, heavyset person.

kibarua* (vi-) (*dimin. of* **barua**) 1. (*also* **kijibarua**) slip of paper, card. 2. irregular employment. **kazi ya —.** work by the day. 3. worker who has no permanent employment, day laborer. 4. employment *(in gen.)*. **siku hizi hana —.** He has no employment at present, is unemployed.

kibatari* [*Pers.*] (vi-) small oil lamp.

kibatobato (vi-) *see* [1]**batobato.**

kibavu, kibavubavu, kiubavubavu *adv.* on/at/to the side, sideways. *Cf.* **ubavu.**

kibe (—) *rare* noise, shouting. (= **ukelele.**)

kibeberu 1. (vi-) *dimin. of* **beberu.** 2. **—a —.** *adj.* dictatorial, imperialistic. *Cf.* **beberu, ubeberu.**

kibemasa (—) children's game (hide-and-seek).

kibepari* [*Ind.*] (vi-) (petty) bourgeoisie. *Cf.* **bepari, ubepari.**

kiberenge* (vi-) 1. small locomotive *(narrow-gage)*. 2. *fig.* deceiver, dishonest person. 3. *rare* prostitute.

kiberiti* (—) *see* **kibiriti.**

kibete (vi-) *see* **kibeti.**

kibeti, kibweti, kibete (vi-) person or animal of less than normal size, dwarf, midget, bantam, pygmy.

kibia (vi-) (*dimin. of* [1]**bia**) 1. small earthenware pot. 2. lid of such a pot.

kibibi* [*Pers.*] (vi-) (*dimin. of* **bibi**) 1. young mistress *(eldest daughter of the house)*. 2. *liter.* princess. 3. young hen, peahen, female parrot; *(in gen.)* peacock (= **tausi**). 4. numbness, going to sleep *(of the feet)*.

kibinadamu*: **–a –.** *adj.* human, natural. *Cf.* **binadamu, ubinadamu.**

kibindo (vi-), **bindo** (ma-) fold of the loin-cloth used for carrying money or tobacco.

kibinja (vi-) whistle *(sound or instrument)*. *Cf.* **ubinja.**

kibiongo (vi-) one who stoops when he walks, a person bent over by age or illness.

kibirikizi (vi-) summons, appeal, proclamation. **piga –.** announce, proclaim.

kibiriti*, **kiberiti, kibriti** (vi-) 1. sulfur. 2. match. **ganda la –.** matchbox. **washa –.** strike a match.

kibisi (vi-) *ornith.* kibisi (species of grebe, dabchick).

kibla*, **kibula** (–) 1. *Isl.* direction of prayer *(toward Mecca)*. 2. part of a mosque where the imam stands. 3. north. **nyumba yangu inatazama –.** My house faces north. *Cf.* **kabili.**

kibobwe (vi-) *see* **kibwebwe.**

kibofu (vi-) *anat.* (urinary) bladder. *Cf.* **bofu.**

kibogoshi (vi-) small traveler's bag.

kibogoyo (vi-) 1. toothless person. 2. one who makes others laugh but does not laugh himself, funnyman, humorist *(writer of a humorous column in a newspaper, etc.)*; *(sometimes derog.)* card.'

kiboko* [*Pers.?*] (vi-) 1. hippopotamus. 2. whip made of hippopotamus hide. 3. zigzag embroidery around the neck of a kanzu.

kibole (vi-) *anat.* appendix.

kibonge (vi-) (*dimin. of* **bonge**) *pharm.* tablet, pill, capsule.

kibri* (vi-) *see* **kiburi.**

kibriti* (vi-) *see* **kiberiti.**

[1]**kibua** (vi-) kibua (a small fish).

[2]**kibua** (vi-) 1. something light/pithy. 2. *dimin. of* **bua.**

kibubutu (vi-) *rare* 1. tree-stump. 2. *fig.* stump of an amputated limb. *Cf.* **butu, butua.**

kibudu* *adv.:* **fa –.** die a natural death.

kibuhudi* (vi-) *see* **kibuhuti.**

kibuhuti*, **kibuhudi** (vi-) 1. grief, care, trouble. **shikwa na –.** have troubles. 2. foreboding, presentiment.

kibula* (vi-) *see* **kibla.**

kibuluu* [*Engl.*] 1. (–) kibuluu (kind of manioc). 2. *adj. see* **buluu.**

kibumba, kipumba (vi-) (*dimin. of* **bumba**) lump, ball; (small) package, packet; paper box.

[1]kibunzi (vi-) corncob. (= **gunzi.**)

[2]**kibunzi, kigunzi** (vi-) end of the year, last day of the year.

[3]**kibunzi** (vi-) kibunzi (children's game).

kiburi*, **kibri** (–) pride, arrogance, presumption, conceit. **fanya (onyesha, wa na) –.** be proud/arrogant/conceited. **mtu anaweza kuwa na – bila ya kukionyesha kila siku.** A person can be proud without showing it every day. *Cf.* **takabari.**

kiburu (–) *dial.* = **kibuyu.**

kiburudishaji* (vi-) a cool and refreshing confection served as dessert. *Cf.* **baridi, burudi.**

kiburudisho* (vi-) 1. rest, relaxation, refreshment, recreation, recuperation. 2. relief, alleviation *(of pain).* 3. flavor, savor. *Cf.* **baridi, burudi.**

kiburuta (vi-) (kind of) fan *(usually made of tin and used to fan a fire). Cf.* **burura.**

kibuyu (*dial.* **kiburu**) (vi-) (*dimin. of* **buyu**) (small variety of) calabash.

kibuzi (vi-) *see* **mbuzi.**

kibwana (vi-) (*dimin. of* **bwana**) 1. young master (eldest son of the house). 2. *liter.* prince.

kibwanyenye (vi-) (petty) bourgeoisie.

kibwebwe, kibobwe (vi-) (white) loincloth *(worn by women).*

kibwengo (vi-) 1. evil sea spirit. 2. dance performed in exorcising spirits.

kibweti (vi-) *see* **kibeti.**

kibwiko (vi-) 1. deformed or mutilated foot, clubfoot (= **kiguu**). 2. a person with such a deformity.

kicha (vi-) bunch, bundle *(usually of palm-leaf strips, used for plaiting mats).*

kichaa *sing.* mental disorder, insanity. (= **wazimu.**) **ana –.** He is deranged/insane.

kichaani (vi-) *bot.* kichaani (annual grass, *Striga elegans).*

kichaazi (vi-) kichaazi (variety of banana).

kichaga (vi-), **uchaga, uchala** (–) container for storing grain *(on a raised platform).*

kichaka (vi-) (*dimin. of* [2]**chaka**) 1. thicket, bushes, shrubbery. 2. group of trees, grove.

kichala (vi-) bunch *(of fruit).*

kichali, kichalichali (*rare* **chali**) *adv.* backwards, on the back. **lala –.** lie on one's back.

kichalichali *see* **kichali.**

kichane (vi-) 1. splinter, shaving. 2. bunch *(of fruit). Cf.* [3]**chana.**

kichangamko (vi-) *see* **changamko.**

kichangamsha (vi-): – **kinywa.** a confection *(served before the main part of a meal). Cf.* **changamka.**

kichanganyiko (vi-) *math.* multiplier; product *(of multiplication). Cf.* [1]**changa.**

kichango (vi-) collection *(of money).* **changa –.** contribute to a collection. *Cf.* [1]**changa.**

kichanio (vi-) *see* **kichanuo.**

kichanja (vi-) *dimin. of* [1]**chanja.**

kichanuo, kichanio, kitana (vi-) (*dimin. of* **chanuo**) comb. *Cf.* [3]**chana.**

kichea *sing., rare* 1. dawn. 2. clearing up *(after a rain). Cf.* [3]**cha.**

kicheche (vi-) *dimin. of* [2]**cheche.**

[1]**kichefuchefu** *sing. see* [1]**kitefutefu.**

[2]**kichefuchefu** *sing.* nausea, seasickness. *coll.* **nina –.** I feel sick. *Cf.* **chefua.**

kichekesho (vi-) amusement, entertainment, diversion, fun. *Cf.* [1]**cheka.**

kicheko (vi-) laugh, smile, grin. **angua –.** burst out laughing. *Cf.* [1]**cheka.**

kichele (*dial.* **kichelele**) *adv.* 1. naked, bare, bald. 2. *fig.* well-defined, clear, plain. **ameniambia – sana.** He spoke to me very plainly.

kichelele *see* **kichele.**

[1]**kichelema** (vi-) watery manioc (or potatoes).

[2]**kichelema** (vi-) *see* **kiselema.**

[1]**kichembe** (vi-) *see* **kitembe.**

[2]**kichembe** (vi-) *see* [1]**chembe.**

kichinichini *adv.* underhandedly, secretively, disingenuously. *Cf.* **chini.**

kichinja (vi-): – (*or* **kitinda**) **mimba.** the last child to whom a woman gives birth. **– udhia.** a weed *(Dissotis prostrata)* used as a remedy for headache. *Cf.* **chinja.**

kichinjo (vi-) *see* **mchinjo.**

kichipukizi (vi-) 1. sprout, shoot. 2. *fig.:* **mtu huyu ni – tu.** This person is as yet undeveloped (is still at the beginning of his career). *Cf.* **chipua.**

kicho (vi-) 1. fear, anxiety, timidity. 2. something arousing fear; danger, peril. *Cf.* [2]**cha.**

kichocheo (vi-) 1. poker *(for stirring a fire).* 2. *fig.* a quarrelsome person. *Cf.* **chocha.**

kichocho (vi-) *med.* bilharzia. *Cf.* **chocha.**

kichochoro (vi-), **chochoro** (ma-), **mchochoro** (mi-), **uchochoro** (ma-) narrow passage, alley *(between houses).*

kichogo (vi-) *see* **kisogo.**

kichokoo (vi-) 1. *dimin. of* **mchokoo.** 2. spur *(on a boot). Cf.* **chokoa.**

kichoma (vi-): – **mguu (nguo).** 1. a shrub *(Bidens pilosa, Bidens leucantha).* 2. an annual plant *(Heteropogon contortus). Cf.* [2]**choma.**

kichomi, kichomo (vi-) sharp (pricking/stabbing) pain, twinge, stitch. **ana –.** He has sharp pains/twinges. *Cf.* [1]**choma.**

[1]**kichomo** (vi-) *see* **kichomi.**

[2]**kichomo** (vi-) *rare* (process, manner of) burning, cauterization. *Cf.* [2]**choma.**

kichongochongo *see* **kitongo.**

kichopa (vi-) small bundle. *Cf.* **chopa.**

kichoro (vi-) small, illegible handwriting. *Cf.* [1]**chora, mchoro.**

kichozi (vi-) 1. kichozi (kind of bird: 'palm-wine drinker'). 2. *fig.* heavy drinker, drunkard. *coll.:* **huyu – sana.** He is a heavy drinker. *Cf.* [2]**chozi.**

kichuguu, kisuguu, kisugulu (vi-) ant/termite hill. *Cf.* **chuguu.**

kichujio (vi-) *dimin. of* **chujio.**

kichumba (*dimin. of* **chumba**) (vi-) compartment, cab. – **cha dreva.** cab *(of a locomotive).*

[1]**kichungu:** *coll.* **niliwakuta watu –.** I met a tremendous crowd of people. *Cf.* [3]**chungu.**

[2]**kichungu** *adv.* sharply, bitterly, caustically. *Cf.* [2]**chungu.**

[3]**kichungu, kijungu** (vi-) (*dimin. of* [1]**chungu**) small cooking pot.

[4]**kichungu** (vi-) tuft *(of grass).*

kichwa, kitwa (vi-) 1. head. – **kikubwa.** arrogance, presumption. **jipa (pata) –.** be proud/arrogant/presumptuous. **wa na (fanya) –.** be obstinate/recalcitrant. **ana – (kizuri).** He is intelligent. **nina (naumwa) –** *or* – **kinaniwanga.** I have a headache. *fig.* – **cha gari la moshi.** locomotive. *coll.* – **chini miguu juu.** upside down, topsy-turvy. 2. upper part, top, main part. *loc.* **kichwani.** upper end. – **cha maneno.** book title. – **cha mlima.** top of a mountain. 3. important person, leader. 4. *adv.:* **kichwa kichwa.** headlong, head over heels.

kichwamgomba, kitwamgomba (vi-) somersault.

Kidachi* [*Germ.*] *arch.* 1. *sing.* German language. 2.: **–a –.** *adj.* German. (= **Kijeremani.**) *Cf.* [2]**Dachi.**

[1]kidaka (vi-) coconut *(in the first stages of growth).*

[2]kidaka (vi-) 1. niche. 2. *anat.* throat. – tonge. *anat.* uvula. *Cf.* [2]daka.

kidako (vi-) kidako (kind of fish).

kidalali* (vi-) (*dimin. of* dalali) agent, henchman.

[1]kidamu* (–) *naut., rare* bow (= omo, gubeti.) *Cf.* kadamu.

[2]kidamu* *rare* = takadamu.

kidanga (vi-) 1. unripe fruit. 2. *adj.* mchungwa –. unripe orange.

kidani (vi-) necklace.

kidaraja* (vi-) *sport* steeplechase, hurdle-race, obstacle-race. *Cf.* daraja.

kidari (vi-) breast, breastbone *(usually of animals or birds). coll.* toa –. be conceited/egotistical.

kidato (vi-) 1. notch *(cut in the trunk of a palm-tree as an aid for climbing).* 2. rung *(of a ladder).*

[1]kidau* (vi-) *dimin. of* dau.

[2]kidau* (vi-) *see* kidawa.

kidawa*, kidau (vi-): – cha wino. inkwell.

kidawati* (vi-) *see* dawati.

kidazi *sing.* baldness, bald spot, bald head. (= upaa.)

kidei (–) *see* kideri.

kidemokrasi* [*Engl.*] *adj.:* –a –. democratic. jamhuri ya –. democratic republic. sheria za –. democratic laws.

kideri, kidei (–) 1. cattle plague, rinderpest. 2. disease of chickens.

kidete *adv.* firmly.

kidevu (vi-) *anat.* chin. ndevu za –. goatee. *Cf.* udevu.

kidhabidhabina* (vi-) *see* mdhabidhabina.

kidhi* grant, bestow, lend, present, confer; satisfy. – maombi. grant a request. *appl.* kidhia. *caus.* kidhisha. *pass.* kidhiwa. *Cf.* mkidhi.

kidifu* (vi-) *see* difu.

kidiku (vi-) fragment, scrap.

kidimbwi, kidumbwi (vi-) (*dimin. of* dimbwi) pool, puddle.

[1]kidimu (vi-): – msitu. wild lemon tree.

[2]kidimu (vi-) kidimu (a chicken with ruffled feathers or a bare neck).

kidingapopo (vi-) *med.* dengue fever (tropical intermittent fever).

kidiplomasi* [*Engl.*]: **–a –.** *adj.* diplomatic. **mtume wa –.** diplomatic courier.

kidiri (–) squirrel. (= **kindi.**)

kidirisha* (vi-) ventilator. *Cf.* **dirisha.**

kidividivi (vi-) earring.

kidogo *adv.* a little, some, not much, few. **maji –.** some water, a little water. **ekundu –.** reddish. **bado –.** soon. *red.* **kidogo kidogo, kidogodogo.** very little, not much at all. *Cf.* **dogo.**

kidokezi (vi-) *see* **kidokezo.**

kidokezo, kidokezi (vi-) suggestion, proposal; hint, allusion; advice. *Cf.* **dokeza.**

[1]**kidoko** (vi-) 1. click *(of the tongue).* **piga –.** to click. 2. *ling.* click (consonant). **lugha yenye vidoko.** language with click consonants. 3. hint, sign. *Cf.* **dokeza.**

[2]**kidoko** (vi-) kidoko (kind of fish).

kidole (vi-) finger, toe. *Also:* **– cha mkono.** finger. **– cha mguu.** toe. **– cha gumba.** thumb. **– shahada.** index finger. **– cha kati.** middle finger. **– cha kati ya kando.** ring finger. **– cha mwisho.** little finger. *Cf.* **dole, udole.**

kidomo (vi-) 1. *dimin. of* **mdomo.** 2. daintiness, fastidiousness *(with respect to food).* **mwenye –.** gourmet. 3. *red.* **kidomodomo.** *adv.:* **ana kidomodomo.** He talks continuously.

kidonda (vi-) *see* **donda.**

[1]**kidondo** (vi-) (*usually* **vidondo**) shaving(s); firewood, kindling.

[2]**kidondo** (vi-) sea mussel.

kidonge (vi-) (*dimin. of* **donge**) 1. small piece/lump, globule. 2. *pharm.* tablet, pill.

kidotia, kilotia (vi-) child's cap.

[1]**kidoto** (vi-) 1. blinker, blinder *(fastened over a camel's eyes).* 2. *fig., coll.* **funda –.** follow blindly.

[2]**kidoto** (vi-) (small) drinking cup, goblet.

kidude* (vi-) (*dimin. of* **dude**) 1. trifle; undefinable thing, what's-its-name, thingumbob; gadget, device, instrument, knob. 2. something unknown/mysterious/frightening. **– gani hili?** What in the world is this object?

kidudu*, kijidudu (vi-) (*dimin. of* [1]**mdudu**) microbe, germ.

kidudusi (vi-) 1. spot, speck. 2. *med.* pimple, rash. *Cf.* **duduka.**

kidugu, kindugu 1. (vi-) *dimin. of* **ndugu.** 2. *adv.* in a brotherly way. **pendana –.** love each other like brothers.

kiduka* (vi-) small shop/business. *Cf.* **duka.**

kiduku* [*Afr.*] (vi-) kiduku (duiker, small antelope).

kidumbwi (vi-) *see* **kidimbwi.**

[1]**kidundu** (vi-) forehead. (= [2]**kipaji.**)

[2]**kidundu** (vi-) *see* **dundu.**

kidungadunga (vi-) boring insect, weevil. *Cf.* [1]**dunga.**

kidurango (vi-) *rare* dwarf. (= **mbilikimo, kibeti.**)

kidurazi (vi-) *see* **kidurusi.**

kidurusi, kidurazi (vi-) *dial.* termite hill. (= **chuguu.**)

kidusi (–) 1. acrid odor. (*e.g., of game, fish).* 2. *in gen.* unusual smell/taste.

kiduta (vi-) prominence, height, hill.

kieleaji (vi-) something which floats; *(pl.)* flotsam. *Cf.* **elea.**

kielekezo (vi-) sign, indication, hint. *Cf.* **elea, elekea.**

kielelezo (vi-) *see* **kielezo.**

kielezo, kielelezo (vi-) explanation; pattern, model, form; example, illustration. *Cf.* **elea.**

kiendeleo, kiendelezo (vi-) progress, advance. *Cf.* **enda, endeleo.**

kiendelezo (vi-) *see* **kiendeleo.**

kieneo (vi-) *see* **eneo.**

kienezo (vi-) *see* **chenezo.**

kienge (vi-) *see* **mwenge.**

kienyeji *sing.:* **–a –.** peculiar to or limited to a country, national. **nguo za –.** national dress/costume. **vita vya –.** civil war. *Cf.* **enye, mwenyeji.**

[1]**kifa** (vi-) *mil.* nipple *(of a musket),* firing pin, detonator.

[2]**kifa** (vi-) dying, death. *Cf.* **fa.**

kifaa (vi-) 1. implement, utensil, apparatus, equipment, material. **vifaa vya kuoga** equipment for washing. **vifaa vya nyumbani.** household implements. 2. *(us. pl.)* counter *(small object used in teaching arithmetic, etc.).* *Cf.* **faa.**

kifabakazi (vi-) *bot.* Nandi flame tree *(Spathodea nilotica).*

kifaduro (vi-) *med.* whooping cough.

kifafa (vi-) *med.* convulsion, spasm, fit; epilepsy. **mwenye –.** an epileptic. **amepata (ugua) –.** be epileptic, have a fit of epilepsy.

kifalme *adj. & adv.* royal(ly). **nguo ya –.** regal clothing. *Cf.* **mfalme, ufalme.**

kifandugu (–) *anat.* coccyx.

kifani (vi-) *see* **kifano.**

kifano, kifani (vi-) similar thing, equal, match. **haina –.** It is unequaled/unique *Cf.* **faa, fana, fanana.**

kifaranga* [*Port.*] (vi-) (*dimin. of* ^{2}**faranga**) young bird, chick.

Kifaransa* 1. *sing.* French language. 2.: **–a –.** *adj.* French. *Cf.* **Faransa, Mfaransa, Ufaransa.**

kifarasi* *adj. & adv.* like a horse; at a gallop, galloping. **enda mbio –.** run at a gallop. *Cf.* **farasi.**

kifaru (vi-) (*or augment.* **faru**) 1. rhinoceros. 2. *fig., mil.* tank. **bunduki ya kupigia vifaru.** antitank gun. 3. **–a vifaru.** *adj.* armored. **kikundi cha vifaru.** armored battalion.

kifauwongo (vi-) (*lit.* that which feigns death; *cf.* ^{2}**kifa, uwongo**) 1. mimosa *(Mimosa pudica).* 2. **kifauwongo** (a shrub, *Biophytum sensitivum).* 3. (kind of) weevil *(or other insect which feigns death when touched).*

kifefe* (vi-) 1. = **ufefe.** 2. weak/useless person.

kifia *appl. of* ^{2}**kifu.**

kifichifichi *see* **kifichoficho.**

kifichoficho, kifichifichi *adv.* stealthily, in secret. **maneno ya –.** intrigues. *Cf.* **ficha.**

kifidio* (vi-) *see* **fidia.**

kifijo (vi-) (*usually* **vifijo**) applause, joyful approval, exultation.

kifiko (vi-) time of arrival; place where one arrives, destination. *Cf.* **fika.**

kifisifisi *adv.* like a hyena; *(fig.)* secretly, surreptitiously. *Cf.* **fisi.**

kifo (vi-) death, dying, manner of death. **– chake kilituhuzunisha.** His death has distressed us. *prov.* **– cha wengi arusi.** The dying of many is like a wedding (= the awareness of working in common for a good cause gives one strength). *Cf.* **fa.**

^{1}**kifu** 1. (vi-) something dead (decayed, decomposed), carrion. 2. *adv.* as if dead. **lala –.** sleep very soundly. *Cf.* **fa.**

^{2}**kifu*, kefu** 1. be enough, suffice. **chakula chako kimenikifu.** Your food has satisfied me (I cannot eat any more). *appl.* **kifia. kifia haja.** satisfy someone's desires. 2. *sing.* sufficiency, plenty, abundance.

kifua (vi-) breast, chest *(of men);* breastbone. **hawezi –.** he coughs. **– kikuu.** *med.* tuberculosis. *See also* **mafua.**

kifuasi (vi-) 1. succession, series, sequence *(of numbers)*. 2. even number. *Cf.* **fuata.**

kifudifudi *see* **fudifudi.**

kifufu (vi-) *see* **kifuu.**

kifuka (vi-) *bot.* kifuka (*a shrub, Verononia cinerea*).

kifukizo, kivukizo (vi-) smoking, fumigation, burning of incense; fumigating material, incense. *Cf.* **¹fuka.**

kifuko (vi-) (*dimin. of* **mfuko**). 1. pouch, small bag/sack. – **cha fedha** *or* **cha kutilia fedha.** purse. 2. *anat.* tonsil. 3. *red.:* **kifukofuko.** cocoon *(of an insect)*.

kifuku (vi-) the hot rainy season. *Cf.* **¹fuka.**

kifuli (vi-) *see* **kivuli.**

kifulifuli *see* **fudifudi.**

kifumba (vi-) (*dimin. of* **²fumba**) small sack made of matting.

kifumbazi (vi-) *see* **¹kivumbasi.**

kifumbu (vi-) filter, sieve *(of matting or basketwork)*. *Cf.* **²fumba, kifumba.**

kifumufumu (vi-) *rare* kifumufumu (kind of manioc). (= **muhogo.**)

kifundi: **–a –.** technical. **msaada wa –.** technical assistance. *Cf.* **²funda, fundi.**

kifundo (vi-) (*dimin. of* **fundo**) 1. knot. **piga –.** tie a knot. 2. *anat.* joint. **– cha mkono.** wrist. **– cha mguu.** ankle, heel. *loc.* **kifundoni.** up to the ankles. 3. tassel. *Cf.* **⁴funda, fundika.**

kifunga (vi-) 1. *rare* something used for tying/fastening. **– mbuzi.** a short-lived variety of grass *(Eleusine indica)*. 2.: **– stimu.** *elec.* fuse. (= **fataki.**) *Cf.* **¹funga.**

kifungo (vi-) 1. (act of, method of) fastening. 2. fastener (button, buckle, clasp, *etc.*). 3. confinement, prison; jail sentence. **peleka (tia) kifungoni).** put into prison. 4. *typ.* parenthesis, bracket. **andika vifungoni.** put in parentheses. *Cf.* **¹funga.**

kifungu (vi-) (*dimin. of* **¹fungu**) small portion; paragraph, section, article *(of a law, constitution, etc.); (mus.)* measure.

kifungua (vi-) something that opens or unfastens. **– kopo.** can opener. **– kinywa.** breakfast. **– mimba.** firstborn child. **– mkoba.** *hist.* payment to a medicine man for discovering the cause of an illness **– mlango.** gift made by the bridegroom to those who, on his wedding day, open the door to the room of the bride. *Cf.* **¹funga.**

kifunguo (vi-) 1. *dimin. of* **ufunguo.** 2. skeleton key. *Cf.* **¹funga.**

kifunifuni *see* **fudifudi.**

kifuniko (vi-) 1. cover, lid, screen. – **cha chungu.** potlid. – **cha saa.** case of a watch. – **cha taa.** lampshade, globe. 2. *fig.* concealment, refuge, hiding-place. *Cf.* **funika.**

kifunuo (vi-) uncovering, revealing. *Cf.* **funua.**

kifuo (vi-) kifuo (a pointed stake thrust in the ground, used for stripping off the husks of coconuts). *Cf.* [1]**fua.**

kifupi *adv.* briefly, in brief. *Cf.* **fupi.**

kifusi (vi-) *see* [1]**fusi.**

kifuu, kifufu (vi-) 1. (empty) shell of the coconut. 2. *rare:* – **cha yai.** eggshell. *Cf.* [1]**fuu.**

kifyonza: –(*or* **mfyonza**) **vumbi** (vi-) vacuum cleaner. *Cf.* **fyonza.**

kiga (vi-) *dial.* thigh *(of an animal)*, shank, ham. (= **paja.**)

kigae, kigai (vi-) (*dimin. of* **gae**) small fragment, splinter, potsherd; (roof-)tile.

kigaga (vi-) (*dimin. of* [1]**gaga**) crust, scurf, scab.

kigagazi (vi-) nausea, seasickness.

kigai (vi-) *see* **kigae.**

kigambo (vi-) controversy, controversial question, (point at) issue. *Cf.* [1]**amba.**

Kigana* [*Engl.*]: **–a –.** Ghanaian.

[1]**kiganda** (vi-) *dimin. of* [2]**ganda.**

[2]**Kiganda:** **–a –.** *adj.* pertaining to/characteristic of the Baganda.

kigango (vi-) *dimin. of* **gango.**

kiganja, kiganya (vi-), **ganja** (ma-) palm of the hand. (= [1]**kitanga.**)

kigao (vi-) (*dimin. of* **ngao**) (small) shield, screen.

kigasha (vi-): – **cha mkono.** forearm.

kigawanye, kigawe (vi-) *math.* dividend. **40 ni kigawe cha 10.** Forty is a multiple of ten. *Cf.* **gawa.**

kigawanyo, kigawo (vi-) division, distribution; *(math.)* divisor. *Cf.* **gawa.**

kigawe (vi-) *see* **kigawanye.**

kigawo (vi-) *see* **kigawanyo.**

kigego (vi-) 1. child that develops abnormally *(regarded as unlucky)*. 2. *fig.:* **mtoto huyu ni – sana.** This child is hard to bring up.

kigelegele (vi-) (*also* **ugelegele** *sing.*) shout of joy *(usually of women, on the occasion of a returning, a birth, a wedding, etc.)*. (= **kelele, shangwe, kijijo.**)

kigeni: **–a –.** *adj.* foreign. **maneno ya –.** a foreign language. *Cf.* **geni.**

kigeregenja (vi-) *see* **kigereng'enza.**

kigereng'enza, kigeregenja (vi-) splinter, fragment, chip, shaving.

kigesi, kigezi (vi-), **kugesi** (–) anklet.

kigeugeu (vi-) 1. inconstant/fickle person. 2. chameleon. (= [2]**kinyonga**). 3. *adj. & adv.* inconstant, changeable, vacillating, fickle. **fanyia fulani –.** make someone vacillate/waver. *Cf.* **geua.**

kigezi (vi-) *see* **kigesi.**

kigezo* [*Pers.*] (vi-) 1. pattern *(for cutting clothes).* 2. measuring rod, yardstick. *Cf.* **geza.**

kigingi, kigwingwi (vi-) peg, stake, post *(for tying animals).*

Kigiriki* [*Engl.*] 1. *sing.* (modern) Greek language. 2. *adv.* in the Greek manner. 3.: **–a –.** *adj.* Greek. *Cf.* **Mgiriki, Ugiriki.**

kigo *pl. of* **ukigo.**

Kigoa* [*Ind.*] 1. *sing.* language of the Goanese. 2.: **–a –.** *adj.* Goanese.

kigodo (vi-) kigodo (confection made of rice flour, sugar, and grated coconut).

kigoe (vi-) *see* **kingoe.**

kigogo. 1. (vi-) *dimin. of* **gogo.** 2. *adv.:* **lala (kama) –.** sleep very soundly.

kigogota, kigotagota, kigong'ota, king'oto (vi-) woodpecker. *Cf.* **gogota.**

kigoli, kigori (vi-) young girl *(before menstruation).*

kigoma (vi-) (*dimin. of* **ngoma**) small drum, tambourine.

kigomba (vi-) (*dimin. of* **mgomba**) young banana plant.

kigombegombe (vi-) kigombegombe (kind of fish).

kigongo (vi-) *see* **kijongo.**

kigong'ota (vi-) *see* **kigogota.**

kigono (vi-) resting place, shelter, camp. *Cf.* **gona.**

kigori (vi-) *see* **kigoli.**

kigosho (vi-) bend, crookedness, deformity. **– cha mkono.** deformed arm.

kigotagota (vi-) *see* **kigogota.**

kiguba (vi-) *see* [1]**kikuba.**

kigugu 1. (vi-) *dimin. of* **gugu.** 2. *adv.* wild, in confusion, like weeds. **jenga –.** build in a disorderly fashion *(not in rows).*

kigugumizi, kigugumiza (vi-) stuttering. **ana –.** He stutters. *Cf.* **gugumia.**

kigumba (vi-) arrowhead, barb on an arrowhead.

kigumi (vi-) *see* **kiguni.**

kiguni*, **kigumi** (vi-) (*dimin. of* [1]**guni**) small bag of matting *(for packing dates).*

kigunzi (vi-) 1. *dimin. of* **gunzi.** 2. *fig.* the last day of the year. (= [2]**kibunzi.**)

kiguu (vi-) (*dimin. of* **mguu**) 1. deformed foot, clubfoot. 2. lame person.

kiguzo (vi-) (*dimin. of* **nguzo**) 1. prop, support, stand *(for holding something).* 2. (cricket) stump. 3. comfort, assurance.

kigwaru (*also* **kinyevu**) (vi-) a growth or swelling on the genitals.

kigwe (vi-) (*dimin. of* **ugwe**) string, cord; tape, braid; strap; lace *(of a shoe);* rein.

kigwingwi (vi-) *see* **kigingi.**

kihame (vi-) deserted dwelling place. (= **hame, mahame,** [1]**tongo.**)

kiharusi*, **kiarusi** (vi-) *med.* stroke, spasm, apoplexy.

kiherehere (vi-) confusion, excitement. **– cha moyo.** palpitation of the heart.

kihero (vi-) 1. *dimin. of* **hero.** 2. crib, manger, trough.

kihesabu*: **–a –.** *adj.* mathematical. *Cf.* **hesabu.**

Kihindi* 1. *sing.* Hindustani (language). 2. **–a –.** *adj.* Indian. *Cf.* [1]**Hindi, Mhindi, Uhindi.**

kihongwe, kongwe (vi-) (*also* **punda –**) pack donkey.

[1]**kihori*** (vi-) *rare dimin. of* [1]**hori.**

[2]**kihori*** (vi-) *dimin. of* [2]**hori.**

kihoro (vi-) grief, pain. **tia –.** feel grief/pain.

kihunzi (vi-) thieves' Latin *(a form of concealed speech in which final syllables are put first). Cf.* **kinyume** 1.

kihusiano (vi-) *gramm.* relative afformative *(infix or suffix). Cf.* **husu.**

kiinamizi (vi-) share of meat which the butcher receives for slaughtering an animal. *Cf.* **inama.**

Kiingereza* 1. *sing.* the English language. 2. *adv.* in the English manner. 3.: **–a –.** *adj.* English. *Cf.* **Mwingereza, Uingereza.**

kiingilio, kiingio (vi-) admission fee. *Cf.* **ingia.**

kiingio (vi-) *see* **kiingilio.**

[1]**kiini, kini** (vi-) 1. inside, interior; pith; kernel, nucleus. **– cha matunda.** kernel/stone of fruit. **– cha yai.** yolk of an egg. **– cha jicho.** *anat.* pupil (of the eye). 2. *fig.* substance, essence, gist *(of a*

matter). – **ya hoja.** central issue. 3. *recent* **–a –.** nuclear. **siasa ya –.** *comm.* policy of nuclear blackmail. **silaha za viini.** nuclear weapons. *Cf.* **ini.**

[2]**kiini: – macho** (vi-) (conjuring) trick, sleight of hand.

kiinikizo (vi-) 1. heavy burden. 2. bribery, bribe. *Cf.* **inika.**

kiinua: – mgongo (vi-) extra payment, bonus *(for heavy work);* tip. *Cf.* **inua.**

kiisha* *see* **kisha.**

Kiislamu* 1. *sing.* (religion of) Islam. 2. *adv.* in the Moslem manner. 3.: **–a –.** *adj.* Islamic, Moslem. *Cf.* **Islamu, silimu.**

kiitikio, kiitiko (vi-) response, repetition, refrain. *Cf.* **ita.**

kiitiko (vi-) *see* **kiitikio.**

kijaa (vi-) 1. millstone. 2. a completely filled vessel. *Cf.* [1]**jaa.**

kijakazi (vi-) (*dimin. of* **mjakazi**) *hist.* young slave girl. *Cf.* **ja.**

kijaluba*, kijaruba (vi-) *dimin. of* **jaluba.**

kijamanda* (vi-) 1. *dimin. of* **jamanda.** 2. blinker, blinder *(of basketwork; fastened over the eyes of camels).*

kijambia* (vi-) 1. *dimin. of* **jambia.** 2. gusset *(of a kanzu).*

Kijampani* *sing. & adj.* *see* **Kijapani.**

kijana (vi-) young person, boy, girl, youngster. **wewe – sisi ni watu wazima.** You are a youngster, (but) we are grown-ups. *Cf.* **mwana.**

kijani 1. (vi-) *dimin. of* **jani.** 2. *adv.* like grass. 3. *adj.* **– kibichi.** grass-green.

Kijapani* [*Engl.*] 1. *sing.* the Japanese language. 2.: **–a –.** *adj.* Japanese. *Cf.* **Mjapani.**

kijaruba* (vi-) *see* **kijaluba.**

kijembe (vi-) (*dimin. of* **jembe**) 1. small knife, pocketknife. 2. *fig.* cutting/sarcastic language.

Kijeremani* [*Engl.*] 1. *sing.* German language. 2. **–a –.** *adj.* German. *Cf.* **Mjeremani, Ujeremani.**

kijeshi* 1.: **–a –.** *adj.* military, army... **korti la –.** court-martial. 2. (vi-) military training. *Cf.* **jeshi.**

kijia (vi-) *see* **kinjia.**

kijibanda (vi-) *see* **kibanda.**

kijibwa (vi-) little dog; *(fig.)* lackey, puppet. *Cf.* **mbwa.**

kijicho (vi-) 1. envy, jealousy. 2. malice, spite. 3. malignant/envious glance. **kuwa na –** *or* **kuwa na – rohoni.** be envious/jealous. *Cf.* **jicho.**

kijichumba (vi-) (*dimin. of* **chumba**) cubicle, cabin.

kijidonda (vi-) (*dimin. of* **donda**) pimple, pustule.

kijidudu (vi-) *see* **kidudu.**

kijigari* [*Ind.*] (vi-) (*dimin. of* **gari**) motor scooter.

kijihospitali* [*Engl.*] (vi-) (*dimin. of* **hospitali**) medical station, first aid.

kijiji (vi-) (*dimin. of* **mji**) (small) village, hamlet. (= **kitongoji.**)

[1]**kijiko** (vi-) (dimin. of [1]**mwiko**) spoon (*in gen.*). – **cha chai.** teaspoon. – **cha chakula.** tablespoon. – **cha kupika.** serving spoon.

[2]**kijiko** (vi-) *dimin. of* **jiko.**

kijimbi: – **msitu** (vi-) *ornith.* (species of) kingfisher.

kijimea (vi-) (*dimin. of* **mmea**) bacterium.

kijimo (vi-) dwarf. (= **mbilikimo, kibeti.**)

kijina (vi-) (*dimin. of* **jina**) *gramm.* pronoun.

kijineno (vi-) (*dimin. of* **neno**) prattling (*of children*), tittle-tattle. *Cf.* [1]**nena.**

[1]**kijinga** (vi-) *dimin. of* [2]**kinga.**

[2]**kijinga, kijingajinga** *adj.* stupid, foolish. *Cf.* **jinga.**

kijingajinga *see* **kijinga.**

kijini* (vi-) (*dimin. of* **jini**) *liter.* spirit, fairy, elf.

kijino (vi-) 1. *dimin. of* **jino.** 2. a small fish, whitebait. 3. shrimp.

kijio (vi-) evening meal, dinner. *Cf.* **ja.**

kijiri (vi-) *see* **chichiri.**

kijisanduku* (vi-) (*dimin. of* **sanduku**) mailbox.

kijisehemu* (vi-) (*dimin. of* **sehemu**) *phys.* micron.

kijisu (vi-) (*dimin. of* **kisu**) small knife.

kijitabu* (vi-) (*dimin. of* **kitabu**) 1. pamphlet, brochure. 2. article, essay.

kijiti (vi-) (*dimin. of* [1]**mti**) 1. small tree, bush, shrub. 2. (small) stick, twig, piece of wood, peg.

kijito, kijuto (vi-) (*dimin. of* [1]**mto**) small stream, brook, rivulet.

[1]**kijitu** (vi-) small person; (*often contemptuous*) little man, wretch. *Cf.* **mtu, jitu.**

[2]**kijitu:** **–a –.** *adj.* huge, gigantic. **ameangukiwa na kijitu cha jiwe.** A huge stone fell on him. *Cf.* **jitu.**

kijivi 1. (vi-) (*dimin. of* **mwivi**) thievish person. 2. *adv.* in a thievish/underhanded way. *Cf.* **iba.**

kijivu, kijivujivu *adj.* ash-colored, ashen, gray. *Cf.* **jivu.**

kijiwe (vi-) *see* **kiwe.**

kijogoo 1. (*dimin. of* **jogoo.** 2. (vi-) (species) of) sea-fish. 3. *adv.* like cocks/roosters. *fig.* **shindana —.** fight with each other like cocks. *prov.* **mtu huyu ndiye — wa mji siku hizi.** He is a notorious character. *Cf.* **jogoo.**

Kijomba *sing. arch.* Swahili (language). (= **Kiswahili**; *cf.* **mjomba, Ujomba.**)

kijongo, kigongo (vi-) (*dimin. of* **mgongo**) hump. **mwenye —.** hunchback.

kijoyo (vi-) (*dimin. of* **moyo**) 1. = **kimoyo.** 2. inclination, desire.

kijukuu (vi-) (*dimin. of* **mjukuu**) great-grandchild.

kijumba (vi-) (*dimin. of* **nyumba**) small house, hut; booth. **— cha simu.** telephone booth.

kijumbamshale *sing.* (epithet applied to the) swallow.

kijumbe (vi-) (*dimin. of* **jumbe**) intermediary in arranging a marriage, go-between. *Cf.* **mjumbe, ujumbe.**

kijungu (vi-) *see* **⁴kichungu.**

¹kijusi* (vi-) 1. bad smell. 2. impurity (period of forty days after parturition, during which a woman is considered to be impure). *Cf.* **ujusi.**

²kijusi (vi-) *dimin. of* **¹mjusi.**

kijusu (vi-) *anat.* foetus (of four months).

kijuto (vi-) *see* **kijito.**

kijuujuu *adv.* 1. above, up, upwards, on top. 2. *fig.* superficially. *Cf.* **juu.**

kijuvi 1. *adj. & adv.* impertinent, impudent, insolent. **sema —.** talk impudently. 2. (vi-) an impertinent child. *Cf.* **²jua, juvi.**

kikaango (vi-) (*dimin. of* **kaango**) (cooking-) pot, frying pan.

kikabaila*: **—a —.** *adj.* great, important. **serikali za —.** the great powers. *Cf.* **kabaila.**

kikabila* *adj. & adv.* pertaining to the people. **—a —.** people's ..., popular, national. *Cf.* **kabila.**

kikaimati* (vi-) 1. (kind of) porridge, gruel *(made of wheat meal).* 2. (kind of) pancake, fritter.

kikaka 1. (vi-) haste, hurry, rush; confusion, disorder. 2. *adv.* hurriedly, hastily. *Cf.* **kakakaka.**

kikale *adj. & adv.* ancient, archaic; old-fashioned, obsolete. *Cf.* **kale.**

kikalio (vi-) *coll.* luxury *(cigarettes, tobacco).* *Cf.* **¹kaa.**

kikambo *adv.* like a stepparent. *Cf.* **kambo.**

kikamulio (vi-) press, squeezer *(for extracting juice from fruit).* *Cf.* **²kama.**

kikanda (vi-) *see* **¹kanda.**

kikande (vi-) kikande (fish similar to sole).

kikanza (vi-) 1. (act of) warming up. 2. something which warms. *Cf.* **¹kaanga.**

kikao (vi-) 1. domicile, residence. **– chake Tanga.** He lives/resides in Tanga. 2. duration of one's stay in a place, period of residence. 3. way/style of life; (social) position, standing; conduct, behavior, attitude. **kaa kwa – chema.** live on good terms. 4. section, division, department. 5. session. **– cha Halmashauri.** session of parliament. *Cf.* **¹kaa.**

kikapu (vi-) (*also* **kapu, ma-**) basket. **– cha karatasi.** wastepaper basket.

kikaratasi*, kikartasi (vi-) (*dimin. of* **karatasi**) handbill, broadside, circular.

kikariri* 1. (vi-) repetition, reiteration. 2. *adv.* again, repeatedly, for the umpteenth time, over and over. *Cf.* **kariri.**

kikartasi* (vi-) *see* **kikaratasi.**

kikatoliki* [*Engl.*] 1. *sing.* (Roman) Catholic religion, Catholicism. 2.: **–a –.** *adj.* (Roman) Catholic. *Cf.* **katoliki.**

kikaufu *see* **kikavu.**

kikausha (vi-) *see* **²kausha.**

kikausho (vi-): **–cha wino.** blotting paper. *Cf.* **kauka.**

kikavu, kikauvu 1. *sing.* dryness. 2. *adj. & adv.* dry; *(fig.)* cool, reserved. *Cf.* **¹kavu, kauka.**

kikawaida* **–a –.** *adj.* usual, regular, natural. *Cf.* **kawaida.**

kikawe (vi-) *see* **kiwe.**

kikaza, kikazo (vi-) 1. fastener (clamp, clip, joint, coupling, *etc.*). 2. lintel *(of a door or window).* *Cf.* **kaza.**

kikazo (vi-) 1. = **kikaza.** 2. pressure. 3. *ling.* stress, accent. *Cf.* **kaza.**

kike *sing.* 1. femininity. **–a –.** female, feminine. **mtoto wa –.** girl. **fanya –.** behave like a woman. 2. *adv.* like a woman, in a feminine way. *Cf.* **ke.**

kikero (vi-) nose ring. (= **hazama, kishaufu.**)

kiki* [*Engl.*] (–) *sport.* kick-off *(in football).*

kikiki *adv.* firmly, tightly. **funga –.** fasten tightly.

kikiri* (–) struggling, wrestling; pushing, crowding. *Cf.* **kikirika;** *also* **¹kakara, kukuru.**

kikirika* wrestle, fight; push, shove. *Cf.* **kikiri.**

kikisa speak fast/indistinctly; be confused/incoherent. *appl.* **kikisia.**

kikisia *appl. of* **kikisa.**

¹kiko (vi-) (tobacco) pipe.

²kiko (vi-) *anat.* elbow. (= **¹kivi.**)

³kiko *loc., sing.* he (she, it) is there. **kiti —?** Is the chair there?

¹kikoa (vi-) people doing something in common, a thing done in common *(meal, collection of money)*; group, team. **kula —.** have meals in common.

²kikoa (vi-) *dimin. of* **¹koa, ³koa.**

kikofi (vi-) palm of the hand, handful. *Cf.* **kofi, ukufi.**

kikohozi (vi-) cough, fit of coughing. **aumwa —.** He has a cough. *Cf.* **kohoa.**

kikoi (vi-) white loincloth *(with colored border).*

kikojozi (vi-), **kojozi** (—) person with weak kidneys, bed wetter. **dawa ya —.** diuretic (medicine). *Cf.* **kojoa.**

kikoko (vi-) (*dimin. of* **ukoko**) *rare* scurf, scab.

kikoloni* [*Engl.*]: **—a —.** colonial. **serikali ya —.** colonial administration. *Cf.* **koloni.**

kikomba (vi-): **— cha njaa** *or* **njaa ya —.** ravenous hunger, tremendous appetite. *Cf.* **¹komba.**

kikombe (vi-) 1. cup (mug, goblet, etc.). 2. *elec.* insulator. **vikombe vya simu.** insulators on a telegraph-pole. 3. hub *(of a wheel).* (= **kinu.**) *Cf.* **¹komba.**

kikombo 1. (vi-) bend, curve. 2. (*also* **kikombokombo**) *adv.* in a curved/crooked way. *fig.* unintelligibly. **maneno ya —.** unintelligible words. *Cf.* **¹komba.**

¹kikomo (vi-) (*also* **komo, ma-**) 1. end, conclusion, termination, boundary, goal. **— cha uso.** forehead. 2. place to stop, stand. 3. *gramm.* object. *Cf.* **¹koma.**

²kikomo* (vi-) *dimin. of* **omo.**

kikomunisti*, **kikomyunisti** [*Engl.*]: **—a —.** *adj.* communistic. *Cf.* **mkomunisti, ukomunisti.**

¹kikondo (vi-) kikondo (variety of banana).

²kikondo (vi-) *dimin. of* **mkondo.**

kikondoo 1. (vi-) (*dimin. of* **kondoo**) lamb. 2. *adv.* like a sheep, unresistingly, patiently, meekly. *Cf.* **kondoo.**

kikongo 1. *sing.* Kikongo language. 2.: **—a —.** *adj.* Congolese.

kikongwe 1. (vi-) very old person, one bent and feeble from old age. 2. *adv.*: **enda –.** to walk bent over and with difficulty. *Cf.* [3]**kongwe,** [1]**konga.**

kikono (vi-) 1. stump of an arm, deformed arm. 2. antenna *(of insects). Cf.* **mkono.**

kikonyo (vi-) stalk, stem *(of fruit). Cf.* **mkono, kikono.**

kikope (vi-) 1. *dimin. of* [3]**kope, ukope.** 2. *med.* inflammation of the eyes, conjunctivitis, sty (= **chokea**).

kikopo (vi-): **mtoto –.** ruffian, rascal, cheat. *Cf.* [3]**kopa.**

kikopwe (vi-) *see* **kilopwe.**

kikora *sing., rare* joy, rejoicing. *Cf.* **kora.**

[1]**kikore** (vi-) a newly laid out garden or field. *Cf.* **kore.**

[2]**kikore** (vi-) rich/famous person. *Cf.* **kora.**

kikorokoro (vi-) 1. *rare* thing, piece of equipment, utensil. 2. *(plur.)* goods, chattels, belongings, utensils, appurtenances. (= **makolokolo.**)

kikorombwe (vi-) call, shout *(with the hands cupped around the mouth).* **piga –.** to call/ shout to someone.

[1]**kikoromeo** (vi-) a coconut when almost ripe. *Cf.* [1]**koroma.**

[2]**kikoromeo** (vi-) *anat.* Adam's apple. *Cf.* [2]**koroma.**

kikororo (vi-) water-pipe, hookah. (= **buruma.**)

[1]**kikosi** (vi-) *anat.* nape of the neck. *Cf.* **kosi.**

[2]**kikosi** (vi-) *mil.* unit, troop, squad, platoon. **– cha askari.** a squad of soldiers. **afisa ya vikosi vya jeshi la East Africa.** officer of a unit of the East African army. **– cha askari wapanda farasi.** cavalry squadron.

kikota, kikoto (vi-) stalk of millet (= [2]**kota**).

[1]**kikoto** (vi-) 1. switch, whip *(braided of grass or twigs).* 2. pigtail, braid *(of hair).*

[2]**kikoto** (vi-) *see* **kikotwe.**

[3]**kikoto** (vi-) *see* **kikota.**

kikotwe, kikoto (vi-) kikotwe (kind of fish).

kikozi (vi-) *see* [1]**kozi.**

kikristo*, kikristu [*Port.?*]: **–a –.** *adj.* Christian. *Cf.* **mkristo, Ukristo.**

[1]**kikuba*, kiguba** (vi-) bundle of aromatic plants *(worn by women at the throat).*

[2]**kikuba*** 1. (vi-) *dimin. of* **kuba.** 2.: **–a –.** *adj.* dome-shaped.

kikucha (vi-) *dimin. of* **ukucha.**

kikuchia (vi-) hangnail. *Cf.* **ukucha.**

[1]**kikuku** (vi-) bracelet, anklet. **– cha kupandia farasi.** stirrup.

[2]**kikuku** (vi-) *dimin. of* [1]**kuku.**

kikuli *sing.* fright, terror, dread, horror. (= **hofu kuu.**)

kikulia (vi-) someone who grew up in a place (but was not born there). *Cf.* [1]**kua.**

kikumbatio (vi-) embrace. *Cf.* **kumbatia.**

kikumbo (vi-; *also* **kumbo, ma-**) push, thrust, butt. **piga –.** shove, jostle, butt. *Cf.* [1]**kumba.**

kikumbuko *sing., rare* memory, remembrance. *Cf.* **kumbuka.**

kikumi (vi-) ten-cent piece. *Cf.* **kumi.**

kikunazi* [*Pers.*] (vi-) *anat., vulg.* clitoris (= **kisimi, kinembe**). *Cf.* **kunazi.**

kikundi (vi-) (*dimin. of* **kundi**) 1. (small) group, clique, circle. **vikundi vya muawana.** cooperatives. **vikundi vya kivita.** military circles. 2. *mil.* battalion. **– cha vifaru.** armored battalion. *Cf.* **kundi.**

kikundu (vi-) *med.* hemorrhoid(s). *Cf.* **mkundu.**

kikunja: – jamvi (vi-) court fee, costs. *Cf.* **kunja.**

kikunje (vi-) *see* **kikunjo.**

kikunjo, kikunje (vi-) 1. fold, crease, seam, pleat, edge. 2. *fig.* wrinkle. *Cf.* **kunja.**

kikuta (vi-) (*dimin. of* **ukuta**) stone border, masonry enclosure *(e.g., around a grave).*

[1]**kikuti** (vi-) chance, opportunity; event. *Cf.* [1]**kuta.**

[2]**kikuti** (vi-) *dimin. of* **kuti.**

[1]**kikuto** (vi-) something rolled up, roll.

[2]**kikuto** (vi-) *rare* hyena (= **fisi**).

kikuukuu 1. (vi-) old, worn-out article of clothing. 2. *adj. & adv.* useless, worthless. *Cf.* **kuukuu.**

kikwapa (vi-) 1. *see* **kwapa.** 2. perspiration *(from the armpits).* **ananuka –.** He smells of perspiration. 3. armhole *(of a garment).*

kikwaru (vi-) cock's spur. (= **kipi.**)

[1]**kikwata, kwata** *adv.:* **enda –.** go on foot. *Cf.* **kiatu,** [1]**kwata.**

[2]**kikwata** (vi-) a tall thorny shrub *(Acacia mellifera)* used to form hedges.

kikwato (vi-) *dimin. of* **kwato, ukwato.**

kikwazo (vi-) hindrance, difficulty, impediment. *Cf.* **kwaa.**

kikwe (vi-): **– cha mkono** *rare* elbow. (= **kiko** [**cha mkono**], **kivi.**)

kikwi (**vikwi, zikwi**) 1. crowd, multitude, countless number. 2. *liter.* thousand *(only in tales;* = **elfu**).

kikwifukwifu *sing.* 1. hiccup. 2. sobbing.

kila*, **killa, kula, kulla** 1. *adj.* each, every, all, entire. **– mtu.** every person, all people. **– mji.** every city, the entire city. **– mara.** every time. 2. *adv.* ever *(generalizing).* **– aendako.** Wherever he goes. **– aendapo.** Whenever he goes.

kilabu*, **klabu** [*Engl.*] (vi-) 1. club. **mwanachama wa –.** club member. 2. bar.

kilaji (vi-) food. *Cf.* [1]**la.**

kilalanungu (vi-) *bot.* a hardy creeping plant *(Callopsis Volkensii).*

kilalio (vi-) 1. sleeping-place, bed(stead). 2. evening meal. *Cf.* **lala.**

kilalo (vi-) resting-place, shelter. *Cf.* **lala.**

kilango (vi-) (*dimin. of* **mlango**) 1. narrow passage. **– cha bahari.** strait, channel, narrows, fairway, waterway. **– cha mlima.** ravine, defile, bottleneck. 2. valve.

kile *demon.* **ki-** *cl.* that. **kiti –.** that chair. **kitabu –.** that book.

kilegesambwa 1. (vi-) *anat.* kneecap. (= **pia ya goti.**) 2. *prov., arch.* Everyone can expect to have bad things said about him during his lifetime.

kileji (vi-) kileji (a cake made of wheat or rice meal).

kilele*, **kileleta** [*Pers.*] (vi-) tip, peak, highest point. **– cha mlima.** mountaintop. **– cha mti.** treetop. *Cf.* **kinyangalele.**

kileleta* (vi-) *see* **kilele.**

kilema (vi-) 1. defect, infirmity. **mwenye –.** cripple. **– cha mkono.** a one-armed person. 2. deformed/crippled person. *Cf.* **lemaa.**

kilemba (vi-) 1. turban. **piga –.** put on/wear a turban. **vunja –.** take off a turban. *fig.* **– cha jogoo.** cock's comb. 2. praise, flattery; reputation. *coll.* **usinivike – cha ukambaa (ukoka).** Don't try to flatter me (*lit.:* Don't put a turban of grass on my head). 3. gift *(e.g., that given by a bridegroom to his father-in-law),* gratuity. *Cf.* **mkilemba.**

kilembwa (vi-) termination, tip, point. **– cha titi.** nipple.

kilembwe (vi-) great-great-grandchild.

kilemea: – nembo. (vi-) *bot.* a shrub *(Cremaspora africana).*

kilendo (vi-) kilendo (kind of fish).

kilenga (vi-) foetus *(in the fourth month).* (= **kijusu.**)

kilenge (vi-) kilenge (a children's game).

kileo (vi-) 1. intoxication. 2. intoxicating beverage. *Cf.* **lewa.**

kileti (vi-) 1. handle, (door-)latch, lever. 2. *naut.* thole, rowlock. 3. stick used in rope-making.

kili *pl. of* **ukili.**

[1]**kilifu*** (vi-) *see* **difu.**

[2]**kilifu*** *see* **kalifu.**

kilihafu (vi-) first stomach *(of ruminants).* (= **kisafu.**)

kilili (vi-) *dimin. of* **ulili.**

kilima (vi-) (*dimin. of* **mlima**) hill, knoll.

kilimbili (vi-) wrist; *(rare)* upper arm.

kilimi (vi-) 1. (*dimin. of* **ulimi**) *anat.* uvula. 2. *med.* sore throat. 3. mouthpiece *(of a wind instrument).* 4. *fig.* bad/abusive language. *Cf.* **limi, mlimi, ulimi.**

kilimia *sing., astr.* Pleiades. *Cf.* [1]**lima.**

kilimo (vi-) 1. agriculture, cultivation. 2. produce, crop(s). *Cf.* [1]**lima.**

kilimwengu *sing.* internationalism. **– ya wafanya kazi.** proletarian internationalism. **–a –.** international. **mchafuko wa –.** international crisis. *Cf.* **ulimwengu.**

kilinda (vi-) guard, watchman, protector. *Cf.* **linda.**

kilindi (vi-) place where water is deep, channel. *Cf.* **lindi.**

Kilindini *sing.* Kilindini (the harbor of Mombasa). *Cf.* **kilindi.**

kilindo (vi-) 1. (act of) watching, guarding, protecting *(especially planted fields against birds).* 2. watchman's platform *(on a plantation).* 3. shelter *(from rain, etc.).* 4. storage place. *Cf.* **linda.**

kilinge (vi-) 1. secret meeting-place *(of medicine-men).* 2. *fig.* secretiveness, mystification. **maneno ya –.** mysterious, unintelligible words.

[1]**kilingo** (vi-) (*dimin. of* **ulingo**) platform *(for keeping a watch over planted fields).*

[2]**kilingo** (vi-) 1. notch, cut, mark *(on trees, to show the way).* 2. *fig.* example, model, pattern. *Cf.* [1]**linga.**

[3]**kilingo** (vi-) war drum.

kiliniki* (–) *see* **kliniki.**

kilinzi (vi-) bracelet of beads.

kilio (vi-) 1. sound. 2. cry, scream; weeping, lamentation, mourning. 3. *gramm.* interjection. *Cf.* **[1]lia.**

killa* *see* **kila.**

kilo* [*Engl.*] (–) kilogram.

kilometa* [*Engl.*] (–) kilometer.

kilopwe, kikopwe (vi-) *bot.* kilopwe (shrub, *Jaquemontia capitata).*

kilotia (vi-) *see* **kidotia.**

kilua (vi-) flower of a species of liana. *Cf.* **mkilua.**

kiludhu*, kuludhu (–) velvet.

kilunzi *sing.* kilunzi (a secret language in which the final syllables of words become the first).

kiluwiluwi (vi-) 1. insect larva. 2. tadpole.

[1]kima* (vi-) 1. price, value. **– chake kadiri gani?** How much is it worth? 2. measure; size, stature. *Cf.* **[1]kimo.**

[2]kima (–) kima (kind of monkey, *Cercopithecus pygerythrus).*

[3]kima* [*Pers.*] (–) minced meat.

kimaada* *adj.* right, correct, true; genuine; fitting, proper; due.

kimacho, kimachomacho *adj.* & *adv.* 1. alert, wide awake. **lala –.** lie (stay) awake. 2. open, frank. **alisema naye –.** He spoke frankly with him. *Cf.* **jicho.**

kimachomacho *see* **kimacho.**

kimagamaga *adv.* very fast, in a hurry. **nilipomwona alikuwa anakwenda –.** When I saw him, he was in a great hurry. *Cf.* **magamaga.**

kimaji, kimajimaji *adj.* & *adv.* watery, wet, damp, swampy, misty, steamy. *Cf.* **maji.**

kimajimaji *see* **kimaji.**

kimako *sing.* astonishment, amazement. *Cf.* **[2]maka.**

kimalidadi*, kimaridadi: –a –. *adj.* elegant, fashionable; *(pej.)* overdressed. *Cf.* **malidadi.**

kimanda (vi-) 1. (*rare* **kiwanda**) omelet, scrambled eggs. 2. a trial by ordeal *(the parties are given bread to eat; the guilty person is supposed to be unable to swallow it).* *Cf.* **manda.**

Kimanga* *rare* (= **Kiarabu**) 1. *sing.* the Arabic language. 2. *adv.* in the Arab manner. 3.: **–a –.** *adj.* Arab, Arabic, Arabian. *Cf.* **[2]Manga.**

kimangalingali *see* **kingalingali.**

kimangari (vi-) *bot.* kimangari (hardy plant, *Ramphicarpa veronicaefolia).*

kimango (vi-) round grinding stone *(for grinding flour, etc.)*. *Cf.* **mango.**

kimanjano: -a —. *adj.* yellow. **rangi ya —.** yellow pigment (dye, paint). *Cf.* **manjano.**

kimarekani* *see* **kiamerika.**

kimaridadi* *adj.* *see* **kimalidadi.**

kimashamba* 1. *sing.* language/manners/customs of the agricultural peoples. 2.: **-a —.** *adj.* rural, rustic; rude, crude, rough. *Cf.* **shamba.**

kimasomaso *sing.* pretext, excuse, pretence, evasion, dissimulation, hypocrisy. **fanya —.** be evasive, make excuses, pretend.

kimatu (vi-) young locust. *Cf.* **matumatu, tunutu.**

kimau (vi-) uniform shirt *(with short sleeves)*.

kimavi: — cha kuku. *bot.* variety of weed *(Ageratum conyzoides,* sometimes used as a vegetable).

kimazeru (vi-) *see* **zeru.**

kimba (vi-) 1. *rare* corpse (= **maiti**). **anguka kimba kimba.** lose consciousness, faint. 2. heap of dung/excrement.

kimbaombao (vi-) 1. kimbaombao (kind of chameleon). 2. *coll.* tall, thin person. *Cf.* **bao.**

kimbia run away, take flight, escape. **— mbio.** *coll.* beat a hasty retreat, take to one's heels. **kukimbia kwa kupeana.** relay race. *intr.* **kimbika.** *pass.* **kimbiwa.** *appl.* **kimbilia.** 1. run to someone. 2. run up. **kimbilia roho.** save someone's life. *appl.-caus.* **kimbiliza.** 1. save oneself. 2. *(w. int. force)* hurry, hasten. **kimbiliza kazi.** work fast. **kimbiliza maneno.** talk very fast (and unintelligibly). *caus.* **kimbiza.** 1. put someone to flight. 2. help someone escape, abduct someone. *caus.-refl.* **jikimbiza.** hide, remain in hiding. *Cf.* **kimbilio, kimbio, kimbizi, mkimbiaji, mkimbizi.**

kimbilio (ma-) 1. refuge, hiding-place, shelter. 2. *fig.* help, salvation. *Cf.* **kimbia.**

kimbimbi *sing.* gooseflesh. (= **msisimko.**) **fanya —.** shiver *(from cold)*.

kimbio, kimbiombio *adv.* at full speed, on the double, quickly, hastily. *Cf.* **kimbia.**

kimbiombio *see* **kimbio.**

kimbizi: maji ya —. rushing/turbulent water, torrent. *Cf.* **kimbia.**

kimbugibugi (vi-) *bot.* kimbugibugi (variety of grass, *Dactylotenium aegyptiacum)*.

kimbunga (vi-) 1. storm, whirlwind, hurricane, typhoon. 2. *fig.*: **— cha nyama.** rinderpest, hoof-and-mouth disease.

kimburu (vi-) 1. half-wild cat. (= **shume.**) 2. *rare* mongoose. (= **nguchiro.**)

kimea (vi-) sprouted seed of grain *(used for making beer)*. *Cf.* **mea.**

kimelea (vi-) 1. a parasitic plant. 2. a plant/tree which grows wild. *Cf.* **mea.**

kimene *sing.* pride, arrogance; contempt, disdain. *Cf.* **mena.**

kimenomeno (vi-) disease of the teeth (thrush, pyorrhea). *Cf.* **jino.**

kimerimeti (vi-) *see* **kimeti.**

kimeta, kimete, kimetameta (vi-) 1. radiance, glitter, sparkle, brightness. 2. spark. *Cf.* **[1]meta.**

kimetameta (vi-) *see* **kimeta.**

kimete (vi-) *see* **kimeta.**

kimeti, kimetimeti, kimerimeti (vi-) glowworm, firefly. *Cf.* **[1]meta.**

kimi (—) pay, wage(s). **— cha chini.** minimum wage.

[1]kimia (vi-) 1. (fine) network, netting. 2. net, casting net.

[2]kimia (—) *see* **kimya.**

kimio (vi-) (*dimin. of* **umio**) 1. *anat.* **uvula.** 2. *med.* sore throat, tonsillitis.

kimkumku 1. *sing., rare* madness, insanity, lunacy. (= **wazimu, kichaa.**) 2. (—) *rare* lie, falsehood. (= **uwongo.**)

[1]kimo* (vi-) 1. measure, size; height, stature; altitude. **— cha mtu.** the size/stature/height of a person. 2. tape measure, measuring tape. *Cf.* **[1]kima.**

[2]kimo *loc.* be in something.

kimondo (vi-) *see* **[1]kimwondo.**

kimoyo, kimoyomoyo (vi-) (*dimin. of* **moyo**) 1. grief, sorrow, pain. 2. *med.* heart disease. 3. sweetheart, favorite *(term of endearment).*

kimoyomoyo *see* **kimoyo.**

Kimrima* *sing.* coast language (= **Swahili**). *Cf.* **mrima.**

kimu* 1. *Isl.* begin prayer *(in a mosque).* 2. provide with food/clothing. 3. harp on *(a subject). Cf.* **mkimu.**

kimua *see* **kimwa.**

kimulimuli, kimurimuri (vi-) 1. glowworm, firefly. 2. will-o'-the-wisp. *Cf.* **mulika.**

kimurimuri (vi-) *see* **kimulimuli.**

Kimvita *sing.* Swahili dialect of Mombasa. *Cf.* **Mvita, Mmvita.**

kimwa, kimua 1. fly into a rage, become violent. 2. be out of sorts/discontented. *Cf.* **mkimwa, ukimwa.**

kimwenye, kimwinyi *sing. (rec., comm.)* feudalism. *Cf.* **enye, mwenye.**

kimwezi (vi-) (*dimin. of* **mwezi**) artificial satellite, sputnik (*lit.:* little moon).

kimwinyi *see* **kimwenye.**

kimwitu 1. (vi-) *dimin. of* mwitu. 2. *adv.* in a wild/uncultivated manner. 3.: **-a —.** *adj.* of the jungle, wild.

[1]**kimwondo, kimondo** (vi-) (*also* **— cha nyota**) *astr.* shooting star, meteor.

[2]**kimwondo** (vi-) *rare* stupid person, fool. (= **mjinga.**)

kimya, kimia 1. *sing.* calm, quiet. *prov.* **— kingi kina mshinda mkuu.** Great calm is followed by a great storm. **nyamaza —.** be silent, keep silence. 2. *adv.* (*also* **kimya-kimya**) still, quiet.

kimyakimya *see* **kimya 2.**

[1]**kina** (vi-) (great) depth. **— cha bahari.** deep place in the ocean, a deep. *Cf.* **mwina.**

[2]**kina*** (—) *see* **akina.**

[3]**kina*** (vi-) *liter.* rhyme. **tunga (tia) vina.** make rhymes, write poetry. **shairi la (lenye) vina.** rhyming poem.

kinaa* (—) *see* **kinaya.**

kinaganaga *adv.* 1. personally, oneself. **kuja —.** to come oneself/personally. 2. thoroughly, in detail. **eleza —.** explain in detail.

kinagiri (vi-) (gold) pendant (on a necklace).

kinai* have enough, be satisfied. **wamekula mpaka wamekinai.** They ate until they were satisfied. *fig.* be satiated/surfeited; feel disgust/loathing. **amekinai.** 1. He has had enough (to eat). 2. He is surfeited/has no appetite. *intr.* **kinaika.** *caus.* **kinaisha.** *Cf.* **kinaifu, kinaya, mkinaifu, ukinaifu.**

kinaifu* *adj.* self-contented, complacent. *fig.* proud, arrogant. *Cf.* **kinai.**

kinakilo* *sing.* carbon paper, tracing paper. *Cf.* **nakili.**

kinamasi, kinamassi (vi-) 1. slime, slimy substance *(mucilage, etc.)*. 2. swamp, marsh.

kinamassi (vi-) *see* **kinamasi.**

kinamisa (—) *rare* deep/dead silence.

kinamo *sing.* flexibility, pliancy, plasticity. **udongo wa —.** potter's clay. *Cf.* **nama.**

kinana (vi-) kinana (kind of yam).

kinanasi (vi-) kinanasi (variety of grass).

kinanda (vi-) 1. stringed instrument (a kind of banjo). 2. piano. 3. harmonium, (parlor-) organ. 4. mouth organ. 5.: **— cha rekodi.** record player. 6. *ornith.* (species of) finch (= **binti chuma**).

[1]**kinanga** (—) kinanga (kind of drum).

[2]**kinanga*** (vi-) *dimin. of* **nanga.**

[1]**kinara*** (vi-) 1. *(dimin. of* **mnara***)* candlestick. 2. platform, podium *(usually for Moslem religious observance in the open air)*. *Cf.* **nuru.**

[2]**kinara*** [*Ind.*] (vi-) embroidery *(on the collar of a kanzu).*

kinaya*, kinaa (–) independence, self-sufficiency; *(fig.)* self-content, complacency; arrogance, conceit. *Cf.* **kinai.**

kinda 1. (ma-) (*also* **mkinda, mi-, wa-**) young of animals/birds. *Originally only* **– la ndege.** chick. *Now also* **– la ng'ombe.** calf. **– la farasi.** foal, colt. 2. *adj.* young, immature. **mnazi mkinda.** young coconut palm.

kindakindaki *adv.* above, up(wards), aloft. (= **juujuu.**)

kindana *dial.* object, protest. **aliambiwa ahame lakini alikindana.** He was told that he had to move, but he protested. *Cf.* **kindano;** *also* [1]**kinga, kinza.**

kindanindani *adv.* surreptitiously, furtively, secretly. **cheka –.** laugh furtively. **vita ya –.** partisan warfare. *Cf.* **ndani.**

kindano (ma-) *(dial.)* objection, protest. *Cf.* **kindana.**

kindi (*dial.* **chindi, sindi**) (–) squirrel.

kindoro (vi-) 1. red pigment. 2. red sweet-potato. **muhogo wa –.** sweet manioc. 3.: **kofia ya –.** red cap, fez.

kindu (–) kindu (fruit of the mkindu).

kindugu *see* **kidugu.**

kinegwa, kinega (vi-) *ornith.* swallow.

kinembe (vi-) *anat.* clitoris. (= **kisimi.**)

kinena (vi-) *anat.* groin, mons veneris. *Cf.* [2]**nena, manena.**

[1]**kinga** 1. protect. **ninajikinga macho na jua.** I protect my eyes from the sun. 2. check, obstruct, stop. **nipishe usinikinge.** Don't stand in my way. 3. *fig.* contradict, object, oppose. 4. intercept, catch, collect. **– mvua.** collect rainwater. *caus.* **kingiza.** defend. *refl.-caus.* **jikingiza.** defend one-self. *stat.* **kingama.** be between, be in the way; cut across, intersect. *ass.* **kingana.** protect each other; oppose each other. 5. (–) check, obstruction, means of protection, screen, safety-device; protection, defense, aid. *Cf.* **kingio, kingo, mkinga, mkingaji, mkingamo, mkingiko, ukingo.**

[2]**kinga** (–) 1. piece of firewood, log. 2. fire-brand. *prov.* **– na – ndipo moto uwakapo.** Log after log keeps the fire burning.

[1]**kingaja** (vi-) bracelet *(of grains or seeds or of glass beads).*

[2]**kingaja** (vi-) back of the hand.

kingalingali, kimangalingali *adv.* backwards, on the back. **lala –.** to lie on one's back.

kingama *stat. of* [1]**kinga.**

kingana *ass. of* [1]**kinga.**

Kingazija *sing.* language of the Comoro Islands. *Cf.* **Ngazija, Mngazija.**

kingilizi (–) *see* **kingio.**

kingio, kingo, kingilizi (–, ma-) protection, cover, screen, shield. **– ya taa.** lampshade. *Cf.* [1]**kinga.**

kingiza *caus. of* [1]**kinga.**

kingo (–) 1. *see* **kingio.** 2. threshold, doorstep, sill. 3. *fig., med.* cataract. 4. *pl. of* **ukingo.** *Cf.* [1]**kinga, ukingo.**

kingoe, kigoe (vi-) 1. hooked stick *(for pulling down the branches of fruit trees).* 2. *rec.* golf club. *Cf.* **ngoeka.**

kingojeo (vi-) *see* **kingojo.**

kingojezi (vi-) *see* **kingojo.**

kingojo, kingojeo, kingojezi (vi-) 1. keeping, saving, preservation. 2. watching, guarding. **kaa (linda) –.** keep watch/guard. 3. sentry post, guard station. *Cf.* **ngoja.**

king'ong'o *sing.* talking through the nose. **ana –.** He talks through his nose. *Cf.* [2]**ng'ong'a.**

kingoringori, kinjorinjori *adv.* lengthwise, longitudinally. *Cf.* **njorinjori.**

king'oto (–) *see* **kigogota.**

Kingozi *sing.* Old Swahili *(the language of Malindi and Pate, preserved in poetry).*

kingu* [*Engl.*] (–) king.

kingubwa (vi-) *see* **kingugwa.**

kingugwa, kingubwa (vi-) spotted hyena.

kingune (vi-) stunted tree.

kinguo (vi-) (*dimin. of* **nguo**) small piece *(of cloth),* rag.

Kingwana *sing.* Congo Swahili. (= **kiungwana.**)

[1]**kini*, kinika** be true, be probable. *Cf.* **yakini.**

[2]**kini** (vi-) *see* [1]**kiini.**

kinika* *see* [1]**kini.**

kining'ina, kinying'ina (vi-) great-great-grandchild.

kinini* (–) *see* **kwinini.**

kinjia, kijia, kajia (vi-) (*dimin. of* **njia**) narrow road/street, path. *Cf.* **ja.**

[1]**kinjorinjori, kinjurinjuri, kinjorijori, kinjurijuri** (–) style of cutting the hair (one tuft is left long). *Cf.* **njorinjori.**

[2]**kinjorinjori** *see* **kingoringori.**

kinjuri(n)juri (–) *see* [1]**kinjorinjori.**

kinofu (vi-) (*dimin. of* **mnofu**) piece/bite of meat.

kinokero (vi-) gazelle, impala. (= ^{4}**paa.**)

kinono (vi-) a (young) fatted animal. *Cf.* **nona.**

kinoo (vi-) 1. whetstone, grindstone, knife sharpener. 2. *fig.* bar *(of soap). Cf.* **noa.**

kinsuiri (vi-) *rare* ring finger.

kinu (vi-) 1. mortar, press, mill. **– cha moshi.** steam engine. **– cha taa (stimu).** power plant. **– cha kushindikia mafuta.** mold for pressing butter. **– cha kuchambulia pamba.** cotton gin. 2. hub *(of a wheel, bicycle, etc.).* 3.: **vinu.** *coll.* machinery.

Kinubi* 1. *sing.* Nubian language. **-a –.** Nubian. 2. (vi-) Kinubi (Nubian musical instrument similar to a harp). 3.: **-a –.** *adj.* Nubian, Sudanese. *Cf.* **Mnubi.**

kinuka: – jio (–) kind of flower (four o'clock, *Miribilis jalapa).*

kinundu 1. (vi-) (*dimin. of* **nundu**) (small) lump, hump; tubercle; *(fig.)* pushbutton. 2. (*also* **kinundunundu**) *adj./adv.* bumpy, uneven.

kinundunundu *see* **kinundu.**

kinusi (–) *see* ^{1}**chunusi.**

kinwa (vi-) *see* **kinywa.**

kinyaa (vi-) 1. something which causes disgust: discharge, secretion; excrement; filth. 2. disgust, repugnance. *Cf.* ^{2}**nyara.**

kinyago (vi-) 1. comedy, farce, masquerade. 2. comedian, clown, joker. 3. kind of dance *(performed at the initiation rites of children).* 4. scarecrow. *Cf.* **manyago, unyago.**

kinyakuzi (vi-) *see* **kigwaru.**

kinyama 1. (vi-) *dimin. of* **mnyama.** 2. *adv.* like an animal, in a brutish/coarse way. *Cf.* **mnyama.**

kinyamkela (vi-) wind spirit. **pepo ya –.** whirlwind.

kinyangalele (vi-) point, tip, summit, peak, top. *Cf.* **kilele.**

kinyangalika, kinyangarika *sing.* a nondescript/useless/meaningless thing. *Cf.* **nyangalika, mnyangalika.**

kinyegele, kinyegere (vi-) *see* **nyegere.**

kinyegenyege *sing.* prurience, lasciviousness. *Cf.* **nyega.**

kinyegere (vi-) *see* **nyegere.**

kinyeleo, kinyweleo (vi-); **nyeleo, nyweleo, unyweleo** (ma-) pore *(of the skin). Cf.* **nya, nywa.**

kinyemi, nyemi 1. (–) something good/pleasant. 2. *adj. & adv.* good, pleasant.

kinyenyevu, kinyevunyevu *sing.* moistness, dampness. *Cf.* **nya.**

kinyerenyere *adv.* gently, calmly, slowly.

kinyesi, kinyezi (vi-), **nyesi** (ma-) excreta, excrement, feces. *Cf.* **nya.**

[1]**kinyevu** *sing.* *see* **kinyenyevu.**

[2]**kinyevu** *sing.* tickling, itching; prurience, lasciviousness. *Cf.* [1]**nyea.**

[3]**kinyevu** (vi-) *see* **kigwaru.**

kinyevunyevu (vi-) *see* **kinyenyevu.**

kinyezi *sing.* *see* **kinyesi.**

kinying'inga (vi-) *see* **kining'inga.**

kinyo (vi-) *anat.* anus (= **mkundu**). *Cf.* **nya.**

[1]**kinyonga** (vi-) *med.* lameness caused by disease/injury of the hip. *Cf.* [1]**nyonga, unyonga.**

[2]**kinyonga** (vi-) chameleon. (= **kigeugeu.**)

kinyonge 1. (vi-) misery, wretchedness; depravity. 2. *adv.* miserably, wretchedly. **kaa —.** to live wretchedly/in poverty. **lia —.** to cry piteously. *Cf.* **nyonge.**

kinyongo *sing.* 1. whim, mood; fad; melancholy. **mwenye —.** hypochondriac. 2. qualms, scruples; aversion. *prov.* **mpenzi hana —.** A lover has no scruples. 3. bitterness, vindictiveness. *Cf.* [2]**nyonga, nyonge.**

kinyong'onyo 1. *sing.* fatigue, weariness, weakness. 2. *adv.* weakly, wearily. **enda —.** to walk along wearily. *Cf.* **nyong'onyea.**

kinyozi, mnyozi (vi-) barber, hairdresser. *Cf.* **nyoa.**

kinyuma *see* **kinyume.**

kinyumba (vi-) (*dimin. of* **nyumba**) 1. concubine. **kaa** (*or* **ishi**) **—.** live with a woman. 2. *pl.* household utensils. **-a —.** household..., domestic.

kinyumbu (vi-) *see* **nyumbu.**

kinyume, kinyuma *sing.* 1. back part, rear; background; reversal, inversion. **msemo wa —.** thieves' Latin *(produced by moving the last syllable of each word to the beginning; cf.* **kihunzi**). 2. opposite, contrary; antithesis. **habari ya —.** a contrary report. 3. result, consequence. 4. *adv.* backwards, behind; in the opposite/contrary way. **mpango wa —.** reverse order. *Cf.* [1]**nyuma.**

kinyunga *sing.* dough.

kinyunya (vi-) confection, piece of candy/cake. *Cf.* **nyunyiza.**

kinywa, kinwa, kanwa (vi-) mouth, throat. **kwa —.** orally. **— wazi.** with open mouth. *Cf.* **nywa.**

kinywaji, kinyweo, kinywewa (vi-) beverage, drink. *Cf.* **nywa.**

kinyweleo (vi-) *see* **kinyeleo.**

kinyweo (vi-) 1. *see* **kinywaji.** 2. drinking-vessel. *Cf.* **nywa.**

kinza retort, object, protest; check, obstruct. *ass.* **kinzana. kinzana na mtu.** quarrel with someone. *Cf.* **kinzani, kinzano, mkinzani, ukinzani;** *and also* [1]**kinga.**

kinzani *adj.* obstinate, refractory; quarrelsome. *Cf.* **kinza.**

kinzano (ma-) (*usually* **makinzano**) contradiction, objection, protest; obstruction, obstacle. *Cf.* **kinza.**

[1]**kio** (vi-) *see* [1]**kioo.**

[2]**kio** (vi-) *see* [2]**kioo.**

kioga, kiyoga (vi-) *see* **uyoga.**

kiogajivu (vi-) *ornith.* blue roller.

kiogeo (vi-) bathtub. *Cf.* [1]**oga.**

kioja (vi-) *see* **kiroja.**

kiokosi, kiokozi (vi-) reward given the finder of a lost object. *Cf.* **okota.**

kiokote (vi-) foundling (*child*). *Cf.* **okota.**

[1]**kiokozi** (vi-) (act of) recovering/saving/rescuing. *Cf.* [2]**okoa.**

[2]**kiokozi** (vi-) *see* **kiokosi.**

kiolezo (vi-) pattern, sample, specimen, example; sampler *(sewing, embroidery). Cf.* **oleza.**

kiomo* 1. (vi-) *dimin. of* **omo** (*also* **kikomo**). 2. *adv.* straight ahead.

kiongozi (vi-) 1. leader, guide; conductor *(of a band, orchestra).* 2. leadership, vanguard. *Cf.* **ongoa.**

kiongwe (vi-) *see* **kihongwe.**

kionja (vi-): **– mchuzi.** small beard below the lip, imperial (*lit.:* 'gravy-taster'). *Cf.* **onja.**

kionjo (vi-) taste, sample *(of food, etc.). Cf.* **onja.**

kionyo (vi-) *rare* characteristic, sign, indication, allusion, hint, warning. *Cf.* **ona.**

[1]**kioo, kio** (vi-) (sheet/pane of) glass, (**– cha kujitazamia**) mirror. **– cha dirisha.** windowpane. **– cheupe.** clear glass.

[2]**kioo, kio** (vi-) *rare* fishhook. (= **ndoana.**)

kiopoo (vi-) hook, stick/pole with a hooked end; handle *(of a pump). Cf.* **opoa.**

kiosha (vi-) 1. **– miguu.** (ceremonial washing of the feet *(on the occasion of a marriage).* 2. payment made at a wedding for such ceremonial washing. *Cf.* **osha.**

kiosho (vi-) 1. (act of, place for) washing. 2. what is needed for washing; (*usually* **viosho**) washing utensils. *Cf.* **osha.**

kiota, kioto (vi-) nest, roost *(of fowls). Cf.* [2]**ota.**

kioteo (vi-) *see* [2]**oteo.**

kioto (vi-) *see* kiota.

kiowe (vi-) *see* yowe.

kioza *sing.* decay, rottenness; badness; *(med.)* gangrene. – cha matunda, decay of fruit. *fig.* ana – ndani. He has a bad character. *Cf.* oza.

^{1}**kipa** (vi-) that which gives *(w. foll. n.)*. 1.: – mkono. present given by the bridegroom to the bride before he enters the bedroom for the first time. 2.: – imara *rel.* confirmation. *Cf.* ^{1}pa.

^{2}**kipa*** [*Engl.*] (ma-) doorkeeper, porter; *(sport)* goalkeeper.

^{1}**kipaa** (vi-) (*dimin. of* ^{3}paa) edge, side, slope *(of a roof)*. – cha mbele (nyuma). front (back) slope of a roof. *Cf.* ^{2}paa.

^{2}**kipaa** (vi-) *see* kipara.

kipago (vi-) 1. step, rung *(of a ladder)*. 2. threshold, doorstep, sill.

^{1}**kipaji** (vi-) 1. gift, present, donation. 2. *fig.* ability, talent, endowment. ana – kwa lugha. He has a gift for languages. *Cf.* ^{1}pa.

^{2}**kipaji** (vi-) (*dimin. of* ^{2}paji) 1.: – cha uso. forehead, brow, temple. 2. a cosmetic or beauty patch applied to the forehead or temple.

kipakasa *sing.* gift of the bridegroom to the bride after entering the bedroom. *Cf.* ^{1}kipa.

kipaku (vi-), **paku** (–) 1. spot of color. 2. *adj.* spotted, speckled. *Cf.* ^{1}paka.

kipamba* [*Pers.*] (vi-) (*also* upamba, –) tuft of cotton, (small piece of) lint, wadding, cotton-wool. *Cf.* ^{2}pamba.

kipambio (vi-) *see* kipambo.

kipambo, kipambio (vi-) 1. decoration, ornament. 2. furnishings, appointments *(of a house)*. *Cf.* ^{1}pamba.

kipanda (vi-) *dial.* *see* ^{5}panda.

kipande (vi-) (*also* mpande, mi-) 1. piece, part, portion. – cha nyama. a piece of meat. 2. fragment, splinter. 3. instrument, equipment. – cha kupimia. surveying instrument. 4. *arch.* card on which the daily work of a laborer is recorded kazi ya –. work by the day. *Cf.* ^{1}pande, pandikizi, upande.

kipandikizo (vi-) *see* pandikizo.

kipandio (vi-) rung of a ladder. (= kipago.) *Cf.* ^{1}panda.

kipandisho (vi-) *mus.* sharp sign. *Cf.* ^{1}panda.

^{1}**kipanga** (vi-) kipanga (a bird of prey, *Falco Dickensoni)*.

^{2}**kipanga** (vi-) horsefly.

[3]**kipanga** (vi-) *dimin. of* **upanga.**

kipanya (vi-) (*dimin. of* [1]**panya**) mouse. (= **panya mdogo.**)

kipao (vi-) (act, means, etc., of) ascending/ mounting. *Cf.* [2]**paa.**

kipapa (vi-) 1. trembling, shudder, tremor. 2. *med.* chill, ague. *Cf.* [1]**papa.**

kipapae (vi-) witchcraft, black magic.

kipapatiko, kipapato (vi-) tip of a bird's wing or of a single feather. *Cf.* [1]**papa.**

kipapato (vi-) *see* **kipapatiko.**

kipara, kipaa (vi-) bald spot, bald head; *(rel.)* tonsure. *Cf.* [2]**para.**

kipasha: – mto (vi-) heater, hot plate. *Cf.* **pata.**

kipasuasanda (vi-) kipasuasanda (kind of bird). *Cf.* **pasua, sanda.**

Kipate *sing.* Swahili dialect of the island of Pate.

kipato (vi-) earnings, receipts, pay, wages, salary. **– cha shirika.** *fin.* dividend. *Cf.* **pata.**

[1]**kipawa** (vi-) 1. gift, present. 2. *fig.* talent. *Cf.* [1]**pa.**

[2]**kipawa** (vi-) step, rung *(of a ladder).* (= **kipago, kipandio.**)

[3]**kipawa** (vi-) *dimin. of* **upawa.**

kipee (vi-) *see* **kipele.**

kipele, kipee (vi-) (*dimin. of* **upele**) pimple, pustule; *(pl.)* rash.

kipembe, kipembepembe *adj. & adv.* angular; notched, serrated; bent, crooked. *Cf.* [2]**pembe.**

kipembepembe *see* **kipembe.**

kipendo (vi-) *rare* love, affection, devotion. (= **upendo.**) *Cf.* **penda.**

kipendwa (vi-) *see* **kipenzi.**

kipenga, kipyenga (vi-) *rare* whistle. (= **filimki, uluzi, miunzi.**)

kipenge, kipengee, kipengele, kipengere (vi-) *see* **pengee.**

kipenu (vi-) 1. *see* **upenu.** 2. side cabin *(of a ship).*

kipenyo (vi-) 1. perforation, hole *(through something),* aperture, break *(in a hedge, etc.).* 2. socket. 3. axis *(of a globe, etc.),* diameter *(of a circle).* **nusu-kipenyo.** radius. *Cf.* **penya.**

kipenzi, kipendwa (vi-) favorite, pet. *Cf.* **penda.**

[1]**kipeo** (vi-) 1. apex, vertex, peak, tip. **– cha macho.** horizon. 2. *fig.* ideal. *Cf.* [1]**pea.**

[2]**kipeo** (vi-) *rare* broom, brush. (= **ufagio.**) *Cf.* [2]**pea.**

kipepeo (vi-) 1. fan, *(recent)* ventilator. 2. butterfly. 3. kipepeo (kind of fish, *Zanclus cornutus).* *Cf.* **pepa.**

kipepo 1. *sing.* (gentle) breeze. 2. *adj.* ghostly, ghostlike. **anasema –.** He speaks unclearly/confusedly. *Cf.* **pepa.**

kipera, kiperea (vi-) small canoe *(for two people).*

kiperea (vi-) *see* **kipera.**

kipete (vi-) ferrule, ring. *Cf.* [1]**peta.**

kipeto (vi-) 1. container (bag, box, case). **– cha barua.** 2. *rare* envelope. *Cf.* [1]**peta.**

kipi (vi-) cock's spur. *Cf.* **kipia.**

kipia (vi-) 1. top, tip *(of a mountain, tower).* 2. post, pillar *(supporting a ceiling).* 3. *fig. see* **kipi.**

kipigi, kipiki (vi-) small stick *(thrown to knock down fruit).* *Cf.* **piga,** [1]**pikipiki.**

kipigo (vi-) blow, stroke, thrust, impact. **alipata – kikubwa.** He got a good thrashing. *Cf.* **piga.**

kipiki, kipikipiki (vi-) *dimin. of* [1]**pikipiki.**

kipila (vi-) *ornith.* curlew. (= [3]**sululu.**)

[1]**kipilipili** (vi-) kipilipili (kind of edible fish).

[2]**kipilipili*** [*Pers.*] *adj. & adv.* 1. peppery, peppered; resembling peppercorns. **nywele za –.** *anthr.* peppercorn hair. 2. *fig.* clever, shrewd. *Cf.* **pilipili.**

kipima (vi-) measure(ment), measuring instrument. **– joto.** thermometer. **– utengo.** rangefinder. *Cf.* **pima, kipimo.**

kipimio (vi-) scale *(of a map).* *Cf.* **pima.**

kipimo (vi-) 1. measure(ment), instrument for measuring, gauge. **– cha jasho.** barometer. **– cha homa.** fever thermometer. **– cha volta.** voltmeter. **– cha maji.** water gauge. **– cha urefu.** linear measure. **– cha ujazo (nafasi).** cubic (dry/liquid) measure. **– cha eneo.** square/surface measure. **– cha uzito.** weight measure. **– cha wakati.** measurement of time. 2. size *(of shoes, clothes, etc.).* *Cf.* **upinda.**

kipinda 1. (vi-) (*also* **pindi, pinda, ma-**) cadaver, carcass *(of an animal that has died a natural death).* 2. *adv.:* **kufa –.** die a natural death. *Cf.* **upinda.**

kipindi (vi-) 1. (unit, period of) time, period, moment. **– cha asubuhi.** (in the) morning. **kila –** *or* **– chote.** at all times, always. **kwa vipindi.** periodically, regularly. **–a –.** temporary, for the time being. 2. set time, definite period of time. **– cha masoma.** period of instruction. 3. *med.* attack, fit. **– cha homa.** attack of fever. **homa ya vipindi.** intermittent fever. 4. *sport* time, count. 5. (radio) program. 6. *adv.* for the present, for the time being. *Cf.* **pinda.**

kipindo (vi-) 1. wrapper. 2. fold *(of clothing)*. 3. winding-sheet *(for a corpse)*. 4. bag, pocket, purse. *Cf.* **pinda.**

kipindua (vi-): **– cha reli.** *railw.* switch. *Cf.* **pinda.**

[1]**kipindupindu** (vi-) 1. outbreak; spasm, convulsion. 2. *med.* epidemic, cholera. **– cha nyama.** rinderpest. *Cf.* **pinda.**

[2]**kipindupindu** *adv.* headlong, head over heels. *Cf.* **pinda, pindu.**

kipinga (vi-): **– hatari.** safety precaution/ device. *Cf.* **pinga.**

kipingamizi (vi-) *rare* difficulty, obstacle, impediment. *Cf.* **pinga.**

kipingili, kipingiri (vi-) 1. thickening; joint, node *(of plants)*. 2. portion between two nodes or joints. *fig.* **– cha mkono.** lower arm. **– cha mguu.** shinbone. *Cf.* **pinga, pingua.**

kipingiri (vi-) *see* **kipingili.**

kipingo (vi-) 1. obstruction, barrier, hurdle. 2. peg, bar, bolt. 3. pin. 4. necklace, bracelet *(of beads)*. *Cf.* **pinga.**

kipingu (vi-) *dimin. of* **pingu.**

kipingwa (vi-) bar, bolt *(on a door)*. *Cf.* **pinga.**

kipini (vi-) 1. handle, haft, hilt *(of tool, knife, sword, etc.)*. 2. ornament worn in the ear or nose. *Cf.* **mpini.**

kipito (vi-) means of getting through, passage. *Cf.* **pita.**

kipo *loc.* be there. **kiti – barazani.** The chair is there on the veranda.

kipofu. 1. (vi-) (*rare* **mpofu, wa-**) a blind person. 2. *adj. & adv.* blind(ly), heedless(ly), reckless(ly). *Cf.* **pofua.**

kipokee *adv.* alternately, by turns, in succession. *Cf.* **pokea.**

kipokeo (vi-) *mus.* accompaniment, refrain. *Cf.* **pokea.**

[1]**kipolepole** *see* **polepole.**

[2]**kipolepole** (vi-) kipolepole (kind of butterfly).

[1]**kipondo** (vi-) *dimin. of* **pondo.**

[2]**kipondo** (vi-) *see* **kipondwe.**

kipondwe, kipondo *sing.* a dish prepared of crushed grain and grated coconut. *Cf.* **ponda.**

kiponya (vi-) medicine, remedy. *Cf.* **pona.**

kipooza 1. *sing.* (*also* **upooza**) insensibility; *(med.)* paralysis. 2. *adj. & adv.* paralyzed, helpless. *Cf.* **pooza.**

kipopo (vi-) moth, butterfly. (= **kipepeo** 2.) *Cf.* **popo.**

kipora (vi-) *see* [1]**pora.**

kiporo (vi-) (*also* **uporo**) leftovers *(of food)*.

kiporomoko *see* **poromoko.**

kipozamataza (vi-) *ornith.* clapper lark.

kiprotestanti* [*Engl.*]: **–a –.** *adj.* Protestant.

kipua 1. (vi-) *dimin. of* [1]**pua.** 2. *adv.* through the nose, nasally. **sema –.** speak through the nose/with a nasal twang.

kipuku, kipukupuku *adv.* in great quantity, in abundance, without number. **watu wanakufa – maradhi.** The people perished in great numbers from an epidemic. *Cf.* **pukuta.**

kipukupuku *see* **kipuku.**

[1]**kipukusa** (vi-) 1. falling, dropping *(of leaves, fruit)*. 2. *fig.* downfall, ruin. 3. *med.* epidemic, pestilence. *Cf.* **pukuta.**

[2]**kipukusa** (vi-) wood-boring beetle. *Cf.* **pukuta.**

[3]**kipukusa** (vi-) *see* **kipukute.**

kipukute, kipukusa (vi-) kipukute (variety of banana). *Cf.* [2]**pukusa.**

kipuli (vi-) kipuli (ear-pendant)

kipumba (vi-) *see* **kibumba.**

kipumbu (vi-) *med.* scrotal hernia, orchitis, varicocele. *Cf.* **pumbu.**

kipumziko *sing.* rest(ing-place), recreation, refreshment. *Cf.* **pumua.**

[1]**kipungu** (vi-) 1. eagle. 2. osprey.

[2]**kipungu** (vi-) kipungu (kind of fish).

kipunguo (vi-) 1. reduction, decrease. 2. absence, lack, shortage. *Cf.* [2]**punga.**

kipunguzi (vi-) deduction, discount, rebate. *Cf.* [2]**punga.**

kipunjo 1. (vi-) short weight. 2. *adv.* deceitfully, slyly, craftily. **cheka –.** laugh slyly. *Cf.* **punja.**

kipupa *sing.* (excessive) eagerness, haste. **– cha kula.** greediness, gluttony. **– cha kazi.** zeal in one's work. **kwa –.** eagerly, zealously. *Cf.* **pupa.**

kipupwe (vi-) 1. cool season (June-August). 2. a cool wind blowing during this season.

kipure (–) *ornith.* (variety of) dove *(with red at the throat and beneath the wings)*.

kipusa (vi-) 1. small tusk *(of a rhinoceros)*. 2. *coll.* pretty girl.

kipuzi (vi-) bauble, trinket, worthless thing. *Cf.* [2]**puza.**

kipwa (vi-) dry place *(rock, etc.)* left by the tide, shallow place; *(pl.)* reef, sandbank. *Cf.* **pwa.**

kipwe (–) *ornith.* (species of) shrike *(Dryoscopus senegalensis).*

kipwepwe (vi-) *med.* skin-eruption, rash *(applied chiefly to a symptom of leprosy).*

kipyenga (vi-) *see* **kipenga.**

kirafiki* *adv.* in a friendly manner. *Cf.* **rafiki.**

kirago (vi-) 1. sleeping-mat. 2. *fig.* belongings, (personal) affairs. **funga virago vyake.** pack one's bags, close out one's affairs. *Cf.* **rago.**

kirahi*, ikirahi, karaha (–) aversion, dislike, abhorrence, antipathy; prejudice. *Cf.* **karaha.**

kiraia* 1. *adv.* as/like a citizen. **fanya –.** behave as a citizen. 2.: **–a –.** *adj.* civil. **haki za –.** civil rights. *Cf.* **raia.**

kiraka* 1. (vi-) spot of color. 2. patch. **nguo yenye –.** a patched garment. **shona (tia) –.** apply a patch, patch (up), mend. 3. *adv.* (*also* **kiraraka**) spotted, speckled. *Cf.* **marakaraka.**

kiranja (vi-) title applied to the first boy of a group to be circumcised.

kirauni* [*Engl.*] (–) crown.

kireaktive* [*Engl.*]: **ndege ya –.** jet airplane.

kirehani (vi-) kirehani (variety of sweet potato).

kirembo 1. (vi-) (*dimin. of* **rembo**) ornament, decoration; beauty spot *(line, etc., on the face).* 2. *adv.* elegantly, with fine clothes, all dressed up. *Cf.* **remba.**

Kireno* [*Port.*] 1. *sing.* the Portuguese language. 2.: **–a –.** *adj.* Portuguese. *Cf.* **Reno.**

1**kiri*, kirri** recognize, acknowledge; accept, assent, confirm, ratify; approve, grant, allow; admit, confess. **– kosa** plead guilty. *appl.* **kiria.** *intr.* **kirika.** *caus.* **kirisha.** *pass.* **kiriwa.** *Cf.* **ikirari, ukiri.**

2**kiri** (–) strip of matting *(for plaiting).* (= **ukili.**)

kiriba* (vi-) water-container *(made of hide),* waterskin.

kiridhi* *see* **karidhi.**

kirihi*, kirikhi 1. abhor, feel aversion; be prejudiced. 2. offend, treat discourteously. *appl.* **kirihia.** *intr.* **kirihika.** *caus.* **kirihisha.** *pass.* **kirihiwa.** *Cf.* **karaha.**

kirikhi* *see* **kirihi.**

kirimba (vi-) 1. cage *(for a bird or animal)* (= **kizimba**); *(fig.)* meat safe, refrigerator. 2. frame *(of a door or window)*, sill/lintel.

[1]**kirimu***, **kerimu** 1. entertain, give presents to a person. 2. be hospitable/generous. *appl.* **kirimia**. *intr.* **kirimika**. *pass.* **kirimiwa**. *Cf.* **karama, karamu, karimu, mkarimu, ukarimu.**

[2]**kirimu*** [*Engl.*] (–) cream. **rangi ya –.** cream-colored, pale yellow.

kiroboto (vi-) flea.

kiroho*: **–a –.** *adj.* spiritual. *Cf.* **roho.**

kiroja*, **kioja** (vi-) 1. something astonishing/terrifying (*e.g.*, oddity, monster). 2. rarity, marvel. 3. something that gives pleasure, something amusing/comical. *Cf.* **roja.**

kirokironi*, **kirokoroni** (–) *see* **korokoroni.**

kirri* *see* [1]**kiri.**

kirugu (vi-) 1. top of a wall *(of a house)*. 2. height of a house-wall.

kiruhu*, **kiruu** (–) anger, wrath, rage, fury.

kirukanjia (vi-) 1. *zool.* shrew. 2. *ornith.* nightjar. 3. *fig.* restless/footloose person. *Cf.* **ruka.**

kirukia (vi-) kirukia (parasitic climbing plant). *Cf.* **ruka.**

[1]**kirumbizi, kiumbizi** (vi-) *ornith.* golden oriole.

[2]**kirumbizi, kiumbizi** (vi-) kirumbizi (kind of dance or mock fight with sticks).

Kirumi* 1. *sing.* Latin (language). 2. **–a –.** *adj.* Roman, Latin. **kanisa la –.** the Roman (Catholic) Church. *Cf.* **Rumi, Mruma.**

kirungu (vi-) (*dimin. of* **rungu**) knob *(of a radio, etc.)*.

Kirusi*, **Kirussi** 1. *sing.* Russian language. 2.: **–a –.** *adj.* Russian. *Cf.* **Mrusi, Urusi.**

Kirussi* *sing., adj.* *see* **Kirusi.**

kirusu (–) mixture of millet flour *(prepared for making beer)*.

kiruu* (–) *see* **kiruhu.**

[1]**kisa***, **kissa** (vi-) 1. narrative, report, story. 2. explanation; cause, reason. **nipe – cha kunitukana.** Tell me the reason why you are insulting me. 3. matter, affair, business. **nipe – chako.** Tell me your affair *(i.e., something about yourself)*. 4. *jur.* complaint, charge. *Cf.* **mkasa.**

[2]**kisa** (vi-) kernel of a fruit-stone.

kisababu* (vi-) (*dimin. of* **sababu**) pretext, excuse, evasion.

kisafu (vi-) (first) stomach *(of ruminants)*. (= **kilihafu.**)

[1]kisaga (vi-) a dry measure *(app. one quart).* *Cf.* **saga.**

[2]kisaga (vi-) (species of) weevil.

kisagalima (vi-) an old worn-out hoe. *Cf.* **kiselema.**

kisagaunga (vi-) kisagaunga (species of crab). *Cf.* **saga, [1]unga.**

kisahani* (vi-) (*dimin. of* **sahani**) 1. small plate, saucer. 2. *sport* discus. **tupa –.** throw the discus. 3. (phonograph) record.

kisaki* *adv.* firmly, tightly. **funga –.** tie tight. *Cf.* **saki.**

kisalisali* *sing. med.* gonorrhea; *(rare)* bilharzia *(the two diseases are believed to be the same because their symptons are similar).* (= **kisonosono, kichocho.**)

kisambare (vi-) kisambare (species of grass, *Lobelia fervens*).

kisambo *sing. see* **kisamvu.**

kisamli (vi-) *see* **kitamli.**

kisamvu, kisambo *sing.* vegetable dish *(prepared with manioc leaves and beans).*

kisanamu* (vi-) (*dimin. of* **sanamu**) picture postcard.

kisanduku* (vi-) (*dimin. of* **sanduku**) small box, casket.

kisarawanda (vi-) sheet *(spread over the bed on the wedding night).*

kisasa* 1. *sing.* modern times, the present. 2. *adj. & adv.* new, modern, present-day. up-to-date. *Cf.* **sasa.**

kisase* (vi-) *see* **kisasi.**

kisasi*, kisase (vi-) 1. revenge, retaliation. 2. compensation, indemnification. **toza (fanya) –.** demand compensation.

kisawazisha (vi-): **– joto.** *rec.* thermostat. *Cf.* **sawa, sawazisha.**

kiselema, kichelema (vi-) an implement *(hoe, knife, pencil)* that has been worn down by much use.

kisengesenge *adv.* forward and backward, like a crab. **enda –.** run like a crab.

kiserikali*: **–a –.** *adj.* governmental, state... **karamu ya –.** state banquet. *Cf.* **serikali.**

kisetiri* (vi-) 1. dividing wall, partition, screen. 2. hiding-place. 3. *fig.* toilet, W.C. *Cf.* **stiri.**

kiseyeye *sing.* bleeding of the gums *(from scurvy?).*

kisha*, kiisha *adv.* afterwards, thereafter, then. *Cf.* **[1]isha.**

kishale (vi-) *dimin. of* **mshale.**

kishamba* 1. (vi-) villager, countryman. 2. *sing.* rustic manners/speech. 3. *adj.* (–a –) & *adv.* rustic, countrified (= **kimashamba**). *Cf.* **shamba.**

kisharifu* (vi-), **msharifu** (mi-) *ornith.* (species of) kingfisher. *Cf.* **sharifu.**

kishasi (vi-) *see* **kishazi.**

kishaufu* (vi-) 1. piece of jewelry, trinket, pendant *(on a chain).* 2. nose ring (= **kikero, hazama**). *Cf.* **shaua, shaufu.**

kishaushi (vi-) *see* **kishawishi.**

kishawishi*, **kishaushi** (vi-) temptation, allurement; attraction, lure, bait. *Cf.* **shawishi.**

kishazi*, **kishasi** (vi-) (*dimin. of* **shazi**) string/stick on which fish or fruit are hung.

kishenzi* [*Pers.*] 1. *sing., hist.* language of the inhabitants of the interior. 2. *sing.* wildness, barbarity. 3. *adv.* in a savage/barbarous way. 4.: –a –. *adj.* wild, uncivilized. *Cf.* **shenzi.**

kisheria*: –a –. legal. *See* **sheria.**

kishigino (vi-) *see* **kisigino.**

kishika: – **mkono** (vi-) advance (of money), earnest (money), instalment. *Cf.* **shika.**

kishiki: – **cha buga** (vi-) climbing plant *(Cissampelos pariera).*

kishikizo (vi-): – **herufi** printer's form. *Cf.* **shika.**

kishiko (vi-) *elec.* contact. *Cf.* **shika.**

kishiku* (vi-) 1. (tree) stump, log. – **cha jino.** root of a tooth. 2. wooden block/wedge.

[1]**kishina** (vi-) *see* **shina.**

[2]**kishina** (vi-) kishina (kind of dance).

kishinda (vi-) remainder, residue; dregs *(in a drinking-vessel).* *Cf.* [1]**shinda.**

kishindi (vi-) *see* **ushindi.**

kishindo (vi-) 1 noise, (sound of a) blow, impact, step. 2. *fig.* excitement, uproar. 3. *fig.* disorder, confusion. *Cf.* [1]**shinda.**

kishogo (vi-) *see* **kisogo.**

kishona (= **kichoma nguo.**) (vi-) kind of grass *(Heteropogon contortus).*

kishoroba* (vi-) (*also* **ushoroba** *sing.*) narrow strip of land, patch; path *(in a field).*

kishungi (vi-) toupee. *Cf.* [1]**shungi.**

kishupi (vi-) small bag or basket *(of matting).*

kishutuo (vi-) *see* **kisutuo.**

kishwara* (vi-) loop of rope *(for holding an oar, etc.).*

[1]**kisi***, **kissi** (*rare* **gisi**) 1. presume, surmise, guess; estimate, calculate, consider carefully. *appl.* **kisia.** guess at, estimate *(something).* 2. (ma-) estimate, calculation; proposal. *Cf.* **kisio, makisi.**

[2]**kisi***, **kissi** *naut.* change course, tack, put about.

kisibao* (vi-) *see* **kisibau.**

kisibau*, **kizibau, kisibao, kisibayo** (vi-) open jacket or vest *(worn over the kanzu).*

kisibayo* (vi-) *see* **kisibau.**

kisibiti* (vi-) (*also* **mboga za –**) caraway seed, cumin.

kisichana (vi-) 1. *dimin. of* **msichana.** 2. girl who has not yet reached puberty.

kisicholipwa, kisichotendwa (vi-) debt, arrears. *Cf.* **lipa, tenda.**

kisifa* (vi-) *gramm.* adverb. *Cf.* [1]**sifa.**

kisigino, kishigino (vi-) *anat.:* **– cha mkono.** elbow. **– cha mguu.** heel.

kisiki (vi-) 1. tree-stump. 2. block/chunk of wood, log. 3. *fig.* prostitute. *Cf.* **kishiku.**

kisikusiku, kiusikusiku 1. (vi-) evening, twilight, dusk. 2. *adv.* at night, in the nighttime. *Cf.* [1]**siku, usiku.**

kisima (vi-) water hole, well. *prov.* **mchimba – hutumbika mwenyewe.** Who digs a pit for others falls into it himself.

kisimamleo (vi-) aloe(s). *See also* [1]**udi.**

kisimbo (vi-) *see* **msimbo.**

kisimi (vi-) *coll., anat.* clitoris. (= **kinembe.**)

kisio* (ma-) (*usually* **makisio**) estimate, conjecture; proposal. *Cf.* [1]**kisi.**

kisirani* (–) 1. failure, (bad) omen, misfortune. **atanitia –.** He will bring me bad luck. 2. annoyance, anger. **ana –.** He is vexed/angry. 3. tendency to cause trouble/damage, destructiveness, delinquency, hoodlumism, hooliganism. *Cf.* [2]**mkosi.**

kisiri* (vi-) secret; *(rec., pol.)* secret ballot. **–a –.** secret, covert. *Cf.* [1]**siri.**

kisiwa (vi-) island.

kisogo, kishogo, kichogo (vi-) *anat.* nape of the neck, back of the head. *prov.* **akupaye – si mwenzio.** Whoever turns his back on you is not your friend. **kisogoni.** (what is) behind, the past. *Cf.* [1]**kogo.**

kisomari* (vi-) *see* **kisumari.**

kisombo (= **kisamvu, kisambo.**) (vi-) paste/porridge made of manioc and beans.

kisomo (vi-) instruction, training, education. *Cf.* **soma.**

kisongo (vi-) 1. pressing, pressure. 2. press, vise. 3. *typ.* ligature, logotype. 4. *med.* tourniquet. *Cf.* **songa.**

kisonono, kisunono (vi-) *med.* gonorrhea. **– cha damu.** bilharzia. *Cf.* **sonona.**

kisoshialisti* [*Engl.*] (vi-) socialism. **–a –.** socialist(ic).

kispoti* [*Engl.*] *adj.:* **–a –.** sport ...

kissa* (vi-) *see* [1]**kisa.**

kissi* *see* [1]**kisi,** [2]**kisi.**

kistari* (vi-) (*dimin. of* **mstari**) *punct.* dash, hyphen.

kisu (vi-) knife. **kata kwa –.** cut with a knife. **ukali wa –.** edge of a knife. **– cha kukunja.** pocketknife. *coll.* **wewe – mimi nyama.** Do whatever you want with me (*lit.:* You are the knife, I am the meat). *Cf.* **jisu, kijisu, msumeno.**

kisua* (vi-) 1. garment, suit (of clothes). 2. a well-dressed person.

kisugulu (vi-) *see* **kichuguu.**

kisuguu (vi-) *see* **kichuguu.**

kisukari* 1. (–) kisukari (sweet variety of banana). 2. *adj.:* **–a –.** very sweet, sugary. *Cf.* **sukari.**

kisukumi (vi-) growth or swelling on the genitals. (= **vitio.**) *Cf.* **sukuma.**

kisukumizi (vi-) 1. = **kisukumi.** 2. disease/misfortune transferred by one person to another. *Cf.* **sukuma, msukumizi.**

kisukuu (vi-) *see* **kitukuu.**

kisuli*, kisulisuli, kizuli, kisunzi (vi-) (spell of) dizziness, fainting fit, vertigo, swoon. **upepo wa kisulisuli.** whirlwind. *Cf.* **kisusuli.**

kisumari*, kisomari (vi-) (*dimin. of* **msumari**) pin, peg. (= **pini.**)

kisunono (vi-) *see* **kisonono.**

kisunzi (vi-) *see* **kisuli.**

kisura* (vi-) *sl.* pretty girl. *Cf.* [1]**sura.**

kisusi (vi-) 1. slope of a roof. 2. sloping side of a thatched roof.

kisusui* (vi-) *see* [1]**kisusuli.**

kisusuli*, kisusui (vi-) 1. scorpion. 2. paper kite, windmill *(children's toy).* *Cf.* **kisuli.**

kisutu* (vi-), **msuto** (mi-) kisutu (large piece of printed cotton cloth, used as a woman's garment or as a screen or curtain).

kisutuo, kishutuo (vi-) 1. payment *(especially in kind).* 2. special remuneration for workers, usually in the form of food received during or after the performance of heavy work.

Kiswahili* 1. *sing.* the Swahili language. 2. *adv.* in the Swahili manner. *Cf.* **Swahili, Mswahili, Uswahili.**

[1]**kita, kitakita** prickle, sting, itch.

[2]**kita** 1. be/stand firm *(in the face of danger, etc.).* 2. thrust firmly into the ground *(a spear, etc.),* place firmly.

[1]**kitaa*** (vi-) *dimin. of* **mtaa.**

[2]**kitaa*** (vi-) kitaa (kind of fish).

kitabosha (vi-) kitabosha (pastry made of rice-flour, sugar, and honey).

kitabu* (vi-) 1. book. **— cha ramani.** atlas. **ufuataji wa vitabu tu.** pedantry, dogmatism. 2.: **vitabu.** literature. *Cf.* **katiba, katibu, katabahu, kijitabu, kitiba, maktaba, mkataba, ukatibu.**

kitadali (vi-) *bot.* kitadali (variety of herb, *Euphorbia hirta).*

kitagaa (vi-) 1. dividing, splitting, branching, forking *(of trees, roads).* 2. (rotten) branch *(of a tree).* *Cf.* [2]**taga.**

kitaifa* 1. (vi-) (*dimin. of* **taifa**) small ethnic group, tribe. 2.: **—a —.** *adj.* popular, national. **bima ya — ya afya.** national health insurance.

kitakataka (vi-) (*dimin. of* **takataka**) 1. particle of dust/dirt. 2. *fig.* trifle, bagatelle. *Cf.* [1]**taka.**

kitakita *see* [1]**kita.**

kitakizo (vi-) kitakizo (head or foot of a bedstead). *Cf.* **tako.**

kitako 1. vi-) *anat.* seat, bottom, buttock; perineum. 2. seat, place to sit; base. **mstari wa —.** base line. **kaa —.** seat oneself, be seated, sit. **— cha baisikeli.** saddle of a bicycle. 3. *med.* hemorrhoid(s). 4. *adv.* below, at the bottom, at the lower end. *Cf.* **tako.**

kitale (vi-) kitale (young coconut in the stage of milk-formation).

kitali (vi-) 1. *naut.* sailcloth, canvas. 2. *recent, sport* ring *(for boxing).*

kitalu (vi-) 1. fence, wall. 2. enclosed place *(yard, courtyard, garden).*

kitambaa (vi-), **mtambaa** (mi-) 1. cloth, rag, patch. 2. *med.* bandage. 3. napkin, handkerchief. *Cf.* [2]**tambaa, utambaa.**

[1]**kitambi** (vi-) turban-cloth. *Cf.* [2]**tambaa.**

[2]**kitambi** (vi-) *anat.* 1. peritoneum. 2. mesentery. **— cha nyama.** reticular fat *(of a slaughtered animal).* *fig.* **mwenye —.** corpulent person.

[3]**kitambi: — cha maskini** (vi-) kind of vegetable *(Talinum cuneifolium).*

[4]**kitambi** *sing.* pride, conceit, arrogance. *Cf.* **tamba.**

kitambo (vi-) 1. (short) time, moment. – **kidogo.** after a short time, soon thereafter. – **cha chuo.** school term. 2. (*also* **tambo, utambo**) (short) space, distance, length, height. **hapa na B ni – kidogo.** From here to B is only a short distance.

kitambulisho (vi-) certificate, authentication. *Cf.* **tambua.**

kitamli, kisamli (vi-): **mnazi wa –.** variety of coconut palm *(the nuts are used only for their milk). Cf.* **mkitamli.**

kitana (vi-) *see* **kichanuo.**

kitanda (vi-) 1. bed, bedstead. 2. litter, stretcher. **enda (panda) kitandani.** go to bed. 3.: – **cha mfumi.** (weaver's) loom. *Cf.* **tanda.**

kitandawili (vi-) *see* **kitendawili.**

kitandiko (vi-) cover, blanket. *Cf.* **tanda.**

[1]**kitanga** (vi-) (small, circular) mat, prayer mat. – **cha mkono.** palm *(of the hand).* – **cha mguu.** sole *(of the foot).* – **cha mizani.** pan of a scale/balance. *Cf.* **utanga.**

[2]**kitanga** (vi-): – **cha pepo.** a kind of dance.

[3]**kitanga** (vi-) *dimin. of* [2]**tanga.**

kitangangaya *sing.* kitangangaya (children's game, hide-and-seek).

[1]**kitango** (vi-) idleness, indolence, waste of time, trifling. *Cf.* [1]**tanga.**

[2]**kitango** (vi-) lace, fastener *(e.g., the tufts on a mattress, etc.).*

kitangulizi (vi-) 1. *math.* uneven/odd number. 2.: – **cha jeshi.** vanguard. 3. = **utangulizi.** *Cf.* **tangulia.**

kitanguo (vi-), **mtanguo** (mi-) 1. annulment, cancellation, abolition, suspension, revocation, invalidation, nullification. 2. dismissal, discharge, removal *(from office). Cf.* **tangua.**

kitani* (–) 1. sisal, flax, tow. **shamba la –.** sisal plantation. 2. linen (cloth). 3. string, lace *(of a shoe).*

kitanitani, kitanutanu *adv.* backwards, on the back. **lala –.** lie on one's back.

kitano (vi-) kitano (small coin, 5-cent piece). *Cf.* [1]**tano.**

kitanutanu *see* **kitanitani.**

kitanzi (vi-) (small) loop, noose, eyelet. *Cf.* **tanda, tanzi, utanzi.**

kitapo (vi-) 1. shivering, trembling. 2. *med.* chill, ague. *Cf.* [1]**tapa.**

[1]**kitara*** [*Ind.*] (vi-) scimitar.

[2]**kitara** (–) *dial., rare* 1. kitara (place where a council meets). 2. (law) court.

kitarishi* (vi-) messenger-boy, 'stooge.' *Cf.* **tarishi.**

^{1}**kitasa** (vi-) 1. lock *(on a door, etc.).* 2. buckle.

^{2}**kitasa*** (vi-) *dimin. of* ^{1}**tasa.**

^{1}**kitata*** (vi-) 1. lath, molding. 2. *med.* splint.

^{2}**kitata** (vi-) 1. = **matata.** 2. speech impediment, lisp (= ^{1}**kitembe, utasi**). *Cf.* **tata.**

^{3}**kitata** (vi-): – **cha asali.** honeycomb.

kitatange (vi-) 1. kitatange (sea-fish with spines). 2. *fig.* mischief-maker, insufferable person. *Cf.* **tata.**

kitawa* 1. *sing.* retirement, solitude, seclusion. 2. *adv.* retired, secluded. **kaa –.** live in retirement/seclusion. *Cf.* ^{1}**tawa.**

^{1}**kitawi** (vi-) 1. *dimin. of* **tawi.** 2. kitawi (a kind of weed).

^{2}**kitawi** (vi-) kitawi (implement used in weaving).

kitaya (vi-) *see* **taya.**

kite *sing.* 1. groan, moan, wail, sigh, cry (of pain). 2. suffering, torment, grief. 3. passion. 4. effort, exertion, straining *(as in childbirth).*

kitefu (vi-) *see* ^{2}**kitefutefu.**

kitefute (vi-) *anat.* cheekbone. (= **kituguta.**)

^{1}**kitefutefu, kichefuchefu** (vi-) 1. sobbing, sighing. 2. hiccup.

^{2}**kitefutefu** (*also* **kitefu, kitetefu**) (vi-) something soft/smooth. *Cf.* ^{2}**teke.**

kiteku (vi-) 1. style, burin; chisel. 2. pickax. *Cf.* ^{1}**tekua.**

kitelemsho (vi-) 1. downward movement. 2. *mus.* flat(-sign). *Cf.* **telemua.**

^{1}**kitembe, kichembe** (vi-) speech defect, lisp, indistinct pronunciation, stuttering. **piga/sema –.** speak with a lisp/indistinctly.

^{2}**kitembe** (vi-) *dimin. of* ^{1}**tembe.**

^{1}**kitembwe** (vi-) vegetable fiber. *Cf.* **utembo.**

^{2}**kitembwe** (vi-) kitembwe (kind of fish).

kitendakazi (vi-) determining/decisive factor. *Cf.* **tenda.**

kitendawili, kitandawili (vi-) riddle, puzzle. **tega –.** propound a riddle, pose a problem. *Cf.* **tenda.**

kitende (vi-) surroundings, environment, milieu. *Cf.* **tenda.**

kitendo (vi-) 1. act, action. 2. undertaking, operation. 3. feat, exploit. 4. *gramm.* verb. *Cf.* **tenda.**

kitengele (vi-) 1. band, stripe. 2. small round mat.

kitengeneza: – **uvuke** (**mvuke**) (vi-) *auto.* carburetor. *Cf.* **tengenea.**

kitengo (vi-) (*dimin. of* **mtengo**) *gramm.* preposition. *Cf.* [1]**tenga.**

kiteo (vi-) (*dimin. of* **uteo**) (shallow, dish-shaped) basket *(used for sifting grain).*

[1]**kitete** (vi-) (*dimin. of* [1]**tete**) reed, sedge.

[2]**kitete** (vi-) *dial.* mongoose.

kitetefu *sing. see* [2]**kitefutefu.**

kitetemeko (vi-) *see* **kitetemo.**

kitetemo, kitetemeko (vi-) shivering, trembling, shuddering. *Cf.* **tetema.**

kiteuzi (vi-) *chem.* separator. *Cf.* **teua.**

kitewatewa, kitewetewe (vi-) kitewatewa (small worm).

kitewetewe (vi-) *see* **kitewatewa.**

kithaura* (vi-) *dimin. of* **thaura.**

kithiri* 1. grow, become larger, increase. 2. (*also caus.* **kithirisha**) cause to grow, enlarge, increase. *appl.* **kithiria.**

kiti (vi-) 1. seat, chair. – **cha kifalme.** throne. – **cha farasi.** saddle. 2. *fig.* seat *(in a representative assembly).* **mwenye** –. chairman. 3. headquarters. 4.: – **cha pweza.** starfish.

kitiba* *sing.* essential nature, character, disposition, constitution. *Cf.* **kitabu.**

kitimbakwira (vi-) *pol., comm.* stooge, opportunist.

kitimbi (vi-) deception, deceit, trick, intrigue. *Cf.* **chimvi.**

kitimiri* *sing.* 1. name of an evil spirit. 2. charm to ensure easy childbirth.

kitinda (vi-), **mtinda** (wa-): – **mimba.** last/youngest child. *Cf.* **tindika.**

kitingisha (vi-) earthquake. (= **tetemeko la nchi.**) *Cf.* **tinga.**

kitinitini (vi-) *see* [2]**kititi.**

kitisho, kitusho (vi-) threat, menace, danger; fright, fear, apprehension; confusion. *coll.* **amepata – cha kutosha.** He has really had a scare thrown into him. *Cf.* **tisha.**

[1]**kitita, kititi** *adv.* 1. in great numbers, in abundance. 2. all at once, in cash, cash down. **amelipa pesa –.** He paid in cash. 3. suddenly, unexpectedly.

[2]**kitita** (vi-) *dimin. of* **tita** 3.

[1]**kititi** (vi-) 1. *dimin. of* **titi.** 2. *med.* mastitis (inflammation of the mammary glands).

[2]**kititi, kitinitini** (vi-) small hare.

[3]**kititi** *sing.:* – **cha bahari.** the depths of the ocean.

[4]**kititi** *adv.* 1. *see* **kitita.** 2. upright, in an erect position, vertical(ly). **simama –.** be upright, stand erect.

kititia (vi-) 1. blade, vane *(of a fan, windmill).* 2. windmill *(children's toy).* 3. *fig.* ventilator.

kititimo (vi-) 1. (rolling, reverberating) noise *(like thunder).* 2. disorder, confusion. *Cf.* **titima.**

[1]**kito** (vi-) (*also* – **cha thamani**) precious stone, jewel.

[2]**kito** (vi-) kito (children's game in which objects are hidden and hunted for).

kitoasi, kitoazi (vi-) castanet. *Cf.* **toasi.**

kitobo, kitobwe (vi-) (*dimin. of* **tobo**) 1. small hole, perforation. 2. *fig.* dimple. *Cf.* **toboa.**

kitobwe (vi-) *see* **kitobo.**

kitokono (vi-) (*also* **tokoni, tokono, ma-**) *anat.* coccyx.

kitoleo (vi-) *math.* subtrahend. *Cf.* [1]**toa.**

kitoma (vi-) 1. small round pumpkin. 2. kitoma (the pumpkin shell used as a vessel for milk or water). 3. *med.* orchitis, hydrocele.

kitone (vi-) (*dimin. of* **tone**) drop (of liquid), (ink) blot. *Cf.* **tona.**

kitonge (vi-) small lump, ball, morsel. – **cha wali.** small lump of rice *(taken in the fingers and eaten).*

kitongo, kichongochongo *adv.* from the side, on a slant, diagonally, obliquely. **tazamia mtu –.** look at someone askance/contemptuously. *Cf.* **tongoza.**

kitongoji (vi-) (small) village, hamlet. (= **kijiji.**)

kitongotongo *see* **kitongo.**

kitoria (vi-) kitoria (edible fruit of the East African rubber liana, mtoria).

kitoroli* [*Engl.* lorry *or Germ.* Motorroller?] (vi-) motor scooter.

kitororo (vi-) *ornith.* (species of) barbet.

kitoto 1. (vi-) (*dimin. of* **mtoto**) small child, baby. 2. *adv.* in a childish/foolish way.

kitovu (vi-) 1. *anat.* navel, umbilical cord. 2. middle, center. 3. *fig.* home, place of origin. **enda kitovuni.** go home *(to one's birthplace.).* 4. hub *(of a wheel), (anything that serves as a)* pivot.

kitoweleo (vi-) *see* **kitoweo.**

kitoweo, kitoweleo (vi-), **toweo** (ma-) 1. something added to food *(i.e., vegetables to meat, gravy, sauce, curry, etc.)*, relish. 2. seasoning, condiment, spice. *Cf.* **towea.**

kitreya* [*Engl.*] (vi-) tray.

kitu (vi-) thing, object; matter, substance. **vitu vya starehe.** luxuries. – **kidogo.** trifle, small matter. **hapana –.** nothing.

kitubio (vi-) 1. repentence, atonement; *(rel.)* penance, confession. 2. punishment, retribution. *Cf.* **tubu.**

kituguta (vi-) *anat.* cheekbone. (= **kitefute.**)

kituka (vi-) 1. clump of trees, copse, grove. 2. thicket. (= **kichaka.**)

kituko (vi-) (*usually* **vituko**) 1. fear, terror. **tia fulani vituko.** inspire someone with terror. 2. excitement, confusion, dismay, consternation. **alipokuja akaionyesha vituko vingi.** When he came, he found things in a state of great confusion. *Cf.* **tukia.**

kitukuu, kisukuu (vi-) great-grandchild.

kitulivu *adv.* quietly, calmly, peacefully. *Cf.* **¹tua, tulivu.**

kitulizo (vi-) soothing, relief, alleviation. **dawa hii ni – cha maumivu.** This medicine is a sedative/anodyne. *Cf.* **¹tua.**

kitumbo 1. (vi-) *dimin. of* **tumbo.** 2. (vi-) abnormally large stomach, obesity. *coll.:* **usinitie – uchungu.** Don't annoy me. 3. *adv.* (*also* **kitumbotumbo**) on the stomach, prone. **lala –.** lie prone.

kitumbotumbo *see* **kitumbo** 2.

kitumbua (vi-) (rice) fritter *(fried in fat).* (= **andazi.**)

kitumwa *adv.* in a servile/obsequious way. *Cf.* **tuma.**

kitunda (vi-) 1. pawn *(chess).* 2. *dimin. of* **tunda.**

¹kitunga (vi-): **kofia ya –.** a kind of fez.

²kitunga (vi-) *dimin. of* **²tunga.**

kitungo (vi-) *dimin. of* **mtungo.**

kitungule (vi-) 1. hare. (= **sungura.**) 2. *fig.* sly, crafty person.

kitunguu (vi-) onion, shallot. – **saumu.** garlic.

kituo (vi-) 1. pause, interruption, rest. 2. stopping place. – **cha gari.** railway station. 3. settlement, establishment, post, camp. – **cha kupumzika.** (vacation) resort. – **cha biashara.** trading post, commercial center. – **cha mafuta.** *auto.* filling station. – **cha kivita.** military base. 4. *gramm.* **alama ya –.** punctuation. 5. section, paragraph *(in a book).* *Cf.* **¹tua.**

Kituruki* *sing.* Turkish language. **–a –.** *adj.* Turkish. *Cf.* **Mturuki, Uturuki.**

kitusho (vi-) *see* **kitisho.**

kitutumi (vi-) something causing a rumbling/ growling sound. *Cf.* [1]**tutuma.**

kitwa (vi-) *see* **kichwa.**

kitwamgomba *see* **kichwamgomba.**

kitwana (vi-) (*dimin. of* **mtwana**) 1. *hist.* slave boy. 2. scamp, brat.

kitwea *sing.* solitude, loneliness.

kitwitwi (vi-) *ornith.* sandpiper.

kiu (–) 1. thirst. **ona (wa na) –.** be thirsty. **komesha (kata) –.** quench the thirst. 2. *fig.* dryness, drought. **– ya maji.** water shortage. *Cf.* **kwiu.**

[1]**kiua** (vi-) 1. buttonhole. 2. embroidering on a kofia.

[2]**kiua** (vi-) kiua (kind of fish).

[3]**kiua** (vi-): **– mwitu.** variety of tree.

[4]**kiua** (vi-) something that kills (= kiuaji).

[5]**kiua** (vi-) *dimin. of* [1]**ua,** [2]**ua.**

kiuaji (vi-) 1. deadly weapon. 2. something that has a deadly effect *(snake, poison, etc.).* *Cf.* [3]**ua.**

kiubavubavu *see* **kibavu.**

kiuka step/jump/pass over something. (= **kia, chupa, ruka, vuka.**) *Cf.* **ukiauaji.**

kiuma (vi-) 1. something that stings/bites/ causes pain. **– mbuzi.** a kind of black lizard (*lit.:* 'goat-biter'). 2. fork. *Cf.* **uma.**

kiumambuzi (vi-) 'goat-biter,' kind of lizard. *Cf.* **uma,** [1]**mbuzi.**

kiumanzi (vi-) kiumanzi (small insect that kills flies).

kiumbe (vi-) (*rare* **chumbe, vy-**) creature, (human) being. *Cf.* **umba.**

[1]**kiumbo** (vi-) nature, character, quality. *Cf.* **umba.**

[2]**kiumbo** (vi-) vessel used for holding potter's tools.

kiume 1. *sing.* male sex. **–a –.** male, masculine. **mtoto wa –.** boy. 2. *sing.* masculinity; strength, vigor; heroism. 3. *adv.* in a masculine/manly way. *Cf.* [1]**ume.**

kiunda (vi-) kiunda (a kind of trap). *Cf.* [1]**unda.**

[1]**kiunga** (vi-) 1. suburb(s), environs *(of a town).* 2. garden, fruit-orchard. **– cha minazi (michungwa).** coconut (orange) grove. *Cf.* [2]**unga.**

[2]**kiunga** (vi-) kiunga (kind of fish).

^{1}kiungo (vi-) 1. something serving to connect or join: connection, joint, coupling, etc. 2. *elec.* connection, switch, contact. 3. *anat. & mech.* joint, articulation. 4. *gramm.* conjunction. *Cf.* **^{2}unga.**

^{2}kiungo (vi-) spice, seasoning, condiment *(salt, vinegar, etc.). Cf.* **^{2}unga.**

^{3}kiungo (vi-) palm-leaf *(used as roofing material).*

Kiunguja 1. *sing.* Swahili dialect of Zanzibar *(as contrasted w. the dialect of the coast* [**Kimrima**], *of Mombasa* [**Kimvita**], *and of Lamu* [**Kiamu**]). 2. *adv.* in the manner usual in Zanzibar. *Cf.* **Unguja.**

kiungulia (vi-) 1. stomach upset, indigestion. 2. belching, eructation. **– moyo.** *med.* heartburn, pyrosis. **fanya –.** belch. *Cf.* **^{1}ungua.**

kiungurumo (vi-) *see* **ngurumo.**

kiunguza, kiunguzo (vi-) 1. poison, virus. 2. medicine containing viruses. 3. acid. *Cf.* **^{1}ungua.**

kiunguzo (vi-) *see* **kiunguza.**

kiungwana 1. *sing.* Swahili language *(term used in the back country);* manners and speech of a well-bred person. 2. *adv.* in a well-bred/cultivated manner. 3.: **–a –.** *adj.* cultivated, civilized. *Cf.* **mwungwana, uungwana:** *also* **Kingwana.**

kiuno (vi-) (*also* **chuno, –**) 1. (*us.* **kiunoni**) waist. 2. *anat.* hip, loins. 3. *anat.* rump, buttocks.

kiunza (vi-) a board placed in a grave to protect the corpse from contact with earth and stones. *Cf.* **^{1}unda.**

kiunzi (vi-) wooden frame, scaffolding. *Cf.* **^{1}unda.**

kiusikusiku (vi-, *adv.*) *see* **kisikusiku.**

kiva (–) *rare* harmony, unity; agreement, approval. (= **umoja.**)

kivazi (vi-) dress, clothing; style *(of dress). Cf.* **vaa.**

^{1}kivi (vi-) *anat.* elbow. (= **^{2}kiko.**)

^{2}kivi (vi-) *see* **^{1}kiwi.**

kivimba (vi-) *see* **kivimbe.**

kivimbe, kivimba, kivimbo (vi-) 1. *med.* swelling, tumor. 2. arch, vault(ing). 3. girth, circumference. **– cha dunia.** *rare* equator (= **ikweta**). *Cf.* **vimba, uvimbe.**

kivimbo (vi-) *see* **kivimbe.**

kivinyovinyo 1. (vi-) trembling, quivering. 2. (vi-) confusion, uncertainty, clouding *(of the mind).* 3. *adv.* tremblingly. *Cf.* **vinya.**

kiviringo (vi-) *see* **mviringo.**

kivita *adj.:* **–a –.** warlike, military. **mambo ya –.** matters relating to war, military affairs; military actions/movements. *Cf.* **vita.**

kivivu, kivivuvivu *adv.* in a lazy/indolent/bored manner. **tazama –.** look at something in an indolent/bored way *(with half-closed eyelids). Cf.* **vivu.**

kivivuvivu *see* **kivuvu.**

kivo, kizo (vi-) (great) quantity, abundance; superfluity, surplus. (= [1]**wingi.**)

kivoteo* [*Engl.*] (vi-) vote, ballot.

kivukizo (vi-) *see* **kifukizo.**

kivuko, kivusho (vi-) 1. ford, crossing; ferry. **– kikavu.** isthmus. 2. crossing place, landing stage. 3. ferry time/fare. *Cf.* [2]**vua.**

kivulana (vi-) (*dimin. of* **mvulana**) boy, young man.

kivuli, kifuli (vi-) 1. shadow, shade; shaded place. **lala kivulini.** lie in the shade. 2. vision, phantom, ghost. *Cf.* **mwavuli, uvuli.**

kivumanyuki (vi-) kivumanyuki (hardy plant, *Pentas purpurea).*

kivumanzi (vi-) small bell, cowbell.

kivumbasi, kivumbazi, *(rare)* **kifumbazi** (vi-) kivumbasi (a fragrant wood which, when ground up with oil, is used as a perfume or to keep off mosquitoes).

kivumbazi (vi-) *see* **kivumbasi.**

kivumbi (vi-) 1. dust; vapor, haze. 2. dust-cloud, sandstorm. 3. *fig.* great quantity, large number. 4. *fig., coll.* crowd, noise, confusion. **mjini kulikuwa na –.** There was a great hubbub in the city. *Cf.* **vumbi.**

kivumi, kivumo (vi-) 1. humming, murmuring, rustling. 2. *fig.* rumor, gossip, hearsay. *Cf.* **vuma.**

kivumo (vi-) *see* **kivumi.**

kivunde *adj.* fermented. **ugali (wa) –.** porridge of manioc meal which has begun to ferment. *Cf.* **vunda.**

kivunga (vi-) (*dimin. of* **vunga**): **– cha nywele.** long, thick hair.

kivunjavunja, kivunjajungu (vi-) *zool.* mantis *(so called from the superstition that the person who kills a mantis will break the next thing he touches; cf.* **vunja** *and* **jungu**).

kivunjo (vi-) 1. (act of) breaking, splintering. 2. *med.* fracture. 3. *auto.* breakdown. 4. tool for breaking *(hammer, crowbar, etc.). Cf.* **vunja.**

kivuno (vi-) *rare* 1. harvest, yield. 2. gain, profit. *Cf.* **vuna.**

kivusho (vi-) *see* **kivuko.**

kivyao (vi-) *see* **kizao.**

kivyazi (vi-) *see* **kizao.**

kiwa *adj.* *(of persons:)* poor; solitary, abandoned, outcast; *(of things:)* solitary, isolated. (= **upweke, hame, ganjo.**) *Cf.* **makiwa, mkiwa, ukiwa.**

kiwaa (vi-) *see* [1]waa.

kiwafuwafu *adv., rare* sideways. **anguka –.** fall sideways.

kiwamba (vi-) *see* **kiwambo.**

kiwambamoyo (vi-) *see* **kiwambo.**

kiwambaza (vi-) *see* **kiambaza.**

kiwambo, kiwamba, kiambo (vi-) tension, tautness; something stretched tightly, covering. **– cha ngoma.** drumskin, drumhead. **kiwamba cha moyo** (*or* **kiwambamoyo**) *anat.* diaphragm. *Cf.* **wamba.**

[1]**kiwanda** (vi-) 1. plot of ground, yard. 2. working place, workshop, factory, plant. **– cha jotojoto.** heat-treatment plant. **– cha kufanyia unga wa maziwa.** powdered-milk processing plant. **– cha kutoa nguvu za umeme (katika mto).** (hydro-)electric power station. 3. mine, forge, foundry. 4. *pl.* industry, enterprise(s). *Cf.* **uwanda.**

[2]**kiwanda** (vi-) *rare* *see* **kimanda.**

[1]**kiwango** (vi-) 1. number, quantity. 2. calculating, computing; computation. 3. *fig.* status, (social) position. *Cf.* [3]**wanga.**

[2]**kiwango** (vi-) kiwango (variety of cowrie shell).

kiwanja (vi-) 1. place, plot of land, field. **– cha ndege (eropleni), – cha kutua.** airfield, landing field. **– cha kurusha roketi.** launching pad/platform. **– cha michezo.** playing field, (sports) stadium, arena. 2. forecourt, court(yard). **– cha mwezi.** *astr.* halo of the moon. *Cf.* **uwanja.**

kiwara* (vi-) flat land, plain, savannah.

kiwavi (vi-) 1. larva, grub, caterpillar. 2. chrysalis. 3. (variety of) stinging nettle *(Tragia furialis, Tragia Scheffleri).* *Cf.* **wana.**

kiwe, kawe, kijiwe, kikawe (vi-) 1. *dimin. of* **jiwe.** 2. (**– cha uso**) pimple, rash *(on the face).*

kiweko (vi-) 1. base, support, prop, underpinning. 2. *fig.* basis, foundation. *Cf.* **weka.**

kiwele (vi-) udder, mammary gland *(of animals; cf.* [2]ziwa).

kiweo (vi-) thigh, shank, ham. (= **paja, kiga.**)

kiwete 1. (vi-) lameness, crippling. **enda –.** be lame, limp. 2. (vi-) a lame person, cripple. 3. *adv.* in a limping way, like a cripple. 4.: **–a –.** *adj.* lame, crippled.

kiweto (vi-) hen that does not lay.

kiwewe (vi-) confusion, dismay, astonishment.

[1]**kiwi, kiwiwi, kivi** (vi-) 1. stick set against a door to hold it shut. 2. bolt *(on a door).*

[2]**kiwi** (vi-) 1. (*also* – **cha macho**) blinding, dazzling *(by the sun, etc.).* 2. *fig.* delusion. *Cf.* **ukiwi.**

kiwiko (vi-) *anat.* wrist, ankle. – **cha mkono.** wrist. – **cha mguu.** ankle.

kiwili (vi-) *eth.* community, common interest. **kazi ya –.** cooperative work *(regarded as a social obligation of all village dwellers).*

kiwiliwili (vi-) 1. body, trunk. 2. *fig.* girth, size, volume. *Cf.* **mwili.**

kiwimawima, imaima *adv.* in an upright position, head up, top uppermost; erect, vertical, straight. *Cf.* **wima.**

kiwimbi 1. (vi-) small wave, ripple. 2. *adv./adj.* wavy, undulating. *Cf.* [1]**wimbi.**

kiwiwi (vi-) *see* [1]**kiwi.**

Kiyahudi* 1. *sing.* the Hebrew language. 2. *adv.* in the Jewish manner. 3.: –**a** –. *adj.* Jewish. *Cf.* **Myahudi.**

kiyama*, kiama (–) *Isl.* resurrection, day of judgment. (= **ufufuo,** *which is used in both Moslem and Christian contexts.)*

kiyambaza (vi-) *see* **kiambaza.**

kiyana* (vi-) earthenware dish.

kiyoga (vi-) *dimin. of* **uyoga.**

kiyombo (vi-) bark cloth.

kiyowe (vi-) *see* **yowe.**

Kiyunani* 1. *sing.* (ancient) Greek language. 2. *adv.* in the (ancient) Greek manner. 3. –**a** –. *adj.* (ancient) Greek, Hellenic. *Cf.* **Myunani, Uyunani.**

kiyuyu (vi-) kiyuyu (poisonous shrub, *Synadenium carinatum*).

kiza (–, ma-) *see* **giza.**

kizalia (vi-) kizalia (someone who was born in a particular place, native). **mimi – cha hapa.** I was born here. I am a native of this place. – **cha Tanga.** someone born in Tanga, a native of Tanga. *Cf.* **zaa.**

kizamaji (vi-) something thrown into the water; *(pl.)* jetsam. *Cf.* [2]**zama.**

kizamani* *adv.* in an earlier way, earlier, formerly. *Cf.* **zamani.**

kizamiadagaa (–) kizamiadagaa (kind of bird, kingfisher).

kizao, kivyao, kivyazi (vi-) *rare* 1. produce, production. 2. product. *Cf.* **zaa, zao.**

kizazi (vi-) 1. procreation, reproduction; progeny, offspring. **hana –.** she is childless. She cannot bear children. 2. birth. 3. generation. – **hiki.** the present (living) generation. *Cf.* **zaa, uzazi.**

kizee (vi-) 1. old woman. 2. sorceress, witch. *Cf.* **zee.**

kizembe 1. (vi-) indolent, relaxed posture; *(fig.)* bad behavior. 2. *adv.* in an idle/indolent/negligent manner. *Cf.* **zembe, mzembe, uzembe.**

kizibau (vi-) *see* **kisibau.**

kizibo (vi-) 1. stopper, plug, spigot, tap. 2. (act of) stopping up, filling up. 3. *fig.* stopgap, (temporary) expedient. *Cf.* **ziba.**

kizibuo (vi-) corkscrew. *Cf.* **ziba.**

kizidishe* (vi-) *math.* multiplicand. *Cf.* **zidi.**

kizidisho* (vi-) *math.* multiplier. *Cf.* **zidi.**

kizimba, kizimbi (vi-) 1. birdcage, dovecote. 2. *jur.* witness stand.

kizimbi (vi-) *see* **kizimba.**

kizimwe (vi-) *bot.* blight, smut *(of grains).* *Cf.* **¹zima, zimwe.**

kizimwi (vi-) *liter.* 1. fairy, sorceress. 2. evil spirit. *Cf.* **zimwi, mzimu, kuzimu, wazimu.**

kizinda (vi-) 1. virginity. 2. virgin. **weka —.** preserve virginity. **tomoa —.** deflower. 3. *anat.* hymen. *Cf.* **zinda.**

kizingia (vi-) something that revolves/whirls. **— cha maji.** whirlpool. *Cf.* **zinga.**

kizingiti (vi-) 1. threshold, sill, lintel (= top or bottom piece of a door or window). 2. dam, weir. 3. reef, bar.

¹kizingo (vi-) twist, turn, bend *(of a road, river).* *Cf.* **zinga.**

²kizingo (vi-) sand *(from the seashore).*

¹kizio (vi-) 1. half *(of a round body, e.g., fruit).* 2. *fig., geogr.:* **— cha dunia.** hemisphere.

²kizio (vi-) (*also* **— cha simu**) *elec.* insulator. *Cf.* **³zia.**

kiziwi (vi-) 1. a deaf person. 2. a coconut that has dried up inside *(i.e., shell without meat or milk; compare Germ.* **eine taube Nuss?**). *Cf.* **ziwi, ukiziwi.**

kizo (vi-) *see* **kivo.**

kizuio, kizuizi (vi-) 1. obstacle, impediment. 2. restriction, limitation, curb, prohibition. *Cf.* **zuia.**

kizuizi (vi-) *see* **kizuio.**

kizuizini (vi-) detention *(by police, as in Mau Mau Camps).* *Cf.* **zuia.**

kizuizui (—) kizuizui (children's game, similar to blindman's buff).

kizuka (vi-) 1. apparition, vision. 2. *liter.* fairy, spirit. 3. window. *Cf.* **zua, ¹zuka.**

kizuli (vi-) *see* **kisuli.**

Kizungu 1. *sing.* (collective term for any) European language. **–a –.** *adj.* European. 2. *adv.* in the European manner. 3.: **kizunguni.** *arch.* European quarter in an African town. *Cf.* **zungu,** [1]**mzungu,** [2]**Mzungu,** [2]**Uzungu.**

kizunguko (vi-) *see* **mzunguko.**

kizunguzungu *sing.* dizziness, indisposition. *Cf.* **zungua.**

kizushi (vi-) 1. innovator, revolutionary. 2. intruder. 3. novelty, sensation. *Cf.* **zua,** [2]**zuka.**

kizuu (vi-) kizuu (evil spirit). *Cf.* **zua,** [1]**zuka.**

klabu* (vi-) *see* **kilabu.**

kliniki*, kiliniki [*Engl.*] (–) clinic. **– ya watoto.** children's clinic.

k.m. *abbr. of* **kwa mfano.** for example, *e.g.*

[1]**koa** (ma-) 1. metal ring (worn as an ornament around the neck or on the arm). 2. leather strap/belt.

[2]**koa** 1. be sharp/pointed. **kisu kinakoa.** The knife has a sharp point. 2. *fig.* be attractive.

[3]**koa** (ma-) snail, slug; snail-shell.

koba* (vi-) (*augm. of* **mkoba**): **fanya –.** be convex/bulgy; belly out *(of a sail). Cf.* **kuba, kubaza.**

kobati* [*Engl.*] *sing.* cobalt.

kobe (–) 1. land tortoise. 2. *Isl.* a person who breaks his fast during Ramadhan.

koboa *see* **goboa.**

[1]**kobwe** (–) kobwe (variety of bean).

[2]**kobwe** (–) kobwe (kind of snail).

[3]**kobwe** (–) clapping (with cupped hands).

koche (ma-) koche (fruit of the dwarf palm). *Cf.* **mkoche.**

kocho *adj.* shrewd, experienced, clever, expert. (= **bingwa, hodari, stadi.**)

kochokocho *adv.* in great abundance, numberless.

kodi* 1. rent, lease. *caus.* **kodisha. nimemkodisha fulani shamba.** I have leased a field to X. 2. (–) rent, lease; tax, duty. **taratibu za –.** tax regulation. **mtoza –.** tax-collector. *Cf.* **mkodi, ukodishaji.**

kodoa (*usually* **– macho**) look fixedly, stare. *appl.* **kodolea.** stare at. *caus.* **kodosha.** gape, goggle.

kodolea *appl. of* **kodoa.**

kodwe (–) small stone; piece, man *(in games)*, die. *Cf.* **jiwe, mbwe.**

koeka *see* **ngoeka.**

kofi (**ma-**) 1. (*also* **ukofi**) palm of the hand, handbreadth. **piga makofi.** clap, applaud. 2. (*also* **ukofi**) handful. 3. slap, box on the ear. 4. hand clapping *(with a dance)*. 5. *pl. of* **ukofi.**

kofia* (–) headgear, cap, fez. **– ya bulibuli.** embroidered white cap. **– ya kitunga, – ya kibandiko.** ordinary cap/fez. **– ya zari.** cap decorated with braid.

[1]**koga** (**ma-**) 1. mold, mildew, blight, dry rot. **fanya (ota) –.** moulder, rot, become moldy. **– la meno.** tartar on the teeth. **– ya maji.** seaweed. 2. *fig.* moldiness, mustiness; uncleanliness, foulness. **– la nguo.** slovenliness of dress.

[2]**koga** show, explain, demonstrate. *Cf.* [1]**mkogo.**

[3]**koga** *see* [1]**oga.**

[1]**kogo** (**ma-**, –), **mkogo** (**mi-**) *anat.* the back of the head, occiput.

[2]**kogo** (–) kogo (string of beads worn by women around the loins).

[3]**kogo** (**ma-**) conceit, presumption, arrogance.

[4]**kogo*** [*Engl.* cargo] (–) *rare, naut.* dock. (= **gudi, majahabu.**)

kohl* (–) *min.* antimony, kohl *(for application to the eyes as a cosmetic)*. (= **wanja wa manga.**) *Cf.* **mkahale.**

koho*, korho (–) koho (species of hawk or eagle).

kohoa cough. *caus.* **kohoza.** *refl.* **jikohoza.** clear one's throat *(from embarrassment or to attract attention)*. *Cf.* **kohozi, kikohozi, ukohozi.**

kohoo (**ma-**) *see* **kohozi.**

kohozi, kohoo (**ma-**) 1. cough. 2. expectoration, phlegm, mucus. *Cf.* **kohoa.**

koikoi (**ma-**) 1. evil spirit. 2. heron, stork.

[1]**koja** (–) koja (ornament worn around the neck). **– la dhahabu.** gold necklace.

[2]**koja** (–) koja (metal pot).

kojoa urinate. *appl.* **kojolea.** *caus.* **kojosha/kojoza. dawa ya kukojosha.** diuretic. *Cf* **kojozi, kikojozi, mkojo.**

kojojo (**ma-**) sea slug, bêche-de-mer.

kojozi (–) 1. *see* **kikojozi, mkojo.** 2. kojozi (species of banana with diuretic effect). *Cf.* **kojoa.**

[1]**koka** 1. (*usually* **– moto**) kindle a fire. 2. warm oneself at a fire.

[2]**koka** = **kuoka** (*inf. of* **oka**).

[1]**koko** (**ma-**) 1. bush, thicket, wilderness. 2. *see* **kokwa.**

[2]**koko*** [*Engl.*] (–) cocoa. *Cf.* [2]**mkoko.**

kokoa 1. sweep up/away. 2. wash away. *appl.* **kokolea. maji yameukokolea mchanga.** The water has washed away the sand.

kokoleka, kokoreka *onom.* crow, cackle.

kokomea drive/knock/wedge in. *Cf.* **kongomea.**

kokomoa (*& intr.* **kokomoka**) 1. throw up, vomit. 2. *fig.* blurt out.

kokomoka *intr. of* **kokomoa.**

kokona, sosona wipe oneself with leaves *(after a bowel movement).*

kokoreka *see* **kokoleka.**

kokorocha *see* **korocha.**

kokota draw, pull, drag. **– gari.** pull a wagon. *fig.* **– maneno.** speak slowly or with difficulty. **– roho.** be short of breath, breathe with difficulty. **– kazi.** work slowly. *appl.* **kokotea.** *intr.* **kokoteka.** *caus.* **kokoteza.** *refl.* **jikokota.** drag oneself along, move slowly/with difficulty. *Cf.* **kokotevu, mkokoto.**

kokotevu *adj.* slow, hesitant, dilatory. *Cf.* **kokota.**

kokoto (**ma-**; *us. pl.*) crushed stone. **makokoto ya kupigilia.** (rough) gravel *(for making concrete).* **makokoto ya kutomelea.** paving stones.

kokwa, koko (–, **ma-**) 1. fruit-stone. 2. nut. **– ya jicho.** eyeball. 3. *coll., anat.* (**– za chini/pumba**) testicle.

[1]**kola*** [*Engl.*] (–) *see* [2]**kala.**

[2]**kola** *see* **kora.**

[1]**kole** (**ma-**) coconut-palm branch. *Cf.* [2]**mkole.**

[2]**kole** (**ma-**) hostage *(someone held as surety for another's debt).* *Cf.* **koleza** 2.

kolea 1. season, prepare (foods). 2. *fig.* make something appear attractive *(by arts of persuasion).* *caus.* **koleza.** 1. = **kolea.** 2.: **koleza moto.** start or encourage a fire *(with oil, etc.).*

kolego (**ma-**) spade, shovel.

kolekole (–) kolekole (large fish).

koleo, kweleo (–, **ma-**) 1. tongs, pincers, pliers, forceps, tweezers. 2. koleo (a long pole with a bent end for picking fruit from trees). 3. notch in an arrow.

koleza 1. *caus. of* **kolea.** 2. make someone accountable for another's offense or debt; keep back/withhold something. *Cf.* [2]**kole.**

koli* (–) 1. *naut.* ship's papers. 2. list, index.

kololo (ma-) *see* **[1]kororo.**

koloni* [*Engl.*] (ma-) colony, colonial property. **afisi ya makoloni.** Colonial Office. **uhuru wa watu wa makoloni.** freedom for the colonial peoples. *Cf.* **kikoloni, mkoloni, ukoloni.**

[1]koma stop, end, cease; come to an end, reach a goal/destination. *prov.* **lisilo na mkoma hujikoma lenyewe.** A matter that has not been settled settles itself. *caus.* **komesha.** put a stop to, bring to an end, terminate; cut short, curtail. **amekomeshwa.** He has been compelled to stop. **komesha maneno.** cut off a debate. **komesha vita.** break off hostilities. *Cf.* **[1]kikomo, [3]mkoma, ukomo, ukomeshaji.**

[2]koma (ma-) koma (edible fruit of the mkoma).

[3]koma (ma-) koma (spirit of a deceased person).

[4]koma* [*Engl.*] (–) comma.

komaa 1. be full-grown/mature *(people or animals).* 2. be over-ripe *(fruit).* 3. *fig.* be decayed/ruined; lose strength/vitality; be demoralized. *caus.* **komaza.** 1. aid/promote/encourage development/growth. 2. demoralize, ruin.

komafi (ma-) komafi (fruit of the mkomafi).

komakanga (–) *ornith.* (species of) finch.

komamanga (ma-) pomegranate. *Cf.* **mkomamanga, [2]Manga.**

komanguku (–) komanguku (a wild herb, *Crotalaria senegalensis).*

komanya *rare* know, understand. (= **fahamu.**) *caus.* **komanza.** inform, announce; explain.

komanza *caus. of* **komanya.**

komaza *caus. of* **komaa.**

[1]komba hollow out, scratch out; press out, empty; scrape off, clean out. **– dafu.** scrape out the meat of a coconut. **– chungu.** clean out a pot. *fig.***–fulani mali.** take the money out of someone's pocket, impoverish/ruin someone. *double appl.* **kombelea.** *double appl.-intr.* **kombeleka. amekombeleka.** He has lost his last cent. He is completely ruined. *Cf.* **komboa, [1]kombe, [3]kombe, [1]kombo, [3]kombo, kikomba, kikombe, kikombo, ukombe.**

[2]komba (–) 1. *zool.* galago *(which drinks the sap of the coconut palm).* **– wa Bukini.** lemur. 2. *coll.:* **mlevi kama –.** a heavy drinker (*lit.:* one who drinks like a komba).

[3]komba (–) komba (kind of fish).

kombaini* [*Engl.* combine] (–, ma-) 1. union, alliance, club. 2. *sport* combined team.

kombamoyo (ma-) roof-beam, rafter.

kombamwiko (–) cockroach. (= **mende.**)

kombati (ma-) *see* **kumbati.**

¹**kombe** (–, ma-) 1. a bivalve shellfish. **– ya pwani.** oyster (= **chaza**). 2. dish, plate. 3. *anat.* shoulder-blade, scapula. **– la kichwa.** skull. *Cf.* ¹**komba.**

²**kombe** (–) kombe (a climbing plant yielding poison for arrows).

³**kombe** (–) gouge, scraper. *Cf.* ¹**komba.**

⁴**kombe** (–): **kunywa –.** treatment by a witch doctor *(the witch doctor writes on a plate which is then washed off and the water drunk by the patient).*

kombeo, kumbewe (ma-) sling, catapult. **piga –.** throw by use of a sling.

¹**kombo** (ma-) (*usually* **makombo**) 1. piece, fragment, morsel. 2. leftovers, crumbs. **sili makombo ya mtu mwingine.** I don't eat another man's crumbs. 3. *fig.* trash, junk. *Cf.* ¹**komba.**

²**kombo** (ma-) pardon; reprieve, amnesty. **omba –.** beg pardon. **pa –.** grant pardon. *Cf.* **komboa.**

³**kombo** (ma-) 1. curve, bend, twist; crookedness. 2. hook, hooked implement. 3. *fig.* fault, defect; difficulty. 4. *fig.* fad. *Cf.* ¹**komba.**

komboa 1. get out, scrape out. 2. buy off, redeem, ransom; free, liberate; *(rel.)* save, redeem. **– deni.** pay/settle a debt. *refl.* **jikomboa.** buy oneself off; recover/recoup *(one's losses, in gambling, etc.).* *appl.* **kombolea.** *intr.* **komboka.** *caus.* **komboza.** *Cf.* ¹**komba,** ²**kombo, mkombozi, ukombozi;** *also (dial.)* **gomboa.**

kombora* (ma-) bomb, shell, grenade, rocket. **– dogo.** (hand-)grenade. **– la atomiki.** atomic bomb. **– la hydrogen.** hydrogen bomb.

kombozi (ma-) *see* **ukombozi.**

kome (ma-) pearl oyster *(Cassis madagascariensis).* *Cf.* ¹**kombe.**

komea close, bolt, latch *(a door).* **– mlango.** bolt a door. *appl.* **komelea.** *intr.* **komeka.** *caus.* **komeza.** *inv.* **komoa.** 1. unbolt. 2. *fig.* free, liberate. 3. *fig.* dishonor, bring into disrepute. *Cf.* **komeo.**

komeo (ma-) bar, bolt, latch *(on a door or window).* *Cf.* **komea.**

komishena*, komeshena [*Engl.*] (–) commissioner.

komisheni*, kamisheni [*Engl.*] (–) commission.

komiti*, komitii, kamiti [*Engl.*] (–) committee. **– ya uchaguzi.** *pol.* electoral committee. **– ya kawaida.** standing committee. **– ndogo.** subcommittee.

komitii* (–) *see* **komiti.**

komo (ma-) *see* **kikomo.**

komoa *inv. of* **komea.**

komoo (–) expulsion, exorcism. **– ya koikoi.** exorcising of an evil spirit. *Cf.* **komea.**

¹kompania* [*Port.*] (–) *mil.* company.

²kompania* (–) *see* **kampuni.**

komred* [*Engl.*] (–) comrade.

komwe (ma-) komwe (seeds of the mkomwe; used as counters in playing bao).

¹kona* (–) secret meeting place; a second establishment maintained by a married man for his mistress.

²kona* [*Engl.*] (–) corner.

konda waste away, become thin/emaciated, lose one's strength; pine away, languish. **– kwa njaa.** become emaciated from starvation. *appl.* **kondea.** *caus.* **kondesha.** *refl.-caus.* **jikondesha.** languish, pine away, grieve.

kondakta* [*Engl.*] (ma-) conductor.

kondavi, kondawi (ma-) string of beads worn around the loins by women.

kondawi (ma-) *see* **kondavi.**

¹konde (ma-) fist. **piga – usoni.** strike someone in the face with the fist. *fig.* **piga moyo –.** display courage/manliness. *Cf.* **konzi.**

²konde (ma-) (small) field, cultivated plot of land. **lima –.** cultivate a plot of land.

³konde (ma-) stone, pit *(of fruit).* (= **kokwa.**)

¹kondo (–) *arch., liter.* battle, combat, war. (= **vita.**)

²kondo (–): **– ya nyuma.** afterbirth. **siku ya kondoni.** period of a woman's recovery after childbirth.

kondoo (–) sheep. **– dume.** ram. **– jike.** ewe. **manyoya ya –.** (sheep's) wool, fleece. *Cf.* **kikondoo.**

konesha* [*Engl.*] *sport* throw a corner *(football). Cf.* **²kona.**

¹konga become old/weak/sickly. *caus.* **kongesha.** make old, wear out. *pass.* **kongwa.** *Cf.* **kikongwe, ²kongoka, kongoja, ³kongwe, mkongojo, mkongwe, ukongwe.**

²konga (–) konga (dance).

konge *pl. of* **ukonge.**

kongoa draw (pull, tear, break) out, extract; disconnect. **– msumari (jino).** pull out a nail (tooth). *appl.* **kongolea.** take apart/to pieces. *intr.* **kongoka.** become disconnected, come apart.

kongoja walk unsteadily, stagger, totter. *appl.* **kongojea. fimbo ya kukongojea.** walking stick, cane. *appl.-refl.* **jikongojea.** walk unsteadily with the aid of a cane. *Cf.* [1]**konga, mkongojo.**

kongojo *pl. of* **ukongojo.** *See* **mkongojo.**

[1]**kongoka** *intr. of* **kongoa.**

[2]**kongoka** be old. *Cf.* [1]**konga.**

kongomana 1. come together, assemble, meet, gather. 2. crowd/pack together, pile/heap/stack up; weld together, agglomerate. 3. be joined/united.

kongomea join, put together, fasten, nail, attach, hang up. *Cf.* **kokomea.**

[1]**kongomeo (ma-)** fastening, connection.

[2]**kongomeo (ma-)** *anat.* larynx, Adam's apple. *Cf.* **koromeo.**

kongoni, kuguni (–) *zool.* kongoni (species of antelope: hartebeest, gnu, topi). (= **nyumbu.**)

kongonyoa *see* **konyoa.**

kongoro (–) old bull. *Cf.* [1]**konga.**

kongosho (–) *anat.* pancreas, thymus, sweetbread.

kong'ota, gong'ota 1. beat *(hides, in preparing leather).* 2. hammer *(metals).*

kongoti (ma-) 1. *ornith.* heron, stork. 2. kongoti (a children's game, in which one child walks on stilts and represents a stork).

kongowea *rare* greet *(in a servile way),* salute.

[1]**kongwa (ma-)** *arch.* slave stick *(a pole with a forked end and a cross pin, used for shackling slaves by the neck).*

[2]**kongwa (–)** kongwa (a plant used for animal fodder, *Commelina bracteosa).*

[1]**kongwe (–)** *mus.* soloist, leader of a chorus/choir. **toa –.** lead (singing), start a song (in which others join).

[2]**kongwe (–)** kongwe (a perennial plant, *Aneilema aequinoctale/sinicum).*

[3]**kongwe** *adj.* old, worn-out. **bibi kikongwe.** a very old woman. *Cf.* [1]**konga, mkongwe, kikongwe, ukongwe.**

konje (–) *zool.* konje (species of marten).

konjo (ma-) *see* **konzo.**

kono (mi-) (*augm. of* **mkono**) 1. (fore-)paw. 2. handle, grip. 3.: **– la tembo.** trunk of an elephant. *Cf.* **mkono.**

konoa *see* **konyoa.**

[1]**konokono (ma-, –)** slug, snail. (= [3]**koa.**)

[2]**konokono (–)** konokono (variety of tree, *Annona squamosa).*

konsonanti* [*Engl.*] (–) *phon.* consonant.

kontinenti* [*Engl.*] (–) *geogr.* continent. **– la Afrika.** the continent of Africa.

kontrakta* [*Engl.*] (–, *rare* **ma-**) contractor.

1konya float, hover, swing, rock, wave, flutter. **bendera inakonya.** The flag waves. *caus. see* **konyeza.**

2konya (–) konya (a children's game).

konyeza (*caus. of* **konya**) 1. give a sign/signal; wink, beckon; warn. *ass.* **konyezana.** wink/make a gesture at each other *(as a sign of mutual understanding or as a greeting).* 2. (ma-) *see* **konyezo.** *Cf.* **konyezo, mkonyezo, ukonyezo.**

konyezo, konyeza (ma-) sign, signal; wink; warning. *Cf.* **konyeza.**

konyo (ma-) great number, abundance. **– la nazi.** a great quantity of coconuts.

konyoa, kongonyoa, konoa tear/pluck/pick off. **– maua (matunda).** pick flowers (fruit). **– maungo.** divide/separate into parts.

konzi (–, ma-) 1. fist; a blow with the fist. **piga –.** strike with the fist. 2. the open hand. 3. handful. *Cf.* **1konde.**

konzo, konjo (ma-; *augm. of* **mkonzo**), **ukonzo, ukonjo** (konzo) stick, rod, pole *(with a hardened tip, used as a hunting weapon or in pit traps).*

1koo (ma-) *anat.* throat, Adam's apple, craw.

2koo (ma-) 1. a breeding female animal. **– la kondoo.** brood ewe. **– la kuku.** brooding hen. 2. *fig., coll.* mistress, prostitute.

3koo *pl. of* **1ukoo.**

koongo, korongo (ma-) 1. depression in the earth; drainage, catchment. 2. ravine, gully. 3. hole dug for planting seed.

1kopa (ma-) (*usually* **makopa**) (pieces of dried) manioc.

2kopa* [*Port.*] (ma-) *cards* (suit of) hearts, ace of hearts.

3kopa 1. borrow, take on credit. **nimemkopa rafiki yangu fedha.** I have borrowed money from my friend. *prov.* **kukopa rahisi, kulipa matanga.** Borrowing is pleasure, paying back is pain. *caus.* **kopesha.** lend, extend credit. 2. cheat, defraud. *Cf.* **1kope, kikopo, mkopaji, mkopeshi, mkopo, ukopaji.**

1kope, kopo (ma-) loan, credit. *Cf.* **3kopa.**

2kope (–) burnt end of a wick.

3kope (–, ma-) *anat.* eyelash, eyelid. **kwa – la juu na chini.** in the twinkling of an eye. *Cf.* **kikope, ukope.**

kopesa: **– macho.** blink, wink.

koplo* [*Engl.*] (wa-) *mil.* corporal.

[1]**kopo** (ma-) *see* [1]**kope.**

[2]**kopo*** [*Port.*] (ma-) 1. metal vessel, can; pan, pot. 2.: **samaki ya –.** canned fish. 3.: **– la maji ya mvua.** gutter, eaves, rainspout.

kora, kola *rare* please; be enough/sufficient, suffice. *Cf.* **kikora,** [2]**kikore.**

korani*, kurani (–) Koran.

kore (–) *rare* (cultivated) field, garden, plantation. (= **shamba.**) *Cf.* **kikore.**

korho* (–) *see* **koho.**

korija*, korja [*Ind.*] korija (unit of quantity used in selling: score, 20 units).

korja* (–) *see* **korija.**

koro *adv., rare* altogether, throughout.

[1]**koroboi*** [*Engl.* carbine ?] (–) *arch.* muzzle-loader. (= **gobori.**)

[2]**koroboi*** [*Engl.* carbide ?] (–) small lamp.

[3]**koroboi*** [*Engl.* call a boy *or* crew boy ?] (–) *arch.* native child employed at a mission. *Cf.* **boi.**

korocha, korochakorocha, kokorocha poke, stick, pierce.

korodani* [*Pers.*] (–) 1. sheave (of a pulley). 2. *anat.* scrotum, testicles.

korofi* 1. *adj.* rough, wild, brutal, cruel; unlucky, ominous, disastrous. 2. (–) korofi (a species of bird supposed to bring bad luck). *Cf.* **korofika, mkorofi, ukorofi.**

korofika* be ruined, suffer misfortune. *caus.* **korofisha.** ruin/injure someone, bring someone bad luck/misfortune. *Cf.* **korofi.**

korofindo* [*? Cf. Engl.* carbine, *Germ.* Flinte ?] (–) *arch.* muzzle-loader, musket.

korofisha* *caus. of* **korofika.**

koroga stir (up), mix, shake; *(fig.)* agitate, provoke. **– simu.** *sl.* call someone up on the telephone. (= *more formal* **piga simu**). *Cf.* **mkoroga, mkorogo, ukorogefu.**

korokoni* (–) *see* **korokoroni.**

korokoroni*, korokoni, kirokironi, kirokoroni, karakoli, karakoni [*Turk.*] (–) 1. jail. 2. *rare* guardhouse, police station.

[1]**koroma** (ma-) koroma (coconut when almost ripe). *Cf.* [1]**kikoromeo.**

[2]**koroma** 1. breathe heavily, pant; snore; groan, sigh; purr *(like a cat).* 2. (ma-) (*also* koromo) snore, snoring; groan, sigh; purr(ing). *Cf.* **koromeo,** [2]**kikoromeo, mkoromaji, mkoromo.**

koromeo (ma-) *anat.* 1. larynx. 2. esophagus, gullet. *Cf.* [2]**koroma.**

koromo (ma-) *see* [2]**koroma** 2.

[1]**korongo** (ma-) *see* **koongo.**

[2]**korongo** (ma-) 1. heron, stork. 2. *fig.* long-legged person.

[1]**kororo, kololo** (ma-) *ornith.* crested guinea fowl *(Guttera pucherani).* *Cf.* [1]**kanga.**

[2]**kororo** (ma-) *med.* Basedow's disease, exophthalmic goiter.

[3]**kororo** *sing.* (sound of) heavy breathing, snoring. *Cf.* [2]**koroma.**

korosho (ma-) cashew nut. *Cf.* **mkorosho.**

korota* *rare* snore, pant. *Cf.* [2]**koroma.**

korowai (–) korowai (a variety of rice).

koroweza 1. confuse, embarrass, baffle, disconcert, take aback. 2. *rare* seize, grasp *(by the throat);* catch *(a ball, a thief).* 3. *fig.* rack one's brains *(over something).* *Cf.* **makorowezo.**

korti* [*Engl.*] (ma-) *see* [2]**koti.**

[1]**kosa** 1. err, be mistaken, make a mistake. **nimekosa.** I was mistaken. **haikosi.** undoubtedly, doubtless. 2. do wrong; *(rel.)* sin, commit a sin. 3. lack, be wanting. 4. be unsuccessful, not achieve one's purpose. 5. deviate, go astray; miss one's mark. **– njia.** lose one's way. *pass.* **koswa.** be without a means of escape, get into a *cul-de-sac.* *ass.* **kosekana.** be missing/lacking. 6. (ma-) error, mistake; blame, censure; wrong, offense; sin; lack, deficiency. **tia kosani.** blame, rebuke; accuse. *Cf.* **kosefu, makosekano, mkosaji, ukosekano.**

[2]**kosa** (–) kosa (sheaf of 60 cornstalks).

kosakosa *adv.* almost, nearly.

kosefu *adj.* incorrect, erroneous; faulty, defective. **kazi ni –.** The work is defective. *Cf.* [1]**kosa.**

kosha* [*Ind.*] (–) (sweet) palm wine.

koshi* [*Pers.*] (ma-) slipper.

kosi (ma-) *anat.* (nape of the) neck, cervical vertebra. *coll.* **vunja –.** break one's neck. *Cf.* [1]**kikosi, ukosi.**

[1]**kota** (ma-) curve, bend, hook, crook. **– la njia.** bend in a road.

[2]**kota** (ma-), **kikota** (vi-) (sweet) millet-stalk *(chewed like candy).*

[3]**kota** *inf. of* **ota.**

kotama (–) short, curved knife *(used for slashing the bark of palm trees in order to collect the sap for making palm wine).*

kote (*loc. of* **-ote**) *adv.* 1. everywhere. 2 always 3. *red.* **kotekote: kisu kinakata –.** The knife cuts on both edges.

[1]**koti*** [*Engl.*] (ma-) coat, jacket; (women's) two-piece suit.

[2]**koti***, **korti** [*Engl.*] (ma-) lawcourt (= **baraza, hakumu, sheria**). **– kuu, – rufaa.** court of appeal, supreme court.

[1]**koto** (–) 1. *arch.* obligatory labor *(of a slave).* 2. (*also* **kotokoto**) extra earnings *(from jobs outside of one's regular working-hours).*

[2]**koto** (ma-) large fishhook *(for catching sharks).*

kotokoto (–) *see* [1]**koto** 2.

kotwe (–) (white-backed) duck *(Thalassornis leuconotus).*

kovo (–, ma-) *see* **kovu.**

kovu, kovo (–, ma-) scar. **mwenye –.** a person disfigured by a scar.

kowana (–) kowana (edible fish).

koya *rare* be contented/happy.

koza be bright, shine. **rangi hii imekoza.** This is a very bright color.

[1]**kozi** (–), **kikozi** (vi-) (species of) hawk.

[2]**kozi** (–) pinnule, fibrous sheath *(of the coconut palm).*

krimu* [*Engl.*] (–) cream, salve. *Cf.* [2]**kirimu.**

Kristo*, Kristu [*Port. ?*] Christ. **Yesu –.** Jesus Christ. **– Mfalme.** Christ the King. *Cf.* **kikristo, mkristo, ukristo;** *also* **masihiya.**

[1]**kua** grow, grow up; be increased/enlarged/magnified. *appl.* **kulia.** *caus.* **kuza.** 1. raise, rear, cultivate; *(fig.)* increase, magnify. **magazeti yaliikuza habari hii.** The newspapers have magnified/blown up these reports. 2. *phot.* enlarge. **– picha.** enlarge a photograph. *Cf.* **kuu, kulivu, kikulia, mkulivu, mkuzaji, ukuaji, ukulifu, ukuzaji.**

[2]**kua** *dial. for* **kuwa,** *q.v.*

kuaga, kuagana *sing.* parting, farewell. *Cf.* [1]**aga.**

kuagana *sing.* *see* **kuaga.**

kuamkia *sing.* greeting. *Cf.* **amkia.**

kuba*, kubba, guba, kubla (–, ma-) 1. dome, cupola, vault. 2. *geogr.* gulf, bay. *Cf.* [2]**kikuba.**

kubadhi* (ma-) *see* **kubazi.**

kubali*, kabuli, kibali, takabali agree, consent; acknowledge; admit, approve. *appl.* **kubalia.** *appl.-pass.* **kubaliana.** be of one mind, be on good terms with each other. *intr.* **kubalika.** be acceptable, be deserving of recognition. *caus.* **kubalisha.** persuade, talk over, prevail on someone to agree to something. *Cf.* **ukubali.**

kubaza* [*Pers.*] puff up, swell, be inflated. *Cf.* **kuba.**

kubazi*, **kubadhi** (**ma-**) sandal. (= **kiatu, koshi, mtalawanda, ndara.**)

kubla* (**–, ma-**) *see* **kuba.**

kubwa *adj.* 1. big, large, great. **mji mkubwa.** a big/large city. 2. *fig.* important, significant, influential. **mtu mkubwa.** an important/influential personage. 3. essential, principal; serious, weighty. **neno –.** a weighty utterance. 4. old, dignified. **ndugu mkubwa.** the older brother. 5. strong, heavy. **mvua kubwa.** a heavy rain. 6. loud. **sema kwa sauti –.** speak in a loud voice. 7. real, total, utter; regular, confirmed *(used with a n. or another adj. simply to intensify its meaning, like the adv.* **sana***).* **mwizi mkubwa.** a regular thief. **Mtu huyu ni mlevi mkubwa.** This fellow is a confirmed drunkard. (= **kuu;** *cf. also* **kua, tukuka.**) *Cf.* **makubwa, mkubwa, ukubwa.**

kubwebwe, kumbwebwe, kumbewe (**ma-**) sling. **piga –.** throw with a sling.

[1]**kucha** (*inf. of* [3]**cha**) 1. dawn, (early) morning. (= **pambauko.**) 2. dark(ness). **usika –.** the whole night long. **amelala –.** He slept the whole night through.

[2]**kucha** (**ma-**) (*augment. of* **ukucha**) claw *(of a lion, etc.)*, talon *(of a bird of prey).*

[3]**kucha** *pl. of* **ukucha.**

kuchanganya *sing.* (act of) mixing, mixture. **– chokaa na mchanga.** a mixture of mortar and sand.

kucheza *sing.* *see* **mchezo.**

kuchi (**–**) gamecock, fighting cock.

kuchwa *see* **chwa.**

kudhamini* *sing.* surety, security, bail. *Cf.* **dhamini.**

kudhumani* (**–**) pomegranate (= **komamanga**). *Cf.* **mkudhumani.**

kudra* (**–**) *see* **kudura.**

kudu (**–**) kudu (kind of fish).

kudura*, **kudra** (**–**) *rel. rare* power, might. (= **nguvu, uwezo.**) **– ya Mungu.** the might of God. *Cf.* **makadara.**

kuendesha *sing.* driving. **– motokaa.** automobile driving. *Cf.* **enda.**

kufa *sing.* dying, death. **– ni kubaya.** Dying is bad. *Cf.* **fa.**

kufika (*inf. of* **fika**, *used sometimes like a prep.*) to, as far as. **amesafiri – Tanga.** He traveled to Tanga.

kufuli* (**–, ma-**) padlock.

kufuru* 1. offend, injure. 2. *rel.* abandon a religion, turn apostate. *appl.* **kufuria.** *intr.* **kufurika.** *caus.* **kufurisha.** 3. (**ma-**, *us. pl.*) sacrilege, atheism. **– sakramenti.** sacrilege. *Cf.* **kafiri, makufuru.**

kugesi (**–**) (*also* **kigesi, kigezi, vi-**) anklet.

kuguni (–) *see* **kongoni.**

kuhani* (ma-) *see* **kahini.**

kuhusiana* **na...** *see* **husu, husiana.**

kuhusu* (*inf. of* **husu** *used as prep.*) concerning.

kuingiza *sing., econ.* import(ing), importation. *Cf.* **ingia.**

kujiendesha: –a –. *adj.* automatic. *Cf.* **enda.**

kujitawala* *sing. pol.* self-government, autonomy, independence. *Cf.* **tawala.**

kujitowa *sing.* **– makosa.** self-criticism. *Cf.* [1]**toa, kutowana.**

kujiua *sing.* suicide. *Cf.* [3]**ua.**

kuke, kuuke *sing.* 1. the female side *(of a family).* *loc.* **kukeni.** on one's mother's side. **jamaa ya kukeni.** relatives on one's mother's side of the family. 2. *rare:* **mkono la –.** left hand. *Cf.* **ke.**

kuki (ma-) *see* **mkuki.**

kuko *adv.* there, in/to that place. **– huko.** in that very/same place.

[1]**kuku** (–) poultry, fowl, chicken, hen. **mtoto wa –.** chick.

[2]**kuku** *adv.:* **– huku.** right there, in that very place.

kukurika* 1. be excited/upset/distressed. 2 be sad/depressed/melancholy. 3. fight, wrestle. *Cf.* **kukuru.**

kukuru* (–) 1. excitement, uneasiness. 2. distress, depression. 3. fighting, wrestling. *Cf.* [1]**kakara, kikiri, kukurika.**

kukusa be inattentive/careless/negligent/slovenly.

kukuta 1. shake off *(drops of water).* 2. gasp for breath, breathe with difficulty. *intr.* **kukutika.** be shaken off, be dry/dried off.

kukutaa be hard, be dried up *(e.g., the ground by the sun).* *Cf.* **kukuta, kukutu.**

kukutu *adv.:* **kauka –.** be completely dry. *Cf.* **kukuta, kukutaa.**

kukuu *adj.* *see* **kuukuu.**

kula eat. *Cf.* [1]**la.**

kulabu*, kalubu (–) hook, clamp.

kulasitara* (–) *ornith.* (black) heron. *Cf.* [2]**la, stiri.**

kule *adv.* 1. that, in that place. 2. *adv.* there, in/to that place. *red.* **kulekule.** in that very place. **kule-e-e**! *(in giving directions, etc.)* Way over there! A long way off!

kulea *sing.* upbringing, (traditional) education. *Cf.* **lea.**

kuli* [*Ind.*] (ma-) 1. dock-worker, longshoreman. 2. *fig.* dock, wharf, shipyard.

[1]**kulia** (–) right side. *pol.* the right, right-wing. **–a –.** right. **mkono wa –.** the right hand. *Cf.* **la** *appl.*

[2]**kulia** *appl. of* [1]**kua.**

kulifu *see* **kulivu.**

kulihali* *adv.* in any case, at all events.

kuliko 1. than *(in comparisons).* **mji huu mkubwa – ule.** This city is larger than that one. 2. *rare* as to, as regards.

kulingana na... according to... *Cf.* [1]**linga.**

kulivu, kulifu *adj.* 1. lacking perseverance/grit, slack, indolent, apathetic. 2. oppressive, burdensome, troublesome. 3. tedious, boring. *Cf.* [1]**kua, ukulifu.**

kuliwi (–) kuliwi (species of insect).

kulla* *see* **kila.**

kuludhu* (–) *see* **kiludhu.**

kulula* *rare* be superior, surpass, excel. (= **shinda, pita.**)

[1]**kululu** 1. (ma-) kululu (large kind of cowrie shell of very small value). 2. *fig., adv.* of little value. **amepata –.** He has received something utterly worthless.

[2]**kululu** (ma-) kululu (species of locust).

kulungu, kuungu, kungu (–) kulungu (species of antelope, bushbuck, *Tragelaphus sylvaticus).*

kuma (–) *anat., vulg.* vagina (= **uke**).

[1]**kumba** 1. push, shove, jostle; butt. 2. destroy, do away with. *caus.* **kumbiza, kumbisha.** push someone aside; push something off on someone; force something on someone. **kumbizia fulani kazi.** push a job off on someone. *ass.* **kumbana.** push/shove each other; bump into each other, collide; butt (each other), fight *(cattle, etc.). Cf.* **kikumbo,** [2]**mkumbizi, ukumbaji.**

[2]**kumba** 1. clear out/away, clean/sweep out; bail *(water out of a boat;* = [3]**vua**). 2. make a clean sweep of something, monopolize. *appl.* **kumbia.** *pass.* **kumbwa.** *Cf.* [1]**kumbo,** [1]**mkumbizi, mkumbo,** [1]**ukumbizi.**

[3]**kumba, kumbakumba** *adj.* mixed, miscellaneous, heterogenous.

[4]**kumba** (–) kumba (kind of fish).

kumbakumba *see* [3]**kumba.**

kumbati, kombati (–) pole *(used in building houses).*

kumbatia embrace, take in the arms. *intr.* **kumbatika.** *caus.* **kumbatisha.** *ass.* **kumbatiana. mtoto alikumbatiana na mamaye.** The child and its mother embraced each other.

kumbe *interj. expressing surprise.* **– ni yeye aliyevunja nyumba!** So he is the one who broke into the house. **Ah, – kila mtu ni tayari ila mimi!** So everybody is ready except me!

[1]**kumbewe** (ma-) *see* **kubwebwe.**

[2]**kumbewe** (ma-) *see* **kombeo.**

[1]**kumbi, kumvi** (ma-) 1. vegetable fiber *(usually from coconut palm leaves.* 2. chaff.

[2]**kumbi** (ma-) 1. circumcision hut *(where boys stay before and after being circumcised).* 2. *rare* circumcision.

[3]**kumbi** *pl. of* **ukumbi.**

kumbikumbi (–) winged white ant *(especially when in the edible flying stage).*

[1]**kumbo** (ma-) destruction, devastation, annihilation, depopulation. *Cf.* [2]**kumba.**

[2]**kumbo** (ma-) *see* **kikumbo.**

kumbufu *adj.:* **mtu mkumbufu.** a person with a good memory. *Cf.* **kumbuka.**

kumbuka remember, call to/bear in mind; recognize. *appl.* **kumbukia.** *caus.* **kumbusha.** *Cf.* **kumbufu, kumbuko, kumbukumbu, kumbusho, kikumbuko, mkumbufu, ukumbuko, ukumbusho.**

kumbuko (ma-) 1. memory, recollection, remembrance. 2. reflection, consideration, thought. *Cf.* **kumbuka.**

kumbukumbu (ma-, –) 1. = **kumbusho.** 2. memory. **ana – nzuri.** He has a good memory. *Cf.* **kumbuka.**

kumbusha *caus. of* **kumbuka.**

kumbusho, kumbukumbu (ma-) 1. memory, recollection. 2. memento, souvenir. 3. memorial, monument, statue. **jumba la makumbusho.** museum. *Cf.* **kumbuka.**

kumbwaya (–) 1. kumbwaya (kind of drum which stands on legs). 2.: **ngoma ya –.** kind of dance.

kumbwe (ma-) *coll.* bite, taste, snack. **– na kinyweo.** food and drink.

kumbwebwe (ma-) *see* **kubwebwe.**

kumi 1. ten. **–a –.** tenth. 2. (ma-) decade *(of a month).* **– la kwanza (kati, mwisho).** first (middle, last) decade. 3. a tenth, tithe. *Cf.* **kikumi.**

kumoja (–) one (and the same) kind, uniformity, homogeneity. *Cf.* **moja.**

kumpuni (–) *see* **kampuni.**

kumunta *see* **kung'uta.**

kumunto (ma-) *see* **kung'uto.**

[1]**kumvi** (ma-) *see* [1]**kumbi.**

[2]**kumvi** *pl. of* **ukumvi.**

[1]**kuna** there is/are in that place. **shambani – minazi.** There are coconut-palms in the plantation. **– nini?** What's the matter?

[2]**kuna** scratch, scrape, grate. **– nazi.** remove the meat of a coconut from the shell. *refl.* **jikuna.** scratch oneself. *Cf.* **kuno, mkuno;** *also* **kunyua.**

kunazi* [*Pers.*] **(ma-)** kunazi (fruit of the mkunazi, jujube). *Cf.* **mkunazi, kikunazi.**

[1]**kunda (ma-)** kunda (a kind of vegetable similar to spinach).

[2]**kunda** *see* **kunja.**

kundaa be small/underdeveloped/stunted/dwarfed; shrink, shrivel. **mtu aliyekundaa.** dwarf, pygmy.

kunde *pl. of* **ukunde.**

kundi (ma-) 1. herd. **– la wanyama.** a herd of cattle. 2. swarm, flock. **– la ndege (nyuki).** a flock/swarm of birds/bees. 3. group, band, troupe. **makundi makundi.** in large groups/crowds. **– la manowari.** *naut.* flotilla, squadron. **– la askari.** *mil.* squadron. 4. an unregistered association; *(rare)* (political) party. **– la mbele.** *comm.* vanguard.

kundu (ma-) *anat.* anus. (= **mkundu.**)

[1]**kunga** fold, hem, seam, edge, trim *(with tape).* **– nguo.** hem/trim a garment.

[2]**kunga** 1. instruct, teach *(especially in connection with the initiation of boys and girls when they reach sexual maturity).* 2. **(ma-)** secret. *Cf.* **kungwi,** [1]**mkunga, ukunga, ukungwi.**

[3]**kunga (–): – ya uzazi.** *anat.* umbilical cord.

[1]**kunge (–)** 1. wood-fiber. 2. center of a tree, heart.

[2]**kunge, kungu, kungugu (–)** fog, mist.

[1]**kungu (ma-)** kungu (edible kernel of the mkungu fruit). *Cf.* [2]**mkungu.**

[2]**kungu (ma-)** *see* **jungu.**

[3]**kungu (–)** *see* **kulungu.**

[4]**kungu (–)** *see* [2]**kunge.**

kungugu (–) *see* [2]**kunge.**

kungumanga (–) nutmeg. *Cf.* **mkungumanga;** *also* **basibasi.**

kunguni (–) 1. bug, bedbug. 2.: **– mgunda.** an insect which eats the roots of growing plants.

[1]**kunguru (–)** *ornith.* (species of) crow *(Corvus albus).*

[2]**kunguru (ma-)** blue and white checked cotton cloth.

kung'uta, kumunta 1. shake, shake off. **– mavumbi.** shake off dust. 2. separate, sift, winnow. 3. check carefully, examine, scrutinize. *refl.* **jikung'uta.** shake oneself. *Cf.* **kung'uto, mkung'uto.**

kung'uto, kumunto (ma-) winnowing or sifting basket. *Cf.* **kung'uta.**

kunguwala *see* **kungwala.**

kungwala, kunguwala stumble.

kungwi (ma-), **ngungwi** (–) 1. midwife. 2. assistant at initiation rites. *fig.* **mimi ni – lako.** I understand the matter better than you do. *Cf.* ²**kunga.**

kungwia (–) kungwia (kind of dance).

kuni *pl. of* **ukuni.**

kunja (*dial.* **kunda**) fold (up), close *(e.g., a pocketknife)*, wind up *(string, etc.)*; *(naut.)* furl, take in *(sail)*. *fig.* – **uso.** wrinkle the forehead, make a face. – **uzi.** wind up yarn. *coll.* **mkewe amemkunja.** He is henpecked. *prov.* **samaki mkunje yungali mbichi.** Tie up the fish while it is fresh. *refl.* **jikunja.** crouch, cower. *ass.* **kunjana.** heal (wounds). *stat.* **kunjama.** *stat.-ass.* **kunjamana.** be wrinkled. **kunjamana uso.** wrinkle the forehead, frown. *inv.* **kunjua.** unfold, smooth out, spread out. **kunjua uzi.** unwind a ball of yarn. **kunjua miguu.** stretch out the legs. **kunjua uso.** smile. *inv.-refl.* **jikunjua.** be hospitable/obliging. *Cf.* **kunjo, kunjufu, kikunja, kikunjo, mkunjaji, mkunjo, ukunjufu.**

kunjama *stat. of* **kunja.**

kunjo (ma-) 1. fold, crease. 2. wrinkle. – **la nywele.** lock of hair. *Cf.* **kunja.**

kunjua *inv. of* **kunja.**

kunjufu *adj.* serene, untroubled; frank, honest; friendly, cordial, obliging; cheerful, genial. *Cf.* **kunja** *(inv.)*, **ukunjufu.**

kuno (ma-) 1. scraping, scratching. 2. product of scraping/scratching, that which has been scraped/scratched off. *Cf.* ²**kuna.**

kunradhi* *interj.* Excuse me! Pardon me! *Cf.* **radhi.**

kunvnu (ma-) empty husk/spike *(of grain)*. (= **pepe.**) – **la mawele.** empty/withered ear of millet.

kunusa *sing.* sense of smell. *Cf.* **nuka.**

kunyanzi (ma-) 1. fold, crease. 2. *fig.* wrinkle. *Cf.* **kunja.**

kunyata press, squeeze. *refl.* **jikunyata.** 1. embrace. 2. *fig.* be depressed. **mbona umejikunyata sana?** Why are you so depressed/sad? *Cf.* **kunja.**

kunyua 1. scratch/cut/hurt oneself. 2. warn, give a sign. *appl.* **kunyulia.** *intr.* **kunyuka.** *Cf.* ²**kuna.**

kuo (ma-) 1. furrow; ditch, trench; hole, pit. 2. hole for planting seed, bed. 3. cultivated plot/parcel of land. **nyosha –.** mark out a field.

kuona *sing.* sensation, feeling. – **kwangu.** in my opinion. *Cf.* **ona.**

kupa* (ma-) side-piece of a pulley.

kupanda *sing.* planting-time. (= **wakati wa –.**) *Cf.* ²**panda.**

kupasuliwa *sing., med.* operation. – **kwa moyo.** heart operation. *Cf.* **pasua.**

kupe (–) (cattle-)tick.

kupia 1. wink, blink. 2. nod, doze, nap.

kupita 1. *see* **pita.** 2. than *(in comparisons).* **nyumba hii kubwa – ile.** This house is larger than that one.

kuponi* [*Engl.*] (–) coupon.

kupua 1. shake out/off; drop. **– nguo.** throw off one's clothes. *fig.* **– mali.** waste/ squander property. 2. pour out, spill. **– maji.** spill water. *appl.* **kupulia.** *intr.* **kupuka.** 1. be shaken off; be an outcast/fugitive. 2. *fig.* be depraved/infamous *(in character).* *Cf.* **mkupuo, mkupuzi.**

kura* (–) 1. lot, chance. **piga (tupa) –.** cast/ draw lots. 2. fate, destiny. **– ilimwangukia yeye.** Fate caught up with him. 3. *pol.* voting, balloting. **– ya siri.** secret voting, voting by ballot. **piga –.** cast a vote, vote. 4. a vote *(in an election),* ballot. **kwa – nyingi zaidi.** by majority vote.

kurani* (–) *see* **korani.**

kurasa* *pl. of* **ukurasa.**

kurea (–) *ornith.* kurea (species of kingfisher).

kuro (–) *zool.* kuro (species of antelope, waterbuck).

kuru* (–) (solid) cylindrical object. *Cf.* **mzinga.**

kuruba* (–) curve, bend.

kurubia *see* **karibia.**

kurumbiza (–) *see* **kurumbizi.**

kurumbizi, kurumbiza (–) *ornith.* golden oriole *(Oriolus oriolus).*

kurunzi*, hurunzi (–) 1. flashlight, searchlight. 2. (cigarette-)lighter.

kurupuka be surprised/startled/frightened. *caus.* **kurupusha.** startle/frighten someone. *refl.-caus.* **jikurupusha.** rise with a start, rouse oneself.

kurupusha *caus. of* **kurupuka.**

kururu (–) kururu (white crab).

kuruta smooth, make even. *Cf.* **guruta.**

kurutu* [*Engl.*] (–, ma-) recruit, trainee.

kuruwiji (–) *ornith.* (species of) bulbul.

kusa *caus. of* [1]**kuta.**

kusanya (*double caus. of* [1]**kuta**) collect, gather, assemble, pile up, accumulate. **– mali.** accumulate wealth. **– jeshi.** assemble an army. *intr.* **kusanyika.** *ass.* **kusanyana.** assemble, meet together. *Cf.* **kusanyiko, mkusanya, mkusanyiko.**

kusanyiko, kusanyo (ma-) 1. gathering, assemblage *(without special purpose),* crowd. 2. gathering-place. *Cf.* **kusanya.**

kusanyo (ma-) *see* **kusanyiko.**

kusha *caus. of* [1]**kuta.**

kushoto (–) left side. *pol.* the left, left-wing. **–a –.** left. **mkono wa –.** left hand. **kutoka – kwenda kuume.** from left to right.

kusi*, **kussi** (–) 1. south wind, south monsoon. 2. period of the south-southwest monsoon. (May - October). 3. *loc.* **kusini.** in/from the south.

kusini* *loc.* *see* **kusi.**

kussi* (–) *see* **kusi.**

kustabani*, **kustabini**, **kustubani** (–) *see* **kastabini.**

kusudi*, **kasidi** 1. intend, purpose, have in view, plan, propose. *us. appl.* **kusudia.** *intr.* **kusudika.** *caus.* **kusudisha.** 2. (*also* **kasida**) (ma-) intention, purpose, plan, aim. 3. *adv.* intentionally, on purpose; in order to. **amevunja makusudi.** He broke it intentionally. **amesafiri – akamwone.** He traveled with the intention of seeing him (*or:* in order to see him). (= **shauri, maana, nia, mradi.**) *Cf.* **makusudio.**

¹kusuru* try hard, make an effort, do under difficulties/with great exertion.

²kusuru* shorten, lessen, reduce. *Cf.* **²kasa.**

¹kuta come upon, meet, run across *(someone or something)*. *ass.* **kutana.** meet (each other). *caus.* **kutisha, kusha, kusa.** produce, create. **kutisha mashaka.** create doubts. *Cf.* **kusanya, kutano, ¹kikuti, mkutano, mkuto.**

²kuta appease, satisfy *(hunger)*. (= **shiba.**)

³kuta: – **mayai.** lay eggs. (= **¹taga.**)

⁴kuta *pl. of* **ukuta.**

kutaa dry up, wither. (= **nyauka, kauka.**)

kutana *ass. of* **¹kuta.**

kutano (ma-) (*usually* **mkutano**) 1. meeting, gathering *(with a definite purpose)*. 2. assemblage, crowd. *Cf.* **¹kuta.**

kutawala* *sing.* government, rule. *Cf.* **tawala, utawala.**

kutayarisha* *sing.* preparation. *Cf.* **tayari, tayarisha.**

kuti (ma-) leaf (of the coconut palm). *Cf.* **ukuti.**

kutoingilia(na) *sing., pol.* non-intervention. *Cf.* **ingia.**

kutoka *prep.* from, out of. – **pale.** from there. *Cf.* **²toka.**

kutokana na... according to, as a result of. *Cf.* **tokana (¹toa).**

kutokujua *sing.* ignorance. *Cf.* **²jua.**

kutoshambulia, kutoshambuliana *sing., pol.* non-aggression. **mkataba wa –.** non-agression pact. *Cf.* **shambulia.**

kutota *sing.* degeneration. *Cf.* **tota.**

kutowana *sing.:* – **makosa.** criticism. – **makosa na kujitowa makosa.** *comm.* criticism and self-criticism. *Cf.* **¹toa.**

kutu *sing.* 1. rust. **ingia —.** to rust. 2. (plant) blight.

kutua, gutua 1. jerk, cause a shock, pull (suddenly). 2. *fig.* land *(of airplanes). intr.* **kutuka.** be shocked/startled/frightened. *caus.* **kutusha.** shock, frighten. *Cf.* **mkutuo.**

kutuzi (—) (odor of) perspiration. (= **kikwapa.**)

kutwa *see* **chwa.**

kuu *adj.* 1. large; great, important; distinguished, prominent, eminent, famous. 2. old, experienced. *Cf.* **makuu, mkuu, ukuu;** *also* [1]**kua, kubwa.**

kuuke *sing.* *see* **kuke.**

kuukuu, kukuu *adj.* worn-out, old, useless. *Cf.* **kikuukuu.**

kuume *sing.* 1. male/paternal side *(of a family). loc.* **kuumeni.** on one's father's side. **jamaa ya kuumeni.** relatives on one's father's side. 2. right side. **—a —.** right. **mkono wa —.** right hand. *Cf.* [1]**ume.**

kuuganisha *sing.* collectivization. *Cf.* [2]**unga.**

kuungo (—) kuungo (oval stone, used to smooth the surface of pottery).

kuungu (—) *see* **kulungu.**

kuvu (—, **ma-**) mold, mildew, blight; fungus, lichen.

kuvuli *rare:* **mkono wa —.** right hand.

kuwa (*dial.* **kua**) *conj.* 1.: **ya —.** (so) that, (in order) that. 2.: **kwa —.** because.

kuwadi* (—) *see* **kawadi.**

kuwi (—) kuwi (a fish).

kuwili *adv.* in two ways, in a double way. **kisu chenye makali —.** a double-edged knife. *Cf.* **wili.**

kuyu (—) wild fig. *Cf.* **mkuyu.**

kuza *caus. of* [1]**kua.**

kuzaliwa *sing.* birth. *Cf.* **zaa.**

kuzi (—, **ma-**) water-jug (with one or two handles). (= **mtungi, chombo.**)

kuzika, kuzikani, kuzikwa *sing., rare* burial, funeral (= **maziko**). *Cf.* **zika.**

kuzimu *sing.* realm of the dead, underworld; *(rel.)* limbo. **amekwenda —** (*or:* **kuzimuni**). He is dead. *Cf.* **mzimu, wazimu, zimwe.**

kuzumburu (—) kuzumburu (species of bird, *Colivus leucatis).*

k. v. *abbr. of* **kama vile.** that is, for example *(i.e., e.g.).*

kwa *prep.* 1. with, by means of, by. **safiri — motokaa.** travel by automobile. **andika — Kiswahili.** write in Swahili. 2. because of, as a result of. **walikimbia — hofu.** They fled because of fear. 3. with, to *(a person),* at/to the home of... **kaa — fulani.** live/stay with/at the home of someone. **kwenda – fulani.** go to (see, visit) someone. 4. in, for *(a period of time).* **safiri – miaka mitatu.** be away for three years. **– mwezi miwili.** in two months. 5. according to. **– maoni yao.** in their opinion. 6. *forming adverbs:* **– haraka.** hastily, quickly. **– siri.** secretly, mysteriously. **mara – mara.** again and again. **– moyo.** by heart. **– miguu.** on foot. **– kujua.** deliberately. 7. *forming conjunctions:* **– kuwa.** since, because. **– sababu (ya).** since, because. 8. *interr.* **– nini?** why? 9.: **– heri!** Good-bye!

kwaa (*and refl.* **jikwaa**) bump, stumble (against, over), slip. **– na jiwe.** stumble over a stone. *fig.* 1. be mistaken/wrong. 2. hestitate, falter. 3. be pugnacious/quarrelsome. **amenikwaa.** He is trying to pick a fight with me. *caus.* **kwaza.** *Cf.* [2]**kwao, kikwazo;** *also* **kwama.**

kwadragesima* [*Lat.*] (–) *see* **kwaresima.**

kwaje *interrog.* how? in what way? why?

kwaju (–) tamarind *(fruit of the* **mkwaju).**

kwajuka fade, deteriorate, become ugly, shrivel up.

kwake 1. *see* **–ake.** 2. *loc. poss. 3rd pers. sing.* to/with/at/from him (her), his/her house. **enda –.** go to him/her, go to his/her house.

kwako 1. *see* **–ako.** 2. *loc. poss. 2nd pers. sing.* to/with/from you, to/at/from your house. **ja –.** come to you, come to your house.

kwakura scratch the ground (with the claws).

kwale, kware, kwara (–) *ornith.* partridge.

kwama 1. stick, be stuck/jammed. **amekwamwa na mwiba wa samaki.** A fishbone is stuck in his throat. 2. *naut.* run aground, be stranded. 3. *fig.* be in a difficult situation. *inv.* **kwamua.** loosen, free, extricate. *inv.-appl.* **kwamulia.** *Cf.* **kwaa.**

kwamba (*also* **ya –**) *conj.* 1. that, in order that, in order to. **alisema (ya) ...** He said that... 2.: **kama –.** as if. **alisema kama – ana hakika.** He talked as if he were sure. 3.: **– ... –.** whether ... or. **– ni vizuri au – ni ya vibaya.** whether it is good or bad.

kwamua *see* **kwama** *(inv.) and* **kwamyua.**

kwamyua, kwanyua, kwamua, kwanua pick, pluck, tear off, break off *(fruit, branches).* *appl.* **kwanyulia.** *intr.* **kwanyuka.**

kwanga (–) *zool.* rock rabbit (hyrax, coney).

kwangu 1. *see* **–angu.** 2. *loc. poss. 1st pers. sing.* to/with/from me, to/at my house. **kaa –.** stay with me, stay at my house.

kwangua clean, scrape, scour.

kwani (< **kwa nini**) 1. *conj.* since, because. 2. *interrog.*, *sl. (pronounced* **kwa'**) why, for what reason. (= **kwa sababu, kwa maana, kwa ajili, kwa kuwa.**)

kwanua *see* **kwamyua.**

kwanyua *see* kwamyua.

kwanyulia *appl. of* kwamyua.

kwanza *adv.* first, at first, in the beginning. –a –. *adj.* first. *Cf.* anza.

[1]kwao 1. *see* –ao. 2. *loc. poss. 3rd pers. plur.* to/with/from them, to/at/from their house. kaa –. stay with them, stay at their house. 3. (ma-) birthplace, home.

[2]kwao, kwazo (ma-) obstruction, impediment. njia ya –. a rough, stony road. *Cf.* kwaa.

[3]kwao (–) *ornith.* brown-headed parrot.

kwapa (ma-) *anat.* armpit. chukua (futika) kwapani. carry something under the arm. *Cf.* kikwapa.

kwapua *see* kwepua.

kwara (–) *see* kwale.

[1]kwarara (–) *ornith.* (species of) ibis.

[2]kwarara *pl.* wild fruit.

[1]kware (–) *see* kwale.

[2]kware *adj.* lascivious, lewd, prurient. *Cf.* mkware, ukware.

kwaresima*, kwadragesima [*Lat.*] (–) *rel.* Lent.

kwaru (–) *ornith.* Grosbeak weaver (= yombi-yombi, katadole).

kwaruza 1. scrape, scratch. 2. be rough/gritty/uneven/bumpy. *Cf.* kwaruzo, mkwaruzo.

kwaruzo (ma-) file, rasp. *Cf.* kwaruza.

kwasi *rare* 1. be rich/wealthy/affluent. 2. *adj.* rich, wealthy; extravagant, wasteful. (= tajiri.) *Cf.* mkwasi, ukwasi.

[1]kwata 1. (*also* kikwata) *adv.* on foot. 2. (–) *mil.* drill, review, parade, maneuver. *Cf.* kiatu, kwato, liwato.

[2]kwata (–): – jeupe (jekundo). white (red) sweet potato.

kwato (ma-), ukwato (kwato), kikwato (vi-) hoof *(of an animal). Cf.* [1]kwata.

kwatua clean. – shamba. clear a field, pull weeds. *refl.* jikwatua. clean/spruce oneself up.

kwaya* [*Engl.*] (–) choir, chorus; choral music, anthem.

kwaza *caus. of* kwaa.

kwazi (–) *ornith.* kwazi (variety of fish-eating eagle).

kwazo (ma-) *see* [2]kwao.

kwea 1. climb up on, get on top of, mount. – mnazi. climb a coconut palm. – meli. go on board a ship. 2. mount, cover, copulate with *(of a male animal).* 3. go up, rise, become higher. *appl.* kwelea. *rare:* mawimbi ya kwelea. surf, high seas. *appl.-intr.* kweleka. *caus.* kweza. raise, increase. kweza bei. raise prices. kweza mashua. pull a boat onto the beach. *refl.-caus.* jikweza. exalt oneself, boast, brag. *Cf.* ²kweleo, kwezi, mkweo, mkwezi, ukwezi.

kweche (ma-) old, worn-out vehicle.

kwechi (–) *ornith.* bishop bird. (= chekechea.)

kwekwe (–, ma-) weed.

kweleka *appl.-intr. of* kwea.

¹kweleo (–, ma-) *see* koleo.

²kweleo (ma-) peg (or notch) in a tree-trunk *(to facilitate climbing). Cf.* kwea.

kweli 1. (–) truth; truthfulness, honesty, candor. *coll.* – inauma. The truth hurts. – ikisimama, wongo hujitenga. Where truth is, falsehood must yield. 2. *adv.* indeed, truly, honestly, really. 3.: –a –. *adj.* true. *Cf.* ukweli.

kwembe (ma-) 1. *ornith.* crowned hornbill *(Lophoceros melanoleucos).* – maji. African woolly-necked stork *(Dissoura episcopus).* 2. *fig.:* domo la –. a walking-stick with a handle shaped like the bill of the kwembe.

kweme (–) kweme (seed of the mkweme plant).

kwenda *prep.* (going) to. amesafiri – Tanganyika. He traveled to Tanganyika. – baharini. sea-going *(vessels). Cf.* enda.

kwenu 1. *see* -enu. 2. *loc. poss. 2nd pers. plur.* to/with you, to/at your home.

kwenye *see* enye.

kwenzi (–) *ornith.* starling.

kwepua, kwapua take/snatch away, steal. *Cf.* mkwepuzi.

kwesha fix, fasten.

kweta flounder, flop, struggle.

kwetu 1. *see* -etu. 2. *loc. poss. 1st pers. plur.* to/with us, at our home.

kweu (–) *see* kweupe.

kweupe, kweu (–) light, brightness; bright sky, good weather. leo ni –. There is fine weather today.

kweza *caus. of* kwea.

kwezi *adj.* climbing, twining *(of plants). Cf.* kwea.

kwikwi (–) hiccup, sobbing.

kwingineko *adv.* elsewhere. *Cf.* ingine, pengine.

kwini* [*Engl.*] (–) queen.

kwinini*, kinini [*Engl.*] *sing., pharm.* quinine.

kwisha 1.: –a –. last, final. 2. *adv.* then, subsequently. alikula chakula – akaenda zake. He ate his meal, then he went away. *Cf.* ¹isha.

kwiu (–) (pangs of) hunger, craving *(for meat). Cf.* kiu.

k.w.k. *abbr. of* kadha wa kadha and so forth, etc.

L

[1]la 1. eat. 2. eat up, devour, consume; use up. *fig.*, *dial.* itakula siku nyingi. It will last for many days. 3. eradicate, destroy. *fig.* – fedha. spend money. *appl.* lia. lia viapo. to take oaths. (*lit.* to 'eat' oaths, since various tribes contract oaths by eating sacrificial foods such as the flesh of sheep, cow's blood, etc.). mwiko wa kulia. spoon. *intr.* lika. be edible; be eaten (up), be consumed. tunda hili haliliki. This fruit is not edible. *caus.* lisha. 1. cause to eat, feed, pasture. lisha ng'ombe. put cattle out to pasture. 2. *fig.* bribe, corrupt. *pass.* liwa. *ass.* lana. *rare.* eat together/in company. *usually appl.-ass.* liana. *refl.-appl.* jilia. be selfish; (wilfully) waste, squander. *double caus.* lishisha, lishiza. nourish, support, care for. *Cf.* chakula, kilaji, malaji, malisho, mlisha, mlisho, mla, mlaji, mlo, ulaji, ulio.

[2]la* no, not so. (= siyo, sivyo, hakuna, hapana, hasha.)

[3]la *conn.* ji- *cl.:* tunda – mti. fruit of the tree.

laabu* amuse, entertain (oneself).

laana*, lana (ma-) curse, imprecation; *(rel.)* damnation. ana – la wazee wake. He has been disowned by his parents. *Cf.* laani, laanifu, maleuni, mlaanifu, ulaanifu.

laani*, lani curse, damn, execrate, swear at. *intr.* laanika. *caus.* laanisha. *pass.* laaniwa. *Cf.* laana.

laanifu* *rare, adj.* accursed, damned. *Cf.* laana.

labda*, labuda *adv.* perhaps, possibly, probably.

labe* *see* labeka.

labeka*, lebeka, labe, bee, abe, ebee! *interj.* At your service! Yes, sir (ma'am)! *(formerly used by slaves).*

labuda* *see* labda.

ladha*, laza, ludha (–) 1. odor, aroma, fragrance *(used for either pleasant or unpleasant odors, but rarely for unpleasant;* = onja, harufu). – ya kahawa. the aroma of coffee. 2. taste.

ladu* [*Ind.*] (–) a confection made of peanuts and sugar or meal and syrup.

lafidhi* (–) *see* lafudhi.

lafua 1. be greedy/voracious. 2. be very hungry. *intr.* lafuka *(in an int. sense).* be insatiable. *Cf.* lapa, mlafi, ulafi.

lafudhi*, lafuzi, lafidhi (–) 1. pronunciation, accent. 2. style, manner of speaking. 3. excuse, evasion.

lafuzi* (–) *see* lafudhi.

laghai*, raghai, ragai 1. deceive, cheat; confuse. 2. (ma-; *also* mlaghai, wa-) cheat, swindler. 3. *adj.* false, fraudulent. *Cf.* uragai.

laha* (–) *rare* piece/sheet of paper. (= **ukurasa.**)

laika, ulaika (ma-) 1. body hair *(on the hands, arms; cf.* **vuzi***).* 2. down *(of birds).*

laiki* 1. be suitable/appropriate/proper. 2. (–) suitability, appropriateness, what is fitting/proper. 3. *adj.* suitable, appropriate, proper *(usually in reference to actions/behavior).* **matendo yake yanamlaiki.** His actions are just what you would expect of him.

laini*, leini, lainifu *adj.* 1. delicate, soft, fine, smooth, thin, pliable. 2. *fig.* gentle, good-natured. *Cf.* **lainika, ulaini.**

lainifu* *see* **laini.**

lainika* be soft/delicate/smooth. *fig.:* 1. be soothing/reassuring. 2. be spoiled/pampered. 3. be gentle/good-natured. *caus.* **lainisha.** soften, smooth; *(fig.)* ease, alleviate. *pass.* **lainiwa.** *Cf.* **laini.**

lainisha* *caus. of* **lainika.**

lainzimani* [*Engl.*] (ma-) *sport* linesman.

laisensi* (–) *see* **leseni.**

laiti* *interj.* would that..., if only... **– angalikuja.** If he would only come!

laka* [*Germ.* Lack ?] (–) sealing wax. **tia –.** seal. *Cf.* **lakiri.**

lake *poss. pron. 3rd pers. sing.* **ji-** *cl. see* **-ake.**

¹laki*, lakki [*Ind.*] (–) 1. hundred thousand. 2. great number.

²laki* (go to) meet, greet, welcome.

lakini*, walakini, ilakini *conj.* but, however, nevertheless.

lakiri*, lakri [*Port.*] (–) sealing wax.

lakki* (–) *see* **laki.**

lako *poss. pron. 2nd pers. sing.* **ji-** *cl. see* **-ako.**

lakri* (–) *see* **lakiri.**

lala 1. lie, lie stretched out, be horizontal; lie down. **– macho.** lie awake. **mstari uliolala.** horizontal line. 2. sleep, go to sleep. **– usingizi.** sleep soundly. 3 fall down, collapse. 4. *tr.* sleep with, have sexual intercourse with *(a woman). appl.* **lalia.** sleep on *(in, etc.). intr.* **lalika. kitanda hiki hakilaliki.** This is not a good bed to sleep in. *caus.* **lalisha, laza.** put to bed, put to sleep; *(fig., sport)* defeat, beat. **timu hii imewalaza kwa mabao matano.** The team has beaten them by five goals. *ass.* **lalana.** sleep with each other, have sexual intercourse. *refl.-caus.* **jilaza.** rest, take a rest. **amejilaza apumzike.** He is lying down to take a rest. *Cf.* **kilalio, kilalo, malale, malalo, mlalaji, mlalavi, mlazi, ¹ulalo, ²ulalo.**

lalaika *rare* complain, groan *(from hunger, pain). Cf.* **lalama.**

lalama (*and intr,* **lalamika**) 1. groan, complain, lament, wail, cry out. 2. beg for mercy/

forgiveness. *appl.* **lalamia.** *caus.* **lalamisha.** *pass.* **lalamiwa.** *Cf.* **lalamiko, mlalamishi, ulalamishi;** *also* **lalaika.**

lalamika *see* **lalama.**

lalamiko (ma-) (*usually* **malalamiko**) appeal, entreaty, supplication; request, petition. *Cf.* **lalama.**

lamba, ramba lick. *appl.* **lambia.** *intr.* **lambika.** *caus.* **lambisha.** give someone a taste of something, arouse someone's desire for something. *appl.-cont.-appl.* **lambitia.** make someone's mouth water, arouse strong desire. *Cf.* **mlamba, lambilambi, ulambilambi.**

lambilambi *adj.* soft *(of something that can be licked off). Cf.* **lamba.**

lambitia *appl.-cont.-appl. of* **lamba.**

lambo (ma-) weir, dam, dike.

lami*, lammi (–) 1. glue. 2. pitch, tar. **barabara ya –.** asphalt street. **paka –.** tar something.

lammi* (–) *see* **lami.**

lana* (ma-) *see* **laana.**

[1]**landa, randa** *rare* be like/similar, resemble. **– baba yake.** He looks like his father. *ass.* **landana.** resemble each other, look alike. (= **fanana, lingana, –a sawasawa.**)

[2]**landa* (–)** *see* [2]**randa.**

lango (ma-) (*augment. of* **mlango**) 1. large door, gate, portal. 2.: **malango.** initiation *(of boys and girls at puberty; cf.* **kunga, jando, unyago, mizingu**).

langu *poss. pron. 1st pers. sing.* **ji-** *cl. see* **-angu.**

lani* *see* **laani.**

lao *poss. pron. 3rd pers. pl.* **ji-** *cl. see* **-ao.**

lapa eat greedily/hastily, be famished. *Cf.* **lafua, mlafi, ulafi.**

lapulapu (–) sandals.

lasi* [*Pers.*] **(–)** lasi (kind of silk cloth: pongee, shantung).

latamia 1. *see* **atamia.** 2. *fig.* rear, bring up *(a child).*

latifu* (–) goodness, kindness, gentleness.

latitudo* [*Engl.*] *geogr.* **(–)** latitude.

lauka *intr. of* **lawa.**

laula* *rare:* **kama –.** if not, unless. **Siwezi kumaliza kazi hii – kama nitapata msaada.** I cannot finish this work unless I get help. (= **isipokuwa, ila.**)

laumu* 1. criticize, reproach, blame, accuse. (= **karipia, kemea, suta, shtaki, hatia, nenea.**) *appl.* **laumia.** *intr.* **laumika.** *caus.* **laumisha.** *(also w. int. force:)* scold someone. *pass.* **laumiwa.** *refl.* **jilaumu.** reproach oneself, blame oneself. 2. **(ma-)** *see* **lawama.**

[1]**launi*** (–) *rare.* 1. resemblance, similarity. 2. form, shape. 3. expression *(of the face).*

[2]**launi*** [*Engl.* (make the) rounds] *rare* walk/stroll around.

launilauni* *adv.* different, various. *Cf.* [1]**launi.**

lavani* [*Engl., w. transposition of syllables ?*] (–) vanilla.

lavya *caus. of* **lawa.**

lawa *rare* go out. *refl.* **jilawa** *and intr.* **lauka.** get up/leave one's house early in the morning. *intr.-appl.* **laukia.** get up early for someone (*or* to surprise someone). *caus.* **lavya.** *fig.* disclose, reveal.

lawalawa, lovulovu (–) (kind of) candy, dessert.

lawama* (ma-) 1. criticism, fault-finding, reproach, reprimand, accusation. 2. risk of criticism, responsibility. **hatutajitia – kuandika mambo hayo.** We are not running the risk/taking the responsibility of writing on those matters. *Cf.* **laumu.**

lawiti* practice sodomy/pederasty. (= [2]**fira.**)

[1]**laza** *caus. of* **lala.**

[2]**laza*** (–) *see* **ladha.**

lazima* 1. (–) necessity, obligation, responsibility. **chukua –.** assume a responsibility, be responsible for, vouch/go bail for. 2. *adv.* irrevocably, necessarily. *Cf.* **lazimu.**

lazimu* must, have to, be obligated; be necessary. **maneno yamemlazimu.** The words have obligated him. *appl.* **lazimia.** *intr.* **lazimika.** *pass.* **lazimiwa.** *caus.* **lazimisha** *(also w. int. force).* force, compel, obligate; punish. *refl.-caus.* **jilazimisha na...** take an interest in/devote oneself to something, take full responsibility for something. *Cf.* **lazima.**

[1]**le** *dem. pron.* that, those. **watu wale.** those people.

[2]**le** (< **lake**) *poss. pron.* his/her. **jinale.** his name.

lea rear, bring up, educate; care for, tend. *prov.* **mwana umleavyo ndivyo akuavyo.** As one rears a child, so it grows (As the twig is bent, so the tree inclines). *appl.* **lelea.** *pass.* **lelewa. amelelewa na shangazi yake.** He was brought up in his aunt's house. *Cf.* **malezi,** [1]**mlezi,** [2]**ulezi.**

[1]**leba*** (–) *rare* lie, falsehood, deception. *Cf.* **lebu.**

[2]**leba*** [*Engl.*] (–) *rare* labor. **waziri wa –.** minister of labor.

lebasi*, libasi (–) clothes, clothing. (= **mavazi,** [1]**nguo.**)

lebeka* *see* **labeka.**

lebu* *rare* lie, deceive, cheat. *Cf.* [1]**leba.**

lefti* [*Engl.*] *sing./adj., sport* left (= **kushoto**). **insaidi wa –.** inside left *(football).*

lega, rega, legalega, regarega 1. waver, be unsteady, oscillate, swing, totter. 2. be loose. 3. be indefinite, uncertain. **siku ya safari yangu inalega (legalega).** The day of my departure is indefinite. 4. be slack/limp; *(fig.)* be negligent/careless/idle. *appl.* **legea.** *caus.* **legeza.** loosen, slacken, relax, ease tension; cause to waver/fluctuate. *Cf.* **legevu, mlegevu, ulegevu.**

legalega *see* **lega.**

legeni* (–) legeni (large metal cooking pot).

legevu *adj.* loose, slack, limp, relaxed; *(fig.)* idle, easy-going. *Cf.* **lega, mlegevu, ulegevu.**

legeza *caus. of* **lega.**

Legiko* *see* **Lejiko.**

lehamu* *see* **lehemu.**

lehemu*, lehamu, lahamu, lihamu 1. solder. *appl.* **lehemia. nyundo ya kulehemia.** soldering iron. *intr.* **lehemika.** *caus.* **lehemisha.** *pass.* **lehemiwa.** 2. (–) solder, soldered joint, soldering. **tia –.** to solder.

leini* *see* **laini.**

Lejiko*, Legiko [*Engl.*] Legico *(abbr. of Legislative Council).*

lekea *see* **elekea.**

lekevu *adj.* *see* **elekevu.**

lela*, leli (–) *rare* night. (= **usiku.**)

lele* (ma-) *augment. of* **kilele.**

leli* (–) *see* **lela.**

[1]**lema** (–) *dial.* fish trap *(of basketwork).*

[2]**lema** exorcise a spirit.

lemaa 1. be disfigured/deformed/maimed/mutilated/crippled. 2. be diseased/paralytic; be addicted. **mwenye kulemaa maungo.** a paralytic. **amelemaa kwa kuvuta.** He is addicted to tobacco. *caus.* **lemaza.** disfigure /maim/cripple. 3. (–) defect, blemish, deformity, mutilation. *Cf.* **kilema.**

[1]**lemba** *see* **remba.**

[2]**lemba** (ma-) *see* [1]**kilemba.**

lembea hand/pass something down to someone *(fruit from a tree, etc.).*

lemea, elemea 1. press/weigh down, oppress, crush, overwhelm. **mzigo huu unamlemea.** This load weighs him down. 2. push forward, impel. 3. be burdensome/troublesome/annoying. *pass.* **lemewa.** *ass.* **lemeana.** *caus.* **lemeza.** pile on, load up.

[1]**lenga, linga** aim, take aim. **– shabaha.** take aim at a target. *appl.* **lengea.**

[2]**lenga** cut up into pieces/slices/strips; clip, crop, dock. *appl.* **lengea.** *ass.* **lengana.**

lengalenga be on the point of crying, be tearful/lachrymose.

lengelenge (**ma-**) *med.* blister *(from a burn)*; scar, weal, welt; pockmark.

lengo (**ma-**) aim, target; *(fig.)* goal, objective. *Cf.* [1]**lenga.**

lensi* (–) *see* **lenzi.**

lenu *poss. pron. 2nd pers. pl.* **ji-** *cl.* *see* **–enu.**

lenye *see* **–enye.**

lenyewe *see* **–enyewe.**

lenzi*, **lensi** [*Engl.*] (–) *opt.* lens.

leo 1. (–) the present day/time. *prov.* **juzi na jana si kama –.** Day before yesterday and yesterday are not like today. *coll.* **– ni –.** today is today. 2. *adv.* today. **si –.** a long time ago. **ukoloni mambo –.** neo-colonialism.

lepe (**ma-**) *rare* sleepiness, drowsiness. (*usually* **– la usingizi**; = **usingizi, uzito, sinzia.**)

lesani*, **lisani** (–) *rare* tongue, voice, language. (= **ulimi, usemi, lugha.**)

leseni*, **laisensi**, **lesensi** [*Engl.*] (–) 1. license, permit, **– ya udereva** *or* **– ya kuendeshea motokaa.** driver's license. **– ya bunduki.** gun-license. **omba –.** apply for a license. 2. *rare* patent.

lesensi* (–) *see* **leseni.**

leso* [*Port.*] (–, **ma-**) 1. leso (woman's kerchief or shawl). 2. *rare* handkerchief. 3. scarf, sash.

leta 1. bring, go and get, fetch. **– kiti.** pull up a chair. 2. *fig.* produce, bring about, result in. **vita inaleta uharibifu.** War produces destruction. **– baina.** prove. *ass.* *(rare)* **letana.** *appl.* **letea.** *appl.-pass.* **leteana. leteana barua.** correspond (with each other). *Cf.* **mletaji, uletaji.**

letu *poss. pron. 1st pers. pl.* **ji-** *cl.* *see* **–etu.**

levi *adj.* drunk(en), intoxicated. *Cf.* **lewa.**

levuka (*inv.-intr. of* **lewa**) sober up, become sober.

levya *caus. of* **lewa.**

levyesha *double caus. of* **lewa.**

lewa 1. be/become drunk. 2. (*also red.* **lewalewa**) stagger, reel. *appl.* **lewea.** *caus.* **levya, lewesha.** make someone drunk. *refl.-caus.* **jilevya** get drunk. *double caus.* **levyesha.** *fig.* confuse, turn someone's head. **pesa nyingi zimemlevyesha.** All that money has turned his head. *Cf.* **kileo, mleo, levi, mlevi, ulevi, uleoleo.**

lewalewa *red. of* **lewa.**

lewesha *caus. of* **lewa.**

li *aux. v., arch.* be. **wewe uliye mwalimu.** You who are a teacher.

[1]**lia** make a sound/noise *(in gen., animate or inanimate;* = **toa/paaza sauti, vuma, nguruma, imba,** *etc.):* 1. weep, cry. **mtoto analia.** The child is crying. 2. sing, twitter. **ndege analia.** The bird is singing. 3. make a loud noise, go bang. **bunduki imelia.** The gun is fired. *appl.* **lilia.** weep/mourn for someone. *refl.-appl.* **jililia.** be sorry for oneself. *caus.* **liza. liza bunduki.** fire a gun. *pass.* **liliwa.** *ass.* **liana.** *Cf.* **lio, kilio, malizano, malizi, mlia, mlio, mlizi, ulizi.**

[2]**lia** *appl. of* **la.**

libasi* (–) *see* **lebasi.**

licha (*or* – **ya**) **... hata...** *conj.* not only... but (what is more important)... – **ya Said hata Musa amekuja.** Not only Said but also Musa has come *(Musa being a more important personage).*

liga *rare* 1. (**ma-**) poison. 2. to poison. (= **sumu, sumisha.**)

ligi*, ligu [*Engl.*] (–) league, club, association.

ligu* (–) *see* **ligi.**

lihamu* (–) *see* **lehemu.**

lijamu*, luguamu (–) bit *(part of a bridle).*

lika *intr. of* **la.**

[1]**likiza** dispose of something quickly, finish, dispatch.

[2]**likiza** *rare* 1. give a holiday to someone, let go. 2. dismiss, send away. 3. *fig.* wean (a child). (= **acha, ondosha, ruhusu.**) *Cf.* **likizo.**

likizo (**ma-**) holiday, vacation. *Cf.* [2]**likiza.**

likwama (**ma-**) handcart, wheelbarrow.

lilamu*, lilam [*Ind.?*] (–) public sale, auction.

lile *dem. pron.* **ji-** *cl.* *see* **le.**

[1]**lima** 1. hoe, cultivate land. 2. plow. *appl.* **limia. jembe la kulimia.** a hoe. *intr.* **limika.** be arable. *caus.* **limisha.** *Cf.* **limaji, kilimia, kilimo, malimo, makulima, mkulima, mlimaji, mlimo, ukulima, ulimaji.**

[2]**lima*** (–) wedding feast.

limaji *adj.* engaged in agriculture, agricultural. *Cf.* [1]**lima.**

limao* [*Pers.*] (**ma-**) *see* **limau.**

limatia, lumatia *dial.* hesitate, delay, stay behind; be late. *caus.* **limatisha.** *pass.* **limatiwa.**

limau*, limao [*Pers.*] (**ma-**) lemon. *Cf.* **mlimau.**

limbika 1. wait for something to grow/ripen. – **nywele (kucha).** let the hair (fingernails) grow. – **ndizi.** let bananas ripen. 2. save, store up. 3. *fig.* be indulgent/patient. *Cf.* **mlimbiko.**

limbiko (ma-) *see* **mlimbiko.**

limbua, rimbua 1. eat the first fruits of a new harvest. 2. use for the first time. *caus.* **limbusha.** *intr.* **limbuka.** taste, try out; enjoy an anticipated pleasure. *Cf.* **limbuko.**

limbuka *intr. of* **limbua.**

limbuko (ma-; *us. pl.*), **mlimbuko** (mi-) 1. first fruits/benefits. 2. anticipated enjoyment/pleasure. *Cf.* **limbua.**

limi *adj.* talkative, loquacious. *Cf.* **kilimi, mlimi, ulimi.**

limuka* 1. be sly/cunning. 2. be underhanded/treacherous. *caus.* **limusha.** (= **danganya, hila, hadaa.**) *Cf.* **elimu, limuko.**

limuko* (ma-) cunning, craftiness, deceit. *Cf.* **limuka.**

linda watch over, guard, protect. **– shamba (nyumba).** guard a field (house). *mil.* **– doria.** to patrol. *refl.* **jilinda.** 1. protect/defend oneself. 2. watch out, be on one's guard. *Cf.* **[1]lindo, kilinda, kilindo, mlinda, mlinzi, ulinzi.**

lindi, dindi (ma-) pit, hole; cesspool, drain. **– la kupanda mbegu.** hole for planting seed. **kitovu cha –.** navel. **– la choo.** cesspool. *Cf.* **kilindi.**

[1]lindo (ma-) lookout, guard-post. *Cf.* **linda.**

[2]lindo (ma-) lindo (a cylindrical box made of bark).

[1]linga *rare* make equal/harmonious, adapt, accommodate. *usually ass.* **lingana.** fit, suit, match; be similar; harmonize, agree. **kulingana na ...** according to ... *appl.* **lingania.** *caus.* **linganisha, linganya.** compare; effect agreement/harmony; *(mus.)* tune *(instruments)*; check, collate. *Cf.* **linganifu, linganisho, [2]kilingo, mlingano, ulinganifu, ulinganisho, ulingano.**

[2]linga *see* **[1]lenga.**

linganifu, linganyifu *adj.* fitting, suitable, homogeneous, agreeing, harmonious, symmetrical. *Cf.* **[1]linga.**

linganisho (ma-) comparison. *Cf.* **[1]linga.**

linganyifu *see* **linganifu.**

lingo *pl. of* **ulingo.**

lingwa be tangled up/caught in something; *(fig.)* become confused, be perplexed/disconcerted.

lini *interrog.* when? at what time?

lio (ma-) *augment. of* **mlio.**

lipa 1. pay, pay for. *fig.* **nitakulipa.** I will pay you back (= get even with you). 2. make up for, compensate, indemnify. *caus.* **lipisha, lipiza.** *refl.-caus.* **jilipiza. jilipiza kisasi.** take revenge. *Cf.* **lipizi, lipo, kisicholipwa, majilipo, mlipa, mlipizi, ulipizi.**

lipizi (ma-; *us. pl.*) 1. demand for payment of a debt. 2. extortion, blackmail. 3. retaliation, revenge. 4. *rel.* atonement, penance. *Cf.* **lipa.**

lipo (ma-; *us. pl.*) 1. payment. 2. compensation, reparation. *Cf.* **lipa.**

lipu* [*Ind.*] (–) plaster, stucco.

lipuka, ripuka flare up, burst into flames; explode; *(fig.)* fly into a rage. *caus.* **lipusha.** explode (something). *pass.* **lipuliwa.** *Cf.* **mlipuaji, mlipuko.**

[1]**lisani*** (–) lisani (flap under the opening of a kanzu).

[2]**lisani*** (–) *see* **lesani.**

lisha *caus. of* [1]**la.**

lishiza *double caus. of* [1]**la.**

livu* [*Engl.*] (–) leave, leave of absence; break for rest.

liwa*, luva (–) liwa (variety of sandalwood). *Cf.* **mliwa, msagaliwa.**

liwaa *rare* forget.

liwado (–, ma-) *see* **liwato.**

liwali*, luwali, wali (ma-) liwali (administrative official, headman; generally an Arab appointed by the government to handle relations with the Moslem community).

liwata step/tread on. *Cf.* [1]**kwata, liwato.**

liwato, liwado (–, ma-) 1. flattened grass. 2. spoor, trail *(of an animal).* 3. butt end of something *(i.e., the part put on the ground). Cf.* [1]**kwata, liwata.**

liwaza comfort, calm, reassure; condole, express sympathy. *Cf.* **liwazo, maliwazo.**

liwazo (ma-) *rare* anything that soothes: comfort, sympathy, condolence. *Cf.* **liwaza.**

liza (–) *see* **riza.**

[1]**lo** *det.* **ji-** *cl.:* – **lote.** *indef. relat.* whatever, no matter what. *w. neg.* (nothing) at all. **hakufanya (neno) – lote.** He did nothing at all.

[2]**lo** *see* **loo.**

loa *see* **lowa.**

lodi (–) *see* **rodi.**

loga, roga *arch.* enchant, place under a spell. *inv.* **logoa.** free from a spell. *Cf.* [2]**mlozi, ulozi.**

loja *see* **roja.**

lokalaizesheni* [*Engl.*] *sing.* localization.

lokeshen* [*Engl.*] (ma-) location, native settlement area.

loma (–) ant-bear.

londea, rondea 1. hunt/look for something, want. 2. sponge, live at someone else's expense. *caus.* **londesha.** *pass.* **londewa.**

longitudo [*Engl.*] (–) *geogr.* longitude.

lonjo, ronjo *adj., rare* big, tall *(of persons).* *Cf.* **mlonjo.**

lonyo 1. (–) show, presentation, demonstration; ostentation, showing off, bragging. 2. *adj.* fine, grand, splendid; pretty, smart, chic *(of clothes).* *Cf.* **ona.**

loo, lo *interj. of joy or amazement* oh! well!

lopoka *see* **ropoka.**

lori* [*Engl.*] (ma-) 1. lorry, truck. 2. *railw.* (open) freight car.

lote *see* **ote.**

lovulovu (–) *see* **lawalawa.**

lowa, loa be wet/moist/damp; get wet, be soaked/saturated. *intr.* **loweka.** 1. = **lowa.** 2. make wet, douse, soak, immerse. 3. be confused/at a loss/perplexed, nonplussed. *stat.* **lowama.** be in a condition of dampness, be wet/soaked. *Cf.* **lowefu.**

lowama *stat. of* **lowa.**

lowefu *adj., rare* wet, damp. *Cf.* **lowa.**

lowela settle, establish oneself, remain *(in a certain place).* *Cf.* **mlowezi.**

lozi* (ma-) almond. *Cf.* [1]**mlozi.**

luanga (–) luanga (kind of bird).

ludha* (–) *see* **ladha.**

lugha* (–) language, dialect. **maarifa ya –.** linguistics.

luguamu* (–) *see* **lijamu.**

[1]**luja*** (–) *rare* thief, robber. (= **mwizi, mkwepuzi.**)

[2]**luja*** *sing., rare* deep thought. (= **mawazo, fikira.**) **yumo katika –.** He is deep in thought.

lukuki* [*Ind.*] (–) countless number, myriad.

lukuma* (–) 1. bite, morsel. 2. *fig.* inducement, quid pro quo. **– yako, basi nifanyizie hivi.** Here is something for you, so you do such-and-such for me.

lulu* (–) pearl. **ubamba wa –.** mother-of-pearl (= **lulumizi**).

lulumizi* (–) mother-of-pearl.

lumatia *see* **limatia.**

lumba 1. *rare* question. 2. talk, speak; report; give a (serious, formal) talk/speech. (= **simulia, hadithia, hoji.**) *Cf.* **malumbano, mlumbaji.**

lumbui (–) *see* **lumbwi.**

lumbwi, lumbui (–) chameleon. (= [2]**kinyonga, kigeugeu.**)

lundika, rundika 1. be piled up, be stored. 2. gather, assemble, store up, accumulate. *Cf.* **lundo.**

lundo (ma-) pile, heap, stack. *Cf.* **lundika.**

lungo *arch.* = [2]**ungo.**

lungu *see* **rungu.**

lungula, rungula 1. take by force, rob. 2. threaten, extort. *Cf.* **mlungula.**

Lusiferi* [*Engl.*] *rel.* Lucifer. *Cf.* **Shetani, Ibilisi.**

lusu* (–) *rare* thief, robber. (= [1]**luja.**)

luva* (–) *see* **liwa.**

luwali* (ma-) *see* **liwali.**

luzu* [*?*] *coll.* broke, on the rocks.

M

maabadi* *sing., rel.* place of worship. *Cf.* **abudu.**

maabudu* *sing., rel.* 1. reverence, worship, religious observance/service. 2. object of worship. *Cf.* **abudu.**

maadam* 1. *conj.* when, while, since, as long as. 2. *conj.* since, because. – **umekuja, nitakuambia.** Since you have come, I will tell you. 3.: – **ya...** *prep.* according to, in consequence of.

maadili* *pl.* *see* **adili.**

maadini* (–) *see* **madini.**

maafa* *pl.* *see* **afa.**

maafikiano*, maafikano *pl.* mutual understanding; agreement, settlement, contract, treaty. *Cf.* **afiki.**

maagano *pl.* *see* **agano.**

maagizo *pl.* *see* **agizo.**

maaguzi *pl.* *see* **aguzi.**

maakuli*, makuli *pl., arch.* food, victuals, provisions, provender (= **chakula.**)

maalum*, maalumu 1. *adj.* well-known, famous, acknowledged, esteemed, distinguished. 2. *adj.* special, particular, characteristic. **mwandishi –.** specialist, expert. 3. *adv.* definitely, certainly; regularly, permanently. **leo atakuja Said? –.** Is Said coming today? Definitely.

hana – ya kuja hapa. He does not come here regularly. *Cf.* **elimu.**

maalumu* *see* **maalum.**

maambukizo *pl.* *see* **ambukizo.**

maamkiano *pl.* *see* **maamkio.**

maamkio, maamkiano, maamkizi *pl.* greeting, salutation, bow. *Cf.* **amka, amkia.**

maamkizi *pl.* *see* **maamkio.**

maamuma*, mahamuma (–) stupid person, simpleton, fool. (= **mjinga, baradhuli.**)

maamuzi *pl.* decision, judgment, verdict. *Cf.* [1]**amua.**

maana* (–) 1. meaning, significance. **maneno ya –.** meaningful words. 2. reason, cause, purpose, intention, objective. 3. (*also* **– ya**) *conj.* since, because, in order that. **– yake.** namely, that is to say.

maandalio *pl.* preparation *(of food, etc.).* **– ya mkutano.** preparations for a meeting. *Cf.* **andaa.**

maandamano *pl.* *see* **andamano.**

maandamizi *pl.* *see* **andamizi.**

maandazi *pl.* *see* **andazi.**

maandikio *pl.* *see* **maandiko.**

maandiko *pl.* 1. writing, document; *(pol.)* (written) statement, communiqué. **– Matakatifu.** 2. *rel.* Holy Scriptures. 3. (*also* **maandikio**) preparation, serving *(of food). Cf.* **andika, andiko.**

maandishi *pl.* 1. literature. 2. content, significance, idea *(of a literary work).* 3. theory *(in gen.).* 4. *rare* (style of) handwriting. 5. = **maandiko** 2. 6.: **–a –.** *adj.* theoretical. *Cf.* **andika, mwandishi.**

maangalio *pl.* 1. observation, inspection. 2. examination, investigation. *Cf.* **angaa.**

maangalizi *pl.* 1. attention, attentiveness. 2. observation, supervision, care. 3. *rare* visit. *Cf.* **angaa.**

maangamizi *pl.* destruction, ruin, decay, decline, downfall. *Cf.* **angamia.**

maangamizo *pl.* accident, casualty. *Cf.* **angamia.**

maanguko *pl.* *see* **anguko.**

maanzilisho *pl.* organization, foundation, establishment, introduction. *Cf.* **anza.**

maao *pl.* *see* **maawio.**

maapizo *pl.* *see* **apizo.**

maarasi* (–) *rare* carrying-pole (a pole carried on the shoulder with water in tins hanging from either end). (= **mzegazega, mpika.**)

maarifa* *pl.* 1. knowledge, information, science. – **ya lugha.** linguistics. 2. understanding, insight, discernment, erudition. *Cf.* **arifu.**

maarubu* *pl., rare* (concealed) purpose, (ulterior) motive *(but not necessarily bad).*

maarufu* *adj.* 1. well-known, famous, esteemed, distinguished. 2. *coll.* enthusiastic, inveterate, untiring. **msikilizaji – wa redio.** an inveterate listener to the radio, a great radio fan. *Cf.* **arifu.**

maarusi* *pl.* bride and bridegroom. *coll.* **msiende kama –.** Hurry up! (*lit.:* Don't walk like a bride and bridegroom).

maasi* *pl.* 1. disobedience, insubordination, recalcitrance. 2. revolt, rebellion, insurrection. 3. *mil.* desertion. *Cf.* **asi.**

maasum* (wa-) *see* **mwasi.**

maawio, maweo, maao *pl.* 1. (*also* – **ya jua**) sunrise. 2. east. *Cf.* **²waa.**

maazimio* *pl.* 1. intention, purpose, aim, decision. 2. plan, project, program. *Cf.* **azimu.**

maazimo *pl.* loan, debt. *Cf.* **azima.**

mabadili*, mabadiliko *pl.* *see* **badiliko.**

mabaki *pl.* *see* **baki.**

mabao *pl.* *sport* score. *Cf.* **bao.**

mabaya *pl.* 1. badness, wickedness; spitefulness, malice. 2. bitterness, embitterment. *Cf.* **baya.**

mabembelezo, mapembelezo *pl.* caressing, coaxing, flattery, cajolery. *Cf.* **bemba.**

mabishano *pl.* 1. quarrel, dispute, altercation. 2. contradiction, rejoinder. *Cf.* **bisha.**

mabotea *pl.* plants which come up by chance/ unexpectedly (without seeds having been planted).

Mabruki* *pr. n. masc.*

maburudisho*, maburudu *pl.* 1. distraction, diversion. 2. refreshment, recreation. 3. relief, alleviation, comfort; *(fig.)* repairs. *Cf.* **burudi.**

maburudu* *pl.* *see* **maburudisho.**

maburuzo, maburuzu *pl.* 1. draft, current *(of air).* 2. track, rut *(left by something dragged over the ground).* *Cf.* **burura.**

machachari, macharichari *pl.* 1. restlessness, sleeplessness. 2. awkwardness, clumsiness, ineptitude. 3. harmfulness, destructiveness. *Cf.* **chachari.**

machafuko *pl.* 1. disorder, confusion. 2. violation, infraction *(of a rule or law).* *Cf.* **chafua.**

machaguzi *pl.* *see* **uchaguzi.**

machangamano *pl.* *see* **changamano.**

machanganyiko *pl.* mixture. *Cf.* **[1]changa.**

machanganyo *pl.* mixture, mixing up. *Cf.* **[1]changa.**

macharichari *pl.* *see* **machachari.**

machaza *pl.* leftover rice *(from the evening meal).*

macheko *pl.* *see* **kicheko.**

machela* [*Port.*] (–) 1. litter, stretcher. 2. hammock.

macheleo *pl.* 1. fear, anxiety. 2. trembling, quivering. *Cf.* **[2]cha.**

macheo *pl.* 1. sunrise, dawn. 2. east. *Cf.* **[3]cha.**

[1]Machi*, Marchi [*Engl.*] (month of) March.

[2]machi* [*Engl.*] (–) march, march-music. **enda –.** to march. **piga –.** play march-music.

machinjioni *pl.* *see* **machinjoni.**

machinjo *pl.* **chinjo.**

machinjoni, machinjioni *pl.* (*rare* **chinjoni**) 1. (cutting) edge (*of a knife; cf.* **mafutuni).** 2. slaughtering place, slaughterhouse. *Cf.* **chinja.**

machipukizi *pl.* *see* **chipukizi.**

macho *pl.* *see* **jicho.**

machozi *pl.* *see* **chozi.**

machugachuga *pl.* unrest, excitement, restlessness. *Cf.* **chugachuga.**

machukio, machukizo *pl.* *see* **chukio.**

machumbwichumbwi, machubwichubwi, matubwitubwi *pl.* *med.* mumps.

machunga, machungani *pl.* pastureland, pasturage. *Cf.* **[2]chunga.**

machungu *pl.* *see* **uchungu.**

machwa, machweo *pl.* 1. sunset, dusk. 2. west. *Cf.* **chwa.**

machweo *pl.* *see* **machwa.**

madadi*, madati (–) opium ball *(prepared for smoking).*

madaha* *pl.* self-importance, complacency; boasting, bragging; presumption, arrogance. **ana –.** He is conceited. **fanya/piga –.** show off.

madahili* *see* **[2]dahili.**

madahiro* (–) *rare* 1. politeness, grace, charm. 2. elegance, distinguished manner.

madai* *pl.* *see* **dai.**

madakata *pl.* dry leaves *(fallen or ready to fall).*

madanganyo *pl.* *see* **danganyo.**

madaraja* *pl.* steps, (flight of) stairs, stairway. *Cf.* **daraja.**

madaraka *pl.* *see* **daraka.**

madarasa* *pl.* 1. *see* **darasa.** 2. *rare* school, academy.

madati* (–) *see* **madadi.**

madenda *pl.* saliva (which flows from the mouth during sleep).

madende *pl.* *rare* trill.

madevu *pl.* *see* **udevu, devu.**

madhabahu* (–) 1. place where sacrifices are performed, altar. 2. *rare* slaughterhouse. *Cf.* **dhabihu.**

madhabuha* (–) *rel.* sacrifice, victim. *Cf.* **dhabihu.**

madhali* *conj.* if, in case that; since, because; when, while, since. *Cf.* **mithili, methali.**

madhehebu* *pl.* 1. custom, usage; principle, tenet. **– ya awali.** basic principle. 2. *rel.* creed, denomination, sect. **upendaji wa –.** sectarianism.

madhilifu* *pl.* difficulty, confusion; misfortune. *Cf.* **dhili.**

madhubuti* *adj.* firm, strict; reliable; accurate, precise; *(fig.)* honest, upright. *Cf.* **dhibiti.**

madhumuni* (–) intention, purpose, aim.

madini*, maadini (–) 1. mineral, metal, ore. **– ya chini.** low alloy. 2. metallurgy.

madoadoa 1. *pl.* spot, blot. 2. *adj.* spotted, dappled; varicolored. *Cf.* **doa.**

madoido *pl.* decoration, ornament, embellishment. **– ya muziki.** trill.

madole *pl.:* **– matano** *bot.* (variety of) fern *(Polypodium phymtodes).*

maduhuli* (–) pay, wages; income, revenue.

maduyuni* *pl.* *see* **mdeni.**

maelekeo *pl.* 1. effort, endeavor. 2. tendency, inclination; talent, gift. **– ya maono.** feeling, ideal. *Cf.* **elea, elekea.**

maelezi *pl.* *rare, naut.* anchorage. *Cf.* **elea.**

maelezo *pl.* explanation, description. *Cf.* **elea.**

maendeleo *pl.* *see* **endeleo.**

maendelezo *pl.* *see* **endeleo.**

maeneo *pl.* *see* **eneo.**

maenezo *pl.* tendency, trend. *Cf.* **enea.**

mafa, mava *pl.* burial place, graveyard, cemetery. *Cf.* **fa.**

mafaa, mafao *pl.* benefit, profit, privilege, advantage. *Cf.* **faa.**

mafafanusi *pl.* *see* **ufafanusi.**

mafamba *pl.* secret/underhanded dealings.

mafanikio* *pl.* prosperity, success. *Cf.* **fanaka, fanikia.**

mafao *pl.* *see* **mafaa.**

maficho *pl.* 1. hiding place, ambush. 2. disguise. *Cf.* **ficha.**

mafieko *pl.* *see* **mafyeko.**

mafinyo *pl.* *see* **finyo.**

mafu: **maji —.** neap tide. *coll.* **leo maji —.** Today was not a good day for fishing. *Cf.* **fa.**

mafua *pl.* *med.* bronchitis, congestion of the upper respiratory tract, pains in the chest. **ana —.** He has a bad cold. *Cf.* **kifua.**

mafuatano *pl.* 1. following, escort; accompaniment. 2. succession, series. **— ya sauti.** *mus.* melody. *Cf.* **fuata.**

mafukizo, mavukizo *pl.* *see* **mfukuto.**

mafunde *pl.* *see* **mavunde.**

mafundisho *pl.* 1. teaching, instruction, doctrine. 2. instructions, directions *(for taking medicine, using a device, etc.).* *Cf.* [2]**funda.**

mafungia *pl.* closing, locking, fastening. *Cf.* [1]**funga.**

mafungulia *pl.* (*also* **— ng'ombe**) time when cattle are driven out to pasture (8-9 A.M.). *Cf.* [1]**funga.**

mafunjo *pl.* reeds, sedge, papyrus.

mafunuo *pl.* revelation. *Cf.* **funua.**

mafuriko *pl.* 1. rising (of water). 2. flood, inundation. (= **gharika.**) 3. *naut.* flood-tide. *Cf.* **fura.**

mafusho *pl.* mafusho (something burned in order to drive out an evil spirit). *Cf.* [1]**fuka.**

mafuta *pl.* 1. fat, oil, grease, salve, lubricant. **— Ulaya, — ya taa.** petroleum, kerosine. **— ya motakaa.** gasoline. **— ya uto.** sesame/semsem oil. **tia —.** fill up, refuel. 2. *fig.* ingratiating/oily manner.

mafutu *pl.* anger, rage, fury.

mafutuni *pl.* back of a knife blade *(as opposed to the edge).*

[1]**mafuu** *pl.* folly, stupidity.

[2]**mafuu** *pl. of* [1]**fuu.**

mafya *pl. of* **jifya.**

mafyeko, mafieko *pl.* 1. clearing land, preparing ground for cultivation. 2. weeding. *Cf.* **fyeka.**

[1]**magadi** *pl.* soda.

[2]**magadi*** *pl. of* [1]**gadi,** [2]**gadi.**

magamaga 1. walk with the legs wide apart, straddle, waddle. 2. walk fast. *Cf.* **ki-magamaga.**

magangao, magaogao *pl.* 1. devastation, destruction. 2. ruin, decay, downfall.

magaogao *pl.* *see* **magangao.**

magendo *pl.* selling of crops or other merchandise without keeping records of profits and losses.

magengo *pl.* contingency (something that will happen *if...*); tit for tat, *quid pro quo;* clandestine bargain, illegal transaction; threat, blackmail. **kwa –.** on the black market. **siasa ya – ya kiini.** policy of nuclear blackmail.

mageuko *pl.* *see* **mageuzi.**

mageuzi, mageuzo, mageuko *pl.* change, fluctuation. **mageuzi makuu.** revolution. *Cf.* **geua, mgeuzo.**

mageuzo *pl.* *see* **mageuzi.**

maghaibi* (–) *see* **magharibi.**

magharibi*, maghaibi, mangharibi, ghurubu (–) 1. time of sunset. 2. west. **– ya kusini.** southwest. **nimemtafuta mashariki na –.** I have hunted for him everywhere (*lit.:* in the east and in the west). 3. *Isl.* evening prayer.

maghofira* (–) *rel.* forgiveness, remission. *Cf.* **ghofira, ghofiri.**

magombano *pl.* quarrel, dispute. *Cf.* **²gomba.**

magombezi, magombezo *pl.* 1. contradiction, rejoinder, retort. 2. prohibition. 3. enmity, hostility, antagonism. *Cf.* **²gomba.**

magombezo *pl.* *see* **magombezi.**

magoti *pl.* *see* **goti.**

magubiko *pl.* *arch.* caravan tax *(to be paid when entering a city).* *Cf.* **gubika.**

magugu *pl.* weeds; bush, jungle.

mahaba*, mahuba (–) affection, devotion, inclination, attachment, sympathy. *prov.* **– hayana dawa.** There is no cure for love. *Cf.* **²haba.**

mahabusi*, mahabusu 1. (–) prisoner, condemned person. 2. (–) *rare* prison, jail. (= **korokoroni.**) 3. *adv.:* **amefungwa –.** He has been given a jail sentence.

mahabusu* (–) *see* **mahabusi.**

mahakma* (–) *rare* place of judgment, court, *Cf.* **hukumu, hakimu.**

mahala* (–) *see* **mahali.**

mahali*, mahala (–) place *(in gen.),* situation; area, district. **si ... – (po pote).** nowhere. **– hapa.** there. **kila –.** everywhere. **– pa.** instead of. **– pa kufanya kazi.** place of employment. **– pa kanuni pa kukaa na kulala.** permanent place of residence. **– pa kupigia kura.** electoral precinct. *Cf.* **pahali.**

mahame, mahamo *pl.* deserted place. (= **hame, kihame, [1]tongo.**) *Cf.* **hama, hamaji.**

mahameli* (–) *see* **bahameli.**

mahamia* *pl.* protectorate. *Cf.* **hami.**

mahamo *pl.* *see* **mahame.**

mahamuma* (–) *see* **maamuma.**

maharagwe *pl.* *see* **haragwe.**

maharazi* (–) awl, bradawl.

mahari* (–) bride-money, marriage settlement, dowry. **mke huyu nimeozwa bure, sikulipa –.** I married this woman without making a marriage settlement.

maharimisho* *pl.* ban, prohibition. **– ya silaha.** disarmament. *Cf.* **harimu.**

maharimu* *pl.* blood-relatives *(who are forbidden to marry). Cf.* **harimu.**

mahashumu*, mahushumu (–) respectable/honest person, person of good repute. *Cf.* **heshima, heshimu, muhashamu.**

mahati* (–) scriber, style; (carpenter's marking) gauge *(for scribing lines parallel to the edge of a board).*

mahazamu* *pl.* belt, girdle, sash.

mahindi* *pl.* (grains of) corn/maize. **unga wa –.** cornmeal. *Cf.* **[1]muhindi.**

mahiri* *adj.* 1. skilful, adroit, nimble, agile, dexterous; clever, quick-witted, capable. 2. *fig.* sly, crafty, deceitful. *Cf.* **umahiri.**

mahitaji* *pl.* *see* **hitaji.**

mahluki*, mahluku (–) *rare* human being. *Cf.* **hulka.**

mahoka, masoka *pl.* 1. spirit of an ancestor, evil spirit. **ibada ya – (*or* mizimu).** ancestor worship. 2. delusion, mania, madness. 3. joke, jest. **maneno yake yasikutishe, yeye ni mtu wa – sana.** Don't believe what he says, he is a wag/joker.

mahonyo *adv.* for nothing, gratis, free. **msile matunda yangu –.** Don't eat my fruit without paying.

mahsai* (–) *see* **maksai.**

mahsusi*, maksusi *adj./adv.* special, particular, precise. **mkutano –.** special/extraordinary session. *Cf.* **husu, hususa.**

mahushumu* (–) *see* **mahashumu.**

mahututi* *adj.* serious, difficult. **ugonjwa –.** a serious illness.

maige* [*Pers.*] (–) young locusts.

maili* [*Engl.*] (–) mile.

maingiano *pl.* society, social life. *Cf.* **ingia.**

maingilio, maingiliano *pl.* 1. approach. 2. interference, intervention. **– ya kivita.** armed intervention. *Cf.* **ingia.**

maisha* *pl.* life, lifetime. **nitakaa hapa –.** I will live here forever (my whole life). **– pamoja kwa salama.** peaceful coexistence. *Cf.* **ishi.**

[1]**maishilio*** *pl.* 1. livelihood, subsistence. 2. work, occupation, job. *Cf.* **ishi.**

[2]**maishilio** *pl.* end, limit, goal. *Cf.* [1]**isha.**

maiti*, mayiti (–) dead body, corpse, cadaver. *Cf.* **mauti.**

maiza* (–) (mark of) respect, honor, distinction.

maizi* *coll.* know, be acquainted with, understand; recognize, ascertain, determine.

majadi* *pl.* 1. effort, exertion. 2. yearning, longing, (strong) desire, passion. *Cf.*[2]**jadi.**

majahaba* (–) *see* **majahabu.**

majahabu*, majahaba (–) *naut.* wharf, dock. (= **gudi.**) *Cf.* **jahabu.**

majaliwa *pl., rel.* 1. mercy, grace, favor, aid. 2. (grace of) God. 3. *pr. n. masc. Cf.* **jalia.**

majani *pl.* grass; leaves, herbage, foliage; weeds. **– ya mwaka.** kind of vegetable. **rangi ya –.** green (color). **anavuta – mabichi.** *fig.* He smokes opium. *Cf.* **jani.**

majaribu* *pl., rel.* temptation. *Cf.* **jaribu.**

majembe *pl., naut./av.* screw, propeller (= **rafardha**). *Cf.* **jembe.**

majengo *pl.* *see* **jengo.**

majenzi *pl.* *see* **ujenzi.**

majeruhi* *rare* 1. (–) wounded person. 2. *adj.* wounded. *Cf.* **jeraha, jeruhi.**

majeshi* *pl.* armed forces. *Cf.* **jeshi.**

maji *pl.* 1. water, liquid. **– ya kunywa.** drinking water. **– ya mvua.** rain water. **– chumvi (bahari).** salt water, brine. **mwana –.** sailor. **– makuu.** spring tides. **– mafu.** neap tides. **– kujaa.** high tide. **– kupwa.** low tide. 2. *med.* secretion, discharge. 3. **–a –** (*or* **majimaji**). *adj.* watery, damp; *(techn.)* hydraulic. **mkandamizo wa majimaji.** hydraulic press. *Cf.* **kimaji, umaji.**

majibizano* *pl.* 1. question and answer, assertion and contradiction, give and take. 2. press conference. *Cf.* **jawabu,** [1]**jibu.**

majilio *pl.* *see* **jilio.**

majilipio *pl.* *see* **majilipo.**

majilipo, majilipio, majilipizi *pl.* 1. repayment, amortization *(of a loan, debt).* 2. revenge, retaliation, reprisal, satisfaction. *Cf.* **lipa.**

majilisi *pl., rare* reception room, waiting room, lounge. *Cf.* **jilisi.**

majimaji *see* **maji** 3.

majinuni* *pl.* *see* **majununi.**

majira* (–) 1. (point of) time. **– ya saa.** clock-time. 2. watch, clock. **saa yangu haishiki –.** My watch is not keeping good time. 3. period, season. **– ya masika.** the great rainy season. 4. *naut.* course.

majirani* *pl.* 1. neighborhood. 2. environment, environs. *Cf.* **jirani, ujirani.**

majisifu* *pl.* self-praise, conceit, egotism, bragging, showing off, arrogance. *Cf.* [1]**sifa, sifu, mjisifu.**

majivu 1. *pl.* ashes. *Cf.* **jivu.** 2.: **–a –.** *adj.* gray. **rangi ya –.** of a gray color. *Cf.* **kijivu.**

majivuno *pl.* self-praise, conceit, boasting, showing off, pride, arrogance. **anapotembea ana – sana.** The way he walks shows that he is arrogant. *Cf.* **vuna.**

majonzi*, **mayonzi** [*Ar.?*] *pl.* sadness, sorrow, grief. **fanya/ona –.** be sad.

majuni* (–) majuni (a narcotic confection made of opium or hemp and sugar). (= **afyuni, madadi, kasumba.**)

majununi*, **majinuni** (–) 1. madman, lunatic. 2. clown, buffoon. 3. foolish/silly talk *(causing amusement or provoking ridicule).* 4. *adj.* insane, mad, crazy.

majusi* *pl.* *see* [3]**mjusi.**

majuto *pl.* regret, contrition. *Cf.* **juta,** [1]**juto.**

majuzi, juzijuzi *adv.* a few days ago. *Cf.* **juzi.**

[1]**Maka*** Mecca.

[2]**maka** 1. be surprised/astonished/amazed. 2. utter an exclamation of surprise. *Cf.* **kimako.**

makaa *pl.* 1. coal, charcoal. 2. embers, cinders. *Cf.* [3]**kaa.**

makaakaa *pl.* *see* **kaakaa.**

makaburi* *pl.* graveyard, cemetery. *Cf.* **kaburi.**

makadara*, **makadari** *pl.* 1. *rel., rare* might, power, omnipotence *(with ref. to God; =* **nguvu, uwezo**). 2. Makadara (name of a section of Nairobi). *Cf.* **kudura.**

makadari* *pl.* *see* **makadara.**

makadirio* *pl.* bill, estimate *(of cost),* evaluation. *Cf.* **kadiri.**

makala* *pl.* treatise, article, essay.

makali *pl.* 1. edge, point *(of a knife, sword, spear, etc.:* the sharp part). 2. *fig.* daring, bravery. 3. *fig.* fierceness, cruelty; harshness, severity. *Cf.* **kali.**

makamo* *pl.* **makamu.**

makamu*, **makamo** *pl.* 1. rank, status, dignity, social position. 2. age-class *(of a person).* 3. substitute, deputy. **– wa rais.** vice-president *(Tanzania).* *Cf.* [1]**kaimu, ukaimu.**

makani*, **maskani, masikani** (–) residence, home, settlement. *Cf.* [1]**sakini.**

makanika* [*Engl.*] (–) 1. mechanic. 2. *phys.* mechanics. *Cf.* **umakanika.**

makao *pl.* (place of) residence, home. **– makuu.** headquarters. *Cf.* [1]**kaa.**

makapo *pl.* chaff. *Cf.* [1]**kapi.**

makasi* *pl.* (pair of) scissors. (= **mkasi.**)

makataa* 1. *pl.* (final) arrangement, settlement, decision, conclusion. 2. *adv.* definitely, categorically; firmly, resolutely. *Cf.* [1]**kataa.**

makazi *pl.* 1. residence, settlement; environment. 2. mode of life; condition, situation. 3. occupation, activity. *Cf.* [1]**kaa.**

makeke *pl.* 1. excitement, disturbance. 2. annoyance, vexation. 3. exaggeration, boasting.

makengeza *pl.* squinting. **macho ya –.** squinting eyes. **tazama kwa –.** look askance at, frown on (someone). *Cf.* [1]**kengeza.**

makeruhi* *see* **makuruhi.**

maki* *pl.* 1. thickness. **nguo ya –.** thick cloth. 2. stoutness, heaviness, corpulence. **ana –.** He is heavy (and strong).

makini* 1. *pl.* strength of character, dignity, composure; calmness, attentiveness. **sikiliza kwa –.** listen attentively. 2. *adj.* quietly, calmly, deliberately, with dignity.

makiri* (–) cleat *(for fastening a rope, etc.).*

makisi*, **makisio** *pl.* guess, conjecture, supposition; estimate, approximation; proposal. *Cf.* [1]**kisi.**

makisio* *pl.* *see* **makisi.**

makiwa *pl.* expression of sympathy, condolence. **makiwani!** Condolences! *(formula of greeting when one enters a house where a death has recently occurred).* **hapa pana –.** There has been a death here (in this house). *Cf.* **kiwa, ukiwa.**

makohoo, makohozi *pl.* *see* **kohozi.**

makoko *pl.* crust *(esp. on cooked rice).* *Cf.* **ukoko.**

makolokolo *pl.* 1. bundle, pack, baggage. 2. equipment, utensils. 3. goods, chattels, property. (= **vikorokoro.**)

makomba *pl.* millet gruel *(also used in the preparation of beer).*

makombo *pl.* *see* [1]**kombo,** [2]**kombo,** [3]**kombo.**

makombozi *pl.* *see* **ukombozi.**

makopa *pl.* dried manioc.

makoroa* (–) *naut.* knot tied in an anchor cable. (= **mangrini.**)

makororo *pl.* 1. *med.* swelling of the tonsils. 2. heavy/difficult breathing; death rattle. **vuta –.** breathe with difficulty; have the death rattle.

makorowezo *pl.* 1. confusion. 2. work poorly done, botchwork. *Cf.* **koroweza.**

makosekano *pl.* fault, defect; mistake, oversight. *Cf.* **[1]kosa.**

[1]makoza* *pl., rare, anat.* testicles, scrotum.

[2]makoza *pl., rare* ivory bracelets.

maksai*, mahsai (–) castrated animal. **ng'ombe –.** bullock, ox. **farasi –.** gelding. *Cf.* **[2]hasa, hasi.**

maksi* [*Engl.*] (–) mark, grade *(in a class or course).*

maksusi* *see* **mahsusi.**

maktaba* *pl.* library, reading room. *Cf.* **kitabu.**

makubadhi* *pl.* *see* **makubazi.**

makubazi*, makubadhi *pl.* leather sandals (decorated).

makubwa *pl.* importance, important matter. *Cf.* **kubwa.**

makucha *pl.* *see* **ukucha.**

makufuru* *pl., rel.* unbelief, atheism; sacrilege, blasphemy. *Cf.* **kafiri, kufuru, ukafiri.**

makulaji *pl., coll.* food, provisions, victuals. *Cf.* **[1]la, chakula.**

[1]makuli* *pl.* *see* **maakuli.**

[2]makuli* *pl.* *see* **kuli.**

makulima *pl.* agriculture. *Cf.* **[1]lima.**

makupwa *pl.* beach, sandbank, rock *(exposed at low tide). Cf.* **pwa.**

makuru* (–) 1. salve, ointment. 2. (adhesive) plaster.

makuruhi*, makeruhi *adj.* bad, offensive, disgusting, abominable, nasty. *Cf.* **karaha.**

makusudi* *pl.* *see* **makusudio.**

makusudio*, makusudi *pl.* aim, intention, purpose. **–a makusudi.** intentional, deliberate. **kwa –.** intentionally, on purpose. **bila –.** unintentionally. *Cf.* **kusudi.**

makutano *pl.* *see* **kutano.**

makuu *pl.* 1. pride, arrogance, vanity, conceit. 2. ambition. *Cf.* **kuu.**

makwa *pl.* 1. support, prop, post, pillar. 2. notch, groove *(in wood).*

1malaika* (–) 1. *rel.* angel, messenger. – **mkuu.** archangel. – **mlinzi.** guardian angel. 2. small child, baby. **huyu ni –.** This child is still a baby.

2malaika *pl.* body hair *(usually on the arms and legs).* *Cf.* **laika.**

malaji *pl.* 1. food, foodstuffs. 2. diet, fare. *Cf.* **1la, kilaji.**

malale *pl.:* **ugonjwa wa –.** *med.* sleeping sickness, encephalitis. *Cf.* **lala.**

malalo, malazi, malazo *pl.* 1. sleeping-place, bedding, bed; lair, den *(of animals).* 2. *rec.* housing. *Cf.* **lala.**

malango *pl.* initiation (of boys and girls at puberty). *Cf.* **lango.**

malaya* (–) prostitute. *Cf.* **2umalaya.**

malazi, malazo *pl.* *see* **malalo.**

malele (–) *bot.* litmus, orchilla *(Rocella Montagnei, Rocella tinctoria).*

maleleji, malelezi *pl.* period between the southwest and northeast monsoons, *i.e.*, approx. late March to early April and late November to early December. *Cf.* **lala** (?).

malendalenda, marendarenda *pl.* 1. mucus (discharge). 2. *med.* mucus-like or watery feces.

malenga (wa-) 1. professional singer, leader of singing *(at dances).* 2. unfermented beer. (= **togwa.**)

maleuni*, maluuni 1. (–) accursed/damned person. 2. (–) *rel.* Satan. 3. (–) good-for-nothing. 4. *adj.* accursed, damned. **mtoto huyu ni – sana.** This child is a good-for-nothing. *Cf.* **laana.**

malevi *pl.* *see* **ulevi.**

malezi *pl.* (home) education, upbringing. – **mabaya.** poor upbringing, bad manners. *Cf.* **lea.**

malhamu* (–) *see* **marhamu.**

mali* (–) possessions, property, goods. – **ya kusafirisha.** export goods. – **inayoondoka.** movable possessions, goods and chattels. – **isiyoondoka.** real estate.

malidadi*, mmalidadi, maridadi, mardadi [?] 1. (–) person dressed in up-to-date style. 2. (–) showily dressed person, fop, dandy. 3. *adj. & adv.* modern, stylish; vain, conceited. *Cf.* **kimalidadi, umalidadi.**

1maliki* (–) *see* **malki.**

2maliki* begin/start something, set to work on a job, do the spadework of a project.

malimati*, maliumati (–) *Isl.* 1. ceremony in commemoration of the dead. 2. meal served after the memorial ceremony.

malimbiko *pl.* *see* **mlimbiko.**

malimo *pl.* field work, agriculture. *Cf.* **[1]lima, makulima, ukulima.**

malimwengu *pl., rel.* worldly things, mundane matters. *Cf.* **ulimwengu.**

[1]malindi *pl.* malindi (small apron of beads worn by women).

[2]malindi *pl. of* **lindi.**

malipizi *pl.* *see* **lipizi.**

malipo *pl.* *see* **lipo.**

malisaa*, malisao (–) *see* **marisaa.**

malisha *pl.* *see* **malisho.**

malisho, malisha, malishoni *pl.* 1. pasture, pasturage. 2. fodder. *Cf.* **[1]la.**

malishoni *pl.* *see* **malisho.**

maliumati* (–) *see* **malimati.**

maliwato *pl.* 1. bathroom *(inside a house).* 2. a small open area adjoining a house where one may wash one's hands, face, etc.

maliwazo *pl.* comfort, sympathy, aid. *Cf.* **liwaza, liwazo.**

maliza 1. end, conclude, finish, complete. **– kazi.** complete a job. **– deni.** pay/settle a debt. 2. consume, polish off (food). **– chakula.** completely consume a meal. 3. destroy, exterminate. **ugonjwa huu umewamaliza watu wengi.** Many people have fallen victim to the disease. *appl.* **malizia.** *intr.* **malizika.** *caus.* **malizisha.** *ass.* **malizana.**

malizano *pl.* lamenting, sobbing, weeping, wailing. *Cf.* **[1]lia.**

malizi *pl.* rustling, crackling, rattling. *Cf.* **[1]lia.**

malki*, maliki (–) ruler, monarch, king. *Cf.* **[1]miliki, milki.**

malkia* (–) queen. *Cf.* **malki.**

malu (–) malu (species of antelope, *Strepsiceros strepsiceros).*

malumbano *pl., jur.* cross-examination. *Cf.* **lumba.**

maluuni* (–) *see* **maleuni.**

mama (–) 1. mother. **mamangu** (< **mama yangu**). my mother. 2.: **– mkubwa.** aunt (older sister of one's mother). **– mdogo.** aunt (younger sister of one's mother). 3.: **– wa kambo.** stepmother. 4. a term of polite address used by younger men or women to older women or by *older* men in positions of authority to *younger* women who are their subordinates *(in an office, etc.).* *Cf.* **umama.**

mamanua open, loosen, separate, break apart.

mamba (–) 1. crocodile. 2. kind of poisonous snake. 3. *rare* leech (= **mruba**).

^{1}**mambo** *pl. of* ^{1}**jambo.**

^{2}**mambo** *pl. of* **uwambo.**

mamboleo *adj.* modern, present-day. **ukoloni –.** neo-colonialism. *Cf.* ^{1}**jambo, leo.**

mamlaka* (–) 1. power, rule, government. **– ya kujitawala.** *rare* self-government. 2. *jur.* jurisdiction. 3. right of ownership, property right, possession. **wa na –.** have the right of possession over a thing. 4. (official) position, capacity, status. *Cf.* ^{1}**miliki, malki.**

mamoja *adv.* one and the same, all the same, immaterial. **ukija usije, kwangu ni –.** Whether you come or not is immaterial to me. *Cf.* **moja.**

mamsahib*, memsahib [*Hind.-Ar.-Engl.*] (–) lady, mistress. *Cf.* **sahibu, suhubiana.**

mamwana *pl. of* **mwana** 2.

man* (–) *see* **mani.**

manamba* [*Engl.*] *pl.* crowd *(of people).* *Cf.* **namba.**

manane *pl.:* **usiku wa –.** the dead of night, the small hours (about 2:00 A.M.). (*lit.* 'the eighth hour of night'; *cf.* nane.)

manani* *sing., rel.* Benefactor, the Beneficent (a title of God).

manati* (–) sling, catapult.

manawa (–) *med.* skin disease, herpes *(affecting especially the hands).* *Cf.* **nawa.**

manda (–) manda (a pastry made of rice-flour and grated coconut). *Cf.* **kimanda.**

mandari* (–) entertainment, revel, dance. *Cf.* **mandhari.**

mandhari* (–) (external) appearance, view, scene, sight; prospect, landscape.

mandusi* (–) 1. box, chest (= **ndusi**). 2. trunk, suitcase.

manemane* (–) myrrh *(Commiphora abyssinica).*

manena *pl., anat.* groin. (= **kinena.**)

maneno *pl.* *see* **neno.**

maneva* [*Engl.* maneuver?] (–) pleasure trip, excursion. **tunakwenda –.** We are going on an excursion.

^{1}**manga** eat food plain *(without relish, gravy, etc.).* *Cf.* ^{1}**umanga.**

^{2}**Manga*** (–) 1. Arabia. (= **Uarabu.**) 2. an object of Arabian origin (= **Mwarabu, Arabuni**). **pilipili –.** black pepper. **mkoma –.** pomegranate tree. **njiwa –.** (species of) pigeon. **wanja wa –.** antimony, kohl. *Cf.* **Kimanga, Mmanga,** ^{2}**Umanga.**

mang'amung'amu, mang'ang'amu *pl.* mental derangement; confusion, dismay. *Cf.* **ng'amua.**

manganja *pl.* 1. rattle/bell worn by dancers on the legs. 2. child's rattle.

mangazimbwe *pl.* optical illusion, mirage. (= **mazigazi.**) **usiku –.** dark night.

mangharibi* (–) *see* **magharibi.**

mangili* (–) *naut.* device (cathead) for securing a cable/anchor *(on native boats). Cf.* **mangrini.**

mango (–) (*augment. of* **kimango**) millstone *(upper part of a stone mill).*

mangrini* (–) *naut.* knot tied in an anchor cable. (= **makoroa.**) *Cf.* **mangili.**

mang'ungumu *adv., rare* secretly, surreptitiously, on the sly, confidentially. (= **siri.**)

mangwaji *pl.* ostentation, vanity.

mani*, man (–) man (unit of weight: three pounds, 1.4 kg).

manii* (–) *phy.* semen, sperm. (= **shahawa.**)

manisipaa*, manisipali (–) *see* **munisipali.**

manja (–) *ornith.* Pemba white-eye. (= **shige la manjano.**)

manjali* (–) *naut.* rope of the front sail *(of a native boat).*

manjano (–) 1. turmeric. 2.: **rangi ya –.** yellow pigment. **rangi ya – mabivu.** orange pigment. *Cf.* **kimanjano.**

manjorinjori *pl.* *see* **ujorinjori.**

manju (–) leader of singing *(at dances).*

manoari* [*Engl.*] (–) *see* **manowari.**

manoleo *pl.* 1. metal ring between the blade and handle of a knife. 2. back of a knife blade *(as opp. to the edge;* = **mafutani).** *Cf.* **noa, noleo.**

manong'onezo, manong'ono *pl.* 1. whispering. 2. rumor, gossip. 3. prophecy, prediction. *Cf.* **nong'ona, mnong'ono.**

manong'ono *pl.* *see* **manong'onezo.**

manowari*, manoari [*Engl.*] (–) man-of-war, warship, naval vessel. **kundi la –.** flotilla, squadron.

mansuli* (–) (kind of) woolen cloth, blanket.

manufaa* (–) 1. necessary/useful thing. 2. use(fulness), profit, benefit, advantage. *Cf.* **nafuu.**

manuku* (–) *see* **manukuu.**

manukuu*, manuku (–) *rare* 1. copy, transcript. 2. imitation. 3. translation. *Cf.* **nakili, nakala.**

manuwio*, manuwiyo *pl., rare* intention, aim, purpose *(especially in respect of a visit to a witch doctor or the use of a charm). Cf.* **nuia, nuio.**

manuwiyo *pl.* *see* **manuwio.**

manyago *pl.* initiation ceremony *(for children).* *Cf.* **kinyago.**

manyatta* [*Maasai*] (–) compound.

manyonyota *pl.* fine rain, drizzle. *Cf.* **nyonyota.**

manyoya *pl.* fur, feathers, wool *(of an animal).* *Cf.* **nyoya, sufi.**

manza (–) 1. crime, offense, delict, outrage. 2. legal action, trial.

manzili*, menzili (–) *rel.* something sent by God, revelation.

maokozi *pl.* rescue, deliverance *(from a personal difficulty).* *Cf.* [2]**okoa.**

maombezi *pl.* *see* **maombi.**

maombi, maombo, maombezi, maomvi *pl.* 1. request, entreaty, petition, appeal. 2. mediation, intercession. *Cf.* **omba.**

maombo *pl.* *see* **maombi.**

maombolezo *pl.* 1. wail(ing), lamentation. 2. groaning, moaning. 3. (sound of) mourning, dirge. (= **kilio.**) *Cf.* **omboleza, ombolezo;** *also* **omba.**

maomvi *pl.* *see* **maombi.**

maondokeo *pl.* *see* **ondokeo.**

maondoleo *pl.* 1. removal, elimination. 2. *rel.* forgiveness, absolution. – **ya dhambi.** forgiveness of sins. *Cf.* **ondoa, ondoleo.**

maonevu *pl.* *see* **uonevu.**

maonezi *pl.* oppression. *Cf.* **ona, uonevu.**

maongezi *pl.* 1. conversation, chat. **weka –.** begin a conversation. 2. pastime, amusement. *Cf.* [2]**ongea.**

maongozi *pl.* 1. order, arrangement, regulation. – **ya siasa.** political platform. 2. repair, restoration. 3. management, administration. 4. *rel.* guidance, providence. – **ya Mungu.** God's providence. *Cf.* **ongoa.**

maoni *pl.* view(s), opinion. – **ya wananchi.** public opinion. *Cf.* **ona, ono.**

maono *pl.* thought, feeling, sensation, perception. *Cf.* **ona, ono.**

maonyesho *pl.* exhibition, demonstration. – **ya ukulima.** agricultural exhibition. *Cf.* **ona.**

maonyo *pl.* warning; sign, hint. *Cf.* **ona.**

maoteo *pl.* hiding-place, ambush. *Cf.* [2]**ota.**

maovu *pl.* 1. evil, wickedness. 2. malice, spite. 3. unfairness, injustice. *Cf.* **ovu, uovu.**

maovyo *pl.* trash, rubbish. *Cf.* **ovyo.**

maowidha* *pl.* *see* **mauidha.**

maozi *pl.* marriage arrangements. *Cf.* **oa.**

mapacha *pl.* twins. – **watatu.** triplets. *Cf.* **pacha.**

mapakio, mapakizi *pl.* 1. loading-platform; *(naut.)* loading-crane. 2. *naut.* freight, cargo. 3. freightage. *Cf.* **[1]pakia.**

mapakizi *pl.* *see* **mapakio.**

mapalilio *pl.* *see* **mapalio.**

mapalio, mapalilio *pl.* hoeing, weeding. *Cf.* **[1]paa.**

mapambano *pl.* 1. contact; impact, collision. 2. meeting, (close) touch *(with a person).* 3. *sport* contest, match. **katika – ya timu mbili hizi, Brazil watashinda Chile.** In the contest between the two teams Chile was defeated by Brazil. *Cf.* **pambana.**

mapana *pl.* 1. width, breadth. 2. diameter. *Cf.* **[1]pana, upana.**

mapatano *pl.* *see* **patano.**

mapatilizo *pl.* *see* **upatilivu.**

mapato *pl.* *see* **pato.**

mapayo *pl.* delirium. *Cf.* **payo.**

mapema *adv.* early, in good time. **asubuhi na –.** early in the morning. **– mwaka.** at the beginning of the year.

mapembelezo *pl.* *see* **mabembelezo.**

mapendano *pl.* (reciprocal) affection, fondness. *Cf.* **penda.**

mapendeleo, mapendo *pl.* inclination, liking, partiality, preference, predilection, favor. *Cf.* **penda.**

mapendezi *pl.* friendliness, kindness, politeness, obligingness. *Cf.* **penda.**

mapendo *pl.* *see* **mapendeleo.**

mapenzi *pl.* *see* **penzi.**

mapepe *pl.* 1. chaff, grain-husks. 2. empty/barren ears of grain.

mapepeta *pl.:* **– ya mpunga.** unripe grains of rice (roasted). *Cf.* **pepeta.**

mapesa* [*Port.*] *pl.* money. **– taslimu.** cash, ready money. *Cf.* **[1]pesa.**

mapigano, mapigiano *pl.* fight, conflict, struggle, battle. **– ya kitabaka.** *comm.* class struggle. *Cf.* **piga, pigano.**

mapindu *pl.* somersault. *Cf.* **pinda, pindu.**

mapinduzi *pl.* 1. (radical) change, upheaval. 2. revolution. *Cf.* **pinda.**

mapishi *pl.* cooking, cookery. *prov.* **mchele mmoja – mabalimbali.** There is only one rice, but there are various ways of cooking it. *Cf.* **pika.**

mapiswa *pl.* stupidity, folly, nonsense. *Cf.* **piswa.**

maponea *pl.* food, subsistence, livelihood. *Cf.* **pona.**

maponyea, maponyo *pl.* 1. drugs, medicines. 2. cure, (course of) treatment. *Cf.* **pona.**

maponyo *pl.* *see* **maponyea.**

maposo *pl., rare* 1. courtship, proposal of marriage. 2. arrangements of marriage. *Cf.* **posa.**

mapoza *pl.* drugs, medicines. *Cf.* **poa.**

mapumziko *pl.* 1. rest, relaxation. 2. cessation *(of work),* pause, break. *Cf.* **pumua.**

mapune (–) *med.* a skin disease. *Cf.* **puna.**

mapurendi* [*Engl.*] *pl.* epaulets, gold braid.

mapusa *pl. augment. of* **kipusa.**

mapwa, mapwaji *pl.* shore, coast, beach. *Cf.* **pwa.**

mapyoro *pl.* 1. boasting, giving oneself airs. 2. exaggeration, fraud. *Cf.* **pyora, pyoro.**

mara* 1. (–) time, turn, occasion; series, sequence. 2. *adv.* once; immediately; suddenly, unexpectedly. **– moja.** once. **– mbili.** twice. **– nyingi.** often, frequently. **– kwa –.** again and again, often. **– hii.** immediately, directly.

maraba* *pl.* *see* **mraba.**

maradhi*, marazi (–) illness, sickness, disease; pestilence, epidemic. **– ya ng'ombe.** cattle plague. **– nyogea.** rachitis. **– ya mti.** scrofula.

maradufu*, marudufu, mardufu 1. (–) doubling, duplicate. 2. (*also* **rudufu**) *adj.* double, twofold. *Cf.* **rudufu.**

marahaba* *interj.* 1. good, thank you. 2. very well *(in response to the salutation* **shikamoo**).

marahamu* (–) *see* **marhamu.**

marakaraka* 1. *pl.* spot, patch, stripe. 2. *adj.* spotted, speckled, striped, checked. *Cf.* **kiraka.**

marasharasha* *pl.* 1. sprinkle, shower, spray. 2. sprinkling, moistening. **mvua ya –.** light rain, drizzle. *Cf.* **rasha.**

marashi* (–) perfume. *Cf.* **rasha.**

marazi* (–) *see* **maradhi.**

mardadi* *see* **malidadi.**

mardudi* (–) 1. refusal, denial, rejection, repudiation. 2. *rare* going over something for a second time *(e.g., checking one's arithmetic to make sure there is no mistake).* *Cf.* **rudi.**

mardufu* (–) *see* **maradufu.**

marefu *pl.* length, height, depth. **haina – ya kutosha.** It is not long enough. *Cf.* **refu.**

marehemu* (–) deceased person, the late...; *(pl.)* the dead. **Sikukuu ya – Wote.** All Souls' Day. *Cf.* **rehema, rehemu.**

marekani* *adj.* American.

marendarenda *pl.* *see* **malendalenda.**

marengu *pl.*, *naut.* outrigger.

marhamu*, **marahamu**, **malhamu** (–) 1. grease, paste. 2. salve, ointment, plaster.

maridadi* (–) *see* **malidadi.**

maridhawa* 1. *adj.* much, plenty of, enough, abundant. 2. *adv.* in abundance/profusion. *Cf.* **radhi, ridhi.**

maridhia*, **mridhia** (wa-) 1. polite/charming/nice person. 2. unassuming, unpretentious, modest person. **mke wangu –.** My wife is unassuming. *Cf.* **radhi, ridhi.**

marigedi* (–) marigedi (large copper kettle).

marijani* (–) coral. **– ya fedhaluka** red coral.

marika *pl.* persons of the same age or belonging to the same age group, contemporaries. **hawa ni – yangu.** These people are my contemporaries. *Cf.* **rika.**

marikani* (–) *see* **merikani.**

marimba (–) marimba (kind of wooden xylophone).

marinda *pl.* edge, border; pleat *(of a skirt, etc.).*

maringo *pl.* 1. boasting, arrogance. 2. talebearing. *Cf.* **ringa.**

marini* [?] *adj.* 1. pleasant, attractive. 2. fashionable, elegant. 3. fresh. healthy, good-looking.

marisaa*, **marisawa, marisao, marisau, malisaa, malisao** *pl.* (small) shot, lead. **bunduki ya –.** shotgun. *Cf.* **risasi.**

marisao*, **marisau, marisawa** (–) *see* **marisaa.**

marmar* (–) marble.

marudi*, **marudio** *pl.* 1. return, arrival. 2. requital, punishment; reprimand. *Cf.* **rudi.**

marudio* *pl.* *see* **marudi.**

marudufu* (–) *see* **maradufu.**

marufaa* (–) 1. bookrest *(used for reading the Koran).* 2. candlestick. 3. part of a native loom. *Cf.* **rufaa.**

marufuku* *pl.* 1. prohibition. **– kuvuta hapa.** No smoking. 2. embargo. *Cf.* **rufuku.**

marugurugu *pl.* swelling, lump(s).

marupurupu *pl.* increase, extra compensation; discount, rebate.

masaa, masao, masalio, masalia, masazo *pl.* 1. remains, remainder, vestige, remnant. 2. *rel.* relic. 3. *rare* corpse. (= **maiti.**) *Cf.* **²saa.**

masahaba* *pl.*, *Isl.* companions of Muhammad. *Cf.* **sahibu.**

masahala*, **msaala** (–) question. – **ya siasa (dini).** political (religious) questions. *Cf.* **saili, swali.**

masaibu* (–) 1. *rel.* predestination, divine punishment. 2. grief, distress, misfortune, affliction. *Cf.* **²sibu.**

masakasaka *pl.* dry leaves/twigs.

masala* (–) *rare, Isl.* law.

masalala* (*usually* **lo masalale**) *interj. of amazement.*

masalan* *see* **mathalan.**

masalia, masalio *pl.* *see* **masaa.**

masalkheri* *salutation:* Good evening. *Cf.* **sabalkheri.**

masamaha*, masameho *pl.* *see* **msamaha.**

masango *pl.* thick wire of brass or copper *(used to make ornaments).*

masao *pl.* *see* **masaa.**

masarifu* *pl.* *see* **masurufu.**

masazo *pl.* *see* **masaa.**

masega *pl.:* – **ya nyuki.** honeycomb, honey in the comb.

masengenyo *pl.* slander, calumny. *Cf.* **sengenya.**

mashabo* (–) *see* **mashobo.**

mashairi* *pl.* *see* **shairi.**

mashaka* *pl.* 1. trouble, distress, difficulty. 2. need, privation, misery. *Cf.* **shaka, shuku.**

mashambizo *pl.* mashambizo (cloths used for washing a corpse).

mashapo *pl.* 1. residue, sediment, dregs. 2. *rare* pulp, husks *(of fruit, grain, etc., left after squeezing or pounding).* (= **masira, mashata, masimbi, mashudu.**)

mashariki* (–) 1. sunrise. 2. east. – **ya mbele.** Near East. – **ya kati/katikati.** Middle East. – **ya mbali.** Far East. – **ya kusini.** southeast. 3.: **–a –.** *adj.* eastern, oriental.

masharti* *pl.* *see* **shuruti.**

masharubu* *pl.* moustache. *Cf.* **sharubu.**

mashata* *pl.* lees, residue *(of oil, etc.).*

mashavu *pl.* *see* **shavu.**

mashenaka* *pl., arch.* gallows.

mashendea *pl.* mashendea (thin, watery rice soup).

mashindano *pl.* *see* **shindano.**

mashine*, mashini [*Engl.*] (–) 1. machine, engine. – **ya kuandika.** typewriter. – **ya**

barafu. refrigerator. – ya stimu. electric motor. – za upuraji wa nafaka. thresher. kwa kutumia –. mechanical. 2. *rare* locomotive.

mashini* (–) *see* mashine.

mashitaka* *pl.* *see* mashtaka.

mashitakiano* *pl.* *see* mashtaka.

mashkara* (–) *see* masihara.

mashobo*, mashabo (–) show(iness), ostentation, vanity.

mashono *pl.*, mshono (mi-) 1. sewing, tailoring, dressmaking. 2. manner of dress; style, fashion; dress, clothing. – mpya. modern dress. *Cf.* shona.

mashtaka*, mashtakiano, mashitaka, mashitakiano *pl.* 1. accusation, reproach, imputation. 2. *jur.* charge, indictment, suit, action, prosecution. ameleta – ya uwongo. He was convicted of falsehood. fanya –. accuse, sue. – waziwazi na ya kisiri. overt and covert charges. *Cf.* shtaki.

mashtakiano* *pl.* *see* mashtaka.

mashua* [*Ind.*] (–) boat(s).

mashudu* *pl.* oilcake (residue after seed has been pressed for oil).

mashuhuri*, mashuuri *adj.* famous, well-known, prominent, distinguished. (= maarufu, enye sifa, [1]bayana.)

mashurti*, mashuruti *pl.* *see* shuruti.

mashuuri* *see* mashuhuri.

masia* (–) *rare* walk, stroll. enda –. go walking, go for a walk.

masifu* *pl.* praise, flattery. *Cf.* [1]sifa, sifu.

masihara*, mashkara (–) jest, joke; mockery, derision. –a –. ridiculous.

masihiya*, masiya 1. (–) Messiah, Christ. (= Kristo.) 2. (= mmasihiya, wa-) Christian. (= Mkristo.) 3. *adj.* Christian. *Cf.* umasihiya.

masika *pl.* masika (the great rainy season, approx. April-May).

masikani* (–) *see* makani.

masikitiko *pl.* *see* sikitiko.

masilaha*, masilahi, masuluhu *rare* 1. agreement, concord, harmony. 2. reconciliation, compromise. 3. (final) result (of bargaining, negotiation). *Cf.* suluhu.

masilahi* (–) *see* masilaha.

masimbi *pl.* residue, dregs. (= mashapo, mashudu.)

masingizio *pl.* slander, calumny; hypocrisy. *Cf.* singiza.

masinzi *pl.* *see* masizi.

masira* *pl.* lees *(of wine, beer).*

masiwa, maziwa *pl.* 1. *rare* large island. 2. (small) group of islands. *Cf.* **kisiwa, siwa.**

masiya* (–) *see* **masihiya.**

masizi, masinzi *pl.* soot.

maskani* (–) *see* **makani.**

maskhara* (–) *rare* mask, disguise.

maskini* 1. (–) poor person, beggar. 2. *adj.* poor, indigent, destitute, wretched. *Cf.* **umaskini.**

[1]**masoka** (–) iron/brass wire.

[2]**masoka** *pl.* *see* **mahoka.**

masombo *pl.* belt, girdle, sash.

masomo *pl.* study, studies. **alimaliza – yake.** He completed his studies. **– ya kujifunza.** self-education. *Cf.* **soma.**

mastadi* [*Engl.*] (–) mustard. (= **haradali.**)

mastakimu* (–) environment, surroundings. *Cf.* **stakimu.**

masua*, mazua (–) swoon, fainting spell, dizziness. *Cf.* **mbasua.**

masubutu* (–) *see* **mathubuti.**

masuko, masukosuko *pl.* 1. rocking, tossing *(of a ship).* 2. disturbance, convulsion, excitement, agitation, unrest. *Cf.* [2]**suka.**

masukosuko *pl.* *see* **masuko.**

masuluhu* (–) *see* **masilaha.**

masumbufu *pl.* *see* **masumbuko.**

masumbuko, masumbufo, masumbuo, masumbulizi *pl.* 1. pain, torment. 2. disturbance, difficulty, obstacle. 3. unrest; annoyance, vexation. 4. pursuit, persecution, suppression. *Cf.* **sumbua, sumbufu.**

masumbulizi *pl.* *see* **masumbuko.**

masumbuo *pl.* *see* **masumbuko.**

masuo *pl.* water used for rinsing out the mouth. *Cf.* [1]**sua.**

masurufu*, masarifu *pl.* expenses, expenditure; housekeeping allowance; cost of living. *Cf.* **sarafu, sarifu.**

masuto *pl.* reproach(es), faultfinding, criticism, accusation. *Cf.* [1]**suta.**

mata *pl., rare* bow and arrows. *Cf.* **uta;** *also* **upinde, mshale.**

matabwatabwa *pl.* gruel, paste *(anything pounded until soft and semi-liquid).*

matafuni, matafuno *pl.* 1. chewing, ruminating. 2. something chewed/nibbled at. *Cf.* **tafuna.**

matafuno *pl.* *see* **matafuni.**

matagataga *pl.:* **enda –.** walk with the legs far apart, walk straddle-legged; take long strides. *Cf.* [1]**tagaa.**

[1]mataka, matakwa *pl.* 1. need, wish, desire. 2. inclination, leaning, talent, gift. *Cf.* **[3]taka.**

[2]mataka, matakataka *pl.* refuse, rubbish; dirt, filth. *Cf.* **[1]taka.**

matakataka *pl.* *see* **[2]mataka.**

matako *pl., anat.* buttocks. *Cf.* **tako.**

matakwa *pl.* *see* **[1]mataka.**

matamalaki* *pl.* power, rule, reign, government. *Cf.* **[1]miliki, malki, milki.**

matambuzi *pl.* explanation, clarification. *Cf.* **tambua, tambuzi.**

matamko, matamshi *pl.* pronunciation, articulation, accent. **sema —.** speak with a foreign accent, speak a language with the accent of one's mother tongue. *Cf.* **tamka.**

matamshi *pl.* *see* **matamko.**

matana *pl., med.* leprosy. (= **ukoma.**)

matanga *pl.* 1. *pl. of* **[2]tanga.** 2. (ceremonies of) mourning. *Cf.* **[3]tanga.**

matapishi *pl.* 1. vomit; vomiting, nausea. 2. obscene language, profanity. *Cf.* **tapika.**

matarajio* *pl.* hope, expectation. *Cf.* **taraji.**

matata *pl.* confusion, trouble, mess, commotion, complication, difficulty. *Cf.* **tata.**

matatizo *pl.* business. *Cf.* **tata.**

mataya *pl.* chops, jowls. *Cf.* **[1]taya.**

matayarisho* [*Pers.*] *pl.* 1. preparation(s), precaution. 2. training, education. *Cf.* **tayari, tayarisha.**

matbaa* (—) *rare* (printing-)press. (= **mtambo wa kupiga chapa na kutoa vitabu, kiwanda cha kupiga chapa.**)

mate *pl.* saliva. **tema —.** spit, expectorate. *Cf.* **ute.**

matege *pl.* bow legs. **mwenye —.** bow-legged person. *Cf.* **tege.**

mategu *pl.* typographical error, misprint. *Cf.* **[1]tego.**

mateka *pl.* 1. prey, booty, plunder. 2. captive, prisoner-of-war. *Cf.* **teka.**

matembele *pl.* sweet-potato leaves *(used as a vegetable).*

matembezi *pl.* walking, strolling; gadding about, loitering, loafing; loose living. **— ya wageni.** tourism. *Cf.* **tembea.**

matemo *adj. & adv.* 1. slanting, crooked. 2. deformed, misshapen.

matendo *pl.* activity, occupation, work. *Cf.* **tenda.**

matengano *pl.* sectarianism. *Cf.* **[1]tenga.**

matengemano *pl.* 1. *geogr.* depression. 2. calming down, pacification, return of peace *(after war)*. 3. prosperity, stabilization. *Cf.* **tengemaa.**

matengenezo *pl.* 1. arrangement, disposition. 2. regulation. 3. preparation. *Cf.* **tengenea.**

matengo, matengu *pl.*, *naut.* outrigger.

matengu *pl.* *see* **matengo.**

mateso *pl.* *see* **teso.**

matetezi *pl.* *see* **utetezi.**

mateto *pl.* protest, objection, argument. *Cf.* **teta.**

mathalan*, mathalani, masalan, methalan *adv.* for example. *Cf.* **mithili, methali.**

mathalani* *see* **mathalan.**

mathubuti*, mathubutu 1. (–) proof, evidence. 2. *adj.* firm, hard, durable, stable. 3. *fig.* honest, trustworthy, dependable. *Cf.* **thabiti, thibiti.**

mathubutu* (–) *see* **mathubuti.**

matibwitibwi *pl.*: **maji –.** stale/muddy water. *Cf.* **tibua.**

[1]**matiko** *pl.* tempering *(of metal)*. **tia –.** temper *(metal, by heating)*.

[2]**matiko** *pl. of* **utiko.**

matilaba* *pl.* 1. desire, request. 2. purpose, aim, intention.

matilo* (–) *naut.* stay.

matimutimu *pl.*: – **ya nywele** *or* **nywele za –.** ruffled/unruly hair. *Cf.* [2]**timka.**

matindi *pl.* young maize plant *(before the formation of ears)*. *Cf.* [2]**tindi.**

[1]**matiti** *pl.*: **enda –.** trot *(of animals)*.

[2]**matiti** *pl. of* **titi.**

matlaa* (–) *see* **matlai.**

matlai*, matlaa (–) *rare* 1. sunrise. 2. east (= **mashariki.**) 3. east wind.

matokeo *pl.* 1. event, occurrence, incident, episode. 2. result, outcome, upshot. *Cf.* [1]**toa.**

matoki *pl.* *see* **toki.**

matongo, matongotongo *pl.* (*also* **utongo**) discharge from the eye. *Cf.* [4]**chongo.**

matope *pl.* dirt, mud; swamp. *Cf.* **tope.**

matubwitubwi *pl.* *see* **machumbwichumbwi.**

matukano *pl.* 1. cursing, invective, abuse. 2. quarrel, dispute. 3. terms of abuse, insults. *Cf.* **tukana.**

matuko* [?] (–) grace, charm.

matule* *pl.* 1. vulgarity, baseness, meanness. 2. dishonor, disgrace. 3. misery, distress. *Cf.* **tule.**

matumatu *pl.* grasshoppers, (young) locusts. *Cf.* **kimatu, tunutu.**

matumbawe *pl.* coral (in the stage before complete fossilization).

matumbo *pl.* bowels, intestines, entrails, viscera. *Cf.* **tumbo.**

matumio *pl.* *see* **matumizi.**

matumishi *pl.* service, attention, care. *Cf.* **tuma.**

matumizi, matumio *pl.* 1. use, employment, utilization, exploitation. 2. expenses, expenditures. **– yake ya mapesa ni makubwa.** His expenses are great. He spends a great deal of money. *Cf.* **tuma.**

matunguu *pl., bot.* wild cardamom *(Aframomum angustifolium)*. *Cf.* **kitunguu.**

matusi, matushi *pl.* 1. cursing, insults. 2. quarrel, dispute. 3. terms of abuse. *Cf.* **tusha.**

matwana (–) bus, truck.

maudhiko* *pl.* 1. unrest, disturbance. 2. annoyance, vexation, trouble, grief. *Cf.* **udhi.**

mauguzi *pl.* care of the sick, nursing. *Cf.* **ugua.**

mauidha*, maowidha, mawaidha (–) (good) advice, admonition, instruction.

[1]**mauja*** (–), **muuya, mwuja (miuja)** 1. unrest, excitement, alarm. 2. danger; misfortune, accident.

[2]**mauja*** (–) *rare* wave (= [1]**wimbi.**)

maujudi* (–) *rare* things which are obtainable/available/in one's possession/known from experience.

mauko *pl.* 1. leaving, departure. 2. sending off/away. 3. *euph.* decease, death. *Cf.* **uka.**

maulana* (–) *rel.* Master, Lord (= God).

maulidi* (–) *Isl.* 1. birthday of Muhammad. 2. festivity celebrating Muhammad's birthday.

maulisho (–) cause of death. *Cf.* [3]**ua.**

maulizo *pl.* 1. investigation, interrogation. 2. *jur.* hearing, trial. *Cf.* **uliza.**

maumbile *pl.* 1. nature, environment. 2. (natural) character, constitution. *Cf.* **umba, umbile.**

maume *pl.* manly deeds, strength, prowess. *Cf.* [1]**ume.**

maumivu *pl.* *see* **umivu.**

maundifu *pl.:* **maji –.** flood, tidal wave.

maungo *pl.* body, limbs, extremities. *Cf.* [2]**unga**, [2]**ungo.**

maunzi *pl.* building, construction, erection. *Cf.* [1]**unda.**

mauti* (–) death. – **yalimfika njiani** *or* **alifikwa na – njiani.** Death overtook him on the way. **dhambi ya –.** *rel.* mortal sin. *Cf.* **maiti.**

mauzauza (–) 1. trick(s), deception, illusion, juggling, legerdemain. 2. confusion, bewilderment, embarrassment.

mava *pl.* *see* **mafa.**

mavalio *pl.* decoration, ornament, adornment, finery. *Cf.* **vaa.**

mavazi *pl.* clothing. *Cf.* **vaa.**

mavi *pl.* 1. waste, rubbish, trash. – **ya chuma.** slag. 2. dung, excrement. *prov.* – **ya kale hayanuki.** The bad part of the past is forgotten. (*lit.:* the offal of the past does not smell.) 3. *a coarse term of abuse or contempt:* rot, humbug. *Cf.* **mawe.**

mavilio *pl.* stoppage, cessation, stagnation. – **ya damu.** *med.* bruises, contusions. *Cf.* **via.**

mavu (–) hornet. (= **nyigu.**)

mavukizo *pl.* *see* **mfukuto.**

mavunde, mavundevunde *pl.* 1. (scattered) clouds, overcast sky. 2. *see* **mavune.**

mavundevunde *pl.* *see* **mavunde.**

mavune (*rarely* **mavunde**) *pl.* 1. weariness, weakness. 2. stiffness *(of the joints).*

mavunga *pl.:* – **ya nywele.** thick, unkempt hair.

mavungu *pl.* what one has killed/caught when hunting, bag, catch. (= **mawindo.**)

mavuno *pl.* 1. harvest, harvesttime, crop. 2. *fig.* gain, profit, proceeds. *Cf.* **vuna.**

mavurugano *pl.* 1. unrest, confusion. 2. disagreement, misunderstanding, difference of opinion. *Cf.* **vuruga.**

mavurugo *pl.* confusion, mess. *Cf.* **vuruga.**

mavuzi *pl.* body hair *(armpits, genitals).* – **ya kwapa.** hair in the armpits. *Cf.* **vuzi, uvuzi.**

mawaidha (–) *see* **mauidha.**

mawakili* *pl.* agency. – **wa kutoa habari.** news agency. *Cf.* **wakili.**

mawazo *pl.* *see* **wazo.**

mawe 1. (*pl. of* **jiwe**) stones, stonework. 2. (– **ya mizani**) weights *(of scales).* 3. *fig.* nonsense, foolishness.

[1]**mawele** *pl.* mawele (kind of millet, *Penicillaria spicata or Pennisetum malacochaete).* *Cf.* [2]**mwele**, [1]**uwele.**

[2]**mawele** *pl., arch.* milk. (= [2]**maziwa.**)

maweo *pl.* *see* **maawio.**

mawese *pl.* palm oil *(from the seeds of the* **mchikichi** *palm).*

mawimbi *pl.* breakers, surf. *Cf.* [1]**wimbi.**

mawindo *pl.* bag, catch *(in hunting).* *Cf.* [2]**winda, uwindo.**

mawingu *pl.* clouds. **kumefanya —.** It is cloudy. *Cf.* **wingu.**

mayiti* (–) *see* **maiti.**

mayonzi *pl.* *see* **majonzi.**

mayowe *pl.* *see* **yowe.**

mayugwa *pl.* leaves of the taro *(used as a vegetable).* *Cf.* **myugwa.**

mayungiyungi *pl.* 1. water lily. 2. honeycomb (= **kamba ya asali, masega, mazana**).

mazao *pl.* 1. produce, offspring. 2. profit, gain. 3. *math.* product *(of multiplication).* 4. result, consequence. **taabu anayopata ni – ya upuuzi wake.** The difficulties that he has are the result of his folly. *Cf.* **zaa, zao.**

mazeka* [*Germ.* Musiker?] (**mi-**) trumpeter, horn player, bugler.

mazeruzeru *pl.* *see* **zeruzeru.**

maziada *pl.* *see* **ziada.**

maziga *pl.* 1. vessel for burning incense, censer. 2. earthenware dish/pot. *Cf.* **ziga.**

mazigazi *pl.* optical illusion, mirage. (= **mangazimbwe.**)

maziko *pl.* 1. burial, interment. 2. graveyard, cemetery. 3. funeral service. *Cf.* **zika.**

mazimbwezimbwe *pl.* 1. *rare* darkness. 2. dark/gloomy weather. 3. *fig.* dullness, stupidity.

mazingaombwe, mazingaumbo *pl.* 1. trick, illusion, cheating *(in games).* 2. witchcraft, magic.

mazingaumbo *pl.* *see* **mazingaombwe.**

mazingazinga *pl.* 1. turn, revolution; rounds *(of a policeman, etc.).* 2. deception, misleading. *Cf.* **zinga.**

mazingira, mazingo *pl.* environment, surroundings. *Cf.* **zinga.**

mazingiwa, mazingo *pl.* siege, blockade. *Cf.* **zinga.**

mazingo *pl.* 1. *see* **mazingira.** 2. = **mazingiwa.** 3. circumstances, conditions. *Cf.* **zinga.**

mazishi *pl.* 1. preparations for a burial. 2. articles used in a burial. *Cf.* **zika.**

[1]**maziwa** *pl.* *see* **masiwa.**

[2]**maziwa** *pl.* milk, dairy products. – **mabichi/ya robu.** curdled milk. – **ya kopo.** condensed milk. – **matupu.** powdered milk. *Cf.* [2]**ziwa.**

mazoea *pl.* 1. habit, custom, usage, practice. 2. conduct, behavior. *Cf.* [1]**zoea.**

mazoezi, mazoezo *pl.* exercise, practice, training, experience. *Cf.* [1]**zoea.**

mazoezo *pl.* *see* **mazoezi.**

mazu* *pl.* mazu (variety of banana).

mazua* (–) *see* **masua.**

mazuka *pl.* apparition, ghost. *Cf.* **zua,** [1]**zuka.**

mazunguko *pl.* 1. circular movement, turn, rotation, revolution. 2. round *(of a sentry, policeman, etc.).* *Cf.* **zungua.**

mazungumzo *pl.* 1. conversation, chat, discussion. 2. amusement, pastime. *Cf.* **zungumza, zungumzo.**

mba (–) 1. *med.* acne. 2. dandruff.

mbaa (–) *see* **mbala.**

mbaamwezi (–) *see* **mbalamwezi.**

mbaazi (mi-) *bot.* 1. plant bearing a variety of pea *(Cajanus indicus).* 2. (–) peas from this plant.

mbacha (mi-) old, worn-out mat.

mbadhiri*, mbadhirifu (wa-) swindler, cheat; extravagant person, spendthrift. *Cf.* **badhiri.**

mbadhirifu* (wa-) *see* **mbadhiri.**

mbadilishaji (wa-) changeable/fickle/whimsical/shifty person; *(comm.)* revisionist. *Cf.* **badili, ubadilishaji.**

mbafu be uncouth/unmannerly/stupid.

mbago: enda –. go separately, avoid each other's company, be at outs.

mbaguzi (wa-) racialist, racist. *Cf.* **mbago.**

mbahili* (wa-) *see* **bahili.**

mbala, mbaa (–) *zool.* mbala (species of antelope, bushbuck). (= **mbawala.**)

mbalamwezi, mbaramwezi, mbaamwezi, balamwezi (–) 1. moonlight. 2. full moon.

mbalanga*, balanga (–) *med.* mbalanga (a skin disease). – **nyeupe (nyeusi).** white(black) mbalanga.

mbalasi* (mi-) *see* **balasi.**

[1]**mbale** *pl. of* **ubale.**

[2]**mbale** (mi-) *augment. of* ubale *(smaller than* bale).

mbalehe* (wa-) *see* **balehe.**

mbali 1. *adv.* far, distant, remote; at/from a distance; *(fig.)* aloof. – ya... far from... **Said na mimi tunakaa –.** Said and I live far away from each other. **nilimwona kwa –.** I saw him from a distance. 2. *adv.* long since, for a long time. **niliyajua mambo haya –.** I have known about this matter for a long time. 3. *adv.* *(with the appl. form of v.)* completely, entirely, utterly. **ulia –.** kill outright. 4. *adj.* (*also* **mbalimbali**) separate, different. *Cf.* **umbali.**

mbalimbali *adj.* different, various. *Cf.* **mbali.**

mbalungi* [*Pers.*] (mi-) *bot.* grapefruit tree. *Cf.* **balungi.**

[1]**mbamba** (mi-) *bot.* mbamba (poisonous plant, spurge: *Euphorbia abyssinica*).

[2]**mbamba** (mi-) spade, shovel. *Cf.* [3]**bamba.**

mbambakofi (mi-) *bot.* magnolia tree *(Afzelia quanzensis).*

mbambangoma (–) *bot.* mbambangoma (a shrub with long spines).

mbamia* (mi-) *bot.* okra plant. *Cf.* **bamia.**

mbandarini* [*Pers.*] (wa-) dock worker, longshoreman. (= **kuli.**) *Cf.* **bandari.**

mbande (–) *rare* neap tide. (= **maji mafu.**)

mbandiko (mi-) 1. pasting, gluing; application. 2. something applied/stuck/pasted *(a plaster, etc.).* *Cf.* **bandika.**

mbanduko (mi-) 1. (act of) pulling off, removing. 2. *fig.* decrease; abolition, annulment. *Cf.* **bandika.**

mbangi* (mi-) *see* **bangi.**

[1]**mbango** (–) wild pig, warthog (= **ngiri**).

[2]**mbango** (–) *sl.* money.

mbanjo (mi-) 1. (act of) breaking up, tearing down. 2. damage, injury. 3. *auto.* breakdown. *Cf.* **banja.**

mbano (mi-) 1. (act of) pressing, squeezing. 2. *fig.* pressure, tension; effort, exertion *(physical or mental).* 3. (*also* **kibano**) tongs, pincers, tweezers. 4. hand vise. *Cf.* **bana.**

[1]**mbao** (mi-) *see* **bao.**

[2]**mbao** *pl. of* **ubao.**

mbaraka (mi-) *see* **baraka.**

mbaramba (–) *see* **mramba.**

mbaramwezi (mi-) *see* **mbalamwezi.**

mbarango (mi-) stick, club.

mbarapi (–) *zool.* mbarapi (sable antelope).

mbari (–) *rare* family, clan, tribe.

mbarika (mi-) *bot.* castor-oil plant *(Ricinus communis).* **mbono/kokwa ya –.** seed of the castor-oil plant. **mafuta ya –.** castor oil.

mbaruti (mi-) *bot.* Mexican poppy *(Argemone mexicana).*

mbashiri* (wa-) 1. messenger, one who brings news. 2. prophet. **– dini.** commentator *(on religious matters).* 3. soothsayer, fortune-teller. *Cf.* **bashiri.**

mbasua* (–) 1. spell of dizziness. 2. madness, insanity, mental aberration. *Cf.* **basua, masua.**

mbata (–) fully ripe coconut.

mbati *pl. of* **²uwati.**

mbatilifu* (wa-) one who declares something to be invalid/ineffective. *Cf.* **batili.**

mbatizaji* [*Engl.*] (wa-) one who baptizes. **Mtakatifu Johana Mbatizaji.** St. John the Baptist. *Cf.* **batiza.**

¹mbau (mi-) *see* **bao.**

²mbau *pl. of* **ubao, ubau.**

¹mbavu *pl. of* **ubavu.**

²mbavu (ma-) *see* **¹bavu.**

mbawa *pl. of* **ubawa.**

mbawala, mbawara (–) *zool.* mbawala (kind of antelope, bushbuck). (= **mbala.**)

mbawara (–) *see* **mbawala.**

mbawawa (–) mbawawa (kind of fish).

mbayana* 1. (wa-) well-known/famous person. 2. *adj.* evident, apparent, obvious, well-known. 3. *adv. see* **¹bayana.** *Cf.* **baina, baini, ¹bayana.**

mbayuwayu* [*Pers.*] *ornith.* swallow, swift.

mbazazi* (wa-) *see* **bazazi.**

mbea 1. (wa-) (*also* **mmbea**) slanderer, gossip, talebearer, scandalmonger. 2. (mi-) slander, denunciation. 3. *adj.* false, untrue. *Cf.* **umbea, mmbea.**

mbega (–) mbega (species of monkey, *Colobus vellerosus).*

mbegu (–) 1. seed. **panda –.** sow. 2. germ, bud, shoot, seedling, cutting. 3. race, breed, species.

mbeja* [*Pers.*] (wa-) neat/well-dressed person, one who takes pride in his personal appearance. *Cf.* **ubeja.**

mbeko (–) *see* **mbeleko.**

mbele 1. (–) front. **– yangu.** in front of me. **– ya sheria.** before the law. *loc.* **mbeleni.** *coll.* genitals. 2. *adv.* before, in front, forward; further, beyond; earlier, previously, long ago; later, subsequently, in the future; on the other hand, on thecontrary. *Cf.* **umbele.**

mbeleko, mbeko, ubeleko, uweleko (–) (*also* **beleko, ma-**) mbeleko (cloth sling used for carrying children on the back). *Cf.* **eleka.**

mbelewele (–) *bot.* pollen.

Mbelgiji* [*Germ.?*] (wa-) a Belgian.

[1]**mbembe, mbembelezi, mbembezi** (wa-) 1. flatterer. 2. seducer, tempter. 3. flirt, coquette, immoral woman. *Cf.* **bemba.**

[2]**mbembe** (mi-) *coll.* hunger.

mbembelezi, mbembezi (wa-) *see* [1]**mbembe.**

mbenuko (mi-) roundness, curve, bulge. *Cf.* **benua.**

mbepari* (wa-) *comm.* bourgeois. **wadoezi wa wabepari.** bourgeois hangers-on. *Cf.* **bepari, kibepari, ubepari.**

mbezi (wa-) presumptuous/arrogant/conceited person. *Cf.* **beza.**

mbibo* [*Port.*] (mi-) cashew apple tree (*Anacardium occidentale*). *Cf.* **bibo.**

mbigili, mbigiri (mi-) mbigili (species of thorny shrub, *Tribulus terrestris*).

mbiginyo (mi-) humiliation.

mbigiri (mi-) *see* **mbigili.**

mbiha (mi-) mbiha (a perennial plant, *Abutilum zanzibaricum*).

mbili two. **nyumba –.** two houses. **mara –.** twice. **mbili-tatu.** two or three, several. *Cf.* **wili.**

mbilikimo* (–) 1. dwarf, gnome. 2. pygmy.

mbilimbi, mbirimbi (mi-) cucumber tree (*Averrhoa bilimbi*).

mbilingani* [*Pers.*] (mi-) eggplant (*Solanum melongena*). *Cf.* **bilingani.**

mbinda* [*Ind.*] (mi-) okra, lady's finger (*Hibiscus esculentus*). (= **mbamia.**)

mbingu (*plur. of* **uwingu**) 1. sky, heaven. 2. clouds, cloudiness. 3. *rare* darkness.

mbini* (wa-) 1. blacksmith. 2. forger, counterfeiter. *Cf.* **bini.**

mbinja (*plur. of* **ubinja**) whistle, whistling.

mbinu (–) 1. roundness, curvature. **– ya mkono (mguu).** well-shaped arm (leg). 2. pressure, arm-twisting. 3. trickery, distortion. **fuata –.** follow suit. *Cf.* **benua.**

[1]**mbio** 1. (–) (act of) running, race. **piga/enda –.** to run. 2. *adv.* (*also* **mbiombio**) very fast, in haste, at full speed.

[2]**mbio** (–) mbio (kind of cassava).

mbiomba (–) *rare* maternal aunt. (= **mama mkubwa/mdogo.**)

mbirambi* (–) *see* **rambirambi.**

mbirimbi (mi-) *see* **mbilimbi.**

[1]**mbishi** (wa-) 1. stubborn/obstinate person. 2. argumentative/contentious/cavilling person. 3. mocker, scoffer. *Cf.* **bisha.**

[2]**mbishi** *pl. of* **ubishi.**

mbisho (mi-) *see* **bisho.**

mbisi* (mi-) *see* **bisi.**

mbiu (–) 1. buffalo horn. 2. announcement, proclamation *(to which attention was formerly called by blowing a buffalo horn).* **piga –.** blow the buffalo horn, make an announcement.

mbiya (–) cutting, seedling: **tia –.** transplant seedlings.

[1]**mbizi** (–) dive, diving. **piga –.** to dive. **maji ya –.** deep water. *sport* fancy diving.

[2]**mbizi** (–) mbizi (kind of bird).

mbobo (–) 1. abundance, excess, superfluity. 2. fertility. 3. cheapness.

mboga 1. (–) mboga (large pumpkin, *Cucurbita moschata).* 2. (*also* **mbogamboga,** –) vegetable *(of any kind).* **– ya pwani.** purslane.

mbogamboga (–) *see* **mboga.**

mbogo (–) buffalo (= **nyati.**)

mboji (–) soil moisture.

mbokora (–) beer calabash *(with a narrow neck).*

mbolea (–) 1. manure, fertilizer. 2. richness *(of soil).*

mbomoko (mi-) *see* **bomoko.**

mbomoshi (wa-) 1. one who destroys/ruins. 2. *rec., pol.* revolutionist, radical. *Cf.* **bomoa.**

mbona *interrog.* why? for what reason? *(more polite than* **kwa nini). – umekawia kuja?** Why are you late?

mboni (–) 1. (*also* **– ya jicho**) *anat.* eyeball, pupil. 2. *fig.* something precious, the apple of one's eye. 3. a lost thing, missing person. **mtumwa wa –.** a missing slave. 4. reward for finding a lost object. *Cf.* **ona.**

[1]**mbono** (mi-) mbono (castor-oil plant, *Ricinus communis).* **mafuta ya –.** castor oil. *Cf.* **ubono,** [2]**nyonyo.**

[2]**mbono** (*pl. of* **ubono**) seeds of the castor-oil plant.

mboo, mboro (mi-) *anat., vulg.* penis. (= **dhakari, uume.**)

mboro (mi-) *see* **mboo.**

mboza (mi-) mboza (kind of tree, *Sterculia cinerea).*

mbu (–) mosquito.

mbuai *adj., rare* wild, brutal. **mnyama –.** wild animal. *Cf.* [3]**ua, mwuaji.**

mbuga (—) savannah, steppe, grassland.

mbuge (wa-) a person who is constantly eating. *Cf.* **bugia, ubuge.**

mbugi (—) small bells *(fastened to the legs of children or dancers).*

1mbugu (mi-) mbugu (climbing plant, rubber liana). *Cf.* **1mbungo.**

2mbugu *pl. of* **ubugu.**

mbuguma (—) cow that has calved.

mbuji (wa-) *see* **mmbuji.**

Mbuki (wa-) a Malagasy. *Cf.* **1Buki.**

mbukulia, mbukuzi (wa-) chatterbox, gossip, scandalmonger. *Cf.* **bukua.**

mbukuzi (wa-) *see* **mbukulia.**

mbulia (mi-) mbulia (a wild shrub).

mbulu, mbulukwa (wa-) insane/feeble-minded person.

mbulukwa (wa-) *see* **mbulu.**

mbungati (mi-) mbungati ('sausage tree,' *Kigelia pinnata).*

mbunge (ma-) member of parliament. *Cf.* **bunge.**

1mbungo (mi-) rubber liana *(Landolphia florida).*

2mbungo, mbung'o (—) tsetse fly. (= **chafuo.**)

mbung'o (—) *see* **2mbungo.**

mbungu (—) *zool.* mbungu (species of antelope, eland.) (= **1mpofu.**)

1mbuni* (mi-) coffee bush. *Cf.* **1buni.**

2mbuni* (—) *zool.* ostrich.

3mbuni* (wa-) 1. organizer. 2. inventor; author. *Cf.* **2buni.**

mbura (mi-) mbura (kind of tree with yellow blossoms, *Parinarium curatellaefolium).*

mburuga (mi-) magic for identifying a wrong-doer *(by use of the* **bao,** *q.v.).*

mburugo (mi-) 1. mixing, mixture. 2. *fig.* confusion, disorder, jumble. *Cf.* **buruga.**

mburukenge (—) *zool.* monitor lizard. (= **kenge.**)

mburuzo, mbuuzo (mi-) 1. pulling, dragging. 2. trace, track, mark. — **wa nyoka.** track of a snake. *Cf.* **burura.**

mbuuzo (mi-) *see* **mburuzo.**

mbuya (—) 1. concubine, mistress. 2. prostitute.

mbuyu (mi-) baobab, calabash tree *(Adansonia digitata). Cf.* **buyu, ubuyu.**

mbuzi (—) 1. goat. — **mwitu.** ibex, klipspringer. 2. coconut grater.

mbwa (–) dog. – **wa mwitu.** jackal. – **koko.** wild dog; *(fig.)* bastard. – **ya kuwinda.** hunting dog. *Cf.* **jibwa, kijibwa.**

mbwago (mi-) 1. fall, collapse, slump. – **wa bei.** drop in price. 2. falling off, subsiding *(of interest, etc.).* *Cf.* **bwaga.**

mbwanda (mi-) sword-bean (= **mwingasiafu**). **kula –.** *fig.* be successful, get what one wants, rejoice.

mbwe (–) 1. small stone, pebble. 2. gravel. *Cf.* **jiwe.**

mbwedu 1. (wa-) an unpleasant/dirty/disgusting/malicious person. 2. (mi-) a disgusting/repulsive thing.

mbweha (–) jackal *(Canis mesomelas).* (= **bweha.**)

mbweko (mi-) bark(ing) *(of dogs).* *Cf.* **bweka.**

mbwende (–) mbwende (apron of beads worn by women beneath their normal clothing).

mbweu (–) belch(ing). **piga –.** to belch.

mbwoji (mi-) spring (of water); spout, fountain.

mcha, mchaji (wa-): – **Mungu.** *rel.* a God-fearing person. *Cf.* [2]**cha.**

mchachatochachato (–) slow, deliberate gait.

mchafuko (mi-) 1. something dirty/filthy. 2. disorder, confusion; *(pol.)* crisis. – **wa kilimwengu.** international crisis. 3. breakers, surf. *Cf.* **chafua.**

mchafuzi (wa-) person who creates confusion/disorder; *(pol.)* diversionist, saboteur. *Cf.* **chafua.**

mchago (mi-) *see* [1]**chago.**

mchagua (wa-): *prov.* – **jembe si mkulima.** A poor workman blames his tools. *Cf.* **chagua.**

mchaguo (mi-) choice, selection. *Cf.* **chagua.**

mchaguzi (wa-) 1. fastidious/exacting person. 2. *pol.* voter, elector. *Cf.* **chagua.**

mchai* (mi-) *bot.* 1. tea-plant *(Thea sinensis).* *Cf.* **chai.** 2. lemon grass *(Andropogon citriodorus).*

mchaji (wa-) *see* **mcha.**

mchakacho (mi-) 1. crushing, pounding, pulverizing. 2. crackling, rustling. *Cf.* **chakacha.**

mchakuro (mi-) 1. scratching, scribbling, scrawl; scratch, laceration. 2. *fig.* careful scrutiny, investigation, revision. *Cf.* **chakura.**

mchamvya (mi-) mchamvya (tree with edible fruit, *Pachystela Sacleuxii).* (= **mchocha.**)

mchana *sing.* 1. day. – **kutwa (kuchwa).** the whole day. 2. daytime. – **mdogo.** midday *(period preceding and following noon).* **chakula cha –.** midday meal. 3. daylight.

mchanga *sing.* 1. sand. – **mnene (mwembamba).** coarse (fine) sand. **chembe ya –.** grain of sand. 2. dust, powder. **sukari –.** granulated sugar. *Cf.* [1]**uchanga.**

mchanganuo (mi-) analysis. *Cf.* [1]**changa.**

mchanganyaji (wa-) 1. one who mixes or compounds something. 2.: – **dawa.** druggist, pharmacist. *Cf.* [1]**changa.**

mchanganyiko (mi-) mixture. *Cf.* [1]**changa.**

mchanganyo (mi-) 1. confusion. 2. forgery, imitation. *Cf.* [1]**changa.**

[1]**mchango** (mi-) intestinal worm, maw-worm. (= [2]**chango.**)

[2]**mchango** (mi-) 1. payment, deposit; contribution. 2. collection *(of money); (fin.)* fund. – **wa Kitaifa.** National Provident Fund. 3. *mil.:* – **wa askari.** recruitment of soldiers. *Cf.* [1]**changa.**

mchanjo (mi-) 1. cutting, lopping *(of branches).* 2. cut, wound. 3. *med.* vaccination. *Cf.* [2]**chanja, chanjo.**

mchanyato (mi-) mchanyato (a dish consisting of bananas and manioc). *Cf.* **chanyata.**

mchapa: – **maji.** (wa-) *coll.* drinker. *Cf.* [3]**chapa.**

mchapaji*, mchapishaji (wa-) printer, publisher. *Cf.* [1]**chapa.**

mchapishaji (wa-) *see* **mchapaji.**

mchapo (mi-) 1. blow, cut *(with a whip).* 2. whip. *Cf.* [1]**chapa.**

mchawi (wa-) magician, sorcerer, wizard. *Cf.* **uchawi.**

mche (mi-) 1. seedling, cutting, slip. 2. *fig.* descendant, offspring.

mchea, mcheaji (wa-) timid/timorous person. *Cf.* [2]**cha.**

mcheaji (wa-) *see* **mchea.**

[1]**mcheche** (mi-) spine, quill *(of a porcupine).*

[2]**mcheche** (mi-) spark. (= [1]**cheche.**)

mchegamo (mi-) mat placed under the head of a corpse. *Cf.* **egama.**

mchekecho (mi-) sifting. *Cf.* **chekecha.**

mchekele (mi-) wild olive tree. *Cf.* **mzeituni.**

mchekeshaji (wa-) *see* **mchekeshi.**

mchekeshi, mchekeshaji (wa-) jolly/amusing person, joker, wag, clown. *Cf.* [1]**cheka.**

mcheko (mi-) (manner of) laughing, laughter. *Cf.* [1]**cheka.**

mchele (mi-; *us. collec. sing.*) 1. (husked) rice. 2. (cleaned) grain *(in gen.).* – **wa mtama.** millet grain.

mchelea, mcheleaji (wa-) nervous person. *Cf.* [2]**cha.**

mcheleaji (wa-) *see* **mchelea.**

mchelema (mi-) watery manioc. *Cf.* **chelema.**

mchemko (mi-) *see* **chemko.**

mchengo (mi-) 1. mowing *(grain)*. 2. cutting, felling *(trees)*. *Cf.* **[1]chenga.**

mchenza (mi-) mandarin-orange tree *(Citrus nobilis)*. *Cf.* **chenza.**

mcheshi (wa-) pleasant/affable person. *Cf.* **[1]cheka, [1]cheshi.**

mcheza, mchezi; mchezaji (wa-) 1. player, athlete. **– gozi.** football player. 2.: **– wa michezo ya kuiga.** actor. 3.: **– ngoma.** dancer. **mcheza** *and* **mchezi** *are used generally and without special connotation;* **mchezaji,** *however, implies always that the person is especially skilled or a professional. Cf.* **cheza.**

mchezaji (wa-) *see* **mcheza.**

mchezi (wa-) *see* **mcheza.**

mchezo (mi-) 1. game. 2. sport. **– wa mpira.** football game. **– wa ngumi.** boxing match. 3. dance. 4. entertainment, amusement, fun. **anafanya haya kwa – tu.** He does this only for the fun of it. *Cf.* **cheza.**

mchi (**michi**) 1. pestle, pounding-pole. 2. (**– wa mashine**) piston.

mchicha (mi-) edible plant, spinach *(Amaranthus spinosus)*.

mchikichi (mi-) oil palm *(Elaeis guineensis)*. *Cf.* **mawese.**

mchikicho (mi-) seasoning, flavoring *(for foods)*.

mchimbaji, mchimbuzi (wa-) one who digs for a living: excavation/construction laborer; (**– wa madini**) miner, mine worker. **– dhahabu.** goldminer, gold-digger. *Cf.* **chimba.**

mchimbi, mchimvi, mtimvi (wa-) *arch.* unlucky person, person of ill omen *(one for whom an unfortunate life was foretold at his birth)*. *Cf.* **chimba, chimvi, uchimvi.**

mchimbuzi (wa-) *see* **mchimbaji.**

mchimvi (wa-) *see* **mchimbi.**

mchinja (wa-) *see* **mchinjaji.**

mchinjadamu (mi-) (kind of) banana.

mchinjaji, mchinja (wa-) 1. slaughterer, butcher. 2. executioner, hangman. 3. murderer. *Cf.* **chinja.**

mchinjiko (mi-) cord, rope *(made of the fibers of the baobab; used by nursing mothers to support the breasts)*.

mchinjo (mi-), **kichinjo** (vi-) slaughter, murder, massacre. *Cf.* **chinja.**

mchipukizi (wa-) handsome young woman. *Cf.* **chipua.**

mchiririko (mi-) drainage water *(from the eaves of a house)*. *Cf.* **chiririka.**

mchirizi, mkirizi (mi-) gutter, eaves, pipe, drainage ditch. *Cf.* **chiririka, chirizi.**

mchocha (mi-) mchocha (tree with edible fruit). (= **mchamvya.**)

mchocheaji (wa-) (*usually* – **moto**) stoker, fireman. *Cf.* **chocha.**

mchocheo, mchocho (mi-) 1. (act of) poking, stirring *(a fire)*; push, shove, kick. 2. *fig.* stimulus, impulse, instigation. *Cf.* **chocha.**

mchochezi (wa-) one who stirs up, excites, provokes; agitator. – **wa vita.** warmonger. *Cf.* **chocha.**

mchocho (mi-) *see* **mchocheo.**

mchochoni (mi-) mchochoni (variety of yam; poisonous, but eaten after the poison has been removed).

mchochoro (mi-) *see* **kichochoro.**

mchochota (mi-) *med.* itching dry scab. *Cf.* **chochota.**

mchokocho (mi-) irritation, vexation, annoyance. *Cf.* **chokoa.**

[1]**mchokochore** (mi-) mchokochore (kind of tree).

[2]**mchokochore** (mi-): – **dume** a weed.

mchokoo (mi-) pointed stick. *Cf.* **chokoa.**

mchokozi (wa-) inquisitive/obtrusive/annoying/troublesome person. *Cf.* **chokoa.**

[1]**mchoma:** – **moto** (wa-) stoker, fireman *(on a locomotive)*. *Cf.* [2]**choma.**

[2]**mchoma** (wa-) one who stabs. *Cf.* [1]**choma.**

mchomaji (wa-) arsonist, incendiary. *Cf.* [2]**choma.**

[1]**mchomo** (mi-) 1. (act of) burning. 2. *rare* cooking. *Cf.* [2]**choma.**

[2]**mchomo** (mi-) 1. irritation. 2. *med.* inflammation; (sharp, sudden) pain. 3. stab (wound). *Cf.* [1]**choma.**

mchongelezi (wa-) *see* **mchongezi.**

mchongezi, mchongelezi (wa-) 1. betrayer, talebearer, informer. 2. slanderer, scandalmonger. *Cf.* **chonga.**

mchongo (mi-), **chongo** (–) (act of) cutting, cut, notch. *Cf.* **chonga.**

mchongoma (mi-) mchongoma (thorny shrub, *Flacourtia indica)*.

mchoo (mi-) rainy season *(July to late September)*.

mchopozi (wa-) 1. thief. 2. miser, skinflint. *Cf.* **chopa.**

mchorachora (wa-) 1. poor writer, scrawler. 2. *(in gen.)* one who does something badly, botcher, bungler. *Cf.* [1]**chora.**

mchoraji (wa-) engraver. *Cf.* [1]**chora.**

mchoro (mi-) 1. scratching, inscribing. 2. engraving. 3. carving, sculpture. 4. tattooing. *Cf.* [1]**chora.**

mchorochoro (mi-) 1. scrawling, scribbling, illegible handwriting. 2. arabesque. *Cf.* [1]**chora.**

mchoroko (**mi-**) plant resembling the pea *(Phaseolus mungo)*.

mchoshi, mchovu (**wa-**) annoying/boring person. *Cf.* **¹choka.**

mchoto (**mi-**) small amount, pinch. *Cf.* **chota.**

mchovu (**wa-**) *see* **mchoshi.**

mchovya (**wa-**) a person who dips his finger into the food when eating. *Cf.* **chovya.**

mchovyo (**mi-**) hardening, tempering *(metals)*; plating. **dhahabu ya —.** gold-plating, gilding. *Cf.* **chovya.**

mchu (**michu**) mchu (species of mangrove, *(Avicennia marina)*.

mchukuzi (**wa-**) carrier, bearer, porter. *Cf.* **chukua.**

mchumba (**wa-**) 1. lover, sweetheart. 2. fiancé(e). *Cf.* **chumba, chumbisha, uchumba.**

mchumbururu (**mi-**) swordfish. (= **chuchunge.**)

mchunaji, mchuni (**wa-**) flayer, knacker. *Cf.* **chuna.**

¹mchunga (**wa-**) *see* **mchungaji.**

²mchunga (**mi-**) mchunga (a plant the leaves of which are cooked as a vegetable).

mchungaji (**wa-**) (*rare* **mchunga**) 1. herdsman, shepherd. 2. *fig.* leader; *(rel.)* pastor, priest. *Cf.* **²chunga.**

mchunguti (**mi-**) *see* **²msunguti.**

mchunguzi (**wa-**) 1. inquisitive/impudent person. 2. spy, scout. 3. observer, journalist. *Cf.* **¹chunga.**

mchungwa (**mi-**) orange tree. *Cf.* **chungwa.**

mchuni (**wa-**) *see* **mchunaji.**

mchuruzi (**wa-**) *see* **mchuuzi.**

mchuuzi, mchuruzi (**wa-**) retail merchant, shopkeeper. *Cf.* **²chuuza.**

mchuzi (**mi-**) soup, broth, gravy, sauce, curry. **kionja —.** small beard below the lip, imperial (lit.: 'gravy-taster').

mchwa (**—**) white ant, termite.

mdaa (**mi-**) mdaa (plant used for making a black dye, *Euclea multiflora)*. (= **msirisha.**)

mdaawa* 1. (**wa-**) *jur.* plaintiff, claimant. 2. (**mi-**) = **daawa, dai.** *Cf.* **daawa, dai.**

Mdachi* [*Germ.*] (**wa-**) *rare* a German. (= **Mjeremani.**) *Cf.* **²Dachi.**

mdadisi (**wa-**) inquisitive/impertinent person. *Cf.* **dadisi.**

mdago (**mi-**) mdago (a weed, *Adenium coetaneum)*.

mdahalo* (**mi-**) discussion, debate, exchange of views. *Cf.* **dahili.**

mdai* (wa-) 1. creditor. 2. *jur.* plaintiff, claimant. *Cf.* **dai.**

mdaiwa* (wa-) 1. debtor. 2. *jur.* defendant, accused. *Cf.* **dai.**

mdakale*, mdakali (mi-) stem of an opium pipe. *Cf.* **digali.**

mdakali* (mi-) *see* **mdakale.**

mdakizi, mdakuzi, mdukizi, mdaku 1. (wa-) eavesdropper, gossipmonger, talebearer, slanderer, informer. 2. (mi-) gossip, slander. *Cf.* **¹daka, dukiza.**

mdako (mi-) mdako (children's game played with pebbles). *Cf.* **¹daka.**

mdaku (wa-) *see* **mdakizi.**

mdakulizi (mi-) 1. slanderer, talebearer, informer. 2. someone who habitually contradicts or protests. *Cf.* **¹daka.**

mdakuzi (wa-) *see* **mdakizi.**

mdala (mi-) *dial.* bolt of cloth.

mdalahani* (mi-) *see* **mdarahani.**

mdalasini* (mi-) cinnamon tree *(Cinnamomum zeylanicum),* cinnamon (bark). *Cf.* **dalasini.**

mdambi (–) 1. savannah, grassland. 2. *bot.* heather *(Erica).*

mdanganyi, mdanganyifu (wa-) deceiver, cheat, swindler; traitor. *Cf.* **danganya, danganyifu.**

mdanganyifu (wa-) *see* **mdanganyi.**

mdanzi (mi-) (Seville) orange tree *(Citrus bigaradia).* *Cf.* **danzi.**

mdarabi* [*Pers.*] (mi-) rose-apple tree *(Eugenia jambosa).* *Cf.* **darabi.**

mdarahani*, mdalahani (mi-) mdarahani (soft silk fabric).

mdeke* (mi-) *see* **mdeki.**

mdeki*, mdeke (mi-) *mil.* ramrod.

mdele* (mi-) *see* **mdila.**

mdengu* (mi-) *bot.* lentil plant. *Cf.* **dengu.**

mdeni* (wa-), **maduyuni** (–) debtor. *Cf.* **deni.**

mdewere (mi-) *bot.* spinach.

mdhabidhabina* (wa-), **kidhabidhabina** (vi-) 1. liar, deceiver, cheat, swindler. 2. gossipmonger.

mdhaha*, msaha (–) mockery, joking, teasing.

mdhalimu* (wa-) 1. oppressor, tyrant, despot. 2. unjust/cruel person. *Cf.* **dhalimu.**

mdhamana* (wa-) *see* **mdhamini.**

mdhamini*, mdhamana (wa-) 1. guarantor, trustee, guardian, sponsor. 2. *rare* oppressor. *Cf.* **dhamini.**

mdhana* (–) 1. bad luck, misfortune, calamity. 2. bad omen. 3. thing or person supposed to bring bad luck/misfortune. 4. one who brings others under suspicion, talebearer, informer.

mdila* (mi-) coffeepot. (= **dele.**)

mdimu*, mndimu [*Ind.*] (mi-) lime tree *(Citrus aurantifolia). Cf.* **ndimu.**

mdiria (–) *ornith.* kingfisher.

mdirifu* (wa-) well-to-do person, someone who lives in easy circumstances.

mdodoki* (mi-) *bot.* luffa *(Luffa acutangula). Cf.* **dodoki.**

mdoea (wa-) *see* **mdoezi.**

mdoezi, mdoea, mdoya (wa-) 1. scout, spy. 2. *fig.* parasite, sponger. **wadoezi wa wabepari.** *comm.* bourgeois hangers-on. *Cf.* **doea, doya.**

mdogo (wa-) junior *(in age or rank).* **– wa waziri.** deputy minister. *Cf.* **dogo.**

mdomo (*rare* **mlomo**) (mi-) 1. lip. 2. mouth. **tia nyama mdomoni.** put meat in one's mouth. 3. beak *(of a bird).* 4. mouth of an animal *(snout, maw, etc.),* proboscis *(of an insect).* 5. opening, hole; nozzle, spout; mouthpiece *(of a wind instrument, etc.);* barrel *(of a gun).* **bunduki ya midomo miwili.** double-barrelled gun. 6. mouth of a river, estuary. *Cf.* **domo, kidomo.**

mdongea (mi-) mdongea (kind of shawl or wrap).

mdono (mi-) bite, biting *(of fish at bait). Cf.* **dona.**

mdoriani* (mi-) *see* **mduriani.**

mdoshi (mi-) treadle *(of a loom).*

mdoya (wa-) *see* **mdoezi.**

mduara* 1. *adj.* round, circular. 2. (mi-) *see* **duara.**

mdubira* (wa-) unlucky person, someone who is always unsuccessful.

[1]**mdudu*** (wa-) insect *(any small creeping or flying creature). Cf.* [1]**dudu, kidudu;** *also* **dude** (?).

[2]**mdudu** (mi-) mdudu (shrub with tuberous roots, rarely used for food; *Thylachium africanum).*

mdukizi (wa-) *see* **mdakizi.**

mdukuo (mi-) push, poke, blow, slap, box on the ear. *Cf.* **dukiza,** [1]**daka** (?).

mdumu (mi-) 1. pot, jug *(usually metal).* 2. tin can/box. (= [1]**dumu.**)

mdundo (mi-) 1. sound of a drum. 2. mdundo (kind of drum). *Cf.* **dunda.**

mdundugo (mi-) mdundugo (a charm or amulet supposed to make the wearer invulnerable).

mdunzidunzi (wa-), **dunzi** (ma-) 1. spy, detective. 2. prying person, busybody.

mduriani*, mdoriani [*Mal.*] breadfruit/durian tree *(Durio zibethinus).*

mdusi*, **mdusia** (wa-) parasite. *Cf.* **dusa.**

mea 1. sprout, germinate. 2. grow *(of the hair or fingernails)*. *appl.* **melea.** grow on...; *(intr.)* be overgrown. *caus.* **melesha.** *intr.* **meleka.** *Cf.* **kijimea, kimea, kimelea, mimea, mmea, mmelea.**

[1]**mechi*** [*Engl.*] (–) match, game. **– ya mpira.** football game.

[2]**mechi*** [*Engl.*] (–) *rare* match *(for lighting fires)*. (= **kibiriti.**)

medali* [*Engl.*] (–) medal.

[1]**mede*** (–) small bed/couch *(also used as a seat for guests)*.

[2]**mede*** (–) *sport* 1. goal, winning-post. 2. *rare* goal, point.

mega break off, divide up. **– kwa meno.** bite off. *appl.* **megea.** *intr.* **megeka.** *caus.* **megesha.** *Cf.* **mego, mmego.**

mego (ma-) piece; bite, morsel; slice *(of bread)*. *Cf.* **mega.**

meguka (*us. red.* **megukameguka**) be confused, disjointed, incompletely expressed, unintelligible. **kifungu hiki cha maneno ya sheria kilitafsiriwa na fundi mmoja lakini maana kamili ya kisheria haipo timamu bali imemegukameguka.** This section of law has been translated by an expert, but its true meaning is confused.

Mei* [*Engl.*] (month of) May.

meka 1. blaze/flame up, be red-hot, burn, glow. 2. be red; *(fig.)* turn red, be embarrassed. 3. (**mekameka**) glitter, sparkle.

mekanika* [*Engl.*] (–, ma-) mechanic, workman.

meko *pl. of* **jiko.**

melea *appl. of* **mea.**

meleka *intr. of* **mea.**

meli* [*Engl.* mail] (–) 1. steamship *(in gen.)*. **chumba cha –.** cabin. **ingia (pakia) –.** go on board. 2. cargo. 3. imported goods *(brought by ship)*. **mpunga wa –.** kind of imported rice.

melikora (–) variety of rice.

melimeli*, **melmeli** [*Ind.*] (–) melimeli (kind of thin fabric like muslin).

mema *pl.* goodness, good actions. *prov.:* **– na maovu ndio ulimwengu.** There are both good and evil in the world. *Cf.* [1]**ema.**

memba* [*Engl.*] (–) member.

membe (–) *ornith.* (species of) curlew *(Numenius phaeopus)*.

memeteka, memetuka, meremeta 1. shine, sparkle, glitter, twinkle; give off sparks. 2. *rare* rage, be furious. *Cf.* **umeme, memetuko.**

memetuka *see* **memeteka.**

memetuko (–) shining, glittering, sparkling, twinkling. *Cf.* **memeteka.**

memsahib* (–) *see* **mamsahib.**

mena 1. scorn, disdain, despise. 2. be rude/impertinent/insolent/impudent. *Cf.* **kimene.**

mende (–) 1. *zool.* cockroach. 2. *vulg.* one who practices sodomy.

meneja* [*Engl.*] (–) 1. manager, director, administrator. – **wa sinema.** movie director. 2. *sport* trainer.

mengi *see* **ingi.**

meno *pl. of* **jino.**

mentaa* (–) *see* **mentari.**

mentari*, **mentaa** (–) tweezers *(for depilation).*

menya 1. pull off, peel, husk. – **muhogo (viazi).** peel manioc (potatoes). – **mpunga.** husk rice. 2. beat, pound, pulverize.

menzili* (–) *see* **manzili.**

merekani*, **amerikani**, (–), **mrekani** (mi-) [*Engl.*] rough, unbleached cotton cloth, sheeting.

meremeta *see* **memeteka.**

merikebu* (–) ship, steamship *(always a vessel of European origin;* **chombo** = *native vessel;* **meli** = *steamship only).* *loc.* **merikebuni.** aboard. *Cf.* [1]**rakibu.**

mesenja* [*Engl.*] (–) messenger.

meski* (–) *see* **miski.**

meskiti* (–) *see* **msikiti.**

messi* [*Engl.*] (–) mess, board, dining-hall.

[1]**meta** 1. gleam, glitter, sparkle, shine. 2. *fig.* do very well at something, be successful. *appl.* **metea.** *intr.* **meteka.** *caus.* **metesha.** *Cf.* **kimeta, kimeti;** *also* **memeteka.**

[2]**meta*** [*Engl.*] (–) meter; cubic meter *(of wood, building stone).* **–a –.** metric. **kipimo cha –.** metric system.

methalan* *see* **mathalan.**

methali*, **mithali**, **misali** (–) symbol, emblem; parable, proverb. **tumia – katika mazungumzo.** use proverbs in a conversation. *Cf.* **mithili.**

[1]**meza*** [*Port.*] (–) 1. table. *loc.* **mezani.** dining room. *adv.* at table. 2. counter, (ticket) office/window *(bank, railroad station).* – **ya kuandikia.** (writing-)desk. **kitambaa cha –.** tablecloth. 3.: – **ya Bwana.** *rel.* altar rail.

[2]**meza** swallow (up), devour. *intr.* **mezeka.** *caus.* **mezesha.** *pass.* **mezwa.**

mfaa (mi-) mfaa (center piece of a door).

mfadhili* (wa-) benefactor, donor, contributor *(to a collection of money).* *Cf.* **fadhili.**

mfafanusi (wa-) draftsman, illustrator. *Cf.* **fafanua.**

mfagiaji (wa-) 1. street sweeper. 2. charwoman. *Cf.* **fagia.**

mfagio (mi-) *bot.* mfagio (plant similar to the mallow; used for making brooms: *Sida carpinifolia). Cf.* **fagia.**

mfalme (wa-) ruler, king. *Cf.* **kifalme, ufalme.**

mfano (mi-) 1. sample, model, pattern; *(liter.)* parable. **kama —.** similar, analogous. 2. example. **kwa —.** for example. 3. *liter.* style *(of writing). Cf.* **faa, fana, fanana.**

mfanya, mfanyi (wa-) 1. someone who performs an action or engages in an activity. **— kazi.** worker. **— kazi ya reli.** railroad worker. **— biashara.** businessman, merchant, trader. **— mambo ya magendo.** black-marketeer. **— hiana.** *pol.* renegade. 2. executor. 3. organizer. *Cf.* **faa.**

mfanyaji (wa-): **— kazi.** worker. **— kazi uchukuzi wa magari.** chauffeur. **— kazi wa relwe.** railroad worker. **— kazi wa shamba.** agricultural worker. *Cf.* **faa.**

mfanyi (wa-) *see* **mfanya.**

mfanyizaji (wa-): **— kazi.** worker. *Cf.* **faa.**

Mfaransa* (wa-) Frenchman. *Cf.* **Faransa, Kifaransa, Ufaransa.**

mfariji* (wa-) comforter, consoler. *Cf.* **fariji.**

mfarika* (wa-) young animal *(lamb, calf).*

mfariki*, mfaraka (wa-) lonely/solitary/abandoned person, one who separates himself from his home and relatives; refugee, dislocated person. *Cf.* **fariki.**

mfarishi* (mi-) mfarishi (kind of quilt or quilted mattress).

mfaruku* (wa-) a bereaved person. *Cf.* **fariki.**

mfasa (mi-) *bot.* mfasa (variety of grass with blue blossoms, *Veronica obconica).*

mfasiri* (wa-) 1. interpreter, commentator. 2. translator. *Cf.* **fasiri.**

mfeleji* (mi-) *see* **mfereji.**

mfenesi* (mi-) jack-fruit tree *(Artocarpus integra). Cf.* **fenesi.**

mfereji*, mfeleji (mi-) 1. ditch, sewer, trench, channel. **mifereji ya kutilia maji.** irrigation channels. 2. canal. **— wa Panama.** Panama Canal. 3. water-pipe, water-tap.

mfichachani (mi-) mfichachani (kind of banana).

mfichaji, mfichifichi (wa-) 1. secretive/reserved person. 2. sly/crafty person. *Cf.* **ficha.**

mfichifichi (wa-) *see* **mfichaji.**

mfidhuli* (wa-) 1. insolent/arrogant person. 2. boor, ruffian. *Cf.* **fidhuli.**

mfigili*, mfigiri (mi-) mfigili (species of radish plant, *Raphanus sativus). Cf.* **figili.**

mfiko (mi-) 1. extent, limit *(i.e., the distance that something will extend or can reach);* hence 2.: **— wa risasi.** *mil.* range *(of a bullet, etc.). Cf.* **fika.**

mfilisi* (wa-) 1. wasteful/extravagant person, spendthrift. 2. one who causes financial distress for another person, by legal or illegal means: distrainer, swindler, embezzler, etc. *Cf.* **filisi.**

mfilisika (wa-) ruined/impoverished/bankrupt person. *Cf.* **filisi.**

mfinyanzi (wa-) potter. *prov.:* – **hulia gae.** The potter commonly eats off potsherds. *Cf.* **finyanga.**

mfinyo (mi-) pinch(ing) *(with the fingers). Cf.* **finya.**

mfiraji* (wa-) sodomite, pederast. *Cf.* ²**fira.**

mfisadi* (wa-) *see* **fisadi.**

mfisha, mfishaji (wa-) 1. murderer. 2. fighter *(in a war). Cf.* **fa.**

mfishaji (wa-) *see* **mfisha.**

mfitini* (wa-) troublemaker, agitator. *Cf.* **fitini.**

mfiwa (wa-) orphan, bereaved person. *Cf.* **fa.**

mfiwi (mi-) *bot.* lima-bean plant *(Phaseolus lunatus). Cf.* **fiwi.**

mfo, mvo (mi-) 1. watercourse, stream, torrent. 2. channel/bed of a torrent. – **mkavu.** dry torrent bed.

mfoko (mi-) sudden rush *(of water, etc.),* torrent. *Cf.* **foka.**

mforsadi* (mi-) mulberry tree *(Morus alba). Cf.* **forosadi.**

mfu (wa-) dead body, corpse. (= **maiti.**) *Cf.* **fa.**

mfua 1. (mi-) (*also* **mfuo**) beating, striking, hammering. – **wa mawimbi.** surf, breakers. 2. (wa-) smith, metal-worker. – **dhahabu (fedha).** goldsmith (silversmith). 3.: – **nguo.** washerwoman. *Cf.* ¹**fua.**

mfuasi, mfuataji (wa-) 1. follower, adherent, partisan, disciple. 2. pursuer, persecutor. *Cf.* **fuata.**

mfuataji (wa-) *see* **mfuasi.**

mfuatano (mi-) 1. sequence, series. 2. retinue. *Cf.* **fuata.**

mfufu, mfuu (mi-) mfufu (tree with small edible berries). *Cf.* ²**fuu.**

mfufuaji, mfufuzi (wa-) one who brings back from the dead/revives/resuscitates. *Cf.* **fufua.**

mfufumaji (mi-) mfufumaji (kind of tree).

mfufuzi (wa-) *see* **mfufuaji.**

mfuga, mfugaji (wa-) 1. one who breeds and raises animals or poultry, cattle-breeder, poultry-raiser, *etc.* 2. one who tames, breaks in, or trains animals. *Cf.* **fuga.**

mfugaji (wa-) *see* **mfuga.**

mfugo 1. (mi-) breeding/raising/taming/training of animals. 2. domesticated animal. 3.: **mifugo.** flocks, herds, livestock. *Cf.* **fuga.**

mfujaji (wa-) 1. extravagant person, spendthrift. 2. lazy person, idler, good-for-nothing. 3. bungler, one who does his work badly. *Cf.* **fuja.**

mfuko (mi-) bag, purse; pocket. — **wa barua.** mailbag. — **wa mto.** pillowcase. — **wa kubebea.** carrying-case. *Cf.* [1]**fuko, kifuko.**

mfukuaji, mfukuzi (wa-) one who digs, miner. *Cf.* **fukia.**

mfukuto (mi-) steam, smoke, vapor. *Cf.* [1]**fuka.**

[1]**mfukuzi** (wa-) *see* **mfukuaji.**

[2]**mfukuzi** (wa-) one who banishes, persecutor. *Cf.* **fukuza.**

mfulilizo (mi-) *see* **mfululizo.**

mfulizo (mi-) 1. regular progression, sequence, succession, continuity. — **wa masomo.** a sequence/course of lessons. 2. series. *Cf.* **fuliza,** [1]**fua.**

mfululizo, mfulilizo (mi-) 1. = **mfulizo.** 2.: — **wa milima.** a range of mountains. **kwa —.** one after the other. *Cf.* **fuliza,** [1]**fua.**

mfuma, mfumi, mfumaji (wa-) weaver. *Cf.* [1]**fuma.**

mfumaji (wa-) *see* **mfuma.**

mfumba, mfumbaji (wa-) 1. magician. 2. someone who conceals/makes a secret of his activities. *Cf.* [1]**fumba.**

mfumbaji (wa-) *see* **mfumba.**

mfumbati (mi-) mfumbati (side-piece of a bedstead).

mfumbi (mi-) drainage ditch *(for rain water).*

mfumbua, mfumbuaji (wa-) 1. one who explains/clears up obscurities. 2. *fig.* translator. *Cf.* [1]**fumba.**

mfumbuaji (wa-) *see* **mfumbua.**

mfumi (wa-) 1. = **mfuma.** 2.: **kitanda cha —.** (weaver's) loom. *Cf.* [1]**fuma.**

[1]**mfumo** (mi-) 1. (act of) plaiting, weaving. 2. fabric, cloth. *Cf.* [1]**fuma.**

[2]**mfumo** (wa-) *see* **fumo.**

mfumua, mfumuaji (wa-) 1. spy, informer. 2. slanderer. *Cf.* [1]**fuma.**

mfumuaji (wa-) *see* **mfumua.**

mfundishaji (wa-) 1. = **fundi.** 2. *rare* trainer. *Cf.* [2]**funda.**

mfundo (mi-) 1. thickening, knot. 2. package, bundle. 3. *fig.* difficulty; grudge, malice, ill-humor. 4. *fig.* fad. *Cf.* [4]**funda, fundika.**

mfune, mgude (mi-) mfune (tree with whitish bark, *Sterculia appendiculata).*

mfunga (wa-) 1.: — **hesabu.** one who checks figures/audits accounts. 2. one who fasts. *Cf.* [1]**funga.**

mfungizo (mi-) 1. obstacle, impediment. 2. fastening up. 3. siege, blockade. *Cf.* [1]**funga.**

mfungo (mi-) 1. (act of) fastening/tying/closing. 2. conclusion. 3. tie, bond. 4. *rel.* fasting. *Cf.* [1]**funga.**

mfungua (wa-) one who opens/unfastens. *Cf.* [1]**funga.**

mfunguo (mi-) 1. loosening, unfastening. 2. release, liberation, rescue. 3. *rel.* end of fasting. *Cf.* [1]**funga.**

mfungwa (wa-) captive, prisoner. *Cf.* [1]**funga.**

mfuniko (mi-) 1. cover, lid. 2. case. 3. protection, shelter. *Cf.* **funika.**

mfunzaji (wa-) *see* **fundi.**

mfunzi (wa-) *see* **fundi.**

[1]**mfuo** (mi-) 1. = **mfua** 1. 2. bellows.

[2]**mfuo** (mi-) 1. line, stripe. **karatasi ya —.** lined/ruled paper. 2. furrow, groove, indentation, depression. 3. *rare* (kind of) drill, augur. *Cf.* [1]**fua.**

mfupa (mi-) bone. — **wa bega.** *anat.* collarbone, clavicle. *pl.* **mifupa.** skeleton. *Cf.* **ufupa.**

mfuradi* (mi-) verse, poem.

mfurahivu (wa-) happy/jovial person. *Cf.* **furaha, furahi, furahivu.**

mfure (mi-) wooden plate.

mfuria* (—) mfuria (kind of loose sleeveless coat).

mfurungu* (mi-) mfurungu (citron, shaddock, *Citrus medica). Cf.* [1]**furungu.**

mfuto (mi-) 1. (act of) wiping, cleaning. 2. erasing, obliteration. 3. removal, abolition. 4. a common/plain/inferior article of any kind. **mlango wa —.** a plain door *(without carving or ornamentation).* **mkeka wa —.** a plain/cheap mat. *Cf.* [1]**futa.**

mfuu (mi-) *see* **mfufu.**

mfyatuko (mi-) *see* **fyatuko.**

mfyeka (wa-) one who cuts down trees or clears land. *Cf.* **fyeka.**

mfyonza (mi-) sucking. — (*or* **kifyonza**) **vumbi.** vacuum cleaner. *Cf.* **fyonza.**

mfyozaji, mfyozi (wa-) rude/insolent person. *Cf.* **fyoa.**

mfyozi (wa-) *see* **mfyozaji.**

mfyuso (mi-) (kind of) net, trap. *Cf.* **fyata, fyusa.**

mgaagaa (wa-) restless/lazy person, vagrant. *Cf.* **gaagaa.**

mgahawa* (mi-) *see* **mkahawa.**

mgaidi* (ma-) *see* **²gaidi.**

mgambo (mi-) public proclamation, official announcement. *Cf.* **¹amba.**

¹mganda (mi-) mganda (kind of drum).

²mganda (mi-) bundle, bunch, sheaf *(of grain). Cf.* **ganda.**

mgandisho (mi-) *see* **mgando.**

mgando, mgandisho (mi-) 1. coagulation *(of milk, blood).* 2. hardening, thickening. *Cf.* **ganda.**

¹mganga, mganguzi (wa-) 1. *arch.* witch doctor. 2. *rec.* doctor, physician. *Cf.* **ganga.**

²mganga (mi-) mganga (a kind of shrub yielding a milky latex used as a fish-poison).

mgango (mi-) 1. binding up, splicing, mending. 2. cure, treatment. 3. healing, scarring over *(of wounds). Cf.* **ganga.**

mganguzi (wa-) *rare* *see* **¹mganga.**

mgao, mgawo (mi-) 1. division, distribution. 2. part, share. – **wa faida.** dividend. *Cf.* **gawa.**

mgaragazo (mi-) confusion, disorder. *Cf.* **gaagaa.**

mgawaji, mgawiaji (wa-): – **dawa.** pharmacist, druggist. *Cf.* **gawa.**

mgawanya, mgawanyi (wa-) one who divides or distributes. *Cf.* **gawa.**

mgawanyi (wa-) *see* **mgawanya.**

mgawanyiko (mi-) division, schism; *(comm.)* splittism. *Cf.* **gawa.**

mgawanyo (mi-) division, distribution. *Cf.* **gawa.**

mgawiaji (wa-) *see* **mgawaji.**

mgawo (mi-) *see* **mgao.**

mgema, mgemi (wa-) mgema (maker of palm wine). *prov.:* – **akisifiwa tembo hulitia maji.** If the maker of palm wine is praised for his wine, he adds water to it. *Cf.* **gema.**

mgemi (wa-) *see* **mgema.**

mgemo (mi-) 1. preparation of palm wine. 2. tapping of palms (to obtain the sap for preparing wine). *Cf.* **gema.**

mgeni (wa-) 1. stranger, foreigner. 2. guest, visitor. *Cf.* **geni.**

mgeuzo, geuzo (ma-) (*usually* **mageuzo**) change, alteration, transformation; innovation, reform. – **wa kidemokrasi.** democratic reform. *Cf.* **geua.**

mghafala* 1. (wa-) fool, simpleton. 2. (mi-) simplicity, artlessness; thoughtlessness, absent-mindedness, carelessness, negligence. *Cf.* **ghafula.**

mghalaba* (mi-) rivalry, competition. *Cf.* **ghilibu, ghiliba.**

mghani* (wa-) (professional) singer. *Cf.* **ghani.**

mgiligilani* (mi-) *bot.* coriander plant *(Coriandrum sativum).*

Mgiriki* [*Engl.*] (wa-) a Greek. *Cf.* **Kigiriki, Ugiriki.**

mgodi (mi-) (*usually loc. pl.* **migodini**) mine.

mgogoro (mi-) 1. obstacle, impediment. 2. difficulty, trouble, nuisance. 3. misunderstanding, problem.

mgomaji (wa-) one who goes on a strike, striker. *Cf.* **¹goma.**

¹mgomba (mi-) banana/plantain palm *(Musa sapientum).* *Cf.* **¹gomba, ugomba;** *also* **ndizi.**

²mgomba (wa-) *see* **mgomvi.**

mgombea, mgombeaji (wa-) candidate, applicant, competitor. – **uchaguzi.** candidate in an election. *Cf.* **²gomba.**

mgombeaji (wa-) *see* **mgombea.**

mgombezi (wa-) 1. faultfinder, carper. 2. grumbler, surly person. *Cf.* **²gomba.**

mgombi (wa-) *see* **mgomvi.**

mgomo (mi-) 1. diversion, feint. 2. sabotage, strike. – **baridi.** slow-down strike. *Cf.* **¹goma.**

mgomvi, mgombi, mgomba (wa-) quarrelsome person. *Cf.* **²gomba, ¹gomvi.**

mgongo (mi-) 1. back. 2. backbone, spine. **lala mgongoni.** lie on one's back. 3. hump *(on the back).* – **wa ngamia.** camel's hump. 4. ridge, crest *(hill, mountain).* *Cf.* **²gongo, jongo, kijongo.**

mgoni (wa-) adulterer. *Cf.* **gona.**

mgonjwa (wa-) sick person, patient. *Cf.* **gonjwa.**

mgono (mi-) mgono (fish-trap).

mgoto (mi-) (act or sound of) knocking, tapping, drumming; clap, bang. *Cf.* **gota.**

mgude (mi-) *see* **mfune.**

mgulabi* [*Pers.*] (mi-) mgulabi (litchi tree, *Nephelium lappasceum).* *Cf.* **gulabi.**

mgumba (wa-) 1. sterile person *(man or woman).* 2. solitary/lonely person. 3. something which does not serve its proper purpose *(because of its nature, inadequate treatment, etc.):* (green) wood that gives off smoke rather than heat; beans or maize that have not been completely cooked and are not fit to eat. *Cf.* **gumba.**

mgumio (mi-) *see* **gumio.**

mgunda (mi-) *rare* plantation. (= **shamba.**)

¹mgunga (wa-) a person who must abstain from something *(e.g., observe a diet).* *Cf.* **gunga.**

[2]**mgunga** (mi-) *bot.* (species of) acacia.

mgunguti (mi-) *bot.* (species of) acacia, mimosa.

mguno (mi-), **guno** (ma-) growling, grumbling, complaining, dissatisfaction. *Cf.* **guna.**

mguruguru (mi-) *see* [2]**guruguru.**

mguruka (mi-) *bot.* (species of) mimosa.

mguruti (mi-) *bot.* (species of) mimosa.

mguruto (mi-) (act of) pressing. *Cf.* **guruta.**

mguso (mi-) 1. (an act of) touching/contacting; touch, contact. 2. sense of touch. *Cf.* **gusa.**

mgutusho (mi-) 1. fright, astonishment, shock. 2. *fig.* (electric) shock. *Cf.* [1]**gutua.**

mguu (mi-) leg, foot. **enda kwa miguu.** go on foot. **shika miguu.** show respect, greet someone respectfully; be in a subordinate position. *loc.* **miguuni.** foot end of a bedstead. *Cf.* **guu, kiguu, mjiguu.**

mgwaru* [*Ind.*] (mi-) mgwaru (bean plant, *Cyamopsis psoraloides). Cf.* **gwaru.**

mgwisho (mi-) 1. tuft of horse hair. 2. fly switch.

Mhabeshi* (wa-), **Habeshi** (ma-) Abyssinian, Ethiopian. *Cf.* **Uhabeshi.**

Mhadimu* (wa-) one of the original inhabitants of Zanzibar. *Cf.* **hadimu.**

mhaini* (wa-) *see* **haini 2.**

mhajiri* (wa-) emigrant. *Cf.* **hajiri.**

mhali* (–) *see* **muḥali.**

mhamaji (wa-) *see* **mhamiaji.**

mhamiaji, mhamaji (wa-) immigrant, refugee. *Cf.* **hama.**

mhamishi (wa-) 1. homeless person. 2. nomad. 3. *rel., rare* pilgrim. *Cf.* **hama.**

mhanga (wa-) 1. animal killed as an offering. 2. *fig.* sacrifice.

mhanuni* (wa-) *see* **mhina.**

mharabu* (wa-) *see* **harabu.**

mharage* (mi-) *see* **mharagwe.**

mharagwe*, mharage, mharaji [*Pers.*] (mi-) mharagwe (variety of bean plant, *Phaseolus communis). Cf.* **haragwe.**

mharaji* (mi-) *see* **mharagwe.**

mharibifu* (wa-) *see* **harabu.**

mharita*, mwarita [*Ind.*] (mi-) soapberry tree *(Sapindus saponaria). Cf.* **harita.**

mharuma* (mi-) mharuma (colored woolen shawl, worn as a turban).

mhasi* (wa-) 1. castrated person or animal, gelding, eunuch (= **towashi, maksai**). 2. one who castrates. *Cf.* **hasi.**

Mhaya (Wa-) Haya (member of a tribe in Tanganyika).

mhenga (wa-) 1. an older person who instructs boys and girls in the initiation rites. 2. an elder who is a member of a native council. 3. *(in gen.)* one who can be relied on to give good advice.

mheshimiwa* (wa-) *title* excellency *(term of address for high officials and prominent persons, but still used for anyone deserving respect).* *Cf.* **heshimu.**

mhimili* 1. (wa-) patient/forbearing/long-suffering person. 2. (mi-) support: post, prop, beam, girder. **– wa dunia.** axis of the earth. *Cf.* **hamali.**

mhina*, mhanuni (mi-) henna plant *(Lawsonia inermis).* *Cf.* **hina.**

Mhindi*, Muhindi (wa-) Indian. **– mwekundu.** Red Indian, American Indian. *Cf.* [1]**Hindi, Kihindi, Uhindi.**

mhirabu* (mi-) mihrab (apse in a mosque, showing the direction toward Mecca).

mhisani* (wa-) benefactor. *Cf.* **hisani.**

Mhispania* [*Lat. ?*] (wa-) Spaniard.

mhitaji* (wa-) 1. petitioner. 2. applicant, candidate. 3. poor/needy person. *Cf.* **hitaji.**

mhogo* (mi-) *see* **muhogo.**

mhoro (mi-) mhoro (pointed stake in a pit for trapping game).

mhubiri* (wa-) 1. *rel.* preacher. 2. (political) speaker. *Cf.* **habari, hubiri.**

mhuni* (wa-) 1. hooligan, vandal. 2. vagabond, tramp. 3. traitor. 4. outlaw, outcast, pariah. *Cf.* **huni.**

mhunzi, muhunzi (wa-) craftsman who works in metal or stone. **– wa chuma.** blacksmith. **– wa mawe.** stonecutter. *Cf.* **uhunzi.**

mhuri* (mi-, –) *see* **muhuri.**

mia* hundred.

miaa *pl. of* **mwaa.**

miadi*, mihadi (–) promise *(to do something at a set time).* *Cf.* **ahadi.**

mialamu* (–), **mwalamu** (mi-) 1. edge, border. 2. seam, hem 3. stripe *(of color, in cloth).* *Cf.* **alama.**

miayo *pl.* yawn(ing). **piga (enda) –.** to yawn.

michezo *pl.* games, sport. *coll.* **kufanya –.** go in for sports. **– ya Olimpiki.** Olympic Games. *Cf.* **cheza.**

mifugo *pl.* flocks, herds, livestock. *Cf.* **fuga, mfugo.**

mifupa *pl.* skeleton. *Cf.* **mfupa.**

miguuni *see* **mguu.**

mihadi* (–) *see* **miadi.**

miiba *pl. of* **mwiba.**

mikaha* (–) *see* **nikaha.**

mikasi* *pl.* *see* **mkasi.**

mila* (–) usage, custom; tradition; religious prescription. **–a –.** customary, traditional.

milele* 1. *pl.* endlessness, infinity; *(rel.)* eternity. **maisha ya –.** life everlasting. 2.: **–a –.** *adj.* eternal, constant. 3. *adv.* always, constantly. **– na –.** forever. **yadumu – ...!** Long live ...! *Cf.* **umilele.**

milia 1. *pl. of* [2]**mlia.** 2. *adj.* striped. **punda –.** zebra.

[1]**miliki***, **tamalaki, tamaleki** 1. lead, conduct. 2. rule, govern. *appl.* **milikia.** *intr.* **milikika.** *caus.* **milikisha.** 3. (–) *see* **milki.** *Cf.* **malki, mamlaka.**

[2]**miliki*** (–) *see* **milki.**

milioni* [*Engl.*] (–) million.

milki*, **miliki** (–) 1. rule, dominion, power. 2. empire, kingdom. 3. property, prosperity. 4. *econ., rec.* asset(s). *Cf.* [1]**miliki, malki.**

mimba (–) 1. fruit, germ. **fanya –.** germinate, sprout. 2. embryo. 3. conception, pregnancy. **tia –.** fertilize, impregnate. **chukua (wa na, shika) –.** be pregnant. **haribu –.** procure abortion.

mimbari* (–) *rel.* pulpit.

mimea *pl.* vegetation. *Cf.* **mea, mmea.**

mimi *abs. pron. 1st pers. sing.* I, me. **– mwenyewe (nafsi yangu).** I myself. **wangu –.** my own.

mimina pour out, spill; pour in, fill. *appl.* **miminia.** *caus.* **miminisha.** *intr.* **miminika.** *fig.* be present in great number. **watu walimiminika katika mkutano.** There were crowds of people at the assembly. *Cf.* **miminiko.**

miminiko (ma-) 1. pouring out, overflowing. 2. *fig.* (super)abundance, profusion. 3. mold, casting. *Cf.* **mimina.**

min* *prep., rare* from, of. *Cf.* **minajili, minghairi** (*sub* **baghairi**), **mintarafu.**

minajili* 1. *prep.* without; except, apart from, because of, as a result of. 2. *conj.* because, since; so that, in order that, in order to. **kwa (ajili ya) minajili ya.** for the sake of. *Cf.* **min, ajili.**

mindi (–) *zool.* mindi (species of antelope, Abbott's duiker; *cf.* **funo**).

minenguo *pl.* minenguo (kind of dance).

minghairi* *see* **baghairi.**

minika fold, turn up *(the edge of cloth)*, hem.

mintarafu* *prep.* concerning, with regard to, as a result of. *Cf.* **min, tarafa.**

minteen* *see* **miteen.**

minya press, squeeze, crush. *Cf.* **finya.**

minyara (–) minyara (kind of tree, *Euphorbia tirucalli).*

minzani* (–) *see* **mizani.**

mio 1. *pl. of* **umio.** 2. **(ma-)** (*augment. of* **umio)** *anat.* larynx, throat, gullet *(e.g., of an animal).*

miongoni *loc. of* **¹mwongo.**

¹mirabaraba*: **–a –.** *adj.* checked, checkered. *Cf.* **¹mraba.**

²mirabaraba* *pl.* cellulose, synthetic fiber. *Cf.* **²mraba.**

mirathi* (–) 1. inheritance, legacy, bequest. 2. *leg.* division of a legacy. **masala ya –.** *rare* law of inheritance. *Cf.* **rithi.**

mirengu *pl.* *see* **mrengu.**

misa*, missa [*Lat.*] (–) *rel.* mass. **adhimisho la – takatifu.** celebration of the mass. **– ya kimya.** low mass. **– kubwa ya kiaskofu.** pontifical high mass. **– kubwa ya sherehe.** solemn high mass. **– ya wafu.** requiem mass.

misali* (–) *see* **methali.**

misheni* [*Engl.*] (–) 1. *rel.* mission. **skuli ya –.** missionary school. 2. (official) mission, detached service.

misili* (–) *see* **mithili.**

misioni* [*Engl.*] (–) mission, parish.

misitumisitu *red. pl. of* **msitu.**

miski*, meski (–) musk. **panya –.** muskrat.

Misri* Egypt. *Cf.* **Mmisri.**

missa* (–) *see* **misa.**

mita* [*Engl.*] (–) meter.

miteen*, minteen, miteni *arch.* two hundred.

miteni* *see* **miteen.**

mithali* (–) *see* **methali.**

mithili*, misili 1. (–) similarity, resemblance. 2. *adv.* similarly, like. **amekuja kimya kimya – ya mwizi.** He came stealthily like a thief. *Cf.* **madhali, mathalan, methali, mithilisha.**

mithilisha* compare. *Cf.* **mithili.**

miti (*pl. of* **¹mti)** framework *(of a house, etc.)*

mitu (–) *ornith.* Indian cockatoo.

miuja* (–) danger; misfortune, accident. *Cf.* **mauja.**

miungano *pl.* combination. **– ya namba mbalimbali.** combination of numbers. *Cf.* **²unga.**

miunzi *pl.* (*sing.* **mwunzi** *rare*) whistle. **piga –.** to whistle.

mivua *pl.* bellows. *Cf.* **vukuta, mvua.**

miwa *pl.* *see* **muwa.**

miwani* (–) (eye) glasses, spectacles. **– ya jua.** sunglasses.

miyaa *pl.* *see* **mwaa.**

miye *see* **mimi.**

mizani*, **minzani** (–) 1. balance, scales. *fig.* **– ya nguvu.** balance of forces. 2. pendulum, balance *(of a clock, watch).* 3. *astr.* (the constellation) Libra. *Cf.* **uzani.**

mizigo *pl.* baggage. *Cf.* **mzigo.**

mja (wa-) *rare* 1. newcomer, stranger. 2. foreigner. 3. *hist., liter.* slave. *Cf.* **ja.**

mjadala* 1. (wa-) opponent. 2. (mi-) *pol.* opposition.

mjafari* (mi-) mjafari (kind of tree, *Erythrina tomentosa).*

mjakazi (wa-) *liter.* female slave. *Cf.* **ja, mja 3.**

mjali (mi-) *see* **ujali.**

Mjampani (wa-) *see* **Mjapani.**

mjane (wa-) 1. solitary/lonely person. 2. unmarried person: bachelor, spinster. 3. widow, widower. *Cf.* **ujane.**

mjango (mi-) a fruitless/unsuccessful visit. *Cf.* **[1]janga.**

mjanja (wa-) deceiver, swindler. *Cf.* **janja.**

Mjapani*, **Mjampani** [*Engl.*] (–) a Japanese. *Cf.* **Kijapani.**

mjari*, **mjarari** (mi-) *see* **ujari.**

mjaribati* *adj.* *see* **jarabati.**

mjaribu* (wa-) person who tries out/tests something. **– wa ndege.** *av.* test pilot. *Cf.* **jaribu.**

mjasiri* (wa-) brave/daring/foolhardy person. *Cf.* **jasiri.**

mjasusi*, **mjasusu, jasusi** (wa-) 1. spy, traitor. 2. detective, plainclothesman. 3. inquisitive person. *Cf.* **jasisi.**

mjasusu* (wa-) *see* **mjasusi.**

mjeledi* (mi-) strap, whip. **piga/tia –.** to whip. *Cf.* **[1]jalidi.**

mjenga, mjengaji (wa-) *see* **mjenzi.**

mjengo (mi-) 1. (act of) building. 2. style/method of building. 3. structure, building. *Cf.* **jenga.**

mjenzi, mjengaji, mjenga (wa-) builder, architect. *Cf.* **jenga.**

Mjeremani*, **Mjerumani** [*Engl.*] (wa-) a German. *Cf.* **Kijeremani, Ujeremani.**

Mjerumani* (wa-) *see* **Mjeremani.**

[1]**mji** (mi-) 1. settlement. 2. village; town, city. **– mkuu.** capital (city). *Cf.* **kijiji.**

[2]**mji** (mi-) *anat.* 1. placenta, afterbirth. 2. (**–wa uzazi**) *rare* womb (= **tumbo** [**la uzazi**]).

mjiari*, **mi-** *see* **ujari.**

mjibu* (wa-) pleasant/affable person. *Cf.* **wajibu.**

mjiguu 1. (mi-) *augment. of* **mguu.** 2. (wa-) a person with very large feet.

mjiko (mi-) 1. *anat.* rectum. 2. *med.* hemorrhoids. *Cf.* [1]**jika.**

mjima (wa-) helpful person. *Cf.* **ujima.**

mjimbi (vi-) *see* [2]**jimbi.**

mjinga (wa-) stupid person, fool. *Cf.* **jinga.**

mjio (mi-) coming, arrival. *Cf.* **ja.**

mjisifu* (wa-) braggart, conceited person. *Cf.* **sifu, majisifu.**

mjoho* (mi-) mjoho (velvet apple tree).

mjohoro (mi-) mjohoro (ironwood tree, *Cassia siamea*).

mjoja, mjoo (mi-) 1. mjoja (kind of tree the wood of which is used for building boats). 2. a small boat similar to a canoe *(made of the wood of this tree)*.

mjoli* [*Ind.*] (wa-) *arch.* comrade, fellow-slave. *Cf.* **ujoli.**

mjomba (wa-) 1. (maternal) uncle. 2. uncle *(in gen.)*. 3. nephew, niece (child of one's sister). 4. polite term of address (for people of the older generation). 5. native of the Swahili-speaking area around Mombasa. *Cf.* **Kijomba, Ujomba.**

mjombakaka (–) mjombakaka (kind of large lizard).

mjombo (mi-) mjombo (kind of sea-fish).

mjoo (mi-) *see* **mjoja.**

mjuba* (wa-) 1. courageous person. 2. impatient/boisterous person. 3.: **moto huyu ni – sana.** This child is very ill-mannered/naughty. *Cf.* **ujuba.**

mjukuu (wa-) 1. grandchild. 2. *(in gen.)* relative (on the paternal side) of the second generation, e.g., grandnephew. *Cf.* **kijukuu.**

mjumbe (wa-) 1. messenger, envoy. 2. *pol., rec.* deputy, delegate, representative. **– wa serikali.** representative of the government, chief of state. *Cf.* **ujumbe;** *also* **jumbe, kijumbe.**

mjume* (wa-) 1. engraver, carver. 2. gunsmith. *Cf.* **mjumu, ujume.**

mjumu*, (mi-), **njumu** (–) *rare* inlay work, incrustation. *Cf.* **mjume.**

[1]**mjusi** (mi-) 1. lizard. 2. mjusi (lizard-shaped ornament on a kanzu).

[2]**mjusi** (mi-) nosebleed.

[3]mjusi (wa-) magician, astrologer. (= **mjuzi** ?)

mjuvi (wa-) presumptuous/impudent person. *Cf.* **[2]jua, juvi.**

mjuzi (wa-) connoisseur, expert. *Cf.* **[2]jua, ujuzi.**

[1]mkaa, mkaaji, mkazi (wa-) 1. inhabitant, resident. 2. *fig.* stay-at-home. *Cf.* **[1]kaa.**

[2]mkaa (mi-) mkaa (kind of tree the bark of which is used as a medicine).

mkaaji (wa-) *see* **[1]mkaa.**

mkabala* *adv.* 1. on the contrary. **– wa ...** facing, opposite, contrasting. 2. face to face. *Cf.* **kabili.**

mkabidhi* (wa-) 1. trustee, administrator, guardian. 2. frugal person, miser. *Cf.* **kabidhi.**

mkadamu* (wa-) *see* **kadamu.**

mkadi* (mi-) mkadi (kind of tree, screw pine, *Pandanus Kirkii/tectorius).*

mkagua, mkaguaji, mkaguzi (wa-) overseer, inspector. **– shamba.** farm inspector. **– wa hesabu.** comptroller. *Cf.* **kagua.**

mkaguaji (wa-) *see* **mkagua.**

mkaguo (mi-) examination, inspection. **– wa skuli.** inspection of a school. *Cf.* **kagua.**

mkaguzi (wa-) 1. = **mkagua.** 2. inspector; *(liter.)* reviewer. *Cf.* **kagua.**

mkahaba* (wa-) *see* **kahaba.**

mkahale* (mi-) pencil for applying kohl to the eyes. *Cf.* **kohl.**

mkahawa*, mgahawa (mi-) café, restaurant. *Cf.* **kahawa.**

mkaidi* (wa-) stubborn/argumentative person. *Cf.* **kaidi.**

mkaja (mi-) 1. bandage worn by women after childbirth. 2. gift given by the family of the bridegroom to the mother of the bride.

mkaka (mi-) mkaka (variety of rubber tree, *Acacia Verek).*

mkakamavu (wa-) sly/shifty person. *Cf.* **kakamavu.**

[1]mkakasi (mi-) (round) metal box with a lid *(for perfumes, cosmetics, etc.).*

[2]mkakasi (mi-) *see* **mkasasi.**

mkakaya* (mi-) mkakaya (kind of tree, royal poinciana, *Delonix regia).*

mkalamu* (mi-) *arch.* mkalamu (kind of reed or bamboo used for making pens). *Cf.* **kalamu.**

mkale (wa-) ancestor, forebear, ancient. *Cf.* **kale.**

mkalimana (mi-) mkalimana (kind of banana).

mkalimani* (wa-) interpreter. (= **mfasiri.**) *Cf.* **kalima, ukalimani.**

mkalimu* (wa-) *rare* teacher, educator. *Cf.* **kalima.**

mkalio (mi-) 1. gift given by the bridgegroom to the bride's attendants. 2. gift given by a young man to a girl's maternal uncle, who then presents it to the girl's father as evidence of a proposal of marriage. *Cf.* **¹kaa.**

mkamachuma (mi-) mkamachuma (kind of tree).

mkamasi (mi-) mkamasi (a fruit tree, *Cordia latifolia).*

¹mkamba (—) *med.* tracheal catarrh.

²mkamba (mi-) *see* **²kamba.**

mkambaa (mi-) *see* **mkambala.**

mkambala, mkambaa (mi-) mkambala (species of acacia).

mkamshe* (mi-) *see* **mkamshi.**

mkamshi*, mkamshe [*Ind.*] (mi-) wooden spoon/ladle.

mkana (wa-) one who denies/disavows. *rel.* — **Mungu.** atheist. *Cf.* **¹kana.**

mkanda (mi-) *rare* strap, belt. (= **ukanda.**)

mkandaa (mi-) variety of mangrove *(Ceriops candolliana).*

mkandaji (wa-) masseur. *Cf.* **³kanda.**

mkandamizo (mi-) press. — **wa maji maji.** hydraulic press. *Cf.* **³kanda.**

¹mkando (mi-) (act of) kneading, massaging; massage. *Cf.* **³kanda.**

²mkando (mi-) bar *(of gold, silver).*

mkangaja (mi-) (species of) orange tree. *Cf.* **¹kangaja.**

mkangazi (mi-) mahogany tree *(Khaya nyasica/senegalensis).*

mkanju* [*Ind.*] (mi-) mkanju (cashew apple tree, *Anacardium occidentale).* (= **mbibo, mkorosho.**) *Cf.* **kanju.**

¹mkano (mi-), **ukano** (—) *anat.* sinew, tendon.

²mkano (mi-) *see* **mkanyo.**

mkanya (wa-) one who rebukes/finds fault with other people. *Cf.* **¹kana.**

mkanyo, mkano (mi-), **kanyo** (ma-) 1. prohibition, refusal, repudiation. 2. rebuke, reproach, reprimand. *Cf.* **¹kana.**

mkapitalisti* [*Engl.*] (wa-) capitalist. *Cf.* **ukapitalisti.**

mkarabaka (mi-) mkarabaka (kind of tree, *Encephalartos villosus*).

mkarafuu* (mi-) clove tree. *Cf.* **karafuu.** — **maiti.** camphor tree. *Cf.* **kafuri.**

¹mkaragazo (mi-) downpour of rain, heavy shower.

²mkaragazo (mi-) an inferior quality of tobacco.

mkarakala (mi-) *see* **mtututu.**

mkarati, mkuruti (mi-) mkarati (kind of tree, *Baphia Kirkii*).

mkaribishaji* (wa-) hospitable/generous person. (= **mkarimu.**) *Cf.* **karibia.**

mkarimu* (wa-) host, hospitable person. *Cf.* **¹kirimu, karimu.**

mkasa* (mi-) *rare* 1. event, occurrence, incident. 2. (piece of) news. *Cf.* **¹kisa.**

¹mkasama* (mi-), **kasama** (—) 1. part, share. 2. division, partition, distribution. 3. *math.* division. *Cf.* **kasimu.**

²mkasama* (mi-) mkasama (kind of manioc).

mkasasi*, mkakasi (mi-) mkasasi (kind of tree).

mkasi*, mkassi (mi-) (*also* **makasi,** *pl.*) (pair of) scissors.

mkasiri (mi-) mkasiri (shrub the bark of which is used to make a black dye).

mkassi* (mi-) *see* **mkasi.**

mkata* (wa-) 1. poor person. 2. boaster, braggart. *Cf.* **¹kata, ukata.**

mkataa* 1. (—) decision, undertaking directed toward a goal. 2. *adv.* definitely, finally, irrevocably, unalterably. *Cf.* ¹kataa.

mkataba* (mi-) 1. agreement, settlement. 2. *jur., pol.* contract, deed, charter, treaty, pact; statute. **— wa amani.** peace treaty. **— wa urafiki.** treaty of friendship. **— wa kutoshambuliana.** nonaggression pact. 3. *mil.* regulations. *Cf.* **kitabu.**

mkataji*, mkati (wa-) cutter *(tailor, etc.). Cf.* **¹kata.**

mkatale* (mi-) stocks, foot-shackles.

mkatani* (mi-) sisal hemp plant *(Agave sisalana).* (= **¹mkonge.**) *Cf.* **katani.**

mkatavu (wa-) stubborn/quarrelsome person. *Cf.* **¹kataa, katavu.**

mkate* (mi-) 1. loaf of bread. 2. (**— mtamu**) cake. 3. compact/pressed piece of something. **— wa tumbako.** pressed/plug tobacco. **— wa nyuki.** honey in the comb. *Cf.* **¹kata.**

mkati (wa-) *see* **mkataji.**

mkatili* (wa-) 1. cruel person. 2. aggressor. *Cf.* **katili.**

mkatizo* (mi-) interruption, pause, break. *Cf.* **¹kata.**

mkato* (mi-) 1. (act of) cutting, felling *(trees).* 2. cut, incision. 3. section, division, compartment; (**— wa duara**) arc (of a circle). 4. cutting down, shortening, reduction. **njia ya —.** shortcut. 5. *med.* amputation. 6. *fig.* firmness, decisiveness, determination. **maneno ya —.** resolute words. *Cf.* **¹kata.**

mkavu: — wa macho (wa-) rude/insolent person. *Cf.* **¹kavu, kauka.**

mkazi (wa-) *see* [1]**mkaa.**

mkazo (mi-), **kazo** (ma-) 1. fastening, securing, strengthening. 2. pressing, compressing. 3. pressure. 4. emphasis, stress. — **wa sauti.** accent *(on a syllable).* 5. *fig.* steadfastness, constancy; stability, durability. *Cf.* **kaza.**

mke (wa-) wife. *Cf.* **ke.**

mkebe* [*Ind.*] (mi-), **kebe** (ma-) 1. pot, can. 2. box, case.

mkeka (mi-) (sleeping) mat.

mkeketo (mi-) something/someone of the same size/height *(as something/someone else). Cf.* **keketa.**

mkekewa (mi-) mkekewa (a weed). (= **mkwangwachara.**)

mkereza (wa-) 1. one who uses a lathe, turner. 2. *pol.* timeserver, opportunist. *Cf.* **kereza.**

mkero (wa-) importunate/meddlesome person. *Cf.* **kera.**

[1]**mkesha** (mi-) clearing up *(after a rain).*

[2]**mkesha** (mi-), **kesha** (ma-) night-watch, vigil. *Cf.* **kesha.**

mkewe (wa-) *arch.* (= **mke wake**) his wife.

mkia (mi-) 1. tail. **la** —. be last. 2. feeler, antenna *(of an insect).* 3. — **wa mjusi.** lines of embroidery on a kanzu, proceeding from the mjusi (*see* [1]**mjusi** 2).

mkichaa (wa-) *rare* = **mwenye kichaa.** insane person, madman, lunatic.

mkidhi* (wa-) *rel.* the granter (of benefactions) (= God). *Cf.* **kidhi.**

mkiki (—) mkiki (kind of fish).

mkilemba (wa-) mkilemba (someone who has earned the right to wear a turban; *see* [1]**kilemba**); *(fig.)* successful candidate, prizewinner.

mkilua (mi-) mkilua (species of liana the flowers of which are used to make perfume). *Cf.* **kilua.**

mkilungwana (mi-) mkilungwana (kind of rubber tree, *Landolphia Kirkii*).

mkimbiaji, mkimbizi (wa-) *sport* halfback. *Cf.* **kimbia.**

mkimbizi (wa-) 1. fugitive, deserter. 2. pursuer, persecutor. 3. = **mkimbiaji.** *Cf.* **kimbia.**

mkimu* (wa-) 1. provider, supporter *(one who supplies someone else with the necessities of life).* 2. careful/attentive person. 3. one who harps on a subject. *Cf.* **kimu.**

mkimwa (wa-) unfriendly/ill-humored person. *Cf.* **kimwa.**

mkinaifu* independent/self-sufficient person. *Cf.* **kinai, kinaifu.**

[1]**mkinda** (mi-) mkinda (dance at the initiation ceremony for girls).

[2]**mkinda** (wa-) *see* **kinda.**

mkindani (wa-) *see* **mkinzani.**

mkindu (mi-) mkindu (wild date palm, *Phoenix reclinata).* *Cf.* **kindu, ukindu.**

mkinga 1. (mi-) obstruction, obstacle, barrier. **– wa maji.** dam, dike. 2. (wa-) person who obstructs/impedes others. *Cf.* **[1]kinga, mkingamo.**

mkingaji (wa-) defender, protector. *Cf.* **[1]kinga.**

mkingamo (mi-) 1. obstacle, impediment. **njia ya –.** roundabout way, detour; crossing, crossroads. 2. resistance, opposition. *Cf.* **[1]kinga.**

mkingiko (mi-) cross-beam, roof-beam *(of a house).* *Cf.* **[1]kinga, mkinga.**

mkingiri (mi-) mkingiri (a shrub the bark of which is used as a remedy for snakebite).

mkingu (mi-) mkingu (kind of tree, *Albizzia lebbek*).

mkinzani, mkindani (wa-) opponent, adversary. *Cf.* **kinza, kinzani.**

mkiristo (wa-) *see* **mkristo.**

mkirizi (mi-) *see* **mchirizi.**

mkitamli (mi-) mkitamli (coconut palm, *Cocos mucifera*). *Cf.* **kitamli.**

mkiwa (wa-) 1. poor/destitute person, beggar. 2. solitary/lonely person. *Cf.* **kiwa.**

mkizi (mi-) 1. cuttlefish. 2. sepia.

mkoba* (mi-) bag, pouch, purse. **– wa kike.** handbag. *Cf.* **koba, kuba, kubaza.**

mkoche, mkoma (mi-) (species of) dwarf palm *(Hyphaene coriacea).* *Cf.* **koche.**

[1]mkodi (mi-) mkodi (a spirit).

[2]mkodi* (wa-) one who rents/leases. *Cf.* **kodi.**

mkoe (mi-) mkoe (kind of liana, *Pergularia extensa).*

[1]mkogo (mi-) show, display, demonstration. *Cf.* **[1]koga.**

[2]mkogo (mi-) *see* **[1]kogo.**

mkojo, mkojozi (mi-) 1. urine. **mwaga –.** urinate. 2. = **kikojozi.** *Cf.* **kojoa.**

mkojozi (mi-) *see* **mkojo.**

[1]mkoko (mi-) mkoko (species of mangrove, *Rhizophora mucronata.* The wood is used for house building; the bark, for the soles of sandals).

[2]mkoko* [*Engl.*] (mi-) cocoa tree. *Cf.* **[2]koko.**

mkokoto (mi-) 1. pulling, dragging. 2. the track left when something is dragged through the sand. *Cf.* **kokota.**

[1]mkole (mi-) mkole (kind of tree).

2mkole (mi-) bundle, bunch. – **wa nuzi.** a bunch of coconuts. – **wa mvua.** *rare* rainbow. (= **upinde**). *Cf.* **1kole.**

mkoloni* [*Engl.*] (wa-) colonialist. *Cf.* **koloni, ukoloni.**

1mkoma (mi-) *see* **mkoche.**

2mkoma (wa-) *rare* leper. (= **mwenye ukoma.**)

3mkoma (wa-) one who stops doing something. *Cf.* **1koma.**

mkomafi (mi-) mkomafi (kind of tree, *Carapa moluccensis*).

mkomamanga (mi-) pomegranate tree (*Punica granatum*). *Cf.* **komamanga, 2Manga.**

mkomba (wa-) *coll.* drunkard. (= **mlevi.**) *Cf.* **2komba** 2.

mkombo (mi-) *naut.* rudder-handle, tiller.

mkombozi (mi-) 1. rescuer, liberator. 2. *rel.* Saviour, Redeemer. *Cf.* **komboa.**

mkombwe, mkomwe (mi-) 1. mkombwe (twining plant, *Coesalpinia bonducella*). 2. seeds of the mkombwe (*used in a board game*). 3. mkombwe (a powder used in charms, made from these seeds).

mkomo (mi-) *rare* end, limit, boundary. (= **kikomo.**)

mkomoka (mi-) mkomoka (kind of manioc).

mkomunisti* [*Engl.*] (wa-) communist. *Cf.* **kikomunisti, ukomunisti.**

mkomwe (mi-) *see* **mkombwe.**

mkondo (mi-) 1. flow, course, run, current. – **wa mto.** bed of a river. *prov.* **maji hufuata – wake.** The water follows its course/runs in its bed. 2. track (*of an animal*). – **wa simba.** the track of the lion. 3. wake (*of a ship*). 4. *elec.*: – **wa stimu.** electric current.

mkonga (mi-) trunk (*of an elephant*). (= **mkono, mwiro.**)

1mkonge (mi-) sisal plant. *Cf.* **ukonge.**

2mkonge (–) mkonge (kind of sea-fish with poisonous spines).

mkongojo (mi-), **ukongojo** (**kongojo**) stick, staff, cane, crutch. *Cf.* **1konga.**

mkongwe (wa-) sickly/feeble person. *Cf.* **3kongwe, 1konga**

mkonjo (mi-) *see* **mkonzo.**

mkono (mi-) 1. arm, hand. – **wa kuume (kushoto).** right (left) hand. – **wa ndizi.** a hand of bananas. 2. unit of length (*from the fingertips to the elbow, 45 cm*). 3. handle. – **wa chungu.** handle of a pan. 4. signature. **tia –.** sign (*a letter, document*). 5. inlet (*of the sea*), branch (*of a river*). 6. (– **wa tembo**) trunk (*of an elephant*); (*fig.*) variety of banana. *Cf.* **kikono, kono, ukono.**

mkonyezo (mi-) sign, signal; wink, hint; warning. *Cf.* **konyeza.**

mkonzo, mkonjo (mi-) pointed stick, hunting spear. *Cf.* **konzo.**

mkoo (wa-) dirty/untidy person. *Cf.* **ukoo.**

mkopaji, mkopi (wa-) 1. debtor. 2. *rare* swindler. *Cf.* **³kopa.**

mkopeshi (wa-) 1. lender, creditor. 2. usurer. *Cf.* **³kopa.**

mkopi (wa-) *see* **mkopaji.**

mkopo (mi-) 1. loan, credit. **– bila ya faida.** interest-free loan. **– wenye faida ya chini kabisa.** low-interest loan. **ununuzi wa –.** purchase on the instalment plan. 2. trickery, swindling. *Cf.* **³kopa.**

mkorofi* (wa-) 1. cruel/brutal person. 2. one who brings bad luck. *Cf.* **korofi.**

mkoroga, mkorogaji (wa-) troublemaker, agitator, insurgent, revolutionary. *Cf.* **koroga.**

mkorogaji (wa-) *see* **mkoroga.**

mkorogi (wa-) *see* **mkorogo** 2.

mkorogo 1. (mi-) agitation, trouble-making, discord, confusion. 2. (wa-) (*also* **mkorogi**) quarrelsome/pugnacious person. *Cf.* **koroga.**

mkoromaji (wa-) one who habitually snores. *Cf.* **²koroma.**

mkoromo (mi-) 1. snoring, snorting. 2. purring *(of a cat)*. *Cf.* **²koroma.**

mkorosho (mi-) mkorosho (cashew apple tree, *Anacardium occidentale*). *Cf.* **korosho.**

mkosaji, mkosefu, mkosi (wa-) 1. one who violates the law, offender, criminal. 2. *rel.* sinner. *Cf.* **¹kosa.**

mkosefu (wa-) *see* **mkosaji.**

¹mkosi (wa-) *see* **mkosaji.**

²mkosi* (–) bad omen, bad luck. *Cf.* **kisirani.**

mkota (mi-) mkota (species of sweet sorghum, *Sorghum saccharatum*).

mkowa (mi-) mkowa (bandage worn by women during pregnancy; *cf.* **mkaja**).

mkristo*, mkristu, mkiristo [*Port.* ?] (wa-) Christian. *Cf.* **kikristo, Ukristo.**

mkubwa (wa-) 1. leader. 2. director, manager; superior, employer. *Cf.* **kubwa.**

mkudhumani* (mi-) pomegranate tree (= **mkomamanga**). *Cf.* **kudhumani.**

mkufu (mi-) (ornamental) chain. **– wa shingo.** necklace. **– wa mguuni.** anklet.

mkufunzi, mkurufunzi (wa-) 1. leader. 2. skilled workman, journeyman. 3. *rare* teacher, educator. *Cf.* **²funda.**

mkugenzi, mkurugenzi (wa-) *rare* pioneer, leader; superior, boss, manager. *Cf.* **ukurugenzi.**

mkuki (mi-) spear, lance.

[1]**mkuku** (mi-) *naut.* keel *(of a boat, ship).*

[2]**mkuku** (mi-) mkuku (a kind of climbing plant).

mkule (mi-) mkule (kind of sea-fish).

mkulima (wa-) agricultural worker, farmer. *Cf.* [1]**lima.**

mkulivu (wa-) 1. idle/lazy person. 2. boring/ tiresome person. *Cf.* [1]**kua, kulivu.**

mkulo, mkuro (mi-) filter, strainer *(for straining grated coconut).*

[1]**mkumbi** (mi-) mkumbi (a shrub, *Ochna alboserrata.* The bark is used to prepare a yellow dye). (= [2]**mwungamo.**)

[2]**mkumbi** (mi-) track, traces *(of an animal or a person).*

[1]**mkumbizi** (wa-) one who cleans up/makes a clean sweep of something; gleaner. *Cf.* [2]**kumba.**

[2]**mkumbizi** (wa-) one who pushes/jostles, rough/inconsiderate person. *Cf.* [1]**kumba.**

mkumbo (mi-) 1. destruction, devastation. 2. loss. *Cf.* [2]**kumba.**

mkumbufu (wa-) person with a good memory. *Cf.* **kumbuka.**

mkumbuu (mi-) 1. belt, sash. 2. sling, bandage. 3. *mil.* shoulder strap.

mkunazi* [*Pers. ?*] (mi-) mkunazi (kind of tree, *Zizyphus jujuba*). *Cf.* **kunazi, kikunazi.**

mkundaji (–) mkundaji (kind of fish).

mkunde (mi-) bean plant *(Phaseolus vulgaris).* *Cf.* **ukunde.**

mkundu (mi-) *anat.* anus. *Cf.* **kikundu.**

[1]**mkunga** (wa-) 1. midwife (= **mzalishi**). 2. confidential (female) adviser, older woman friend who makes arrangements for a marriage. *Cf.* [2]**kunga, ukunga.**

[2]**mkunga** (mi-) (species of) marine eel.

[1]**mkungu** (mi-) 1. cooking pot, frying pan. 2. lid of a cooking pot. *Cf.* [1]**chungu.**

[2]**mkungu** (mi-) (species of) almond tree *(Terminalia catappa).* *Cf.* [1]**kungu.**

[3]**mkungu** (mi-) fruit stem of the banana plant *(with the entire bunch of fruit).*

mkunguma (mi-) mkunguma (kind of tree, *Sorindeia usambaraensis*).

mkungumanga (mi-) nutmeg tree *(Myristica fragrans).* *Cf.* **kungumanga.**

[1]**mkunguni** (wa-) lazy person, idler. *Cf.* **ukunguni.**

[2]**mkunguni** (mi-) mkunguni (species of almond tree, *Terminalia Fatraea*).

[3]**mkunguni** (mi-) a long, stout stick.

mkunguru, ukunguru *sing.* seasoning fever, newcomer's fever *(due to difficulty in adjusting to a change of climate or diet).*

mkung'uto (mi-) 1. shaking, sifting, winnowing. 2. refuse, rubbish. *Cf.* **kung'uta.**

mkunjaji (wa-) one who bends/folds something; folder. **— uso.** one who makes faces, clown. *Cf.* **kunja.**

mkunjo (mi-) 1. folding, creasing. 2. fold, crease. **suruali yenye —.** trousers with a pressed crease. 3. wrinkle. *Cf.* **kunja.**

mkuno (mi-) (act of) scratching, scraping, grating. *Cf.* [2]**kuna.**

mkunungu (mi-) mkunungu (kind of tree the leaves of which are eaten as a vegetable).

mkuo (mi-) 1. heap, lump. 2. bar, ingot *(of metal).*

mkupuo (mi-) 1. push, shove, blow. 2. *(act of)* shaking off, pushing aside, getting rid of something. *Cf.* **kupua.**

mkupuzi (wa-) one who is given to pushing/hitting/horseplay. *Cf.* **kupua.**

mkuranga (mi-) arid region, desert. (= **jangwa.**)

mkuro (mi-) *see* **mkulo.**

mkuru (wa-) *see* **mkuu.**

mkurufunzi (wa-) *see* **mkufunzi.**

mkurugenzi (wa-) *see* **mkugenzi.**

mkurungu (mi-) mkurungu (kind of tree, *Pterocarpus chrysothrix*).

mkururo (mi-) line, procession *(of people).*

mkuruti (mi-) *see* **mkarati.**

mkuruzo, mkuruzu (mi-) drawstring *(cord, etc., for closing a bag, a garment at the neck, etc.)*

mkuruzu (mi-) *see* **mkuruzo.**

mkusanya, mkusanyi (wa-) one who collects/gathers/assembles. *Cf.* **kusanya.**

mkusanyi (wa-) *see* **mkusanya.**

mkusanyiko, mkusanyo (mi-) 1. heap, quantity. 2. accumulation, collection. 3. gathering, assembly; crowd, throng; tumult. 4. set, kit. *Cf.* **kusanya.**

mkusanyo (mi-) *see* **mkusanyiko.**

mkutano (mi-) 1. meeting. **— wa umma.** mass meeting. **— hadharani.** open meeting. 2. consultation, discussion, conference, session. **— wa waandishi/wanagazeti.** press conference. 3. contest, competition. *Cf.* [1]**kuta.**

mkuto (mi-) 1. (act of) meeting, running across, finding. 2. fold, bend, curve. *Cf.* **[1]kuta.**

mkutuo (mi-) jerk, impact, shock. *Cf.* **kutua.**

mkuu, mkuru (wa-) 1. superior, manager, director, head. – **wa skuli.** school principal. 2. leader, chairman. – **wa chama (kiti).** party leader. 3. *mil.* commander. 4. president. – **wa serikali/dola.** chief of state. 5. *comm.* cadre. *Cf.* **kuu.**

mkuwadi*, mkwadi (wa-) 1.(sexual) impotence. 2. = **kawadi.**

mkuyati* (–) *med.* (sexual) restorative, tonic; aphrodisiac.

mkuyu (mi-) wild fig tree. *Cf.* **kuyu.**

mkuzaji (wa-) livestock breeder. *Cf.* **[1]kua.**

mkwachuro (mi-) mkwachuro (disease of coconuts).

mkwadi* (wa-) *see* **mkuwadi.**

mkwaju (mi-) tamarind tree *(Tamarindus indica). Cf.* **kwaju.**

mkwakwa, mkwakwara (mi-) mkwakwa (climbing plant bearing edible fruit, *Landolfia florida).*

mkwakwara (mi-) *see* **mkwakwa.**

mkwamba (mi-) mkwamba (kind of thorny shrub).

mkwangwachare (mi-) mkwangwachare (species of liana, *Smilax Kraussiana*). (= **mkekewa.**)

mkwao (wa-) fellow villager, fellow countryman. *Cf.* **[1]wao.**

mkwara (mi-) mkwara (kind of tree, *Millettia Bussei*).

mkware (wa-) 1. sensual/lascivious person. 2. prostitute. 3. female animal in heat. *Cf.* **[2]kware, ukware.**

mkwaruzo (mi-) 1. scratching, scraping, grating *(action, sound).* 2. scraper. 3. scratch, surface wound, abrasion. 4. track, trail *(of a snake, etc.). Cf.* **kwaruza.**

mkwasi (wa-) wealthy/well-to-do person. *Cf.* **kwasi, ukwasi.**

mkwe (wa-) relative by marriage: father- (mother-) in-law, son- (daughter-) in-law, brother- (sister-) in-law.

mkweme (mi-) mkweme (species of liana, *Telfairia pedata*). *Cf.* **kweme.**

mkweo (mi-) 1. (act of) climbing, mounting. 2. climb, ascent. *Cf.* **kwea.**

mkwepuzi (wa-) *rare* thief. (= **mwivi.**) *Cf.* **kwepua.**

mkwezi 1. (wa-) one who climbs/mounts; one who make a business of climbing coconut trees to knock down the nuts. 2. (mi-) climbing plant, creeper, liana. *Cf.* **kwea, kwezi.**

[1]mkwiji (mi-) bag, pouch, purse.

[2]mkwiji (wa-) *rare* = **gwiji.**

mkwiro (mi-) drumstick.

mla (wa-) eater, consumer. **mla riba.** usurer. *liter.:* – **watu.** cannibal. *Cf.* **¹la.**

mlaanifu*, mlaanizi (wa-) 1. one who curses/swears. 2. accursed person. *us. pl.* **walanifu.** *rel.* the damned. *Cf.* **laana, laani.**

mlaanizi* (wa-) *see* **mlaanifu.**

mladi* (mi-) mladi (stick used by weavers to tighten threads).

mlafi (wa-) one who eats greedily/voraciously, glutton. *Cf.* **lapa, lafua.**

mlaghai* (wa-) deceiver, cheat, swindler. *Cf.* **laghai.**

mlai* [*Engl.*] (wa-) *see* **¹mlei.**

mlaji (wa-) (great) eater, one who likes to eat certain things. *Cf.* **¹la.**

mlala (mi-) mlala (species of dwarf palm). (= **mkoche, mwaa.**)

mlalafi (wa-) *see* **mlalavi.**

mlalaji (wa-) late sleeper, sleepyhead. *Cf.* **lala.**

mlalamishi (wa-) *jur., rare* plaintiff. (= **mdai.**) *Cf.* **lalama.**

mlalangwa (mi-) mlalangwa (kind of tree, *Ficus Bussei*).

mlalavi, mlalafi (wa-) 1. restless sleeper *(one who twists and turns in his sleep).* 2. quarrelsome/irritable person. *Cf.* **lala.**

mlalazamu* (wa-) watchman, guard. *Cf.* **lala, zamu.**

¹mlamba (wa-) one who licks / has a sweet tooth. *Cf.* **lamba.**

²mlamba (mi-) *see* **mramba.**

mlamu (wa-) *see* **mwamu.**

mlandawa (mi-) banyan tree.

mlangali (mi-) mlangali (kind of tree, *Euphorbia*).

mlangamia (mi-) mlangamia (parasitic plant growing on cloves, etc.; *Cassytha filiformis*).

mlango (*rare* **mwango**) (mi-) 1. door, gate, entrance. *fig.* **milango ya maarifa.** the five senses. 2.: – **wa mto.** mouth of a river. – **wa bahari** (*or sometimes* **mlangobahari**). strait, channel. – **wa Suez.** the Suez Canal. 3. (mountain) pass, defile; bottleneck. 4. genealogy. 5. *liter.* chapter. 6. goal *(football).* *Cf.* **lango, kilango.**

mlariba* (wa-) moneylender, usurer. *Cf.* **mla, riba.**

mlazi 1. (wa-) children's nurse *(lit.: one who puts to sleep).* 2. (mi-) cradle. *Cf.* **lala.**

mle *dem. pron. (also adv.)* in that, inside there, within.

mlegevu (wa-) 1. weak, sickly person. 2. depressed/dejected person. *Cf.* **lega, legevu.**

[1]**mlei, mlai** [*Engl.*] (wa-) layman; *(pl.)* lay-people, laity.

[2]**mlei** (wa-) (children's) nurse, baby-sitter. *Cf.* [1]**mlezi.**

mleli (mi-) tail-feathers of a bird *(often used as ornament).* **toa —.** put out a tail-feather = *(fig.)* show signs of prosperity.

mlembe (mi-) mlembe (the honey bird, *Indicator indicator*).

mlenge (mi-) mlenge (game played by throwing sticks).

mlengu (mi-) *naut.* outrigger.

mleo (mi-) 1. staggering, reeling *(as a drunken person).* 2. swaying, rocking, wavering. 3. concussion, vibration. 4. rolling *(of a ship).* *Cf.* **lewa.**

mletaji (wa-) 1. messenger, deliverer, bearer. 2. sender *(of a letter).* 3. porter. *Cf.* **leta.**

mlevi (wa-) heavy drinker, drunkard, alcoholic. *Cf.* **lewa, levi.**

[1]**mlezi, mlei** (wa-) 1. nurse, children's maid. 2. governess, tutor. 3. *jur.* guardian. *Cf.* **lea.**

[2]**mlezi** (mi-) *med.* swelling of the neck glands, scrofula.

[3]**mlezi** (mi-) (species of) millet plant. *Cf.* [1]**ulezi.**

[1]**mlia** (wa-) one who cries (*e.g.*, a child). *Cf.* [1]**lia.**

[2]**mlia** (mi-) 1. colored stripe. 2. striped pattern *(of cloth).* *Cf.* **milia.**

mlilana (mi-) mlilana (kind of mangrove, *Sonneratia caesolaria/acida*).

mlima (mi-) mountain, large hill; steep climb. **— wa moto.** volcano. **milima, safu ya milima.** mountain range. *Cf.* **kilima.**

mlimaji (wa-) *rare* agricultural worker, farmer. (= **mkulima.**) *Cf.* [1]**lima.**

mlimao* (mi-) *see* **mlimau.**

mlimau*, mlimao [*Pers.*] (mi-) lemon tree *(Citrus limonum).* *Cf.* **limau.**

mlimbiko (mi-), **limbiko** (ma-) 1. supply, reserve; *(econ.)* reserve fund. 2. thrift, economy. *Cf.* **limbika.**

mlimbolimbo (mi-) mlimbolimbo (a thorn bush, *Euphorbia cuneata*). *Cf.* **ulimbo.**

mlimbuko (mi-) *see* **limbuko.**

mlimi (wa-) 1. chatterer, gossip, talebearer. 2. boaster, braggart. *Cf.* **limi, kilimi, ulimi.**

mlimo (mi-) cultivation, agriculture, farming, tillage. *Cf.* [1]**lima, kilimo.**

mlimwengu, mwulimwengu (wa-) 1. inhabitant of the earth, human being. 2. easy-going/happy-go-lucky person. *Cf.* **ulimwengu.**

mlinda, mlindaji (wa-) 1. watchman, guard, keeper, caretaker. **— ndege.** one who watches over a planted field *(scares away birds, etc.).* 2. *mil.* guard, sentry. *Cf.* **linda.**

mlindaji (wa-) *see* **mlinda.**

mlingano (mi-) 1. resemblance, similarity. 2. harmony, unison. 3. *geom.* symmetry. 4. (*or* **mlinganyo**) *math.* equation. *Cf.* **[1]linga.**

mlinganyo (mi-) *see* **mlingano** 4.

mlingoti (mi-) 1. (ship's) mast. **— wa maji.** bowsprit. **— wa mbele.** foremast. **— wa galme.** mizzenmast. **— wa bendera.** flagstaff. 2. *vulg.* penis.

mlinzi (wa-) 1. watchman, guard, caretaker; shepherd. 2. protector, defender. 3. *jur.* guardian. *Cf.* **linda.**

mlio (mi-) 1. sound *(in gen.).* 2. bang, report. **— wa bunduki.** rifle shot. 3. cry *(of a person or animal),* roar, bellow, etc. **— wa ng'ombe.** lowing of cattle. *Cf.* **[1]lia.**

mlipa, mlipaji, mlipi (wa-) one who pays, payer. *Cf.* **lipa.**

mlipaji (wa-) *see* **mlipa.**

mlipi (wa-) *see* **mlipa.**

mlipizi (wa-) one who exacts payment. **— kisasi.** avenger. *Cf.* **lipa.**

mlipuaji (wa-): **— baruti.** minesweeper, explosives expert. *Cf.* **lipuka.**

mlipuko (mi-) explosion, detonation. *Cf.* **lipuka.**

mlisha, mlishi (wa-) one who feeds/cares for *(people or animals).* *Cf.* **[1]la.**

mlishi (wa-) *see* **mlisha.**

mlisho (mi-) 1. feeding, nourishment. 2. *Isl.* month of the Muhammadan year *(preceding Ramadhan).* *Cf.* **[1]la.**

mliwa* (mi-) mliwa (kind of tree, *Spirostachys africana*). *Cf.* **liwa.**

mlizabu* (mi-) *see* **mrizabu.**

mlizamu* (mi-) spout, eaves, gutter, pipe. *Cf.* **mrizabu.**

mlizi (wa-) 1. one who cries/screams/whines. 2. one who causes someone/something to make a noise. *Cf.* **[1]lia.**

mlo (mi-) 1. food, diet; provender, fodder. 2. banquet. *Cf.* **[1]la.**

mlomo (mi-) *see* **mdomo.**

mlonge (mi-) mlonge (kind of tree the leaves of which are eaten as a vegetable).

[1]mlongo (mi-) *see* **[1]mwongo.**

[2]mlongo (wa-) *see* **[2]mwongo.**

mlonjo (mi-) stilt *(used in various games).* *Cf.* **lonjo.**

mlowezi (wa-) settler. *Cf.* **lowela.**

[1]**mlozi*** **(mi-)** almond tree. *Cf.* **lozi.**

[2]**mlozi** (wa-) magician, sorcerer. *Cf.* **loga.**

mlumbaji (wa-) speaker, orator, eloquent person. *Cf.* **lumba.**

mlungula, mlungura 1. (wa-) thief, robber, swindler, extortionist. 2. **(mi-)** bribery, corruption; bribe. *Cf.* **lungula.**

mlungura (wa-, **mi-**) *see* **mlungula.**

mluzi *sing.* *see* **uluzi.**

mluziluzi **(mi-)** mluziluzi (a kind of tree; the seed pods make a whistling noise in the wind; *cf.* **uluzi**).

mmalidadi* (wa-) *see* **malidadi.**

Mmanga* (wa-) Arab. *Cf.* [2]**Manga.**

mmasihiya*, mmasiya (wa-) Christian (= **mkristo**). *Cf.* **masihiya.**

mmasiya* (wa-) *see* **mmasihiya.**

mmbea (wa-) 1. chatterer, gossip, scandalmonger. 2. inquisitive/curious person. *Cf.* **mbea, umbea.**

mmbuji*, mbuji (wa-) well-dressed/elegant person. *Cf.* **umbuji.**

mmea **(mi-)** sprout, shoot; *(pl.)* vegetation. *Cf.* **mea, kijimea.**

mmego **(mi-)** 1. breaking, biting. 2. ripping, tearing (up, to pieces). *Cf.* **mega.**

mmelea **(mi-)** creeping/climbing plant, parasite plant. *Cf.* **mea, kimelea.**

mmisionari* [*Engl.*] (wa-) missionary.

Mmisri (wa-) Egyptian. *Cf.* **Misri.**

mmoja (wa-) a (certain) person, someone. **kila —.** each (and every) one. *Cf.* **moja.**

mmoyomoyo, mmwaka **(mi-)** mmoyomoyo (a shrub, *Sapindus saponaria*).

mmrima* (wa-) coast dweller *(i.e., inhabitant of the coastal area where Swahili is the native language)*. *Cf.* **mrima.**

mmumunye, mmung'unye **(mi-)** bottle-gourd plant *(Lagenaria vulgaris)*. *Cf.* **mumunye.**

mmung'unye **(mi-)** *see* **mmumunye.**

mmunina* (wa-) *see* **muminina.**

Mmvita (wa-) inhabitant of Mombasa. *Cf.* **Mvita, Kimvita.**

mmwaka **(mi-)** *see* **mmoyomoyo.**

mmwambao (wa-) *rare* one who lives on the coast. *Cf.* **ambaa, mwambao.**

mna, muna 1. *2nd pers. pl.* you have. 2. (in it) there is...

mnaanaa **(mi-)** *see* **mnanaa.**

mnada* **(mi-)** 1. sale, auction. **piga (uza kwa) —.** auction off. 2. *rare, rec.* chamber of commerce. *Cf.* **nadi.**

mnadi* (wa-) 1. auctioneer. 2. announcer. – **sala.** *Isl.* one who calls to prayer, muezzin. *Cf.* **nadi.**

mnafiki* (wa-) deceiver, hypocrite, liar. *Cf.* **unafiki.**

mnajimuu*, mnajimu (wa-) 1. astrologer. 2. astronomer. *Cf.* **unajimu.**

mnajisi* (wa-) unclean/impure/profane person. *Cf.* **najisi.**

mnamo *adv.* about, approximately.

mnana (mi-) 1. *ornith.* finch, golden weaver. 2. yellow dye *(used for staining the strips from which mats are made).*

mnanaa*, mnaanaa (mi-) *bot.* mint plant *(Mentha viridis/piperita).* *Cf.* **nanaa.**

mnanasi* [*Pers.*] (mi-) pineapple plant *(Ananas sativa/comosus).* *Cf.* **nanasi.**

mnandi (wa-) *ornith.* mnandi (cormorant, *Phalacrocorax*).

mnara* (mi-) 1. tower. – **wa taa.** lighthouse. 2. minaret, steeple. *Cf.* **nuru.**

mnaso (mi-) 1. (act of) catching, trapping. 2. trap. 3. what is caught (in a trap), catch. *Cf.* **nasa.**

mnavu (mi-) *bot.* nightshade *(Solanum nigrum/nodiflorum).*

mnawili* (–) mnawili (an agreement for shipping goods). *Cf.* **nauli.**

mnazaa* 1. (wa-) quarrelsome person; one who does a shameful/disgraceful thing. 2. (mi-) quarrel, dispute, ill-feeling. *Cf.* **nazaa.**

mnazi (mi-) coconut palm *(Cocos nucifera).* *Cf.* **nazi.**

mndege (wa-) *see* **mwana.**

mndimu* (mi-) *see* **mdimu.**

mndunga (mi-) mndunga (bitter species of manioc).

mnena (wa-) eloquent, confident speaker. – **watu.** popular speaker, demagogue. – **uwongo.** liar. *Cf.* [1]**nena.**

mnenaji, mneni (wa-) 1. talkative person, gossip. 2. = **mnena.** *Cf.* [1]**nena.**

mnenea (wa-) 1. defender, advocate, proponent. 2. critic. 3. opponent. *Cf.* [1]**nena.**

mneni (wa-) *see* **mnenaji.**

mng'ago (mi-) *see* **mng'aro.**

mng'ao (mi-) *see* **mng'aro.**

mng'ariza (wa-) 1. a person with very bright/piercing eyes. 2. wicked person, sorcerer. *Cf.* **ng'aa.**

mng'arizo (mi-) brightness, gleam, glitter, glare, glow. – **wa macho.** shining/piercing eyes. *Cf.* **ng'aa.**

mng'aro, mng'ao, mngago (mi-) 1. brightness. 2. *fig.* clarity, lucidity, intelligibility. *Cf.* **ng'aa.**

Mngazija (wa-) inhabitant of the Comoro Islands. *Cf.* **Ngazija.**

mng'oaji (wa-) *(usually with a following object)* one who pulls ... out/up. **– meno.** dentist. *Cf.* **ng'oa.**

mngoja, mngoje, mngojaji (wa-) watchman, guard, keeper, attendant. *mil.* guard, sentry. **– mlango.** doorkeeper, porter. *Cf.* **ngoja.**

mngojaji (wa-) *see* **mngoja.**

mngoje (wa-) *see* **mngoja.**

mngojezi (wa-) 1. guard, protector. 2. observer. 3. steward, housekeeper. *Cf.* **ngoja.**

mnguri (mi-) wooden hammer, mallet *(used by shoemakers).*

mngurumizi (wa-) 1. one who roars/growls/bellows. 2. grumbler, faultfinder. *Cf.* **nguruma.**

mngwana (wa-) *see* **mwungwana.**

mnili* (mi-) indigo plant *(Indigofera tinctoria).* *Cf.* **nili.**

mnimbi (–) mnimbi (a large fish).

mninga (mi-) mninga (a tree providing good lumber).

mnjugumawe (mi-) Madagascar/Bambara peanut plant. *Cf.* **njugu.**

mnjugunyasa (mi-) peanut plant *(Arachis hypogaea).* *Cf.* **njugu.**

mno *adv.* very much; too much, inordinately, excessively; unusually; very. *(Sometimes used in conjunction with other words of similar senses:* **sana –, – ajabu,** *etc.).*

mnofu (mi-) flesh, lean meat *(without fat or bones).* *Cf.* **nofu, kinofu, nofoa.**

mnoga (mi-) green tobacco leaf.

mnong'onezi, mnong'oni (wa-) whisperer, prompter. *Cf.* **nong'ona.**

mnong'oni (wa-) *see* **mnong'onezi.**

mnong'ono (mi-) 1. whispering. 2. (idle) talk, rumor. *Cf.* **nong'ona.**

Mnubi* (wa-) a Nubian. *Cf.* **Kinubi.**

mnukauvundo (mi-) mnukauvundo (a shrub, *Cassia occidentalis*).

mnukio (mi-) aromatic substance, perfume. *Cf.* **nuka.**

mnuko (mi-) smell, odor *(either pleasant or unpleasant).* *Cf.* **nuka.**

mnuna, mnunaji, mnuni (wa-) grumbler, faultfinder, malcontent. *Cf.* **nuna.**

mnunaji (wa-) *see* **mnuna.**

mnunda (wa-) *see* **nunda.**

mnuno (mi-) grumbling, complaining, faultfinding. *Cf.* **nuna.**

mnunuzi (wa-) buyer, purchaser, customer. *Cf.* **nunua.**

mnyama (wa-) 1. animal, beast. 2. *fig.* coarse/stupid person. *Cf.* **nyama, kinyama, unyama.**

mnyamavu (wa-) taciturn/uncommunicative person. *Cf.* **nyamaa, nyamavu.**

mnyampara, mnyapara (wa-) head, headman, leader *(esp. of a caravan or an expedition).*

mnyangalika (wa-) nondescript/useless/hopeless person; stupid person, fool. *Cf.* **nyangalika.**

mnyang'anyi (wa-) 1. robber, plunderer, brigand, burglar. 2. invader, conqueror. *Cf.* **nyang'anya.**

mnyanya (mi-) tomato plant *(Lycopersicum cerasiforme).* *Cf.* [2]**nyanya.**

mnyanyuko (mi-) uprising, insurrection. **— wa silaha.** armed uprising. *Cf.* [1]**nyanya.**

mnyapa (mi-) mnyapa (a plant, spurge).

mnyapara (wa-) *see* **mnyampara.**

mnyaufu *sing.* (process of) drying up, withering/wasting away. *Cf.* **nyauka.**

mnyefu (mi-) *see* **unyefu.**

mnyegea (mi-) mnyegea (kind of tree, *Kigelia pinnata*).

mnyenyekeo (mi-) 1. honor, respect, esteem, devotion. 2. deference, servility, humility, reverence. *Cf.* **nyenya.**

mnyenyekevu (wa-) quiet, humble person. *Cf.* **nyenya, nyenyekevu.**

mnyeo (mi-) 1. tickling, itching. 2. craving, yearning. *Cf.* [1]**nyea.**

mnyevu (mi-) dampness, moisture, vapor. *Cf.* **nya.**

mnyevunyevu *adj.* wet, moist, damp. *Cf.* **nya.**

mnyima, mnyimaji (wa-) miser, skinflint. *Cf.* **nyima.**

mnyimaji (wa-) *see* **mnyima.**

mnyimo (mi-) stinginess, miserliness. *Cf.* **nyima.**

mnyiri (mi-) feeler, arm, tentacle *(of a cuttlefish, etc.).*

mnyo (mi-) 1. (act of) discharging urine/feces. 2. shower *(of rain).* *Cf.* **nya.**

mnyofu (wa-): **mtu —.** honest/honorable person. *Cf.* [1]**nyoka, nyofu.**

mnyongaji (wa-) hangman, executioner. *Cf.* [2]**nyonga.**

mnyonge (wa-) 1. weak/sickly person. 2. mean/malicious person. *Cf.* **nyonge.**

mnyonywaji (wa-): **— damu.** bloodsucker, exploiter. *Cf.* **nyonya.**

[1]**mnyoo** (mi-) *see* **mnyororo.**

[2]mnyoo (mi-) roundworm, intestinal worm.

mnyororo, mnyoo (mi-) 1. chain, fetter. **– wa baisikeli.** bicycle-chain. 2. jail, confinement.

mnyozi (wa-) *see* **kinyozi.**

mnyunyo (mi-) sprinkling, moistening. *Cf.* **nyonyota.**

mnywa, mnywaji (wa-) drinker. *Cf.* **nywa.**

mnywanywa (mi-) mnywanywa (a shrub, *Pluchea dioscorides*).

mnywo (mi-) 1. swallow of water. 2. mnywo (an alcoholic beverage). *Cf.* **nywa.**

mo 1. *relat. pron.* 2. *adv.:* **– mote.** wherever, no matter where, everywhere.

modeli* [*Engl.*] (–) model, type.

moduleta* [*Engl.*] (–) *mus.* modulator.

mofa (–) 1. small (clay) oven. 2. (*also* **mkate wa –**) round loaf of bread (of millet flour) baked in a mofa.

mofti* [*Engl.*] *adj./adv.* *see* **mufti.**

mogo (mi-) *see* **mwogo.**

moja 1. *num.* one. **kumi na –.** eleven (= ten and one). **mia kwa –.** one percent. **– kwa –.** straight away, without delay, immediately. **amesikia ati mama yake mgonjwa akaondoka – kwa –.** News reached him that his mother was ill and he left immediately. **moja moja.** one after another, one by one, one each. **walikuja mmoja mmoja.** They came one at a time. **uhusiano wa – na –.** one-to-one correspondence. **pamoja.** together. 2. an individual, a certain one. **mtu mmoja.** a certain person. **mmoja wetu.** one of us. **mojawapo.** someone or other. 3. uniform, homogeneous. **moyo mmoja.** harmony (*lit.:* one heart). **watu si wamoja.** People are not all alike. *Cf.* **kumoja, mamoja, mmoja, pamoja, umoja.**

mojawapo *see* **moja** 2.

mola* *sing., Isl.* Lord (= God).

[1]moma be spread out/spilled/scattered; to spread (*of fire, water, disease*). *appl.* **momea** (**momia**).

[2]moma (ma-) moma (kind of snake, *Bitis gabonica*).

momonyoa *see* **monyoa.**

monyoa, momonyoa break off, tear off; pick (*fruit*). *appl.* **monyolea.** *caus.* **monyosha.** *intr.* **monyoka, momonyoka.** break off, become eroded, crumble away, fall into ruin.

[1]mori (–) young animal. **– ya ng'ombe.** calf, heifer. **– ya farasi.** colt, filly.

[2]mori* (–) (animal) fat, tallow.

[3]mori* (–) 1. excitement, anger, ferocity (*e.g., of male animals fighting over females, and fig.*). 2. mori (a medicine which is supposed to produce anger and ferocity).

morita*, **morta** (–) (short) span (distance from thumb to forefinger when the hand is fully opened). *Cf.* **shibiri.**

Moroko* Morocco.

morta* (–) *see* **morita.**

moshi (**mi-**) 1. smoke. **pazia la –.** *recent, pol.* smokescreen. 2. soot. 3. vapor, steam. **gari la –.** locomotive. *prov.* **palipo na – pana moto.** Where there is smoke there is fire. *Cf.* **joshi.**

mosi *arch.* 1. *num.* one. **Jumamosi.** Saturday (the first day of the week). **mwezi –.** the first day of the month. 2. *rare, adv.* first. **– lazima niende, pili...** First I must go, secondly...

mota* [*Engl.*] (–) motor. *rare* **baisikeli ya –.** motor scooter.

motaboti* [*Engl.*] (–) motorboat.

motakaa*, **motokaa, motakari, motokari** [*Engl.*] (–) automobile. **– ya abiria.** bus, taxi.

motakari* (–) *see* **motakaa.**

mote, mwote *indef. pron. (agreeing w. nouns w. suff.* **-ni***)* all, whole, entire. **nyumbani –.** in all the houses. **mjini –.** in the whole city. **mo –.** wherever, in all places, everywhere. *Cf.* **ote.**

¹**moto** (**mioto**) 1. fire, flame. **washa –.** light/kindle a fire. **zima –.** put out/extinguish a fire. **ota –.** warm oneself at the fire. **pata –.** become hot. **tia –.** set a fire *(arson)*. *fig., recent.* take off *(of airplanes)*. *prov.:* **dawa ya – ni –.** The remedy for fire is fire. **– wa milele.** *rel.* hell. 2. burning, glowing. **makaa ya –.** glowing coals. 3. heat, warmth, temperature. **maji –.** hot water. 4. *fig.* zeal, energy, exertion. **kazi –.** hard/taxing work. 5. *rare, elec.* current. **–a –.** charged, live. **isiyo na –.** without current. 6. *adv.:* – *or* **motomoto. mkate huu u motomoto.** This bread is very fresh. *Cf.* **joto, ujotojoto, umoto, vimoto;** *also* ²**ota.**

²**moto** (**mioto**) marks/welts (made by beating). *Cf.* ⁴**ota.**

motobaiki* [*Engl.*] (–) *coll.* motorbike, motorcycle.

motokaa* (–) *see* **motakaa.**

motokari* (–) *see* **motakaa.**

motomoto *see* **moto.**

moyo (**mioyo**; *dial.* **nyoyo**) 1. heart, feeling, conscience, character. 2. interior, center, middle. **– wa mnazi.** core at the top of the coconut tree *(favored as a delicacy)*. **– wa jipu.** core of an abscess. *fig.* **kujifunzu kwa –** (*or* **kujifunza**). study hard. **kimoyomoyo.** learn by heart. 3. *fig.* courage, determination, willpower. **tia (kuza) –, jipa –, piga – konde.** take heart, pluck up courage. **– za kithaura.** *comm.* revolutionary fervor. 4. *fig.* favorite, pet, sweetheart. **huyu ndiye – wake.** This one is his favorite. *Cf.* **choyo, kijoyo, kimoyo, uchoyo.**

Mozambiki Mozambique.

mpagani* [*Engl.*] (wa-) pagan, heathen.

mpagazi (wa-) carrier, bearer, porter. *Cf.* **pagaa.**

mpaji (wa-) 1. generous person. 2. benefactor, donor. *rel.* – **Mungu.** God is the giver. *Cf.* [1]**pa.**

[1]**mpaka** (mi-) 1. boundary, border, limit, barrier. **piga (weka) –.** set/establish a boundary, draw a limit. **ruka –.** cross a boundary-line, trespass, invade *(a country).* – **mmoja.** bordering, neighboring, contiguous. 2. (time) limit, term. – **wa mwisho.** the latest date, deadline. 3. *prep.* until. – **lini?** until when? how long? – **sasa.** until/up to now. **toka ... –.** from ... to. *Cf.* [2]**paka.**

[2]**mpaka, mpakaji, mpaki** (wa-) one who spreads or applies something. – **chokaa.** plasterer. – **rangi.** painter. *Cf.* [1]**paka.**

mpakaji (wa-) *see* [2]**mpaka.**

mpakato (mi-) something applied: patch, plaster, etc. *Cf.* [1]**paka.**

mpaki (wa-) *see* [2]**mpaka.**

mpakizi (wa-) packer, loader, stevedore. *Cf.* [1]**pakia.**

mpako (mi-) 1. spreading, smearing. – **wa chokaa.** plastering. – **wa rangi.** painting. 2. plaster, stucco, whitewash. *Cf.* [1]**paka.**

mpakuzi (wa-) 1. one who unloads, *(usually)* stevedore, longshoreman. 2. *rare* one who serves food. *Cf.* [1]**pakia.**

mpalilio, mpalio (mi-) 1. hoeing, weeding. 2. hoeing time. *Cf.* [1]**paa.**

mpalilizi (wa-) *see* **mpalizi.**

[1]**mpalio** (mi-) rising of the gorge, choking. *Cf.* [2]**paa.**

[2]**mpalio** (mi-) *see* **mpalilio.**

mpalizi, mpalilizi (wa-) one who hoes or pulls weeds. *Cf.* [1]**paa.**

[1]**mpamba*** [*Pers.*] (mi-) cotton plant *(Gossypium sp.).* *Cf.* [2]**pamba.**

[2]**mpamba, mpambaji, mpambi** (wa-) decorator. *Cf.* [1]**pamba.**

mpambaji (wa-) *see* [2]**mpamba.**

mpambanisho (mi-) 1. contest. 2. bankruptcy. *Cf.* **pambana.**

mpambano (mi-) 1. encounter, meeting *(sport, pol.).* 2. *mil.* skirmish, engagement. 3. *rare* collision *(of vehicles).* *Cf.* **pambana.**

mpambauke (mi-) mpambauke (a shrub, *Lippia asperifolia*).

mpambe, mpambi (wa-) 1. *eth.* mpambe (girl who attends a bride at the wedding ceremony). 2. *rec.* well-dressed young girl. *Cf.* [1]**pamba, pambe.**

[1]**mpambi** (wa-) *see* [2]**mpamba.**

[2]**mpambi** (wa-) *see* **mpambe.**

[1]**mpanda, mpandaji, mpandi, mpanzi** (wa-) planter, sower. *Cf.* [2]**panda.**

[2]**mpanda, mpandaji** (wa-) 1. (mountain-)climber. – **baisikeli.** bicycle rider. – **farasi.** (horseback) rider. 2. *fig.* sponger, sycophant. *Cf.* [1]**panda.**

[3]**mpanda** (mi-) *see* [3]**panda.**

mpandaji (wa-) *see* [1]**mpanda,** [2]**mpanda.**

mpande (mi-) *see* **kipande, upande.**

mpandi (wa-) *see* [1]**mpanda.**

[1]**mpando** (mi-), **pando** (ma-) 1. (act, time, method of) planting, sowing. 2. row of plants. 3. furrow, bed. *Cf.* [2]**panda.**

[2]**mpando** (mi-) (act of) climbing, mounting. *Cf.* [1]**panda.**

mpanga (wa-) *see* [1]**mpangaji,** [2]**mpangaji.**

[1]**mpangaji, mpanga** (wa-) arranger. – **herufi.** typesetter. – **viti (meza).** one who arranges the chairs (tables) at a feast. *Cf.* [1]**panga.**

[2]**mpangaji, mpanga** (wa-) 1. renter, tenant, lessee *(of a house, field).* 2. *rare* employer. *Cf.* [2]**panga.**

mpangishaji, mpangishi (wa-) landlord, lessor. *Cf.* [2]**panga.**

mpangishi (wa-) *see* **mpangishaji.**

[1]**mpango** (mi-) 1. arrangement, apportionment, classification, order. 2. list, plan. 3. *pol.* program, platform, constitution. *Cf.* [1]**panga.**

[2]**mpango** (mi-) 1. (act of) renting, leasing. 2. rent. *Cf.* [2]**panga.**

mpanje (mi-) mpanje (kind of banana).

mpanzi (wa-) *see* [1]**mpanda.**

mpapai*, mpapayu [*Ind.*] (mi-) papaya tree *(Carica papaya).* – **mwitu.** wild papaya *(Melochia melissifolia).* *Cf.* **papai.**

mpapatiko (mi-), **papatiko** (ma-) 1. beating, throbbing, fluttering, palpitation, pulsation, vibration. 2. *med.* spasm, convulsion. *Cf.* [1]**papa.**

mpapayu (mi-) *see* **mpapai.**

mpapindi (mi-) mpapindi (kind of palm, *Cycas Thouarsii*).

mpapuro (mi-) 1. scratching, scraping. 2. scratcher, scraper *(an implement).* 3. trace left by a scratch or scrape; scratch, surface wound. 4. *fig.* scribble, scrawl. *Cf.* **papura.**

mparamuzi (mi-) mparamuzi (kind of tree, *Sterculia appendiculata*).

mparuzi (wa-) 1. idler, lazybones. 2. bungler, blunderer. – **wa karatasi.** scribbler, poor writer. *Cf.* [1]**paa, parua.**

mparuzo (mi-) 1. scratching, scraping. 2. scratch. 3. botchwork. *Cf.* [1]**paa, parua.**

mpasi (wa-) ambitious person, go-getter. *Cf.* **pata.**

mpasua (wa-) one who cuts/splits. – **mbao.** one who saws boards, sawmill worker. *Cf.* **pasua.**

mpasuasanda (–) *(ornith.)* nightjar.

mpasuka (mi-) *see* **mpasuko.**

mpasuko, mpasuka, mpasuo (mi-) 1. tear, split. 2. bursting, breaking. 3. explosion, detonation. **mipasuko ya bomu la atomiki.** atomic bomb explosions. *Cf.* **pasua.**

mpasuo (mi-) *see* **mpasuko.**

mpatanishi (wa-) mediator, negotiator, arbitrator. *Cf.* **pata.**

[1]**mpato** (mi-) 1. = **kipato.** 2. procurement, acquisition. 3. gain, profit. *Cf.* **pata.**

[2]**mpato** (mi-) float *(on fishnets).* (=[1]**chelezo.**)

mpayukaji (wa-) chatterbox, gossip. *Cf.* **paya.**

mpea* (mi-) *see* **mpera.**

[1]**mpekecho, mpeketo** (mi-) 1. (act of) twisting, twirling, stirring. 2. disturbance, excitement. 3. agitation, trouble-making. *Cf.* **pekecha.**

[2]**mpekecho, mpeko** (mi-) mpekecho (two sticks used for producing fire). *Cf.* **pekecha.**

mpeketevu (wa-) vain/arrogant person. *Cf.* **pekecha, peketevu.**

mpeketo (mi-) *see* [1]**mpekecho.**

mpeko (mi-) *see* [2]**mpekecho.**

mpekuzi (wa-) inquisitive person. *Cf.* **pekua, pekuzi.**

mpelekwa (wa-) 1. messenger, courier. 2. envoy, delegate. *Cf.* **peleka.**

mpelelezi (wa-) 1. observer, scout, spy. 2. pursuer, persecutor. *Cf.* **peleleza.**

[1]**mpemba** (mi-) mpemba (kind of manioc).

[2]**mpemba** (wa-) *coll.* ignorant/ill-bred person.

mpenda, mpendi, mpendao (wa-) *(usually w. foll. obj.)* one who is fond of something. – **kula.** glutton. – **michezo.** sports fan. – **raha.** easy-going person. **wapendao vita.** warmongers. *Cf.* **penda.**

mpendao (wa-) *see* **mpenda.**

mpendelevu (wa-) one who favors/shows favoritism. *Cf.* **penda, pendelevu.**

mpendevu, mpendezi (wa-) agreeable/congenial person. *Cf.* **penda, pendevu.**

mpendezi (wa-) *see* **mpendevu.**

mpendi (wa-) *see* **mpenda.**

mpendwa (wa-) 1. favorite, pet. 2. youngest child. *Cf.* **penda.**

mpenyezi (wa-) 1. smuggler. 2. secret agent. 3. traitor. *Cf.* **penya.**

mpenyezo (mi-) 1. penetration. 2. smuggling. 3. bribe, bribery. *Cf.* **penya.**

mpenzi (wa-) favorite; lover, sweetheart. *Cf.* **penda.**

mpepea (mi-) breeze, draft. *Cf.* **pepa.**

mpepetaji, mpetaji (wa-) one who sifts/winnows *(grain).* *Cf.* **pepa.**

mpera*, mpea [*Port.*] (mi-) guava tree *(Psidium guajava).* – **wa kizungu.** myrtle tree *(Jambosa vulgaris).*

mpetaji (wa-) *see* **mpepetaji.**

mpevu (wa-) full-grown person, adult. **huyu si mtoto mchanga ni –.** This person is no longer a child but an adult. *Cf.* **pevua, pevu.**

mpevushi (wa-) one who tempts/perverts/seduces. *Cf.* **pevua.**

mpiga, mpigaji, mpigi (wa-) *(always w. foll. obj.)* one who strikes/makes/produces something. – **picha.** photographer. – **simu.** telegrapher. – **chapa.** printer. – **muziki.** musician. – **ramli.** soothsayer, fortune-teller. – **kura.** voter. – **maji.** *coll.* drinker. – **ngoma.** drummer. – **nyama.** hunter. – **kelele.** noisy child. – **filimbi.** *sport.* umpire, referee. *Cf.* **piga.**

mpigaji (wa-) 1. = **mpiga.** 2.: – **ngumi.** boxer. – **bendi.** orchestra musician. *Cf.* **piga.**

mpiganaji, mpigani (wa-) warrior, fighter. *Cf.* **piga.**

mpigani (wa-) *see* **mpiganaji.**

mpiganisho (mi-) impact, collision; encounter; conflict, combat. *Cf.* **piga.**

mpigano (mi-) *see* **pigano.**

mpigi (wa-) *see* **mpiga.**

mpigo (mi-) striking, hitting, beating; blow. *Cf.* **piga.**

mpigwa (wa-) 1. defeated/beaten person. 2. *rare* person killed in combat, casualty. *Cf.* **piga.**

mpikaji (wa-) *rare* cook. (= **mpishi.**) *Cf.* **pika.**

[1]**mpiko** (mi-) cooking, preparation of food. *Cf.* **pika.**

[2]**mpiko** (mi-) 1. carrying-pole; supporting bar of a hammock. 2. lever.

mpilipili* [*Pers.*] (mi-) pepper plant (Capsicum annuum). – **manga.** black-pepper plant *(Piper nigrum).* – **hoho.** African pepper plant *(Capsicum frutescens).* *Cf.* **pilipili.**

mpima, mpimaji (wa-) one who measures, surveyor. *Cf.* **pima.**

mpimaji (wa-) *see* **mpima.**

mpimo (mi-) (act of) measuring, surveying, weighing. *Cf.* **pima.**

mpindani (wa-) a person bent/deformed by disease. *Cf.* **pinda.**

mpindanifu (wa-) unshakable/resolute person. *Cf.* **pinda, pindani.**

mpindano (mi-) 1. stiffening, straining, pressing. 2. *med.* cramp. *Cf.* **pinda.**

mpinduzi (wa-) 1. disturber of the peace, rioter. 2. lawbreaker. 3. rebel, agitator. *Cf.* **pinda.**

mpinga (wa-) one who obstructs. **– maendeleo** *pol.* reactionary. **– thaura.** counter-revolutionary. *Cf.* **pinga.**

mpingaji, mpingani, mpinzani (wa-) 1. opponent, adversary. 2. mischief-maker. *Cf.* **pinga.**

mpingani (wa-) *see* **mpingaji.**

mpingi (mi-) mpingi (kind of thorn tree, *Ximenia americana*).

[1]**mpingo** (mi-) ebony tree *(Diospyros ebenum).*

[2]**mpingo** (mi-) *see* **pingo.**

mpini (mi-) (*augment. of* **kipini**) (handle *of a knife, etc.*).

mpinzani (wa-) 1. = **mpingaji.** 2. stubborn person. *Cf.* **pinga.**

mpira (mi-) 1. rubber tree. 2. rubber. **– wa gurudumu.** (bicycle, automobile) tire. **– wa ndani.** inner tube. **– wa nje.** (tire) casing. 3. (rubber) ball, football. **kucheza –.** play football. 4. elasticity. **nyama hii ngumu kama –.** This meat is tough.

mpishi (wa-) cook. (= *rare* **mpikaji.**) *Cf.* **pika.**

mpita, mpitaji (wa-) 1. (*also* **– njia**) passer-by. 2. *rare* traveler, passenger. *Cf.* **pita.**

mpitaji (wa-) *see* **mpita.**

mpito (mi-) crossing, passage. *Cf.* **pita.**

mpoa, mpua (mi-) distant country. **– wa bahari.** seacoast.

[1]**mpofu, pofu** (–) eland *(Boselaphus canna).*

[2]**mpofu** (wa-) *rare* *see* **kipofu.**

mpokea, mpokeaji, mpokezi (wa-) one who receives/collects. **– kodi.** tax collector. *Cf.* **pokea.**

mpokeaji (wa-) *see* **mpokea.**

mpokezi (wa-) *see* **mpokea.**

mpomoshi (wa-) one who destroys. *Cf.* **poromoa.**

mponda (wa-) 1. *(always w. foll. obj.)* one who pounds/crushes/pulverizes. – **mawa.** stonemason. 2. *fig., coll.* – **mali (fedha).** one who squanders property (money). *Cf.* **ponda.**

[1]**mpondo** (mi-) (act of) crushing, grinding, pulverizing. *Cf.* **ponda.**

[2]**mpondo** (mi-) *see* **pondo.**

mponyeshaji, mponyi (wa-) 1. one who cures, physician. 2. quack. *Cf.* **pona.**

mponyi (wa-) *see* **mponyeshaji.**

[1]**mpopoo*, mpopo** [*Pers.*] (mi-) mpopoo (kind of palm, *Areca catechu*). *Cf.* **popoo.**

[2]**mpopoo** (mi-) (act of) knocking something down *(w. a stick/stone)*. *Cf.* **popoa.**

mpororo (mi-) 1. single file, Indian file. 2. row of tribal markings down the nose.

Mportugesi* [*Engl.*] (wa-) *rare* a Portuguese. (= **Mreno.**)

mposa (wa-) *see* **mposaji.**

mposaji, mposa, mposi (wa-) one who proposes marriage, suitor. *Cf.* **posa.**

mposeaji (wa-) person who acts on behalf of another in proposing marriage, matchmaker. *Cf.* **posa.**

mposi (wa-) *see* **mposaji.**

mposo (mi-) proposal of marriage, courtship. *Cf.* **posa.**

mposta* [*Engl.*] (wa-) *rare* post-office employee. (= **mtu wa posta**). *Cf.* **posta.**

mpotefu (wa-) *see* **mpotevu.**

mpotevu, mpotefu, mpotezi (wa-) spendthrift, wastrel, libertine. – **wa mali (fedha).** one who squanders property (money). – **wa maneno.** windbag, chatterbox, one who talks illogically. *Cf.* **potea, potevu.**

mpotezi (wa-) *see* **mpotevu.**

mpoto (mi-) (act of) twisting, braiding, knitting. *Cf.* **pota.**

mpotoe, mpotwe, mpotovu, mpotofu (wa-) stubborn/capricious/unprincipled person. *Cf.* **pota.**

mpotofu, mpotovu, mpotwe (wa-) *see* **mpotoe.**

mpozi (wa-) one who cures/heals, physician. *Cf.* **poa.**

mpujufu (wa-) mean/vile/shameless person. *Cf.* **pujua, pujufu.**

mpukuti (wa-) *coll.* money. *Cf.* **pukuta.**

mpumbavu, mpumbafu (wa-) stupid person, fool. *Cf.* **pumbaa, pumbavu.**

mpunga (mi-) rice plant *(Oryza sativa)*, (grains of) rice *(while the plant is still standing in the field)*. *See also* **mchele, wali.**

mpungate, mpungati (mi-) mpungate (species of cactus, *Opuntia ficus*).

mpungufu (wa-) person with a defect, one lacking in some respect. **mtu huyu – wa akili.** This person is stupid/foolish/ mentally defective. *Cf.* [2]**punga, pungufu.**

mpupu (mi-) mpupu (species of bean plant, *Mucuna pruriens* or *Canavalia ensiformis).*

mpurukushani (wa-) 1. careless/negligent/ slipshod person. 2. carefree/lighthearted person. *Cf.* **purukusha, purukushani.**

mpurule (mi-) mpurule (a shrub, *Chenopodium sp.*)

mpururo (mi-) 1. (act of) rubbing/stripping off, shelling *(peas, beans, etc.).* 2. spinning/paying out *(thread through the fingers).* 3. a single file *(of people, etc.) Cf.* **pura.**

mpuzi (wa-) 1. silly/frivolous person. 2. chatterbox, gossip. 3. nagger, faultfinder. *Cf.* [2]**puza.**

mpwa (wa-) nephew, niece *(= child of one's sister).*

[1]**mpweke** (wa-) lonely/solitary person *(without relatives). Cf.* **peke.**

[2]**mpweke** (mi-) 1. mpweke (kind of hardwood tree). 2. short, thick stick or truncheon *(made from the wood of the mpweke tree).* 3. *fig.* difficulty.

mpyo (mi-) rubber liana *(Landolphia Kirkii).*

mpyoro (wa-) 1. user of obscene language. 2. one who exaggerates: boaster, talebearer; hypocrite, liar. 3. one who shows off by using many English words or difficult and unusual Swahili words. *Cf.* **pyora, pyoro.**

[1]**mraba*, maraba** 1. (mi-) square, rectangle, cube. **–a –.** square, rectangular, perpendicular. **mistari ya –.** perpendicular lines. 2. *adj.* right *(of an angle).* **pembe –.** right angle. **pembetatu mraba.** right-angled triangle. *Cf.* **mirabaraba.**

[2]**mraba*, maraba** (mi-) preserves, jam, marmalade. **– wa tangawizi.** candied ginger. **njugu za –.** peanut brittle.

mrabaha* (mi-) *hist.* trading tax *(collected by the chief of a particular place for the right to trade in that place).*

mradi* 1. (mi-) (*also* **muradi**) intention, plan, decision; desire, ambition, goal; *(rare)* whim. **sasa ni mwalimu na ametimiza – wake.** Now he is a teacher and has achieved his ambition. 2. *conj.* and so, accordingly; since, because; provided that. **– amelala msimwamshe.** Since he is asleep do not wake him. 3. *adv., rare* intentionally.

mrajis* (ma-) *see* **rais.**

mrama* (mi-) *naut.* pitching, rolling *(of a ship).* **enda –.** pitch, roll; *(fig.)* take a wrong direction, go the wrong way. **mipango yetu imekwenda –.** Our plans have gone awry.

mramba, mbaramba, mlamba (–) *ornith.* mramba (kind of starling). – **mweupe.** golden oriole.

mranaa*, mranaha, mrenaha (ma-) 1. mranaa (kind of tree, *Datura metel & Datura fastuosa).* 2. *rare* = **mwegea,** *q.v.*

mranaha* (mi-) *see* **mranaa.**

1**mrao*** (mi-) 1. wick. 2. *arch., mil.* match, fuse. **bunduki ya –.** matchlock gun.

2**mrao*** [*?*] (mi-) mrao (cool season, harvest time).

mrarua (wa-) one who tears something. *Cf.* **rarua.**

mraruasanda (–) *ornith.* nightjar (*lit.:* 'shroud-tearer.'). (= **pwaju.**)

mraruo (mi-) (act of) tearing, rending. *Cf.* **rarua.**

mrasharasha*, mrasho (mi-) sprinkling. – **wa mvua, mvua ya rasharasha.** sprinkle, drizzle *(of rain). Cf.* **rasha.**

mrashi* (mi-) 1. scent-bottle, spray. 2. scent, perfume. *Cf.* **rasha.**

mrasho (mi-) *see* **mrasharasha.**

mratabu* (mi-) mratabu (species of plum tree, *Achras zapota*).

mregaa* (–) *see* **mrejaa.**

mrehani*, mrihani (mi-) *bot.* (sweet) basil *(Ocimum basilicum).*

mrejaa*, mregaa (–) commission business, commission. **biashara ya –.** commission business. *Cf.* **rejea, rejareja.**

mrekani* [*Engl.*] (mi-) *see* **merekani.**

mreli* [*Engl.*] (wa-) *rare* railroad worker, railwayman. *Cf.* **reli.**

mrembe (mi-) 1. wooden spear with a sharp point. 2. *arch.* German military helmet, Pickelhaube (Tanganyika).

mrembo 1. (wa-) person who pays much attention to his dress; fashion plate, fop. 2. (mi-) ornament, decoration (= **rembo**). *Cf.* **remba.**

mrenaha (mi-) *see* **mranaa.**

mrengu (mi-) *naut.* outrigger.

mreno* [*Port.* **reino**] (wa-) a Portuguese. *Cf.* **Reno.**

mrera (mi-) mrera (embroidered ornamentation on the collar of a kanzu).

mreteni (mi-) *bot.* juniper.

mriba (mi-) mriba (leaf of the sweet potato plant, eaten as a vegetable).

mridhia* (wa-) *see* **maridhia.**

mrihani* (mi-) *see* **mrehani.**

mrihi, mriti (mi-) mrihi (kind of tree producing good lumber for building purposes).

mrija (mi-) 1. mrija (kind of reed, used for making musical instruments and as a drinking tube). 2. pipe, flute *(musical instrument).* 3. *rare* pipe, tube *(in gen.).* 4. *rec., elec.* tube *(radio, etc.).* 5. *(in gen.)* tube, straw *(for drinking).*

mrili (mi-) mrili (kind of tree, used for making dugout canoes).

mrima* (mi-) 1. coast, coastal region, littoral. 2. continent, mainland *(as opp. to islands). Cf.* **Kimrima, mmrima.**

mrithi* (wa-) heir. *Cf.* **rithi.**

mrithisha*, mrithishi (wa-) executor *(of a will, estate). Cf.* **rithi.**

mrithishi* (wa-) *see* **mrithisha.**

mriti (mi-) *see* **mrihi.**

mrizabu*, mlizabu (mi-) 1. channel, drain, pipe. 2. water tap, faucet. *Cf.* **mlizamu.**

mroho* (wa-) glutton, greedy person *(one who eats more than his share). Cf.* **roho.**

mronge (mi-) mronge (horse-radish tree, *Moringa pterigosperma).*

[1]**mrongo** (wa-) young person of either sex who has been through the initiation rites, one who is experienced in matters of sex. *Cf.* **msungo.**

[2]**mrongo** (wa-) *dial.* liar, swindler. *See also* **mwongo.**

mrua*, murua 1. (–) politeness, courtesy, obligingness, good behavior; respect, deference. 2. (wa-) courteous, well-bred person.

mruba (mi-), **ruba** (ma-) leech.

mrugaruga, rugaruga (wa-) 1. *mil.* irregular soldier, guerrilla. 2. robber, plunderer.

mrukaji (wa-) 1. *sport* jumper. 2. *av., rare* flier, pilot. *Cf.* **ruka.**

mruko (mi-) 1. jumping, jump. 2. flight. *Cf.* **ruka.**

Mruma*, Mrumi (wa-) Roman. *Cf.* **rumi, kirumi.**

Mrusi* (wa-) a Russian. *Cf.* **Kirusi, Urusi.**

mrututi*, mrututu [*Ind.*] (–) *chem.* copper sulphate, blue vitriol.

mrututu* (–) *see* **mrututi.**

msaada* (mi-) help, aid, assistance, support. – **wa fedha.** financial assistance/support. – **wa iktisadi.** economic aid. – **wa kifundi.** technical assistance. *Cf.* **saidia.**

msaajaji* (wa-) *see* **msaidizi.**

msaala* (–) *see* **masahala.**

msadikifu* (wa-) 1. trusting/friendly person. 2. trustworthy/reliable person. *Cf.* **sadiki, sadikifu.**

msafa* (mi-) *see* **safu.**

msafara* (mi-) 1. caravan. 2. journey, expedition. 3. crowd of people. **nimekutana na – wa watu wakitoka mpirani.** I met a big crowd of people coming from the football game. *Cf.* **safiri, safari.**

msafihi*, msafii (wa-) impudent/insolent/rude/ill-bred person. *Cf.* **safihi.**

msafii* (wa-) *see* **msafihi.**

msafiri* (wa-) traveler. *Cf.* **safiri.**

msafirishaji* (wa-): **– mali.** *econ.* exporter. *Cf.* **safiri.**

msafishaji* (wa-) 1. cleaner, charwoman **– choo.** latrine cleaner. 2. medical orderly. *Cf.* **safi.**

msafu* (mi-) *see* **msahafu.**

msaga, msagi (wa-) miller. *Cf.* **saga.**

msagaliwa (wa-) an impotent male who acts as a servant to women, eunuch (*lit.* grinder of sandalwood; *cf.* **saga, liwa**).

msagi (wa-) *see* **msaga.**

[1]msago (mi-) grinding *(of meal, flour).* *Cf.* **saga.**

[2]msago *adv.* *see* **[2]sago.**

[1]msaha* (mi-) 1. crowbar. 2. spade, shovel.

[2]msaha* (–) *see* **mdhaha.**

msahafu*, msafu (mi-) 1. book *(us. the Koran).* 2. *rare* page, leaf. 3. *rare* Bible. *Cf.* **sahifa.**

msahala* (mi-) *med.* laxative, purgative.

msahau*, msahaulifu, msahaulizi (wa-) forgetful/absent-minded person. *Cf.* **sahau.**

msahaulifu* (wa-) *see* **msahau.**

msahaulizi* (wa-) *see* **msahau.**

msaidia* (wa-) *see* **msaidizi.**

msaidizi*, msaidia (wa-) 1. helper, assistant. **– wa hospitali.** nurse's aid. 2. accomplice. *Cf.* **saidia.**

msaji* (mi-) teak tree *(Tectona grandis).*

msaka (wa-) *see* **msakaji.**

msakaji, msaka, msasi (wa-) driver, hunter. *Cf.* **saka.**

Msakalawa* (wa-) inhabitant of (the west coast of) Madagascar.

msakamo (mi-) sticking, jamming. *Cf.* **sakama.**

msako (mi-) hunting, trapping. *Cf.* **saka.**

[1]**msala*** (mi-) 1. *Isl.* prayer mat. 2. *(in gen.)* oval/round mat. *Cf.* **sala.**

[2]**msala*** (mi-) toilet, W.C. **enda msalani.** go to the toilet.

msalaba* (mi-) *hist., rel.* cross. **ishara ya —.** sign of the cross. **Chama cha Msalaba Mwekundu.** Red Cross Society. *Cf.* **sulibi.**

msalata*, msaliti (wa-) 1. traitor, slanderer; one who makes a false accusation. 2. despot. *Cf.* **salata.**

msalheri* *salutation* Good morning, etc. *Cf.* **heri.**

msalihina*, msalikhina (wa-) (*also* **salihina,** wa-) 1. honest/incorruptible person. 2. pious/devout person. *Cf.* **salihi.**

msalikhina* (wa-) *see* **msalihina.**

msalimina*, msalimu (wa-) 1. pious/devout person *(of any faith).* 2. *rare* Moslem (= **Mwislamu**). *Cf.* **silimu.**

msalimu* (wa-) *see* **msalimina.**

msaliti* (wa-) *see* **msalata.**

msamaha*, msamehe (mi-), **masamaha** *pl.* 1. forgiveness, pardon. (= **ghofira.**) 2. liberation, deliverance, salvation. *Cf.* **samehe.**

msamba (mi-) *anat.* perineum. (= **kitako.**)

msambale (mi-) msambale (flowering shrub, *Lobelia fervens*).

msambia (mi-) msambia (kind of tree with edible fruit).

msameha* (wa-) *see* **msamehaji.**

msamehaji*, msameha (wa-) forgiving/indulgent person. *Cf.* **samehe.**

msamehe* (mi-) *see* **msamaha.**

msamilo (mi-) msamilo (a kind of wooden headrest or pillow).

[1]**msana** (mi-) *dial.* passage, corridor. (= **ukumbi.**)

[2]**msana*** (wa-) metal worker, smith. **— chuma.** blacksmith. *Cf.* [2]**sana.**

msanaa*, msani, msanii (wa-) skillful/competent craftsman, specialist. *Cf.* **sanaa.**

msanaka (mi-) msanaka (species of pine, *Pandanus sp.).*

msanapichi, msanapiti (mi-) frangipane/jasmine tree (*Plumeria acuminata).*

msandali* (mi-) sandalwood tree. *Cf.* **sandali.**

msandarusi* (mi-) (gum-)copal tree. *Cf.* **sandarusi.**

msangao (mi-) *see* **mshangao.**

msani* (wa-) *see* **msanaa.**

msanii*, msanifu (wa-) 1. = **msanaa.** 2. *fig.* one who invents and spreads lies. *Cf.* **sanaa, sanifu.**

msapata* [*Port.*] (mi-) msapata (kind of dance).

msaro (mi-) msaro (species of thorn tree).

msasa (mi-) 1. msasa (*Ficus sp.*, the leaves of which are used for smoothing wood). 2. sandpaper, emery paper. **meza hii haikupigwa – vizuri.** This table is not smooth (has not been well sanded).

msasi (wa-) *see* **msakaji.**

msazo (mi-) 1. remainder, remains, remnant. 2. *fig., rare* remains, corpse. *Cf.* [2]**saa.**

msegese (mi-) msegese (kind of tree, *Bauhinia Thonningii;* the wood is used for making bedsteads, and a remedy for bronchitis is prepared from the roots).

mseja (wa-) 1. unmarried man, bachelor. *Cf.* [2]**useja.** 2. a necklace of small beads. *Cf.* [1]**useja.**

msema (wa-) *see* **msemaji.**

msemaji, msema (wa-) 1. narrator, speaker, orator. 2. *recent, pol.* information officer, spokesman. **– wa mkutano huu.** the speaker at this meeting. 3. commentator. 4. = **msemi.** *Cf.* **sema.**

msemi (wa-) 1 = **msemaji.** 2. speaker *(parliament).* 3. spokesman. **– wao.** their spokesman. **yeye ni – wa chama cha kikomunisti katika baraza la kufanya sheria.** He is the spokesman of the communist group in the legislative body. *Cf.* **sema.**

msemo (mi-) 1. speech, address. 2 conversation. 3. dialect; *(rare)* language. 4. utterance; saying, maxim; expression, idiom. 5. slogan, watchword. *Cf.* **sema.**

msengenya (wa-) *see* **msengenyi.**

msengenyaji (wa-) 1. underhanded assailant, calumniator. 2. *fig., rel.* the devil, Satan. *Cf.* **sengenya.**

msengenyano (mi-) talebearing, backbiting; dissension, quarrel, dispute. *Cf.* **sengenya.**

msengenyi, msengenya (wa-) gossip, talebearer. *Cf.* **sengenya.**

msengenyo (mi-) rumor, gossip, slander, calumny. *Cf.* **sengenya.**

msetiri (wa-) *see* [1]**mstiri.**

mseto (mi-) 1. mseto (a porridge made of beans cooked together with various grains, maize, or rice). 2. *fig.* a mixture. *pol.:* **serikali ya –.** a government including the representatives of various tribes/parties, coalition government. *Cf.* **seta.**

msewe (mi-) 1. msewe (a kind of bush bearing pods which are used as rattles). 2. msewe (rattles worn by dancers). 3. child's rattle. 4. kind of large drum.

mshabaha* (mi-) similarity, resemblance. *Cf.* [1]**shabaha.**

mshabiki* (wa-) enthusiast. **mtu huyu – sana wa karata.** He is an enthusiastic/inveterate cardplayer.

mshadhari* (–) *see* **mshazari.**

mshahara* (–, mi-) payment, remuneration; (monthly, weekly) salary, wages; income.

mshairi* (wa-) poet. *Cf.* **shairi, ushairi.**

mshakiki*, mshikaki (mi-) 1. spit, skewer. 2. piece of meat roasted on a skewer.

mshale (mi-) 1. arrow. **– wa sumu.** poisoned arrow. 2. *fig.* ray. **– wa nuru.** ray of sunlight. 3. sting *(of a bee, etc.).* 4. hand, pointer, indicator.

mshamo (mi-) 1. stick for digging holes. 2. crowbar. 3. *naut.* marline spike.

mshangao, msangao (mi-) (*also* **ushangao**) 1. astonishment, amazement. 2. confusion, speechlessness. *Cf.* **shangaa.**

msharafu* (wa-) an honored/respected person. *Cf.* **sharifu.**

msharasi (mi-) awl.

mshari* (wa-) an unlucky person, jinx *(someone who causes misfortune or injury to other people).* *Cf.* [1]**shari.**

msharifu* (mi-) *see* **kisharifu.**

msharika* (wa-) *see* **mshirika.**

mshaufu* (wa-) 1. shameless/ill-mannered person. 2. frivolous/ostentatious person. *Cf.* **shaua, shaufu.**

mshauri* (wa-) 1. advisor, counsellor. **– wa mambo ya sheria.** legal advisor, counsel. 2. *pol.* representative, deputy, delegate. **– wa upande wa serikali.** government delegate. *Cf.* **shauri.**

mshawishi* 1. (wa-) tempter, seducer. 2. (mi-) *rare* = **shawishi.** 3. *pol.* agitator. *Cf.* **shawishi.**

mshazari*, mshadhari 1 (–) tape, cord, string; edging, braid; hem 2. (–) twist, bend, curve, slant. **mstari wa –.** oblique line. 3. *adv.* slanting, oblique; lopsided, crooked; cylindrical. *fig.:* **mambo yake siku hizi yanakwenda –.** His affairs are not in order at present (have not gone well, turned out badly). 4. (wa-) *fig.* deformed person.

mshelisheli* [< Seychelles] (mi-) mshelisheli (species of breadfruit tree).

mshemali* (wa-) an Arab from Muscat.

mshenga (wa-) 1. go-between, matchmaker *(one who arranges a marriage for someone else).* 2. messenger, agent, confidant.

mshenzi* [*Pers.*] (wa-) 1. aboriginal, native *(from the interior).* 2. savage, barbarian. 3. (*also* **mtu –**) uncouth/uncivilized/nondescript person. 4. *interj.* **– we!** You scoundrel! *Cf.* **shenzi.**

mshihiri* (wa-) an Arab from Sheher (South Arabia).

mshika, mshiki (wa-) (*always w. foll. obj.*) one who holds something. **– sukani.** 1. *naut.* helmsman. 2. driver *(of an automobile).* 3. pilot *(of an airplane).* **– filimbi.** *sport, rare* referee, umpire. **– duru.** leader of the duru ceremony (drinking by turn). *Cf.* **shika.**

mshikaki* (mi-) *see* **mshakiki.**

mshikano (mi-) 1. mass, accumulation, group. 2. cluster, bunch *(of fruit, etc.).* *Cf.* **shika.**

mshiki (wa-) *see* **mshika.**

mshikilizo, mshikizo (mi-) (act of) tacking/basting together *(in dressmaking).* *Cf.* **shika.**

mshikizo (mi-) *see* **mshikilizo.**

mshinda, mshindi (wa-) 1. victor. 2. winner *(sport).* *Cf.* **¹shinda.**

mshindaji, mshindi (wa-) 1. victor, conqueror. 2. rival, competitor. *Cf.* **¹shinda.**

mshindani, mshindanizi (wa-) 1. opponent, adversary, rival. *prov.* **asiyekubali kushindwa si –.** The man who is not willing to be beaten is no adversary. 2. participant in a contest. 3. stubborn/contentious person. *Cf.* **¹shinda.**

mshindano (mi-) *see* **shindano.**

mshinde (wa-) *see* **mshindwa.**

mshindi (wa-) *see* **mshinda, mshindaji.**

mshindikizo (mi-) 1. accompaniment. 2. escort *(for protection),* guard. 3. retinue, attendants. *Cf.* **¹shinda.**

mshindilio (mi-) 1. (act of) pushing, forcing, stuffing *(e.g., clothes into a suitcase).* 2. *mil.* loading *(a gun, cannon).* *Cf.* **¹shinda.**

mshindio (mi-) 1. (act of) working the woof/weft into the warp in weaving. 2. woof/weft. *Cf.* **¹shinda.**

mshindo (mi-) 1. (sudden, loud) noise: crash, bang, rumble, etc. **– wa miguu ya farasi.** the trample of horses. **– wa ngoma.** beating of a drum. 2. shouting, outcry, din. **– wa watu walio (katika mkutano) mkutanoni.** noise of people in a crowd. 3. *phy.* orgasm. *Cf.* **¹shinda.**

mshindwa, mshinde (wa-) one who is defeated/beaten/conquered. *Cf.* **¹shinda.**

mshipa (mi-) *anat.* 1. vein, artery. 2. pulse. **– unapiga.** the pulse beats. 3. nerve. 4. muscle, sinew, tendon. 5. any illness involving the nerves or muscles. **maradhi ya –.** neuralgia, sciatica. 6. (**– wa utumbo kutokeza**) hernia. 7.: **– wa maji.** hydrocele.

mshipi (mi-) 1. band, cord, strip (of cloth). 2. belt. 3. suspenders, braces. 4. fishing-line.

Mshirazi* (wa-) a descendant of Persians from Shiraz.

mshirika*, mshiriki, msharika 1. (wa-) partner, joint-owner. **– biashara.** business partner. 2. (mi-) partnership. *Cf.* **shiriki.**

mshiriki* (wa-, mi-) *see* **mshirika.**

mshirikina* (wa-) superstitious person *(one who believes in magic and sorcery). Cf.* **shiriki.**

mshitaki* (wa-) *see* **mshtaki.**

mshitakiwa* (wa-) *see* **mshtakiwa.**

mshitiri* (wa-) *see* **mshtiri.**

mshokishoki (mi-) mshokishoki (kind of tree bearing edible fruit, *Nephelium lappaceum). Cf.* **shokishoki.**

mshona (wa-) *(always w. foll. obj.)* one who sews. **– nguo.** tailor, dressmaker. **– viatu.** shoemaker. *Cf.* **shona.**

mshonaji (wa-) *see* **mshoni.**

mshongo (wa-) passionate person *(usually in a sexual sense). Cf.* **shonga.**

mshoni, mshonaji (wa-) one who sews. **– wa nguo.** tailor. **– wa viatu.** shoemaker. *Cf.* **shona.**

mshono (mi-) 1. sewing. 2. seam, suture. 3. ready-made clothing. *Cf.* **shona, mashona.**

mshtaka* (mi-) complaint, accusation, charge. *Cf.* **shtaki.**

mshtaki*, mstaki, mshitaki (wa-) 1. talebearer, informer. 2. *jur.* plaintiff. *Cf.* **shtaki.**

mshtakiwa*, mshitakiwa (wa-) *jur.* accused, defendant. *Cf.* **shtaki.**

Mshtarii* (–) *astr.* Jupiter.

mshtiri*, mshitiri, mstiri (wa-) 1. buyer *(usually at auction).* 2. *jur.* client.

mshtuko, mstuko (mi-) 1. sudden fright, convulsion, wincing, flinching. 2. shock, stroke. 3. sprain. 4. *fig., elec.* (electrical) shock. *Cf.* **shtua.**

mshtuo, mstuo (mi-) cause of fright/shock. *Cf.* **shtua.**

mshubiri (mi-) *see* **msubili.**

mshuko (mi-) 1. descent, lowering, decline. 2. sinking. **– wa jua.** sunset. 3. *fig., rare* end, conclusion. *Cf.* **shua.**

mshuku* (mi-) chewing tobacco.

mshulu* (mi-) *see* **shuru.**

mshumaa* (mi-) candle. **washa (zima) –.** light (extinguish) a candle. **kinara cha –.** candlestick.

mshupavu (wa-) 1. tough/hardy/courageous person. 2. energetic/resolute person. 3. obstinate/persevering person. *Cf.* **shupaa, shupavu.**

mshuru* (mi-) *see* **shuru.**

mshurutisho* (mi-) pressure, force, compulsion. *Cf.* **shuruti.**

mshushio (mi-) *see* **mshusho.**

mshusho, mshushio (mi-) 1. (act of) lowering, discharging. 2. *phy.* ejaculation, orgasm. *Cf.* **shua.**

msia, mzia (mi-) msia (kind of fish similar to an eel).

msiba* (mi-) 1. misfortune, affliction, distress; accident, disaster, calamity. *prov.* **hakuna – usio mwenziwe.** A misfortune seldom comes alone. 2. poverty. 3. sadness, grief; mourning. **shikwa (patwa) na – mkuu (mkubwa).** be overcome by great sorrow. **pa mkono wa –.** condole with someone, express sympathy. **nguo za –.** mourning dress. *Cf.* ²**sibu.**

¹**msibu*** (wa-) one who causes sorrow/misfortune. *Cf.* ²**sibu.**

²**msibu*** (wa-) one who foretells, prophet. *Cf.* ⁴**sibu.**

msichana (wa-) young girl *(who has reached puberty). Cf.* **kisichana.**

msifu* (wa-) flatterer, eulogist. **– mno.** toady, sycophant, lickspittle. *Cf.* ¹**sifa, sifu.**

msiga (mi-) msiga (kind of tree, *Dobera loranthifolia;* twigs from this tree are used for cleansing the teeth).

msikiaji (wa-) listener, auditor. *Cf.* **sikia.**

msikilivu, msikivu (wa-) tractable/docile/obedient person. *Cf.* **sikia, sikilivu.**

msikilizaji, msikizi (wa-) 1. listener, auditor. 2. attentive person. *Cf.* **sikia.**

msikilizano (mi-) 1. audibility. 2. *fig.* (mutual) understanding. *Cf.* **sikia.**

msikiti*, meskiti (mi-) *Isl.* mosque.

msikivu (wa-) *see* **msikilivu.**

msikizi (wa-) *see* **msikilizaji.**

msikundazi (mi-) msikundazi (kind of tree; the wood is used for building boats).

msikwao (wa-) (< si + ¹**kwao**) 1. homeless person, wanderer, vagrant. 2. *fig., pol.* cosmopolitan.

msilimu* (wa-) *see* **mwislamu.**

msimacho (wa-) (< si + **macho**) obtuse person, wilfully blind person.

msimamizi (wa-) 1. overseer. 2. superintendent, manager, administrator. 3. advocate, defender; attorney. 4. *rare* protector. *Cf.* **simama.**

msimbo (wa-), **kisimbo** (vi-) 1. bad reputation/character. 2. assumed name, pseudonym *(to disguise a name of bad repute)*.

msimiko (mi-) *phy.* erection. *Cf.* **simama.**

msimu*, **musimu** (mi-) 1. northeast monsoon. 2. msimu (season of the northeast monsoon). 3. *(in gen.)* period, season *(esp. w. ref. to agriculture)*. **sasa ni – wa embe.** Now is the mango-harvesting season. 4. *rec.* semester.

msimulizi* (wa-) 1. narrator, storyteller. 2. *rec.* reporter, correspondent. *Cf.* [1]**simulia, simulizi.**

msindi (mi-) *see* **msinzi.**

msindikizo (mi-) (act of) accompanying/speeding a departing guest. *Cf.* [1]**shinda, shindikizo** 3.

msindusi (mi-) msindusi (kind of tree).

msinga (mi-) msinga (kind of hardwood tree).

msingefuri (mi-) *see* **mzingefuri.**

msingi, mzingi, msinji (mi-) 1. ditch, trench, pit, drain. 2. foundation. **jenga –.** lay the cornerstone/foundation. 3. *fig.* basis, essence, substance *(of a thing)*. 4. *mus.* key, clef.

msinji (mi-) *see* **msingi.**

msinzi, msindi, msizi (mi-) msinzi (species of mangrove, *Rhizophora mucronata;* a red dye is prepared from the bark, and the trunk is used for boat-building).

msio (mi-) msio (soft coral stone, used for massaging the skin).

msiri* (wa-) 1. confidant, intimate friend. 2. secret agent, accomplice. *Cf.* [1]**siri.**

msirisha (mi-) msirisha (a plant from which a black dye is made, *Euclea multiflora)*. (= **mdaa.**)

msisimko (mi-) gooseflesh, tingling *(from fright or excitement)*. (= **kimbimbi.**) *Cf.* **simua.**

msitamu*, **mstamu** (mi-) *naut.* keelson.

msitiri* (wa-) *see* [1]**mstiri.**

msitu (mi-) land covered with low, shrubby vegetation, bush. *red.* **misitumisitu.** brushwood, undergrowth, thicket. *Cf.* **mwitu.**

msiwana (wa-) (< **si** + **wana**) childless person. *Cf.* **mwana.**

msizi (mi-) *see* **msinzi.**

msoa (mi-) large gathering/company *(of people)*.

msokoto (mi-) 1. (act of) twisting, twining *(thread, etc.)*. 2. *something twisted:* curl, braid. 3. *fig.:* **– wa tumbo.** stomachache, colic. *Cf.* **sokota.**

msolo (mi-) msolo (kind of thorny bush, *Caesalpinia cristata*). *Cf.* **solo.**

[1]**msoma** (wa-) (*always w. foll. obj.*) one who reads. – **gazeti.** reader *(of a newspaper)*. *Cf.* **soma.**

[2]**msoma** (mi-) msoma (kind of dance).

msomaji, msomi, msomeshaji (wa-) reader, lecturer. *Cf.* **soma.**

msomeshaji, msomeshi (wa-) 1. *rare* = **msomaji.** 2. teacher, tutor. *Cf.* **soma.**

msomeshi (wa-) *see* **msomeshaji.**

msomi (wa-) *see* **msomaji.**

msomo (mi-) 1. (act of) reading. 2. reading matter. 3. studying. 4. subject *(of study)*. 5. *rare* class, lesson (= **masomo**). *Cf.* **soma.**

msonde (*rare* **msondo**) (mi-) msonde (large drum). *Cf.* **msondo.**

msondo (mi-) 1. *rare* = **msonde.** 2. msondo (a dance performed at the initiation rites for girls). 3. msondo (a kind of tall fez, formerly worn by police). 4. loud, booming noise *(of a drum, cannon)*.

msonga, msongi (mi-) *(always w. foll. obj.)* one who pushes/urges. – **mbele.** one who presses forward. *Cf.* **songa.**

msongano, msonge (mi-) 1. (act of) pushing/shoving/crowding. 2. crowd, mass *(of people or things)*. *Cf.* **songa.**

msonge (mi-) *see* **msongano.**

msongi (mi-) *see* **msonga.**

msongo (mi-) 1. (act of) twisting/squeezing/compressing. 2. crowd, throng, mass. 3. *fig.* confusion, disorder. *Cf.* **songa.**

msongora (wa-) *coll.* policeman.

msono, msonyo (mi-) msono (a whistling intake of breath, indicating contempt or derision). *Cf.* **fyonya.**

msonobari* (mi-) *see* **msunobari.**

msonyo (mi-) *see* **msono.**

Mspain* [*Engl.*] (Wa-) Spaniard.

mstaarabu* (wa-) 1. civilized/cultivated person. 2. *pl.* intelligentsia. *Cf.* **staarabu.**

mstadi* (wa-) skilled craftsman; specialist, expert. *Cf.* **stadi.**

mstafeli* [*Ind.*] (mi-) mstafeli (soursop tree, *Annona muricata*). 2. = **mtopetope.**

mstahifu* (wa-) *see* **mstahivu.**

mstahivu*, mstahifu (wa-) 1. a person who respects/esteems others. 2. a person who is respected/esteemed. *Cf.* **stahi, stahivu.**

mstaki* (wa-) *see* **mshtaki.**

mstamu* (wa-) *see* **msitamu.**

mstarehe* (–) *see* **mustarehe.**

mstari* (mi-) 1. line, row. **– wa kitako.** base line. **karatasi ya mistari.** lined/ruled paper. **piga –.** draw a line. **–a –.** lined/ruled. 2. ruler. *Cf.* **kistari.**

mstatili* (mi-) oblong, rectangle.

[1]**mstiri*, msitiri, msetiri** (wa-) one who hides/conceals/makes a secret of something. *Cf.* **stiri.**

[2]**mstiri*** (wa-) *see* **mshtiri.**

mstuko* (mi-) *see* **mshtuko.**

mstuo (mi-) *see* **mshtuo.**

Msuaheli* (Wa-) *see* **Mswahili.**

msuaki*, mswaki (mi-) 1. a twig or stick used to clean the teeth. 2. *rec.* toothbrush.

msuani (mi-) msuani (shroud for women).

msubili*, mshubiri (mi-) aloe plant. *Cf.* **subili.**

msubukuo (mi-) (act of) poking (with the finger, as a sign of contempt). **piga –.** poke, nudge. *Cf.* **subukua.**

msufi* (mi-) kapok tree *(Bombax rhodognaphalon). Cf.* **sufi, usufi.**

[1]**msuka** (wa-) *(always w. foll. obj.)* one who plaits/braids. **– miketa.** mat-weaver. **– nywele.** hair-braider. *Cf.* [1]**suka.**

[2]**msuka** (mi-) 1. the part of a tool which fits into the handle. 2. the spike of a (native) hoe.

msukani* (wa-) 1. *naut.* helmsman. 2. driver *(of a vehicle). Cf.* **usukani.**

[1]**msukano** (mi-) quarrel, disagreement, dissension. *Cf.* [2]**suka.**

[2]**msukano** (mi-) *see* **msukwano.**

msuki (wa-) *see* **msusi.**

[1]**msuko, msukosuko** (mi-) 1. (act of) braiding, plaiting, twisting. 2. braid, pigtail; plaited work. 3. *fig.* unrest, movement; disorder, fracas, riot. 4. *fig., naut.* rolling, tossing *(of a ship). Cf.* [1]**suka,** [2]**suka.**

[2]**msuko** (mi-) msuko (kind of tree; the leaves are used to prepare a medicine).

msukosuko (mi-) *see* **msuko.**

msukumano (mi-) pushing, shoving; crowd, throng. *Cf.* **sukuma,** [2]**suka.**

msukumizi (wa-) 1. one who incites/causes trouble. 2. unfair/impetuous person. *Cf.* **sukuma,** [2]**suka.**

msukwano*, **msukano** (**mi-**) 1. shaft of a drill. 2. pouch in which a drill is kept.

msuli* (**wa-**) *hist.* Arab trader from the Persian Gulf *(who arrives in his dhow with the Northeast Moonsoon and returns with the Southwest Moonsoon).*

msuluhifu* (wa-) *see* **msuluhivu.**

msuluhisha* (wa-) *see* **msuluhivu.**

msuluhishi* (wa-) *see* **msuluhivu.**

msuluhivu*, **msuluhifu**, **msuluhisha**, **msuluhishi** (wa-) conciliator, arbitrator, mediator, peacemaker. – **wa vita.** negotiator at a peace conference. *Cf.* **suluhu.**

msumari*, **msomari** (**mi-**) 1. sting(er) *(of an insect).* 2. nail, peg, pin. **pigilia** (**ng'oa**) **–.** drive (pull out) a nail. 3.: – **wa parafujo.** *rare* screw. 4. spur *(of a boot).*

Msumbiji* Mozambique.

msumbufu (**wa-**) 1. annoying/importunate person, one who causes exasperation in others. 2. one who is exasperated/angry. *Cf.* **sumbufu, sumbua.**

msumeno (**mi-**) saw. **piga** (**kata kwa**) **–.** to saw. – **wa kitanda.** bow-saw, frame-saw. **unga wa –.** sawdust. *Cf.* **kisu, jino.**

msungo (**wa-**) boy or girl who has not been through the initiation rites, a person inexperienced in matters of sex. *Cf.* [1]**mrongo, usungo.**

msungululu (**mi-**) msungululu (poisonous plant used for medicinal purposes, *Strophanthus eminii).*

[1]**msunguti** (**mi-**) msunguti (kind of tree, *Acokanthera longiflora*).

[2]**msunguti, mchunguti** (**mi-**) something strong/highly flavored *(tobacco, coffee, etc.). Cf.* [2]**chungu** (?).

msunobari*, **msonobari** (**mi-**) 1. (imported) pine, fir (timber). 2. *rare* kind of tree (flamboyant, ironwood).

msuraki, msuruaki (**mi-**) wooden peg on a clog or sandal *(passing between the toes and holding the clog on the foot).*

msuruaki (**mi-**) *see* **msuraki.**

msusi, msuka, msuki (**wa-**) one who braids/twists. **msuka mikeka.** mat-weaver. **msusi wa nywele.** (women's) hairdresser. *Cf.* [1]**suka.**

[1]**msusu** (**mi-**) tail feathers *(of a bird).*

[2]**msusu** (**mi-**) msusu (kind of tree; the roots are used to prepare a medicine).

[1]**msuto** (**mi-**) charge, accusation. *Cf.* [1]**suta.**

[2]**msuto*** (**mi-**) *see* **kisutu.**

msuzo (**mi-**) wooden handle (by which the upper stone of a hand-mill is turned).

Mswahili*, **Msuaheli** (wa-) a speaker of Swahili. *Cf.* **Swahili, Kiswahili, Uswahili.**

mswaki* (mi-) *see* **msuaki.**

mtaa* (mi-) 1. district, quarter *(of a city).* **kaa – mmoja.** live in the same part of town, be neighbors. 2. *rare* state *(as an administrative or territorial unit).*

mtaala* (mi-) learning, study. *Cf.* **taali.**

mtaalamu* (wa-) 1. educated person, scholar, scientist. 2. *rec.* intellectual. **mwandishi –.** special correspondent. *Cf.* **taalamu, elimu.**

mtaawa* (wa-) *see* **mtawa.**

mtabibu* (wa-) *see* **tabibu.**

mtabiri* (wa-) 1. one who reports *(news, events).* 2. commentator. 3. prophet, soothsayer. 4. forecaster. **– wa hewa.** weather forecaster, meteorologist. *Cf.* **tabiri.**

mtafara* (mi-) *see* **mtafura.**

mtafaruku* (mi-) *rare* disagreement, difference of opinion, quarrel, dispute.

mtafitafi* (wa-) gossip, talebearer. *Cf.* **tafiti.**

mtafiti* (wa-) inquisitive/impertinent person. *Cf.* **tafiti.**

mtafuni (wa-) one who chews. *Cf.* **tafuna.**

mtafuno (mi-) (act of) chewing. *Cf.* **tafuna.**

mtafura*, **mtafara** (mi-) crupper (leather loop passing under the horse's tail and buckled to the saddle).

mtafutaji* (wa-) one who searches. *Cf.* **tafuta.**

mtago (mi-) (act of) laying *(eggs).* *Cf.* **[1]taga.**

mtaguso (mi-) *dial.* council, assembly, debate. **– mkuu.** *rel.* ecumenical council.

mtahamari* (wa-) *rare* drunkard. (= **mlevi.**)

mtahini* (wa-) one who tests, examiner. *Cf.* **mtihani.**

mtai (mi-) 1. scratch, abrasion, (superficial) wound. 2. (small) incision. **piga –.** to scratch.

mtaimbo, mtalimbo (mi-) iron bar, crowbar, lever, handspike.

mtajaji (wa-) *pol.* candidate *(for election to public office).* *Cf.* **taja.**

mtajiri* (wa-) *see* **tajiri.**

mtaka, mtakaji (wa-) one who asks for something: applicant, petitioner. *prov.:* **– yote hukosa yote.** He who asks for everything receives nothing. *Cf.* **[3]taka.**

mtakadamu* (wa-) *see* **kadamu.**

mtakaji (wa-) *see* **mtaka.**

mtakalamu* (wa-) *see* **mutakalamu.**

mtakaso (mi-) 1. cleansing, purification. 2. *fig.* menstruation. *Cf.* **takata.**

mtakatifu (wa-) 1. a pure/clean person. 2. *rel.* saint. *Cf.* **takata, takatifu.**

mtakawa (mi-) mtakawa (kind of tulip tree, *Thespesia populnea*).

mtalaleshi* (wa-), **talaleshi** (ma-) 1. prostitute. 2. procurer, procuress. 3. slanderer, talebearer. *Cf.* **utalaleshi.**

mtalawanda (mi-) 1. species of tree. 2. (wooden) clog.

mtali (mi-) (silver) anklet.

mtalimbo (mi-) *see* **mtaimbo.**

[1]**mtama** (mi-) mtama (kind of millet, kafir corn, sorghum). – **mtindi.** half-grown sorghum. – **mtete.** sorghum which has not quite ripened. *prov.* **penye kuku wengi usimwage –.** Where there are many chickens one should not spill millet.

[2]**mtama** (mi-) *see* [5]**tama.**

mtamani* (wa-) 1. ambitious/pushy person. 2. greedy/lustful person. *Cf.* **tamani.**

mtamba (mi-) female animal which has not yet produced young. – **wa ng'ombe.** heifer.

[1]**mtambaa** (wa-) *(usually w. foll. adjunct)* creeper, crawler. – **chini.** *coll.* snake. – **jongoo.** kind of tree (the wood is used to make hoe handles). – **miti.** a climbing plant. *Cf.* [1]**tambaa.**

[2]**mtambaa** (mi-) *see* **kitambaa.**

mtambaazi (–) *see* **mtambazi.**

mtambatamba (wa-) braggart, show-off. *Cf.* **tamba.**

mtambazi, mtambaazi (–) 1. insect. (= **mdudu**). 2. (**mnyama –**) reptile. *Cf.* [1]**tambaa, tambazi.**

mtambika (wa-) *see* **mtambikaji.**

mtambikaji, mtambika (wa-) one who makes offerings/performs sacrifices. *Cf.* **tambika.**

mtambiko (mi-) act of making an offering to propitiate the spirits of the dead. *Cf.* **tambika.**

mtambo (mi-) 1. *arch.* (spring) trap. 2. spring, compression spring. – **wa bunduki.** lock/action of a gun. 3. mechanism, drive. – **wa saa.** works of a watch/clock. – **wa stimu.** *elec.* switch, commutator. 4. machine, motor, engine. *(in gen.)*. – **wa kupiga chapa.** (printing-)press. – **wa reli.** *railw.* switch, points. – **wa kurushia maneno.** radio transmitter. 5. factory, plant.

mtambua (wa-) *see* **mtambuzi.**

mtambuu* [*Ind., Pers.*] (mi-) betel plant *(Piper betel)*. *Cf.* **tambuu.**

mtambuzi, mtambua (wa-) 1. knowledgeable/well-informed person. 2. interpreter, commentator. *Cf.* **tambua, tambuzi.**

mtanashati* (wa-) well-dressed person, one with good taste in clothing. *Cf.* **tanashati.**

mtanda, mtandi (wa-) *(always w. foll. obj.)* one who spreads. **– miongo.** spreader of lies, gossip, talebearer. *Cf.* **tanda.**

mtande (mi-) 1. something spread out. 2. a strip of meat or fish laid out to dry. 3. (weaver's) loom (= **kitanda cha mfumi**). *Cf.* **tanda.**

mtandi (wa-) *see* **mtanda.**

mtandio (mi-) mtandio (kind of shawl worn by women). *Cf.* **tanda.**

mtando (mi-) 1. (act of) spreading. 2. expansion, extension. *Cf.* **tanda.**

Mtanganyika (wa-) inhabitant of Tanganyika.

mtangatanga, mtanga (wa-) 1. wanderer, tourist. 2. vagabond. *Cf.* **¹tanga.**

mtangawizi (mi-) ginger plant *(Zingiber officinale)*. *Cf.* **tangawizi.**

mtangazaji (wa-) *see* **mtangazi.**

mtangazi, mtangazaji (wa-) 1. one who publicly announces or proclaims something. 2. commentator, announcer *(radio)*. *Cf.* **tangaa.**

mtange (mi-) beam *(of scales, balance)*.

¹mtango (mi-) cucumber plant. *Cf.* **²tango.**

²mtango (mi-) wandering, idling, loitering, vagrancy. *Cf.* **¹tanga.**

mtangulizi (wa-) one who precedes/leads the way: leader; herald, harbinger; forerunner, precursor, predecessor; *(rel.)* John the Baptist. *Cf.* **tangulia.**

mtanguo (mi-) *see* **kitanguo.**

mtani* (wa-) 1. member of a family/clan/tribe. 2. relative. 3. fellow countryman, compatriot, conational. 4. close friend *(of one's own age-group)*. **hawezi kukasirika, kwa sababu ni – wangu.** He can't be angry; he is my mtani. *Cf.* **tania, utani, watani.**

mtapishi (mi-) *med.* emetic. *Cf.* **tapika.**

mtapisho (mi-) mtapisho (a kind of shrub used in preparing an emetic). *Cf.* **tapika.**

¹mtapo (mi-) mtapo (kind of palm, *Cycas Thouarsii)*.

²mtapo (mi-) ore *(iron, gold, silver)*.

3mtapo (mi-) shivering, trembling (= **kitapo**). *Cf.* **1tapa.**

mtapta* [*Engl.*] (wa-) *coll.* interpreter, translator. (= **mfasiri.**)

mtaro (mi-) 1. *agr.* terrace, terracing. 2. ditch.

mtasbihi* (mi-) mtasbihi (kind of plant, *Canna indica;* the seeds are used for Moslem rosaries). *Cf.* **tasbihi.**

mtashi (wa-) one who asks/begs/pleads earnestly/importunately. *Cf.* **3taka.**

mtata (mi-) 1. mtata (an ornamental plant, also used to make torches). 2. a torch (made from this plant).

mtatago (mi-) 1. small bridge *(usually consisting of a tree trunk).* 2. (act of) crossing; walking with long strides. *Cf.* **tataga.**

mtatio (mi-) 1. coiling, winding *(cord, thread).* 2. *fig.* confusion, complication, obscurity. 3. *fig.* something confusing/puzzling/intriguing. *Cf.* **tata.**

mtatizo (mi-) *see* **tatanisho.**

mtawa*, **mtaawa** (wa-) 1. religious/pious person. 2. a person living in seclusion, recluse, hermit. 3. girl who enters a convent. 4. *fig.* stay-at-home. 5. *rare* priest, missionary. *Cf.* **1tawa.**

mtawala*, **mtawalaji**, **mtawali** (wa-) ruler, governor. – **mmoja.** autocrat, absolute monarch. *Cf.* **tawala.**

mtawalaji* (wa-) *see* **mtawala.**

mtawali* (wa-) *see* **mtawala.**

mtawalia*, **mtawalio** *adv.* continuously, persistently; consecutively, in succession.

mtawanya (wa-) one who spends lavishly, generous person. *Cf.* **tawanya.**

mtawanyo (mi-) 1. (act of) scattering, strewing. 2. sowing. *Cf.* **tawanya.**

mtazamaji (wa-) spectator, observer. *Cf.* **tazama.**

mtazamo (mi-) observation, inspection. *Cf.* **tazama.**

mteba (mi-) mteba (a climbing plant, *Flagellaria guineensis).*

mtega (wa-) *see* **mtegaji.**

mtegaji, **mtega** (wa-) one who sets traps/ *(fig.)* ensnares/deceives. *Cf.* **tega.**

mtego (mi-) 1. trap, snare. 2. *fig.*, *mil.* mine. **fichia –.** lay mines. *Cf.* **tega.**

mteja, **mteji** (wa-) 1. one who is exorcised *(by a mganga).* 2. assistant of the mganga *(in exorcising spirits).*

mteka (*rare* **mtekaji**) (wa-) *(always w. foll. obj.)* one who takes away. **— maji.** water-carrier, one who draws water. **— mateka.** marauder, plunderer. *Cf.* **teka.**

mtekaji (wa-) *rare* *see* **mteka.**

mteketeo, mteketezo (mi-) 1. great fire, holocaust. 2. *fig.* destruction, devastation. *Cf.* **teketea.**

mteketezo (mi-) *see* **mteketeo.**

mtelemko, mteremko (mi-) 1. (act of) going down, descending. 2. declivity, slope. *Cf.* **telemua.**

[1]**mtema** (wa-) *see* [1]**mtemi.**

[2]**mtema** (wa-) *see* [2]**mtemi.**

mtemba (mi-) tobacco pipe.

mtembezaji (wa-) *see* **mtembezi.**

mtembezi, mtembezaji (wa-) 1. walker, stroller. **mwanamke —.** *coll.* girl of easy morals, prostitute. 2. tourist. **— sana.** He travels a great deal. 3. *fig.* idler, vagrant. *Cf.* **tembea.**

mtembo (mi-) 1. bud, shoot *(for planting).* 2. *med.* fistula *(usually a crack in the sole of the foot caused by yaws).* 3. *(rare)* scar.

[1]**mtemi, mtema** (wa-) one who cuts, woodcutter, carver. *Cf.* [2]**tema.**

[2]**mtemi, mtema** (wa-) one who spits out/expectorates/coughs up blood. *Cf.* [1]**tema.**

[3]**mtemi** (wa-) *arch.* mtemi (title of a chief in Tanganyika).

[1]**mtemo** (mi-) (act of) cutting (up, off), carving; slash. *Cf.* [2]**tema.**

[2]**mtemo** (mi-) 1. (act of) spitting out/expectorating/coughing up. 2. *rare* matter spit out/coughed up, phlegm, etc. *Cf.* [1]**tema.**

mtenda (wa-) *(always w. foll. obj.)* one who does something. **— kazi.** *rare* worker. **— dhambi.** *rel.* sinner. *Cf.* **tenda.**

mtendaji (wa-) 1. energetic/enterprising person. **— kazi.** working man, workman. 2. *comm.* activist. *Cf.* **tenda.**

mtende (mi-) date palm. *Cf.* [2]**tende.**

mtendo (mi-) doing, acting, performing; accomplishing. *Cf.* **tenda.**

[1]**mtenga** (wa-) 1. one who separates *(himself from the community),* solitary person, recluse. 2. *pol.* separatist. *Cf.* [1]**tenga.**

[2]**mtenga** (mi-) mtenga (carrying-pole, carried on the shoulders of two men with the load hung in the middle).

mtengano (mi-) *pol.* split, faction, separatism. *Cf.* [1]**tenga.**

mtenge (mi-) *naut.* outrigger.

mtengenezaji, mtengezaji (wa-) 1. arranger, organizer, producer. 2. editor. 3. compiler. *Cf.* **tengenea.**

mtengezaji (wa-) *see* **mtengenezaji.**

mtengo (mi-) (act of) separating, dividing off; withdrawing, removing. – **katika kazi.** dismissal, discharge *(from a position/job).* *Cf.* **¹tenga, kitengo.**

mtengwa (wa-) 1. one who is separated/set apart. 2. one who is removed/dismissed. 3. one who is devoted to something *(his work, a cause).* *Cf.* **¹tenga.**

mtenzi (wa-) *rare:* (– **wa kazi**) worker, workman, tradesman. *Cf.* **tenda.**

mteo *adv.* by boiling. **pika –.** bring to a boil, parboil.

mtepe (mi-) mtepe (native sailing vessel).

mtepetevu (wa-) lazy person, idler. *Cf.* **tepetea.**

mteremeshi, mteremezi (wa-) friendly/cheerful/good-natured person. *Cf.* **terema.**

mteremezi (wa-) *see* **mteremeshi.**

mteremko (mi-) *see* **mtelemko.**

mteremo (mi-), **nderemo** (–) joy, happiness; cheerfulness, contentment, comfort; lightheartedness, freedom from care; amusement. *Cf.* **terema.**

mteremuko (mi-) *see* **mtelemko.**

mtesa (wa-) *see* **mtesi.**

mtesaji (wa-) *see* **mtesi.**

mtesi, mtesa, mtesaji (wa-) 1. one who causes trouble, quarrelsome/contentious person. 2. persecutor, oppressor. *Cf.* **tesa.**

mteta (wa-) *see* **mtetaji.**

mtetaji, mteta, mtetea, mtetezi (wa-) troublemaker, intriguer, schemer. *Cf.* **teta.**

mtete (mi-) mtete (kind of reed, *Phragmites communis*). (= **utete.**)

mtetea, mteteaji, mtetezi (wa-) 1. = **mtetaji.** 2. defender. 3. opponent, adversary. 4. quarrelsome/argumentative person; politician. *Cf.* **teta.**

mtetemeko (mi-) *see* **mtetemko.**

mtetemko, mtetemeko, mtetemo (mi-) trembling, quivering; vibration. – **wa nchi.** earthquake. – **wa meno.** chattering of the teeth. *Cf.* **tetema.**

mtetemo (mi-) *see* **mtetemko.**

mtetezi (wa-) *see* **mtetea, mtetaji.**

mteua, mteuzi (wa-) 1. one who chooses/selects. 2. fastidious/fussy person, faultfinder. *Cf.* **teua, teuzi.**

mteule (wa-) one who is chosen/picked out *(for some quality or skill)*, excellent/outstanding person. *Cf.* **teue, teule.**

mteuo (mi-) choice, selection. *Cf.* **teua.**

mteuzi (wa-) *see* **mteua.**

mtezaji, mtezi (wa-) *see* **mtesi.**

[1]**mti** (mi-) 1. tree. **miti ya matunda.** fruit-trees. 2. wood. 3. (cricket) stump. **merikebu ya –.** wooden boat. **– mkavu.** dry wood. **kaa la –.** charcoal. 4. post, pole, shaft, bar. **– wa simu.** telegraph pole. *Cf.* **jiti, kijiti, ujiti, uti.**

[2]**mti** *sing.* (*us.* **maradhi/uele ya/wa –**) (scrofulous/gangrenous) sore.

mtia, mtiaji (wa-) *(always w. foll. obj.)* one who applies/employs something. **– rangi.** painter. **– dawa.** one who prescribes medicines. **– jalada.** bookbinder. *Cf.* **tia.**

mtiaji (wa-) 1. = **mtia.** 2.: **– moto.** incendiary, arsonist. *Cf.* **tia.**

mtihani* (mi-) 1. test, examination. **– wa udaktari.** doctoral examination. **fanya –.** take an examination. **pita (shindwa na) –.** pass (fail) an examination. 2. *fig.* trial, ordeal, difficult situation. **kutana na –.** get into a difficult situation. *Cf.* **mtahini.**

mtii (wa-) *see* **mtiifu.**

mtiifu*, mtiivu, mtii (wa-) obedient/tractable/obsequious person. *Cf.* **tii.**

mtiivu (wa-) *see* **mtiifu.**

mtikiso (mi-) (act of) shaking; concussion, shock, stroke. *Cf.* **tikisa.**

mtikiti (mi-) watermelon vine. *Cf.* [1]**tikiti.**

mtima (mi-) *rare, liter.* (= **moyo**) 1. heart. 2. feeling, emotion. 3. *rel.* soul.

mtimbi (wa-) *see* **chimvi.**

mtimvi (wa-) *see* **mchimbi.**

mtinda (wa-) *see* **kitinda.**

mtindi (mi-), **tindi** (ma-) 1. (*usually* **– wa maziwa** *or* **maziwa ya –**) buttermilk. 2. intoxicating (alcoholic) beverage *(in gen.)*.

[1]**mtindo** (mi-) 1. form, pattern, model. 2. kind, sort. 3. quality. **nguo hizi ni – wa zile.** These clothes are of the same kind as those.

[2]**mtindo** (mi-) *rare* end, conclusion. *Cf.* **tindika.**

mtini* (mi-) fig tree *(Ficus carica)*. *Cf.* **tini.**

mtipitipi, mturituri (mi-) mtipitipi (climbing plant, *Abrus precatorius*).

mtiriri (wa-) 1. sensuous/lascivious person *(male or female)*. 2. restless/lively/irresponsible child. 3. a person in whom one can have no confidence.

mtiririko (mi-) 1. flowing, trickling, seeping *(of water)*. 2. gliding *(of snakes, etc.)*. 3. mark, track *(left by a snake, etc.)* 4. traces left by flowing or trickling water: channel, rill. *Cf.* **tiririka.**

mtishaji (wa-) one who frightens/intimidates others. *Cf.* **tisha.**

mtiti (mi-) *ornith.* mtiti (species of owl).

mtitio (mi-) (act of) sinking, tottering, shaking, rocking, collapsing. *Cf.* **tita.**

[1]**mto** (mi-) river, stream. **bonde la –.** river bed. **mkono wa –.** branch, tributary *(of a river)*. **– wa mkono.** delta. **– wa bahari.** inlet, bay. **– wa barafu.** glacier. **fuata –.** go downstream. **kata –.** go upstream. *Cf.* **jito, kijito.**

[2]**mto** (mi-) pillow, cushion.

mtoa (wa-) *(always w. foll. obj.)* one who issues/dispenses. **– dawa.** pharmacist, druggist. **– gazeti.** editor/publisher of a newspaper. *Cf.* [1]**toa.**

mtoaji (wa-) editor. **– wa gazeti.** editor of a newspaper. *Cf.* [1]**toa.**

mtobwe (mi-) mtobwe (kind of shrub, *Strophanthus courmonti*).

mtofaa*, **mtofaha** (mi-) rose apple/Malay apple tree *(Eugenia jambosa/malaccensis)*. *Cf.* **tofaa.**

mtofaha* (mi-) *see* **mtofaa.**

mtohara* (wa-) 1. *Isl.* circumcised person. 2. *Isl.* ritually clean person. 3. *fig.* clean/neat/well-dressed person. *Cf.* **tohara.**

mtoki (mi-) (*also* **matoki** *pl.*) *med.* 1. swollen lymph gland. 2. inflamed sore, tumor. *Cf.* [1]**toa.**

mtokoso (mi-) 1. boiling, cooking *(by boiling)*. 2. frying *(in fat/butter)*. *Cf.* **tokota.**

mtokwe (mi-) mtokwe (kind of tree, *Annona senegalensis*).

mtolilio (mi-) sweet-potato leaf *(used as a vegetable)*.

mtombo, mtomboro (mi-) *ornith.* cuckoo.

mtomo (mi-) 1. (act, method of) reinforcing plaster with stone work. 2. paving *(a road/street)* with stone. *Cf.* **tomea.**

mtomoko (mi-) *see* **mtopetope.**

mtomondo (mi-) mtomondo (Malay apple tree, *Eugenia malaccensis*). (= **mtofaa.**) *Cf.* [1]**tomondo.**

mtondo (mi-) the day following the day after tomorrow, the third day from today. **kushinda – *or* – goo.** the fourth day from today.

[1]**mtondoo** (mi-) mtondoo (kind of tree, *Calophyllum inophyllum*). *Cf.* [1]**tondoo.**

[2]**mtondoo** (mi-), **tondoo** (ma-) thimble. (= **kastabini.**)

mtongotongo (mi-) *bot.* mtongotongo (euphorbia, spurge, *Euphorbia abyssinica).*

mtongoza (wa-) *see* **mtongozi.**

mtongozaji (wa-) *see* **mtongozi.**

mtongozi, mtongoza, mtongozaji (wa-) seducer. *Cf.* **tongoza.**

mtopetope, mtomoko (mi-) mtopetope (custard-apple tree, *Annona squamosa*).

mtoria (mi-) mtoria (species of rubber liana, *Landolphia petersiana*). *Cf.* **kitoria.**

mtoro (wa-) 1. deserter, truant, runaway; refugee. 2. *pr. n., masc. Cf.* **toroka, utoro.**

mtoto (wa-) 1. offspring, descendant, child. **— mwanamume (mwanamke).** boy (girl). **— mchanga.** infant, baby. **— wa ng'ombe.** (small) calf. **— wa kuku.** chick. **— wa mgomba.** banana shoot/sprout. 2. dependent/subordinate person *(irrespective of age).* 3. subordinate/less important/ smaller part or adjunct of a thing. **— wa meza.** drawer. **— wa mto.** *rare* branch, tributary. *Cf.* **toto, kitoto, utoto.**

mtovu (wa-) person who lacks something or falls short in some respect. **huyu ni — wa heshima.** This is a person who shows too little respect (where it is due). *Cf.* [2]**toa, tovu.**

mtoza (wa-) *(always w. foll. obj.)* one who gathers/collects. **— kodi (ushuru).** tax-collector. *Cf.* [1]**toa.**

mtozaji, mtozi (wa-) collector *(of taxes). Cf.* [1]**toa.**

mtu (watu) 1. human being, person, individual. **— mume (mke).** man (woman). **— mzima.** grown person, adult. **mimi mtumtu tu.** I am only a simple/ordinary person. **mapato kwa mtu.** per capita income. 2. someone, somebody. **hakuna —.** No one is there. 3.: *pl.* **watu.** people, population. **— wa nchi hii.** the population of this country. **—a watu.** *adj.* popular, people's... *(chiefly comm.).* **jamhuri ya watu.** People's Republic. *Cf.* **jitu, kijitu, utu.**

mtua, mtula, mtunguja (mi-) *bot.* wild egg-plant *(Solanum bojeri),* nightshade.

mtubwi (mi-) yam.

mtuchi (mi-) *med.* mtuchi (a disease of the stomach).

mtukufu (wa-) a dignified/respected/important person, notable, dignitary. *rel.* **Mungu —.** the Most High. *Cf.* **tukuka, tukufu.**

mtukutu (wa-) 1. active/mischievous child. 2. restless/nervous/troublesome person. *Cf.* **tukuta, tukutu.**

mtula (mi-) *see* **mtua.**

mtule* (wa-) poor/destitute/miserable person. *Cf.* **tule.**

mtulinga (mi-) *anat.* clavicle, collarbone, scapula.

mtulivu (wa-) quiet/reserved person. *Cf.* [1]**tua, tulivu.**

mtumainifu* (wa-) one who inspires confidence, dependable/reliable person. *Cf.* **tumaini, tumainifu.**

mtumba (mi-) 1. bale, bundle, bolt *(of cloth).* 2. burden, load *(for one man).* – **nguo.** a load of cloth. *Cf.* [1]**tumba.**

mtumbako* [*Ind.*] (mi-) tobacco plant. *Cf.* **tumbaku.**

mtumbuizi (wa-) one who sings/hums under his breath *(to calm his nerves or to soothe a child).* *Cf.* **tumbuika.**

mtumbuu (mi-) mtumbuu (kind of small sea fish, sprat).

mtumbwi (mi-) log canoe (dugout, without outriggers). *Cf.* **tumbua.**

mtume (mi-) 1. messenger, envoy. 2. courier. – wa **kidiplomasi.** diplomatic courier. 3. *rel.* apostle *(Christ.),* prophet *(Isl.).* *Cf.* **tuma.**

mtumi (wa-) *see* **mtumishi.**

mtumiki (wa-) *see* **mtumishi.**

mtumishi, mtumi, *(rare)* **mtumiki** (wa-) 1. paid domestic servant. *Cf.* **mtumwa.** 2. *(in gen.)* one who serves/is employed, employee. – wa **moto.** fireman *(on a locomotive).* 3.: – wa **serikali.** civil servant. *Cf.* **tuma.**

mtumo (mi-) use, employment, utilization, application. *Cf.* **tuma.**

mtumwa (wa-) 1. slave. – **mwanamke.** female slave. 2. *pr. n. masc.* *Cf.* **tuma.**

mtumwaji (wa-) 1. *rare* messenger, envoy. 2. someone in another person's employ, agent. *Cf.* **tuma.**

mtundu* [*Pers.*] (wa-) 1. sly/crafty person. 2. spoiled/pampered/precocious child. *Cf.* [2]**tundu.**

mtunduizi (wa-) secret agent; spy; *(mil.)* scout. *Cf.* **tunduia, tunduizi.**

mtunga, mtungaji (wa-) 1. one who arranges/constructs/compiles/designs. – **mashairi.** poet. – **kitabu.** author. – **nyimbo.** composer *(of music).* 2. designer, inventor. *Cf.* [1]**tunga.**

mtungi (mi-) earthenware water jug/pitcher.

mtungo (mi-) 1. compilation, construction, arrangement, composition. – wa **habari.** essay, composition, theme. 2. (act of) arranging in a row *(on a string, stick, etc.),* the things so arranged. – wa **samaki.** a string of fish. *Cf.* [1]**tunga.**

mtunguja (mi-) *see* **mtua.**

mtungule (mi-) tomato plant. (= **mnyanya.**) *Cf.* **tungule.**

mtunguo (mi-) ready-made article of clothing. *Cf.* **[1]tunga.**

mtunza (wa-) protector, keeper; curator *(in a museum, etc.)* — **hazina/fedha.** treasurer. *Cf.* **tunza.**

[1]mtupa (wa-) *(always w. foll. obj.)* one who throws/hurls something. — **mkuki.** spear-thrower. *Cf.* **[1]tupa.**

[2]mtupa (mi-) mtupa (a general designation for various poisonous plants). *Cf.* **utupa.**

mtupio (mi-) (act of) throwing down/away. **vazi la —.** worn-out clothing. *Cf.* **[1]tupa.**

mtupo (mi-) 1. (act of) throwing/hurling. 2. distance a thing can be thrown, throwing distance. *Cf.* **[1]tupa.**

mturituri (mi-) *see* **mtipitipi.**

Mturki* (wa-) *see* **Mturuki.**

Mturuki*, Mturki (wa-) Turk. *Cf.* **Kituruki, Uturuki.**

mtutu (mi-) barrel *(of a gun).* (= **kasiba, mwanzi.**)

mtutumo (mi-) deep, rumbling sound. — **wa ngurumo (bahari).** rumble/roar of thunder (the sea). — **wa tumbo.** growling *(of the stomach).* — **wa mvua.** noise of rain. *Cf.* **[1]tutuma.**

mtututu, mkarakala (mi-) mtututu (kind of tree, *Bridelia zanzibarensis).*

mtwa (wa-) dwarf, pigmy.

mtwaa, mtwaaji (wa-) one who carries off/takes away. *Cf.* **[1]twaa.**

mtwaaji (wa-) *see* **mtwaa.**

[1]mtwana (wa-) 1. *hist.* (young) slave. 2. rogue, rascal. 3. uncouth/unmannerly person. *Cf.* **twana, kitwana.**

[2]mtwana (mi-) *naut.* a pole strengthening the mast *(in native vessels).*

mtwango (mi-) (act, manner, etc. of) crushing, grinding, pulverizing *(with mortar and pestle).* *Cf.* **twanga.**

mtwanzi (wa-) one who pounds/pulverizes *(grain).* *Cf.* **twanga.**

mtweto (mi-) panting, puffing, gasping, difficulty in breathing. *Cf.* **tweta.**

mua (miua-) *see* **muwa.**

muaa (miuaa) *see* **mwaa.**

muamuzi (wa-) *see* **mwamua.**

muawana* (—) help, support, assistance. *Cf.* **auni.**

mubalighi* (wa-) *pol.* speaker *(in the legislative assembly).* (= **mutakalamu.**)

muda* (–) 1. period *(of time).* – **wa saa nne.** a period of four hours. **kwa – (wa).** in the course of... – **wa.** during. – **(wa) kitambo.** moment. **homa ya –.** *med.* intermittent fever. 2. term, set period of time. **taka –** (*better:* **wakati**). ask for a delay/extension. *Cf.* **mudu.**

mudiri* (wa-) *dial.* administrative official *(in districts of Zanzibar).* *Cf.* **mudiria.**

mudiria* (–) *dial.* (administrative) district *(Zanzibar).* *Cf.* **mudiri.**

mudu* stretch, extend. *us. refl.* **jimudu.** stretch oneself, move first one limb then another *(when waking up; after an illness).* *fig.* be temperate, exercise self-control; be in moderate circumstances/fairly well-off. *appl.* **mudia.** *intr.* **mudika.** *Cf.* **muda.**

muflisi* *sing., jur.* bankruptcy. *Cf.* **filisi.**

mufti*, **mofti** [*Engl.*] *adj./adv., coll.* modern, elegant, fashionable, stylish *(of clothes).* **vaa nguo –.** wear modern/stylish clothes.

muhali*, **mhali, umhali** (–) something very difficult/unobtainable/unreasonable/impossible, impossibility, impracticability, unobtainability, unreasonableness. **anitaka –.** He is asking the impossible of me. **kutoka nje wakati wa baridi naona – sana.** To go outside in the cold is for me absolutely impossible.

muharamu* (–) muharram (the fourth month of Muhammadan year).

muhariri* (wa-) journalist, correspondent, editor.

muhashamu*, **muheshamu** *(in letters)* a very formal salutation: Esteemed Sir. *Cf.* **heshima, heshimu.**

muhebi*, **muhibu** *(in letters)* a salutation used to those whom one knows rather well but not intimately *(older friends, teachers, etc.)*: Dear... *Cf.* [1]**hebu**, [2]**haba.**

muhibu* *see* **muhebi.**

muhimu* 1. (–) an important/urgent matter. 2. *adj.* important, urgent. 3. *adv.* especially, particularly; significantly. *Cf.* **hima.**

muhina* (–) bleeding from the nose.

[1]**muhindi*** (mi-) 1. maize/corn plant *(Zea mays).* 2. a grain of corn. *Cf.* **hindi, mahindi.**

[2]**Muhindi*** (wa-) *see* **Mhindi.**

muhogo*, **mhogo** [*Tupi-Port.*] (mi-) (*also,* **hogo,** ma-) 1. manioc/cassava plant. 2. manioc root.

muhtasari*, **mutasari** (–) (brief) outline, extract, précis, survey, résumé, conspectus; table of contents. – **ya mafundisho.** program, schedule *(of studies).*

muhula* (–) 1. *rare* period (of time). 2. intermission, break, rest period.

muhunzi (wa-) *see* **mhunzi.**

muhuri*, mhuri (mi-, —) 1. seal, stamp. **tia —.** to seal/stamp. **hati hii si kwela kwa sababu haina — wa serikali.** This document is not vàlid because it does not have the official stamp. 2. visa.

mujibu*, muujibu 1. *sing.* what is proper and fitting (morally and socially) according to tradition and custom; legal/official action. 2. *adv.* in accordance with, according to. **— wa sheria.** according to the law. *Cf.* **wajibu.**

mukafaa*, mukofu (—) *econ.* extra dividend, bonus.

mukofu* (—) *see* **mukafaa.**

mulika shine, gleam, beam. *prov.* **anayekumulika mchana usiku atakuunguza.** Who gives you light by day will burn you by night. *appl.* **mulikia.** *caus.* **mulikisha.**

mumbi (mi-) *see* **mwumbi.**

mume (waume) husband. *Cf.* [1]**ume.**

mumiani* [*Pers.*] **(ma-)** mumiani (a gumlike substance used as a medicine both internally, *e.g.*, against cramps, and externally for fractures, etc.).

muminina*, mmunina (wa-) *Isl.* an orthodox Moslem, a true believer. *Cf.* [1]**amini.**

mumo (*also* **— humo**) *adv.* in(side) here.

mumu: — humu. *adv.* in this very place.

[1]**mumunya, munya, munyamunya, mung'unya** chew, masticate; gnaw. *intr.* **mumunyika.** be chewed/broken up; be eroded, crumble away *(plaster, etc.)*.

[2]**mumunya (ma-)** *see* **mumunye.**

mumunye, mung'unye, mumunya (ma-) kind of gourd, calabash, vegetable marrow. *Cf.* **mmumunye.**

muna *see* **mna.**

[1]**munda (miunda)** harpoon. (= **chusa.**)

[2]**munda (miunda)** plank, board *(used in housebuilding)*.

mundu (miundu) sickle, machete, billhook. **— na nyundo.** *comm.* hammer and sickle.

mungu, muungu 1. **(miungu)** a god. 2. **Mungu** *sing.* (*also* **Jicho la Mungu**) God. 3. **(miungu)** fate, destiny, providence. *Cf.* **uungu, umungu.**

mung'unya *see* [1]**mumunya.**

mung'unye (ma-) *see* **mumunye.**

mungwana (wangwana) *see* **mwungwana.**

munisipaa* (—) *see* **munisipali.**

munisipali*, manisipali, munisipaa, manisipaa [*Engl.*] **(—)** city government, municipal administration. **kodi za nyumba zitalipwa katika afisi ya –.** House taxes are paid at the municipal administration offices.

munya *see* **[1]mumunya.**

munyu *sing., rare* salt. *Cf.* **chumvi, chunyu.**

muo (miuo) stick with an iron tip *(for digging up stones).*

muombaji (wa-) *see* **mwombaji.**

muradi* (mi-) *see* **mradi.**

muru *sing.* muru (a root from which is prepared a medicine for stomach disorders). *Cf.* **mviru.**

murua*, muruwa 1. (wa-, mi-) = **mrua.** 2. *adj.* polite, gracious, amiable; elegant, pretty.

mushkeli* (–) uncertainty, obscurity; difficulty, problem. **ugonjwa huu umeniletea –.** This complaint is giving me trouble. *Cf.* **shaka, shuku.**

musiki* (–) *see* **muziki.**

musilimu* (wa-) *see* **mwislamu.**

musimu* (mi-) *see* **msimu.**

muslimu* (wa-) *see* **mwislamu.**

mustarehe*, mstarehe (–) 1. rest, quiet, repose. **raha –.** absolute repose/comfort. 2. relaxation, recreation. *Cf.* **raha, starehe.**

musuli* [*Engl.*] (mi-) muscle. **– mwingi.** strong muscles.

mutakalamu*, mtakalamu (wa-) *pol.* speaker *(in the legislative assembly).* (= **mubalighi.**)

mutasari* (–) *see* **muhtasari.**

mutribu* (–) one who plays the gambusi or zeze *(q.v.). Cf.* **tarabu.**

muufi* (wa-) *rare* potter. (= **mfinyanzi.**)

muujibu* *sing.* *see* **mujibu.**

muujiza* (mi-) *see* **mwujiza.**

muumba, mwumba, mwumbaji (wa-) 1. originator, founder. 2. *rel.* Creator (= God; *us.* **– yote** Creator of All Things). *Cf.* **umba.**

muumbuzi (wa-) one who destroys/annihilates. *Cf.* **umba.**

muumishi, mwumikaji, mwumishi, mwumizi (wa-) one skilled in medicine *(esp. one who cups/bleeds people). Cf.* **umika.**

muunda (wa-) *see* **mwunda.**

[1]muundi (miundi) 1. (*us.* **– wa miguu**) *anat.* shinbone, tibia. 2. *rare* leg.

[2]muundi (wa-) *see* **mwunda.**

muundo (mi-) *see* **mwundo.**

muungamo (mi-) *see* **mwungamo.**

muungano (mi-) *see* **mwungano.**

muungo, mwungo (mi-) 1. (act of) connecting, joining; connection, joint. 2. something joined; *(fig.)* seam. *Cf.* **[2]unga.**

muungu (mi-) *see* **mungu.**

muuya* (mi-) *see* **mauja.**

muuzaji (wa-) *see* **mwuzaji.**

muwa, mua (miwa) sugarcane.

muweka *see* **mweka.**

muwi (miwi) muwi (kind of mangrove, *Bruguiera gymnorrhiza*).

muyombo (mi-) *see* **myombo.**

muziki*, musiki [*Engl.*] *sing.* music.

mvao, mviko (mi-) manner of dress; style, fashion. *Cf.* **vaa.**

[1]mvi (—) (*also* **nywele za —**) gray hair. **mwenye —.** gray-haired person.

[2]mvi (mi-) *arch.* arrow.

mviko (mi-) 1. = **mvao.** 2. clothing, garment, dress. *Cf.* **vaa.**

mvinjari* (wavinjari, wamevinjari) loafer, unemployed person. *Cf.* **vinjari.**

mvinje (mi-) mvinje (cassowary/beefwood tree, *Casuarina equisetifolia*).

mvinyo* [*Port.*] **(—)** 1. spirits *(in gen.)*. 2. *rare* wine (= **divai**).

mviringano (mi-) something round/circular/spherical. *Cf.* **viringa, mviringo, uviringo.**

mviringo (mi-), kiviringo (vi-) 1. circle, roundness; circumference. 2. sphere, globe, ball. 3. *adj.:* **-a —.** circular, round, spherical. **mpira una umbo la —.** A ball is spherical. *Cf.* **viringa, mviringano, uviringo.**

mviru (mi-) mviru (kind of tree. A remedy for stomach complaints is prepared from its roots). *Cf.* **muru.**

Mvita *sing.* Mombasa *(city and island)*. *Cf.* **Mmvita, Kimvita.**

mvivu (wa-) lazy person, idler, loafer. *Cf.* **vivu, uvivu.**

mviziaji (wa-): — faida. *fin.* speculator. *Cf.* **via.**

mvo (mi-) *see* **mfo.**

mvongonya, mvungunya (mi-) mvongonya (sausage tree, *Datura metel*).

[1]mvua (—) rain. **— inanyesha.** It is raining. **— ya mawe.** hail. **upinde wa —.** rainbow. **wakati wa —.** rainy season. **— kubwa (nyingi).** heavy rain, cloudburst. **— ya mwaka.** light rain *(us. in August)*.

[2]mvua, mvuo, mvukuto (mi-) *(us. pl.)* bellows. **vukuta mivua.** blow/work bellows. *Cf.* **vukuta.**

[3]mvua (wa-) *see* **mvuvi.**

mvuke (–) (*also* **uvuke, vuke**) 1. steam, steam-power. 2. (intense, humid) heat. 3. vaporization, evaporation. 4. moisture, dampness, humidity. 5. *rec.* gas. *Cf.* **[1]fuka.**

mvuko (mi-) ford, crossing, ferry. *Cf.* **[2]vua.**

mvukuto (mi-) *see* **[2]mvua.**

mvulana, mvuli (wa-) unmarried young man, bachelor. *Cf.* **kivulana, uvulana.**

mvule (mi-) (species of) teakwood tree *(Chlorophora excelsa).*

[1]mvuli (wa-) *see* **mvulana.**

[2]mvuli (mi-) 1. = **kivuli.** 2. = **vuli.**

[1]mvuma (wa-) *see* **mvumi.**

[2]mvuma (mi-) *see* **[1]mvumo.**

mvumanyuki (mi-) mvumanyuki (kind of shrub, *Premna chrysoclada*).

mvumatiti (–) *see* **vumatiti.**

mvumbasi (mi-) mvumbasi (kind of plant with aromatic leaves, *Ocimum sp.*).

mvumi, mvuma (wa-) grumbler, faultfinder. *Cf.* **vuma.**

[1]mvumo, mvuma (mi-) 1. humming, rustling, rumbling. – **wa mvua.** the pounding of rain. 2. roaring, growling, bellowing *(of various animals, usually wild).* 3. *fig.* echo, reverberation. 4. *fig.* rumor. *Cf.* **vuma.**

[2]mvumo (mi-) mvumo (kind of palm, *Borassus flabellifera*).

mvunaji, mvuni (wa-) reaper, harvester. *Cf.* **vuna.**

mvungu (mi-) 1. hollow, cavity. 2. space under something. – **wa meza (kitanda).** space under a table (bed). *prov.* **mpenda cha mvunguni sharti ainame.** Whoever wants to get something from under the bed must stoop over (i.e., good things are not easily obtained). *Cf.* **vungu.**

mvungunya (mi-) *see* **mvongonya.**

mvuni (wa-) *see* **mvunaji.**

mvunja (wa-) *(always w. foll. obj.)* one who breaks something. – **mawe.** stonemason. – **mapesa.** money-changer. *Cf.* **vunja.**

mvunjaji (wa-) one who breaks something. – **wa sheria.** lawbreaker. *Cf.* **vunja.**

mvunjiko (mi-) *see* **mvunjo.**

mvunjo (mi-) 1. (act of) breaking, destruction, demolition. 2. (*also* **mvunjiko**) break, fracture. *Cf.* **vunja.**

[1]mvuo (mi-) (act of) undressing. *Cf.* **vaa.**

[2]mvuo (mi-) 1. (act of) fishing. 2. catch, haul *(of fish).* 3. (good) place for fishing. *Cf.* **[1]vua.**

mvuruga (wa-) *see* **mvurugaji.**

mvurugaji, mvuruga (wa-) one who causes destruction/dissension/confusion, troublemaker, agitator. *Cf.* **vuruga.**

mvurugo (mi-) 1. (act of) stirring, mixing. 2. strife, dissension. 3. confusion, disorder. *Cf.* **vuruga.**

mvushaji, mvushi (wa-) 1. ferryman. 2. *rare* preserver, savior. *Cf.* [2]**vua.**

mvushi (wa-) *see* **mvushaji.**

mvuta (wa-): – **tumbako.** smoker. *Cf.* **vuta.**

mvuto (mi-) 1. (act of) drawing, pulling. 2. *fig.* influence. 3. *fig.* persuasion, conviction. *Cf.* **vuta.**

mvuvi, mvua (wa-) (*also* – **samaki**) fisherman. *Cf.* [1]**vua.**

mvyele (wa-) *rare* old woman. (= **kizee.**)

mwa *conn.:* **nyumbani – mchuuzi.** in the house of the shopkeeper.

mwaa, muaa (**miaa, miwaa, miyaa**) 1. dwarf palm. 2. leaf of the dwarf palm. 3. strip of leaf from the dwarf palm *(used for plaiting mats).*

mwaandishi (wa-) *see* **mwandishi.**

mwabudu* (wa-) *rel.* worshipper. – (wa) **sanamu.** idolator. *Cf.* **abudu.**

mwadhini* (wa-) *Isl.* muezzin. *Cf.* **adhini.**

mwafaka* (mi-) 1. acceptability. 2. unanimity, accord. 3. agreement, bargain, pact, contract. 4. conspiracy. *Cf.* **afiki.**

Mwafrika* [*Engl.*] (wa-) an African. *Cf.* **Afrika.**

mwafu* (mi-) *bot.* wild jasmine *(Jasminum mauritianum). Cf.* [1]**afu.**

mwaga pour out, empty, spill. *intr.* **mwagika.** 1. be poured out/spilled. *prov.* **maji yaliyomwagika hayazoleki.** Spilled water cannot be picked up (*e.g.*, something once said cannot be retracted). 2. *fig.* scatter, disperse, break up. **baada ya mkutano watu walimwagika.** After the meeting the people dispersed. *Cf.* **mwagano,** [2]**mwago.**

mwagano, mwago (mi-) dismissal. *Cf.* **mwaga.**

[1]**mwago** (mi-) *see* **mwagano.**

[2]**mwago** (mi-) (act of) pouring out, spilling. *Cf.* **mwaga.**

[3]**mwago** (mi-) mwago (gift given by a husband to his first wife when she agrees to his taking a second wife). *Cf.* [2]**aga.**

[4]**mwago** (mi-) (act, manner, etc., of) leave-taking. *Cf.* [1]**aga.**

mwaguzi (wa-) 1. soothsayer, diviner. *Cf.* **agua.** 2. = **mwuguzi.**

Mwajemi* (wa-) a Persian. *Cf.* **Kiajemi, Uajemi.**

mwaka (miaka) year. **kila –, – kwa –.** yearly, annual. **– uliopita, – (wa) jana.** last year. **– ujao, – (wa) kesho.** next year. **– (wa) juzi.** year before last. **siku ya – mpya.** New Year's Day. **mwakani.** in the course of a year, in a year's time; *(fig.)* sooner or later.

mwake *poss. pron. 3rd pers. sing.* *see* **-ake.**

[1]**mwako** (mi-) 1. flame, blaze. 2. blazing, burning. 3. heat, ardor; temperament. *Cf.* [1]**waka.**

[2]**mwako** *poss. pron. 2nd pers. sing.* *see* **-ako.**

mwalamu* (mi-) *see* **mialamu.**

mwale (mi-) raffia palm.

[1]**mwali, mwari** (wali) 1. a boy or girl before or during the initiation ceremony. 2. (*also* **mwanamwali,** *pl.* **wanawali**) a girl who menstruates for the first time.

[2]**mwali*** (nyali) (tongue of) flame.

[3]**mwali, mwari** (wa-) *ornith.* pelican.

[1]**mwaliko** (mi-) (*also* **jaliko,** ma-) 1. call, summons. 2. invitation, challenge. *Cf.* [2]**alika.**

[2]**mwaliko** (mi-) cracking (noise), clapping, snapping *(of the fingers)*. *Cf.* [1]**alika.**

mwalimu* (wa-) 1. educated person, scholar, scientist. 2. teacher, tutor. **– mkuu.** professor. 3. *rel.* Master (= Christ). 4. *rare, naut.* steersman, pilot. *Cf.* **elimu.**

[1]**mwalishi** (wa-) one who invites *(to a feast, etc.)*, host. *Cf.* [2]**alika.**

[2]**mwalishi** (wa-) one who makes a cracking/snapping noise. *Cf.* [1]**alika.**

mwamali* (wa-) 1. one who has a share in something, sympathizer, participant. 2. accomplice. (mi-) 1. interest, sympathy, participation. 2. activity, action. *Cf.* [1]**amali.**

mwamana* (wa-) one willing to trust others. **mtu yule hana –.** That person does not trust/have confidence in anybody else. *Cf.* **amana,** [1]**amini.**

mwamba (mi-), **kiamba** (vi-) 1. rock, crag, reef. 2. ridge-pole, roof-tree. 3. *fig.* steadfast/courageous person. 4. *sport, coll.* boxer.

mwambaji, mwambi (wa-) 1. gossip, slanderer. 2. nagger, faultfinder. *Cf.* [1]**amba.**

mwambao (mi-) *rare* coast, coastline, shore. **safari ya –.** *naut.* coastal shipping. *Cf.* **ambaa.**

mwambi (wa-) *see* **mwambaji.**

mwambo (mi-) financial straits. **siku za –.** *coll.* the last few days of the month *(before payday)*. *Cf.* **wamba.**

mwambula (mi-) *bot.* mwambula (a bush with poisonous roots, *Plumbago zeylanica*).

Mwamerika* [*Engl.*] (wa-) an American.

mwamini*, mwaminifu, mwumini (wa-) 1. trustworthy/reliable person. 2. a person in whom one has confidence, confidant, confidential agent. 3. devout/religious person, (true) believer. **waamini.** the faithful. *Cf.* **¹amini.**

mwaminifu* (wa-) *see* **mwamini.**

mwamizi* (wa-) one who watches a planted field (and frightens away birds). *Cf.* **amia.**

mwamu, mlamu (wa-) relative by marriage: brother/sister-in-law.

mwamua, mwamuzi (wa-) mediator, peacemaker, go-between, arbitrator, umpire. *Cf.* **¹amua.**

mwamuzi (wa-) *see* **mwamua.**

mwamvuli (mi-) *see* **mwavuli.**

mwana 1. (wana, waana) child *(with respect to relationship:* son, daughter). **mwanadamu.** human being. **– haramu.** illegitimate child. **– maji.** seaman, sailor. **– hewa.** aviator, pilot. **– komiti.** member of a committee. 2. (mamwana) lady, mistress. 3. adopted child, dependent. *Cf.* **³jana, kijana, uana, ujana.**

mwanaanga (wanaanga) cosmonaut.

mwanachama (wa-) member *(of an organization, party, etc.).* **yeye ni – cha wafanya kazi.** He is a member of a labor union. **– asiye wa desturi.** alternate member. *Cf.* **uanachama.**

mwanachuo (wa-) one who learns/studies, student.

mwanadamu (wa-) human being. *Cf.* **mwana, adamu.**

mwanafunzi (wa-) pupil, apprentice, student. *Cf.* **²funda.**

mwanagazeti* [*Engl.*] (wana ...) newspaperman.

mwanahewa* (wa-) aviator, pilot. *Cf.* **uanahewa.**

mwanajeshi* (wana...) soldier, serviceman. *Cf.* **jeshi, uanajeshi.**

mwanamaji (wanamaji) sailor, seaman.

mwanamimba (wana..., waana...) 1. pregnant woman. 2. ailment of women (pains in the uterus, chiefly in cases of premature births).

mwanamizi (wa-) hermit crab, sea urchin.

mwanamji (wa-) townsman, city-dweller.

mwanamke (wanawake) woman; *(pl.)* female sex, womenfolk. **– mtembezi.** *coll.* girl of easy morals, prostitute. *Cf.* **ke.**

mwanamume (wanaume) man; lover, paramour; *(pl.)* male sex, menfolk. *Cf.* **mwana, ¹ume.**

mwanamwali (wa-) *see* **¹mwali.**

mwananchi (wananchi) inhabitant *(of a country),* citizen. *Cf.* **uwananchi.**

mwanasesere (wa-), **sesere** (–) doll *(child's toy)*.

mwanashanga *sing.* northwest wind.

mwanasheria* (wa-) lawyer, attorney, jurist. *Cf.* **uanasheria.**

mwanasiasa* (wa-) politician, political figure. – **mhamaji.** political emigrant/refugee.

mwanathaura* (wa-) revolutionist.

mwandaji (wa-) *see* mwandaliaji.

mwandaliaji, mwandaji (wa-) 1. one who prepares/arranges something *(sets the table, etc.)*. 2. *rare* cook. *Cf.* **andaa.**

mwandamano (mi-) 1. suite, entourage, retinue. 2. procession. *Cf.* **andama.**

mwandamizi (wa-) 1. one who follows/accompanies someone. 2. successor. *Cf.* **andama.**

mwandamo (mi-) 1. (act of) following/accompanying. 2. succession, heritability. 3. file, line *(of people)*. *Cf.* **andama.**

mwandani (wa-) 1. follower, companion. 2. ally. *Cf.* **andama.**

mwandao (mi-) preparation, arrangement. (= **andao.**) *Cf.* **andaa.**

mwandazi (wa-) 1. servant *(who sets the table)*. 2. pastry cook. *Cf.* **andaa.**

mwande (mi-): **la –.** get nothing, be disappointed.

mwandikaji, mwandiki (wa-) 1. clerk, copyist. 2. secretary. 3. writer, author. *Cf.* **andika.**

mwandiki (wa-) *see* **mwandikaji.**

mwandiko (mi-) 1. writing, written matter. 2. manner of writing, style. – **wa michoro.** cursive writing. – **wa chapa.** printing. 3. script, handwriting; manuscript. 4. inscription, address. *Cf.* **andika.**

mwandishi (wa-) 1. writer, author; newspaper reporter; correspondent. 2. secretary. – **mkuu.** secretary-general. *Cf.* **andika.**

[1]**mwanga** 1. (mi-) (*also* **mwangaza**) light, lightness, radiance, clarity. 2. (wa-) (*also* **mwangavu, mwangazi**) enlightened/cultivated/educated person. *Cf.* [2]**anga, angaa.**

[2]**mwanga** (mi-) mwanga (kind of rice).

[3]**mwanga** (mi-) mwanga (species of arrowroot, *Tacca pinnatifida*).

mwangachaa (mi-) mwangachaa (kind of tree, *Cerbera Manghas*).

mwangalifu, mwangalizi (wa-) observant/attentive person. *Cf.* **angaa.**

mwangalizi (wa-) 1. = **mwangalifu.** 2. observer. 3. caretaker, overseer; proctor *(in schools)*. *Cf.* **angaa.**

mwangamizi (wa-) one who destroys/ruins. *Cf.* **angamia.**

mwangao (mi-) mwangao (species of clove).

mwangati (mi-) (kind of) cedar tree *(Juniperus procera).*

mwangavu (wa-) *see* **[1]mwanga 2.**

mwangaza (mi-) 1. hole admitting light, (small) window. 2. ray of light, brightness. 3. *fig.* clarity. 4. *fig.* enlightenment, culture, education. **pata (shikwa na) —.** receive enlightenment/culture. 5. *fig.* publication, announcement. 6. *fig.* expedient, solution *(of a difficulty). Cf.* **[2]anga, angaa.**

mwangazi (wa-) *see* **[1]mwanga 2.**

[1]mwango (mi-) mwango (kind of tree, *Rauwolfia sp.*).

[2]mwango (mi-) *rare* *see* **mlango.**

[3]mwango (mi-) *augment. of* **kiango.**

mwangu *poss. pron. 1st pers. sing.* *see* **-angu.**

mwangushi, mwanguzi (wa-) 1. one who destroys/ruins something. 2. one who lets something fall/drop. 3. *fig.* fruit-picker *(by occupation).* **— wa nazi.** coconut gatherer. *Cf.* **angua.**

mwanguzi (wa-) *see* **mwangushi.**

mwangwi (mi-) echo.

mwani (miani) seaweed.

mwanya (mi-) split, crack, cleft, crevice, notch, gap, small hole/aperture. **— wa meno.** gap between the teeth. **meno yake yana —.** He is missing some teeth.

mwanzi (mi-) 1. mwanzi (kind of bamboo). 2. mwanzi (kind of flute made of bamboo). 3. *(in gen.)* tube, pipe. **— wa pua.** nostril. **— wa bunduki.** barrel of a gun.

mwanzilishi, mwanzilizi, mwanzishaji (wa-) initiator, originator, author; founder, pioneer. *Cf.* **anza.**

mwanzilizi (wa-) *see* **mwanzilishi.**

mwanzishaji (wa-) *see* **mwanzilishi.**

mwanzo 1. (mi-) start, beginning. 2. *adv.* in/from the beginning. *Cf.* **anza.**

[1]mwao (miao) 1. piece of wood used as a support/prop. 2. boards in the bottom of a dhow *(protecting the cargo from the bilge).*

[2]mwao *poss. pron. 3rd pers. pl.* *see* **[1]-ao.**

mwapaji (wa-) one who swears an oath. *Cf.* **apa.**

mwapizi (wa-) one who habitually curses. *Cf.* **apa.**

Mwarabu* (Waarabu) an Arab. *Cf.* **Arabu, [1]Arabuni, Kiarabu, Uarabu;** *also* **[2]Manga.**

mwari (wa-) *see* **[3]mwali.**

mwaridi* (ma-) rosebush *(Rosa damascena). Cf.* **waridi, halwaridi.**

mwarita*, **mharita** [*Ind.*] (**mi-**) soapberry tree *(Sapindus saponaria)*.

mwasha (**wa-**) *(always w. foll. obj.)* one who lights/kindles/turns on *(a fire, light)*. – **moto.** one who lights/kindles a fire. – **stimu.** one who turns on a light. *Cf.* [1]**waka.**

mwasherati* (**wa-**) immoral person, adulterer *(one who violates the Islamic code of marriage morals)*. *Cf.* **asherati.**

mwashi (**waashi**) mason. *Cf.* [2]**aka.**

mwashiri* (**mi-**) *naut.* mwashiri (longitudinal beam supporting the mast of a native vessel).

mwasi*, **maasum** (**wa-**) disobedient/intractable person; rebel, insurgent. *Cf.* **asi.**

Mwasia* [*Engl.*] (**wa-**) an Asiatic.

mwata (–) mwata (kind of worm used as fishing bait).

mwatuko (**mi-**) crack, fissure *(in the ground, etc.)*. *Cf.* **atua.**

mwavi (**mi-**) 1. mwavi (kind of tree with poisonous bark). 2. *arch.* a trial by ordeal (the suspect drinking a poison prepared from the bark of the mwavi tree).

mwavuli, **mwamvuli**, **mwemvuli** (**mi-**) umbrella, parasol. – **wa kuchuka.** parachute. *Cf.* **kivuli, uvuli.**

mwawadhi* (**wa-**) *see* **mwawazi.**

mwawazi*, **mwawadhi** (**wa-**) Almighty (= God). *Cf.* **awadha.**

mwayo (**miayo**) *(us. pl.)* yawn. **piga miayo.** to yawn.

mwaza (**wa-**) *see* **mwazaji.**

mwazaji, **mwaza**, **mwazi** (**wa-**) thoughtful/imaginative/creative person. *Cf.* **waza.**

mwazi (**wa-**) *see* **mwazaji.**

mwazimo (**mi-**) (act of) lending/borrowing, loan. *Cf.* **azima.**

mwega (**mi-**) *see* **mwegamo.**

mwegamo 1. (**mi-**) (*also* **mwega**) support, prop, post. 2. (**wa-**) one on whom a feeble person leans. *Cf.* **egama.**

mwegea (**mi-**) mwegea (sausage tree).

mwehu (**wehu**) madness, lunacy. *Cf.* **ehuka.**

mweka, **mwekaji** (**we-**) *(always w. foll. obj.)* one who keeps/preserves. – **fedha/hazina/mapesa.** treasurer. *Cf.* **weka.**

mwekaji (**we-**) 1. = **mweka.** 2. owner, proprietor. *Cf.* **weka.**

mweko (**mi-**) (act of) keeping, preserving, putting aside *(savings)*. *Cf.* **weka.**

[1]**mwele** (**waele, wawele**) invalid, cripple. *Cf.* **uele.**

[2]**mwele** (mi-) mwele (kind of millet plant, *Penicillaria spicata*). *Cf.* **mawele, [1]uwele.**

mwelekeo (mi-) attitude, tendency, trend. *Cf.* **elekea.**

mweleko (mi-) 1. mweleko (cloth sling, for carrying children on the back). 2. rifle-sling. *Cf.* **eleka.**

mwelewa (wa-) intelligent/perceptive/quick-witted person. *Cf.* **elea, elewa.**

mwelezaji (wa-) 1. one who explains. 2. guide *(for tourists)*. *Cf.* **elea.**

mwelezo (mi-) 1. explanation; directions, instructions. 2. mark, sign. 3. index *(of a book)*. 4. program. *Cf.* **elea, elezo.**

mwembe* [*Ind.*] (mi-) mango tree. *Cf.* **embe.**

mwemvuli (mi-) *see* **mwavuli.**

mwenda (wa-) one who goes/walks, passer-by. **– kwa miguu.** pedestrian. **– wazimu.** madman *(or someone who acts like one)*. *Cf.* **enda.**

mwendeleo (ma-) (forward) movement, advancement, improvement, progress. *Cf.* **enda.**

mwendelezi (wa-) 1. one who makes things move/progress, a progressive person. 2. imitator. *Cf.* **enda.**

mwendesha (wa-) *(always w. foll. obj.)* one who makes something go. **– gari.** wagon driver. **– gari la moshi.** locomotive engineer. **– ndege.** aviator, pilot. *Cf.* **enda.**

mwendeshaji, mwendeshi (wa-) driver *(of any vehicle)*. **– (wa) ndege.** aviator, pilot. *Cf.* **enda.**

mwendo, mwenendo (mi-), **wenendo** *sing.* 1. movement. 2. march. **– wa siku.** a day's march. 3. course, route. 4. pace. **kaza –.** speed up one's pace. *fig.* **– wa pigo.** rhythm. 5. tempo, (rate of) speed. **– wa meli hii ni maili 30 kwa saa moja.** This ship makes thirty miles an hour. 6. distance *(from something)*. 7. *elec., meteor. (rare)* current. 8. *fig.* behavior, conduct. **anajifunza sana lakini – wake si mzuri.** He learns well, but his conduct is bad. *Cf.* **enda.**

mwene (wa-) *rare* *see* **mwenye.**

mwenea (wa-): **– pote.** *rel.* the Omnipresent (= God). *Cf.* **enea.**

mwenendo (mi-) *see* **mwendo.**

mwenenzi (wa-) 1. passer-by. 2. traveler. *Cf.* **enda.**

mweneza, mwenezaji, mwenezi (wa-) one who distributes/bestows *(often* = God*)*. **– habari.** publicity-man, public-relations man. *Cf.* **enea.**

mwenezaji (wa-) *see* **mweneza.**

mwenezi (we-) 1. = **mweneza.** 2. *rec.:* **katibu –.** secretary for propaganda/publicity. *Cf.* **enea.**

mwenge (mi-) (*rare* **kienge,** vi-) 1. tuft of straw, etc., used for starting a fire. 2. torch. *fig.:* **– wa jua.** sunlight.

mwengero (mi-) 1. mwengero (palm wine in the fermenting stage). 2. mwengero (the portion of palm wine due the owner of a tree who allows others to tap it).

mwenu *poss. pron. 2nd pers. pl.* *see* **-enu.**

mwenye, mwenyewe, mwenyi, mwinyi (wenye) owner, proprietor *(usually w. foll. obj.)*. **— nyumba (chombo).** owner of a house (ship). **— deni.** debtor. **— kudhamini.** guarantor, bondsman. **— kuhozi.** monopolist. **— wazimu.** madman. **— juhudi.** *comm.* activist. *Cf.* **enye, mwenyeji, umwinyi.**

mwenyeji (wenyeji) 1. (regular) owner, proprietor. 2. master of a house, host. 3. native (of a place), resident, inhabitant. *Cf.* **enye, mwenye, kienyeji.**

mwenyekiti (wenyekiti) 1. chairman, president. 2. member (of parliament, etc.).

mwenyewe (wenyewe) 1. -self. **mimi — nimemwona.** I have seen him myself. 2. *rare* = **mwenye.**

mwenyezi (<mwenye ezi) (—) *rel.* possessor of power (= God). **— Mungu.** God Almighty.

mwenzi (wenzi) 1. friend, acquaintance, companion, comrade, colleague. *us. w. poss. suff.* **mwenzangu.** my friend. **mwenzio.** your friend. **mwenziwe.** his friend. 2. associate, partner *(in a business)*. 3. accomplice. *Cf.* **enda.**

mwere (mi-) mwere (species of wild cotton-plant).

mwerevu (wa-) clever/cunning/deceitful person, fox, cheat. *Cf.* **erevu.**

mwerezi* (mi-) cedar tree *(Pygeum africanum)*.

mwetu *poss. pron. 1st pers. pl.* *see* **-etu.**

mwewe (—) *ornith.* African kite.

mweza (we-) *(always w. foll. obj.)* one who has power over something/someone. **— nchi.** ruler of a country. **— mwenyewe.** one who is his own master, a self-reliant/capable person. **Mweza yote.** Almighty (= God). *Cf.* **weza.**

mwezekaji (we-) thatcher, roofer. *Cf.* **ezeka.**

mwezeko (mi-) (act of) thatching (a roof). *Cf.* **ezeka.**

mwezi (mi-) 1. moon. **— mkubwa.** full moon. **— mchanga** (*or* **mwandamo**). new moon. **— umepatwa.** eclipse of the moon. 2. month. **— mkubwa.** month of thirty days. **— mpungufu.** month of twenty-nine days. **kila —.** monthly. 3. *rec.* artificial satellite, sputnik. 4. *rare* menstruation. *Cf.* **kimwezi.**

mwia (wa-) someone who lends money/gives credit, creditor. *Cf.* **2wia.**

mwiba (miiba) 1. thorn, barb, sting. **seng'enge yenye miiba.** barbed wire. **— wa nyuki.** sting of a bee. **— wa samaki.** fishbone. 2. *fig.* needle, pin. 3. spur *(on a boot)*.

mwibaji (wa-) *rare* *see* **mwizi.**

mwiga (wa-) *see* **mwigaji.**

mwigaji, mwiga, mwigishaji (wa-) (exact, careful) imitator, mimic; actor. *Cf.* **iga.**

[1]**mwigo (mi-)** 1. (act of) imitating, imitation. 2. counterfeiting, forging, forgery. *Cf.* **iga.**

[2]**mwigo (wa-)** *ornith.* mwigo (large dove).

[1]**mwiko (miiko)** 1. (large) spoon, ladle. 2. (mason's) trowel. *Cf.* **kijiko.**

[2]**mwiko (miiko)** 1. (act of) abstention; thing abstained from, taboo. **– wa nyama.** food taboo. **shika (vunja) –.** observe (break) a taboo. 2. *med.* regimen, diet. **– wa mganga.** doctor's orders.

mwiku *sing.* leftovers *(of food, saved from the evening meal for the following morning).*

mwili (miili) 1. body *(human or animal).* 2. trunk *(excluding the head).* 3. *fig., av.* fuselage. *Cf.* **kiwiliwili;** *also* **wili** (?).

mwima (wa-) 1. a person who carries himself erect/has good posture. 2. **(mi-)** a party of women who are making arrangements for a funeral. (= **maziko.**) *Cf.* **wima.**

mwimba, mwimbaji (wa-) singer. **waimbaji.** chorus, choir. *Cf.* **imba.**

mwimbaji (wa-) *see* **mwimba.**

mwimbishi (wa-) singing teacher; conductor, director *(of a chorus).* *Cf.* **imba.**

mwimo (miimo) (door-) post, (window-) frame. *Cf.* **wima.**

mwina (mi-) cavity, pit. *Cf.* [1]**kina.**

mwinamishi (wa-) 1. one who forces others to bend, oppressor, tyrant. 2. one who submits to others. *Cf.* **inama.**

mwinamo (mi-) 1. bending, stooping. 2. declivity, slope. *Cf.* **inama.**

mwinda (wa-) *see* **mwindaji.**

mwindaji, mwinda, mwinzi (wa-) hunter. *Cf.* [2]**winda.**

mwingamo (mi-) *see* [2]**mwungamo.**

mwingasiafu, mbwanda (mi-) mwingasiafu (kind of bean, *Canavalia ensiformis).*

Mwingereza* (Waingereza) Englishman. *Cf.* **Kiingereza, Uingereza.**

mwingi (wingi) *see* **-ingi.**

mwingilizi (wi-) mwingilizi (a man who marries the wife of his deceased brother, in accordance with the practice of levirate). *Cf.* **ingia.**

mwingine (wingine) *see* **-ingine.**

mwingizaji, mwingizi (we-) one who introduces something *(a custom, etc.).* *Cf.* **ingia.**

mwinjilisti* [*Engl.*] **(we-)** *rel.* evangelist.

mwinuko (mi-) 1. (act of) raising, lifting, elevation. 2. prominence, hill. *Cf.* **inua.**

mwinyi (we-) *see* **mwenye.**

mwinzi (we-) *rare* *see* **mwindaji.**

mwiro (mi-) (*us.* – **wa tembo**) trunk of an elephant. (= **mkono, mkonga.**)

mwisho. 1. (mi-) end, conclusion. **siku ya –** (*or* **kiyama**). last day, day of judgment. 2. completion, goal. 3. result, outcome. 4. destruction, death. 5. *adv.* (*also* **mwishoni, mwishowe**) finally, conclusively, irrevocably. 6. **–a –.** *adj.* final. *Cf.* [1]**isha.**

mwishowe *adv.* *see* **mwisho 5.**

Mwislamu*, **Msilimu, Muslimu, Musilimu** (wa-) Moslem, Mohammedan. *Cf.* **silimu, Islamu.**

mwita (wa-) *see* **mwitaji.**

mwitaji, **mwita** (wa-) one who calls/summons. *Cf.* **ita.**

mwito (mi-) (*also* **wito**) 1. call, summons; invitation. **itikia –.** reply to/accept an invitation. 2. slogan, watchword. 3. calling, vocation; inclination, proclivity. *Cf.* **ita.**

mwitu (mitu, miitu) forest, jungle. **mnyama wa –.** wild animal. **– mnene, gongo la –.** dense forest, jungle. *Cf.* **kimwitu, msitu.**

mwivi (wevi) (*also* **mwizi, mwibaji**) thief, robber. *Cf.* **iba.**

mwivu (waivu) envious/jealous person. *Cf.* **wivu.**

mwiwa (wa-) debtor. (= **mdeni.**) *Cf.* [2]**wia.**

mwizi (wezi) *see* **mwivi.**

[1]mwoga (wa-) timid/timorous person, coward. *Cf.* [2]**oga.**

[2]mwoga (wa-) *see* **mwogaji.**

mwogaji, **mwoga** (wa-) bather. *Cf.* [1]**oga.**

mwogeleaji (wa-) swimmer. *Cf.* [1]**oga.**

mwogo, **mogo** (mi-) bathing. **siku ya –.** day on which boys bathe for the first time after circumcision. *Cf.* [1]**oga.**

mwogofyo (mi-) threat, intimidation *Cf.* [2]**oga.**

mwoka (wa-) *see* **mwokaji.**

mwokaji, **mwoka** (wa-) baker. *Cf.* **oka.**

mwoko (mi-) baking, roasting. *Cf.* **oka.**

mwokosi, **mwokoti** (wa-) 1. (*also* **mwokotaji**) one who picks up/gathers something. 2. finder *(of a lost object)*. *Cf.* **okota.**

mwokotaji (wa-) 1. = **mwokosi.** 2. *fig.* tax-collector. *Cf.* **okota.**

mwokoti (wa-) *see* **mwokosi.**

mwokozi (wa-) 1. one who saves/rescues. 2. *(also rel.)* deliverer, savior, preserver. *Cf.* [2]**okoa.**

mwomba (wa-) *see* **mwombaji.**

mwombaji, muombaji, mwomba, mwombi (wa-) 1. one who asks for/requests something, petitioner. 2. beggar. 3. *rel.* one who (regularly, habitually) prays. *Cf.* **omba.**

mwombelezi (wa-) 1. *rare* suppliant, petitioner. 2. mourner. *Cf.* **omba, omboleza.**

mwombezi (wa-) intercessor, advocate. *Cf.* **omba.**

mwombi (wa-) *see* **mwombaji.**

mwonevu (wa-) bully; tyrant, despot. *Cf.* **ona, onevu.**

mwongeza (wa-) *see* **mwongezi.**

mwongezi, mwongeza (wa-) 1. fluent/eloquent person, good conversationalist. 2. gossip, chatterbox. *Cf.* **2ongea.**

1mwongo, mlongo (mi-) 1. number. **yuko katika miongo yao.** He is one of them. *loc.* **mwongoni** (*us.* **miongoni**) **mwa...** in the midst of..., from a number of... 2. decade *(division of a month).* **– wa kwanza.** first decade. **– wa kati.** second (middle) decade. **– wa mwisho.** third (last) decade. 3. (*us.* **–a miongo**) decimal. **hesabu za miongo.** decimal arithmethic, decimals.

2mwongo, mlongo (waongo, wawongo) liar, deceiver. *Cf.* **1wongo, uwongo.**

mwongofu (wa-) (*us. w. foll. obj.)* one who is directed/guided to something. **– wa dini.** *rel.* a convert. **– wa kazi.** clever/skilful person, specialist, expert. *Cf.* **ongoa.**

mwongozi (wa-) guide, leader. **– mwenye madaraka.** responsible leader. *Cf.* **ongoa.**

mwongozo (mi-) 1. guidance, direction. 2. instruction, advice. 3. commentary. 4. manual, textbook. *Cf.* **ongoa.**

mwonjaji (wa-) taster, one who tastes/tries food, etc. *Cf.* **onja.**

mwonjo (mi-) 1. (act of) tasting/trying. 2. test, trial. 3. experience. *Cf.* **onja.**

mwonyeshaji (wa-) demonstrator, illustrator. *Cf.* **ona.**

mwonzi (mi-) sunbeam, ray of light.

mwosha (wa-) *see* **mwoshaji.**

mwoshaji, mwosha (wa-) 1. one who washes *(in gen.).* 2.: **– maiti.** person who makes a business of washing corpses, undertaker. *Cf.* **osha.**

mwosho (mi-) (act, manner, place of) washing. *Cf.* **osha.**

mwote *see* **-ote.**

mwozi (wa-) one who performs the marriage ceremony. *Cf.* **oa.**

mwua (wa-) *see* **mwuaji.**

mwuaji, mwua (wa-) murderer. *Cf.* **3ua.**

mwuguzi, mwaguzi (wa-) medical attendant, nurse, orderly. *Cf.* **ugua.**

mwuja* (mi-) *see* **mauja.**

mwujiza*, mwujizi, muujiza (mi-) 1. something remarkable/supernatural. 2. *rel.* miracle. 3. surprise.

mwulimwengu (wa-) *see* **mlimwengu.**

mwumba, mwumbaji (wa-) *see* **muumba.**

mwumbi, mumbi (mi-) *ornith.* mwumbi (a large bird resembling the bittern).

mwumikaji (wa-) *see* **muumishi.**

mwumini (wa-) *see* **mwamini.**

mwumishi (wa-) *see* **muumishi.**

mwumizi (wa-) 1. someone who causes pain. 2. = **muumishi.** *Cf.* **uma, umika.**

mwunda, muunda, muundi (wa-) *(always w. foll. obj.)* one who builds/constructs something *(us. of wood).* **— chombo.** shipbuilder. *Cf.* **[1]unda.**

mwundaji, mwundi, mwunzi (wa-) carpenter. *Cf.* **[1]unda.**

mwundi (wa-) *see* **mwundaji.**

mwundo, muundo (mi-) 1. building, structure. 2. pattern, model. 3. form, shape. **kwa kufuata —.** according to pattern. *Cf.* **[1]unda.**

mwungama, mwungamaji (wa-) 1. one who admits/confesses that he has done wrong. 2. *rel.* penitent, one who confesses/goes to confession. 3. prophet. (*us.* = **Muḥammad**). *Cf.* **[1]ungama.**

mwungamaji (wa-) *see* **mwungama.**

mwungamishi (wa-) 1. one who receives/elicits/forces a confession. 2. *rel.* confessor. *Cf.* **[1]ungama.**

[1]mwungamo, muungamo (mi-) 1. admission, acknowledgment, recognition *(of an obligation, etc.).* 2. *rel.* confession. *Cf.* **[1]ungama.**

[2]mwungamo, mwingamo (mi-) *bot.* mwungamo (a tree from the bark of which a yellow dye is prepared; = **[1]mkumbi**). *Cf.* **[2]ungamo.**

mwunganisho (mi-) *see* **mwungano.**

mwungano, mwunganisho, muungano (mi-) connection, union, combination, alliance, coalition. **— wa nchi za Amerika.** United States of America. *Cf.* **[2]unga.**

mwungo (mi-) *see* **muungo.**

mwungwana, mngwana, mungwana (**waungwana, wangwana**) 1. *hist.* free man *(as opp. to* **mtumwa**, *q.v.).* 2. polite/cultivated/well-bred person, gentleman. *Cf.* **kiungwana, Kingwana, uungwana.**

[1]mwunzi (mi-) *see* **mwundaji.**

[2]mwunzi *sing., rare* *see* **uluzi, miunzi.**

mwuo (**miuo**) pointed stick used for digging.

mwuza (wa-) *see* **mwuzaji.**

mwuzaji, mwuza, muuzaji (wa-) seller, salesman, trader. *Cf.* **uza.**

m.y. = **maana yake.** that is to say, i.e. *See* **maana.**

Myahudi* (wa-) Jew. *Cf.* **Kiyahudi.**

myombo, muyombo (mi-) myombo (kind of tree; the bark is used for making cloth).

myugwa (mi-) *bot.* taro plant. *Cf.* **mayugwa, 2jimbi.**

Myunani* (wa-) (ancient) Greek, Hellene. *Cf.* **Kiyunani, Uyunani.**

mzaa (wa-) 1. one who gives birth/begets, parent. 2. *coll.* mother. – **bibi.** great-grandmother. *Cf.* **zaa.**

mzaanyuma, mzalianyuma (mi-) mzaanyuma (variety of spurge/euphorbia; the roots are used to prepare a medicine for treating gonorrhea).

mzabibu* (mi-) grapevine. – **mwitu.** wild grapevine. **shamba la mizabibu.** vineyard. *Cf.* **zabibu.**

mzabuni* (wa-) buyer, purchaser, bidder *(at auction). Cf.* **zabuni.**

mzaha* (mi-) 1. joke, jest. **jina la –.** nickname. **fanya –.** joke, tease. 2. (act of) laughing at/deriding someone. **fanyizia –.** laugh at/deride someone.

mzalia (wa-) *see* **mzaliwa.**

mzalianyuma (mi-) *see* **mzaanyuma.**

mzalisha, mzalishi, mzalishaji (wa-) midwife. *Cf.* **zaa.**

mzaliwa, mzalia, mzawa (wa-) 1. a person born *(in a certain place, etc.)*, native, inhabitant *(of a place)*. – **mbele.** first-born. – **hapa.** someone born here. 2. a native/local plant. *Cf.* **zaa.**

mzama, mzamaji (wa-) drowning person. *Cf.* **2zama.**

mzamaji (wa-) 1. = **mzama.** 2. diver *(occupation or sport). Cf.* **2zama.**

mzambarau* (mi-) mzambarau (species of plum tree. *Cf.* **zambarau.**

mzamia (wa-) one who dives for something. – **lulu.** pearl-diver. *Cf.* **2zama, mzamaji 2.**

mzamio, mzamo (mi-) (act of) diving. *Cf.* **2zama.**

mzamishi (wa-) 1. one who submerges. 2. person who employs divers. *Cf.* **2zama.**

mzamisho (mi-) employment of divers. *Cf.* **2zama.**

mzamo (mi-) *see* **mzamio.**

mzandiki* (wa-), **zandiki** (ma-) liar, deceiver, hypocrite. *Cf.* **zandiki, uzandiki.**

1mzao (wa-) 1. child, descendant, offspring *(of a human being or an animal)*. 2. (wazao) progeny, issue. *Cf.* **zaa.**

[2]mzao (mi-) birth, delivery. *Cf.* zaa.

mzawa (wa-) *see* mzaliwa.

mzazi (wa-) 1. one who gives birth/begets. 2. fertile woman/female animal. 3. parent. baba (mama) —. real father (mother). 4.: wazazi. parents. *Cf.* zaa.

mzee (wa-) 1. old man/woman. 2. respected/dignified man. 3. elder. 4.: wazee. parents. 5. ancestor. 6. *liter.:* — ndovu. the old elephant. *Cf.* zee.

mzegazega* 1. (wa-) water-carrier *(who carries two water-tins suspended from either end of a carrying pole).* 2. (mi-) water-tin.

mzeituni* (mi-) (cultivated) olive tree. *Cf.* zeituni; *also* mchekele.

mzembe (wa-) 1. negligent/slovenly person. 2. careless/indifferent/superficial person. *Cf.* zembe, kizembe, uzembe.

mzengwe (mi-) secret meeting/council.

mzeze (mi-) mzeze (kind of tree). *Cf.* [2]zeze.

mzia (mi-) *see* msia.

mzibo (mi-) 1. (act of) closing, stopping. 2. stopper, plug, bung. 3. (electric) plug. 4. *fig.* obstruction, stoppage. 5. *fig.* bolt *(on a door).* *Cf.* ziba.

mzigo (mi-) 1. load, burden. funga —. pack/tie up a load. — wa bidhaa. load of merchandise. mizigo. baggage. 2. *fig.* sorrow, loss.

mziko (mi-) burial, interment. *Cf.* zika.

mzikoziko (mi-) *pharm.* ipecac(uanha).

[1]mzima 1. (wa-) grown-up person, adult. 2. (wa-) healthy person. *Cf.* [2]zima, uzima.

[2]mzima (wa-) *(always w. foll. obj.)* one who extinguishes. — moto. fireman. *Cf.* [1]zima.

mzimu (mi-) *myth.* 1. soul/spirit of a dead person/ancestor. 2. place where offerings are made to the spirits of ancestors. *Cf.* kuzimu, wazimu, zimwi.

mzinduko, mzinduo (mi-) 1. sudden awakening. 2. formal opening, inauguration ceremony. *Cf.* zindua.

mzinga (mi-) 1. (hollow) cylindrical object. (*Cf.* kuru.) — wa nyuki. beehive. 2. *mil.* cannon (barrel). piga —. fire a cannon. mizinga ya salamu. salute. mizinga ya kupigia eropleni. antiaircraft artillery. *Cf.* zinga.

mzingatifu (wa-) *see* mzingativu.

mzingativu, mzingatifu (wa-) 1. someone with a good memory. 2. sensible/thoughtful person. 3. person without rigid opinions, unprejudiced/liberal-minded person. *Cf.* zingatia.

mzingefuri*, msingefuri (mi-) kind of plant (anatta, from which an orange dye is prepared). *Cf.* zingefuri.

[1]mzingi *see* msingi.

[2]mzingi (**mi-**) *ornith.* weaverbird.

mzingile (**mi-**) labyrinth, maze. — **mwambaji.** *rare* puzzle. *Cf.* **zinga.**

mzingo (**mi-**) 1. circle, curve, bend. 2. circumference, periphery. 3. environment, neighborhood. 4. *mil.* encirclement, investment. *Cf.* **zinga.**

mzinifu*, **mzinzi** (**wa-**) lecherous/immoral person, adulterer. *Cf.* **zini, zinifu.**

mzinzi* (**wa-**) *see* **mzinifu.**

mzio (**mi-**) prohibition, ban, taboo *(for medical or magical reasons). Cf.* **[1]zia.**

mzira (**mi-**) mzira (kind of fish, barracuda). (= **sansuri.**)

mzishi (**wa-**) one who attends to a burial *(either a friend who looks after the details of the ceremony or a professional undertaker, gravedigger, etc.). Cf.* **zika.**

mziwanda, mzuwanda (**wa-**) last child (that a woman is capable of bearing).

mziwaziwa (**mi-**) mziwaziwa (a swamp plant, *Cyperus flabelliformis*).

mzizi (**mi-**) 1. root, root-fiber. 2. medicinal root. — **wa fitina.** *coll.* the root of the trouble.

mzizimi, mzizimizi (**wa-**) 1. adventurer, globetrotter. 2. swindler, confidence man. *Cf.* **[2]zizima.**

mzizimizi (**wa-**) *see* **mzizimi.**

mzizimo (**mi-**) coolness, freshness. *Cf.* **[1]zizima**

mzo* (**mi-**) 1. mzo (unit of weight, 160 kg). 2. *rare* sixty. 3. large number, great amount.

mzoea, mzoevu (**wa-**) one who is familiar with/accustomed to something. — **wa bahari.** experienced seafarer. *Cf.* **[1]zoea, zoevu.**

mzoevu, mzoefu (**wa-**) *see* **mzoea.**

mzofafa* *adv.:* **enda —.** walk on tiptoe; *(fig.)* strut, show off.

mzoga (**mi-**) dead body, corpse *(usually that of the victim of an accident, found outside the home; cf.* **maiti***);* carrion, carcass.

mzomari*, **mzumari** (**mi-**) mzomari (a kind of grass; the roots are used for making a perfume).

mzomeo (**mi-**) abusive/sarcastic speech/remark, insult. *Cf.* **zoma.**

mzonazanje (**—**) mzonazanje (kind of snake).

mzozo (**mi-**) quarrel, dispute, difference of opinion; nagging, fault-finding. *Cf.* **zoza.**

mzuhali*, **mzohari** (**wa-**) someone who is habitually late/unpunctual, who is never on time.

mzuka (**wa-, mi-**) spirit, ghost, phantom, vision. *Cf.* **zua, [1]zuka.**

[1]mzumai* (**mi-**) mzumai (kind of millet).

²mzumai* (mi-) flotsam and jetsam, driftwood.

³mzumai* (mi-) lemon grass, khuskhus grass. (= **mchai.**)

mzumari* (mi-) *see* **mzomari.**

mzumbao *sing.* 1. astonishment, amazement. 2. embarrassment, confusion. **pigwa (shikwa) na —.** be astonished/embarrassed/ nonplussed.

¹mzungu (mi-) 1. something remarkable/ amazing/rare. 2. talent, ability. 3. skill, dexterity. 4. trick, feat. 5. instinct *(of an animal).* 6. **mizungu** *ethn.* instructions given to girls at the age of puberty. *Cf.* **zungu, kizungu, uzungu.**

²Mzungu (wa-) 1. a European. 2. *cards:* **— wa mbili.** queen. **— wa tatu.** jack, knave. **— wa nne.** king. *Cf.* **zungu, Kizungu, ²Uzungu.**

mzunguko (mi-), **kizunguko** (vi-) 1. circular movement. 2. turn, bend. **njia ya —.** roundabout way, detour. 3. whirlpool, vortex, eddy. 4. surroundings, environment. 5. *astr.* course, orbit *(of a planet).* 6. *fig.* outline, contour. *Cf.* **zungua.**

mzungumzaji (wa-) amusing person, good conversationalist. *Cf.* **zungumza.**

mzungushi (wa-) someone who twists/distorts. **— maneno.** 1. someone who twists words. 2. loquacious person. *Cf.* **zungua.**

mzungusho (mi-) 1. round, circuit. 2. a forced turning back/return. *Cf.* **zungua.**

mzushi (wa-) *see* **mzuzi.**

mzuwanda (wa-) *see* **mziwanda.**

mzuza (wa-) *arch.* one who visits a witch doctor/who believes in magical powers. *Cf.* **zua, ²zuka.**

mzuzi, mzushi (wa-) 1. innovator, inventor, reformer. 2. slanderer, talebearer. *Cf.* **zua, ²zuka.**

¹mzuzu (wa-) 1. someone who is dejected/ shocked/dismayed. 2. simpleton, greenhorn. *Cf.* **zuzu, zuzua.**

²mzuzu (mi-) mzuzu (kind of tree, the roots are used for preparing a medicine).

³mzuzu (mi-) mzuzu (kind of banana which is cooked when unripe).

N

na 1. with, and. **yeye na baba yake.** he and his father (*lit.:* with his father). **pamoja —.** together with. 2. *in expressions equivalent to Engl.* 'have,' 'be': **alikuwa na fedha.** He had money. **fedha aliyo nayo.** the money which he had. **hana budi.** He has no alternative. He must. *loc.* **pana, kuna, mna (muna).** There is... (*lit.:* the place with...). 3. by *(expressing the agent w. the pass.)*. **chakula kilipikwa na mke.** The food has been cooked by the woman. 4. also, but, however. **alisafiri kufika Tanga hakukutana na mwenziwe.** He took a trip to Tanga but did not find his friend.

naam* 1. *affirm. part.* yes, certainly, of course. 2. *interr. part.* I'm sorry? (would you mind repeating what you said, I didn't understand).

nabihi* understand, notice, perceive, remember, be fully aware of. *intr.* **nabihika.** *caus.* **nabihisha.** *Cf.* **tanabahi.**

nabii* (ma-) *rel.* prophet.

nadhari* (—) 1. (power of) judgment, discretion, good sense. 2. perspicacity, penetration, discernment. 3. decision, choice. **wa na (hana) —.** He has the (no) choice. 4. look, gaze, glance. *Cf.* **tanadhari.**

nadhifisha* clean up, put in good order, arrange. *Cf.* **nadhifu.**

nadhifu* *adj.* clean, neat, orderly, well kept. *Cf.* **nadhifisha, unadhifu.**

nadhiri* (—) oath, vow *(often rel.)*. **weka —.** take an oath. **ondoa —.** keep a vow.

nadi* 1. make known, announce, proclaim. 2. *fig.* offer for public sale, auction off. *appl.* **nadia.** *caus.* **nadisha.** *pass.* **nadiwa.** *Cf.* **mnada, mnadi.**

nadra* *adj.* rare, scarce, uncommon, unusual.

nafaika*, nufaika be successful, have an advantage, prosper, win. *caus.* **nafaisha, nufaisha.** *caus.-ass.* **nafaishana, nufaishana.** be mutually profitable. *Cf.* **nafuu.**

nafaka* (—) grain, cereal *(in gen.)*.

nafasi* (—) 1. room, space, facilities. 2. spare time, leisure. 3. opportunity, possibility. **wa na —.** have an opportunity. 4. (*also mus.*) period of time, interval. *Cf.* **nafsi, nafisi, tanafusi.**

nafasika*, nafasisha *see* **nafisi*.**

nafidhi* 1. preserve, protect. 2. help, rescue.

nafisi* (*us. caus.* **nafisisha, nafasisha**) support, maintain, provide for *(with money)*, help out. *intr.* **nafisika, nafasika.** be well off/in easy circumstances. *refl.-caus.* **jinafisisha.** make oneself comfortable, take it easy. *Cf.* **nafasi.**

nafsi* (—) 1. breath, vital essence, soul. 2. self, individuality, personality. **— yangu.** I myself. **anajipenda —.** He loves himself. *Cf.* **nafasi.**

nafuu* (–) 1. advantage, benefit, gain. *prov.* **kuvuja pakacha – ya mchukuzi.** If something falls out of the (heavy) basket, that is a benefit to the carrier. 2. increase, growth, increment. 3. *fig.*, *fin.* profit. **pata –.** to profit. 4. *fig.*, *med.* improvement, recuperation. **amepata –.** He is improving/getting better. *Cf.* **manufaa, nafaika.**

nahau* (–) 1. explanation. 2. excuse, evasion, pretext. 3. grammar, syntax. 4. *rare* meaning.

nahodha* (ma-) 1. *naut.* captain. *prov.* **chombo cha manahodha wengi huzama.** A ship with many captains is liable to sink (= Many cooks spoil the broth). 2. *zool.* heron, cormorant.

naibu* (ma-), **niabu, niaba** (–) representative, deputy, delegate. **kwa niabu ya...** in the place of, on behalf of, in the name of. *Cf.* **unaibu.**

nailoni* [*Engl.*] (–) nylon.

nairuzi* (–) *see* **nauruzi.**

naizesheni benefiting from the effects of...

najisi* 1. (–) (ritual) uncleanness; filth, disorder. 2. *adj.* unclean, impure, dirty, filthy; *(fig.)* profane. 3. *v.* *(also caus.* **najisisha**) soil, pollute, defile; *(fig.)* profane, desecrate; violate, ravish *(a woman).* *Cf.* **mnajisi, unajisi.**

nakala*, nuku, nakili (–) 1. copy. **– ya pili.** duplicate. 2. issue, number *(of a periodical).* 3. article *(in a periodical).* *Cf.* **manukuu, nakili.**

nakawa* *adj.* 1. pure, clean. 2. *fig.* immaculate, faultless; good-looking. *Cf.* **jinaki.**

nak'di*, nakudi (–) cash, payment in cash.

nakili*, nakulu 1. copy. 2. translate. *appl.* **nakilia.** *intr.* **nakilika.** *caus.* **nakilisha.** 3. (–) = **nakala.** 4. (–) translation. *Cf.* **manukuu, nakala, kinakilo.**

nakisi* 1. lessen, reduce, curtail. 2. (–) reduction, cut *(in pay);* deficit, shortage; flaw, blemish.

nako (<**na huko**) and here.

nakshi*, nakishi 1. carve, engrave, decorate *(with carving, embroidery, etc.).* *appl.* **nakshia.** *intr.* **nakshika.** 2. (–) carving, engraving, (carved) ornamentation.

nakudi* (–) *see* **nakidi.**

nakulu* *see* **nakili.**

nama 1. be flexible/pliable. 2. *adj.* flexible, pliable, elastic, plastic. **kijiti kinama.** flexible stick. *Cf.* **kinamo.**

namba*, nambari [*Engl.*] 1. (–) number. **– kwanza.** first quality. **– ya simu.** telephone number. **tia –.** to number **– tasa.** *math.* prime number. 2. (ma-) quantity. **manamba.** (great) crowd *(of people).*

nambari* [*Engl.*] (–, ma-) *see* **namba.**

nambawani* [*Engl.*] (ma-) *rare* acknowledged leader, victor, first-class man; a thing of first quality.

nami (< **na mimi**) and I, I too.

namna* [*Pers.*] (–) 1. kind, sort, quality. **kila –.** of all sorts, various, heterogeneous. **– gani?** of what kind? **dukani kwake kuna viatu – kwa –.** In his store there are shoes of every kind. 2. pattern, model, example. 3. form, tabulation, paradigm.

namua take out, remove, set free, extricate.

nanaa* *pl.* mint (leaves). *Cf.* **mnanaa.**

nanasi* [*Pers.*] (**ma-**) pineapple. *Cf.* **mnanasi, unanasi.**

nane eight. **–a –.** eighth. *Cf.* **manane.**

nanga* [*Pers.*] (–) *naut.* anchor. **tia –.** cast anchor. **ng'oa –.** weigh anchor.

nang'anika be fat/greasy/oily.

nangonango (–) worm *(in the bowels).*

nani? *interrog. pron.* who? **–a –.** whose?

nanigwanzula (–) nanigwanzula (a small lizard).

nanua break/split open, open by force. *intr.* **nanuka.** be split open.

nanyi (< **na ninyi**) and you *(pl.),* you too.

nao (< **na wao**) and they, they too.

napukia be flexible/limber/elastic.

nargisi* (–) narcissus.

nasa seize, grasp; catch, hold on to. **mnyama amenaswa katika mtego.** The animal has been caught in the trap. *appl.* **nasia.** *intr.* **nasika.** *caus.* **nasisha.** *inv.* **nasua.** set free, release *(from a trap).* *Cf.* **mnaso;** *also* **nata.**

nasaba* (–) 1. lineage, descent. 2. genealogy, family tree. 3. relations, relatives, kinsfolk. **sina – naye.** I am not related to him. *Cf.* [2]**nasibu.**

nasaha* (–) request for forgiveness/pardon. *Cf.* **nasihi.**

[1]**nasi** (< **na sisi**) and we, we too.

[2]**nasi*** [*Engl.*] (–, **ma-**) nurse.

nasibisha* *see* [2]**nasibu.**

[1]**nasibu*** (–) 1. (*us.* **bahati –**) luck, chance. **kwa –.** by chance, perhaps. 2. fate, destiny. 3.: **bahati –.** lottery.

[2]**nasibu*, nasibisha** trace someone's genealogy. *Cf.* **nasaba.**

nasiha* (–) 1. true/sincere friend. 2. wise/reliable adviser. *Cf.* **nasihi.**

nasihi* 1. advise, give (good) advice. 2. beg for forgiveness/pardon. *Cf.* **nasaha, nasiha.**

nasua *inv. of* **nasa.**

nasuri* (–) *med.* fistula.

nata 1. be sticky/viscous. 2. stick/spread on. 3. *fig.:* **jinata.** boast. *Cf.* **nasa.**

natija* (–) result.

nauli* 1. hire, pay fare. 2. pay freight. *caus.* **naulisha.** make arrangements for shipping, charter. 3. (–) freight(age) *Cf.* **mnawili.**

nauruzi*, nairuzi, neruzi [*Pers.*] (–) Nauruz (Persian New Year's Day, 22 March).

navya *caus. of* **nawa.**

nawa wash *(hands, face, feet). caus.* **nawisha, navya.** provide with water for washing *(before a meal). appl.* **nawia. maji ya kunawa.** water for washing. *Cf.* **manawa.**

nawe (< **na wewe**) and you *(sing.)*, you too.

nawiri* shine, glow *(of the face:* have a healthy appearance, pleasant expression). *Cf.* **nuru.**

naye (< **na yeye**) and he (she, it), he (she, it) too.

nazaa* 1. quarrel, dispute. *appl.* **nazia.** *appl.-ass.* **naziana.** quarrel with each other. 2. (–) quarrel, dispute, dissension, hostility. *Cf.* **mnazaa.**

nazi (–) (ripe) coconut. *prov.* – **mbovu harabu ya nzima.** A bad coconut destroys the good one. *Cf.* **mnazi.**

ncha (–) 1. tip, point. – **ya kalamu.** point of a pencil. 2. end, extremity, peak. – **ya kaskazini (kusini).** *geogr.* north (south) pole. 3. strand *(of a rope, etc.)*. 4. (final) result, outcome.

nchi, inchi (–) 1. country. – **yetu** (*or* **ya kwetu**). our country, our homeland. – **za Afrika.** the countries of Africa. – **kubwa.** the great powers. **ndugu wa – moja.** compatriot, fellow countryman. **fukuza katika –.** deport, exile *(from a country)*. 2. land, earth. – **kavu.** dry land *(as opp. to* **bahari**). – **sawa.** level country. 3. *rare* district, region.

ndago (–) ndago (a weed, 'nut grass,' *Cyperus rotundus*). – **mwitu.** papyrus grass.

ndakaka (–) ndakaka (long thin pole used in thatching roofs).

ndala (–) *see* **ndara.**

ndama (–) 1. calf. 2. young of some other animals. – **ya mbuzi.** kid.

ndani 1. (–) inner part, inside. 2. *adv.* inside, within. – **ya...** inside of... **alifika mpaka –.** He came all the way inside. **aliingia –.** He went in. 3. inwardly, secretly. **anadhani – ya moyo wake.** He thought in his innermost heart. *Cf.* **kindanindani, undani.**

ndara, ndala (–) ndara (leather sandal without decoration).

ndaro (–) boasting, bragging. **sema maneno ya –.** make boastful statements.

ndau (–) dipper, bailer *(used for bailing out boats)*. *Cf.* **ndoo.**

[1]**ndege, dege,** *(arch.)* **nyuni** (–) 1. bird. 2. *fig.* (*also* – **ulaya**) airplane. – **yenye kutua majini** (*or* – **yenye magalawa**). seaplane. – **ya jet.** jet airplane. – **ya upelelezi.** reconnaissance plane.

[2]**ndege** (–) sign, omen. – **njema (mbaja).** a good (bad) sign/omen.

ndema (–) *see* **dema.**

ndere (–): **uganga wa –.** (kind of) powder *(regarded as a love-charm).*

nderemo (–) *see* **mteremo.**

nderi (–) *ornith.* nderi (large bird of prey similar to a condor).

ndevu *pl.* 1. beard, whiskers. 2. *fig.* awn, beard *(of grain).* 3. wattle *(of birds). Cf.* **udevu.**

ndewe, njewe (–) 1. *anat.* lobe of the ear. 2. hole pierced in the lobe of the ear *(to receive an earring).*

[1]**ndezi** (–) sleepiness, drowsiness; indolence, laxity.

[2]**ndezi** (–) ndezi (kind of rat).

ndia (–) *see* **njia.**

ndiga (–) ndiga (kind of wild grass, *Dioscorea dumetorum*).

ndigano (–) ndigano (disease of cattle especially prevalent on the east coast of Africa, 'east-coast fever'). **katika wilaya hiyo iko –.** The east-coast fever has appeared in these districts.

ndilo (< **ni hilo**) *(emph.)* That is it!

[1]**ndimi** (< **ni mimi**) *(emph.)* That is me! I'm the one!

[2]**ndimi** *pl. of* **ulimi.**

ndimo (< **ni humo**) *(emph.)* In there is where it is!

ndimu* [*Ind.*] (–) lime *(fruit). Cf.* **mdimu.**

ndinyi (< **ni ninyi**) *(emph.)* You *(pl.)* are the ones! Especially you!

[1]**ndio** (< **ni wao**) *(emph.)* They are the ones! Especially them!

[2]**ndio** *see* **ndiyo.**

ndipo (< **ni hapo**) *(emph.)* It is there/then (that...). **aliufunga mlango – akaenda zake.** He first locked the door and then he went his way.

ndiposa *conj., dial.* therefore, consequently.

ndisi (< **ni sisi**) *(emph.)* We are the ones! Especially us!

ndivyo (< **ni hivyo**) *(emph.)* It is in this/that way (that...). **kama –.** If that is the way it is. **– hivyo.** in this very way.

ndiyo, ndio (< **ni hiyo**) *(emph.)* That is the way it is! Yes!

ndizi (–) banana, plantain (fruit of the [1]**mgomba**, *q.v.*).

ndoa (–) marriage, wedding, matrimony. **funga –.** conclude a marriage. **vunja –.** break up a marriage. *Cf.* **oa.**

ndoana (–) fishhook.

ndoero (–) *ornith.* ndoero (kind of bird, crab-plover).

ndogoro (–) *zool.* ndogoro (species of antelope, waterbuck).

ndole *pl. of* **udole.**

ndondi *adv.* with the fist(s). **pigana –.** fight with the fists, box.

ndongoa (–) ndongoa (custom of killing an animal [goat, ox] in front of the house of a deceased person).

ndonya (–) ndonya (wooden disc/plug inserted in a woman's upper lip [Makonde, Wiha, Nyasa]).

ndoo (–) 1. bucket, pail; dipper, bailer, scoop. 2. bucket of a dredger, one of the receptacles on a conveyor belt.

ndorobo (–) tsetse fly. (= **mbung'o, chafuo.**)

ndoto (–) 1. dream(ing). 2. *rare* sleep, drowsiness. *Cf.* ³**ota.**

ndovu (–) *dial.* elephant. (= ²**tembo.**)

nduara (–) nduara (a sea-fish).

ndubi (–) *naut.* outrigger.

ndugu (–) 1. relative of the same generation: brother, sister, cousin. **– mume.** brother. **– mke.** sister. **– mzazi.** blood brother. **– tumbo moja.** child of the same mother, half brother/sister. **– wa kunyonya.** foster brother. 2. friend, fellow tribesman. 3. *fig.* citizen, conational. 4. *fig.* birthmark. *Cf.* **kidugu, udugu.**

ndui *pl., med.* smallpox (a single pustule = **udui**). **mgonjwa wa –.** victim of smallpox. **chanja –.** vaccinate for smallpox.

nduli (–) 1. cruel/brutal person, ruffian, thug. 2. murderer. 3. *rel.* angel of death.

ndumakuwili (–) *zool.* blindworm *(which is popularly believed to have a mouth at either end; cf.* **uma, kuwili***).*

ndume (–) 1. *see* **uume.** 2. male *(of animals).* 3. strong/vigorous man. *Cf.* ¹**ume.**

ndumiko, umiko (–) instrument (horn) used for cupping/bleeding. *Cf.* **umika.**

nduni (–) novelty, latest fashion/rage.

nduruku *adj., coll.* thin, light, weak; small, undersize *(of persons).*

ndusi* (–, ma-) box *(us. covered with rawhide; used by women for clothing, personal ornaments, etc.). Cf.* **mandusi.**

nduu (–) *dial.* = **njugu.**

nduvi *pl. of* **uduvi.**

ndwele (–) *dial.* = **uele.**

ndweo (–) pride, arrogance.

neema* (–) 1. *rel.* (divine) favor, grace, blessing, benefaction. 2. well-being, comfort. 3. wealth, prosperity, abundance. 4. generosity, aid, support. *Cf.* **neemeka, neemevu, uneemevu.**

neemefu* *adj.* *see* **neemevu.**

neemeka* 1. be in comfortable circumstances/well-off, own property. 2. be generous/charitable. 3. make a good profit. *Cf.* **neema.**

neemevu*, **neemefu** *adj.* plentiful, abundant; in comfortable circumstances, prosperous; generous, charitable. *Cf.* **neema, neemeka.**

nektai* [*Engl.*] (–) necktie.

neli* [*Ind.*] (–) tube, pipe.

nema *rare* bend *(intr.)*. *caus.* **nemesha.** *intr.* **nemeka.** dance gracefully.

nembo (–) tribal mark/tattoo. *Cf.* **rembo, urembo.**

nemsi* (–) *rare* good name, honorable reputation.

[1]**nena** 1. speak, talk, articulate. – **vizuri, usiseme puani.** Articulate clearly, don't talk through the nose. 2. mention, speak of, talk about. **Unayemnena na mfahamu.** I know the person you are talking about. 3. name, designate; declare. **makamu amemnena waziri wa ukulima.** The president has named the minister of agriculture. *caus.* **nenesha, neneza.** *appl.* **nenea.** speak against, contradict someone. *appl.-ass.* **neneana.** speak against each other, argue, blame/accuse each other. recriminate. *Cf.* **neno, kijineno, mnena, mnenaji, mnenea, unenaji.**

[2]**nena** (ma-) *anat.* groin. *Cf.* **kinena.**

nenda *see* **enda.**

nene *adj.* 1. thick, broad; fat *(of persons or animals)*, corpulent. 2. complete, full. 3. *fig.:* **sauti –.** a deep voice. *Cf.* **nenepa, unene;** *also* **nona.**

nenepa become fat/corpulent/unwieldy *(of persons; see* **nona***)*. *caus.* **nenepesha.** *Cf.* **nene.**

neneza *caus. of* [1]**nena.**

neno (ma-) 1. word, expression, utterance. – **la kweli.** a true word. 2. *pl., rare* language, dialect. 3. *pl.* discussion, debate. 4. statement, assertion. 5. (important) matter, affair, (matter for) concern. – **hili limetukasirisha.** This matter has annoyed us. – **siri.** secret. 6. objection. **sina –.** I have no objection. *Cf.* [1]**nena.**

nepa bend down, sink, dip, sag *(of a tree branch, etc.)*. *caus.* **nepesha.** bend down, press down.

neruzi* (–) *see* **nauruzi.**

nesa 1. bend, sag *(as a branch)*. *(Cf.* **nepa.***)* 2. strike, beat.

neva* [*Engl.*] (–) *anat.* nerve.

ng'aa, ng'ara, ng'ala shine, gleam, glitter, sparkle. *caus.* **ng'aza, ng'ariza, ng'aliza.** *Cf.* **mng'ariza, mng'arizo, mng'aro, ung'aro.**

ngabu (–) chisel, gouge (= **bobari**).

ngadu (–) ngadu (kind of crab).

ng'akia growl, snarl, show the teeth *(dogs, etc).*

ng'ala *see* **ng'aa.**

ngalawa, galawa (–) *naut.* native boat with outriggers.

ng'aliza *caus. of* **ng'aa.**

[1]**ngama** (–) ngama (kind of white clay).

[2]**ngama** (–) hold (of a vessel), bilge (= **banduru**).

ng'amba (–) 1. (kind of) turtle. 2. (**chuma cha** –) tortoise-shell.

ngambi (–) communal work, mutual assistance *(organized by a group of people living together).* *Cf.* [2]**amba.**

ng'ambo (–) 1. either of two opposite sides. – **ya huku.** this side. 2. (– **ya pili**) other/opposite side *(of a river, etc.).* 3. *prep.:* – **ya...** on the other side of... 4. *rec.* abroad.

ngamia* (–) 1. camel. 2. *fig., coll.:* **ana shingo ya –.** She has a camel neck *(of a girl with a long, slim neck, regarded as a mark of beauty).*

ng'amua find out, learn about, discover, unravel; disclose *(a secret).* *Cf.* **mang'amung'amu.**

[1]**ng'anda** (–) handful.

[2]**ng'anda, ng'andu** *sing., astr.* Venus.

[3]**ng'anda** (–) *cards* pip, spot.

ng'andu *sing.* *see* [2]**ng'anda.**

ng'ang'ama seize, grasp, catch hold of, hold fast *(something moving, swinging: a branch, etc.).*

ng'ang'anaa 1. become dry/hard *(from the effects of the sun).* 2. wilt, wither.

ng'ang'ania 1. *rare* beg, implore, entreat, plead *(persistently and urgently for something one wants).* 2. vie for, contest *(the possession of something).* *Cf.* **ng'ang'anivu.**

ng'ang'anivu *adj.* persistent, importunate. *Cf.* **ng'ang'ania.**

[1]**ngano** (–) *rare, liter.* story, tale, fable.

[2]**ngano** (–) wheat.

ngao (–) (*also* **gao, ma-**) 1. shield. 2. house-front, façade.

ngapi *interrog. pron.* how many? **saa –?** What time is it?

[1]**ngara** (–) ngara (male blossom of maize).

[2]**ngara** (–) *rare* 1. skin, hide, leather (= **ngozi**). 2. ngara (a leather headband worn by chiefs).

ng'ara *see* **ng'aa.**

ng'arange (–) heartwood *(of a tree).*

ngariba (ma-) professional circumciser.

ng'ariza *caus. of* **ng'aa.**

ngavu *pl. of* **ugavu.**

ngawa (–) *zool.* civet cat, serval.

ngazi (–) ladder, steps, (flight of) stairs. *fig.:* – **ya noti.** (musical) scale.

Ngazija *sing.* Great Comoro Island. *Cf.* **Kingazija, Mngazija.**

nge (–) *see* **ng'ge.**

ngedere (–) ngedere (small black monkey).

ngema *dial.* *see* **njema.**

ngeu (–) 1. red ochre. 2. mark, line (made by native carpenters with red ochre). 3. *fig.* bleeding from a head wound.

ng'ge, nge (–) scorpion.

ngimbi *pl. of* **ugimbi.**

ngiri (–) 1. warthog. 2. *rare* wild boar. (= **nguruwe wa mwitu**). **mshipa wa –.** swollen scrotum, scrotal hernia.

ngisi (–) cuttlefish. **wino wa –.** sepia.

ng'o, ng'oo *interj. expressing contempt, derision, refusal.*

ngoa (–) 1. desire, lust. **timiza –.** satisfy desire. 2. envy, jealousy.

ng'oa 1. tear out, pull/dig up. **– mzizi.** pull up a root. *fig., coll.* **– mzizi wa fitina.** remove the roots of an evil. **– jino.** pull a tooth. 2. raise, hoist. **– tanga.** *naut.* set sail. *fig.* **– safari.** set out on a journey. *Cf.* **mng'oaji.**

ngoe (–) *augment. of* **kingoe.**

ngoeka (*rare* **koeka**) get hold of something *(fruit, etc.)* with a hook *(forked stick, etc.). Cf.* **kingoe, ugoe.**

ng'ofu (–) fish-roe.

ngogo (–) ngogo (small fish).

ngoja 1. wait (for). 2. stay, remain behind, stop. *appl.* **ngojea.** *appl.-ass.* **ngojeana.** wait for each other; wait together. *caus.* **ngojeza.** postpone, adjourn; keep someone waiting. 3. guard, be on guard, keep watch. 4. (–) *rare (red., w. int. force):* **ngoja-ngoja yaumiza tumbo.** Long waiting hurts the stomach. *Cf.* **ngojo, kingojo, mngoja, mngojezi, ungojaji.**

ngojamaliko (–) *ornith.* (species of) heron, bittern.

ngojo (–) 1. stopping-place, station. 2. waiting room. 3. guarding, surveillance. 4. *mil.* patrol. *Cf.* **ngoja.**

ngole (–) string, twine.

ngoma (–) (*rare* **goma, ma-**) 1. drum. **piga –.** beat a drum. 2. dance. **cheza (ingia) –.** take part in a dance. 3. music.

ng'ombe (–), **gombe** (ma-) 1. cow, ox, cattle. **– dume.** bull. **– jike.** cow. **– maksai.** ox, bullock. **kama –.** milk a cow. **ndama ya –.** calf. *prov.* **wawili hula –.** Two can eat an ox. 2. *fig.* stupid person.

ngome (–) 1. fort, fortress. 2. fortification, escarpment.

ng'onda 1. to dry fish. 2. (–) dried fish.

[1]**ng'ong'a** (–) 1. war horn. 2. the sound of such a horn.

[2]**ng'ong'a** 1. hum, buzz. 2. to make a contemptuous noise with tongue and lips (the 'raspberry'). *Cf.* **king'ong'o.**

ng'ongo *pl. of* **ung'ongo.**

ng'ong'ona gnaw.

ngongongo (–) *(onom.)* freight train.

ngono *pl.* 1. sexual intercourse. 2. bedtime, nighttime. 3. *polyg.* a wife's turn for sleeping with her husband. *Cf.* **gona.**

ng'oo *see* **ng'o.**

ng'ota, ng'uta 1. gnaw. 2. tap, rap *(as a woodpecker).* 3. pound, beat *(pillows, rugs).* 4. shake, sift.

[1]**ngovi** (–) *see* **govi.**

[2]**ngovi** (–) *see* **ngozi.**

ngozi, ngovi (–) 1. skin, hide, leather. 2. *fig., sport* football, football game.

nguchiro (–) mongoose.

ngumbaru (–) middle-aged/older person *(over 45).*

ngumbi (–) ngumbi (winged white ant; *cf.* **kumbikumbi**).

ngumi (ma-) fist. **piga –.** strike with the fist. **mpiga –.** *sport* boxer.

ng'ungwe (–) 1. furrow (prepared for planting seeds). 2. a piece of land allotted to someone for cultivation.

ngungwi (–) *dial.* *see* **kungwi.**

[1]**nguo** (–) 1. cloth, fabric, material. **– za kitanda.** bedclothes. **fuma –.** weave cloth. 2. garment, clothing, dress. **vaa (vua) –.** dress (undress) oneself. **vika –.** dress/clothe someone. 3. loincloth.

[2]**nguo** (–) nguo (a kind of bird regarded as a bringer of misfortune).

nguri (–) wooden hammer *(used by shoemakers).*

nguru (–) nguru (a large edible fish).

nguruma rumble, thunder, growl, roar, bellow *(indicating any loud, deep sound).* *prov.*

angurumapo simba nani achezaye? When the lion roars, who dances then? *Cf.* **ngurumo, mngurumizi.**

ngurumo (–), **kingurumo** (vi-) *any loud, deep sound:* rumbling, thundering, growling, roaring, bellowing. – **ya simba.** the roaring of a lion. – **ya radi.** the rumbling of thunder. *Cf.* **nguruma.**

nguruwe (–) 1. swine, hog, pig. – **mwitu.** wild pig. – **jike.** sow. 2. (*also* **nyama ya** –). pork.

nguruzi (–) plug, peg.

ng'uta *see* **ng'ota.**

nguu (–) mountaintop, peak.

nguva (–) dugong, manatee.

nguvu (–) 1. strength, power, force, energy. **tia nguvuni.** arrest, place in custody. – **ya umeme.** electricity. – **za atom.** atomic energy. – **za kubuni.** creative forces. 2. power, ability, influence, authority. 3. importance, seriousness. 4. passion, vehemence. **kwa** –. 1. strongly, energetically; with authority; earnestly; passionately, vehemently. 2. by force, under compulsion, reluctantly.

nguyu (–) *anat.* ankle bone.

nguzi (–) nguzi (hole in the bottom of a boat to let out water).

nguzo (–) 1. prop, post, pillar, column, beam, girder. 2. *fig., Isl.:* – **za Uislamu.** the five articles of Muhammadan faith. 3. *fig.* basis, support, proof, corroboration; comfort, assurance. 4. monument. *Cf.* **kiguzo.**

ng'wafua snatch, snap at something *(of an animal).*

1**ngwe** (–) 1. row/bed of plants. 2. plot, parcel *(of land).* 3. the piece of land that a man is allotted or assigned to work in a day.

2**ngwe** *pl. of* **ugwe.**

ngwea 1. be exhausted/emaciated. 2. be wilted/parched.

ngwena (–) *dial.* crocodile. (= **mamba.**)

ni *aux. v.* be *(serving as a copula).* **yeye ni mgonjwa.** He is ill.

nia* 1. (–) aim, goal, intention, purpose. **kwa** –. intentionally. **bila** –. unintentionally. 2. (–) thought, idea; conscience. 3. *v.* have in mind, intend; decide. 4. *v.* consider, reflect. *Cf.* **ania, nuia, nuio, manuwio.**

niabu*, **niaba** (–) *see* **naibu.**

nidhamu* (–) order, discipline. **endesha** –. maintain discipline.

nie nie [*Germ.* niemand?] no one at all.

nikaha*, **mikaha, nikahi** (–) *Isl.* marriage, wedding. **fungisha** –. solemnize a marriage, perform the wedding ceremony.

nikwata (–) nikwata (a species of small lizard which lives in houses).

nili* (–) indigo (the dye; *cf.* **mnili**).

[1]**nina** (–) *liter.* mother.

[2]**nina** *aux. v. 1st pers. sing.* I have.

ninga (–) 1. ninga (species of pigeon). 2. Ninga *(pr. n., fem.)*.

ning'inia move back and forth, swing, sway, rock. *caus.* **ning'iniza, ning'inisha.**

nini *interrog. pron.* what? **kwa –?** why? *(more emphatic than* **mbona**, *q.v.)*. **ya – (hii).** Why (that)? What for? **una –?** What's the matter with you? **– maana yake?** What is the meaning of that? **hujambo –?** How are you?

ninyi, nyinyi *abs. pron. 2nd pers. pl.* you *(pl.)*.

nipo *see* **po.**

nira* (–) (ox-)yoke.

nisha*, nishaa (–) *rare* starch(-flour). (= [1]**wanga.**)

nishaa* (–) *see* **nisha.**

nishani* (–) medal, badge; order, decoration.

nishati* (–) *rare* strength, exertion, energy.

njaa (–) 1. hunger, appetite. **nina (naona) –.** I am hungry. 2. food shortage, famine. **– ilikuwa katika nchi hii.** There was a famine in this country.

njaanjaa (–) papyrus grass.

njama (–) 1. secret society. 2. secret meeting. 3. secret message/communication.

njari* *pl. of* **ujari.**

nje *adv.* 1. outside. **– ya...** outside of..., on the surface of... **– ya maji.** on the surface of the water. 2. *sport* offside.

njegere (–) (small variety of) pea, pigeon pea.

njeku (–) undersized bull.

njema, *(dial.)* **ngema** 1. *adj.* = [1]**ema.** 2. *interj.* Good! Certainly! *Cf.* **vema.**

njenje (–) *coll.* money.

njewe (–) *see* **ndewe.**

njia, ndia (–) 1. way, route; road, street, path. **– kuu.** highway. **– ya reli.** railway track. **– ya kuzunguka.** roundabout way, detour. **– ya kukata.** shortcut. **– panda.** crossroads. *loc.* **njiani.** on the way, en route. 2. *elec.*: **– kuu.** (power) main. 3. *fig.* way, means; method. **tumia – zote uwezavyo umtoe jelani.** Use any means to get him out of jail. **umetumia – gani?** What kind of method are you using? *Cf.* **ja.**

njiti (–) 1. = **kijiti.** 2.: **– za kibiriti.** match. 3. *rec.* spoke of a bicycle wheel.

njiwa (–) pigeon, dove.

njombo (–) njombo (kind of fish).

njongwanjongwa *adv.* softly, quietly, stealthily, surreptitiously, on tiptoe.

njorinjori 1. (ma-) a very tall man *(often w. ref. to Nubians).* 2. *adj.* tall. *Cf.* **kingoringori. kinjorinjori.**

njozi (–) phantom, apparition, ghost.

njuga (–) njuga (a little bell, worn as an ornament and by dancers).

njugu (–) peanut. **njugunyasa.** (ordinary) peanut (= **karanga**). **njugumawe.** a hard variety of peanut (Madagascar/Bambara peanut). *Cf.* **mnjugunyasa, mnjugumawe.**

njukuti *pl.* *see* **uchukuti.**

njumu*, njumunjumu (–) (metal) inlay work, studding. *Cf.* **mjume, mjumu.**

njumunjumu (–) *see* **njumu.**

njuti* [*Ind.*] (–) shoe *(of European style).*

n.k. *abbr.* = **na kadhalika.** and so forth. *(etc.).*

nne *num.* four. **watu wanne.** four people. **–a –.** fourth.

[1]**noa** sharpen, whet, hone. **– kisu.** sharpen a knife. *fig.* **– meno.** welcome, approve. *appl.* **nolea. jiwe la kunolea.** whetstone. *intr.* **noleka.** *caus.* **nolesha.** *Cf.* **noleo, kinoo, manoleo.**

[2]**noa** *see* [2]**nyoa.**

Noeli* [*Fr.-Engl.*] (–) Christmas.

nofoa, nyofoa, nyafua pull off, strip off *(meat from bones).* *Cf.* **mnofu.**

nofu (–) (piece of) lean meat. *Cf.* **mnofu.**

noga be tasty/sweet, taste sweet. *appl.* **nogea.**

nokoa* [*Pers.*] (ma-) 1. observer, spectator. 2. sub-overseer, assistant *(on a plantation).* 3. *comm.* flunky, stooge, serf.

noleo (ma-) 1. *something used for sharpening:* whetstone, knife-sharpener, razor strop, etc. 2. metal ring, ferrule *(between the blade and handle of a knife).* *Cf.* **noa.**

nomi* *adv.* brimful.

nona become fat *(of animals).* *appl.* **nonea.** *caus.* **nonesha.** fatten (up). *Cf.* **nono, kinono, unono;** *also* **nene, nenepa.**

nondo (–) 1. (kind of) moth. 2. *liter.* dragon.

nonea kiss. *ass.* **noneana.** kiss each other.

nonga be troublesome/importunate/disagreeable. *caus.* **nonza.** 1. = **nonga.** 2. bore someone, exhaust someone's patience. *Cf.* **nongwa.**

nongo (–) 1. sweat, perspiration. 2. dirt on perspiring skin.

nong'ona whisper. *int.* **nong'oneza.** whisper something to someone. *Cf.* **manong'onezo, mnong'onezi, mnong'ono, nong'onong'o, unong'onezi.**

nong'onong'o (ma-) 1. whispering. 2. *fig.* rumor, gossip. *Cf.* **nong'ona.**

nongwa (–) 1. unpleasantness, annoyance, trouble. 2. malice, spite. *Cf.* **nonga.**

nono *adj.* fat, plump, well-fed. *Cf.* **nona.**

nonza *caus. of* **nonga.**

noo (ma-) *augment. of* **kinoo.**

noti* [*Engl.*] (–) 1. banknote, bill. 2. *mus.* note.

notisi* [*Engl.*] (–) 1. *jur.* notice, summons. **– ya masaa 24.** 24 hours' notice. 2. handbill.

Novemba* [*Engl.*] November.

nso (–) *anat.* 1. kidney. (= **²buki, figo.**) 2. *rare* liver. (= **ini.**)

nswi (–) *arch.* fish. (= **samaki.**)

nta (–) wax. **– ya nyuki.** beeswax.

nti (–) nti (ear-ornament).

nufaika* *see* **nafaika.**

nufaishana* *caus.-ass. of* **nafaika.**

nuhusi* (–) *see* **nuksi.**

nuia* 1. think, believe, assume. 2. have in mind, intend, resolve. *appl.* **nuilia.** *intr.* **nuika. nuiza:** 1. *caus.* inculcate, instruct. 2. *int.* concentrate one's thoughts on something *(a particular desire, etc.)*, make a wish. *Cf.* **nia 2, manuwio.**

nuio* (–) aim, intention, purpose. *Cf.* **nia 1, nuia, manuwio.**

nujumu* (–) *see* **jumu.**

nuka 1. give off a bad smell, stink. 2. nauseate. *appl.* **nukia.** smell good/sweet. *double appl.-int.* **nukilia** (*caus.* **nukiliza**). smell out, follow a scent, sniff, snuffle. **nukilia vizuri.** detect/notice a pleasant odor *(of perfume, food, etc.)*. *caus.* **nusa, nukiza.** have something/someone traced/hunted. *Cf.* **nukato, nuko, mnukio, mnuko.**

nukato (ma-) (*usually* **manukato**) something having or producing a smell (*us.* pleasant), scent, perfume. *Cf.* **nuka.**

nukiza *caus. of* **nuka.**

nuklia* [*Engl.*] *adj.* nuclear.

nuko (ma-) smell *(either good or bad)*. **– hilo mbaya limetokea wapi?** What is causing that bad smell? **manukato ya aina hii yana – nzuri sana.** This kind of perfume smells very good. *Cf.* **nuka.**

nuksani* (–) *see* **nuksi.**

nuksi*, nuksani, nuhusi (–) misfortune, bad luck, failure, disappointment.

nukta* (–) 1. dot, point, mark. 2. punctuation mark. 3. diacritical mark, vowel sign *(Arabic)*.

— **mbili.** colon. 4. *fig.* moment, second. — **moja.** Just a moment. — **tano.** five seconds.

nuku* *see* **nakili.**

numbi (—) 1. throwing out a net *(in fishing).* 2. catch/haul *(of fish).*

nuna sulk, act sullen; be discontented, grumble, complain; be unfriendly. *appl.* **nunia.** be discontented/complain about something (to someone); be cross with someone. *appl.-ass.* **nuniana.** grumble to each other, complain about each other. *caus.* **nunisha.** *Cf.* **mnuna, mnuno, ununaji.**

nunda (—), **mnunda** (wa-) 1. wild animal, beast of prey. 2. half-wild domestic cat. 3. *fig.* cruel, bloodthirsty person. 4. *fig.* something very heavy.

nundu (—) bump, lump; hump *(of native cattle, etc.).* **nundunundu.** *adj. & adv.* lumpy, hunchbacked. *Cf.* **kinundu.**

nundunundu *see* **nundu.**

nunge (—) leper colony.

nungu, nungunungu (—) 1. porcupine. 2. nungu (globe fish, = **bunju**).

nung'unika grumble, complain, pout. *appl.* **nung'unikia.** *caus.* **nung'unisha.** *Cf.* **nung'uniko.**

nung'uniko (ma-) 1. grumbling, pouting. 2. dissatisfaction, complaint. *Cf.* **nung'unika.**

nung'unisha *caus. of* **nung'unika.**

nungunungu (—) *see* **nungu.**

nunu *pl. of* **ununu.**

nunua buy, purchase; bargain over, make a bid on. *appl.* **nunulia.** *intr.* **nunulika.** *caus.* **nunuza.** *Cf.* **mnunuzi, ununuzi.**

nunulia *appl. of* **nunua.**

[1]**nunuza** rub the gums of a child to encourage teething.

[2]**nunuza** *caus. of* **nunua.**

nurisha* 1. light up, illuminate, brighten. 2. reflect. *Cf.* **nuru.**

nuru* (—) 1. light, illumination. **tia —.** light up, illuminate, brighten; *(fig.)* clear up, elucidate. **toa —.** emit light, shine. 2. brightness, radiance. *fig.:* **uso wa —.** a bright/cheerful/friendly face. 3. bright color. *Cf.* **nawiri, nurisha,** [1]**kinara, mnara.**

nusa *caus. of* **nuka.**

nusra* (—) *see* [1]**nusura,** [2]**nusura.**

nusu* 1. (—) half. — **saa.** half an hour. **saa u —.** an hour and a half. — **kipenyo.** radius *(of a circle).* **gawa — kwa (bi) —.** divide in half, halve. **bunduki ya nusu mtombo.** submachine gun. 2. (—) part, piece. — **kidogo.** a small piece. **nusu ... nusu.** partly ... partly. 3. *adv.* in small number. **wamekuja — tu.** Only a few people came.

nusudunia* (—) hemisphere.

[1]**nusura***, **nusra** (–) help, aid, support, protection. *Cf.* **nusuru.**

[2]**nusura***, **nusra** *adv.* almost, nearly; about, approximately. **aliugua – afe (kufa).** He was so sick he almost died.

nusurika *intr. of* **nusuru.**

nusuru* help, support; guard, protect, defend. *intr.* **nusurika.** be saved from/spared a difficulty. *Cf.* [1]**nusura.**

nusushilingi* [*Ar.-Engl.*] (–) 50-cent piece, half a shilling.

nwa *see* **nywa.**

nya (*also* **inya**) 1. drop, discharge. **– mvua.** rain. **inakunya.** It is raining. 2. (*coll. also* **– mavi**) defecate, urinate. *appl.* **nyea.** *prov.* **anayesifu mvua imemnyea.** Whoever praises rain is rained upon. *Cf.* **nyevu, kinyeleo, kinyenyevu, kinyesi, kinyo, mnyevu, mnyevunyevu, mnyo, unyaji, unyesi, unyevu.**

nyaa (–) *rare* nail *(of finger or toe).* (= **ukucha.**)

nyafua *see* **nofoa.**

nyagonyago (–) *coll.* howling, wailing, yelling.

nyaka (& *inv.* **nyakua**) 1. snatch, grab; filch. 2. pluck, pull up *(plants).*

nyakanga (–) nyakanga (person in charge of initiation rites, chief of the kungwi, *q.v.*).

nyakati* *pl. of* **wakati.**

nyakua *inv. of* **nyaka.**

nyala* *pl. of* [2]**ala.**

[1]**nyalio** (*pl. of* [2]**walio**) 1. a fish-trap. 2. sticks laid inside a cooking-pot to keep the food from burning.

[2]**nyalio** (–) welt, weal. *Cf.* [3]**walio.**

nyama (–) 1. = **mnyama.** 2. flesh, meat. **– ya ng'ombe (nguruwe).** beef (pork). **– ya matunda.** flesh of a fruit. **– ya nazi.** meat of a coconut. 3. substance, matter. *Cf.* **mnyama.**

nyamaa 1. be silent/still/quiet. 2. suppress expression of pain. *appl.* **nyamalia.** *caus.* & *int.* **nyamaza.** be (quite) still, keep (perfect) silence. *imp. sing.* **nyamaza!** *pl.* **nyamazeni!** Be still! Keep quiet! *Cf.* **nyamavu, mnyamavu, unyamavu.**

[1]**nyamafu** *see* **nyamavu.**

[2]**nyamafu** (–) dead animal, carrion. *Cf.* **nyama, fu.**

nyamavu, nyamafu *adj.* 1. still, quiet, silent. 2. *fig.* reserved, taciturn. *Cf.* **nyamaa.**

nyambua 1. tear apart/to pieces, crumble; peel off *(in strips).* 2. *fig.* find fault, rebuke, criticize. *appl.* **nyambulia.** *intr.* **nyambuka.**

nyambuo (–) nyambuo (a small fish).

[1]**nyanda** *pl. of* [1]**wanda.**

[2]**nyanda** *pl. of* **uwanda.**

nyangalika *adj.* unheard-of, nondescript, impossible, useless; *(of persons)* irresponsible, hopeless. **nguo hii ni kinyangalika haivaiki.** This dress is so old that I cannot wear it any more. **mtu huyu ni kinyangalika.** This person is irresponsible/hopeless. *Cf.* **kinyangalika, mnyangalika.**

nyang'amba (–) nyang'amba (a confection made of arrowroot).

nyang'anya take away by force, rob, plunder; abduct, kidnap; annex. *Cf.* **mnyang'anyi, unyang'anyi.**

nyangumi (–) whale.

nyani (–) ape, baboon. – **mkubwa.** baboon.

[1]**nyanya** 1. stretch oneself, raise oneself. 2. come into prominence, put oneself forward. *appl.* **nyanyia.** try to get something by underhanded means. *inv.* **nyanyua.** 1. = **nyanya.** 2. raise, lift. *Cf.* **mnyanyuko, unyanya.**

[2]**nyanya** (–) tomato. *Cf.* **mnyanya.**

[3]**nyanya** (–) grandmother.

nyanyasa tease, bother, annoy.

nyanyua *inv. of* [1]**nyanya.**

nyapa, nyapanyapa stalk *(game)*, follow stealthily, sneak up on.

nyapanyapa *see* **nyapa.**

nyapo *pl. of* [1]**uapo.**

[1]**nyara** 1. rob, take by force, abduct; take into captivity, imprison. 2. (–) plunder, booty, stolen goods.

[2]**nyara** be ashamed/embarrassed/humiliated. *Cf.* **nyarafu, kinyaa, unyaa, unyarafu.**

nyarafu feel aversion/repugnance/disgust. *appl.* **nyarafia.** *Cf.* [2]**nyara, unyarafu.**

nyaraka* *pl.* *see* **waraka.**

nyasi 1. **ma-** grass *(in gen.)*. 2. *pl. of* **unyasi.**

nyata walk quietly/stealthily, steal/sneak along. *appl.* **nyatia.** – **mnyama.** stalk an animal. – **mtu.** creep up on a person. *inv.* **nyatua.** walk unsteadily *(with short, quick steps, as a child first learning to walk)*. *Cf.* **nyatunyatu.**

nyati (–) buffalo. (= **mbogo.**)

nyatua *inv. of* **nyata.**

nyatunyatu *adv.* quietly, stealthily. *Cf.* **nyata.**

nyauka 1. dry up, wither. 2. be distorted *(in the process of drying)*. *caus.* **nyausha. jinyausha.** act/talk in a misleading way, give a wrong impression. **Watu nchini wana njaa sana, bado serikali yajinyausha ati mipango ya ukulima imendelea.** The government gives the impression that agricultural development is increasing; yet people are still suffering from hunger. *Cf.* **mnyaufu, unyaufu.**

nyayo *pl. of* **wayo, unyayo.**

[1]nyea 1. itch, tickle. 2. scratch oneself. *appl.* **nyelea.** *caus.* **nyeza.** *pass.* **nyewa.** feel itchy, be irritated; be excited sexually. *Cf.* **[2]kinyevu, mnyeo, unyeo;** *also* **nyega.**

[2]nyea *appl. of* **nya.**

nyega arouse desire *(us. sexual). caus.-int.* **nyegesha, nyegeresha, nyengeresha.** *Cf.* **[1]nyea, nyege, kinyegenyege.**

nyege, unyege *sing.* 1. desire *(us. sexual); (of animals)* heat, rut. 2. *med., rare* irritation, stimulation. 3. *fig., rare* exasperation, vexation. *Cf.* **nyega.**

nyegere (–), kinyegere, kinyegele (vi-) nyegere (an animal similar to a skunk).

nyegeresha *caus.-int. of* **nyega.**

nyekenya 1. decompose *(from natural decay or applied chemical action).* 2. *med.* become necrotic/gangrenous.

[1]nyele *pl. of* **unywele.**

[2]nyele *pl. of* **[1]uwele.**

nyeleo (ma-) *see* **kinyeleo.**

nyemelea steal up on, take by surprise, catch unawares.

nyemi (–) *see* **kinyemi.**

nyendea creep up on, stalk, follow on the sly.

nyendo (–) activity, movement; expedient. **– ya Umoja wa Afrika na Asia.** Afro-Asian Solidarity Movement. **– ya hila.** technical expedient. *Cf.* **enda.**

[1]nyenga *rare* interrogate, pump *(a person),* force someone to talk, extort an admission. *appl.* **nyengea.** *intr.* **nyengeka.** *caus.* **nyengesha.** *Cf.* **nyenya.**

[2]nyenga (–) nyenga (large flat fish).

nyengeresha *caus. of* **[1]nyenga.**

nyenje, nyenze (–) nyenje (species of cricket).

nyenya 1. interrogate, pump *(with questions);* extract information from a person, make someone admit something; ferret out. 2. talk someone into something, persuade. *appl.* **nyenyea.** *double appl.* **nyenyelea.** find out a secret. *double appl.-caus.* **nyenyeleza.** let someone in on a secret. *intr.* **nyenyeka.** be talked into something, yield to pressure. *intr.-appl.* **nyenyekea.** subordinate oneself to someone, be polite/obsequious to a person, show respect. *intr.-caus.* teach someone politeness/humility; humiliate a person. *pass.* **nyenywa.** *Cf.* **nyenyekevu, mnyenyekeo, mnyenyekevu, unyenyekevu.**

nyenyekevu *adj.* modest, humble, unassuming; servile, obsequious. *Cf.* **nyenya, mnyenyekevu, unyenyekevu.**

nyenze (–) *see* **nyenje.**

nyenzo *pl. of* **wenzo.**

nyerere (–) 1. nyerere (bracelet of brass/copper wire). 2. Nyerere *(pr. n. fem.)*.

nyerereza 1. hide, conceal; deceive, cheat. 2. disguise, camouflage.

nyesi (–) *see* **kinyesi.**

nyeta 1. be proud/arrogant/boastful. 2. be rude/ill-mannered/insolent. 3. be dissatisfied/hard to please/insufferable. *appl.* **nyetea.** behave insolently toward someone. *caus.* **nyetesha.** *Cf.* **unyeti.**

1**nyetea** *appl. of* **nyeta.**

2**nyetea** *see* **jetea.**

nyevu *adj.* moist, damp, wet. *Cf.* **nya.**

nyewa *pass. of* 1**nyea.**

nyiga (ma-) *see* **nyigu.**

nyigu, nyiga (ma-) hornet, wasp.

nyika (ma-) 1. uninhabited place, barren land, wasteland. 2. open, treeless region.

nyima 1. refuse, withhold. **tutamnyima chakula.** refuse to give someone food. 2. hold back, repress. *refl.* **jinyima. lazima ujinyime nafsi yako.** You must restrain yourself somewhat. *Cf.* **nyimivu, mnyima, mnyimo, unyimivu.**

nyiminyimi *see* **nyimivu.**

nyimivu, nyiminyimi *adj.* 1. frugal, stingy. 2. poor, shabby, scanty. *Cf.* **nyima.**

nyinyi *see* **ninyi.**

nyinyiha 1. shine *(as if smeared with grease)*. 2. shine up, polish.

nyinyirika, nyiririka glide, slide, slip. *Cf.* **tiririka.**

nyiririka *see* **nyinyirika.**

nyiza (ma-) strip of dried palm-leaf *(for plaiting mats)*.

1**nyoa** 1. pull/strip off, remove. 2. shear *(sheep)*. 3. shave, cut/dress the hair. *appl.* **nyolea.** *Cf.* **kinyozi, unyozi.**

2**nyoa, noa** straighten, correct; draw out, stretch; extract. *intr.* **nyoka.** be/become straight, be stretched out (to full length).

nyoe (–) *see* 2**nyonye.**

nyofoa *see* **nofoa.**

nyofu *adj.* 1. straight, stretched out, extended. 2. *fig.* straightforward, honest. *Cf.* 1**nyoka.**

nyoga *pl. of* **uyoga.**

nyogea (–) *see* **nyongea.**

1**nyoka, nyooka, nyoroka** be straight/straightened; *(fig.)* be frank/outspoken/honest. **mstari ulionyoka.** a straight line. *caus.* **nyosha, nyoosha, nyorosha.** straighten; *(fig.)* teach/bring up to be honest. *refl.-caus.* **jinyosha.** rest, take one's afternoon rest. *Cf.* **nyofu, mnyofu, unyofu.**

^{2}**nyoka** (–) 1. snake. 2. worm *(in gen.)*.

nyoko! *interj. a vulgar term of abuse (arch.,* 'Your mother'*)*.

^{1}**nyonga** 1. (–) *anat.* hip. 2. *pl. of* **unyonga.**

^{2}**nyonga** 1. squeeze (out), press, wring. 2. choke, strangle, throttle. 3. twist, wind, coil. 4. *fig.* irritate, annoy. *appl.* **nyongea.** *intr.* **nyongeka.** *caus.* **nyongesha.** *refl.* **jinyonga.** strangle/hang oneself. *inv.* **nyongoa.** 1. smoothe out, straighten out *(twists, kinks in something)*. 2. stretch oneself *(after having been in a bent/cramped position)*. *Cf.* **nyonge, nyongea, kinyongo, mnyongaji.**

nyonge *adj.* 1. low, mean, base, vile. 2. weak, sickly, decrepit. 3. slight, insignificant. 4. spurious, degraded, debased. *Cf.* **kinyonge, mnyonge, unyonge;** *also* ^{2}**nyonga, nyongea.**

nyongea, nyogea (–) *med.* rachitis, rickets. *Cf.* ^{2}**nyonga, nyonge.**

nyongeza (–) (*pl. of obs.* **uongeza**) 1. addition, supplement, increase, increment. 2. addendum, appendix. *Cf.* ^{1}**ongea.**

nyongo (–) 1. bile. 2. gallbladder.

nyongoa *inv. of* ^{2}**nyonga.**

nyong'onyea 1. be weak/feeble/slack/languid. 2. be depressed/downcast. *Cf.* **kinyong'onyo, unyogovu.**

nyono (–) the breathing of a sleeping person. *Cf.* **gona.**

nyonya suck *(of small children and animals)*. **ndugu wa kunyonya.** foster brother. *caus.* **nyonyesha.** suckle, feed at the breast. *Cf.* **nyonye, mnyonywaji.**

^{1}**nyonye, nyonyo** (–) mother's breasts *(in the speech of small children)*. *Cf.* **nyonya.**

^{2}**nyonye, nyoe** (–) nyonye (green grasshopper).

^{1}**nyonyo** (–) *see* ^{1}**nyonye.**

^{2}**nyonyo** (–) seed of the castor-oil plant. *Cf.* ^{1}**mbono, ubono.**

nyonyoa pull out *(hair)*, pluck *(feathers)*. *appl.* **nyonyolea.** *intr.* **nyonyoka.** *caus.* **nyonyosha.** *fig.* nag, find fault, criticize; annoy, torment.

nyonyota, nyotanyota, nyunya trickle, drizzle *(of light rain)*. *Cf.* **manyonyota, mnyunyo.**

nyonyotoa break into small pieces, crumble. *intr.* **nyonyotoka.** fall apart, disintegrate *(of overcooked food, etc.)*.

nyoo! *interj. of derision or contempt.*

nyooka *see* ^{1}**nyoka.**

nyoosha *see* ^{1}**nyoka.**

nyoroka *see* ^{1}**nyoka.**

nyorora become thin/emaciated/sickly/exhausted *(from disease)*. *Cf.* **ororo.**

nyorosha *see* ^{1}**nyoka.**

nyota (–, **ma-**) 1. *astr.* star. – **yenye baridi.** planet. 2. *fig.:* **hana – nzuri.** He does not have a good star (= He has no luck).

nyotanyota *see* **nyonyota.**

nyote (**ninyi** –) all of you. – **lazima mfike.** You should all come. All of you should come.

nyotoa 1. become exhausted/weak *(from pain).* 2. feel a sharp pain.

nyoya (**ma-**) 1. hair, feather, strand of wool. 2. *pl. of* **unyoya.**

nyoyo *pl., dial.* = **mioyo.** *Cf.* **moyo.**

nyua *pl. of* [2]**ua.**

nyufa *pl. of* **ufa.**

nyuga *pl. of* [1]**uga.**

nyugo *pl. of* **ugo.**

nyugwe *pl. of* **ugwe.**

nyuka hit, strike, beat. (= **piga.**)

nyuki (–) bee. **asali ya –.** honey. *Cf.* **uki.**

nyukua pinch, pluck.

[1]**nyuma** 1. (–) back, rear, reverse. **mlango wa –.** back door. – **ya ...** behind, after. – **yangu.** behind/after me. 2. (–) the past. **mambo ya –.** (things which occurred in) the past. 3. *adv.* behind. **kwa –.** from behind. 4. *adv.* back, backwards. **rudi –.** go back. *Cf.* **kinyume.**

[2]**nyuma** *pl. of* **uma** 4.

nyumba (–) 1. house, dwelling-place. – **ya udongo.** clay house. – **ya mawe.** stone house. 2. building. – **ya dawa.** drugstore, pharmacy. – **ya simu.** telegraph office. – **ya ghorofa.** apartment house. 3. *fig.* group of related families. *Cf.* **chumba, jumba, kinyumba, unyumba.**

nyumbu (–) (*also* **kinyumbu, vi-**) 1. mule. (= **baghala.**) 2. nyumbu (some kinds of antelope: hartebeest, topi, gnu; = **kongoni.**).

nyumbua stretch, bend, flex *(something elastic, without breaking). intr.* **nyumbuka.** be flexible/elastic. *Cf.* **nyumbufu, unyumbufu.**

nyumbufu *adj.* flexible, elastic. *Cf.* **nyumbua, unyumbufu.**

nyundo (–) hammer. *Cf.* [1]**unda.**

nyundu *pl. of* **undu.**

nyungo *pl. of* [3]**ungo.**

[1]**nyungunyungu** (–) *med.* inflamed/ulcerous fissures between the toes.

[2]**nyungunyungu** (–) earthworm.

nyuni (–) *arch.* = [1]**ndege.**

nyunya *see* **nyonyota.**

nyunyiza sprinkle. *Cf.* **nyonyota, nyunyu, kinyunya.**

nyunyu (**ma-**) (*us.* **manyunyu**) light rain, drizzle, sprinkle, spray. *Cf.* **nyonyota, nyunyiza.**

nyuo *pl. of* **uo.**

nyupo *pl. of* **upo.**

nyushi *pl. of* **ushi, unyushi.**

nyusi *pl. of* **usi.**

nyuso *pl. of* **uso.**

nyuta *pl. of* **uta.**

nyuti *pl. of* **uti.**

nyuzi, nyuzinyuzi (*pl. of* **uzi**) threads, fibers. – **zibuniwazo na watu.** synthetic fibers.

nyuzio *pl. of* **uzio.**

nywa, nwa (*inv. of* **nya** ?) drink, suck up, absorb. *appl.* **nywea.** *intr.* **nyweka.** *caus.* **nywesha.** give to drink, provide with water. **nywesha wanyama maji.** water livestock. **nywesha** (**nyweshea**) **mashamba.** water/irrigate fields. *Cf.* **jinywa, kinywa, kinywaji, kinyweo, mnywa, mnywo, unywaji.**

1**nywea** contract, shrivel/curl up; recoil *(from fright).*

2**nywea** *appl. of* **nywa.**

nywele *pl. of* **unywele.**

nyweleo (**ma-**) *see* **kinyeleo.**

nywesha *caus. of* **nywa.**

nzige (–) locust.

nzigunzigu (–) butterfly.

O

oa, owa take a wife, marry *(of a man). appl.* **olea.** *intr.* **oleka.** 1. be married *(of a woman).* 2. be marriageable/nubile. *pass.* **olewa.** be/get married *(of a woman). caus.* **oza.** 1. cause/allow to marry, marry off. **amemwoza mtoto wake kwa mtu mzee.** He has married off his daughter to an old man. **nioze mtoto wako.** Permit me to marry your daughter. 2. make preparations for a wedding, perform the marriage ceremony. *ass.* **oana.** intermarry *(of families). Cf.* **maozi, mwozi, ndoa, uozi.**

ofisa*, afisa [*Engl.*] (**ma-**) 1. official. 2. *mil.* officer. *Cf.* **uafisa.**

ofisi* [*Engl.*] (–) 1. (business) office. 2. (government) bureau, institution.

ofisiboi* [*Engl.*] (ma-) office boy, errand boy, messenger.

ofusaidi* [*Engl.*] (–) *sport* offside.

[1]**oga** (*also* **koga**) wash *(the body)*, bathe, take a bath. *appl.* **ogea.** *caus.* **ogesha.** bathe someone *(e.g., a child).* *double appl.* **ogelea.** 1. swim. 2. *fig.* turn up, appear, arise *(a question)*, occur *(an event).* *double appl.-intr.* **ogeleka.** **baharini hapa hapaogeliki.** It is not possible to bathe in this sea. *double appl.-caus.* **ogeleza, ogelesha.** cause/teach to swim. *Cf.* **kiogeo, mwogaji, mwogeleaji, mwogo.**

[2]**oga** *adj.* cowardly, timorous, fainthearted, pusillanimous; timid, shy, nervous. *Cf.* **ogofyo, ogopa, mwoga, mwogofyo, woga, mogofya.**

[3]**oga** (–) *rare* *see* **woga.**

ogeleka *double appl.-intr. of* [1]**oga.**

ogeleza *double appl.-caus. of* [1]**oga.**

ogofisha *double caus. of* **ogopa.**

ogofya *caus. of* **ogopa.**

ogofyo (ma-) 1. danger. 2. threat, menace. *Cf.* [2]**oga.**

ogopa be afraid/terrified/startled. *caus.* **ogofya** & *double caus.* **ogofisha.** frighten, terrify; startle; endanger, jeopardize; threaten, menace. *Cf.* [2]**oga.**

oka 1. roast, bake. – **mkate.** bake bread. – **nyama.** roast meat. 2. dry *(fruit).* 3. fire *(pottery).* *caus.* **okesha, okeza.** *inv.* **okoa.** take away from the fire, remove from the oven/kiln. *inf. (rare)* **koka** (= **kuoka**). *Cf.* **joko, mwokaji, mwoko, uokaji.**

[1]**okoa** *inv. of* **oka.**

[2]**okoa** 1. save, preserve, rescue, deliver, help out of a difficulty/predicament. **ametuokoa katika taabu zetu.** He has helped us out of our difficulties. **ameniokoa na hatari ya mamba.** He rescued me from a crocodile *(lit.:* from the danger of a crocodile). *appl.* **okolea.** *intr.* **okoka.** *caus.* & *int.* **okoza.** 1. rescue someone. 2. get oneself out of a difficult situation. *Cf.* [1]**kiokozi, maokozi, mwokozi, uokozi, wokovu.**

okota 1. pick up, gather; find. 2. come upon by chance/unexpectedly. 3. obtain something without effort. *appl.* **okotea.** *intr.* **okoteka.** be capable of being picked up. *prov.* **maji yaliyomwagika hayaokoteki.** Spilled water cannot be picked up. *caus.* **okotesha.** *Cf.* **kiokosi, kiokote, mwokosi, mwokotaji, uokosi, uokotaji.**

oktavo* [*Engl.*] (–) *mus.* octave.

Oktoba* [*Engl.*] October.

ola *rare* look at, observe. *Cf.* **oleza,** [1]**kioo** (?).

ole* (–) 1. fate, lot, destiny. 2. woe, grief. **mwenye –.** despondent/melancholy person. 3. *interj.:* – **wangu!** Woe is me!

oleleza *see* **oleza.**

olewa *pass. of* **oa.**

oleza, oleleza make even/level; make something like something else, imitate, copy. *Cf.* **kiolezo;** *also* **ola** (?).

omba 1. ask, beg, be a beggar. 2. pray. 3. implore, entreat, beseech. *appl.* **ombea.** plead/intercede for someone; ask/demand something of someone. *intr.* **ombeka.** *caus.* **ombesha, ombeza.** 4. (ma-) request, entreaty, petition. *Cf.* **ombokeza, omboleza, ombolezo, maombi, maombolezo, mwombaji, mwombezi, mwombelezi, uombaji, uombezi.**

ombasha* [*Turk.*] (ma-) *mil., arch. (approx.)* corporal.

ombojea be soft/overripe/overcooked.

ombokeza repeat the words of the formula before swearing an oath. *Cf.* **omba.**

omboleza 1. bewail, lament, mourn. 2. beseech, request urgently. *Cf.* **omba.**

ombolezo (ma-) (*us.* **maombolezo**) 1. lament, weeping/wailing. 2. ceremonial song of mourning, dirge. 3. earnest entreaty, urgent request. *Cf.* **omboleza.**

ombwe (–) 1. edge, margin, brink. 2. shore.

omeka unpack, spread out, lay out, display *(wares, objects). appl.* **omekea.** *int.* **omekeza.** pile up, arrange objects by stacking them one on the other.

omo* (ma-) *naut.* bow *(of a ship). Cf.* **kiomo.**

omoa 1. open. 2. dig up, break up *(soil).* 3. *(fig.)* stir up, disturb, cause unrest/disorder. 4. *fig.* reveal, bring to light, display. *appl.* **omolea.** *intr.* **omoka.** *caus.* **omosha.**

omolea *appl. of* **omoa.**

ona 1. see, notice. **nionavyo.** as I see it, in my opinion. 2. feel, sense. – **njaa (kiu).** feel hunger (thirst), be hungry (thirsty). – **furaha (huzuni).** feel joy (sorrow). **waonaje?** How do you feel? How are you? 3. think, believe. **naona utaona ajabu.** I think you will be amazed. 4. perceive *(hear, smell).* – **kishindo.** hear a noise. – **harufu.** detect an odor. – **ladha.** perceive a taste. 5. recognize, acknowledge. *refl.* **jiona.** 1. feel. **jiona na nguvu.** feel strong. 2. *fig.* be conceited/proud/arrogant. *ass.* **onana.** see/meet each other (again). *appl.* **onea.** 1. look at someone. 2. feel... *(a certain emotion, usually hostility)* toward someone. **onea fulani chuki.** feel hatred for someone. **onea kijicho.** envy someone. **onea wivu.** be jealous of someone. 3. look down on someone. 4. mistreat, persecute, oppress. *intr.* **oneka** & *intr.-ass.* **onekana.** 1. be visible/apparent/obvious, seem/appear to be. 2. be acceptable. *caus.* **onya.** 1. cause/permit to see, show, explain. 2. warn, admonish, deter, restrain. 3. criticize, disapprove of. *caus.-intr.* **onyeka.** be warned. *caus.-ass.* **onyana.** warn each other, exchange warning signals. *double caus.* **onyesha.** 1. show, indicate, point out, explain, clarify, demonstrate. 2. display, exhibit, disclose. *Cf.* **kionyo, lonyo, maonezi, maoni, maono, maonyo, maonyesho, mboni, mwonevu, mwonyeshaji, oneo, onevu, ono, onyesho, onyo, uonevu, wonyesho, wonyeshano.**

ondoa 1. take away, remove, get rid of, eliminate. 2. put an end to, abolish; conclude, terminate. – **matanga.** conclude the burial ceremony. 3. *fig.* release, relieve of. – **madaraka.** release from obligations. *appl.* **ondolea.** remove from, rid of, relieve of. **ondolea mashaka.** relieve of doubts. *pass.* **ondolewa.** be relieved of *(doubts)*, be absolved from *(sins)*. *intr.* **ondoka.** get up, rise; set out, start; leave, depart, withdraw. **ondoka katika ulimwengu.** *euph.* die *(lit.: depart from the world)*. *liter.:* **paliondoka.** Now it came to pass... *(at the beginning of a story)*. *intr.-appl.* **ondokea.** make progress, prosper, be successful; develop, grow; swell, protrude; stand out, be prominent. *intr.-double appl.* **ondokelea.** get up and leave *(a place)*. *caus.* **ondosha.** cause to leave, send away, dismiss. **ondosha nanga.** weigh anchor. **ondosha mtu kazini.** discharge a worker. *Cf.* **ondokeo, ondoleo, maondoleo.**

ondoka *intr. of* **ondoa.**

ondokelea *double appl. of* **ondoa.**

ondokeo (ma-) (*us.* **maondokeo**) 1. departure, start *(of a journey)*. 2. prospering, success, advancement. 3. *rare* progress. *Cf.* **ondoa.**

ondolea *appl. of* **ondoa.**

ondoleo (ma-) (*us.* **maondoleo**) 1. removal, elimination, dismissal. **maondoleo ya mashaka.** removal of doubts. 2. shifting, transposition. 3. change of residence. *Cf.* **ondoa.**

ondosha *caus. of* **ondoa.**

onea *appl. of* **ona.**

onekana *intr.-ass. of* **ona.**

oneo (ma-) (*us.* **maoneo**) mistreatment, cruelty, bullying, persecution. *Cf.* **ona.**

onevu *adj.* cruel, malicious, oppressive, violent. *Cf.* **ona, mwonevu, uonevu.**

[1]**ongea** *rare* grow, increase. *us. caus.* **ongeza.** 1. grow, increase. 2. add to, enlarge, augment, expand, fill up. **ongeza mali.** add to property. **ongeza upana.** widen, broaden, expand. *caus.-appl.* **ongezea.** *caus.-intr.* **ongezeka.** be increased/enlarged/expanded. **chama hiki kinaongezeka katika nchi nzima.** This organization is spread over the entire country. *Cf.* **ongezo, nyongeza.**

[2]**ongea** 1. talk, converse, chat. 2. waste time. *ass.* **ongeana.** chat with each other, pass the time together. *Cf.* **maongezi, mwongezi.**

ongeza *caus. of* [1]**ongea.**

ongezeko (ma-) *see* **ongezo.**

ongezo, ongezeko (ma-) (*us.* **maongezo, maongezeko**) increase, growth, addition, enlargement, expansion. *Cf.* [1]**ongea.**

ongoa 1. precede, go straight ahead. 2. lead, guide. 3. instruct, train. 4. make right, correct, improve, reform. 5. cause someone to change his views, *(rel.)* convert. 6. be successful, prosper. *appl.* **ongolea.** 1. = **ongoa.** 2. *liter.* rhyme. *intr.* **ongoka.** 1. be put on a straight course. 2. be reformed/converted. **ongoka nafsi.** change one's ways, turn a new leaf. *caus.* **ongoza.** 1. promote, advance, expedite. 2. show the way. 3. instruct, teach, train. **ongoza maneno.** give a good turn to a conversation. *caus.-ass.* **ongozana.** follow each other, move together in the same direction/toward a common goal. *Cf.* **ongofu, kiongozi, maongozi, mwongofu, mwongozi, mwongozo, uongozi, wongofu.**

ongofu *adj.* 1. straightened out, reformed, corrected. 2. successful, prosperous. *Cf.* **ongoa.**

ongofya *caus. of* **ongopa.**

ongopa 1. lie, deceive. 2. slander, make false statements. *caus.* **ongofya.** 1. = **ongopa** *w. int. force.* 2. lead astray, mislead. *Cf.* [1]**wongo, mwongo, uwongo.**

onja 1. try, test. 2. taste *(foods). fig.* **ameonja mapesa.** He loves money. 3. examine, investigate. *appl.* **onjea.** *intr.* **onjeka.** *caus.* **onjesha.** *Cf.* **onjo, kionja, kionjo, mwonjaji, mwonjo, uonjaji.**

onjesha *caus. of* **onja.**

onji (ma-) *see* **onjo.**

onjo, onji (ma-) trial, test, investigation. *Cf.* **onja.**

ono (ma-) 1. perception, sensation, feeling. 2. thought, opinion, impression. *Cf.* **ona.**

onya *caus. of* **ona.**

onyana *caus.-ass. of* **ona.**

onyeka *caus.-intr. of* **ona.**

onyesha *double caus. of* **ona.**

onyesho (ma-) *(us. pl.)* display, demonstration, exhibition. **maonyesho ya vita.** military review. *Cf.* **ona.**

onyo (ma-) (*us.* **maonyo**) 1. warning, advice, exhortation, hint. 2. indication, mark, index. 3. indicator *(on a machine). Cf.* **ona.**

onza 1. wound, hurt, do harm to, damage. 2. *fig.* torment, annoy.

opoa 1. take/pull out. 2. *fig.* save, rescue, extricate *(from difficulties). appl.* **opolea.** *pass.* **opolewa.** *intr.* **opoka.** *caus.* **oposha, opoza.** *Cf.* **kiopoo.**

orda* [*Engl.*] (–) order *(for something).* **mchukuaji – wa chakula.** one who takes orders at the table, waiter.

orodha*, oroza, worodha (–) 1. list, register, inventory. **– ya biashara.** commercial register. **– ya majina.** roll, roster. 2. bill, invoice. 3. catalog, program. **– ya masomo.** timetable, schedule.

orofa*, ghorofa, gorofa (–) (upper) floor, story. **– ya pili.** third floor. **nyumba ya – nne.** a four-story house.

ororo *adj.* soft, smooth, tender, delicate, sensitive. **ufupa mwororo.** gristle, cartilage. *Cf.* **nyorora.**

oroza* (–) *see* **orodha.**

osha wash *(us. objects, clothes, etc.)*, wash off, rinse. *appl.* **oshea.** *intr.* **osheka.** be washable. **haiosheki.** It is not washable. *caus.* **osheza.** *Cf.* **josho, kiosha, kiosho, mwoshaji, mwosho, uoshaji.**

¹ota grow *(of hair, nails; rarely of plants).* *appl.* **otea.** *intr.* **oteka.** *caus.* **otesha.** *Cf.* **¹oteo, uotaji, ¹woto.**

²ota sit, squat, crouch *(us. in order to warm oneself).* – **moto.** warm oneself at the fire. *appl.* **otea.** 1. = **ota.** 2. lie in wait/ambush for someone. *intr.* **oteka.** *caus.* **otesha.** *stat.* **otama.** be in a sitting/squatting position. *stat.-appl.* **otamia, atamia, latamia, tamia.** sit on eggs, brood. **kuku anaatamia mayai.** The hen is sitting on eggs. *Cf.* **²oteo, kiota;** *also* **¹moto.**

³ota 1. dream. – **ndoto.** have a dream. 2. be half awake, doze, be in a trance. 3. *fig.* daydream, indulge in reveries, talk foolishly. *appl.* **otea.** dream about. *intr.* **oteka.** *ass.* **otana.** dream about each other. *Cf.* **ndoto.**

⁴ota 1. mark, designate. 2. make a mark, leave marks *(us. welts from blows).* *Cf.* **²moto.**

otama *stat. of* **²ota.**

otamia *stat.-appl. of* **²ota.**

otana *ass. of* **³ota.**

ote 1. *indef. pron.* all, whole. **watu wote.** all people. **nchi yote.** all countries. **sisi sote.** all of us. **nyumba yote.** the whole house. **–ote –wili.** both. 2. *indef. relat.* **mtu ye yote.** anyone whatever. *Cf.* **mote.**

otea *appl. of* **¹ota, ²ota, ³ota.**

¹oteo (ma-) growth. *Cf.* **¹ota.**

²oteo (ma-), **kioteo** (vi-) hiding-place, ambush. *Cf.* **²ota.**

ovataimu* [*Engl.*] (–) overtime.

ovu 1. (ma-) (*us.* **maovu**) badness, wickedness; injustice. *coll.* **mema na maovu ndio ulimwengu.** There are both good and bad in the world. 2. *adj.* bad, evil, wicked, wrong, depraved; malicious, spiteful. *Cf.* **maovu, uovu.**

ovyo 1. *adj.* worthless, inferior; *(fig.)* superficial, careless. 2. *adv. (also* **ovyoovyo***)* haphazardly, aimlessly, carelessly, at random. **fanya kazi ovyoovyo tu.** do one's work carelessly/in a slipshod way. *Cf.* **maovyo.**

oya (ma-) handful. (= **ukofi, konzi, ¹gao.**)

¹oza turn bad, decay, rot, decompose. **matunda yameoza.** The fruit is rotten. *prov.* **samaki akioza ni mtungo pia.** One bad fish spoils the whole string. (*Cf.* **mtungo.**) *appl.* **ozea.** *intr.* **ozeka.** *caus.* **ozesha.** spoil/ruin *(something, someone).* *Cf.* **kioza, wozo.**

²oza *caus. of* **oa.**

P

[1]**pa** 1. give. – **mkono.** give the hand *(to express congratulation/condolence);* lend a helping hand. – **mgongo (uso).** turn the back (face). – **shauri.** give a piece of advice. – **ruhusa.** give permission, allow. 2. carry out, perform, accomplish. – **mchezo.** play out a game. – **hadithi.** tell a story. *refl.* **jipa.** 1. give oneself, have oneself provided with. 2. *fig.* make oneself out to be, act as if, pretend to be. **jipa ujinga.** play the fool, feign stupidity. **jipa mali.** play the great man, put on airs. *appl.* **pea** (*rare* **pia**). *ass.* **pana.** give each other something. *appl.-ass.* **peana.** make an agreement/bargain with each other; exchange greetings. **peana zawadi.** exchange presents. **kukimbia kwa kupeana.** relay race. *pass.* **pewa.** **amepewa zawadi.** He has been given a present. *Cf.* [1]**paji,** [1]**kipa,** [1]**kipaji,** [1]**kipawa, mpaji,** [2]**uapo, upaji.**

[2]**pa** *conn.* **mahali – uhalifu.** on the scene of the crime.

[1]**paa, para** 1. scrape/scratch (off). – **magamba ya samaki.** scale fish. – **moto.** stir the fire (and take out burning coals). 2. paw (the ground). **farasi anapaa.** the horse is pawing. 3. *fig.:* – **karata.** win a game of cards. *appl.* **palia, paria.** 1. = **paa.** 2. rake, gather up *(leaves);* weed *(a field). double appl.-caus.* **paliliza.** 1. employ someone to pull weeds. 2. *fig.* stir up, agitate someone. *caus.* **paaza, paraza.** grind coarsely, pound *(w. mortar and pestle),* pulverize. *intr.* **palika.** *ass.* **paana.** *Cf.* **palizi,** [2]**para,** [3]**para, parua, paruparu, mapalio, mpalilio, mpalizi, mparuzi, mparuzo.**

[2]**paa** 1. rise, get up. 2. go up, rise, ascend, mount. *appl.* **palia. wali umenipalia.** *coll.* I choked over the rice (i.e., it went down the wrong way). *appl.-caus. (also int.).* **paliza.** raise, lift. **paliza sauti.** raise the voice, speak loudly. *caus.* **paaza, paza. paaza ugomvi.** goad someone on, start a quarrel with someone. *Cf.* [3]**paa,** [1]**pao,** [1]**kipaa, kipao,** [1]**mpalio.**

[3]**paa (ma-)** sloping side of a native thatched roof. *Cf.* [2]**paa.**

[4]**paa (–)** paa (kind of gazelle, impala). (= **kinokero.**)

paana *ass. of* [1]**paa.**

paanda (–) *see* [4]**panda.**

paaza *caus. of* [1]**paa,** [2]**paa.**

pacha 1. **(ma-)** twin, one of twins. **watoto hawa ni (ma)pacha.** These children are twins. 2. **(ma-)** something closely resembling something else: double, counterpart. **njia –.** crossroads, (street) crossing. **ndizi –.** two bananas that have grown together. 3. *red.* **pachapacha, pachipachi.** *adj., adv.* similar, of the same nature; twinned *(of rice or millet heads, etc.),* growing in clusters. 4. *v.* produce more than one plant from a single seed; grow in clusters *(bananas, etc.). ass.* **pachana.** grow in clusters.

pachapacha *see* **pacha** 3.

pachika fasten, secure, stick in. – **kisu kipinini.** fasten a knife-blade in the handle. *refl.* **jipachika.** 1. interfere/meddle in a matter. 2. sit with legs spread, sit astride of something. *appl.* **pachikia.** *intr.* **pachikika.** *inv.* **pachua.** take/draw out, separate, remove.

pachipachi *see* **pacha 3.**

pachua *inv. of* **pachika.**

pachuri*, pachori, pacholi [*Ind.*] (–) pachuri (a perfume).

padiri* (ma-) *see* **padre.**

padre*, padri, padiri [*Port.*] (ma-) clergyman (priest, pastor, minister; either Roman Catholic or Protestant; = **kasisi**). *Cf.* **upadre.**

padri* (ma-) *see* **padre.**

pafu, bafu (ma-) *anat.* lung. (= **buhumu, pumu.**) **ugonjwa wa mapafu.** disease of the lungs.

pagaa 1. carry *(a burden, on head or shoulders; an amulet).* 2. *ethn. (us. pass.* **pagawa***)* be possessed (by a spirit). **amepagawa na pepo.** He is possessed by a spirit. *caus.* **pagaza.** 1. employ someone as a bearer/porter. 2. *ethn.* cause someone to be possessed by an evil spirit, bring evil/misfortune upon someone. 3. strike someone dumb *(from amazement),* astound, dumbfound. **alitupagaza kwa maneno yake.** He dumbfounded us with his words. *Cf.* **pagao, mpagazi, upagazi.**

pagao, pagaro (ma-) charm, amulet *(against evil spirits or dangers). Cf.* **pagaa.**

pagaro (ma-) *see* **pagao.**

pagawa *pass. of* **pagaa.**

pagaza *caus. of* **pagaa.**

pagua *see* **pogoa.**

pahala* (–) *see* **pahali.**

pahali*, pahala (–) (proper, expected) place, situation, position. – **pa kupumzika.** resting-place. – **pa kupikia.** cooking-place. – **po pote.** in all places, everywhere. *Cf.* **mahali.**

¹painti* [*Engl.*] (–) pint.

²painti* [*Engl.*] *adj.* painted, colored.

paipu*, peipu [*Engl.* pipe] (–) (automobile) horn, (ship's) siren, warning horn. **piga –.** sound/blow an automobile horn.

paja (ma-), **upaja (paja)** *anat.* 1. thigh, ham *(of a human being or an animal).* 2. *(us.* **pajani***)* lap.

¹paji (ma-) 1. gift, present. 2. sacrifice, offering. *Cf.* **¹pa.**

²paji (ma-): – **la uso.** forehead. *Cf.* **²kipaji, panja.**

¹paka, pakaa spread/smear/paint on, apply. – **udongo.** plaster (the wall of a house with mud). – **chokaa.** whitewash. *fig., cul.:* **samaki wa kupaka.** breaded fish. – **rangi.** paint, stain, dye. – **mafuta.** rub (the body) with oil. **dawa ya kupaka.** salve, ointment. *appl.* **pakia.** *caus.* **pakaza.** apply *(a bandage, splint). Cf.* **kipaku, ²mpaka, mpakato, mpako, upakizi.**

²**paka** *rare* border on, adjoin, be contiguous. *us. ass.* **pakana.** border on each other, lie side by side. **nchi zetu zinapakana.** Our countries are adjacent. *ass.-caus.* **pakanisha.** set boundaries, delimit. *Cf.* **¹mpaka.**

³**paka** (–) cat. – **mwitu.** wild cat.

pakaa *see* **¹paka.**

¹**pakacha** (ma-) light basket. *prov.* – **kuvuja, nafuu ya mchukuzi.** A punctured basket is advantageous to the carrier.

²**pakacha** (–) *see* **pakaja.**

pakaja, pakacha (–) footpad, highwayman, robber.

pakana *ass. of* **²paka.**

pakanga (–) wormwood, rue.

pakanisha *ass.-caus. of* **²paka.**

pakanya (ma-) compensation, indemnification *(in money or an equivalent present).*

pakari (–) tongs, (flat-nosed) pliers.

pakasa twist *(thread, rope).*

pakata hold, carry. – **mtoto.** carry a child *(in one's arms). intr.* **pakatika. mtoto huyu hapakatiki.** This child cannot be held *(i.e., is wild/unruly). Cf.* **¹paka.**

pakaza *caus. of* **¹paka.**

paketi*, pakiti, pakti [*Engl.*] (–) packet, pack, package. – **ya sigara.** a pack of cigarettes.

pake his, her. **pahali –.** his/her place. *Cf.* **ake.**

paki* [*Engl.*] park *(a car).*

¹**pakia** 1. load, pack, stow. 2. put on board, ship. 3. *fig.* export. **mwenye kupakia mali.** exporter. *pass.* **pakiwa. mali ipakiwayo, bidhaa zipakiwazo.** export goods/merchandise/articles. *appl.* **pakilia.** load/stow something; pile up. *caus.* **pakiza, pakisha.** have something packed/loaded. **pakiza gari.** have a wagon/car loaded. *refl.-caus.* **jipakiza.** 1. go on board (a ship); book passage. 2. *fig.* accept a responsibility. *inv.* **pakua.** 1. unload, discharge. 2.: *us.* **pakua chakula.** transfer food from a cooking pot to plates, dish up, serve. *Cf.* **mapakio, mpakizi, mpakuzi, upakizi, upakuzi.**

²**pakia** delimit, fix the limits/bounds of... – **ngwe.** mark out a field for tilling.

pakilia *appl. of* **¹pakia.**

pakio (ma-) *see* **upakio.**

pakiti* (–) *see* **paketi.**

pakiza *caus. of* ^{1}**pakia.**

pakti* (–) *see* **paketi.**

paku (ma-) *see* **kipaku.**

pakua *inv. of* ^{1}**pakia.**

pakulalia (–) (= **mahali pa kulalia**) sleeping-place.

pakulia (–) (= **mahali pa kulia**) eating-place.

pakuogea, pakogea (–) (= **mahali pa kuogea**) washing-place, bathroom, swimming pool.

palahala (–) palahala (sable antelope, *Hippotragus niger*).

palama *see* **parama.**

pale 1. *demon.:* **mahali pale.** in that place. 2. *adv.* there; then, afterwards. **palepale.** in that very place, in the same place.

^{1}**palia** *appl. of* ^{1}**paa,** ^{2}**paa.**

palika *intr. of* ^{1}**paa.**

palikuwa *liter.* Once upon a time... *(at the beginning of a story).*

paliliza *double ass.-caus. of* ^{1}**paa.**

palipo *loc., rare* (place) where there is... **palipoinuka.** highland. *Cf.* **inua.**

palizi (ma-) weed *(in a cultivated field). Cf.* ^{1}**paa.**

^{1}**pamba** 1. decorate, ornament. 2. prepare, arrange. – **maiti.** prepare a corpse for burial. 3. *fig.* furnish *(a room, house).* **chumba chake kimepambwa vizuri.** His room is well furnished. *refl.* **jipamba.** adorn oneself, dress well. **anapenda kujipamba.** He likes to be well dressed. *appl.* **pambia.** 1. decorate for something/someone. 2. set a table. *intr.* **pambika.** *caus.* **pambisha.** *inv.* **pambua.** 1. remove an ornament/decoration. 2. move out furniture, prepare to change residence. 3. deface, disfigure. *inv.-appl.* **pambulia.** *inv.-intr.* **pambulika.** *Cf.* **pambe, pambo, kipambo,** ^{2}**mpamba, mpambe, upambo.**

^{2}**pamba*** [*Pers.*] (–) 1. cotton. **kitambaa cha –.** cotton cloth. 2. cotton wool, wadding. *Cf.* **kipamba,** ^{1}**mpamba.**

^{3}**pamba** (ma-) *see* **pambo.**

^{4}**pamba** (–) large number/quantity, multitude.

^{5}**pamba** *pl. of* ^{1}**upamba,** ^{2}**upamba.**

pambaja 1. embrace, clasp. 2. (–) an embrace. **piga –.** embrace.

pambana 1. come together, meet *(in a hostile or competitive sense),* compete. *sport:* **timu za miji hii zitapambana kesho.** The teams of these cities will meet/clash tomorrow. 2. collide *(of ships). appl.* **pambania.** compete for something. **Ali na Juma wanapambania kiti cha Mombasa.** Ali and Huma are running for election to the seat for Mombasa. **Nita-pambania nambari ya kwanza darasani mwangu.** I will compete for the first place in my class. *caus.* **pambanisha, pambanya.** 1. bring together, put side by side, exhibit. 2. compare, contrast. 3. bring into conflict. 4. contradict, oppose, vote against. *inv.* **pambanua.** separate *(for purposes of comparison)*, distinguish; pick out, select; compare. *inv.-appl.* **pambanulia.** *inv.-intr.* **pambanuka.** *Cf.* **mapambano, mpambanisho, mpambano, upambano, upambanuzi.**

pambano *see* **mapambano.**

pambanua *inv. of* **pambana.**

pambanuka *inv.-intr. of* **pambana.**

pambanulia *inv.-appl. of* **pambana.**

pambanya *caus. of* **pambana.**

pambauka, pambazuka get light, dawn. *Cf.* **pambauko, pambazua.**

pambauko, pambazuko (ma-) *(us. pl.)* dawn, daybreak. *Cf.* **pambauka.**

pambazua make clear/plain, explain. *intr.* **pambazuka.** *only fig.* = **pambauka.**

pambazuko (ma-) *see* **pambauko.**

pambe *adj.* decorated, dressed up. *Cf.* [1]**pamba.**

pambizo, pembizo (ma-) 1. edge, margin, end. – **la meza.** the edge of the table. 2 (room for) play, clearance, margin. 3. outskirts, environs, periphery. 4. suburb.

pambo, pamba (ma-) 1. furnishing, decoration *(of a room, house).* 2. ornament, adornment. *prov.* **mke mzuri ni – la nyumba.** A beautiful wife is the adornment of the house. *Cf.* [1]**pamba.**

pambua *inv. of* [1]**pamba.**

pamoja *adv.* together, at the same time, in the same place. – **na...** together with... – **na hayo.** nevertheless, in spite of everything. **–a –.** *adj.* joint, united, collective. **taarifa ya –.** joint communiqué. **umbele mkubwa wa –.** *pol.* a broad united front. **uongozi wa –.** collective leadership. *Cf.* **moja.**

pampu* [*Engl.*] (–) pump. – **ya maji.** water pump. (= **bomba.**)

[1]**pana, panapana** *adj.* 1. broad, wide. **bahari panapana.** the open sea. 2. flat, level. *Cf.* **panua, mapana, upana.**

[2]**pana** *aux. v.* there is, it has. *Cf.* **na.**

panapana *adj.* *see* [1]**pana.**

panapo *relat.* 1. where there is/are... 2. when it is... – **saa tisa.** When it is three o'clock.

[1]**panda** 1. get (up) on, mount, ride on. – **farasi.** get on/mount a horse. – **baisikeli.** get on a bicycle. – **motokaa.** get into an automobile. 2. climb, ascend. – **mlima (mti).** climb a mountain (a tree). 3. mount, cover, copulate *(with a female; of a male animal).* 4. rise, increase *(in number, weight, quantity, price).* *appl.* **pandia.** *intr.* **pandika.** *caus.* **panza, pandisha.** raise, hoist; increase. *fig.*

amepandishwa cheo. He obtained a degree. – **tanga.** set/hoist sail. *ass.* **pandana.** lie across/overlap/cross each other. *Cf.* **pandio, kipandio, kipandisho, 2mpanda, 2mpando, 2upandaji.**

2panda sow, plant; grow, raise *(plants)*. *intr.* **pandika.** *intr.-int.* **pandikiza.** plant out, transplant *(seedlings)*. *Cf.* **pandikizo, 1mpanda, mpando, 1upandaji.**

3panda (–, ma-) (& **mpanda, mi-**) 1. division, separation. 2. fork(ing), bifurcation. **njia –.** forking of a road. – **ya mto.** branching of a river. – **ya mti.** branches of a tree. 3. *fig.* catapult, slingshot.

4panda, paanda (–) *mus.* horn, trumpet. **piga –.** blow a horn/trumpet.

5panda (ma-), kipanda (vi-) *dial.:* – **la uso.** forehead. *Cf.* **2paji.**

pandana *ass. of* **1panda.**

1pande (*also* **pandepande**) **(ma-, –)** (*augment. of* **kipande**) 1. large piece, lump, chunk, block. – **la chuma.** bar/pig of iron. *fig.* – **la mtu.** large person, giant. 2. part, section. – **hizi hatuna nazi.** In this part of the country there are no coconuts.

2pande: piga –. be out of sorts/in a bad humor.

3pande *pl. of* **upande.**

pandekizi *see* **pandikizi.**

pandepande (ma-) *see* **1pande.**

pandikiza *intr.-int. of* **2panda.**

pandikizi, pandekizi (ma-) 1. large piece, lump, block. 2. *fig.:* – **la mtu.** large person, giant. *Cf.* **1pande.**

pandikizo (ma-), kipandikizo (vi-) 1. (act of) planting out, transplanting. 2. seedling, slip. *Cf.* **2panda.**

pandio (ma-) pandio (a notch cut in a tree-trunk to facilitate climbing). *Cf.* **1panda.**

pando (ma-) *see* **1mpando.**

1panga 1. put in order, line up, set up, arrange. – **askari.** draw up, dress ranks. – **kambi.** set up camp. – **makundi.** group. 2. *fig., liter.:* compose, write *(a book, poem)*. 3. form, conclude. – **udugu.** conclude a friendship (which implies a relation of kinship). 4. classify, organize. *refl.* **jipanga.** put oneself in position, straighten oneself up. *appl.* **pangia.** *double appl.* **pangilia.** set up in rows/lines, set out *(plants)*. *caus.* **pangisha.** take care of the (proper) arrangement/order *(of guests at table, etc.)*, seat. **pangisha watu karamuni.** seat guests at a feast. *inv.* **pangua.** create disorder, disarrange; *(fig.)* fall out, quarrel. *Cf.* **pangilio, 1mpangaji, 1mpango.**

2panga 1. rent, lease. – **nyumba.** rent/lease a house. 2. *fig., coll.* live together without being married. *caus.* **pangisha.** rent/lease *(something to someone)*. *Cf.* **2mpangaji, mpangishaji, 2mpango, upangaji.**

[3]**panga** (**ma-**) (*augment. of* **upanga**) 1. long knife, machete. 2.: **mapanga.** screw, propeller *(of ship, airplane)* (= **majembe**).

[4]**panga** (**ma-**) panga (kind of fish, with prickly skin).

[5]**panga** (**–**): **– za wazuka** (a prickly plant, *Achyranthes aspera*).

[6]**panga** *pl. of* **upanga.**

pange (**ma-**) gadfly, horsefly.

pangilio (**ma-**) (*us.* **mapangilio**) 1. succession, sequence, alternation. **mapangilio ya matunda.** rotation of crops. 2. layer, stratum. *min.* **– la madini.** vein/lode of metal. *Cf.* [1]**panga.**

pangisha *caus. of* [1]**panga,** [2]**panga.**

pango (**–, ma-**) 1. hole, hollow, recess. 2. cave, cavern. 3. lair, den *(of animals)*. 4. *fig.*: **ana –.** He has a protruding tooth.

[1]**pangua** *inv. of* [1]**panga.**

[2]**pangua** knock off/down *(with a single blow)*.

pangusa wipe/rub off, dry off, dust off.

pania lift up, tuck/turn up *(clothing, to protect it from dirt or damp)*. **– kanzu.** tuck up the kanzu. **– suruali.** turn up the trouser-legs.

panja (**ma-**), *also* **– la uso.** *anat.* temple, forelock. *Cf.* [2]**paji,** [2]**kipaji.**

panju (**–**) panju (kind of fish).

panua open up, spread apart, expand, broaden. **– miguu.** spread the legs, take long steps. *fig.* **– akili.** broaden one's mind, enlarge the range of one's ideas. *appl.* **panulia.** *intr.* **panuka.** *Cf.* [1]**pana, upanuzi.**

[1]**panya** (**–**) mouse, rat. *prov.* **paka akiondoka – hutawala.** When the cat is away the mouse rules.

[2]**panya** 1. make an incision/notch. 2. *ethn.* file the teeth *(as a family or tribal mark)*.

[1]**panza** *caus. of* [1]**panda.**

[2]**panza** (**–**) panza (the residue of coconut left after the white part has been scraped out of the shell).

[1]**panzi** (**–**) grasshopper.

[2]**panzi** (**–**), *also* **– bahari.** flying fish.

[1]**pao, pau** (**–**) 1. pao (a thin pole carrying the thatch in native houses). 2. framework (of a roof). 3.: **– la chuma.** iron bar/rod. 4. *pl. of* **upau.**

[2]**pao*** [*Port.*] (**–**) *cards* club(s).

[1]**papa** 1. beat, throb *(heart, pulse)*. 2. *fig.* tremble, quiver, shudder. 3. *fig.* be worried/upset. *appl.* **papia.** be in a hurry over something, do something in haste/hastily. **papia chakula.** eat hastily. **papia kazi.** work hurriedly. *cont., arch.* **papata.** *cont.-intr.*

papatika. flutter, twitch. *Cf.* papara, papio, [1]papo, kipapa, kipapatiko, mpapatiko.

[2]papa be porous/permeable. – maji. let water through, permit water to pass.

[3]papa: – hapa. in this very place; at this very time, now.

[4]papa (–) shark. – upanga. swordfish.

papai* [*Ind.*] (ma-) papai (a melon-like fruit, papaya, pawpaw). *Cf.* mpapai.

papara (–) haste, hurry; hastiness, rashness. • *Cf.* [1]papa.

papasa 1. stroke, touch. 2. grope, feel one's way. kipofa anapapasa. A blind man feels his way.

papasi (ma-) tick. homa ya –. *med.* spirillum tick fever.

papatika *cont.-intr. of* [1]papa.

papatiko (ma-) *see* mpapatiko.

papatua remove husk/shell/rind *(fruits, vegetables).* – maganda. remove husks/rinds. *refl.* jipapatua. slough *(the skin; of snakes). appl.* papatulia. *intr.* papatuka. 1. be clean; be bright, shine. 2. *fig., interj.:* nipapatuke! Go away! Let me alone! (*lit.:* Cleanse me of you!)

papayuka *intr. of* paya.

papi *pl. of* upapi.

papio (ma-) 1. haste, hurry, hastiness, restlessness. 2. avarice, greediness. *Cf.* [1]papa.

paplini* [*Engl.*] (–) poplin.

[1]papo (ma-) 1. beating, pulsing. – la moyo. heartbeat. 2. *fig.* stimulation, excitement. 3. *rare, naut.* surf, breakers. *Cf.* [1]papa.

[2]papo: – hapo *adv.* in that very place, at that very time/moment.

papua *rare* *see* papura.

papura (*rare* papua) 1. tear, rip, claw, scratch, lacerate, tear to pieces *(of wild animals and birds of prey).* – kwa makucha. scratch/rend with the claws/talons. 2. *fig.* quarrel, dispute. *Cf.* mpapuro.

papuri* [*Ind.*] (ma-) papuri (flat cake made of bean meal).

[1]para *see* [1]paa.

[2]para (–) 1. scratch, superficial wound. 2. bald spot, baldness. *Cf.* [1]paa, kipara, upaa.

[3]para (–) 1. gnashing, grinding *(the teeth).* 2. scratching, pawing *(e.g., of a horse; us. red.* parapara*). Cf.* [1]paa.

[4]para (ma-) para (kind of cake).

parafujo* [*Port.*] (–) 1. screw. 2. *rare* screwdriver (= bisibisi.)

paraga climb *(a tree, etc., using arms and legs).*

parago (ma-) 1. parago (a stick on which one props oneself when picking cloves). 2. *naut.* balancing-pole (used in dugout canoes).

parakacha (–) rustling sound (made by dry leaves).

parama, palama 1. be lacking/deficient. **– usingizi.** fail to get enough sleep. 2. be sterile/barren *(esp. of trees). appl.* **paramia.** *used in an inv. sense; see* **paramia** *below.*

paramende* (ma-) *see* **peremende.**

paramia (*appl. of* **parama,** *but used in an inv. sense ?)* 1. climb/clamber up something (quickly). **simba alipotokea mtu aliparamia mti.** When the lion appeared the man quickly scrambled up a tree. 2. climb onto/get on *(vehicles).* 3. grasp, take hold of *(an opponent in fighting); (fig.)* assail someone *(with words),* have an argument with someone.

parange (ma-) broad-bladed knife, machete.

parapanda (–) parapanda (trumpet used for special ceremonies). *rel.* the last trump.

parare, barare (–) large grasshopper.

paraza *caus. of* [1]**paa.**

paredi* [*Engl.*] (–) *mil.* parade, review.

paria *appl. of* [1]**paa.**

parokia* [*Port.*] (–) parish.

paroko* [*Port.*] (–) parish priest.

paru (ma-) paru (a confection made of sugar and opium).

parua, parura scrape, scratch. *coll.* **– kazi.** do slipshod work. *int.* **paruza.** 1. rub on something. **paruza kibiriti.** strike a match. 2. be rough/harsh; *(fig.)* be rude/abrupt. *Cf.* [1]**paa, paruparu, mparuzi, mparuzo.**

paruparu 1. *adj.* rough, coarse; *(fig.)* rude, uncivil. 2. *adv.* perfunctorily, in a slipshod/hit-or-miss way. *Cf.* [1]**paa, parua.**

parura *see* **parua.**

pasa (*caus. of* **pata** ?) concern, affect; be necessary; be unalterable/irrevocable. **imepasa, yapasa.** It is right/fitting. It is necessary. One must... **imempasa aende.** He had to go. *ass.* **pasana.** be mutually obligated, be intimately concerned with each other. *caus.* **pasisha.** obligate someone, impose/inflict something on someone, coerce someone. *Cf.* **pata.**

Pasaka* [*Port.*] (–) Easter.

pasha *caus. of* **pata.**

[1]**pasi*** [*Ind.*] (–, ma-) flatiron. **piga –.** iron *(clothes).*

[2]**pasi*** [*Engl.*] (–, ma-) 1. *sport* pass *(football).* 2. pass *(in an examination).*

[3]**pasi*, paspoti, passipoti** [*Engl.*] (–, ma-) pass, passport. **usiingie hapa bila ya –.** One cannot enter this country without a pass(port).

[4]**pasi** *see* **pasipo.**

[5]**pasi** *adj., rare* avaricious, grasping; pushing, ambitious. *Cf.* **pata, mpasi.**

pasia*, pasira [*Engl.*] *sport* 1. to pass *(football).* 2. concede the championship to someone. *Cf.* [2]**pasi.**

Pasifiki* [*Engl.*] *geogr.* Pacific (Ocean).

pasipo, pasi, *(rare)* **pasi na** *prep.* without. **– shaka.** without doubt. **– hofu.** without fear. **– nia.** without intention, unintentionally. **ameondoka – kuniambia.** He left without telling me (that he was going).

pasira *see* **pasia.**

paspoti* (–) *see* [3]**pasi.**

passipoti* [*Engl.*] (–) *see* [3]**pasi.**

pasta* [*Engl.*] (ma-) *rare* pastor. *Cf.* **mchungaji.**

pasua 1. tear (into pieces). 2. cut open, split. **– mti.** split a tree. **– kuni.** split firewood. 3. eviscerate, remove entrails *(of an animal).* 4. *med.* operate. 5. tear open. **– barua.** open a letter. 6. burst, explode. *appl.* **pasulia.** operate on (someone). *appl.-pass.* **pasuliwa.** *intr.* **pasuka. bomu imepasuka.** The bomb has exploded. *Cf.* **mpasua, mpasuko.**

pata 1. get, obtain, receive. **– fedha (faida).** receive money, make a profit. 2. reach, attain, achieve. **– nguvu.** gain strength, become strong. **– nchi.** reach/arrive in a country. *fig.:* **anapata miaka kumi.** He is about ten years old. 3. find, hit upon. **– sababu.** find a reason. **– njia.** find a way/method. 4. happen, occur. **kupata.** As it happened... *(at the beginning of stories).* 5. *(in conj. w. other verbs)* can, be able, succeed in doing. **– kufanya kazi.** He was able to work. **– kusikia.** He succeeded in hearing. 6. suffer, be the victim of. **– (patwa na) homa.** have a fever. **– ugonjwa.** suffer an illness. **– baridi.** suffer cold, catch a cold. *appl.* **patia.** procure, secure. *double appl.* **patilia.** *intr.* **patika,** *us. intr.-ass.* **patikana.** be procurable/obtainable. **bidhaa hizi hazipatikani sasa.** These goods are not obtainable now. **patikana na hatia.** be found guilty. **njia inapatikana kwa upesi.** The way could quickly be found. *pass.* **patwa. patwa na ugonjwa.** be seized by an illness. **patwa na taabu.** be overtaken by difficulties. *ass.* **patana.** 1. agree, strike a bargain. 2. be reconciled, reach an understanding. 3. work well/harmoniously together. *caus.* **pasha, patisha, patiza.** cause to get/have. **– moto.** warm up, heat. *ass.-caus.* **patanisha.** 1. pacify, appease. 2. reconcile. *Cf.* **pasa,** [5]**pasi, patanisho, patano, pato, kipasha, kipato, mpasi, mpatanishi,** [1]**mpato, upasi, upataji, upatanisho, upatikanaji, upatilivu.**

patanisho (ma-) (*us.* **mapatanisho**) 1. agreement. 2. reconciliation. *Cf.* **pata.**

patano (ma-; *us. pl.*) 1. agreement (= **patanisho** 1). 2. understanding, settlement, contract, treaty. **fanya mapatano.** conclude a contract/treaty. **mapatano ya biashara.** commercial treaty. **– la kuridhiana.** compromise. 3. alliance. 4. conspiracy. *Cf.* **pata.**

patashika *pl.* jeans, slacks.

patasi* (–) chisel.

pati* [*Engl.*] (–) 1. party, social gathering. 2. *rare* (political) party.

patilizo (ma-) *see* **upatilivu.**

pato (ma-) (*also* **upato,** ma-; *us.* **mapato**) 1. acquisition; proceeds, return. 2. earnings, income. **mapato kwa mtu.** per capita income. 3. profit. **biashara ya nazi haina –.** Dealing in coconuts is not profitable. 4. achievement, enrichment. *Cf.* **pata, kipato, 1mpato.**

patu* [*Ind.*] 1. *pl. of* **upatu.** 2. (ma-) *augment. of* **upatu** 1.

pau (ma-) *see* **1pao.**

paua construct the roof of a native house. **nyumba imekwisha lakini haijapauliwa.** The house is finished, but the roof has not yet been constructed.

paundi* (–) *see* **pauni.**

pauni*, paundi, poundi [*Engl.*] (–) pound *(unit of currency or weight).*

pawa *pl. of* **upawa.**

paya, payapaya 1. chatter, talk nonsense. 2. divulge *(a secret),* blab. 3. rave, be delirious. *intr.* **payuka, payukapayuka, papayuka.** 1.: **alishikwa na homa kali akapayuka.** He had a high fever and was delirious. 2.: **siku zote anapayuka ovyo.** He always talks nonsense. *caus.* **payusha.** 1. loosen someone's tongue, get someone to talk (and divulge secrets). 2. bombard someone with questions. *Cf.* **payo, mpayukaji, upayukaji.**

payapaya *see* **paya.**

payo (ma-) *(us. pl.)* 1. chatter, blabbing. 2. nonsense. 3. delirium. *Cf.* **paya.**

payuka *intr. of* **paya.**

payukapayuka *intr. of* **paya.**

payusha *caus. of* **paya.**

paza *caus. of* **2paa.**

pazi (ma-) village elder/headman.

pazia* (ma-) curtain, screen. **– la tumbo.** *rare, anat.* diaphragm. **– la moshi.** *recent, pol.* smokescreen.

1pea 1. be fully developed/mature; be completely ripe *(fruit).* 2. *fig.* attain the peak of perfection. 3. look well/healthy. *Cf.* **1kipeo, upeo;** *also* **pevua.**

2pea *rare* sweep. (= **fagia.**) *Cf.* **2kipeo.**

3pea (–) *rare* rhinoceros. (= **kifaru.**)

4pea *appl. of* **pa.**

pecha *adv.* like a cripple. **enda –.** limp, be lame.

peipu* (–) *see* **paipu.**

peke, pekee, pweke (–) solitude, isolation, uniqueness. **– ya.** alone. **– yangu.** I alone. **– yao.** they alone. **–a peke yake, –a pekee.** alone, single, unique; individual, personal. **hukumu ya pekee.** personal judgment. *Cf.* ^{1}**mpweke, upweke.**

pekecha, peketa 1. twist, twirl, stir, drill. **– mashimo.** drill holes. **– moto.** produce fire by twirling one stick in a hole in another. 2. spoil, damage, ruin. 3. *fig.* hurt, ache. **mifupa yangu inanipekecha.** My bones ache. 4. annoy/exasperate/bore someone. 5. confuse, disorganize. *intr.* **pekecheka, peketeka.** 1. be drilled/perforated. 2. be well stirred, be of a pasty consistency. 3. be damaged. 4. be disorganized/in a state of confusion. 5. *fig.* be arrogant/overbearing/impudent. *intr.-appl.* **pekechekea, peketekea.** treat someone with scorn/contempt. *Cf.* **peketevu,** ^{1}**mpekecho,** ^{2}**mpekecho, mpeketevu, upekecho, upeketevu;** *also* ^{1}**pekua.**

pekecheka *intr. of* **pekecha.**

pekecho (ma-) *see* **upekecho.**

pekee (–) *see* **peke.**

pekesheni* [*Engl.*] 1. (–) inspection, investigation, search. **nyumbani kwake polisi walifanya –.** The police searched his house. 2. *v.* investigate, search; eavesdrop.

peketa *see* **pekecha.**

peketeka *intr. of* **pekecha.**

peketekea *intr.-appl. of* **pekecha.**

peketevu, pekutevu *adj.* 1. mixed/stirred up, well stirred, thick, mushy. 2. annoying, troublesome; scornful, contemptuous, defiant, arrogant. *Cf.* **pekecha, mpeketevu, upeketevu.**

pekua 1. scratch *(of hens)*; paw *(the earth; of horses)*. 2. *fig.* search, investigate; be inquisitive. *appl.* **pekulia.** hunt for *(someone, something)*; pry into *(someone's affairs)*. *intr.* **pekulika.** *red.* **pekuapekua** *(w. int. force)*. search diligently, investigate intensively. 3. *coll.* run away. *Cf.* **pekuzi, mpekuzi, upekuzi.**

pekutevu *adj.* *see* **peketevu.**

pekuzi *adj.* curious, inquisitive. *Cf.* **pekua, mpekuzi, upekuzi.**

pele *pl. of* **upele.**

pelea *appl. of* ^{2}**pea.**

peleka 1. take (to a particular place or person), convey, transport. 2. send, transmit, deliver. **– simu.** telegraph, wire. 3. lead, conduct, escort. *appl.-caus.* **pelekeza.** cause to send, have someone send something. **pelekeza kidole.** point with the finger. *Cf.* **mpelekwa, upelekaji.**

^{1}**pelele** (–) pelele (species of rabbit, hyrax).

^{2}**pelele** (–) pelele (disc inserted in the lip).

peleleza 1. observe, examine *(surreptitiously)*; pry into/be curious about. 2. spy (out), reconnoiter. **– siri.** pry into secrets. *Cf.* **mpelelezi, upelelezi.**

pelezi (ma-) blunt place, nick *(in the edge of a cutting tool).*

[1]pemba 1. get hold of *(with a hook).* **– minazi.** pull down coconuts. 2. knock off/down *(with a stick).* 3. *fig.* trick, deceive, cheat. 4. *fig., rare* lick, taste *(with the tongue). Cf.* **upembo.**

[2]Pemba Pemba (an island near Zanzibar, famous for its cloves).

[1]pembe (–, ma-) 1. horn *(of an animal or the substance).* **piga –.** strike with the horns, butt *(cattle, goats, etc.;* = **[1]kumba**). 2. elephant's tusk, ivory. 3. *mus.* horn. 4. powder-horn/flask. 5. wing *(of a building, army).*

[2]pembe (–) 1. corner. **– nne za chumba (nyumba).** the four corners of the room (house). *loc.* **pembeni.** in the corner. 2. *geom.* angle. **pembemraba.** right angle. **pembekali.** acute angle. **pembebutu.** obtuse angle. **pembetatu.** triangle. 3. corner-post; *(fig.)* prominent feature. 4.: **– za mwaka.** seasons of the year. *Cf.* **kipembe, upembe.**

pembea (*rare* **bembea**) 1. swing, rock, oscillate. *appl.* **pembelea.** *intr.* **pembeka.** *caus.* **pembeza. pembeza mtoto.** rock a child to sleep. 2. (–) swing, seesaw, trapeze. **kiti cha –.** rocking chair.

pembeja 1. persuade, cajole, talk someone into something. 2. play the hypocrite, flatter.

pembejo (ma-) *anat.* thigh; *(rare)* hip.

pembenne (–) quadrilateral, rectangle. *Cf.* **[2]pembe.**

pembetatu (–) triangle. *Cf.* **[2]pembe.**

pembizo (ma-) *see* **pambizo.**

pembo *pl. of* **upembo.**

pembua 1. sift, winnow. 2. sort out, cull, select. *appl.* **pembulia.** *intr.* **pembuka.**

penalti* [*Engl.*] (–) *sport* penalty kick.

penda 1. like, love, be fond of. 2. want, wish; choose, prefer. **upendavyo.** as you like. **kwa kupenda kwako.** for your sake. *intr.* **pendeka.** be likeable/popular. *intr.-caus.* **pendekeza.** attract attention. *refl.-intr.-caus.* **jipendekeza.** ingratiate oneself, curry favor. *double appl.* **pendelea.** have a predilection/propensity for, be partial to, favor. *double appl.-caus.* **pendeleza.** cause to be partial, win favor for, recommend. *caus.* **pendeza.** 1. cause to like/love, be popular/attractive. 2. be refreshed/pleased. 3. appease, placate. *ass.* **pendana.** love each other. *ass.-caus.* **pendanisha.** reconcile, make peace between. *Cf.* **pendevu, pendelevu, kipendo, kipenzi, mapendano, mapendeleo, mapendezi, mpenda, mpendelevu, mpendevu, mpendwa, mpenzi, pendekezo, pendeleo, penzi, upendaji, upendano, upendeleo, upendelevu, upendezi, upendo, upendwa.**

pendekezo (ma-) 1. wish, desire. 2. decision. 3. prescription. *Cf.* **penda.**

pendeleo (ma-) (*us.* **mapendeleo**) affection, goodwill, attachment, favor. *Cf.* **penda.**

pendelevu *adj.* partial, biased, prejudiced *(in favor of someone). Cf.* **penda.**

pendevu *adj.* kind, affectionate, friendly. *Cf.* **penda.**

pene* (ma-) *see* **peni.**

penesilini* [*Engl.*] *sing.* penicillin.

penga 1. blow the nose. 2. puff, pant, breathe heavily.

pengee (ma-) (*also* **kipengee, kipenge, kipengere, kipengele,** vi-) 1. side-path, byway, indirect route. 2. detour, bypass. 3. evasion, excuse, subterfuge. **maneno ya mapengee.** excuses. 4. *fig.* indiscretion, escapade. 5. branch, tributary, affluent *(of a river,* — **cha mto).**

pengi *adv.* in many places. *Cf.* **ingi.**

pengine *adv.* at another place, elsewhere; at another time, sometime; (*us. red.* **pengine pengine**) sometimes. — **na** —. in any event, perhaps. *Cf.* **ingine.**

pengo (—, ma-) 1. nick, notch, cut. 2. gap. **ana** —. He is missing a tooth. 3. *fig.* flaw, defect.

peni*, pene [*Engl.*] (ma-) penny.

penseli* [*Engl.*] (—) *see* **pensili.**

pensheni* [*Engl.*] (—) pension.

pensili*, penseli [*Engl.*] (—) *rare* (lead) pencil. (= **kalamu.**)

[1]**penu** *see* **-enu.**

[2]**penu** *pl. of* **upenu.**

penya 1. penetrate, make one's way through/into. — **mwituni.** make one's way through the forest. 2. *fig.* arouse desire/greed. **ndizi zimempenya.** He is greedy for bananas (*lit.:* Bananas penetrate into him). *caus.* **penyeza, penyesha.** put in (by force), force in; smuggle. — **fedha.** force money on someone, bribe. **penyeza desturi (kawaida).** introduce new customs/practices without considering those previously observed. *refl.-caus.* **jipenyeza.** insinuate oneself, steal/slip in. *Cf.* **penyenye, kipenyo, mpenyezi, mpenyezo, upenyaji.**

penye (< **pa** + **-enye**, *q.v.*) *(always w. following obj.):* — **tangi.** filling station. *prov.:* **Penye urembo ndipo penye urimbo.** Where there is beauty there is also a trap.

penyenye (ma-) 1. *rare* (secret) passage, means of access. 2.: **mapenyenye.** secret matters/affairs. *Cf.* **penya.**

penyewe *see* **-enyewe.**

penyezi *see* **upenyaji.**

penyo (ma-) *augment. of* **kipenyo.**

penzi (ma-) (*us.* **mapenzi**) 1. love, favor, inclination. 2. desire, wish. *Cf.* **penda.**

peo *pl. of* **upeo.**

pepa 1. swing, shake, wave, fan. 2. stagger, totter, reel. *appl.* **pepea, bebea.** swing/wave/shake something. **pepea vitambaa.** swing cloths, fan. **pepea moto.** fan a fire. **mvua inapepea.** the rain beats/drives. *double appl.* **pepelea. pepelea fulani chakula.** cool the food for someone *(by fanning). double appl.-intr.* **peperuka** (< **pepeluka**). fly away, be carried away. **karatasi imepeperuka.** the paper is blown away *(by the wind). double appl.-caus.* **peperusha.** blow away. **peperusha bendere ya...** fly the flag of... *caus.* **pepesa. pepesa macho.** blink/squint the eyes. *caus.-inv. (w. int. force).* **pepesua.** cause to stagger/stumble. *caus.-(inv.-)intr.* **pepesuka.** 1. stagger, stumble, reel, lurch. 2. shake. *cont.* **pepeta** (*also* **peta**). sift, winnow, separate. *cont.-inv.* **pepetua** = **pepeta** *(cf. also* **papatua***). inv.* **pepua** = **pepeta.** *Cf.* **pepe, pepeo, pepeta, 1pepo, kipepeo, kipepo, mpepea, mpepetaji, upepeo, upepezi, upepo.**

pepe (**ma-**) empty/barren ear of grain. *Cf.* **pepa.**

pepelea *double appl. of* **pepa.**

pepeo (**ma-**) (*augment. of* **kipepeo**) 1. (large) fan *(for fanning fires, etc.).* 2. *fig.* ventilator. 3. *zool.* butterfly. 4. *pl. of* **upepeo.** *Cf.* **pepa.**

peperuka *double appl.-intr. of* **pepa.**

peperusha *double appl-caus. of* **pepa.**

pepesa *caus. of* **pepa.**

pepesua *caus.-inv. of* **pepa.**

pepesuka *caus.-intr. of* **pepa.**

pepeta 1. *cont. of* **pepa.** 2. (**–**): **– za mpunga.** pulverized grains of rice. *Cf.* **pepa.**

pepetua *cont.-inv. of* **pepa.**

1pepo (**–**) 1. spirit. **– mwema (mbaya).** a good (evil) spirit. **ingiwa/shikwa/pagawa na –.** be possessed by a spirit. **punga/toa –.** exorcise a spirit. **mwenye –.** one possessed by a spirit. 2. dwelling-place of spirits, world of spirits, abode of the dead (spirits of ancestors). 3. (*also* **– za kesho** *or loc.* **peponi**). the other world, the hereafter. **– ya leo.** the present world, the world of the living. 4.: **– punda.** evil spirit; *(med.)* tetanus. *Cf.* **pepa.**

2pepo *pl. of* **upepo.**

peponi *loc. see* **1pepo.**

pepua *inv. of* **pepa.**

pera* [*Port.*] (**ma-**) guava *(fruit of the* **mpera***).*

perema (**–**) *med.* mumps. (= **machumbwichumbwi.**)

peremende*, perementi, paramende [*Engl.*] (**ma-**) peppermint, hard candy.

1pesa* [*Port.*] (**ma-**) 1. *arch.* pice. 2.: **mapesa.** money. **hana mapesa.** He has no money.

2pesa *caus. of* **1peta.**

[1]**peta** 1. bend, curve. **– uzi.** bend a wire. **– mguu.** bend the leg. 2. turn/roll up. **– nguo.** tuck up a garment. *fig.* **– uso.** wrinkle the brow, make a face. *caus.* **petesha.** bend round, make a ring of something. *ass.* **petana.** *appl.-stat.-ass.* **petemana.** be bent round, be formed into a ring. *appl.-stat.-ass.-caus.* **petemanisha.** bend round, form into a ring/hoop, give a curve *(to something)*. *caus.* **pesa.** wink, blink *(the eyes; cf.* **pepesa***)*. *inv.* **petua.** turn around/over, upset, turn upside down. *inv.-appl.* **petulia.** *inv.-intr.* **petuka.** *inv.-caus.* **petusha.** *Cf.* **pete** [1]**peto, kipete, kipeto, upeto.**

[2]**peta** *cont. of* **pepa.**

pete (–, **ma-**) 1. ring, circle, hoop. *coll.* **siku hizi wamekuwa chanda na –.** They are now like ring and finger (*i.e.*, close friends). 2. hasp, staple *(for securing a door)*. 3. hole pierced in a woman's ears *(for inserting earrings or ornaments)*. **toga mapete.** pierce the ears. *Cf.* [1]**peta.**

petemana *appl.-stat.-ass. of* [1]**peta.**

petemanisha *appl.-stat.-ass.-caus. of* [1]**peta.**

[1]**peto** (**ma-**) 1. bag, sack *(made of matting)*. 2.: **mapeto.** chains, fetters. *Cf.* [1]**peta.**

[2]**peto** *pl. of* **upeto.**

petroli* [*Engl.*] (–) petrol, gasoline. **mafuta ya –.** gasoline, fuel.

petu *see* **-etu.**

petua *inv. of* [1]**peta.**

petuka *inv.-intr. of* [1]**peta.**

petulia *inv.-appl. of* [1]**peta.**

petusha *inv.-caus. of* [1]**peta.**

pevu *adj.* full grown, mature, adult. *Cf.* **pevua, mpevu, upevu.**

pevua 1. develop fully, mature, ripen. 2. overstimulate, pervert, corrupt. *intr.* **pevuka.** be fully developed/mature; reach a climax/culmination. **ugonjwa wake sasa umepevuka.** His illness has reached its final stage /culmination. *caus.* **pevusha.** 1. allow to ripen/mature. 2. corrupt, ruin. *refl.* **jipevua.** put on airs, show off, be conceited. *Cf.* **pevu, mpevu, mpevushi, upevu;** *also* [1]**pea.**

pewa *pass. of* **pa.**

pezi (**ma-**) fin *(of a fish)*.

pi *interrog.* 1. which? what? **mtu yupi?** Which person? **kiti kipi?** Which chair? 2. *encl.* how? **atafanyapi?** How will he do it? 3. (= **wapi**) where? to what place? **unakwendapi?** Where are you going?

[1]**pia** *adv.* 1. completely, totally, without exception. 2. also, even.

[2]**pia** (–) 1. reel, spool, spindle. 2. top *(child's toy)*. 3. *fig., anat.:* **– ya goti/mguu.** kneecap. (= **kilegesambwa.**) 4. *fig.:* **anazunguka kama –.** He is always on the move (*lit.:* like a top).

picha [*Engl.*] (–) 1. picture, drawing. **andika –.** draw (a picture). 2. photograph. **piga –.** photograph, take a snapshot.

piga strike, hit, beat. *used. w. a variety of direct objects to form verbal expressions:* **– mhuri.** stamp. **– chapa.** print. **– simu.** telephone, telegraph. **– taipu.** type (= write with the typewriter). **– muziki.** play music. **– ngoma.** beat the drum. **– tarumbeta.** blow the trumpet. **– kengele.** ring a bell. **– bunduki.** shoot *(a gun).* **– hema.** pitch a tent. **– pasi.** iron *(clothes).* **– msumeno.** saw *(wood).* **– burashi.** brush. **– mstari.** draw a line. **– picha.** draw *(pictures),* take photographs. **– stati.** start *(a car).* **– fundo.** tie a knot. **– sindano.** vaccinate. **– kelele.** yell, scream. **– vita.** wage a war. **– mbio.** run. **– mbizi.** dive. **– kura.** vote. **– hodi.** ask admission, knock. **– magoti.** kneel. **– fatiha.** perform a ceremony. **– makuu.** put on airs, be arrogant. *red.* **pigapiga.** whip *(eggs, etc.).* *appl.* **pigia. pigia kura.** elect someone. **pigia simu.** call someone up *(on the telephone),* send a wire to someone. *double appl.* **pigilia.** 1. strike in, drive home. **pigilia msumari.** drive a nail. 2. ram down, tamp. *intr.* **pigika.** *caus.* **pigisha.** *ass.* **pigana.** strike each other, fight. *ass.-appl.* **pigania.** fight for something. *Cf.* **kipigi, kipigo, mapigano, mpiga, mpigaji, mpiganaji, mpiganisho, mpigo, mpigwa, pigano, pigo, upigaji, upiganaji, upigano.**

pigano (ma-) (*us.* **mapigano;** *also* **mpigano, mi-**) fight, battle, engagement, skirmish; quarrel. *Cf.* **piga.**

pigipigi (ma-) *see* [1]**pikipiki.**

pigo (ma-) 1. blow, stroke. **– la ngoma.** beat of a drum. **mapigo ya moyo.** pulsebeat. 2. hardship, misfortune, accident. *Cf.* **piga.**

pika 1. prepare food, cook. 2. boil. *Cf.* **mapishi, mpishi,** [1]**mpiko, upishi.**

piki (ma-) *see* [1]**pikipiki.**

[1]**pikipiki, piki, pigipigi (ma-), kipiki, kipikipiki (vi-)** stick used for knocking down fruit.

[2]**pikipiki (–)** *onom.* motorcycle.

piku* [*Port.*] 1. *cards* win *(a trick or the game).* 2. cheat *(at cards).* 3. *coll.* excel, surpass, outdo (= **shinda**). **ananishinda kwa masomo ya hesabu, lakini na mimi kwa somo la jiografia nimempiku.** He did better than I did in mathematics but I beat him in geography. 4. **(ma-)** cheating *(at cards).*

pilau*, bilau [*Pers.*] **(–)** pilau (boiled rice with raisins and ghee).

[1]**pili** *num.* two. **–a –.** second. **ya –.** secondly, next, following. **mara ya –.** for the second time.

[2]**pili, piri (–)** pili (kind of adder).

pilipili* [*Pers.*] (–) pepper. **– manga (hoho).** black (red) pepper. *Cf.* **kipilipili, mpilipili.**

pilka-pilka (–) viewfinder *(of a camera).*

pima 1. measure, weigh, test. **– upana.** measure the width. **– viazi.** weigh potatoes. **– joto.** take a person's temperature. 2. consider critically, form an estimate, criticize. **nimeyapima maneno yake nimeyaona si kweli.** I have weighed his words and found that they are untrue. *appl.* **pimia. kitu cha kupimia.** measure. 3. (–) fathom, two yards. *fig., coll.* toa macho —. stare into space. *Cf.* **pimamaji, kipima, kipimio, kipimo, mpima, mpimo, upimaji.**

pimamaji (*rare* **pimasharazi**) (–) 1. water level, stage. 2. water gauge. 3. spirit level. *Cf.* **pima, maji.**

pimasharazi (–) *see* **pimamaji.**

pimo (ma-) *see* **kipimo.**

pinda 1. twist, bend, curve. **– uzi.** twist a thread. **mstari uliopinda.** curve(d line). 2. fold. **– upindo/mshono.** turn down a seam *(on a garment). ass.* **pindana.** be folded/fitted together; *(fig.)* be tense/strained; have a cramp; be stubborn, assert dogmatically. *stat.-ass.* **pindamana.** be twisted together/entangled/gnarled; *(fig.)* be convulsed. *inv.* **pindua.** turn around, overturn, reverse; change direction. **pindua ukarasa wa kitabu.** turn the page of a book. **pindua meli.** change the course of a ship. *refl.-inv.* **jipindua.** turn around *(of a person)*; change one's mind. *inv.-appl.* **pindulia.** *intr.* **pinduka.** be turned around, be changed, take a new direction. *inv.-intr.-appl.* **pindukia.** climb over something *(a wall, etc.). caus.* **pinduza.** *Cf.* **kipindi, kipindo, kipindupindu, mpindani, mpindanifu, mpindano, mpinduzi, pindani, 1pindi, pindo, pindu, pinduani, pinduli, pinduo, pindupindu, mapindu, mapinduzi, upindani, upinde, upinduzi.**

pindamana *stat.-ass. of* **pinda.**

pindani *adj.* stubborn/obstinate/unyielding. *Cf.* **pinda.**

pinde, pindi *pl. of* **upinde, upindi.**

1pindi (ma-, –) 1. bend, twist, curve, turn. **– ya mto.** bend of a river. 2. (division or interval of) time, time for something. **– za mchana.** the times (= divisions) of the day. **– ya chakula.** mealtime. **– za mti.** annual rings *(of a tree).* 3. lapse, course, period *(of time).* **tutaonana – mwakani.** We shall see each other again in the course of the year. 4. *conj.* (at the time) when; if, although, supposing. *Cf.* **pinda.**

2pindi *see* **pinde.**

3pindi, pinda (ma-) = **kipinda.**

pindo (ma-) edge, border, hem. *Cf.* **pinda.**

pindu 1 (ma-) (sudden) turn, somersault, cartwheel. 2. *adv.* upside down. **kichwa –.** head over heels. *Cf.* **pinda.**

pindua *inv. of* **pinda.**

pinduani (ma-) 1. stubborn/determined person. 2. revolutionist, radical. *Cf.* **pinda.**

pinduka *inv.-intr. of* **pinda.**

pinduli (ma-) something which produces a change of direction/radical change/revolution, cause of change. *Cf.* **pinda.**

pindulia *inv.-appl. of* **pinda.**

pinduo (ma-) 1. (radical, drastic) change, transformation, alteration. 2. *pol.* revolution. *Cf.* **pinda.**

pindupindu 1, (–) convulsion, fit, seizure. 2. *adv.* head over heels. **anguka –.** fall down head over heels. *Cf.* **pinda.**

pinga (& *caus.* **pinza**) 1. lock, fasten. **– mlango.** fasten a door *(with a bar).* 2. block, obstruct. **– njia.** block a road. 3. *fig.* oppose, counteract, check, frustrate, thwart. **– nia ya fulani.** thwart someone's plans. 4. *fig.* refute, revoke, contradict. 5. *fig.* bet, lay a wager. *ass.* **pingana.** thwart/contradict each other; make a bet with each other; challenge/defy each other. *stat.* **pingama** & *stat.-ass.* **pingamana.** be opposed/in opposition to something. *stat.-ass.-caus.* **pingamanisha** *(w. int. force).* deliberately obstruct/frustrate something. *inv.* **pingua.** remove, carry away; unfasten *(a door);* cut open, cut up *(fruit, wood). inv.-appl.* **pingulia.** *Cf.* **pingamizi, pingani, pingo, pingu, kipinga, kipingamizi, kipingili, kipingo, kipingwa, mpinga, mpingaji, mpinzani, upingaji, upingamishi, upinzani.**

pingama *stat. of* **pinga.**

pingamizi (–) impediment, obstacle; disturbance, interruption, difficulty. **tunataka kufanya amani lakini kuna – nyingi.** We want to make peace, but there are many difficulties. *Cf.* **pinga.**

pingani *adj. (of persons)* obstructive, contrary, troublesome, difficult. *Cf.* **pinga.**

[1]**pingili** (ma-) *augment. of* **kipingili.**

[2]**pingili** (–) (*augment. of* **kipingili**) piece, section *(e.g., of sugarcane, between joints).* **nipe – tatu za mua.** Give me three pieces of sugarcane.

pingo (ma-) (*also* **mpingo, mi-**) obstruction, barrier, bolt *(on a door). Cf.* **pinga.**

pingu (–, ma-) 1. fetter, shackle; handcuff. 2. a loop of rope used as an aid in climbing trees. 3. a disc of wood (ebony) worn in the lobe of the ear. 4. a charm protecting against evil spirits. *Cf.* **pinga.**

pingua (*inv. of* **pinga**) cut into pieces/lengths *(e.g., sugarcane). Cf.* **kipingili.**

pingulia *inv.-appl. of* **pinga.**

[1]**pini** (ma-) *augment. of* **kipini.**

[2]**pini*** [*Engl.*] (–) pin.

pinki* [*Engl.*] *adj.* pink.

pinza *caus. of* **pinga.**

pipa* [*Port.*] (ma-) barrel, cask, water-container, tank. **– la maji ya moto.** hot-water tank. **– la mafuta ya petroli.** fuel tank.

piramidi* [*Engl.*] (ma-) pyramid.

piri (–) *see* **²pili.**

pirikana be well developed/muscular.

pisha *caus. of* **pita.**

pishi (–) pishi (a measure of capacity or weight: half a gallon, 6 lb.).

pisho (ma-) (act of) cauterizing (or the mark left).

pistola* (–) *see* **bastola.**

piswa 1. speak confusedly/foolishly *(like a feeble-minded or senile person).* 2. (ma-) = **mapiswa.**

pita 1. go past, pass (by); go on, proceed. **– mji.** pass by a town. **mto wapita.** the river flows past. **mwaka uliopita.** the past year. 2. go beyond, surpass, excel, exceed; distinguish oneself; be better than... **kitabu hiki ni kizuri kupita kile.** This book is better than (*lit.:* surpasses) that one. *appl.* **pitia.** go past, pass by *(something, someone)*, be forgotten. *pass.* **pitiwa.** forget. **nilipitiwa.** I have forgotten. I cannot recall/remember. *double appl.* **pitilia** *(w. int. force).* **nimepitiliwa.** I have completely forgotten. *appl.-ass.* **pitiana.** be in constant touch/association with each other, be on familiar terms *(of social or business relationships).* *caus.* **pisha, pitisha.** 1. lead, guide, conduct; allow to pass, make room for. **pitisha hewa safi.** ventilate. **pisha sheria.** pass/promulgate a law. 2. miss, neglect; waste. **pitisha wakati.** pass/waste time. *Cf.* **pito, kipito, mpita, mpito.**

pito (ma-) (*augment. of* **kipito**) (act, means of) passing, passage. *Cf.* **pita.**

plagi* [*Engl.*] (–) 1. plug, stopper, bung. 2. (electric) plug.

plau* [*Engl.*] (–) plow. **lima kwa (na) –.** to plow.

plen* [*Engl.*] *adj.* plain, simple, understandable.

po *det.:* **pote, popote.** wherever, everywhere.

poa 1. cool off, become cool. **chai imepoa.** the tea has cooled. 2. recover *(from an illness)*, get well. **amepoa ugonjwa.** He has recovered from the illness. 3. cool off, calm down. **hasira yake imepoa.** His anger has calmed down. *appl.* **polea.** *caus.* **poza.** 1. cool something (off). 2. calm, console. **nitakwenda kumpoza.** I will go to console him/calm him down. 3. cure, heal. *Cf.* **mapoza, mpozi.**

pochi* [*Ind.?*] (ma-) pochi (kind of bracelet).

poda* [*Engl.*] (–) powder. *Cf.* **podea.**

podea* [*Engl.*] powder (a baby, etc.). *refl.* **jipodea.** powder oneself/one's face. *Cf.* **poda.**

podo (ma-) quiver, case for arrows.

¹pofu *adj.* blind. *Cf.* **pofua.**

[2]pofu (–) *see* [1]**mpofu.**

pofua damage, destroy, ruin. – **macho.** blind (*lit.:* destroy the eyes). *appl.* **pofulia.** *intr.* **pofuka.** *caus.* **pofusha.** *Cf.* **pofu, kipofu, upofu.**

pofuka *intr. of* **pofua.**

pofulia *appl. of* **pofua.**

pofusha *caus. of* **pofua.**

pogo 1. (ma-) lopsidedness, irregularity, asymmetry. **mapogo ya macho.** squinting. 2. *adv.* sideways, in a crooked/lopsided way. **enda –.** limp. **tazama –.** squint, look sideways. *Cf.* **pogoa.**

pogoa, pokoa, pagua lop, prune *(bushes, trees)*, cut off *(branches)*. *appl.* **pogolea. kisu cha kupogolea.** pruning knife. *caus.* **pogosha** *Cf.* **pogo, pogoo, upogo.**

pogoo (ma-) branch cut off a tree. *Cf.* **pogoa.**

pointi* [*Engl.*] (–) point, dot.

[1]**pojo** (–) pojo (kind of bean, *Phaseolus mungo*). (= **choroko.**)

[2]**pojo** (–) pojo (kind of vetch).

poka (& *inv.* **pokua**) take away, appropriate *(by force)*, snatch; rob, steal. *ass.* **pokana.** steal from/rob each other. *inv.-caus.* (?) **pokonya** = **poka.** *Cf.* **upokonyaji.**

pokea 1. accept, receive; obtain. – **barua.** receive a letter. 2. take in, welcome *(as a guest)*. **wametupokea vizuri.** They have given us a good reception. 3. acknowledge, approve, admit; consent, agree. – **maneno.** acknowledge/admit words/ statements. *appl.* **pokelea.** *appl.-caus.* **pokeleza.** *caus.* **pokeza.** cause to receive, hand out, issue. **jana alitupokeza mshahara.** Yesterday he issued the wages to us. *caus.-ass.* **pokezana** & *caus.-ass.-caus.* **pokezanya.** alternate/take turns *(at doing something)*, take/get something by turns. **pokezana/pokezanya mizigo.** take turns carrying burdens. **wafanya kazi wanapokezana kazi kila saa nne.** The workers relieve each other on the job every four hours. *Cf.* **pokezi, kipokee, kipokeo, mpokea, upokeaji.**

pokelea *appl. of* **pokea.**

pokeleza *appl.-caus. of* **pokea.**

pokeo (ma-) *see* **pokezi, mapokezi.**

pokezana *caus.-ass. of* **pokea.**

pokezanya *caus.-ass.-caus. of* **pokea.**

pokezi, pokeo (ma-) (*us.* **mapokezi**) 1. that which is received. 2. acceptance, reception. 3. *fig.* tradition, custom, usage. 4. *fig.* superstition. *Cf.* **pokea.**

pokoa *inv. of* **poka.**

pokonya *inv.-caus. of* **poka.**

[1]**pole, polepole** *adj./adv.* 1. calm, cautious, careful, slow. **sema pole(pole)!** Speak slowly. **(kwa) polepole.** gradually. 2. mild, gentle, kind. *Cf.* **upole.**

[2]**pole** *interj.* 1. *expressing sympathy/compassion (on occasions of misfortune, troubles, illness, death).* 2. Sorry! Excuse me!

polea *appl. of* **poa.**

polisi* [*Engl.*] 1. **(ma-)** (*also* **askari –**) policeman. 2. **(–)** police force.

pombe **(–)** pombe (an intoxicating drink prepared from millet, bananas, and sugarcane).

pombo **(–, ma-)** 1. *(in gen.)* the leaf of any plant used as a vegetable. 2. pombo (a kind of vegetable gruel used to thicken gravies).

pomboo **(ma-)** porpoise.

[1]**pomoka** = **bomoka** *intr. of* **bomoa.**

[2]**pomoka** *see* **poromoa.**

pomoni *adv.* chock-full, crowded.

pona 1. flee, run away *(from danger).* 2. be rescued/saved. 3. make a living; live, exist. 4. improve; get better *(from an illness). appl.* **ponea.** 1. be saved by. 2. live off, be dependent for one's livelihood on something. *caus.* **ponya** & *double caus.* **ponyesha.** 1. cause to flee/run away. 2. rescue, save. 3. heal, cure. **mgonjwa ameponywa na mganga.** The sick person was cured by the doctor. *caus.-intr.* **ponyeka. haiponyeki.** It is incurable. *refl.-caus.* **jiponya.** save oneself. *Cf.* **kiponya, maponea, maponyea, mponyeshaji, uponyi.**

ponda 1. pound, ram, tamp. **– udongo.** ram/tamp clay. 2. pound to pieces, grind, pulverize. 3. destroy, overwhelm, annihilate. 4. *fig.* run over *(w. a vehicle).* **amepondwa na motokaa.** He was run over by an automobile. *appl.* **pondea. pondea pilipili kinuni.** grind up pepper in a mortar. *caus.* **ponza** & *caus.-appl.* **ponzea.** 1. have something pounded/ground. 2. expose someone to a danger, risk something. **ametuponzea tukafungwa.** He got us into a dangerous situation, and we were arrested. *Cf.* **pondeo, pondo, kipondwe, mponda,** [1]**mpondo.**

pondeo **(ma-)** pondeo (wooden hammer/mallet used by shoemakers). *Cf.* **ponda.**

pondo **(ma–), mpondo** **(mi-), upondo** **(–), kipondo** **(vi-)** *naut.* punting pole, boathook. *Cf.* **ponda.**

pongea 1. *rare* bring something difficult to a conclusion. 2. *rare* recover *(from an illness). caus.* **pongeza.** congratulate *(someone who has recovered from an illness). Cf.* **pongezi.**

pongezi **(–, ma-)** congratulations. *Cf.* **pongea.**

pongono (**ma-**) quiver.

pongoo *pl. of* **upongoo.**

poni* [*Engl.*] 1. (–) pledge. (= **rahani.**) **weka –.** leave as a pledge, pawn. 2. *v.* pledge, pawn.

pono (–) pono (a kind of sluggish fish that lives among coral). *prov.* **mtu huyu ana usingizi kama –.** This man sleeps like a pono.

ponoa 1. pull/strip off *(the bark from a tree, etc.).* 2. wipe off *(the hands). appl.* **ponolea.**

ponta* [*Port.*] (–) back stitch, quilting seam.

ponya *caus. of* **pona.**

ponyeka *caus.-intr. of* **pona.**

ponyesha *double caus. of* **pona.**

ponyoka slip away, escape (unexpectedly, inadvertently). **– maneno.** make a slip of the tongue, say the wrong thing.

ponza *caus. of* **ponda.**

pooza 1. be incompletely developed. **tunda hili limepooza.** This fruit is unripe. 2. be paralyzed/crippled; *(fig.)* be impotent. **mkono umepooza.** the arm is paralyzed/crippled. **mwenye kupooza.** a cripple; *(fig.)* an impotent man. 3. *fig.* feel lonely/abandoned. **tangu ameondoka tumepooza.** Since he is gone we feel abandoned. *caus.* **poozesha.** cripple, mutilate, deform, paralyze. 4. (**ma-**) something undeveloped/immature; premature birth. 5. *adj.* undeveloped, immature. *Cf.* **kipooza, upooza.**

popo (**ma-**) 1. *zool.* bat. 2. *rare* (*us.* **kipopo**) butterfly, moth.

popoa knock fruit off a tree with a stick/stone. *appl.* **popolea.** *Cf.* **2mpopoo.**

popoo* [*Pers.*] (*rare* **bobo**) (–) areca/betel nut. *Cf.* **1mpopoo.**

popota *see* **pota.**

popote *see* **po.**

popotoa *inv. of* **pota.**

1pora (**ma-**) young cock/rooster.

2pora *coll.* snatch *(at something).* **mwivi amempora mfuko wake.** The thief snatched her purse.

pori* (**ma-**) wilderness, uninhabited region *(without trees).*

poroja, porojo 1. (–) porridge, gruel; a mixture of a watery consistency. 2. *v.* be pasty/watery.

1porojo (**ma-**) 1. small talk, chitchat, idle/empty talk. 2. *pol.* propaganda.

²porojo (–) *see* **poroja.**

poromoa (& *caus.* **poromosha,** *rare* **pomosha)** slide/roll down. *intr.* **poromoka** (*rare* **pomoka, boromoka). mjenzi ameporomoka kwenye paa la nyumba.** The builder fell off the roof of the house. **mvua iliporomoka.** The rain poured down *(e.g., in a cloudburst). Cf.* **poromoko.**

poromoko (*us.* **maporomoko)** (ma-) 1. steep slope, precipice. 2. fall, crash. **maporomoko ya mvua.** cloudburst. **maporomoko ya maji.** waterfall. **maporomoko ya mto.** cataract. 3. landslide, avalanche. *Cf.* **poromoa.**

portangi* [*Ind.*] (–) (paper) kite. (= **tiara.**)

posa 1. ask to marry *(a girl)*, propose; woo, be a suitor. *appl.* **posea. mali ya kuposea.** money for wedding preparations. *ass.* **posana.** reach an agreement on a marriage. 2. (–) *see* **poso.** *Cf.* **maposo, mposaji, mposeaji, mposo.**

posha support, maintain, provide with food. *appl.* **poshea.** *caus.* **posheza.** *Cf.* **posho.**

posho (–, ma-) 1. daily rations (e.g., of corn meal, issued to workers on plantations). 2. *(in gen.)* maintenance, support; means of subsistence, livelihood. *Cf.* **posha.**

poso, posa (–) (*also* **uposo, uposa)** 1. suit, proposal of marriage. **peleka –.** send a proposal of marriage *(from the parents of the man to the parents of the girl).* 2. wedding preparations. 3. wedding present. *Cf.* **posa.**

posta* [*Engl.*] (–) post office *(building and services).* **tikiti ya –.** postage stamp. **kwa –.** by mail. **karani wa –.** postal employee. **nyumba ya –.** post office (building). **idara ya –.** post-office department. **benki ya akiba kwa njia ya –.** postal savings bank.

pota (*rare* **popota)** twist. **– uzi.** twist/twine thread. **– miguu.** cross the legs. *inv.* **potoa, popotoa.** 1. = **pota.** 2. ruin, spoil *(work)*; distort, pervert. **potoa maneno.** pervert words. *refl.-inv.* **jipotoa.** ruin oneself *(by drinking, immoral conduct). inv.-appl.* **potolea.** *inv.-intr.* **potoka.** 1. be twisted/crooked. 2. *fig.* be perverse/eccentric/whimsical. 3. *fig.* be stubborn/obstinate. *inv.-caus.* **potosha.** distort; pervert, lead astray, spoil. *Cf.* **potea, potoe, mpoto, mpotoe, upote, upotovu.**

¹pote *see* **–ote.**

²pote *pl. of* **upote.**

potea (*appl. of* **pota)** 1. disappear, be/get lost. **– njia.** lose one's way. **– akili.** lose one's head/senses, become excited/confused. **– maneno.** say the wrong thing, make a slip of the tongue. 2. be mistaken, be in the wrong. 3. perish, be ruined. *appl.* **potelea.** *pass.* **potewa.** incur/suffer a loss. **amepotewa na mapesa yake.** He has lost his money. *caus.* **poteza.** 1. lose. 2. throw away. 3. ruin/corrupt/abuse someone. *ass.* **poteana.** lose each other, be separated/scattered. *Cf.* **potevu, mpotevu, upotevu.**

potevu *adj.* 1. lost, strayed. 2. destructive. 3. disastrous, ruinous. 4. wasteful, extravagant. *Cf.* **potea, mpotevu, upotevu.**

potoa *inv. of* **pota.**

potoe, potovu 1. *adj.* bent, crooked, askew; deformed, distorted; ruined, depraved, demoralized; stubborn, eccentric. 2. *rare* (–) obstinacy, wilfulness, caprice. *Cf.* **pota.**

potoka *inv.-intr. of* **pota.**

potolea *inv.-appl. of* **pota.**

potosha *inv.-caus. of* **pota.**

potovu *see* **potoe.**

poundi* (–) *see* **pauni.**

povu (ma-) bubble; lather, foam, froth; scum; effervescence. **fanya –.** foam, bubble, effervesce.

poza *caus. of* **poa.**

prediketo* [*Engl.*] (–) *rare, gramm.* predicate.

¹pua (–) 1. nose. **piga –.** snort; blow the nose. **tundu la –, mwanzi wa –.** nostril. **sema puani** *or* **sema na –.** talk through the nose, nasalize. 2. sense of smell. 3. nozzle, spout. *Cf.* **kipua.**

²pua* [*Pers.*] (–) (*us.* **chuma cha –**) tempered iron, steel. **tia –.** harden, temper.

³pua *see* **puna.**

⁴pua *see* **pura.**

puchari*, buchari [*Ind.*] (–) large knife.

puchua *see* **pujua.**

pugi (–) *ornith.* wood dove *(Turtur afer).*

pugikikombe (–) *ornith.* tambourine dove *(Tympanistria tympanistria).*

pujua, puchua 1. scratch, scrape. 2. pull/strip off. **– embe.** peel a mango. **– muhindi.** strip off the grains of an ear of maize. 3. *rare* skin, flay. *Cf.* **chuna.** 4. separate grain from the chaff. *appl.* **pujulia.** *intr.* **pujuka.** *pass.* **pujuliwa.** *refl.* **jipujua.** 1. scratch oneself. 2. *fig.* undress, strip. 3. *fig.* expose oneself, be shameless/immodest. *Cf.* **pujufu, mpujufu.**

pujufu, pujuzi *adj.* shameless, immodest; wasteful. *Cf.* **pujua.**

pujuzi *adj.* *see* **pujufu.**

puku (–) field mouse/rat.

pukuchua, pukutua *inv. of* **pukuta.**

pukuchulia dehydrate *(foods).* *Cf.* **pukuta.**

pukupuku *see* **kipukupuku.**

[1]**pukusa** *caus. of* **pukuta.**

[2]**pukusa** (–) pukusa (kind of banana). *Cf.* **pukuta.**

pukuso (ma-) gift, present *(on festive occasions) Cf.* **pukuta.**

pukuta, pukucha shake off *(water),* shake down *(fruit, etc.),* strip off. – **mahindi.** strip off the grains *(from an ear of maize). intr.* **pukutika.** fall off *(in great numbers, like leaves). fig.* **watu walipukutika.** People have fallen like flies *(as victims of an epidemic). caus.* **pukutisha.** 1. crumble something. 2. let fall, allow to drip. **pukutisha jasho.** drip with sweat. *caus.* **pukusa.** 1. shake off/down. **pukusa mwembe mzima.** shake down the fruit of the mango tree. 2. *fig.* pour out, hand out *(presents);* congratulate. *inv.* **pukutua, pukuchua** = **pukuta.** *Cf.* [2]**pukusa, pukuso, pukute, kipuku,** [1]**kipukusa,** [2]**kipukusa, mpukuti.**

pukute (–): **wali wa** – *or* – **ya wali.** rice cooked in such a way that the grains are separate. *Cf.* **pukuta.**

puleki*, puluki [*Pers.?*] (–) 1. tinsel, spangle, trinket. 2. pinchbeck, sham, shoddy.

pulika *rare* listen, obey. *caus. & int.* **pulikiza.** *ass.* **pulikana.**

puliza (*rare* **puza**) 1. blow, blow up, inflate. – **mpira.** inflate a ball. 2. blow/fan *(a fire). appl.* **pulizia,** *(rare)* **puzia.** *intr.* **pulizika.**

puluki* (–) *see* **puleki.**

pululu (ma-) wilderness, desolate/uninhabited place.

puma beat, pulse *(of the heart). Cf.* **pumua.**

[1]**pumba** (–, ma-) 1. lump; (small) ball, bundle. 2. chaff. 3. *med.* excretion *(under the foreskin).*

[2]**pumba** (–, ma-) *see* **bumba.**

pumbaa 1. be speechless *(from astonishment);* gape, stare, be nonplussed. 2. be dull-witted/stupid/ignorant. 3. be careless/thoughtless/absentminded/lazy. – **kazi.** do one's work carelessly/in a slipshod fashion; *(fig.)* take it easy, amuse oneself. *caus.* **pumbaza.** 1. render someone speechless, embarrass/nonplus someone. 2. delude someone, make a fool of someone. *refl.-caus.* **jipumbaza.** feign stupidity. *caus.-intr.* **pumbazika.** be deluded/deceived/cheated. *Cf.* **pumbavu, mpumbavu, upumbavu.**

pumbavu *adj.* dull-witted, stupid, foolish, ignorant. *Cf.* **pumbaa, mpumbavu, upumbavu.**

pumbo (ma-) *see* **pumbu.**

pumbu, pumbo (ma-) 1. *anat.* scrotum. 2. (*us.* **mapumbu**) testicle. 3. *med.* disease of the scrotum *(orchitis, hernia, etc.)*. *Cf.* **kipumbu.**

pumu (ma-) 1. *anat.* lung (= **pafu, buhumu**). 2. *med.* difficulty in breathing, asthma. *Cf.* **pumua.**

pumua (*inv. of* **puma**?) 1. breathe. 2. take a deep breath, catch one's breath *(after strenuous effort)*. **sasa naweza kupumua.** Now I can catch my breath/take a rest. *caus.* **pumuza.** *caus.-intr.* **pumzika** (< **pumuzika**). 1. take a rest. 2. be pensioned off, retire. *caus.-intr.-appl.* **pumzikia. mahali pa kupumzikia.** resting place. *double caus.* **pumzisha.** allow someone to rest, give someone peace; *(fig.)* calm/soothe someone. *Cf.* **pumu, pumzi, pumziko, kipumziko, mapumziko.**

pumuza *caus. of* **pumua.**

pumuzi (–) *see* **pumzi.**

pumuzika *caus.-intr. of* **pumua.**

pumzi, pumuzi (–) (*also* **upumuo, upumzi** *sing.*) 1. breath, breathing. **pandisha (vuta) –.** breathe in, inhale. **toa (shusha) –.** breathe out, exhale. **hewa ya –.** oxygen. 2. rest, break. **fanya kazi kutwa bila –.** work the entire day without a break. *Cf.* **pumua.**

pumzika *caus.-intr. of* **pumua.**

pumzikio (ma-) *see* **pumziko.**

pumziko, pumzikio (ma-) 1. rest, relaxation. 2. place/time for rest/relaxation/recreation, holiday resort. 3.: **mapumziko.** vacation. *Cf.* **pumua.**

pumzisha *double caus. of* **pumua.**

puna, pua 1. scrape/strip off. **– magome ya mti.** strip the bark off a tree. 2. wipe off *(sweat from the face, etc.)*. *caus.* **punisha.** *inv.* **punua** = **puna.** *Cf.* **mapune, punyeto.**

punda (–) ass, donkey. **– kihongwe.** pack donkey (*in contr. w.* **– Maskati.** riding donkey). **– milia.** zebra. **pepo –.** *med.* tetanus, lockjaw.

punde *adv.* a little; soon, in a little while. **tulikuwa tunamngoja, na – akaja.** We waited for him, and he soon came. **– si –.** in a moment, directly. **– kwa –.** little by little, gradually.

[1]**punga** 1. swing, wave; fan. **– mikono.** swing the arms, give a signal. 2. *fig.* drive away *(by waving the arms, gesticulating)*. **– pepo.** exorcise a spirit. 3. *fig.*: **– upepo/hewa.** get a change of air, take a trip *(for recreation)*. *Cf.* **pungwa.**

[2]**punga** decrease, diminish, let up; shorten *(a dress, etc.)*. **jua limepunga.** the heat of the sun is decreasing *(toward sunset)*. *inv.* **pungua.** decrease, diminish *(in quantity)*. *inv.-intr.* **punguka.** grow less, diminish,

abate. *inv.-caus.* **punguza.** make less, reduce, shorten, lower *(prices). Cf.* **pungufu, punguani, kipunguo, kipunguzi, mpungufu, upungufu.**

[3]**punga** *pl. of* **upunga.**

[1]**pungu** (–) pungu (species of eagle).

[2]**pungu, pungo** (–) pungu (a large sea fish).

[1]**pungua** (–) pungua (kind of drum).

[2]**pungua** *inv. of* [2]**punga.**

punguani (ma-) 1. feebleminded person, idiot. 2. half-breed. *Cf.* [2]**punga.**

pungufu 1. *adj.* reduced, shortened; wanting, defective, imperfect, incomplete; on the wane. **mwezi mpungufu.** an incomplete month *(of 29 days).* **pesa hizi ni –.** It is not the right amount of money *(i.e., is too little).* 2. (ma-) *rare* deficiency, defect. *Cf.* [2]**punga, mpungufu, upungufu.**

punguka *inv.-intr. of* [2]**punga.**

punguo (ma-) *see* **upungufo.**

punguza *inv.-caus. of* [2]**punga.**

pungwa (–) *ethn.* pungwa (a ceremony/dance for exorcising a spirit). *Cf.* [1]**punga.**

punja deceive, cheat, swindle. **alinipunja ratli nzima.** He cheated me by a whole pound. *Cf.* **kipunjo.**

punje (ma-) (single) grain *(of wheat, maize, etc.).*

punju, punyu (–) *ethn.* punju (a medicine for snakebite).

punua *inv. of* **puna.**

punyeto *sing.* masturbation. *Cf.* **puna.**

punyu (–) *see* **punju.**

puo (ma-) *see* **puzo.**

pupa *sing.* eagerness, zeal, avidity; haste, hurry. **fanya – ya...** be eager/in a hurry to do something. *Cf.* **kipupa.**

pura, pua, purura 1. strike, beat, pound. **– nguo.** wash/pound clothes. 2. knock down *(fruit from a tree with a stick or stone).* 3. strip off *(grains of corn, etc.),* shell *(peas, beans).* 4. thresh *(grain). intr.* **pururika** (*rare* **purika**). 5. *refl.* **jipura.** masturbate. 6. *ass.* **purana.** fight; have sexual intercourse. *Cf.* **mpururo.**

pure* [*Ind.*] (–) pure (a dish of maize and beans).

purendi* [*Engl.*] (ma-) *see* **mapurendi.**

purukusa *see* **purukusha.**

purukusha (*rare* **purukusa**) behave carelessly/frivolously. **– maneno (sikio).** talk (listen) heedlessly/inattentively. *refl.* **jipurukusha.** be frivolous/superficial/inattentive. *Cf.* **purukushani, mpurukushani, upurukushaji.**

purukushani (ma-) carelessness, superficiality, frivolity, negligence, contempt. **kwa —.** carelessly, negligently. **fanya —.** act carelessly/negligently. **dereva ameiendesha motokaa kwa —.** The driver drove the car negligently. *Cf.* **purukusha.**

purupuru *adj.* gay, playful.

pururа *see* **pura.**

pururika *intr. of* **pura.**

[1]**pusa** gradually cease, abate, let up. **mvua imepusa.** The rain has let up.

[2]**pusa** (ma-) *augment. of* **kipusa.**

puta, buta beat, whip. **— zulia.** beat a rug.

puuza *see* [2]**puza.**

[1]**puza** *see* **puliza.**

[2]**puza, puuza** talk nonsense; be silly/foolish. **— kazi.** do one's work in a foolish way. *intr.* **puzika** = **puza.** *caus.* **puzisha.** confuse/bewilder someone *(with nonsensical talk). Cf.* **puzo, kipuzi, mpuzi, upuzi.**

puzia *appl. of* **puliza.**

puzo, puo (ma-) nonsense; stupid/inept speech/behavior. *Cf.* [2]**puza.**

pwa become dry, dry up. **maji yamekupwa.** The water has dried up. **maji ya kupwa.** ebb tide. *appl.* **pwea** & *double appl.* **pwelea.** 1. *fig.* have a dry throat. **sauti imempwea.** He has a hoarse voice. 2. *naut.* run aground, be stranded. *appl.-pass.* **pwelewa. amepwelewa.** *fig.* He had no arguments left *(i.e., had to be satisfied). caus.* **pwesha, pweza.** allow to dry up *(a sore). double appl.-caus.* **pweleza.** *naut.* run aground, strand *(a ship). Cf.* **pwani, kipwa, mapwa, makupwa.**

pwaga pound, grind. **— mpunga kinuni.** grind rice in a mortar.

pwagu (—) *see* **pyagu.**

pwaguzi (—) *see* **pyagu.**

pwaju (—) *ornith.* nightjar.

pwani (—) coast (land), littoral. **— na bara.** coast and interior. **panda —.** run aground, be stranded. *Cf.* **pwa.**

pwata *see* **pweteka.**

pwaya hang loose, dangle, be loose. **koti hili linampwaya.** This coat/suit is too big for him.

pwea *appl. of* **pwa.**

pweke *see* **peke.**

pweleza *double appl.-caus. of* **pwa.**

pwesha *caus. of* **pwa.**

pweteka: jipweteka *or* **jipweteka pwata.** throw oneself down in a sitting position.

[1]pweza (–) cuttlefish, squid. *prov.* **mimi si – kujipalia makaa.** I will not get myself into difficulties (i.e., I will not contribute to my own discomfiture, like the cuttlefish, which, when roasted on the fire, spasmodically pulls coals onto its own body). **– mkubwa.** octopus. **kiti cha –.** starfish.

[2]pweza *caus. of* **pwa.**

pwita beat, throb, pulsate.

pya *adj.* new, fresh; modern, up-to-date. *Cf.* **upya.**

pyagu, pyaguzi, pwagu, pwaguzi (–) thief. *prov.* **pyagu na pyaguzi wamekutana.** A clever thief and a still more clever one met each other.

pyora 1. boast, exaggerate, lie. 2. use obscene language. *Cf.* **pyoro.**

pyoro, pyororo *adj.* 1. boastful, deceitful. 2. obscene. *Cf.* **pyora, mapyoro, mpyoro.**

R

rabi* (–) *rel.* master, lord *(used by Moslems in reference to God (creator) and by Christians in reference to Christ (savior);* = **Bwana wangu, Mungu wangu).**

rabishi* 1. throw into confusion, disarrange. 2. confuse, nonplus, distract *(a person). appl.* **rabishia.** bungle/make a mess of something. *intr.* **rabishika.** be in disorder/confusion. *Cf.* **rabsha.**

rabsha* (–) 1. disorder, confusion. 2. noise, tumult. *Cf.* **rabishi.**

rada* (–) retribution, punishment. *Cf.* **rudi.**

radhi* 1. forgiveness, pardon. **niwie –!** Pardon me! **taka –.** beg pardon. 2. satisfaction, approval, blessing. **mpango huu mimi si – nao.** This arrangement does not meet with my approval. **amekosa – ya baba yake.** He has been disowned by his father (does not have his father's blessing). 3. *adj.* satisfied, approving, willing. 4. *v.* (*also* **ridhi, taradhia**) forgive, pardon; satisfy. **kumradhi!** Pardon me! *Cf.* **ridhi.**

radi* (–) (clap of) thunder, lightning. (= **mngurumo, umeme.**) **– imepiga.** It is thundering. **pigwa na –.** be struck by lightning.

radio* [*Engl.*] (–) *see* **redio.**

rafardha* [?] (–) *naut., av.* (ship's) screw, propeller. (= **majembe.**)

rafiki* (–) friend, comrade. *Cf.* **kirafiki, urafiki.**

[1]**rafu*** (–) drawer, shelf.

[2]**rafu*** [*Engl.*] *adj.* rough, *(sport)* not fair. **timu ya K. ilicheza – sana.** The team from K. played very unfairly.

ragai*, raghai *see* **laghai.**

rago (ma-) camp. **piga –.** pitch camp. *Cf.* **kirago.**

raha* (–) rest, peace, quiet; comfort, contentment; enjoyment, entertainment; happiness. **ona –.** find peace/contentment. **kaa – mustarehe.** be in very good circumstances. *Cf.* **starehe, starehevu, mustarehe.**

rahamani* (–) *see* **ramani.**

rahani*, rehani (–) pledge, loan, mortgage. **weka/tia –.** mortgage, pawn. **weka nyumba –.** mortgage a house. **komboa –.** redeem a pledge, pay off a mortgage.

rahimu* *adj.* the Merciful (= God). *Cf.* **rehema, rehemu.**

rahisi* 1. *adj.* cheap. **bidhaa –.** cheap goods. 2. easy, simple. **kazi –.** easy work. **lugha –.** an easy language (= one easy to learn). **njia –.** a simple method. 3. *v.* be cheap; lessen, reduce *(the value of something)*, debase; scorn, belittle, deprecate. *intr.* **rahisika. bei zimerahisika.** The prices have been reduced. *caus.* **rahisisha.** cheapen, make cheaper. **tajiri hakurahisisha bei ya bidhaa.** The shopkeeper has not reduced the prices of the goods. *prov.* **rahisi inavunja upishi.** 'Cheap' spoils cookery. *Cf.* **urahisi.**

rahisisha* *caus. of* **rahisi.**

[1]**rai*, rairai** flatter, play the hypocrite. *pass.* **raiwa.** *intr.* **raika.** *Cf.* **urai.**

[2]**rai*** *rare* give someone something to eat, feed someone.

[3]**rai*** (–) 1. opinion, point of view, standpoint. **msimtume huyu kwenye mkutano maana hana –.** Don't send him to the assembly, for he has no opinion (of his own). **kwa – ya...** in the opinion of... 2. proposal, suggestion, advice.

[4]**rai*** (–) 1. health, vigor. 2. self-assurance.

raia* (ma-, –) citizen *(of a country)*, subject, national *Cf.* **kiraia, uraia.**

rairai* *see* [1]**rai.**

rais*, mrajis (–, ma-) chairman, president.

raiti* [*Engl.*] *sing./adj., sport* right. (= **kuume.**) **insaidi wa –.** inside right *(football).*

rajabu*, rajab (–) 1. seventh month of the Muhammadan year. 2. *pr. n., masc.*

rajamu* (–) *rare* mark, stamp *(of a business firm)*, trademark. (= [1]**chapa.**)

[1]**rajua*** change one's mind, be undecided; postpone, delay.

[2]**rajua*** (–) hope. **wa na –.** to hope, have hopes.

raka* (**ma-**) *augment. of* **kiraka.**

rakaa* (–) *Isl.* bow *(with the hands on the knees, during prayer).* **enda –.** to make such a bow.

rakibisha* *caus. of* [1]**rakibu.**

[1]**rakibu*, rekibu, rekebu** mount, ride on *(a horse, etc.). appl.* **rakibia.** *intr.* **rakibika.** *caus.* **rakibisha, rekibisha.** 1. cause to mount/ride; put on top of. 2. put together, assemble, finish; organize, simplify. 3. be directed toward..., be headed for... **ndege ilirakibishwa kuelekea Nairobi.** The airplane is headed for Nairobi. 4. *rare* mend, repair. 5. *rare* set (a watch or clock). *caus.-intr.* **rakibishika.** *Cf.* [2]**rakibu, rekebisho, tarakibu, urekebisho;** *also* **merikebu.**

[2]**rakibu** (–) good rider. *Cf.* [1]**rakibu.**

ramadhani* (–) 1. Ramadhan (the last month of the Muhammadan year, a month of fasting between dawn and sunset). 2. *pr. n. masc.*

ramani*, rahamani (–) 1. sketch, diagram, plan, drawing. 2. map. **kitabu cha –.** atlas.

[1]**ramba*** [*Malagasy* **lamba**] (–) ramba (a kind of striped cloth made of finely plaited grass).

[2]**ramba*** [*Ind.*] ramba (shoemaker's knife).

[3]**ramba** *see* **lamba.**

rambaza *naut.* cruise around (in search of fish).

rambirambi* (–) (*also* **mbirambi**) words of condolence. **– zako.** My sincere condolence.

rambitia, lambitia *see* **lamba.**

ramia* (–) *mil.* bullet, round *(of ammunition).* (= [2]**kiasi, risasi.**)

ramisi* [*Pers.*] amuse/enjoy oneself. *Cf.* **ramsa.**

ramli* (–) ramli (telling fortunes from markings on sand). **piga –.** tell fortunes. **mpiga –.** fortune-teller. **– yake inaona (haioni).** His prophecy came true (did not come true).

ramsa* [*Pers.*] (–) a place where people are entertaining themselves *(at a fair, etc.). Cf.* **ramisi.**

[1]**ramu*** (–) sorrow, grief.

[2]**ramu*** [?] building lot. (= **kiwanja.**)

ramuka attack (each other). (= **shambulia.**)

[1]**randa, randaranda** 1. dance *(a dance symbolizing courage or strength).* 2. *fig.* boast, show off, act big.

[2]**randa***, **landa** [*Pers.*] (–) (carpenter's) plane. **piga –.** to plane.

[3]**randa** *see* [1]**landa.**

randaranda *see* [1]**randa.**

rangi* [*Ind.*] (–) color, pigment, dye. **tia (paka) –.** color, paint. **geuka –.** change color. **– nyekundu (nyeusi).** red (black) pigment/dye. **enye –.** colored. **enye rangirangi.** varicolored. **–a –.** colored. **nyeupe ao ya –?** White or colored? **ubaguzi wa –.** racial discrimination.

ranki* [*Engl.*] (–) rank.

rarua tear, rip (to pieces). *appl.* **rarulia.** *intr.* **raruka. kitambaa hiki hakiraruki.** This cloth will not rip. *ass.* **raruana.** *fig.* abuse each other, speak ill of each other. *Cf.* **raruo, mrarua, mraruo.**

rarulia *appl. of* **rarua.**

raruo (ma-) 1. tear, rip. 2. *fig.* rage, fury. *Cf.* **rarua.**

ras* (–) *see* **rasi.**

rasha*, **rasharasha** 1. smear/daub on, paint, whitewash. 2. do something carelessly/superficially. *appl.* **rashia.** 1. daub on something. 3. sprinkle. **rashia maji.** sprinkle with water. *Cf.* **marasharasha, marashi, mrasharasha, mrashi, urasharasha.**

rasharasha* 1. = **rasha.** 2. (ma-) drizzle *(of rain).*

rasi*, **ras** (–) 1. cape, promontory. 2. leader, chief.

rasilimali* (–) *see* **rasilmali.**

rasilmali*, **rasilimali, raslimali** (–) 1. *econ.* capital, assets, principal. 2. *(in gen.)* property, wealth.

rasimu* 1. set a price; make an opening bid *(at an auction).* 2. *rare* copy, imitate. 3. (–) design, plan, drawing.

rasisi* plate with tin. *appl.* **rasisia.** *intr.* **rasisika.** *caus.* **rasisisha.** *Cf.* **risasi, marisaa.**

raslimali* (–) *see* **rasilmali.**

rasmi* *adj.* official, legal; formal. **fanya karamu –.** give an official reception. **nguo za –.** uniform.

rasuli* (–, ma-) prophet, apostle, messenger.

ratibu*, **ratibisha** put in order, coordinate. *appl.* **ratibia.** *intr.* **ratibika.** *Cf.* **taratibu.**

ratili* (–) *see* **ratli.**

ratli*, **ratili** (–) ratli (a unit of weight, 1 lb., 450 g).

raufu* *adj.* gentle, well-bred. *Cf.* **uraufu.**

rauka, lauka *see* **lawa.**

rausi* *naut.* trim sail.

re* (ma-) *see* **ree.**

reale*, **riale**, **riali** [*Ar.-Span.*] (–) *liter.* riyal, piaster, dollar. **– ya mzinga.** Spanish dollar. **– ya Sham.** Maria Theresa dollar.

redio*, **radio** [*Engl.*] (–) radio.

ree*, **re** [*Port.*] (**ma-**) *cards* ace.

refarii*, **referii**, **rifarii**, **rifirii** [*Engl.*] (–) *sport* referee.

refu *adj.* long, tall; high, deep. **mti mrefu.** a tall tree. **kisima kirefu.** a deep well. **kisu kirefu.** a long knife. **muda mrefu.** a long period of time. *Cf.* **refusha, marefu, urefu.**

refusha make long, lengthen, extend. **– mstari.** extend a line. *Cf.* **refu.**

rega *see* **lega.**

rehani* (–) *see* **rahani.**

rehe* (–) *see* **riahi.**

rehema* (–) 1. pity, mercy; sympathy, compassion; generosity, magnanimity. 2. *rel.* indulgence. *Cf.* **rahimu, rehemu, marehemu**; *also* **huruma** (?).

rehemu* take pity on, show mercy to, feel sympathy for. *appl.* **rehemia.** *intr.* **rehemika.** *caus.* **rehemisha.** please someone with something, make someone a present of something. *Cf.* **rehema.**

rejareja* 1. *adj.:* **biashara ya –.** retail trade, commission business. 2. *adv.* by/on commission. **biashara yake ni ya –.** He is in the retail business. *Cf.* **rejea.**

rejea* 1. return, go back, begin again. **– nyuma.** retreat. 2. refer to (something). **– sarufi.** refer to the grammar. *intr.* **rejeka.** *caus.* **rejesha, rejeza.** take/give back; correct someone. *caus.-appl.-ass.* **rejesheana, rejezeana. rejesheana fedha.** pay back money to each other. *Cf.* **rejareja, rejeo, mrejaa.**

rejeo* (**ma-**) (*us.* **marejeo**) return. **baada ya marejeo yake.** after his return. *Cf.* **rejea.**

rejesheana* *caus.-appl.-ass. of* **rejea.**

rejeza* *caus. of* **rejea.**

rejista* [*Engl.*] (–) registered letter.

rekabisho* (**ma-**) *see* **rekebisho.**

rekebisha* *caus. of* [1]**rakibu.**

rekebisho*, **rekabisho** (**ma-**) 1. repair. 2. organization. *Cf.* [1]**rakibu.**

rekebu*, **rekibu** *see* [1]**rakibu.**

rekodi* (–) *see* **rikodi.**

reli* [*Engl.*] (–) railway, railroad. **njia ya –.** railroad line. **idara ya –.** railroad company.

relwe* [*Engl.*] (–) railway.

remba make beautiful/handsome/attractive, decorate, ornament. *appl.* **rembea.** *intr.* **rembeka.** *caus.* **rembesha.** *inv.* **rembua.** destroy the beauty of something, disfigure, ruin. *inv.-appl.* **rembulia.** *inv.-intr.* **rembuka.** *inv.-caus.* **rembusha.** *Cf.* **rembo, kirembo, mrembo, urembo.**

rembo (ma-) ornament, design, pattern. *Cf.* **remba.**

rembua *inv. of* **remba.**

rembulia *inv.-appl. of* **remba.**

renga fool, hoax, cheat. *pass.* **rengwa.**

rengu (ma-) (*us.* **marengu**) *naut.* outrigger.

Reno* [*Port.* **reino**] *adj.* Portuguese. *Cf.* **Kireno, Mreno, Ureno.**

resheni* [*Engl.*] (–) ration, portion, helping.

resipi* [*Engl.*] (–) prescription.

rewa (–) rewa (signal drum).

rezolusheni* [*Engl.*] resolution. **pitisha –.** adopt a resolution.

riahi*, rihi, rehe (–) bloating, flatulence.

riale*, riali (–) *see* **reale.**

riaria* *rare* hunt for; watch, observe.

riba* (*rare* **iriba**) (–) 1. usury. 2. avarice, greed *(for money)*. **la –.** practice usury. **mla –.** usurer.

ridhaa* (–) satisfaction; agreement, approval. *Cf.* **ridhi.**

ridhi* be satisfied/pleased. *appl.* **ridhia.** 1. please someone. 2. accept. *intr.* **ridhika.** *caus.* **ridhisha.** please, satisfy. *ass.* **ridhiana. patano la kuridhiana.** compromise. *Cf.* **radhi, ridhaa, maridhawa, maridhia, taradhia, uradhi.**

rifarii*, rifirii [*Engl.*] (–) *see* **refarii.**

rifrijireta* [*Engl.*] (–) refrigerator.

riha* (–) odor, fragrance, aroma.

rihani* (–) *bot.* basil.

rihi* (–) *see* **riahi.**

rijali* (–) *rare, liter.* man.

rika (ma-) *ethn.* contemporary, member of the same age-group. **hawa ni marika.** They are of the same age.

rikebu* (–) *see* **merikebu.**

rikodi*, rekodi [*Engl.*] 1. (–) (phonograph) record; tape(-recorder); *(sport)* record. **weka –.** set/establish a record. 2. *v.* record, make a (tape) recording.

riksha* [*Jap.-Engl.*] (–) rickshaw.

rima (ma-) pit trap *(for animals).*

rimbua *see* **limbua.**

rimende* (–) *see* **rumande.**

rinda *see* **marinda.**

rindima 1. roar, rumble, boom *(of thunder, waterfalls, drums).* 2. *rare* strike, hit. *Cf.* **rindimo.**

rindimo (ma-) roaring, thundering. *Cf.* **rindima.**

ringa 1. act important, put on airs, swagger. 2. irritate, provoke. 3. set one's cap for someone. *Cf.* **maringo.**

rinksho* *see* **riksha.**

ripea* [*Engl.*] (–) repair.

ripota* [*Engl.*] (ma-) reporter.

ripoti* [*Engl.*] 1. (–) report, information. 2. *v.* report, inform.

ripuka *see* **lipuka.**

risala* (–) 1. message. 2. summary *(of a speech, etc.),* epitome, précis. 3. *rare* letter.

risasi*, **lisasi** (–) 1. solder *(tin, lead).* **tia –.** to tin-plate. 2. bullet. **tia –.** load a rifle. *Cf.* **²kiasi, rasisi, marisaa.**

risavu*, **rizavu** [*Engl.*] 1. (–) reserve, supply; (tribal) reservation. 2. (ma-) *sport* reserve player.

rishai* 1. be wet/damp/moist. 2. exude *(moisture, perspiration). Cf.* **warishai.**

risiti* [*Engl.*] (–) receipt.

ritadi* 1. deviate, swerve *(from one's principles, etc.),* backslide. 2. *rel.* apostacize. *Cf.* **rudi.**

ritani* [*Engl.*] (–) return, profit, income.

rithi* inherit, fall heir to. **– mali nyingi.** inherit a great deal of property. *appl.* **rithia.** *caus.* **rithisha.** 1. leave, bequeath something. 2. divide up the property of a deceased person. *Cf.* **mirathi, mrithi, mrithisha, urithi, warithi.**

riza*, **liza** (–) door chain.

rizavu* (–, ma-) *see* **risavu.**

riziki* (–) means of subsistence, food, nourishment. **tangu asubihi hajapata –.** He has had nothing to eat since morning. *Cf.* **ruzuku.**

robo* (–) 1. fourth, quarter. **kasa –.** three quarters. **saa mbili kasa –.** 7:45 o'clock. 2. (*also* **roboo**) *coll.* one shilling.

robota* (ma-) bundle, bale. **– la pamba.** a bale of cotton.

robu* (–): **maziwa ya –.** curdled milk, curds.

roda* [*Port.*] (–) (sheave of a) pulley.

rodi*, lodi [*Engl.* lord] (_) 1. pompous/arrogant person; talebearer. 2. monocle.

roga *see* **loga.**

rogoa, logoa *inv. of* **loga.**

roho* (–) 1. soul, spirit, life. **– Mtakatifu.** *rel.* Holy Ghost. 2. breath. 3. throat. 4. disposition. 5. character, personality, individuality. **ana – njema.** He has good character. 6. (*also* **uroho**) greed, gluttony; avarice, miserliness. *Cf.* **kiroho, mroho.**

roja*, loja be astonished/amazed. *Cf.* **kiroja.**

rojorojo 1. *adj.* thick, gelatinous *(of foods)*. 2. (–) gravy.

roketi* [*Engl.*] (–) rocket. **kiwanja cha kurusha –.** launching pad/platform.

roku* [*Engl.*] *recent* dance the rock-and-roll.

rondea *see* **londea.**

rongaronga 1. beseech, implore. 2. carry with great care *(something fragile or damaged)*.

rongera (–) rongera (native beer before fermentation).

ronjo *see* **lonjo.**

ropoka, lopoka talk nonsense, speak without thinking. *appl.* **ropokea.** *caus.* **ropokesha.**

roshani* [*Pers.*] balcony, veranda.

ruba (ma-), **mruba** (mi-) leech; *(fig.)* usurer.

rubani* (ma-) 1. *naut.* pilot, helmsman. 2. *av.* pilot. 3. leader, director. **– la kwaya.** choir leader.

rubuni* deceive, cheat, lead astray. *appl.* **rubunia.**

rudi* 1. come back, return **– katika safari.** return from a journey. 2. give/take/send back. 3. reply, respond. 4. find fault, reprove, correct. **– (kwa) makosa.** correct mistakes. *appl.* **rudia. amemrudia mkewe.** He went back to his wife *(after a separation)*. **rudia neno.** contradict. *appl.-ass.* **rudiana.** 1. return to each other. 2. reprimand/correct each other. *intr.* **rudika.** *caus.* **rudisha.** give/send back, return, restore. *caus.-intr.:* **hairudishiki.** It is irrevocable. *Cf.* **marudi, mardudi, rada, ritadi, urudishaji.**

rudufu* 1. to double. *intr.* **rudufika.** *caus.* **rudufisha, rudufya.** 2. *adj.* = **maradufu** 2.

rufaa*, rufaani, rufani (–) freight, cargo. *Cf.* **rufai, marufaa.**

rufai* 1. mount. 2. *rare* go away quickly; get rid of something quickly *(by throwing it away)*. *Cf.* **rufaa.**

[1]**rufani*** (–) *jur.* appeal. **taka (chukua) –.** appeal *(a case).* **batilisha –.** dismiss an appeal. **kubali –.** allow an appeal.

[2]**rufani*** (–) *see* **rufaa.**

rufuku* 1. *rare* forbid, prohibit; deter. (= **kataza.**) *appl.* **rufukia.** *caus.* **rufukisha.** 2. (ma-) *see* **marufuku.**

rugaruga (wa-) *see* **mrugaruga.**

ruhsa* (–) *see* **ruhusa.**

ruhusa*, ruhsa, rukhsa (–) 1. permission. **omba –.** ask for permission. **toa –.** give permission. 2. vacation, holiday. 3. dismissal. 4. *econ.* permit, license. 5. *v.* permit, allow. *appl.* **ruhusia.** *intr.* **ruhusika.** *caus.* **ruhusisha.**

rujumu* kill by stoning. *appl.* **rujumia.** *intr.* **rujumika.** *caus.* **rujumisha.**

ruka 1. jump, hop. **bao la kuruka.** diving board, trampoline. **– juu.** *av.* take off. **kuruka kwa mbali.** broad jump. **kuruka na mti.** pole-vault. 2. pass over/beyond, cross; transgress, trespass. **– mpaka.** exceed a limit, go beyond bounds. 3. fly. 4. swell. **wali umeruka.** The rice has swelled up. *appl.* **rukia.** attack someone *(in a conversation).* *intr.* **rukika.** *caus.* **rusha.** cause to jump/fly, throw up/off; launch *(a rocket, etc.).* **rusha akili.** cause someone to lose his head, startle. **rusha ndege.** fly an airplane. *pass.* **rukwa: rukwa na akili.** lose one's head. *Cf.* **ruko, rusho, kirukanjia, kirukia, mrukaji, mruko, urukaji.**

rukhsa* (–) *see* **ruhusa.**

ruko (ma-) 1. jump, hop. 2. *fig.* transgression, trespass. 3. *fig.* omission. *Cf.* **ruka.**

rukudhu* 1. lose one's way; enter without authorization, trespass. 2. *fig.* insult someone.

rukuu* *Isl.* bow with the hands on the knees *(in prayer).*

rukwama (–) truck, van.

rula* [*Engl.*] ruler.

Rum* *arch.* Turkey. **sultani –.** the sultan of Turkey. **Bahari ya –.** Mediterranean.

rumada* [*Port.*] (–) *naut.* rudder-pivot.

rumande*, rumenda, rimende [*Engl.*] (–) remand, arrest, imprisonment. **weka –.** arrest.

rumbi (–) rumbi (large water-jug).

rumenda* (–) *see* **rumande.**

rumi* *adj.* Roman. *Cf.* **kirumi, Mruma.**

runda 1. be retarded in development, be stunted. 2. be crippled. 3. *fig.* be bad-tempered/surly.

rundika *see* **lundika.**

runga *rare* collect, gather.

rungu, lungu (–) knobbed stick. *Cf.* **kirungu.**

rungula *see* **lungula.**

rupia* [*Ind.*] (–) rupee (1£ = 13 rupees).

rupu *see* **marupurupu.**

rusha *caus. of* **ruka.**

rusho (ma-) (act of) throwing off/away. *Cf.* **ruka.**

rushwa* (–) bribe. **toa –.** to bribe. **la –.** accept a bribe.

rusu* (–) layer, tier, row *(of piled objects);* stratum, level.

rutuba* (–) dampness, moisture; fertility. **ardhi ina –.** The soil is fertile. *Cf.* **rutubika.**

rutubika* 1. be moist/damp. 2. be fertile. *caus.* **rutubisha.** make moist/fertile. **kwa kutia mbolea sasa shamba limerutubishwa.** This manure has made the field fertile. 3. *fig.* be refreshed/invigorated. *Cf.* **rutuba.**

ruwaza* (–) sample, model, pattern.

ruya* (–) dream, vision.

ruzu* get into difficulties; be impoverished; abandon hope. *appl.* **ruzia.** *intr.* **ruzika.**

ruzuku*, tarazaki provide for, support, maintain; preserve, store up. *Cf.* **riziki.**

ruzuna* (–): *us.* **dawa ya –.** a medicine for whooping-cough.

S

¹saa* (–) 1. hour, (period of) time. **– ngapi?** What time is it? (*lit.:* what kind of an hour?) **nusu –.** half an hour. 2. watch, clock. **– ya mkono.** wristwatch. **– ya mfuko.** pocket watch. **– ya ukuta.** wall-clock.

²saa* remain, be left (over). *fig.* stay, linger. *appl.* **salia** = **saa.** *caus.* **saza.** 1. leave (over/behind). 2. leave out, omit; leave undone/unfinished/unsaid. *Cf.* **masaa, msazo.**

³saa *interj. of impatience or amazement.* **sema –.** Well, say something, will you?

¹saada* (–) *see* **seyyida.**

²saada* (–) *see* **msaada.**

saanda* (–) *see* **sanda.**

saari* (–) 1. *rare* price, value. (= **bei, thamani, ¹kiasi, ¹kima.**) 2. *econ.* face value *(of money, etc.).*

saba* 1. *num.* seven. **–a –.** seventh. 2. (–) *coll.* week. **– mbili.** two weeks. *See also* **Saba-Saba.**

sababisha*, **sabibisha** give as the reason for..., regard as the cause of... *pass.* **sabibishwa.** be caused by. *Cf.* **sababu.**

sababu* (–) cause, reason, motive. **kwa –.** because, since. **kwa – ya...** because of... **(kwa) – gani?** why? **ndio –.** for that reason, therefore. **bila (pasipo) –.** without reason. **toa –.** give a reason. *Cf.* **sababisha. kisababu.**

sabaha* (ma-) successor *(in an office). Cf.* **usabaha.**

sabahi*, **sabihi** wish someone good morning, pay a morning call on someone. *Cf.* **asubuhi.**

sabaini* *see* **sabini.**

sabalheri* (–) *see* **sabalkheri.**

sabalkheri*, **sabalheri, subalkheri** *salutation:* Good morning. *Cf.* **masalkheri.**

Saba-Saba 7 July, the Anniversary of TANU (= Tanzania National Union).

sabasi* (–) enmity, hostility, ill-will, dissension.

sabatashara* *arch. num.* seventeen. (= **kumi na saba.**) **–a –.** seventeenth.

sabibisha* *see* **sababisha.**

sabidi* arrange, settle *(a debt).*

[1]**sabihi*** = **sabahi.**

[2]**sabihi*** be face to face with someone. **nilimsabihi yeye mwenyewe.** I have met him personally.

sabiki* 1. (–) cause, reason, supposition. 2. *v.* go before, lead.

sabili* 1. make way/room for, allow to pass. 2. remove, clear away. 3. permit, allow, admit. 4. have patience with someone. 5. loosen, relax, relieve. *appl.* **sabilia.** *intr.* **sabilika.** 6. (–) removal; permission; relief, relaxation. 7. *adj.* free, mobile, unimpeded, relaxed.

sabini*, **sabaini** *num.* seventy.

sabiti* *rare* = **thabiti.**

sabmarini* [*Engl.*] (–) submarine.

sabuni* (–) soap **povu la –.** suds, lather.

saburi*, **subiri** 1. be patient/calm/resigned. 2. wait (*more polite than* **ngoja**). **nisaburi.** wait for me. *appl.* **saburia.** *caus.* **saburisha.** calm, pacify. 3. (*also* **subira**) (–) patience, forbearance, resignation. *prov.* **– yavuta heri.** Patience brings blessing. *coll.* **kutokuwa na – ni kubaya.** To be impatient is bad.

sadaka* (–) 1. alms, charity. 2. *rel.* offering, sacrifice. *Cf.* **sadaki, sadiki.**

sadaki* 1. give alms. 2. make a sacrifice. *Cf.* **sadaka.**

sadifu* 1. be true/right/proper/exact. 2. *adj.* true, right, proper, correct, exact.

sadiki* believe, trust. *appl.* **sadikia.** *intr.* **sadikika.** be credible/trustworthy. *caus.* **sadikisha.** win confidence; justify, confirm; convince; *(w. int. force)* believe firmly, trust implicitly. *Cf.* **sadikifu, msadikifu, suduku;** *also* **sadaka, sadaki.**

sadikifu* *adj.* 1. trusting, credulous. 2. credible, trustworthy; dependable, reliable, honest. *Cf.* **sadiki.**

sadoka, sotoka (–) *dial.* cattle plague, rinderpest.

safari* (–) 1. journey, trip, expedition; departure. 2. *see* **msafara.** 3. time, moment. **– hii sitasema naye.** This time I shall not talk with him. **– nyingine.** at another time. *Cf.* **safiri.**

safi* 1. (*also* **swafi**) *adj.* clean, pure, clear, bright; transparent; true, honest, candid, unselfish; real, genuine. **hewa –.** fresh air. **sema Kiswahili –.** speak good/pure Swahili. 2. (*us. caus.* **safisha**) *v.* clean, purify; clarify, put in order; correct; defecate. **safisha picha (filmu).** develop a film. *appl.* **safia.** *intr.* **safika.** *Cf.* **msafishaji, usafi, usafishaji.**

safidi*, tasifida [*Pers.*] clean, put in order, arrange. *appl.* **safidia.** *intr.* **safidika.** *caus.* **safidisha.** *Cf.* **safi, usafidi.**

safihi*, safii 1. offend, insult, abuse; treat with scorn/contempt/derision. 2. be rude/insolent/impudent. 3. (–) boor, lout, impudent person. 4. *adj.* rude, offensive, insolent. *Cf.* **msafihi, usafihi.**

safii* *see* **safihi.**

safika* *intr. of* **safi.**

safina* *sing.* (*orig.* boat, ship; *now only:*) *rel.* Noah's ark.

safiri* travel, set out on a journey/expedition. *appl.* **safiria.** *intr.* **safirika.** *caus.* **safirisha.** 1. make preparations for a journey. 2. send off/out, transport. 3. *econ.* export. *Cf.* **safari, msafara, msafiri, msafirishaji, usafiri, usafirishaji.**

safisha* *caus. of* **safi.**

safu* (–, **ma-**), **msafa** (**mi-**) row, line, series. **– ya milima.** range of mountains. **weka (panga) –.** put/set in a row. **jipanga –.** *mil.* form ranks.

safura* (–) *med.* 1. jaundice. 2. anemia. 3.: **–a –.** *adj.* pale, pallid.

saga 1. grind, pulverize. **– meno.** grind/gnash the teeth. 2. *fig.* oppress. *appl.* **sagia. kinu cha kusagia kahawa.** coffee mill. 3. (*& ass.* **sagana**) commit an act of female homosexuality/lesbianism. *Cf.* **²sago** (?), **¹kisaga, msaga, msagaliwa, ¹msago.**

sagai* (–) (short) spear, assegai.

sagama *rare* = **sakama.**

¹sago*, sagu [*Ind.*] (–) sago.

²sago, msago *adv.* without interruption, continuously. *Cf.* **saga** (?).

sagu* (–) *see* **[1]sago.**

sagua laugh at, deride. *Cf.* **saguo.**

saguo (ma-) (act of) laughing at someone, derision, mockery. *Cf.* **sagua.**

sahala* *adj.* light, easy. *Cf.* **sahalia, tasihili.**

sahalia* be light/easy. *caus.* **sahalisha.** lighten, facilitate. *Cf.* **sahala.**

sahalisha* *caus. of* **sahalia.**

sahani* (–) 1. dish, plate. **– za kaule.** (imported) earthenware, china. 2. *fig.:* **– ya santuri.** (phonograph) record. 3. cavity, depression. *Cf.* **kisahani.**

sahau* 1. forget, not remember; fail to do something; be careless/inattentive. *appl.* **sahaulia.** *intr.* **sahaulika.** *caus.* **sahaulisha.** 2. *n.* failure to remember something, lapse of memory. *Cf.* **sahaulifu, msahau, usahaulifu.**

sahaulifu* *adj.* forgetful, absentminded, inattentive. *Cf.* **sahau.**

sahib* (–, ma-) *see* **sahibu.**

sahibu*, sahib, suhuba (–, ma-) 1. friend. 2. master, sir. *Cf.* **suhubiana, masahaba, mamsahib.**

sahifa*, sahifu (–) *rare* page *(of a book).* (= **ukurasa.**) *Cf.* **msahafu.**

sahihi* 1. (*us. caus.* **sahihisha**) correct, read proof; attest, authenticate, prove; sign. *appl., rare,* **sahihia,** *us.* **sahihishia.** *intr.* **sahihika.** 2. (–) correction, revision; proof; attestation, security, guarantee. 3. signature. **– yako.** your signature. **tia –.** sign *(a document)* (*see also* **saini**). 4. *adj. & adv.* (*also* **sahihifu**) right, correct, true, genuine, valid. *Cf.* **sahihisho, usahihi.**

sahihisho* (ma-) correction, revision; attestation, authentication, confirmation. *Cf.* **sahihi.**

saidi*, sayidi (ma-) 1. *hist.* lord, master, ruler. 2. *pr. n. masc.* *Cf.* **seyyedia, seyyid, seyyida.**

saidia* help, assist, aid, support; favor, promote; protect, defend; approve, sanction. *intr.* **saidika.** *caus.* **saidiza.** *pass.* **saidiwa.** *Cf.* **msaada, msaidizi.**

saikoloji*, saikolojia, sikolojia [*Engl.*] (–) psychology.

saili* ask, inquire; investigate, examine. *appl.* **sailia.** *caus.* **sailisha.** *ass.* **sailiana.** *Cf.* **swali, masahala.**

saini* [*Engl.*] (–) signature, sign, mark. **tia/weka –.** to sign. *See also* **sahihi.**

[1]sairi* 1. paddle, loll about *(in the water).* 2. *fig., naut.* hug the shore.

[2]sairi* pound a residue on the side of a mortar.

saisi* (**ma-**) groom, coachman.

saiti* [*Engl.*] (–) *auto.* turn-signal. **dereva hakutoa –.** The driver did not give a turn-signal.

saizi* [*Engl.*] (–) size.

sajin* [*Engl.*] (**ma-**) *mil.* sergeant.

saka chase, hunt *(wild animals by driving);* catch *(in a trap).* *caus.* **sakiza.** *Cf.* **msakaji, msako, usasi;** *also* **sakama.**

sakafu* (–) 1. floor *(of hard-packed mud or concrete).* 2. roof *(of a flat-roofed clay or stone building).* *Cf.* **sakifu.**

sakama (*rare* **sagama**) stick, be caught *(e.g., of an animal in a trap).* **mwiba wa samaki umemsakama kooni.** The fishbone stuck in his throat. *fig.* **maneno yao yametusakama moyoni.** Their words made a lasting impression on us (*lit.:* stuck in our hearts). *caus.* **sakamisha.** fasten, secure. *Cf.* **saka, msakamo.**

sakara* (*us. intr.* **sakarika**) 1. be exhausted/debilitated *(by hunger, thirst, heat).* 2. overeat *(with resulting sluggishness).*

sakata 1. strike, hit, beat. (= **piga.**) 2. devour, eat up, finish off.

saki* 1. press, squeeze, be tight. **njaa inasaki.** I am dying of hunger. 2. *fig.* have a profound influence, affect deeply, move. *appl.* **sakia.** *intr.* **sakika.** *caus.* **sakisha.** *pass.* **sakiwa.** *Cf.* **kisaki.**

sakifu* pack mud, make a (hard-packed) mud or concrete floor. *appl.* **sakifia.** *intr.* **sakifika.** *caus.* **sakifisha.** *pass.* **sakifiwa.** *Cf.* **sakafu.**

sakimu* *rare* be ill/ailing. (= **ugua.**)

[1]**sakini*** settle down, stay in a place. *Cf.* **makani.**

[2]**sakini** (–) *see* **sekini.**

sakiti* 1. reduce, diminish. 2. *fig.* soothe, appease.

sakitu* (–) (white) frost, hoarfrost. *Cf.* **jalidi.**

sakubimbi, chakubimbi (–) troublemaker, gossip, talebearer, sneak. (= **mfitini, mdakuzi.**)

sala* (–) *rel.* prayer. **– ya Bwana.** the Lord's Prayer. **– ya kupunga pepo wabaya.** exorcism. *Cf.* **sali, msala.**

salaam* (–) *see* **salama, salamu.**

saladi* [*Engl.*] (–) salad.

[1]**salala*, sarara** (–) chine, sirloin, fillet.

[2]**salala*** *interj. of surprise.*

salama*, salaam 1. (–) peace, tranquillity, security; health, well-being. 2. *adj.* peaceful, calm, safe, unharmed; favorable, satisfactory. **mwisho –.** a favorable outcome. 3. *adv.* (*also* **salama salimini**). (quite) safely, in perfectly good order. *Cf.* **salamu, salimu, usalama.**

salamu*, salaam 1. (–) greeting, salutation; bow. **toa (pa) –.** greet, salute. **mizinga ya –.** salute *(by firing guns).* **pokea –.** accept a greeting. **peana –.** greet each other. 2. *adj.* safe and sound, prosperous, flourishing. *Cf.* **salama, salimu, taslimu, usalama.**

salasila* (–) *see* **silasila.**

salata* (–) harshness, want of consideration, ruthlessness; sharpness, sarcasm. *Cf.* **2saliti, msalata, tasliti.**

sali* *Isl.* pray. *appl.* **salia.** *caus.* **salisha.** *ass.* **saliana.** *Cf.* **sala.**

1salia* *appl. of* **sali.**

2salia* *appl. of* **2saa.**

salihi* *adj.* good, in good condition, sound; honest, upright, of good character; useful, proper, suitable. *Cf.* **msalihina.**

salihina* (–) *see* **msalihina.**

salili (–) (various species of) duck. (= **bata.**)

salimini* *adv.* *see* **salama.**

salimu* 1. greet, salute; congratulate; bow. 2. hand over, deliver; entrust; capitulate. *fig.* **– roho.** give up the ghost, die. 3. save, rescue. *appl.* **salimia.** 1. greet someone, give someone regards. **ukimwona fulani nisalimie.** If you meet X, give him my regards. 2. entrust something to someone. *intr.* **salimika.** *caus.* **salimisha.** *refl.-caus.* **jisalimisha.** surrender (oneself), give oneself up. *Cf.* **salama, salamu.**

salio (ma-) *see* **masaa.**

1saliti* put together, mix. **ukisaliti jinsi mbili za mchanga huu utapata mchanga mzuri.** If you mix these two kinds of sand together, you will get good sand.

2saliti* 1. be sharp/sarcastic. 2. irritate, stir up, disturb, annoy, confuse. 3. betray, falsify, deceive, cheat. 4. set at variance, alienate. **mgeni ndiye aliyetusaliti.** It was a stranger who alienated us. *appl.* **salitia.** *Cf.* **salata.**

saluti* [*Engl.*] (–) salute, greeting. **pokea –.** accept a greeting, be made welcome.

sama* stop up, choke; stick in the throat.

samadari* [*Ind.*] (–) bedstead *(iron or wood)*

samadi* (–) fertilizer *(natural manure mixed with ashes).* *Cf.* **simadi.**

samaha* (ma-) *see* **msamaha.**

samaki* (–) fish *(in gen.)* **– mbichi (mkavu).** fresh (dried) fish. **vua –.** to fish. **tunga –.**

string fish on a stick *(for drying). prov.* **— mmoja akioza, wote wameoza.** One bad fish infects all the rest.

samani* [*Ind.*] (–) instrument, implement, tool, utensil; piece of (movable) property, article of furniture. **— za mwashi.** stonemason's tools.

samawari* [*Russ.-Ar.*] (–) (coffee-)urn *(with brazier).*

samawati*, samawi (–) 1. sky. 2.: **rangi ya —.** sky-blue, azure.

samawi* (–) *see* **samawati.**

sambaa be spread/scattered. *appl.* **sambalia.** *intr.* **sambalika.** *caus.* **sambalisha.**

sambamba *adv.* side by side, shoulder to shoulder; parallel; simultaneously. **mistari iliyo —.** parallel lines.

sambaratika disintegrate.

sambusa* [*Pers.*] sambusa (a pastry made of meat, onions, and pepper).

samehe* 1. forgive, pardon, remit, pass over *(mistakes, offenses, etc.).* **— makosa.** pass over/overlook mistakes (failings). 2. give up, stop trying. **nimeitafuta sikuiona, kwa hiyo nimeisamehe.** I have hunted for it, but did not find it; so I have given up. 3. *rare* save, rescue. *Cf.* **msamaha, msamehaji.**

samesame* (–) 1. samesame (red glass bead). 2. samesame (a kind of red ant).

samli* (*rare* **samuli**) (–) clarified butter, ghee *(used only for cooking).*

sampuli* [*Engl.*] (–) sample, model, example.

samu* (–) *see* **saumu.**

samuli* (–) *rare see* **samli.**

[1]**sana*** *adv.* very, very much, to a high degree, to a great extent. **tazamia —.** examine carefully. **lia —.** weep copiously. **la —.** eat heavily. **asante —.** many thanks. **sema —.** speak loudly/emphatically.

[2]**sana*** hammer, forge *(something). Cf.* [2]**msana, usani.**

sanaa* 1. (–) (work of) skilled craftsmanship, art. 2. *v.* (*also* **sanii**) make, construct, fabricate. *appl.* **sanalia.** *Cf.* **msanaa.**

sanamaki* (–) senna *(used as a purgative).*

sanamu* (–) 1. image, idol. **ibada ya —.** idolatry. 2. statue. **chora —.** make a statue. **mchonga —.** sculptor. 3. picture, painting, photograph; figure, diagram. *Cf.* **kisanamu.**

sanati*, sene (–) *arch., liter.* year *(in dating letters).*

sanda*, saanda, shanda (–) burial cloth, shroud.

sandali* (–) sandalwood. **mafuta ya –.** sandalwood oil. *Cf.* **msandali.**

sandarusi* (–) gum copal. *Cf.* **msandarusi.**

sanduku* (–, ma-) box, chest, trunk. **– la kupiga kura.** ballot box. **– la posta.** mailbox; letters to the editor *(in a newspaper).* *Cf.* **kijisanduku.**

sangaa *see* **shangaa.**

sangara (–) sangara (red ant).

sangaza *caus. of* **shangaa.**

sanifu* work skilfully, invent, compose, write. *Cf.* **usanifu.**

sanii* *see* sanaa 2.

sanjari*, **shanjari**, **chanjari** [*Pers.*] 1. accompany, escort; follow in succession, move in a line or column *(ships, etc.).* 2. *adv.* in single file, in line/column formation.

sansuri* (–) 1. sansuri (kind of fish, barracuda). (= **mzira.**) 2. a large knife with a blunt edge.

santuri*, **senturi** (–) 1. santuri (a musical instrument resembling a zither). 2. *fig.* phonograph, barrel organ *(or other devices).*

sao (ma-) *see* **masalio.**

sapa (*us. red.* **sapasapa**) 1. tout, spiel *(to attract customers).* 2. take everything one has, make a clean sweep.

1**sapatu*** [*Port.*] (–) (house-)slipper.

2**sapatu** (–, ma-) sapatu (plaited cording to support a bed).

sarabi* (–) mirage, fata morgana.

sarafa* (ma-) *see* **sharafa.**

sarafu*, **sarufu**, **sarifu**, **sarifa** (–) 1. coin, (small) change. 2. (rate of) exchange. *Cf.* 1**sarifu**, **masurufu.**

saraka* [*Pers.*] (–) drawer *(of a chest of drawers or a table/desk).*

sarakasi* [*Engl.*] (–) circus.

sarara* (–) *see* **salala.**

1**sare** (–) the incision made in the ritual of blood brotherhood.

2**sare** (–) *sport* draw, tie.

3**sare** *adv.* at the same time, simultaneously. (= 2**sululu.**)

4**sare** (–) 1. (= **jina la –**) the name given to a child immediately after birth. 2. nickname.

sari* [*Ind.*] sari (woman's garment).

sarifa* (–) *see* **sarafu.**

[1]**sarifu*, serifu** 1. exchange money. 2. arrange, put in order; have a good command of a language. **– maneno (mwandiko) kwa uzuri.** speak (write) correctly/well. *Cf.* **sarafu.**

[2]**sarifu*** (–) *see* **sarafu.**

sarufi* (–) grammar. **kitabu cha –.** a grammar (book).

sarufu* (–) *see* **sarafu.**

[1]**saruji*, seruji** (–) 1. cement, concrete. **tia –.** to cement (a floor). 2. rubble.

[2]**saruji*, seruji** (–) saddle.

sasa* 1. *adv.* now, at present, nowadays. **– hivi.** at once, immediately; now. **–a –** *or* **–a kisasa.** modern, up-to-date, fashionable. 2. *interj. of surprise* Well, what do you know? *Cf.* **kisasa.**

sataranji* (–) 1. chess. 2. a kind of sleeping-mat.

satini* (–) satini (kind of cloth).

satua* [?] (–) *rare* possibility, chance.

saujika* *see* **sawajika.**

[1]**saumu*, tumu** 1.(–) *Isl.* fasting. 2. to fast.

[2]**saumu, samu, thumu, tumu** (–): **kitunguu –.** garlic.

sauti* (–) 1. voice, sound, noise. **– moja.** unanimity; *(mus.)* unison. **– ya kiume.** deep (male) voice. **– ya kitoto.** high (treble, soprano) voice. **kwa – kubwa.** in a loud voice. **paza –.** raise the voice. 2. *fig., parl.* vote. **tutawapa – wanachama wa chama chetu.** We will give our vote to the members of our party. *fig.* **– ya Tanganyika.** The Voice of Tanganyika (the radio company).

sawa* 1. (–) 1. likeness, similarity. 2. (–) *geogr.* plain. 3. *adj.* alike, the same, similar, equal; right, exact; fair, just, impartial. 4. *adj.* level, flat, straight. **nchi –.** flat country. 5. *adv.* (*also* **sawasawa**) equally, fairly, (just) the same, exactly. **fanya –.** make even, equalize; act fairly. **gawia –.** divide into equal parts. **saa hii inakwenda –.** This watch is running right. **mtoto huyu na baba yake ni –.** This child resembles his father. *coll.:* **– kama sahani na kawa.** getting on together like a dish and its cover. *Cf.* **sawia, sawazisha, kisawazisha, usawa, usawanisho.**

sawadi* (–) *see* **zawadi.**

sawajika*, saujika 1. be exhausted/debilitated/emaciated *(from illness, hunger).* 2. be disfigured/crippled.

sawanyisha* *see* **sawazisha.**

sawasawa* *see* **sawa 3.**

sawazisha* (*rare* **sawanyisha**) make even, equal, similar; compare. *Cf.* **sawa, kisawazisha.**

sawia* *adv.* then, at that time; at that very time/moment. **naye akafika —.** He arrived too at that very time. *Cf.* **sawa.**

sawidi* make black; *(fig.)* calumniate, slander, besmirch.

sawiri* form, shape; draw a picture.

sayansi* [*Engl.*] (–) science.

sayari* (–) *astr.* planet.

sayidi* **(ma-)** *see* **saidi.**

saza* *caus. of* ²**saa.**

sazo **(ma-)** *see* **masaa.**

sebeha* *rare* to breakfast.

sebule* (–) reception room, antechamber, hall, porch.

sebusebu* refuse, reject (unwillingly, regretfully); relinquish, forgo.

sedeka*, seteka be long/protracted *(of an illness).*

sefu* [*Engl.*] (–) 1. safe. 2. refrigerator.

sefule!* *interj. see* ¹**kefu.**

¹**sega** **(ma-)** (*us. pl.*) honeycomb.

²**sega** lift, turn up *(skirt, trousers, to keep them clean).* **— nguo.** tuck up a dress. *appl.* **segea.** *intr.* **segeka.**

segele, shegele (–) string of beads worn around the loins by children. *Cf.* **kondavi.**

segua *see* **sekua.**

sehelea *see* ¹**selea.**

sehemu* (–) 1. part, share. **— ya mwenzangu.** my friend's share. 2. fraction, instalment. **— ya kumi.** a tenth. **— za kumi.** tenths, decimals. **— za mia.** hundredths, percentages. 3. section, paragraph. 4. *mil.* unit, detachment. 5.: **— ya mtambo.** part/element of a machine. 6. region, district. **— inayojitawala wenyewe.** autonomous region. *Cf.* **kijisehemu.**

sekeneka be infected *(by syphilis),* waste away. *Cf.* **sekeneko.**

sekeneko (–) *rare, med.* syphilis. (= **kaswende.**) *Cf.* **sekeneka.**

sekini, sakini (–) *eth.* sekini (shaving the head so that only a tuft or strip is left in the middle).

sekua, segua push, shove (along, aside).

sekunde* (–) *see* **sekundi.**

sekundi*, **sekunde** [*Engl.*] second *(of time).*

selaha* (–) *see* **silaha.**

Selani* [*Engl.*] Ceylon.

[1]**selea**, **sehelea** (& *appl.* **selelea**) 1. stay, continue to live in (a place that one visits and finds attractive), join (a new group). 2. be attracted/attached to something.

[2]**selea** (–) *see* **seleha.**

seleha, **selea** (–) seleha (a red glass bead).

selehi* *see* **suluhi.**

selo* [*Engl.* Sail ho!] (–) signal *(of arrival or departure of a ship/train).* – **ya kuingia haijapanda.** The signal of arrival has not yet been given.

sema 1. speak, talk, say. – **na...** speak with... 2. *rare* converse; tell, narrate. *appl.* **semea.** *intr.* **semeka** (*or intr.-ass.* **semekana**). be pronounceable; be said/reported to; be usual/customary. *fig.* **hasara iliyopatikana haisemeki.** The loss incurred is tremendous (*lit.:* unspeakable). **inasemekana ya kuwa haji tena.** It is said (= it is probable) that he will no longer come. *caus.* **semesha, semeza.** *ass.* **semana.** scold/abuse each other, speak ill of each other. *Cf.* **semezano, msemaji, msemo, usemaji, usemi.**

sembuse *conj. & adv.* apart from, not to mention, to say nothing of, let alone. **Senti moja sikupi sembuse shilingi.** I will not give you a single cent, let alone (much less, to say nothing of) a shilling.

semezano (ma-) *rare* conversation. *Cf.* **sema.**

semifainali* [*Engl.*] (–) *sport* semifinal.

semsem*, **simsim** (–) sesame. (= **ufuta** 1.)

sena (–) 1. sena (kind of sugarcane). 2. sena (kind of sweet potato). 3. sena (kind of rice).

sene* (–) *see* **sanati.**

senea be dull/blunt *(of a knife, etc.).* *caus.* **seneza, seza.** make dull; smooth *(with an adze).* *Cf.* **senezo.**

seneta* [*Engl.*] (ma-) senator.

seneza *caus. of* **senea.**

senezo, sezo *rare* adze. *Cf.* **senea.**

senge* *coll., adj.* 1. unmarried. 2. homosexual.

seng'enge (–) (iron) wire. – **yenye miiba.** barbed wire.

sengenya 1. slander, calumniate, speak ill of someone. 2. abuse, insult, deride. *ass.* **sengenyana.** *Cf.* **masengenyo, msengenyaji, msengenyano, msengenyi, msengenyo.**

senta* [*Engl.*] (–) *sport* center *(football); also geom.* **– ya pembetatu.** center of a triangle. **enye – moja.** concentric. **duara zenye – moja.** concentric circles.

senti* [*Engl.*] (–) cent. **leo sina –.** Today I don't have a cent.

senturi* (–) *see* **santuri.**

seperuka *see* **sepetuka.**

sepeto* [*Engl.*] (–) spade, shovel.

sepetuka, seperuka reel, stagger; stumble, trip, slip.

Septemba* [*Engl.*] September.

[1]**sera*** (–) fort, fortification.

[2]**sera** (–) beeswax.

serahangi*, serangi, serehangi [*Pers.*] (ma-) *naut.* 1. boatswain, mate. 2. foreman *(of dock workers).*

serangi* (ma-) *see* **serahangi.**

seredani* [*Pers.*] (–) (charcoal) brazier.

serehangi* (ma-) *see* **serahangi.**

seremala*, sermala (ma-) carpenter, cabinet-maker, joiner. *Cf.* **useremala.**

serifu* *see* [1]**sarifu.**

serikali* [*Pers.*] (–) 1. government, (public) authority. **– ya mseto.** coalition government. **– ya kibeberu, – ya nguvu.** dictatorship. *prov.* **– ina mkono mrefu.** The government has a long arm. 2. administration. **amri ya –.** a directive of the administrative officials. **jimbo lenye – yake.** autonomous territory/region. *Cf.* **kiserikali.**

sermala* (ma-) *see* **seremala.**

seruji* (ma-) *see* [1]**saruji,** [2]**saruji.**

sesere (–) *see* **mwanasesere.**

sesereka, seseteka, sesetuka reel, stagger.

seseteka *see* **sesereka.**

sesetuka *see* **sesereka.**

seta 1. crush, squeeze, mash. 2. shove, crowd, jostle. *appl.* **setea.** *intr.* **seteka.** *caus.* **setesha.** *Cf.* **mseto.**

seteka* *see* **sedeka.**

[1]**seti*** [*Port.*] (–) *cards* seven.

[2]**seti*** (–) *coll.* a wealthy Indian.

[3]**seti*** [*Engl.*] (–) set *(of something).*

setiri* *see* **stiri.**

setla* [*Engl.*] (ma-) settler.

seyyedia* *adj.* lordly, grand. *Cf.* **saidi.**

Seyyid* title of the Sultan of Zanzibar. *Cf.* **saidi.**

seyyida*, saada *hist., liter. (in direct address)* lady, mistress. *Cf.* **saidi.**

seza (= **seneza**) *caus. of* **senea.**

[1]**sezo (ma-)** *see* **senezo.**

[2]**sezo (ma-)** *see* [1]**tezo.**

shaabani* (–) *see* **shabani.**

shaba* (–): **– nyekundu.** copper. **– nyeupe.** brass. *prov.* **wengine – huidhani dhahabu.** Many people mistake brass for gold.

shababi* (–) youth, young man. *Cf.* **ushababi.**

shababu* (–) storm.

[1]**shabaha*** 1. (–) similarity, resemblance. 2. *adv.* like, same as. **mtunda – embe.** a fruit like/resembling the mango. *Cf.* **shabihi, mshabaha.**

[2]**shabaha*** (–) mark, target. **pata –.** hit the mark. **twaa (piga, shika) –.** aim, take aim, sight. **ana – sana.** He is a good shot.

[1]**shabaki*** (–) fishing-net, weir-basket.

[2]**shabaki*, shabuka** (–) 1. a quarrelsome/deceitful person. 2. (*us.* **shabuka**) exaggeration, excess. **kila neno kwake ni –.** He makes much of every trifle. 3. trap, snare; trick. *Cf.* **ushabaki.**

shabani*, shaabani 1. eighth month of the Muhammadan year *(preceding Ramadhan).* 2. *pr. n. masc.*

shabihi* 1. (–) (external) appearance, behavior. 2. *adv.* = [1]**shabaha** 2. 3. (*also ass.* **shabihiana**) be like/similar, resemble. **mtoto huyu amemshabihi** (*or* **anashabihiana na**) **mama yake sana.** This child greatly resembles his mother. *Cf.* [1]**shabaha.**

shabu* (–) alum.

shabuka* (–) *see* [2]**shabaki.**

shada* (–, ma-) 1. bunch, cluster. **– la maua.** a bunch of flowers, bouquet. **– la nywele.** a tuft of hair *(tied up at the back of the head).* 2. string *(of beads, etc.),* necklace. **– la ushanga.** a pearl necklace. 3. tassel, fringe. 4. kite *(a child's toy).*

shafaka* (–) *see* **shufaka.**

shaghala*, baghala [?] *adv.* at random, haphazardly, indiscriminately, any old way.

shaha*, sheha, shehe (ma-) 1. chief, leader. 2. minstrel, storyteller, composer of ballads. 3. king *(chess).* *Cf.* **sheikh, usheha.**

shahada* (–) 1. obligation, liability. 2. *Isl.* shahada (the Moslem confession of faith).

3. covenant, testament. 4. testimony, evidence. 5. certificate, diploma, document. *Cf.* **shahidi, shuhuda, shuhudu, ushahidi.**

shahamu* (–) (animal) fat, grease, lard, tallow.

shahara* (–) *rare* *see* **mshahara.**

shahawa* (–) *phy.* semen, sperm. (= **manii.**)

shahidi* (ma-) 1. witness, guarantor. 2. (– **wa dini**) martyr. *Cf.* **shahada, ushahidi.**

shaibu* (–) old man/woman.

shairi* (ma-) 1. poem, line of poetry, verse, rhyme. 2.: **mashairi.** poetry, versification. **tunga mashairi.** write poetry. *Cf.* **mshairi, ushairi.**

shaitani* (–) *see* **shetani.**

shajara* [?] (–) (pocket) diary, notebook.

shaka* (ma-) 1. doubt, uncertainty. **wa na –.** be in doubt, be perplexed. **bila –.** doubtless. 2. difficulty, concern, uneasiness. **amekutana na mashaka.** He had a series of problems to solve. *Cf.* **shakawa, shake, shuku, mashaka, mushkeli.**

shakawa* (–) difficulty, problem, anxiety. *Cf.* **shaka.**

shake* (ma-) grief, misery. **ingiwa na – la kulia.** weep and sob. *Cf.* **shaka.**

shakevale (–) shakevale (species of hawk). *Cf.* **hajivale.**

shakiri* be satisfied/sated. *Cf.* **shukuru.**

shakwe (ma-) *ornith.* gull, tern.

shalaka* (–) 1. loop, noose. 2. hole in the gunwale of a boat holding a loop of rope serving as an oarlock. *See also* **kishwara.** *Cf.* **shaliki.**

shali* (–) shawl.

shaliki* tie/fasten loosely, tie in a bow. *Cf.* **shalaka.**

Sham* Syria. **bahari ya –.** the Red Sea. **reali ya –.** Maria Theresa dollar.

shamari* (–) *bot.* fennel.

shamasi*, shemasi (ma-) 1. *rel.* deacon. 2. an older person (not necessarily a clergyman) who gives advice on religious matters. *Cf.* **ushamasi.**

shamba* [*prob.* < *Fr.* champ] (ma-) 1. (cultivated) field, plantation, garden, farm. **– la Mungu.** cemetery. 2. country *(as opp. to town).* **nakaa –** (*or* **mashamba**). I live in the country. **watu wa –.** country folk. **–a mashamba.** rustic, countrified, rough (= **–a kishamba, –a kimashamba**).

shambiro* *adv.* for common use, without regulation or restriction.

shambulia attack (suddenly), invade; bombard. *ass.* **shambuliana.** attack each other. *pass.* **shambuliwa.** *Cf.* **shambulio, ushambulizi, kutoshambulia.**

shambulio **(ma-)** (sudden) attack, raid, invasion. *Cf.* **shambulia.**

shamili* **(ma-)** earring, pendant.

shamiri* 1. load a gun. 2. fit together *(in carpentry, cabinetmaking).*

shamrashamra hustle and bustle.

shamua, chemua sneeze, snort. *appl.* **shamulia.** *caus.* **shamulisha.**

shanda* **(–)** *see* **sanda.**

shanga *pl. of* **ushanga.**

shangaa, sangaa 1. stare. 2. be astonished/amazed/dumbfounded/perplexed/stupefied/shocked. 3. be thrilled/enraptured/filled with enthusiasm. 4. admire. *caus.* **shangaza, sangaza.** astonish/confuse someone. *Cf.* **mshangao.**

shangama **(–)** shangama (short-sleeved shirt).

shangaza *caus. of* **shangaa.**

shangazi **(ma-)** 1. paternal aunt, sister of one's father. 2. aunt *(in gen).*

shangilia, shangalia receive *(with joy, enthusiasm),* greet, welcome, congratulate. **wamemshangalia.** they received/greeted him joyfully. *pass.* **shangiliwa.** be given a festive reception. *Cf.* **shangilio.**

shangilio **(ma-)** *rare* rejoicing, festive reception, ovation; congratulations. *Cf.* **shangilia.**

shangwe **(–)** 1. rejoicing, ovation. **walimpokea kwa –.** They greeted him joyfully. 2. festivity; hubbub, commotion. **arusi hii haina –.** This wedding was quiet (without commotion).

shani* **(–)** 1. (rare, unexpected) occurrence, event. 2. marvel, novelty, curiosity, adventure. 3. mishap, accident, catastrophe. 4. important/notable event. **karamu hii imetia – kuliko ile ya jana.** This party was a more notable event than the one of yesterday.

shanjari* *see* **sanjari.**

shanta* **(–)** knapsack.

shanuo **(–)** *see* **chanuo.**

shapa **(ma-)** raft, ferry. **– la nyuki.** honeycomb.

shapo **(ma-)** *see* **mashapo.**

sharabeti*, sherbeti, shebeti, sharubati **(–)** sherbet, syrup; soft drink, soda water. *Cf.* **sharabu.**

sharabu* 1. drink (alcoholic beverages). 2. **(–)** alcoholic/intoxicating beverage. *Cf.* **sharabeti.**

sharaf* *sing.* honor, status.

sharafa*, sarafa (ma-): – **la ndevu** *or* **ndevu za –.** a long, flowing beard.

[1]**shari*** 1. (–) malice, hatred, spite; harm, mischief, bad luck, disaster. **taka –.** defy, challenge. 2. (–) misery, distress, illness, poverty. 3. *adj.* evil, malicious; miserable; bad, depraved *(of character). Cf.* **mshari.**

[2]**shari*** (–) watch spring. (= **kamani.**)

sharia* (–) *see* **sheria.**

sharifu*, sherifu 1. treat respectfully, respect, regard. 2. (ma-) a respected person. 3. *adj.* respectable, honorable, highly regarded/ esteemed, excellent. *Cf.* **kisharifu, msharafu, usharifu.**

sharika* (ma-) *see* **shirika.**

shariki* *see* **shiriki.**

shariti* lie; twist, distort; evade, make excuses, talk oneself out of something.

sharti*, shurti, shuruti, sherti (ma-) 1. necessity, obligation. – **uje (kuja).** You must come. 2. (*us.* **masharti**) stipulations, terms, conditions; binding agreement, contract. **kwa –.** by agreement, as stipulated. **fanya –.** make an agreement, conclude a contract. *pol.* **masharti ya chama.** statutes of a party/organization. 3. bet, wager, stake. *Cf.* **shuruti.**

sharubati* (–) *see* **sharabeti.**

sharubu*, shuarub, shuarubu (ma-) moustache.

shashi*, chachi (–) 1. thin, white muslin; gauze. 2.: **karatasi ya –.** tissue paper.

shashimamishi* *adj.* proud, arrogant, contemptuous, conceited.

shasira* (ma-) *see* **shazia.**

shata* (ma-) *(us. pl.)* shata (the solids remaining after coconut meat has been boiled to produce oil).

shati* [*Engl.*] (ma-) shirt, blouse.

shatoruma* [*Pers.*] (–) a broad sash or shawl worn around the waist.

shau* *see* **shaua, shaufu.**

shaua*, shau 1. be pleasing, arouse (unsatisfied) desire. 2. deceive, delude, disappoint. *appl.* **shaulia.** *intr.* **shauka.** *caus.* **shausha.** *Cf.* **shaufu, kishaufu, mshaufu, ushaufu.**

shaufu*, shau *adj.* delusive, pretentious, showy; frivolous, of easy morals. *Cf.* **shaua, mshaufu, ushaufu.**

shauku* (–) desire, longing, passion; eagerness, impatience. **ana – nao.** He longs for them. – **ya michezo.** a passion for sports. *Cf.* **ashiki.**

shauri* (–) 1. advice, suggestion. **uliza –.** ask for advice. **toa –.** give (a piece of) advice. 2. intention, plan, project; problem *(on which one needs advice).* **una –?** Do you have a problem? – **yako.** It is your affair/ business. **mwenye –.** a helpless person *(who constantly needs the advice of others).* 3. discussion, debate, negotiations. 4. opinion, voice *(in a matter).* 5. telephone conversation. **– moja, kwa –.** unanimously. 6. *v.* take counsel, consult, confer; ask for advice. *appl.* **shauria.** *caus.* **shaurisha, shauriza.** *ass.* **shauriana.** *Cf.* **mshauri, halmashauri.**

1shaushi* [*Turk.*] (ma-) *mil.* noncommissioned officer, corporal.

2shaushi* *see* **shawishi.**

shauwa* *see* **shawali.**

shavu (*rare* **chavu, chafu**) (ma-): **– la uso.** cheek. **– la mkono.** biceps. **– la mguu.** calf *(of the leg).* **– la samaki.** gill *(of a fish).* **– la jogoo.** wattles *(of a cock).*

shawali*, shauwi (–) tenth month of the Muhammadan year.

shawishi*, shaushi 1. entice, lure, tempt. 2. persuade, talk someone into something. 3. *pol.* agitate. *appl.* **shawishia.** *intr.* **shawishika.** *caus.* **shawishisha.** 4. (ma-) temptation, enticement, persuasion. *Cf.* **kishawishi, mshawishi, ushawishi.**

shayiri* *sing.* barley.

shaza* (–) *see* **chaza.**

shazasi* (–) sal ammoniac.

shazi* (ma-), **kishazi** (vi-) bunch, cluster *(of fruit);* string *(of fish).*

shazia* (ma-) (large) needle, bodkin *(used in making mats).*

shebeti* (–) *see* **sharabeti.**

shegele (–) *see* **segele.**

sheha* (ma-) *see* **shaha.**

shehe* (ma-) *see* **sheikh, shaha.**

shehena* (–) freight, cargo. *Cf.* **sheheni.**

sheheni* be loaded, have cargo (on board). *Cf.* **shehena.**

sheikh*, shehe, shekhe, sheki (ma-) important/ influential person, leader, chief, ruler.

sheitani* (ma-) *see* **shetani.**

shekhe* (ma-) *see* **sheikh.**

sheki* (ma-) *see* **sheikh.**

1shela* (ma-) shela (black veil worn by Arab women).

2shela* (–) shela (sword dance).

shelabela* *adv.* indiscriminately; *(of merchandise)* as a lot, 'as is.'

sheleli* *rare* sew, stitch. (= **shona.**)

shemali* (–) *liter.* 1. left hand. 2. north, north-wind.

shemasi* (ma-) *see* **shamasi.**

shembea* (–) knife with a curved blade. (= **jambia.**)

shemeji* (–) relative by marriage, brother/sister-in-law.

shemeri* (–) nose ring *(for cattle).*

shemshi*, shumusi (–) *rare* sun. (= **jua.**)

shenga *see* **¹chenga.**

shenzi* [*Pers.*] *adj.* savage, barbarous, uncouth, uncivilized, ill-mannered; pagan, heathen. *Cf.* **kishenzi, mshenzi, ushenzi.**

sherbeti* (–) *see* **sharabeti.**

shere* (–) *see* **sheri.**

sherehe* (–) 1. rejoicing, merriment. 2. celebration, ceremony, festival. 3. pomp, magnificence, display. *Cf.* **sherehekea.**

sherehekea* celebrate. *Cf.* **sherehe.**

sheresi* (–) *see* **sherisi.**

sheri*, shere (–) joke, fun; derision, mockery. **cheza/fanya –.** joke; mock, ridicule, deride.

sheria*, sharia (–) 1. law, prescription, regulation. **– na utengamano.** law and order. **baraza la kufanya –.** legislative body. **– haina kwao.** The law knows no favorites (*lit.:* has no home). 2. legal proceedings, justice. *loc.* **sheriani.** (law) court. **peleka sheriani.** prosecute. **mwana –.** lawyer. 3. *pol.* constitution. **– ya jamhuri.** republican constitution. 4.: **–a (ki)sheria.** *adj.* legal.

sherifu* *see* **sharifu.**

sherisi*, sherizi, sheresi (–) glue.

sherizi* (–) *see* **sherisi.**

sherti* (–) *see* **sharti.**

sheshe (–) beauty. **– ya nchi.** the beauty of the country.

shetani*, sheitani, shaitani (ma-) *rel.* devil, demon, supernatural power. **punga –.** exorcise.

shetri* (–) *naut.* stern, poop.

shiba* 1. be satisfied/sated/appeased. **utashiba chakula hiki?** Will this be enough for you to eat? **mimi ninashiba nikila viazi.** When I eat potatoes I am satisfied. 2. *fig.* be filled with/absorbed in *(a subject, etc.).* **– masomo.** be absorbed in one's studies. *appl.* **shibia.** *caus.* **shibisha.** satisfy/sate someone; *(fig.)* fill someone with enthusiasm. *Cf.* **shibe.**

shibe* *sing.* 1. satisfaction, satiation. 2. appeasement *(of hunger, thirst).* *Cf.* **shiba.**

shibiri*, shubiri (–) shibiri (unit of length, span; about 9 inches).

shida* (–, ma-) 1. trouble, hardship, distress, difficulty. **patwa na (wa na, ingia) –.** have trouble/difficulty. **kwa –.** with difficulty. 2. lack, scarcity, shortage. **ni – kumwona.** He is rarely to be seen. **chuma ni –.** There is a shortage of iron. **kwa –.** seldom, rarely.

shifta* [*Engl.*] (–) shifter (member of a troublesome nomadic group in Kenya).

shige (–): – **la manjano.** *ornith.* Pemba white-eye.

shika 1. grasp, seize, hold on to, keep; *(mil.)* occupy (= **shikilia,** *below*). 2. follow, observe, comply with. – **sheria (desturi).** observe the law (custom). 3. persist in, insist on. – **bei.** insist on a price, bargain, haggle. – **njia.** follow a road, hold to an established course. 4. hold, carry on (= do, make something). – **mazungumzo.** carry on a conversation. – **miguu ya...** greet someone (respectfully). *appl.* **shikia.** *double appl.* **shikilia.** hold onto *(stubbornly, resolutely),* keep permanently, occupy. *intr.* **shikika.** *prov.* **maji hayashikiki.** Water cannot be held fast. *caus.* **shikisha, shikiza. shikisha mkono.** guide the hand *(e.g., of a child learning to write). ass.* **shikana.** 1. be good friends. 2. wrestle with each other. *stat.* **shikama.** *stat.-ass.* **shikamana.** stick tight, form a bond, set *(of mortar, etc.). stat.-ass.-caus.* **shikamanisha.** join *(firmly),* fasten together. *pass.* **shikwa.** be grasped/seized. **shikwa na homa.** have a fever. **shikwa na hofu.** be seized by terror, be afraid. **shikwa na kazi.** be very busy. *Cf.* **shikamuu, shikio, shikizo, kishika, kishikizo, kishiko, mshika, mshikano, mshiikilizo, ushikimano.**

shikamoo, shikamu *see* **shikamuu.**

shikamuu, shikamu, shikamoo *formula of salutation, lit.* I grasp (your) feet *(orig. used only by young people to older persons or, in general, in addressing an elder or chief). Cf.* **shika.**

shikilia *double appl. of* **shika.**

shikio (ma-) 1. handle. **mashikio ya chungu.** the handles of a pot. 2. *naut.* rudder. *Cf.* **shika.**

shikizo (ma-) 1. support, prop, post. 2. tack(ing stitch) *(in sewing). Cf.* **shika.**

shiku (ma-) *augment. of* **kishiku.**

shilamu* [*Ind.*] (–) stem of a hookah.

shilingi* [*Engl.*] (–) shilling.

shimbi, simbi (–, ma-) lees of palm-wine *(used as yeast).*

shimbika tie, fasten *(a fishhook to a line). caus.* **shimbikisha, shimbisha.** *Cf.* **shimbiko.**

shimbiko (ma-) 1. act of fastening a hook to a line. 2. thread used for this purpose. *Cf.* **shimbika.**

shime! *interj. of encouragement to increased effort.* **haya –, tusaidiane.** Come on now, let's all pull together!

shimiri*, simiri fit, be suitable/useful. **mavazi yake hayamshimiri.** His clothes do not fit/become him.

shimo (ma-) 1. hole, cavity, rut; hollow, depression, cave, excavation. – **la sahani.** the hollow of a plate. 2. pit, trench; tunnel. 3. shaft, well, mine. – **la almasi (dhahabu).** diamond (gold) mine. – **la kaa.** vertical shaft *(mining).*

[1]**shina** (ma-) (*also* **kishina, vi-**) 1. tree-trunk *(from root to top).* 2. *fig.* source, origin.

[2]**shina** (ma-) *agr.* hole for planting seed.

[1]**shinda** 1. conquer, overcome, overpower, subdue. – **adui.** conquer the enemy. 2. outdo, surpass, be better than. – **mtihani.** pass an examination. **yule mrefu kushinda mimi.** He is taller than I. **kushinda jana.** day before yesterday. 3. win. – **mchezo.** win a game. 4. bear, endure. – **maumivu.** endure pain. 5. be left, remain. **anashinda nyumbani.** He is always at home/is a stay-at-home. *appl.* **shindia.** *double appl.* **shindilia.** press (down). **shindilia nguo sandukuni.** pack clothes in a chest. **sindilia chakula kinywani.** stuff food into one's mouth. **shindilia bunduki.** load a gun. *intr.* **shindika, sindika.** 1. be defeated/overpowered/subjugated. 2. *(trans.)* do something forcibly, apply force to something. **shindika miwa.** press/crush sugarcane. 3. feign, sham. *intr.-int.* **shindikiza, sindikiza.** 1. = **shindika.** 2. see a guest to the door (or go part of the way with him). *caus.* **shindisha, shindiza.** 1. cause/help to conquer (excel, win). 2. cause to remain, take in a guest/lodger; hinder, impede. *caus-intr.* **shindizika.** be hindered/impeded; be blunted *(of a tool).* *ass.* **shindana.** 1. try to defeat each other, fight. 2. dispute, fall out with each other. 3. compete, contend. **shindana mpira.** settle a football contest. **shindana sawasawa.** be well/evenly matched. *ass.-appl.* **shindania.** strive/struggle for something. **shindania fedha.** haggle over a price. *stat.* **shindama.** *rare, us. stat.-ass.* **shindamana.** be firmly pressed/packed together, be compact. *pass.* **shindwa.** be defeated/outdone, capitulate. **shindwa na mzigo mzito.** be overloaded, try to carry too heavy a load (*lit.:* be defeated by a heavy burden). **shindwa na lugha.** be defeated by a language (admit that it is too much for one). *inv.* **shindua, sindua.** release pressure; open; be open to *(arguments, persuasion);* reveal, give vent to. **shindua maneno.** give vent to utterances, argue, persuade. *inv.-appl.* **shindulia.** *inv.-intr.* **shinduka.** **maji yameshinduka.** The flood has receded. *Cf.* [2]**shinda, shindani,** [1]**shindano, shindikizo, shindo, kishinda, kishindo, mshinda, mshindaji, mshindani, mshindikizo, mshindilio, mshindio, mshindo, mshindwa, msindikizo, ushinda, ushindani, ushinde, ushindi, ushindwaji.**

[2]**shinda** (ma-, –) remainder, residue. – **la kinu.** residue in a mortar. *Cf.* [1]**shinda.**

shindama *stat. of* [1]**shinda.**

shindamana *stat.-ass. of* [1]**shinda.**

shindani *adj.* competitive, contentious, hostile. *Cf.* [1]**shinda.**

shindania *ass.-appl. of* [1]**shinda.**

[1]**shindano** (ma-) (*us.* **mashindano;** *also* **mshindano, mi-**) competition, contest; comparison. – **ya mpira.** football match. *Cf.* [1]**shinda.**

[2]**shindano** (ma-) *see* [1]**sindano.**

shindikiza *intr.-int. of* [1]**shinda.**

shindikizo, sindikizo (ma-) 1. (act of) pressing, pressure. 2. press, mill *(for pressing oil, fruit, etc.).* 3. **sindikizo:** escorting, accompanying *(a departing guest).* *Cf.* [1]**shinda,** [2]**sindikiza.**

shindilia *double appl. of* [1]**shinda.**

shindiza *caus. of* [1]**shinda.**

shindizika *caus.-intr. of* [1]**shinda.**

shindo (ma-): enda kwa – (*or* **mashindo).** trot *(of horses). Cf.* [1]**shinda, mshindo.**

shindua *inv. of* **shinda.**

shingo (–, ma-) neck. *fig., geogr.* **– la nchi.** isthmus. **mwenye – ngumu.** a stiff-necked/ stubborn person.

shinikiza, sinikiza press, crush, pulverize. (= **shindikiza** 1. *Cf.* [1]**shinda.**) *appl.* **shinikizia.**

shinikizo, sinikizo (ma-) 1. (act of) pressing, crushing. 2. press, mill. (= **shindikizo.** *Cf.* [1]**shinda.**)

shira* **(–)** *rare* sail. (= [2]**tanga.**)

shiraa* **(–)** *astron.* Sirius.

shirika*, sharika 1. **(ma-)** partnership, community of interests, cooperation; organization. **mali yetu ni –.** We own our property jointly. **fanya –.** do something in common, go shares. 2. **(ma-)** share. **tia –.** share, divide up. 3. *adv.* in common, jointly, together. *Cf.* **shiriki.**

shiriki*, shariki 1. participate, have a part in; be partners, act in common. 2. be associated, unite, combine, join. **– katika biashara.** combine for business purposes. 3. be devoted/ addicted to. **– ulevi.** be addicted to drink. **– kazi.** be heart and soul in one's work. **– karata.** be a confirmed cardplayer. **– sanamu.** *rel.* worship an idol. *appl.* **shirikia.** *intr.* **shirikika.** *caus.* **shirikisha, shirikiza.** give someone a share in something, allow to participate, make a member of a society. *ass.* **shirikiana.** be partners together, cooperate, join forces; be jointly responsible/ liable. *Cf.* **shirika, shirikisho, mshirika, mshirikina, ushirika, ushirikina.**

shirikisho* **(ma-)** union, federation, association. **– la Ulimwengu la Vijana wa Kidemokrasi.** World Federation of Democratic Youth. **– la Ulimwengu la Wanawake wa Kidemokrasi.** Women's International Democratic Federation. **soko la –.** common market. *Cf.* **shiriki.**

shisha* **(–)** hourglass.

shitaka* **(ma-)** *see* **mashtaka.**

shitaki* *see* **shtaki.**

[1]**shiti*** **(ma-)** cotton print (cloth).

[2]**shiti*** [*Engl.*] **(–, ma-)** (bed)sheet.

shitua* *see* **shtua.**

shituko* **(ma-)** *see* **shtuko.**

shoga* **(ma-, –)** 1. a woman (or older girl) who instructs a girl who has reached the age of puberty. 2. term of endearment used between women. 3. an impotent man who acts as a servant to women. 4. catamite. *Cf.* **ushoga.**

shogi*, **sogi** (ma-) saddlebag, packsaddle.

shogoa* (–) *see* **shokoa.**

shoka, choka (ma-) ax.

shokishoki (ma-) shokishoki (fruit of the mshokishoki, *q.v.*).

shokoa*, **shogoa** [*Pers.*] (–) 1. compulsory labor. 2. compulsory military service, universal conscription, draft. **kamatwa –.** be subject to forced labor/military service.

shombo (–) (natural, sharp) odor of fresh fish. *Cf.* **vumba.**

shomoro (–) *ornith.* shomoro (bird similar to the sparrow).

shona sew, stitch. *appl.* **shonea. sindano ya kushonea.** sewing-needle. *intr.* **shoneka.** *caus.* **shonesha.** have sewn, have (clothes) made. **shonesha nguo.** have clothes made. *inv.* **shonoa.** unsew, undo, take out stitches, unravel. *inv.-appl.* **shonolea.** *inv.-intr.* **shonoka.** *inv.-caus.* **shonosha.** *Cf.* **mashono, mshona, mshoni, mshono, shono, ushoni, ushono.**

[1]**shonde** (ma-) 1. dung *(of animals)*, manure. 2. (cake of) dried dung *(used for fuel)*.

[2]**shonde** (–) grudge, resentment, vindictiveness. **ingawa tumegombana usiniwekee –.** Even though we have quarrelled, don't be vindictive/don't hold a grudge against me.

shonesha *caus. of* **shona.**

shonga (ma-) persuasion, seduction, incitement, enticement. *Cf.* **mshongo.**

shoni (ma-) *see* **shono.**

shono, shoni (ma-) (*us.* **mashono**) 1. (act/method of) sewing. 2. sewing equipment. *Cf.* **shona.**

shonoa *inv. of* **shona.**

shonoka *inv.-intr. of* **shona.**

shonolea *inv.-appl. of* **shona.**

shonosha *inv.-caus. of* **shona.**

shore (–) *ornith.* (species of) bulbul. **– kishungi.** paradise flycatcher. **– wanda.** (species of) sparrow.

shoroba* (ma-) (*augment. of* **kishoroba**) path, passage.

shoti* (–) gallop. **enda (piga) –.** to gallop.

shoto 1. (ma-) left hand/side; left-handedness. **mwenye –.** left-handed person. 2. (*also* **shotoshoto**) *adv.* in a left-handed way, awkwardly, backwards. **anafanya kazi –.** He does his work clumsily.

shtaka* (ma-) *see* **mashtaka.**

shtaki*, **shitaki** 1. make a complaint, blame, accuse. 2. *jur.* charge, sue, bring action against. *appl.* **shtakia.** *intr.* **shtakika.** *caus.* **shtakisha, shtakiza.** *refl.* **jishtaki.** accuse/blame oneself. *refl.-appl.* **jishtakia.** complain about someone. *Cf.* **mashtaka, mshtaka, mshtaki, mshtakiwa, ushtaki.**

shtiri* make the final (successful) bid *(at an auction). Cf.* **rasimu.**

shtua, shitua, stua 1. move suddenly/violently; *(fig.)* wrench, sprain. – **mguu.** sprain one's foot. 2. surprise, startle, shock. 3. remove quickly. – **chungu.** take a pot off the fire (to keep the contents from burning). 4. *elec.* receive a shock. *appl.* **shtulia.** *intr.* **shtuka.** 1. be alarmed/startled. 2. be sprained. *caus.* **shtusha.** *Cf.* **shtuko, mshtuko, mshtuo;** *also* **jituka** (?).

shtuka *intr. of* **shtua.**

shtuko, shituko (ma-) jerk, twitch, shudder; *(elec.)* shock. *Cf.* **shtua.**

shtusha* *caus. of* **shtua.**

shua lower, let down *(e.g., a boat into the water). appl.* **shulia.** *intr.* **shuka** *(often w. inv. & int. force).* 1. disembark, land; alight, get out. **shuka motokaa.** get out of an automobile. 2. fall (to the ground), collapse. 3. be steep/precipitous. 4. be humbled/humiliated/depressed. *intr.-appl.* **shukia.** get down from/out of something. *caus.* **shusha** (& *caus.-appl.* **shushia**). 1. lower, bring/take down, discharge *(cargo, etc.).* **shusha bendere.** haul down a flag. 2. have an orgasm *(in coitus).* 3. *av.* land. *Cf.* **mshuko, mshusho.**

shuarub*, shuarubu (ma-) *see* **sharabu.**

shubaka* (ma-), kishubaka (vi-) 1. peephole, porthole, small opening/window. 2. hiding-place, niche. 3. *mil.* loophole, embrasure. 4. (shelved) recess in a wall.

shubiri* (–) *see* **shibiri.**

shudu* (ma-) residue (of seeds, when oil is pressed), oil cake.

shufaka*, shafaka (–) sympathy, compassion, pity. (= **huruma.**)

shufu* 1. perceive, notice, detect, see. 2. watch, observe, look at.

shufwa* (–) *math.* even number. *Cf.* **witiri.**

shughuli* (–) 1. duty, task, occupation, business, affairs, work, function, career. **ana – muhimu.** He has an important task/piece of business. **kwa –.** in the line of business, professional(ly). **– za nchi.** public affairs. 2. worry, trouble; excitement, disturbance. *Cf.* **shughulika.**

shughulika* 1. be busy/active, have much to do. 2. be worried/disturbed/harassed. *caus.* **shughulisha.** give work, employ; overburden someone; disturb, harass. *refl.-caus.* **jishughulisha.** be busy; be worried/agitated; pretend to be busy, make excuses *(for not doing the work at hand). Cf.* **shughuli.**

shuhuda* (ma-) proof, evidence; testimonial, diploma. *Cf.* **shahada, shuhudu.**

shuhudia* *appl. of* **shuhudu.**

shuhudika* *intr. of* **shuhudu.**

shuhudisha* *caus. of* **shuhudu.**

shuhudu* prove, confirm, attest, corroborate, certify, verify. *appl.* **shuhudia.** *intr.* **shuhudika.** *caus.* **shuhudisha.** *Cf.* **shahada, shahidi.**

shuhuli* (–) rear part of a house.

shujaa* 1. (ma-) hero, warrior, brave man. **Mashujaa wa Uhuru.** Freedom Fighters. 2. *adj.* brave, courageous. *Cf.* **ushujaa.**

[1]**shuka** (–, ma-) 1. loincloth. 2. shuka (piece of calico about two yards in length, commonly worn as a loincloth; hence a unit of measure).

[2]**shuka** *intr. of* **shua.**

shuke (–) *see* **suke.**

[1]**shukia*** *appl. of* **shuku.**

[2]**shukia** *intr.-appl. of* **shua.**

shukiwa* *pass. of* **shuku.**

shukrani* (–) thanks, gratitude. (= **asante.**) *Cf.* **shukuru.**

shuku* 1. doubt, have doubts/misgivings/scruples, suspect. *appl.* **shukia.** have doubts about something. *pass.* **shukiwa.** be doubted/suspected/suspect. 2. (ma-) doubt, suspicion. *Cf.* **shaka.**

shukuru* 1. thank, be grateful. **tulimshukuru kwa wema wake.** We have thanked him for his kindness. 2. console oneself, be contented/resigned. *Cf.* **shukrani, ushukuru;** *also* **shakiri.**

shule* [*Germ.*] (–, ma-) *rare* school, academy. (= **chuo, skuli.**)

shulu*, shuru 1. sew, stitch; whip, overcast, oversew. 2. (ma-) (*also* **mshulu, mshuru,** mi-) stitch, seam; backstitch.

shumberere*, shumbulele [*Port.*] (ma-) sombrero.

shumbi* (–) 1. deep water. 2. heap. – **ya mchanga.** heap of sand.

shumbulele* (ma-) *see* **shumberere.**

shume (ma-): **paka –.** large, half-wild tomcat.

shumua *rare inv. of* **choma.**

shumusi* (–) *see* **shemshi.**

shundi (–) shundi (kind of bird, coucal). (= **dudumizi, tipitipi.**)

shundwa (–) shundwa (large striped hyena).

shunga 1.: – **ng'omba.** tend/drive cattle. (= [2]**chunga.**) 2. *rare* drive (chase, scare) away. (= **fukuza.**) – **ndege.** scare away birds.

[1]**shungi** (ma-) 1. tress, tuft, plait, lock *(of hair)*; mane *(of a lion)*. 2. crest, plume, comb *(of a cock)*. 3. fringe, tassel. *Cf.* **kishungi, ushungi.**

[2]**shungi** *pl. of* **ushungi.**

shupaa 1. be strong, vigorous, tough, hardy. 2. be stubborn, obstinate, unyielding. – **maneno.** affirm, insist. – **mwili.** be muscular. *caus.* **shupaza.** strengthen, harden, toughen; support, confirm. *ass.* **shupana.** *Cf.* **shupavu, mshupavu, ushupavu.**

shupatu (ma-) plaited strip (of grass/palm-leaf fiber) used as lacing for beds.

shupavu *adj.* firm, hard, tough; stubborn, unyielding. *Cf.* **shupaa, mshupavu, ushupavu.**

[1]**shupaza** *caus.* *of* **shupaa.**

[2]**shupaza*** [*Port.*] (–) *cards* spades.

shura*, **chora** [*Pers.*] (–) saltpeter.

shuri* (ma-) *anat.* steatopygia.

shurti* (–) *see* **sharti.**

shuru* *see* **shulu.**

shurua* (–) *see* **surua.**

shuruti* 1. oblige, compel, necessitate. *appl.* **shurutia.** *caus.* **shurutisha, shurutiza.** oblige, compel (= **shuruti**); demand, insist on. *ass.* **shurutiana.** obligate/make terms with each other; make a bet/wager. 2. (ma-) = **sharti.** *Cf.* **sharti, shurutisho, mshurutisho.**

shurutisho* (ma-) compulsion, pressure; stipulation. *Cf.* **shuruti.**

shusha *caus.* *of* **shua.**

shuta break wind. *Cf.* **shuzi.**

shuti* [*Engl.*] (–) 1. shooting, firing. 2. *sport* shot, stroke, drive.

shutumu* 1. scold, nag; abuse, insult; reproach, find fault. *appl.* **shutumia.** *intr.* **shutumika.** *caus.* **shutumisha.** 2. (ma-) insult, abuse, reproach, reprimand, rebuke.

shuzi (ma-) (*us.* **mashuzi**; *also* **ushuzi**) breaking wind, flatulence; stench. *prov.* **shukrani za punda ni mashuzi.** The donkey's gratitude is stench. *Cf.* **shuta.**

shwari* (–) *naut.* calm.

si *adv.* (is/are) not; non-. – **vema.** (It is) not good. **wao** – **wagonjwa.** They are not ill. – **mwanachama.** non-member.

[1]**sia** plant *(rice, in holes)*; transplant, set out in rows.

[2]**sia** drive away ants *(with burning grass).*

siafu (–) siafu (kind of brown ant).

siagi* (–) butter, cream.

siaha* (–) loud cry/scream. *Cf.* [2]**sihi.**

siala* (ma-) *see* **swali.**

siasa* (–) 1. politics, political activity. 2. policy. – **ya fungamana.** policy of alignment. **chama cha** –. political party. **maongozi ya** –. political platform. **mtu wa** –. politician. **-a** –. political. 3. attentiveness, carefulness, accuracy; tact. **mtu mwenye** –. a tactful/diplomatic person. **hana** –. He is tactless/indiscreet. 4. *adv.* careful, orderly, meticulous.

sibabi* *see* [1]**sibu.**

sibia *appl. of* ^{1}**sibu**, ^{2}**sibu**, ^{3}**sibu**.

^{1}**sibu***, **sibabi** abuse, insult, revile; slander. *appl.* **sibia.**

^{2}**sibu*** distress, afflict, cause pain, bring misfortune. *appl.* **sibia.** *intr.* **sibika.** *Cf.* **masaibu, msiba, msibu, subiani.**

^{3}**sibu*** happen, occur, take place. **ilikusibu lini?** When did it happen to you? *appl.* **sibia.** *intr.* **sibika.** *caus.* **sibisha.**

^{4}**sibu***, **subu** prophesy, foretell the future.

sidiboi* [?] **(ma-)** native member of the crew of a warship.

sidiria* (–) 1. *arch.* sidiria (cloth worn by native women to support the breasts). 2. *(recent)* brassiere. (= **kanchiri.**)

sidukia* *intr. of* **suduku.**

^{1}**sifa***, **sifu** (–) 1. praise, commendation; applause; recommendation. 2. reputation, character. – **zake njema.** He has a good reputation. 3. *gramm.* adjective. *Cf.* **sifu, kisifa.**

^{2}**sifa*** [*Port.*] (–) shark-oil *(used for caulking boats).*

sifia* *appl. of* **sifu.**

sifongo*, **sifonjo, sifunjo** (–) sponge.

sifonjo* (–) *see* **sifongo.**

sifu* 1. praise, recommend. 2. flatter. *appl.* **sifia.** *intr.* **sifika.** *caus.* **sifisha.** *pass.* **sifiwa. amesifiwa kwa nguvu zake.** He was praised for his strength. *refl.* **jisifu.** praise oneself, boast. 3. (–) = ^{1}**sifa.** *Cf.* ^{1}**sifa, msifu, masifu, majisifu, mjisifu.**

sifunjo* (–) *see* **sifongo.**

^{1}**sifuri***, **sufuri** (–) *math.* zero.

^{2}**sifuri*** (–) copper, brass. (= **shaba.**) *Cf.* **sufuria.**

sigara* (–) *see* **sigereti.**

sigareti* (–) *see* **sigereti.**

sigereti*, **sigareti, sigara** [*Engl.*] (–) cigarette, cigar.

sigida* (–) *see* **sijida.**

signali* [*Engl.*] (–) 1. signal. 2. *naut.* heliograph.

siha* (–) strength, good constitution, health.

^{1}**sihi*** be acceptable/appropriate/suitable.

^{2}**sihi*** call, cry; beg, beseech, implore. *appl.* **sihia.** *intr.* **sihika.** *Cf.* **siaha.**

sihia* 1. transfer. – **mali.** transfer (ownership of) property. 2. = *appl. of* ^{2}**sihi.**

sihiri* 1. enchant, bewitch, fascinate. *appl.* **sihiria.** 2. (–) witchcraft, magic. 3. charm, talisman. *Cf.* **usihiri.**

sijafu* [*Pers.*] (–) cuff *(of a coat, etc.)*.

sijambo *see* **jambo.**

sijida*, sigida (–) sijida (a calloused place on the foreheads of Muhammadans caused by the traditional prostrations at prayer). *Cf.* **sujudu.**

siki* [*Pers.*] (–) vinegar.

sikia 1. hear. 2. listen, pay attention. 3. notice, understand. 4. obey. **mtoto huyu hasikii.** This child does not obey. 5. perceive, detect. **nasikia harufu.** I notice/detect a smell. *appl.* **sikilia.** listen to/for something. *intr.* **sikika.** be audible/perceptible/noticeable. *caus.* **sikiza.** make someone understand/obey. *appl.-caus. (us. w. int. force)* **sikiliza.** listen intently. *appl.-caus.-ass.* **sikilizana.** listen to each other, come to an understanding. *caus.-ass.* **sikizana.** be intelligible to each other, understand each other's languages. *Cf.* **sikilivu, sikio, sikizano, msikiaji, msikilivu, msikilizaji, msikilizano, usikilizaji, usikivu, usikizano.**

sikilivu, sikivu *adj.* be attentive, obedient, docile, teachable. *Cf.* **sikia.**

sikio (ma-) 1. ear. **tega –.** listen carefully. **tia –.** remember. **toga –.** pierce the earlobe *(for earrings)*. 2. *rare* feeling, sensation. 3. *fig.:* **– la simu.** telephone receiver. *Cf.* **sikia.**

sikitika be sorry, regret; grieve, mourn for, miss. *appl.* **sikitikia.** *caus.* **sikitikisha, sikitisha.** grieve (someone), make sorry, sadden. *Cf.* **sikitiko.**

sikitiko (ma-) grief, sorrow; cause of sorrow/regret; object of pity. *Cf.* **sikitika.**

sikivu *see* **sikilivu.**

sikizano (ma-) (*us.* **masikizano**) mutual understanding, agreement. **pata –.** reach an understanding. **hali ya amani na masikizano.** peaceful coexistence. *Cf.* **sikia.**

sikolojia* [*Engl.*] (–) *see* **saikoloji.**

[1]**siku** (–) day (= period of 24 hours). **– zote** (*or* **sikuzote**). always. **– hizi.** now, at this time; nowadays, at present. **– za kale.** formerly, in ancient times. **kila –.** every day, daily. **– kwa –.** from day to day. **– hata –.** day after day. **– ya mwaka mpya.** New Year's Day. *Cf.* **sikukuu. usiku.**

[2]**siku** *pl. of* **usiku.**

sikukuu (–) holiday, festival. *Cf.* [1]**siku.**

sikuzote *see* [1]**siku.**

sila* [*Pers.*] (–) dipper, scoop, bailer. (= **ndoo,** [2]**kata.**)

silabi*, silabu [*Engl.*] (–) syllable.

silabu* (–) *see* **silabi.**

[1]**silaha*, selaha** (–) weapon. **twaa (shika) –.** arm oneself, take up arms. **– za viini.** nuclear weapons.

[2]**silaha*** (ma-) *see* **masilaha.**

silasila*, salasila, silisila (–) chain, anchor-chain.

silika*, **sirika** (–) 1. character, nature, disposition. **ana – mbaya.** He has a bad character. 2. instinct.

silimu* be converted to Islam, turn Muhammadan. *intr.* **silimika.** *caus.* **silimisha.** *Cf.* **Islamu, Kiislamu, msalimina, Mwislamu.**

silinda* [*Engl.*] (ma-) cylinder.

silingi*, **slingi** [*Engl.* sling] (–) windlass, winch, derrick, crane.

silisila* (–) *see* **silasila.**

sima (–) *dial.* sima (a thick porridge made of flour and water; = **ugali**).

simadi* to manure *(a field, etc., with natural fertilizer; cf.* **samadi***)*.

simama stand, be in an upright position; stand up, rise; stand still, stop, be stationary; *(fig.)* be steady/steadfast/immovable. *appl.* **simamia.** 1. confront/oppose someone. 2. supervise, superintend, direct, manage. *intr.* **simamika, simika.** 1. stand, be upright (= **simama**). 2. be erect *(of the penis)*, have an erection. 3. set up, establish, appoint. *caus.* **simamisha.** 1. cause to stand, make steady, stabilize. 2. (cause to) stop, obstruct. 3. put up (a candidate for election). **simamisha bei.** stabilize prices. *inv.* **simua.** move from a vertical to a horizontal position, lower, lay down, overturn. *inv.-appl.* **simulia.** *inv.-intr.* **simulika.** *Cf.* **msimamazi, msimiko, usimamao, usimamizi, usimeme.**

simanga 1. exult, triumph *(over something)*. 2. gloat over, take a malicious pleasure in *(another's misfortune, discomfiture)*; mock, deride. *ass.* **simangana.** reproach/blame each other. *Cf.* **usimango.**

simango (ma-) *see* **usimango.**

simanzi (–) sorrow, sadness, grief, distress.

simba (–, ma-) 1. lion (*also* **– dume**). **– jike.** lioness. **– mrara.** large spotted hyena. 2. *fig.* brave person, courageous warrior. 3. *fig.* cruel/bloodthirsty person. 4. *fig.* fine, healthy child.

[1]**simbi** (–) simbi (small cowry shell).

[2]**simbi** (–, ma-) *see* **shimbi.**

simbu *see* [1]**sumba.**

sime (ma-) 1. large knife. 2. short (double-edged) sword.

simika (= **simamika**) *intr. of* **simama.**

simile*, **sumile, similla**! (< **bismillahi**, *q.v.*) *interj.* Make way! Gangway!

similla!* *see* **simile.**

simiri* *see* **shimiri.**

[1]**simo*** [*Pers. ?*] (–) 1. something remarkable/noteworthy, event, news. 2. *rare* kind, sort, quality. 3. *adj.* new, novel, strange.

[2]**simo** *neg. 1st pers. sing. det.* 1. I am not (in) there. 2. *fig.* It is no concern of mine.

simsim* (–) *see* **semsem.**

[1]**simu*** [*Pers.*] (–) 1. telegraph, telegraphy. **uzi wa –.** telegraph wire. **– ya upepo.** wireless (telegraphy). 2. telegram. **peleka –.** send a telegram, wire. **pata –.** receive a telegram. 3. telephone, telephone conversation. **piga/sema kwa –.** to telephone, call up. **pigiwa –.** be called up.

[2]**simu** (–) simu (kind of small fish, sprat). (= **dagaa.**)

simua *inv. of* **simama.**

[1]**simulia***, **sumulia** tell *(a story)*, relate, narrate, report, give an account of. *appl.* **simulika.** *caus.* **simulisha.** *ass.* **simuliana.** converse, carry on a conversation. *Cf.* **simulizi, msimulizi.**

[2]**simulia** *inv.-appl. of* **simama.**

simulika *inv.-intr. of* **simama.**

simulizi* (ma-) (*us.* **masimulizi**) 1. news, report. 2. story, legend. *Cf.* [1]**simulia.**

[1]**sina** *neg. auxil. v. 1st pers. sing.* I do not have.

[2]**Sina*** *sing.* *see* [2]**Sini.**

sinasina be on the verge of tears, be ready to cry.

[1]**sindano, shindano** (ma-) 1. needle. 2. *med.* injection, vaccination, shot. **piga –.** give an injection/shot, vaccinate. **dawa ya –.** vaccine, serum. 3. magnetic needle. 4.: **– ya santuri.** phonograph-needle.

[2]**sindano** (–) sindano (kind of rice).

sindi (–) *dial.* *see* **kindi.**

sindika, shindika *intr. of* [1]**shinda.**

[1]**sindikiza, shindikiza** *intr.-int. of* [1]**shinda.**

[2]**sindikiza** go part of the way with someone *(e.g., a departing guest)*, give *(someone)* a send-off *(prob. a specialized sense of* [1]**sindikiza**; *cf.* [1]**shinda***)*.

sindikizo (ma-) *see* **shindikizo.**

sindua, shindua *inv. of* [1]**shinda.**

sine* (ma-) *anat.* gum(s) *(of the teeth)*. (= **ufizi.**)

sinema* [*Engl.*] (–) 1. cinema, motion pictures, movies, movie theater. 2. *fig., coll.* spectacle, occurrence, episode. **hapo sokoni tuliona –, wanawake wawili walipigana.** In the market we witnessed the spectacle of two women fighting.

sineri* [*Ind.*] (–) (gold, silver) foil/leaf.

[1]**singa** rub/massage with an aromatic substance. **– kwa sandali.** massage with sandalwood oil.

[2]**singa** *pl. of* **usinga.**

singafuri* (–) *see* **singefuri.**

singe* [*Turk.*] (–) bayonet. (= **beneti.**)

singefuri*, **singafuri** (–) *see* **zingefuri.**

singiza (*us. appl.* **singizia**) 1. accuse falsely, slander, calumniate. 2. pretend, feign. **walinisingizia.** I have been falsely accused. *appl.-refl.* **jisingizia. amejisingizia ugonjwa.** He pretended to be ill. *Cf.* **singizio.**

singizio (ma-) (*us.* **masingizio**) 1. false accusation, slander, calumny. 2. pretense, sham, make-believe, pretext. *Cf.* **singiza.**

[1]**sini*** (–) appearance, features *(of the face).*

[2]**Sini***, **Sina** *sing.* China. (= **China, Chaina.**)

sinia* (–, ma-) tray.

sinikiza *see* **shinikiza.**

sinikizo (ma-) *see* **shinikizo.**

sinua turn/push over; uproot, tear out. *intr.* **sinuka.** *intr.-appl.* **sinukia.** lie every which way/in confusion/pell-mell. *intr.-caus.* **sinukisha.** turn something upside down.

sinyaa 1. wither, shrivel, become wrinkled. 2. fade *(of colors)*, become discolored. *appl.* **sinyalia.**

sinzia 1. doze, daydream. 2. *fig.* be absent-minded/inattentive. 3. *fig.* be indolent/indifferent/negligent. 4. *fig.* lose strength, become weaker. **taa inasinzia.** The light is getting weaker/fainter. *appl.* **sinzilia. kwa macho ya kusinzilia.** with dreamy eyes. *caus.* **sinzisha.** put/lull to sleep. *Cf.* **usingizi.**

sio (–) grog (powdered potsherds, mixed with clay for making new pots).

-siofaa impotent *(sexually).* (= **hanithi.**) *Cf.* **faa.**

sipitali* (–) *see* **hospitali.**

sira* (ma-) (*us. pl.*) residue, lees, dregs. **– la pombe.** residue formed when beer is brewed. (= **masimbi.**)

siraji* (–) *rare* lamp, candlestick, torch. (= [2]**taa.**)

[1]**siri*** 1. (–) secret, secrecy; mystery. **maneno ya –.** mysterious/unintelligible words. **mwandiko wa –.** code, cipher. **kwa –.** secretly, mysteriously. 2. *v., rare* secrete, hide. *us. refl.* **jisiri.** secrete oneself. *appl.* **siria.** *Cf.* **msiri.**

[2]**siri*** *rare* become, turn/change into.

siridado* *sing.* dry rot.

sirika* (–) *see* **silika.**

[1]**sirima*** make someone wait, try a person's patience by letting him wait; *(fig.)* torture.

[2]**sirima** *rare* *see* [1]**sisima.**

sirinji* [*Engl.*] (–) *med.* syringe.

sisi (*rare* **siye**) *abs. pron. 1st pers. pl.* we. **– sote.** all of us. **– tunakwenda.** We shall go.

[1]**sisima** (*rare* **sirima**) smooth a surface; oil, grease, lubricate.

[2]**sisima** *see* **sisimua.**

sisimizi (–) sisimizi (small black ant).

sisimka *intr. of* **sisimua.**

sisimsha *caus. of* **sisimua.**

sisimua, sisima tremble *(with fright) appl.* **sisimulia.** *intr.* **sisimuka, sisimka.** be excited/stimulated *(also sexually)*, have gooseflesh *(from fear). caus.* **sisimusha, sisimsha.** frighten, terrify; excite, stimulate, arouse interest. *Cf.* **msisimko.**

sisitiza 1. say emphatically, emphasize. 2. advise, urge, warn (repeatedly). *ass.* **sisitizana.** give each other good advice.

sista* [*Engl.*] (ma-) sister, nurse.

[1]**sita, sitasita** 1. walk/move slowly or uncertainly; dawdle. 2. be uncertain/perplexed, hesitate, waver, vacillate. **bila kusita.** without hesitation, constantly.

[2]**sita*** *num.* six. **–a –.** sixth.

sitaha* (–) *see* [2]**staha.**

sitashara* *num., arch.* sixteen.

sitasita *see* [1]**sita.**

sitawi*, stawi bloom, flourish, prosper; be in good condition, be successful, live in easy circumstances. **miti imesitawi.** The trees are thriving. *caus.* **sitawisha.** cause to prosper, help to succeed, encourage, promote, further. **jumuiya ya kusitawishi Kiswahili.** Society for the Promotion of the Swahili Language. *Cf.* **usitawi.**

siti* (–) *rare, liter.* lady (of the house); *(in address)* madam. (= **bibi, mwana.**)

sitima* (–) *see* **stima.**

sitini* *num.* sixty.

sitiri* *see* **stiri.**

sitoo* (ma-) *see* **stoo.**

sivyo, siyo no.

[1]**siwa** (ma-) *augment. of* **kisiwa.**

[2]**siwa*** (ma-) *arch.* horn, trumpet (of wood or ivory; emblem of a chief).

siyara* (–) nature, character; behavior, conduct.

siye *rare* *see* **sisi.**

siyo *see* **sivyo.**

-siyoepukika unavoidable, inevitable. **mahanga isiyoepukika.** inevitable sacrifices. *Cf.* **epa.**

sizi (mi-, ma-) *(us. pl.)* 1. soot. 2. piece of charcoal.

skati*, sketa [*Engl.*] (–) skirt, coattail.

skauti* [*Engl.*] (**ma-**) scout, spy.

skeli* [*Engl.*] (**–**) *mus.* scale. **– ya do.** major scale. **– ya la.** minor scale.

sketa* (**–**) *see* **skati.**

skrubu*, skurubu [*Engl.*] (**–**) screw, bolt; corkscrew.

skuli* [*Engl.*], *rare* **shule** [*Germ.*] (**–**) school. **– ndogo.** *rare.* elementary school. **– ya kati.** intermediate school. (= **chuo.**)

skurubu* (**–**) *see* **skrubu.**

skuta* [*Engl.*] (**–**) (motor-)scooter.

skweya* [*Engl.*] (**–**) (carpenter's, mason's) square.

skwota* [*Engl.*] (**ma-**) squatter *(on land).*

slingi* (**–**) *see* **silingi.**

1**soda*** [*Engl.*] (**–**) soda, soda water, mineral water.

2**soda*** (**–**) dejection, melancholy.

sodawi* *adj.* proud, arrogant. *Cf.* **usodawi.**

sodo* (**–**) sodo (cloth used during menstruation).

sofa [*Engl.*] (**–**) 1. sofa, couch. 2. seat (of an automobile).

1**soga*** (**ma-**) chat, conversation.

2**soga** (**–**) *ethn.* blood-brotherhood.

1**sogea, songea** move *(closer, further away).* **– mbali!** Go away! **– karibu!** Come here! *appl.* **sogelea.** *caus.* **sogeza.** move someone (closer, further away). *appl.-ass.* **sogeleana.** come nearer to each other, draw together.

2**sogea** (**–**) sogea (kind of manioc).

sogi* (**ma-**) *see* **shogi.**

sogonea wipe oneself (with grass, etc., after going to the toilet).

sogora (**ma-**) sogora (a skilful drummer).

soka* [*Engl.*] (**–**) *rare* soccer.

sokisi* (**–**) *see* **soksi.**

soko* (**–, ma-**) (established) market, market-place, trading center. **– la shirikisho.** common market.

sokota 1. twist, twine, spin, roll *(e.g., a cigarette, the hair),* wind. 2. *fig.* have colic pains. *appl.* **sokotea.** *intr.* **sokoteka.** *caus.* **sokotesha.** *Cf.* **sokoto, msokoto.**

sokoto (**ma-**) 1. something twisted, twine, rope. 2. *med.* colic. *Cf.* **sokota.**

soksi*, sokisi [*Engl.*] (**–**) socks, stockings. **– ndefu.** stockings.

sokwe (**–**) chimpanzee.

[1]soli* [*Turk.*] (–) *mil., arch.* sergeant major.

[2]soli *adv.* unexpectedly, face to face.

[3]soli* [*Engl.*] (–) sole (of a shoe).

solo, soro (–) solo (seeds of the msolo tree, used as counters in games).

soma 1. read; read aloud, recite. – **kitabu.** read a book. – **shairi.** recite a poem. 2. learn by heart. 3. go to school, receive education. **mtoto huyu anasoma.** This child goes to school/can read. **umesoma nini skuli?** What did you learn at school? 4. study. *appl.* **somea.** *intr.* **someka.** be decipherable/legible. *caus.* **somesha.** send to school, teach to read; instruct. *Cf.* **[1]somo, kisomo, masomo, [1]msoma, msomaji, msomeshaji, msomo, usomaji.**

somba carry, transport, convey. – **mchanga.** transport sand.

sombea, sombera 1. climb *(a tree, etc.).* 2. = **sota.**

sombera *see* **sombea.**

sombo (ma-) *see* **masombo.**

[1]somo (ma-) 1. something to read, reading matter. 2. lesson. 3. education, study. 4. section, paragraph. *Cf.* **soma.**

[2]somo (ma-) 1. (intimate, confidential) friend. 2. a women who instructs a young girl in sexual matters; assistant at initiation rites. 3. namesake.

sonara* [*Ind.*] (–) jeweler, goldsmith, silversmith.

songa 1. press, compress, squeeze. 2. crowd, throng. 3. apply pressure, close (by exerting pressure); choke, throttle. – **roho.** strangle. 4. *fig.* oppress, weigh down, overwhelm. **taabu zinanisonga.** My troubles are weighing me down. 5. press forward, make progress. 6. twist, braid. – **nywele.** braid the hair. *appl.* **songea.** *intr.* **songeka.** *caus.* **songesha.** *stat.* **songama.** *ass.* **songana.** push/jostle each other *(in a crowd);* oppress with taxation. *stat.-ass.* **songamana.** be rolled/pressed together; writhe, wriggle. *stat.-caus.* **songamiza.** disgrace/embarrass publicly; accuse publicly. *inv.* **songoa.** twist, wring. **songoa nguo.** wring out clothes. **songoa kuku.** wring a chicken's neck. *inv.-appl.* **songolea.** *inv.-intr.* **songoka.** *inv.-ass.* **songona.** *inv.-ass.-caus.* **songonyoa** *(w. int. force).* press tightly together, pack tight *(one thing on top of another). inv.-stat.-int. (rare).* **songomeza.** roll up, coil. **nyoka anajisongomeza.** The snake is coiling itself up. *Cf.* **songo, kisongo, msonga, msongano, msongo.**

[1]songea *see* **[1]sogea.**

[2]songea *appl. of* **songa.**

songo (ma-) 1. twisting, writhing. 2. loop, noose. 3. twist, coil, braid. – **la nywele.** a braid of hair. *Cf.* **songa.**

songomeza *inv.-stat.-int. of* **songa.**

soni (–) shame, modesty, timidity.

sonoa harm, injure (someone), cause pain; disturb, annoy, irritate, bore. *Cf.* **sonona.**

sonona, sununa grieve, regret, mourn; feel sorrow/pain. *appl.* **sononea.** *intr.* **sononeka.** be sorrowful/depressed/gloomy/melancholy/out-of-sorts. *caus.* **sononesha.** cause someone pain/sorrow; annoy/irritate someone. *Cf.* **sonoa, sononeko, kisonono, usononi.**

sononeko (ma-) sorrow, trouble, care, grief, suffering; unrest, excitement. *Cf.* **sonona.**

sonya *see* **fyonya.**

soro (–) *see* **solo.**

sororo (–) sororo (edible sea fish).

soshialisti* [*Engl.*] socialist.

sosi* [*Engl.*] (–) sauce.

sosona *see* **kokona.**

sota, sowera slide, drag oneself *(on the buttocks, as one who has lost the use of his legs).*

sote *see* **ote, sisi.**

sotoka (–) *see* **sadoka.**

sowera *see* **sota.**

soza 1. reach (one's destination), arrive. *naut.*: – **pwani.** land. *fig.* be high and dry/without resources. 2.: – **kidole.** point with the finger. *appl.* **sozea.** *intr.* **sozeka.** 1. be suitable for a landing *(of a place).* 2. have landed; be beached/run ashore. *caus.* **sozesha.** *ass.* **sozana.** 1. approach/accost someone. 2. bump against each other, collide.

spaki* [*Engl.*] (–) spark, flame.

spesheli* [*Engl.*] *adj./adv.* special(ly).

spidi* [*Engl.*] (–) speed.

spika* [*Engl.*] (–) speaker *(in parliament, of a radio, etc.).*

spiringi*, springi [*Engl.*] (–) *mech.* spring. **kitanda cha –.** spring bed. **–a –.** springy, resilient.

spoki* [*Engl.*] (–) spoke *(of a wheel).*

spoti* [*Engl.*] (–) sport.

springi* (–) *see* **spiringi.**

spuni* [*Engl.*] (–) *rare* spoon. (= [1]**kijiko,** [1]**mwiko.**)

staajabu*, taajabu 1. be astonished/amazed. *appl.* **staajabia.** *intr.* **staajabika.** be amazed/speechless. *caus.* **staajabisha.** astonish, amaze. 2. (ma-) (*us.* **mastaajabu**) astonishment, amazement; an amazing thing, wonder, miracle. *Cf.* **ajabu.**

staamani* *see* **amini.**

staarabika* *see* **staarabu.**

staarabu* (*us. intr.* **staarabika**) 1. *(originally)* be Arabized, live according to Arab customs.

2. *fig.* adopt Western/European ways, be civilized/cultivated, show good manners/ breeding. *caus.* **staarabisha.** 3. *adj.* civilized, wise. *Cf.* **mstaarabu, ustaarabu.**

stadi* 1. **(ma-)** experienced/capable/skilful person. 2. *adj.* experienced, capable, skilful. *Cf.* **mstadi, ustadi.**

stafeli* [*Ind.*] (–, **ma-**) 1. fruit of the mstafeli, *q.v.* 2. cinnamon (= **mdalasini.**)

[1]**staha*, sitaha** (–) *naut.* deck.

[2]**staha*** (–) honor, respect, esteem, reverence, deference. **toa –.** show respect. *Cf.* **stahi.**

stahabu*, stahiba, stehebu like, prefer, favor. *Cf.* [1]**hebu,** [2]**haba.**

stahi* honor, respect, revere. *appl.* **stahia.** *ass.* **stahiana.** *intr.* **stahika.** *Cf.* [2]**staha, stahivu, mstahivu, ustahivu.**

stahiba* *see* **stahabu.**

stahika* be upright/worthy/respected. *Cf.* **haki.**

stahiki* 1. be fitting/proper/suitable; be worthy/ deserving of; be obligatory. 2. *adj.* worthy, deserving; respected, honorable. *Cf.* **haki.**

stahili* 1. merit, deserve. **Juma, wee mkaidi sana siku hizi, wastahili kupigwa.** Juma, you are very naughty these days; you deserve a beating. 2. be fitting/proper; be due, be obligatory. **Amepata kazi nzuri sana, si – yake.** He has a very good job; in fact it is too good for him. *appl.* **stahilia.** *intr.* **stahilika.** *caus.* **stahilisha.** 3. (–) (*also* **astahili**) merit, worthiness. 4. *adj.* worthy, deserving; suitable, qualified; obligatory. *Cf.* **ustahili.**

stahimili* endure, suffer, stand, put up with; be patient, persevere. *appl.* **stahimilia.** *intr.* **stahimilika.** be patient/long-suffering; be persevering/persistent. *Cf.* **hamali.**

stahimilivu* *adj.* persevering, persistent, tenacious, stubborn; patient, long-suffering. *Cf.* **hamali.**

stahivu* *adj., rare* deserving respect, estimable, honorable. *Cf.* **stahi.**

staili* [*Engl.*] (–) style, manner.

staka* (–) sandal.

stakabadhi* 1. turn over/deliver *(for safekeeping/ deposit).* **– pesa.** turn over/entrust/deposit money. 2. (–) (*also* **istakabadhi**) care, safekeeping, deposit; (acknowledgement of) receipt, quittance. *Cf.* **kabidhi.**

stakimu* thrive, prosper, be successful. *Cf.* **mastakimu.**

stampa* [*Engl.*] (–) *rare* (rubber, metal) stamp, punch; mark, stamp. (= [1]**chapa, muhuri.**)

stampu*, stempu [*Engl.*] (–) (postage) stamp.

standi*, stendi [*Engl.*] (–) *rare* stand, stopping-place, bus stop.

stara* 1. (–) cover, concealment. 2. (place of) refuge, asylum. 3. *fig.* modesty, reticence, reserve. 4. proper covering *(of the genitals)*. *Cf.* **stiri.**

starehe* 1. (–) rest, peace, ease. 2. *(in response to the greeting* **karibu**! Come in!) Don't disturb yourself! Keep your seat! 3. comfort, well-being, prosperity. **vitu vya –.** luxuries. 4. *recent* welfare, recreation. 5. *v.* live quietly/peacefully; be in comfortable circumstances/well off. **siku hizi amestarehe.** At present he is living in comfortable circumstances. *caus.* **starehesha.** make comfortable, relieve, give aid to. *Cf.* **raha, starehevu, mustarehe.**

starehefu* *adj.* *see* **starehevu.**

starehevu*, starehefu *adj.* quiet, peaceful; comfortable. *Cf.* **raha, starehe.**

stashahada* (–) evidence, testimony, deposition; certificate, receipt; bill, account. *Cf.* **shahada.**

stati* [*Engl.*] (–) start. **tia (piga) –.** start *(a car)*. **alipopiga – ile motokaa haikuwaka.** When he stepped on the starter the engine didn't turn over.

stawi* *see* **sitawi.**

stedi* [*Engl.*] *adj.* steady, firm, hard.

stehebu* *see* **stahabu.**

steling* (–) *rare* *see* **stiringi.**

stempu* (–) *see* **stampu.**

stendi* [*Engl.*] (–) *see* **standi.**

steringi* [*Engl.*] (–) *rare* *see* **stiringi.**

stesheni* [*Engl.*] (–) station, stop(ping-place). **– ya mafuta/petroli.** gas station. **– ya redio.** radio station. **– za mabomba ya kuvutia maji.** pumping station.

stichi* [*Engl.*] (–) 1. stitch. 2. loop, eyelet, catch.

stihizai*, stihizaya *see* [1]**hizi.**

stima*, sitima [*Engl.*] (–) 1. steamer, steamship. 2. electricity, electric light (= **umeme**); utilities. **Wizara ya Kazi na Stima.** Ministry of Public Works and Utilities.

stimu* [*Engl.*] (–) 1. *arch.* steam. 2. current *(of air)*. 3. *now rare* electricity (= **umeme**). **taa za –.** electric light. **– ya njia kuu.** main (electrical) line. **majiko ya –.** electric stove/cooker. **– kubwa.** high tension/voltage.

stiri*, sitiri, setiri 1. hide, conceal. 2. cover (up). 3. *fig.* protect, preserve. *appl.* **stiria.** *intr.* **stirika.** be concealed, keep oneself hidden; be safe/not to be found/out of harm's way. *caus.* **stirisha.** hide/conceal someone, keep safe. *Cf.* **stara, kisetiri,** [1]**mstiri.**

stiringi*, steringi, steling [*Engl.*] (–) steering wheel.

stoa* (–) *see* **stoo.**

stoki*, stokingi [*Engl.*] (–) *rare* stocking(s). (= **soksi** [**ndefu**].)

stoo*, **sitoo, stoa** [*Engl.*] (–) 1. store, shop. 2. storehouse, warehouse. 3. stock, supply.

stovu* [*Engl.*] (–) stove.

stua *see* **shtua.**

stuka, shtuka *intr. of* **shtua.**

stusha *caus. of* **shtua.**

¹**sua** eject, spit out. – **maji.** spit out water *(after rinsing the mouth). refl.* **jisua.** retch, vomit. *Cf.* **masuo.**

²**sua** clean, rub, brush. – **meno.** clean the teeth.

³**sua** *see* **sulika.**

subahiya* (–) *see* **subaya.**

subalkheri* (–) *see* **sabalkheri.**

subana* (–) 1. (*also* **subano**) thimble. (= **kastabini.**) 2. small piece of meat.

subano* (–) *see* **subana.**

subaya*, subahiya (–) cloth covering a bier, pall.

subiani* (ma-) an evil spirit. *Cf.* ²**sibu.**

subili* (–) subili (species of aloe). *Cf.* **msubili.**

subira*, subiri *see* **saburi.**

¹**subu*** cast, mold *(metals). appl.* **subia.** *intr.* **subika.** *caus.* **subisha.**

²**subu*** *see* ⁴**sibu.**

subukua jab someone with the finger *(as a sign of contempt). Cf.* **msubukuo.**

sudi* (–) *rare* good luck, success.

suduku* (*us. intr.* **sudukia, sidukia**) 1. confirm, verify, make sure, prove. 2. admit, accept, agree, concur. *Cf.* **sadiki.**

sudusi* (–) *see* **sudusu.**

sudusu*, sudusi (–) a sixth.

sufi*, sufu (–) (*also* **usufi** *sing.*) 1. kapok. *Cf.* **msufi.** 2. *(commercial)* wool, woolen cloth.

sufii* (–) hermit, pious/saintly person. *Cf.* **usufii.**

sufu* (–) *see* **sufi.**

sufuri* (–) *see* ¹**sifuri.**

sufuria* (–, ma-) (metal) cooking-pot. *Cf.* ²**sifuri.**

sugu (–) 1. callous, callosity; corn *(on the foot);* wart. 2. *fig.* callousness, want of feeling, insensitivity, heartlessness, apathy. **mtu –.** a coarse/unfeeling person. *Cf.* **sugua, usugu.**

sugua rub, scour, clean, polish. – **meno.** clean the teeth. – **kisu.** whet a knife *(by stroking it against an earthenware pot).* – **sakafu.**

smooth a cement floor. *intr.* **suguika.** be/ become hard/insensitive. *appl.* **sugulia.** *appl./caus.* **sugulisha.** *Cf.* **sugu, suguo, usugu.**

suguo (–) 1. (coarse) whetstone, strop. 2. scraper. *Cf.* **sugua.**

suheli* *sing.* (in the) south. (= **kusini.**)

suhuba* (–, ma-) *see* **sahibu.**

suhubiana* (*rare* **suhubu**) be good friends, be on intimate terms. *Cf.* **sahibu, mamsahib, usuhuba.**

suhubu* *see* **suhubiana.**

sujudu* prostrate oneself, bow down, worship; implore. *appl.* **sujudia.** *intr.* **sujudika.** *caus.* **sujudisha.** cause someone to bow down; convert *(to Islam).* *Cf.* **sijida.**

¹suka twist, plait, braid. – **nywele.** braid the hair. – **mkeka.** plait a mat. *inv.* **sukua.** untwist, loosen. **sukua nazi.** remove a coconut from its shell. *Cf.* **¹msuka, ¹msuko, msusi, ususi.**

²suka move quickly back and forth, shake, rock. – (*us.* **sukasuka**) **mkia.** wag the tail. – **maziwa.** churn milk. – **kichwa.** shake the head. *red.* **sukasuka.** 1. = **suka.** 2. cause someone trouble, disturb, worry. *appl.* **sukia. mashine ya kusukia maziwa.** centrifuge, (cream) separator. *Cf.* **masuko, ¹msukano, ¹msuko.**

sukani* (ma-) *see* **usukani.**

sukari* (–) sugar. – **mchanga/cheucheu/ chembechembe.** granulated sugar. – **ya mawe.** lump sugar. *Cf.* **kisukari.**

suke, shuke (–) ear *(of grain).*

sukua *inv. of* **¹suka.**

sukuma 1. push, shove; push aside, crowd, jostle. **haifai kusukuma wazee.** One should not push elderly people aside. 2. urge on, incite, spur on, stimulate, encourage. *appl.* **sukumia.** *intr.* **sukumika.** *int.* **sukumiza.** drive on, push forward; drive back, ward off; incite, stimulate. **sukumiza gari.** drive a car fast. **sukumiza taabu.** ward off difficulties. *ass.* **sukumana.** shove/crowd each other. **kwa kusukumana.** with much crowding/ jostling. *Cf.* **²suka, kisukumi, kisukumizi, msukumizi, msukumano, usukumizi.**

sukutu* 1. *rare* be still/quiet/silent. 2. *interj.:* **askut!** Be still! Silence!

sukutua 1. rinse the mouth, gargle *(before and after meals).* **dawa ya kusukutua.** mouthwash, gargle. 2. *rare, fig.* eat.

sulibi*, sulubu 1. force, compel. 2. torment, torture. 3. *rel.* crucify. *appl.* **sulibia.** *intr.* **sulibika, sulubika.** be forced *(to work);* be accustomed to hard work; be strong/hard/ firm. *caus.* **sulibisha** = **sulibi.** *pass.* **sulibiwa.** *Cf.* **¹sulubu, msalaba.**

sulika* (*rare* **sua**) feel unwell, be dizzy/faint, be subject to vertigo. *Cf.* **sulisuli.**

sulisuli* (–) dizziness, vertigo. *Cf.* **sulika.**

sultani* (ma-) sultan, ruler, monarch. *Cf.* **usultani.**

sulu *adv.:* **piga —.** rub, polish, scour.

sulubika* *intr. of* **sulibi.**

1**sulubu*** (—) (*also* **usulubu** *sing.)* 1. (power of) resistance, strong constitution, stamina. 2. strength, energy; exertion, effort. **kazi ya kuchimba makaa ni ya — sana.** Coal-mining is very hard work. *Cf.* **sulibi.**

2**sulubu*** *see* **sulibi.**

suluhi*, suluhu, selehi 1. improve, perfect. 2. reconcile; adapt, adjust, accommodate; effect an understanding/agreement; come to terms, reach a compromise. *appl.* **suluhia.** *appl.-ass.* **suluhiana.** make peace with each other, become adjusted to each other. *intr.* **suluhika.** be reconciled; be adaptable. *caus.* **suluhisha.** bring into harmony, reconcile, conciliate. **katika vita wanaoshindwa huomba suluhisha.** In the war the conquered asked for a cessation of hostilities. 3. **suluhu, isilahi** (—) reconciliation, agreement, compromise, peace; *(sport)* tie. **taka/omba —.** ask for peace, capitulate. **unanidai sh. 100 (shilingi mia moja), lakini kwa kuwa nimevunya kinanda chako, sasa suluhu yako ni sh. 25 (shilingi ishirini) na tano tu.** You owe me a hundred shillings, but since I have broken your record player, you now owe me only twenty-five shillings *Cf.* **suluhivu, masilaha, msuluhivu, usuluhi.**

suluhivu* *adj., rare* conciliatory, peaceable. *Cf.* **suluhi.**

suluhu* *see* **suluhi.**

1**sululu, sururu** (—) 1. pickax. 2. *zool.* swordfish.

2**sululu** *adv.* at the same time, simultaneously. (= **sare.**)

3**sululu** (—) *ornith.* curlew. (= **kipila.**)

sumaku* (—) magnet. **—a —.** magnetic.

1**sumba, simbu** light, ignite, kindle *(a fire).*

2**sumba** sell at a much reduced price *(under pressure of circumstances).*

3**sumba: ana kichwa cha msumba.** He is annoyed/worried.

sumbivi (—) crisis. *Cf.* **sumbua, sumbufu.**

sumbua 1. worry, upset, disconcert, distress, torment, harass, annoy, tease. 2. oppress, subjugate. *appl.* **sumbulia.** *appl.-ass.* **sumbuliana.** get on each other's nerves. *intr.* **sumbuka.** be distressed/harassed/exhausted. *caus.* **sumbusha.** *(w. int. force)* annoy/torment someone (constantly, intentionally). *Cf.* **sumbufu, sumbulio, sumbuo, masumbuko, msumbufu, usumbufu.**

sumbufu *adj.* annoying, troublesome, vexatious, distressing. *Cf.* **sumbua, msumbufu, usumbufu.**

sumbuko (ma-) *see* **sumbuo.**

sumbulio (ma-) 1. = **sumbuo** 1, 2. 2. persecution, oppression, subjugation. *Cf.* **sumbua.**

sumbuo, sumbuko (ma-) 1. unrest, disquiet, anxiety. 2. trouble, annoyance, vexation, teasing. 3. hindrance, obstacle, difficulty. *Cf.* **sumbua.**

sumile!* *see* **simile!**

sumisha* *caus. of* **sumu.**

sumu* 1. poison. – **mshale.** to poison an arrow. *appl.* **sumia.** *intr.* **sumika.** *caus.* **sumisha.** 2. (–) poison, venom, virus. **lisha –.** give poison (to someone). **kwa –.** poisonous. – **ya kuambukiza.** *med.* virus.

sumughu* (–) gum(-arabic).

sumulia *see* **[1]simulia.**

suna* 1. (–) = **[2]suni.** 2. *adj.* commendable, creditable, praiseworthy, meritorious.

sunagogi* [*Engl.*] (–) synagogue.

sungua sweep up the chaff *(after winnowing grain).*

sungura (–) 1. hare. 2. *fig.* a shrewd/cunning person.

sungusungu (–) sungusungu (large black ant).

[1]suni* (–) *Isl.* Sunnite. **yeye ni –.** He belongs to the Sunnite sect.

[2]suni*, suna (–) 1. good tradition. 2. commendable achievement. 3. (piece of) good advice.

sunobari* (–) sunobari (kind of pine wood). *Cf.* **msunobari.**

sununa *see* **sonona.**

sunza 1. part with reluctantly, give grudgingly; move hesitantly/uncertainly. – **mguu (mkono).** grope one's way (in the dark). – **teo (kombea).** throw with a sling. 2. tease, annoy.

sunzu (–) sunzu (a tuft of hair left when the rest of the head is shaved).

supu* [*Engl.*] (–) soup, gravy. **nywa –.** eat *(lit.:* drink) soup.

[1]sura* (–) 1. look, appearance, expression *(of the face).* **ana – nzuri.** She is attractive in appearance/makes a pleasing impression. 2. similarity, resemblance. **Ana sura kama ya mama yake.** She looks like her mother. 3. surface. – **ya nchi.** surface of the earth. (= **uso.**) *Cf.* **kisura.**

[2]sura* (–) 1. *Isl.* surah of the Koran. 2. *(in gen.)* chapter *(of a book).*

suria* (ma-) *hist.* 1. female servant (who lives as a concubine with her master). 2. concubine. *Cf.* **suriama, usuria.**

suriama* (ma-) 1. suriama (child of a concubine). 2. half-caste. *Cf.* **suria.**

surua*, shurua, churua [*Pers.*] (–) *med.* measles.

suruali*, surwali (–) trousers. – **fupi/kipande.** shorts (= **kaputula**). – **ndefu.** long trousers.

[1]**sururu** (–) *see* [1]**sululu.**

[2]**sururu** (–) sururu (kind of beetle which destroys coconut palms).

surwali* (–) *see* **suruali.**

sus* (–) *see* [1]**susu.**

[1]**susa*** (–) 1. tartar *(on the teeth).* 2. *med.* decay, caries.

[2]**susa** (& *appl.* **susia**) refuse *(food, etc., in a pout),* have nothing to do with, despise, disdain; *(recent)* boycott, sabotage. **– amri.** boycott a regulation.

susia *see* [2]**susa.**

[1]**susu***, **sus** (–) licorice.

[2]**susu** (–) 1. clothes-rack, shelf, *(etc., on a wall).* 2. hammock, (child's) cot.

susuika 1. withdraw an accusation when confronted by the person accused, back down. 2. bring false charges (against someone). 3. question intensively, give the third degree.

susurika wander around, loiter; waste time. *Cf.* **zurura.**

susuwaa become dry/hard, dry up.

[1]**suta** confront, accuse, make open charges against a person. *ass.* **sutana.** accuse each other. *pass.* **sutwa. amesutwa mbele ya watu.** He has been publicly accused. *Cf.* **masuto, msuto, suto.**

[2]**suta** (–) spendthrift, bankrupt person.

suti* [*Engl.*] (–) suit *(of clothes).*

suto (ma-) (*also* **msuto, mi-**) (public), accusation, indictment; rebuke, reprimand. *Cf.* [1]**suta.**

suuza *see* **suza.**

suza, suuza rinse (off). **– nguo.** rinse clothes. **– mikono.** rinse off the hands *(to remove the soap).*

swafi* *see* **safi** 1.

swaga drive *(cattle).*

Swahili* *sing.* the Swahili coast. *Cf.* **Kiswahili, Mswahili, Uswahili.**

[1]**swala, swara** (–) swala (impala, Grant's gazelle).

[2]**swala** (ma-) *see* **swali.**

swali*, swala, siala (ma-) question. **nina –.** I have a question. *Cf.* **saili.**

swara (–) *see* [1]**swala.**

sweta* [*Engl.*] (–) sweater.

swichi*, swisi [*Engl.*] (–) switch *(railw., elec.).*

swila (–) (spitting) cobra. (= [1]**fira.**)

swisi* (–) *see* **swichi.**

T

[1]**taa** (–) 1. obedience, discipline. 2. devotion, submissiveness, humility. *Cf.* **tii.**

[2]**taa** (–) lamp. **washa (zima) –.** light (extinguish) a lamp. **– ya umeme.** 1. electric lamp. 2. *rare* electric light bulb. **– za mbele, – kubwa.** searchlight, headlight *(of an automobile).* **kinu cha –.** electric power plant.

[3]**taa** (–) taa (kind of fish: skate, ray).

[4]**taa** *see* **taala.**

[5]**taa** *pl. of* **utaa.**

taabika* 1. be in difficulty/distress. 2. be worried/perturbed. *caus.* **taabisha.** distress, trouble, worry; oppress. *Cf.* **taabu.**

taabu (–) 1. difficulty; toil, trouble, hardship. 2. inconvenience, annoyance. 3. want, privation, misery, distress. *Cf.* **taabika.**

taadabu* *see* **adibu.**

taadhima* (–) 1. fame, splendor, glory. 2. respect, esteem, honor. *Cf.* **adhama, taadhimika.**

taadhimika* 1. be glorious/majestic/exalted. 2. be honored/respected. *Cf.* **adhama, taadhima.**

taadi* *see* **tadi.**

taahari* delay, procrastinate, be late. *Cf.* **ahiri.**

taahira* (–) delay, postponement; respite. *Cf.* **ahiri.**

taajabu* *see* **staajabu.**

taala*, taa *Isl.* be exalted. **Allah –.** God is most high.

taalamu* be learned; be well educated/well informed. *Cf.* **elimu, maalum, utaalamu.**

taali* learn, study. *Cf.* **mtaala.**

taalimu*, taaluma (–) 1. education, culture. 2. instruction, study. *Cf.* **elimu.**

taaluma* (–) *see* **taalimu.**

taamali* think, reflect, ponder. *Cf.* **taamuli.**

taamamu* take a chance, avail oneself of an opportunity.

taamuli* (–) thought, reflection, meditation. *Cf.* **taamali.**

taanasa* 1. be a pleasure seeker, lead a life of luxury. 2. (–) = **anasa.**

taanisi* *see* **anisi.**

taaraa* *see* **taraa.**

taaradhi*, taaradhia 1. interfere/meddle *(in other people's affairs);* concern oneself with, become involved in *(a matter).* 2. disturb; obstruct, impede.

taaradhia* *see* **taaradhi.**

taarifa*, taarifu (–) report, statement *(written or spoken); (pol.)* communiqué. – **ya pamoja.** joint communiqué. *Cf.* **arifu.**

taarifu* (–) *see* **taarifa.**

taashira* (–) *see* **ishara.**

taataa* 1. move restlessly; toss, writhe *(in pain).* 2. be confused/bewildered, talk incoherently.

taathiri* (–) effect, influence. *Cf.* **athari.**

taba, tabu, tabutabu (–) 1. piece, fragment, scrap. 2. strip of palm leaf *(for plaiting baskets). Cf.* **tabua.**

tabahani* be learned/well-educated.

tabaka* (–, **ma-**) 1. cover, lid. *fig.* – **moja.** side by side, close together, nearby. 2. lining *(of a garment).* 3. fold, crease. – **ya suruali.** (ironed) crease *(in trousers).* 4. layer, stratum; class *(of society).* – **za makaa (madini).** bed/deposit of coal (ore). – **ya tanuu.** charge/batch *(in a lime kiln).* **mapigiano ya kitabaka.** *comm.* class struggle. *Cf.* **tabiki.**

tabakelo* [*Port.*] (–) tobacco-case, snuffbox.

tabakwa be/become poor/impoverished, fall upon evil days.

tabana *arch.* pronounce magic formulas/incantations *(in preparing medicines). caus.* **tabanya.**

tabangatabanga spoil *(by mixing with something of an inferior quality),* adulterate.

tabanya *caus. of* **tabana.**

tabaradi*, tabaridi, tabarudu *see* **burudi.**

tabaruki*, tabaruku 1. *Isl.* gather for prayer. 2. gather for social purposes *(conversation, etc.).* 3. dedicate. – **kanisa.** dedicate a church. *Cf.* **baraka.**

tabaruku* *see* **tabaruki.**

tabasamu* 1. smile. (= [1]**cheka.**) 2. *fig.* be hypocritical, feign innocence. 3. (–) smile, grin, smirk. (= **kicheko.**)

tabasuri* (–) *see* **busara.**

tabawali*, dabaulo *rare* urinate. (= **kojoa.**)

tabia* (–) 1. (natural) environment, (geographical, climatic) features/conditions. 2. nature, character, disposition *(of people),* property *(of a thing).*

[1]**tabibia*** treat *(medically),* cure, nurse back to health. (= [1]**tibu.**) *intr.* **tabibika.** *pass.* **tabibwa.** *Cf.* [1]**tiba,** [1]**tibu, tabibu.**

[2]**tabibia*** (–) *see* **tiba.**

tabibu*, mtabibu (**wa-**) doctor, physician. (= **mganga.**) *Cf.* [1]**tiba,** [1]**tibu,** [1]**tabibia, utabibu.**

tabii* become accustomed to something, contract a habit.

tabiki* 1. lie directly on top of something, adhere to, cover, line. 2. be folded/creased. 3. be/become attached to, grow fond of *(a person)*. *appl.* **tabikia.** *ass.* **tabikiana.** be close friends. *caus.* **tabikisha.** put on top of, cover; fold; paste/glue together; *(fig.)* establish friendly contacts. *Cf.* **tabaka.**

tabiri* foretell, predict, tell fortunes, interpret dreams; *(in gen.)* explain, interpret. *appl.* **tabiria.** *intr.* **tabirika.** *caus.* **tabirisha.** *Cf.* **mtabiri, utabiri.**

tabu (–) *see* **taba.**

tabua break/tear off, pluck. *appl.* **tabulia.** *intr.* **tabulika.** *Cf.* **taba.**

tabulia *appl. of* **tabua.**

tabura* (–) *mil.* training, drill.

tabutabu (–) *see* **taba.**

tadaraki*, tadariki *see* **diriki.**

tadhibiri*, tadubiri 1. put in order, mend, repair, revise. 2. look/hunt for, search.

tadi*, taadi 1. transgress, violate, not observe, fail to comply with *(customs, laws)*. 2. offend *(someone)*, mistreat, abuse, bully. 3. attack. *appl.* **tadia.** 4. (–) (*also* **utadi,** *sing.*) violation, infraction; offense, insult; attack.

tadubiri* *see* **tadhibiri.**

tafadhali* 1. please, do a favor, be so kind *(as to do something)*. 2. *interj.* Please (do me the favor). Would you please be so kind. *Cf.* **fadhili.**

tafakari* *see* **fikiri.**

tafaraji*, tafaruji enjoy/amuse oneself, find relaxation. *Cf.* **tafrija.**

tafaruji* *see* **tafaraji.**

tafauti* (–) *see* **tofauti.**

tafi (–) *see* [1]**tasi.**

tafiti* 1. interfere, meddle, pry. 2. be inquisitive/critical. *Cf.* **fatiisha, tafuta, mtafitaji, mtafiti, utafiti.**

taflisi* (–) bankruptcy. (= **ufilisi.**)

tafrija*, tafriji (–) entertainment, amusement, relaxation, diversion; party, reception; concert. *Cf.* **tafaraji.**

tafsiri* 1. explain, interpret, comment on. 2. translate, interpret. 3. (ma-) explanation, interpretation, commentary; translation. *Cf.* **fasiri.**

tafuna chew, gnaw, nibble. *Cf.* **matafuni, mtafuni, mtafuno.**

tafuta* 1. look/hunt for, search. – **vitu.** hunt for things. – **ugomvi.** look for trouble, pick a fight. – **maneno.** try to find words. 2. find, discover. *appl.* **tafutia.** search out, look for (something/someone). *caus.* **tafutisha.** *red.* **tafutatafuta** *(w. intr. force)* hunt everywhere. *Cf.* **fatiisha, tafiti, mtafutaji, utafutaji.**

[1]taga (*us.* – **yai**) lay *(an egg). pass.* **tagwa** *caus.* **tagisha.** *Cf.* **tago, mtago.**

[2]taga, tagaa (**ma-**) (*also* **utagaa** *sing.*, **kitagaa, vi-**) branching, forking *(of a tree, a road). Cf.* **[1]tagaa.**

[1]tagaa 1. walk fast *(with long steps)*, stride. 2. straddle, sit straddle-legged. 3. waddle (= **bata, magamaga**). *Cf.* **[2]taga, [1]kitagaa, matagataga.**

[2]tagaa (**ma-**) *see* **[2]taga.**

taghafali* 1. be taken unawares, be surprised/amazed. 2. be distracted/absentminded/inattentive; act thoughtlessly/imprudently. *caus.* **taghafalisha.** *pass.* **taghafaliwa.** *Cf.* **ghafula.**

tagio (**ma-**) *see* **tago.**

tago, tagio (**ma-**) place where a hen lays eggs, nest. *Cf.* **[1]taga.**

tahadhari* *frequently the imperative of* **hadhari:** – **mbele ya simba!** Beware of the lion!

tahafifu* *adj.* *see* **hafifu.**

tahalili* (–) *see* **tahlili.**

tahamaki* 1. pay heed to, notice, observe. 2. *interj. (imper.)* Look! Behold! 3. *adv.* suddenly. **tulipokwenda njiani,** – **akatokea chui.** While we were on our way, a leopard suddenly appeared.

taharaki*, taharuki 1. be in a hurry, be busy. 2. be excited. *appl.* **taharukia.** *caus.* **taharukisha.** *Cf.* **haraka.**

taharizi* (–) side pieces of a kanzu. *Cf.* **badani.**

taharuki* *see* **taharaki.**

tahayari* 1. (*& intr.* **tahayarika**) be ashamed; by shy/bashful; be humiliated. *caus.* **tahayarisha.** put to shame, humiliate. 2. (–) = **[1]haya.** *Cf.* **[1]haya, tahayuri.**

tahayuri* (–) 1. shame, humiliation, disgrace. 2. embarrassment, confusion. *Cf.* **[1]haya, tahayari.**

tahidi* *see* **jitahidi.**

tahiri* 1. purify (ritually). 2. *eth.* circumcise. 3. *med.* operate. *pass.* **tahiriwa. mtoto huyu ametahiriwa.** This child has been circumcised. *caus.* **tahirisha.** 4. (–) *rare* circumcision; *(usually:)* a ritually pure person. *Cf.* **tohara.**

tahlili*, tahalili (–) song of mourning, dirge.

tahyati* *interj.(in salutation)* (I wish you) a long life! *Cf.* **hai.**

[1]tai* (–) tai (a small pastry).

[2]tai* [*Engl.*] (–) (neck)tie.

[3]tai (–) tai (a large bird of prey: eagle, vulture).

taibika* *intr. of* **taibu.**

taibu*, tayibu 1. be good/kind/obliging. 2. be well/in good health. *intr.* **taibika.** be happy/contented. 3. *adv.* good, well, right(ly). 4. *interj.* **tayib!** Good! Very well!

taifa* **(ma-)** 1. race, (large) tribe. 2. *rec., pol.* nation. **Umoja wa Mataifa.** the United Nations. **mataifa makuu.** the Great Powers. **– a mataifa mbalimbali.** international. *Cf.* **kitaifa, utaifa.**

taifod* **(–)** *see* **taifoid.**

taifoid*, taifod [*Engl.*] **(–)** *med.* typhoid (fever).

taileni, tailetai, tawireni *interj., ethn.* Help! *(a cry introducing and concluding the ceremony for exorcising spirits).*

tailetai *see* **taileni.**

taili* *see* **talii.**

taimu* [*Engl.*] **(–)** *sport* time.

taipu* [*Engl.*] **(–)** typewriter. **piga –.** to type. **kwa maandiko ya –.** typewritten.

tairi* [*Engl.*] **(–)** (automobile) tire.

¹taiti* be in (financial) need, be poverty-stricken, be hard up. *Cf.* **utaiti.**

²taiti* [*Engl.*] **(–)** tight/close-fitting dress, sheath.

taja 1. name, mention. **– jina.** call by name. 2. *rare* nominate *(for election).* (= **chagua.**) *intr.* **tajika.** be worthy of mention. *pass.* **tajwa.** be mentioned/reported/quoted. *Cf.* **mtajaji.**

tajamala* **(–)** 1. favor, kindness. 2. approval, agreement. *Cf.* **jamala.**

tajamali* show favor/kindness, do a favor to someone, help, assist. *Cf.* **jamala, tajamala.**

taji* **(–)** crown, diadem, coronet.

tajiri* 1. (*also* **tijara**) engage in commerce, become rich. *appl.* **tajiria.** *intr.* **tajirika.** *caus.* **tajirisha.** *refl.* **jitajirisha.** enrich oneself. 2. **(ma-)** (*also* **mtajiri, wa-**) rich man, (wholesale) merchant, capitalist. *prov.* **– na maliye, maskini na mwanawe.** A rich man and his property are like a poor man and his son. *Cf.* **utajiri.**

tajwa *pass. of* **taja.**

¹taka, takataka (ma-) 1. dirt, rubbish, garbage. 2. a worthless thing, junk, trash. *Cf.* **kitakataka, ²mataka.**

²taka* **(–)** bolt (of cloth/calico, about 30 yards).

³taka 1. want, wish. 2. ask for, request, inquire about. **– shauri.** ask for advice. 3. need. 4. have a tendency to..., incline to... 5. intend, be going to..., be about to..., be on the verge of... **inataka kunyesha.** It is going to rain. *appl.* **takia.** *intr.*

takika, *us. intr.-ass.* **takikana.** be desired/desirable. **haitakikani.** It is not desirable. *ass.* **takana.** desire each other (sexually). *Cf.* **[1]mataka, mtaka, mtashi, utashi.**

takabadhi* 1. *see* **kabidhi.** 2. *caus.* **takabadhisha.** entrust someone with something. – **fedha.** entrust someone with money. *Cf.* **kabidhi.**

takabali* *see* **kubali.**

takabari* (*also refl.* **jitakabari**) be proud/arrogant, show off. *Cf.* **kiburi.**

takadamu* 1. go forward, precede, lead the way. 2. lead, guide, escort. 3. *(of timepieces)* go (too) fast. *Cf.* **kadamu.**

takalifu* 1. go to trouble, take pains; obligate oneself. 2. (–) difficulty, trouble, inconvenience; disorder, disturbance. *Cf.* **kalifu.**

takamali* be complete/perfect. *Cf.* **kamili.**

takaramu* (–) *see* **karama.**

takarimu* *see* **karimu, karama.**

takasa *caus. of* **takata.**

takata 1. be clean/pure. **nguo yangu imetakata kwa sababu nimeifua na sabuni bora.** My dress is clean/white because I washed it with good soap. 2. be clear/bright. **kumetakata.** It is clear/has cleared up *(the weather).* 3. *rel.* be holy/sanctified/consecrated. *intr.* **takatika.** *caus.* **takasa.** 1. clean, cleanse, purify. 2. make clear, clear up. 3. purify ritually *(e.g., after menstruation). Cf.* **takatifu, takato, mtakaso, mtakatifu, utakaso, utakatifu.**

takataka (ma-) *see* **[1]taka.**

takatifu *adj.* 1. clean, pure, clear. 2. *rel.* holy, sanctified. *Cf.* **takata, mtakatifu, utakatifu.**

takato (ma-) 1. cleaning, cleansing, purification. 2. cleanness, purity. 3. carefulness, neatness. 4. *fig.* innocence, chastity. *Cf.* **takata.**

takbira* *Isl.* to repeat the formula 'Allah akbar,' Allah is great.

[1]takia (ma-) (*us.* **matakia**) request, demand, claim.

[2]takia* (ma-) large cushion.

[3]takia *appl. of* **[3]taka.**

takikana *intr.-ass. of* **[3]taka.**

takilifu* *see* **takalifu** 2.

tako (ma-) 1. *(us. pl.)* seat, buttocks. 2. butt-end (of something), base. – **la mkuki.** the butt(-end) of the spear. **mstari wa (ki)tako.** base line. 3. end, main point. *Cf.* **kitakizo, kitako, matako, utako.**

takriban* *adv.* almost, nearly. *Cf.* **karibu, karibia.**

takshi* (–) fez, tarboosh. (= **tarbushi.**)

taksiri* (–) fault, defect; shortage, deficit; offense, crime.

[1]**takua** (–) pride, arrogance, ostentation.

[2]**takua** *dial.* scratch, scrape. **kuku wanapotafuta chakula hutakua mchanga.** When chickens hunt for food they ordinarily scratch in the sand.

takwimu* (–) calendar, almanac.

taladadi* *see* **taradadi.**

talaka* (–) divorce. **kumpa fulani –.** grant someone a divorce. *Cf.* **taliki.**

talakeki*, talakaki (–) powderhorn. (= **pembe.**)

talakim* (–) *Isl.* burial prayers. (= **uradi.**)

talaleshi* (**ma-**) *see* **mtalaleshi.**

talasimu* (**ma-**) talisman, amulet, charm.

tale (**ma-**) *see* **kitale.**

talibisi* (–) talibisi (mat protecting cargo on a heavily loaded dhow).

talii*, taili 1. investigate, examine. **ameenda kwenye safari ya kutalii nchi.** He is touring the country. 2. teach, instruct.

taliki* divorce, annul a marriage. **alimtaliki mkewe.** He has divorced his wife. *pass.* **talikiwa.** be divorced. **mke alitalikiwa.** The woman has been divorced. *Cf.* **talaka.**

taliza* smear, plaster *(a wall with clay, mortar).*

[1]**tama*** 1. be ended, come to an end. 2. (–) end, conclusion, final stage; (final) decision. 3. *adv.* final, conclusive, decisive. *Cf.* **tamati.**

[2]**tama*, dama** (–) 1. dirt, rubbish. 2. a worthless thing, trash, trifle; nonsense.

[3]**tama** *rare* move, change one's residence; emigrate. (= **hama.**)

[4]**tama** (–): **shika –.** to rest the head on one's hands.

[5]**tama:** – (*or* **mtama**) **la bibi.** *ornith.* (species of) cuckoo.

tamaa* (–), **tamani** (**ma-**), **tamanio** (**ma-**) 1. longing, yearning, striving, desire, ambition. **wa na (fanya) –.** desire, wish. 2. hope. **shika –.** live in hope. **kata (ondoa) –.** give up hope. 3. avarice, greed. **– ya mapesa.** greed for money. **ana –.** He is avaricious. 4. (sexual) desire, lust. *Cf.* **tamani, mtamani, tamauka, tumaini.**

tamaduni* become refined/civilized. *Cf.* **utamaduni.**

tamalaki*, tamaleki *see* [1]**miliki.**

tamani* 1. yearn, desire, strive. **natamani kurudi nyumbani.** I yearn to return home. 2. hope. *intr.* **tamanika** be worth striving for; be attractive/absorbing. *caus.* **tamanisha.** arouse desire; attract, fascinate. 3. (ma-) = **tamaa.** *Cf.* **tamaa, mtamani, utamanifu.**

tamanio (ma-) (*us.* **matamanio**) *see* **tamaa.**

tamasha* (–, ma-) 1. festival, entertainment, festivity. **sikukuu ya uhuru ilikuwa na – nyingi.** The independence holiday was celebrated with great festivity. 2. show, pageant, spectacle.

tamati* (–) *liter.* finis, end *(of a story or performance).* *Cf.* [1]**tama.**

tamauka* be satisfied/appeased *(of desires).* *Cf.* **tamaa.**

tamba 1. dance, leap *(as in the triumphal dance of warriors).* 2. *fig.* strut, swagger. 3. boast *(of a success, one's prowess, personal appearance, etc.),* be exultant, glory (in something). **Mariamu alikuwa wa kwanza darasani, mwetu na sikuhizi anatamba ajabu.** Mary was first in our class, and she boasts a lot these days. *Cf.* [1]**tambo,** [4]**kitambi, mtambatamba.**

[1]**tambaa** 1. creep, crawl, move forward unsteadily. **mtoto anatambaa.** The child crawls around. 2. crawl, wriggle *(of reptiles). fig.* **ugonjwa utambaao.** a creeping sickness. 3. twist, twine. **mimea inayotambaa.** creeping/twining plants. 4. stretch, extend. **pori linatambaa.** The savannah stretches out a long way. 5. fawn, curry favor. *appl.* **tambalia.** creep up to. *caus.* **tambaza** (*rare* **tambarisha**). drag. **tambaza maneno.** speak slowly, drawl. *Cf.* **tambazi,** [1]**mtambaa, mtambazi, utambazi.**

[2]**tambaa, tambara** (ma-) 1. a piece/length/strip/scrap of cotton cloth (calico). 2. an old article of clothing, piece of old cloth, rag. *Cf.* **kitambaa, utambaa.**

tambara (ma-) *see* [2]**tambaa.**

tambarajika 1. be old/worn-out. 2. *fig.* be feeble/decrepit. *Cf.* [2]**tambaa.**

tambarare (–) *geogr.* plain. **nchi ya –.** level land.

tambarisha *caus. of* [1]**tambaa.**

tambaza *caus. of* [1]**tambaa.**

tambazi 1. *adj.* creeping, crawling. 2. (ma-) *med.* a spreading skin-disease, phlegmon. *Cf.* [1]**tambaa, mtambazi, utambazi.**

[1]**tambi** (–) noodle, macaroni. *Cf.* **utambi.**

[2]**tambi** *pl. of* **utambi.**

tambika *ethn.* make a sacrifice/offering to propitiate the spirits of the dead (mizimu). *Cf.* **tambiko, mtambikaji, mtambiko.**

tambiko (ma-) 1. a sacrifice/offering *(animals, fowls, beer, cloth)* made to propitiate the spirits of the dead. **mara nyingi watu wakiisha tambika, hunywa pombe ya –.**

Often when people have made sacrifices, they are accustomed to drink the tambiko beer. 2. tambiko (a totem). *Cf.* **tambika.**

[1]**tambo (ma-), utambo (–)** strutting, swaggering; prancing, rearing *(of horses)*. *Cf.* **tamba.**

[2]**tambo (–), utambo** *sing.* length, width; height, tallness, stature; distance. *Cf.* **kitambo.**

[3]**tambo (ma-)** 1. riddle, enigma. 2. secret language. *Cf.* **tambua.**

[4]**tambo (ma-)** strength, vigor. **ana –.** He is powerful/muscular.

tamboa (ma-) *anat.* testicle. (= **pumbu, korodani.**)

tambua 1. recognize. 2. remember. 3. perceive, understand. **asitambuke.** be unknown, be unrecognized, remain incognito. *appl.* **tambulia.** *intr.* **tambulika.** be well-known/remarkable. *intr.-ass.* **tambulikana.** be recognizable/memorable/understandable/distinctive. *caus.* **tambulisha.** make known, determine; explain; point out, identify; guess, make out, decipher. *ass.* **tambuana. baada ya kukutana walitambuana.** After they had met they recognized each other. *Cf.* **tambuzi, kitambulisho, matambuzi, mtambuzi, utambulisho, utambuzi.**

tambuu*, dhambu [*Ind., Pers.*] (–) betel. **jani la –.** betel leaf. **tafuna –.** chew betel. *Cf.* **mtambuu.**

tambuza forge, weld, hammer.

tambuzi *adj.* intelligent, clever. *Cf.* **tambua.**

tamfu *adj.* easily pronounceable. **herufi –.** vowel. *Cf.* **tamka.**

tamia, atamia, otamia, *(rare)* **latamia** 1. sit on eggs, brood, hatch. 2. *fig., rare* bring up a child. *caus.* **tamisha.** put eggs under a hen. *Cf.* [2]**ota.**

tamka 1. pronounce, articulate. **analitamka neno hili vibaya.** He does not pronounce this word well. 2. accent, stress, emphasize. 3. express something publicly, declare, announce. *Cf.* **tamfu, tamko, matamko.**

tamko, tamshi (ma-) (*us.* **matamko, matamshi**) 1. pronunciation, articulation. **ana matamko ya kigeni.** He has a foreign (incorrect) pronunciation. 2. accent, stress. 3. *rare* declaration, announcement, statement. *Cf.* **tamka.**

tamshi (ma-) *see* **tamko.**

tamthili* (–) similarity, analogy.

tamu* *adj./adv.* 1. sweet. **maji matamu.** sweet water *(in contr. w. salt water)*. 2. pleasant, agreeable; appetizing, good *(of foods)*. **maneno matamu.** pleasant words. **chakula kitamu.** tasty/appetizing foods *(not necessarily sweet)*. 3 mild, gentle. **upepo mtamu.** a gentle breeze. 4. *adv.* in a pleasant way. **anasema**

utamu. He speaks pleasantly. 5. (–; *also* **tamutamu**) candy, confectionery, dessert. *Cf.* **utamu.**

tamutamu (–) *see* **tamu** 5.

tamvua (**ma-**), **utamvua** *sing.* fringe, tassel. *Cf.* **chambua.**

[1]**tana** (**ma-**) bunch of bananas. *Cf.* [1]**chana.**

[2]**tana** *see* [3]**chana.**

tanabahi* 1. pay attention, notice, observe. 2. be awake/alert/on one's guard/ready. 3. understand. *Cf.* **nabihi.**

tanadhari* be on one's guard, take care, be cautious. *Cf.* **nadhari.**

tanafusi* breathe, catch one's breath; sigh. *Cf.* **nafasi, nafsi.**

tanaki* [*Engl.*] (**ma-**) *see* **tangi.**

tanasara* be converted to Christianity. *caus.* **tanasarisha.** convert someone to Christianity.

tanashati* *adj.* clean, neat, pretty, well-dressed. *Cf.* **mtanashati, utanashati.**

tanboi* [*Engl.*] (**ma-**) *see* **taniboi.**

tanda 1. cover. **kumetanda.** It is overcast/cloudy. *fig.* strike, beat. **ametandikwa fimbo nne.** He has received four blows with a stick. 2. spread out, extend. *refl.* **jitanda. jitanda nguo.** cover oneself with a garment. *intr.* **tandika** = **tanda. tandika kitanda.** make a bed. **tandika mikeka.** spread mats. **tandika punda.** harness a donkey. *caus.* **tandaza, tandisha.** spread out, stretch out (*often* = **tanda**). **tandaza mtama.** spread out millet (to dry). *stat.* **tandama.** lie stretched out. **mamba anatandama juani.** The crocodile is lying stretched out in the sun. *stat.-ass.* **tandamana.** be extended/drawn out full length. *inv.* **tandua.** take off, uncover. **tandua kitanda.** strip a bed. **tandua punda.** unharness a donkey. *inv.-appl.* **tandulia.** *inv.-intr.* **tanduka.** *inv.-caus.* **tanduza.** *Cf.* **tandaa, tandabui, tandiko, tando, tanzi, kitanda, kitandiko, kitanzi, mtanda, mtande, mtandio, mtando, utando, utanzi.**

tandaa 1. be spread out/scattered over a large area. 2. be wide/open *(a plain, etc.). Cf.* **tanda.**

tandabelua* (–) *see* **tanta.**

tandabui (–) 1. spider web. 2. a membrane sometimes covering the head of an infant at birth. 3. *fig.:* **macho yangu yameingia –.** I cannot see clearly. My eyes are clouded over. (*lit.:* My eyes are covered by a membrane.) *Cf.* **tanda, buibui.**

tandala (–) *zool.* tandala (greater kudu).

tandama *stat. of* **tanda.**

tandarua (–) *see* **chandalua.**

tandawaa 1. be silent/taciturn. 2. be thoughtful/pensive/melancholy. *appl.* **tandawalia.**

tandaza *caus. of* **tanda.**

tandiko (ma-) 1. cover(ing). **matandiko ya kitanda.** bedding, bedclothes. 2. mat, mattress, carpet. 3. saddlery. *Cf.* **tanda.**

tando 1. (ma-) (*also* **tandu**) something spread out. **– la buibui.** spider web (= **tandabui**). **– la macho.** *med.* cataract (*lit.:* eye membrane). 2. (ma-) tando (kind of fungus). 3. (–) swarm, pack. *Cf.* **tanda.**

[1]**tandu*** [*Pers.*] (–) centipede.

[2]**tandu** (ma-) *see* **tando.**

tandua *inv. of* **tanda.**

[1]**tanga, tangatanga** be idle, waste time; wander about aimlessly, loiter, lounge around. **siku hizi hana kazi anatangatanga ovyo.** He has no work at present and lounges around. *caus.* **tangisha, tangaza.** 1. cause to be idle. 2. = **tanga.** *Cf.* [1]**tango,** [1]**kitango, mtangatanga,** [2]**mtango.**

[2]**tanga** (ma-) *naut.* sail. **tweka –.** set sail. **tua/kunja –.** lower/take in sail.

[3]**tanga** (ma-) (*us.* **matanga**) (period of formal) mourning (3-10 days, during which friends of the deceased sleep in the house of mourning). **weka (kaa) matanga, lala –.** to observe (this practice of) mourning.

[4]**tanga** *pl. of* **utanga.**

tangaa be spread/circulated, become (widely) known. **habari hizi zimetangaa ulimwengu mzima.** These reports have been spread over the entire world. *caus.* **tangaza.** make known, spread, publish, propagate. **tangaza biashara.** advertise. *caus.-appl.* **tangazia.** make something known. *caus.-ass.* **tangazana.** make acquainted with each other. *Cf.* **tangazo, mtangazi, utangazaji.**

tangamana, changamana *stat.-ass. of* [1]**changa.**

tangamano (ma-) *see* **changamano.**

tangambili (–) *rare* period of changing winds (between the southwest and the northeast monsoons; *lit.* two sails). (= **maleleji.**)

tangatanga *see* [1]**tanga.**

tangawizi (–) ginger. *Cf.* **mtangawizi.**

[1]**tangaza** *caus. of* [1]**tanga.**

[2]**tangaza** *caus. of* **tangaa.**

tangazo (ma-) 1. announcement, proclamation, publication. **– la serikali.** government proclamation. 2. notice, advertisement. **– la biashara.** business advertisement. 3. information, advertising, propaganda, publicity. *Cf.* **tangaa.**

tangi*, tanki, tanaki [*Engl.*] (ma-) tank, reservoir. **– la mafuta (maji).** oil (water) tank.

[1]tango **(ma-)** idling, loitering, loafing, vagrancy. *Cf.* **[1]tanga.**

[2]tango **(ma-)** (kind of) cucumber. *Cf.* **[1]mtango.**

[3]tango **(ma-)** gutter, eaves.

tangu *prep.* (= **toka, kutoka.**) 1. since. **– lini?** since when? **– miezi mitano.** for five months. 2. from. **– lini mpaka lini?** from when to when? **– leo.** from now on, in future. **– hapo mbeleni.** in the past, a long time ago.

tangua do away with, abolish, cancel, annul, revoke, suspend, invalidate. **– deni.** pay off/amortize a debt. **– sheria.** repeal a law. **– urafiki.** break off a friendship. *intr.* **tanguka.** *Cf.* **tanguko, kitanguo.**

tanguko, tanguo **(ma-)** abolishment, cancellation, annulment, suspension, abolition, abrogation, repeal, revocation. **– la ndoa.** divorce. *Cf.* **tangua.**

tangulia 1. go before, precede. 2. lead, take the lead. 3. anticipate, forestall. **alitangulia kuniambia.** He was the first to tell me. **amenitangulia jua.** He was born before me (is older than I). *caus.* **tanguliza.** cause to go before, give precedence/preference to. *caus.-refl.* **jitanguliza.** put oneself forward, look out for one's own interests, defend oneself. *Cf.* **tangulifu, kitangulizi, mtangulizi, utangulizi, yaliyotangulia.**

tangulifu *adj.* 1. leading, eminent; important, significant. 2. early, premature. *Cf.* **tangulia.**

tanguo **(ma-)** *see* **tanguko.**

[1]tani, tanitani *adv.:* **kwa –.** on the back, backwards, sideways, askew. *Cf.* **chali.**

[2]tani* [*Engl.*] (–) ton. *fig.:* **ana – sana.** He is very strong.

tania* be on familiar terms with someone, treat someone as a friend or relative. *ass.* **taniana.** *Cf.* **mtani, utani, watani.**

taniboi*, tanboi [*Engl.*] **(ma-)** helper (on a bus, truck), loader, unloader (one who loads or unloads baggage or merchandise on a bus or truck and who sits in the back, not with the driver). *Cf.* **[2]tani, boi.**

tanitani *see* **[1]tani.**

tanki* **(ma-)** *see* **tangi.**

[1]tano (*rare* **tanu**) *num.* five. **–a –.** fifth. **Jumatano.** Wednesday. *Cf.* **kitano.**

[2]tano* (–) *see* **tanuu.**

tanta*, tantabelua, tandabelua [*Ind.*] (–) noise, row, disturbance.

tantabelua* (–) *see* **tanta.**

[1]tanu *see* **[1]tano.**

[2]tanu* (–) *see* **tanuu.**

tanua open wide, widen, expand, increase, enlarge. **– kinywa.** open the mouth wide. **– miguu.** take long steps. *appl.* **tanulia.** *intr.* **tanuka.**

tanuri* (–) *see* **tanuu.**

tanuru* (–) *see* **tanuu.**

tanuu*, tanuru, tanuri, tanu, tano (–) lime-kiln, furnace. **choma –.** burn lime. **– la kuba.** cupola furnace.

tanzi (–, **ma-**) (*also* **kitanzi,vi-**) noose, loop, slipknot; snare, trap *(controlled by a cord).* **– la samaki.** catch/haul of fish. **ametiwa –.** He was hanged. *Cf.* **tanda, kitanzi, utanzi.**

tanzia* (–) funeral announcement, death-notice. **amepata –.** He has received a death-notice. **pa mkono wa –.** pay someone a visit of condolence, express one's sympathy (on the occasion of a death).

¹**tanzu** (**ma-**) *rare* branch, bough. (= **tawi.**)

²**tanzu** *pl. of* **utanzu.**

tanzua 1. open. **– macho.** open the eyes. 2. uncover, expose, detect. **– jambo gumu.** explain a difficult thing. **– siri.** reveal a secret. *intr.* **tanzuka.** 1. be opened/exposed/revealed. **jambo halitanzuki.** The matter has been cleared up. 2. be clear. **kumetanzuka.** It is clear (= not cloudy).

tao (**ma-**) 1. bend, twist, curve. **– la mto.** bend of a river. **– la njia.** curve of a road. **piga (fanya) –.** bend, twist. 2. arch, vault. 3. *math.* arc, sector *(of a circle).*

¹**tapa, dapa** (*us. red.* **tapatapa, dapadapa**) 1. shudder, tremble, shiver, quiver. 2. be startled, take fright. 3. make excuses, talk evasively/confusedly. **– kwa hofu (baridi).** tremble from fright (cold). *refl.* **jitapa.** shake, have a chill/ague; hop/jump around. *appl.* **tapia.** 1. run away *(from fear).* 2. be eager/greedy for something. *Cf.* **kitapo,** ³**mtapo.**

²**tapa** (**ma-**) tapa (leaf of the mvumo or mnazi, sometimes used as a protection against rain).

tapakaa be scattered/spread. **ugonjwa umetapakaa nchi nzima.** The disease has spread over the entire country. *Cf.* **tapanya, tawanya.**

tapanya 1. scatter, disperse. 2. waste, squander. 3. allow to go bad/spoil. **– mapesa.** waste money. **– chakula.** allow food to spoil. *intr.* **tapanyika. nchi imetapanyika.** The country is inundated. *intr.-ass.* **tapanyikana.** scatter/disperse in various directions. *caus.* **tapanyisha.** *Cf.* **tapakaa, tawanya.**

tapatapa *see* ¹**tapa.**

tapika 1. vomit, be nauseated. *caus.* **tapisha.** 2. *fig.* pour out a torrent of grievances or abuse; orate vociferously. *Cf.* **tapishi, tapisho, matapishi, mtapishi, mtapisho, utapishi.**

tapishi, tapisho (**ma-**) 1. nausea, vomiting. 2. *fig.* abusive/obscene language, profanity. *Cf.* **tapika.**

tapisho (ma-) 1. = **tapishi.** 2. *pharm.* emetic. *Cf.* **tapika.**

[1]**tapo*** [*Turk.*] (ma-) 1. crowd, host *(of people)*; herd *(of animals)*. 2. *mil.* division.

[2]**tapo** (ma-) tapo (kind of nut).

tapureta* [*Engl.*] (–) *rare* = **taipu.**

taraa*, taaraa *conj., rare* if. – **akija.** if he comes.

taraba* rule by force/despotically.

tarabe* (–): **mlango wa –.** double door.

tarabu* (–) tarabu (instrumental music with singing). *Cf.* **mutribu.**

taradadi*, taladadi 1. wander around, walk about aimlessly. 2. hesitate, be uncertain, be perplexed/at a loss. 3. (–) indecision, vacillation.

taradhia* 1. warn, remonstrate; give advice. 2. reproach, reprimand. 3. *see* **radhi.**

tarafa*, tarafu (–) 1. district. 2. part, share; business, duty. 3.: **min –, mintarafu.** *prep.* concerning, regarding, about.

tarafu* (–) *see* **tarafa.**

taraja* (–) hope, expectation, wish. *Cf.* **taraji.**

tarajali* (ma-) *rare* apprentice, trainee. (= **mwanafunzi.**)

taraji* (& *appl.* **tarajia**) wish, desire; hope for, expect. *intr.* **tarajika.** *Cf.* **taraja, matarajio.**

taraju* [*Pers.*] (–) *rare* 1. scales, balance. (= **mizani.**) 2. *fig.* equilibrium, harmony.

tarakanya* search for.

tarakibu* (–) plan, design, pattern, model; sample. *Cf.* [1]**rakibu.**

tarakiki* *adj., rare* narrow, slender, slim. (= **embamba.**)

tarakimu* (–) (written) number, figure, numeral; digit. – **za kirumi.** Roman numerals.

tarare (–) wild plant *(which has seeded itself)*.

taratibu* (–) 1. (*also* **utaratibu**) order, organization; system, structure; method, procedure. – **ya masomo.** class schedule. – **ya lugha.** linguistic structure. 2. composure, collectedness, self-possession. 3. *adv.* (*also* **kwa –**) in an orderly fashion, systematically; composed, self-possessed. **sema –!** Speak slowly! *Cf.* **ratibu.**

taraweha* (–) *see* **tarawehi.**

tarawehi*, taraweha (–) *Isl.* tarawehi (a long prayer pronounced after sunset during Ramadhan).

taraza*, **tarizo, daraza** (–) (embroidered) border/edging. *Cf.* **tarizi.**

tarazaki* *see* **ruzuku.**

tarazia* (–) tarazia (kind of dance).

tarazo* (–) *see* **darizi.**

tarbushi* (–) tarboosh, fez.

tarehe*, **tarihi** (–) 1. date; date of birth. 2. chronology; chronicle, history. **bitarehe...** dated... *(in letters).*

[1]**tari*** [*Pers.*] (–) 1. small drum, tambourine. 2. tari (a dance for exorcising spirits).

[2]**tari*** *pl. of* **utari.**

tarigia* (–) *rare* periodical, magazine. (= **gazeti.**)

tarihi* (–) *see* **tarehe.**

tariki* (–) *rare* road, street, highway. (= **njia.**)

tarishi* (ma-) messenger, courier; postman. *Cf.* **utarishi.**

tarizi*, **darizi** weave a border, make an embroidered edging. *Cf.* **taraza.**

tarjisi* *sing., rare* education, training.

[1]**taruma*** (ma-) support, cross-beam, prop; *(naut.)* rib *(of a ship)*; spoke *(of a wheel)*; *(railw.)* tie, sleeper.

[2]**taruma*** (ma-) *eth.* tattooing of the face *(as a tribal mark).*

tarumbeta* [*Engl.*] (ma-) 1. trumpet. 2. danger signal.

[1]**tasa*** (–) tasa (a metal bowl or basin used for washing the hands before and after meals). *Cf.* **bakuli.**

[2]**tasa*** 1. *adj.* barren, sterile. 2. *sing.* (*also* **utasa**) sterility.

[3]**tasa** *dial. (always w. neg.)* not yet *(+ another verb).* **sitasa kufanya kazi.** I have not yet finished the work.

[4]**tasa** *caus. of* **tata.**

tasawari* 1. be capable/competent. 2. (–) practicability, feasibility; competence.

tasbihi* (–) *Isl.* 1. prayer-beads, rosary. **sala –.** say prayers by a rosary. 2. praise. 3.: **maua ya –.** a kind of flower. *Cf.* **mtasbihi.**

tashtiti* 1. annoy, tease, provoke. 2. (–) provocation, incitement, instigation.

tashwishi* (–) doubt, uncertainty, confusion. **shikwa (patwa) na –.** have doubts/misgivings. *Cf.* **shawishi.**

[1]**tasi, tafi** (–) tasi (a kind of clamp used for smoothing rope after it has been twisted).

[2]**tasi** (–) tasi (kind of fish). (= [1]**chafi.**)

tasifida* *see* **safidi.**

tasihili* 1. *adv.* quickly, speedily, hastily. 2. (–) words of farewell *(before leaving on a journey). Cf.* **sahala.**

taslimu* 1. (–) (payment in) cash. 2. *adv.* in cash. **lipa –.** pay in cash. **nunua –.** buy for cash. *Cf.* **salamu, salimu.**

tasliti* 1. betray, deceive, lead astray. 2. annoy, incite, stir up trouble. **– hata wata wanagombana.** stir things up until people begin to quarrel. *Cf.* **salata, saliti.**

tasua *caus.-inv. of* **tata.**

taswira* (–) 1. drawing, picture, portrait. 2. *fig.:* **– ya dunia.** surface of the earth. *Cf.* **sawiri.**

tata 1. complicate, tangle, confuse, make difficult. *intr.* be confused/in confusion. *appl.* **tatia.** confuse, complicate; wrap, wind. **tatia kilemba.** wind a turban. *ass.* **tatana.** be tangled/interlaced; *(fig.)* be dumbfounded/speechless. *ass.-caus.* **tatanisha.** confuse/perplex/astound someone. *caus.* **tasa** (& *appl.-caus.* **tatiza**). perplex, astound (= **tatanisha**); intrigue, meddle, stir up. *inv.* **tatua.** untangle, unwind, loosen; solve; tear up, pull apart, split, rip. *inv.-appl.* **tatulia.** *inv.-intr.* **tatuka.** be unwound/untangled/solved; be torn apart/split. *inv.-caus.* **tatulisha.** *caus.-inv.* **tasua.** explain, clarify; display. *ass.-inv.* **tatanua.** unwind, unravel; clear up *(a misunderstanding, disagreement),* solve *(a problem).* 2. (ma-) (*us.* **matata**) complication, difficulty, annoyance; confusion, disorder. **– la maneno.** a confused comment. *Cf.* **tatanisho, matata, matatizo, mtatio, utasi, utata.**

tataga 1. cross *(a street, river).* 2. cross, fold *(the arms).* 3. walk quickly/with long strides. *Cf.* **mtataga.**

tatai* *adj.* sly, wily, cunning, deceitful.

tatanisha *ass.-caus. of* **tata.**

tatanisho, tatizo (ma-) (*also* **mtatizo, mi-**) confusion, complexity, difficulty; crisis. **tatizo la uchumi.** economic crisis. *Cf.* **tata.**

tatanua *ass.-inv. of* **tata.**

tatarika 1. crackle, snap. 2. *fig.* chatter, babble.

tatiza *appl.-caus. of* **tata.**

tatizo (ma-) *see* **tatanisho.**

tatu *num.* three. **–a –.** third. **Jumatatu.** Monday. *Cf.* **utatu.**

tatua *inv. of* **tata.**

tatuka *inv.-intr. of* **tata.**

tatulisha *inv.-caus. of* **tata.**

taufiki* (–) *rel.* grace *(of God).*

taulo* [*Engl.*] (–) towel. **pangusa kichwa kwa –.** dry the head with a towel.

taumu* (ma-) *naut.* prop, shore.

tauni* (–) *med.* 1. cholera, (bubonic) plague. 2. *in gen.* epidemic. **– ya mnyama.** cattle plague, hoof-and-mouth disease.

taurati* (–) *see* **torati.**

tausi*, dausi (–) peacock.

[1]**tawa*** 1. stay at home/indoors; live in retirement/seclusion; be isolated. 2. lead a pious/religious life; lead a quiet/moral/exemplary life. *caus.* **tawisha.** keep someone at home. **anamtawisha mkewe.** He keeps his wife at home. 3. *adj.* retired, secluded, solitary; religious, pious, devout. *Cf.* **kitawa, mtawa, utawa.**

[2]**tawa*** (–) frying pan.

[3]**tawa** (–) tawa (kind of fish).

tawadha* *rel.* wash ceremonially *(esp. the feet:* **– miguu).**

tawafa* (–) candle; candlestick, candelabrum.

tawakali* 1. hope, have hopes of something. 2. trust, rely on, have confidence in. *Cf.* **wakala, wakili.**

tawala* rule, govern; come to power. **kujitawala.** *pol.* self-government. **sehemu inayojitawala wenyewe.** autonomous region. **vikundi vinavyotawala.** governmental/official circles. *appl.* **tawalia.** *caus.* **tawaza, tawalisha.** cause to rule, put in power; install in office, inaugurate. *caus.-pass.* **tawazwa.** *Cf.* **kujitawala, mtawala, utawala, ujitawala.**

tawanya 1. strew, scatter. **– mbegu.** sow seeds. 2. *fig.* throw away, waste, squander. **– mali.** waste/dissipate property. *intr.* **tawanyika.** *pass.* **tawanywa. wafanya kazi walitawanywa na polisi.** The workers were dispersed by the police. *red.* **tawanyatawanya** *(w. int. force).* disperse, scatter, break up. *Cf.* **tawanyiko, mtawanya, mtawanyo;** *also* **tapanya.**

tawanyiko (ma-) 1. (act of) scattering, throwing away, wasting. 2. *fig.* devastation. *Cf.* **tawanya.**

tawasifu* provide information *(on a person's character, etc.).* *Cf.* **wasifu.**

tawasufi* (–) 1. moderation, abstinence. 2. *rel.* pious/secluded life. *Cf.* **wasifu.**

tawaza* *caus. of* **tawala.**

tawi (ma-), **kitawi** (vi-), **utawi** (tawi & ma-) 1. branch, frond, bough. **matawi.** branches. 2. cluster, bunch. **– la mwembe.** bunch of bananas. 3. *fig.* branch, division, section. **– jipya la chama lafunguliwa.** A new section of the party has been started.

tawili* *adj., rare* long, tall. (= **refu.**) *Cf.* **tawilisha, tuili.**

tawilisha* lengthen, prolong. – **mkutano.** prolong a meeting (unnecessarily). *Cf.* **tawili.**

tawireni* *interj.* *see* **taileni.**

[1]**taya** (ma-), **kitaya** (vi-), **utaya** (taya) *anat.* jaw, jawbone.

[2]**taya*** blame, rebuke, reproach. *Cf.* **tayo.**

tayari* [*Pers.*] *adj.* ready, prepared. **fanya –.** make ready, prepare. **weka –.** provide, furnish, make available. **saa –.** The time is up. *Cf.* **tayarisha, matayarisho, utayari.**

tayarisha* [*Pers.*] make ready, prepare. *Cf.* **tayari.**

tayibu* *see* **taibu.**

tayo* (ma-) reproach, rebuke, criticism. *Cf.* [2]**taya.**

taz (*abbr. of* **tazama**) look at! see!

tazama 1. look (at), observe, see. 2. examine, investigate; try, test. – **mtego.** look at a trap *(to see if anything has been caught).* – **nyama.** inspect meat. *appl.* **tazamia.** look into, investigate (something); *(eth.)* consult a divining board, take omens; scrutinize, check on. **kitu cha kutazamia.** something that one looks through *(e.g., a telescope).* **tazamia kazi.** check over work. *intr.* **tazamika.** be good/pleasant to look at; be worth looking at/noteworthy. *caus.* **tazamisha.** attract attention, be attractive. *refl.* **jitazama.** look at oneself *(in a mirror).* *Cf.* **tazamo, mtazamaji, mtazamo.**

tazamo (ma-) look, glance, gaze. *Cf.* **tazama.**

tebo* [*Engl.*] (–) table. – **ya kujumlisha.** *arith.* addition table.

teende (ma-) *see* [1]**tende.**

tefu *adj.* soft, tender. **nyama –.** tender meat. **chakula kitefu.** soft food.

tega 1. set up, prepare, put in position. – **mtego.** set a trap. – **uchumi.** invest *(money).* – **sikio.** prick up one's ears, (get ready to) listen. 2. entrap, catch; *(fig.)* deceive, plot, intrigue. 3. prepare a charm/spell, perform witchcraft. – **kitendawili.** ask a riddle. **kitendawili!** – **tega!** Here is a riddle! – Go ahead and ask it! *appl.* **tegea.** *intr.* **tegeka.** *caus.* **tegesha.** *inv.* **tegua.** 1. remove/release something that has been put in position/prepared to go off. **tegua mtego.** release a trap, let it go off. **tegua chungu.** take a pot off the fire. **tegua uchawi.** take off/lift a spell, make a charm ineffective. 2. sprain *(the ankle, etc.).* *inv.-app.* **tegulia.** *inv.-intr.* **teguka.** *Cf.* [2]**tego,** [2]**tezo, mtegaji, mtego.**

tege, chege (ma-) crookedness, curvature. **ana – la miguu.** He is bowlegged. *Cf.* **matege.**

tegemea 1. support/prop oneself on something, lean against. – **mkongojo.** support oneself with a stick. 2. take a rest, relax. 3. rely/depend on someone; receive support from someone; be dependent on someone. **anamtegemea baba yake.** He is dependent on his father. 4. confide in a person, take someone into one's confidence. *ass.* **tegemeana.** depend on each other, be interdependent. *caus.* **tegemeza.** support/protect someone; make someone a protégé/favorite. *pass.* **tegemewa.** *Cf.* **tegemeo.**

tegemeo (ma-) prop, support; protection, patronage. *Cf.* **tegemea.**

tegemeza *caus. of* **tegemea.**

[1]**tego, tegu** (ma-) 1. *med.* tapeworm. 2.: **ma-tegu.** *rec.* typographical error, misprint.

[2]**tego** (ma-) (dangerous) charm, magic. *Cf.* **tega.**

tegu (ma-) *see* [1]**tego.**

tegua *inv. of* **tega.**

[1]**teguka** *inv.-intr. of* **tega.**

[2]**teguka** *see* [1]**teuka.**

tegukiwa *see* [1]**teuka.**

[1]**tehemu*** 1. be debilitated/emaciated *(by sickness).* 2. be unable to do something.

[2]**tehemu*** *see* **tuhumu.**

teitei* [*?*] (ma-) (fashionable) frock/gown, evening gown.

teka 1. take up and carry away. – **maji kisimani.** draw water from a well. 2. plunder, pillage. – **mji.** plunder a city *appl.* **tekea.** *pass.* **tekwa, tekewa. tekewa akili.** lose one's mental powers. *caus.* **tekeza, tekeleza.** attract, bewitch, hold spellbound. 3. (ma-; *us. pl.*) booty, captive. *Cf.* **mateka, mteka.**

tekanya: – **miguu.** cross the legs.

[1]**teke** (ma-) kick. **piga –.** to kick.

[2]**teke** (*us.* **teketeke, tikitiki**) *adj.* 1. soft. **matunda mateke.** soft fruit. 2. pliable, flaccid, flabby. 3. yielding, compliant, without character. **mtu mteke.** a weak/spineless person.

tekea *appl. of* **teka.**

tekelea 1. arrive at, reach. 2. be achieved/attained/brought to a conclusion; be fulfilled/carried out. **ahadi imetekelea.** The promise was kept. *caus.* **tekeleza, tekeza.** fulfill, accomplish; bring to a conclusion. *pass.* **tekelewa.** *Cf.* **tekelezo.**

tekeleza *caus. of* **tekelea.**

tekelezo (ma-) fulfillment, completion, realization. *Cf.* **tekelea.**

[1]**tekenya** tickle, itch. *ass.* **tekenyana.** *pass.* **tekenywa.**

[2]**tekenya** (ma-) *see* [1]**tekenywa.**

[1]**tekenywa, tekenya** (ma-) sand flea, chigger. (= [1]**funza.**)

[2]**tekenywa** *pass. of* [1]**tekenya**

teketa 1. grind/gnash the teeth, crunch. 2. gnaw, gnaw through. 3. hollow out, enlarge a hole *(by twisting a knife or tool)*.

teketea 1. be used up/consumed. 2. be (completely) destroyed *(us. by fire)*. **nyumba hii imeteketea.** This house has burned down. *caus.* **teketeza.** consume, destroy, ruin. **watu wameteketezwa na vita.** Many people were wiped out in the war. *Cf.* **mteketeo, uteketevu, uteketezo.**

teketcke *see* [2]**teke.**

tekeza *caus. of* **teka.**

teksi* [*Engl.*] (–) taxi.

[1]**tekua** break up, destroy, ruin; undermine. *Cf.* **kiteku.**

[2]**tekua** *inv. of* [1]**teleka.**

tele* 1. (–) (large) quantity, plenty, abundance. 2. *adj.* much, many, abundant, plenty of. 3. *adv.* in great quantity/number, in abundance. **kwetu chakula –.** We have food in abundance. **kikombe hiki kimejaa –.** The cup is brimfull. (= **ingi, maridhawa.**)

telea 1. slide, slip, skid. 2. come down, descend. *caus.* **teleza.** slide, slip (= **telea**); (*intr.*) be slick/slippery. **mimi nimeteleza.** I slipped and fell. **barabara inateleza.** The street is slick. **samaki anateleza.** The fish is slippery. *Cf.* **utelezi;** *also* **telemua.**

telefoni* [*Engl.*] (–) *rare* telephone. (= [1]**simu.**) **piga –.** to telephone.

[1]**teleka** 1. put on the fire. **– chungu.** put a pot on the fire. 2. boil, cook. *appl.* **telekea.** *caus.* **telekeza.** 1. = **teleka.** 2. have a meal prepared. *inv.* **telekua,** *(us.)* **tekua.** take off the fire.

[2]**teleka** (–) *ornith.* swallow.

telekeza 1. *caus. of* [1]**teleka.** 2. leave (behind). **tumemtelekeza.** We have left him behind.

telemka *intr. of* **telemua.**

telemko, telemuko, teremko, teremuko (ma-) slope, declivity, (abrupt) descent. *Cf.* **telemua.**

telemsha *caus. of* **telemua.**

telemua, teremua (cause to) go down/sink/slip/fall. *intr.* **telemuka, teremuka, telemka, teremka.** go down, descend, slope; slip/slide *(down a steep slope)*; land *(intr.)*. *caus.* **telemusha, teremusha, telemsha, teremsha.** cause to descend, let down, lower; land *(goods, troops)*. *Cf.* **telea, telemko, kitelemsho, mtelemko.**

telemuka *intr. of* **telemua.**

telemuko (ma-) *see* **telemko.**

telemusha *caus. of* **telemua.**

televishen* [*Engl.*] (–) television.

teleza *caus. of* **telea.**

teli* [*Pers.*] (–) gold (or silver) thread/braid.

telki*, dalki [*Ind.*] *adv.* quickly, at a trot. **enda –.** go at a trot, run.

[1]**tema** spit (out), expectorate. **– mate (kikohozi).** spit out saliva (phlegm). *appl.* **temea.** *intr.* **temeka.** *caus.* **temesha.** *Cf.* [2]**mtemi,** [2]**mtemo.**

[2]**tema** cut (up, into strips), chop. **– kuni.** chop firewood. **– nakshi.** carve. *appl.* **temea.** *intr.* **temeka.** *caus.* **temesha.** *Cf.* [1]**mtemi,** [1]**mtemo.**

[1]**tembe** (–) chicken, hen.

[2]**tembe** (–) house with a flat roof.

[3]**tembe** (–) dosage, pill.

tembea 1. go walking, walk around, stroll. 2. go on a trip, make a tour. **– kwa motokaa.** take an automobile trip. 3. wander, gad about, lead an irregular life. *appl.* **tembelea.** go to visit, call on someone. *appl.-refl.* **jitembelea.** go on a pleasure trip; go for a stroll, saunter about. *appl.-ass.* **tembeleana.** visit each other. *caus.* **tembeza.** 1. take for a walk. 2. hawk, display, advertise *(merchandise). Cf.* **matembezi, mtembezi, tembezi, utembezi.**

tembezi (ma-) (*us.* **matembezi**) walk, stroll; trip, tour; wandering, gadding about; irregular/immoral living; vagrancy. *Cf.* **tembea.**

[1]**tembo** (–) palm wine (made from the fermented sap of the coconut palm).

[2]**tembo** (–) elephant. **mkonga wa –.** trunk of the elephant.

temsi* (–) filigree work *(in metal).*

tena* adv. 1. then, next, further, afterwards, in addition. 2. again, repeatedly. **nimesema – na –.** I have said it again and again.

tenda 1. make, do, act, carry out, perform, accomplish. 2. do something to someone *(us. something bad or unfavorable).* **amenitenda.** He has done something (harmful) to me. *refl.* **jitenda.** 1. claim something for oneself. 2. pretend, feign. *appl.* **tendea.** *intr.* **tendeka.** be done/accomplished; be feasible/practicable. *caus.* **tendesha, tendeza.** *intr.-caus.* **tendekeza.** make feasible/possible. *refl.-intr.-caus.* **jitendekeza.** 1. make an effort, strive. 2. complete something successfully; graduate *(from school). Cf.* **tendo, kitendakazi, kitendawili, kitende, kitendo, matendo, mtenda, mtendaji, mtendo, mtenzi, utendaji, utende, utenzi.**

[1]**tende, teende** (ma-) *med.* elephantiasis.

[2]**tende** (–) date (fruit of the date palm, mtende).

tendegu (ma-) leg of a bedstead.

tendeti (–) tendeti (a kind of pastry made of rice and coconut juice).

tendo (ma-) act, action, deed; cause, effect; efficacy, influence. *Cf.* **tenda.**

[1]**tenga** 1. divide off, separate, split off. 2. delay, postpone. 3. put aside, remove. 4. dismiss, discharge *(from a position).* 5. avert, prevent. 6. confiscate. 7. *rel.* excommunicate. *refl.* **jitenga.** 1. seclude oneself. **amejitenga na wenzake.** He has secluded himself from his friends. 2. deviate from a route/course. 3. move aside, get out of the way. *appl.* **tengea.** *intr.* **tengeka.** *caus.* **tengesha.** *inv.* **tengua.** 1. *often* = **tenga.** 2. *(w. int. force)* reduce to small pieces, chop up. **tengua kitabu.** read proof. 3. put aside, remove, eliminate. **tengua maneno.** refute arguments. **tengua mtu.** push aside/oust someone. *inv.-intr.* **tenguka.** fall over on one side; be derailed *(of a train).* *Cf.* **kitengo, matengano, [1]mtenga, mtengano, mtengo, mtengwa, utengano, utengo.**

[2]**tenga** (ma-) tenga (a very large flatfish; a sea monster).

[3]**tenga** (ma-) a carrying-net/basket.

[4]**tenga** *rare* descend, alight *(of birds, insects).* (= **tua.**)

tengamaji (ma-) watershed, divide. *Cf.* **[1]tenga, maji.**

tenge (–) 1. curve, crookedness. 2. *fig.* confusion, excitement, bewilderment.

tengea *see* **tengenea.**

tengemaa (*also ass.* **tengemana**) settle down, be restored to peace *(e.g., of a country after a natural catastrophe or a war).* *Cf.* **tengemano, matengemano, utengemano.**

tengemano (ma-), **utengemano** *sing.* peace, tranquillity, stabilization, normalcy, (restored) prosperity. *Cf.* **tengemaa.**

tengenea (*rare* **tengea**) 1. be in order, be in good shape. **mashauri yake sasa yametengenea.** His affairs are now in order. 2. be usable/suitable, be ready for use. 3. be regular/steady. **Upepo umetengenea.** The wind is steady. *caus.* **tengeneza.** 1. put in order/good shape; regulate, correct; mend, repair; edit *(a book, etc.).* **tengeneza baisikeli (redio).** repair a bicycle (radio). 2. settle, reach a decision (on something). **baraza haitengenazi mashauri haya.** The council does not make decisions on these matters *(i.e., does not have jurisdiction).* *caus.-intr.* **tengenezeka. saa imetengenezeka.** The watch has been repaired. *Cf.* **tengenezo, kitengeneza, matengenezo, mtengenezaji, utengenezaji, utengevu.**

tengenezo (ma-) (*us.* **matengenezo**) arrangement, regulation; repair. *Cf.* **tengenea.**

tengo (ma-) (*us.* **matengo**) *naut.* outrigger.

tengua *inv. of* ^{1}**tenga.**

tengura disdain, scorn; offend, insult, debase, dishonor.

tenisi* [*Engl.*] (–) *sport.* tennis. **cheza –.** play tennis.

^{1}**teo** (–) sling *(for throwing stones).*

^{2}**teo** *pl. of* **uteo.**

^{1}**tepe*, utepe** [*Engl.*] (ma-) tape, ribbon, braid, chevrons *(on uniforms, etc.).*

^{2}**tepe, tepetepe** *adj.* many, numerous.

tepeta *see* **tepetea.**

tepete, tepetevu *adj.* slack, flabby, flaccid, limp; listless, languid, indolent. *Cf.* **tepetea.**

tepetea (*rare* **tepeta**) be limp/listless/weak-willed/indolent. *Cf.* **tepete, mtepetevu, utepetevu.**

tepetepe *see* ^{2}**tepe.**

tepetevu *see* **tepete.**

terafini* [*Ind.*] (–) turpentine.

terema be carefree/cheerful/happy. *appl.* **teremea** *and intr.* **teremeka** = **terema.** *caus.* **teremesha.** 1. make someone carefree/happy. 2. receive someone hospitably. *Cf.* **mteremeshi, mteremo.**

teremesha *caus. of* **terema.**

teremka *intr. of* **telemua.**

teremko (ma-) *see* **telemko.**

teremsha *caus. of* **telemua.**

teremua *see* **telemua.**

teremuka *intr. of* **telemua.**

teremuko (ma-) *see* **telemko.**

teremusha *caus. of* **telemua.**

tesa distress, hurt, trouble, torment, tease, persecute. *appl.* **tesea.** *intr.* **teseka.** *caus.* **tesesha.** *ass.* **tesana.** *ass.-caus.* **tesanya.** cause dissension/strife, make people hostile toward each other, stir up trouble. *Cf.* **teso, mtesi, utesi.**

tesanya *ass.-caus. of* **tesa.**

teso (ma-) (*us.* **mateso**) suffering, pain, anxiety; persecution, harassment; misfortune, misery, adversity; *(rel.)* passion. *Cf.* **tesa.**

teta 1. take energetic action, speak out forcibly, assert strongly. 2. dispute, oppose, protest, contradict. **tumeteta na.** We disputed with them. 3. speak ill of someone, talk behind someone's back, slander. *appl.* **tetea.** speak out strongly for or against someone; attack, contradict; support, defend *(in a dispute).* *double appl.* **tetelea.** *double appl.-caus.* **teteleza** cause strife/conflict, provoke opposition. *intr.* **teteka.** *caus.* **tetesha.** *ass.* **tetana.** be enemies, quarrel. *Cf.* **teto, mateto, mtetaji, mtetea, utetezi, uteto.**

[1]**tete** (ma-) reed.

[2]**tete** (–) grain that is formed but not yet fully ripe. – **za mtama.** a grain of millet that has not fully ripened.

[3]**tete** *pl. of* **utete.**

tetea cackle *(of hens).*

tetekuwanga, tetewanga, tetemaji (–) *med.* chicken pox.

tetelea *double appl. of* **teta.**

tetema (& *intr.* **tetemeka**) tremble, quiver, shake. – **kwa homa (hofu, hasira).** tremble from fever (fear, anger). *Cf.* **tetemeko, kitetemo, mtetemko.**

tetemaji (–) *see* **tetekuwanga.**

tetemeko, tetemo (ma-) trembling, shaking, tremor, convulsion. – **la nchi** (*or* **la ardhi**). earthquake. *Cf.* **tetema.**

tetemo (ma-) *see* **tetemeko.**

tetere (–) *ornith.* (species of) dove *(Streptopelia capicola).*

tetereka 1. swing, sway; stagger. 2. be uncertain/irresolute. 3. be a little injured/damaged, suffer a slight accident.

tetesi (ma-) whisper(ing); rumor, gossip.

tetewanga (–) *see* **tetekuwanga.**

teto (ma-) (*often* **mateto**) 1. argument, plea. 2. objection, protest. 3. excuse, evasion. *Cf.* **teta.**

teua 1. pick out, select, choose. 2. (*also intr.* **teulika**) be fussy/hard to please/critical. *pass.* **teuliwa.** *Cf.* **teule, teuzi, kiteuzi, mteua, mteule, mteuo, uteuzi.**

[1]**teuka, teguka, tegukiwa** be sprained/dislocated. **mguu wangu umeteuka.** My leg is sprained.

[2]**teuka** belch, burp, bubble *(mostly of infants after feeding).*

teule *adj.* select, choice, of the finest quality. *Cf.* **teua.**

teuzi *adj.* choosy, fastidious, dainty; critical. *Cf.* **teua.**

[1]**tezi*** [*Pers.*] (ma-) *naut.* stern, poop *(of a ship).*

[2]**tezi** (ma-) *med.* swelling, tumor, goiter.

[1]**tezo** (ma-) adze.

[2]**tezo** (ma-) harm, injury *(caused by sorcery).* *Cf.* **tega.**

thabiti* (*rare* **sabiti**) *adj.* 1. firm, strong, secure. 2. steadfast, reliable, of strong character. 3. genuine, true. *Cf.* **thibiti, thubutu, mathubuti, uthabiti, uthubutifu.**

thama* *adv., rare* then, after that; also, likewise, similarly.

thamani* (–) value, price. **– yake nini?** What is the value/price? **–a –.** valuable, precious. **amevaa nguo za –.** She wears expensive clothes. *fig.:* **hana –.** He is of no value/is good for nothing. *Cf.* **thamini.**

thamini* 1. price, evaluate, appraise, assess, estimate; *(fig.)* respect, appreciate. **– nyumba.** appraise a house. 2. *fig.* form an estimate *(of a person)*, characterize. *intr.* **thaminika.** *caus.* **thaminisha.** *pass.* **thaminiwa.** *Cf.* **thamani.**

thamra* (–) thamra (cloves in the first stage of growth).

thari* (–) moisture, dampness.

thaura*, thawra (–), **kithaura** (vi-) 1. tribal warfare, raiding. 2. *pol., recent* revolution. **–a –.** revolutionary. **moyo za –.** revolutionary fervor. **mpinga –.** counterrevolutionary.

thawabu* (–) 1. reward, recompense, gift. 2. *fig., rel.* retribution, punishment.

thawra* (–) *see* **thaura.**

thelatha* *num., rare* three. (= **tatu.**)

thelathashara* *num., rare* thirteen. (= **kumi na tatu.**)

thelathini* *num.* thirty.

theluji* (–) snow.

theluthi*, thuluthi *num.* a third.

themani*, themanya *num., rare* eight. (= **nane.**)

themanini* *num.* eighty.

themantashara* *num., rare* eighteen. (= **kumi na nane.**)

themanya* *see* **themani.**

themuni*, thumni, thumuni *num.* an eighth.

thenashara* *num., rare* twelve. (= **kumi na mbili.**)

theneen* *num., rare* two. (= **mbili, wili.**)

thibiti* 1. be firm/strong/hardy/durable. 2. *fig.* be steadfast/of strong character/inflexible. 3. be brave/courageous/bold. 4. be truthful/honest/upright. *intr.* **thibitika.** *caus.* **thibitisha.** 1. strengthen, make secure. 2. encourage, renew. 3. maintain, affirm, prove, establish, guarantee. *Cf.* **thabiti, thibitisho.**

thibitika* *intr. of* **thibiti** *and* **thubutu.**

thibitisha* *caus. of* **thibiti** *and* **thubutu.**

thibitisho* (ma-) 1. guarantee, assurance. 2. proof, evidence. *Cf.* **thibiti.**

thubutu* venture, risk, dare, have the courage/ audacity to do something. **hathubutu kuifanya mbele ya wazee wake.** He doesn't dare to do it before his parents. *imp.* **thubutu!** I dare you to... *intr.* **thubutika, thibitika.** *caus.* **thubutisha, thibitisha.** *Cf.* **thabiti, thibiti, mathubuti, uthubutifu.**

thuluthi* *see* **theluthi.**

thumni* *see* **themuni.**

thumu*, **saumu, tumu** (–) garlic.

thumuni* *see* **themuni.**

thurea* (–) 1. chandelier. 2. *astr.* the Pleiades (= **kilimia**).

tia 1. put, set, lay, place. – **nanga.** cast anchor. – **chumvi.** salt *(food).* – **mbolea.** fertilize, manure. – **adabu.** teach good manners. – **kazini.** set to work seriously. – **rangi.** dye, stain. – **saini.** sign *(a document).* – **alama.** mark, designate. – **jeraha (kijeraha).** inflict a wound. 2. apply, use, bring to bear. – **dawa.** apply medicine. – (*or* **tilia**) **nguvu.** strengthen, encourage. – **nguvuni.** arrest, place in custody. – **moyo.** encourage. – **moyoni.** reflect, consider seriously. 3. produce, cause. – **ugonjwa.** cause an illness. – **mashaka.** raise doubts. – **hofu.** inspire fear. – **furaha (huzuni).** cause joy (sorrow). – **mimba.** make pregnant. *refl.* **jitia.** 1. devote oneself to, occupy oneself with. 2. adapt oneself to. 3. pretend, feign. **jitia ugonjwa.** feign illness. *appl.* **tilia.** *double appl.* **tililia. tililia uzi.** mend, darn. *intr.* **tilika.** *caus.* **tilisha.** *pass.* **tiwa. tiwa katika taabu.** get into trouble. *Cf.* **mtia, mtiaji.**

tiabu* (–) tiabu (a game played with sticks).

tiara* (–) kite (children's toy).

^{1}**tiba***, **tabibia** (–) medicine. *Cf.* **utabibu.** ^{1}**tibu,** ^{1}**tabibia, tabibu, utabibu.**

^{2}**tiba*** *sing.* a term of endearment: dear, beloved.

^{1}**tibu*** treat medically, heal, cure. (= ^{1}**tabibia.**) **mganga amenitibu.** The doctor has cured me. *appl.* **tibia.** *intr.* **tibika. ugonjwa huu hautibiki.** This disease is incurable. *caus.* **tibisha.** *Cf.* ^{1}**tiba, tabibia, tabibu.**

^{2}**tibu*** (–) tibu (a perfume prepared from powdered sandalwood, rose water, and oil of cloves).

tibua 1. mix, stir up. *intr.* **tibuka.** be muddy *(of water).* 2. *fig.* provoke, excite. *Cf.* **matibwitibwi.**

tifu 1. (ma-) dust, fine sand. 2. (*also* **tifutifu**) crumbly, loose, friable, dusty, pulverized. *Cf.* **tifua.**

tifua make the dust rise, shake, stir up; pulverize; rummage about. *appl.* **tifulia.** *intr.* **tifuka.** *caus.* **tifusha.** *Cf.* **tifu.**

tifutifu *see* **tifu 2.**

tii* 1. obey, submit, subordinate oneself. **yapasa watoto kutii wazee wao.** Children must obey their parents. *intr.* **tiika.** be obedient/submissive/docile. *caus.* **tiisha.** subjugate, subdue, dominate. *pass.* **tiiwa.** (= **sikia, tumikia, nyenyekea.**) 2. *adj.* = **tiifu.** *Cf.* [1]**taa, tiifu, mtiifu, utii.**

tiifu*, tii *adj.* obedient, submissive; loyal, disciplined. *Cf.* **tii.**

tiika* *intr. of* **tii.**

tiisha* *caus. of* **tii.**

tija* (–) 1. income, earnings, profit. **kazi hii haina –.** This kind of work is unprofitable. 2. wealth, prosperity. *Cf.* **tijara.**

tijara* 1. = **tajiri.** 2. (–) wares, merchandise; profit.

tike*, dike 1. *adv.* exactly, precisely. 2. *interj.* good! right!

tikisa 1. shake, move back and forth. **– mti.** shake a tree. 2. *fig.* agitate, disturb, excite, shock. **– mtu kwa taabu.** bother someone with difficulties. *appl.* **tikisia.** *intr.* **tikisika. nchi yote ilitikisika watu waliposikia kuwa kuna vita.** The whole country was excited when people heard that there was war. *caus.* **tikisisha.** *Cf.* **mtikiso.**

[1]**tikita** 1. grind, pound, pulverize; masticate (thoroughly). 2. *fig.* **– usingizi.** have a sound sleep. *appl.* **tikitia.** *int.* **tikitiza.** 1. grind up fine. 2. roll the hips.

[2]**tikita** *see* **chikicha.**

[1]**tikiti** (–, ma-) watermelon. *Cf.* **mtikiti.**

[2]**tikiti*, tikti** [*Engl.*] (–) ticket, pass. **– ya posta.** postage stamp.

tikitiki *see* [2]**teke.**

tikiza endure, suffer, put up with, bear *(pain, grief).*

tikti* [*Engl.*] (–) *see* [2]**tikiti.**

tilatila *adj.* well mixed, variegated. **chakula cha –.** various foods mixed together.

tilia *appl. of* **tia.**

tilifika *intr. of* **tilifu.**

tilifisha *caus. of* **tilifu.**

tilifu 1. destroy, ruin. 2. give up, get rid of, terminate. *intr.* **tilifika.** become less, decrease, be lost. *caus.* **tilifisha** = **tilifu.**

tililila *double appl. of* **tia.**

tilisika *see* **tiririka.**

timamu* 1. (–) completion, conclusion; completed state. 2. *adj.* completed, finished; present *(in full strength, with perfect attendance).* **je watu wote –?** Are all the people present *(with no absences)? Cf.* [1]**timu.**

timazi* (–) plummet, plumb bob; (sounding-) lead; pendulum.

[1]**timba** (–) string of beads, necklace.

[2]**timba** (–) sprouted grain *(for making beer)*.

[3]**timba** *dial.* = **chimba.**

timbe (–) lump of metal, (rough) casting.

[1]**timbi** (ma-) *see* **chimvi.**

[2]**timbi** (–) bracelet (of silver globules).

timbua stir up (maize or millet, when being pounded in a mortar, to keep it from sticking). *Cf.* **tibua.**

timia *appl. of* [1]**timu.**

timilifu* *adj.* complete, finished; perfect, faultless. *Cf.* [1]**timu.**

timiliza *appl.-caus. of* [1]**timu.**

timiza *caus. of* [1]**timu.**

[1]**timka, titimka, timuka** 1. go at a trot, run *(of animals)*. 2. run away, flee. **simba alipolikaribia lile kundi ng'ombe wote walitimka.** When the lion approached that herd, all the cattle ran away.

[2]**timka, timuka** be ruffled/dishevelled *(of feathers, hair)*. *caus.* **timsha.**

[1]**timu*** 1. be completed/finished/concluded; be complete/perfect. 2. contain, be included. *us. appl.* **timia. fedha hazikutimia.** Not all the money was there *(i.e., the sum was not complete)*. **watu wote wametimia.** All the people are included *(in a conversation or discussion)*. *caus.* **timiza.** complete, finish; include. *double appl.-caus.* **timiliza.** carry out, perform, execute *(e.g., a contract, judgment)*. *Cf.* **timamu, timilifu, utimilifu.**

[2]**timu*** [*Engl.*] (–) *sport* team. **– zote mbili zilicheza kwa bidii sana.** Both the teams played with great concentration.

timuka *see* [1]**timka,** [2]**timka.**

[1]**tinda** (ma-) string of beads, necklace.

[2]**tinda** *see* **chinja.**

tindanga 1. make one's way, push through *(e.g., dense undergrowth or water)*, traverse *(with difficulty, against resistance)*. 2. shine through, barely show through *(open places in thick vegetation)*.

[1]**tindi** (ma-) spoke (of a bicycle wheel).

[2]**tindi** *adj.* unripe, not fully grown *(of grain)*.

[3]**tindi** (ma-) *see* **mtindi.**

tindiga (–) tindiga (a thorny swamp plant).

tindika 1. cut/clip/lop off *(plants)*. 2. end, conclude. 3. fail, run out, run short. *appl.* **tindikia.** run short of something, be deficient. **tindikia chakula.** run short of food, have a food shortage. *caus.* **tindikisha.** *ass.* **tindikana.** be cut off/separated/isolated from each other; be dispossessed.

tindikali* [*Pers.?*] (–) solder. (= **lehemu.**)

tindo (–) chisel.

tine (ma-) *anat.* glans penis.

tineja* [*Engl.*] teen-ager.

tinga (*rare* **tingatinga**) 1. shake, roll, toss, bob up and down, vibrate. 2. defeat, overcome, get the better of. *intr.* **tingika.** *caus.* **tingisha.** *pass.* **tingwa. ametingwa na kazi.** He is very busy/overworked. 3.: **tingatinga** (ma-) *arch.* tractor (= **trekta**). *Cf.* **tingetinge, kitingisha.**

tingatinga (ma-) *see* **tinga 3.**

ting'ating'a (ma-) 1. tractor. 2. police car *(with siren)*. 3. tunnel.

tinge (–) tinge (kind of dance).

tingetinge, tingitingi (–) bridge. *Cf.* **tinga.**

tingitingi (–) *see* **tingetinge.**

tini* (–) fig. *Cf.* **mtini.**

tipati* [*Engl.*] (–) *rare* tea party.

tipitipi (–) *ornith.* (species of) coucal. (= **dudumizi.**)

tipwa, tipwatipwa *adj.* strong, vigorous, sturdy, healthy.

tipwatipwa *see* **tipwa.**

tiringa cut notches, notch, score.

tiririka, tilisika 1. glide, slide, slither *(e.g., of a snake)*. 2. flow, trickle, drip. *Cf.* **mtiririko.**

tisa* *num.* nine. **–a –.** ninth.

tisaini* *rare* *see* **tisini.**

tisashara*, tisatashara *num., rare* nineteen. (= **kumi na kenda.**)

tisatashara* *see* **tisashara.**

tisau* *num.* a ninth.

tisha 1. frighten, scare, intimidate, threaten. 2. be timid/timorous/nervous. *appl.* **tishia.** *intr.* **tishika.** *ass.* **tishana.** *Cf.* **tisho, kitisho, mtishaji, utisho.**

tishali* (ma-) *see* **tishari.**

tishari*, tishali (ma-) *naut.* barge, lighter; tug.

tisho (ma-) (*also* **kitisho,** vi-) terror, scare, threat, menace, danger. *Cf.* **tisha.**

tisini* (*rare* **tisaini**) *num.* ninety.

tisti* *adv.* firmly, immovably. **simama —.** stand firm.

tisu* [*Engl.* tissue?] (—) (fine) muslin.

tita 1. tie up in a bundle. 2. carry a bundle. *appl.* **titia.** walk in a stooped position, be bowed down *(under a burden)*; be arched/raised; stagger, break down *(under a burden)*, collapse. **hapa ardhi imetitia.** In this place the earth is mounded up. *intr.* **titika.** have a heavy burden *(also fig.)*. *caus.* **titisha.** put a (heavy) burden on someone; cause to stagger/collapse. 3. **(ma-)** bundle *(of grass, firewood)*. *Cf.* **mtitio.**

titi **(ma-)** *anat.* nipple, teat. (= **chuchu.**)

titiga 1. hit, beat. 2. stir vigorously, whip.

titima roll, rumble, rattle, clatter.

titimka *see* **¹timka.**

tiva (—) *ornith.* (species of) shrike (bou-bou, puffback).

to— not, non- *(forming the negative of infinitives; cf.* **²toa**).

¹toa, towa 1. put/take/give out, give off, issue, emit, produce, publish. **— amri.** give an order. **— habari.** give a report. **— hotuba.** give a speech; *(rel.)* preach. **— saiti.** give a signal. **— maua.** bloom. **— machozi.** cry, weep. **— nuru.** shine, gleam. **— pumzi.** exhale. **— shauri.** give (a piece of) advice. 2. show, display. **— meno.** show the teeth. **— ukali.** show courage/severity. 3. take out, remove; save *(from something)*. **— kazini.** discharge from a job. **— makosa.** correct errors. **— hatarini.** save from a danger. 4. take away, reduce; *(math.)* subtract. **kumi kutoa tano ni tano.** 10–5 = 5. *refl.* **jitoa.** 1. refuse, renounce, disavow. 2. give in, yield, surrender; come down a peg. *appl.* **tolea, tolia.** 1. give to. 2. take away/remove from; save from. *refl.-appl.* **jitolea.** make sacrifices, volunteer. *appl.-ass.* **toleana.** 1. give to each other. 2. take away from each other. *pass.* **tolewa.** be given out/published; be driven away/expelled. *intr.* **toka.** 1. come/go out; get out, quit. **nimetoka kazini.** I am coming from work; I have quit my job. 2. come/be from *(a place)*, originate in. **ametoka Unguja.** He is from Zanzibar. 3. come away from, be rid of, recover from. **toka ugonjwani.** recover from an illness. *intr.-appl.* **tokea.** 1. come out, appear, happen. 2. be saved from something. 3. result from, be a result/consequence of. *intr.-caus.* **tokeza.** 1. cause to come out, make prominent. 2. *(intr.)* project, be prominent. *intr.-caus.-refl.* **jitoleza.** put oneself forward, introduce oneself. *caus.* **toza.** extract, impose, collect. **toza kodi.** collect taxes. **toza adabu.** impose a fine. *ass.* **tokana.** 1. leave/part from each other. 2. result from, be caused by. **taabu nyingi zimetokana na mtu yule.** Many difficulties have been caused by that man. *Cf.* **²toka, tokeo, tolatola, toleo, kitoleo, matokeo, mtoa, mtoaji, mtoki, mtoza, mtozaji, utoaji, utokezo, utoko, utolewaji.**

[2]toa 1. be lacking. *The simple form occurs only as an auxil. v. forming the negative of the infinitive, usually in the shortened form* **kuto-** (< **kutoa**). **kutofanya.** not do. **kutosema.** not speak. **siasa ya tofungamana.** policy of non-alignment. *intr.* **toweka.** be lacking/absent, disappear; be beside oneself. *caus.* **towesha.** put out of the way; ruin, destroy; dissipate, scatter. 2. (–) lack, want; fault, defect. *Cf.* [1]**tovu, mtovu, utovu.**

toamini* lack faith, distrust. *Cf.* [2]**toa** & [1]**amini.**

toasi, toazi, tuwazi (ma-) *mus.* cymbal. *Cf.* **kitoasi.**

toazi* (ma-) *see* **toasi.**

toba* (–) 1. regret, remorse, repentance, contrition. 2. *rel.* confession, penance. **omba –.** ask forgiveness. **siku za –.** day of forgiveness.

tobo, tobwe (ma-) hole, opening. *Cf.* **toboa.**

toboa 1. make a hole, pierce, penetrate, break through. **ameingia nyumbani kwa kutoboa ukuta.** He got into the house by breaking through the wall. 2. *fig.* make a way/passage, force one's way through something. 3. *fig.* maintain, assert, insist. *appl.* **tobolea.** *intr.* **toboka.** *caus.* **tobosha.** *Cf.* **tobo, kitobo.**

tobosha *caus. of* **toboa.**

[1]**tobwe** (ma-) wood of the mtobwe shrub.

[2]**tobwe** (ma-) stupid person, fool.

[3]**tobwe** (ma-) *see* **tobo.**

tochi* [*Engl.*] (–) 1. (electric) torch, flashlight. 2. (cigarette) lighter.

tofaa* (ma-) fruit of the rose-apple tree (**mtofaa**, *q.v.*).

tofali*, tufali (ma-) brick. **matofali ya kuchoma.** fired brick. **matofali ya kuanika.** mud brick, adobe. **udongo wa matofali.** clay for brick-making.

tofauti, tafauti (–) 1. difference, distinction; discrepancy. **hapana –.** There is no difference. 2. difference of opinion, quarrel, dispute. **ana – nao.** His opinion differs from theirs. 3. fault, defect. **nunua samaki hawana –.** Buy these fish, they are good *(have no faults).* 4. *adj./adv.* different, dissimilar; not exactly what one expected/wanted, not up to standard.

tofautiana *ass. of* **tofautisha.**

tofautisha 1. distinguish, make a distinction. **ni lazima utofautishe kati ya mtu na mtu usiwaamini wote.** You must make a distinction among people; you cannot believe everybody. 2. be different. *ass.* **tofautiana.** be different from each other. **siasa zao zinatofautiana.** They are pursuing different policies.

tofoa, tofua 1. = **pofua.** 2. stick, stab. **amemtofoa jicho na kalamu yake.** He stabbed him in the eye with his pencil.

tofua *see* **tofoa.**

toga pierce (the ears, for earrings). **– mtoto masikio.** pierce the lobes of a child's ears. *pass.* **togwa.**

[1]togwa (–) togwa (an unfermented beverage made of various grains with water and sugar). **hii si pombe ni –.** This is not beer but togwa.

[2]togwa *pass. of* **toga.**

tohara* (–) 1. *Isl.* ritual purity *(us. through circumcision).* **hana –.** He is impure *(i.e., cannot enter a mosque).* 2. circumcision. 3. *Christ.* purgatory. *Cf.* **tahiri, mtohara, utohara.**

tohe, toi (–) tohe (kind of wild goat).

toi (–) *see* **tohe.**

toja 1. make an incision, tattoo. **– mshipa.** open a vein, bleed *(a person).* 2. *rare* drip. (= **tona.**) *Cf.* **tojo.**

tojo (ma-) 1. incision, cut, slash, gash; tattoo(ing). 2. *rare* drop. (= **tone.**) *Cf.* **toja.**

[1]toka *intr. of* **[1]toa.**

[2]toka, tokea, kutoka *prep.* from, out of, away from; since. **– huku.** from there to here. **amekwenda – nyumbani.** He went away from the house. **– hapo.** from this time on. **– jana.** since yesterday. **– leo.** from today on. **– zamani.** for a long time. *Cf.* **[1]toa.**

tokana *ass. of* **[1]toa.**

[1]tokea *intr.-appl. of* **[1]toa.**

[2]tokea *prep.* *see* **[2]toka.**

tokeo (ma-) (*us. pl.*) 1. appearance, occurrence. **– la Bwana.** Epiphany. 2. result, consequence. 3. apparition, vision. *Cf.* **[1]toa.**

toki (–) *see* **mtoki.**

tokomea 1. disappear, vanish. **ametokomea msituni.** He disappeared in the bush. 2. be completely destroyed. 3. arrive, enter a place *(with much noise and confusion).* *caus.* **tokomeza.** 1. destroy, annihilate. 2. scatter, spread. *Cf.* **utokomeaji.**

tokomeza *caus. of* **tokomea.**

tokoni, tokono (ma-) *anat.* coccyx.

tokosa *caus. of* **tokota.**

tokota be boiled/cooked/fried. *caus.* **tokosa.** boil, cook, fry. **mayai ya kutokosa.** boiled eggs. *Cf.* **mtokoso.**

tola* [*Ind.*] (–) tola (unit of weight for precious metals and perfumes; about ½ ounce or 14 grams).

tolatola *adj., rare* selected, choice. *Cf.* **[1]toa.**

tolea *appl. of* **[1]toa.**

toleana *appl.-ass. of* **[1]toa.**

toleo (ma-) that which goes out/is delivered, etc.; *(rec.)* production. *Cf.* **[1]toa.**

toli* (–) thread, cord, braid.

toma thrust (in). **jitoma.** burst in. *Cf.* **[1]choma.**

tomasa press, squeeze (gently), feel (something soft), knead. **ukitaka kununua embe, kwanza huitomasa uitazame kama ni mbichi au imeiva.** When you want to buy a mango you feel/squeeze it first to see if it is ripe or not.

tomba copulate *(of a male animal, and vulg.). ass.* **tombana.** *pass.* **tombwa.** *Cf.* **[1]panda, kwea.**

tombo, tomboo, tomboro, tomboroko (–) *ornith.* quail.

tomboo (–) *see* **tombo.**

tomboro (–) *see* **tombo.**

tomboroko (–) *see* **tombo.**

tomea 1. reinforce/surface *(a wall, etc.)* by coating with mortar mixed with small stones. 2. roughcast, plaster. *caus.* **tomesha.** *Cf.* **mtomo.**

[1]tomesha egg on, sic on *(a dog, etc.)*; urge/encourage to attack, incite, stir up.

[2]tomesha *caus. of* **tomea.**

tomoa 1. *rare* break through, pierce. 2. deflower *(a virgin).*

tomoko (ma-) custard apple (fruit of the mtomoko/mtopetope).

[1]tomondo (ma-) tomondo (fruit of the mtomondo, *q.v.*).

[2]tomondo (–) *dial.* hippopotamus. (= **kiboko.**)

tona drip. *appl.* **tonea.** *intr.* **toneka.** *caus.* **tonesha.**

tondo (–) tondo (species of snail).

[1]tondoo (–) tondoo (fruit of the [1]mtondoo, *q.v.*).

[2]tondoo (ma-), **mtondoo** (mi-) *rare* thimble. (= **kastabini, [1]subana.**)

tondoti *pl. of* **utondoti.**

tone (ma-) drop *(of a liquid).* **– la maji (damu).** drop of water (blood). **nimepigwa na – la mvua.** I felt a drop of rain (= It is beginning to rain). *Cf.* **tona.**

tonesha *see* **tonosha.**

tonga (ma-) 1. basket. 2.: **– la dafu.** coconut in the final stage of development.

tonge (–) (*augment. of* **kitonge**) lump, ball *(of rice, etc.). Cf.* **donge.**

[1]tongo (ma-) a deserted settlement/village. (= **hame, kihame, mahame.**)

[2]tongo (ma-) tongo (variety of banana; = **[1]mgomba**).

[3]tongo (–): – **kanga/pofu/simba.** *ornith.* (various species of) finch, mannikin.

tongoza lead astray, seduce *(a woman). appl.* **tongozea.** *caus.* **tongozesha.** *ass.* **tongozana.** *Cf.* **mtongozi, utongozaji.**

toni* [*Engl.*] (–) *mus.* tone.

[1]tonoka, tononeka, tononoka get fat, put on weight; flourish, prosper; regain strength/health; become healthy/vigorous. *caus.* **tonokesha, tononosha.**

[2]tonoka *intr. of* **tonosha.**

tonokesha *caus. of* **[1]tonoka.**

tononoka *see* **[1]tonoka.**

tononosha *caus. of* **[1]tonoka.**

tonosha, tonesha hurt someone by inadvertently bumping a sore or wound. *intr.* **tonoka.**

top* [*Engl.?*] *adv.* extremely, to a high degree.

topas* [*?*] (ma-) scavenger, street sweeper, latrine cleaner.

tope (ma-) (*us.* **matope**) 1. mud, dirt. 2. *rare* great number (of people), crowd. **watu wengi kama –.** a great throng of people. *Cf.* **topea?**

topea sink into something, be plunged/submerged/steeped in something; get into trouble, be overwhelmed/swamped with difficulties. **mtu yule ugonjwa wa ukoma umemtopea.** That man has been seized by leprosy. *caus.* **topeza.** cause something to sink in, press/push/plunge (something into something else).

topetope (ma-) topetope (fruit of the mtopetope. = **tomoko**).

topeza *caus. of* **topea.**

topito* [*Engl.*] (–) 1. torpedo. 2. slingshot, catapult *(for shooting birds).*

topoa 1. pull out, extricate *(from difficulties)*, rescue *(from a difficult or unpleasant situation).* 2. counteract *(a poison, etc.).* 3. *arch.* set free/release *(from a magic spell). appl.* **topolea.** *intr.* **topoka.**

topolea *appl. of* **topoa.**

[1]tora* [*?*] spear with a narrow head.

[2]tora* (–) *rare* regularity, orderliness.

[3]tora cackle *(of hens).*

[4]tora *see* **chora.**

[5]**tora** *rare:* – **meno.** pick the teeth. (= **chokoa.**) *Cf.* **totora.**

torati*, taurati (–) *rel.* the Pentateuch.

toria (**ma-**) toria (kind of liana).

toroka run away, flee, escape; play truant. **wafungwa wawili walitoroka jela.** Two prisoners have escaped from the jail. *caus.* **torosha.** *Cf.* **mtoro, utoro.**

torosha *caus. of* **toroka.**

[1]**tosa** 1. (**ma-**) fruit that is beginning to ripen or is nearly ripe. 2. *adj.* ripening, nearly ripe. **embe –.** a ripening mango.

[2]**tosa** *caus. of* **tota.**

tosha be enough/sufficient/adequate/satisfactory, suffice. **–a kutosha.** enough, sufficient. **haitoshi.** it is not enough. *appl.* **toshea.** *double appl.* **toshelea.** *double appl.-caus.* **tosheleza.** satisfy, give satisfaction; fulfill *(the terms/requirements of someth.).* **kazi yake inatosheleza.** His work is satisfactory.

toshea *appl. of* **tosha.**

tosheleza *double appl.-caus. of* **tosha.**

tosi *pl. of* **utosi.**

tota 1. sink; be drowned, drown; go down, founder *(of ships).* **meli imetota.** The ship has sunk. 2. lose irrecoverably. **nimempa fedha yangu, lakini imetota.** I have given him my money, but I don't expect to see it again. 3. become wet/soaked. **nguo zangu zimetota.** My clothes are soaked. 4. sink in; be ruined/destroyed. *stat.* **totama.** *caus.* **tosa.** throw into the water, submerge (something/someone); *(fig.)* waste, squander. **walizitosa mali zetu baharini.** They have wasted our property *(lit.* thrown it into the sea). *caus.-refl.* **jitosa.** throw oneself into the water.

toto (**ma-**) 1. *augment. of* **mtoto.** 2. part *(of a whole).*

totoma 1. wander about. 2. *rare* get lost. *appl.* **totomea.**

totora pick the teeth. (= **chokoa.**) *Cf.* [5]**tora.**

[1]**tovu** *adj.* lacking, missing. *Cf.* [2]**toa, mtovu, utovu.**

[2]**tovu** (**ma-**) *augment. of* **kitovu. tungu –.** protruding navel.

towa *see* [1]**toa,** [2]**toa.**

towashi* [*Pers.*] (**ma-**) eunuch.

towe (–) potter's clay. (= **udongo.**)

towea add to, put into *(food)*; flavor, season. *appl.* **towelea.** flavor/season *(food with something)*, eat with... **towelea wali kwa mchuzi.** flavor rice with gravy. **nimenunua nyama ili nikatowelee na ugali wangu.** I have bought meat to eat along with my porridge. *caus.* **toweza, towesha.** *Cf.* **kitoweo.**

toweka *intr. of* **2toa.**

toweo (**ma-**) *see* **kitoweo.**

1towesha *caus. of* **2toa.**

2towesha *caus. of* **towea.**

toweza *caus. of* **towea.**

1toza (**ma-**) pipe bowl.

2toza *caus. of* **1toa.**

trakta* (**ma-**) *see* **trekta.**

transista* [*Engl.*] (–) *elec.* transistor.

trekta*, trakta [*Engl.*] (**ma-**) tractor. **kilimo kipya cha sasa ni kwa matrekta.** In modern agriculture tractors are used.

treni* [*Engl.*] (–) *rare* (railroad) train.

tropiki* [*Engl.*] *geogr.* tropic(s). **–a –.** tropical.

tu *adv.* only, just, merely, nothing but; utterly, completely. *Cf.* **tupu(?). kidogo –.** just a little. **ni fungu –.** It is only a part. **mtoto –.** a mere child, nothing but a child. **giza –.** utter darkness.

1tua 1. put/set down. **– mzigo.** put down a burden. 2. settle (down); set *(of the sun).* **jua limetua.** The sun has set/gone down. 3. land. **ndege imetua kiwanjani.** The airplane has landed on the flying field. 4. come to rest, take a rest, settle down, stop. **lazima atue kama maji ya mtungi.** He ought to take to a more regular existence (*lit.* He should settle down like the water in a jug). 5. calm down, satisfy. *appl.* **tulia.** 1. calm down, become/be quiet/tranquil. **bahari imetulia.** The sea has become calm. 2. be satisfied. **moyo umemtulia.** He is satisfied. 3. settle down, stay in one place, have an established residence. *imp.* **tulia!** Calm yourself! Calm down! *intr.* **tulika.** convey, forward, transport. *caus.* **tuliza.** bring to rest, ease, allay, relieve *(pain);* pacify, comfort, reassure. **dawa hii inatuliza maumivu.** This medicine relieves the pain. **lazima nimtulize.** I must comfort/reassure him. *caus.-ass.* **tulizana.** comfort/pacify each other; live on good terms with each other, get along well together. *double appl.-ass.* **tuliliana.** reach a satisfactory agreement/settlement. *stat.* **tuama.** 1. lead a settled existence, be a permanent resident. 2. settle *(of muddy water, etc.). ass.* **tuana.** settle down together, reach an agreement. *Cf.* **tuli, tulivu, tulizo, kitulivu, kitulizo, kituo, mtulivu, utulivu, utuvu.**

2tua* (–) 1. fate, destiny. 2. blemish, disgrace, stigma. 3. libel, calumny, slander.

3tua *see* **1chua.**

tuama *stat. of* **1tua.**

tuana *ass. of* **1tua.**

tubu* regret, repent, feel remorse. **ametubu makosa yake.** He repents of his shortcomings. *appl.* **tubia.** *caus.* **tubisha.** *Cf.* **kitubio.**

tufali* (ma-) *see* **tofali.**

tufani* (–) storm, hurricane, typhoon.

tufe* (–) 1. ball, ballgame (= **mpira**). 2. *math.* sphere. **– nzima.** a solid sphere.

tuguu (ma-) tuguu (a mat on which grain is ground).

tuhuma* (–) suspicion, accusation. *Cf.* **tuhumu.**

tuhumu* (*rare* **tehemu**) suspect, throw suspicion on, accuse, charge with something. *appl.* **tuhumia.** *intr.* **tuhumika.** *caus.* **tuhumisha.** *appl.-ass.* **tuhumiana.** *Cf.* **tuhuma.**

tui (–) tui (strained coconut juice).

tuili* 1. be prolonged/delayed/postponed. *caus.* **tuiliza, tuilisha.** prolong, delay, make late; put off, postpone, defer. 2. *adj.* lengthy, protracted, prolonged, dilatory, delayed, belated. *Cf.* **tawili.**

tuilisha *caus. of* **tuili.**

tuiliza *caus. of* **tuili.**

tuka (–) post, prop, support. (= **nguzo.**)

tukana 1. curse, swear. 2. abuse, revile, insult. *appl.* **tukania.** *intr.* **tukanika.** *ass.* **tukanana. watu wametukanana.** The people were using abusive language to each other. *caus.* **tukanisha.** 1. *(w. int. force)* treat someone with the greatest contempt; avoid someone's company. 2. give someone a bad name, expose someone to ridicule, make someone a public laughingstock. **ukienda nchi ya mbali usitukanishe taifa lako.** When you visit a foreign country, behave yourself properly (*lit.* do not disgrace your people). *Cf.* **matukano.**

tukano (ma-) (*us.* **matukano**) swearing, abusive language, abuse, insults. *Cf.* **tukana.**

tukia happen, occur, take place; appear, present itself; turn out. **jambo baya limenitukia leo.** A terrible thing happened to me today. **ilitukia jinsi alivyosema.** It turned out just as he said. *caus.* **tukiza.** *Cf.* **tukio, kituko.**

tukio (ma-) 1. occurrence, event, incident. 2. accident. *Cf.* **tukia.**

tukiza *caus. of* **tukia.**

tukufu *adj.* great, important; glorious, magnificent; majestic; generally recognized, widely known. *Cf.* **tukuka, mtukufu, utukufu.**

tukuka be great/important/famous/generally recognized. **mashine mpya imetukuka mahali pengi duniani.** The new machine is well known in many parts of the world. *caus.* **tukuza.** make famous/prominent, bring into the foreground, give publicity to. **viongozi wa chama hiki wametukuzwa sana katika magazeti.** The leaders of this party have been given a great deal of publicity in the newspapers. *Cf.* **tukufu, mtukufu, utukufu.**

tukusha *caus. of* **tukuta.**

tukuta 1. be restless/nervous. 2. be impatient/bad-tempered/moody. 3. be worried/alarmed. *intr.* **tukutika.** 1. be irritable/excitable. 2. tremble, quiver; be jumpy, start up *(with fright). intr.-caus.* **tukutiza.** cause restlessness/excitement. *caus.* **tukusha.** make someone nervous/restless; annoy, torment. *Cf.* **tukutiko, tukutu, mtukutu, utukutu.**

tukutiko, tukuto (ma-) trembling, tremor, shuddering; nervousness, excitement, nervous emotion. *Cf.* **tukuta.**

tukutiza *intr.-caus. of* **tukuta.**

tukuto (ma-) *see* **tukutiko.**

tukutu *adj.* 1. restless, nervous, irritable; annoying, troublesome; nagging, querulous. 2. fidgety, mischievous *(of a small child). Cf.* **tukuta, mtukutu, utukutu.**

tukuza *caus. of* **tukuka.**

tule* *adj.* poor, wretched, miserable. *Cf.* **matule, mtule, utule.**

tuli *adj., adv.* quiet, still; reserved. *Cf.* **[1]tua.**

tulia *appl. & imp. of* **[1]tua.**

tuliliana *double appl.-ass. of* **[1]tua.**

tulivu *adj.* quiet, still, peaceful. *Cf.* **[1]tua, kitulivu, mtulivu, utulivu.**

tuliza *caus. of* **[1]tua.**

tulizo (ma-) 1. quieting, soothing; relief, comfort. 2. sedative, anodyne. **mgonjwa amelala baada ya kupewa —.** After taking a sedative the patient slept. *Cf.* **[1]tua.**

tuma 1. send, dispatch *(a person).* 2. give work to, put to work, employ. **— fulani kwa kazi.** give someone work. *appl.* **tumia.** 1. use, make use of, utilize, employ *(either person or thing).* **tumia taratibu** (*or* **kwa kadiri**). use sparingly, be sparing/frugal. 2. have sexual relations with... 3. *(intr.)* menstruate. *double appl.* **tumilia.** utilize (fully), use (up). **tumilia mbali.** use up completely, consume. *double appl.-refl.* **jitumilia.** waste, squander; waste time, loiter, loaf. *intr.* **tumika.** 1. have work, be employed. **anaitumikia skuli yetu.** He works at our school. 2. be usable, be available *(for use/employment).* **pesa za Wareno hazitumiki tena Afrika Mashariki.** Portuguese money is no longer used in East Africa. *intr.-appl.* **tumikia.** work for (someone), serve, be a servant (of someone); be useful/available to (someone); obey; *intr.-appl.-pass.* **tumikiwa.** **anapenda sana kutumikiwa.** He is very fond of being waited on. *intr.-caus.* **tumikisha.** take as a servant/employee. *caus.* **tumisha, tumiza.** 1. send off, dispatch. 2. *(w. int. force)* assign someone a special/urgent task/duty. *pass.* **tumiwa.** *ass.* **tumana.** *Cf.* **tume, kitumwa, matumishi, matumizi, mtume, mtumishi, mtumo, mtumwa, mtumwaji, utume, utumishi, utumizi, utumwa.**

tumai* *see* **tumaini.**

tumaini*, tumai 1. wish, desire, yearn for. 2. hope for, expect. 3. trust, have confidence in, rely on, believe. **tunamtumaini mtu huyu.** We trust this man. *appl.* **tumainia.** *intr.* **tumainika.** *caus.* **tumainisha.** raise someone's hopes, give someone assurance. 4. **(ma-)** (*us.* **matumaini**) desire; belief, faith, confidence, trust; hope, expectation. 5. *adj.* confident, hopeful. *Cf.* **tumainifu, mtumainifu;** *also* **tamaa, tamani.**

tumainifu* *adj.* 1. trusting, confident, hopeful. 2. trustworthy, reliable. *Cf.* **tumaini.**

[1]**tumba (ma-)** (*augment. of* **mtumba**) cover, container, case; package, bag, bundle, bale. **– la nguo.** bundle of clothes. **– la ua.** bud. **– la kitabu.** cover of a book. **– la mwezi.** halo of the moon. *Cf.* **tumbua, tumbo.**

[2]**tumba (ma-)** *arch.* tumba (calabash containing a magic potion).

tumbako* **(–)** *see* **tumbaku.**

tumbaku*, tumbako [*Ind.*] (–) tobacco. **vuta –.** smoke. **nusa –.** take snuff. **– ya kunusa.** snuff (= **ugolo**). **tafuna/bugia –.** chew tobacco. *Cf.* **mtumbako.**

tumbasi* **(–)** *med., rare* abscess. (= **jipu.**)

tumbawe (ma-) coral rag *(i.e., coral in the state before complete petrifaction; hence light, and used for lime burning). Cf.* **marijani.**

tumbili, tumbiri (–) tumbili (species of small monkey). *Cf.* **kima, nyani, ngedere.**

tumbiri (–) *see* **tumbili.**

tumbo (–) 1. stomach, belly; abdomen. **matumbo.** bowels, viscera. 2. **(– la uzazi)** womb. **ndugu – moja.** children of a single mother. **ngoja ngoja yaumiza –.** Waiting is painful (*lit.* hurts the stomach). 3. pain or complaint in the stomach or abdomen. stomachache, colic. **– la kuhara.** diarrhea. **– la kuhara damu.** dysentery. 4. *fig.* interior of something (*e.g.*, hold of a ship), capacity. **– la merikebu.** tonnage of a ship. 5. protuberance, swelling. *Cf.* **kitumbo, utumbo.**

tumbua 1. eviscerate, draw *(poultry).* 2. open up, cut open, make a hole *(in something).* **– jipu.** lance a boil. 3. dissect. *appl.* **tumbulia. tumbulia macho.** open the eyes wide, stare. *intr.* **tumbuka, tumburujika.** be opened up/cut open, break open. *intr.-appl.* **tumbukia.** rush/burst/fall/tumble into something. **tumbukia kisimani.** tumble into a well. *prov.* **mchimba kisima hutumbukia mwenyewe.** Who digs a pit for others falls into it himself. *intr.-appl.-caus.* **tumbukiza.** cause to fall into, push into something. *caus.* **tumbuza.** force a way through something *(forest, etc.);* look at fixedly, glare at. *Cf.* **¹tumba, tumbo, mtumbwi, utumbavu, utumbo.**

tumbuika be soothed/calmed/pacified/consoled. *caus.* **tumbuiza.** soothe, calm, appease; delight, amuse. **tumbuiza kwa maneno mazuri.** soothe/placate with pleasant words. **walitutumbuiza kwa muziki wao.** They have amused us with their music. *Cf.* **tumbuizo, mtumbuizi, utumbuizi.**

tumbuiza *caus. of* **tumbuika.**

tumbuizo (ma-) 1. lullaby, soothing song. 2. refrain *(of a song)*. *Cf.* **tumbuika.**

tumbuka *intr. of* **tumbua.**

tumbulia *appl. of* **tumbua.**

tumbuo*, tumbuu [*Pers.?*] (–) metal fastener for a door or window *(consisting of a chain securing a hasp and staple)*.

tumburujika 1. be decayed/rotten/useless; *(fig.)* be corrupted. 2. = **tumbuka** *(intr. of* **tumbua).**

tumbuu* (–) *see* **tumbuo.**

tumbuza *caus. of* **tumbua.**

tume (–) 1. messenger; *(Isl.)* apostle (= Muhammad). 2. employee, servant; representative, agent. 3. errand, task; business, occupation. *Cf.* **tuma.**

tumia *appl. of* **tuma.**

¹tumu*, saumu (–) fasting, time of fasting. **mwezi wa –.** month of fasting, Ramadhan.

²tumu* (–) *see* **thumu.**

tuna 1. puff up, swell out. **– mashavu.** puff up the cheeks. 2. *fig.* put on airs, act high and mighty. **anapenda sana kutuna.** He likes to act big. 3. be annoyed/out of humor. *refl.* **jituna.** put on airs, be arrogant. *appl.* **tunia.** *intr.* **tunika.** *caus.* **tunisha.** 1. dress up. 2. blow up, exaggerate; flatter. 3. anger/offend someone.

¹tunda 1. (ma-) (piece of) fruit. **– bivu (bichi).** unripe (ripe) fruit. **matunda.** fruit *(coll.); (fig.)* result, outcome, product. **haya ni matunda ya tabia zako.** This is the result of your disposition. 2. *v. dial.* pluck, gather *(fruit)* (= **²chuma).**

²tunda (–) tunda (belt of beads, worn by women).

tundama 1. accumulate, settle *(e.g., of water in a hole)*. 2. stand in line, queue up. **watu wametundama tangu mlangoni mpaka barabarani.** The people were lined up from the door to the street.

tundawaa, tunduaa be motionless, still, quiet; freeze *(in a certain position)*. *caus.* **tundawaza.**

tundawaza *caus. of* **tundawaa.**

tundika hang up, suspend. *appl.* **tundikia.** *caus.* **tundikisha.** *Cf.* **²tundua, tunduo.**

tundiza begin to ripen *(fruit).*

[1]**tundu** 1. (–) hole *(in gen.),* aperture, passage, hollow; leak. **– ya pua.** nostril. **– ya sindano.** eye of a needle. **– ya bunduki.** muzzle of a gun. 2. (ma-) a hollow receptacle, *e.g.:* den, lair *(of an animal),* nest *(of a bird),* cage, pocket, basket.

[2]**tundu*** [*Pers.*] *adj.* 1. ill-bred, insolent, impudent, stubborn. 2. troublesome, mischievous *(child).* 3. worthless, good-for-nothing. *Cf.* [1]**tundua, mtundu, utundu.**

[1]**tundua*** [*Pers.*] spoil, pamper *(a child). Cf.* [2]**tundu.**

[2]**tundua** take/get down *(something hanging/suspended). Cf.* **tundika, tunduo.**

tunduaa *see* **tunduwaa.**

tunduia keep an eye on, watch, guard, spy on, investigate. *appl.* **tundulia. anamtundulia sana mkewe.** He keeps a close eye on his wife. *caus.* **tunduiza.** have someone watched/investigated. *Cf.* **tunduizi, mtunduizi, utunduizi.**

tunduiza *caus. of* **tunduia.**

tunduizi (ma-) watcher, guard, spy. *Cf.* **tunduia, mtunduizi.**

tunduo (ma-) (act of) taking down *(something suspended). Cf.* **tundua, tundika.**

[1]**tunga** put together, tie/string together; arrange, put in order; put in a row, line up; form, compose, construct, make. **– maua.** make a bouquet. **– uzi katika shindano.** thread a needle. **– samaki.** string fish *(for drying).* **– ushanga.** string beads. **– usaha.** form matter, suppurate *(a sore).* **– kitabu.** write a book. **– mashairi.** write poetry. **– nyimbo.** compose songs. *appl.* **tungia.** *intr.* **tungika.** 1. be joined/tied together. 2. be hung up/suspended. 3. be dependent on *(something or someone).* *caus.* **tungiza.** 1. put in order. 2. cause to follow, lead *(people in a single file),* draw/pull *(as a locomotive pulls cars).* *stat.* **tungama.** 1. be firm/stable/durable. 2. become thick, congeal. *stat.-ass.* **tungamana.** 1. hold together, be in agreement/harmony. **watu wametungamana.** The people present a united front. 2. be packed together/crowded. *stat.-ass.-caus.* **tungamanisha.** cause to agree/harmonize. *inv.* **tungua.** 1. get out of order, disarrange. 2. separate, interrupt. 3. lower, reduce *(prices).* 4. take down *(e.g., from a hook); (fig.)* buy clothing ready-made. **suti hii umeshonesha ao umetungua?** Did you have this suit made to order or did you buy it ready-made? *inv.-appl.* **tungulia.** *inv.-intr.* **tunguka.** *Cf.* **tungizi, mtunga, mtungo, mtunguo, utungaji, utungo.**

[2]**tunga** (–) tunga (a round, flat basket used for winnowing grain).

tungama *stat. of* [1]**tunga.**

tungi (ma-) *augment. of* **mtungi.**

tungika *intr. of* [1]**tunga.**

tungiza *caus. of* [1]**tunga.**

tungizi (**ma-**) (*us.* **matungizi**) 1. invention. 2. (act of) inventing/devising. *Cf.* [1]**tunga.**

tungo (**ma-**) *augment. of* **mtungo.**

[1]**tungu** (**ma-**) 1. species of large calabash. 2. *fig.* (*also* – **tovu**) protruding navel.

[2]**tungu** (–) wood file, rasp.

tungua 1. *inv. of* [1]**tunga.** 2.: – **usingizi.** fall into a deep sleep.

tunguja (–) 1. tunguja (fruit of the mtunguja; *cf.* **mtua**). 2. *rare* (European) tomato (= [2]**nyanya, tungule**).

tungule (–) tomato. (= [2]**nyanya.**) *Cf.* **mtungule.**

tunguri (–) (small) gourd/calabash.

tunguridi (–) *ornith.* (species of) finch.

tuni* [*Engl.*] (–) tune.

tunu 1. (–) something rare/valuable; rarity; (valuable) gift, keepsake, souvenir. 2. *adj.* rare, valuable; *(fig.)* dear, precious. *Cf.* **tunuka.**

tunuka, chunuka be very fond of, set great store by; yearn for, have one's heart set on; finally obtain something long desired, receive a special honor/distinction, pay a high price for something. *appl.* **tunukia.** have a special liking for something; make a present to someone, show someone an honor. **ametunukiwa na serikali.** He has received a decoration from the government. *ass.* **tunukana.** *Cf.* **tunu, utunu.**

tunutu, funutu (–) young locust.

tunza 1. care for, take care of, mind, tend; guard, protect. – **mtoto.** look after/mind a child. 2. do something carefully/attentively. 3. make a present, show an honor (= **tunukia**), make an award. **ametunzwa.** He has been (signally) honored/has received an award. *appl.* **tunzia.** look after/keep an eye on/take care of (something/someone). *intr.* **tunzika. kitabu hiki kimetunzika.** This book has received very favorable notice. *caus.* **tunzisha.** 4. (**ma-**) = **tunzo.** *Cf.* **tunzo, mtunza, utunzaji;** *also* **tuza.**

tunzo, tunza, utunzo (–, **ma-**) care, attention; protection; honor, award, distinction. **amepewa –.** He has received a distinction. *Cf.* **tunza;** *also* **tuzo.**

[1]**tupa** 1. throw, cast, hurl. – **chini.** throw to the ground. – **macho.** cast the eyes on something. 2. throw away, repudiate, abandon, desert. **amemtupa mkewe.** He has deserted his wife. **ametutupa mkono.** He has died (*lit.* He has thrown us his hand). *appl.* **tupia.** 1. throw away. 2. throw something at/to (someone); *(fig.)* speak to (someone), refer (something to someone). *intr.* **tupika.** be thrown down/away (carelessly); *(fig.)* escape the

attention. *refl.* **jitupa kitandani.** throw oneself down on one's bed, be completely exhausted. *pass.* **tupwa. ametupwa.** He has been repudiated/has emigrated. *Cf.* **¹mtupa, mtupio, mtupo.**

²tupa (*also* **dupa**) (–) rasp, file. **piga –.** to rasp/file. **kata kwa –.** file through something. **– ya tunga.** rasp, wood file. **– ya chuma.** (metal-)file.

tupu *adj.* 1. naked, bare, bald. **kwa miguu mitupu.** with bare feet, barefoot. 2. empty; *(fig.)* meaningless, worthless. **mkono mtupu haurambwi.** An empty hand is not welcomed (*lit.* is not licked). **maneno matupu.** empty (= meaningless) words. 3. mere, pure, sheer, downright. **uwongo mtupu.** a downright/barefaced lie. *Cf.* **utupu.**

turbali*, turubai (–) *see* **turubali.**

turubali*, turbali, turubai [*Engl.*] (–) 1. tarpaulin, sailcloth. 2. oilcloth, waxed paper.

¹turufu* scorn, despise, disdain; ignore, neglect.

²turufu* [*Port.*] (–) *cards* trump(s). **hii ndiyo karata ya –.** This is the trump card.

turuhani* [*Pers.*] (–) tare *(allowance for packing, when weighing); (fig.)* something extra *(thrown in w. a sale)*, bonus.

Turuki* (ma-) *see* **Mturuki.**

turuma* (mi-) *rare* molding, panelling, wainscoting.

turusi* [*Engl.*] (–) *rare* truss, supporting framework; window frame.

tusha annoy, irritate; treat with contempt, humiliate, degrade, abase. *appl.* **tushia.** *intr.* **tushika.** *refl.* **jitusha.** abase oneself, submit, yield; disgrace oneself. *inv.* **tushua** = **tusha.** *Cf.* **tushi, matusi.**

tushi, tusi, tusu (ma-) (*us.* **matushi**) abuse, insult, offensive language/behavior. **ametumia lugha ya matushi.** He used offensive language. **kuingia katika nyumba bila ya kupiga hodi ni matushi.** To enter a house without knocking is impolite. *Cf.* **tusha.**

¹tusi (–) palanquin, litter; *(rare)* stretcher (= **kitanda**).

²tusi (ma-) *see* **tushi.**

tusu (ma-) *see* **tushi.**

¹tuta 1. pile/heap up *(fruit, grain)*. 2. carry. *appl.* **tutia.** fill up with something. pour on, throw into a heap. **tutia majani.** sweep up leaves. **tutia kaburi.** close a grave. *intr.* **tutika** *(w. tr. force)*. carry off *(one load of something after another)*.

²tuta (ma-) 1. bed *(for planting)*. **– la kupanda mbegu.** seedbed. **piga/chimba –.** dig up a bed. 2. *fig., coll.* grave.

³tuta *rare* beat *(of the heart)*, pulsate.

¹tutu (–) tutu (kind of drum).

[2]**tutu** (–) *ornith.* tutu (species of wild dove).

[3]**tutu** (–) *med.* swelling, tumor. *Cf.* **tutuu, tutuka.**

[4]**tutu** *interj.* Restrain yourself! Leave it alone!

tutuka, tutumka, tutuma 1. swell (up). 2. bubble/boil (up). 3. *fig.* get excited, become angry; be puffed up *(w. pride). inv.* **tutumua** (*us. refl.-inv.* **jitutumua**). 1. strain oneself, make a strong effort. 2. puff oneself up, boast. **usitutumke.** Don't brag/put on airs/act so big. *caus.* **tutuza.** *caus.-intr.* **tutuzika.** take a rest, catch one's breath. *Cf.* **tutuo, tutuu.**

[1]**tutuma** rumble, growl. *Cf.* **kitutumi, mtutumo.**

[2]**tutuma** *see* **tutuka.**

tutumka *see* **tutuka.**

tutumua *inv. of* **tutuka.**

tutuo (ma-) 1. hurry, haste, impatience. 2. boasting. *Cf.* **tutuka.**

tutusa grope *(for something)*, feel one's way. *intr.* **tutusika.** *med.* be infected.

tutuu, tuutuu (ma-) *med.* (hard) growth, swelling; wart. *Cf.* **tutuka.**

tutuza *caus. of* **tutuka.**

tutuzika *caus.-intr. of* **tutuka.**

tuutuu (ma-) *see* **tutuu.**

tuwanyika (–) tuwanyika (kind of snake).

tuwazi* (ma-) *see* **toasi.**

tuza 1. give a present/reward. 2. do honor to, show respect/appreciation. *pass.* **tuzwa.** be given a present/honored/rewarded. *inv.* **tuzua.** disgrace, humiliate. 3. (–) = **tuzo.** *Cf.* **tunza.**

tuzo, tuza (ma-) gift, present; reward; honor, distinction; award, prize. *Cf.* **tunzo.**

tuzua *inv. of* **tuza.**

twa *see* **chwa.**

[1]**twaa** 1. take, take away from. 2. get, receive, accept. **– jina jingine.** take/assume a different name. 3. *mil.* take, capture, occupy. 4. have sexual intercourse with *(a woman).* **– bikira.** deflower. *appl.* **twalia.** take away from someone, rob. *intr.* **twalika.** *ass.* **twaana** & *caus.-ass.* **twazana.** 1. have sexual intercourse *(of man and woman).* 2. be on intimate terms. 3. resemble each other. *pass.* **twaliwa, twawa.** 1. be taken/seized/received. 2. be robbed, have something stolen. *Cf.* **mtwaa.**

[2]**twaa** *adv.* quietly, silently. **lala –.** sleep peacefully.

twaana *ass. of* [1]**twa.**

twalika *intr. of* [1]**twa.**

twaliwa *pass. of* [1]**twa.**

twana (ma-) 1. *augment. of* [1]**mtwana.** 2. rascal, swindler. 3. ill-bred/impolite person.

twanga 1. pound/clean/husk grain *(in a mortar).* 2. *fig.* drive a hard bargain, beat down *(the price of something).* 3. beat, defeat. **katika mashindano hayo timo yetu iliwatwanga.** In this game our team won. 4. snap *(a photograph). appl.* **twangia.** *intr.* **twangika.** *caus.* **twangisha.** *Cf.* **mtwango, mtwanzi.**

twawa *pass. of* [1]**twaa.**

twaza be complacent/proud/arrogant, show off, boast; deceive.

twazana *caus.-ass. of* [1]**twaa.**

tweka, twika raise, hoist. **merikebu imetweka matanga.** The ship has set/hoisted sail. **– bendera.** hoist a flag. *appl.* **twekea.**

twesha *see* **tweza** & [1]**twisha.**

tweta pant, gasp, breathe heavily/with difficulty. **bado anatweta.** He is still breathing *(of a dying person). appl.* **twetea.** *Cf.* **mtweto.**

tweza (*rare* **twesha**) 1. disgrace, dishonor, humiliate. 2. offend, injure.

twiga (–) giraffe. **– mdogo.** species of gazelle (gerenuk).

twika 1. = **tweka.** 2. place a load on the head or shoulders. *refl.* **jitwika.** place a load on one's head. *caus.* **twisha.** *Cf.* **twisho.**

[1]**twisha, twesha** 1. wish someone good night. 2. pay someone an evening visit. 3. invite guests for the evening.

[2]**twisha** *caus. of* **twika.**

twisho (ma-) twisho (a pad used when carrying a load on the head). *Cf.* **twika.**

twisti* [*Engl.*] dance the twist.

U

[1]**ua** (ma-) flower, blossom. **toa maua.** bloom. **chuma –.** pick flowers. **shada ya maua.** bouquet.

[2]**ua** (nyua) 1. (open) court (behind a house), backyard. **ninakwenda uani.** I am going into the backyard (= to the toilet). 2. fence, hedge, enclosure. **jenga –.** build/put up a fence.

3ua kill, murder; destroy. *appl.* **ulia.** *ass.* **uana.** *pass.* **uawa.** *refl.* **jiua.** commit suicide. *Cf.* **kiuaji, maulisho, mwuaji, uuaji.**

uabudiwaji* *sing.* worship, cult. – **wa mtu maalamu.** cult of the individual. *Cf.* **abudu, ibada.**

uadhimishaji* *sing.* festival, ceremony. *Cf.* **adhama, adhimu.**

uadilifu* *sing.* justice, honesty, integrity. *Cf.* **adili.**

uadui* *sing.* (*also* **maadui, adawa**) enmity, hostility, ill-will. *Cf.* **adui.**

uafisa*, uofisa [*Engl.*] *sing.* status (rank, duties, pay, etc.) of an official/officer. *Cf.* **ofisa.**

uagizaji *sing.* request; order, commission. *Cf.* **2aga.**

uaguzi *sing.* 1. interpretation, explanation, commentary. 2. prophecy, prediction. 3. *med.* diagnosis. *Cf.* **agua.**

uaili* *sing.* accusation, blame, reprimand, censure. *Cf.* **aili.**

uajazi* *sing.* *see* **uajizi.**

Uajemi*, Agami, Ajemi *sing.* Persia, Iran. *Cf.* **Kiajemi, Mwajemi.**

uajenti* [*Engl.*] *sing.* position (duties, pay, etc.) of an agent/manager. *Cf.* **ajenti.**

uaji *sing.* *see* **uuaji.**

uajizi*, uajazi *sing.* weakness, feebleness; flabbiness; slowness, sluggishness; hesitation, indecision; lateness, delay, procrastination. *Cf.* **ajizi.**

ualimu*, uwalimu *sing.* teaching; teaching profession, education; instruction. *Cf.* **elimu, mwalimu.**

uambukizo (**ma-**) (*us.* **maambukizo**) *med.* infection, contagion. *Cf.* **ambua.**

uamini* *sing.* *see* **uaminifu.**

uaminifu*, uamini *sing.* 1. trust, confidence, reliance. **fulani hana –.** So-and-so enjoys no confidence. **amevunja – wake.** He has broken his confidence. 2. trustworthiness, veracity, credibility, honesty, accuracy, reliability, dependability, certainty. *Cf.* **1amini.**

uamuzi *sing.* judgment, decision, verdict; arbitration. *Cf.* **1amua.**

1uana *sing.* childhood. *Cf.* **mwana.**

2uana *ass. of* **3ua.**

uanaadamu *sing.* *see* **ubinadamu.**

uanachama *sing.* membership *(in an organization). Cf.* **mwanachama.**

uanadamu *sing.* *see* **ubinadamu.**

uanafunzi *sing.* (period of) apprenticeship, studies. *Cf.* **2funda.**

uanahewa* *sing.* aviation. *Cf.* **mwanahewa.**

uanajeshi* *sing.* military affairs. *Cf.* **mwanajeshi.**

uananchi, uwananchi *sing.* citizenship, patriotism. *Cf.* **mwananchi.**

uanasheria* *sing.* legal matters, (the practice of) law. *Cf.* **mwanasheria.**

uanauke *sing.* *see* **uke.**

uanaume *sing.* *see* **uume.**

uanda (nyanda) *see* **uwanda.**

uandamano (ma-) (*us.* **maandamano**) procession. *Cf.* **andama.**

uandamizi (ma-) (*us.* **maandamizi**) 1. dependence, linking. 2. sequence, continuation. *Cf.* **andama.**

uandikishaji *sing.* registration. *Cf.* **andika.**

uandishi *sing.* manner of writing, style. *Cf.* **andika.**

uangafu *sing.* *see* **uangavu.**

uangaliaji *sing.* guarding, supervision, care, protection. *Cf.* **angaa.**

uangalifu, uangalizi *sing.* attention, carefulness, circumspection. *Cf.* **angaa.**

uangalizi *sing.* *see* **uangalifu.**

uangamio *sing.* collapse. *Cf.* **angamia.**

1uangamizi (ma-) (*us.* **maangamizi**) 1. collapse, ruin, destruction. 2. loss, disappearance. **mvua hii imeleta maangamizi makubwa.** This rain has caused great devastation. *Cf.* **angamia.**

2uangamizi *sing.* stockpiling. **– ya silaha za viini.** stockpiling of nuclear weapons. *Cf.* **angama.**

uangavu, wangavu, uangafu, wangafu *sing.* 1. glow, luster, brightness, clearness, transparency. **nje leo kuna –.** The weather is fair today. 2. *fig.* clarity, intelligence, discernment, penetration. *Cf.* **2anga, angaa.**

uanzishaji *sing.* 1. beginning, origin, inception. 2. foundation, establishment. *Cf.* **anza.**

1uapo (nyapo) (self-imposed) oath, vow. *Cf.* **apa.**

2uapo, wapo (–) *rare* gift. *Cf.* **1pa.**

Uarabu* *sing.* Arabia. *Cf.* **Mwarabu.**

uasherati*, washerati *sing.* 1. immorality, profligacy, debauchery. 2. adultery. *Cf.* **asherati.**

uashi *sing.* stonemason's craft, masonry, building trade; mason's wages. *Cf.* **2aka.**

uasi*, **wasi**, **uwasi**, **uhasi** (ma-) *(us. pl.)* 1. insurrection, rebellion, mutiny. **fanya —.** rebel, resist. 2. disobedience. 3. hesitation, misgivings *(when requested to do something).* **vunja —.** agree, accede *(to a request, etc., after a period of doubt or hesitation),* (finally) give in. *Cf.* **asi.**

uaskari* *sing.* military service/pay, military profession. *Cf.* **askari.**

uaskofu* *sing., rel.* episcopate, bishopric. *Cf.* **askofu.**

uati (**mbati**) *see* ²**uwati.**

uawa *pass. of* ³**ua.**

uayo (**nyayo**) *see* **wayo.**

uazimaji *sing.* obligation, commitment; loan *(for a fixed period of time).* **maktaba ya —.** lending library. *Cf.* ²**azima.**

ubaba *sing.* paternity, fatherhood. *Cf.* ¹**baba.**

ubabaiko *sing.* 1. murmuring, whispering. 2. incoherent/meaningless speech, stammering. *Cf.* **babaika.**

ubadhiri* *sing.* *see* **ubadhirifu.**

ubadhirifu*, **ubadhiri** *sing.* 1. waste, extravagance, prodigality. 2. immoderation, lack of restraint. *Cf.* **badhiri, badhirifu.**

ubadili* *sing.* *see* **ubadilifu.**

ubadilifu*, **ubadili**, **ubadiliko** (ma-) 1. change, exchange; changeableness. **tumepata mapumziko, lakini hatuoni mabadiliko.** Although we have had a rest, we do not notice any change. 2. substitution. *Cf.* **badili, badilifu.**

ubadiliko* (ma-) *see* **ubadilifu.**

ubadilishaji* *sing.* changeableness, fickleness; *(pol.)* revisionism. *Cf.* ¹**badala, badili, mbadilishaji.**

ubaguzi *sing.* different treatment, discrimination, segregation. **— wa rangi.** racial discrimination. *Cf.* **bagua.**

ubaharia* *sing.* navigation, shipping, seamanship. **anajifunza kazi ya —.** He is learning the seaman's trade. *Cf.* **bahari, baharia.**

ubahili* *sing.* avarice, miserliness. *Cf.* **bahili.**

ubaini* *sing.* *see* **ubainifu.**

ubainifu*, **ubaini**, **ubayana** *sing.* proof, evidence, certainty, notoriety. **— umetolewa.** The proof has been furnished. *Cf.* **baina, baini, bainifu.**

ubakuaji *sing.* dominance, exploitation. *Cf.* **bakwia.**

ubale (**mbale**) strip, piece, slice. *Cf.* **bale,** ²**mbale.**

ubaleghi* *sing.* *see* **ubalehe.**

ubalehe*, ubalehi, ubaleghi (–) (sexual) maturity, puberty, marriageable age. *Cf.* **balehe.**

ubalehi* *sing.* *see* **ubalehe.**

ubali *sing.* *see* **umbali.**

ubalozi* *sing.* embassy, legation, consulate; diplomatic/consular affairs. *Cf.* **balozi.**

ubamba (–) 1. metal foil, tinsel. 2. = [3]**bamba.**

ubambo (ma-) 1. = [3]**bambo.** 2. strip of plaited grass *(used for making mats).*

[1]**ubango** (ma-) husk of the betel nut.

[2]**ubango** (ma-) ubango (kind of reed).

[1]**ubani*** *sing.* frankincense.

[2]**ubani*** *sing.* customary fee *(e.g., that paid by a father to the man who teaches his son a trade, a doctor's fee, etc.).*

ubao, ubau (mbao) 1. board, plank, timber, beam. 2. blackboard. *Cf.* **bao.**

ubapa *sing.* 1. = **bapa.** 2. *geogr.* plain. 3. flatness.

ubaradhuli*, ubardhuli *sing.* stupidity, foolishness, gullibility. *Cf.* **baradhuli.**

ubaramaki* (–) 1. ruse, trickery. 2. foolish mistake, boner.

ubardhuli* *sing.* *see* **ubaradhuli.**

ubaridi* *sing.* 1. coldness, coolness; cooling. 2. *fig.* reserve, self-control. 3. *fig.* indifference, apathy. 4. *fig.* gentleness, kindness. *Cf.* **baridi.**

ubashiri* *sing.* 1. prophecy, prediction. 2. announcement, proclamation. *Cf.* **bashiri.**

ubati (–) *rare* outbuilding, shed; addition to a house, wing; lean-to.

ubatili*, ubatilifu *sing.* uselessness, futility, emptiness, worthlessness. *Cf.* **batili.**

ubatilifu* *sing.* *see* **ubatili.**

ubatizo* [*Engl.*] *sing., rel.* baptism. *Cf.* **batiza.**

ubau (mbau) *see* **ubao.**

ubavu (mbavu) 1. *anat.* rib. 2. (mbavu) side *(of the body and in gen.); (mil.)* flank. – **wa mlima.** slope of a mountain. **mbavuni.** alongside, on the side(s). *Cf.* **bavuni, kibavu.**

ubavuni *see* **bavuni.**

ubawa (mbawa) 1. wing *(of a bird);* (wing) feather. 2. *rec.* (*us.* – **za ndege**) wing *(of an airplane).*

ubawabu* *sing.* position/work/wages of a doorkeeper. *Cf.* **bawabu.**

ubaya (ma-) badness, wickedness, meanness, depravity. *Cf.* **baya.**

ubayana* *sing.* *see* **ubainifu.**

ubazazi* (ma-) 1. *rare* retail trade. 2. cheating, fraud, trickery. 3. speculation. **fanya —.** cheat, defraud; speculate, have wild money-making schemes. *Cf.* **bazazi.**

ubeberu *sing.* dictatorship, imperialism. *Cf.* **beberu.**

ubeja* *sing.* 1. smartness, elegance *(of clothing).* 2. athletic build *(of a man).* *Cf.* **mbeja.**

ubele *sing.* *see* **umbele.**

ubeleko (–) *see* **mbeleko.**

ubembe *sing.* *see* **ubembelezi.**

ubembelezi, ubembe *sing.* 1. frivolity, flightiness. 2. allurement, coaxing. 3. prostitution. *Cf.* **bemba.**

ubepari* [*Ind.*] *sing.* bourgeoisie, capitalism. *Cf.* **bepari, kibepari.**

ubeti* (beti) 1. verse, strophe. 2. section, paragraph. *Cf.* **[1]beti.**

ubiashara* *sing.* *see* **biashara.**

ubichi *sing.* rawness, unripeness; *(fig.)* immaturity, shallowness, banality. *Cf.* **bichi.**

ubikira* *sing.* 1. virginity, celibacy. 2. *anat.* hymen (= **kizinda**). *Cf.* **bikira.**

ubilisi* *sing., rel.* temptation. *Cf.* **bilisi, ibilisi.**

ubinadamu, uanaadamu, uanadamu *sing.* humanity, human nature. *Cf.* **binadamu.**

ubinafsi* *sing.* personality. **ibada ya —.** *pol.* personality cult. *Cf.* **binafsi.**

ubinda*, uwinda [?] (ma-) ubinda (type of loincloth worn by Indian traders, but not by Africans). *prov.* **ukimtaka Baniani umtake na – wake.** If you like something you must take it in its entirety (even if some part does not please you).

ubingwa *sing.* skill, proficiency, capability, expertness; qualification. *Cf.* **bingwa.**

[1]ubini* *sing.* forgery, counterfeiting. *Cf.* **bini.**

[2]ubini* (–) family name. **tunajua kuwa anaitwa Ali lakini – wake hatuujui.** We know that his (given) name is Ali, but we do not know his family name. *Cf.* **bin.**

ubinja, uwinja (mbinja, winja) whistle, whistling. *Cf.* **kibinja.**

ubishi (**ma-** & **mbishi**) quarrelsomeness, argumentativeness; opposition; excuse, evasion; mockery, derision, (malicious) joke. *Cf.* **bisha.**

ubivu *sing.* 1. ripeness *(of fruit, etc.).* 2. maturity *(of character, conduct). Cf.* **bivu.**

uboi* [*Engl.*] *sing.* function/activity of a house-servant, errand-boy. *Cf.* **boi.**

ubongo *sing.* 1. brain, brain substance. 2. marrow. *Cf.* **bongo.**

ubono (**mbono**) seed of the castor-oil plant. *Cf.* [1]**mbono.**

ubora* *sing.* excellence, superiority; (high) quality, merit, advantage. *Cf.* **bora.**

ubovu *sing.* rottenness, putrefaction; *(fig.)* unhealthiness, weakness; badness, corruption. *Cf.* **bovu.**

ubozi* *sing.* idleness, laziness, indolence; stupidity, folly. *Cf.* **bozi.**

ubua (–) *see* **bua.**

ububu *sing.* dumbness, muteness. *Cf.* [1]**bubu.**

ubuge *sing.* greed(iness), gluttony. **ana mambo ya –.** He has nothing but food on his mind. *Cf.* **bugia, mbuge.**

ubugu (**mbugu**) the stem of any creeping plant *(used as cord or for plaiting).*

ubukuzi *sing.* gossiping, talebearing, scandalmongering. *Cf.* **bukua, mbukulia.**

ubure* *sing.* uselessness, futility, folly. *Cf.* **bure.**

uburudisho* *sing.* coolness, refreshment, rest, recreation. *Cf.* **baridi.**

ubutu *sing.* dullness *(of a knife, etc.).* *Cf.* **butu.**

ubuyu *sing.* the kernel or the powdered pith of the baobab nut. *Cf.* **buyu, mbuyu.**

ubwabwa *sing.* 1. thin rice gruel. 2. *coll.* cooked rice *(in gen.).*

ubwana *sing.* 1. mastership, position (rights, etc.) of a master. 2. lordliness, arrogance, overbearing/domineering ways. *Cf.* **bwana.**

ubwete *sing.* idleness, laziness, indolence.

ucha *sing.* *see* **uchaji.**

uchache *sing.* 1. slightness, scantiness, meagerness. 2. want, lack, deficiency, scarcity, shortage. **– wa akili.** lack of intelligence, imprudence, rashness. *prov.* **– wetu si wingi wao.** Our lacks are not your greatness (= you are no better than we are). *Cf.* **chache.**

uchachu *sing.* sourness, sour/sharp taste. *Cf.* [3]**chacha, chachu.**

uchafu *sing.* 1. dirt(iness), uncleanliness. 2. nastiness, indecency, obscenity. 3. baseness, vileness. *Cf.* **¹chafu, chafua.**

uchafuko *sing.* disorder(liness), confusion, mess. *Cf.* **chafua, mchafuko.**

uchafuzi *sing.* confusion, disorder; *(pol.)* diversion, sabotage. *Cf.* **chafua.**

uchaga, uchala (–) *see* **kichaga.**

uchago (chago) *see* **¹chago.**

uchaguo *sing.* *see* **uchaguzi.**

uchaguzi, uchaguo *sing.* 1. selectiveness, discrimination; choice, selection. 2. *pol.* election, voting. **– wa nafsi (unaibu).** direct (indirect) election. **– mkuu.** general elections. *Cf.* **chagua.**

uchaji, ucha *sing.* fear, awe, reverence, respect. *Cf.* **²cha.**

uchakacho *sing.* rustling, crackling, crunching *(sound). Cf.* **chakacha.**

uchala (–) *see* **kichaga.**

uchale *sing.* cut, incision, slash, scratching, scoring. **chanja –.** make incisions in the skin, tattoo. **undugu wa –.** blood brotherhood. *Cf.* **¹chale.**

¹uchanga *sing.* grain of sand. *Cf.* **mchanga.**

²uchanga *sing.* unripeness; immaturity, infancy. *Cf.* **³changa.**

uchangamfu *sing.* good-humor, liveliness, gaiety, exuberance, exhilaration. *Cf.* **changamka, changamfu.**

uchanganuo *sing.* analysis. *Cf.* **¹changa.**

uchango (–) 1. = **uchengelele.** 2. = **¹mchango.**

uchao, uche, ucheachea *sing., rare* dawn, daybreak. *Cf.* **³cha.**

uchapaji* *sing.* 1. printing business, typography. 2. edition, printing. *Cf.* **¹chapa.**

uchapishaji* *sing.* publication. *Cf.* **¹chapa.**

uchavushi *sing., bot.* pollination.

uchawi *sing.* witchcraft, sorcery, magic. *Cf.* **mchawi.**

uche *sing., rare* *see* **uchao.**

ucheachea, uteatea *sing.* 1. = **uchao.** 2. brightening, clearing up *(of the weather). Cf.* **³cha.**

uchechefu *sing.* 1. fewness, small number. 2. *rare* = **uchache.**

uchekeshi, uchekeshaji *sing.* *see* **ucheshi.**

uchelewaji *sing.* lateness, tardiness, delay. *Cf.* **³cha.**

uchengelele, ujengelele, uchango *sing., anat.* small intestines; *(fig., vulg.)* penis.

ucheo, ucheu, uchoo *sing.* plot of land, field *(prepared for cultivation).*

uchepechepe *sing.* moisture, dampness. **ardhi ya hapa ni ya – na nzuri kwa miwa tu.** The soil is good only for sugarcane because it contains very much moisture. *Cf.* **chepechepe.**

ucheshi, uchekeshi, uchekeshaji *sing.* gaiety, exuberance; humor, wit. *Cf.* **[1]cheka, [1]cheshi.**

ucheu *sing.* *see* **ucheo.**

uchezaji *sing.* playing, playing/fooling around. **mwalimu akiingia darasani watoto wasifanye –.** When the teacher enters the classroom, the children are supposed to stop fooling around. *Cf.* **cheza.**

uchi *sing.* 1. nakedness, nudity. **yu –.** He is naked. **enda – wa nyama.** go stark naked. 2. *coll.* genitals.

uchifu* [*Engl.*] *sing.* position (function, activities, etc.) of a chief/leader, leadership, direction, management. *Cf.* **chifu.**

uchimbaji *sing.* mining, output, production *(of ore, coal).* *Cf.* **chimba.**

uchimvi, utimvi, utimbi *sing.* 1. intrigue, machinations, plotting. 2. bad luck. *Cf.* **chimba, chimvi, mchimbi.**

uchipuko *sing.* sprout, shoot. *Cf.* **chipua.**

uchochezi *sing.* provocation, agitation; revolt, sedition, mutiny. *Cf.* **chocha.**

uchochoro (ma-) *see* **kichochoro.**

uchokezi *sing.* *see* **uchovu.**

uchokozi (ma-) teasing, nagging, annoyance; obtrusiveness, insolence, impudence. *Cf.* **chokoa.**

uchomaji *sing.* (*us.* **– wa moto**) arson, incendiarism. *Cf.* **[2]choma.**

uchomozi *sing.*, *rare* rising, (sudden) appearance *(of sun, moon).* *Cf.* **[1]choma.**

uchongelezi *sing.*, *see* **uchongezi.**

uchongezi, uchongelezi, uchongezo *sing.* slander, defamation, backbiting, insinuation, talebearing, informing. *Cf.* **chonga.**

uchongezo *sing.* *see* **uchongezi.**

uchongo *sing.*, *med.* condition of being one-eyed. *Cf.* **[3]chongo.**

uchoo *sing.* *see* **ucheo.**

uchoraji *sing.* sketching, drawing. *Cf.* **[1]chora.**

uchovu (*rare* **uchokezi**) *sing.* 1. weariness, fatigue, exhaustion. **– wa mwili.** state of exhaustion. 2. boredom, ennui, tedium. **ana –.** It is boring for him. *Cf.* **[1]choka.**

uchoyo *sing.* 1. greed(iness), avarice, covetousness. 2. *rare* haste, hurry. *Cf.* **choyo.**

uchu *sing.* 1. longing, craving. **ana – sana wa nyama.** He has a great craving for meat. 2. *vulg.* passion, (sexual) desire.

uchujo *sing.* filtering, straining. *Cf.* **chuja.**

uchuki *sing.* uchuki (small-grained rice).

uchukivu, uchukizo *sing.* aversion, repugnance, loathing, disgust. *Cf.* **chuki, chukia.**

uchukizo *sing.* *see* **uchukivu.**

uchukuti (chukuti), ujukuti, unjukuti (njukuti) 1. central vein or stem of the coconut-palm leaf 2. *fig.* spoke *(of a bicycle wheel).*

uchukuzi *sing.* (means, system, cost, etc. of) transport, transportation, porterage. *Cf.* **chukua.**

uchumaji *sing.* gathering, picking *(of fruit).* *Cf.* [2]**chuma.**

uchumba *sing.* 1. relationship of lovers, wooing, courtship. 2. a gift given by a suitor to a girl's father. *Cf.* **chumba, mchumba.**

uchumi *sing.* (*also* **uchumo**) 1. earnings, income; gain, profit, proceeds. **tega –.** invest *(money).* 2. occupation, employment. 3. *(rec.)* commerce, industry, economy. **–a –.** economic. **tatizo la –.** economic crisis. *Cf.* [2]**chuma.**

uchumo *sing.* *see* **uchumi** 1.

uchungaji *sing.* herding, tending, pasturing. *Cf.* [2]**chunga.**

uchungu, utungu (ma-) 1. bitterness, bitter taste. 2. *fig.* vexation, annoyance, resentment. 3. pain, anguish. *prov.* **– wa mwana aujuaye mzazi.** Only one who has borne a child knows how painful it is. **– wa kuzaa.** labor-pains. 4. dejection, homesickness. *Cf.* [2]**chungu.**

uchunguzi *sing.* curiosity, inquisitiveness. *Cf.* [1]**chunga.**

uchuro *sing.* 1. bad luck, ill omen. 2. incitement, provocation. *Cf.* **chira, churo.**

uchuruzi *sing.* *see* **uchuuzi.**

uchusichusi, utusitusi *sing.* cloudiness, darkness.

uchuuzi (*rare* **uchuruzi**) *sing.* business (status, earnings, etc.) of a small shopkeeper or a dealer in second-hand goods. *Cf.* [2]**chuuza.**

Udachi* [*Germ.*] *sing.*, *arch.* Germany (= **Ujeremani**). *Cf.* [2]**Dachi.**

udadisi *sing.* curiosity, inquisitiveness; indiscretion. *Cf.* **dadisi.**

udago (ndago) udago (kind of reed, *Cyperus rotundus*).

udakaji *sing.* seizing, grasping, snatching. *Cf.* [1]**daka.**

udaktari* [*Engl.*] *sing.* 1. (profession, art, fees, etc. of) medicine. 2. doctor's degree. *Cf.* **daktari.**

udaku *sing.* 1. objection, protest; retort, rejoinder. 2. gossip(ping), rumor(-spreading). *Cf.* **¹daka.**

udakuzi *sing.* rumor-spreading, talebearing. *Cf.* **¹daka.**

udalali* *sing.* 1. (business, fees, etc. of) auctioneering. 2. (salesman's) fee, commission. *Cf.* **dalali.**

udamisi* *sing.* gaiety, joviality, sociability; fun. *Cf.* **damisi.**

udanganyifu *sing.* deceitfulness, trickery, fraud, imposture; treachery. *Cf.* **danganya, danganyifu.**

udekuaji *sing.* sureness of aim, expertness *(in shooting or throwing)*. *Cf.* **dekua.**

udelele, udende *sing.* saliva, slaver. **mtoto akitokwa na – mdomoni mama lazima amfute.** If saliva flows from a child's mouth, the mother must clean it up.

udende *sing.* *see* **udelele.**

udereva* [*Engl.*] *sing.* (activity of, competence in) driving *(a motor vehicle)*. **leseni ya –.** driver's license. *Cf.* **dereva.**

udevu (**ndevu**; *also* **madevu**) 1. hair on the face/of the beard. 2. *fig.* feeler, antenna *(of an insect)*. *Cf.* **kidevu.**

udhahiri* *sing.* *see* **udhahirifu.**

udhahirifu*, udhihirifu, udhahiri *sing.* 1. manifestation, demonstration. 2. plainness, obviousness, clarity, certainty. 3. testimony, evidence. *Cf.* **dhahiri, dhihiri.**

udhaifu* *sing.* 1. weakness, feebleness, infirmity. 2. weakness of character, meanness, baseness. 3. insignificance, paltriness. *Cf.* **dhaifu.**

udhalifu* *sing.* *see* **udhalilifu.**

udhalilifu*, udhalifu, udhilifu *sing.* humiliation, abasement; abjectness, submissiveness. *Cf.* **dhili.**

udhalimu* *sing.* 1. wrong, injustice. 2. oppression, tyranny. 3. aggression. *Cf.* **dhalimu.**

udhamini* *sing.* guarantee, surety, pledge; sponsorship, tutelage, trusteeship. *Cf.* **dhamini, dhamana.**

¹udhani*, udhanifu *sing.* guess, suspicion, supposition, assumption; opinion, view. *Cf.* **dhana, dhani.**

²udhani* *sing., rare* *see* **uzani.**

udhanifu* *sing.* *see* **¹udhani.**

udhi* 1. hurt, offend. 2. annoy, vex, disturb, worry. 3. tire, bore. *appl.* **udhia.** *intr.* **udhika.** be annoyed/disturbed/worried. *caus.* **udhisha.** *Cf.* **¹udhia, maudhiko.**

[1]udhia*, udhiko *sing.* 1. annoyance, difficulty, trouble, worry. 2. disorder, confusion, uproar. *Cf.* udhi.

[2]udhia* *appl. of* udhi.

udhibiti* *sing.* control. *Cf.* dhibiti.

udhihirifu* *sing.* *see* udhahirifu.

udhiki* *sing.* 1. narrowness, lack of space, cramped quarters. 2. straitened circumstances, want, distress. *Cf.* dhiki.

udhiko* *sing.* *see* [1]udhia.

udhilifu* *sing.* *see* udhalilifu.

udhu* *sing., Isl.* (condition of) ritual purity. kaa kwa –. live a respectable/orderly life.

udhuru* *sing.* 1. excuse, pretext. toa/jipa –. excuse oneself, make an excuse. 2. reason, cause. bila –. groundless, without reason/cause. 3. *v., rare* make excuses.

[1]udi* (–) aloe wood.

[2]udi* (–) udi (a musical instrument similar to a banjo).

udibaji* *sing.* 1. decoration, ornament(ation). 2. (mere) form *(as opp. to substance)*, show, ostentation. 3. elegance, refinement. *Cf.* dibaji.

udikteta* [*Engl.*] *sing.* dictatorship. (= ubeberu.) *Cf.* dikteta.

udobi* [*Ind.*] *sing.* occupation (pay, etc.) of a laundryman. *Cf.* [1]dobi.

udodi (dodi) *see* dodi.

udogo *sing.* 1. smallness. 2. insignificance. 3. childhood, youth. *Cf.* dogo.

udohudohu, udohodoho 1. *sing., rare* cheapness, insignificance. 2. *adv.* cheaply, sparingly, economically. nunua –. buy economically.

udole (ndole) 1. *rare* = kidole. 2. *rare* fingernail, toenail; claw *(of an animal)* (= ukucha). 3. slender/fragile person.

udongo *sing.* 1. (plowed) earth. 2. soil, clay; potter's clay (– wa kinamo). ponda –. ram/tamp clay. – (*or* dongo) Ulaya. cement.

udresa* [*Engl.*] *sing.* work (pay, etc.) of an orderly/nurse's aid. *Cf.* dresa.

udufu* *sing.* 1. inferior quality, worthlessness. 2. insipidity, tastelessness; foolishness. *Cf.* dufu.

udugu, undugu *sing.* kinship, brotherhood; friendship. fanya –. form a friendship. *Cf.* ndugu.

udui (ndui) pustule *(of small pox); (pl.)* smallpox.

udusi *sing.* *see* ujusi.

uduvi (nduvi, –) shrimp, prawn.

uele, uwele (maele) (*dial.* ndwele, –) illness, sickness. *Cf.* [1]mwele.

ueleano *sing.* explanation, clarification. *Cf.* **elea.**

uelekeo, welekeo (ma-) direction. – **wa mazunguko.** direction of rotation. *Cf.* **elea, elekea.**

uelekevu, welekevu, wekevu, uwekevu *sing.* (power of) comprehension, intelligence, ingenuity, aptitude. *Cf.* **elea, elekea.**

uelekezo *sing.* instruction, direction, guidance. *Cf.* **elea, elekea.**

uelezaji *sing.* explanation, elucidation. *Cf.* **elea.**

uendeleo (ma-) *see* **endeleo.**

uendelezo, wendelezo *sing.* 1. continuation. 2. spelling. *Cf.* **enda.**

uendeshaji *sing.* 1. guiding, steering, piloting. – **wa ndege.** the piloting of an airplane. 2. *rare* growth, increase; advance, prosperity, success. 3. *recent* secretariat. *Cf.* **enda.**

uenyekiti* *sing.* *see* **uenyikiti.**

uenyemali* *sing., rare* property, fortune. *Cf.* **enye, mali.**

uenyikiti*, uenyekiti *sing.* chairmanship, presidency. *Cf.* **mwenyekiti.**

ufa (nyufa) opening, tear, split, crack, break. **tia –.** tear, split, crack, burst. **ziba –.** fill in a crack.

ufadhili* *sing.* 1. kindness, kindheartedness. 2. affection, partiality, good-will, favor. 3. privilege. 4. obligation. *Cf.* **fadhili.**

ufafanusi *sing.* *see* **ufafanuzi.**

ufafanuzi, ufafanusi (ma-) 1. explanation, interpretation. 2. announcement, revelation. 3. certainty, definiteness. Cf. **fafanua.**

ufagio (–) 1. (small) broom (made of twigs, etc.). 2. (large) brush, scrub brush. *Cf.* **fagia.**

ufahami *sing.* *see* **ufahamivu.**

ufahamikiano* *sing., rare* mutual understanding. *Cf.* **fahamu.**

ufahamivu*, ufahamu, ufahami *sing.* 1. understanding, intelligence. 2. memory. 3. perspicacity, penetration, quick-wittedness. *Cf.* **fahamu.**

ufahamu* *sing.* *see* **ufahamivu.**

ufalme (falme) 1. chieftainship; kingship, royalty; kingdom. 2. rule, dominion. *Cf.* **mfalme.**

ufananaji, ufanani *sing., rare* 1. similarity, resemblance, analogy. 2. comparison. *Cf.* **faa, fanana.**

ufanani *sing., rare* *see* **ufananaji.**

ufanikivu*, ufanisi *sing., rare* well-being, prosperity. *Cf.* **fanaka, fanikia.**

ufanisi *sing., rare* *see* **ufanikivu.**

ufanyaji *sing.* 1. execution, realization. – **kazi wa pamoja.** 2. *comm.* collectivization. *Cf.* **faa, fanya.**

Ufaransa* *sing.* France. *Cf.* **Faransa, Kifaransa, Mfaransa.**

ufarisi* *sing.* capability, competence, expertness; experience. *Cf.* **farisi.**

ufasaha*, ufasihi *sing.* 1. eloquence, facility. 2. clarity *(of pronunciation);* lucidity, purity *(of style).* 3. elegance, good taste. *Cf.* **fasaha.**

ufasihi* *sing.* *see* **ufasaha.**

ufasiki* *sing.* 1. immorality, vice, debauchery. 2. fornication, adultery. *Cf.* **fasiki.**

ufatani* *sing.* *see* **ufitina.**

ufaulu* *sing.* success. *Cf.* **faulu.**

ufedhuli* *sing.* *see* **ufidhuli.**

ufefe* *sing., rare* weakness, worthlessness. *Cf.* **kifefe.**

ufidali* [*Engl.*] *sing., comm.* feudalism.

ufidhuli*, ufedhuli *sing.* insolence, impudence, presumption, arrogance. *Cf.* **fidhuli.**

ufidio*, ufidiwa *sing., rare* ransom, redemption; deliverance, salvation. *Cf.* **fidi.**

ufidiwa* *sing.* *see* **ufidio.**

ufifi, ufifilizi *sing.* playing deaf, feigning absentmindedness (or incomprehension). *Cf.* **fifia.**

ufifilizi *sing.* *see* **ufifi.**

ufilisi *sing., rare* bankruptcy, insolvency. (= **muflisi.**) *Cf.* **filisi.**

ufingirishaji *sing.* (act, business of) rolling. – **wa chuma cha pua.** steel-rolling. *Cf.* **fingirika.**

ufinyangi *sing.* *see* **ufinyanzi.**

ufinyanzi, ufinyangi *sing.* work (methods, wages, etc.) of a potter. *Cf.* **finyanga, mfinyanzi.**

ufinzi *sing., rare* *see* **ufizi.**

ufisadi* *sing.* vice, corruption. *Cf.* **fisadi.**

ufitina*, ufatani *sing.* quarrel(ing), discord, dissension; agitation, intrigue; rebellion, revolt. *Cf.* **fitina.**

ufito (fito) 1. stick, rod, bar, lath. – **wa chuma.** iron rod/bar. – **wa kutembelea.** walking stick. 2. ufito (a present given by a father to the teacher when a boy enters school).

ufizi, ufinzi (fizi) *anat.* gum *(of the teeth).* (= **sine.**)

ufo (–) *see* **ufu.**

ufu, ufo (nyufu) *rare* 1. death (= **mauti**). 2. *fig.* deadness, numbness (= **ganzi**). *Cf.* **fa.**

ufuaji *sing.* 1. business (method, cost, etc.) of washing clothes; *(rare)* washing, laundry. 2. trade (skills, wages, etc.) of a smith. – **wa fedha (dhahabu).** goldsmith's (silversmith's) work. *Cf.* [1]**fua.**

ufuasi *sing.* 1. accompaniment, escort. 2. condition of a follower/retainer/adherent/disciple. 3. imitation. *Cf.* **fuata.**

ufuataji *sing.* (act of) following, complying. – **wa vitabu tu.** pedantry, dogmatism. *Cf.* **fuata.**

ufuatano (fuatano & ma-) 1. succession, sequence. 2. file, line *(of people). Cf.* **fuata.**

ufufuko, ufufuo *sing.* 1. renewal, restoration, revival. 2. *rel.* resurrection *(Isl. or Christ.;* = *Isl.* **kiyama***). Cf.* **fufua.**

ufufuo *sing.* *see* **ufufuko.**

ufugaji *sing.* breeding, rearing, taming *(of animals). Cf.* **fuga.**

ufukara* *sing.* poverty, distress, misery; begging. *Cf.* **fakiri.**

ufukizo, uvukizo *sing.* burning of incense, fumigation; fragrance of burning incense. *Cf.* [1]**fuka.**

ufuko, ufukwe, ufuo *sing.* (*us. loc.* **ufukoni, ufukweni**) beach, shore.

ufukuto, uvukuto *sing.* exhalation, effluvia, vapor; smell of perspiration. *Cf.* [1]**fuka.**

ufukwe *sing.* *see* **ufuko.**

ufukweni *sing. loc. of* **ufuko.**

ufumbi (ma-) *rare* hollow, depression, valley. (= **bonde.**)

ufumbulio *sing., rare* *see* **ufumbuzi.**

ufumbuo *sing.* *see* **ufumbuzi.**

ufumbuzi, ufumbuo, ufumbulio *sing.* unfolding, clearing up, solution. – **wa kitendawili.** solving of a puzzle. *Cf.* [1]**fumba.**

ufumwale *sing.* fiber *(of the raffia palm).*

ufundi *sing.* 1. position (status, quality, etc.) of a master of a craft/trade/art. 2. craft, skill, dexterity, proficiency, qualification. **pata –.** qualify as a craftsman. 3. *rec.* technology. *Cf.* [2]**funda.**

ufunga (funga) (stone) seat, bench *(in front of a house, for receiving guests).*

ufungu *sing.* 1. connection, relationship. 2. *collec.* relations, relatives. **hawa wako – (fungu) gani?** What connection (relationship) do they have with each other?

ufunguaji *sing.* opening. – **wa maonyesho (mkutano).** the opening of an exhibition (meeting). *Cf.* [1]**funga.**

ufunguo, ufunguzi (funguo, funguzi) key. *Cf.* [1]**funga.**

ufunguzi (funguzi) *see* **ufunguo.**

ufunuo *sing.* revealing, revelation. – **wa Mtakatifu Joane.** the Apocalypse/Revelation of St. John. *Cf.* **funua.**

¹ufuo *sing., eth.* ufuo (a hole dug underneath a bier to drain off the water when the corpse is washed).

²ufuo *sing.* 1. = **ufuko.** 2. source, origin, beginning.

ufupa *sing.* 1. osseous/cartilaginous state. 2.: - **mwororo.** gristle, cartilage. *Cf.* **mfupa.**

ufupi *sing.* shortness, brevity, terseness, compactness. *Cf.* **fupi.**

ufupisho *sing.* shortening, abbreviation; summary, extract, résumé. *Cf.* **fupi, fupika.**

ufurahi* *sing., rare* joy, pleasure, delight. *Cf.* **furaha, furahi.**

ufurufuru *sing.* anger, fury. *Cf.* **fura.**

ufusho *sing.* *see* **mafusho.**

ufusio *sing.* (concrete) foundation *(of a house).* *Cf.* **¹fusa.**

ufuta (–) 1. sesame. 2. roselle.

ufuu *sing., rare* hard inner shell of a coconut (= **nyama ya nazi**). *Cf.* **¹fuu, kifuu.**

ufyekwaji *sing.* elimination. *Cf.* **fyeka.**

ufyozi *sing.* insolence, impudence. *Cf.* **fyoa, fyozi.**

¹uga (**nyuga**) 1. open place (in front of or around a house), yard; square, field. 2. threshing-floor. – **wa ngoma.** dancing-place.

²uga bellow *(of bulls).*

ugaga, ugwagwa *sing.* tartar *(on the teeth).* (= **¹gaga.**)

ugaidi* *sing.* 1. underhanded/nefarious practices, thievery. 2. *rec.* guerrilla activity/warfare. *Cf.* **²gaidi.**

ugale *sing.* (*also* **gale, ma-**) the soft, white part of a tree-trunk.

ugali *sing.* porridge, paste, pap. – **wa mahindi (mtama).** corn (millet) porridge. **songa –.** prepare porridge.

ugandamano *sing.* (process of) coagulation. *Cf.* **ganda.**

ugandisho *sing.* quality causing coagulation. *Cf.* **ganda.**

ugando *sing.* *see* **mgando.**

uganga (*rare* **uganguzi**) *sing.* 1. (profession, fees etc. of) medicine, doctoring, healing, curing. 2. medicine, medicament, remedy. 3. *arch.* charm, magic potion. *Cf.* **ganga.**

uganguzi *sing., rare* *see* **uganga.**

ugavu (**ngavu**) net (for fishing or trapping animals). *Cf.* **wavu.**

ugawa *sing.* *see* **ugawaji.**

ugawaji, ugawanyaji (*rare* **ugawa**) *sing.* dividing up, division; distribution, issue. **– huu wa fedha haukuwa wa haki.** The division of the money was unfair. **benki ya –.** bank of issue. *Cf.* **gawa.**

ugawanyaji *sing.* 1. = **ugawaji.** 2. part, share. *Cf.* **gawa.**

uge, ugea *sing.* fat/grease adhering to a pot or pan.

ugea *sing.* *see* **uge.**

ugege *sing.* having one's teeth set on edge *(from eating something sour). See also* **ukakasi.**

ugelegele *sing.* *see* **kigelegele.**

ugema, ugemi *sing.* (act, method, etc. of) tapping palms, preparation of palm wine. *Cf.* **gema.**

ugemi *sing.* *see* **ugema.**

ugemo *sing* ugemo (a short knife used for making incisions in the bark of palm trees in order to drain off the sap for making wine). *Cf.* **gema.**

ugeni *sing.* 1. strangeness, foreignness. 2. foreign country. **safiri ugenini.** travel to a foreign country. *Cf.* **geni.**

ugeufu *sing.* *see* **ugeuzi.**

ugeuko *sing.* *see* **ugeuzi.**

ugeuzaji *sing.* *see* **ugeuzi.**

ugeuzi, ugeuzaji, ugeuzo, ugeko, ugeufu (**geuzi, mageuzi**) change, alteration, transformation, modification. *Cf.* **geua.**

ugeuzo *sing.* *see* **ugeuzi.**

ughaibu* *sing.* state of being absent/missing/ unobtainable, absence, remoteness. *Cf.* **ghaibu.**

ughoshi*, ughushi *sing.* adulteration. **– wa tembo kwa maji.** adulteration of wine with water. *Cf.* **ghoshi.**

ughushi* *sing.* *see* **ughoshi.**

ugimbi (**ngimbi**) (*also* **gimbi, –**) intoxicating beverage, beer.

Ugiriki* [*Engl.*] *sing.* Greece. *Cf.* **Kigiriki, Mgiriki.**

ugo (**nyugo**) enclosure, fenced-in area; fence. *Cf.* **²ua.**

ugoe, goe, goya *sing.* (act of) hooking a foot around an opponent's leg *(in wrestling),* tripping someone up. *Cf.* **ngoeka.**

ugoigoi *sing.* inactivity, indolence. *Cf.* **goigoi.**

ugolo, ugoro *sing.* snuff, chewing tobacco.

ugomaji (*rare* **ugomeaji**) *sing.* strike, boycott. **amua ya kuwa kuweko – wa kazi.** call a strike. *Cf.* **¹goma.**

ugomba (**ma-**) fiber of the banana plant. *Cf.* **¹gomba, ¹mgomba, ugomba.**

ugombo (–) ugombo (a musical instrument resembling a banjo).

ugombozi (*dial.* = **ukombozi**) *sing.* liberation. *Cf.* gomboa.

ugomeaji *sing.* *see* **ugomaji.**

ugomvi (**gomvi, ma-**) 1. quarrel, dispute. 2. quarrelsomeness; grumbling, faultfinding. 3. a quarrelsome/argumentative person. *Cf.* **²gomba, ¹gomvi.**

ugoni, ugono *sing.* 1. sexual intercourse. 2. extramarital relations, adultery. 3. assault, rape. **shikwa –.** be caught with another man's wife, be accused of adultery. **fedha ya –.** fine imposed for adultery. *Cf.* **gona.**

ugonjwa (*rare* **gonjwa**) (**ma-**) illness, sickness, disease, malady, complaint. **– wa ukoma.** leprosy. **– wa baridi yabisi.** rheumatism. **– wa ndui.** smallpox. **– wa puma.** asthma. **– wa malale/usingizi).** sleeping sickness. *Cf.* **gonjwa.**

ugono *sing.* *see* **ugoni.**

ugoro *sing.* *see* **ugolo.**

ugoya *sing., arch.* *see* **unyoya.**

ugozi *sing.* algae, green scum *(on stagnant water).*

ugua fall ill, be in pain, feel sick. *appl.* **ugulia.** *pass.* **uguliwa. ninauguliwa.** I am not feeling well. *intr.* **uguka.** be sick. *caus.* **uguza.** 1. allow to become ill. 2. tend the sick, nurse; be careful of, favor *(an injured limb, etc.).* **niauguza mguu wangu.** I favor my injured leg. *Cf.* **mauguzi, mwuguzi, uuguzi.**

ugumu *sing.* 1. hardness, firmness, solidity. 2. *fig.* severity; stubbornness; steadfastness, resoluteness; hard-heartedness, heartlessness. *Cf.* **gumu.**

ugundi *sing.* ugundi (a powder prepared from the stem of the coconut leaf and used to treat sores).

uguzi *sing., dial.* purchase, sale, barter.

ugwagwa *sing.* *see* **ugaga.**

ugwe (**ngwe, nyugwe**) string, twine, cord; fishing line; strap. *Cf.* **kigwe.**

uhaba* *sing.* fewness, scantiness; inadequacy, deficiency; poor quality, paltriness, insignificance. *Cf.* **¹haba.**

Uhabeshi* *sing.* Abyssinia. *Cf.* **Mhabeshi.**

uhafifu* *sing.* 1. = **uhaba.** 2. trash, junk, rubbish; poor quality; worthlessness, insignificance. 3. old/unsaleable merchandise, drug on the market. *Cf.* **hafifu.**

uhai* *sing.* life, existence. **anakumbuka – wake.** He is reviewing his life(-history). *Cf.* **hai.**

uhaini* *sing.* deceit, treachery, perfidy, disloyalty. **fanya –.** commit (an act of) treachery. *Cf.* **haini.**

uhaji*, uhaja *sing.* need, necessity. *Cf.* **haja.**

uhakikisho* *sing.* confirmation, corroboration; guarantee, security. *Cf.* **hakiki.**

uhali *sing.* *see* **hali.**

uhalifu* **(–, ma-)** 1. transgression, contravention, violation, fault, offense. 2. disobedience. 3. *rare* rebellion, revolution. *Cf.* [1]**halifu.**

uhamaji, uhamiaji *sing.* 1. (regular) migration *(e.g., of birds).* 2. emigration, immigration. *Cf.* **hama, hamaji.**

uhamiaji *sing.* *see* **uhamaji.**

uhamisho *sing.* 1. move, removal, resettlement. 2. ejection, eviction. 3. transfer. **amepata – kwenda ofisi nyingine.** He has been transferred to a different office. *Cf.* **hama.**

uharabu* *see* **uharibifu.**

uharamia* *sing.* robbery, brigandage, piracy. *Cf.* **haramu, haramia.**

uharamu* *sing.* 1. unlawfulness, illegality. 2. violation of religious precepts. *Cf.* **haramu.**

uharara* *sing.* 1. heat, warmth. 2. *fig.* passion, vehemence; temperament. 3. *fig.* ardor, zeal, diligence. *Cf.* **harara.**

uharibifu*, uharabu *sing.* 1. destruction, devastation, vandalism. 2. plundering, pillage. 3. damage, loss. 4. wastefulness, prodigality, extravagance. *Cf.* **harabu, haribu, haribifu.**

uhasama*, uhusuma *sing.* (*also* **hasama**) quarrel, dispute; dissension, ill-will, enmity, hostility, antagonism, antipathy. **deni hili limeleta – baina ya rafiki wawili.** These debts have caused bad feeling between the two friends. *Cf.* **hasimu, husuma, husumu.**

[1]**uhasi*** *sing.* castration, condition of being a gelding/eunuch. *Cf.* **hasi, hasua.**

[2]**uhasi** *sing.* *see* **uasi.**

uhasidi*, uhusuda *sing.* envy, spite, ill-will, hostility. *Cf.* **hasidi, husuda.**

uhawara* *sing.* 1. debauchery, fornication, prostitution. 2. cohabitation *(of unmarried persons).* **hawakuoana wanakaa pamoja kwa – tu.** They are not married, they only live together. *Cf.* **hawara.**

uhawilishaji* **(ma-)** *jur.* conveyance. *Cf.* **hawili, hawala.**

uhayawani* *sing.* 1. stupidity, ignorance. 2. dullness, brutishness. *Cf.* **hayawani.**

uhenga *sing., arch.* (history of) ancient times, antiquity.

uheri* *sing.* good fortune, happiness. *Cf.* **heri.**

uhiana* *sing.* meanness, baseness; faithlessness, disloyalty, treachery, malice, cunning. *Cf.* **hiana.**

Uhindi* *sing.* India. *Cf.* [1]**Hindi, Mhindi, Kihindi.**

uhitaji* **(hitaji, ma-)** *(us. pl.)* 1. need, want, desire, necessity. **alinunua mahitaji ya nyumbani.** He has bought what is necessary for the household. 2. poverty, indigence. *Cf.* **hitaji.**

uhodari* *sing.* 1. ability, competence, industry, aptitude, fitness. 2. energy, vigor, endurance, stability, durability. 3. courage, bravery. *Cf.* **hodari.**

uhondo *sing.* 1. feast, entertainment. 2. something extra given without charge, bonus, premium. 3. *rare* gift.

uhuni* *sing.* 1. vagrancy. 2. lawlessness, disorderly conduct, vandalism, hooliganism. **vijana wasiokuwa na kazi wakipatiwa kazi labda na – mjini utapungua.** If work were provided for the unemployed young people, the disorderly conduct in the city would probably cease. *Cf.* **huni.**

uhunzi *sing.* 1. trade (skills, pay, etc.) of a smith. 2. metalwork *(engraving, chasing, etc.).* *Cf.* **mhunzi.**

uhuru* *sing.* freedom, liberation, independence. *Cf.* **huri, huria, huru.**

uhusiano *sing.* 1. connection, relation(ship). **– wa mataifa.** international relations. **hatuna – mzuri na Serikali yao kwa sababu wamemfukuza balozi wetu.** We do not have good relations with their government because they had our ambassador recalled. 2. correspondence. **– wa moja na moja.** one-to-one correspondence. 3. relevancy, competence. 4. admissibility. *Cf.* **husu.**

uhusuda* *sing.* *see* **uhasidi.**

uhusuma* *sing.* *see* **uhasama.**

uigaji, uigizaji *sing.* imitation. *Cf.* **iga.**

uigizaji *sing.* *see* **uigaji.**

uimara* *sing.* firmness, solidity, stability, durability. *Cf.* **imara.**

uimarisho *sing.* 1. strengthening, securing. 2. establishment, installation. 3. determination, fixing; decision, resolution. *Cf.* **imara, imarika.**

uimbo *sing.* *see* **wimbo.**

Uingereza* *sing.* England, Great Britain. *Cf.* **Mwingereza, Kiingereza.**

uingiaji *sing.* entrance, entry. **fedha za –.** entrance fee. *Cf.* **ingia.**

uingiliaji *sing.* intervention. *Cf.* **ingia.**

uingizaji *sing.* importation *(of merchandise).* *Cf.* **ingia.**

uinjinia* [*Engl.*] *sing.* engineering. *Cf.* **injinia.**

Uislamu* *sing.* Islam. *Cf.* **silimu.**

uizi *sing.* stealing, theft, robbery. *Cf.* **iba, wivi.**

uja *sing., arch., liter.* slavery, captivity, servitude, bondage. *Cf.* **mja.**

uhajili*, **ujuhula** *sing.* 1. heartlessness, mercilessness, cruelty. 2. violence, crime of violence. 3. ignorance, foolishness. *Cf.* **jahili.**

[1]**ujaji*** [*Engl.*] *sing.* position (duties, pay, etc.) of a judge, judgeship. *Cf.* [1]**jaji.**

[2]**ujaji** *sing., rare* coming, arrival. *Cf.* **ja.**

[1]**ujaka** *sing.* ujaka (kind of spinach).

[2]**ujaka** *sing.* ujaka (kind of mushroom). *Cf.* **uyoga.**

ujali* [*Ind.*] *sing.* (*also* **mjali, mi-**) lampwick. (= [1]**utambi.**)

ujalifu *sing.* *see* **ujalivu.**

ujalivu, ujalifu (*also* **ujazi**) *sing.* 1. fullness, satiety. 2. *fig.* corpulence, obesity. *Cf.* [1]**jaa.**

ujamaa*, ujamii *sing.* 1. (blood) relationship, consanguinity; kin, family; brotherhood, fellowship. 2. *rec.* socialism. – **uliodhihirika.** scientific socialism. – **wa domo.** demagogic socialism. – **wa mila.** traditional socialism. – **wa shiriki.** cooperative socialism. *Cf.* **jamii, jamaa.**

ujambo, hujambo, hajambo *sing.* well-being, good state of health; improvement. **mgonjwa wetu hana hujambo yoyote.** There is no improvement in the condition of our patient. *Cf.* [1]**jambo.**

ujamii *sing.* *see* **ujamaa.**

ujamu* *sing.* rope *(for leading an ox).* *Cf.* **lijamu.**

ujana *sing.* youth; youthfulness, sprightliness, youthful appearance. *Cf.* **mwana.**

ujanadume *sing.* manliness, courage, bravery. *Cf.* **mwana,** [1]**ume.**

ujane *sing.* unmarried state, condition of one not yet married or of one who has lost husband or wife: bachelorhood, spinsterhood, widowhood, widowerhood. *Cf.* **mjane.**

ujanja *sing.* 1. slyness, cunning, craftiness; deceit, fraud, peculation. **amenifanyia –.** He has cheated me. **kwa –.** with intent to deceive, under false pretenses. 2. strategem, maneuver. *Cf.* **janja.**

ujari* (**njari**) (*rare* **mjari, mjiari, mjarari, mi-**) *naut.* tiller rope.

ujasiri*, ujasirishaji *sing.* daring, bravado, temerity, foolhardiness, recklessness; *(comm.)* adventurism. *Cf.* **jasiri.**

ujasusi* *sing.* 1. curiosity, inquisitiveness. 2. disloyalty, breach of faith, treachery. *Cf.* **jasisi.**

ujazi *sing.* 1. fullness, abundance. 2. generosity, liberality. 3. = **ujalivu.** *Cf.* [1]**jaa.**

ujengaji (ma-) *see* **ujenzi.**

ujengelele *sing.* *see* **uchengelele.**

ujenzi, ujengaji (ma-) 1. style of building, architecture. 2. erection, construction. 3. structure, building, installation. *Cf.* **jenga.**

Ujeremani* [*Engl.*] (*rare* **Ujerumani**) *sing.* Germany. *Cf.* **Mjeremani, Kijeremani.**

Ujerumani* *sing.* *see* **Ujeremani.**

ujeuri* *sing.* *see* **jeuri.**

uji *sing.* soup, gruel, porridge. **– wa mtama (mchele).** millet (rice) soup.

ujia (–) passage(way), alley *(between two houses).* *Cf.* **ja.**

ujihamu* *sing.* self-defense. *Cf.* [2]**hamu.**

ujima *sing.* communal work, mutual aid, neighborhood cooperation *(in field work, house-building); (comm.)* collective. **duka la –.** cooperative store. *Cf.* **mjima.**

ujinamizi (ma-) *see* **jinamizi.**

ujinga *sing.* stupidity, ignorance, folly. *Cf.* **jinga.**

ujini* *sing.* 1. cunning, guile, wickedness. 2. diabolical art, magic, sorcery. 3. *arch.*. **ujinini** *loc.* home of evil spirits. *Cf.* **jini.**

ujio (ma-) (action, manner, time of) coming, arriving. *Cf.* **ja.**

ujira* *sing.* pay, wages, salary, fee. **kazi hii ni bure, haina –.** This work is gratis; there is no charge. *Cf.* **ajiri.**

ujirani* *sing.* 1. neighbors, neighborliness. 2. neighborhood, vicinity, environs. *Cf.* **jirani, majirani.**

ujitahidi* *sing., rare* *see* **jitihadi.**

ujitawala* *sing.* self-government, autonomy. *Cf.* **tawala.**

ujiti (njiti) 1. tall, slender tree. 2.: **– wa kiberiti.** a match. *Cf.* [1]**mti.**

ujogoo *sing., rare* daring, boldness, bravado. *Cf.* **jogoo.**

ujoli* *sing., arch.* solidarity, fellow-feeling *(of slaves).* *Cf.* **mjoli.**

[1]**ujomba** *sing.* relationship between maternal uncles and nephews. *Cf.* **mjomba.**

[2]**Ujomba** Ujomba (the Swahili-speaking area around Mombasa). *Cf.* **Mjomba, Kijomba.**

ujotojoto *sing., rare* heat, warmth. *Cf.* **joto,** [1]**moto.**

ujuba* *sing.* 1. boldness, courage, fearlessness. 2. *rare* tyranny, oppression. *Cf.* **mjuba.**

ujuhula* *sing.* *see* **ujahili.**

ujuizi *sing.* *see* **ujuzi.**

ujukuti (njukuti) *see* **uchukuti.**

ujumbe *sing.* 1. delegation, deputation. **peleka –.** send a delegation. 2. message. **– wako nimeufikisha.** I have received your message. 3. petition. *Cf.* **mjumbe;** *also* **jumbe, kijumbe.**

ujume*, **ujumi** *sing.* 1. (trade, methods, pay, etc. of) metalworking. 2. locksmith's trade. *Cf.* **mjume.**

ujumi* *sing.* *see* **ujume.**

ujumla* *sing.* 1. large quantity, great number. 2. totality. **kwa —.** in totality, in general. *Cf.* **jumla.**

ujusi*, **udusi** *sing.* 1. ujusi (the ritual impurity of a new-born child until it has been ceremonially washed). 2. (natural) smell *(of animals)*. 3.: **fa —.** die a natural death *(of animals); (fig. of persons)* want something very much, yearn for. 4. matter, pus. *Cf.* **kijusi.**

ujuu *sing.* height, eminence; top, peak. *Cf.* **juu.**

ujuvi *sing.* impudence, insolence, boorishness, rudeness. **maneno ya —.** impudent language. **fanya —.** be impudent/rude. *Cf.* [2]**jua, juvi.**

ujuzi, ujuizi *sing.* wisdom, intelligence; science, knowledge; experience; skill, competence. **— wa matumizi ya nguvu za umeme.** electrical engineering. *Cf.* [2]**jua, mjuzi.**

uka *rare* go away, depart. *appl.* **ukia.** *caus.* **usha.** *Cf.* **mauko.**

ukaa *sing., rare* *see* **ukaaji.**

ukaaji (*rare* **ukaa, ukao**) *sing.* manner of living, way of life. *Cf.* [1]**kaa.**

ukaango (—) 1. (large) cooking-pot. 2. *rare* (action of) frying, cooking. *Cf.* [1]**kaanga.**

ukabaila* *sing.* importance, prominence, high social standing. *Cf.* **kabaila.**

ukabidhu*, **ukabidhi** *sing.* 1. hoarding. 2. thriftiness, economy. *Cf.* **kabidhi.**

ukabila* *sing.* 1. nationality, citizenship. 2. tribalism, racism. *Cf.* **kabila.**

ukadiri* *sing.* *see* **ukadirifu.**

ukadirifu*, **ukadiri** *sing.* 1. estimate, appraisal, evaluation. 2. calculation, computation, settlement *(of accounts)*. 3. *fig.* estimation, judgment. 4. moderation, temperance. *Cf.* **kadiri, kadirifu.**

ukafiri*, **ukufuru** *sing., Isl.* unbelief, infidelity; sacrilege, blasphemy. *Cf.* **kafiri, kufuru.**

ukafu *sing.* *see* **ukavu.**

ukago *sing., arch.* protection *(by means of magic)*. *Cf.* [1]**kaga,** [1]**kago.**

ukaguzi *sing.* inspection, check(ing), examination. **— wa skuli.** school inspection. **— wa kitabu.** examination of a book *(before printing)*. *Cf.* **kagua.**

ukahaba* *sing.* prostitution. *Cf.* **kahaba.**

ukaidi* *sing.* stubbornness, obstinacy; disobedience, recalcitrance, insubordination. *Cf.* **kaidi.**

ukaimu* *sing.* position of a substitute/representative/deputy/agent. *Cf.* [1]**kaimu, makamu.**

ukakamavu *sing.* cunning, deceit, treachery. *Cf.* **kakamavu.**

ukakasi *sing.* (*also* **kakasi, –**) 1. grinding/gnashing *(of the teeth).* 2. = **ugege.**

ukakaya *sing.* extent, range.

ukali *sing.* 1. sharpness *(of a knife, etc.).* 2. acidity, sourness, bitterness *(to the taste).* 3. strength, intensity. **– wa jua.** intense heat of the sun. 4. *fig.* severity, strictness, austerity, harshness. 5. *fig.* cruelty, fury; tyranny. 6. *fig.* daring, bravery. 7. *fig.* passion, temperament. *Cf.* **kali, makali.**

ukalifu* *sing.* 1. = **ukali.** 2. tension, intensity. *Cf.* **kalifu.**

ukalimani* *sing., arch.* interpreting, translating. *Cf.* **kalima, mkalimani.**

ukambaa* (–) cord, rope *(made of plaited strips of leaves).* *Cf.* ¹**kamba.**

ukambi *sing., med., rare* measles. (= **surua.**)

ukame *sing.* 1. wilderness, desert. 2. barrenness *(of land).* *Cf.* **kame.**

ukamili* *sing.* *see* **ukamilifu.**

ukamilifu*, ukamili *sing.* 1. completeness, perfection. 2. fulfilment, accomplishment, consummation. 3. *fig.* unity. *Cf.* **kamili.**

ukamio *sing.* 1. threatening, menacing. 2. extortion. *Cf.* ²**kama.**

ukanda (kanda) 1. thong, strap, belt. 2. lace *(of a shoe).* 3. *fig., geogr.* zone. **– wa mvua.** rainy/tropical zone.

ukandamizwaji *sing.* suppression. *Cf.* ³**kanda.**

ukando *sing.* *see* **kando.**

ukano (–) *see* ¹**mkano.**

ukao (ma- & kao) 1. residence, domicile; housing. 2. seat, headquarters. **makao makuu ya chama hiki.** headquarters of this party. 3. *rare* = **ukaaji.** *Cf.* ¹**kaa.**

ukapitalisti* [*Engl.*] *sing.* capitalism. *Cf.* **mkapitalisti.**

ukarani* *sing.* position (duties, pay, etc.) of a clerk/secretary. *Cf.* **karani.**

ukarimu* *sing.* generosity, liberality; hospitality; beneficence, charity. *Cf.* ¹**kirimu, karimu.**

ukashifu* *sing.* slander, defamation, libel. *Cf.* **kashifu, kashifu.**

ukasisi* *sing., rel.* priesthood. *Cf.* **kasisi.**

ukata* *sing., rare* privation, need, poverty. *Cf.* ¹**kata, mkata.**

ukatavu* *sing., rare* 1. renunciation, abandonment. 2. obstinacy, sullenness. *Cf.* ¹**kataa, katavu.**

ukatazaji* *sing., rare* prohibition. (= **makatazo.**) *Cf.* ¹**kataa, kataza.**

ukatibu* *sing.* position (duties, pay, etc.) of a clerk/secretary. *Cf.* **kitabu, katibu.**

ukatili* *sing.* 1. cruelty, bloodthirstiness. 2. massacre, atrocity. *Cf.* **katili.**

ukavu, ukafu *sing.* 1. dryness. 2. *fig.* wit, humor. 3. *fig.:* – **wa macho.** impudence, nonchalence. **usiniletee – wa macho.** Don't treat me so impudently. *Cf.* **1kavu, kauka.**

ukawa *sing.* *see* **ukawiaji.**

ukawiaji, ukawio, ukawa *sing.* delay, lateness, postponement. *Cf.* **3kawa.**

ukawio *sing.* *see* **ukawiaji.**

ukaya (kaya) *arch.* ukaya (women's headdress, kind of turban).

ukazi (ma-) residence, home. *Cf.* **1kaa.**

uke (*rare* **uanauke**) *sing.* 1. womanhood, femininity; the female sex. 2. condition of being a wife. 3. *anat.* vagina (= *vulg.* **kuma**). 4.: *loc.* **ukeni.** (relatives on) the mother's side of the family. **huyu ni jamaa kwa ukeni kwetu.** He is a relative of ours on our mother's side. *Cf.* **ke.**

ukelele (–, ma-) cry, shout(ing), noise, uproar. *Cf.* **kelele.**

ukemi (–) call, cry, shout. *Cf.* **kemea.**

ukengee *sing.* *see* **kengee.**

ukengefu *sing.* deviation *(from a proper course),* disloyalty, desertion, backsliding, apostasy. *Cf.* **kengeua.**

uketo *sing.* depth; chasm, abyss.

uki *sing.* (*dial.* **woki**) honey. *Cf.* **nyuki.**

ukigo (kigo) enclosure, fence, hedge.

ukili (kili) a strip of coconut-palm leaf *(used for weaving mats).*

ukilia 1. intend, purpose, have in view; be intent upon, have designs on. 2. decide on, bring about.

ukimwa *sing.* ill humor, bad temper, moodiness, sulkiness. *Cf.* **kimwa.**

ukinaifu* *sing.* 1. satisfaction, contentment. 2. self-satisfaction, complacency; conceit, presumption, arrogance. 3. self-sufficiency, independence. *Cf.* **kinai, kinaifu.**

ukindani *sing.* *see* **ukinzani.**

ukindu *sing.* ukindu (fibers from the leaf of the wild date palm; used for weaving mats, etc.). *Cf.* **kindu, mkindu.**

ukingo (kingo) 1. protection, shelter; defense. 2. edge, margin, border, brink. – **wa mto.** edge of a river. – **mnyofu.** straightedge (= ruler). 3. parapet, balustrade, rail, banister. 4. screen, curtain, awning. *Cf.* **1kinga.**

ukinzani, ukindani (–, ma-) 1. objection, protest, rejoinder, contradiction, opposition. **upande wa –.** opposition in parliament. 2. obstructiveness, obstinacy, contentiousness. *Cf.* **kinza, kinzani.**

ukiri* *sing.* 1. recognition, acceptance, acknowledgment, assent, approval. 2. admission, confession. **– wa makosa.** admission of errors. 3. acknowledgment of receipt. *Cf.* **1kiri.**

ukiuaji *sing.* transition. *Cf.* **kiuka.**

ukiwa *sing.* 1. solitude, loneliness, abandonment. 2. condition of an orphan/widow, bereavement. 3. *fig.* poverty, want, distress. **nchi hii imepata/imeingiliwa na –.** Great distress has come upon this country. 4. *fig.* desolation, destruction, devastation. *Cf.* **kiwa, makiwa.**

ukiwi *sing.* condition of being dazzled/blinded *(by strong light).* *Cf.* **2kiwi.**

ukiziwi, uziwi *sing.* deafness. *Cf.* **ziwi, kiziwi.**

uko *auxil. v.* 1. you are there. **– wapi?** Where are you? 2. it is there.

ukoa (–) = **1koa.**

ukodishaji* *sing.* (payment of) rent, rental. *Cf.* **kodi.**

ukofi, ukufi (kofi, kufi) 1. (upturned) palm of the hand. 2. handful *(i.e., the amount of anything that will lie on the palm of the hand).* *Cf.* **kofi.**

ukoga *sing.* 1. deposit, incrustation. **– wa meno.** tartar on the teeth. **– wa maji.** foam/scum on water. 2. mold, mildew, blight. 3. *bot.* lichen.

ukohozi (ma-) (*us.* **makohozi**) 1. coughing, respiratory disease. 2. phlegm, sputum. *Cf.* **kohoa.**

ukoja *sing.* bead necklace. *Cf.* **1koja.**

1ukoka *sing.* ukoka (a kind of creeping grass used for fodder).

2ukoka *sing.* distinction, award, honorary degree. **yeye hakuwa daktari kweli ila alivikwa kilemba cha – tu.** He did not earn his doctor's degree, it was given to him (to flatter him).

ukoko *sing.* hard crust, (caked or burnt) deposit *(of foods, us. rice).* **amekula chakula kizuri, mimi akaniachia – tu.** He has eaten all the good food, and left only the (burned) residue (at the bottom of the pot) for me. *Cf.* **kikoko.**

ukoloni* [*Engl.*] *sing.* colonialism. **wakati wa –.** colonial times, period of colonialism. **– mambo leo.** neo-colonialism. **– wa mlango wa nyuma.** back-door colonialism, neo-colonialism. *Cf.* **koloni, mkoloni.**

ukoma *sing.* *med.* leprosy. **mwenye –, mgonjwa wa –.** leper.

ukomba (–) *see* **ukombe.**

ukombe, ukomba (–) 1. scraper *(tool for hollowing out mortars, dugout canoes, etc.).* 2. *rare* (small) spoon. 3. *rare* claw, talon. *Cf.* **1komba.**

ukombo (**kombo**) 1. *rare* bend, curve. 2. ukombo (fee paid by a father to the teacher upon completion of a boy's schooling). *Cf.* **[1]komba, komboa.**

ukomboleo *sing.* *see* **ukombozi.**

ukomboo *sing.* *see* **ukombozi.**

ukombozi, ukomboo, ukomboleo *sing.* (*also* **kombozi, ma-**) 1. rescue, deliverance. 2. redemption, ransom(ing). 3. *rel.* redemption, salvation. 4. fine. 5. *recent* money owed for a service. **suti yangu imekwisha kushonwa, sasa bado – tu.** My suit is finished; now I have to pay for it. *Cf.* **komboa.**

ukomeshaji *sing.* (act of) bringing to an end, termination, curtailment. – **wa silaha kwa nchi zote.** general disarmament. *Cf.* **[1]koma.**

ukomo *sing.* 1. end, goal, termination. 2. *euph.* death. *Cf.* **[1]koma.**

ukomunisti* [*Engl.*] *sing.* communism. *Cf.* **kikomunisti, mkomunisti.**

ukonge (**konge**) sisal fiber. *Cf.* **[1]mkonge.**

ukongojo (**kongojo**) *see* **mkongojo.**

ukongwe *sing.* advanced old age, feebleness, decrepitude. *Cf.* **[3]kongwe, [1]konga.**

ukonjo *sing.* *see* **konzo.**

ukono *sing.*, *bot.* tendril. *Cf.* **mkono.**

ukonyezo (**konyezo**) (*us.* **mkonyezo, mi-**) 1. wink, sign, signal, warning. 2. hint, allusion. *Cf.* **konyeza.**

ukonzo, ukonjo *sing.* *see* **konzo.**

[1]ukoo (**koo**) 1. (blood) relationship, family. 2. descent, pedigree, lineage. 3. clan.

[2]ukoo, ukowo *sing.* dirt, filth, uncleanliness. *Cf.* **mkoo.**

ukopaji, ukopi *sing.* 1. credit, loan, advance. 2. *rare* deception, fraud. *Cf.* **[3]kopa.**

ukope (–) eyelash, eyelid. *Cf.* **[3]kope.**

ukopi *sing.* *see* **ukopaji.**

ukorofi* *sing.* ill-temper, malignity, hostility; roughness, coarseness; brutality, tyranny. *Cf.* **korofi, mkorofi.**

ukorogefu, ukorogo *sing.* mixing, mixture; disorder, confusion; disturbance. *Cf.* **koroga.**

ukorogo *sing.* *see* **ukorogefu.**

ukosa, ukosefu, ukosekanaji *sing.* *see* **ukosekano.**

ukosekano, ukosekanaji, ukosefu, ukosa *sing.* fault, defect; lack, want, absence; deficiency, deficit, shortage; failure; mistake, error. *Cf.* **[1]kosa.**

ukosi (–) 1. *rare* nape of the neck. 2. collar. – **wa koti (shati).** coat (shirt) collar. *Cf.* **kosi.**

ukowo *sing.* *see* ²**ukoo.**

Ukristo* [*Port.*] *sing.* Christianity. *Cf.* **Kikristo, Mkristo.**

ukuaji *sing.* growth. *Cf.* ¹**kua.**

ukubali* *sing.* (*also* **kabuli, kibali, ikibali**) 1. assent, agreement, approval, concurrence. – **wake utatusaidia.** His approval will help us. 2. concord, harmony. *Cf.* **kubali.**

ukubwa *sing.* 1. size, dimensions, capacity, volume. 2. greatness, significance, importance. 3. power, authority. – **wa jeshi.** army command. 4. manhood, prime. *loc.* **ukubwani.** in one's prime. *Cf.* **kubwa.**

ukucha 1. (**kucha**) fingernail, toenail. 2. (**ma-**) claw, talon, hoof. **piga –.** scratch. *Cf.* ²**kucha, kikuchia.**

ukufi (**kufi**) *see* **ukofi.**

ukufuru* *sing.* *see* **ukafiri.**

ukukwi (**kukwi**) ukukwi (a species of harmless snake).

ukulifu, ukulivu *sing.* lack of perseverance/courage/grit, slackness, remissness, indolence, carelessness, apathy, resignation. *Cf.* ¹**kua, kulivu.**

ukulima *sing.* agriculture, farming, field work. *Cf.* ¹**lima.**

ukulivu *sing.* *see* **ukulifu.**

ukumbaji, ukumbizi *sing.* pushing, shoving, jostling. *Cf.* ¹**kumba.**

ukumbi (**kumbi**) 1. front room of a house, vestibule, hall, anteroom. 2. porch, veranda. 3. corridor. 4. tribal initiation rites.

¹**ukumbizi** *sing.* sweeping up/away, removal, elimination. *Cf.* ²**kumba.**

²**ukumbizi** *sing.* *see* **ukumbaji.**

ukumbizo *sing.*, *rare* open veranda. *Cf.* **ukumbi.**

ukumbuko *sing.* memory, recollection. *Cf.* **kumbuka.**

ukumbuo (–) *see* **ukumbuu.**

ukumbusho *sing.* reminder, souvenir; memorial, monument. *Cf.* **kumbuka.**

ukumbuu, ukumbuo (–) strip of cloth, scarf, sash; bandage, sling.

ukumvi (–) (empty) husk, chaff, bran.

ukunde (**kunde**; *us. pl.*) (kind of) bean. *Cf.* **mkunde.**

ukunga *sing.* 1. midwifery, obstetrics. **anafanya kazi ya —.** She is employed as a midwife. 2. fee paid a midwife. *Cf.* **²kunga, ¹mkunga.**

ukungu (**kungu** & **ma-**) 1. mold, mildew; fungus, lichen. 2. damp, moisture; mist, fog.

ukunguni *sing.* laziness, indolence, idleness. *Cf.* **¹mkunguni.**

ukunguru *sing.* *see* **mkunguru.**

ukungwi *sing.* the work (methods, pay, etc.) of a kungwi, *q.v.* *Cf.* **²kunga.**

ukuni (**kuni**) piece of firewood.

ukunjufu *sing.* good spirits, cheerfulness, geniality, gaiety, exuberance. *Cf.* **kunja, kunjufu.**

ukurasa* (**kurasa**) sheet (of paper), page/leaf *(of a book),* leaflet.

ukurugenzi *sing., rare* leadership, pioneering spirit. *Cf.* **mkurugenzi.**

ukuruti *sing.* *see* **ukurutu.**

ukurutu, ukuruti *sing., med.* itch, rash, acne.

ukuta (**kuta**) stone wall. *Cf.* **kikuta.**

ukuti (**kuti**) single frond of a coconut-palm leaf (*cf.* **kuti**), palm branch.

ukuu *sing.* 1. greatness, eminence, distinction. 2. superiority. *Cf.* **kuu.**

ukuzaji *sing.* (stock) raising/breeding, domestication *(of animals);* cultivation *(of plants).* *Cf.* **¹kua, mkuzaji.**

ukwaju (**kwaju**) tamarind *(used in tanning).* **chakula kina —.** The food has turned sour. *Cf.* **kwaju, mkwaju.**

ukware *sing.* sensuality, lasciviousness, lust. *Cf.* **²kware, mkware.**

ukwasi *sing., rare* wealth, luxury, comfort. *Cf.* **kwasi, mkwasi.**

ukwato (**kwato**) *see* **kwato.**

ukwe *sing.* 1. relationship through one's wife, relatives of one's wife. **ninakwenda ukweni.** I am going to visit my wife's family. 2. *(in gen.)* relationship/relatives by marriage, in-laws. *Cf.* **mkwe.**

ukweli *sing.* truth, truthfulness, frankness. *Cf.* **kweli.**

ukwezi *sing.* work (methods, pay, etc.) of a climber (= **mkwezi**, one who makes his living by gathering coconuts). *Cf.* **kwea.**

ulaanifu*, ulaanizi *sing.* cursing, damnation. **acha kufanya mambo ya —.** Cease doing things which are damnable. *Cf.* **laana, laanifu.**

ulaanizi* *sing.* *see* **ulaanifu.**

ulabibu* *sing.* endurance, perseverance, persistency, pertinacity, stubbornness.

ulafi *sing.* greed(iness), gluttony. **usile kwa —.** Don't eat so greedily. *Cf.* **lapa, lafua.**

ulaga *dial., arch.* strike dead, kill.

ulaghai* *sing.* *see* **uragai.**

ulaika (ma-) *see* **laika.**

ulaini*, ulainifu *sing.* 1. softness. **matunda haya hayana – wa kutosha.** This fruit is not soft enough. 2. *fig.* gentleness. *Cf.* **laini.**

ulainifu* *sing.* *see* **ulaini.**

ulaiti* *sing.* *see* **ulayiti.**

ulaji *sing.* 1. (act, manner of) eating, nourishment, sustenance, food and drink. 2. = **ulafi.** Cf. **[1]la.**

ulalamishi, ulalamizi *sing.* 1. appeal, supplication, plea. 2. groaning, moaning. *Cf.* **lalama.**

ulalamizi *sing.* *see* **ulalamishi.**

ulalo (ma-) 1. *rare* (place, manner, etc. of) lying down/sleeping. 2. something laid down *(e.g., a log across a stream).* *Cf.* **lala.**

ulamali* *sing.* *see* **uramali.**

ulambilambi, urambirambi *sing.* ulambilambi (early stage in the growth of the coconut, when the meat is still quite soft; also the meat itself at this stage). *Cf.* **lamba, lambilambi.**

ulanga *sing.* mica, talc. *Cf.* **[2]anga, angaa.**

Ulaya* *sing.* 1. Europe. *Cf.* **ulayiti.** 2. district (= **wilaya**).

ulayiti*, ulaiti *sing.* 1. ulayiti (unbleached cotton cloth of European manufacture). 2. *(in gen.)* something of European manufacture. *Cf.* **Ulaya.**

ule *dem. pron. of the* **m-** *and* **u-** *classes* that.

uledi* (–) 1. *naut.* cabin boy. 2. *pr. n. masc.*

ulegeo *sing.* *see* **ulegevu.**

ulegevu, ulegeo *sing.* 1. exhaustion, slackness, limpness, weakness, enervation. **msipofanya – kazi yetu tutaimaliza mapema.** If you don't go limp we'll finish our work ahead of time. 2. laziness, carelessness, inattentiveness. *Cf.* **lega, legevu.**

uleoleo *sing.* state of half-consciousness. *Cf.* **lewa.**

ulesi *sing., rare* *see* **ulezi.**

uletaji *sing.* delivery, supply. *Cf.* **leta.**

ulevi *sing.* (*also* **malevi** *pl.*) 1. drunkenness, intoxication, dipsomania. 2. *(in gen.)*

mania, weakness. **sigara ndio – wake.** He is a confirmed smoker (*lit.* cigarettes are his mania/weakness). 3. spirits, alcohol. *Cf.* **lewa, levi.**

¹ulezi (*rare* **ulesi**) **(ma-)** (kind of) millet. **pombe ya –.** millet beer. *Cf.* **³mlezi.**

²ulezi (ma-) (*us.* **malezi**) (work, methods, pay, etc. of) caring for/nursing/educating *(children).* **amewapa watoto wake malezi mazuri.** He has brought his children up well. *Cf.* **lea.**

ulia *appl. of* **³ua.**

ulili (ma-) 1. ulili (a wooden bedstead). 2. *ethn.* ulili (a shrine where offerings are made to spirits).

ulimaji *sing.* (work, methods, pay, etc. of) cultivation, agriculture. *Cf.* **¹lima.**

ulimbo, urimbo *sing.* ulimbo (the sticky sap of various plants used as birdlime or glue). *prov.:* **Penye urembo ndipo penye urimbo.** Where there is beauty there is also a trap.

ulimbwende *sing.* 1. elegance, fashionable dress. 2. undue attention to dress.

ulimi (ndimi) *anat.* tongue. **ana – mzito.** He lisps/does not pronounce clearly. **mtoto ana – mzito.** The child is having trouble learning to talk. **kama – na mate.** They are inseparable (friends) (*lit.* like tongue and saliva). *Cf.* **limi, kilimi, mlimi.**

ulimwengu (ma-) 1. world, universe. **ndiyo –.** That is the way of the world. **–a –.** universal. 2. sky. 3. environment, surroundings, living conditions. **ana – mgumu.** He has a hard life. *Cf.* **kilimwengu, malimwengu, mlimwengu.**

ulindi *sing.* ulindi (the 'female' of a pair of firesticks; *cf.* **wimbombo, upekecho).**

ulinganifu, ulinganyifu *sing.* 1. agreement, conformity, harmony. 2. equilibrium, symmetry. *Cf.* **¹linga, linganifu.**

ulinganisho *sing.* comparison, adaptation, accommodation. *Cf.* **¹linga.**

ulingano *sing.* likeness, similarity. *Cf.* **¹linga.**

ulinganyifu *sing.* *see* **ulinganifu.**

ulingo (lingo & ma-) platform *(for the watchman guarding a field).* **amelala juu ya – apate kulinda mihogo yake.** He slept on the platform in order to guard his manioc plants. *Cf.* **kilingo.**

ulinzi *sing.* 1. guarding, watching, surveillance. 2. supervision, control. 3. defense. **Chama cha – cha UNO.** Security Council of the UN. *Cf.* **linda.**

ulio (–) *rare* dish, platter. *Cf.* **¹la.**

ulipizi (ma-) (*us.* **malipizi**) 1. enforced payment, exaction, extortion. 2. repayment; *(fig.)* retaliation, revenge. *Cf.* **lipa.**

ulishaji *sing.* causing to eat, feeding. — **wa viapo.** administering of an oath. *Cf.* [1]**la.**

ulitima*, ultima, uritima [*Port.*] *sing.* 1. *rare* unemployment, inactivity. 2. poverty, distress. 3. *cards* the last trump card in the game of Arbastini.

uliwali* *sing.* position (duties, pay, etc.) of a liwali, *q.v.*

uliza ask (about), inquire, question, interrogate. *appl.* **ulizia.** *intr.* **ulizika. mambo yenyewe hayauliziki.** One should not ask questions about this matter. *Cf.* **ulizo.**

ulizi (**ma-**) crying, screaming *(of a child). Cf.* [1]**lia.**

ulizo (**ma-**) (*us.* **maulizo**) question, inquiry, investigation, interrogation. *Cf.* **uliza.**

ulozi *sing.* magic, witchcraft. *Cf.* **loga.**

ultima* *sing.* *see* **ulitima.**

uluzi, uruzi (*also* **mluzi, mwunzi**) *sing.* whistle, whistling. **piga —.** to whistle.

uma 1. bite. **nimeumwa na mbwa.** I have been bitten by a dog. **njaa inamwuma.** He is very hungry (*lit.* hunger bites him). 2. hurt, be painful. **kidonda hiki kinaniuma.** This wound hurts me. 3. sting. **wadudu hawa wanauma.** These insects sting. *appl.* **umia** (*& pass.* **umwa**). hurt/sting (someone). **nimeumia** (**nimeumwa**) **mkononi.** I have been stung on the arm. *ass.* **umana.** hurt each other. *prov.* **meno ya mbwa hayaumani.** A dog's teeth do not bite each other. *caus.* **umiza.** injure, cause pain. 4. (**uma, nyuma, mauma**) pointed implement (awl, punch, etc.); fork, rake; *(rare)* sting (of an insect; = **msumari, mwiba**). *Cf.* **kiuma, mwumizi, umivu, umizi.**

umaarufu* *sing., rare* fame, renown. *Cf.* **arifu, maarufu.**

umahiri* *sing.* 1. skill, cleverness, deftness. 2. tact. *Cf.* **mahiri.**

umaji, umajimaji *sing.* 1. fluid/liquid state. 2. damp, moisture. 3. vapor. *Cf.* **maji.**

umajimaji *sing.* *see* **umaji.**

umakanika*, umekanika [*Engl.*] *sing.* work (methods, pay, etc.) of a mechanic. *Cf.* **makanika.**

[1]**Umalaya*** [*Engl.*] *sing.* Malaya.

[2]**umalaya*** *sing.* prostitution. *Cf.* **malaya.**

umalidadi*, umaridadi *sing.* 1. care, neatness, elegance *(of dress).* 2. fashionable clothing. 3. excessive attention to one's appearance, overdressing. *Cf.* **malidadi.**

umama *sing.* motherhood, maternity. *Cf.* **mama.**

[1]**umana** *ass. of* [1]**uma.**

[2]**umana** 1. close, fit together *(of doors, windows, etc.).* 2. form a line, queue up. **watu wameumana toka sokoni mpaka posta.** People were lined up from the market to the post office.

umande *sing.* mist, fog, dew; cool/damp *(of morning or evening).*

[1]**umanga** (–) plain food *(without relish).* *Cf.* [1]**manga.**

[2]**Umanga*** *sing., rare* Arabia, the Arabian Peninsula. (= **Uarabu.**) *Cf.* [2]**Manga.**

umaridadi* *sing.* *see* **umalidadi.**

umasihiya* *sing.* Christianity. (= **Ukristo.**) *Cf.* **masihiya.**

umasikini* *sing.* *see* **umaskini.**

umaskini*, umasikini *sing.* poverty, distress, misery. **ana – wa roho.** He has a bad disposition. He is unfriendly/unpleasant. *Cf.* **maskini.**

umathubuti* *sing.* firmness, hardness, solidity, stability, durability. *Cf.* **thabiti, uthabiti.**

umati* *sing.* 1. large gathering, crowd. **tumekuta – wa watu.** We found a large crowd of people. 2. followers, adherents. **– wa Nabii Muhamadi.** followers of Muhammad, Muhammadans.

umba form, shape, make, *(rel.)* create. **– vyungu.** form/make clay pots. *appl.* **umbia.** *intr.* **umbika** & *pass.* **umbwa. ameumbika/ameumbwa vizuri.** He is attractive in appearance/is handsome. *inv.* **umbua.** 1. disfigure, deform, distort, mutilate. 2. spoil, destroy. 3. kill. 4. corrupt, demoralize. *inv.-appl.* **umbuliwa.** *inv.-intr.* **umbuka.** *inv.-ass.* **umbuana.** revile/insult/slander each other. *Cf.* **umbile, kiumbe,** [1]**kiumbo, maumbile, muumba, muumbuzi.**

umbali (*rare* **ubali**) *sing.* distance, remoteness. **enye – sawa.** equidistant. *Cf.* **mbali.**

umbea *sing.* talebearing, scandalmongering, gossip. *Cf.* **mbea, mmbea.**

umbele, ubele *sing.* 1. the future. 2. advancement, progress. 3. = **mbele.** 4. *pol.* front. **– mkubwa wa pamoja.** a broad, united front. **– wa kuikombowa nchi.** National Liberation Front. 5. *rare* forwardness, presumption. *Cf.* **mbele.**

[1]**umbia** soar, glide *(of birds)*; flare up *(a fire).*

[2]**umbia** *appl. of* **umba.**

umbile, umbo (ma-) (*us.* **maumbile**) 1. (natural, original) condition, shape, form, figure, appearance. **sheria ya maumbile.** natural law. 2. quality, property, feature. 3. forming, fashioning. 4. *rel.* creation. *Cf.* **umba.**

umbo *sing.* *see* **umbile.**

umbu *sing., arch.* (*dial.* **dumbu**) umbu (term of address used between brother and sister).

umbua *inv. of* **umba.**

umbuji* *sing.* 1. elegance, grace, distinction *(us. in external appearance).* 2. good manners. *Cf.* **mmbuji.**

[1]**ume** *adj.* 1. male, masculine. 2. *fig.* virile, courageous, strong. 3. *fig., of things* big, strong, firm, solid. *Cf.* **dume, kiume, kuume, maume, mume, mwanamume, ndume, uume.**

[2]**ume** *sing.* *see* **uume.**

umekanika* *sing.* *see* **umakanika.**

umeme *sing.* 1. lightning. 2. irradiation. 3. electricity. *Cf.* **memeteka.**

umhali* (–) *see* **muhali.**

umika 1. bleed *(a person)* by cupping, cup *(for blood).* 2. make an incision. 3. fasten a vessel below a gash in a palm tree *(in order to catch the sap),* tap a palm tree. 4. put a vessel to one's lips *(in order to drink);* take a long draft/drink. *appl.* **umikia. pembe ya kuumikia.** an instrument for cupping *(us. the horn of a goat). inv.* **umua.** take off a bleeding cup. *inv.-intr.* **umuka.** *Cf.* **muumishi, ndumiko, uumikaji.**

umiko *sing.* *see* **ndumiko.**

umilele* *sing.* eternity, perpetuity, permanence. *Cf.* **milele.**

umio (**mio**) *anat.* 1. throat, larynx. 2. *rare* esophagus, trachea. *Cf.* **kimio, mio.**

umito *sing.* swelling (of the feet of a pregnant woman).

umivu (*rare* **umo**) (**ma-**) (*us.* **maumivu**) pain, ache, sting; torment, suffering. *Cf.* **uma.**

umiza *caus. of* **uma.**

umizi (**ma-**) (*us.* **maumizi**) harm, injury. *Cf.* **uma.**

umka *intr. of* **umua.**

[1]**umo** (**maumo**) *see* **umivu.**

[2]**umo** *auxil. v. det.* 1. *2nd pers. sing.* you are in (the previously mentioned...) 2. *3rd pers. sing.,* **m-** *and* **u-** *cl.* he (she, it) is in (the previously mentioned...)

umoja *sing.* 1. oneness, unity, union. **kwa –.** unanimously. **– wa Mataifa.** United Nations. **– wa nchi za Afrika (UNA).** Organization for African Unity (OAU). **unda –.** form a union. *prov.* **– ni nguvu.** Union is strength. 2. concord, harmony, agreement. 3. identity. 4. *gramm.* (**jumla ya –**) singular. *Cf.* **moja.**

umoto, umotomoto *sing.* 1. warmth, heat. 2. *fig.* passion, temperament. *Cf.* [1]**moto.**

umotomoto *sing.* *see* **umoto.**

umri* *sing.* 1. age *(of a person).* **hana – wa kutosha.** He is not yet very old.

hana – wa kuendelea. He cannot live much longer. 2. time, period. **siwezi kungoja mpaka – kiyama.** I can't live forever.

umua 1. take/steal away, deprive of; confiscate. 2. cause fermentation, put yeast in bread flour. 3. *inv. of* **umika.** *intr.* **umuka, umka.** 1. swell up, ferment. 2. *inv.-intr. of* **umika.**

[1]**umuka** *intr. of* **umua.**

[2]**umuka** *inv.-intr. of* **umika.**

umungu *sing.* deity, divinity (of God, Allah). *Cf.* **mungu, uungu.**

umwene *sing.* *see* **umwinyi.**

umwinyi (*dial.* **umwene**) *sing.* 1. office (status, duties, etc.) of a chief. 2. *rec., comm.* feudalism. *Cf.* **mwenye.**

[1]**una** *auxil. v.* 1. *2nd pers. sing.* you have. 2. *3rd pers. sing.,* **m-** *and* **u-** *cl.* he (she, it) has.

[2]**una** (–) una (kind of fish).

unadhifu* *sing.* cleanliness, neatness, orderliness. *Cf.* **nadhifu.**

unafiki* *sing.* deceit, hypocrisy, dissimulation. *Cf.* **mnafiki.**

unaibu* *sing., rare* deputyship. *Cf.* **naibu.**

unajimu* *sing.* astronomy, astrology. *Cf.* **mnajimu.**

unajisi* *sing., Isl.* (ritual) impurity, uncleanliness; desecration, defilement. *Cf.* **najisi.**

unanasi* [*Pers.*] *sing.* fiber of the pineapple plant *(used as thread)*. *Cf.* **mnanasi.**

[1]**unda** build, make, construct, fit together, assemble, form. **– stima.** build a ship. **– injini.** construct a machine. *prov.* **ukikiona (chombo) kikielea kimeundwa.** Keep a thing in good condition; then it will stay good. *Cf.* **kiunda, kiunza, kiunzi, mwunda, mwundaji, mwundo, nyundo, uundaji, uunzi.**

[2]**unda** remove honey from a beehive.

undani *sing.* 1. (secret) grudge, hatred. **ukigombana naye habari huisha pale pale, hana – (tena).** When people dispute about a matter it should be gradually settled and not leave a grudge behind. 2. innermost feelings. **toa –.** reveal one's innermost feelings. **azimio ya –.** ulterior motive. *Cf.* **ndani.**

undu (**nyundu**) cock's comb.

uneemefu* *sing.* *see* **uneemevu.**

uneemevu*, uneemefu *sing.* plenty, abundance, profusion. *Cf.* **neema, neemevu.**

unenaji, uneni *sing.* 1. (power of) speech, speaking. 2. fluency, eloquence. 3. turn of speech, manner of speaking. – **wake hatukuupenda.** His manner of speaking did not impress us. *Cf.* [1]**nena.**

unene *sing.* stoutness, fatness, corpulence. *Cf.* **nene.**

uneni *sing.* *see* **unenaji.**

[1]**unga** 1. meal, flour. – **wa mtama.** millet flour. – **wa mahindi.** cornmeal. **kanda –.** knead dough. 2. anything ground fine or pulverized, powder. – **wa mbao.** sawdust.

[2]**unga** 1. mix. – **mchuzi.** stir soup. 2. join, connect, fasten together. – **mbao.** join boards/planks. – **mfupa.** set a bone. – **mkono.** support. 3. *fig.:* – **hesabu.** count/add up. 4. secure, consolidate, establish. **siku hizi ameunga.** His (financial) situation is secured. *ass.* **ungana.** 1. mix together. 2. join/fit together. 3. unite, combine. *ass.-intr.* **unganika.** be combined/united. *ass.-caus.* **unganisha.** bring together, join, glue together; combine. *stat.* **ungama.** *stat.-ass.* **ungamana.** be connected/cohesive/coherent/interdependent. *inv.* **ungua.** separate, take apart, detach, disconnect. *inv.-appl.* **ungulika.** be separable/divisible/detachable. *Cf.* [2]**ungo,** [1]**kiunga, kiungo, maungo, miungano, muungo, uunganishaji.**

[1]**ungama** 1. admit, grant, concede, confess *(also rel.).* 2. allow, acknowledge, recognize. *appl.* **ungamia.** *caus.* **ungamisha.** cause to confess, *(rel.)* hear a confession. *Cf.* [1]**ungamo, mwungama, mwungamishi,** [1]**mwungamo, uungamaji.**

[2]**ungama** *stat. of* [2]**unga.**

[1]**ungamo** (**ma-**) admission, confession. *Cf.* [1]**ungama.**

[2]**ungamo** *sing.* a yellow pigment. *Cf.* [2]**mwungamo.**

unganisho (**ma-**) union, association, federation. *Cf.* [2]**unga.**

ung'aro *sing., rare* brightness, luster. *Cf.* **ng'aa.**

[1]**ungo** *sing.* 1. *anat.* hymen. **vunja –.** begin to menstruate. 2. virginity.

[2]**ungo, ungu** (**ma-**) (*arch.* **lungo;** *us.* **maungo**) 1. joint. 2. member *(of the body).* 3. back, backbone. 4. (**maungo**) (entire) body. **maungo yote yanamwuma.** His entire body aches. *Cf.* [2]**unga.**

[3]**ungo** (**nyungo** & **ma-**) ungo (a flat basket used for winnowing grain).

ungojaji, ungoje, ungojezi *sing.* position (duties, pay, etc.) of a watchman or guard. *Cf.* **ngoja.**

ung'ongo (**ng'ongo**) strip of palm leaf *(used for weaving baskets).*

[1]**ungu** (**ma-**) *see* [2]**ungo.**

[2]**ungu** (**nyungu**) *see* [1]**chungu.**

[1]**ungua** be burnt/baked/scorched/singed/hardened/damaged *(by fire)*. **– moto.** be damaged by fire. *fig.:* **anaungua rohoni.** It affected him very deeply *(lit.* scorched his soul). *appl.* **ungulia.** 1. apply fire to something, burn, bake, fire *(pottery)*. 2. *fig.* have heartburn *(from indigestion)*. *caus.* **unguza.** burn, scorch, singe, sear. *Cf.* **unguzo, kiungulia, kiunguza.**

[2]**ungua** *inv. of* [2]**unga.**

Unguja *sing.* Zanzibar. *Cf.* **Kiunguja.**

unguza *caus. of* [1]**ungua.**

unguzo *sing., rare* (act of) burning, baking, scorching, searing. *Cf.* [1]**ungua.**

ungwana *sing.* *see* **uungwana.**

unjukuti *see* **uchukuti.**

unong'onezi *sing., rare* whispering, rumor. *Cf.* **nong'ona, mnong'ono.**

unono *sing.* 1. fatness *(of animals)*. 2. *fig.* comfort, luxury. *Cf.* **nona.**

ununaji,ununo *sing.* sullenness, bad temper, discontentment; complaining, grumbling. *Cf.* **nuna.**

ununo *sing.* *see* **ununaji.**

ununu **(nunu)** ununu (fiber from the stalk of the coconut-palm leaf).

ununuzi *sing.* 1. buying, purchasing. 2. price, offer, bid, quotation. **– wa ng'ombe umekatazwa.** The quotation on cattle has gone down. *Cf.* **nunua.**

unyaa *sing.* 1. filth, excrement. 2. *fig.* disgust, repugnance. *Cf.* [2]**nyara, kinyaa.**

unyago *sing., ethn.* unyago (ceremonies and dances marking the initiation of children as adult members of a tribe). *Cf.* **kinyago, manyago.**

unyaji *sing.* evacuation *(of the bowels)*, urination. *Cf.* **nya.**

unyakuzi *sing., rare* *see* **unyang'anyi.**

unyama *sing.* 1. nature/behavior of an animal. 2. *fig.* brutishness, beastliness, bestiality; stupidity; coarseness, brutality. **amefanya –.** He behaved like a beast/was brutal. 3. *fig., chem.* protein. *Cf.* **mnyama.**

unyamafu *sing.* *see* **unyamavu.**

unyamavu, unyamafu *sing., rare* quiet, silence, taciturnity. *Cf.* **nyamaa, nyamavu.**

unyang'anyi (*rare* **unyakuzi**) *sing.* seizure, plundering, robbery, brigandage, depredation, extortion. *Cf.* **nyang'anya.**

unyanya *sing.* feeling of superiority, arrogance, disdain, contempt, aloofness. *Cf.* [1]**nyanya.**

unyao *sing.* *see* **unyayo.**

unyarafu *sing.* 1. disgust, repugnance. *Cf.* [2]**nyara, nyarafu.** 2. *rare* = **unyanya.**

unyasi (**nyasi** & **ma-**) (blade of) grass, reed, straw *(used for thatching). Cf.* **nyasi.**

unyaufu *sing.* drying up, shrivelling, wasting away, languishing. *Cf.* **nyauka.**

unyayo, unyao (**nyayo**) trace, footprint, track *(of an animal). Cf.* **wayo.**

unyefu *sing.* *see* **unyevu.**

unyege *sing.* *see* **nyege.**

unyele (**nywele**) *see* **unywele.**

unyeleo (**nyeleo**) *see* **kinyeleo.**

unyeme *sing.* noise, uproar.

unyende, unyenje *sing.* cry, call.

unyenje *sing.* *see* **unyende.**

unyenyekeo *sing.* *see* **unyenyekevu.**

unyenyekevu, unyenyekeo *sing.* 1. modesty, reticence. 2. humility, deference, obsequiousness, servility. *Cf.* **nyenya, nyenyekevu.**

unyenyevu *sing.* *see* **kinyenyevu.**

unyenyezi *sing.* 1. mist, fog, haze. 2. haziness, vagueness, indistinctness.

unyeo *sing.* tickling, itching. *Cf.* [1]**nyea.**

unyesi, unyezi (**ma-**) (*us.* **kinyesi**) 1. excretion, elimination. 2. excrement, urine. *Cf.* **nya.**

unyeti *sing.* 1. conceit, vanity, arrogance, presumption, impudence, insolence. 2. irritability, sensitiveness. *Cf.* **nyeta.**

unyevu, unyefu *sing.* (*also* **mnyefu, mi-**) dampness, humidity, moisture. **ardhi hapa ina – sana.** The earth is very damp here (*lit.* has dampness). *Cf.* **nya.**

unyezi (**ma-**) *see* **unyesi.**

unyimivu *sing.* stinginess, miserliness. *Cf.* **nyima, nyimivu.**

unyo, unyounyo *adv.* close together, in close order. **simama –.** stand close together.

unyofu *sing.* 1. straightness. 2. straightforwardness, honesty, integrity. *Cf.* [1]**nyoka, nyofu.**

unyogofu *sing.* *see* **unyogovu.**

unyogovu, unyogofu, unyong'onyevu *sing.* sluggishness, languidness, slowness; weariness, exhaustion; weakness. *Cf.* **nyong'onyea.**

unyonga (**nyonga**) 1. *anat.* hip, thigh, side. 2. = [1]**kinyonga.** 3.: **enda –.** *rare* limp, hobble (= **enda chopi**). *Cf.* [1]**nyonga.**

unyonge *sing.* 1. weakness, feebleness *(due to illness).* **rafiki yetu mwenye –**

yu hali gani? How is our ailing friend? 2. worthlessness, insignificance. 3. lowness, meanness, baseness. **naona – kufanya jambo hili.** It seems to me a mean trick to do this. *Cf.* **nyonge.**

unyong'onyevu *sing.* *see* **unyogofu.**

unyonyaji *sing., fig.* exploitation. *Cf.* **nyonya.**

unyounyo *adv.* *see* **unyo.**

unyoya (nyoya *or* **ma-)** feather; (single strand of) down, (animal) hair, wool.

unyozi *sing.* 1. work (methods, pay, etc.) of a barber, hairdresser; haircutting, shaving, etc. 2. (style of) haircut, coiffure. **– wake ni mbaya.** He (she) does not have a good haircut (coiffure). *Cf.* **nyoa.**

unyumba *sing.* 1. household, housekeeping, domesticity. 2. married state, married life, relation of man and wife. **pa –.** fulfill one's marital duties. **mvunja –.** adulterer. *Cf.* **nyumba.**

unyumbufu *sing.* flexibility. *Cf.* **nyumbua, nyumbufu.**

unyushi, unyusi (nyushi) (single hair of the) eyebrow. *Cf.* **ushi.**

unyusi *sing.* *see* **unyushi.**

unywaji *sing.* 1. (manner of) drinking, absorbing. **– wa pombe siku hizi umezidi.** Beer-drinking is on the increase today. 2. liquid, beverage. 3. *rare* dampness, moisture, humidity. *Cf.* **nywa.**

unywele, unyele (nywele, nyele) (a single human) hair. **nywele za singa.** long, straight hair *(like that of Europeans).* **nywele za kipilipili.** hair in wooly tufts, 'peppercorn' hair.

unyweleo (ma-) *see* **kinyeleo.**

uo (nyuo) cover *(of a book, etc.)*; envelope, wrapper; case, sheath *(of a knife)*, scabbard.

uofisa* [*Engl.*] *sing.* *see* **uafisa.**

uoga *sing.* *see* **woga.**

uogeleaji *sing.* bathing, swimming. *Cf.* **¹oga.**

uokaji *sing., rare* roasting, baking, culinary art. *Cf.* **oka.**

uokosi *sing.* reward *(for finding a lost object).* *Cf.* **okota.**

uokotaji *sing.* 1. finding, picking up. 2. find, discovery. 3. = **uokosi.** *Cf.* **okota.**

uokozi, wokozi *sing.* saving, rescue, deliverance, salvation. *Cf.* **²okoa.**

uombaji *sing.* (habitual, professional) begging, mendicancy. *Cf.* **omba.**

uombezi, uombi *sing.* entreaty, supplication; petition, application. *Cf.* **omba.**

uombi *sing.* *see* **uombezi.**

uonevu (*rare* **uonezi, uono, uonyo**) (ma-) 1. warning, notification, exhortation. **–a –.** ominous. 2. bullying, oppression. 3. *rec.:* **– wa kitaifa.** chauvinism. **– wa kitaifa wa nchi kubwa.** great-power chauvinism. *Cf.* **ona.**

uonezi (ma-) *see* **uonevu.**

uongo *sing.* *see* **uwongo.**

uongofu *sing.* *see* **wongofu.**

uongozi *sing.* leadership, management. *Cf.* **ongoa.**

uonjaji *sing.* 1. sense of taste. 2. tasting, sampling, testing. *Cf.* **onja.**

uono (ma-) *see* **uonevu.**

uonyesho (ma-) *see* **wonyesho.**

uonyo *sing.* *see* **uonevu.**

uoshaji *sing.* 1. *rare* washing *(clothes).* 2. preparation of a corpse for burial. *Cf.* **osha.**

uotaji, uoto *sing.* growing, growth *(of plants).* **– wa pamba.** the growth of the cotton. *Cf.* **[1]ota.**

uoto *sing., rare* *see* **uotaji.**

uovu (ma-) badness, wickedness, evil, corruption, immorality, viciousness, wrong. **walitufanyia mambo ya – sana.** They have done us a great wrong. *Cf.* **ovu.**

uozi (ma-) *rare* marriage ceremony, wedding. *Cf.* **oa, ndoa.**

upaa, upara *sing.* 1. baldness, bald spot. 2. crown of the head. 3. *rec.* (use of) cosmetics, makeup. *Cf.* **[2]para.**

upadre* [*Port.*] *sing.* (Roman Catholic) priesthood, holy orders. *Cf.* **padre.**

upagazi *sing.* 1. work (duties, pay, etc.) of a porter, transport (business). 2. witchcraft. *Cf.* **pagaa.**

upaja (paja) *see* **paja.**

upaji *sing.* 1. *us. rel.* gift (of God) 2. *in gen.* generosity, liberality, hospitality. *Cf.* **[1]pa.**

upakiaji *sing.* *see* **upakizi.**

upakio *sing.* *see* **upakizi.**

upakizi, upakiaji, upakio *sing.* 1. loading, putting on board *(a ship)*, stowing cargo. 2. cargo, freight. 3. (loading) crane. 4. shipping cost, freight, carriage. 5. plastering, stucco work. *Cf.* **[1]pakia, [1]paka.**

upakuzi *sing.* 1. unloading, discharging *(cargo, freight).* 2. serving *(of food).* *Cf.* **[1]pakia.**

[1]**upamba** **(pamba)** 1. upamba (a knife or billhook used for tapping palm trees). 2. sickle. 3. small hoe (used for weeding).

[2]**upamba** **(pamba)** tusk *(of a boar).*

[3]**upamba*** [*Pers.*] (–) *see* **kipamba.**

upambano *sing.* 1. comparison. 2. collision, conflict, disagreement. *Cf.* **pambana.**

upambanuzi *sing.* 1. selecting, sorting out. 2. (power of) discrimination. *Cf.* **pambana.**

upambo **(ma-)** (*us.* **mapambo**) decoration, furnishing *(of a house);* furniture. *Cf.* [1]**pamba.**

upana 1. **(ma-)** breadth, width; diameter. 2.: **mapana** *adv.* far and wide; thoroughly, inside out. **anaijua nchi – na –.** He knows the country inside out. *Cf.* [1]**pana.**

[1]**upandaji, upanzi** *sing.* sowing, planting; time for planting. *Cf.* [2]**panda.**

[2]**upandaji** *sing.* ascending, climbing. *Cf.* [1]**panda.**

upande **(pande)** (*also* **mpande, mi-**) 1. side. **pande zote.** on all sides. **– huu (ule) wa mto.** this side (the other side) of the river. 2. direction. **– wa kaskazini (kuzini).** northerly (southerly) direction. 3. part, section, district *(of a country/city).* 4. wing *(of a building/army).* 5. *prep.* by, near, beside. 6. *adv.* aside; sideways, awry. *Cf.* **kipande.**

upanga **(panga)** 1. sword. **makali (maungo) ya –.** edge (back) of a sword. *fig.* **– wa jogoo.** cock's comb. **– wa suruali.** crease of trousers. 2. a wooden implement used by weavers to tighten threads.

upangaji *sing.* 1. (act, terms, etc. of) hiring, renting, leasing. 2. (money paid for) rent, hire. *Cf.* [2]**panga.**

upanuzi *sing., rare* widening, broadening, expansion. *Cf.* [1]**pana, panua.**

upanzi *sing.* *see* [1]**upandaji.**

upao **(pao)** *see* **upau.**

upapasa *sing.* upapasa (pastry made of manioc flour and coconut juice).

upapi **(papi)** 1. long thin strip of wood or metal, beading, stripping. **papi za msumeno.** sawblade strips. **papi zenye magololi.** bearing strips. 2. gore, gusset *(in clothing).*

upara 1. apply makeup *(powder, lipstick, etc.).* 2. *sing.* = **upaa.**

upasi *sing.* trouble, annoyance, difficulty. **fanzia –.** cause trouble for someone. *Cf.* **pata.**

upataji *sing.* 1. value, price. 2. purchasing power. *Cf.* **pata.**

upatanisho *sing.* reconciliation, arbitration, pacification. *Cf.* **pata.**

upatano *sing.* *see* **patano.**

upatikanaji *sing., rare* obtaining, procuring, receipt, delivery. *Cf.* **pata.**

upatilivu, upatilizo **(ma-)** *rare* blame, reproach, accusation, punishment. *Cf.* **pata.**

upatilizo **(ma-)** *see* **upatilivu.**

upato **(ma-)** *see* **pato.**

upatu* [*Ind.*] **(patu)** 1. gong. 2. gifts presented on a tray to the bride and groom at a wedding.

upau, upao **(pau, pao)** one of the poles laid across the rafters of a native hut to support the thatch. (= ^{1}**pao.**)

upawa **(pawa)** 1. a ladle made of coconut shell. 2. *in gen.* (wooden) ladle.

upayukaji *sing.* indiscretion *(in talking);* incoherence, inconsistency. *Cf.* **paya.**

upekecho **(–)** (*also* **pekecho, ma-**) 1. (act of) drilling, boring. 2. making fire by twirling one fire-stick in a hole in the other. 3. one of such fire-sticks (either 'male' or 'female'; *cf.* **wimbombo, ulindi**). 4. *fig.* annoyance, vexation. 5. *fig.* persistent ache/pain. *Cf.* **pekecha.**

upekee *sing.* *see* **upweke.**

upeketevu *sing.* contempt, disdain; arrogance. *Cf.* **pekecha, peketevu.**

upekuzi *sing.* 1. curiosity, inquisitiveness. 2. search, inquiry, investigation. 3. fault-finding, criticism. *Cf.* **pekua, pekuzi.**

upele **(pele)** *med.* itch, skin-rash/eruption, acne, scabies.

upelekaji *sing., rare* delivery, transmittal, conveyance. *Cf.* **peleka.**

upelelezi *sing.* spying, espionage, reconnaissance. **ndege za –.** reconnaissance plane. *Cf.* **peleleza.**

upembe **(pembe)** 1. *naut.* the upper corner of a triangular sail. 2. *fig.:* **ananitazama kwa –.** He looks askance at me. *Cf.* ^{2}**pembe.**

upembo **(pembo)** upembo (a hooked stick for pulling down fruit). *Cf.* ^{1}**pemba.**

upendaji **(ma-)** inclination, propensity, predilection, partiality, special liking for something. **– wa madhehebu.** sectarianism. *Cf.* **penda.**

upendano **(ma-)** liking for each other, mutual affection, congeniality. *Cf.* **penda.**

upendeleo **(ma-)** 1. favoritism, bias, patronage. 2. indulgence, consideration. 3. = **upendaji.** *Cf.* **penda.**

upendelevu **(ma-)** 1. = **upendeleo.** 2. state of being liked/favored, charm, attractiveness. *Cf.* **penda.**

upendezi (ma-) 1. agreeableness, amiability, kindness, charm. 2. pleasure *(over something)*, delight, happiness. 3. = **upendo**. *Cf.* **penda**.

upendo, upenzi (*rare* **upendezi**) (ma-) love, affection, liking. *Cf.* **penda**.

upendwa *sing.* state of being liked/loved. *Cf.* **penda**.

upenu (**penu**) space covered by the projecting roof of a house, (small) addition to a house, lean-to.

upenyaji, upenyezi (ma-, **penyaji, penyezi**) secret/surreptitious/underhanded action, smuggling, bribery; insinuation. *Cf.* **penya**.

upenyezi *sing.* *see* **upenyaji**.

upenzi (ma-) *see* **upendo**.

upeo (**peo**) 1. extremity, limit, furthest/highest point, apex, peak, summit. **— wa macho**. horizon. **pita —**. beyond measure, out of all bounds. 2. *adv.* to the utmost, thoroughly. **piga —**. give a sound beating. *Cf.* [1]**pea**, **kipeo**.

upepeaji (ma-) *see* **upepezi**.

upepeo (**pepeo**) fan, ventilator. *Cf.* **pepa**.

upepezi, upepeaji *sing.* (act of) fanning; gentle breeze. *Cf.* **pepa**.

upepo (**pepo**) wind, current of air, draft. **— wa bahari**. sea breeze. **— unavuma, — unaanguka**. the wind is changing. **punga —**. 1. get fresh air, go for a change of air. 2. fan oneself. *Cf.* **pepa**.

upesi 1. *sing.* speed, velocity; haste. 2. *adv.* quickly, speedily, fast. **fanya kazi —**. work fast. **sema —**. talk fast. *Cf.* **epesi, wepesi**.

upeto (**peto**) 1. fold, roll. 2. something folded/rolled: package, bundle. *Cf.* [1]**peta**.

upevu *sing.* ripeness, maturity. *Cf.* **pevua, pevu**.

upi *see* **pi**.

upigaji, upigiaji *sing.* 1. striking, beating, blows. 2.: **— wa picha**. photography. **— (wa) kura**. casting votes, voting. *Cf.* **piga**.

upiganaji *sing.* 1. fight, battle. 2. rivalry, competition, contest *(sport, etc.)*. *Cf.* **piga**.

upigano 1. *sing.* fighting; contest, rivalry. 2. (ma-) conflict, struggle, battle. *Cf.* **piga**.

upigiaji *sing.* *see* **upigaji**.

upikaji *sing., rare* cooking, cookery, culinary art. (= **upishi**.) *Cf.* **pika**.

upimaji *sing.* 1. measuring, weighing. 2. registration, recording. 3. criticism, assessment, evaluation. *Cf.* **pima**.

upinda *adv.:* fa —. die a natural death. *Cf.* **kipinda.**

upindani *sing.* 1. stiffness. 2. stubbornness, obstinacy, contentiousness. *Cf.* **pinda.**

upinde, upindi (**pinde**) 1. *rare* bending, bend, something bent. 2. bow *(for shooting).* **— wa mvua.** rainbow. **— wa jua.** spectrum. *Cf.* **pinda.**

upindi (**pindi**) *see* **upinde.**

upindo *sing.* *see* **pindo.**

upinduzi (**ma-**) overturning, upsetting; (**mapinduzi**) revolution. *Cf.* **pinda.**

upingaji *sing.* 1. resistance, opposition. **chama cha —.** opposition party. 2. blocking, barring *(of one's way, etc.).* *Cf.* **pinga.**

upingamishi, upingamizi *sing.* (active) opposition, antagonism, obstructionism. (= **upinzani.**) *Cf.* **pinga.**

upinzani *sing.* 1. spirit of contradiction, obstructionism. 2. obstruction, obstacle, difficulty. 3. *pol.* opposition (party). *Cf.* **pinga.**

upishi *sing.* (*rare* **upikaji**) work (methods, pay, etc.) of a cook; cookery, art of cooking. *Cf.* **pika.**

upo (**nyupo**) upo (dipper for bailing out a boat).

upofu *sing.* blindness. *Cf.* **pofua.**

upogo (**pogo**) 1. lopsidedness; squinting/cockeyed condition. 2. *red.:* **upogoupogo.** *adv.* from side to side, in a zigzag manner. *Cf.* **pogoa.**

upokeaji, upokezi *sing.* collecting, receiving; receipts. *Cf.* **pokea.**

upokezi *sing.* *see* **upokeaji.**

upokonyaji, upokonyo *sing.* seizure, confiscation; robbing, plundering; extortion. *Cf.* **poka.**

upokonyo *sing.* *see* **upokonyaji.**

upole *sing.* kindness, gentleness, amiability, good nature, easy-going disposition. *Cf.* [1]**pole.**

upondo (—) *see* **pondo.**

upongoo (**pongoo**) central stem of a palm leaf.

uponyi *sing.* saving, deliverance, rescue; cure. *Cf.* **pona.**

upooza *sing.* 1. numbness, paralysis. (= **kipooza 1.**) 2. dumbness, speechlessness. *Cf.* **pooza.**

uporo *sing.* *see* **kiporo.**

uposa, uposo *sing.* *see* **poso.**

upote (**pote**) thong *(of a whip, etc.);* bowstring. *Cf.* **pota.**

upotevu *sing.* 1. loss. 2. impoverishment, destitution. 3. destruction, destructiveness, vandalism. 4. wastefulness, extravagance. 5. immoral life. *Cf.* **potea, potevu.**

upotoe *sing.* *see* **upotovu.**

upotovu, upotoe *sing.* 1. capriciousness, wrongheadedness. 2. stubbornness, obstinacy. 3. wickedness, degeneracy, corruption, perversion. *Cf.* **pota.**

upumbavu *sing.* stupidity, folly, ignorance, thoughtlessness. *Cf.* **pumbaa, pumbavu.**

upumuo, upumzi *sing.* *see* **pumzi.**

upunga (**punga**) 1. upunga (stage of growth of a plant which is in full flower and just beginning to form fruit). 2. *pl.* male flowers of the coconut palm.

upunguaji *sing.* *see* **upungufu.**

upungufu, upunguo, upunguaji (–, **ma-**) 1. decrease, reduction. 2. defect, fault. 3. deficiency, inadequacy, insufficiency. 4. need, privation. 5. disability, handicap. *Cf.* **²punga, pungufu.**

upunguo *sing.* *see* **upungufu.**

upupu *sing.*, *bot.* upupu (cowage, mucuna bean).

upuraji *sing.* beating, threshing. **mashine ya – wa nafaka.** thresher. *Cf.* **pura.**

upurukushaji, upurukushani, upurukusho *sing.* inattentiveness, carelessness, negligence. *Cf.* **purukusha.**

upurukushani, upurukusho *sing.* *see* **upurukushaji.**

upuuzi *sing.* *see* **upuzi.**

upuzi, upuuzi *sing.* nonsense, foolishness, foolish talk, gossip. *Cf.* **²puza.**

upweke, upekee *sing.* solitude, loneliness; seclusion, retirement. *Cf.* **peke.**

upya (**ma-**) 1. newness, novelty. **hayo ni mapya hayo.** This is a novelty for me. 2. *adv.* anew, afresh, again. **wameijenga nyumba yao –.** They have rebuilt their house. *Cf.* **pya.**

uradhi* *sing.* 1. satisfaction, contentment. 2. fulfilment of desires/claims. 3. assent, approval, sanction. *Cf.* **ridhi.**

uradi*, auradi *sing.*, *Isl.* prayers pronounced at a burial.

urafiki* *sing.* friendship. **fanya (vunja) –.** form (break off) a friendship. *Cf.* **rafiki.**

uragai*, ulaghai *sing.* deception, fraud, swindle, imposture. *Cf.* **laghai.**

urahisi* 1. cheapness, low price, bargain. 2. *adv.* cheaply, easily. *Cf.* **rahisi.**

urai* *sing.* flattery, servility, adulation; cunning. *Cf.* [1]**rai.**

uraia* *sing.* citizenship. *Cf.* **raia.**

uraibu* *sing.* uraibu (a mixture of areca nut and tobacco, with lime, cloves, and a red gum, prepared for chewing). (= **tambuu.**)

uramali*, ulamali *sing.* black magic. *Cf.* **ramli** (?).

urambirambi *sing.* *see* **ulambilambi.**

urari* *sing.* evenness, proportion, balance. **— wa hesabu.** balancing an account. **fanya —.** strike a balance.

uraro *sing.* *see* [2]**ulalo.**

urasharasha* (ma-) drizzle, sprinkle, light rain. *Cf.* **rasha.**

uraufu* *sing.* gentleness, sympathy, compassion. *Cf.* **raufu.**

urefu (ma-) length, height, altitude, depth. **— wa kwenda juu (chini).** height (depth). *Cf.* **refu.**

urekebisho* *sing.* 1. repair. 2. adjustment, orientation. *Cf.* [1]**rakibu.**

urembo (ma-, —) ornamentation, adornment, decoration; finery; ornamental markings *(on the face). Cf.* **remba, rembo;** *also* **nembo.**

Ureno* [*Port.*] *sing.* Portugal. *Cf.* **reno.**

urimbo *sing.* *see* **ulimbo.**

urithi* *sing.* inheritance, bequest, legacy, heritage. **mambo ya —.** matters/business relating to inheritance. *Cf.* **rithi.**

uritima* *sing.* *see* **ulitima.**

uroho* *sing.* greed, avarice, gluttony. (= **roho** 6.)

urongo *sing.* *see* **uwongo.**

uru* [*Port.*] *sing., cards* diamonds.

urudishaji* *sing.* reconstruction, restoration, rehabilitation. *Cf.* **rudi.**

urujuani*, urujuwani [*Pers.*] *sing.* violet *(color).*

urujuwani* *sing.* *see* **urujuani.**

urukaji *sing.* 1. jump(ing). 2. *av.* takeoff. *Cf.* **ruka.**

urukususu* *sing., pharm.* cough medicine.

urumo* *sing.* poverty, need, distress. **shikwa/patwa na —.** be reduced to poverty, be in straitened circumstances, fall upon hard times.

Urusi* *sing.* Russia, Soviet Union. *Cf.* **Kirusi, Mrusi.**

uruzi *sing.* *see* **uluzi.**

usabaha* *sing., rare* succession *(by inheritance, in office). Cf.* **sabaha.**

usafari* *sing.* *see* **usafiri.**

usafi* *sing.* 1. cleanliness, purity. 2. orderliness, neatness. 3. frankness, truthfulness. *Cf.* **safi.**

usafidi* [*Pers.*] *sing.* 1. cleanliness, neatness. 2. friendliness, pleasantness. 3. dexterity, agility. *Cf.* **safidi.**

usafihi* *sing.* impudence, insolence; abuse, affront; presumption, pride, arrogance. *Cf.* **safihi.**

usafiri*, **usafari** *sing.* travel(ing), journey, trip. **– wa wageni.** tourism. *Cf.* **safiri.**

usafirisha* *sing.* *see* **usafirishaji.**

usafirishaji*, **usafirisha** *sing.* 1. sending off, dispatch. 2. conveyance, transport, transportation; communications. 3. customs, duty. 4.: **– wa bidhaa.** export. *Cf.* **safiri.**

usafishaji* *sing.* cleaning, purification. *Cf.* **safi.**

usaha* *sing.* pus, matter. **toka –.** discharge matter, suppurate *(a sore, etc.).*

usahaulifu* *sing.* forgetfulness, absentmindedness. *Cf.* **sahau, sahaulifu.**

usahibu* *sing.* *see* **usuhuba.**

usahihi* *sing.* 1. rightness, correctness, faultlessness. 2. accuracy, precision, punctuality. 3. truthfulness. *Cf.* **sahihi.**

usakaji *sing.* *see* **usasi.**

usalama* *sing.* safety, security. **halmashauri/baraza/chama ya – (ya UNO).** Security Council (of the UN). *Cf.* **salamu, salama.**

usani* *sing.* forging, work (methods, pay, etc.) of a (black)smith. *Cf.* [2]**sana.**

usanifu* *sing.* 1. skill. 2. art, craft. *Cf.* **sanifu.**

usare *sing.* blood brotherhood. *Cf.* [1]**sare, uchale.**

usasi, usakaji *sing.* (methods, pay, etc. of) hunting. *Cf.* **saka.**

usawa* *sing.* 1. likeness, similarity, equality; evenness, fairness, balance. 2. level. **– wa bahari.** sea level. 3. *sport* tie. *Cf.* **sawa.**

usawanisho* *sing.* 1. arrangement *(in a row, line),* alignment. 2. marking out/off, delimiting, demarcation. *Cf.* **sawa.**

[1]**useja** *sing.* useja (a necklace or collar of beads).

[2]**useja** *sing.* unmarried state, bachelorhood. *Cf.* **mseja.**

usemaji *sing.* 1. eloquence, public speaking. **– wake haukutusaidia.** His eloquence did not help us. 2. loquaciousness, talkativeness, garrulousness. 3. pronunciation. **– wake hautoshi.** His pronunciation is faulty. *Cf.* **sema.**

usemi *sing.* 1. speech, address. **alipomaliza – wake.** when he had finished his speech. 2. conversation. 3. diction, style, manner of expression. 4. *gramm.* word. 5. *fig.* attitude, position *(on a matter).* – **wa serikali.** the position of the government. *Cf.* **sema.**

useremala* [*Pers.*] *sing.* (craft, pay, etc. of) carpentry, cabinetmaking. *Cf.* **seremala.**

usha *caus. of* **uka.**

ushababi* *sing.* youth(fulness). *Cf.* **shababi.**

ushabaki* *sing.* 1. cleverness, cunning. 2. snare; trick, trickery, strategem. *Cf.* **²shabaki.**

ushahidi*, ushuhuda *sing.* 1. proof, confirmation; *(jur.)* evidence, testimony. 2. *rel.* martyrdom. *Cf.* **shahada, shahidi, shuhudu.**

ushairi* *sing.* 1. poetry, art of poetry. 2. *fig.* beauty, high skill. *Cf.* **mshairi, shairi.**

ushamasi*, ushemasi *sing., rel.* diaconate. *Cf.* **shamasi.**

ushambulizi *sing.* aggression. *Cf.* **shambulia.**

ushanga (**shanga** & **ma-**) bead; *(us. pl.)* (string of) beads. – **wa kuteremesha.** belt of beads *(worn by women).*

ushangao *sing.* *see* **mshangao.**

usharifu* *sing.* excellence, dignity, respectability. *Cf.* **sharifu.**

ushaufu* *sing.* deception, something misleading or disappointing *(display, promise),* delusion. *Cf.* **shaua, shaufu.**

ushawishi* *sing.* enticement, allurement, temptation; *(pol.)* agitation. *Cf.* **shawishi.**

usheha* *sing.* 1. position of/status as a chief/councillor. 2. respected social position. 3. *ethn.* place reserved for elders at a funeral. *Cf.* **shaha, sheikh.**

ushenzi* [*Pers.*] *sing.* savagery, barbarism; uncouthness, unmannerliness; paganism, heathenism. *Cf.* **shenzi.**

ushi (**nyushi**) 1. eyebrow, eyebrow ridge. 2. *fig. (in gen.)* ridge, projection *(ledge, cornice, brink of a well, etc.).* *Cf.* **unyushi.**

ushikimano *sing.* (quality of) holding together, tenacity. *Cf.* **shika.**

ushimbu (–) shrimp (= **uduvi**).

ushinda *sing., rare* residue, remainder, refuse. *Cf.* **shinda.**

ushindani *sing.* 1. rivalry, competition, emulation. 2. contest, match. 3. fight (ing). 4. dispute, altercation, argument. 5. *rare* (legal) action, lawsuit. *Cf.* **¹shinda.**

ushinde *sing.* defeat. *Cf.* **¹shinda.**

ushindi *sing.* 1. cause of a dispute, point at issue, bone of contention. 2. victory; conquest, success. *Cf.* **¹shinda.**

ushindwaji *sing.* defeatism. *Cf.* [1]**shinda.**

ushirika*, ushiriki, ushirikiano, ushirikisho *sing.* 1. partnership; cooperation, collaboration. **chama cha –.** cooperative. 2. community of interests. 3. association, society, organization. *Cf.* **shiriki.**

ushirikiano*, ushirikisho *sing.* *see* **ushirika.**

ushirikina* (–) superstition. *Cf.* **shiriki, mshirikina.**

ushoga* *sing.* friendship *(between women, etc.; cf.* **shoga).**

ushombwe *sing., arch.* a magic potion.

ushonaji *sing.* *see* **ushoni.**

ushoni, ushonaji *sing.* occupation (craft, pay, etc.) of a tailor/seamstress; sewing, needlework, tailoring, dressmaking. *Cf.* **shona.**

ushono *sing.* style/method of sewing. *Cf.* **shona.**

ushoroba* *sing.* *see* **kishoroba.**

ushtaki* *sing., jur.* legal action, accusation, arraignment, prosecution. *Cf.* **shtaki.**

ushuhuda* *sing.* *see* **ushahidi.**

ushujaa* *sing.* 1. bravery, courage, heroism. 2. act of heroism, great exploit. *Cf.* **shujaa.**

ushukuru* *sing.* 1. thanks, gratitude (= **shukrani).** 2. resignation, humility. *Cf.* **shukuru.**

ushungi (shungi) 1. (women's) headcloth. 2. tuft of hair, (plaited) knot of hair. 3. *rare* cock's comb. *Cf.* [1]**shungi.**

ushupavu *sing.* 1. hardness, toughness, solidity, durability. 2. strength, vigor, energy. 3. endurance, tenacity, perseverance, resoluteness. 4. fanaticism, bigotry, dogmatism. 5. stubbornness, obstinacy. *Cf.* **shupaa, shupavu.**

ushuru* *sing.* 1. taxation, tax, duty. **– wa forodha.** custom duty, customs. 2. rent. **toa/lipa –.** pay taxes/rent. **toza –.** collect taxes/rent.

ushuzi *sing.* breaking wind. *Cf.* **shuta.**

ushwa *sing.* *see* **wishwa.**

usi (nyusi) usi (kind of grass).

[1]**usia*, wosia** 1. order, direct, instruct, commission. **ninakuusia usisahau kununua vitu hivi.** I expressly instructed you not to forget to buy these things. 2. make one's last will and testament, bequeath something to someone. **alimwusia mali yake.** He bequeathed his property to him. *appl.* **usilia.** *intr.* **usika.** *caus.* **usisha.** *pass.* **usiwa.** *Cf.* **wasia, wasii.**

[2]**usia*** *sing.* *see* **wasia.**

usihiri* *sing.* magic, witchcraft. *Cf.* **sihiri.**

usikilivu *sing.* *see* **usikivu.**

usikilizaji *sing.* make oneself understood *(at a distance).* *Cf.* **sikia.**

usikivu, usikilivu, usikizi *sing.* 1. attentiveness, attention, interest. 2. intelligence, teachability. 3. tractability, obedience. *Cf.* **sikia, sikilivu.**

usikizano *sing.* mutual understanding, agreement, harmony. *Cf.* **sikia.**

usikizi *sing.* *see* **usikivu.**

usiku 1. **(siku)** night, nighttime *(from* 6 *p.m. to* 6 *a.m.).* **wa manane.** midnight. **– na mchana.** night and day. *prov.* **moyo wa mwenzio ni – wa giza.** The heart of your friend is deep night (= one does not really know even one's friends). 2. *adv.* (*us.* **usiku usiku**) at night. **– hata/kwa –.** night after night. *Cf.* **¹siku, kisikusiku.**

usilia* *appl. of* **¹usia.**

usimamao *sing.* state of being erect/upright, upright/vertical/erect position. *Cf.* **simama.**

usimamizi *sing.* 1. supervision, superintendence, control. 2. position (duties, pay, etc.) of an overseer/superviser/superintendent/manager. 3. supervisory body/authority, administration, management, direction. 4. *fig.* protection, assistance, aid. *Cf.* **simama.**

usimango, usimanga, simango (ma-) (*us.* **masimango**) derision, mockery; malicious pleasure taken in another person's misfortune, schadenfreude. *Cf.* **simanga.**

usimeme *sing., rare* firmness, stability; steadfastness. *Cf.* **simama.**

usinga (singa) (single) hair *(us. of an animal).*

usingizi *sing.* sleep. **shikwa na –.** be overpowered by sleep. **lala –.** go to sleep. **ondoka usingizini.** wake up. **ugonjwa wa –.** sleeping sickness. **dawa ya –.** soporific, narcotic. *Cf.* **usingizisha;** *also* **sinzia.**

usingizisha *med.* anesthetize. *Cf.* **usingizi.**

usiniombe (–) usiniombe (kind of manioc).

usira *sing., arch.* usira (dried and powdered skin of animal or reptile, used as a charm or medicine).

usiri* 1. stay, tarry, linger, delay, lose time, be slow/late. *appl.* **usiria.** *intr.* **usirika.** be held up/delayed/detained; be arrested. *caus.* **usirisha.** delay/detain someone. 2. *sing.* delay, lateness. **mtu huyu ana mambo ya –.** This man has time-consuming business to do; this man does everything very slowly.

usita (–) *rare* way, road, path. (= **njia.**)

usitawi*, usitawishi, usitawishaji *sing.* 1. prosperity, progress, success. **tangu**

kupata uhuru umeingia – mkubwa katika nchi yetu. Since independence our country has made considerable progress. 2. growth, development, vitality. – wa miti unategemea rutuba ya ardhi. The growth of trees depends on the fertility of the soil. *Cf.* sitawi.

usitawishaji *sing.* *see* usitawi.

usitu (–) usitu (strip of plaited grass or palm-leaf fiber for making mats).

uskani* (–) *see* usukani.

uso (nyuso) 1. face; expression (of the face), appearance. – wa kutulia. a kind/friendly face. sina –. I am ashamed (*lit.* I have no face). kunja –. wrinkle the forehead *(from worry/annoyance).* kunjua –. smile. – kwa –. face to face. usoni. what is ahead, the future. *Cf.* kisogoni. 2. front, forward part; exterior; surface. usoni mwa nyumba kuna duka. There is a shop in the front part of the house. – wa dunia (mwezi). the surface of the earth (moon).

usodai* *sing.* *see* usodawi.

usodawi*, usodai *sing.* pride, arrogance; contempt, disdain. *Cf.* sodawi.

usoka (ma-) brass wire.

usomaji *sing.* reading, reading matter. *Cf.* soma.

usoni *see* uso.

usono *sing.* 1. rest, relaxation. 2. friendship.

usononi, usununo *sing.* 1. pain, grief, care. 2. bad humor, irritability. 3. sadness, melancholy. *Cf.* sonona.

uss! usu! *interj.* hush! quiet!

ustaarabu* *sing.* civilization, refinement; education; good manners. *Cf.* staarabu.

ustadi* *sing.* 1. skill, dexterity, cleverness. 2. expert knowledge, ability, competence. 3. cunning, craftiness. *Cf.* stadi.

ustahifu* *sing.* *see* ustahivu.

ustahiki* *sing.* worthiness, respect, honor, esteem, regard. *Cf.* haki.

ustahili* *sing.* merit, worthiness, deservingness. *Cf.* stahili.

ustahimili* *sing.* *see* ustahimilivu.

ustahimilivu*, ustahimili *sing.* perseverance, pertinacity, endurance; patience. *Cf.* hamali.

ustahivu*, ustahifu *sing.* politeness, courtesy; respect, consideration, deference; attention, attentiveness. *Cf.* stahi, stahivu.

usubi (–) gnat, sandfly.

usufi*, **usufu** *sing.*, **sufi** (–) 1. (*us.* **sufi ya mti**) kapok. 2. (*us.* **sufi ya kondoo**) wool. 3. cotton wool, wadding, swab. *Cf.* **msufi.**

usufii* *sing.* life (character, conduct, etc.) of a dervish/hermit, seclusion, retirement, solitary/lonely existence. *Cf.* **sufii.**

usufu* *sing.* wool. *Cf.* **usufi, sufi.**

usugu *sing.* 1. callousness, insensitivity. 2. stubbornness, obstinacy. 3. stupidity, folly. *Cf.* **sugua, sugu.**

usuhuba*, **usahibu** *sing.* friendship (= **urafiki**). *Cf.* **suhubiana, sahibu.**

usukani*, **uskani** (–) (*also* **sukani, ma-**) 1. *naut.* rudder. 2. *(in gen.)* steering gear, steering wheel *(of an automobile)*, handlebar *(of a bicycle, etc.)*. *Cf.* **msukani.**

usuki *sing.*, *rare* *see* **ususi.**

usukumizi *sing.* 1. urging, instigation, incitement; stimulus, encouragement. 2. roughness, rudeness. 3. abruptness, (sudden) anger, (violent) temper. *Cf.* **sukuma.**

usultani* *sing.* sultanship, sultanate. *Cf.* **sultani.**

usulubu* *sing.* *see* **sulubu.**

usuluhi*, **usuluhifu** *sing.* 1. agreement, concord. 2. mediation, reconciliation, satisfaction. *Cf.* **suluhu.**

usuluhifu* *sing.* *see* **usuluhi.**

usumba *sing.* usumba (cleaned coconut fiber, ready for use in making cord, etc.).

usumbufu *sing.* 1. annoyance, vexation. 2. disturbance, excitement, agitation. 3. *med.* irritation, inflammation. *Cf.* **sumbufu, sumbua.**

usungo *sing.* inexperience *(in matters of sex)*, lack of knowledge of tribal tradition *(on the part of young people who have not yet been initiated)*. *Cf.* **msungo.**

usununo *sing.* *see* **usononi.**

usuria* *sing.* concubinage. *Cf.* **suria.**

ususaji, ususiaji *sing.* refusal; boycott, sabotage. *Cf.* [2]**susa.**

ususi (*rare* **usuki**) *sing.* braiding, plaiting *(hair, mats)*. *Cf.* [1]**suka.**

ususiaji *sing.* *see* **ususaji.**

ususu *sing.* hall, passage, corridor.

Uswahili* *sing.* the coastal area of East Africa where Swahili is spoken as a native language. *Cf.* **Swahili, Kiswahili, Mswahili.**

uta (**nyuta**) bow (and arrows). *Cf.* **mata.**

utaa (**taa**) *dial.* utaa (platform for drying and storing grain).

utaalamu* *sing., rare* learning, education, knowledge. *Cf.* **elimu, taalamu.**

utabibu*, utibabi *sing.* (profession, methods, fees, etc. of) medicine, medical science/practice, treatment. *Cf.* **[1]tiba, [1]tibu, tabibu.**

utabiri* *sing.* soothsaying; interpretation, explanation; prediction, forecast; announcement. **– wa hewa.** weather forecasting, meteorology. *Cf.* **tabiri.**

utadi* *sing.* (*also* **tadi, –**) violation, infraction; offense, insult, rudeness; attack, aggression. *Cf.* **tadi.**

utafiti* *sing.* curiosity, inquisitiveness, indiscretion, meddling. *Cf.* **tafiti.**

utaftishi* *sing.* *see* **utafutaji.**

utafutaji*, utafutishi, utaftishi *sing.* search, investigation; research. *Cf.* **tafuta.**

utagaa *sing.* *see* **[2]taga.**

utaifa* *sing.* nationality. *Cf.* **taifa.**

utaiti* *sing., rare* poverty, need, distress. *Cf.* **[1]taiti.**

utaji* [*Pers.*] *sing.* head covering, headcloth, veil.

utajiri* *sing.* wealth, property; business enterprise, capital. *Cf.* **tajiri.**

utakalifu* *sing.* weariness, fatigue; disgust, aversion; indisposition. *Cf.* **kalifu, takalifu.**

utakaso *sing.* cleansing, purifying. *Cf.* **takata.**

utakatifu *sing.* cleanliness, purity *(literal or figurative)*; morality; *(rel.)* sanctity, holiness. *Cf.* **takata, takatifu.**

utako *sing.* 1. = tako. 2. *naut.* anchorage.

utalaleshi* *sing.* 1. slander, talebearing. 2. viciousness, corruptness, immorality. 3. lasciviousness, lust. *Cf.* **mtalaleshi.**

utalii* *sing.* tourism. *Cf.* **talii.**

utamaduni* *sing.* refinement, good taste; civilization, culture. **–a –.** cultural. **ujumbe wa –.** cultural delegation. *Cf.* **tamaduni.**

utamani* *sing.* *see* **utamanifu.**

utamanifu*, utamani *sing., rare* longing, covetousness; desire, lust(fulness). *Cf.* **tamani.**

utambaa (tambaa) 1. = **kitambaa.** 2. textiles. *Cf.* **[2]tambaa, kitambaa.**

utambazi (–) 1. crawling *(of insects, reptiles)*. 2. track, trail *(left by a snake, etc.)*. 3. *fig.* obsequiousness, servility. 4. *plur.* = **tambazi.** *Cf.* **[1]tambaa.**

¹utambi (**tambi**) 1. wick (of a lamp). 2. fuse. *Cf.* **¹tambi.**

²utambi *sing.* turban-cloth.

³utambi *sing.* *see* **²kitambi.**

utambo (–) 1. = **kitambo.** 2. = **¹tambo.** 3. handle, bail *(of a bucket, pot).*

utambulifu *sing.* *see* **utambuzi.**

utambulisho *sing.* 1. explanation *(of a problem).* 2. mark, characteristic. *Cf.* **tambua.**

utambulizi *sing.* *see* **utambuzi.**

utambuzi, utambulizi, utambulifu *sing.* 1. quickness of wit/perception, intelligence. 2. recognition, understanding. 3. intelligibility. 4. explanation, answer, solution. *Cf.* **tambua, tambuzi.**

utamu* *sing.* 1. flavor, taste. 2. sweetness. 3. candy, sweets, dessert. 4. *fig.* pleasantness, kindness, charm. *Cf.* **tamu.**

utamvua *sing.* *see* **tamvua.**

utanashati* *sing.* cleanness, neatness *(of dress).* *Cf.* **tanashati.**

utando, utandu (–) 1. something spread/stretched out. **– la buibui.** spiderweb. 2. covering, veil; film, scum, crust. **– wa macho.** a film over the eyes, clouded vision. 3. swarm *(of bees, locusts).* 4. *rare* plain. *Cf.* **tanda.**

utandu *sing.* *see* **utando.**

utanga (**tanga**) utanga (a mat on which grain is ground; = **tuguu**). *Cf.* **¹kitanga.**

utangazaji *sing.* 1. announcement, proclamation. **– wa redioni.** radio transmission/broadcasting. 2. public relations, publicity. *Cf.* **tangaa.**

utangule *sing.* utangule (strips of palm leaf, used for plaiting).

utangulizi *sing.* foreword, introduction, preface. *Cf.* **tangulia.**

utani* *sing.* 1. membership in a family/clan/race, kinship. 2. utani (familiarity, jesting, etc. permissible between persons of mtani relationship). **nimefanya – tu.** I was just joking. I didn't mean any harm. *Cf.* **tania, mtani, watani.**

utaniboi* [*Engl.*] *sing.* work (duties, pay, etc.) of a helper/assistant. *Cf.* **taniboi.**

utanzi *sing.* loop, noose, eyelet. *Cf.* **tanda, tanzi, kitanzi.**

utanzu (**tanzu** & **ma-**) *rare* branch *(of a tree).* (= **tawi.**)

utapishi *sing.* 1. vomiting. 2. emetic. *Cf.* **tapika.**

utaratibu* *sing.* *see* **taratibu.**

utari* (**tari**) string *(of a musical instrument);* cord, rope.

utarishi* *sing.* position (duties, pay, etc.) of a messenger/postman; courier service. *Cf.* **tarishi.**

utasa* *sing.* 1. sterility, barrenness. 2. *fig.* uselessness, worthlessness. *Cf.* **²tasa.**

utashi *sing.* 1. importunity, obtrusiveness. 2. (urgent) request, desire, plea, petition. **usiniletee —.** Don't press me with requests. *Cf.* **³taka.**

utasi *sing.* 1. inability/unwillingness to speak; speech defect/impediment. (= **²kitata.**) 2. = **utata** 2. *Cf.* **tata.**

utata *sing.* 1. utata (wicker fish trap). 2. *anat.* frenum *(of the tongue, etc.)*. *Cf.* **tata.**

utatu *sing.* 1. state of being triple/threefold. 2. *mus.* trio. 3. *rel.* trinity. *Cf.* **tatu.**

utawa* *sing.* 1. retirement, seclusion *(esp. of women in Moslem households)*. 2. strict morality/piety. 3. religious order. **nyumba ya —.** monastery, convent. *Cf.* **¹tawa.**

utawala*, utwala *sing.* 1. ruling, governing; reign, rule, government, administration; power. **— wa chama kimoja.** one-party rule. 2. form of government. 3. direction, management; discipline *(in a classroom, etc.)*. *Cf.* **tawala, mtawala.**

utawi (**tawi** & **ma-**) *see* **tawi.**

utaya (**taya**) *see* **taya.**

utayari* [*Pers.*] *sing.* readiness, preparedness, willingness. *Cf.* **tayari.**

ute (**mate**) thick/sticky/viscous fluid: mucus, saliva, mucilage, *etc.* **— wa yayi.** white of egg. **tema —.** expectorate.

uteatea *sing.* *see* **ucheachea.**

utegemeano *sing.* interdependence. *Cf.* **tegemea.**

uteketevu *sing.* destruction *(by fire)*. *Cf.* **teketea.**

uteketezo *sing.*, *rare* burning, destruction, damage by fire. *Cf.* **teketea.**

utelezi (**—, ma-**) slipperiness, slipping, sliding. *Cf.* **telea.**

utembe *sing.* utembe (the expectorated remains of chewed betel mixture; = **mate ya tambuu**).

utembezi (**ma-**) 1. (act, methods, etc. of) offering for sale, advertising, merchandising; advertisement. 2. walking around, loitering (= **matembezi**); *(coll.)* prostitution. 3. tourism. *Cf.* **tembea.**

utembo, utembwe *sing.* palm-leaf fiber. *Cf.* **¹kitembwe.**

utendaji *sing.* activity, energy, diligence, industry; work, performance, accomplishment, productivity. *Cf.* **tenda.**

utende *sing.*, *rare* magical powers, sorcery. *Cf.* **tenda.**

utendi *sing.* *see* **utenzi.**

utengamano *sing.* *see* **utengemano.**

utengano *sing.* separation, withdrawal; *(pol.)* division, factionalism. *Cf.* **[1]tenga.**

utengemano, utengamano *sing.* settling down, recovery *(after disorders, war);* peace, *(restored)* prosperity. **sheria na –.** law and order. *Cf.* **tengemaa.**

utengenezaji *sing.* mending, repairing, correcting; preparing, editing *(of books, etc.).* *Cf.* **tengenea.**

utengevu *sing.* accomplishment, performance, execution. *Cf.* **tengenea (tengea).**

utengo (ma-) *rare* 1. separation, withdrawal, removal. 2. shelter, refuge, hiding place. *Cf.* **[1]tenga.**

utenzi, utendi *sing.* 1. = **utendaji.** 2. (religious) poem, epic. **Utenzi wa Liongo.** the Lay of Liongo. *Cf.* **tenda.**

uteo (teo) uteo (a plaited basket or tray used for sifting grain).

utepe* [*Engl.*] **(ma-)** *see* **[1]tepe.**

utepetevu *sing.* limpness, lassitude; indifference, apathy; indolence, carelessness, negligence. *Cf.* **tepetea.**

utesaji *sing.* *see* **utesi.**

utesi, utesaji *sing.* 1. quarrelling, strife, discord. 2. annoyance, irritation, agitation; persecution. 3. distress, trouble, misfortune. *Cf.* **tesa.**

utetaji *sing.* *see* **uteto.**

utete (tete & ma-) stalk of grass, reed *(used as a pipestem or musical instrument).*

utetezi *sing.* (*also pl.* **matetezi**) 1. argumentation *(for or against);* intercession, advocacy, *(jur.)* defense; opposition, objection; obstructiveness. 2. *pol.* representative body. *Cf.* **teta.**

uteto, utetaji *sing.* 1. quarrel, dispute, debate. 2. slander, backbiting. *Cf.* **teta.**

uteuzi *sing.* 1. choice, selection. 2. selectiveness, choosiness, fastidiousness. 3. good taste. *Cf.* **teua, teuzi.**

uthabiti* *sing.* 1. firmness, strength, solidity, stability, rigidity, reliability. 2. steadfastness, courage. 3. veracity, authenticity. *Cf.* **thabiti, thibiti.**

uthubutifu* *sing.* certainty, conviction; self-confidence. *Cf.* **thabiti, thubutu.**

uthubutu* *sing.* *see* **uthabiti.**

uti (nyuti) 1. trunk, stem *(of a tree, etc.).* 2.: **– wa mgongo.** *anat.* backbone, spine. 3. shaft *(of a spear).* 4. chip, splinter, shaving. *Cf.* **[1]mti.**

utibabi* *sing.* *see* **utabibu.**

utii*, utiifu *sing.* 1. obedience, tractability, reliability. 2. discipline. 3. subservience, servility. *Cf.* **tii.**

utiifu* *sing.* *see* **utii.**

utiko (ma-) ridge *(of a thatched roof).*

utiliaji *sing.* adding, introducing, applying, supplying. *Cf.* **tia.**

utimbi *sing.* *see* **uchimvi.**

utimilifu* *sing.* completion, consummation, fulfilment, accomplishment, execution; conclusion. *Cf.* **¹timu, timilifu.**

utimvi *sing.* *see* **uchimvi.**

utingo (ma-) 1. conductor *(on a motorbus).* 2. driver's mate *(on a taxi, truck),* apprentice driver.

utiriri *sing.* elusiveness, evasion *(of an answer, difficulty).* *Cf.* **tiririka.**

utisho (–) (act of) frightening, terrifying; fright, scare, panic. **pata –.** take fright, be given a scare. *Cf.* **tisha.**

utitiri *sing.* cattle tick, chicken louse.

uto *sing.* (vegetable) oil. **mafuta ya –.** semsem oil.

utoaji, utowaji *sing.* (act of) issuing, output; publishing, publication; distribution. **– wa bidhaa.** volume of production. **ofisi ya utoaji wa habari.** office of information. **– wa maji.** distribution of water, irrigation. *Cf.* **¹toa.**

utohara* *sing.* 1. (ceremonial) purity, cleanliness (= **tohara**); *(us.)* circumcision. 2. *rare* menstruation. *Cf.* **tohara.**

utokezo (ma-) (act of) issuing; utterance, explanation; publication, appearance. *Cf.* **¹toa.**

utoko *sing.* mucus *(from the vagina).* *Cf.* **¹toa.**

utokomeaji *sing.* disappearance. *Cf.* **tokomea.**

utolewaji *sing.* issue, delivery, distribution *(of a publication, etc.).* *Cf.* **¹toa.**

utomvu *sing.* 1. juice, sap *(of a plant).* 2. mucilage, glue.

utondoti (**tondoti**) 1. an old-fashioned ornament worn by women: a necklace of many strands of copper wire from which a Maria Theresa dollar is suspended. 2. *fig., rare* repeated action, repetition.

utongo (ma-) = **matongo.**

utongozaji, utongozi *sing.* 1. immorality, lasciviousness. 2. seduction *(of a woman).* *Cf.* **tongoza.**

utongozi *sing.* *see* **utongozaji.**

utope *sing.* *see* **tope.**

utoro *sing.* 1. flight, desertion; truancy. 2. treachery, betrayal, disloyalty, apostasy. *Cf.* **toroka, mtoro.**

utosi (tosi) 1. crown (of the head); fontanel *(of an infant).* 2. *fig.* top, tip, peak.

utoto *sing.* 1. childhood, infancy, youth. 2. *fig.* youthfulness, vigor. 3. dependence. *Cf.* **mtoto.**

utotole *sing.* reward *(given for finding something lost).* *Cf.* [1]**toa** (?).

utovu *sing.* lack, want, absence. *Cf.* [2]**toa, tovu.**

utowaji *sing.* *see* **utoaji.**

utu *sing.* 1. humanity, human nature. **– ume.** manhood. **– uke.** womanhood. 2. good human qualities, goodness, kindness. **onyesha –.** show kindness/consideration. *Cf.* **mtu.**

utukufu *sing.* greatness, grandeur, glory; eminence, prominence, fame. *Cf.* **tukuka, tukufu.**

utukutu *sing.* restlessness, excitability, nervousness; fluster, haste; liveliness, exuberance; mischievousness, naughtiness *(of children).* *Cf.* **tukuta, tukutu.**

utule *sing.* poverty, need, distress, wretchedness. *Cf.* **tule.**

utulivu *sing.* rest, quiet(ness), peacefulness, composure; forbearance; carefulness, attention. **fanya kazi yako kwa –.** Do your work carefully. *Cf.* [1]**tua, tulivu.**

utuma *sing.* *see* **utume.**

utumbavu *sing.* swelling, bulging. *Cf.* **tumbua,** [1]**tumba, tumbo.**

utumbo (tumbo & ma-) 1. *(us. pl.)* intestines, entrails, viscera. 2. gut *(the substance).* *Cf.* **tumbua, tumbo.**

utumbuizi, utumbuizo *sing.* (singing of a) lullaby; (singing of a) refrain *(during the performance of a dance).* *Cf.* **tumbuika.**

utume, utuma *sing.* (act of) sending (off), dispatch; delegation, deputation. *Cf.* **tuma.**

utumi, utumiaji *sing.* *see* **utumizi.**

utumishi, utumizi *sing.* 1. position (duties, pay, etc.) of a servant; employment, service. **– wa kiaskari.** military service. 2. religious service, worship. *Cf.* **tuma.**

[1]**utumizi, utumiaji, utumi, utumo** *sing.* (*us.* **matumizi**) use, employment, utilization. **fedha ya –.** pocket money. **kitu cha –.** useful article, tool, utensil. *Cf.* **tuma.**

[2]**utumizi** *sing.* = **utumishi.**

utumo *sing.* *see* **utumizi.**

utumwa *sing.* 1. servitude, slavery, exploitation. 2. *recent* instructions, directions. **nimeutimiza/nimeufanya – wako.** I have followed your instructions/carried out your orders. *Cf.* **tuma.**

utunda (tunda) girdle of beads *(worn by women)*. (= **kondavi.**)

utundu* [*Pers.*] *sing.* 1. mischief, troublesomeness, capriciousness; mischievousness, wilfulness, precocity *(of a child)*. 2. slyness, craftiness. *Cf.* **²tundu.**

utunduizi *sing.* 1. watchfulness, alertness. 2. watching, spying. *Cf.* **tunduia.**

utungaji, utungo *sing.* (act of) putting in order, arranging, composing, compiling. **– wa sheria.** drafting of laws. *Cf.* **¹tunga.**

utungo *sing.* 1. = **utungaji.** 2. (literary) composition, essay, poem. **– wa sauti.** melody. 3. draft, plan, idea, proposal. 4. invention, fabrication, lie. 5. line, series, succession. *Cf.* **¹tunga.**

utungu *sing.* *see* **uchungu.**

utunu *sing.* rarity, value, preciousness. *Cf.* **tunuka, tunu.**

utunzaji, utunzi *sing.* (act of) caring for, tending, protecting; care, attention, protection. **– wa matunda.** care/tending of plants. *Cf.* **tunza.**

utunzi *sing.* *see* **utunzaji.**

utunzo *sing.* *see* **tunzo.**

utupa *sing.* utupa (poisonous juice of mtupa plants; *cf.* **²mtupa**).

utupu *sing.* 1. nakedness, bareness, nudity. **enda –.** go naked. 2. *fig.* simplicity, purity (= not mixed/adulterated). 3. emptiness, meaninglessness, worthlessness. 4. *coll.* genitals. *Cf.* **tupu.**

uturi* *sing.* attar, scent, perfume.

Uturuki* *sing.* Turkey. *Cf.* **Mturuki, Kituruki.**

utusitusi *sing.* *see* **uchusichusi.**

utuvu *sing.* gentleness, politeness, civility, good manners. *Cf.* **¹tua.**

utwala* *sing.* *see* **utawala.**

uuaji, uaji *sing.* murder(ousness), slaughter, massacre. *Cf.* **³ua.**

uuguzaji *sing.* *see* **uuguzi.**

uuguzi, uuguzaji *sing.* (occupation, methods, etc. of) nursing, caring for the sick. *Cf.* **ugua.**

uume, ume, uanaume *sing.* 1. masculinity, **uumeni.** on the male side. **watu hawa ni uumeni/kuumeni kwangu.** These people are relatives on my father's side. 2. *anat.* penis. (= **dhakari, mboo**). *Cf.* **¹ume.**

uumikaji, uumizi *sing.* (act/method of, fee charged for) cupping, blood-letting. *Cf.* **umika.**

uumizi *sing.* *see* **uumikaji.**

uundaji *sing.* construction, structure, organization. *Cf.* **¹unda.**

uungamaji *sing.* confession, admission, acknowledgment. *Cf.* **¹ungama.**

uunganishaji *sing.* (act of) uniting, joining, combining. *Cf.* **²unga.**

uungu *sing.* deity, divinity *(in gen.). Cf.* **mungu, umungu.**

uungwana, ungwana *sing.* 1. *rare* status of a free man *(as opp. to a slave).* 2. civilization, education, good breeding/manners. 3. friendliness, kindness, goodwill. *Cf.* **mwungwana, kiungwana.**

uunzi (ma-) building, carpentry, construction. *Cf.* **¹unda.**

uuzaji *sing.* (business of) selling, salesmanship. *Cf.* **uza, mwuzaji.**

uvi (ma-) (kind of) wasp.

uvimbe *sing.* 1. swollen condition, tumescence. 2. swelling, protuberance. 3. *fig.* distention, enlargement, expansion; inflation, exaggeration. 4. girth, circumference (= **kivimbe**). *Cf.* **vimba.**

uvimbizi *sing.* thatching *(of a house). Cf.* **vimba.**

uvinjari* *sing.* vigilance. *Cf.* **vinjari.**

uviringo *sing.* roundness, curvature, rotundity. *Cf.* **viringa, mviringo, mviringano.**

uvivu *sing.* idleness, laziness; carelessness, negligence; indifference; scorn, contempt. *Cf.* **vivu.**

uvoo *sing.* bracelet, armlet *(of ivory, beads).*

uvoteshaji* [*Engl.*] *sing.* (election) campaign. *Cf.* **votesha.**

uvuguvugu *sing.* 1. tepidity, lukewarmness. **maji haya si moto yana — tu.** This water is not hot, it is just lukewarm. 2. closeness, stuffiness *(of a room, etc.).* 3. confusion, discomposure, consternation. *Cf.* **vuguvugu.**

uvuke *sing.* *see* **mvuke.**

uvuko *sing., rare* *see* **uvushi.**

uvukuto *sing.* *see* **ufukuto.**

uvulana *sing.* 1. youth(fulness). 2. bachelorhood, life of a bachelor. **fuata mambo ya —.** live like a bachelor. *Cf.* **mvulana.**

uvuli *sing.* shade, shadiness, shadowiness. *Cf.* **kivuli, mwavuli.**

uvumba *sing.* uvumba (a fragrant gum).

uvumbi *sing.* 1. (particle of) dust. 2. dustiness. 3. *fig.* (mortal) remains. *Cf.* **vumbi, kivumbi.**

uvumbuaji, uvumbuzi *sing.* discovery, exploration. *Cf.* **vumbua.**

uvumbuzi *sing.* *see* **uvumbuaji.**

uvumi *sing.* 1. (low, indistinct) sound, noise (rumbling, humming, buzzing, murmuring). 2. *fig.* stir, sensation; approval. 3. rumor. *Cf.* **vuma.**

uvumilivu *sing.,* **vumilio (ma-)** patience, tolerance; perseverance, persistence, fortitude; gentleness, meekness, humility. *Cf.* **vuma.**

uvumo (ma-) = **uvumi 1.**

uvundo *sing.* bad smell, stink *(of bad meat, etc.). Cf.* **vunda.**

uvungu, uvurungu *sing.* 1. hollowness, vacuum. 2. cavity. *Cf.* **mvungu.**

uvunjaji, uvunjifu, uvunjo *sing.* 1. (act, manner, etc. of) breaking, destroying, wrecking. 2. destructiveness, vandalism. 3. *(result:)* wreck, ruin, ruinous state. 4. abolition, annulment. *Cf.* **vunja.**

uvunjifu, uvunjo *sing.* *see* **uvunjaji.**

uvuno (ma-) (*us.* **mavuno**) reaping, gathering, picking, harvesting; *(fig.)* make a profit. *Cf.* **vuna.**

uvunzovunzo *sing.* worn condition *(of clothing)*, state of showing much use *(a tool, etc.)*; fragility *(of something which is likely to tear or break unless carefully handled). Cf.* **vunja.**

uvurungu *sing.* *see* **uvungu.**

uvushi, uvusho, uvuko *sing.* 1. work (methods, means, pay, etc.) of a ferryman. 2. = **kivuko.** *Cf.* [2]**vua.**

uvusho *sing.* *see* **uvushi.**

uvutaji *sing.* smoking. *Cf.* **vuta.**

uvutano *sing.* (mutual) attraction/influence. **nguvu ya —.** power of attraction. *Cf.* **vuta.**

uvuto *sing.* attraction, influence. *Cf.* **vuta.**

uvuvi *sing.* (act, method, etc. of) fishing; work (pay, etc.) of a fisherman. *Cf.* [1]**vua.**

uvuvio *sing.* 1. (act of) blowing. 2. *fig.* vanity, conceit, arrogance. *Cf.* **vivia.**

uvuzi (ma-) (*us.* **mavuzi**; *also* **vuzi**) body hair *(armpits)*, pubic hair.

uvyazi *sing.* *see* **uzazi.**

uwaasi* *sing.* *see* **uasi.**

uwahi* *sing.* promptness, alacrity. *Cf.* **wahi.**

uwakala* *sing.* *see* **uwakili.**

uwakfu* *sing.* dedication, consecration. *Cf.* **wakef.**

uwakili*, uwakala *sing.* 1. representation, stewardship, agency. **simama katika —.** represent, act as the agent of. 2. (= **hati ya —**) power of attorney. 3. administration, government business. *Cf.* **wakili.**

uwalimu*, ualimu *sing.* education *(as a science)*, pedagogy. *Cf.* **elimu, mwalimu.**

uwambo (mambo) 1. = **kiwambo.** 2. cording *(of a native bedstead).* 3. pegs *(used for stretching something out, tent-pegs, etc.). Cf.* **wamba.**

uwananchi, uananchi *sing.* patriotism, nationalism. *Cf.* **mwananchi.**

uwanda, uanda (nyanda), *also* **wanda** *sing.* 1. open area, (town) square, plaza. 2. open country, plain. **— wa juu.** plateau. *Cf.* **1kiwanda.**

uwanga *sing.* starch. (= **1wanga.**)

uwanja (wanja) 1. enclosed area, court(yard). 2. *sport* (playing-)field, stadium. 3. *av.:* **— wa ndege.** landing field, airfield, airport. *Cf.* **kiwanja.**

1uwasho *sing.* lighting, illumination. *Cf.* **2waa, 1waka.**

2uwasho *sing.* irritation, inflammation. *Cf.* **wawa.**

uwasi (ma-) *see* **uasi.**

1uwati *sing., med.* skin-eruption, boil.

2uwati, uati (mbati) side-post/pole *(supporting the rafters of a native house).*

uwatu *sing.* uwatu (a kind of herb, fenugreek, *Trigonella foenum-graecum).*

uwazi *sing.* clarity, plainness, intelligibility, cogency. *Cf.* **wazi.**

uwaziri* *sing.* status (function, pay, etc.) of a minister, ministry. *Cf.* **waziri, wizara.**

uwazo *sing.* meditation, reflection; imagination, fancy. *Cf.* **waza.**

uwekaji (*rare* **weko**) **(ma-)** (act of) putting aside, saving; (bank) deposit. *Cf.* **weka.**

1uwekevu, uelekevu *sing.* power of comprehension, perceptiveness, penetration, acumen, intellect. *Cf.* **elea, elekea.**

2uwekevu, wekevu *sing.* thrift(iness), frugality, economy. *Cf.* **weka.**

1uwele (ma-, nyele) (grain of) bulrush millet. *Cf.* **2mwele.**

2uwele *sing.* *see* **uele.**

uweleko (—) *see* **mbeleko.**

uweza *sing.* *see* **uwezo.**

uwezekano *sing.* possibility, feasibility. *Cf.* **weza.**

uwezo, uweza *sing.* 1. ability, power, capacity, capability, competence, talent. **kila mtu kwa — wake.** each according to his abilities. 2. possibility, opportunity. **sina —.** I have no opportunity. 3. energy, intensity. 4. supreme power *(of the state). Cf.* **weza.**

uwili *sing.* doubleness, duality. *Cf.* **wili.**

uwima *sing.* uprightness, verticality, perpendicularity. *Cf.* **wima.**

uwimbi (wimbi) (single grain of a variety of) millet *(used for making beer). Cf.* **mtama.**

uwinda *sing.* 1. = **uwindaji.** 2. *anat.* perineum. 3. = **ubinda.**

uwindaji, uwinda (*rare* **uwinzi**) *sing.* (occupation, methods, equipment, pay, etc. of) hunting. *Cf.* **2winda.**

uwindo (ma-) (*us.* **mawindo**) what is obtained by hunting; prey, bag, booty, quarry. *Cf.* **2winda.**

uwingu (mbingu) 1. sky, heavens, firmament. 2. clouding, cloudiness. *Cf.* **wingu.**

uwinja, ubinja (mbinja, winja), *also* **kibinja (vi-)** whistle. **piga —.** to whistle.

uwinzi *sing.* *see* **uwindaji.**

uwivi *sing.* *see* **wivi.**

uwivu *sing.* *see* **wivu.**

uwizi *sing.* *see* **wizi.**

uwongo, wongo, uongo, urongo *sing.* 1. lie, falsehood, untruth. 2. deception, fraud; pretence, dissimulation. 3. illusion, delusion. 4. falsity, spuriousness. **kiapo cha —.** perjury. *Cf.* **1wongo, ongopa, 2mwongo.**

uya *dial.* come back, return. (= **rudi.**)

uyabisi* *sing.* 1. dryness, hardness *(of the soil, etc.).* 2. dry, hot climate. 3. drought. 4. *fig.* roughness, rudeness; reserve, taciturnity. *Cf.* **yabisi.**

uyoga (nyoga), *also* **kiyoga (vi-) & yoga (ma-)** fungus, mushroom, toadstool.

Uyunani* *sing.* (ancient) Greece. *Cf.* **Kiyunani, Myunani.**

uza sell, vend, offer for sale. *appl.* **uzia.** *intr.* **uzika.** be for sale. *appl.-ass.* **uziana.** sell to each other. *caus.-ass.* **uzanya.** be for sale. *pass.* **uzwa.** *Cf.* **mwuzaji.**

uzalishaji *sing.* *see* **uzazi.**

uzalishi *sing.* 1. = **uzazi.** 2.: **hospitali ya —.** maternity hospital. *Cf.* **zaa.**

uzandiki* *sing.* deceit, hypocrisy, cunning. *Cf.* **zandiki, mzandiki.**

uzani*, wizani, winzani *sing.* weighing, weight. *Cf.* **mizani.**

uzanya *caus.-ass. of* **uza.**

uzao (ma-) 1. product, production. 2. progeny, offspring. 3. descent, extraction *(through 5 or 6 generations).* *Cf.* **zaa.**

uzazi, uvyazi, uzalishaji *sing.* 1. reproduction, procreation, propagation. **tumbo/mji la/wa —.** womb. 2. childbirth, delivery, confinement; *(fig.)* birthday. 3. descent, parentage. 4. *(degree of)* kinship, relationship. 5. fertility. **kosa (kuwa na) —.** be sterile (fertile). *Cf.* **zaa.**

uzee *sing.* old age, senility. *Cf.* **zee, mzee.**

uzembe *sing.* idleness, laziness; carelessness, negligence; indifference; contempt. *Cf.* **zembe, kizembe, mzembe.**

uzi (nyuzi) 1. thread, yarn. **sokota —.** spin. 2. string, cord. **— wa timazi.** plumbline *(used by masons).* 3. wire. **— wa chuma.** iron wire. **— wa simu.** telegraph wire. 4.: **nyuzi** (*also* **nyuzinyuzi**) threads, fibers. **—a nyuzinyuzi.** fibrous.

uzima *sing.* 1. life, vitality; health, vigor, energy. 2. *rare* lifetime. **— wote.** one's entire lifetime. 3. full development, maturity, adulthood. 4. *fig.* completeness, perfection. 5. *fig.* existence, reality. *Cf.* ²**zima, mzima.**

uzimbezimbe *sing.* slackness, weakness; uselessness, worthlessness; impotence. *Cf.* **zembe.**

uzindusho *sing., rare* warning, admonition. *Cf.* **zindua.**

uzinge (ma-) (iron) armband, bracelet. *Cf.* **zinga.**

uzingo, uzungo *sing.* roundness, something round; encirclement, *(astr.)* orbit. *Cf.* **zinga, zungua.**

uzini* *sing.* *see* **uzinzi.**

uzinifu* *sing.* (sexual) immorality, lechery, lasciviousness. *Cf.* **zini, zinifu.**

uzinzi*, uzini *sing.* illicit sexual intercourse, fornication, adultery. (= **zinaa.**) *Cf.* **zini.**

uzio (nyuzio) fish trap.

uzishi (ma-) (*us.* **mazishi**) (act, method, cost, etc. of) burying, burial, interment. *Cf.* **zika.**

uzito *sing.* 1. heaviness, weight. 2. *fig.* difficulty, trouble; sorrow, depression. 3. slowness, slackness; carelessness, stupidity. 4. harshness, severity. 5. *coll.* pregnancy. *Cf.* **zito.**

uziwa *sing., rare* sea, ocean. *Cf.* ¹**ziwa.**

uziwi *sing.* *see* **ukiziwi.**

uzohari* *sing.* hastiness, overhaste, rush *(in working, etc.).*

uzua* *see* **uzulu.**

uzuhali* *sing.* 1. friendliness, obligingness. 2. gentleness, delicacy.

uzuiaji, uzuwiaji, uzuizi, uzuio, uzuivu *sing.* 1. (act of) hindering, checking, obstructing; hindrance, obstacle, check. 2. *med.* prophylaxis. *Cf.* **zuia.**

uzuio, uzuivu, uzuizi *sing.* *see* **uzuiaji.**

uzuka *sing.* state of mourning/seclusion *(of a widow after her husband's death).* *Cf.* **zua,** ¹**zuka.**

uzulu*, uzuru, uzua 1. remove *(from a position),* dismiss, discharge, depose; reduce in rank, demote. *appl.* **uzulia.** *intr.* **uzulika.** *caus.* **uzulisha.** *pass.* **uzuliwa.** *refl.* **jiuzulu.** resign, retire, abdicate. 2. (ma-) removal, dismissal, discharge, deposition; abdication, resignation.

uzungo *sing.* *see* **uzingo.**

¹**uzungu** *sing.* strangeness, unusualness, novelty, peculiarity. **anapenda —.** He has a fondness for the novel/unusual. *Cf.* **zungu.**

²**Uzungu** *sing.* Europe. *Cf.* **zungu, Kizungu,** ²**Mzungu.**

uzuri *sing.* 1. beauty, elegance. 2. decoration, ornament; cosmetic(s). *Cf.* [1]zuri.

uzuru* *see* **uzulu.**

uzushi, uzuzi *sing.* 1. appearance, emergence. 2. discovery, invention; innovation, novelty. 3. rumor, gossip. **ni – mtupu.** That is a pure fabrication. *Cf.* **zua,** [2]**zuka.**

uzuwiaji *sing.* *see* **uzuiaji.**

uzuzi *sing.* *see* **uzushi.**

uzuzu *sing.* 1. ignorance, inexperience, strangeness *(to a place, etc.)*. 2. embarrassment, perplexity. *Cf.* **zuzu.**

V

vaa dress, get dressed, put on *(clothes)*. **amevaa nguo ya kisasa.** She wears up-to-date clothes. *appl.* **valia.** dress oneself in something, put on something; dress elegantly/ fashionably. **amevalia leo.** He is wearing his best clothes today. *pass.* **valiwa.** 1. be worn/shabby *(of things)*. 2. be dressed *(of persons)*. *caus.* **visha, valisha, vika.** dress someone. **mvike mtoto nguo!** Dress the child! *inv.* **vua.** 1. undress, get undressed, strip. 2. *fig.* rob, plunder. *inv.-appl.* **vulia.** *inv.-pass.* **vuliwa.** *inv.-intr.* **vuka.** *inv-caus.* **vulisha.** make someone undress. *inv.-ass.* **vuana.** *Cf.* **valio, vao, vazi, vulio, kivazi, mavalio, mavazi, mvao, mviko,** [1]**mvuo.**

valia *appl. of* **vaa.**

valio (ma-) ornament, accoutrement, accessory. *Cf.* **vaa.**

valisha *caus. of* **vaa.**

vama lie (heavy) on, weigh down on; cut into *(e.g., of a tight cord)*, go in deep, penetrate *(as a plant into the soil)*. *appl.* **vamia.** 1. = **vama.** 2. pounce on (someone). **simba amemvamia.** The lion pounced on him.

vao (ma-) 1. clothing. 2. style of clothing/ dressing. *Cf.* **vaa.**

varanga (–) *rare* noise, din, confused sound of voices. *us. red.:* **varangavaranga.** interrupt, butt in on a conversation; introduce a discordant note into a previously enjoyable conversation.

vazi (ma-) (*us.* **mavazi**) 1. clothing, garment, apparel, attire, costume. **mavazi ya arusi.** wedding apparel. 2. *mil.* uniform. 3.: **mavazi ya misa.** *rel.* vestments. *Cf.* **vaa.**

vema, vyema *adv.* well, properly, correctly. *Cf.* [1]**ema.**

vena* [*Engl.*] (–) *anat.* vein.

vepa* [*Engl.*] (–) vapor, steam; exhaust fumes. (= **mvuke.**)

v.h. *abbr. of* **vivi hivi, vivyo hivyo.**

via 1. be undeveloped/stunted/atrophied *(used of anything which has not reached the state normally expected).* **mguu wake umevia.** His leg is withered/deformed. **chakula kimevia.** The food is underdone. 2. stand still, stagnate, congeal. *appl.* **vilia.** stagnate, congeal. **damu imevilia ndani.** The blood has congealed. *caus.* **viza.** check the development of something, impede, interrupt, retard. **kuku huyu ameviza mayai yote.** This hen lays only addled eggs. *caus.-appl.* **vizia.** 1. spoil, frustrate, thwart, balk; impede, stunt. 2. waylay, ambush, be 'out to get' someone, harass. *Cf.* **vilio, ²viza, mviziaji.**

vibaya *adv.* badly, wickedly. *Cf.* **baya.**

viboko *plur.* fancywork, fine embroidery. *Cf.* **²kiboko.**

vidondo *plur.* kindling.

vifaa *plur.* necessaries, (personal) belongings; material(s), utensils; commodities. *Cf.* **faa, kifaa.**

vifijo *plur.* whistling, shouts *(of approval),* applause.

vigumu *adv.* hardly, with difficulty. **ni vigumu kusadiki mambo hayo.** It is hard to believe those things. *Cf.* **gumu.**

vijimea *pl.* (*dimin. of* **mmea**) bacteria.

vijiwe *plur., med.* acne. *Cf.* **kiwe.**

vika *caus. of* **vaa.**

viko *loc., pl.* they are there.

vikope *plur.:* **ana –.** He has bleary eyes. *Cf.* **³kope, kikope.**

vikorokoro *pl.* goods, chattels, belongings; utensils, appurtenances. *Cf.* **kikorokoro, makolokolo.**

vile 1. *dem. pron.,* vi- *class.* those. **vitu –.** those things. 2. *adv.* (*also* **vile vile**) also, too; likewise, in the same way. **mwite Ali vile vile.** Call Ali too. **shati hili lishone vile vile.** Sew this shirt in the same way. **fanya vile vile.** follow suit.

vilia *appl. of* **via.**

vilio (ma-) *(us. pl.)* stoppage, stagnation. **– la damu.** bruise, contusion. *Cf.* **via.**

¹vimba swell, swell up, expand, be swollen. **kidole nilichojiumiza kimevimba.** The finger that I hurt is swollen. *appl.* **vimbia.** be swollen/bloated/stuffed; have digestive difficulties. *caus.* **vimbisha.** *caus-refl.* **jivimbisha.** overeat. *pass.* **vimbiwa. amekula mpaka akavimbiwa.** He has eaten so much that he has stomach trouble. *Cf.* **vimbizi, kivimbe, uvimbe.**

²vimba, fimba roof/thatch *(a house).* (= **ezeka.**) *inv.* **vimbua.** remove thatch. (= **ezua.**)

vimbizi (**ma-**) overeating, stomach pains *(from overeating)*. *Cf.* **¹vimba.**

vimo *auxil. v. det.* vi- *class* be in something.

vimoto *adv.* heatedly, hastily, energetically, excitedly. **sema –.** talk excitedly/fast. *Cf.* **¹moto.**

vingi 1. *see* **ingi.** 2. *adv.* in great numbers, in abundance.

vingine 1. *see* **ingine.** 2. *adv.* (**kwa –**) differently, otherwise, in another way, variously.

vinginevyo 1. *see* **ingine.** 2. *adv.* differently, otherwise, in some other way, specially.

vinginyika *see* **finginyika.**

vingirika *see* **fingirika.**

vinjari* 1. go back and forth; loiter/loaf around; have nothing to do, be unemployed. (= **tangatanga.**) **mbona unavinjari hapa?** Why do you keep walking up and down here? 2. *naut.* cruise. **manowari ya kuvinjari.** cruiser. 3. be on the watch, search. *Cf.* **uvinjari.**

vinya, vinyavinya 1. shake, swing, rock. 2. crush, mash *(food)*. 3. move back and forth, wag, quiver. *Cf.* **kivinyovinyo.**

vinyavinya *see* **vinya.**

vipele *pl.* rash *(on the skin)*. (= **ukurutu.**) *Cf.* **kipele.**

vipi *see* **pi.**

vipo *auxil. v. det.* vi- *class* they are there.

vipwa *pl.* reef, sandbank. *Cf.* **pwa, kipwa.**

viringa, biringa 1. roll up, wind up. **– uzi katika kidonge.** wind thread on a ball. 2. become round, be rounded/curved. *intr.* **viringika.** *ass.* **viringana.** 1. be round. 2. *fig.* be healthy/well nourished. *caus.* **viringisha.** 1. make round, round off. 2. twist something around. *Cf.* **mviringano, mviringo, uviringo.**

¹virugu *pl.* 1. anger, excitement. 2. roughness *(of the skin)*.

²virugu *pl. of* **kirugu.**

visha *caus. of* **vaa.**

vita (*rare* **zita**) (**–**) 1. war, battle. 2. *fig.* contest, dispute. **piga/fanya –.** make war, wage a war. **leta –.** attack, raid, invade. **alika –.** challenge to battle, declare war. **– vya kienyeji.** civil war. **– kuu (kubwa) ya pili duniani.** the Second World War. **mchezo wa –.** maneuver. **ngoma ya kivita.** war dance. *Cf.* **kivita.**

vitakataka *pl.* trifles, odds and ends, miscellany. **ana biashara ya – tu.** He carries on only a small retail business. *Cf.* **¹taka.**

vitamini [*Engl.*] (–) vitamin.

vitio *pl.* growth or swelling on the genitals. (= **kisukumi.**)

vitumbuizo *pl.* entertainment. *Cf.* **tumbuika.**

vivi *adv.* – **hivi.** just so, in this very way.

vivia, vuvia 1. blow *(with the mouth),* blow up. 2. *coll.* cheat, swindle, dupe. *Cf.* **uvuvio.**

vivinyuka *see* **finginyuka.**

vivu *adj.* 1. slow, idle, lazy; careless; languorous, indifferent, apathetic. 2. dull, blunt (= **butu**). *Cf.* **kivivu, mvivu, uvivu.**

vivyo *adv.:* – **hivyo.** in just the same way (as before).

1viza *caus. of* **via.**

2viza *adj. & n.* (ma-): **yai (la)** –, – **la yai.** spoiled/addled egg. *Cf.* **via.**

vizuri *adv.* nicely, beautifully; properly, correctly. *Cf.* **zuri.**

vokali* [*Germ.*] (–) vowel.

voliboli* [*Engl.*] (–) volleyball.

volkeno* [*Engl.*] (–) volcano.

volta* [*Engl.*] (–) *elec.* volt, voltage.

vongonya, vungunya (ma-) vongonya (fruit of the mvongonya, *q.v.*).

vote* [*Engl.*] *rare* vote (= **kura**). *Cf.* **votesha, uvoteshaji.**

votesha* [*Engl.*] get out the vote, conduct an election campaign. *Cf.* **vote.**

1vua (*or* – **samaki**) fish, (try to) catch fish. – **kwa mshipi.** fish with a line (or trap). *appl.* **vulia. ndoana ya kuvulia.** fishhook. *Cf.* **vuo, 2mvuo, mvuvi, uvuvi.**

2vua save, keep, preserve, get/keep out of trouble. *intr.* **vuka.** 1. be saved/preserved; escape. 2. pass (safely) through; cross, pass over, be ferried across. **vuka mto katika ngalawa.** cross a stream in an outrigger canoe. *fig.* **nimevuka katika taabu hii.** I have overcome these difficulties. *caus.* **vusha** & *intr.-caus.* **vukisha.** cause to cross, ferry over. *Cf.* **kivuko, mvuko, mvushaji, uvushi.**

3vua bail *(water out of a boat;* = **2kumba**).

4vua *inv. of* **vaa.**

5vua: – **macho.** cast a glance, raise the eyes.

vuata put/hold in the mouth; chew tobacco.

vuaza 1. cut, pierce. 2. *fig.* hurt, cause pain. **amevuazwa na kisu.** He has been cut with a knife. **maneno haya yamemvuaza sana.** These words hurt/offended him very much (cut him to the quick).

vue (—, **ma-**) clump/thicket of long grass.

vugaza *dial.* close partially, put to, leave ajar *(a door).*

vugo (**ma-**) vugo (a kind of horn, musical instrument).

vuguta *dial.* = **vukuta.**

vuguvugu *adj.* lukewarm, tepid; stuffy *(of a room). Cf.* **uvuguvugu.**

vuja leak, ooze *(of a liquid);* be leaky, let in water *(of a roof, wall). appl.* **vujia.** *intr.* **vujika.** *appl.-pass.* **vujiwa. leo nimevujiwa.** It rained in on me today.

[1]**vuka** *see* [1]**fuka.**

[2]**vuka** *intr. of* [2]**vua.**

[3]**vuka** *inv.-intr. of* **vaa.**

vuke (**ma-**) *see* **mvuke.**

vukizo (**ma-**) *see* **fukizo.**

vukuta, fukuta (*dial.* **vuguta**) blow/work bellows. *Cf.* [2]**mvua.**

vukuto (**ma-**) *see* **fukuto, mfukuto.**

vuli *sing.* vuli (the short rainy season: November and December in Zanzibar).

vulio (**ma-**) something laid aside or cast off: cast-off clothing; the sloughed-off skin of a snake. *Cf.* **vaa.**

vulisha *inv.-caus. of* **vaa.**

vuma 1. roar, growl, howl *(wind, water, wild animals);* hum, buzz *(insects);* roll, rumble *(thunder).* 2. *fig.* be a subject of conversation/the talk of the town. 3. work hard *(carpenters, etc.).* 4. lose at cards. *double appl.* **vumilia.** endure, tolerate, put up with; persevere. *intr.* **vumika.** be much talked about/famous/notorious. *caus.* **vumisha.** 1. make a noise, cause a commotion. 2. cause to be talked about, make well-known/famous. 3. win at cards. *Cf.* **vumi, vumilivu, kivumi, mvumi,** [1]**mvumo, uvumi, uvumilivu.**

vumatiti, mvumatiti (—) 1. vumatiti (species of owl). 2. *med.* convulsions *(of children).*

vumba (**ma-**) (bad) smell of fish.

vumbi (**ma-**) (*also* **fumbi,** —) 1. dust, sweepings; sediment *(in water).* **chumba – tele.** The room is very dusty. 2. powder. 3. chaff. 4. *phys.* particle. *Cf.* **kivumbi, uvumbi.**

vumbika 1. cover up, hide, conceal. 2. bury fruit for ripening. **ndizi hizi hazikuiva zenyewe, ni ndizi za kuvumbika.** These bananas did not ripen naturally, they were artificially ripened. 3. bake (*potatoes, etc.).* 4. *fig.* keep close to home, confine to the house. *double appl.* **vumbilia.** stir up, excite, provoke *(trouble, war). Cf.* **vumbua.**

vumbu (**ma-**) lump *(in flour, rice).*

vumbua, zumbua uncover, bring to light; study, examine; find, invent, discover; explore. **– nchi.** explore a country. **– vita.** begin war. *appl.* **vumbulia.** *intr.* **vumbuka.** *caus.* **vumbusha.** *Cf.* **[1]fumba, vumbika.**

vumburuka be startled *(of a sleeping animal). caus.* **vumburusha.** startle, start up, scare.

vumi, vumo (ma-) a dull/indistinct/rumbling noise: roar, growl, rumble, hum, buzz. *Cf.* **vuma.**

vumilia (*double appl. of* **vuma**) endure, tolerate, put up with; persevere. *Cf.* **vumilivu, uvumilivu.**

vumilio (ma-) *see* **uvumilivu.**

vumilivu *adj.* patient, forbearing; steadfast, courageous. *Cf.* **vuma.**

vumo (ma-) *see* **vumi.**

vuna, funa 1. gather, pick, reap, harvest. **– matunda.** pick fruit. 2. *fig.* gain, profit, derive an advantage. *refl.* **jivuna.** boast, brag, be conceited/insolent. *Cf.* **kivuno, majivuno, mavuno, mvunaji, uvuno.**

vunda spoil, sour, decompose, be high *(of meat)*; stink. *caus.* **vundisha** & *intr.-int.* **vundikiza.** cause decomposition, produce a bad smell/stench. *Cf.* **vunde, kivunde, uvundo.**

vunde 1. (ma-) something decomposed/putrid/stinking; meat that has become high. 2.: **vundevunde** *adj.* cloudy, overcast. *Cf.* **vunda.**

vundevunde *adj.* *see* **vunde.**

vunga, vunge (ma-) bunch, bundle, bale. *Cf.* **kivunga.**

vungavunga 1. break up/into small pieces, crumble. **– mkate.** crumble up bread. 2. crumple, rumple, wrinkle *(clothing)*. **– nguo.** wrinkle up a garment. 3. confuse, perplex.

vunge (ma-) *see* **vunga.**

vungu *adj.* hollow, concave. *Cf.* **mvungu.**

vungunya (ma-) *see* **vongonya.**

vunja 1. break (*in gen.:* up, through, into, to pieces, *etc.*). 2. tear down, demolish; spoil, damage, destroy. **– nyumba.** pull down a house. 3.: **– ungo.** reach puberty, menstruate for the first time. 4. *fig.* interrupt, delay. **– safari.** interrupt a journey. 5. diminish, reduce. **– mapesa.** change money. 6. unfold. **– kilemba.** take off a turban. 7. *fig.:* **– moyo.** discourage, dishearten, intimidate. 8. *fig.:* **– uso.** humiliate, insult publicly. *appl.* **vunjia, vunjilia.** *appl.-pass.* **vunjiwa. vunjiwa mwiko.** violate a taboo. *intr.* **vunjika.** *Cf.* **vunjifi, vunjifu, kivunjavunja, kivunjo, mvunja, mvunjaji, mvunjo, uvunjaji, uvunzovunzo.**

vunjajungu (–) *see* **kivunjavunja.**

vunjifi *adj.* broken, ruined, destroyed. *Cf.* **vunja.**

vunjifu *adj.* destructive. *Cf.* **vunja.**

vunjilia *appl. of* **vunja.**

vuno **(ma-)** *see* **mavuno.**

[1]**vuo** **(ma-)** catch *(of fish).* (= [2]**mvuo** 2.) *Cf.* [1]**vua.**

[2]**vuo** (–) vuo (a medicine prepared from various roots and herbs for use in a vapor bath or for inhalation).

vura pull/take out *(of a bundle).*

vuru, vuruvuru *adv.* with a humming/whirring sound *(e.g., of a spinning top).*

vuruga, vurugavuruga 1. stir, stir up, mix. **– maji.** stir up/trouble water. **– mkate.** crumble bread. 2. disarrange, disorganize, create disorder; rumple, wrinkle. **– nguo.** wrinkle a dress. 3. *fig.* stir up, excite, incite, agitate. *intr.* **vurugika.** 1. be stirred up/mixed. 2. be decayed/decomposed. *ass.* **vurugana.** *Cf.* **mavurugano, mavurugo, mvurugaji, mvurugu, vuruguvurugu;** *also* **buruga.**

vurugavuruga *see* **vuruga.**

vuruguvurugu **(ma-)** disorder, confusion. *Cf.* **vuruga.**

vuruma 1. = **vuruga.** 2. *caus.* **vurumisha, vurumiza.** throw (away), hurl (a long distance); *(fig.)* send (far) away. **vurumisha jiwe.** throw a stone. **fulani amevurumishwa mbali sana.** X. has been sent a long way off. *refl.-caus.* **jivurumisha.** put on airs, boast, brag.

vurumai **(ma-)** *rare* disorder, destruction, chaos.

vuruvuru *see* **vuru.**

vusha *cause. of* [2]**vua.**

vuta 1. draw, pull, drag. **– makasia.** row *(a boat).* **– gari.** pull a wagon. **– tumbako (sigara, bangi).** smoke tobacco (a cigarette, hashish). **– pumzi.** inhale, take a deep breath. **– mtambo wa bunduki.** pull the trigger of a gun. **– maji.** draw water. 2. stretch, prolong, protract. **– maneno.** protract a speech. 3. *fig.* attract, fascinate; influence. **mkutano umevuta watu wengi sana.** The meeting attracted a great many people. **– macho.** attract attention. *appl.* **vutia. vutia roho.** struggle for breath. *ass.* **vutana.** *Cf.* **mvuta, mvuto, uvutano, uvuto, uvutaji.**

vuvi (–) vuvi (a large snake).

vuvia *see* **vivia.**

vuvumka develop well, grow fast, thrive *(of children, plants).* *caus.* **vuvumsha.** encourage growth or development, feed well, fatten *(animals).*

vuvuwaa 1. be lukewarm/tepid. 2. be silent/taciturn/reserved. 3. have no opinions of one's own.

vuzi (ma-) (*us.* navuzi) body hair *(armpits, pubic; cf.* laika).

vya *conn.* vi- *class:* vidole – mkono. the fingers of the hand.

vyaa *dial.* *see* zaa.

vyake *see* -ake.

vyako *see* -ako.

vyakula *pl. of* chakula.

vyamba *pl. of* 1chamba.

vyambo *pl. of* chambo.

vyanda *pl. of* 2chanda.

vyangu *see* –angu.

vyao *see* –ao.

vyaro *pl. of* charo.

vyema *see* vema.

vyenu *see* -enu.

vyeo *pl.* 1. *see* cheo. 2.: – vya juu katika elimu. the highest academic rank.

vyero (–) fish trap.

vyeti* [*Ind.*] *pl. of* cheti.

vyetu *see* -etu.

vyo *det.* vi- *class* – vyote. whatever (you please).

vyoga step/tread/stamp on, trample, crush. *appl.* vyogea. *intr.* vyogeka.

vyombo *pl. of* chombo.

vyoo *pl. of* choo.

vyote *see* –ote.

vyuma *pl.* 1. *see* 1chuma. 2. *coll.* money.

vyuo *pl. of* 1chuo, 2chuo.

vyura *pl. of* 1chura.

W

1**wa** 1. be, become, exist. – na... be with... (= have). – na imani. have confidence. – na kazi. have work. – na shaka. have doubt. – na shida. have difficulty. – na umoja. agree. – sawasawa na. be the same as, match, correspond. 2. happen, occur. palikuwa, alikuwako, palikuwako. once upon a time *(at the beginning of tales). appl.* wia, wea. 1. give someone something. uniwie radhi! Excuse me! 2. be ... to (a person). mambo haya yataniwia magumu. These things will be very hard on me. *See also sub* wea, wia. *pass.* wiwa.

2wa* *conj., rare* and.

3wa *conn.* m-/wa- *cl.* **mwalimu – darasa.** the teacher of the class. **watu – mji.** the people of the city. **mfuko – mke.** the woman's purse. **uzito – mzigo.** the heaviness of the burden.

1waa (ma-) (*also* **kiwaa, vi-**) 1. spot, speck, patch *(of color).* **nyama mwenye –.** spotted/speckled animal. 2. *fig.* stain, blot, blemish, stigma. 3. indication, characteristic, criterion.

2waa shine, gleam; blaze, burn, flame. *Cf.* **1waka, maawio;** *also* **wawa.**

waadhi*, widhaa (–) (*also* **maudhia**) *rare* sermon, speech.

waaidha* *see* **aidha.**

waama* *conj.* afterwards, then; further, moreover.

waana *pl. of* **mwana.**

waba* (–) *rare* pestilence (*us.* cholera). (= **1kipindupindu.**)

wabadahu* *conj., rare* and now *(introducing the body of a letter, after the salutation).*

wadhifa* (–) *rare* position, job.

1wadi* (–) *rare* son. **– Ali.** son of Ali. *arch.* **wadinasi.** a well-born man (the son of free parents).

2wadi* (–) *rare* wadi (dry stream-bed); ravine, defile.

3wadi* 1. (*us. appl.* **wadia**) be high time to... **saa yake ya kusafiri imewadia.** It is high time for him to start on his journey. 2. (–) appointed time, proper time *(to leave).*

wafiki* be suitable/appropriate, agree, correspond, be the same. *appl.* **wafikia.** *ass.* **wafikiana.** be equivalent/synonymous. *Cf.* **afiki.**

wahabu* *sing., liter.* god of love.

wahadi* (–) *see* **ahidi.**

wahed* *see* **wahedi.**

wahedi*, wahed *num., rare* one. (= **moja.**)

wahedu* *adv.* only, solely.

wahi* 1. be on time, be prompt; reach, arrive (on time, at the right time). **alitaka kuwahi gari la moshi.** He wanted to reach the train at the right time. 2. be ready (to do something). **aliwahi kufanya kazi.** He was ready to work. *appl.* **wahia.** *pass.* **wahiwa.** *Cf.* **uwahi.**

waima*, waina *conj., rare* if not, otherwise.

wajadili* (–) *rare* opposition.

wajibia* *appl. of* **wajibu.**

wajibu* 1. *sing.* duty, responsibility, task, obligation; proper behavior *(us. in a moral sense).* **ni – wako kuwaheshimu wazee wako.** It is your (moral) duty to respect your parents. 2. *v.* be a duty, be obligatory/proper. *appl.* **wajibia.** *caus.* **wajibisha.** obligate, force, compel. *Cf.* **mjibu, mujibu.**

wajihi* 1. appear; meet *(face to face)*, present oneself; go to see, visit; greet, salute. *appl.* **wajihia.** *ass.* **wajihiana.** meet (each other) face to face. 2. *sing.* (external) appearance, exterior, surface. **– wa mtu (kitu).** the appearance of a person (thing). 3. *sing.* visit, reception.

wajomba *plur.* wajomba (one's male relatives on one's mother's side). *Cf.* **mjomba.**

[1]**waka** 1. burn, catch fire, be in flames. **mti unawaka upesi.** Wood catches fire quickly. *fig., elec.* **taa inawaka.** The lamp is turned on. 2. shine, gleam. 3. *fig.* be inflamed, be painful. 4. *fig.* be excited/angry. *appl.* **wakia.** catch fire (accidentally). *caus.* **washa.** cause to burn, set fire to, light; *(fig.)* turn on (an electric light); start (an automobile); cause pain, sting, hurt. **dawa hii katika kidonda inawasha sana.** This medicine burns/stings very much in the wound. *Cf.* [2]**waa, wawa,** [1]**mwako, mwasha,**[1]**uwasho.**

[2]**waka** 1. = **aka.** 2. lay a floor (of hard-packed earth or cement) in a house.

wakaa* (–) *see* **wasaa.**

wakala* (–) representation; proxy, power of of attorney; appointment; agency. *Cf.* **wakili.**

wakati* (**nyakati**) 1. time *(in gen.)*, period, season. **– wa mavuno.** harvest time. **– wa kulala.** bedtime. **– wa alasiri.** during the afternoon. **– huu.** (during) this time. **– ule.** at that time, then. **– ujao (upitao).** the future (past). 2. point of time, fixed time, moment. **– haujafika bado.** It is not yet the right time/moment. 3. chance, opportunity. **huu ni – wako, angalia!** Watch out, this is your chance!

wake *see* **-ake.**

wakef*, wakf, wakfu, wakifu (–) *Isl.* 1. endowment *(land, money)* made to a mosque, trust, settlement. **weka –.** make an endowment/bequest (to a mosque). 2.: **– ya makaburi.** a burial plot acquired during one's lifetime. 3. *rel.* consecration. **weka –.** consecrate. *Cf.* **uwakfu.**

wakf* (–) *see* **wakef.**

wakfu* (–) *see* **wakef.**

wakia* (–) ounce (unit of weight: one-sixteenth of a ratli).

[1]**wakifu*, akifu** 1. stop, curb, limit *(prices, etc.)*, have a fixed price. 2. refuse, reject. *appl.* **wakifia.** estimate, evaluate, fix the price *(to charge someone). caus.* **wakifisha.** prevent, stop; reduce.

[2]**wakifu*** (–) *see* **wakef.**

wakili* 1. represent, act as representative/agent. *appl.* **wakilia.** *caus.* **wakilisha.** appoint as representative/agent/deputy, empower, authorize, commission. 2. **(ma-)** representative, agent, deputy; *(jur.)* attorney, lawyer; *(pol.)* representative, delegate; *(pl.)* agency. **– wa kutoa habari.** news agency. *Cf.* **wakala, mawakili, tawakali, uwakili.**

wakina* **(–)** *see* **akina.**

¹wako *see* **-ako.**

²wako *auxil. v. det.* 1. they are there. 2. he (she, it) is there.

wakwe *pl.* parents-in-law. *Cf.* **mkwe.**

wala* *conj.* and not, but not, nor. **wala ... wala.** neither ... nor. **Hakuweza kusema – Kiingereza – Kifaransa.** He could speak neither English nor French.

walahi* *interj.* really, indeed. **– nitakwenda.** I will indeed go.

walakini* *conj.* but, however, nevertheless, notwithstanding. *Cf. also* **lakini.**

walau*, alau 1. *adv.* even, at least, at any rate, anyhow. 2. *conj., rare* although.

wale *dem. pron.* **wa-** *cl.* those. **watu –.** those people.

¹wali* *sing.* (cooked) rice. **– kwa nyama (mchuzi)** rice with meat (curry).

²wali* **(ma-)** *see* **liwali.**

walii* **(ma-)** *Isl.* saint.

¹walio (nyalio) *see* **¹nyalio 2.**

²walio (nyalio) *see* **¹nyalio 1.**

³walio (nyalio) welt, weal, scar.

wallahi!*, wallai! *interj.* By God!

wallai!* *see* **wallahi!**

wama (*us. appl.* **wamia**) 1. lie down on one's stomach. 2. bend over something *(e.g., a fire).*

wamba 1. spread/stretch over, cover. **– ngoma.** cover a drum with a skin. 2. be cloudy/overcast/foggy. **ukungu umewamba.** It is foggy. *appl.* **wambia.** *caus.* **wambisha.** *Cf.* **kiambaza, kiwambo, mwambo, uwambo;** *also* **²amba.**

wambe *sing.* dust from threshing/winnowing grain.

wambiso *sing.* adherence, attachment. *Cf.* **²amba.**

wamevinjari *pl.* the unemployed. *Cf.* **vinjari, mvinjari.**

wamia *appl. of* **wama.**

¹wana *auxil. v.* **wa-** *class* they have. **– nyumba nzuri.** They have pretty houses.

[2]wana *pl. of* **mwana.**

wanaume (*pl. of* **mwanamume**) male sex, menfolk.

wanawake (*pl. of* **mwanamke**) female sex, womenfolk.

[1]wanda (**nyanda**) 1. *arch.* finger. (= **kidole.**) 2. the thickness of a finger *(about an inch).* 3. *adv.* as thick as one's finger. *Cf.* **[2]chanda.**

[2]wanda 1. get fat, put on weight. 2. grow well, thrive *(of plants).* *caus.* **wandisha.**

[3]wanda *sing.* *see* **uwanda.**

[1]wanga (–) arrowroot, starch.

[2]wanga 1. cut (open). 2. wound, injure, hurt. **kichwa kinaniwanga.** I have a headache.

[3]wanga *rare* count, calculate. (= **hesabu.**) *Cf.* **[1]kiwango.**

[4]wanga *arch.* stay up at night; practice magic, conjure.

wangafu, wangavu *sing.* *see* **uangavu.**

wangi *rare* *see* **ingi.**

wangine *rare* *see* **ingine.**

wangu *see* **angu.**

wangwa (**nyangwa**) wasteland, wilderness, desert; tidal flats.

wangwana *pl.* *see* **mwungwana.**

[1]wanja *pl. of* **uwanja.**

[2]wanja *sing.:* – **wa manga.** antimony *(used as a cosmetic).* (= **kohl.**)

wano (**ma-**) 1. shaft *(of a spear, arrow).* 2. *(pl.)* sticks used for fortune-telling.

wao *see* **ao.**

wapi 1. *see* **pi.** 2. *interrog.* where? **yuko –?** Where is he? 3. to what avail? without success. **Nilijaribu, nikajaribu tena, lakini wapi?** I tried and tried again, but without success (what good did it do me?).

wapilia* smell (too) strongly of perfume.

[1]wapo *auxil. v.* **wa-** *cl.* they are there.

[2]wapo (–) *see* **kiapo.**

[3]wapo (–) *see* **[2]uapo.**

waraka* (**nyaraka**) 1. letter, document, certificate; *(rel.)* epistle. 2. cigarette paper. 3. *pol., rec.:* – **wa serikali.** white paper. – **wa Baba Mtakatifu.** Papal encyclical.

wardi* (–) *see* **waridi.**

wargi*, warigi *sing.* wargi (locally distilled African gin, Nubian gin).

[1]wari* [*Pers.*] (–) wari (unit of measure, about a yard).

[2]wari* [*Engl.*] (–) 1. valve *(of a bicycle or automobile tire).* 2. inner tube.

waria* [*Ind.*] (–) (skilled) worker, journeyman. *Cf.* **mwanafunzi** *(apprentice)*, **fundi** *(master)*.

waridi*, wardi (–, ma-) rose. **ua la –.** rose blossom. **mafuta ya –.** attar of roses. **maji ya –.** rosewater. *Cf.* **mwaridi, halwaridi.**

warigi* *sing.* *see* **wargi.**

warishai* (–) water-cooler, vessel for storing drinking water. *Cf.* **rishai.**

warithi* 1. (ma-) *rare* heir. (= **mrithi.**) 2. *sing., rare* inheritance, heritage, legacy. (= **urithi.**) *Cf.* **rithi.**

[1]wasa* (–) wasa (sticks or laths used to fill up the spaces in the framework of a native house prior to plastering).

[2]wasa (–) drizzle *(of rain).*

[3]wasa *see* **asa.**

wasaa*, wakaa (–) 1. (established) time (for something). 2. free time, leisure. 3. favorable time, opportunity.

wasalam!* *interj., Isl.* formula of greeting and conclusion in letters.

washa *caus. of* **[1]waka & wawa.**

washerati* *sing.* *see* **uasherati.**

wasi (ma-) *see* **uasi.**

wasia*, usia, wusia, wosia *sing.* will, last will and testament.

wasifu* 1. describe, explain. 2. *sing.* description, explanation. *Cf.* **tawasifu, tawasufi.**

wasii* (ma-) executor *(of a will)*, trustee, guardian. *Cf.* **usia, wasia.**

wasili* 1. reach, arrive, appear. **– kwake.** arrive at his house. *appl.* **wasilia.** *caus.* **wasilisha.** send something, write to. *caus.-appl.* **wasilishia.** send something to someone, write to someone. 2. *sing.* arrival; receipt *(of something);* receipts, credits, income.

wasiwasi* *sing.* 1. doubt, misgiving, scruple. **fanya –.** have doubts/misgivings. 2. confusion. **tia –.** confuse, embarrass. 3. perplexity, uncertainty, irresolution, vacillation. 4. critical situation, crisis. **nchi hii ina –.** This country is in a state of crisis.

wastani*, wasta 1. *sing.* average, mean. 2. *adj.* average, medium, moderate. **kimo – tu.** of average/medium height. 3. *adv.:* **kwa –.** on the average, about, approximately. **wanafunzi wana kwa – umri wa miaka kumi.** The pupils are about ten years old on the average.

watani* *sing.* home, birthplace; native country, fatherland. *Cf.* **tania, mtani, utani.**

watu (*pl. of* **mtu**): **–a watu.** *adj.* 1. belonging to other people, other people's *(property, etc.).* 2. *(chiefly comm.)* popular, people's... **Jamhuri ya watu.** People's Republic.

wavi (**ma-**) *augment. of* **kiwavi.**

wavu (**nyavu**) net *(in gen.).* **tega –.** fish with a net. **tanda –.** spread/set a net. **– wa kulalia.** *rare* hammock. *Cf.* **ugavu.**

wawa 1. itch. 2. (*also intr.* **waka**) burn, smart, be inflamed/irritated; be sunburned. *caus.* **washa.** *Cf.* **kiwavi,** [2]**uwasho**; *also* [2]**waa,** [1]**waka.**

[1]**waya** (**nyaya**) earthenware dish *(for baking cakes).*

[2]**waya*** [*Engl.*] (–) wire *(of an electrical appliance).*

[3]**waya** *sing.* lack of something, inability to afford something. **Watu wengine wanashindwa kula hata ratili tatu za nyama kwa mwaka. Wao sio ugonjwa, lakini waya.** Some people cannot consume even three pounds of meat in a year, not because they are sick, but because they cannot afford it.

wayawaya 1. sway, stagger *(under a load),* be loaded down *(a tree with fruit, etc.).* **mti umewayawaya.** The tree is bent down *(by its burden of fruit).* 2. *fig.* be uncertain, vacillate, have no firm opinions. *Cf.* **wayowayo.**

wayo, uayo (**nyayo**) 1. sole of the foot. 2. footprint, track. **nyayo za mnyama.** tracks/spoor of an animal. *fig.* **anafuata nyayo za baba yake.** He is following in his father's footsteps.

wayowayo (**ma-**) swaying, staggering; uncertainty, indecision. *Cf.* **wayawaya.**

waza, aza 1. think, consider, reflect, meditate. 2. suppose, imagine, assume, conjecture. *appl.* **wazia.** think about/consider/reflect on something. *intr.* **wazika.** **–a kuwazika tu.** abstract. *caus.* **wazisha.** 1. get someone to think about something, put someone in a reflective frame of mind. 2. *(w. int. force)* think over carefully, ponder. *Cf.* **wazo, mwazaji, uwazo.**

wazi, waziwazi *adj.* 1. opened, open; *(fig.)* overt. **mlango –.** an open door. **mashtaka waziwazi na ya kisiri.** overt and covert charges. 2. uncovered. **kichwa –.** bareheaded. 3. *fig.* clear, plain; frank, candid, sincere. **maneno yake –, hayana kificho.** He gives his opinion frankly, without concealing anything. *Cf.* **uwazi.**

wazimu 1. madness, insanity. **wa (na) –.** be mad/insane. **tia –.** drive mad. **ingiliwa –.** go mad. **mwenye –.** insane/crazy person, lunatic, maniac. 2. mania, hallucination, delusion. *Cf.* **mzimu, kuzimu, zimwi.**

wazira* *see* **wizara.**

waziri* (ma-) statesman, secretary of state, minister. **waziri mkuu.** prime minister, premier. **waziri wa elimu (ulimaji).** minister of education (agriculture). **waziri wa mambo ya nchi ngeni.** foreign minister, minister of foreign affairs. **– bila ya wizara.** minister without portfolio. *Cf.* **uwaziri, wizara.**

waziwazi *see* **wazi.**

wazo (ma-) (*us.* **mawazo**) 1. thought, idea. 2. opinion, view. 3. assumption, supposition, conjecture, hypothesis. 4. reflection. **wa (kaa) katika mawazo.** be lost/absorbed in thought. *Cf.* **waza.**

–we (< **wake**) *poss. pron. 3rd pers. sing.* his, her, its. **mkewe.** his wife.

wea 1. affect, concern; suit, be good for/useful to. 2. have a claim on, be a creditor of. *appl.* **welea.** *Cf.* **1wa, wia.**

wee (< **wewe**) *rare abs. pron. 2nd pers. sing.* you.

wehu* (–) madness, insanity, lunacy. *Cf.* **mwehu.**

weka 1. put, place, set, lay. **– saini.** sign, place one's signature upon. **– tayari.** make ready, prepare. **– pamoja.** put together. **– chini.** underestimate. **– juu.** overestimate. 2. put down, lay aside. **– mzigo.** put down a burden. **– silaha.** lay down arms, surrender. **– msingi.** lay a cornerstone. 3. lay aside, save, deposit. **– fedha.** save money. **– akiba.** store up, keep in reserve. **– wakifu.** make a donation/endowment. 4. introduce, establish, put into effect. **– sheria.** put a law into effect. **– desturi.** introduce a custom. 5. install *(in an office)*. **– waziri.** install a minister. 6. put off, delay, defer. **– hukumu.** delay judgment, put off a trial. 7. found, open. **– duka.** open a business. *appl.* **wekea.** put, place, *etc.* for someone. **wekea amana.** trust/rely on someone. **wekea fedha.** save money for someone. *appl.-ass.* **wekeana. wekeana heshima.** treat each other with respect. *intr.* **wekeka. chakula hiki kinawekeka mpaka kesho.** This food will keep until tomorrow. *caus.* **wekesha, wekeza.** *Cf.* **1wekevu, 1weko, kiweko, mweka, mwekaji, mweko, uwekaji, 2uwekevu.**

1wekevu *adj.* thrifty, frugal, miserly. *Cf.* **weka.**

2wekevu *see* **2uwekevu.**

3wekevu *sing.* *see* **uelekevu.**

1weko (ma-) 1. place for putting something, storage place, storehouse, repository (stand, base, shelf, drawer, etc.). 2. = **uwekaji.** *Cf.* **weka.**

2weko (ma-) metal used for welding. **tia –.** to weld.

wekua *see* **ekua.**

wekundu *sing.* redness, red color. *Cf.* **ekundu.**

[1]**wele** (**ma-**) *see* **kiwele.**

[2]**wele** (**ma-**) grain of millet. *Cf.* [2]**mwele.**

weledi* 1. (–) skill, art, ability. 2. *adj.* skilful, clever, adept.

weleka *see* **eleka.**

welekevu *sing.* *see* **uelekevu.**

welfeya* [*Engl.*] (–) welfare, prosperity.

wema *sing.* goodness, excellence, kindness. *Cf.* [1]**ema.**

wembamba *sing.* thinness, slenderness; delicacy. *Cf.* **embamba.**

wembe (**nyembe**) razor; very sharp knife. *prov.* **mtoto akililia – mpe.** When a child cries for a knife, give it to him. *Cf.* **jembe.**

wembembe (–) wild bee.

wendelezo *sing.* *see* **uendelezo.**

wendo (**nyendo**) 1. = **mwendo.** 2. *plur.:* **nyendo zake.** *coll.* his character. *Cf.* **enda.**

wenendo *sing.* *see* **mwendo.**

wenga have certain foods disagree with one; break out in a rash; *(fig.)* dislike, feel abhorrence for; refuse, reject.

wengi *see* **-ingi.**

wengine *see* **-ingine.**

wengu (**ma-**) *anat.* spleen. (= **bandama.**)

weni (–) weni (medicinal plant).

wenu *see* **-enu.**

wenye *see* **-enye.**

wenyewe *see* **-enyewe.**

wenzi 1. *plur. of* **mwenzi.** 2. *sing.* friendship, friendliness; companionship, society, company.

wenzo (**nyenzo**) (*us. pl.*) 1. lever, roller. **mti huu hauendi ila kwa nyenzo.** This piece of wood cannot be moved without the help of rollers. 2. *fig.* (natural) resources, products; raw materials. **– za nchi.** the natural resources of a country. *Cf.* **enda.**

wepesi *sing.* 1. lightness *(in weight);* ease, agility *(of movement, etc.).* 2. speed, haste. *Cf.* **epesi, upesi.**

werevu *sing.* 1. shrewdness, cleverness; intelligence, reasoning power; acuteness, penetration. 2. adroitness, adaptability. 3. deceit, cunning, craftiness. *Cf.* **erevu.**

wetu *see* **-etu.**

weu (**nyeu**) open place, clearing *(in a forest).*

weuo *sing.* 1. (ritual) purification. 2. *fig.* menstruation. *Cf.* **eua.**

weupe *sing.* 1. whiteness, white/gray color. 2. paleness, pallor. 3. lightness, brightness. 4. *fig.* simplicity, naiveté, ingenuousness, innocence. *Cf.* **eupe.**

weusi *sing.* blackness, black color; gloom, darkness. *Cf.* **eusi.**

wevi *plur. of* **mwivi.**

wewe (*rare* **wee, weye**) *abs. pron. 2nd pers. sing.* you.

wewedeka *rare see* **weweseka.**

weweseka, wewedeka, ewedeka talk in one's sleep, have nightmares; talk deliriously. *caus.* **wewesesha.** make one talk in one's sleep, give one nightmares.

weye *rare see* **wewe.**

weza 1. can, be able; be strong/well; have power. **mtoto anaweza kuandika.** The child can write. 2. *neg.* be ill/sick. **hawezi tumbo.** He has stomach trouble. 3. overpower, overwhelm. **ametuweza.** He has overpowered us. 4. endure, bear, put up with. **– taabu.** bear up under difficulties. *refl.* **jiweza.** 1. be independent/self-sufficient. 2. have self-control. *appl.* **wezea.** *intr.* **wezeka,** *us. intr-ass.* **wezekana.** be possible/feasible. **haiwezekani.** It is impossible. **hawezekani.** He is invincible/uncontrollable/intolerable. *caus.* **wezesha.** empower, authorize; make it possible for someone to do something. *Cf.* **mweza, uwezekano, uwezo.**

wezi *plur. of* **mwizi.**

wi *adj., arch.* bad, evil, wicked.

¹wia become warm, (begin to) get hot, start to boil *(water)*, seethe.

²wia have a claim on someone *(for money owed)*, be a creditor. **mwenye kuwia.** creditor. **mwenye kuwiwa.** debtor. *ass.* **wiana.** owe/be indebted to each other. **namba inayowiana.** *math.* rational number. *pass.* **wiwa.** be in someone's debt, owe *(money)*. *Cf.* **¹wa, wea, mwia, mwiwa.**

³wia *appl. of* **¹wa.**

wiana *ass. of* **²wia.**

wibari* (–) wild rabbit, hyrax.

widhaa (ma-) *see* **waadhi.**

wifi (ma-) sister-in-law *(brother's wife, husband's sister)*.

wika 1. crow *(a cock)*. *prov.* **likiwika lisiwike kutakucha.** The day breaks whether the cock crows or not. 2. *fig.:* **siku hizi katika siasa ya Afrika Bwana X. ndiye anayewika.** Mr. X. has recently been creating a stir in African politics. *Cf.* **wiko.**

wiki* [*Engl.*) (–) week. **– ujao.** next week. **– jana.** last week.

wikiendi* [*Engl.*] (–) weekend.

wiko (ma-) (*or* – la jogoo) cockcrow; (mawiko) the morning crowing of cocks. *Cf.* **wika.**

wilaya* (–) district. *Cf.* **Ulaya.**

wili *num.* two. **-ote -wili.** both. *Cf.* **kuwili, mbili, uwili.**

wima (*rare* **ima**) 1. *sing.* state of being upright/erect/vertical/perpendicular. *(fig.)* uprightness, honesty. 2. (–) prop, support, post, upright. 3. *v.* stand upright, be erect/vertical/straight. 4.: **–a –.** *adj.* upright, vertical, straight. **mistari ya –.** vertical lines. **simama –.** stand upright. *Cf.* **kiwimawima, mwima, mwimo, uwima.**

wimbaji *sing.* (profession, manner, etc. of) singing. *Cf.* **imba.**

[1]**wimbi** (ma-) 1. wave *(in water);* (mawimbi) surf, swell. 2. *fig.* excitement. *Cf.* [1]**kiwimbi,** [2]**kiwimbi.**

[2]**wimbi** *pl. of* **uwimbi.**

wimbo (nyimbo) song, hymn, anthem. **– wa dini.** hymn. **– wa Tanganyika.** the (national) anthem of Tanganyika. *Cf.* **imba.**

wimbombo *sing.* wimbombo (the 'male' of a pair of firesticks; *cf.* **ulindi, upekecho**).

winchi* (*rare* **winji**) [*Engl.*] winch, crane, windlass.

[1]**winda** (–) *see* **ubinda.**

[2]**winda** 1. hunt, chase. 2. *fig.* pursue, search (for). *ass.* **windana.** 1. hunt together/in large numbers. 2. hunt/pursue each other. *Cf.* **mwindaji, uwindaji, uwindo.**

windo (ma-) *see* **uwindo, uwindaji.**

winga drive/chase away, expel.

[1]**wingi** *sing.* 1. large number/quantity, much, a great deal. **– si hoja.** Quantity is not the important thing (= Quality is more important than quantity). 2. *gramm.* plural. **–a –.** *adj.* plural. 3. majority. **– zaidi.** absolute majority. *Cf.* **ingi.**

[2]**wingi*** [*Engl.*] (ma-) *sport, pol.* wing.

wingu (ma-) cloud. **– la mvua.** rain cloud. **– la moshi.** cloud of smoke. *coll.* **pamepiga – la mvua.** It has rained. **kumefanya mawingu.** It is cloudy. *Cf.* **uwingu.**

winja *pl. of* **uwinja.**

winji* (–) *see* **winchi.**

wino* *sing.* ink. **– mwekundu.** red ink. **doa la –.** inkspot, blot.

winzani* *sing.* *see* **uzani.**

wishwa, wiswa, ushwa *sing.* chaff, bran.

wiswa *sing.* *see* **wishwa.**

witiri*, **wituri** (–) *math.* odd number. *Cf.* **shufwa.**

[1]**wito** *sing., med.* infection, contagion. (= **ambukizo.**) **pata (shikwa na) –.** be infected, catch *(a disease).*

[2]**wito** *sing.* *see* **mwito.**

[3]**wito** (–) mold, casting.

wituri* (–) *see* **witiri.**

wiva *see* **iva.**

wivi, wizi (–) (*also* **uwivi, uwizi**) theft, robbery, burglary. *Cf.* **iba.**

wivu 1. *sing.* (*also* **uwivu**) envy, jealousy, ill will. 2. *adj.* envious, jealous, spiteful, malicious. *Cf.* **mwivu.**

[1]**wiwa** *pass. of* [1]**wa.**

[2]**wiwa** *pass. of* [2]**wa.**

wizani* *sing.* *see* **uzani.**

wizara*, wazira (–) ministry. **waziri bila ya –.** minister without portfolio. *Cf.* **waziri, uwaziri.**

wizi (–) *see* **wivi.**

woga, uoga *sing.* (*also* **oga,** –) 1. cowardice, faintheartedness, pusillanimity, fear. **pata (ingiwa, shikwa na, ona) –.** be afraid. 2. timidity, shyness, nervousness. *Cf.* [2]**oga, ogopa.**

wogofya, wogofyo (**ma-, nyogofya**) something terrifying, threat, menace. *Cf.* [2]**oga, ogopa, woga.**

wogofyo *see* **wogofya.**

woki (–) *see* **uki.**

wokofu *sing.* *see* **wokovu.**

wokovu, wokofu *sing.* 1. rescue, deliverance, salvation. 2. reward for finding something lost. *Cf.* [2]**okoa.**

wokozi *sing.* *see* **uokozi.**

wole (–) *see* **ole.**

[1]**wongo** *adj., rare* lying, untrue, false, deceitful (= **–a uwongo.**). *Cf.* **ongopa,** [2]**mwongo, uwongo.**

[2]**wongo** *sing.* *see* **uwongo.**

wongofu *sing.* 1. rightness, correctness. 2. righteousness, uprightness, honesty. 3. justness, fairness, justice. 4. legal matter. 5. *rel.* conversion. *Cf.* **ongoa.**

wonyeshano *sing.* showing, demonstration, exhibition. *Cf.* **ona.**

wonyesho (**maonyesho**) 1. = **wonyeshano.** 2. show, display; parade; exhibition. **– wa biashara.** commercial exhibition/exposition/fair. *Cf.* **ona.**

worodha* (–) *see* **orodha.**

[1]wosia* *see* [1]usia.

[2]wosia* *see* wasia.

wote *see* -ote.

[1]woto *sing.* growth, development; vegetation. *Cf.* [1]ota.

[2]woto *sing.* warming (oneself), basking; warmth. *Cf.* [2]ota.

wozo *sing.* 1. decay, putrefaction, decomposition. – wa matunda. decay of fruit. – wa meno. tooth decay, caries. 2. *fig.* decline, deterioration, corruption, ruin. *Cf.* [1]oza.

wusia* *sing.* *see* wasia.

Y

ya *conn.* 1. mi- *cl.* mizizi – miti. the roots of the trees. 2. ma- *cl.* maji – mito. the water of the rivers. *isolated:* – nini? Why? – kwamba, ya kama. *conj.* that, in order that. 3. n- *cl.* nyumba – mwarabu. the house of the Arab.

yaa!* *interj.* oh! *us. in the expr.:* – Rabi! O God!

yaani*, yani *conj.* that is (to say).

yabis* *see* yabisi.

yabisi*, yabis 1. dry, hard. ardhi –. dry earth. 2. stiff, rigid. baridi –. rheumatism. 3. *fig.* inflexible, rude, difficult. mtu huyu ni – sana. He is a very difficult person (to deal with). 4. *v.* (*us. intr.* yabisika) be dry/hard. *caus.* yabisisha. *Cf.* uyabisi.

yadi*, yard [*Engl.*] (–) yard *(unit of measure).*

yadumu milele...! Long live...! *Cf.* [2]dumu.

yahe* (–) 1. (*also* ahi, aki) *rare* brother, friend. 2. *pl.* common people, rabble.

yahom* *adv., naut.* straight ahead, with the wind.

Yahudi* (ma-) Jew.

yai, yayi (ma-) 1. egg. ute wa –. white of egg, albumen. kiini cha –. yolk. ganda la –. eggshell. – bichi. fresh/uncooked egg. taga –. lay an egg. atamia (tamia) mayai. hatch eggs. namna ya –. egg-shaped, oval. 2. *fig.:* mayai ya pumbu. *anat.* testicles. 3. *sport* nothing, zero *(in giving the score of a game).*

yaika *see* yeyuka.

[1]yakama *sing.* 1. runoff (election). 2. majority, quorum.

[2]**yakama** *conj.* *see* [1]**kama.**

yake *see* **-ake.**

yakini* 1. (*also intr.* **yakinika**) be true/sure/certain. **imeyakinika ya kuwa amekufa.** It is certain that he is dead. *appl.* **yakinia.** be sure about something; decide, make up one's mind. **ameyakinia kuja kwetu.** He has decided to come to us. *caus.* **yakinisha.** 2. (–) truth, certainty, definiteness. **– ya habari.** the definiteness of the report. 3. *adj.* true, certain, actual, definite. 4. *adv.* certainly, definitely. **ni – kuwa atakuja.** It is certain that he is coming. **kwa – jambo hili halifai.** This matter is certainly not good. *Cf.* [1]**kini.**

yako *see* **-ako.**

yakuti* (–) ruby, sapphire. **– ya samawi.** sapphire. **– ya kimanjano.** topaz.

yale *dem. pron.* **ma- & n-** *cl.* that, those. **maneno –.** those words. **nyumba –.** that house.

yaliyomo, yaliomo, zilizomo *pl.* (*lit.* which are within) (table of) contents *(of a book).* (= **faharasa.**)

yaliyotangulia (–) preamble, preface, prologue. *Cf.* **tangulia.**

[1]**yamini*** (–) 1. right hand. 2. *fig.* oath. **– ya uwongo.** perjury. **apa (twaa, la, toa) –.** swear an oath.

[2]**yamini** *rare* *see* [2]**amini.**

yamkini*, yumkini 1. be possible/probable. *intr.* **yamkinika. hayamkiniki.** It is impossible/out of the question. 2. possibility, probability, eventuality. 3. *adj.* possible, likely, probable. 4. *adv.* possibly, perhaps.

yamo *auxil. v., det.* **mi-, ma-, n-** *cl.* it is/they are in there.

yana *auxil. v.* **mi-, ma-, n-** *cl.* has/have.

yangeyange (–) *ornith.* (small) heron, egret.

yangu *see* **-angu.**

yani* *see* **yaani.**

yao *see* **-ao.**

yapata *adv.* perhaps, maybe; about, approximately.

yapi *see* **-pi.**

yapo *auxil. v.* **mi-, ma-, n-** *cl.* it is/they are there.

yard* (–) *see* **yadi.**

yasi* (–) yasi (a yellow powder used as a cosmetic).

yasimini* (–) *see* **yasmini.**

[1]**yasini*** *interj. of scorn or disdain.* What's the use? Why should I? I want nothing to do with it!

[2]**yasini*** (–) yasini (a charm made from the 36th sura of the Koran, so-called from the two Arabic letters *ya* and *sin* which appear at the beginning of the sura).

yasmini*, **yasimini**, **jasmini** (–) jasmine.

yatima* (**ma-**) orphan. **nyumba ya mayatima.** orphanage.

[1]**yavuyavu** (**ma-**) *anat.* lung (*us. of animals*), lights.

[2]**yavuyavu** (–) jellyfish.

[1]**yaya*** [*Ind.*] (**ma-**) (children's) nurse.

[2]**yaya** *det.:* – **haya.** these very things.

yayi (**ma-**) *see* **yai.**

yayo *det.:* – **hayo.** these very things (that we have mentioned).

yayuka *see* **yekuka.**

ye 1. *relat. pron.* **m-** *cl.* 2. *rare abbr. of* **yake.** *Cf.* **-ake.**

yee *rare* = **yeye.** *abs. pron. 3rd pers. sing.* he, she, it.

yenu *see* **-enu.**

yenye *see* **-enye.**

yenyewe *see* **-enyewe.**

yetu *see* **-etu.**

yeye *abs. pron. 3rd pers. sing.* he, she, it.

yeyuka, **yayuka**, **yaika** flow, melt, dissolve, liquefy. **siagi imeyeyuka yote.** The butter has completely melted. *caus.* **yeyusha.** melt, dissolve (something); *(fig.)* – **fulani furaha.** spoil someone's pleasure in something.

yo 1. *relat. pron.* **mi-**, **ma-**, **n-** *cl.* 2. *rare abbr. of* **yako.** *Cf.* **-ako.**

yoga (**ma-**) *augment. of* **uyoga.**

yombiyombi (–) *ornith.* Grosbeak weaver.

yonga, **yuga**, **yongayonga**, **yugayuga** 1. move back and forth, swing, sway. 2. stagger, walk unsteadily. *appl.* **yongea.** *caus.* **yongesha.**

yongayonga *see* **yonga.**

yongo (–) *med.* nettle rash, urticaria.

yongoa, **yongoya** be carried on someone's back *(e.g., initiates after the ceremony).*

yongoya *see* **yongoa.**

yote *see* **-ote.**

yowe*, **iowe** (–) (*also* **kiyowe**, **kiowe**, **vi-**) cry, shout, scream *(esp. for help).* **piga –.** call for help.

yoyomea arrive/enter with much noise and confusion.

yua (*us. red.* **yuayua**) move unsteadily, wobble, waver; miss one's aim.

yuga *see* **yonga.**

yugayuga *see* **yonga.**

yuko *auxil. v. det.* **m-** *cl.* he (she, it) is there.

yule *dem. pron.* **m-** *cl.* that. **mtu —.** that person.

yumba, yumbayumba 1. sway, stagger, stumble. 2. *naut.* roll *(of ships).* 3. *fig.* be undecided, vacillate.

yumbayumba *see* **yumba.**

yumkini* *see* **yamkini.**

yumo *auxil. v. det.* **m-** *cl.* he (she, it) is in there.

yungayunga (—) (intestinal) worm.

yungiyungi (—, **ma-**) *bot.* (species of) water lily.

yunifomu* [*Engl.*] (—) *rare* uniform.

yupi *see* **-pi.**

yupo *auxil. v. det.* **mi-** *cl.* he (she, it) is there.

yuranimu* [*Engl.*] *sing.* uranium.

yusi*, yuzi [*Engl.*] (**ma-**) youth. **— wingi.** Youth Wing (of KANU).

Z

za *conn.* **n-** *cl.* **nyumba — mji.** the houses of the city.

zaa (*dial.* **vyaa**) 1. beget, give birth. **amezaa mtoto.** She has given birth to a child. 2. bear fruit. **miti hii imezaa sana.** These trees are bearing much fruit. *appl.* **zalia. mkewe amemzalia mtoto.** His wife has borne him a child. *pass.* **zaliwa** (*arch.* **zawa**). be born; be a native of a place. **siku ya kuzaliwa.** birthday. **amezaliwa hapa.** He is a native of this place (*i.e.*, was born here). *ass.* **zaliana** (*arch.* **zaana**). breed, multiply. *caus.* **zalisha.** 1. beget, fertilize, engender. 2. assist in childbirth, act as midwife. 3. produce, generate. *Cf.* **zalio, 1zao, zazi, kizalia, kizao, kizazi, mzaa, mzalisha, mzaliwa, 1mzao, 2mzao, mzazi, uzalishi, uzao, uzazi.**

zaana *arch. ass. of* **zaa.**

zaba* strike *(in the face),* slap. **— makofi.** box the ears.

zabadi* (–) musk, civet *(used in making perfumes). Cf.* **zabidi.**

zabibu* (–) grape, raisin **– kavu.** raisin. *Cf.* **mzabibu.**

zabidi* take civet (from the civet cat). *pass.* **zabidiwa** *Cf.* **zabadi.**

zabuni* bid *(at an auction) appl.* **zabunia.** *intr.* **zabunika.** *pass.* **zabuniwa.** *Cf.* **mzabuni.**

zaburi* (–) *rel.* psalm.

zafarani*, zafrani (–) saffron.

zafe* (–) slipperiness, slime.

zafrani* (–) *see* **zafarani.**

zagaa* 1. shine, gleam, glitter. 2. *coll.* spread, extend. **mchungwa wake umezagaa machungwa.** He has very many oranges. *appl.* **zagalia.** *caus.* **zagasha.** *pass.* **zagawa.**

zagaazagaa obstruct, clutter up. **– majiani.** clutter up the paths.

Zahali* *sing.* *see* **Zohari.**

zahama*, zahimu (–) 1. annoyance, vexation, distress. 2. noise, uproar, confusion. 3. (police-)raid.

zahimu* (–) *see* **zahama.**

zaidana* (–) *see* **zaidi 2.**

zaidi* 1. *adv.* more, in greater number. **– ya...** more than... 2. besides, in addition. **– ya hayo.** besides this, moreover. 3. (–) (*also* **zaidana**) increase, increment. **– ya habari.** further reports.

zaini* *rare* deceive, cheat, dupe, lead astray.

[1]**zaka*** (–) pipe-bowl.

[2]**zaka*, zakati** (–) *rel.* tithe *(given as alms).*

[3]**zaka*** (–, **ma-**) (*arch* **ziaka**) quiver *(for arrows).* (= **podo.**)

zakati* (–) *see* [2]**zaka.**

zake *see* **-ake.**

zako *see* **-ako.**

zalia *appl. of* **zaa.**

zalio (**ma-**) *anat.* placenta. *Cf.* **zaa.**

zalisha *caus. of* **zaa.**

zaliwa *pass. of* **zaa.**

[1]**zama*** (–) *see* **zamani.**

[2]**zama** 1. sink, be immersed in, plunge into; be drowned, perish. *fig.:* **– katika kitabu.** be immersed in a book. 2. dive for something. **– lulu.** dive for pearls. *appl.* **zamia.** *caus.* **zamisha.** sink, immerse (something); engage someone as a driver. *Cf.* **mzama, mzamaji, mzamia, mzamio, mzamishi, mzamisho.**

zamani*, **zama** 1. (–) time, period (of time), age, epoch. **– za kale.** ancient times, antiquity. **– za vita.** at the time of the war. **– zetu (hizi).** our times/age. **alitawala – gani?** At what period did he rule? 2. *adv.* earlier, long ago; already, before. **nimemwona –.** I have seen him before. *Cf.* **kizamani.**

zambarau* 1. (–) zambarau (kind of plum). 2. *adj.* purple. *Cf.* **mzambarau.**

zamburu (ma-) zamburu (kind of fish occurring in swamps).

zamu* (–) 1. (six-hour period of) duty, stint, shift, turn; (period of) guard duty, watch. *mil.* sentry, patrol. **ngoja (shika, linda) –.** keep watch; *(mil.)*, stand guard/sentry. 2. relief, change (of guards, etc.). **– ya kazi** change of (work) shifts. **kwa –.** by turns.

zana* (–) 1. apparatus, instrument, device; equipment, fittings. 2. supplies. **– za vita.** military supplies, munitions.

zandiki* 1. play the hypocrite, lie, deceive. 2. (ma-) = **mzandiki.** *Cf.* **mzandiki, uzandiki.**

zangefuri* (–) *see* **zingefuri.**

zangu *see* **-angu.**

zani* 1. (–) (sexual) immorality, debauchery, fornication; adultery. 2. (ma-) prostitute. *Cf.* **zini.**

1**zao** (ma-) (*us.* **mazao**) 1. product, production, produce, yield, output. 2. offspring. 3. *math.* result, product. 4. result *(in gen.)*. **taabu anayopata ni mazao ya upuuzi yake.** The difficulties that he has are the result of his foolish behavior. *Cf.* **zaa.**

2**zao** *see* **-ao.**

zaraa* (–) *rare* agriculture. (= **kilimo.**)

zarambo* [*Pers.*] (–) zarambo (an alcohol distilled from palm wine).

zari* [*Pers.*] (–) gold/silver braid/lace.

zartari* (–) zartari (a herb added as flavoring to tea).

zatiti* prepare, make ready, arrange, put in order. **– vyombo vya safari.** prepare what is needed for a journey.

zawa *arch. pass. of* **zaa.**

zawadi* (–, ma-) 1. present, memento, keepsake. 2. prize.

zawaridi* (–) *ornith.* zawaridi (kind of sparrow).

zazi *adj.* fruitful, fertile. **yeye si mzazi, ndio maana hawana mtoto.** He/she is sterile, so they have no children. *Cf.* **zaa.**

ze *abbr. of* **zake** (*see* **-ake**). **nduguze.** his brothers.

zebaki* (–) quicksilver, mercury.

zee *adj.* old, aged. *Cf.* **kizee, mzee, uzee.**

zefe* (–) row, line. **panga –.** arrange in rows.

zege* (–) 1. concrete, cement. **matofali ya –.** concrete blocks. **piga –.** mix concrete. 2. *rare* dome, cupola. 3. *rec.* (arched) bridge.

zeituni* (–) olive. *Cf.* **mzeituni.**

zelabia*, zilabia (–) zelabia (a light pastry).

zema *see* **ema.**

zembe *adj.* idle, lazy, negligent. *Cf.* **kizembe, mzembe, uzembe;** *also* **uzimbezimbe.**

zengea 1. hunt/search for. 2. observe, inspect, make a tour of. **– hapa hapa.** See the sights of a locality.

zenu *see* **-enu.**

zenye *see* **-enye.**

zenyewe *see* **-enyewe.**

zeri* (–) balm, balsam.

zeru, zeruzeru (ma-) (*also* **kimazeru, vi-**) albino.

zeruzeru (ma-) *see* **zeru.**

zetu *see* **-etu.**

¹zeze (–) zeze (stringed instrument similar to a banjo).

²zeze (ma-) pod of the mzeze tree.

¹zia, zira 1. hate, detest, abhor, feel an aversion for. 2. abstain from something, observe a taboo. *caus.* **ziza.** forbid someone to eat certain foods, impose a taboo; prescribe a diet for someone, put on a diet. *Cf.* **mzio.**

²zia drive away with fire, burn out, smoke out. **– siafu.** smoke out ants.

³zia waste away, wither, shrink, languish. *caus.* **ziza.** 1. cause/allow to waste away. 2. *fig.* ruin, destroy. *Cf.* **²kizio.**

ziada*, ziyada (ma-) 1. increase, increment, supplement, addition. 2. gain, profit. *Cf.* **zaidi.**

ziaka* (ma-) *arch.* quiver *(for arrows).* (= **³zaka.**)

ziara*, ziyara (ma-) *Isl.* 1. grave, burial place, tomb, monument. 2. place of pilgrimage, shrine. *Cf.* **zuru.**

ziba close up, fill/stop up, plug, cork. **– chupa.** cork a bottle. *ass.* **zibana** & *intr.* **zibika.** be closed/plugged/corked. *caus.* **zibisha.** *inv.* **zibua.** open (up), uncork. *inv.-appl.* **zibulia.** *inv.-intr.* **zibuka.** *inv.-pass.* **zibuliwa.** *Cf.* **kizibo, kizibuo, mzibo.**

zibo (ma-) *see* **kizibo.**

zibua *inv. of* **ziba.**

zibuka *inv.-intr. of* **ziba.**

[1]**zidi*** 1. increase, become larger/greater/longer, grow, multiply. 2. exceed, outstrip, be too much for. **kazi imemzidi.** The work was too much for him. 3. *w. foll. inf.:* **anazidi kwenda.** He is going faster/farther (*lit.* He increased to go). **azidi kujua.** He knows better. **– kufikiri (kutafuta).** think over (search) carefully. *appl.* **zidia.** *intr.* **zidika.** *caus.* **zidisha.** 1. increase something. **zidisha bei.** raise the price. 2. *math.* multiply. *Cf.* **zaidi, kizidishe, kizidisho.**

[2]**zidi*, zidio, zidisho** (ma-) *see* **ziada.**

zidua pull out *(nails, etc.),* extract.

ziga (ma-) ziga (a vessel containing hot coals, for warming invalids, etc.). *Cf.* **maziga.**

zika bury, inter; attend a funeral. **siku ya kuzika.** day of burial. *caus.* **zisha.** prepare for a burial; pay funeral expenses. *Cf.* **maziko, mazishi, mziko, mzishi, uzishi.**

ziki* (–) white embroidered collar (of a kanzu).

ziko *auxil. v. det.* **n-** *class* they are there.

zikri* (–) *see* **dhikiri.**

zikwi *rare pl. of* **kikwi.**

zilabia* (–) *see* **zelabia.**

zile *demon. pron.* **n-** *class.* those.

zilebia* (–) *see* **zelabia.**

zilia 1. refuse something *(in a pout, fit of temper, etc.).* 2. take amiss, be offended. (= [2]**susa.**)

zilizomo *pl.* *see* **yaliyomo.**

[1]**zima** put out, extinguish, quench. **– moto (taa).** extinguish a fire (lamp). **– njaa.** satisfy hunger. **– kiu.** quench thirst. **– ugomvi.** settle a quarrel. *appl.* **zimia.** extinguish something; *(fig.)* lose consciousness, faint (= **zimia roho**). *pass.* **zimwa.** *inv.* **zimua** *(us. w. int. force).* reduce the strength or intensity of something, cool down, temper, dilute, etc. **zimua maji ya moto.** cool down hot water. **zimua tembo.** dilute palm wine. *coll.* **kwenda kuzimua.** treat a hangover by drinking again. *Cf.* [2]**mzima, zimwe, kizimwe.**

[2]**zima** *adj.* 1. entire, whole, complete. **nchi nzima.** the entire country. **mkate mzima, sio kipande tu.** a whole loaf of bread, not just a piece. **namba nzima.** *math.* whole numbers. 2. full-grown, adult. **mtu mzima asifanye mambo ya kitoto.** A grown-up person does not behave like a child. 3. sound, healthy. **alikuwa mgonjwa, lakini sasa mzima kabisa.** He was ill, but now he is

quite well again. 4. live, alive, unhurt. **samaki mzima.** live fish. 5. solid, massive. **tufe nzima.** a solid sphere. *Cf.* **1mzima, uzima.**

zimbaa be surly/sullen/sulky.

zimda* (–) zimda (medicine for diarrhea).

zimeo (ma-) *see* **zomeo.**

zimo *auxil. v. det.* **n-** *class.* they are in...

zimua *inv. of* **1zima.**

zimwe (ma- *or adj.*) (something) extinguished/quenched/lifeless. **makaa –.** extinguished coals. **nazi mazimwe.** coconut without meat or milk. *Cf.* **1zima, kizimwe.**

zimwi (ma-) spirit, ogre, demon. *prov.* **– likujualo halikuli likakuisha.** A demon who knows you won't eat you up. *Cf.* **kizimwi, mzimu, kuzimu, wazimu.**

1zina *auxil. v.* **n-** *class* they have.

2zina* (–) *see* **zinaa.**

zinaa*, zina (–) sexual immorality, illicit sexual intercourse, fornication, adultery. (= **uzinzi.**) *Cf.* **zini.**

zinara* (–) 1. flange, lip *(of a pot, etc.).* 2. molding, cornice. 3 (embroidered) belt. 4. *naut.* waterline.

zinda *rare* be hard/firm/resistant, stick fast; be steady/steadfast/resolute. *Cf.* **kizinda;** *also* **zindika, zindua.**

zindika protect with a charm/magic, ward off evil spirits. *appl.* **zindikia.** *Cf.* **zindiko;** *also* **zinda, zindua.**

zindiko (ma-) protective magic *(us. charms buried at the entrance of a house to secure it from evil spirits). Cf.* **zindika.**

zindua take away, remove; free from a spell. **– usingizini.** wake someone up suddenly. *appl.* **zindulia.** *intr.* **zinduka** & *intr.-ass.* **zindukana.** be awakened suddenly, wake up with a start from a sound sleep. *caus.* **zindusha.** *Cf.* **zinduo, mzinduko, uzindusho;** *also* **zinda, zindika.**

zinduka *intr. of* **zindua.**

zinduo (ma-) 1. opening, inauguration. 2. = **zindiko.** *Cf.* **zindua.**

zinga 1. turn, change, veer *(of wind, etc.).* 2. move in a circle; *(fig.)* wander about aimlessly. 3. encircle, surround. **– mji.** surround/invest a city. 4. roll up, wind up. **– uzi.** wind up thread on a ball. *pass.* **zingwa.** be surrounded. *appl.* **zingia, zingira.** *stat.-ass.* **zingamana.** be twisting/winding *(a river, etc.),* be twisted/tangled. **fungua kamba iliyozingamana.** Unravel this string which is all tangled up. *inv.* **zingua.** 1. unroll, unwind, untangle. 2. free from a charm/illness *(by means of magic),* exorcize. *Cf.* **zingio, zingo, zinguo, kizingia, kizingo, mazingazinga, mazingira, mazingiwa, mazingo, mzinga, mzingile, mzingo, uzinge, uzingo;** *also* **zungua.**

zingamana *stat.-ass. of* **zinga.**

zingatia 1. remember, keep in mind. 2. hold tight, hold on to. **ulichokishika kizingatie huu ni ulimwengu wa kunyang'anyana.** Hold on to what you have; it is a thievish world. *Cf.* **mzingativu.**

zingefuri*, zangefuri, singefuri, singafuri (–) *min.* cinnabar. *Cf.* **mzingefuri.**

zingio (ma-) (act of) surrounding; *(mil.)* investment, siege. *Cf.* **zinga.**

zingira *appl. of* **zinga.**

zingizi, jingizi (–) 1. pains at the beginning of menstruation. 2. pains after childbirth.

zingo (ma-) turn, twist; rotation, revolution. **– la maji.** eddy, whirlpool. *Cf.* **zinga.**

zingua *inv. of* **zinga.**

zinguo, zunguo (ma-) (act of) exorcizing, magic formula, charm; cure effected by magic. *Cf.* **zinga.**

zini* have illicit sexual intercourse, fornicate, commit adultery *(of either man or woman).* *appl.* **zinia.** *refl.-appl.* **jizinia** & *refl.-caus.* **jizinisha.** indulge in debauchery, lead a dissolute life. *Cf.* **zani, zinaa, zinifu, mzinifu, uzinifu, uzinzi.**

zinifu* *adj.* (sexually) immoral, lecherous, adulterous. *Cf.* **zini.**

zinza 1. display *(goods, for sale).* 2. exhibit a thief or malefactor in public *(to be hissed at by the crowd).*

[1]**zio** (ma-) post (used in building native huts). (= **nguzo.**)

[2]**zio** (ma-) = [1]**kizio.**

zipi *see* **pi.**

zira hate, have an aversion for/grudge against. *ass.* **zirana.** take a dislike to each other, be at outs with each other. *Cf.* [1]**zia.**

zirai* lose consciousness, faint.

zita (–) *rare* *see* **vita.**

zito *adj.* 1. heavy. **mfuko mzito.** a heavy bag. 2. thick, dense, impenetrable. **mwitu mzito.** a dense forest. 3. difficult, troublesome, serious. **swali –.** a difficult question. 4. deep, sound. **usingizi mzito.** a deep sleep. 5. pregnant. *Cf.* **uzito.**

ziua *see* **zua.**

[1]**ziwa** (ma-) pond, pool, lake. *Cf.* **uziwa.**

[2]**ziwa** (ma-) 1. (woman's) breast. **nyonyesha –.** nurse a child. 2. *rare* udder (= **kiwele**). *Cf.* [2]**maziwa.**

ziwi *adj.* deaf. *Cf.* **kiziwi, ukiziwi.**

ziwia *rare* *see* **zuia.**

ziyada* (ma-) *see* **ziada.**

ziyara* (–) *see* **ziara.**

ziza *caus. of* [1]**zia** & [3]**zia.**

[1]zizi (ma-) enclosure for animals: yard, pen, fold, stable, paddock.

[2]zizi *dem. pron.* n- *class:* – hizi these very...

[1]zizima 1. become cool/cold, cool off. chai hii imezizima. The tea has cooled off/is cold. 2. *fig.* be calm/collected/composed. mji umezizima. The city is perfectly quiet. moyo umezizima. be inwardly content. *appl.* zizimia. *intr.* zizimika. *caus.* zizimisha. cool something off, make (very) cold; *(fig.)* calm down, pacify. *inv.* zizimua. 1. take the chill off something, warm up, become warm. 2. *(w. int. force)* cool off suddenly; *(fig.)* scare off. 3. *fig.* be excited/stirred/moved. *Cf.* [1]zima, mzizimo.

[2]zizima, didima sink down, be swallowed up, disappear. *appl.* zizimia. *caus.* zizimisha. *Cf.* mzizimi.

zo 1. *relat. pron.* n- *class.* 2. = zako. *Cf.* ako.

zoa gather up, sweep up, pick up. – matakataka. sweep up rubbish in a pile. *appl.* zolea. fagio la kuzolea. broom/brush for sweeping up rubbish. *intr.* zoleka. *caus.* zolesha. *pass.* zolewa.

[1]zoea be used to/in the habit of, become accustomed to, be familiar with. *ass.* zoeana. *appl.* zolea. get used to something, become acclimatized. *appl.-intr.* zoeleka. be customary/usual. *caus.* zoeza, zoelesha, zoeleza. 1. get someone used to something. 2. make familiar with, train, break in. *refl.-caus.* jizoeza. train oneself, practice, make oneself familiar with something. *Cf.* zoevu, zoezi, mazoea, mazoezi, mzoea.

[2]zoea (ma-) *see* zoezi.

zoevu, zoefu, zoelefu *adj.* accustomed (to), familiar (with), experienced (in). yeye ni mzoevu wa hapa. He is well acquainted with this locality. *Cf.* [1]zoea.

zoezi, zoea (ma-) (*us.* mazoezi, mazoea) 1. habit, custom, familiarity. 2. instruction, practice, exercize, training. *Cf.* [1]zoea.

Zohari*, Zahali (–) *astr.* Saturn.

zolea *appl. of* zoa.

zoleka *intr. of* zoa.

zolesha *caus. of* zoa.

zolewa *pass. of* zoa.

zoloto* (–) *anat.* larynx, Adam's apple. (= [2]kikoromeo.)

zoma *rare* groan *(in derision/contempt),* hoot, mock. *appl.* zomea. groan/hoot at someone, mock, deride. *caus.* zomesha. *pass.* zomewa. *Cf.* zomeo, mzomeo.

zomari*, zumari (–) zomari (a kind of woodwind instrument).

zomeo, zimeo (ma-) 1. call/cry (of derision/disapproval). 2. war cry. *Cf.* **zoma.**

zonga, zongazonga 1. wind, twist, coil (around something); *(fig.)* embrace, enclose, surround. **nyoka amezonga mti.** The snake has coiled itself around the tree. 2. confuse, perplex. *appl.* **zongea.** *stat.-ass.* **zongamana.** 1. be rolled up/coiled. 2. be surrounded. *inv.* **zongoa.** unwind, unroll. *inv.-stat.-caus.* **zongameza.** 1. wind/coil/tie around. 2. = **zongamana.**

zongazonga *see* **zonga.**

zote *see* **ote.**

zoza grumble, complain, nag. **usinizoze!** Don't nag at me! *ass.* **zozana.** nag at each other. *Cf.* **mzozo.**

zua, ziua 1. make a hole, bore through, pierce, perforate. **– tundu.** bore a hole. 2. *fig.* be engrossed in something, meditate, reflect. 3. *fig.* bring to light, discover, obtain information, find out, ascertain. *appl.* **zulia.** tell lies about someone. **amenizulia.** He has accused me falsely. *intr.* **zuka, zulika.** 1. appear suddenly, emerge, pop up. (*See also sub* **2zuka.**) 2. be discovered/found out. *caus.* **zusha, zulisha.** 1. think up something, invent. 2. fabricate, make up (and spread) lies. **ametuzusha wongo.** He has made up lies about us. *Cf.* **1zuka, 2zuka, zulio, kizuka, kizushi, kizuu, mazuka, mzuka, mzuza, mzuzi, uzuka, uzushi.**

zubaazubaa loiter, hang around. **– bure.** loaf around aimlessly.

zubu* (–) *anat.* penis. (= **mboo, uume.**)

zugezuge (ma-) imbecile, idiot, fool.

zuhura* (–) *astr.* Venus.

zuia, zuwia 1. prevent, hinder, hold back, withhold, check, restrain, limit, deter, detain. 2. support, protect. *refl.* **jizuia.** restrain/control oneself, hold back. *appl.* **zulia.** *intr.* **zuika.** *caus.* **zuiza.** *pass.* **zuiwa.** *Cf.* **zuio, kizuio, kizuizini, uzuiaji.**

zuika *intr. of* **zuia.**

zuio, zuizi, zuizo (ma-) obstruction, hindrance, limitation, detention; support, protection. *Cf.* **zuia.**

zuiwa *pass. of* **zuia.**

zuiza *caus. of* **zuia.**

zuizi, zuizo (ma-) *see* **zuio.**

1zuka (ma-) ghost, apparition, vision. *Cf.* **zua, 2zuka, kizuka, mazuka, mzuka, uzuka.**

2zuka (*intr. of* **zua**) appear suddenly, emerge, pop up. **vita imezuka.** War has suddenly broken out. **umezuka kutoka wapi?** Where did you come from so suddenly? *appl.* **zukia.** *caus.* **zusha.** produce (suddenly). *Cf.* **zua, 1zuka, kizuka, mazuka, mzuka, uzuka.**

1zulia* (ma-) carpet, rug.

[2]zulia *appl. of* **zua.**

[3]zulia *appl. of* **zulu.**

[1]zulika *intr. of* **zua.**

[2]zulika *intr. of* **zulu.**

zulio **(ma-)** (*us.* **mazulio**) 1. false statement/accusation. 2. *rare* information, statement, indication; advice, notice. *Cf.* **zua.**

[1]zulisha *caus. of* **zua.**

[2]zulisha *caus. of* **zulu.**

zulizuli* **(–)** dizziness; confusion, perplexity. *Cf.* **zulu.**

zulu* 1. feel dizzy. 2. be confused/bewildered. **– akili.** go out of one's mind. *appl.* **zulia.** *intr.* **zulika.** *caus.* **zulisha.** drive crazy. *pass.* **zuliwa.** be confused, be driven crazy.

zuma contradict, interrupt.

zumaradi* **(–)** *see* **zumaridi.**

zumari* **(–)** *see* **zomari.**

zumaridi*, zumaradi [*Pers.*] **(–)** emerald.

zumbua *see* **vumbua.**

zunga **(–)** *anat.* foreskin, prepuce (= **govi**). **mwenye –.** uncircumcised man.

zungu *adj.* 1. strange, peculiar, extraordinary, remarkable. 2. European. *Cf.* **[1]mzungu, [2]mzungu, kizungu, uzungu.**

zungua 1. turn around, twist around, rotate. 2. go around, encircle. 3. *fig.* evade, avoid. *intr.* **zunguka.** 1. *(w. trans. force)* go around something, round *(a corner)*; patrol. 2. *(intr.)* revolve, rotate; *(fig.)* wander about aimlessly, waste time. *intr.-appl.* **zungukia.** circumvent, outwit. *caus.* **zungusha.** 1. encircle, close in **zungusha boma.** put up a fence around something. 2. turn around/round and round, rotate (something). 3. lead around, take for a walk. 4. put someone off, keep someone waiting/in suspense. **zungusha maneno.** talk ambiguously. *caus.-ass.* **zungushana.** 1. avoid each other, keep out of each other's way. 2. keep each other waiting; *(fig.)* try to get the better of each other, cheat/outwit each other. *Cf.* **zungusho, kizunguzungu, mazunguko, mzunguko, mzungushi, mzungusho;** *also* **zinga.**

zunguka *intr. of* **zungua.**

zunguko **(ma-)** *see* **zungusho.**

zungumza 1. carry on a conversation, chat. 2. amuse oneself, pass the time. *refl.* **jizungumza.** 1. amuse oneself, occupy one's time. 2. take up someone else's time. *appl.* **zungumzia.** *Cf.* **zungumzo, mzungumzaji.**

zungumzo **(ma-)** (*us.* **mazungumzo**) conversation, gossip; amusement, pastime. *Cf.* **zungumza.**

zunguo (ma-) *see* **zinguo.**

zungusha *caus. of* **zungua.**

zungusho, zunguko (ma-) (act of) turning, revolving; turn, bend *(of a river, etc.)*; eddy, whirlpool; enclosure, fence, fencing. *Cf.* **zungua.**

[1]**zuri** *adj.* beautiful, handsome, pretty; good, fine, nice; excellent, splendid; *(of food)* delicious, tasty. *Cf.* **uzuri.**

[2]**zuri*, azur** (–) 1. perjury. 2. *v.* commit perjury.

zuru* 1. visit a grave. 2. *(in gen.)* visit, pay a visit. **amezuru nchi yetu.** He has paid a visit to our country. *caus.* **zuruza.** have someone pay a visit, invite. *Cf.* ziaria.

zurura wander around, loaf around, waste time. **usizurure ovyo.** You shouldn't just loiter around aimlessly. *intr.* **zururuka** = **zurura.**

zururuka *intr. of* **zurura.**

zuruza *caus. of* **zuru.**

zusha *caus. of* **zua** & [2]**zuka.**

zuwia *see* **zuia.**

zuzu *adj.* inexperienced, ignorant, foolish. *Cf.* **zuzua, mzuzu, uzuzu.**

zuzua make a fool of/play tricks on someone, embarrass. **sema maneno ya kweli usijizuzue.** Tell the truth and don't make a fool of yourself. *intr.* **zuzuka.** be fooled, be deceived/confused/at a loss. *appl.* **zuzulia.** *caus.* **zuzulisha.** *Cf.* **zuzu, mzuzu.**

zuzuka *intr. of* **zuzua.**

zuzulia *appl. of* **zuzua.**

For Warren and Betty

With fondest regards and all good wishes.

Charles

This is about the last of its kind. A new edition is in preparation.